LABOUR AND EMPLOYMENT LAW

Cases, Materials, and Commentary

NINTH EDITION

COMPILED BY A GROUP OF TEACHERS OF LABOUR AND EMPLOYMENT LAW KNOWN AS

The Labour Law Casebook Group

Labour and Employment Law: Cases, Materials, and Commentary, ninth edition
© Irwin Law Inc., 2018

All rights reserved. No part of this publication may be reproduced, stored in a retrieval system, or transmitted, in any form or by any means, without the prior written permission of the publisher or, in the case of photocopying or other reprographic copying, a licence from Access Copyright (Canadian Copyright Licensing Agency), 56 Wellesley St W, Suite 320, Toronto, ON, M5S 2S3.

Every effort has been made to seek copyright permission, where required, from copyright holders. If there are any omissions, they will be corrected in subsequent editions.

Published in 2018 by
Irwin Law
14 Duncan Street
Suite 206
Toronto, Ontario
M5H 3G8
www.irwinlaw.com

ISBN: 978-155221-486-2
e-book ISBN: 978-1-55221-487-9

Cover and interior design by Heather Raven

Library and Archives Canada Cataloguing in Publication

Labour and employment law: cases, materials and commentary / compiled by a group of teachers of labour and employment law known as the Labour Law Casebook Group. — Ninth edition.

Includes bibliographical references.
Issued in print and electronic formats.
ISBN 978-1-55221-486-2 (softcover).—ISBN 978-1-55221-487-9 (PDF)

1. Labor laws and legislation—Canada—Cases. I. Labour Law Casebook Group, editor

KE3109.L315 2018	344.7101	C2018-903845-4
KF3320.ZA2L33 2018		C2018-903846-2

Printed and bound in Canada.

1 2 3 4 5   22 21 20 19 18

The Labour Law Casebook Group

Pnina Alon-Shenker, Ryerson University
Bruce Archibald, Dalhousie University
Kevin Banks, Queen's University
Tim Bartkiw, Ryerson University
Stephanie Bernstein, Université du Québec à Montréal
Adelle Blackett, McGill University
Bruce Curran, University of Manitoba
Gillian Demeyere, Western University
David Doorey, York University
Brian Etherington, University of Windsor
Brian Langille, University of Toronto
Michael Lynk, Western University
Michael Mac Neil, Carleton University
Ravi Malhotra, University of Ottawa
Sarah Marsden, Thompson Rivers University
Claire Mummé, University of Windsor
Kerry Rittich, University of Toronto
Supriya Routh, University of Victoria
Sara Slinn, York University
Gilles Trudeau, Université de Montréal

Summary Table of Contents

        Preface *xxv*

Chapter 1: **Introduction** *1*

Chapter 2: **International and Transnational Labour Law** *119*

Chapter 3: **The Contract of Employment** *219*

Chapter 4: **Status Under Collective Bargaining Legislation** *336*

Chapter 5: **The Right to Join a Union** *409*

Chapter 6: **The Acquisition and Termination of Bargaining Rights** *475*

Chapter 7: **Negotiating a Collective Agreement** *538*

Chapter 8: **Industrial Conflict** *598*

Chapter 9: **The Collective Agreement and Grievance Arbitration** *692*

Chapter 10: **The Individual Employee Under Collective Bargaining** *778*

Chapter 11: **The Trade Union and Its Members** *821*

Chapter 12: **The Constitutionalization of Collective Bargaining Law** *870*

Chapter 13: **Statutory Minimum Standards** *993*

Chapter 14: **Equality and Human Rights in Employment** *1064*

        Table of Cases *1187*

Detailed Table of Contents

PREFACE *xxv*

CHAPTER 1: INTRODUCTION *1*

1:100   **Our Objectives** *1*

1:200   **Historical Development and Sources of Labour and Employment Law** *2*
- 1:210   **The Contract of Employment in Canadian Common Law and Quebec Civil Law** *3*
  - Alan Fox, *History and Heritage: The Social Origins of the British Industrial Relations System* *4*
- 1:220   **Collective Bargaining** *6*
  - Donald D Carter et al, *Labour Law in Canada* *6*
- 1:230   **Direct Statutory Regulation** *12*
  - 1:231   **Employment Standards Legislation** *12*
    - Federal Labour Standards Review Commission, *Fairness at Work: Labour Standards for the 21st Century* *12*
  - 1:232   **Human Rights Codes** *13*
    - Kevin Banks, Roberta Nunin, & Adriana Topo, "The Lasting Influence of Legal Origins: Workplace Discrimination, Social Inclusion and the Law in Canada, the United States and the European Union" *13*
  - 1:233   **Occupational Safety and Health Legislation** *14*
  - 1:234   **Privacy Legislation** *15*
- 1:240   **The *Canadian Charter of Rights and Freedoms*** *16*
- 1:250   **International Law** *17*
  - Kevin Banks, "The Role and Promise of International Law in Canada's New Labour Law Constitutionalism" *18*
- 1:260   **The Institutional Distinctiveness of Quebec** *19*
  - Jacques Belanger & Gilles Trudeau, "The Institutional Specificity of Quebec in the Context of Globalization" *19*

1:300   **Values and Market Ordering** *23*
- Brian Langille, "Labour Law's Back Pages" *24*
- 1:310   **Market Models** *29*
  - Armen A Alchian & William R Allen, *University Economics* *29*
  - Richard Posner, *Economic Analysis of Law* *30*
  - Steven L Willborn, "Individual Employment Rights and the Standard Economic Objection: Theory and Empiricism" *33*
  - Alan Manning, *Monopsony in Motion: Imperfect Competition in Labour Markets* *42*
  - Paul Weiler, *Governing the Workplace* *46*

Richard Freeman & James Medoff, "The Two Faces of Unionism" 48

1:320 Normative Defences and Critiques of Market Ordering 55

Milton Friedman, *Capitalism and Freedom* 55

CB Macpherson, "Elegant Tombstones: A Note on Friedman's Freedom" 56

Max Weber, "Freedom and Coercion" 58

David Beatty, "Ideology, Politics and Unionism" 60

Paul Weiler, *Reconcilable Differences: New Directions in Canadian Labour Law* 61

1:400 The Changing World of Work and of Workplace Law 62

1:410 Market Pressures and the Reorganization of Production 62

Federal Labour Standards Review Commission: *Fairness at Work: Labour Standards for the 21st Century* 62

David Weil, *The Fissured Workplace: Why Work Became So Bad for So Many and What Can Be Done to Improve It* 65

Kevin Banks, "Workplace Law Without the State?" 70

1:420 The Changing Position of Unions 71

Peter Ackers, "Trade Unions as Professional Associations" 71

John Kelly, "Trade Union Power and Membership in Comparative Perspective" 74

1:430 Diversity, Inclusion, and Inequality 75

Adelle Blackett & Colleen Sheppard, "Collective Bargaining and Equality: Making Connections" 75

Federal Labour Standards Review Commission: *Fairness at Work: Labour Standards for the 21st Century* 77

1:431 The Growth of Precarious Work 78

Wayne Lewchuk, "The Political Economy of Precarious Employment: Will it Be No Work or Precarious Employment?" 78

1:432 The Persistence of Unequal Opportunity 82

Melissa Moyser, "Women and Paid Work" 82

Elizabeth Shilton, "Family Status Discrimination: 'Disruption and Great Mischief' or Bridge over the Work–Family Divide?" 85

Jeffrey Reitz & Rupa Bannerjee, *Racial Inequality, Social Cohesion, and Policy Issues in Canada* 85

K Banks, R Chaykowski, & G Slotsve, "The Accommodation Gap in Canadian Workplaces: What Does it Mean for Law, Policy and an Aging Population?" 87

1:433 The Growth of Income Inequality 88

David A Green, W Craig Riddell, & France St-Hilaire, "Income Inequality in Canada: Driving Forces, Outcomes and Policy" 88

Seth Klein & Armine Yalnizyan, *Better Is Always Possible: A Federal Plan to Tackle Poverty and Inequality* 92

1:440 Renewing Workplace Law and Policy 92

1:441 The Changing Roles of Legislation and Collective Bargaining 93

Judy Fudge, "Reconceiving Employment Standards Legislation: Labour Law's Little Sister and the Feminization of Labour" 93

Morley Gunderson, "Social and Economic Impact of Labour Standards" 94

Kevin Banks, "Workplace Law Without the State?" 96
1:442 Beyond Regulating Employment 99
David Weil, *The Fissured Workplace: Why Work Became So Bad for So Many and What Can Be Done to Improve It* 99
Elizabeth Shilton, *Empty Promises: Why Workplace Pension Law Doesn't Deliver Pensions* 100
K Banks, R Chaykowski, & G Slotsve, "The Accommodation Gap in Canadian Workplaces: What Does It Mean for Law, Policy and an Aging Population?" 103
Joanne Conaghan & Kerry Rittich, "Introduction: Interrogating the Work/Family Divide" 106
1:443 The Changing Role of the State 107
Harry Arthurs, "Labour Law Without the State" 107

1:500 The Constitutional Division of Powers 110
1:510 The Division of Powers Between the Federal and Provincial Governments 111
Federal Labour Standards Review Commission, *Fairness at Work: Federal Labour Standards for the 21st Century* 111
Tessier Ltée v Quebec (Commission de la santé et de la sécurité du travail) 112
1:520 Aboriginal Self-Government 117

CHAPTER 2: INTERNATIONAL AND TRANSNATIONAL LABOUR LAW 119

2:100 Connecting Labour and Employment Law at Home and Abroad 119
Kerry Rittich & Guy Mundlak, "The Challenge to Comparative Labor Law in a Globalized Era" 120
Adelle Blackett & Anne Trebilcock, "Conceptualizing Transnational Labour Law" 121
2:200 Understanding Work, Social Welfare, Globalization, and International Law: Four Periods 122
2:210 Period I: Globalization, Work, and the Origins of the ILO 122
Werner Sengenberger, "Restructuring at the Global Level: The Role of International Labour Standards" 122
Adelle Blackett, "'This is Hallowed Ground': Canada and International Labour Law" 125
2:220 Period II: Embedded Liberalism and the Keynesian Welfare State 126
Robert Howse, "From Politics to Technocracy—and Back Again: The Fate of the Multilateral Trading Regime" 127
Kerry Rittich, "The Right to Work and Labour Market Flexibility: Labour Market Governance Norms in the International Order" 130
2:230 Period III—Globalization, Rise of the Washington Consensus, and Labour Responses 131
2:231 Globalization 131
Kerry Rittich & Guy Mundlak, "The Challenge to Comparative Labor Law in a Globalized Era" 131
David Harvey, *Spaces of Global Capitalism: Towards a Theory of Uneven Geographical Development* 132
World Bank, *World Development Report 2013: Jobs* 132
2:232 The Rise of the Washington Consensus 133

John Williamson, "A Short History of the Washington Consensus" *133*
David Harvey, *Spaces of Global Capitalism: Towards a Theory of Uneven Geographical Development* *135*
Robert Howse, "From Politics to Technocracy—and Back Again: The Fate of the Multilateral Trading Regime" *135*

2:233 Labour Responses *136*

Marion Jansen & Eddy Lee, *Trade and Employment: Challenges for Policy* *136*
Chantal Thomas, "Labour Migration as an Unintended Consequence of Globalization in Mexico, 1980–2000" *139*
Québec (Commission des droits de la personne et des droits de la jeunesse) c Centre maraîcher Eugène Guinois JR inc *140*

2:240 Period IV: The Financial Crisis and its Aftermath *143*

Goran Therborn, "Dynamics of Inequality" *143*
Peter Temin, *The Vanishing Middle Class: Prejudice and Power in a Dual Economy* *144*
Cynthia Estlund, *A New Deal for China's Workers?* *145*
Fay Faraday, "Made in Canada: How the Law Constructs Migrant Workers' Insecurity" *147*
Aristea Koukiadaki & Damian Grimshaw, *Evaluating the Effects of the Structural Labour Market Reforms on Collective Bargaining in Greece* *149*
Dani Rodrik, *Straight Talk on Trade: Ideas for a Sane World Economy* *150*
Judith Butler, "Trump Is Emancipating Unbridled Hatred" *150*

2:300 Labour Law from Reaction to Response *151*

2:310 Attempts to Renew International Labour Law *151*

2:311 Labour Standards and the Multilateral Trading System *151*

OECD, *Trade, Employment and Labour Standards* *151*
WTO, *Singapore Ministerial Declaration* *152*

2:312 The ILO Declaration on Fundamental Principles and Rights at Work *153*

Hilary Kellerson, "The ILO Declaration of 1998 on Fundamental Principles and Rights: A Challenge for the Future" *153*
Brian Langille, "The ILO and the New Economy: Recent Developments" *155*

2:313 Regional and Bilateral Trade and Labour Agreements *158*

North American Agreement on Labor Co-operation Between the Government of the United States of America, the Government of Canada and the Government of the United Mexican States *159*
OECD, *Trade, Employment and Labour Standards* *160*
International Brotherhood of Teamsters et al, "Violations of NAALC Labor Principles and Obligations in the Case of the St-Hubert McDonald's Restaurant" *162*
Lance Compa, "NAFTA's Labor Side Agreement and International Labor Solidarity" *164*
Employment and Social Development Canada, *Review of Public Communication CAN 2016-1—Report issued pursuant to the Canada-Colombia Agreement on Labour Cooperation* *166*
Comprehensive Economic and Trade Agreement (CETA) between Canada and the European Union and its Member States *169*

    Comprehensive and Progressive Agreement for Trans-Pacific Partnership (CPTPP) 170
    Franz Christian Ebert, "The Comprehensive Economic and Trade Agreement (CETA): Are Existing Arrangements Sufficient to Prevent Adverse Effects on Labour Standards?" 171

2:320 The Emergence and Roles of Transnational Labour Regulation 175
  Adelle Blackett & Anne Trebilcock, "Conceptualizing Transnational Labour Law" 175
  Bob Hepple, *Labour Laws and Global Trade* 175
  Alan Hyde, "Game Theory and Labour Standards" 177

2:330 Transnational Uses of International Labour Law 178
  2:331 Vignette — International Labour Law in Canadian Jurisprudence 178
    Convention (No 87) Concerning Freedom of Association and Protection of the Right to Organize 178
    Convention (No 98) Concerning the Application of the Principles of the Right to Organize and to Bargain Collectively, 1961 179
    Adelle Blackett, "'This is Hallowed Ground': Canada and International Labour Law" 180
    Saskatchewan Federation of Labour v Saskatchewan 183
    Report of the Committee of Experts on the Application of Conventions and Recommendations 185
  2:332 Vignette — The ILO and Maritime Labour in Canada 185
    Canada, Employment and Social Development Canada, *Canadian Position with Respect to the Maritime Labour Convention, 2006* 185
    Moira L McConnell, "The Maritime Labour Convention, 2006 — Reflections on Challenges for Flag State Implementation" 187
    "Government of Canada Settles SIUC Lawsuits" 187
  2:333 Vignette — Decent Work for Domestic Workers 188
    Convention (No 189) Concerning Decent Work for Domestic Workers 188
    CN v The United Kingdom 189

2:340 Self-Regulatory Initiatives 191
  Kevin Kolben, "Transnational Private Labour Regulation, Consumer-Citizenship and the Consumer Imaginary" 192
  Resolution Concerning Decent Work in Global Supply Chains 194
  Adelle Blackett, "Global Governance, Legal Pluralism and the Decentered State: A Labor Law Critique of Codes of Corporate Conduct" 194
  2:341 Vignette — Rana Plaza 196
    Juliane Reinecke & Jimmy Donaghey, "After Rana Plaza: Building Coalitional Power for Labour Rights between Unions and (Consumption-Based) Social Movement Organisations" 196
    Janelle Diller, "Pluralism and Privatization in Transnational Labour Regulation: Experience of the International Labour Organization" 198
    Aruna Kashyap, "The April 24 Ritual — Rana Plaza's Unfinished Legacy" 200
    Committee on Economic, Social and Cultural Rights, *Concluding observations on the initial report of Bangladesh* 202

2:342   Vignette—The Guiding Principles on Business and Human Rights and Global Supply Chains 203
    John Ruggie, *Guiding Principles on Business and Human Rights: Implementing the United Nations "Protect, Respect and Remedy" Framework* 203
    Penelope Simons & Audrey Macklin, *The Governance Gap: Extractive Industries, Human Rights and the Home State Advantage* 204

2:350   The Jurisdiction of Canadian Courts in Transnational Litigation 206
    Garcia v Tahoe Resources Inc 207
    Chevron Corp v Yaiguaje 208

2:400   **Migrant Labour: Legal Regulation and Construction of Vulnerability** 211
    Fay Faraday, *Profiting From the Precarious: How Recruitment Practices Exploit Migrant Workers* 211
    Fay Faraday, *Made in Canada: How the Law Constructs Migrant Workers' Insecurity* 213
    PN v FR & MR and another (No 2) 214

2:410   Human Trafficking for Work 216
    Prabha Kotiswaran, "From Sex Panic to Extreme Exploitation: Revisiting the Law and Governance of Human Trafficking" 216

CHAPTER 3: THE CONTRACT OF EMPLOYMENT 219

3:100   Introduction 219
    Otto Kahn-Freund, "A Note on Status and Contract in British Labour Law" 221
    Alan Fox, *Beyond Contract: Work, Power and Trust Relations* 222
    Christie v York Corp 224
    Pierre Verge, "Le contract de travail selon le *Code civil du Québec*: pertinence ou impertinence?" 225

3:200   **Employment Status: Who Is an Employee and Who Is an Employer?** 226
    David Weil, *The Fissured Workplace: Why Work Became So Bad for So Many and What Can Be Done to Improve It* 226

    3:210   **Who Is an Employee?** 228
        Otto Kahn-Freund, "Servants and Independent Contractors" 228
        Brian A Langille & Guy Davidov, "Beyond Employees and Independent Contractors: A View from Canada" 229
        Carter v Bell & Sons (Canada) Ltd 235
        McKee v Reid's Heritage Homes Ltd 236
        Jeremias Prassl & Martin Risak, "Uber, Taskrabbit, And Co.: Platforms as Employers? Rethinking the Legal Analysis of Crowdwork" 240

    3:220   **Who Is an Employer?** 243
        Downtown Eatery (1993) Ltd v Her Majesty the Queen in Right of Ontario 244

3:300   **The Terms of the Contract of Employment** 247
    3:310   Express Terms 248
        3:311   Interpretational Approach 248
            Ceccol v Ontario Gymnastic Federation 248

3:312   **Incorporating Terms** 253
    Ellison v Burnaby Hospital Society 253
3:314   **Restrictive Covenants** 256
    Elsley v JG Collins Ins Agencies 256

3:320 **Common Law Implied Terms** 261
  3:321   **The Employer's Managerial Prerogative and the Employee's Duty of Fidelity** 262
  3:322   **Reasonable Notice of Termination** 263
  3:323   **The Duty of Honesty in Contractual Performance** 264
      Bhasin v Hrynew 265
  3:324   **Fiduciary Employees** 268
      GasTOPS Ltd v Forsyth 268

3:400 **Terminating the Contract of Employment** 273
  3:410 **Wrongful Dismissal** 273
  3:420 **Cause for Dismissal** 273
      McKinley v BC Tel 274
  3:430 **Constructive Dismissal** 283
      Potter v New Brunswick Legal Aid Services 284
      Hill v Peter Gorman Ltd 289
      Lloyd v Imperial Parking Ltd 290

3:500 **Remedies for Wrongful Dismissal** 295
  3:510 **Reinstatement** 295
      Geoffrey England, "Recent Developments in the Law of the Employment Contract: Continuing Tension Between the Rights Paradigm and the Efficiency Paradigm" 295
  3:520 **Extent of Financial Compensation** 297
    3:521   **The Assessment of Reasonable Notice Damages** 297
        Cronk v Canadian General Insurance Co 298
        Bartlam v Saskatchewan Crop Insurance Corp 304
        Anderson v Haakon Industries (Canada) Ltd 308
    3:522   **Mitigation** 311
        Evans v Teamsters Local Union No 31 312
  3:530 **Other Damages** 318
      Wallace v United Grain Growers Ltd 318
      Honda Canada Inc v Keays 326

CHAPTER 4: STATUS UNDER COLLECTIVE BARGAINING LEGISLATION 336

4:100 **Introduction** 336

4:200 **Who Is an Employee?** 339
  4:210 **Dependent Contractors** 340
      International Alliance of Theatrical Stage Employees, Moving Picture Technicians, Artists and Allied Crafts, Local 849 v Egg Films Inc 340
  4:220 **Near-Employees** 349

4:300 **Excluded Employees** *349*
    4:310   **Professionals** *350*
    4:320   **Public Employees** *350*
    4:330   **Managerial Employees** *351*
        Re Burnaby (District) and CUPE, Local 23   *351*
        Captains and Chiefs Association v Algoma Central Marine   *352*
        Children's Aid Society of Ottawa-Carleton   *364*
    4:340   **Confidential Employees** *372*
        Grande Prairie Roman Catholic Separate School District No 28 v CEP, Local Union No 328   *372*

4:400 **Qualified Trade Unions** *375*
    4:410   **The Union as an Organization** *375*
        Ontario Workers' Union v Humber River Regional Hospital   *375*
        Smith & Rhuland Ltd v Nova Scotia   *379*
    4:420   **Employer Influence** *381*

4:500 **The Employer for Purposes of Collective Bargaining** *382*
    4:510   **Identifying the Employer** *382*
        C Michael Mitchell & John C Murray, Changing Workplaces Review: Special Advisors' Interim Report   *382*
        Pointe-Claire (City) v Quebec (Labour Court)   *385*
    4:520   **Related Employers** *392*
        White Spot Ltd v British Columbia (Labour Relations Board)   *392*
    4:530   **Successor Employers** *396*
        Hospitality & Service Trades Union, Local 261 v Service Star Building Cleaning Inc   *397*
    4:540   **Contracting Out** *400*
        Re Canada Post Corp and CUPW   *401*

CHAPTER 5: THE RIGHT TO JOIN A UNION   *409*

5:100 **Introduction** *409*
    Stanley Hanson, "Estevan 1931"   *409*
    Human Rights Watch, *Unfair Advantage: Workers' Freedom of Association in the United States under International Human Rights Standards*   *413*
    Paul Weiler, "Promises to Keep: Securing Workers' Rights to Self-Organization under the NLRA"   *414*

5:200 **Non-Motive Unfair Labour Practices** *416*
    Canadian Paperworkers Union, Canadian Labour Congress and Its Local 305 v International Wallcoverings, a Division of International Paints (Canada) Limited   *416*
    Canadian Broadcasting Corp v Canada (Labour Relations Board)   *423*

5:300 **Alteration of Working Conditions: The Statutory Freeze** *431*
    Simpsons Limited v Canadian Union of Brewery, Flour, Cereal, Soft Drink and Distillery Workers   *433*
    Ontario Public Service Employees Union v Royal Ottawa Health Care Group   *436*
    National Labor Relations Board v Exchange Parts Co   *439*

5:400	**Employer Speech** 439	
	United Steelworkers of America v Wal-Mart Canada 440	
5:500	**Solicitation on Employer Property** 450	
	Canada Post Corporation 450	
5:600	**Union Unfair Labour Practices** 456	
5:700	**Remedies for Interference with the Right to Organize** 457	
	National Bank of Canada and Retail Clerks' International Union 460	
	National Bank of Canada v Retail Clerks' International Union et al 461	
	5:710	**Interim Relief** 462
	5:720	**Remedial Certification** 463
	5:730	**What if the Employer Closes Down the Workplace?** 465
		United Food and Commercial Workers, Local 503 v Wal-Mart Canada Corp 465
	5:740	**Criminal Law Penalties** 469
		R v K-Mart Canada Ltd 469
5:800	**The Professional Responsibility of Lawyers** 470	
	Law Society of Upper Canada v Rovet 471	

CHAPTER 6: THE ACQUISITION AND TERMINATION OF BARGAINING RIGHTS 475

6:100 **The *Wagner Act* Model and the Principle of Exclusivity** 475
  Roy Adams, "Union Certification as an Instrument of Labor Policy: A Comparative Perspective" 475
  Harry Arthurs, "Reinventing Labor Law for the Global Economy" 477
  David Weil, *The Fissured Workplace: Why Work Became So Bad for So Many and What Can Be Done to Improve It* 478

6:200 **The Appropriate Bargaining Unit** 480
  6:210 **Bargaining Unit Determination: General Principles** 480
  6:220 **Voluntary Delineation of the Bargaining Unit** 482
    6:221 **Delineation of the Bargaining Unit by a Labour Relations Board** 483
      Metroland Printing, Publishing and Distributing Ltd 484
    6:222 **Bargaining Unit Delineation and Part-Time Employees** 488
      Canadian Imperial Bank of Commerce (Powell River Branch) v British Columbia Government Employees' Union 489
  6:230 **Bargaining Unit Determination and the Organizing Drive** 491
    Elizabeth Lennon, "Organizing the Unorganized: Unionization in the Chartered Banks of Canada" 491
    Service, Office and Retail Workers' Union of Canada [SORWUC] v Canadian Imperial Bank of Commerce 493
    United Steelworkers of America v TD Canada Trust in the Greater City of Sudbury 498
    United Rubber, Cork, Linoleum & Plastic Workers of America, Local 1028 v Michelin Tires (Canada) Ltd 503

Brian Langille, "The Michelin Amendment in Context" 504

6:240 Labour Relations Board Powers to Amend the Scope of the Bargaining Unit Post-certification 506

C Michael Mitchell & John C Murray, *Changing Workplaces Review: Special Advisors' Interim Report* 506

6:300 Determining Employee Support 507

Paul Weiler, "Promises to Keep: Securing Workers' Rights to Self-Organization under the NLRA" 508

6:400 Timeliness of Certification and Decertification Applications ("Open Seasons") 512

6:500 Decertification Applications 513

Employees of Kelly's Ambulance (1982) Ltd and Canadian Union of Public Employees v Kelly's Ambulance (1982) Ltd 514

International Association of Machinists and Aerospace Workers and Courtesy Chrysler 517

6:600 Alternatives to the *Wagner Act* Model 519

    6:610 Minority and Occupational Unionism 520

    Clyde Summers, "Unions without Majority: A Black Hole?" 521

    Roy Adams, "Bringing Canada's Wagner Act Regime into Compliance with International Human Rights Law and the *Charter*" 522

    Dorothy Sue Cobble, "Making Postindustrial Unionism Possible" 523

    6:620 Broader-Based Bargaining 525

    C Michael Mitchell & John C Murray, *Changing Workplaces Review: Special Advisors' Interim Report* 526

        6:621 Broader-Based Bargaining in Quebec 530

        Patrice Jalette, "When Labour Relations Deregulation Is Not an Option: The Alternative Logic of Building Services Employers in Quebec" 530

    6:630 Alternative Worker Voice Mechanisms: Workplace Councils? 535

    Rafael Gomez & Juan Gomez, *Workplace Democracy for the 21st Century: Towards a New Agenda for Employee Voice and Representation in Canada* 536

    6:640 Alternative Worker Voice Mechanisms: Protecting "Concerted Activities" of Non-unionized Workers? 536

CHAPTER 7: NEGOTIATING A COLLECTIVE AGREEMENT 538

7:100 Introduction 538

7:200 The Statutory Timetable 538

7:300 The Bargaining Freeze 540

7:400 The Duty to Bargain in Good Faith 541

    7:410 Purposes of the Duty to Bargain 541

    Archibald Cox, "The Duty to Bargain in Good Faith" 541

    7:420 Content of the Duty to Bargain 543

    United Electrical, Radio and Machine Workers of America v DeVilbiss (Canada) Ltd 543

Graphic Arts International Union Local 12-L v Graphic Centre (Ontario) Inc 544
Canadian Association of Industrial, Mechanical and Allied Workers v Noranda Metal Industries Ltd 545
Simon Fraser University v CUPE, Local 3338 548

7:421 Substantive and Procedural Obligations Imposed by the Duty to Bargain 552

United Steelworkers of America v Radio Shack 552
Canadian Union of United Brewery, Flour, Cereal, Soft Drink & Distillery Workers, Local No 304 v Canada Trustco Mortgage Company 559
Brian Langille & Patrick Macklem, "Beyond Belief: Labour Law's Duty to Bargain" 562
Royal Oak Mines v Canada (Labour Relations Board) 566
National Automobile, Aerospace Transportation and General Workers Union of Canada (CAW-Canada) and its Local 2224 v Buhler Versatile Inc 568
United Food & Commercial Workers Canada, Local 175 v WHL Management Limited Partnership 571

7:422 Disclosure of Decisions or Plans Substantially Affecting the Bargaining Unit 575

Brian Langille, "Equal Partnership in Canadian Labour Law" 576
International Woodworkers of America, Local 2-69 v Consolidated Bathurst Packaging Ltd 578

7:500 Remedies for Violating the Duty to Bargain 584

Royal Oak Mines v Canada (Labour Relations Board) 584
International Alliance of Stage Employees, Local 849 v Egg Films, Inc 589

7:600 First Contract Arbitration 592

Yarrow Lodge Ltd v Hospital Employees' Union 593
Communications, Energy and Paperworkers Union of Canada, Local, 87-M v Ming Pao Newspapers (Canada) Ltd 594
Bradley R Weinberg, "A Quantitative Assessment of the Effect of First Contract Arbitration on Bargaining Relationships" 595
Susan Johnson, "First Contract Arbitration: Effects on Bargaining and Work Stoppages" 597

CHAPTER 8: INDUSTRIAL CONFLICT 598

8:100 Industrial Pluralism and Industrial Conflict 598

Paul Weiler, *Reconcilable Differences: New Directions in Canadian Labour Law* 599

8:200 The Constitutional Right to Strike 603

8:300 Legal Forums Regulating Industrial Conflict: An Overview 603

8:400 The Role of Labour Relations Boards in Regulating Industrial Conflict 605

8:410 Regulating Strike Activity 605
8:411 Defining "Strike" Activity 605
8:412 Actions Constituting a Strike: Common Action or Concerted Activity 606

Communications, Electronic, Electrical, Technical and Salaried Workers of Canada v Graham Cable TV/FM 606

British Columbia Terminal Elevator Operators' Association on Behalf of the Saskatchewan Wheat Pool v Grain Workers' Union, Local 333 610

8:413 The Strike Prohibition and Sympathetic Action 610

Local 273, International Longshoremen's Association v Maritime Employers' Association 611

Unilux Boiler Corp v United Steelworkers of America, Local 3950 613

Nelson Crushed Stone and United Cement, Lime & Gypsum Workers' International Union, Local Union 494 v Martin 613

8:414 The Strike Prohibition and Political Protests 614

8:420 Regulating Economic Sanctions Available to the Employer 615

8:421 Regulating Lockouts 615

8:422 Changes to the Employment Contract Without Union Consent 616

United Steelworkers 1-2693 v Neenah Paper Company of Canada 616

8:423 Employer Economic Weapons, the Duty to Bargain, and Unfair Labour Practices 619

Westroc Industries Ltd v United Cement, Lime and Gypsum Workers International Union 620

8:430 Labour Board Remedies 623

National Harbours Board v Syndicat national des employés du Port de Montréal 624

8:500 The Role of the Courts 627

8:510 Criminal Jurisdiction 627

8:520 Civil Jurisdiction 628

8:521 Pleading a Cause of Action: Tort Illegalities 628

8:522 The Legal Capacity of Trade Unions to Sue and Be Sued 632

8:523 Civil Remedies: Damages and Injunctions 633

St Anne Nackawic Pulp & Paper Co Ltd v Canadian Paper Workers Union, Local 219 637

8:600 The Role of Arbitrators in Industrial Conflict 644

8:610 Awards of Damages by Arbitrators 644

Re Oil, Chemical & Atomic Workers & Polymer Corporation 644

8:620 Employer Disciplinary Action against Strikers 646

Rogers Cable TV (British Columbia) Ltd, Vancouver Division et al v International Brotherhood of Electrical Workers, Local 213 647

8:700 The Regulation of Picketing 648

8:710 Regulatory Schemes Governing Picketing 649

8:711 The British Columbia Approach 649

Canex Placer Limited (Endako Mines Division) v Canadian Association of Industrial, Mechanical and Allied Workers, Local 10 650

8:712 Other Regulatory Approaches: Ontario and Alberta 651

8:720 Primary and Secondary Picketing 653

        8:721   **Primary Picketing** *653*
                      Harrison v Carswell *654*
                      Cancoil Thermal Corp v Abbott *656*
        8:722   **Secondary Picketing and the "Modified *Hersees*" Approach** *660*
                      Hersees of Woodstock Ltd v Goldstein *660*
        8:723   ***Pepsi-Cola* and the "Wrongful Action Model"** *663*
                      Retail, Wholesale and Department Store Union, Local 558 v Pepsi-Cola Canada Beverages (West) Ltd *663*
        8:724   **The Impact of *Pepsi-Cola Canada*** *669*
                      Telus Communications Inc v Telecommunications Workers' Union *671*

8:800   **Job Rights of Strikers** *672*
        8:810   **Employee Status During a Strike** *672*
                R v Canadian Pacific Railway Co *673*
                Canadian Air Line Pilots' Association [CALPA] v Eastern Provincial Airways Ltd *675*
        8:820   **Replacement Worker Laws** *678*
                Seeking a Balance: Canada Labour Code Part 1 Review *680*

8:900   **Alternatives to Strikes?** *684*
        8:910   **Essential Services Legislation** *685*
        8:920   **Interest Arbitration** *687*
                Allen Ponak & Loren Falkenberg, "Resolution of Interest Disputes" *687*
                Robert Hebdon & Maurice Mazerolle, "Regulating Conflict in Public Sector Labour Relations: The Ontario Experience (1984–1993)" *691*

CHAPTER 9: THE COLLECTIVE AGREEMENT AND GRIEVANCE ARBITRATION *692*

9:100   **Introduction** *692*
        9:110   **The Common Law View of Collective Agreements** *693*
                Young v Canadian Northern Railway *694*
        9:120   **Grievance Arbitration as a Distinctive Form of Adjudication** *695*

9:200   **The Role of Grievance Arbitration in Our Collective Bargaining Regime—A Story of Transformation** *696*
        9:210   **Different Visions of the Role of Arbitration** *696*
                Paul Weiler, "The Role of the Labour Arbitrator: Alternative Versions" *696*
                David Beatty, "The Role of the Arbitrator: A Liberal Version" *705*
        9:220   **Management Rights** *708*
        Re United Steelworkers of America and Russelsteel Ltd *708*
        Communications, Energy and Paperworkers Union of Canada, Local 30 v Irving Pulp & Paper, Ltd *712*

9:300   **Sources of Arbitral Law and Reasoning** *715*
        9:310   **The Collective Agreement—Contract Interpretation** *715*
                Paul Weiler, *Reconcilable Differences: New Directions in Canadian Labour Law* *715*
            9:311   **Negotiation History** *716*

Re Noranda Metal Industries Ltd, Fergus Division v International Brotherhood of Electrical Workers 716

    9:312   Past Practice 719

International Association of Machinists v John Bertram & Sons Co 719

9:320   Promissory Estoppel 720

Nor-Man Regional Health Authority Inc v Manitoba Association of Health Care Professionals 720

9:330   General Public Law: Employment-Related Statutes 722

Parry Sound (District) Social Services Administration Board v Ontario Public Service Employees Union, Local 324 722

9:340   General Public Law: The *Canadian Charter of Rights and Freedoms* and the Common Law 733

    9:341   Arbitral Authority to Give *Charter* Remedies 733

Weber v Ontario Hydro 734

    9:342   Arbitral Authority to Apply the Common Law 736

9:400   Remedial Jurisdiction of Arbitrators 736

    9:410   Damages 736

Re Polymer Corp and Oil, Chemical & Atomic Workers 736

    9:420   Reinstatement 740

William Scott & Company Ltd v Canadian Food and Allied Workers Union, Local P-162 740

New Dominion Stores (cob Great Atlantic & Pacific Co of Canada) v Retail Wholesale Canada Canadian Service Sector, Division of USWA, Local 414 (McCaul Grievance) 744

    9:430   Rectification 749

9:500   The Institutional Framework: Competing Models for Allocating Jurisdiction Among Multiple Forums 750

    9:510   Arbitration and Civil Actions Concerning *Charter* and Common Law Claims 750

Weber v Ontario Hydro 750

Michel Picher, "Defining the Scope of Arbitration: The Impact of *Weber*: An Arbitrator's Perspective" 754

    9:520   Arbitration and Other Statutory Tribunals 758

Quebec (Commission des droits de la personne et des droits de la jeunesse on behalf of Morin et al) v Quebec (Attorney General) 758

    9:530   Criminal Courts Versus Arbitrators 765

        9:531   Arbitrators Versus Other Administrative Tribunals 766

9:600   Judicial Review of Arbitration 768

Dunsmuir v New Brunswick 769

9:700   The Future of the Grievance Resolution Process 774

CHAPTER 10: THE INDIVIDUAL EMPLOYEE UNDER COLLECTIVE BARGAINING 778

10:100   Introduction 778

10:200   The Primacy of the Collective Agreement 780

Detailed Table of Contents

    10:210   Bargaining with other Unions or with Individual Employees   780
    10:220   The Eclipsing of the Individual Contract of Employment   781
             McGavin Toastmaster Ltd v Ainscough   781
    10:230   The Pre-eminence of Grievance Arbitration   784
             Bisaillon v Concordia University   785

10:300   The Duty of Fair Representation   789
         Steele v Louisville & Nashville Railroad Co   790
    10:310   The Duty of Fair Representation in the Negotiation of a Collective Agreement   792
             Bukvich v Canadian Union of United Brewery, Flour, Cereal, Soft Drink and Distillery Workers, Local 304 and Dufferin Aggregates   793
             Atkinson v CLAC, Local 66   798
    10:320   The Duty of Fair Representation in the Administration of a Collective Agreement   801
             Rayonier Canada (BC) Ltd v International Woodworkers of America, Local 1-217   801
             Lucyshyn v Amalgamated Transit Union, Local 615   806
             Bernard Adell, "Collective Agreements and Individual Rights: A Note on the Duty of Fair Representation"   813
             Judd v CEP, Local 2000   816
             Ontario Labour Relations Board, "Duty of Fair Representation Applications"   820

CHAPTER 11: THE TRADE UNION AND ITS MEMBERS   821

11:100   Trade Union Structures   821
         Stephanie Ross, Larry Savage, Errol Black, & Jim Silver, *Building a Better World: An Introduction to Trade Unionism in Canada*   821

11:200   Union Liability for Actions of Members   825
         Fullowka v Pinkerton's of Canada Ltd   825

11:300   The Legal Protection of Union Membership Rights   829
         Michael Mac Neil, Michael Lynk, & Peter Engelmann, *Trade Union Law in Canada*   829
         Berry v Pulley   830
         Michael Mac Neil, Michael Lynk, & Peter Engelmann, *Trade Union Law in Canada*   837
    11:310   The Protection of Local Union Officers When Representing Members   840

11:400   Union Security and Union Discipline   842
    11:410   Union Security Clauses   845
         Speckling v Communications, Energy and Paperworkers' Union of Canada, Local 76   847
         Birch v Union of Taxation Employees, Local 70030   851

11:500   Union Security Provisions and the Role of Unions in Society   856
         Lavigne v Ontario Public Service Employees' Union   857
         R v Advance Cutting & Coring Ltd   860

11:600   The Union's Right to Communicate With Its Members   865
         Bernard v Canada (Attorney General)   866

CHAPTER 12: THE CONSTITUTIONALIZATION OF COLLECTIVE BARGAINING LAW 870

12:100 Introduction 870

12:200 Freedom of Association 871
- **12:210** The First Trilogy (1987): The *Alberta Reference*, *PSAC*, and *RWDSU* 871
  - *Reference Re Public Service Employee Relations Act (Alberta)* 871
- **12:220** The Second Trilogy (2001–2011): *Dunmore*, *Health Services*, and *Fraser* 891
  - *Dunmore v Ontario (Attorney General)*, 1997 891
  - *Dunmore v Ontario (Attorney General)*, 2001 893
  - **12:221** The *Health Services* Decision 900
    - *Health Services and Support—Facilities Subsector Bargaining Association v British Columbia* 900
  - **12:222** The Final Case of the Second Trilogy: *Fraser v Ontario (Attorney General)* 925
    - *Fraser v Ontario (Attorney General)* 925
    - *Ontario (Attorney General) v Fraser* 933
- **12:230** The Third Trilogy (2015): *MPAO*, *Meredith*, and *Sask Fed* 946
  - **12:231** *Mounted Police Association of Ontario v Canada (Attorney General)* 946
    - *Mounted Police Association of Ontario v Canada (Attorney General)* 947
  - **12:232** *Saskatchewan Federation of Labour*: The Right to Strike 970
    - *Saskatchewan Federation of Labour v Saskatchewan* 972
  - **12:233** *Meredith v Canada (Attorney General)* 984
    - *Meredith v Canada (Attorney General)* 984
- **12:240** Conclusion: What Is the Current and Future Legal Content of Section 2(d)? 986
  - *British Columbia Teachers' Federation v British Columbia* 988

CHAPTER 13: STATUTORY MINIMUM STANDARDS 993

13:100 Introduction 993
- Barry J Reiter, "The Control of Contract Power" 994
- Judy Fudge, "The New Workplace: Surveying the Landscape" 997

13:200 An Overview of Modern Employment Standards Legislation 1000
- Leah F Vosko, Eric Tucker, Mark P Thomas, & Mary Gellatly, "New Approaches to Enforcement and Compliance with Labour Regulatory Standards: The Case of Ontario, Canada" 1000

13:300 Coverage: The Meaning of "Employee" Under Employment Standards Legislation 1003
- *Renaud (Re)* 1004
- *Girex Bancorp Inc v Lynette Hsieh* 1009
- *New Jenny Nail & Spa v Qiurong Cao Jane and Director of Employment Standards* 1012

13:400 The Enforcement of Employment Standards 1016
- Kevin Banks, *Employment Standards Complaint Resolution, Compliance and Enforcement: A Review of the Literature on Access and Effectiveness* 1016

C Michael Mitchell & John C Murray, *The Changing Workplaces Review—Final Report* 1023
Leah F Vosko, "'Rights Without Remedies': Enforcing Employment Standards in Ontario by Maximizing Voice Among Workers in Precarious Jobs" 1028

13:500 Statutory Minimums, the Contract of Employment, and the Common Law 1031
Machtinger v HOJ Industries Ltd 1031

13:600 Statutory Protection of Non-unionized Employees Against Dismissal for Cause 1037
Wilson v Atomic Energy of Canada Ltd 1039

13:700 Hours of Work, Overtime, Family Care, and Flexibility 1047
Harry W Arthurs, *Fairness at Work: Federal Labour Standards for the 21st Century* 1050

13:800 Low Pay and the Statutory Minimum Wage 1054
Mark Thompson, *Rights and Responsibilities in a Changing Workplace: A Review of Employment Standards in British Columbia* 1054
Jennifer Wells, "McJobs: Is Minimum Wage a Good Idea?" 1056
Don Pittis, "Ontario's Experiment With Minimum Wage Could Transform Canada's Economy" 1058

13:900 Termination Pay Under Employment Standards Legislation 1060
  13:910 Entitlement to Individual and Mass Termination Pay 1060

13:1000 The Interface Between the Employment Standards Forum, Collective Bargaining, and Common Law Litigation 1062

CHAPTER 14: EQUALITY AND HUMAN RIGHTS IN EMPLOYMENT 1064

14:100 Introduction 1064

14:200 The Concept of Equality 1064
  14:210 Theoretical Development of the Concept 1064
  14:220 Application of the Concept of Equality by the Courts 1066
    Vriend v Alberta 1067
  14:230 Establishing Discrimination Under Human Rights Laws 1071
  14:240 The "Unified Approach" to Discrimination 1075
    British Columbia (Public Service Employee Relations Commission) v BCGSEU 1075

14:300 Some Major Employment-Related Equality Issues 1086
  14:310 Sex Discrimination 1086
  14:320 Sexual Harassment 1088
    14:321 Sexual Harassment as Sex Discrimination 1088
      Janzen v Platy Enterprises Ltd 1088
    14:322 Defining Sexual Harassment 1089
      Shaw v Levac Supply Ltd 1090
  14:330 Racial Discrimination 1091
    McKinnon v Ontario (Ministry of Correctional Services) (No 3) 1091
  14:340 Discrimination on the Basis of Disability 1093

Michael Lynk, "Disability and the Duty to Accommodate" 1093
Shuswap Lake General Hospital v British Columbia Nurses' Union (Lockie Grievance) 1094
Hydro-Québec v Syndicat des employées de techniques professionnelles et de bureau d'Hydro-Québec, section locale 2000 (SCFP-FTQ) 1099

14:350 Who Is Under a Duty to Accommodate? 1105
Central Okanagan School District No 23 v Renaud 1106

14:360 Systemic Discrimination 1111
Statistics Canada, "Earnings and Incomes of Canadians over the Past Quarter Century, 2006 Census" 1112
Derek Hum & Wayne Simpson, "Revisiting Equity and Labour: Immigration, Gender, Minority Status, and Income Differentials in Canada" 1113
Canadian National Railway v Canada (Human Rights Commission) 1115

14:370 Pay Equity 1122
Walden v Canada (Social Development) 1125

14:400 The Future of Equality 1130
  14:410 Economic Inequality 1130
  14:420 Equality in the Interface Between Welfare and Work 1133
  Natasha Kim & Tina Piper, "*Gosselin v. Quebec*: Back to the Poorhouse ..." 1133
  14:430 Gender and Economic Discrimination 1136
  Diane Elson, "Labor Markets as Gendered Institutions: Equality, Efficiency and Empowerment Issues" 1136
  Richard Posner, *Economic Analysis of Law* 1137
  14:440 Evolving Boundaries of Discrimination 1140
    14:441 Family Status and Caregiving Responsibilities 1140
    Canada (Attorney General) v Johnstone 1140
    14:442 Gender Identity and Gender Expression 1149
    14:443 Accommodation of Age-Related Needs 1149
    14:444 Intersectionality 1149
  14:450 Questions of Scope, Coverage, and Classifications 1150
  Robichaud v Canada (Treasury Board) 1150
  United Steelworkers obo others v Tim Hortons and others (No 2) 1155
  McCormick v Fasken Martineau DuMoulin LLP 1159

14:500 Some Other Human Rights Issues in the Workplace 1163
  14:510 Drug Testing 1163
  Entrop v Imperial Oil Ltd 1164
  14:520 The Right to Privacy at Work 1168
  R v Cole 1170
  Jones v Tsige 1173
  14:530 Off-Duty Conduct on Social Media 1184
  14:540 Freedom from Bullying and Psychological Harassment 1185

TABLE OF CASES 1187

Preface

This is the latest edition of a book initially published in 1970 as the first Canadian law school casebook prepared by a national group of academics—the Labour Law Casebook Group. Labour and employment law has evolved considerably over the decades, and the book has changed accordingly. Beginning with the fourth edition in 1986, we moved away from an almost exclusive focus on collective labour law, adding chapters on the individual contract of employment and on statutory regulation, as well as an introductory chapter on the historical and normative foundations of labour and employment law. The growing importance of the *Canadian Charter of Rights and Freedoms*, and of equality issues more generally, led to providing a greater emphasis on those subject areas in the fifth edition, in 1991. In the sixth edition, published in 1998, we added a final chapter on the impact of globalization, the liberalization of trade, and the changing role of the state. By the time the seventh edition came out in 2004, statutory regulation and *Charter*-based jurisprudence (as exemplified by the Supreme Court of Canada decisions in *Advance Cutting and Coring*, *Pepsi-Cola Canada*, and *Parry Sound*) had become more prominent across the entire spectrum of workplace relations, and so had the consequences of the globalization of the economy. Our work on the eighth edition convinced us that it was no longer pedagogically or logistically advisable for us to try to deal with *Charter* issues in any depth in the context of the particular area of collective bargaining law to which they related (for example, the determination of employee status or the regulation of picketing). We therefore decided to consolidate them in a new chapter, titled "The Constitutionalization of Collective Bargaining Law." The years following the publication of the eighth edition saw the Supreme Court decide *Fraser*, *Meredith*, *Mounted Police Association of Ontario*, and *Saskatchewan Federation of Labour*. As a result, that chapter has become one of the weightiest in this volume.

For this edition, we have made two structural changes. Both reflect the view of casebook group members who feel that the study of Canadian labour and employment law increasingly requires a grasp of the social and economic environment changes that both shape and challenge its defining aims, structures, boundaries, and models of governance. In light of this, we have updated and moved our treatment of what was described in the eighth edition as the "new economy"—but is not so new anymore and is now simply referred to as the "Changing World of Work and Workplace Law"—from the closing to the introductory chapter. Second, reflecting the growing influence of globalization, international law, and transnational law on Canadian workplace regulation, we have expanded and updated our treatment of these issues, and moved them from the conclusion of the casebook to its second chapter. Chapter 2 enables students and teachers to extend their consideration of issues raised in the introduction, delving into the evolution of globalization and its impact on workers, employers, labour laws, and states, and to examine how international and transnational law has responded.

In addition to or in conjunction with those structural changes, we have made a great many changes throughout the book in response to the many developments in labour and employment law since 2011. The most high-profile of those developments has been the set of *Charter* decisions mentioned above, which extended the *Charter* protection of freedom of association to include the right to choose an independent bargaining agent and the right to strike, and which relied significantly on international labour standards in doing so. However, developments in a number of other areas have arguably been just as important. We have responded to the emergence of internet platform work and the proliferation of contracting networks that have, in David Weil's evocative phrase, fissured workplace relations; we have provided examples of caselaw and policy discussions grappling with the reach of legal responsibility to workers in these new relationships; and we have deepened the treatment of the rights of dependent contractors at common law and under labour and employment legislation. With the continued decline of collective bargaining coverage in the private sector, there has been a growing emphasis on a range of substantive statutory labour standards, instructively canvassed in Harry Arthurs's *Fairness at Work* 2006 report to the federal government, and more recently in the 2017 final report of the *Changing Workplaces Review* by Justice John Murray and arbitrator Michael Mitchell. We have deepened our treatment of what rules employment standards establish and how they are enforced, and extended our treatments of emerging statutory and common law privacy rights in the workplace, and of recent major developments of contractual good faith obligations at common law. We have also expanded our treatment of the interfaces between the various forums that enforce labour and employment law. These remain complex and perhaps as confused as ever, despite (or because of) the considerable amount of recent jurisprudence that has come in the wake of the *Weber* and *Parry Sound* cases.

Where a case or other source that was included in the eighth edition also appears in this edition, it should not be assumed that the particular excerpt from that source remains the same; many excerpts have been condensed or otherwise changed in an effort to make them fit better with newer material. As in the eighth edition, the notes or other passages we have written ourselves to provide transition between or within excerpts are identified by the use of a sans serif typeface. Although the book continues to be primarily designed for law school courses, a significant proportion of users in recent years have been in other university faculties and in community colleges. We have therefore tried to make the material more digestible for readers without legal training.

As well as spanning most of the country geographically, the Labour Law Casebook Group includes scholars with a wide range of perspectives on labour and employment law, and more generally on the role of law in society. Harry Arthurs was the group's initiator more than four decades ago, and served as its long-time guiding spirit and taskmaster. The seventh edition was the first in which he did not participate, but his seminal influence remains clear throughout. For the seventh and eighth editions, the only founding member still in the group, Bernie Adell, took on the role of coordinating editor. He did an admirable job of ensuring that the casebook gave concise expression to its guiding vision, while adapting to the changing legal landscape. With Bernie's untimely passing in 2014, members of the casebook group asked Kevin Banks and Michael Mac Neil to serve as coordinating editors, and they agreed to do so. As in the past, we have again tried to defy reality by attempting to make the book read as if it were not written by a committee.

The first six editions of this book were published by the Queen's Industrial Relations Centre. The seventh, eighth, and ninth editions have been published by Irwin Law. We are very grateful for the encouragement, support, and patience of Jeff Miller at Irwin Law, for the painstaking work that Lesley Steeve has done in the final polishing of the manuscript, for the proofreading by Queen's Centre for Law in the Contemporary Workplace Research Assistant Heather Bonnell, and for logistical support from the Centre through the work of Natalie Moniz-Henne.

Labour Law Casebook Group
June 2018

Chapter 1: Introduction

1:100   OUR OBJECTIVES

This casebook has two purposes. One is to provide some familiarity with the legal regimes that purport to regulate workplace relations, and with the normative foundations of those regimes. The other, undoubtedly more important in the long run, is to encourage reflection on whether changes in the organization of work, and changes in the capacity of governments to regulate employment relations in Canada and elsewhere, are outstripping labour and employment law as we know it and undermining its effectiveness.

In recent decades, it has become clear that collective bargaining cannot be relied on to provide as much protection as was once expected of it. According to Statistics Canada, as of 2018, 30.4 percent of workers belonged to a union or were covered by a collective agreement, and unionization rates varied significantly by province, from about 25 percent in Alberta to almost 40 percent in Quebec. This means that close to 70 percent of Canadian workers remain beyond the reach of collective bargaining. That is so for historical, social, and economic reasons, and because of the length and difficulty of the legal procedures for setting up collective bargaining relationships. Those factors will become apparent in the chapters that follow. At this point it is enough to note that the factors limiting the spread of collective bargaining through the workforce have proved to be very persistent and not easily remedied by changes in collective bargaining legislation or in the interpretation and application of that legislation by labour relations boards. Even where collective bargaining has been able to penetrate hard-to-organize sectors of the workforce, the balance of economic power in those sectors often remains such that unions cannot negotiate terms that are considered minimally acceptable in our society. In addition, even long-standing collective bargaining relationships commonly fail to come to grips with important but often overlooked issues such as health and safety in the workplace and the persistence of unacceptable forms of employment discrimination.

Canadian labour lawyers, and those in many other countries as well, have long understood labour law as constituted in a certain way. They have had a narrative about the reality of the working world and how the law applies to that world. The narrative has explained and provided a framework for the details of the various labour laws which apply to work, and has made them part of a more or less coherent whole. This received wisdom evolved in the twentieth century against the backdrop of the economic and social organization which prevailed throughout much of that century. Most productive activity was organized through continuing employer-employee relationships: employers (firms) entered into long-term contracts of employment, giving employees security and stability in return for being subordinated to

CHAPTER 1: INTRODUCTION

the control of the firm. The law that applied to employees and employers was understood at its most general level as seeking to achieve justice in the contractual relationship known as employment. This is a familiar, if controversial, picture for lawyers—re-regulating contract power in the name of justice. A problem with that understanding of labour law, however, is that it often overlooked the lack of bargaining power of specific groups of workers (agricultural and domestic workers, for example), some of whom have been the subject of long-standing and tenacious exclusions from legal protection and collective bargaining. More generally, discrimination embedded in how work is organized and remunerated has also undermined the role of labour and employment law in the quest for justice at work.

Changes in technology and in the social and economic organization of productive activity, as well as the increasingly integrated nature of global systems of consumption and production, have altered the reality that labour law seeks to comprehend and address. As we will see, the resulting problems are quite fundamental. Are the basic categories of employment law's subjects ("employee" and "employer") still relevant? Has the existing paradigm in fact brought justice, in any accepted meaning of that term? Are there any new paradigms which might do so? Is the state regulation of labour markets still viable? In short, has labour law lost its grip on what it was meant to take hold of? Can it get a grip?

In this chapter, we will begin with a look at the historical development and sources of labour and employment law. Next, we will explore the controversies, both normative and empirical, which arise out of the received wisdom in this area of law. Then we set out some reflections on the changing world of work and how labour and employment law might respond to it. We end the chapter with an overview of constitutional divisions of powers relating to labour and employment relations.

In planning this casebook, a basic pedagogic decision we had to make was whether to treat the three regimes together, by considering how all three deal with a particular substantive question (for example, the types of workers that are considered to be employees), then moving on to see how all three treat another such question (for example, the principles that govern the termination of employment). This approach would have had the virtue of putting into the same chapter all of the law on a particular substantive question, but at the cost of obscuring the overall structure of each of the three regimes and making it hard to discern their distinctive features. We judged this cost to be too high. Therefore, after the next chapter, in which we consider international and transnational labour and employment law, we will proceed through each of the three regimes in the roughly chronological order in which they are arranged by the received wisdom: the common law first, then collective bargaining law, and finally, direct statutory regulation.

1:200 HISTORICAL DEVELOPMENT AND SOURCES OF LABOUR AND EMPLOYMENT LAW

Labour relations and employment law in Canada are conventionally seen as consisting of three closely interrelated regimes that regulate the employer-employee relationship. Outside of Quebec, the first of those regimes is the common law of employment, which treats employers and employees as free and equal contracting parties in the buying and selling of labour. It is based on the notion of a contract of employment between employer and employee, formed by negotiation between individuals and enforced by the courts, much like the classic commercial contract. The common law of employment is the subject matter of Chapter 3 of this book. In Quebec, which is governed by civil rather than common law, legislation codifies contractual obligations of employers and employees. Quebec's labour and employment law system is distinct in other ways as well. We briefly consider these in Section 1:260, below.

Collective bargaining, which is examined in Chapters 4 to 12, is the second regime. It is based on the realization that the usually inferior economic position of the employee *vis-à-vis* the employer keeps the individual employment contract from being a satisfactory regulatory mechanism. For the negotiation of terms and conditions between individual employers and employees, the collective bargaining regime substitutes collective negotiation between union and employer or between groups of unions and groups of employers. The individual employment contract is replaced by the collective agreement. When adjudication is needed under collective bargaining, it is usually done by specialized administrative tribunals (labour relations boards and arbitration tribunals) rather than by the courts.

Direct statutory regulation is the third regime governing the employer-employee relationship and is the subject of Chapters 13 and 14. Chapter 13 deals with employment standards legislation on such matters as minimum wages, limitation of working time, and health and safety. Legislation of this sort has existed for a long time to protect employees against some of the excesses of the individual contract regime. Until fairly recently, such legislation was seen as having a very subordinate role—as being little more than a stop-gap to provide basic protection for employees who remained outside the reach of collective bargaining or whose bargaining power, even when marshalled collectively, was insufficient to secure minimally acceptable employment terms. Chapter 14 deals with what has been the fastest-growing aspect of labour and employment law in recent years: legislation designed to advance human rights and equality in the workplace.

In recent years, Canadian courts interpreted and applied constitutional freedoms under the *Canadian Charter of Rights and Freedoms* so as to protect worker rights to organize, bargain collectively and strike. Further, courts have increasingly had recourse to international law in interpreting and applying such Charter protections. Constitutional and international law have thus become additional important sources of labour and employment law.

1:210 The Contract of Employment in Canadian Common Law and Quebec Civil Law

Working for wages under a negotiated contract is a relatively recent historical phenomenon, and took several centuries to emerge. In feudal times, production was based on status relations: servants owed duties of fealty to their masters, who had complete control over them. In the eighteenth century, new contract doctrines that facilitated the use of free wage labour emerged. Sir Henry Maine acclaimed the evolution of modern contract as a marvellously progressive development. The following excerpt suggests, however, that the principles of individual freedom and equal treatment embodied in the common law contract of employment were infused with paternalistic elements, and operated within an overarching system of unequal power.

CHAPTER 1: INTRODUCTION

Alan Fox, *History and Heritage: The Social Origins of the British Industrial Relations System* (London: George Allen and Unwin, 1985) at 7, 14–15, and 51

> Strains of both paternalist control and individualism were evident in English society from early times, but attempts towards the former strengthened during the sixteenth and early seventeenth centuries. On labour questions both elements of the paternalist equation—authoritarian control and some profession of solicitude—were visible: the first more obviously than the second. Whether or not the superior was punctilious in discharging his own obligations, inferiors were held to theirs. The *Statute of Artificers of 1563*—little more than an attempt to apply, on a national scale, laws, guild rules and municipal regulations going back to the Middle Ages—applied, among other things, the medieval notion of the universal obligation to work by making labour compulsory when employment was offered.... It also enabled local justices to punish by imprisonment craftsmen who 'left work unfinished'—a convenient counter to strikes. Vagrancy legislation was particularly revealing of the control element. The essence of the whole paternalist strategy as a mode of social control was that everyone must come under the tutelage, guidance, responsibility and control of some person of superior status. 'No man without a lord' was the phrase which expressed this principle whereby all subjects of the realm were bound within a pyramidal structure of reciprocal obligations of protection and obedience. Given such a conception, 'masterless men'—that is, men lacking any personal and reciprocal bonding of submission to a superior—were a threat to social order and discipline, for they were outside that network of responsible dependencies which was deemed to hold society together. They were accordingly legislated against with extreme ferocity. Successive statutes from the sixteenth century decreed, for 'sturdy beggars,' vagrants and men refusing to work, such punishments as whipping, branding, imprisonment and, during one period, slavery and death.... These statutes, which sought both to compel the idle to work and to force them back into the structure of control, remained legally binding until the beginning of the eighteenth century....
>
> [The] emergence of the treatment of labour as a commodity to be bought and sold like any other, though not yet elevated to the status of formally acknowledged proposition in received economic doctrine, became specially apparent in the widespread 'outworking' industries, such as clothmaking, the metal trades, footwear, and others. In these might be found quite sizeable establishments, though large numbers worked in their own homes or in small workshops heavily dependent upon a principal employer or large-scale merchant. This was the outcome of strong economic pressures bursting the bonds of urban monopoly and promoting the growth of so-called 'domestic' industry in the countryside beyond the reach of guild authority....
>
> The growth of individualism had differing impacts upon the dependent lower orders. For those still contained within a traditionally regulated, custom-dominated sector, it might seem only a distant, though potentially disruptive, threat. For those who had come to be directly controlled by it, it could often appear as a disastrous deviation from traditional patterns of personalised control—an abandonment of that diffuse bonding by which, as a reciprocal of their coming under the employer's comprehensive governance, there could be pinned upon him some degree of responsibility for their general welfare.

Even though it might be demonstrated that paternalist obligations were more ignored than honoured, there remains significance in the expectation, which bulked large in popular consciousness, that certain social duties of property would be discharged. Men of spirit reacted collectively with outrage when their masters failed them, appealing to principles of 'time immemorial' as leverage against authority and not invariably failing.

What was never abandoned, of course, was the employer's demand for their obedience in the workplace, where the courts invariably supported him. But it was a feature of the growing free labour market, increasingly pervaded by a sharper and more specific conception of contract, that it should be undermining the old notion of each person being contained within a linked pyramid of tutelage, control and diffuse responsibility. Employers were increasingly disposed to throw off such traditional encumbrances in so far as they had survived—for given the English strand of individualism and the lack of a forceful state apparatus to uphold them they had long been more precarious than in some Continental countries. These beginnings of an abdication by those of superior status of their paternalist social control never ceased to disturb some sections of ruling-class opinion and were to excite vocal alarm in the nineteenth century when large-scale consequences began to become apparent. Long before that, they violated the expectations of substantial groups of artisans who appealed to Parliament, town corporations or justices for protection under paternalist statutes and customs only to have quoted at them the tenets of market individualism. But even for them there was not only loss. Instructed by their masters to become independent, many of them took the lesson to heart and became so—not as isolated individual agents, as intended, but as collectives, culturally and socially as well as economically. In these ways the changing English scene was unintentionally weakening, for some groups of workers, such habituated bonds of obedience and deference as there were. Repudiation by their masters of paternalist responsibility left a larger social space within which they could construct a larger independence of spirit and aspiration....

[T]he repudiation of paternalist obligations was revealing ever more clearly ... that the labour market itself, given the growing disparity of power between employer and individual worker, was an instrument of coercive duress. Of this fact the courts refused to take cognisance. In other spheres of contract the courts had come to accept that 'a contract made by duress or extortion—that is, by actual or threatened violence or imprisonment—could not be upheld.' This was seen as valid morally as well as legally. But ever since 'the devastating analysis by Marx it has been generally realised that this definition of duress as consisting only of threatened violence or imprisonment is impossibly narrow. The formal freedom of the contracting parties can conceal a fundamental inequality of bargaining power which can effectively restrict freedom of choice, even though no physical duress is employed.' The common law courts of the seventeenth century had already made sure, however, that no charge of coercive duress could be read into the dependent position of the individual wage-earner *vis-à-vis* his employer. By concentrating solely on physical coercion the courts made 'no allowance for the various forms of economic coercion which might lead a man "freely" to contract for work for low wages or to pay high prices for food, when loss of life was as much the alternative as it would have been had the agreement been made at the point of a pistol'.... In such ways did the old hierarchical structure of power continue to exert itself within what was increasingly proclaimed an open market order of free and equal agents.

[Reprinted with permission.]

The notion of using the criminal law to enforce individual contracts of employment persisted in early Canadian legislation. The *Master and Servant Act* of the Province of Canada, 1847, c 23, applicable in what was formerly Upper Canada, provided (in section 2) that it was an offence for anyone who had "engaged to perform any service or work" to, among other things, "refuse to go to work," refuse to obey the employer's "lawful commands," or "neglect the service or injure the property of such employer...." In addition (under section 3), "any tavern keeper, boarding-house keeper or other person" who "shall induce or persuade any servants or labourers to confederate for demanding extravagant or high wages" was subject to forfeiture of his licence and to fine or imprisonment (repealed by SC 1877, c 35). See generally Paul Craven, "Canada, 1670–1935" in Douglas Hay & Paul Craven, eds, *Masters, Servants and Magistrates in Britain and the Empire, 1562–1955* (Chapel Hill and London: U of North Carolina Press, 2004) c 5.

Today, the only vestige of this rigorous enforcement of employment contracts is found in section 422 of the *Criminal Code*, which makes any person "who wilfully breaks a contract" guilty of an offence when he or she knows or reasonably ought to know that the breach will "endanger human life ... cause serious bodily injury ... expose valuable property ... to destruction or serious injury," or disrupt a public utility or railway service. A saving provision permits a work stoppage by employees engaged in a collective bargaining dispute, provided that all relevant labour legislation is complied with.

In Quebec, the contract of employment has historically been regulated through the *Civil Code*, and therefore by the legislature, through the codification process. The 1866 Civil Code of Lower Canada included the relationship between master and servant in a small number of separate provisions inspired by the French Civil Code of 1804. The nineteenth-century provisions on the "lease and hire of work" were replaced with the entry into force of the 1994 *Civil Code of Quebec*, which devotes an entire chapter to a more modern approach to employment relations (Chapter VII, "The contract of employment," ss 2085–97, which includes provisions on notice of termination, the renewal of determinate term employment contracts, non-competition clauses, and the effects of the sale and transfer of undertakings on the continuation of the individual employment contract). (For a more detailed analysis of the Quebec's regulatory framework for work and employment, see Section 1:260, below.)

1:220 Collective Bargaining

Donald D Carter et al, *Labour Law in Canada*, 5th ed (Deventer: Kluwer; Markham: Butterworths, 2002) at 48–54

> The beginnings of the Canadian labour movement antedate the establishment of the Canadian Confederation in 1867. As early as 1794 employees of the North West Fur Trading Company went on strike for higher wages. However, only with the introduction of industry at the beginning of the nineteenth century was a true labour movement begun. Journeymen and craftsmen in the few urban areas, particularly in the building, printing, clothing and shoe trades, began to organize for the purpose of mutual aid and

protection and to achieve by united action such objectives as the ten hour day, higher wages and better working conditions. In 1830, for example, the journeymen shoemakers in Toronto went on strike against 'scanty wages ... beds of straw ... and tyrannical oppression.' The union movement grew slowly before 1840 owing to depression and labour surpluses but gained momentum in the years prior to Confederation, a period which was further characterized by the affiliation of Canadian unions with their British and American counterparts. This growth brought unionism into collision with the law.

Union organizers were subject to prosecution for the common law crime of conspiracy. The freedom of workers to associate and to alter conditions of work was restricted by legislation modelled upon the English *Combinations Act* of 1800, such as the Nova Scotia statute of 1816, which prohibited unlawful meetings and combinations for the purpose of regulating wages. Union organizational activities were interdicted as well. In the old Province of Canada, the Master and Servant Act declared the persuasion of labourers 'to confederate for demanding extravagant or high wages' to be unlawful. The common law prohibition against restraint of the course of free trade also affected the civil status of unions. As a result of common law prohibitions, the trade unions were unable to use the courts to enforce any contractual rights they may have achieved, or to protect their property.

In the years following Confederation, labour began to develop a new assertiveness and unity. Local labour councils sprang up in the cities and in 1873, representatives of thirty-five unions formed the first central labour council, the Canadian Labour Union. The C.L.U. resolved to promote union membership, to bring unorganized workers into the C.L.U., and to provide financial assistance to striking unions. Realizing that efforts in these directions would be in vain in view of the existing state of the law, it resolved further to:

> ... agitate such questions as may be for the benefit of the working classes, in order that we may obtain the enactment of such measures by the Dominion or local legislatures as will be beneficial to us, and win the repeal of all oppressive laws now existing.

This organization petered out in 1877, but it must be credited with arousing in government an awareness of the grievances and aspirations of this segment of the electorate.

In the 1870s the federal government intervened to limit the availability of criminal sanctions to inhibit trade unionism. In part, this reflected the evolution of English law, in part, local political realities. Popular working class support for the nine hour day movement in 1872, and public reaction against the arrest of the strike committee of the Toronto Typographical Union on conspiracy charges, moved Parliament to enact legislative reforms. Trade unions were encouraged to register under a new *Trade Unions Act*, and thereby to escape the taint of illegality which the common law had assigned them as 'conspiracies in restraint of trade.' The *Criminal Law Amendment Act* of the same year legalized all strikes except those in which the means employed were calculated to coerce the employer or to prevent him carrying on his business. However, these reforms were not nearly so far reaching in practice as they were held out to be. Whilst the legislation provided that the common law doctrines of criminal conspiracy and restraint of trade did not apply to registered trade unions, the vast majority of trade unions did not register under the federal legislation. Moreover, common law tort doctrines, initially developed in England, were available to restrain trade union activity where the criminal law no longer operated.

However, further amendments in 1875 and 1876 narrowed the definition of criminal conspiracy for the purposes of trade combinations to the performance of acts expressly punishable by law. In 1890, the refusal to work with a workman or for an employer was expressly legalized. By the end of the nineteenth century, the doctrine of criminal conspiracy had ceased to be of practical significance in relation to ordinary labour-management disputes, although it has become, and remains, a central theme in relation to the regulation of business competition.

Another significant development of the 1870s was the definition of the permissible limits of picketing, or 'watching and besetting' as it is called in the *Criminal Code*. From the outset, violent and coercive conduct was outlawed while the peaceful communication of appeals was permitted. However, when the *Criminal Code* of 1892 was enacted, the peaceful picketing proviso was omitted. Until it was restored in 1934, the courts tended to deal severely with all forms of picketing, no matter how innocuous.

If the 1870s were a period of legal reform and symbolic advance for the cause of trade unionism the next two decades were to represent a considerable setback. The 'long depression' (mid-1870s to mid-1890s), and the growth of manufacturing on an industrial scale, combined to create abysmal working conditions and nullify the bargaining power of the individual employee. By 1889, as the report of the Royal Commission on the Relations of Capital and Labour disclosed, employers deemed it their prerogative to discipline workers by administering beatings, by imprisonment and by fines; factories were often unsanitary; employees were required to sign agreements to work on religious holidays; the 60 hour week prevailed; and the penalty for joining a union was dismissal and blacklisting. These practices stimulated the growth of unionism in the worst years of the depression, and led to the establishment of the Trades and Labour Congress of Canada and the more militant Knights of Labour. By the end of the century, then, it was becoming clear that the repeal of criminal prohibitions against unionism did not automatically place labour organizations on an equal footing with employers.

Unions grew as resource development and national transportation were emphasized as key elements in the emerging national economy. Several provincial governments enacted legislation authorizing third party intervention in order to resolve disputes in industries considered essential for the fragile provincial economies—typically, coal mines, railways and public utilities. These provincial experiments in third party arbitration and conciliation were modelled on legislation enacted in other Commonwealth jurisdictions, and proved to be unsuitable for resolving industrial disputes in Canada prior to the turn of the century. For example, much of this legislation became operative only with the consent of both parties—a condition which usually led the stronger party (typically the employer) to refuse consent.

Industrial disputes in the Western provinces which threatened the federal government's policy of western settlement led to the enactment of three federal statutes—the *Conciliation Act* [in 1900], the *Railway Labour Disputes Act* [in 1903], and the *Industrial Disputes Investigation Act, 1907*. The first authorized voluntary third party conciliation of industrial disputes, the second enabled one of the parties to initiate conciliation and investigation of the dispute by an *ad hoc* tripartite board which was required to issue a normative report, and the third, borrowing the main features of its immediate predecessor, added a prohibition against industrial action by the disputants during the *ad hoc* board's investigation. Like its provincial antecedents, the *Industrial Disputes Investigation Act* was directed to industries considered to be essential for the Canadian economy. However, unlike the provincial statutes the federal legislation introduced features of Canadian labour relations policy which continue to exist to date—in particular, the requirement that the parties refrain from using economic sanctions until the conciliation board has exhausted its investigation. Furthermore, this statute clearly signalled a conscious policy choice on the part of the federal government to avoid the use of compulsory and binding interest arbitration to settle labour disputes.

Although weakened by constitutional attack, the *Industrial Disputes Investigation Act* dominated Canadian labour relations policy until the end of the Second World War. In theory the legislation provided for the legitimacy of collective bargaining and the propriety of even-handed government intervention to assist in the establishment of a permanent, bilateral relationship. However, in practice, the *Industrial Disputes Investigation Act* neither forced employers to bargain with trade unions nor established the terms and conditions of employment. Under this legislation collective bargaining and its outcomes were viewed as essentially private matters between employers and employees.

During the first third of the twentieth century the Canadian economy described a cyclical pattern of growth and recession. The strength and size of the Canadian labour movement tended to ebb and flow with the economy. Moreover, the trade union movement was weakened by internal controversies over international versus national unionism, over the issue of social reform versus higher wages as prime union objectives, over organization of unskilled industrial workers versus organization of skilled craftsmen. Rival labour organizations were formed.

Throughout this period Canada experienced a large increase in industrialization. Foreign investment attracted by extensive natural resources provided the capital required to stimulate economic growth while immigration opened up the West, swelled the unskilled labour force and created larger domestic markets for industry. Between 1901 and 1915 capital investment in Canadian manufacturing quadrupled and, as the capital requirements of industrial enterprises expanded, these enterprises became organized increasingly along corporate lines. In these same years, the number of workers employed in manufacturing rose from 340,000 to 600,000. Labour organization grew even more dramatically, especially during World War I, as union membership swelled from 50,000 in 1901 to 175,000 in 1915 to 250,000 in 1919.

The First World War proved to be extremely important for the Canadian trade union movement. Workers exploited their new-found strength (which was attributable to the brief period of full employment caused by the surge in war production) by engaging in industrial action. The number of workers involved in strikes grew from 43,000 in 1912 to 150,000 in 1919. When the war ended workers were determined to ensure that employers did not take advantage of the changed economic conditions to roll back their collective bargaining gains. This resulted in widespread confrontations between workers, employers and public authorities.

The postwar discontent and conflict is symbolized by the Winnipeg General Strike of 1919. The vast majority of the city's workers demanded union recognition, collective bargaining and the maintenance of working conditions obtained during the war. The entire city was brought to a virtual standstill until the federal government intervened to break the strike. Not only did the federal government use its immigration and criminal powers to deport and imprison strike leaders, it called in armed mounted police reinforced by federal troops. In the end the strike was crushed, as was labour militancy across the country. Throughout the 1920s substantial segments of the industrial work force remained unorganized and little improvement in working conditions was achieved. Working conditions deteriorated during the depression of the 1930s as the massive unemployment caused the power of the unions (together with their membership) to decline dramatically. Unprotected by collective organizations, the lives of individual workers and their families grew increasingly desperate.

Throughout these two decades, the federal legislation—the 1907 *Industrial Disputes Investigation Act*—had limited impact. The fundamental problem of industrial relations remained the gross disparity of bargaining power as between employers and employed. Given this disparity, employers could ultimately afford to ignore conciliation efforts, to disregard concessions sought, and occasionally secured, by workers in favourable market conditions, and even to make it impossible for workers to bargain collectively. Workers who joined unions were threatened with discharge and then fired; they were easily replaced from the ranks of the unemployed. When unions were formed, employers simply refused to deal with them. And when strikes occurred, either to secure union recognition or for better conditions, employers were almost always able to replace the strikers and to outlast them in any endurance contest.

Increasingly, in the 1930s, industrial strife began to centre on the very basic issue of whether workers would be prevented from associating together for purposes of collective bargaining—not by legislation as in the early days, but by the harsh economic realities. As this issue was being thrashed out on picket lines and street corners throughout North America, unions and employers both began to resort increasingly to coercive and violent tactics. Added to the debilitating effects of the depression, this industrial warfare was doubly damaging.

In 1935 the US Congress passed the *National Labour Relations Act* (also called the '*Wagner Act*' after its sponsor, Sen. Wagner of New York) which exerted a profound, if somewhat delayed, influence on Canadian labour relations policy. This statute explicitly recognized the right of employees to belong to the trade union of their choice and to participate in the process of collective bargaining through that union. To make effective these rights, the statute forbade certain unfair labour practices commonly practised by employers to thwart unionization and imposed upon employers the duty to bargain in good faith with the union selected by their employees.

These elements of the *Wagner Act* did not come to Canada for almost a decade. In the interim, Canadian unionists continued to struggle against both intransigent governments and employers for the basic right of association and for the fruits which could be won through the practice of collective bargaining. Perhaps the most dramatic episode in this struggle came in 1937 when the Premier of Ontario threatened to use the provincial police to end a strike at the General Motors plant in Oshawa where the company refused to recognize the newly-organized United Automobile Workers. This threat, in turn, precipitated both a cabinet crisis and considerable public protest. In the end, a face-saving compromise emerged in which the union gained some of its demands, but not formal recognition. The incident, however was regarded as a moral victory for industrial unionism and a spur to further organization.

From the mid-1930s onwards there was an attempt by the recently established industrial union movement to organize the semi-skilled workers employed in the new mass production industries on an industrial basis. Between 1935 and 1937 union membership increased from 280,000 to 383,000. Moreover, organized labour began to pressure both the federal and provincial governments for legislative protection of the freedom of association. Between 1937 and 1939 a number of provinces enacted statutes which announced the basic right of association and attempted to protect employees from employer retaliation on the basis of trade union membership. In 1939 the federal government followed suit by amending the *Criminal Code* to prohibit discrimination or discharge of workers because of their union membership. However, these statutes proved ineffective as they were enforceable only through criminal prosecution. Both the federal and provincial enactments deviated from the *Wagner Act* in that they failed to provide an administrative tribunal whose function it was to police the provisions of the statute.

The Second World War was a period of rapid industrialization and trade union growth. Trade union membership almost doubled from 362,000 in 1940 to 711,000 in 1945, as the labour shortage and general economic recovery proved conducive to trade union organization. Initially the federal government responded to the increased demand for legislative recognition of trade unions and collective bargaining by issuing exhortary regulations declaring the freedom of association and extolling the benefits of collective bargaining. However, employers refused to bargain with trade unions unless compelled to do so by the union's economic sanctions. As the war continued the failure of the federal government to provide legislative backing for union representation and collective bargaining led to repeated outbursts of industrial unrest. In 1943 the crisis reached its peak as the steel industry was shut down by a nation-wide walkout and one out of every three workers was on strike.

The need to move to an American-style statute became increasingly obvious. In 1943, Ontario became the first jurisdiction to adopt a fully-fledged collective bargaining statute, although its enforcement was entrusted to the Ontario Labour Court (a division of the High Court of Justice), rather than to an administrative board. Experience under the Ontario statute was short-lived, as the federal government pre-empted the field of collective bargaining in 1944 by enacting P.C. 1003, regulations made under the *War Measures Act*, which covered virtually all significant industry and economic activity. The federal regulations welded features of the *Wagner Act* to the long-established Canadian policy of third party conciliation and investigation during a compulsory cooling off period. In particular, P.C. 1003 established a representative tribunal (the National War Labour Relations Board) to administer a regime of collective bargaining which included bargaining unit determination and certification, unfair labour practices and a ban on industrial action during the currency of a collective bargaining agreement. Following the repeal of the federal wartime regulations in 1948, virtually all provinces (and the federal government) adopted *Wagner-style* labour relations statutes, covering all employees in the private sector.
[© Reprinted with permission from Kluwer Law International.]

For a comparison of regimes across the country, see Mark Thompson, Joseph B Rose, & Anthony E Smith, eds, *Beyond the National Divide: Regional Dimensions of Industrial Relations* (Montreal-Kingston: McGill-Queen's University Press, 2003).

1:230 Direct Statutory Regulation

Statutory frameworks have been implemented at the provincial and federal levels to establish minimum employment standards and norms governing occupational health and safety and human rights in the workplace. These areas of regulation will be dealt with in some detail in Chapters 13 and 14 of this book. Their evolution has been fairly similar across the country, although some significant differences do exist. In Quebec in particular, minimum standards legislation has been more extensively used to regulate the results of collective bargaining—for example, through the prohibition of psychological harassment in the workplace, the prohibition of mandatory retirement at a certain age, and the imposition of restrictions on the negotiation of two-tier clauses, which would deprive new hires of the benefit of previously-bargained working conditions.

1:231 Employment Standards Legislation

Employment standards legislation (also commonly referred to as "labour standards" legislation) establishes minimum terms and conditions of employment with respect to wage levels, modes of payment, access to leaves (paid and unpaid) and vacation, minimum rest periods, when premium "overtime" rates must be paid for hours worked above daily or weekly thresholds, and a range of other issues. The following excerpt outlines the origins, aims and regulatory methods of such legislation, providing examples from Part III of the *Canada Labour Code*, which sets employment standards in the federal jurisdiction. (For a discussion of the division between federal and provincial jurisdiction, see Part 1:500 below.)

Federal Labour Standards Review Commission, *Fairness at Work: Labour Standards for the 21st Century* (Gatineau, QC: Department of Human Resources and Skills Development, 2006) at 5–6

> "Labour standards" is not a precise term. In their inception in the United Kingdom, early in the Industrial Revolution, labour standards reflected widespread public sentiment, given force by legislation, that no employer should be allowed to impose, and no worker should be obliged to endure, working conditions that fell below the standard that a decent society would tolerate. The decent societies of the time were particularly concerned with the plight of women and child workers; later they became concerned with adult male workers as well. They were initially concerned with safety issues and hours of work; they ultimately became concerned with wages, leaves, vacations and other benefits.
>
> As the provisions of Part III suggest, the concerns of decent societies continually evolve. Part III is still concerned with hours of work, minimum wages, statutory holidays and annual vacations. But it now deals as well with statutory leaves (maternity, parental, compassionate care, bereavement and sick leave), with the termination of employment (mass terminations, termination of injured workers or workers whose pay has been garnisheed, unjust dismissal) and, to a limited extent, with human rights in the work-place (pay equity, sexual harassment).

The development of early labour standards legislation also involved a series of experiments in public administration. Initially, compliance was entrusted to employers themselves, and to a body of "visitors", often clergymen, with no legal powers. However, this approach permitted unscrupulous employers to compete against those who were more enlightened by ignoring the statutory requirements, thus creating pressures for all employers to do the same. It soon became clear that standards would have to be enforced across the board if they were to be effective. Accordingly, factory and mine "inspectors" were given the power to enter premises, to require the production of records, to compel the adoption of safe equipment and detailed working rules, to determine whether violations had occurred, to make remedial and stop-work orders, to impose fines, and to conduct prosecutions of serious offences. As appears below, the need for further experiments with techniques for securing compliance continues.

Finally, Part III—like most such legislation—exhibits symptoms of inner turmoil. It requires that legislated labour standards "apply notwithstanding any other law or any custom, contract or arrangement." However, Part III specifically allows derogation from some provisions under emergency conditions and from others for good reasons related to the operational realities of particular enterprises or industries ("custom"). When derogation is permitted, it usually requires the agreement of individual workers or their union or some other collective expression of employee wishes ("contract"); however, it sometimes requires ministerial approval in the form of regulations or permits ("arrangement"). And of course deviations from the statutory terms are freely permitted so long as they are enhancements or improvements rather than derogations. In fact, many enhancements—paid vacations or maternity leave, for example—begin life as enlightened management policies or pioneering provisions in collective agreements, and then are enacted into law as "labour standards" as they become more commonplace.

This suggests that although the state is formally committed to decent standards for all workers, it also defers—tacitly or explicitly—to the tendency of employers to apply the standards that they deem practical or desirable in particular sectors and circumstances. In short, labour standards often turn out to be more flexible in practice than they seem in principle.

1:232   Human Rights Codes

Kevin Banks, Roberta Nunin, & Adriana Topo, "The Lasting Influence of Legal Origins: Workplace Discrimination, Social Inclusion and the Law in Canada, the United States and the European Union" in Matthew Finkin & G Mundlak, eds, *Comparative Labor Law* (Cheltenham, UK: Edward Elgar Publishing, 2015) 220 at 224

Canadian provinces began to enact comprehensive statutes, commonly referred to as 'human rights codes' around the same time as civil rights struggles in the U.S. bore fruit in the Civil Rights Act. Between the early 1960s and the mid 1970s all Canadian jurisdictions enacted such laws. One of the first to do so was Ontario .... Ontario's legislation and the debates surrounding it were influential elsewhere in Canada. The movement for legal protection against discrimination in Ontario was led by a loose coalition of religious, labour, and ethnic community organizations. At the centre of this movement were Jewish organizations aiming to change the pervasive anti-semitic practices of Post

World War II Canadian society. Jewish leaders saw the protection of democracy and the elimination of discrimination against religious and racial minorities as inextricably linked. Many saw the pursuit of these aims as essential to ensuring that Canadian society would not again react with indifference to the persecution of Jews at home or abroad. They also saw that the project of eliminating anti-semitism entailed seeking greater acceptance of all religious, racial and ethnic minority rights. Labour leaders joined the cause in part because they viewed the elimination of racial, religious and ethnic prejudice as making for a more egalitarian society in which the aims of the labour movement would find a better reception in local and national politics. Black-white race relations were also an important aspect of the animating concerns of Ontario reformers and legislators. Racial segregation not that different from that found in the southern U.S. was practiced in some places in Ontario. But it is fair to say that such concerns were intermingled with the struggle for religious and ethnic equality and with efforts to construct what would later become known as a 'multicultural' society, rather than being overriding as they were in the U.S. The Canadian post-World War II human rights project, though sharing important common threads with its U.S. counterpart, has a distinct character, one which eventually favoured the development of a very different theory of the purposes of anti-discrimination law, and thus of the concept of discrimination itself. [Reproduced with permission of the Licensor through PLSclear.]

1:233 Occupational Safety and Health Legislation

The compensation of workers who are personally injured in the course of their employment was one of the very first issues addressed by labour legislation in Canada. Today, all provinces have a statute providing for a compensation system under which injured employees receive compensation without having to establish that their employer or fellow employees are at fault. This no-fault system is based on the employer's collective liability. Employers covered by the statutes are grouped by industry, and each employer pays a contribution to the system determined by the collective accident experience of the particular group of industries the employer belongs to. The compensation available generally includes lump sum payments to cover non-economic loss and pensions in the case of partial or total permanent impairment. Most provincial regimes also provide for the reinstatement of the injured employee in their former job when their functional abilities allow it. In return, the injured employee is deprived of their right to sue the employer for damages in court. In each province, an administrative agency, usually a workers' compensation board, administers the scheme, calculates the contribution each employer has to pay to the system, and determines what compensation each injured employee is entitled to.

This compensation system has, however, done little to prevent work injuries or illnesses from happening. Preventive mechanisms were traditionally left to the private parties and collective bargaining, whereas specific statutes imposed penalties on breaching standards externally set for dealing with specified pieces of equipment or dangerous working conditions. It was not until the last decades of the twentieth century that more comprehensive health and safety legislation was enacted in Canada. Today, in all jurisdictions, an occupational health and safety act or similar legislation, typical of which is Part II of the *Canada Labour Code*, establishes a set of rights and obligations on both employers and employees to achieve a certain degree of safety in the workplace. Thus, the employer is made responsible for protecting the health and ensuring the safety of its employees. This general duty relates to more detailed obligations and requirements stemming from a web of regulations on specific hazards or types of work issued by the government, usually following the recommendations of a health and safety agency. The agency is also given the authority, with the aid of an inspectorate, to enforce the applicable safety standards. This generally includes consulting with the employer, the employees and their representatives; performing investigations and inspections; making recommendations; instituting prosecutions for violation of the act; and, in case of immediate danger, totally or partially shutting down the production process or the workplace.

Occupational health and safety legislation in Canada generally provides employees with three basic rights. The first is the right to be informed of known or foreseeable safety hazards in the workplace and to be provided with the proper information and instruction to protect one's safety and physical well-being. Being consulted with and participating in identifying and correcting job-related health and safety issues constitutes the second right. This is usually done through worker health and safety representatives or joint health and safety committees. For instance, Part II of the *Canada Labour Code* requires that such a committee be established in workplaces where there are twenty employees or more, and that a health and safety representative selected by employees must be appointed in workplaces with fewer employees. Finally, employees are given the right to refuse to perform work that they honestly and reasonably believe is dangerous to them. Accordingly, they are protected against any disciplinary or retaliatory action for a genuine and reasonable refusal of work. In some jurisdictions, more specific rights are also given to employees, such as the right to cease to perform a job that the *Canada Labour Code* confers to an employee who is pregnant or nursing, if that employee believes that her job poses a risk to her health or to that of the fetus or child.

1:234 Privacy Legislation

More than ever before, the protection of employees' privacy has become a major concern in Canada. Due to advances in information technology, not only can almost every action of an employee be easily tracked by the employer through a camera, a computer, a cellphone, or another surveillance device, but personal and sensitive information is readily available simply by consulting an employee's personal website or Facebook page. This raises the pressing and delicate question of the proper balance to be achieved between the employer's right to manage its employees and to have access to the relevant personal information about them, and employees' rights to privacy.

Despite its utmost importance, there is no single source of workplace privacy law in Canada. Rather, the matter is regulated through myriad overlapping provincial and federal laws, mainly aimed at restricting the processing and the sharing of personal information that a government body or a private employer is allowed to collect. For instance, at the federal level, the *Privacy Act*, RSC 1985, c P-21, regulates the processing of personal information by government bodies, including public sector employers, and grants individuals the right to challenge the record-keeping practices of these organizations. Similarly, the *Personal Information Protection and Electronic Documents Act* (PIPEDA), SC 2000, c 5, requires that private sector organizations in the federal domain only collect, use, or disclose personal information for purposes that a reasonable person would consider appropriate in the circumstances. While all Canadian provinces have legislated a privacy protection policy for the personal information detained by government agencies, only Alberta, British Columbia, and Quebec have passed legislation similar to PIPEDA.

In addition to these statutory developments, it is worth mentioning that Canadian common law has recently evolved in such a way that it could be relied upon by employees to protect their privacy at work. These developments are briefly considered in Chapter 14. Given its civil law tradition, Quebec has a different stance on the question since both its *Civil Code* and its *Charter of Human Rights and Freedoms* expressly state that every person has a right to the respect of his or her privacy (or for his or her private life). Being considered as fundamental, this right is not only inalienable but also applies in the workplace. Furthermore, section 2858 of the *Civil Code*, which provides that "courts shall ... reject any evidence obtained under such circumstances that fundamental rights and freedoms are violated and whose use would tend to bring the administration of justice into disrepute," has greatly helped privacy rights at work to be respected.

Finally, it must be pointed out that a right to privacy has been drawn from the *Canadian Charter of Rights and Freedoms*, which states, in section 8 that "everyone has the right to be secure against unreasonable search or seizure." However, given that the protection of the *Charter* applies to government action, only public sector employees may directly claim its protection.

1:240 The *Canadian Charter of Rights and Freedoms*

The *Canadian Charter of Rights and Freedoms* was included in the Canadian Constitution in 1982 when Canada, a former British dominion, repatriated its constitution so that it would henceforth come under Canadian jurisdiction. The *Charter* guarantees several fundamental rights and freedoms to everyone, including the freedom of expression and association, as well as the equality of every individual before and under the law, without discrimination based on individual factors such as sex, colour, religion, or other similar factors. These fundamental rights and freedoms are guaranteed "subject only to such reasonable limits prescribed by law as can be demonstrably justified in a free and democratic society."

As part of the Constitution, the *Charter* applies only to the state and its agencies, and no private employer is directly subject to its provisions. Except where the state acts as employer, the Constitution is not a source of law operating directly upon the parties like the common law, labour relations statutes, or labour standards legislation. Constitutional rules apply to the state and their primary role is to delimit and organize legislative and governmental powers.

The Constitution has nonetheless become a prominent source of labour and employment law. *Charter* cases in labour and employment law have mostly involved the rubrics of freedom of association under section 2(d); freedom of expression under section 2(b); and the right to equality before and under the law under section 15(1). The nature and impact of *Charter* jurisprudence on labour and employment law will be referred to in some detail in several chapters of this book. Suffice it here to mention that the Supreme Court set aside the legal rules that traditionally severely restricted or prohibited secondary boycotts and picketing in Canada since they were considered to be an unjustified limitation on unions' freedom of expression (see *United Food and Commerce Workers, Local 1518 v Kmart Canada Ltd*, [1999] 2 SCR 1083; *Allsco Building Products Ltd v United Food and Commerce Workers, Local 1288P*, [1999]

2 SCR 1136; and *Retail, Wholesale and Department Store Union, Local 558 v Pepsi-Cola Canada Beverages (West) Ltd*, [2002] 1 SCR 156). Similarly, labour unions' freedom of expression was invoked to shield some union control over the crossing of a picket line against the provisions of the *Personal Information Protection Act* of Alberta (*Alberta (Information and Privacy Commissioner) v United Food and Commercial Workers, Local 401*, 2013 SCC 62, [2013] 3 SCR 733). In addition, as more extensively considered in Chapter 12 of this book, the jurisprudence on the relation between freedom of association and collective bargaining has had a profound effect on labour law in Canada. In its 1987 trilogy, the Supreme Court of Canada first held that the right to bargain collectively and the right to strike were not implicitly included in the freedom of association protected by section 2(d) of the *Charter*. Adopting a narrow definition of freedom of association, the Court stated that neither collective bargaining with respect to working conditions nor the right to strike were fundamental rights in Canada (*Reference Re Public Service Employee Relations Act (Alberta)*, [1987] 1 SCR 313; *PSAC v Canada*, [1987] 1 SCR 424; *RWDSU v Saskatchewan*, [1987] 1 SCR 460). In 2007, the Supreme Court did an about-face, holding that freedom of association included the right to collective bargaining. In *Health Services and Support—Facilities Subsector Bargaining Assn v British Columbia*, [2007] 2 SCR 391, the Court invalidated legislation from British Columbia that, for the purpose of addressing the budgetary difficulties of the provincial health system, rendered void any provisions of collective agreements applicable to health sector workers relating to certain sensitive working conditions and prohibiting negotiation on these issues. This time the Court decreed that the freedom of association guaranteed by the *Charter* protects the capacity of members of labour unions to engage in collective bargaining on fundamental issues. In concrete terms, it means that employees have the right, without any substantial interference, to unite, to present demands to their employer collectively, and to engage in discussions in an attempt to achieve workplace-related goals. The issue of the right to strike, which the Court had expressly left open in 2007, was addressed in 2015. In *Saskatchewan Federation of Labour v Saskatchewan*, 2015 SCC 4, the Supreme Court, once again overturning its 1987 precedent, declared that the right to strike constituted an essential and indispensable component of a meaningful process of collective bargaining and needed to be constitutionalized. Therefore, any statutory limit on the right to strike that substantially interferes with collective bargaining represents a violation of the freedom of association recognized in section 2(d) of the *Charter*.

1:250   International Law

The Supreme Court of Canada has drawn upon international law to determine the meaning of rights and freedoms protected in Canada's *Charter*. The Court has repeatedly reaffirmed that it seeks to "ensure consistency between its interpretation of the *Charter*, on the one hand, and Canada's international obligations and the relevant principles of international law, on the other," and that "the *Charter* should be presumed to provide at least as great a level of protection as is found in the international human rights documents that Canada has ratified." See, for example, *Saskatchewan Federation of Labour v Saskatchewan*, 2015 SCC 4 at para 64. The influence of international law on the Court's approach to freedom of association is made evident in Chapter 11. In the field of labour and employment law, the relevant international human rights documents include the *International Covenant on Civil and Political Rights* (999

UNTS 171), the *International Covenant on Economic Social and Cultural Rights* (993 UNTS 3), the *Charter of the Organization of American States* (Can TS 1990, No 23), and the Constitution and Conventions of the International Labour Organization, overviewed immediately below. Canada's international legal obligations will receive more detailed treatment in Chapter 2.

Kevin Banks, "The Role and Promise of International Law in Canada's New Labour Law Constitutionalism" (2012) 16:2 *Canadian Labour & Employment Law Journal* 233 at 253–57

> [T]here are four ... sources [which define Canada's international commitments]. The first source is the text of the international treaties ratified by Canada. They are binding on Canada under international law, and they include ratified [International Labour Organization] (ILO) conventions and the ILO Constitution. The second source is the ILO's landmark *1998 Declaration on Fundamental Principles and Rights at Work*, interpreting member state obligations under the ILO Constitution. Such interpretive declarations can be read as expressions of the intent of the parties to a treaty, and therefore as providing authoritative guidance on the meaning of the treaty. The *1998 Declaration* offers at least a persuasive and quite likely a binding interpretation of Canada's obligations under the ILO Constitution.
>
> The third and fourth sources are the accumulated decisions of the two committees established by the ILO to advise its Governing Body and Conference, respectively, on the application of ILO conventions and constitutional principles: the Committee on Freedom of Association (the CFA) and the Committee of Experts on the Application of Conventions and Recommendations (the Committee of Experts). Neither of these committees is empowered under the ILO Constitution to issue legally binding decisions, but they have nonetheless emerged as the primary vehicles for elaborating on the meaning of ILO conventions on freedom of association.
>
> The better known of the two committees is the CFA, which is a tripartite body with government, worker and employer representatives and an independent chair. It examines complaints received directly from worker and employer representatives (mainly worker representatives) around the world. Since its establishment in 1951, the CFA has made recommendations to the Governing Body on more than 2,800 complaints, and it has built up a detailed and coherent set of principles on freedom of association and collective bargaining under the ILO Constitution and under ILO conventions, recommendations and resolutions. The CFA's persuasive authority is based on its specialized, impartial, tripartite and experienced composition, and on the balance achieved through its consensus-based decision-making process.
>
> The other committee, the Committee of Experts, submits comments to the Conference of the ILO on reports provided by member states regarding measures taken by those states to implement ratified conventions. The Committee of Experts consists of about 20 distinguished jurists, including retired and active judges and legal academics. Each year it issues a general survey of its comments on the application of conventions in a particular subject area. It has issued six general surveys on freedom of association and the right to bargain collectively, the last in 1994. Like the CFA, the Committee of Experts

owes its persuasive authority to its impartiality and specialization, but its expertise is more juridical than that of the CFA.

A remarkable convergence in how the Committee of Experts and the CFA interpret freedom of association and the right to bargain collectively can be seen by comparing the Committee of Experts' 1994 *General Survey* with the CFA's *Digest of Decisions*. The work of each committee informs that of the other; the CFA often cites the Committee of Experts' general surveys, and the Committee of Experts has referred to the accumulated principles of the CFA as "a veritable international law on freedom of association." The juridical authority of the Committee of Experts and the more practical, consensus-based authority of the CFA have thus come to buttress each other.

Nonetheless, one must proceed with some caution in drawing guidance from the jurisprudence of either committee .... [T]he CFA, again consistent with its promotional mandate, will often seek to conciliate disputes. In so doing, it may issue hortatory declarations based not on legal obligations but on ILO recommendations or on what it sees as good practice in light of the experience of its members. For this reason, in reading CFA reports and digests, it is again important to pay close attention to whether the relevant ratified convention imposes obligations which relate to the CFA principle in question. Finally, as both committees have only persuasive (and not binding) authority, their jurisprudence should yield where the reasoning behind it is not convincing in the context in which it is sought to be applied.

[Originally published in (2012) 16:2 CLEJ 233. Reproduced with the permission of Lancaster House.]

1:260   The Institutional Distinctiveness of Quebec

Jacques Belanger & Gilles Trudeau, "The Institutional Specificity of Quebec in the Context of Globalization" (2009–10) 15:1 *Canadian Labour & Employment Law Journal* 49 at 56–63

> Quebec's regulatory framework for work and employment is hybrid in nature.... This hybridity is essentially due to the interface between French-based civil law, which governs individual employment relations, and the American and Canadian model of collective labour relations....
>
> (a) Individual Employment Relations and Civil Law
> The employment relationship is usually formed by the negotiation of a contract on an individual basis between the worker and the employer. The relevant legal rules come mainly from the general law of contract, from which the legislator can depart in order to establish rules for particular situations. In Quebec, the law of general application to private matters (that is, relations between individuals, including contractual relations) derives from the *Civil Code of Quebec*. In contrast, in the other Canadian provinces and in the United States, the general law of contract is found in the common law, which is of English origin. This difference has deep historical roots. In the *Quebec Act* of 1774, the British Parliament decreed that in private matters, the French civil law, as it existed in New France before the Conquest, would apply thereafter in Quebec. That law was systematized and codified in 1866 in the *Civil Code of Lower Canada*, the form and much

of the content of which were drawn from the French *Civil Code* that Napoleonic France had adopted some 60 years earlier. In contrast, the English common law was implanted in the rest of the British colonies in North America, including those that subsequently rebelled to form the United States of America. The 1866 *Code* was replaced in 1994 by the *Civil Code of Quebec*, which is based on the same civil law tradition.

It is interesting to observe that although the general civil law rules which apply today to the employment relationship in France and Quebec share common legal roots and also (by and large) common ideological roots in nineteenth-century liberalism, they differ markedly. The very different sociopolitical contexts in which those rules have evolved in the two states clearly appear to have had a structural effect on their content, in a way that transcends the similarities in the underlying civil law system. Furthermore, the general rules of contract law which govern the employment relationship are roughly the same in Quebec and in the rest of Canada but differ significantly from those in the United States, despite the fact that the U.S. shares the English common law tradition with the rest of Canada.

It must also be pointed out that Quebec is not solely a civil law state. Its entire body of public law — i.e., the law on the organization of the state and its relations with its citizens — has been based on the English common law ever since the Royal Proclamation of 1763. Moreover, the Quebec judicial system is based on the British model, as is the judicial system in Canada as a whole. The organization, jurisdiction and procedures of the Quebec courts, as well as the characteristics of judicial decision-making in Quebec, are similar to those in the British system and substantially different from the French model. Although Quebec labour law in general is more a part of private than of public law, its content and operation have been coloured by close proximity to the common law.

Nevertheless, the fact that the general rules underlying Quebec's employment law are based mainly in the civil law tradition is not without consequence. The rule of law is given effect to in different ways in the civil law and in the common law. In the civil law, the law of general application is enacted by the legislator and written down in a code — a body of rules structured in accordance with a logical and predetermined classification. Those rules, which are stated in general terms and are meant to apply to all situations, are liberally interpreted by the courts. Great deference is shown to legislation as a source of law, because it represents the sovereign will of a democratically elected branch of government. In contrast, in the common law tradition, the rules forming the law of general application are not defined and systematized in advance by the legislator, but are inferred from case law — the body of judicial decisions known as precedent. Judges are bound to follow and apply existing case law, to ensure stability and continuity in the legal system.

(b) Labour Legislation, Collective Labour Relations and the Hybrid Quebec System

At least with regard to collective labour relations, Quebec's institutional specificity in the area of labour and employment is mainly due to the blending of a law of general application grounded in the civil law tradition and a body of labour legislation largely based on the American model. Like many industrialized countries, however, Quebec has designed its regulatory framework on employment to give a crucial role to the protection of freedom of association and collective bargaining. The Quebec law on workers' collective action, which dates back to the early years of industrialization, has evolved along the same lines as elsewhere in the western world. Such action was once considered illegal, before being decriminalized and then tolerated. In the early twentieth century, Quebec and federal legislators, who were concerned to maintain labour peace, provided mechanisms for conflict resolution, such as mediation or arbitration, and in some cases, imposed those mechanisms before the parties to collective bargaining could resort to economic pressure tactics.

Quebec's policy on collective labour relations was radically changed by the adoption in 1944 of the *Labour Relations Act*. Quebec thus imitated some other Canadian provinces and, in particular, the federal government, which in the same year adopted Order in-Council PC 1003 under the *War Measures Act*. From then on, the Canadian and Quebec governments, inspired by the American *Wagner Act* of 1935, promoted the collective negotiation of working conditions as their main employment relations policy. The main characteristics of the legal regime of collective bargaining were derived from the industrial relations system developed in the United States, which by international standards is unique. Considerable economic integration had already been achieved between the United States and Canada, and the fact that much of the Canadian labour movement was made up of locals of major American trade unions favoured the transposition of the American model to Canadian and Quebec soil. As a result, although Quebec's law of general application in private matters continued to be based in the civil law, Quebec emulated the rest of Canada and the United States in its collective labour law.

The principal features of the model established by the *Labour Relations Act* still prevail today with regard to collective Labour relations in Quebec. That Act was reformulated into the *Labour Code* in 1964, and although it has often been amended since then, it has maintained its core foundations. It is essentially limited to protecting freedom of association, to specifying procedures for collective bargaining, and to dealing with the legal effects of collective agreements. For groups of workers who choose to invoke the *Labour Code*, it replaces the law of general application and the individual contract of employment, and it gives precedence to the terms and conditions embodied in the collective agreement.

However, the Quebec system of collective labour relations is distinguished somewhat from its counterparts in other Canadian provinces by the fact that it bears the marks of a higher degree of state intervention. This can be shown by a number of specific examples. Counting the number of workers who have joined a union remains the usual method of assessing its representative status in Quebec; the secret ballot is used much less than elsewhere in Canada. As soon as a union is certified as the bargaining agent in Quebec, it automatically benefits from compulsory dues check-off. In the event of a deadlock in the negotiation of a first collective agreement after certification, either party can ask the Minister of Labour to appoint an arbitrator who, if he or she deems it appropriate, can determine the content of the collective agreement and impose it on the parties for a maximum of three years. During a legal strike, a Quebec employer can under no circumstances have the strikers' work done by any other persons except managers at the establishment affected by the strike. A system of juridical extension of the scope of a collective agreement—the decree system—still exists in Quebec alongside the *Labour Code*, although its impact is now marginal. Furthermore, the Quebec construction industry is subject to a specialized and highly centralized labour relations regime, which requires all employees in the industry to join one of a number of employee associations declared to be representative.

In addition to the general law grounded in the *Civil Code of Quebec* and the legislation on collective labour relations, the regulatory framework of the employment relationship also includes a number of statutes regulating working conditions or imposing other standards on the parties to employment contracts and collective agreements. Here again, Quebec is distinguished from the United States and from English Canada by the fact that, in line with the continental European tradition, its employment legislation is broader, more varied and more interventionist. In its early form, in the late nineteenth century, the Quebec legislation sought only to curb the worst abuses of capitalism, particularly in relation to health and safety and the protection of women and children. In these areas, Quebec relied mainly on the British experience, even though its first legislative incursions on working conditions drew on broader European developments. Later on, during the early decades of the twentieth century, Quebec statutes imposed a range of minimum labour standards, especially with respect to wages, hours of work and annual leave, as a response to the commitments made by Canada to the International Labour Organization.

Only in the last three decades has the Quebec legislature, like many others in the western world, gone beyond the mere imposition of minimum labour standards and intervened more intensively in the direct determination of working conditions. Among the areas addressed in this more recent wave of legislation are equal opportunities and employment equity, occupational health and safety, workforce training, job security and the use of the French language at work. Clearly, collective bargaining no longer holds the privileged position that it once held in the implementation of state policies on labour and employment.

Although the content of labour standards legislation has at times been based on foreign experience, it has much that is truly specific to Quebec. For example, in addition to being able to challenge a dismissal on grounds that are expressly prohibited by law, including those set out in human rights legislation, any employee (other than a high-level manager) with two or more years of service in the same enterprise can challenge a dismissal for the absence of good and sufficient cause. That right is enforceable in an adjudicative forum which is very similar to grievance arbitration, and a remedy of reinstatement with full compensation for lost wages is available. It should be noted that the government agency which administers this process provides the employee with free legal representation before the adjudicative body. Moreover, Quebec's *Act respecting labour standards* now requires the employer—and this is a first for North America—to provide a work environment free from psychological harassment. Parental leave is paid for by the public, compulsory Quebec parental insurance plan, which is funded through employee and employer contributions. This plan ensures partial remuneration for up to 18 weeks of maternity leave and 32 weeks of parental leave. Finally, another Quebec innovation, the *Act to foster the development of manpower training*, requires regulated employers to devote one percent of their payroll to workforce training, either for their own employees or through contribution to a national fund set up for this purpose.

It is also important to note the deep penetration of fundamental human rights into the workplace and into the law that governs it. This development has been part of a broader trend toward the international recognition of human rights, and Quebec has been in the forefront of this trend, in particular through its *Charter of human rights and freedoms,* passed in 1975. The integration of human rights law has led to a marked evolution in Quebec labour law, and has reinforced its specificity.

[Originally published in (2009–10) 15:1 CLEJ 49. Reproduced with the permission of Lancaster House.]

The socio-historical context adds additional layers of difference to the regulation of industrial relations law in Quebec. The Quebec system of legislative decrees, adopted in 1934, reflected the Roman Catholic influence on continental European approaches to labour regulation. Vestiges of that system remain today in the *Collective Agreement Decrees Act,* RLRQ, c D-2. The early links between the sovereignty movement, which encompassed political parties and trade unions, translated into electoral success in the 1970s and the adoption of several important pieces of legislation. The diversity within the union movement in Quebec, and the comparatively high rate of unionization, are in part attributable to greater labour militancy and to public acceptance of principles of social justice. For a history of unionism in Quebec, see Jacques Rouillard, *Le syndicalisme québécois : deux siècles d'histoire* (Montreal: Boréal, 2004). On the evolution of the legal regulation of the contract of employment, and of labour law more generally in Quebec, see Marie-France Bich, "Droit du travail québécois: Genèse et génération" in H Patrick Glenn, ed, *Droit québécois et droit français: Communauté, autonomie, concordance* (Cowansville: Yvon Blais, 1993) 515, and Pierre Verge, Gilles Trudeau, & Guylaine Vallée, *Le Droit du travail par ses sources* (Montreal: Thémis, 2006).

1:300 VALUES AND MARKET ORDERING

As some of the prior readings suggest, labour law emerges in response to economic and political pressures. Those pressures change over time, and so do the discourses used to justify particular responses.

The common law is rooted in the notion of contract, private ordering, and the values that underlie the market—self-reliance, individualism, liberty for atomistic individuals, and the separation of the private and public spheres. Some of the values that underlie collective bargaining are the same as those that underlie the common law contract of employment, but some are not. Collective bargaining departs from the individualistic principles of the market insofar as it allows for concerted action by employees with a view to both a fairer market process and a fairer distribution of the fruits of the market. Nevertheless, collective bargaining is above all a procedural mechanism. Although it introduces a new collective party on the employee side and sometimes on the employer side as well, it ultimately relies on the market to set terms and conditions of employment. In contrast, statutory regulation involves direct governmental intervention in the market/contract process. It is obvious that the appropriate scope and interrelationship of the common law, collective bargaining, and statutory regimes cannot be discussed without asking basic questions about such concepts as liberty and equality, fairness and efficiency.

Help in resolving some of the basic issues in labour and employment law and labour relations can be found by seeking answers to empirical questions, such as the effect of collective bargaining on incomes and the impact of minimum wage legislation. These empirical questions can only be fully answered if we go beyond the language of the legislation or the intricacies of legal doctrine and look to the law in action. However, many of the most important issues cannot be resolved by empirical methods—by collecting more facts—because at a basic level they are ethical or political issues. The earlier readings are enough to indicate that different actors use different theoretical, ideological, and methodological tools in approaching those issues—and the readings that follow will only reinforce that indication. People have different ways of looking at the world, proceed from different premises, and rely on different types of information.

What is to be done? Are we left with unprincipled venting of our intuitions? How are choices to be made? These fundamental questions of moral and political choice arise in many areas of legal and social policy. All we can do is try to advance our understanding of those questions in the context at hand—that of labour and employment law.

The materials that follow attempt to do this in several ways. First, bringing to light some of the claims—factual and normative—made about the employment relationship and its regulation can perhaps clarify our own thinking. Second, understanding those claims may help us understand what is happening in the most controversial areas of Canadian labour and employment law, where debate on fundamental issues inevitably percolates to the surface and influences legislative and adjudicative events. Third, looking at the materials that follow against the historical backdrop sketched out previously helps us realize that concepts such as justice, fairness, and efficiency are essentially contested, and that the meanings we give to them may depend on our position in the web of social relations at a particular historical moment. This is a book on law and not on economics, political philosophy, or ethics, but we cannot avoid the important multidisciplinary issues that are very much at play in labour and employment law. The first of the readings below sketches the central narrative concerning those issues that has come to inform Canadian labour and employment law.

Brian Langille, "Labour Law's Back Pages" in Guy Davidov & Brian Langille, eds, *Boundaries and Frontiers of Labour Law* (Oxford: Hart Publishing, 2006) 20 at 20–26

> For Canadian labour lawyers the story of labour law, the narrative which both delineates and justifies the field, has evolved over time since Laskin first introduced labour law into the law school curriculum. But it has been reasonably secure for the past 25 or 30 years. Many very distinguished Canadian labour law academics, of whom Harry Arthurs would be the acknowledged Dean, have spent much of the last decade or so pointing out the threat which 'globalisation' poses for the system constructed and held together by this narrative. But there is no doubt that the system so constructed is the system under threat.
>
> For Laskin and those who immediately followed him, the subject matter of labour law was collective labour relations, that is, the relationship between firms and unions. It subsequently became much broader. Laskin studied law in Toronto but pursued his graduate work at Harvard in the late 1930s. This was in the immediate glow of the New Deal in general and the passing of the Wagner Act in particular. Laskin's return to Canada from Harvard was soon followed by the importation of the Wagner Act model, with some very important local innovations, into Canada. These were heady days. The

common law was hostile to collective worker action, and in its normal analysis of working relations still did not blink in using the labels of a dead social order, 'master' and 'servant,' to describe them. The break with this common law past offered by the new legislative and administrative regime was radical and must have been truly exhilarating. Moreover this new system of labour law was given coherence and content by the comprehensive statutory scheme itself, which started at the beginning, defining the eligible players (employees, employers, unions etc.), then constructing a chronology, and, implicitly, a narrative about life for those players in the new world of labour law. The chronology begins with the right to organise and legal protection thereof ('unfair labour practices'), then how to convert union organisation into union recognition via the new 'certification' process. Next, how this leads to the imposition of a 'duty to bargain in good faith' upon employers and unions following certification, then to the law of strikes and lockouts when negotiations fail, and finally to the law of 'labour arbitration' when a collective agreement is reached and the law is applied in the daily life of a functioning collective agreement. Then the statute shows how the system repeats itself, possibly *ad infinitum*. All of this administered by new tripartite entities, such as the labour relations and labour arbitration boards, which were specifically not courts and which administered a world from which the common law contract of employment was banished. This was the world of labour law in which I grew up as a law student in the 1970s.

But by then there were changes underway. Law faculties, following Innis Christie's lead, began to offer courses in what became called 'employment law.' The subject matter here is somewhat more difficult to describe, but we would say now that it is all of the rest of labour law lying outside collective bargaining law. This has two components—the common law of the employment relationship (most critically the law of the contract of employment and of 'wrongful dismissal') and the vast and expanding world of statutory regulation of the contract of employment including health and safety laws, human rights codes, employment standards legislation (meaning minimum wage, maximum hours, holiday and vacation regulation, etc.), pension regulation, and so on. In the United States this turn to employment law was also a turn away from collective labour law driven by the radical decline in the union density rates and the de-centring of collective bargaining in that country. In Canada this was not the motivation. The initial interest in employment law is best explained by simply the existence, and in the case of most of the statutes recent creation, of much new law which applied to many people. But there was a problem in giving a meaningful account of employment law. The common but erroneous account was that collective bargaining law was for organised workers and employment law for the unorganised. This was commonly said, but clearly wrong, for most of the statutory component of employment law applies across the board to all workers. This problem of how to give a meaningful account of employment law could be, and was, resolved only when employment law and labour law were seen as one coherent system of law organised around not simply the comprehensive set of statutory novelties which dominated the emergence and account of labour law as collective bargaining law which Laskin offered, nor (poorly) organised around the idea of labour law for the unorganised on the other, but on a reading of the two as parts of a whole greater than the simple sum of these two parts. This was achieved gradually and finally explicitly around 25 years ago. And the narrative which stitches these subject matters together is the narrative we are after. It is labour law's foundational framing and justificatory account of itself.

There are many dimensions of, and possible routes into, this compelling story, but let me start with the idea of contract. The labour law narrative takes the category of contract law as prior and primitive. In one way the entire story can be seen as a story of the 'real life of contract law,' as opposed to the abstract and general rules of general contract law. It is what happens when the rubber of contract law hits the real and hard road of the working life. Part of the reasoning here is 'historical.' (A word of caution here—the history revealed here is not meant to be taken as accurate, although some or even all of it might be. The claim to accuracy is, rather, about the structure of the narrative.) Labour lawyers know that contract is a relatively modern category of legal thinking. They know that productive activity is possibly, and was long, organised on other lines. And labour lawyers, as are all lawyers, are familiar with Sir Henry Maine's famous dictum that

> The movement of all progressive societies is one from status to contract.

I am also quite certain that our labour lawyer will be very familiar with many pronouncements of which the following from the Supreme Court of Canada is merely representative:

> The common law views mutually agreed upon employment relationships through the lens of contract. ...

But our modern labour lawyer will not actually need to know any specific milestones on the road to modern labour law because a very general history suffices to underwrite what follows. Nonetheless this idea of the emergence of contract, of a chronology, is of importance to the credibility of the received wisdom. The entire narrative makes its way in the world by taking this idea of historical development and seeing the emergence of our current law as a reaction to it, combined with a justificatory account of why these developments are important. At its core this account is one of law constraining, or humanising, or softening, or resisting contract in the name of justice, democracy, fairness, and equality. It is an account of justice against, or as resistance to, markets.

How does the constituting narrative construct itself upon this foundation of the emergence of contract as the dominant legal category relevant to labour law? As we have noted, labour lawyers understand that productive relations can be organised, and historically have been organised, by different principles. Nonetheless they accept that the overwhelmingly important mode of engaging in productive relations in modern society, at least in North America, is through the mechanism of contract and specifically the contract of employment. On this view employees and employers are seen as participants in the labour market, and they are engaged in the exercise of contracting, that is, the formation of individual contracts of employment. Here, all of the conceptual apparatus appropriate to private market ordering is understood to apply. Nonetheless, labour lawyers see the development of labour law, certainly within recent memory, as one of the elaboration and remedying of a series of disenchantments with this contractual reality. Labour law is thus primarily conceived as a set of interventions in the labour market, that is, in the negotiation process for contracts of employment. The point of all this is, of course, 'justice' in this part of our lives, that is, in employment relationships. The idea of justice does not need, for most labour lawyers, a complete theoretical account. The more sophisticated will likely be able to draw upon ideas elaborated by John Rawls or Ronald Dworkin about a liberal theory of justice containing two elements, sometimes expressed as, 'concern' and 'respect.' Others may now draw upon the human development approach elaborated by Sen. But the core normative claim which the received wisdom makes is that justice for employees will never be completely secured as long as the relationship is analysed in purely (common law) contractual terms. (As a result the very idea of a contract of employment separates out those who are employees from those who are simply independent commercial contractors—those who need protection from those who do not.) When employees negotiate contracts of employment they suffer from an 'inequality of bargaining power.' As a result, they will not obtain just outcomes. We should pause to note that the claim about 'inequality of bargaining power' is famously controversial. From the point of view of economic theory, any discussion of 'inequality of bargaining power' can be viewed as a form of economic nonsense. This is not a point which dismays many labour lawyers. But it does call for some clarification. It may well be that on certain views of economic theory a discussion of 'inequality of bargaining power' in the labour market is a form of economic nonsense. This may indeed be at least partly true if it is meant to be understood as a comment within economic theory (because the idea is meant to go beyond correcting for market failures). But I think the best understanding of the idea of 'inequality of bargaining power' is that it is not meant to be taken as a comment from within economic theory. Rather, it is meant to offer a critique external to that theory. It has the form of another famous slogan: 'property is theft.' When Proudhon offered this remark he did not intend it to be taken as a comment 'within' the legal theory of property. Rather, it was meant to be an external critique of the idea of property. An interesting feature of the slogan, and whence it derives its rhetorical force, is, as John Searle has pointed out, that it uses concepts from within the theory being criticised in order to make a criticism of the theory.

Labour law then continues its self-constituting narrative in the following way. If our aim is to secure justice for employees, and employees will not secure justice because the employment relationship is a contractual one and employees suffer from inequality of bargaining power in the contracting process, then there are two possible responses. These two responses are two possible modes of 'consumer protection.' Labour law is to be understood on a par with other interventions in other market places in the name of defending 'weaker parties.' The law protects those in need of protection in the market place. The first mode of intervention is procedural. If the problem is that we are not securing justice for employees through this contractual bargaining relationship, because of inequality of bargaining power on the part of employees, then we must simply adopt the procedural device of turning up the bargaining power on the side of the employee. Our primary mechanism for achieving this is through the device of collective bargaining. Here we permit workers to secure whatever additional substantive rights and benefits they can in the contracting process by making available to them whatever increases in bargaining power will accrue through collective representation by unions. This approach is, at least in theory, purely procedural. There is no guarantee that employees will be able to secure much benefit by acting collectively. The essence of collective bargaining law is to remove legal obstacles to collective action and to compel the employer to deal with the union as the collective representative of the employees. The accepted wisdom is that collective bargaining is entirely procedural in the sense that the substance of the bargain to be is still left open to the parties to determine through the exercise of their now restructured bargaining power relationship. The employer's freedom *to* contract with whom it wishes is taken away, and it is compelled to bargain with the collective representative. But the employer's freedom *of* contract is maintained.

Most labour lawyers acknowledge that this is a deeply problematic condition to sustain. But the important point is that collective bargaining guarantees no substantial results. It is the device of procedural justice. If employees are located in labour markets such that collective action does improve their bargaining position, then they will achieve results. But for other employees collective bargaining may be no guarantee at all of any improvement in their substantive conditions of work.

But labour law consists in more than simply procedural intervention through collective bargaining. There is a second response to our problem of securing justice in employment relationships. This second response is substantive in nature. The logic here is as follows. If our problem is that we will not secure justice in employment relationships because these relationships are analysed in contractual terms, and employees suffer from inequality of bargaining power in the negotiation of such contracts, then we should simply rewrite the resulting bargain. This we do via human rights codes, employment standards legislation, occupational health and safety regulation, and so on.

Thus at the end of the day labour law ends up being constituted by three legal regimes — the 'original' common law of the contract of employment, collective bargaining, and what we can refer to as 'direct statutory intervention' — all organised by the story we have just told. There are many places where the Supreme Court of Canada has articulated this narrative, often piecemeal. But a very comprehensive rendition of the whole narrative can be found in the following words of Madame Justice Wilson:

> Collective bargaining is a mechanism by which individual employees come together and form a union to represent their interests. The whole purpose of unionization is to strengthen the position of these employees in order to offset the countervailing power of employers. Rather than simply enacting legislation aimed solely at protecting individual workers by controlling employer abuses (eg minimum wage, occupational health and safety, and workers' compensation legislation), government established our current regime of collective bargaining. The purpose of this system is also to curb the excesses of the common law of the employment relationship and to thereby assuage industrial tensions.
>
> This is achieved, not through legislative protectionism, but rather through the promotion of the self-advancement of working people. Thus, these two systems differ in respect of the mechanisms they adopt to achieve their ends, but both individual employment law and collective employment law aim to advance the interests of a vulnerable group, the individual employees.

Although not in perfect order, almost all of the elements of the package which is the received wisdom are nicely stated here.

It will be apparent that every element of the received wisdom is contestable and controversial. But the point of the narrative is not so much that it resolves our controversies, or generates a consensus about them, but rather that it gives us a way of understanding and ordering those controversies as being the very controversies which constitute labour law. At its heart, of course, is the central dilemma of its claims about 'justice' or lack thereof in market ordering. Labour lawyers may actually disagree among themselves as to whether the claims made by labour law, along the lines just outlined, actually do advance the cause of justice, in whole or in part. But they will be in agreement that this is the way that labour law, that is the law that we actually do have, is to be understood. (It may be wrongheaded, but this is what labour law is.) The result is a unified account of all of our labour law, that is, all three legal regimes, including the previously bifurcated subjects of labour law and employment law. Part of the narrative's value added, from the normative and pedagogical points of view, is precisely that it opens up the different sets of normative underpinnings of each of the three constituting legal approaches. The normative underpinnings of procedural intervention, that is, of collective bargaining ('self advancement of working people') are to be distinguished from the paternalistic normative underpinnings of much substantive legal intervention ('legislative protectionism'). And both substantive and procedural re-regulation of the bargaining relationship stand in sharp contrast to the values underlying common law market ordering (with its 'excesses'). What is opened up to us is the possibility of seeing common problems 'solved' in different ways by the three different legal approaches. So too there is much value added in our ability to see the normative tensions played out in decision-making under each of the three separate regimes. There is, in addition, much detailed legal controversy about the proper institutional, let alone the substantive, relationships between the three regimes. But the great achievement of the constituting narrative is that it provides a chronology, a justification, and a delineation of the field in a concise and compelling manner.
[Reprinted with permission.]

1:310 Market Models

Central to the controversies described in the previous reading are differing understandings of how labour markets work. The following readings introduce some of the most influential theories and sources of evidence that shape those understandings.

Armen A Alchian & William R Allen, *University Economics*, 3d ed (Belmont, CA: Wadsworth, 1972) at 407 and 443

'Labor is not a commodity' is a battle cry of some labor groups. Whatever its emotional appeal, the assertion is misleading. Labor service is bought and sold daily....

Economic analysis denies that, in the absence of legal protection for labor, employers would grind wages down to the minimum survival level. An analogy will suggest why. Why are rents on land not ground down by renters to zero? The demands by those who would use the land bid up the rents. Simple supply and demand are in operation. And so it is with labor. The alternative uses and values to which labor could be put are determined by all who compete for it. Potential employers, faced with the available supply, bid wages to whatever level enables them to get an amount of labor that can be put to profitable use. That may be a very high level, if labor is relatively scarce given its productivity function. The price of labor, like that of every other good, depends upon demand and supply forces.

... All the considerations in interpreting the demand and supply analysis of price and output effects are applicable to labor services.... Suffice it to say, demand-and-supply analysis of open-market determination of wages and employment is similar in principle to that for any other good. Underlying is the assumption that people are free agents and can quit or change jobs when they wish, and that at least some will change jobs when knowledge of more attractive openings is available. Employees who entertain offers to look for opportunities elsewhere also permit their current employers to make a counter-bid.

An employer, then, if he is to retain his employees, must detect and match offers of other employers. The employer who does so (through periodic wage and salary reviews and raises), without forcing his employees to seek offers and then ask for a raise, will have to pay no higher wages than if he waited for each employee to initiate negotiations. Job comparison is costly for employees; so the employer who is known to take the initiative in anticipating or matching market offers will find more employees willing to work for him than for one who tries to impose all the costs of job comparison on employees. [Copyright © 1972. By permission of South-Western College Publishing, a division of International Thomson Publishing Inc., Cincinnati, OH 45227.]

Richard Posner, *Economic Analysis of Law*, 7th ed (New York: Aspen Publishers, 2007) at 341–48 [citations omitted]

In the nineteenth century, the main question of antitrust policy was whether labor unions should be suppressed as unlawful combinations in restraint of trade. The classical economists thought not, but neither did they believe that workers' combinations could be distinguished from combinations of employers to lower wages or of sellers to raise prices. The main purpose of a union, most economists have long believed, is to limit the supply of labor so that the employer cannot use competition among workers to control the price of labor (wages). The common law was thus on solid economic ground when it refused to enforce agreements to join unions, enjoined picketing—an attempt to interfere with contractual relations between the picketed firm and its customers, workers, or other suppliers—and enforced yellow dog contracts (whereby workers agree not to join unions during the term of their employment). Regarding the last, the worker presumably would demand compensation for giving up his right to join a union—and if he was not compensated generously, this was not a social loss, since any compensation for not combining with other workers to create a labor monopoly is itself a form of monopoly gain.

Maybe, though, this picture of an efficient common law of labor relations rests on unrealistic assumptions about nineteenth-century American labor markets. Employers would have monopsony power if workers were ignorant of their alternative employment opportunities or had very high relocation costs, or if employers conspired to depress wages. All three conditions may have been common in the nineteenth century, when there was much immigrant labor, the level of education was much lower than today, the mobility of labor was also lower, firms had less competition because the cost of transportation was higher, and the antitrust laws were not enforced against conspiracies to depress wages. Against all this are the facts ... that the great era of immigration to this country after the Civil War was a response to a surging labor demand, that wages were always higher in America than in other countries, and that Americans have always been highly mobile. Moreover, even if labor monopsonies were a problem, labor monopolies are not an attractive solution. The situation is one of bilateral monopoly. With both sides trying to limit the supply of labor, though for different reasons, supply will not reach the competitive level, although wages will be higher than if there is just monopsony....

If we set aside labor monopsony, which is not a serious problem in this country today, we can say with some confidence (but shall entertain a contrary suggestion in § 11.3 *infra*) that the effect of unionization is to reduce the supply of labor in the unionized sector. The higher wages obtained by the union will induce the employer to substitute capital for labor and also to substitute cheaper for costlier labor (for instance, by relocating his business to a region where unions are weak) and white-collar for blue-collar workers. Thus some workers benefit from unionization—those who are paid higher wages in the unionized industries and those newly employed by employers seeking substitutes for union labor. So do some shareholders—of firms whose competitors formerly paid lower wages than they did but are compelled as a result of unionization to pay the same wage. And so do consumers of the products of nonunionized firms (why?). The losers are consumers in unionized industries (for the employers in those industries will pass along to consumers a portion, at least, of their higher labor costs ...), stockholders and suppliers in those industries, workers who lose their jobs because of the reduction in the demand for labor caused by union wage scales, workers in the nonunionized sector because the supply of workers in that sector is now larger, and consumers in general, because labor inputs are being used less efficiently throughout the economy.

The point about the effect on the wages of the workers in the nonunionized sector requires qualification, however. Suppose the unionized sector is highly capital intensive. When wages rise in that sector, prices will rise and output will fall. There will be some substitution of capital for labor, but if the output effect dominates the substitution effect there may be a net capital outflow from the unionized to the nonunionized sector, resulting (why?) in increased labor productivity in the latter sector. The wage increase due to this increased productivity conceivably could dominate the wage decrease due to the increased supply of labor, resulting in a net increase in wages in the nonunionized sector. The result would be to benefit all workers, although at the expense of all (or at least most) consumers and the social welfare as a whole, since both capital and labor would be employed less efficiently than if no part of the economy had been unionized ...

But as we know from the preceding chapter, monopolies and cartels carry within them the seeds of their own destruction. Union wage premia (including union-negotiated fringe benefits and job protections) force up the marginal costs of unionized firms, causing them to lose business to nonunionized firms and resulting eventually, as has occurred in the United States and other advanced economies in recent decades, in a steep decline in the percentage of the workforce that is unionized. Today, fewer than

8 percent of privately employed workers in the United States are unionized, though more than a third of publicly employed workers are. The disparity reflects the fact that public employees are voters; that public agencies are less strongly motivated to minimize cost since they don't compete in the marketplace; and that partly because of the lack of competitive pressure, nepotism, cronyism, and political favoritism are rife in public employment and so employees believe, often rightly, that they need a union to protect themselves against arbitrary employment practices. A private employer is less likely to engage in such practices because they reduce productivity....

The key to understanding the economics of strikes is the bilateral monopoly of employer and union. A producers' cartel will reduce output but of course not to zero. If, however, the customers banded together into a buyers' cartel, or if there were a single customer, it or he might respond to the sellers' cartel by threatening to stop buying from the cartel in the hope that the threat would induce the cartel to back down. An employer is, in effect, the sole buyer of the labor services controlled by the union. If the union announces that it wants a higher price for those services, the employer can refuse, in effect threatening to buy nothing; and then the union, if it is to maintain credibility, must call the employer's bluff by calling the workers out on strike....

Since a strike imposes costs on both parties—forgone wages for the workers, and forgone profits for the employer (unless there is a large supply of replacement workers)—it might seem that the parties would always be better off negotiating a settlement. The problem, familiar from our discussion of predatory pricing in the last chapter, is that the terms of the settlement depend on the credibility of the parties' respective threats. The willingness of the employer to take an occasional strike, and of the union to call an occasional strike, may yield each party (ex ante) long-term benefits in enhanced credibility that exceed the short-term costs of the strike. Because "talk is cheap," "putting your money where your mouth is" is the more credible form of signalling. This implies that strikes are likeliest early in the bargaining relationship or, if later, when there is some dramatic change in circumstances. In both cases the parties will tend to lack good information about each other's reservation price and it will be difficult for them to obtain good information without calling each other's bluff. The employer will have a hard time knowing whether the union's threat to strike is empty unless it refuses to yield, and likewise the union will have a hard time knowing whether the employer's threat to take a long strike is empty unless the union calls for a strike.

Unions and Productivity

Some economists have speculated that unionization may enhance productivity, perhaps completely offsetting its monopolistic effects. Collective bargaining contracts generally establish a grievance machinery for arbitrating workers' complaints and also give workers job security—not absolute security, for they can be laid off if the firm's demand for labor declines, but security against being fired other than for good cause (determined by means of the grievance machinery). Without grievance machinery, it is argued, employers would not discover that their foremen were mistreating the workers until they noticed that job turnover was abnormal, and older workers would refuse to share their experience with younger ones, fearing that the younger ones might replace them.

But the theory does not explain why, if grievance machinery and job security reduce costly turnover and enhance worker efficiency, employers do not adopt these devices without waiting for a union to come on the scene. (Some of course do.) If only one employer in an industry tumbled to their advantages, competition would force the others to follow suit. Maybe, though, for the grievance machinery or job-security provisions to be credible to the workers, third-party enforcement would be necessary. But an employer could easily arrange this. Even if the only credible third parties were unions, employers would unionize voluntarily if unionization increased the productivity of their workforce, provided that competition among unions compressed the price for their services to their marginal cost.

The most telling evidence against the theory is that it cannot explain the decline of the unionized sector. If unionization enhances productivity, that sector should be growing. [Reprinted from *Economic Analysis of Law*, 7th edition, with the permission of Aspen Publishers.]

Steven L Willborn, "Individual Employment Rights and the Standard Economic Objection: Theory and Empiricism" (1988) 67 *Nebraska Law Review* 101 at 104–33

I. PRICE THEORY, MINIMAL TERMS, AND THE STANDARD OBJECTION

A. The Price Theory Model of the Labor Market

The price theory model of the labor market is a specific instance of the more general neoclassical economic model in which the price of a commodity in a competitive market is determined by its supply and demand. The price theory model describes how the labor market would operate in a perfectly competitive environment. Although by now the basic outline of the model should be familiar to most lawyers, it may be helpful to begin by examining the model in broad relief.

Under the price theory model, the supply of labor and the demand for labor determine the equilibrium wage and the quantity of labor utilized. A basic understanding of labor supply and demand, then, is essential to an understanding of the price theory model.

Figure 1.

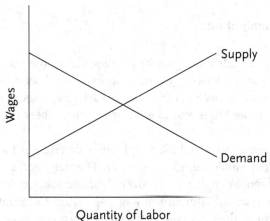

CHAPTER 1: INTRODUCTION

As indicated in Figure 1, the demand curve for labor generally slopes downward. That is, assuming a fixed supply of capital, the marginal value of each unit of labor to employers declines as the quantity of labor utilized by employers increases. The downward slope of the demand curve for labor makes sense intuitively. Consider, for example, the demand for manual labor to dig a ditch. One worker using a large shovel may be able to dig 100 feet per day; two workers using medium-sized shovels might be able to complete 150 feet per day; three workers with tiny shovels might be able to complete 180 feet per day; and so on until there are many men with small trowels. The *marginal* product of each unit of labor decreases as more units of labor are added, assuming once again that capital is held constant. The marginal product of the first worker is 100 feet, of the second worker fifty feet, of the third worker thirty feet, and so on. Employer demand for labor depends on the marginal product of labor. An employer might be willing to pay the first worker the equivalent of 100 feet of ditch (the first worker's marginal product), but the second worker is only worth the equivalent of fifty feet of ditch, the third worker only thirty feet, and so on. If we graphed this phenomenon, the marginal product for ditch diggers (which would determine the demand for that type of labor) would slope downward like the demand curve in Figure 1.

Figure 2.

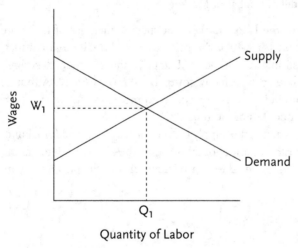

Quantity of Labor

The supply curve for labor indicates the quantity of labor that is available at a particular wage rate. The supply curve for labor generally slopes upward, as indicated in Figure 1. Once again, the slope is intuitively sensible because a higher wage would tend to encourage workers to work more hours and to encourage non-workers to enter the labor force.

The intersection of the demand curve and the supply curve determines the equilibrium wage and quantity of labor employed. (See Figure 2). The wage and quantity of labor are in equilibrium in the sense that that level is the only stable position. Employers have no incentive to pay more than the equilibrium wage; as Figure 3 illustrates, they can attract sufficient labor to meet their demand at W_1. Indeed, the employer demand for labor at a higher wage, W_2, is only Q_3. Since there is an excess supply of labor at that wage level, (with Q_2 willing to work, but employers only willing to hire Q_1), workers will be unemployed, which should result in competition between workers for the available jobs, which should drive the wage down toward W_1, the equilibrium wage. In much the same way, as indicated in Figure 4, if employers pay a lower-than-equilibrium wage, employers will demand Q_2 workers, but only Q_3 workers will be available. The resulting competition between employers for the available workers should drive the wage up toward W_1. As a result, when wages are higher or lower than equilibrium, there are forces which drive the wages toward equilibrium. In contrast, when wages are at the equilibrium level, these forces are absent. The equilibrium wage is stable because, at that wage, employers can hire the optimal amount of labor given the demand for their products, while workers can optimally balance their demands for work and leisure.

Figure 3.

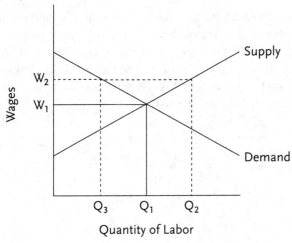

Figure 4.

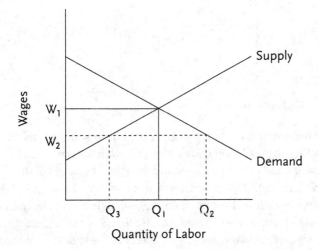

This formal and bloodless picture of the labor market describes only how the market would operate in a perfectly competitive environment. In such an environment, employers and workers would have full, perfect and costless knowledge of the market, including information on wage rates and job openings; employers and workers would be entirely rational, with employers attempting to maximize their profits and workers responding to wage differences and attempting to optimally balance their desires for work and leisure; there would be no externalities; workers would be perfectly mobile and able to change jobs without any costs, and would not act in concert, and employers would be numerous, they would not act in concert, and none would be so large that its decisions would affect the market as a whole. Obviously, these conditions are seldom, if ever, met. Nevertheless, the model is a useful starting point for discussion. When the conditions affect the analysis, as they inevitably do, the discussion can be advanced by easing the conditions.

B. Minimal Terms and the Standard Objection

Minimal terms are non-waivable, minimum substantive terms of employment which are required by the government. They come in a wide variety of forms. The government might require employers to pay minimum wages, to provide a certain level of maternity rights, to provide a safe workplace, to supply information about plant closings, to pay severance pay, to make certain provisions for retirement and possible unemployment, to provide a certain level of health insurance, and so on.

Figure 5.

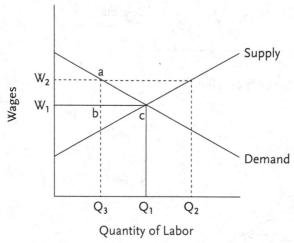

Quantity of Labor

In the abstract, effective minimal terms provide a benefit to workers and impose a cost on employers. All other things being equal, when a minimal term is added to the wage package, both the wage cost to the employer and the effective wages of the workers go up. Minimal terms, at least in the short run, are the equivalent of a wage increase.

The standard objection to minimal terms, then, begins with a consideration of the effects of an exogenous wage increase (i.e., a wage increase that is not the result of changes in labor supply or demand) on the labor market. The effects in the short run should be as indicated in Figure 5. The intersection of the supply and demand curves determines the equilibrium wage, W_1. A minimal term imposed by the government would have the effect of a wage increase, raising the wage to W_2. The wage increase, in turn, would result in a reduction in the quantity of labor utilized from Q_1 to Q_3. One part of the standard objection to minimal terms, then, is that minimal terms do not confer any benefits on workers as a class. Any benefits received by one set of workers are paid for (and often more than paid for) by other workers in unemployment. The effects of minimal terms illustrated in Figure 5, however, are not stable. The excess supply of labor creates competition between workers for the available jobs and, as a result, tends to force the wage level back down to equilibrium. Whether the wage actually moves back to (or at least closer to) the equilibrium level depends on whether the employer can avoid the minimal term which effectively raised the wage level by making a compensating change in another part of the wage package. That is, an employer may be able to avoid a minimal term by offsetting the effective wage increase caused by the minimal term with an effective wage decrease in another part of the wage package. For example, a minimal term requiring employers to pay workers for maternity or paternity leave would be avoidable if employers reduced the wages of workers by an amount equivalent to the cost of the required leave program. Some minimal terms may not be avoidable. Minimum wage laws, for example, effectively apply only to low-wage, low-benefit jobs, so offsetting the wage increase by an effective wage decrease in another part of the wage package may not be possible. Most minimal terms, however, should be avoidable, at least in the long run. Even if employers cannot make compensating changes immediately, as in the maternity or paternity leave example, they should be able to do so in the long run, for example, by reducing the rate of increase in wages. When minimal terms are avoidable through compensating changes, wages and quantity of labor should tend to move back to equilibrium.

Another part of the standard objection to minimal terms, then, is that workers and employers will find ways to counteract the desired effects of minimal terms and, indeed, that there are economic forces which drive the parties to do so. Since minimal terms are effective wage increases, they can be counteracted by actual or effective wage decreases in other parts of the wage package. The excess supply of labor encourages the counteraction. A corollary of this objection is that when wages and quantity of labor move back to equilibrium in reaction to a minimal term, both employers and workers are worse off than they would have been if the minimal term had never been imposed. Using the maternity or paternity leave example again, if the wages and quantity of labor move back to equilibrium, the overall wage package is worth the same as the overall wage package before the minimal term was imposed, but its components are different. Before the minimal term, the package provided no maternity or paternity leave, but a higher wage; after the minimal term was imposed, the package provided maternity or paternity leave, but a lower wage. By hypothesis, the ex post position leaves the parties worse off. In a world with perfect competition, if the parties had wanted that wage package, they would have bargained for it ex ante. Since they did not, imposition of the minimal term frustrates the wage package preferred by the parties.

The standard economic objection to minimal terms, then, is that any perceived benefits to workers are merely illusory. Because imposition of minimal terms is the equivalent of a wage increase and because an exogenous wage increase reduces the demand for labor, any benefits to workers from minimum terms in the short run are paid for by other workers in unemployment. In the long run, minimal terms can usually be avoided by offsetting the effective wage increase from imposition of the minimal terms with wage decreases elsewhere in the wage package. When minimal terms are avoided, employers and workers are worse off than they would have been if minimal terms had not been required in the first place ...

III. JUSTIFICATIONS FOR MINIMAL TERMS WITHIN THE PRICE THEORY MODEL

Employers and individual workers face a difficult problem when they wish to enter into a relationship. A number of uncertainties exist which may affect the relationship—uncertainties about the precise work the employer needs done, the ability of the worker to perform it, the employer's long-term need for the work, other work opportunities which may present themselves to the worker, the worker's continued good health, the safety of the workplace, and so on. The proposed relationship is also quite complex—what arrangements should be made for the worker's retirement, for the possibility of a work-related injury, for health insurance, and so on.

Minimal terms can be viewed as a set of ready-made contract terms which deal with many of these difficult issues. The government, for example, requires a certain minimum amount to be set aside for retirement and requires certain safeguards if greater amounts are reserved. To the extent the parties would have included the same or very similar terms in the employment contract even if they had not been required by the government, the minimal terms are efficient. They spare the parties the time and expense of having to negotiate the terms. This effect of minimal terms should be uncontroversial.

Governments generally enact minimal terms, however, not merely to save transaction costs, but to change the substance of the employment arrangement. That is precisely why minimal terms are nonwaivable. It is this goal—to change the employment contract—which runs into the standard objection. When minimal terms are required and they change the arrangements the parties would otherwise have made, the standard objection leads to the conclusion that the parties are necessarily made worse off.

This section considers circumstances in which minimal terms might not be subject to the standard objection but, rather, may enhance efficiency or lead to a more desirable distribution of resources.

A. Efficiency Justifications

1. Collective Terms

Some terms of employment are collective in nature; that is, if they are supplied to one worker, they must also be supplied to other workers. Terms may be collective by their very nature or they may be collective for practical reasons. Health and safety terms, for example, are often collective by their very nature. If an employer supplies clean air or good lighting to one worker, other workers are usually able to share in the benefits. More often, however, terms are collective for practical reasons. When workers work together closely, an eight hour day for one worker may mean an eight hour day for other workers. When one worker demands and receives a new vending machine in the cafeteria, it is likely that other workers will be allowed to use it. When an employer establishes a disciplinary system for a few workers, it may be efficient to use it for all workers.

Collective terms are likely to be underproduced. That is, the terms will often not be offered even though the cost to the employer of providing the terms is less than the value the workers place on the benefits of the terms. To illustrate why this is the case, consider an employer who employs ten workers and who could install Equipment A at a cost of one, which would clean the air in the plant a bit or Equipment B at a cost of twenty, which could clean the air in the plant quite a bit. Assume that each worker would value the cleaner air produced by Equipment A at two and the cleaner air produced by Equipment B at five (i.e., each worker would be willing to accept a reduction in pay of two and five, respectively, in return for the cleaner air). From an efficiency standpoint, the employer should install Equipment B. At a marginal cost of nineteen, the employer can produce cleaner air with a marginal value of thirty ... both the employer and the workers would be better off if the employer installed Equipment B and reduced the workers' aggregate wages by an amount between twenty and twenty-nine.

Because of strategic behavior and information imperfections, however, Equipment B will not always be installed and, indeed, even Equipment A may not be installed in some instances. Consider the calculations of each individual worker who is deciding whether to accept lower wages for cleaner air. Clearly the best outcome for an individual worker would be to refuse to accept lower wages, but to have the equipment installed because other workers accepted lower wages.

In that situation, the worker would be a free rider; she could share in the benefits of the clean air, but would not have to pay for it. If all of the workers engaged in this type of strategic behavior, neither Equipment A nor Equipment B would be installed. Thus, one reason the efficient outcome may not be achieved is that individual workers may engage in strategic behavior designed to position themselves as free riders....

2. Imperfect Information

Imperfect information is a common justification for governmental intervention in markets of various kinds, including labor markets. Various forms of the argument provide weak and strong justifications for minimal terms.

The conventional argument from imperfect information is that workers cannot enter into optimal employment contracts if they do not have all of the information necessary, to evaluate their options. Consider again the worker who is attempting to decide whether to accept a wage reduction in return for a "for cause" provision which would provide some protection against discharge. If the worker believes that she has some protections against discharge even without a "for cause" provision, when in fact she does not, she is likely to underestimate the value of the provision and, as a result, may fail to buy it even though she should. Other workers may understand the limitations of their protections in the absence of a "for cause" provision and yet fail to purchase the provision because they underestimate the risk of discharge and, hence, underestimate the provision's potential benefits. Once again, this information failure could lead to an inefficient result—the worker may not buy the "for cause' provision even though it is worth more to her than the wages.

Imperfect information does not justify intervention, however, merely because individual workers make mistakes. Intervention is justified only if the labor market fails to produce optimal terms because workers make decisions based on imperfect information. Even if many workers make mistakes because of imperfect information, optimal terms may be produced. If some workers seek optimal terms and if employers both wish to attract those workers and cannot distinguish between them and the workers making mistakes, the market should produce optimal terms. In essence, those workers who demand optimal terms protect other workers from the consequences of their limited information.

On the other hand if insufficient numbers of workers seek optimal terms, or if employers do not wish to attract those workers, or if employers can distinguish between those workers and workers with imperfect information, the labor market may fail to produce optimal terms.

Intervention in the labor market is justified, then, if the labor market fails to produce optimal terms because workers make decisions on the basis of imperfect information. This provides only a weak justification for minimal terms, however, because there are other, less intrusive options for remedying this type of information failure. Ensuring that workers receive fuller information on the "for cause" provision, either by requiring the employer to provide it or by having the government provide it, would remedy the information failure and lead to a more fine-tuned result than simply requiring the "for cause" provision. It would permit those workers who prefer higher wages even when they have knowledge of the true value of the "for cause" provision, to continue to receive higher wages.

Another type of information failure provides a stronger justification for minimal terms. If there is information failure not because of limited information, but because workers cannot rationally evaluate the available information, the less intrusive remedial option of providing information may not be effective. Minimal terms may be required to correct the suboptimal choices made by workers.

Information overload and cognitive dissonance are two reasons workers may not be able to effectively evaluate the information necessary to make a choice. Evidence from outside the employment context suggests that there is a point at which additional information becomes dysfunctional; that is, the additional information does not contribute to a better decision because the people to whom it is provided are "overloaded" and simply cannot process it. To the extent information overload occurs, one would expect it to occur in the employment context. Employment contracts cover a broad range of topics, many of them quite complex; they are often expected to remain in effect for long periods of time; and workers are often poorly equipped to evaluate them. Thus, minimal terms may be justified when there is evidence of information failure and when it is likely that the failure cannot be remedied simply by providing additional information.

Cognitive dissonance may also interfere with the ability of workers to evaluate additional information. Stated generally, cognitive dissonance means that people are uncomfortable when they simultaneously hold two conflicting ideas. People prefer to view themselves as smart and if new information indicates that a prior belief was in error, the new information tends to undermine the preferred self-image. As a consequence, people tend to reject, ignore or accommodate information that conflicts with prior beliefs.

Cognitive dissonance may also justify minimal terms. To illustrate, consider workers who when they first choose a job, choose an industry that is hazardous, but necessarily hazardous because no safety equipment is available to correct the hazards. Over time, cognitive dissonance may lead the workers to believe that the job is really fairly safe. (Smart workers would not work at a hazardous job, therefore the workers must either view themselves as not smart or their jobs as not hazardous. Viewing the jobs as safe is less threatening to the workers' self-image.) If cost-effective safety equipment then becomes available, the workers will not purchase the equipment (by accepting a reduction in their wages). Because of cognitive dissonance, they have come to believe that their jobs are safe even without the equipment. As a result, they are unable to evaluate fairly the value of the newly available equipment. A minimal term which required the equipment to be installed would be necessary to achieve the efficient outcome.

Minimal terms may also correct for information failure from the other side of the ledger—they may increase efficiency by improving the information base of employers. Employers can learn about worker perceptions of the compensation package they offer workers (and, indeed, about worker ideas on ways in which work can be reorganized to enhance productivity) in one of two ways. They can learn when workers quit to take other jobs (exit) or they can learn when workers tell them what they think about the compensation package (voice). Clearly, learning through voice has several advantages for both employers and workers: the costs of job search and transfer are minimized; the investment in job-specific training is not lost; the message is clearer since the communication is direct and the employer need not infer worker perceptions from numerous exits; and so on. Nevertheless, voice is likely to be underutilized:

> [W]orkers ... are unlikely to reveal their true preferences to an employer, for fear the employer may fire them. In a world in which workers could find employment at the same wages immediately, the market would offer adequate protection for the individual, but that is not the world we live in. The danger of job loss makes expression of voice by an individual risky.

Because of this, a minimal term which encourages voice may be efficient. A minimal term requiring cause for discharge, for example, would be likely to cause workers to increase the use of voice to communicate with the employer (because they would be less fearful of discharge when they expressed displeasure), and to decrease correspondingly the use of exit. Thus, the minimal term should result in gains both because the employer has obtained better and quicker feedback from workers which should enable it to make productivity-enhancing changes in the workplace, and because the costs of exit (job search costs, loss of training investment, etc.) can be minimized. If these gains outweigh the costs of administering the "for cause" system, the minimal term would be efficient.

Minimal terms may lead to a more efficient outcome, then, in several circumstances related to information imperfections. Minimal terms may be efficient when workers do not have the information necessary to evaluate the value of an employment term, when workers are intellectually or psychologically unable to value accurately an employment term, or when employers operate with poor information because workers are reluctant to exercise voice.

3. External Cost

Minimal terms may also be justified when employment terms impose costs on third parties, that is, when there are "external" costs that are not weighed by employers and workers when they negotiate the employment contract. Consider an employer that hires a worker who smokes. In a price theory world, the employer would pay the worker less than a worker who does not smoke by an amount equal to the extra costs imposed on the employer by smoking. Thus, if smokers are absent from work more often than non-smokers, the employer should pay a lower wage to a worker who smokes to compensate for the costs to the employer of the extra absences. Considering only the employer and the smoking worker, the price theory world would optimally balance the desire of workers to smoke and the employment costs associated with smoking. A worker would smoke if she valued smoking more than the decrease in pay caused by her smoking. An employer would hire smokers if they would agree to work for an amount sufficiently less than non-smokers to compensate the employer for its increased costs.

Some of the costs of smoking in the workplace, however, may be external, that is, they may be imposed on parties other than the employer and the smoking worker. Fellow workers, health and life insurance companies, social welfare agencies, and others may all bear some of the costs of smoking. To the extent this occurs, the efficient result may not be achieved. The costs of smoking are actually higher than the amount by which the employer reduces the pay of smokers; the employer reduces the pay only enough to recapture its losses, not enough to recapture *all* losses associated with smoking. As a result, some workers will continue to smoke even though they would not if they had to accept a reduction in pay sufficient to cover all of the costs of smoking. There will be "too much" smoking in the workplace.

Minimal terms can be used to correct for this type of overproduction. The test of efficiency is what the market would have produced if all the costs of workplace smoking were considered. A minimal term which prohibited workplace smoking, or which taxed employers or workers for workplace smoking, would reduce the amount of workplace smoking and may produce an amount of smoking which closer approximates the efficient ideal.

[Reprinted by permission].

Alan Manning, *Monopsony in Motion: Imperfect Competition in Labour Markets* (Princeton: Princeton University Press, 2003) at 3–6, 13–14, 351–52, and 360–64

What happens if an employer cuts the wage it pays its workers by one cent? Much of labor economics is built on the assumption that all existing workers immediately leave the firm as that is the implication of the assumption of perfect competition in the labor market. In such a situation an employer faces a market wage for each type of labor determined by forces beyond its control at which any number of these workers can be hired but any attempt to pay a lower wage will result in the complete inability to hire any of them at all. The labor supply curve facing the firm is infinitely elastic.

In contrast, this book is based on two assumptions about the labor market. They can be stated very simply:

- there are important frictions in the labor market;
- employers set wages.

The implications of these assumptions can also be stated simply. The existence of frictions means that there are generally rents to jobs: if an employer and worker are forcibly separated one or, more commonly, both of the parties would be made worse off. This gives employers some market power over their workers as a small wage cut will no longer induce them to leave the firm. The assumption that employers set wages then tells us that employers exercise this market power. But, with these two assumptions, it is monopsony, not perfect competition, that is the best simple model to describe the decision problem facing an individual employer. Not monopsony in the sense of there being a single buyer of labor, but monopsony in the sense of the supply of labor to an individual firm not being infinitely elastic. The actions of other employers (notably their choice of wages) in the market will affect the supply of labor to an individual firm so, if one wants to model the market as a whole, models of oligopsony or monopsonistic competition are what is needed. The usefulness of the monopsonistic approach rests on the two assumptions so they need some justification.

That important frictions exist in the labor market seems undeniable: people go to the pub to celebrate when they get a job rather than greeting the news with the shrug of the shoulders that we might expect if labor markets were frictionless. And people go to the pub to drown their sorrows when they lose their job rather than picking up another one straight away....

[The] view that the relationship between the employer and worker is onesided has a long tradition. In the *Wealth of Nations*, Adam Smith wrote that "in the long run the workman may be as necessary to his master as his master is to him; but the necessity is not so immediate." And Alfred Marshall in his *Principles of Economics* wrote that "labour is often sold under special disadvantages arising from the closely connected group of facts that labour power is 'perishable', that the sellers of it are commonly poor and have no reserve fund, and that they cannot easily withhold it from the market." To these arguments that a worker is typically more desperate for work than an employer is desperate for that particular worker, Sidney and Beatrice Webb added the argument that the manual worker is, from his position and training, far less skilled than the employer ... in the art of bargaining itself. This art forms a large part of the daily life of the entrepreneur, whilst the foreman is specially selected for his skill in engaging and superintending workmen. The manual worker, on the contrary, has the smallest experience of, and practically no training in, what is essentially one of the arts of the capitalist employer. He never engages in any but one sort of bargaining, and that only on occasions which may be infrequent, and which in any case make up only a tiny fraction of his life.

The view that the relationship between employer and worker is not one of equals was the origin of pro-labor legislation in many if not all countries. Section 1 of the US National Labor Relations Act of 1935 says "the inequality of bargaining power between employees who do not possess freedom of association or actual liberty of contract, and employers who are organized in the corporate and other forms of ownership association substantially burdens and affects the flow of commerce." Our assumption that employers set wages is in this tradition....

CHAPTER 1: INTRODUCTION

Many labor economists find the claim that labor markets are pervasively monopsonistic inherently implausible. It is doubtful that anyone would claim literally that the labor supply curve facing a firm is, in the short run, infinitely elastic as the perfectly competitive model assumes. Almost certainly, most labor economists think of the elasticity as "high" and that the competitive model provides a tolerable approximation to reality.

But, once one concedes that the competitive model is not literally true, it becomes an empirical matter just how good an approximation it is. The claim of this book is that, for many questions, the competitive model is not a tolerable approximation, and that our understanding of labor markets would be much improved by thinking in terms of a model where the labor supply curve facing the firm is not infinitely elastic.

The belief that the elasticity of the labor supply curve facing a firm is infinitely elastic is not based on any great weight of accumulated empirical evidence. The number of papers written about the elasticity of the labor supply curve at firm level can almost be counted on the fingers of one hand.... Rather, it is introspection (or revelation) which is the source of the faith of many labor economists in the irrelevance of monopsony.

There are a number of sources of this faith. First, there is the belief that large employers are necessary for employers to have some market power and that the vast majority of employers are small in relation to their labor market.... But the approach developed [here] does not require employers to be "large" in relation to their labor market. It only requires that a wage cut of a cent does not cause all workers to leave employment immediately.

Secondly, some labor economists argue that labor turnover rates are so high that workers cannot be thought of as "tied" to firms. But, the *level* of labor turnover is irrelevant: the issue is the *sensitivity* of labor turnover rates to the wage. Existing studies of this find that separations are related to the wage but that the elasticity is not enormous....

Some other labor economists think that the supply of labor to a firm is irrelevant because they believe that the normal state of affairs is that employers are turning away workers who want a job at prevailing wages. Involuntary unemployment might be taken as one piece of evidence in this respect, low vacancy rates as another. But ... the existence of monopsony and involuntary unemployment are essentially orthogonal issues. Employers have market power over their workers whenever the elasticity of the supply of workers that the employer might consider employing is less than infinite, while involuntary unemployment exists when the supply of the workers that the employer would want is less than the supply who would like to work at the going wage.... [L]ow vacancy rates and durations are perfectly consistent with the existence of labor supply being a constraint on employers. As job creation is costly, firms will not create jobs they do not expect to be able to fill. Hence, one should think of vacancies as "accidents" and a low vacancy rate is perfectly consistent with employers having some monopsony power.

Thus, the faith that so many labor economists have in the irrelevance of monopsony or oligopsony is not based on hard evidence, and the throwaway arguments sometimes heard are not as compelling as generations of labor economists have been led to believe....

[E]mployers have non-negligible market power over their workers and ... our understanding of labor markets would be markedly improved by an explicit recognition of this fact....

It is frictions, broadly defined, that give employers monopsony power in the labor market. The most important sources of these frictions are:

- ignorance among workers about labor market opportunities;
- individual heterogeneity in preferences over jobs;
- mobility costs ...

[S]keptics might more legitimately wonder whether the extent of monopsony power in the labor market is large....

There are two ways to address these doubts. First, one can try to provide direct evidence on the extent of monopsony power. This means trying to obtain estimates of the elasticity of the labor supply curve facing individual employers.... [T]his simple aim is not so easy to achieve in a credible way. The estimates we have that are based on the most persuasive methodology ... show the elasticity to be very low. But, there is scope for a lot more work here.

The second way of providing evidence on the extent of monopsony power is more indirect: to provide evidence on the predictions of monopsony and to emphasize how monopsony can provide a much better explanation of a wide range of labor market phenomena.... The market power of employers is large enough to explain, among other things, why:

- there is substantial wage dispersion in the labor market;
- there is an employer size wage effect;
- separation rates are lower for high-wage workers;
- employers pay higher wages to more senior workers even if productivity is no higher;
- more experienced displaced workers suffer larger earnings losses ... ;
- part of the gender pay gap exists;
- equal pay legislation does not harm the employment of women;
- "good" employers pay more;
- it is hard to find evidence of compensating wage differentials;
- lower-wage workers are more likely to be looking for another job;
- low-wage employers find it harder to fill vacancies;
- employers are prepared to pay for the general training of their workers;
- it is so hard to find evidence of job losses associated with the minimum wage;
- non-union employers pay higher wages in more unionized labor markets.

But, it is important to retain a sense of perspective on what monopsony can and cannot explain....

How important is the value-added of monopsony depends on the issue one is considering. If one wants to understand the gap in wages between a chief executive and the person who cleans their office then, although there are arguments in favor of the view that the labor market for cleaners is more monopsonistic than that for chief executives (e.g., a much higher fraction of cleaners is likely to be recruited directly from non-employment), this is not the first-order effect. Demand and supply factors are almost certainly the more important components of the explanation....

But, one should not be carried away by this particular example to imagine that monopsony power is so small as to be ignorable. The frontier of labor economics is not concerned with answering easy questions like "why are chief executives paid more than cleaners?" It is about trying to answer trickier questions about the causes of changes in wage inequality, the impact of minimum wages. And, here, the impact of monopsony is of a size that labor economists cannot ignore. Few estimates of the elasticity of the labor supply curve to an individual employer exceed 5 and [this] then implies that wages will be 17% below marginal products, a similar order of magnitude to the union wage mark-up ... and to estimates of how much minimum wages raise the earnings of the lowpaid. [Republished with permission of Princeton University Press; permission conveyed through Copyright Clearance Center, Inc.]

Paul Weiler, *Governing the Workplace* (Cambridge: Harvard University Press, 1990) at 136–52

A major premise of this book is that there are fundamental differences between the market for the labor of a human being and markets for other commodities, including the labor of a robot; these differences are (and should be) manifested throughout the entire employment relationship, not only with respect to exceptional concerns such as workplace safety. As good a way as any to appreciate the nature and significance of such differences is to reflect briefly on some peculiar features of contemporary employment, features that are widespread in the real world but anomalous in neoclassical economic theory.

Rigidity of Wages

Perhaps the most widely noted such phenomenon is that when the general demand for labor drops in the economy, the wages and benefits paid to workers usually do not drop; indeed, nominal compensation typically continues to rise. It is true that when severe drops occur in the demand and consequently in the price for particular product lines, special (and usually traumatic) wage concessions may be negotiated in the affected industries (say, in steel or airlines), so that the firms' costs of production can be brought into line with their shrunken revenues. But a general decline in economic activity coupled with a substantial increase in unemployment in the overall labor market is rarely used by employers as a reason to reduce wages to a level which would be sufficient to attract and keep workers who are in surplus supply. Instead, the standard way in which firms adjust to a reduction in consumer demand is to lay off workers and reduce production rather than cut employee wages in order to reduce consumer prices and thereby maintain sales and production.... Whatever may be the source or the cure of such inflexibility in wage levels, what is significant here is the sharp contrast between the labor market and the market for nonhuman commodities. A slump that hits the economy will have a downward impact on the price paid by firms such as General Motors to almost all its suppliers (including vendors of robots), who will themselves have a surplus of product to sell, and to whom GM will feel no obligation to continue paying pre-slump prices or maintain the suppliers' income. Although it is not unique, the labor market is very much a special case in this respect.

Distribution of Wages

Not only are rates of pay not particularly influenced by changes in short-term demand for labor, but they are not strongly correlated with the long-term productivity of the individual worker. Within the firm, the distribution of wages among employees is far more compressed than is the range of differences in their relative productivity, even where such differences can be individually metered. The larger, more sophisticated firms use job evaluation programs that establish rates of pay for the job, not for the individual; and as we saw earlier, progress along that salary scale is based more on length of service than on apparent 'merit.' Though the outside market becomes relevant when the firm must decide where to peg its internal wage structure in the community pay spectrum, surveys conducted of local wage patterns find that there is still a wide disparity in wages paid by different firms for the same type and quality of work. Even more curious, there is a systematic tilt in this pay range under which the larger, more capital-intensive, more profitable firms pay considerably higher wages (and benefits) for the same workers than do their smaller counterparts. The implication, then, is that employees as a group are allowed to share in the overall economic success of their employers even if their individual performance is no better than that of workers in less successful firms; and these wages are distributed in a relatively egalitarian manner within this group of employees, rather than related strongly to individual productive merit. The other side of the coin is that large powerful firms like General Motors and IBM, which can command a discount on almost everything else they buy (money and raw materials as well as robots), pay a premium when they buy labor from human beings.

Internal Labor Market

The allocation of attractive jobs in the more successful firms is done in accordance with what has been called an internal labor market. The selection of workers to be promoted, for example, is made by posting the job vacancy to solicit applications from current employees, then picking one of the internal contenders to fill the position. Only if no suitable candidate can be found inside the firm will the search be broadened to look at outside applicants. To the extent promotion is based on relative ability, it can serve as a substitute for merit pay in that it motivates workers to do better in their present job in order to improve their chances in the competition for better positions. Most firms rely not simply on incumbency, but also to a considerable extent on seniority as a criterion for promotion decisions (seniority counts very heavily for layoffs), thus reducing the level of competition even among workers in the firm. Whatever may be the range and mix of administration and market inside the work force, incumbent employees in these firms are almost entirely insulated from the outside market in the allocation of jobs: they need not worry greatly about an outsider's persuading the company that he will do better in filling a vacancy, and they need worry hardly at all about an outsider's offering to do the work more cheaply in the case of a surplus of employees in a recession. Again, this pattern is almost totally limited to the purchase and sale of human labor, by contrast with the market for almost any other commodity.

Career Employment

These standard features of contemporary employment are closely connected to the phenomenon I described earlier: the long-term career relationship of the worker to the firm.

Indeed that kind of relationship is likely to be induced and reinforced by this pattern of administration of job opportunities, wages, and benefits. The implication I drew from the earlier discussion was that an individual's present job becomes more and more valuable to him as he commits more and more of his working life to it while working his way up the internal labor ladder; and that this presents a compelling case for some kind of protection against arbitrary dismissal from the firm and expulsion into the outside market. The crucial point is that the pattern of workers committing themselves to jobs and becoming locked into relationships that can last for decades reduces and inhibits the play of market forces that function most effectively in settings where there is flexibility and mobility in the competition for services.

A number of general comments can be made about these features of the world of work. First, I do not suggest that they are inevitable and universal. Indeed, as we shall see, this employment pattern is of relatively recent vintage. There are many contemporary examples of occupations marked by more casual relationships and more influenced by standard market forces; jobs that range in quality from the migrant farm laborer to the entertainment personality in theater, television, sports, and so on. But the majority of jobs filled by people who are committed to stay in the labor force take the form of this structured career arrangement: in such jobs internal administrative regulation has much more influence than does conventional supply and demand from the external market.

Nor can we bracket these observations from our analysis by assuming these practices to be the hallmark primarily of unionized or union-like public employers—organizations that are supposedly less productive than they might be because they are not required by the market to be efficient in their use of labor. It is fair to say that the origins and impetus of this kind of employment structure are to be found in collective bargaining, and that they continue to remain more pronounced in the union sector. However, administration of employment along the lines I have sketched is also a visible and regular characteristic of nonunion firms; and, even more significantly, of the more successful, more profitable nonunion firms that other employers try to learn from and to emulate. In other words, employers like IBM, General Motors, and the federal government behave very differently in their purchase of labor than in their purchases of other commodities in the marketplace. [Reprinted by permission of the publisher, Harvard University Press, Copyright © 1965, 1971, 1990 by the Presidents and Fellows of Harvard College.]

Richard Freeman & James Medoff, "The Two Faces of Unionism" (1979) 57 *The Public Interest* 69 at 70–93

Our research demonstrates that [the] view of unions as organizations whose chief function is to raise wages is seriously misleading. For in addition to raising wages, unions have significant non-wage effects which influence diverse aspects of modern industrial life. By providing workers with a voice both at the workplace and in the political arena, unions can and do affect positively the functioning of the economic and social systems. Although our research on the non-wage effects of trade unions is by no means complete and some results will surely change as more evidence becomes available, enough work has been done to yield the broad outlines of a new view of unionism.

UNIONS AS COLLECTIVE VOICE

One key dimension of the new work on trade unionism can best be understood by recognizing that societies have two basic mechanisms for dealing with divergences between desired social conditions and actual conditions. The first is the classic market mechanism of exit and entry, individual mobility: The dissatisfied consumer switches products; the diner whose soup is too salty seeks another restaurant; the unhappy couple divorces. In the labor market, exit is synonymous with quitting, while entry consists of new hires by the firm. By leaving less-desirable jobs for more-desirable jobs, or by refusing bad jobs, individuals penalize the bad employer and reward the good—leading to an overall improvement in the efficiency of the social system. The basic theorem of neoclassical economics is that, under well-specified conditions, the exit and entry of persons (the hallmark of free enterprise) produces a "Pareto-optimum" situation—one in which no individual can be made better off without making someone worse off. Economic analysis can be viewed as a detailed study of the implications of this kind of adjustment and of the extent to which it works out in real economies. As long as the exit-entry market mechanism is viewed as the only efficient adjustment mechanism, institutions such as unions must necessarily be viewed as impediments to the optimal operation of a capitalist economy.

There is, however, a second mode of adjustment. This is the political mechanism, which Albert Hirschman termed "voice" in his important book, *Exit, Voice, and Loyalty*. "Voice" refers to the use of direct communication to bring actual and desired conditions closer together. It means talking about problems: complaining to the store about a poor product rather than taking business elsewhere; telling the chef that the soup had too much salt; discussing marital problems rather than going directly to the divorce court. In a political context, "voice" refers to participation in the democratic process, through voting, discussion, bargaining, and the like....

In the job market, voice consists of discussing with an employer conditions that ought to be changed, rather than quitting the job. In modern industrial economies, and particularly in large enterprises, a trade union is the vehicle for collective voice—that is, for providing workers as a group with a means of communicating with management.

Collective rather than individual bargaining with an employer is necessary for effective voice at the workplace for two reasons. First, many important aspects of an industrial setting are "public goods," which affect the well-being (negatively or positively) of every employee. As a result, the incentive for any single person to express his preferences, and invest time and money to change conditions (for the good of all), is reduced. Safety conditions, lighting, heating, the speed of a production line, the firm's policies on layoffs, work-sharing, cyclical-wage adjustment, and promotion, its formal grievance procedure and pension plan—all obviously affect the entire workforce in the same way that defense, sanitation, and fire protection affect the entire citizenry. "Externalities" (things done by one individual or firm that also affect the well-being of another, but for which the individual or firm is not compensated or penalized) and "public goods" at the workplace require collective decision-making. Without a collective organization, the incentive for the individual to take into account the effects of his or her actions on others, or express his or her preferences, or invest time and money in changing conditions, is likely to be too small to spur action. Why not "let Harry do it" and enjoy the benefits at no cost? This classic "free-rider" problem lies at the heart of the so-called "union-security" versus "right-to-work" debate.

A second reason collective action is necessary is that workers who are not prepared to exit will be unlikely to reveal their true preferences to their bosses, for fear of some sort of punishment.... Since the employer can fire a protester, individual protest is dangerous; so a prerequisite for workers' having effective voice in the employment relationship is the protection of activists from being discharged ...

The collective nature of trade unionism fundamentally alters the operation of a labor market and, hence, the nature of the labor contract. In a non-union setting, where exit and entry are the predominant forms of adjustment, the signals and incentives to firms depend on the preferences of the "marginal" worker, the one who will leave (or be attracted) by particular conditions or changes in conditions. The firm responds primarily to the needs of this marginal, generally younger and more mobile worker and can within some bounds ignore the preferences of "infra-marginal," typically older workers, who—for reasons of skill, knowledge, rights that cannot be readily transferred to other enterprises, as well as because of other costs associated with changing firms—are effectively immobile. In a unionized setting, by contrast, the union takes account of the preferences of all workers to form an average preference that typically determines its position at the bargaining table. Because unions are political institutions with elected leaders, they are likely to be responsive to a different set of preferences from those that dominate in a competitive labor market.

... When issues involve sizeable fixed costs or "public goods," a calculus based on the average preference can lead to a contract which, ignoring distributional effects, is socially more desirable than one based on the marginal preference—that is, it may even be economically more "efficient."

As a voice institution, unions also fundamentally alter the social relations of the workplace. Perhaps most importantly, a union constitutes a source of worker power in a firm, diluting managerial authority and offering members a measure of due process, in particular through the union innovation of a grievance and arbitration system.... More broadly, the entire industrial jurisprudence system—by which many workplace decisions are based on negotiated rules (such as seniority) instead of supervisory judgment (or whim), and are subject to challenge through the grievance/arbitration procedure—represents a major change in the power relations within firms. As a result, in unionized firms workers are more willing and able to express discontent and to object to managerial decisions.

Thus, as a collective alternative to individualistic actions in the market, unions are much more than simple monopolies that raise wages and restrict the competitive adjustment process. Given imperfect information and the existence of public goods in industrial settings, and conflicting interests in the workplace and in the political arena, unionism provides an alternative mechanism for bringing about change. This is not to deny that unions have monopolistic power nor that they use this power to raise wages for a select part of the workforce. The point is that unionism has two "faces," each of which leads to a different view of the institution: One, which is at the fore in economic analysis, is that of a monopoly; the other is that of "a voice institution," i.e., a socio-political institution. To understand fully what unions do in modern industrial economies, it is necessary to examine both faces....

EFFECTS ON EFFICIENCY

In the monopoly view, unions reduce society's output in three ways. First, union-won wage increases cause a misallocation of resources by inducing organized firms to hire fewer workers, to use more capital per worker, and to hire higher quality workers than is socially efficient. Second, union contract provisions—such as limits on the loads that can be handled by workers, restrictions on tasks performed, featherbedding, and so forth—reduce the output that should be forthcoming from a given amount of capital and labor. Third, strikes called to force management to accept union demands cause a substantial reduction in gross national product.

By contrast, the collective-voice/institutional-response model directs attention to the important ways in which unionism can raise productivity. First of all, unionism should reduce "quits." As workers' voice increases in an establishment, less reliance need be placed on the exit and entry mechanism to obtain desired working conditions. Since hiring and training costs are lowered and the functioning of work groups is less disrupted when "quit" rates are low, unionism can actually raise efficiency.

The fact that senior workers are likely to be relatively more powerful in enterprises where decisions are based on voice instead of exit and entry points to another way in which unions can raise productivity. Under unionism, promotions and other rewards tend to be less dependent in any precise way on individual performance and more dependent on seniority. As a result, in union plants feelings of rivalry among individuals are likely to be less pronounced than in non-union plants and the amount of informal training and assistance that workers are willing to provide one another is greater. (The importance of seniority in firms in Japan, together with the permanent employment guaranteed many workers there, have often been cited as factors increasing the productivity of Japanese enterprises.) It is, of course, also important to recognize that seniority can reduce productivity by placing individuals in jobs for which they are not qualified.

Unionism can also raise efficiency by pressuring management into tightening job-production standards and accountability, in an effort to respond to union demands while maintaining profits ... [M]odern personnel practices are forced on the firm and traditional paternalism is discarded.... Most of the econometric analysis of unions has focused on the question of central concern to the monopoly view: How large is the union wage effect? In his important book, *Unionism and Relative Wages*, H. Gregg Lewis summarized results of this analysis through the early 1960s, concluding that, while differing over time and across settings, the union wage effect averages on the order of 10 to 15 percent. That is, as a result of collective bargaining, a union member makes about 10 to 15 percent more than an otherwise comparable worker who is not a member. Later work, using larger data files which have information permitting more extensive controls and employing more complex statistical techniques, tends to confirm Lewis's generalization. While unions in some environments raise wages by an enormous amount, the average estimated union wage effect is by no means overwhelming....

THE EVIDENCE ON QUITS AND PRODUCTIVITY

One of the central tenets of the collective-voice/institutional-response model is that among workers receiving the same pay, unions reduce employee turnover and its associated costs by offering "voice" as an alternative to exit. Our own research ... shows that, with diverse factors (including wages) held constant, unionized workers do have significantly lower quit rates than non-union workers who are comparable in other respects....

Our analyses ... suggest that the monopoly view of unions as a major deterrent to productivity is erroneous. In some settings, unionism leads to higher productivity, not only because of the greater capital intensity and *higher* labor quality, but also because of what can best be termed institutional-response factors....

[U]nionism may increase productivity in some settings and decrease it in others. If the increase in productivity is greater than the increase in average unit costs due to the union wage effect, then the profit rate will increase; if not, the rate of profit will fall. There is limited tentative evidence that, on average, net profits are reduced somewhat by unionism, particularly in oligopolistic industries, though there are notable exceptions. At present, there is no definitive accounting of what proportion of the union wage effect comes at the expense of capital, other labor, or consumers, and what portion is offset by previously unexploited possibilities for productivity improvements.

Finally, it is important to note that despite what some critics of unions might claim, strikes do not seem to cost society a substantial amount of goods and services.... Even "national emergency" disputes—those that would be expected to have the largest repercussions on the economy—do not have major deleterious impacts. Though highly publicized, the days idle because of the direct and indirect effects of strikes represent only a minuscule fraction of the total days worked in the U.S. economy....

PERSONNEL PRACTICES AND EMPLOYEE BENEFITS

[...]

Data on the remuneration of individual workers and on the expenditures for employees by firms show that the proportion of compensation allotted to fringe benefits is markedly higher for organized blue-collar workers than for similar non-union workers. Within most industries, important fringes such as pensions, and life, accident, and health insurance are much more likely to be found in unionized establishments.... The greatest increases in fringes induced by unionism are for deferred compensation, which is generally favoured by older, more stable employees. This is consistent with the view that unions are more responsive to senior, less-mobile workers....

One of the most important personnel decisions made by a firm is how to adjust its employment and wages in response to swings in economic demand: by temporary layoffs, cuts in wage growth, reduced hours, or voluntary attrition. The evidence indicates that the layoff mechanism is used to a much greater extent in unionized than in non-union establishments. It is important to note, however, that the vast majority of these layoffs are temporary, in that the laid-off members await rehire and are recalled after a short spell of unemployment....

Why do temporary layoffs dominate alternative adjustment mechanisms to a much greater extent in firms that are unionized than in those that are not? The most reasonable explanation is that under the provisions of most union contracts—which specify that junior workers will be laid off before those with more company service—senior workers, who can be expected to have greater power in organized firms, will generally prefer layoffs over the alternatives.

THE DISTRIBUTION OF INCOME

One of the striking implications of the monopoly view, which runs counter to popular thought, is that union wage gains increase inequality in the labor market. According to the monopoly model, the workers displaced from unionized firms as a result of union wage gains raise the supply of labor to non-union firms, which can therefore be expected to reduce wages. Thus in the monopoly view unionized workers are likely to be made better off at the expense of non-union workers. The fact that organized blue-collar workers would tend to be more skilled and higher paid than other blue-collar workers even in the absence of unionism implies further that unionism benefits "labour's elite" at the expense of those with less skill and earning power. Since many people have supported unions in the belief they reduce economic inequality, evidence that unions have the opposite effect would be a strong argument against the union movement.

In fact, the collective-voice/institutional-response model suggests very different effects on equality than does the monopoly view. Given that union decisions are based on a political process, and given that the majority of union members are likely to have earnings below the mean (including white-collar workers) in any workplace, unions can be expected to seek to reduce wage inequality. Union members are also likely to favor a less-dispersed distribution of earnings for reasons of ideology and organizational solidarity. Finally, by its nature, collective bargaining reduces managerial discretion in the wage-setting process, and this should also reduce differences among similarly situated workers.

Two common union wage policies exemplify unions' efforts to reduce economic inequality. The first is the long-standing policy of pushing for "standard rates"—uniform rates for comparable workers across establishments, and for given occupational classes within establishments. While many large non-union enterprises today also employ formal wage-setting practices, personal differentials based on service, performance, favoritism, or other factors are more common in the non-union than in the union sector.... Overall, according to Slichter, Healy, and Livernash, "the influence of unions has clearly been one of minimizing and eliminating judgment-based differences in pay for individuals employed on the same job" and of "removing ability and performance judgments as a factor in individual pay for job performance." One important potential result of these policies is a reduction of inequality, possibly at the expense of efficiency, which may be lessened because the reward for individual effort is reduced. Another important potential result of this policy is that wage discrimination against minorities is likely to be less in unionized than in non-unionized settings.

Union policies favoring seniority in promotion, and job-posting and bidding systems in which workers are informed about new openings and can bid for promotions, can also be expected to have egalitarian consequences. The possibility that arbitrary supervisory judgments will determine the career of a worker is greatly reduced by the development of formal rules which treat each worker identically....

EXPLAINING MANAGERIAL OPPOSITION

If, in addition to its negative monopoly effects, trade unionism is associated with substantial positive effects on the operation of the economy and on the performance of firms, why do so many U.S. firms oppose unions so vehemently? There are in fact several reasons.

First, the bulk of the economic gains that spring from unionism accrue to workers and not to owners or managers. Managers are unlikely to see any personal benefits in their subordinates' unionization, but are likely to be quite aware of the costs: a diminution of their power, the need to work harder, the loss of operating flexibility, and the like.

Second, though productivity might typically be higher in union than in otherwise comparable non-union work settings, so too are wages. It would seem, given the objectives and actions of most unions, that the rate of return on capital would be lower under collective bargaining, although there are important exceptions. Thus, there is risk in unionization; the firm may be able to rationalize operations, have good relations with the union, and maintain its profit rate—or it may not. In addition, while the total cost of strikes to society as a whole has been shown to be quite small, the potential cost to a particular firm can be substantial. Since managers—like most other people—dislike taking risks, we would expect opposition to unions even if on average the benefits to firms equal the costs. Moreover, given the wide-ranging differences in the effects of unions on economic performance, at least some managerial opposition surely arises from enterprises in which the expected benefits of collective bargaining are small but the expected costs high. Even the most vocal advocate of the collective-voice/institutional-response view of unionism would admit that, though functional in many industrial settings, unions are not functional in others—and one must expect greater managerial opposition in the latter cases.

Third, management may find unionism expensive, difficult, and very threatening in its initial stages, when modes of operation must be altered if efficiency is to be improved. New and different types of management policies are needed under unionism, and these require either changes in the behavior of current management, or—as appears to be the case in many just-organized firms—a new set of managers.

Finally, U.S. management has generally adopted an ideology of top-down enlightened control, under which unions are seen as both a cause and an effect of managerial failure. In this view, unions interfere with management's efforts to carry out its social function of ensuring that goods and services are produced efficiently. In addition, because unions typically come into existence as a result of management's mistakes in dealing with its workforce, managers frequently resent what unionization implies about their own past performances.

[Reprinted with permission of the authors and *The Public Interest*, Number 57, Fall 1979, pp. 69–93 © 1979 by National Affairs, Inc.]

1:320 Normative Defences and Critiques of Market Ordering

Milton Friedman, *Capitalism and Freedom* (Chicago: University of Chicago Press, 1962) at 12–15

The basic problem of social organization is how to co-ordinate the economic activities of large numbers of people. Even in relatively backward societies, extensive division of labor and specialization of function is required to make effective use of available resources. In advanced societies, the scale on which co-ordination is needed, to take full advantage of the opportunities offered by modern science and technology, is enormously greater. Literally millions of people are involved in providing one another with their daily bread, let alone with their yearly automobiles. The challenge to the believer in liberty is to reconcile this widespread interdependence with individual freedom.

Fundamentally, there are only two ways of co-ordinating the economic activities of millions. One is central direction involving the use of coercion—the technique of the army and of the modern totalitarian state. The other is voluntary cooperation of individuals—the technique of the market place.

The possibility of co-ordination through voluntary co-operation rests on the elementary—yet frequently denied—proposition that both parties to an economic transaction benefit from it, *provided the transaction is bi-laterally voluntary and informed*.

Exchange can therefore bring about co-ordination without coercion. A working model of a society organized through voluntary exchange is a *free private enterprise exchange economy*—what we have been calling competitive capitalism.

In its simplest form, such a society consists of a number of independent households—a collection of Robinson Crusoes, as it were. Each household uses the resources it controls to produce goods and services that it exchanges for goods and services produced by other households, on terms mutually acceptable to the two parties to the bargain. It is thereby enabled to satisfy its wants indirectly by producing goods and services for others, rather than directly by producing goods for its own immediate use. The incentive for adopting this indirect route is, of course, the increased product made possible by division of labor and specialization of function. Since the household always has the alternative of producing directly for itself, it need not enter into any exchange unless it benefits from it. Hence, no exchange will take place unless both parties do benefit from it. Co-operation is thereby achieved without coercion.

Specialization of function and division of labor would not go far if the ultimate productive unit were the household. In a modern society, we have gone much farther. We have introduced enterprises which are intermediaries between individuals in their capacities as suppliers of service and as purchasers of goods. And similarly, specialization of function and division of labor could not go very far if we had to continue to rely on the barter of product for product. In consequence, money has been introduced as a means of facilitating exchange, and of enabling the acts of purchase and of sale to be separated into two parts.

Despite the important role of enterprises and of money in our actual economy, and despite the numerous and complex problems they raise, the central characteristic of the market technique of achieving co-ordination is fully displayed in the simple exchange economy that contains neither enterprises nor money. As in that simple model, so in the complex enterprise and money-exchange economy, co-operation is strictly individual and voluntary provided: (a) that enterprises are private, so that the ultimate contracting parties are individuals and (b) that individuals are effectively free to enter or not to enter into any particular exchange, so that every transaction is strictly voluntary.

It is far easier to state these provisos in general terms than to spell them out in detail, or to specify precisely the institutional arrangements most conducive to their maintenance. Indeed, much of technical economic literature is concerned with precisely these questions. The basic requisite is the maintenance of law and order to prevent physical coercion of one individual by another and to enforce contracts voluntarily entered into, thus giving substance to 'private.' Aside from this, perhaps the most difficult problems arise from monopoly—which inhibits effective freedom by denying individuals alternatives to the particular exchange—and from 'neighbourhood effects'—effects on third parties for which it is not feasible to charge or recompense them....

So long as effective freedom of exchange is maintained, the central feature of the market organization of economic activity is that it prevents one person from interfering with another in respect of most of his activities. The consumer is protected from coercion by the seller because of the presence of other sellers with whom he can deal. The seller is protected from coercion by the consumer because of other consumers to whom he can sell. The employee is protected from coercion by the employer because of other employers for whom he can work, and so on. And the market does this impersonally and without centralized authority.

Indeed, a major source of objection to a free economy is precisely that it does this task so well. It gives people what they want instead of what a particular group thinks they ought to want. Underlying most arguments against the free market is a lack of belief in freedom itself. [© 1962 by The University of Chicago. Reprinted by permission.]

CB Macpherson, "Elegant Tombstones: A Note on Friedman's Freedom" in *Democratic Theory: Essays in Retrieval* (New York: Oxford University Press, 1973) 143 at 145–47

Professor Friedman's demonstration that the capitalist market economy can co-ordinate economic activities without coercion rests on an elementary conceptual error. His argument runs as follows. He shows first that in a simple market model, where each individual or household controls resources enabling it to produce goods and services either directly for itself or for exchange, there will be production for exchange because of the increased product made possible by specialization. But 'since the household always has the alternative of producing directly for itself, it need not enter into any exchange unless it benefits from it. Hence no exchange will take place unless both parties do benefit from it. Co-operation is thereby achieved without coercion.' ... So far, so good. It is indeed clear that in this simple exchange model, assuming rational maximizing behaviour by all hands, every exchange will benefit both parties, and hence that no coercion is involved in the decision to produce for exchange or in any act of exchange.

Professor Friedman then moves on to our actual complex economy, or rather to his own curious model of it:

> As in [the] simple model, so in the complex enterprise and money-exchange economy, co-operation is strictly individual and voluntary *provided*: (a) that enterprises are private,

so that the ultimate contracting parties are individuals and (b) that individuals are effectively free to enter or not to enter into any particular exchange, so that every transaction is strictly voluntary....

One cannot take exception to proviso (a): it is clearly required in the model to produce a co-operation that is 'strictly individual.' One might, of course, suggest that a model containing this stipulation is far from corresponding to our actual complex economy, since in the latter the ultimate contracting parties who have the most effect on the market are not individuals but corporations, and moreover, corporations which in one way or another manage to opt out of the fully competitive market. This criticism, however, would not be accepted by all economists as self-evident: some would say that the question who has most effect on the market is still an open question (or is a wrongly posed question). More investigation and analysis of this aspect of the economy would be valuable. But political scientists need not await its results before passing judgement on Friedman's position, nor should they be tempted to concentrate their attention on proviso (a). If they do so they are apt to miss the fault in proviso (b), which is more fundamental, and of a different kind. It is not a question of the correspondence of the model to the actual: it is a matter of the inadequacy of the proviso to produce the model.

Proviso (b) is 'that individuals are effectively free to enter or not to enter into any *particular* exchange,' and it is held that with this proviso 'every transaction is strictly voluntary.' A moment's thought will show that this is not so. The proviso that is required to make every transaction strictly voluntary is *not* freedom not to enter into any *particular* exchange, but freedom not to enter into any exchange *at all*. This, and only this, was the proviso that proved the simple model to be voluntary and non-coercive; and nothing less than this would prove the complex model to be voluntary and *non-coercive*. But Professor Friedman is clearly claiming that freedom not to enter into any particular exchange is enough: 'The consumer is protected from coercion by the seller because of the presence of other sellers with whom he can deal.... The employee is protected from coercion by the employer because of other employers for whom he can work....'

One almost despairs of logic, and of the use of models. It is easy to see what Professor Friedman has done, but it is less easy to excuse it. He has moved from the simple economy of exchange between independent producers, to the capitalist economy, without mentioning the most important thing that distinguishes them. He mentions money instead of barter, and 'enterprises which are intermediaries between individuals in their capacities as suppliers of services and as purchasers of goods' ... as if money and merchants were what distinguished a capitalist economy from an economy of independent producers. What distinguishes the capitalist economy from the simple exchange economy is the separation of labour and capital, that is, the existence of a labour force without its own sufficient capital and therefore without a choice as to whether to put its labour in the market or not. Professor Friedman would agree that where there is no choice there is coercion. His attempted demonstration that capitalism co-ordinates without coercion therefore fails.

Since all his specific arguments against the welfare and regulatory state depend on his case that the market economy is not coercive, the reader may spare himself the pains (or, if an economist, the pleasure) of attending to the careful and persuasive reasoning by which he seeks to establish the minimum to which coercion could be reduced by reducing or discarding each of the main regulatory and welfare activities of the state. None of this takes into account the coercion involved in the separation of capital from labour, or the possible mitigation of this coercion by the regulatory and welfare state. Yet it is because this coercion can in principle be reduced by the regulatory and welfare state, and thereby the amount of effective individual liberty be increased, that liberals have been justified in pressing, in the name of liberty, for infringements on the pure operation of competitive capitalism.

[© Oxford University Press 1973. Reprinted by permission of Oxford University Press.]

Max Weber, "Freedom and Coercion" in M Rheinstein, ed, *Max Weber on Law in Economy and Society*, translated by E Shils & M Rheinstein (Cambridge: Harvard University Press, 1954) 188 at 188–91

The formal right of a worker to enter into any contract whatsoever with any employer whatsoever does not in practice represent for the employment seeker even the slightest freedom in the determination of his own conditions of work, and it does not guarantee him any influence on this process. It rather means, at least primarily, that the more powerful party in the market, i.e., normally the employer, has the possibility to set the terms, to offer the job 'take it or leave it,' and, given the normally more pressing economic need of the worker, to impose his terms upon him. The result of contractual freedom, then, is in the first place the opening of the opportunity to use, by the clever utilization of property ownership in the market, these resources without legal restraints as a means for the achievement of power over others. The parties interested in power in the market thus are also interested in such a legal order. Their interest is served particularly by the establishment of 'legal empowerment rules.' This kind of rule does no more than create the framework for valid agreements which, under conditions of formal freedom, are officially available to all. Actually, however, they are accessible only to the owners of property and thus in effect support their very autonomy and power positions.... The increasing significance of freedom of contract and, particularly, of enabling laws which leave everything to 'free' agreement, implies a relative reduction of that kind of coercion which results from the threat of mandatory and prohibitory norms. Formally it represents, of course, a decrease of coercion. But it is also obvious how advantageous this state of affairs is to those who are economically in the position to make use of the empowerments. The exact extent to which the total amount of 'freedom' within a given legal community is actually increased depends entirely upon the concrete economic order and especially upon the property distribution. In no case can it be simply deduced from the content of the law....

The private enterprise system transforms into objects of 'labor market transactions' even those personal and authoritarian-hierarchical relations which actually exist in the capitalistic enterprise. While the authoritarian relationships are thus drained of all normal sentimental content, authoritarian constraint not only continues but, at least under certain circumstances, even increases. The larger a structure whose existence depends in some specific way on 'discipline,' for instance a capitalistic industrial plant, the more relentlessly can authoritarian constraint be exercised in it, at least under certain conditions. It finds its counterpart in the shrinkage of the circle of those in whose hands the power to use this type of constraint is concentrated and who also hold the power to have that former power guaranteed to them by the legal order. A legal order which contains ever so few mandatory and prohibitory norms and ever so many 'freedoms' and 'empowerments' can nonetheless in its practical effects facilitate a quantitative and qualitative increase not only of coercion in general but quite specifically of authoritarian coercion.

[Reprinted by permission of the publisher, Harvard University Press, Copyright © 1954 by the Presidents and Fellows of Harvard College, Copyright © renewed 1982 by Edward J Shils.]

* * * * *

These excerpts from MacPherson and Weber reveal one of the most long-standing and controversial aspects of the debate on the normative validity of market ordering and contract as the basis for the ordering of labour. The question of whether the relationship between employers and employees is one that maximizes or promotes liberty and is free of coercion is a central element in a Marxist critique of capitalist labour arrangements.

This is an issue of great importance. The reality is that the employment relationship in Canada is heavily regulated. There are, as already noted, two major components in the current system of regulation—regulation of the substance of the bargain struck by workers and employers (in the form of minimum wage and other labour standards legislation) and regulation of the process of bargaining (through collective bargaining legislation). The orthodox justification for such regulation of the contract of employment is found in the commonplace slogan "inequality of bargaining power," which is a troubling but important notion. What is to be made of it?

A starting point is to note that Adam Smith, in *The Wealth of Nations*, perceived that it would be the employer who would have an upper hand in bargaining with employees:

[I]t is not ... difficult to foresee which of the two parties must, upon all ordinary occasions, have the advantage in the dispute, and force the other into compliance with their terms .... In all such disputes the masters can hold out much longer. A landlord, a farmer, a master manufacturer, or merchant, though they did not employ a single workman, could generally live a year or two upon the stocks which they have already acquired. Many workmen could not subsist a week, few could subsist a month, and scarce any a year without employment. In the long run the workmen [sic] may be as necessary to his master as his master is to him; but the necessity is not so immediate. [(1776) vol. 1 at 81.]

But of what normative significance was this insight? The excerpt from Friedman, above, appears to deny that coercion exists in a system of market ordering.

Some other (more egalitarian) critiques of collective bargaining have focused on the concern that because it enhances the position of some employees, it accentuates the structural inequality between better-off and worse-off employees.

David Beatty, "Ideology, Politics and Unionism" in K Swan & K Swinton, eds, *Studies in Labour Law* (Toronto: Butterworths, 1983) 299 at 301–14

> I argue that collective bargaining does practically nothing to remedy many of the disabilities and inequities generated by the common law system of individual bargaining and actually fosters different injustices of its own.... My purpose is to make clear that the system of collective bargaining that has been advocated by unions for the past fifty years systematically discriminates against some of the most disadvantaged and deprived employees in our society. Not only is it a scheme of employment regulation which is neither legally nor practically available to large segments of our employed population but, as critically, it is one which generally rewards those individuals who are already better off with more humane, dignified and fair working conditions.
>
> [I]n an 'order of labour' (to borrow Renner's phrase) regulated by a law of collective bargaining, we are looking at a continuum on which each occupational group can, to varying degrees, negotiate a package of material and social advantages different from what they would achieve as individuals in a 'pure' or individualized market solution. How different, of course, depends on the relative strength of their bargaining power. Certain groups, as I have noted, predictably and consistently do well. Indeed some collectives of employees, for example policemen or firemen, are so absolutely certain of completely monopolizing the process because of the importance of the services that they render that we prohibit them from even engaging in collective bargaining. For others, collective bargaining has meant very little; personal service workers in hotels, restaurants, retail trade and clothing are traditionally among our lowest paid workers, notwithstanding the presence of collective bargaining.
>
> The positions of these two groups of workers on a continuum measuring the outcomes generated by the collective bargaining system reveal horizontal and vertical inequities which are endemic to the institution.... The gulf that divides these two industrial states tells us that how a group of employees will fare in a system of employment regulated by a law of collective bargaining will depend largely on a set of circumstances over which the individual has little if any control and which are, as a result, highly arbitrary from a moral or social justice point of view ... [T]he system is perverse in the sense that to those with relatively rare endowments and skills, who provide services of relatively constant desire, collective bargaining delivers not only the jobs, but the rewards as well. By contrast, to the unskilled, in the secondary labour markets, collective bargaining can scarcely generate an adequate level of income to meet the official poverty standards.
>
> ... Both the law of collective bargaining, which permits an occupational group to monopolize the provision of a service, and the law of property which sanctions the monopolization by the professional of the scarcity of her labour, are social constructs which have little to do with moral worth or desert. While there is an obvious incentive justification in recognizing the property a woman possesses in her labour, and even a sense of justice in rewarding her effort, unless severe constraints are imposed to guarantee all employees access to a sufficient property to sustain themselves, even such a property right in one's person is without moral justification. Indeed, unless one denies the assertion that the endowments of people, upon which the skills which stratify the supply of labour are

developed, are themselves not deserved, then the argument in favour of merit and meritocracy, of rewarding socially useful effort, leads naturally to the adoption of a much more egalitarian system of rewards than that which is generated by collective bargaining....

In effect, by failing to be sensitive to this argument, and by mimicking the distribution effected by the market, collective bargaining stands condemned of rendering 'morally arbitrary facts [into] ones of great social significance.'

... But it is not just on its inverted system of rewards and target inefficiencies that collective bargaining founders. Collective bargaining prejudices the position of many of the worst-off individuals in our society in other ways as well. Specifically, there is strong theoretical support and some empirical evidence to confirm what is for economists the commonplace hypothesis: that the gains secured by those for whom collective bargaining is a powerful instrument for controlling their employment are made at the expense of the lower income groups in our society. There are two logical ways this can be expected to happen. In the first place there will be occasions when the 'supra-competitive' employment benefits that are secured by a group of employees as a result of their bargaining collectively together will be paid for by those at the lower end of the income scale in the form of higher prices....

Alternatively, if the effects of collective bargaining's successes are alleviated by a reduction in the amount of labour that is hired, which will more commonly be the case where our demand for the product or that labour is not insatiable, the worst-off members in the nation's distribution of goods will be adversely affected in a different way. In this event, to the extent that those who are laid off to counteract the increased cost of the collective bargain seek to find employment in alternative markets, as some must inevitably do, there will be a further depression in the terms and conditions of employment that will be paid in these secondary, unorganized markets.
[Reprinted by permission.]

Debate on the normative value of collective bargaining as an alternative to the individual contracting model has not been confined to its economic and distributive impact. Indeed, traditional defences of collective bargaining may rely heavily on other normative assumptions.

Paul Weiler, *Reconcilable Differences: New Directions in Canadian Labour Law* (Toronto: Carswell, 1980) at 30–32

The economic function is the beginning, not the end, of the case for collective bargaining. The role performed by trade unions has never been narrowly pecuniary. Most industrial relations scholars believe that the true function of economic bargaining consists in its civilizing impact upon the working life and environment of employees.

... Management is challenged to spell out the principles on which it deals with the employee in her daily life. The employees have a vehicle through which they can forcefully voice their objections when any such standards appear to override their interests without compelling reasons. Once the employer has written into a collective agreement the rules by which it will govern the workplace, then any supervisory or departmental edict may be challenged before a neutral arbitrator to test its compliance with these contract standards. An apt way of putting it is to say that good collective bargaining tries to subject the employment relationship and the work environment to the 'rule of law.' Many theorists of industrial relations believe that this function of protecting the employee from the abuse of managerial power, thereby enhancing the dignity of the worker as a person, is the primary value of collective bargaining, one which entitles the institution to positive encouragement from the law....

... Collective bargaining is not simply an instrument for pursuing external ends, whether these be mundane monetary gains or the erection of a private rule of law to protect the dignity of the worker in the face of managerial authority. Rather, collective bargaining is intrinsically valuable as an experience in self-government. It is the mode in which employees participate in setting the terms and conditions of employment, rather than simply accepting what their employer chooses to give them (which, if the employer happens to be benevolent, may be just as generous compensation, just as restrained supervision). If one believes, as I do, that self-determination and self-discipline are inherently worthwhile, indeed, that they are the mark of a truly human community, then it is difficult to see how the law can be neutral about whether that type of economic democracy is to emerge in the workplace.
[Reprinted by permission.]

1:400 THE CHANGING WORLD OF WORK AND OF WORKPLACE LAW

As we indicated at the outset of this chapter, the demands of a changing economy and an increasingly diverse society have radically altered the situation of Canadian labour and employment law. These demands have expanded the range of issues that the law is called upon to address, while at the same time placing pressures on its effectiveness and reach. They have increasingly called upon policy makers to concern themselves not only with workplace justice, but also with economic competitiveness. In this section, we first outline the nature of market pressures generated by the reorganization of enterprises, by the relationship between financial and productive capital, and by globalization. Then we consider the changing position of unions within this altered economic environment. Next, we identify issues for labour and employment law's capacity to foster social inclusion and equality for an increasingly diverse Canadian workforce. We outline the growth of what has come to be known as "precarious work" in the Canadian labour market, and the persistence of unequal opportunity. Finally, we provide a brief introduction to various arguments about how Canadian workplace law can or should respond to these changes to renew its approach to pursuing its central aims.

1:410   Market Pressures and the Reorganization of Production

Federal Labour Standards Review Commission: *Fairness at Work: Labour Standards for the 21st Century* (Gatineau, QC: Department of Human Resources and Skills Development, 2006) at 24–28

It is now a commonplace to say that we live in a "new economy." While the term is ambiguous and sometimes controversial, it is widely understood that we are indeed experiencing the effects of several inter-connected trends, each of which has significant implications for labour markets and labour policy.

First, markets have become more competitive. The deepening and broadening of international economic integration has fostered greater competition for investment and market shares. Since 1991, exports have grown as a share of the Canadian economy from 25% to nearly 38%. We have also seen a similar growth in imports. Because about 84% of our merchandise export trade is with the United States, we are particularly aware of developments in that country that may have an impact on Canada's economy and labour markets. The growing importance of international capital flows has only reinforced this awareness. Moreover, deregulation has opened up many Canadian markets that were once largely closed to new entrants, which in turn has fostered increased price competition and put new pressures on operating costs, including labour costs. These pressures are especially severe where goods or services can be sourced directly from abroad.

The second trend, as noted earlier, is for firms to increasingly rely upon skills and knowledge and their application through technology for a competitive advantage. This has led to greater demand for skilled and knowledge workers, and to fewer opportunities for the unskilled, at least in relatively high wage labour markets such as Canada's. It has also led in some sectors to shortages of skilled workers (partly due to the aging of the workforce), which are not easily remedied because of lags in training policy and increased worldwide demand.

Third, competition has become more time-sensitive. Because many firms now do business on a continental or global basis, they are required to respond to customer demands on a 24/7 basis. Consequently, many employers have been asking their existing workforce to accept more flexible, less sociable and sometimes longer work schedules. They have also asked workers to be on call if needed to work off-site in their "non-working" hours, which technology now allows them to do. Through these strategies, employers have been able to not only avoid the costs of hiring and training additional workers but, to some extent, to actually lower their labour costs.

The fourth trend is that currency, commodity and product markets are becoming more volatile. This has in turn led employers to respond by seeking greater flexibility in introducing technology, in acquiring needed supplies and services and in gaining access to new distribution channels and markets. However, the increasing pace of technological change and global integration also means that competitive advantages may prove to be more short-lived than they once were. One result is that many firms change the size and deployment of their workforce with increasing frequency and rapidity, which in turn leads them to experiment with contractual arrangements that give them greater freedom to do so.

Finally, many firms have reorganized their competitive and operational strategies, partly in response to market competitiveness and volatility, partly in order to exploit new technologies and partly to take advantage of gaps in legal regulations that exist at the boundaries of labour law. Specifically, firms have restructured their production into core and contingent elements, using outsourcing strategies—including supply chain contracting, often with smaller enterprises in a position of economic dependence—in order to reduce costs, focus on core competencies, and achieve greater flexibility to cut back, expand or redeploy the workforce in the face of market changes. Many firms have also sought greater flexibility and/or profitability by expanding their use of part-time, agency and temporary workers....

CHAPTER 1: INTRODUCTION

The emergence of this new economy—even allowing for jurisdictional and sectoral variations—has had important implications for workers.

First, the new economy has transformed working time practices. Flexible schedules and longer hours, now much more common than in the 1960s and 1970s, can impinge dramatically on workers' personal lives, especially if they are required rather than voluntary. In many cases this adds to the pressures already faced by two-income and single parent families. There is evidence that long and unpredictable work hours are taking a toll on the health, well-being and productivity of workers, and there is reason to believe that they are having harmful effects on family and civic life as well.

Second, the rise of the new economy has coincided with a significant increase in income inequality. During the period of considerable economic growth between 1980 and 2000, median real household incomes rose because more of them contained two earners, and those earners were working longer hours. But median real individual incomes did not rise. The proportion of low income earners (less than $10 per hour in today's terms) remained the same—about 16% of the national workforce—but their share of GDP declined. On the other hand, top income earners significantly increased their share, with the greatest increases at the very top. Even within the lower- and middle-income tiers, inequality increased. Wages of young workers and new hires—especially among men both more and less educated—fell significantly relative to other workers, and have not been rising more steeply with experience to offset this. The real annual earnings of less educated males fell sharply. These trends place greater pressure on Canadian workers seeking opportunities to enter high-paying niches within the economy to acquire the necessary knowledge and credentials. But finding the opportunity, time and resources to do so is not easy under current conditions.

The third implication, and perhaps the most important given the traditional focus of labour standards legislation, is that the rise of the new economy has been accompanied by a rise in what can be termed "precarious work." Precarious work combines relatively low pay with one or more of the following: an unstable or at-risk source of income, few or no benefits, limited or inaccessible legal protections, and uncertain prospects for future advancement, profit, or other compensatory opportunities or advantages....

The increase is largely accounted for by very significant growth in temporary employment and own-account self-employment. Not all of these people are in precarious work; some have voluntarily chosen it for lifestyle or other reasons, and some are in fact entrepreneurs. However, it appears that as many as 75% of temporary employees would prefer permanent employment, as would about 25% of own-account self-employed workers. About 25% of part-time workers would prefer full-time work.

The disadvantages of precarious work are often multiple and overlapping. Compared to full-time permanent workers, who now make up just over 60% of the workforce, temporary full-time workers are much more likely to have low incomes and no access to benefits; own-account self-employed workers are much more likely to have low incomes and no access to benefits; and low income workers generally are far less likely to have insurance or pension benefits or to be unionized. Research tends to show that temporary workers have significantly higher rates of employment strain than other workers due to uncertainty of employment and earnings, among other things. Employment strain, in turn, leads to health problems, tension and exhaustion. Moreover, for many people, precarious work is persistent, not transitory. For example, about 50% of workers earning less than $10 per hour find themselves in the same situation five years later. Finally, it is worth noting that workers experiencing disadvantages are more likely to be young, women, recent immigrants, members of visible minorities or some combination of these characteristics.

The underlying causes of these labour market trends continue to be debated. However, a number of them are apparently linked to features of the new economy itself. It is widely accepted that globalization and technological change have increased the demand in Canada for skilled workers relative to unskilled, which would account for the decline in the relative incomes of the latter. The growth of precarious work and the rise in pay inequality also appear to result from workers being relegated to the contingent workforce rather than finding places at the core. These are not the only causes of precariousness: declining rates of private sector unionization and the presence on the job market of immigrants lacking basic language proficiency or negotiable credentials also play a role. Moreover, precariousness and vulnerability become self-perpetuating ... [W]orkers are often vulnerable precisely because the law provides them no protection, and when it does, because they are vulnerable, they often lack the means, confidence or knowledge to enforce their rights.

David Weil, *The Fissured Workplace: Why Work Became So Bad for So Many and What Can Be Done to Improve It* (Cambridge, MA: Harvard University Press, 2014) at 7–20

The modern workplace has been profoundly transformed. Employment is no longer the clear relationship between a well-defined employer and a worker. The basic terms of employment—hiring, evaluation, pay, supervision, training, coordination—are now the result of multiple organizations. Responsibility for conditions has become blurred. Like a rock with a fracture that deepens and spreads with time, the workplace over the past three decades has fissured. And fissuring has serious consequences for the bedrock that people depend upon from employment: the share of the economic pie available to workers and their families; their exposure to health and safety and other risks each day at work; and the likelihood that their workplaces comply with the standards set out by law....

In 1960 most hotel employees worked for the brand that appeared over the hotel entrance. Today, more than 80% of staff are employed by hotel franchisees and supervised by separate management companies that bear no relation to the brand name of the property where they work. Twenty years ago, workers in the distribution center of a major manufacturer or retailer would be hired, supervised, evaluated, and paid by that company. Today, workers might receive a paycheck from a labor supplier or be managed by the personnel of a logistics company, while their work is governed by the detailed operating standards of the nationally known retailer or consumer brand serviced by the facility. And whereas IBM in its ascendency directly employed workers from designers and engineers to the people on the factory floor producing its computers, Apple can be our economy's most highly valued company while directly employing only 63,000 of the more than 750,000 workers globally responsible for designing, selling, manufacturing, and assembling its products.

CHAPTER 1: INTRODUCTION

A Seismic Shift in the Focus of Employment

During much of the twentieth century, the critical employment relationship was between large businesses and workers. Large businesses with national and international reputations operating at the top of their industries (which will be referred to as "lead businesses" ...) continue to focus on delivering value to their customers and investors. However, most no longer directly employ legions of workers to make produces or deliver services. Employment has been actively shed by these market leaders and transferred to a complicated network of smaller business units. Lower-level businesses operate in more highly competitive markets than those of the firms that shifted employment to them.

This creates downward pressure on wages and benefits, murkiness about who bears responsibility for work conditions, and increased likelihood that basic labor standards will be violated. In many cases, fissuring leads simultaneously to a rise in profitability for the lead companies who operate at the top of industries and increasingly precarious working conditions for workers at lower levels.

But the fissured workplace is not simply the result of employers seeking to reduce wages and cut benefits. It represents the intersection of three business strategies, one focused on revenues, one on costs, and one on providing the "glue" to make the overall strategy operate effectively. Its components begin not with employment, but with the demands by capital markets that lead companies focus on core competencies that produce value for investors and consumers. This means building brands, creating innovative products and services, capitalizing on true economies of scale and scope, or coordinating complex supply chains. But focusing on the core also has come to mean shifting activities once considered central to operations to other organizations in order to convert employer-employee relationships into arm's-length market transactions. Finally, fissuring weds these potentially contradictory activities through the glue of the creation, monitoring, and enforcement of standards on produce and service delivery, made available through new information and communication technologies and enabled by organizational models like franchising, labor brokers, and third-party management.

The result is businesses and industries wired in fundamentally new ways. Wage setting and supervision shift from core businesses to a myriad of organizations, each operating under the rigorous standards of lead businesses but facing fierce competitive pressures. Although lead businesses set demanding goals and standards, and often detailed work practice requirements for subsidiary companies, the actual liability, oversight, and supervision of the workforce become the problem of one or more other organizations. And by replacing a direct employment relationship with a fissured workplace, employment itself becomes more precarious, with risk shifted onto smaller employers and individual workers, who are often cast in the role of independent businesses in their own right....

Having It Both Ways

The fissured workplace gives rise to a basic contradiction in many industries and in the policies of major businesses. In focusing on core competencies, businesses seek to expand their margins and their markers, thereby improving the profitability of their operations. At the same time, by shedding nonessential activities, they seek to push out activities that would be more costly if maintained within the boundaries of the firm.... To do the latter while protecting the integrity of the central business model (that is, protecting the brand or the other sources of core competencies), businesses rely on the promulgation and enforcement of myriad standards through a variety of organizational and technological methods. This final piece of the fissured workplace model is fundamental: it explains why many of the forms of fissured work are possible and prevalent now but not in the past, and represents an intrinsic but under-acknowledged element of many business models....

Yet many of the businesses that rely on the close enforcement of such standards create an artificial distance from subordinate organizations when it comes to employment obligations. While a major restaurant brand may set out standards and guidelines that dictate to a minute degree the way that food is prepared, presented, and served, and specify cleaning routines, schedules, and even the products to be used, it would recoil from being held responsible for franchisees' failure to provide overtime pay for workers, for curbing sexual harassment of workers by supervisors, or for reducing exposure to dangerous cleaning materials. Similarly, a lead electronics company in a supply chain may specify all aspects of product quality and production, set a price, and specify delivery standards but blanch at the notion of responsibility for the consequences of those parameters on the ability to pay people the legally required minimum wage....

In light of all these factors, the spread of the fissured workplace creates an economy that is wired differently than the traditional model it has gradually replaced. The economic system for much of the twentieth century was dominated by large corporations where economic value creation, power, and employment were concentrated. The fissured economy still is powerfully affected by large businesses with their concentration of value creation and economic power. But employment now has been split off, shifted to a range of secondary players that function in more competitive markets and are separated from the locus of value creation. The consequences for employment and working conditions and the functioning of the economy as a whole are enormous.

Twin-Edged Sword...

The widespread adoption of new forms of organization in markets is often a sign of a superior method of allocating resources. It signals that a set of outputs (goods and services) can be produced at a lower cost through a new way of organizing production. Economists would be quick to point out that this makes society overall better off: if fewer resources can be used to produce the same bundle of goodies, more resources are released for use elsewhere. The drivers behind the fissured workplace must improve outcomes for someone—why else would they become so pervasive?

There are indeed positive aspects of the reorganization of production for companies, investors, and consumers, and finding new ways to organize production can enhance social welfare. Focusing on core competencies and the benefits of specialization, facilitated by flexible organizational forms, can lead to the development of new and better products available at lower prices. But reorganization can also have real social consequences if the businesses undertaking it do not fully weigh the costs and consequences of their actions.

CHAPTER 1: INTRODUCTION

Fissured Work, Vulnerable Employment
Although the fissured workplace plays out in different ways across industries, its consequences for workplace conditions are similar. By shifting the provision of service or parts of production to other employers, lead businesses create markets for services that are usually very competitive, thereby creating downward pressure on the marginal price for them. This means that the employers competing for that work face significant pressures on the wages and conditions they can offer their workforce, particularly in industries where there is an elastic supply of labor, skill requirements are relatively low, and labor costs represent a significant part of overall costs. . . .

There is abundant evidence that the majority of workers in the United States face an increasingly difficult workplace—and did so even before the Great Recession of 2007–2009. Falling real wages, declining benefits, reduced employment security, and a stifled ability to complain about problems describe a growing part of the employment landscape. . . .

Many of the industries where researchers in recent years have found high rates of violations of basic labor standards and worsening employment conditions coincide with industries where fissuring is most advanced. These include restaurant and hospitality sectors, janitorial services, many segments of manufacturing, residential construction, and home health care. But fissuring also is present in retailing, telecommunication and IT sectors, hospitals, public schools, auto supply, transportation, and logistics/distribution services. Accounts of fissuring of paralegal and legal jobs, accounting, journalism, and professional services are also increasingly common. In fact, employment fissuring represents an organizational format that has been adopted across many sectors of the economy, assuming many different forms.

There are three reasons we should worry about the social consequences of the fissured workplace. First, it often undermines compliance with basic labor standards. Second, chopping employment into pieces makes production coordination harder and results in a problem economists call externalities that can result in accidents, injuries, and fatalities. Third, there are distributional consequences of the fissured workplace, shifting surplus generated by businesses away from the workforce and to investors.

Obeying the Law
. . . Large companies . . . often paid wages to even unskilled workers in excess of the minimum wage or provided pensions or medical leave because of a desire to keep valued workers or to maintain morale and meet standards of fairness inside the firm. . . . Other times, large businesses complied because they perceived that their scale made them particularly vulnerable to inspections, penalties, or public scrutiny.

By shedding employment to other subordinate businesses, fissured employment altered those incentives. Lead businesses that, for example, shed janitorial and security work to contractors or franchised service providers no longer faced the responsibility for compliance with minimum wage or overtime standards, or even ensuring that payroll, unemployment, or workers' compensation insurance taxes were being paid for those workers. Activities that are shed by lead organizations are often taken up by smaller businesses. Given the competitive markets in which they operate, smaller employers face intense pressure to reduce costs. Noncompliance with a gamut of workplace standards is often the end result.

Some of the highest rates of violations of basic labor standards occur in industries where fissuring is common....

Creating External Costs

To understand the second social problem associated with the fissured workplace—externalities—take the classic case of a manufacturer that makes, say, plastic containers. When it does so, it considers all the labor, material, and capital costs it faces in setting its production goals, weighed against the price it thinks it can charge for the containers. If it also creates air and water pollution in the process of making containers but does not face a cost for that pollution, it will act as if that cost is zero—in other words, it will ignore the costs of pollution it imposes on society. As a result, its prices will not reflect the total social costs of production, and its market price will be too low. That will lead consumers, responding to the lower price, to consume too many containers, resulting in too much pollution. The pollution externality will leave society worse off than if the container manufacturer, as well as consumers, were forced to include the cost of pollution in their decisions.

Significant externalities arise from fissuring. By fragmenting the employment relationship, certain important decisions that do not directly affect the costs of any of the employers involved fall through the cracks....

Dividing the Pie

... Large firms employing a wide spectrum of workers—from highly trained engineers and professional managers, to semiskilled production workers, to janitors and groundskeepers—characterized the workplace of the midtwentieth century. An important consequence of having people with diverse skills and occupations working under one roof was that companies shared the gains received from their market position with the workforce. They did so through how wages were set—in both union and nonunion workplaces. While some businesses shared gains out of corporate beneficence, many did so because of what might be called enlightened self-interest. Because feelings about fairness affect employee morale, fairness considerations have an impact on human resource policies, including wage determination. In particular, perceptions about what one is paid depend in part on what others are paid. If a large company employed executives, secretaries, engineers, mechanics, and janitors, it therefore needed to be cognizant of how the structure of wages was perceived among all those working underneath the common corporate umbrella. As a result, janitors' wages were pulled up because of the wages lead employers paid their factory workers.

Fissured employment fundamentally changes the boundaries of firms—whether through subcontracting, third-party management, or franchising. By shifting work from the lead company outward—imagine the outsourcing of janitorial or security workers—the company transforms wage setting into a pricing problem.... [T]his pushes wages down for workers in the businesses now providing services to the lead firm, while lowering the lead business's direct costs. Fissuring results in redistribution away from workers and toward investors. It therefore contributes to the widening income distribution gap.

[THE FISSURED WORKPLACE: WHY WORK BECAME SO BAD FOR SO MANY AND WHAT CAN BE DONE TO IMPROVE IT by David Weil, Cambridge, Mass.: Harvard University Press, Copyright © 2014 by the President and Fellows of Harvard College.]

CHAPTER 1: INTRODUCTION

Kevin Banks, "Workplace Law Without the State?" in S Archer, D Drache, & P Zumbansen, eds, *The Daunting Enterprise of Law: Essays in Honour of Harry W Arthurs* (Montreal; Kingston: McGill-Queen's University Press, 2017) 233 at 236–38

In internationally integrated industries, employers are often in a position to reproduce both the technological sophistication of production facilities and the training of their workforce in many locations around the world. Compensation costs may matter a great deal at the margin in determining the location of production. The offshoring/de-localization of manufacturing is, of course, well advanced in the industrialized world. The offshoring/de-localization of services has only just begun, and is likely to accelerate with increased Internet connectivity. The growing mobility of investment and production thus enhances employer bargaining power.

These mobility effects are amplified by changes in the relative scarcities of capital and labour in the internationally traded economy. As Richard Freeman points out, the integration of China, India and the former communist *bloc* countries into the international trading system effectively doubled the global labour supply while adding relatively little capital. Emerging economies in which labour is relatively abundant often have significant unit labour cost advantages in particular economic sectors. The forces of supply and demand can, therefore, exert downwards pressure on wages in traded industries.

Furthermore, unions not only find it harder to get more for their members, but also to pursue re-distribution within the workforce. The globalization of production has been accompanied by a wave of skill-biased technological change that generates higher returns to skill, and thus promotes greater dispersion in earnings among workers. These effects may have been compounded in countries with unequal access to higher education, contributing significantly to increased inequality within the workforce.

Not surprisingly then, the globalization of production appears to be, in part, responsible for the stagnation of middle class incomes, increased income inequality and an increase in capital's share of national income in the industrialized world. The effects of the globalization of production on the workplace bargain are further compounded by three developments elsewhere that have left less money on the table for employers and workers to divide up. First, recent decades have witnessed what Thomas Picketty has termed the rise of the "super-manager" in the Anglo-American world. There, changes in the norms and practices governing executive compensation have enabled top managers at major private corporations to capture a very disproportionate share of the gains from economic growth in recent decades, and are the primary reason for increased income inequality in recent decades. Second, long-term declines in demographic and economic growth in the industrialized world have caused an increase in the ratio of the capital stock to national income, while technological advances continue to enable capital to be put to a growing number of valuable purposes. As a result, capital's share of national income will tend to increase. Since ownership of capital is highly unequal, and negligible in the bottom half of the income distribution, these long-term developments stand to increase income inequality dramatically. Finally, financial globalization, and the resulting mobility of finance capital are associated with reductions in the wage share of national incomes. While the reasons for this require more study, it appears

that, in the industrialized world, they include the switch in the 1980s to corporate governance systems based upon maximizing shareholder value and the rise of aggressive returns-oriented institutions, including private equity funds, hedge funds and institutional investors that put pressure on firms to increase profits, especially in the short term. As a result, a greater share of corporate profits is paid out as dividends. These last two developments are good candidates to be most significant causes of a decline in the share of national income accruing to labour (and a corresponding increase in the share accruing to capital) across the industrialized world.
[Banks, Kevin. "Workplace Law without the State?" *The Daunting Enterprise of Law*. Eds. Simon Archer, Daniel Drache and Peer Zumbansen. Montreal: MQUP, 2017. Print.]

1:420   The Changing Position of Unions

As noted on the first page of this chapter, according to Statistics Canada, as of 2018, 30.4 percent of Canadian workers belonged to a union or were covered by a collective agreement, meaning that close to 70 percent of Canadian workers remain beyond the reach of collective bargaining. These figures represent a point on a long-term trend of decline. From 1981 to 2012, Canada's unionization rate fell from 38 percent to 30 percent. During that time, the percentage of men in unionized jobs fell from 42 percent to 29 percent, while the percentage of unionized women hovered around 30 percent. Unionization rates declined in all provinces during this period. These trends appear to have been driven by the private sector, where unionization rates have been on a long-term path of decline, hitting 15.9 percent by January 2018. By contrast, public sector unionization rates have held steady near 70 percent in recent decades. See Diane Galarneau and Thao Sohn, *Long Term Trends in Canadian Unionization* (Statistics Canada, 2013). Similar declining trends, varying considerably in magnitude, have been observed across the industrialized world. The following excerpt discusses some of the reasons for these international trends.

Peter Ackers, "Trade Unions as Professional Associations" in S Johnstone & P Ackers, ed, *Finding a Voice at Work? New Perspectives on Employment Relations* (Oxford Scholarship Online, 2015) at 7–11

> Three related trends are taking place everywhere across the globe, albeit at greatly variable speeds. First, trade union membership and the coverage of collective bargaining are in steady decline. Second, unions are losing political influence—especially outside continental Europe— either as corporate actors or militant mobilization organizations. Third, and perhaps most important, unions are becoming marginal to the way we talk and think about work and society. They are no longer part of the 'spirit of the age'. Why? One pat radical answer is *neoliberalism*. In other words, free market political policies that have spread around the world from Thatcher and Reagan in the 1980s, inspired by the writing of Hayek and Friedman, have de-legitimized and stigmatized trade unions as enemies of freedom and prosperity. The threat is real, but begs the further question: why have these ideas been so successful that, in Marx's words, they have become a 'material force' in contemporary global society? I will consider six partial explanations for why trade unions are being marginalized. Three concern *external material changes* related to the structure of industry and the role of markets. Then two others relate to

external ideological changes in the way people—the state, employers, employees, and the general public—think about unions and work. The sixth centres on the way unions reposition their traditional role in this new global context.

One external material change in Western societies is the development of *post-industrial society*. Modern Britain has about 10 per cent of the workforce in manufacturing and an increasingly white-collar economy. As late as the 1970s, trade unions with a manual workforce in primary and secondary industries, such as coal, steel, and engineering, were considered the *real* trade unions.... Clearly the changing shape of the workforce in the West, away from the era of industrial society, has contributed to the anachronism of phrases like the 'labour movement'. Even so, it is often among middle-class, white-collar workers in the public sector that trade unions are strongest, while, in Britain, several large supermarket chains and banks are unionized. The old 'industrial' unions were largely male and the new service economy is highly feminized; but, overall, British women are now as well represented by trade unions as men. Other features of the new service economy, such as smaller workplace size and more temporary and part-time workers don't help union organization. However, small-scale employers and casualization were also characteristics of the late Victorian world from which trade unions began their great twentieth-century expansion. And general unions of the poor have declined much more rapidly than professional or skilled organizations. Most tellingly, there has been no rapid unionization of the new industrial workforces in the developing world. In short, there is no simple or inevitable connection between the class and gender characteristics of a given workforce and trade union membership.

A second trend, *globalization*, has grave implications for trade unions. Mobile transnational capital is much harder for nation states to regulate while international competition over labour costs undermines the effectiveness of the national unions of the low paid. In the past, unions organized local labour markets.... Working with responsible employers they established industry agreements that set minimum rates and prevented cut-price competition from those with poor labour practices. Global free trade and high levels of international migration make these local standards difficult to maintain, such that we now find even the Swedish construction industry struggling to protect national labour standards. Skilled, well-trained employees may be able to cushion themselves against low-cost competition and easy replacement, but low skilled workers cannot. Despite radical rhetoric about trade union internationalism and the existence of organizations like the European Trade Union Confederation (ETUC) and the International Labour Organization (ILO), trade unions are essentially national organizations and have few serious strategies beyond the national to deal with these problems. Organizing a mobile, unskilled, global workforce is like herding cats—and just as hopeless. So any credible union strategy must entail insulating employees from the lowest global market price by upgrading the status of jobs for a given occupation. This is the strategy of *professionalization*.

The emergence of *the flexible firm* is closely related to the problem of globalization. For not only do companies compete in increasingly competitive product markets and price down wages by tapping low-cost labour, but they also have developed new structures that are inimical to the old forms of trade union action, most notably strikes.... One likely explanation for this is the development of complex, just-in-time supply chains and subcontracting arrangements, whereby any disruption of work would lead rapidly to workplace closure and job loss. Thus the unionized warehousing and haulage company that supplies a major supermarket chain would see its contract moved elsewhere; while the turbulent manufacturing plant, owned by a large multinational, would see production relocated; and even the small, independent firm would lose its market. Here, old forms of collective economic power are simply too toxic to use. The effect would be instant, dramatic, and suicidal.

However, neither fragmented workplaces nor cut-throat market competition are new to trade unions. And this suggests that there are clear limits to purely material explanations for union decline. Something else is going on and two external ideological changes suggest themselves. One possibility is *post-modern affluence and consumer capitalism*, with the suggestion of different cultural identities to those found in the working-class communities of the early twentieth century.... More recently, there is the suggestion that people construct their identity around consumption rather than production. There is also evidence of a wider decline of associational forms in society, such as churches, political parties, clubs, and so on.... Yet, people probably spend more time in paid work than ever, while some employers have turned workplaces into leisure centres and professional forms of organization remain strong. Overall then, it is oversimplistic to suggest that society is so individualized and consumer-orientated that there is no scope for trade unions. Rather this suggests that old appeals to economic interests need to be complemented by a stronger emphasis on values and identities.

Another candidate is *the end of the Cold War* and the associated decline of socialism as a major world ideology. Indeed, there is a remarkable correlation between the fall of the Berlin Wall in 1989 and the declining salience of trade unionism as a popular idea, notwithstanding the contribution made by the Polish 'Solidarity' union to the collapse of communism. In narrower terms, this may be interpreted as the death of one of the most determined sponsors of trade unionism in the capitalist world, responsible for the largest confederations in France, Italy, India, and many other countries. Without communist organization and activism one brand of trade unionism lost its vital impetus. Other socialist activists often worked with or against communists and the broader demise of any sense of an alternative socialist society, worth fighting against capitalism for, further corroded this variety of politicized union commitment. On the other side, free of the Cold War need to compete with communism, sponsors of alternative liberal and conservative models of trade unionism, such as the CIA or the Catholic Church, have tended to fade from the scene. Politics no longer needs the 'labour movement' and the impetus to plant your union brand all over the world is lost. So today the USA has many criticisms of human rights in China, but a lack of independent trade union representation rarely figures very high among them.
[By permission of Oxford University Press.]

* * * * *

Canada has been particularly affected by the shifts in the composition of employment from manufacturing, a traditional stronghold of union organizing, to service employment, where unions have had greater difficulty organizing new members. In 1976, manufacturing accounted for 19.1 percent of Canadian employment. By 2014, it accounted for no more than 9.6 percent. During that time, the share of the service sector in total employment grew from 65 to 78 percent (see André Léonard, "Employment Trends, Seasonality and Cycles in Canada" (Ottawa, ON: Library of Parliament, 2015)). In addition to the shift in the composition of Canadian employment, changes to and the inherent limitations of Canada's distinctive regime of labour law appear to have also contributed to the decline in the rate of unionization in Canada. See the discussion in Chapter 6, Section 6:300.

Unions in Canada have responded to these changed conditions in a variety of ways, including most notably by mergers and consolidation, and renewed emphasis on organizing (see Sara Slinn, "Whither Wagner? Reconsidering Labour Law and Policy Reform" (2014) 98 *Minnesota Law Review* 1805). These efforts have produced some successes. In 2017, roughly 20,000 part-time workers at Ontario's colleges voted to join the Ontario Public Service Employees' Union. In the private sector, employees at Vice Canada and other digital media companies have recently voted to unionize, as have personal trainers at Goodlife gyms. However, a gap in representation persists, with 40 percent of Canadians stating they desire union representation, which is about 10 percentage points higher than the coverage observed in 2016: see Rafael Gomez, *Employee Voice and Representation in the New World of Work: Issues and Options for Ontario* (Toronto: Queen's Printer for Ontario, 2016) at 16–17. This gives rise to question about whether unions need to pursue (and labour law needs to facilitate) new models of worker representation better aligned with pressures of globalization and new flexible organization of production. Research and debate with respect to these questions are canvassed in Chapter 6, Section 6:600.

Some see economic and social conditions within industrialized democracies as containing the raw materials for a renewal of union movements. Do you agree? Consider the changing distributions of income and opportunity in Canada, discussed in the next section, below.

John Kelly, "Trade Union Power and Membership in Comparative Perspective" (2015) 26 *The Economic and Labour Relations Review* 526 at 539–51

> The trade union movement in the advanced capitalist world is both smaller and weaker in 2015 than at the end of the world strike wave of 1968–1974. This position has been reached despite a host of strategic innovations, in organizing, in the reconstruction of trade unions to advance the interests of women and ethnic minority workers and through mobilisations, protests and general strikes against government austerity policies. It is true that unions remain strong in the public sectors of many countries, and that professional workers with a strong sense of occupational identity continue to be highly organised. Yet generally, the pattern is one of widespread decline in membership, power and influence.
>
> At the same time, however, the world's major capitalist economies display a number of features and tendencies which could provide the foundations for union revitalisation centred on a "narrative" of injustice and exclusion. First, average earnings have declined or stagnated for many workers in many countries, particularly since 2008....
>
> ... With many workers on low and stagnating incomes, the dramatic increase in reward packages at the top end of the distribution has led to a substantial rise in income inequality....

Wage stagnation, the growing contrast between rich and poor ... can all be interpreted as signs of fundamental flaws in national systems of wage determination.... Unions may therefore be able to position themselves both as the champions of wage growth and income equality and as part of the solution to the problems arising from egregious forms of exploitation.... Unions in the UK, the USA and New Zealand have also acted in concert with other organisations, running campaigns to persuade large private and public sector employers to pay a 'Living Wage'.... This type of coalition building with community and faith groups does not necessarily produce many additional union members but it does, albeit indirectly, extend the reach of unions into areas of the labour force where they have few members and little or no collective bargaining presence.

Living wage campaigns have often involved unions moving up the supply chain, away from the contractors who employ low wage workers, in cleaning or food processing, for example, and towards the powerful, and often highly profitable, corporations that place the contracts and largely set their terms. Campaigns to improve terms and conditions within low pay firms have often collided with the employers' claims that their scope for improvement is limited by the stringent terms in their contracts. Targeting large finance companies or food retailers has sometimes proved a more effective method of boosting pay and conditions further down the supply chain. It does, however, depend in part on the susceptibility of the contracting firm to the reputation damage associated with campaigns connecting the firm to low pay.

[Copyright © 2015. Reprinted by Permission of SAGE Publications, Ltd.]

1:430   Diversity, Inclusion, and Inequality

The Canadian workforce is far more diverse than when the foundational stones of the modern labour and employment law system were laid in the post–World War II era. It has become more inclusive of women; members of ethnic, religious, and racial minorities; and of persons with disabilities. Yet major barriers to equal opportunity for these groups remain. Further, long-term increases in precarious employment and growing economic inequality have reduced the access of many workers of all social groups to opportunities to better their lot and that of their families, or even to access decent working conditions. The developments pose new challenges to the capacity of workplace law to deliver on some of its most fundamental objectives.

The following passage describes systemic practices embedded in the twentieth-century Canadian industrial economy (and in those of other industrialized countries) that effectively excluded many workers from equal opportunity in the labour market. Consider, in light of recent evidence (presented below in this section), to what extent such barriers may persist today. Have new ones emerged in the twenty-first century?

Adelle Blackett & Colleen Sheppard, "Collective Bargaining and Equality: Making Connections" (2003) 142 *International Labour Review* **419 at 422–27**

Fordism functioned in an era of mass production in large workplaces, which spurred on an industrial model of employment. It combined with Taylorist scientific management approaches, leading to industrial de-skilling, since the components of any given production process could be broken down into individual repetitive tasks that most labourers could perform; their execution could be timed and monitored by employers along an assembly line. Since employers and workers were likely to be based in a given factory located within the same country for which production was destined, the workers were essentially also the consumers. Consequently, there was incentive for employers to pay workers good, rising wages, to enable them in turn to buy the products that they produced. They also needed leisure time so that they could exercise their purchasing power, and consume the goods they bought. These workplace gains were consolidated by Keynesian macroeconomic policies that encouraged governments to spend in the creation of a welfare state. Liberal economic policies were increasingly embedded in society.

[M]any fictions of Fordism have resulted in a number of de facto exclusions from the effective recognition and exercise of collective bargaining rights. One was that women did not have to work because men were the family breadwinners. Though women had worked outside the home long before, throughout, and since the height of Fordism, their work was mostly in precarious conditions and for low wages; they were a reserve labour force to be drawn upon when men were not available. Accordingly, there was no need to pay women a family wage, as men were the breadwinners. Women were also penalized in that social benefits were often tied to employment, so the male breadwinner also controlled access to social safety nets, including health benefits and retirement pensions....

In its preoccupation with production, Fordism excluded women's reproductive work, as well as the associated "non-productive," "invaluable" labour of love in the home, assumed to be without value in the labour market. When the wife/mother's labour was replaced, the work was performed by women (and some men) from disadvantaged groups—earlier through slavery or indentured servitude, later through restrictive migration schemes or bonded labour. Thus, the inadequate value attributed to the work was reinforced. It is a testament to the depth of this dichotomy that domestic work is traditionally excluded from many collective bargaining systems. The exclusions, coupled with the limits placed on women's participation even when they are unionized, compound the exclusionary effects....

Fordism also assumed away other divergences from the "norm." Thus, job applicants with disabilities were simply not hired; "accommodation" of persons with disabilities, by modifying the workplace or enabling the worker to undertake different tasks or the same tasks differently, came much later. Workers who developed work-related disabilities sometimes simply lost their jobs after prolonged absence from work. Entitlement to some limited compensation, through long-term disability pay and to some extent accommodation through more flexible approaches to otherwise rigid seniority and job classification systems, was only gradually achieved. Production schedules were organized in shifts; although those shifts recognized dominant norms (e.g. Sundays off in traditionally Christian societies), the religious beliefs of workers outside the dominant social groups were not readily recognized and accommodated. In their emphasis on transparency through "colour-blind" seniority and merit-based job classification, Fordist hiring, promotion and disciplinary practices were potentially able to foster greater racial and ethnic integration rather than accentuating difference. Yet in fact workers from the dominant social groups benefited disproportionately from these facially neutral rules and for many reasons, including past discrimination, hostile work environments, harassment, job segregation based on traditional roles for women, interruptions for child-rearing and recent workplace attachments linked to immigration status. In particular, systemic discrimination resulting in labour market segregation and in some cases in exclusion from the labour market meant that workers from certain racial or ethnic groups were effectively excluded from access to collective bargaining that recognized their rights and interests. The categories of worker who tended to be excluded, expressly or implicitly, during the Fordist era largely correspond to the categories enumerated in Convention No. 111 as requiring protection from discrimination.

[D]omestic workers are predominantly women from racial and other minority backgrounds; to exclude (in law or on a de facto basis) domestic work from the reach of collective bargaining has a particularly marked impact on these vulnerable women. Similarly, agricultural workers, notably in industrialized countries, are disproportionately racial minority and foreign workers; therefore their exclusion from collective bargaining legislation in some countries has a disparate impact in terms of race, national and ethnic origin. Workers in the informal economy, atypical, part-time and precarious contractual workers, and workers facing occupational segregation are predominantly women, workers from racial, ethnic and religious minorities, immigrants, workers with disabilities, and young people.

Moreover, even if all the express exclusions from collective bargaining regimes were reversed, this would not solve the problem of unequal access to collective bargaining, because access to trade unions and collective bargaining is much more difficult in certain sectors of the economy. Workers' inadequate bargaining power is an important explanation for the difficulty of unionizing workers in certain sectors. Even if unions manage to secure a foothold within a particular workplace or industry and begin collective bargaining, they often encounter a second layer of difficulty in negotiating favourable working conditions. If the union cannot achieve any significant gains through collective bargaining because of inadequate bargaining power, of course, its support will gradually wither away.

Where the legal and socio-economic realities of certain kinds of work render collective organization difficult and where workers lack sufficient bargaining power despite being organized, collective bargaining reveals its limited ability to ensure equality at work. Indeed, it may even accentuate the gap between workers with effective bargaining power and those without it.

[Originally published in the International Labour Review, vol 42 (2003) No 4, pp 422–27.]

Federal Labour Standards Review Commission: *Fairness at Work: Labour Standards for the 21st Century* **(Gatineau, QC: Department of Human Resources and Skills Development, 2006) at 18–19**

The Canadian workforce is radically different from what it was ... in 1965. First and foremost, it is more diverse. Women have entered the workplace in dramatic numbers. In 2004, 58% of all women aged 15 and over were part of the paid workforce, up from 42% in 1976. Women accounted for 47% of the employed workforce in 2004, up from 37% in 1976. Today, the two-income household has become the norm. In 1961, 68% of households were supported by a single breadwinner—usually male; in only 19% did both partners work.

By 2001, in 62% of all households both partners were in the workforce while in only 15% was the male partner the sole breadwinner. Family structures have also become more diverse. In 2001, one in five families with children was headed by a female single parent, double the proportion in 1971. Immigration has transformed the ethnic, racial, cultural and religious make-up of Canadian society and its workplaces. According to Statistics Canada, immigration represents close to 70% of current population growth, up from under 20% in 1976. Nearly three quarters of recent immigrants are members of a visible minority. Today, about 44% of Torontonians are members of visible minorities, one of the largest percentages in the western world. The pattern is being repeated in many of Canada's large cities and their suburbs. Finally, other groups that have for a very long time been underrepresented in Canada's workplaces are now present in more significant numbers. Aboriginal peoples are one such group; disabled persons are another. . . .

1:431   The Growth of Precarious Work

Wayne Lewchuk, "The Political Economy of Precarious Employment: Will it Be No Work or Precarious Employment?" *Canadian Labour and Employment Law Journal* **[forthcoming in 2018]**

The decades following World War II saw the spread of a form of employment known as the Standard Employment Relationship involving stable, long-term, full-time employment with one employer as a norm in many parts of the economy. Most workers bargained collectively through trade unions. This is not to say that all workers enjoyed the benefits of employment stability, decent wages and generous benefit packages. On average, Canadian-born white men fared better than women, racialized workers and immigrants. . . .

. . . In the 1960s and 1970s, the majority of male workers were in permanent full-time full-year jobs with benefits. This was not a guarantee of employment for life, but it was a commitment to ongoing employment subject to the risk of job loss inherent in a market-based economy. For most workers, the terms of employment were set by long-term contractual agreements, many of which were renegotiated by unions. For those workers who did lose their jobs, government programs provided short-term relief until they could find new employment. . . .

The percentage of workers employed full-time has declined since 1976 when just under 88 percent of all employees reported working thirty or more hours a week. By 2016, fewer than 81 percent were employed full-time. . . .

As fewer workers find full-time employment, more are employed in part-time jobs, through temporary employment agencies, on short-term contracts, or through self-employment. Most of these workers are not represented by unions and must negotiate the terms and conditions of employment as individuals. For most, legislated labour standards become a more important determinant of the terms of employment. Part-time employment increased from under 13 percent of all employees in 1976 to almost 20 percent by 2016. The share of women working part-time grew from under 24 percent in 1976 to over 26 percent in 2016. The percentage of men working part-time more than doubled in the same period from around 6 percent to over 12 percent in 2016.

There has also been a dramatic growth in self-employment. The number of Canadians reporting they are self-employed without employees increased from around 6 percent of all employment in 1976 to 11 percent in 2016. Many of today's freelancers and "gig" workers would be classified as self-employed without employees.

Data on the prevalence of temporary employment is limited as Statistics Canada only began collecting this data in 1997, when it started asking workers if they were employed on a contract with a fixed end date including employment that was seasonal, temporary, term or casual. Vosko (2009), in a special report, estimated that about 7 percent of Canadians aged 15–64 were in temporary or contract employment in 1989. By 2016, Statistics Canada was reporting that over 13 percent of employed Canadians were in temporary or short-term contract employment.

The data collected by Statistics Canada on the prevalence of full-time employment, part-time employment, self-employment and temporary employment provides only a partial picture of the extent of precarious employment in the Canadian economy ... [A] permanent job today has become less of a guarantee of a permanent job tomorrow as the pace of technical change increases and corporate reorganizations become a fact of life for more and more workers.

Measuring Precarity

Recognizing the limitation of existing data in assessing the true extent of employment precarity in the contemporary labour market, the Poverty and Employment Precarity in Southern Ontario (PEPSO) research group developed new instruments to assess employment insecurity in the Greater Toronto-Hamilton labour market. This includes an instrument that determines who is in a Standard Employment Relationship and an *Employment Precarity Index* that provides a single measure of employment precarity on a scale of 0–100 by combining ten different indicators of insecurity. Together, these two new research instruments provide a more nuanced picture of the state of the Canadian labour market and allow us to explore the social consequences of less secure employment....

The survey asked participants to identify the form of their employment relationship including whether they were employed casually, on a short-term contract, self-employed, in permanent part-time employment, or in permanent full-time employment. We also asked a series of questions detailing the characteristics of employment relationships. We used some of these questions to assess who was in a Standard Employment Relationship and who was not. To be in a Standard Employment Relationship, participants had to state they were in a permanent full-time position, that they expected that job to last at least 12 months, that they had a single employer and that the employer provided some supplemental benefits beyond a wage.

To offer a more accurate measure of employment precarity, we combined 10 survey questions into the *Employment Precarity Index* (EPI). Each question was assigned the same weight in the Index. Index scores range from 0 to 95. The mean score was 23.7 and the standard deviation was 21.4. The questions that make up the Index include:

- Do you usually get paid if you miss a day's work?
- I have one employer, whom I expect to be working for a year from now, who provides at least 30 hours of work a week, and who pays benefits.

- In the last 12 months, how much did your income vary from week to week?
- How likely will your total hours of paid employment be reduced in the next six months?
- In the last three months, how often did you work on an on-call basis?
- Do you know your work schedule at least one week in advance?
- In the last three months, what portion of your employment income was received in cash?
- What is the form of your employment relationship (short-term, casual, fixed-term contract, self-employed, permanent part-time, permanent full-time)?
- Do you receive any other employment benefits from your current employer(s), such as a drug plan, vision, dental, life insurance, pension, etc.?
- Would your current employment be negatively affected if you raised a health and safety concern or raised an employment rights concern with your employer(s)?

Scores on the *Employment Precarity Index* are used to divide the sample into four relatively equal sized employment security categories. Those categories are: *Secure, Stable, Vulnerable,* and *Precarious.* There are substantial differences in average Index scores between the categories from a low of 0.6 for those in the *Secure* category to 53.4 for those in the *Precarious* category.

Just over 70 percent of PEPSO survey participants aged 25-65 reported they were in permanent full-time employment....

The employment relationship characteristics of workers in a Standard Employment Relationship differed from those in other forms of employment. Those differences are as follows:

- Over 80 percent of workers in Standard Employment Relationships reported being enrolled in a company pension plan compared to less than one-third of those not in a Standard Employment Relationship.
- All workers in Standard Employment Relationships received some supplementary benefits compared to less than one-quarter of those not in a Standard Employment Relationship.
- Workers not in a Standard Employment Relationship were five times as likely to report their income varies from week to week and four times as likely to report their hours might be reduced in the next six months compared to those in Standard Employment Relationships.
- Men were marginally more likely than women to be in a Standard Employment Relationship.
- White workers were more likely than racialized workers to be in a Standard Employment Relationship.
- Workers with a university degree were more likely than those without a degree to be in a Standard Employment Relationship.

Turning now to the *Employment Precarity Index* we can begin to get a clearer picture of who the precarious are in the economy defined as the 25 percent of our sample who scored the highest on the EPI.

- Temporary agency workers (9 percent) and permanent part-time workers (16 percent) represent a small share of the *Precarious* category.

- The most frequent type of employee found in the *Precarious* category were the own-account self-employed who represented 29 percent of the category and those on short-term contracts who represented another 22 percent of the category. These two categories capture the growing number of workers who are employed as freelancers or are working as part of the gig economy.
- Of equal interest is that nearly one in four in the *Precarious* category reported they were in permanent full-time employment. The large number of nominally permanent workers in the *Precarious* category captures the changing nature of full-time employment under the conditions of the fissured workplace as described by Weil (2014). These workers describe themselves as permanent and full-time yet they work without any benefits beyond a basic wage, or they are uncertain if their employment is likely to last at least 12 months.

Precarity was widely spread in our sample.

- Approximately one in four men and women were in *Precarious* employment. Women were marginally more likely to be in *Secure* employment (25 percent) compared to men (21 percent).
- There were more significant differences by race. About one in four white workers was in *Precarious* employment while closer to one in three racialized workers was in *Precarious* employment.
- There was a significant difference in who was in *Secure* employment by race with just over one in four white workers in *Secure* employment while fewer than one in five racialized workers was in *Secure* employment.
- Having a university degree was associated with how workers were employed. There were small differences amongst the university educated, with just under 23 percent of those with a degree in *Precarious* employment while just over 28 percent were in *Secure* employment. Not having a degree sharpened the differences. Of those without a degree, nearly one in three found themselves in *Precarious* employment but less than one in five found *Secure* employment.
- Workers in *Precarious* employment earned about half of what those in *Secure* employment earned. Limiting the comparison to those working at least 30 hours per week, those in *Precarious* employment earned about 60 percent of what those in *Secure* employment earned.
- Workers in *Precarious* employment lived in households with household earnings that were about two-thirds of the household income of a worker in *Secure* employment. This difference was unaffected by limiting the comparison to workers who reported living with someone else.

There were large differences in the probability of a worker obtaining benefits depending on their employment category. For example, all the workers in *Secure* employment received at least some supplemental health benefits, such as a drug plan, compared to less than 10 percent of those in *Precarious* employment. In addition, all workers in *Secure* employment received some sort of employer paid pension plan compared to over 15 percent of those in *Precarious* employment.

There were distinct differences in the prevalence and type of training by employment category.... Over half of those in *Secure* employment received training provided by their employer while fewer than one in five of those in *Precarious* employment were provided with training from their employer. Fewer than one in ten workers in *Secure* employment had to pay for their own training while more than one in four workers in *Precarious* employment paid for their own training.

Workers in *Precarious* employment were more likely to be working without the benefit of a union. Fifteen percent of those in *Precarious* employment were unionized compared to almost 34 percent of those in *Secure* employment. The impact of this lack of union representation was reflected in the question we asked about concern over raising an employment standards issue or health and safety issue and how this might affect future employment. None of the workers in *Secure* employment replied that raising such an issue at work might negatively affect their future work prospects while 35 percent of those in *Precarious* employment expressed some concerns and over one in five thought it was likely that raising such as issue would have a negative effect.

[Originally published in (2018) CLEJ [forthcoming]. Reproduced with the permission of Lancaster House.]

1:432 The Persistence of Unequal Opportunity

Gender Inequality — Occupational Segregation and Unequal Pay

Melissa Moyser, "Women and Paid Work" (Ottawa, ON: Statistics Canada, 2015) at 26–28

Since the 1960s, through the Public Service Commission of Canada, and later the *Employment Equity Act* as well, the federal government has endeavored to make its workforce representative of the national population by providing employment opportunities to qualified Canadians who have historically been disadvantaged in this regard, including women. Beyond federal employment equity legislation, seven provinces have employment equity policies that pertain to provincial public servants: Nova Scotia, New Brunswick, Prince Edward Island, Quebec, Manitoba, Saskatchewan and British Columbia (Ontario repealed its employment equity legislation in 1995, two years after its creation). Partly as a result of these efforts, gender parity now exists in the public sector with respect to women's representation in leadership positions ... in 2015, 54.0% of legislators and senior government managers and officials were women. This represents an improvement over 1987, when the proportion of women in the top public sector positions was 17.2 percentage points less, at 36.8%. In contrast, in 2015, 25.6% of senior managers in the private sector were women — 11.3 percentage points more than in 1987....

The gender pay gap is a matter of intense scholarly and popular interest, often being seen as indicative of the broader state of gender equality in society. The size of the gender pay gap depends on the measure of earnings that is used. Traditionally, academics (and Statistics Canada) have used the annual earnings of full-time, full-year workers. According to that metric, women aged 25 to 54 earned an average of $52,500 in 2014, while their male counterparts earned an average of $70,700. These figures correspond to a gender earnings ratio (women: men) of 0.74, meaning that women earned $0.74 for every dollar earned by men. Yet annual earnings are a problematic measure of gender-based pay inequality, as women work fewer hours on average than men, even on a full-time, full-year basis, typically due to their family responsibilities. Put differently, when the gender pay gap is measured from the annual earnings of full-time, full-year workers, it is confounded by gender differences in work hours. While annual earnings reflect both the price of labour and its quantity, the hourly wages of full-time workers reflect only the price of labour, and they are therefore closer to the issue of gender-based discrimination. Women earned an average of $25.38 per hour in 2014, while their male counterparts earned an average of $28.92. It follows that women earned $0.88 for every dollar earned by men. Thus, the male-female pay gap calculated on the basis of average hourly earnings is $0.14 smaller than the one calculated on the basis of average annual earnings, as it is not confounded by gender differences in work hours.

The current gender wage ratio represents considerable improvement over previous decades.... In 1981, women earned an average of $0.77 for every dollar earned by men. The gender wage ratio hovered around the mid- to high-0.70 range until 1994, when it reached 0.82. From the mid-1990s to the early 2000s, the gender wage ratio remained in the low 0.80 range. In 2004, it reached 0.85, and has stayed in that vicinity to date. In 2015, women were $0.10 closer to every dollar earned by men than their counterparts in 1981.

One of the factors that has contributed to the improvement of the gender wage ratio over time is the increase in women's educational attainment. Gender-based pay inequality tends to diminish with increasing levels of education, and women have sustained a long-term trend toward higher education. Between 1991 and 2015, the proportion of women with a university degree increased by 21.1 percentage points, from 14.0% to 35.1%. The proportion of men with a university degree also increased during this period, but to a lesser extent: 11.2 percentage points, from 17.4% in 1991 to 28.6% in 2015. Yet women have not been able to educate themselves out of gender differences in pay entirely. Even when they had a university degree above the Bachelor's level, women earned an average of $0.90 for every dollar earned by men in 2015.

The gender pay gap partly owes to the differential allocation of female and male workers across occupations. Women are over-represented in low-paying occupations and under-represented in high-paying ones. In 2015, 21.2% of women who worked full-time had occupations with average hourly wages in the bottom 20% of the wage distribution, compared to 17.3% of their male counterparts. Conversely, 25.9% of men who worked full-time had an occupation with average hourly wages in the top 20% of the wage distribution, compared to 18.3% of their female counterparts. Put differently, women are more likely to have an occupation in the bottom 20% of the wage distribution than they are in the top 20%; the reverse is true for men.

Differences in how female-dominated occupations are valued, relative to male-dominated jobs, also contribute to the gender-based pay inequality. Female-dominated occupations tend to be compensated at lower wage rates than male-dominated occupations — even when they involve the same skill level. Employment and Social Development Canada organizes NOC occupations according to the skill level they usually require: A: university education; B: college education or apprenticeship training; C: secondary school and/or occupation-specific training; and D: on-the-job training. Within these skill levels, women earn less in female-dominated occupations than men do in male-dominated occupations. For example, professional occupations in nursing and professional occupations in natural and applied sciences are dominated by women and men, respectively, and both usually require a university education. Even so, the average hourly wage for professional women working in nursing was $35.37 in 2015, while the average hourly wage for professional men working in natural and applied sciences was $39.85—a difference of $4.48. Similarly, administrative and financial supervisors and administrative occupations and industrial, electrical and construction trades are dominated by women and men, respectively, and both usually require a college education or apprenticeship training. The average hourly wage for women in administrative occupations was $25.11, compared to $29.76 for men in construction-related trades. Given female-dominated occupations largely resemble work women have traditionally performed in the household, the fact that women in these occupations tend to have lower wages than men in male-dominated occupations at the same skill level speaks to the devaluation of women's work in both the private and public spheres.

Sexual Harassment

Women disproportionately bear the brunt of sexual harassment in the workplace. High-profile cases of workplace sexual harassment in many industries, along with the #metoo movement, have recently brought the issue to the fore in public discourse. There are few sources of statistical data on the prevalence of workplace sexual harassment, and there are good reasons to think that the problem is under-reported. In an online survey conducted in 2017 by the federal Department of Employment and Social Development, 30 percent of respondents indicated that they had experienced sexual harassment at work. The respondents were self-selected rather than randomly selected, and the sample was not representative of the Canadian population as a whole. Most notably, 1,005 respondents identified as female while 200 identified as male. Among respondents, women were much more likely to report sexual harassment than men. Sixty-five percent of those reporting sexual harassment at work also indicated that there was a high ratio of men in positions of power within the relevant workplace.

Around 75 percent of those who said that they had been sexually harassed took some action by discussing it with a supervisor or other workplace representative, but about half of them said that the matter was not resolved, and 41 percent of them said that no attempt was made to resolve it. Seventy-five percent of those experiencing harassment said that they experienced obstacles while trying to resolve the issue. Commonly reported barriers were that their supervisor or manager did not take their complaints seriously, that their supervisor or manager did not initiate an investigation, and that the employee experienced retaliation from individuals in positions of authority. Fears of retaliation or harm to career prospects were high among reasons cited by those who chose not to come forward. See Employment and Social Development Canada, *Harassment and Sexual Violence in the Workplace—Public Consultations: What We Heard* (online: www.canada.ca/en/employment-social-development/services/health-safety/reports/workplace-harassment-sexual-violence.html).

Another telling measure of the importance of the issue is the value that women tend to place on having a workplace free of harassment and discrimination. As Lowe and Graves observe with respect to their worker survey data: "The biggest gender gap in work values has to do with a workplace free of harassment and discrimination. The fact that almost three quarters of the women we surveyed place high importance and what essentially is a respectful and inclusive work environment—compared with half of the men surveyed—surely reflects the reality that it is women, more so than men, who bear the brunt of these uncivil behaviours in today's workplaces." See Graham Lowe & Frank Graves, *Redesigning Work: A Blueprint for Canada's Future Well-Being and Prosperity* (Toronto: University of Toronto Press, 2016).

Division and Accommodation of Caregiving Responsibilities

Elizabeth Shilton, "Family Status Discrimination: 'Disruption and Great Mischief' or Bridge over the Work–Family Divide?" 14 *Journal of Law & Equality* **[forthcoming in 2018] [footnotes omitted]**

> Family care has only recently been acknowledged as a workplace issue. Within the gendered logic of the male breadwinner family, dominant throughout most of the twentieth century, family care and paid work have belonged in strictly separate spheres. Family care was women's work, relegated to the (unpaid) sphere of social reproduction. Paid work was men's work, generating the financial means to support the family. The male breadwinner model was never as all-pervasive as its myth. Nevertheless, it described many working households in Canada across class lines, and its powerful narrative buttressed the allocation of unpaid care work to women even in households that did not fit its economic mould. Under nineteenth- and twentieth-century industrial capitalism, it provided the essential foundation for the iron rule that family-care issues should not cross the threshold of the workplace.
>
> In twenty-first-century Canada, the male breadwinner family has largely vanished along with the idea of the "family wage"; women are almost as likely as men to belong to the paid workforce. Two constants remain, however. Employers continue to demand an "unencumbered worker," along with the right to organize work without regard to workers' care obligations. And gender roles within families have been slow to change. Care work still needs to be done, and women still bear most of the practical responsibility for doing it. In consequence, women are forced to manage family care without impinging on their work obligations. Their strategies—euphemistically labelled "choices"—often include part-time and precarious forms of work that typically come with lower wages, fewer benefits, fewer promotional opportunities, and minimal or no retirement pensions. The impact on women's economic welfare is compounded by stereotypical assumptions that women do not merit or want more responsible, higher-paying jobs because they will inevitably prioritize family over work. The unequal burden of family care creates and reinforces women's continuing inequality both inside and outside the workplace.
> [Permission given by author.]

Racialized Workers

Jeffrey Reitz & Rupa Bannerjee, *Racial Inequality, Social Cohesion, and Policy Issues in Canada* **(Ottawa: Institute for Research on Public Policy, 2014) at 12–17**

> Four types of evidence are cited in discussions of the extent of discrimination: prejudiced attitudes; evidence of discrimination in human rights cases; field tests of discrimination;

and discrimination as revealed by statistical analysis of earnings gaps in labour market surveys. While each is useful, each is also problematic. Prejudiced attitudes could lead to discrimination, but not necessarily. Human rights case evidence may be persuasive, and the circumstances of a particular case may be suggestive of broader patterns, but it remains case-specific. Field trials show patterns of discrimination but not its consequences in the aggregate for minority inequality. Finally, statistical analyses of labour force data are open to diverse interpretations. However, when considered together, the four types of evidence suggest that the possibility of significant discrimination should be taken seriously. We deal with each in turn.

Attitude research reveals prejudice in Canada and a corresponding potential for discrimination. Not all attitudes toward minorities are negative, of course. Attitudes toward immigration in general tend to be more favourable in Canada than in societies receiving fewer immigrants.... Yet research also makes it clear that racial boundaries are a reality of Canadian social life. For example, while most Canadians deny harbouring racist views, they maintain a "social distance" from minorities—that is, they say they prefer not to interact with members of other racial groups in certain social situations....

The potential impact of racial attitudes on discrimination is complex, however. Although prejudicial attitudes do not necessarily lead to discriminatory behaviour, they may be associated with such behaviour. For example, psychological research ... shows that assessments of foreign qualifications tend to be lower among persons who show other evidence of racial bias or prejudice. Discrimination may be displayed by persons who are not overtly prejudiced because of social pressure. For example, systemic discrimination arises when established practices in an organization exclude minorities.

Field tests have been conducted to find out if there is a variance in employer responses to people from different racial groups applying for the same jobs and presenting the same qualifications, and the results have offered persuasive evidence of discrimination....

A large number of statistical studies show that within the labour force as a whole—relative to measured job qualifications, such as education or work experience, and with differences in knowledge of official languages taken into account—visible minority immigrants have lower earnings than their European counterparts or native-born Canadian workers of European origin.... In either case, the amount of earnings disadvantage varies among minority groups and between genders. For immigrant men, it varies between 10 and 25 percent. Inequalities are greater for Blacks than for some Asian groups. Earnings disadvantages exist for immigrant women, although the amounts are less, as the comparison group is native-born Canadian women, themselves a disadvantaged group compared with men.

Such analyses are useful in identifying potential discriminatory earnings gaps, but the earnings disadvantages of minorities are open to interpretation not just in terms of discrimination but also in terms of deficiencies in qualifications that cannot be measured in the survey data. Foreign-acquired educational qualifications might be of lower quality, foreign experience might not be relevant in Canada or language skills might be deficient in subtle but significant ways....

Regarding the critical question of employment discrimination, analysis of the employment experiences of the children of immigrants has been hampered by statistical problems. One such problem stems from the small size of the second-generation population. Derek Hum and Wayne Simpson suggest that among native-born racial minorities, only Black men suffer employment discrimination. By contrast, Krishna Pendakur and Ravi Pendakur have found that the racial disadvantage for native-born racial minorities is significant, albeit less so than for racial minority immigrants....

Among the various ethnic groups in Canada, racial minorities have the lowest incomes and highest rates of poverty, and many members of these groups believe they have experienced discrimination based on their minority racial origins. Although the economic situation is somewhat better for those who have been in Canada longer and for the Canadian-born generation, the perception that they have been affected by discrimination is more widespread among the latter two groups.

Workers with Disabilities

K Banks, R Chaykowski, & G Slotsve, "The Accommodation Gap in Canadian Workplaces: What Does it Mean for Law, Policy and an Aging Population?" (2013) 17:2 *Canadian Labour and Employment Law Journal* 295

[I]n 2006 (despite the booming economy and tight labour market at the time) about 35% of Canadian employees with disabilities reported not receiving one or more needed forms of workplace accommodation. The Canadian population is aging; among disabled employees, about 60% are now between 40 and 59 years old, and about 40% report that they require at least one type of accommodation. All of this suggests that a large and probably growing number of Canadians do not receive accommodations that they need to reach their productive potential at work, or perhaps even to continue working at all. This is deeply problematic from the standpoints of equity, productivity and public health.

Our research indicates that the older the worker and the more severe his or her activity limitation, the greater the accommodation shortfall. This finding is best understood against the background of earlier studies indicating that economic considerations and stereotypes about age and disability, both of which work to the disadvantage of older workers, do influence employer decisions on whether to accommodate. We add to that background a set of new findings that the shortfall is probably aggravated by certain types of case-specific factors: factors that make an accommodation more costly for the employer (such as the worker's need for individualized accommodation); factors that lower the employer's expected return on an investment in accommodation (such as a worker's non-permanent status, or the onset of the disability in a previous job or outside the workplace); and the fact that certain types of accommodation (such as the provision of modified duties or hours) can conflict with workplace cultural norms. The accommodation gap thus appears to be the product of a confluence of incomplete information, problematic stereotypes and negative economic incentives. These all seem to interact with perceptions of the aging process on the part of employers, co-workers and the public, in ways that can be expected to exacerbate the problem as the population ages. [Originally published in (2013) 17:2 CLEJ 295. Reproduced with the permission of Lancaster House.]

1:433 The Growth of Income Inequality

David A Green, W Craig Riddell, & France St-Hilaire, "Income Inequality in Canada: Driving Forces, Outcomes and Policy" in David A Green, W Craig Riddell, & France St-Hilaire, eds, *Income Inequality: The Canadian Story* (Montreal: The Institute for Research on Public Policy) 1 at 9–27

Inequality measures: A closer look

[B]etween 1982 and 2010 ... real market income of Canadian tax filers rose on average by 13.5 percent. However, that growth was strikingly uneven. The income of the bottom 90 percent increased by a meagre 2 percentage points. In contrast, the income of the top 10 percent increased by more than 75 percent and that of the top 0.01 percent by 160 percent. Among the top 10 percent, the further up the income distribution one goes the larger are the percentage gains in real market income. ...

The top

... Based on data from income tax files, the share of market income received by the top 1 percent increased from 7.6 percent in 1982 to 13.6 percent in 2006, before declining slightly to 12 percent in 2011. Increases in income shares were even more pronounced at the very top of the income distribution, with the share of the top 0.1 percent more than doubling from around 2 percent in the early 1980s to around 5 percent in recent years. In other words, the income of this small group (one taxfiler out of a thousand) went from 20 times average income to 50 times average income over this period. Much of the surge in top incomes occurred in the 1990s, but the trend was evident starting in the 1980s. ...

During the period from the 1920s to the beginning of the Second World War, income was highly concentrated in both countries, with the top 1 percent earning between 15 and 20 percent of all market income. This concentration declined substantially during the postwar period, hovering between 7 and 9 percent in the United States and slightly higher in Canada through the 1950s and into the early 1980s. The sharp increase in the share of market income going to those at the very top of the income distribution since the early 1980s is thus a major departure from earlier trends, marking a return for both countries to levels of income concentration not seen since the "Great Gatsby era" of the 1920s. ...

The steep rise in earnings of Canadians at the very top of the income distribution has far outpaced that of other income earners over the past three decades. Who are Canada's top-income earners, and how has the composition of this group changed over time? ... [S]enior executives and those working in the financial and business services sectors have been driving the growth in top incomes in Canada. As in the United States, these two groups have come to represent a much larger proportion of the top 1 percent over the past three decades, and their incomes have grown much more rapidly than those of other top earners. Senior executives are 19 times more likely and those working in business services and finance are 3 to 4 times more likely than average to be in the top 1 percent. ...

[T]hose with degrees in the natural and applied sciences, including computer science, accounted for barely 1 percent of those in the top 1 percent of earners, whereas the increased presence of computer scientists among the top earners is basically in line with their increased share of earners in general. Although technological changes can affect the earnings of different groups of workers in different ways ... technological change is "only a modest part of the explanation of what has happened at the very top of the distribution" in Canada.

The middle

First, beginning in the 1970s and up to 2005, there was a marked decline in the proportion of middle-class workers among male and FTFY female workers—for instance, the proportion of male workers receiving middle-class earnings dropped from 54 to 42 percent over the period—and a corresponding increase in the proportion of both lower and higher-earning workers, although there is evidence that this trend has subsided since 2005. Second, as of the early 1980s, there was an even larger decline in the share of earnings going to middle-class workers. The earnings share of middle-class FTFY male and female workers fell by 20 and 17 percentage points, respectively, while their higher-earning counterparts saw their share of earnings increase by 13 percentage points. There was little change in the earnings share of lower-earning workers. This shift in earnings from middle-class workers to higher-earning workers is consistent with evidence we have already noted. . . .

The leading explanation of wage and employment polarization is technological change—in particular, the widespread adoption of computers in the workplace. Routine tasks—often found in middle-skill secretarial and clerical occupations—are those most vulnerable to being replaced by computers. In contrast, demand for cognitive task occupations, such as management and the professions, in which worker productivity is enhanced by information technology, is likely to increase with the more widespread use of computers. At the other end of the distribution, low-skill occupations such as sales and services, which entail nonroutine tasks and personal interaction, are not easily replaced by computers and are less likely to be affected by greater use of information technology. This theory predicts rising demand for high-skilled workers, and thus increased employment among those in cognitive-skill occupations and increases in their wages relative to those in middle-skill occupations. Similarly, it predicts declines in both employment and wages for middle-skilled workers. . . .

Canada, the United States and European countries did experience job polarization over the past several decades, which is consistent with the predictions of theory about the effects of technological change. However, employment polarization combined with wage polarization occurred only in the United States in the 1990s and, to a mild degree, in Canada since 2000. The more common pattern in all these countries was job polarization combined with growing wage inequality, which does not accord with the predictions of theory. Rather, the observed outcomes are consistent with rising demand for high-skill occupations—as predicted by the computerization story—but this was accompanied by a combination of falling demand and/or rising supply for low-skill occupations ... one possibility is that job loss in highly paid middle-skill occupations in manufacturing has increased the labour supply for low-skill sales and services occupations.

CHAPTER 1: INTRODUCTION

The bottom

[P]overty levels have been relatively stable or have declined substantially compared with the levels in the mid-1970s.... That the incidence of low income has been stable or has declined is clearly a favourable development. Two cautionary notes, however, should be added. First, there might still be high and persistent levels of poverty among more vulnerable segments of the population.... Second ... both low- and middle-income earners ... have seen little progress in their standard of living over an extended period of lime. The vast majority of the gains from economic growth have gone to a small minority of the population at the very top of the earnings distribution....

... Poverty was also more persistent among vulnerable groups: on average over 9 percent remained in low income for three or more years between 2005 and 2010, compared with only 2.8 percent of nonvulnerable individuals.

... Indeed, the low-income rate among recent immigrants, which in 1980 was 1.4 times that of the Canadian-born, increased to 2.4 times that of the Canadian-born by 2000 and showed no relative improvement in the 2000s, despite declining poverty rates. Thus ... it is primarily the falling rate of poverty among the Canadian-born that explains the decline in the low-income rate at the national level.

Mobility across the income distribution

Our discussion so far has focused on trends over time in aggregate measures of inequality and changes in income shares for different segments of the distribution. But the income mobility of individuals across the distribution is also important. We would evaluate an income distribution in which low-income individuals were stuck at the bottom throughout their lifetimes differently than one that produced the same Gini coefficient but displayed more churning over time. For example, the degree of concern we might attach to the fact that around 12 to 13 percent of Canadian families have incomes that fall below the low-income threshold depends in part on whether that situation is temporary or persistent. As we have seen, poverty in Canada tends to be a transitory state for most individuals, although, of course, it is much more persistent for a non-negligible number of vulnerable individuals. Moreover, notions of equal opportunity in a society are strongly related to intergenerational mobility, that is, the extent to which children are afforded the same life chances regardless of their parents' income status....

[I]ncome mobility is relatively high in Canada overall, but that it appears to have declined in recent years ... the proportion of individuals that remained in the same income decile increased substantially over that period, from 25.7 percent in 1989–94 to 30.1 percent in 1993–98 and to 32.5 percent in 2005-10. This indicates a greater degree of income "immobility," which also suggests that the level of income inequality observed at any point in time is more likely to persist going forward.

Another important indicator of equality of opportunity is the extent of income mobility across generations ... more unequal societies tend to have less intergenerational mobility.... Although this correlation can be interpreted in several ways, it does raise the concern that income inequality not only affects the current distribution of economic well-being of individuals and families; it also might reduce economic opportunity from one generation to the next, particularly among those in the lower half of the income distribution. Indeed, the OECD has found that this is the main mechanism through which inequality affects long-term economic growth. The effects of income inequality on equality of opportunity can be found in the lower levels of educational attainment and skills acquired through education and the higher risk of unemployment of individuals from low-education family backgrounds as inequality rises. In essence, "higher inequality of incomes of parents tends to imply higher inequality of life chances of their children".... With more income inequality among subsequent cohorts of fathers, we can expect declines in intergenerational mobility in Canada....

[W]e believe that a consistent pattern emerges: income inequality (as well as consumption inequality) has increased in Canada, to an important extent because of the dramatic increases in income among top earners over the past 30 years. In contrast, incomes have grown very little among those in the middle and at the bottom of the distribution. The lack of progress in income in the middle combined with a shrinking share of workers receiving midrange earnings has led to considerable angst about the decline of the middle class. The evidence reviewed here indicates that this concern is justified. Poverty rates in Canada have been either flat or declining, but these reflect similarly meagre income gains in the middle and at the bottom of the distribution. Perhaps most important, income mobility across the distribution has declined, and there is every reason to believe that intergenerational mobility is also deteriorating. Thus, middle-class and low-income families face not only a lack of progress in income for themselves, but also a genuine worry that their children will not be able to improve their lot.... The combination of greatly increased concentration of income at the top and reduced chances of getting there for the rest signals a society that is substantially less equitable, inclusive and fair than it was three decades ago. Moreover ... a strong case can be made that the relatively stable level of inequality since the early 2000s is in good part due to the increased demand for lower-skilled workers associated with the resource boom. And with the boom now turning into bust, Canada might very well return to a path of rising inequality....

[T]he question we really need to ask is, What happens in a society when inequality increases continually over time?...

[T]he rising share of income going to top earners is a secular trend that should not be expected to abate without active intervention ... most of the income of the top 1 percent is in the form of labour income, not capital income.... [Osberg posits] a hierarchical labour structure within a firm implies that a few top executives extract substantial rents based on the size of the global market for the firm's output.... Moreover, Osberg argues that there is no inherent mechanism in the system to offset these inequality-driving forces. Indeed, it is the operation of the market that has generated the problem.

Osberg foresees far-reaching consequences for society of having an everincreasing share of output distributed to a small share of its members. Perhaps most important, as the top 1 percent gradually pulls farther away from everyone else in terms of income, they will have a tendency to form a separate society within the broader society. This means that they could also form a different set of preferences about the direction for society from that of their fellow citizens. And with their increased relative income comes an increased ability to influence policy through lobbying and other means. This political economy channel is the one Stiglitz emphasized as both the source and the means of perpetuation of increasing inequality. The troubling implication is a future in which an increasingly disaffected majority suffers from policies made by and for the few.

We share this concern. The inequality trends depicted in this volume have the potential over time to tear at the fabric of our society, not just economically but also in terms of the strength of our democracy and the quality of social interactions....

Those at the top will be inclined to pull up the ladder and jealously guard what they have for fear that they or their children could fall into the stagnant middle or lower parts of the income distribution. And the people in the lower-income echelons, stressed by their lack of progress in a society built on the promise of progress, will find it harder to offer the type of reciprocal assistance to their neighbours on which ... a flourishing society is based. Is there a problem with inequality in Canada when measured against our own past or against other countries? We think the answer is clearly yes.
[Reproduced with permission of the Institute for Research of Public Policy www.irpp.org.]

Seth Klein & Armine Yalnizyan, *Better Is Always Possible: A Federal Plan to Tackle Poverty and Inequality* (Canadian Centre for Policy Alternatives, 2016) at 4–5

[I]nternational research reveals an important link between the two phenomena: the higher the rate of inequality among people, the higher the rate of poverty that is tolerated.

In the past, inequality trends were driven by what happened to people at the bottom of the income spectrum. More recently, it has been shaped by what happens at the top. Inequality used to widen in the wake of economic recessions. Now it widens during good times, too, partly due to the market and partly due to public policies.

While the top 1% in North America has amassed a rising share of total income over time, the same is not true in some industrialized countries such as the Netherlands, France, Japan, and Sweden. Just as poverty can be addressed with good public policy, these countries show us high rates of inequality are also not inevitable....

As inequality increases, the rich bid up the cost of basic goods such as housing, causing affordability problems for lower-income households. The squeeze on household incomes (rising costs plus downward pressure on wages) is being managed through higher household debt and/or reduced spending, which is also bad for business. As the International Monetary Fund (IMF) has pointed out, higher levels of inequality are correlated with fewer and shorter spells of growth. The OECD has identified inequality as a major societal and economic challenge, and recently launched the Centre for Opportunity and Equality (COPE) to explore and showcase ways of accelerating inclusive growth.

1:440   Renewing Workplace Law and Policy

The economic pressures of globalization, the fissuring of production, and the increasing influence of finance capital have generated debate on the scope for intervention in markets and the appropriate policy stance of the state, while at the same time creating new demands for such interventions. Considering how workplace law might respond to such demands raises fundamental questions about the organization of workplace law as a system. The declining role of unions presents the issue of whether the role of legislated standards within the overall system of labour and employment law can or should expand. The fissuring of work has led researchers and policy makers to ask which economic relationships should be regulated in the interests of decent or just working conditions, to what extent employment or other work relationships are an appropriate platform upon which to pursue important social goods like income security, and whether social goods like the accommodation of disabled workers should be pursued through a wider range of strategies than simply through regulation.

1:441 The Changing Roles of Legislation and Collective Bargaining

The readings immediately below consider the limits on the reach of collective bargaining and the potential new role of legislation; whether legislation can serve the aims of equity in the face of market pressures; and the challenges facing workplace legislation and collective bargaining in achieving income equality goals.

Judy Fudge, "Reconceiving Employment Standards Legislation: Labour Law's Little Sister and the Feminization of Labour" (1991) 73 *Journal of Law & Social Policy* 73 at 87–88

> Employment standards legislation should be moved from the margin to the centre of a revised labour policy which consists of a constellation of related pieces of legislation, including collective bargaining, pay and employment equity. The point of reconceptualizing the role of employment standards legislation is to ensure that it is no longer seen as simply an adjunct to collective bargaining: a fall-back mechanism designed to cover inadequacies in collective bargaining legislation. Limiting employment standards legislation to such a secondary role blinds us to the possibility that effective and extensive minimum standards may be a necessary condition for the extension of collective bargaining. It is precisely because employers are able to exploit flexible labour that the collective bargaining norm is threatened.
>
> Employers have argued that they must use flexible forms of labour in order to be more efficient. But the question is whether business is simply exploiting workers by using flexible labour; that is, whether it is simply shifting the burden of economic insecurity further on to workers, rather than adopting more efficient and productive means of employing labour. One way to prevent the former is to impose obligations on employers to provide economic security and flexibility for workers; in other words, employment standards legislation should be designed to ensure that employers internalize the costs of flexible labour rather than shifting it to workers or the state.
>
> ... Effective and extensive standards would help to prevent employers from exploiting flexible labour. Such standards should be devised to include those workers, especially women and visible minorities in non-standard employment in the service sector, who, if not protected, will bear the brunt of economic restructuring. What we need is a new norm of worker and a new norm for the role of labour law. By imposing effective universal standards, protective legislation could help halt the substitution of non-standard work for traditional jobs as employers would no longer obtain the benefit of exploiting unregulated labour. As well, it could help to provide workers with the flexibility to adapt to the process of restructuring. The abolition of service eligibility requirements, and implementation of family responsibility leaves, sick leaves, a reduced work week

and increased vacation time would enable the growing ranks of women workers, in particular, to accommodate both their domestic responsibilities and the exigencies of life. [Reprinted with permission from the author.]

Morley Gunderson, "Social and Economic Impact of Labour Standards," prepared for the Federal Labour Standards Review Commission (2005) at 6–8, 14

[W]orkers tend to be subject to more competitive pressures associated with the vicissitudes of market forces arising from such factors as globalisation, free trade, technological change and industrial restructuring. Such pressures tend to be skill-biased, with an adverse effect on those who are already the most vulnerable and often bypassed by the benefits of the market oriented changes. Just as the demand for labour is a derived demand, derived from the demand for the goods and services produced by firms that are increasingly subject to the vicissitudes of market forces, so is the demand for labour standards a derived demand, derived from the demands of labour that is increasingly subject to market forces.

Risk shifting has occurred from employers to employees. Non-standard employment in various forms has increased, putting substantial numbers beyond the prevue of conventional labour standards protection and raising the issue as to whether and how they should be protected. The issue is of concern especially for vulnerable workers who otherwise have little or no individual or collective bargaining power and who may find themselves at the bottom of an increasing polarized wage distribution.

Labour standards can be particularly important issues for transitions at both ends of the life-cycle: for youths making the transition from school to work, and for older workers making the transition from work to retirement and increasingly from retirement back to the labour market. Standards especially with respect to hours of work and overtime may be particularly important to facilitate work-family balance—an increasingly important issue given the dominance of the two-earner family. Labour standards are often regarded as a basic safety net that provides a modicum of protection, reducing the resistance of workers to otherwise efficient changes associated with free trade, deregulation and technological change. As well, to the extent that union power is declining, the government provision of labour standards is often regarded as a necessary alternative.

We tend to think of labour standards as needed to deal with many of the *downside* adjustment consequences (e.g. termination policies and unjust dismissal to deal with job losses, plant closures, layoffs and low-wages from the wage polarization). This is true, but it is also true that many of the upside effects are also increasing the demand for labour standards (e.g. hours of work regulations to deal with the long hours that are increasingly worked by core employees).

Reduced Ability of Employers and Governments to Supply or Provide Labour Standards
Unfortunately, at the same time as there is an increased need or demand for the protection of labour standards, there is also a reduced ability of employers and governments to supply or provide such labour standards. Many private sector employers are less able to pass any cost increases associated with labour standards to consumers since the prices of goods and services are increasingly set on world markets. They are no longer

protected by tariffs or non-tariff barriers to trade or by regulatory protections that enable them to pass cost increases on as rate increases in formerly regulated industries. Even *if*—and this is a big if—employers wanted to provide more costly labour standards for purely equity oriented reasons, they could risk their survival by doing so under such competitive conditions.

Governments are also under similar pressures that make it difficult for them to provide legislated labour standards. In a world of mobile capital (both financial and physical capital) investment will gravitate towards countries and jurisdictions within countries that have fewer costly regulations, including labour regulations. In such a world, business has a more credible threat of locating its plants and new investments into jurisdictions that are more "open for business." Governments are under increased pressure to compete for such business investment and the jobs associated with that investment.

The phrases used to describe this phenomenon are invariably negative: race to the bottom; harmonization to the lowest common denominator; regulatory meltdown; and social dumping. This need not be the case. Such inter-jurisdictional competition could be healthy competition that dissipates regulations that are excessively costly and which serve mainly to protect already advantaged interest groups. Regulations that are cost-effective and that foster efficient market transactions will survive—and indeed thrive—under such inter-jurisdictional competition. This could be the case, for example, for workers' compensation laws whereby workers are guaranteed no-fault insurance in return for employers being free from the threat of being sued for negligence by injured workers. Statutory protection against "unjust dismissal" can also reduce the use of the costly and lengthy process of tort liability claims through the courts. Advance warning and severance pay in the case of plant closures or mass layoffs can foster efficient job search, and provide new employers with a pool of otherwise redundant workers. They can also save governments the cost of unemployment insurance or other income support during periods of unemployment. Workplaces that are free of harassments and bullyism may be more productive workplaces. Government provision of labour market information can aid efficient job search. The phrase "efficient regulation" need not be an oxymoron.

While some of the costs of labour regulations can be offset by benefits to employers themselves, it is likely wishful thinking that they can "pay for themselves." Otherwise, one would not expect to see employers resist such initiatives as is generally the case. From a policy perspective, all that would be necessary would be to inform employers of these benefits and opportunities they are missing, and they would self-regulate to the benefit of all. The more realistic perspective is that there are some benefits to employers that offset some of the costs; nevertheless, on net, labour standards regulations generally are a cost to employers. As such, governments are under increased pressure to reduce costly labour regulation, and to make sure that the regulation that exists is applied in a cost effective fashion. The call is for smart policy, not no policy.

Unfortunately, pure equity oriented policies that assist the most disadvantaged and vulnerable members of society and that have few if any positive feedback effects on efficiency are the least likely to survive given the competitive pressures on employers and governments. It is simply more difficult to be a "kinder and gentler" employer or government. To a large extent this is the case with labour standards which are designed to protect the most vulnerable who have little individual or collective bargaining power. Their social impacts may be laudatory, but their very existence is jeopardized by the same market forces that are giving rise to the need for such initiatives in the first place.

In essence, the very market oriented forces that are giving rise to a need or demand for labour standards, are making it more difficult for employers and governments to provide or supply such standards. This is the fundamental dilemma facing policy makers in this area today. While "smart" policies will help, this is easier said than done....

Labour Standards and Active Labour Market Adjustment

There is general agreement that active labour market adjustment programs (e.g., training, mobility) are generally preferred to passive income maintenance programs (e.g., unemployment insurance, social assistance). This is part of the transformation of social policy away from providing security or *support to buffer the effect of change*, towards enhancing the *capacity of individuals to adjust to change* largely through a human capital or skills development strategy. This is beneficial for both recipients who prefer to earn their own income if capable of doing so, as well as taxpayers who prefer the "hand-up" over the "hand-out." Active adjustment assistance programs facilitate the reallocation of labour in the direction of basic market forces, from declining sectors and regions to expanding ones. In contrast, passive income maintenance programs encourage the "stay" option, making the adjustments more costly and disruptive when they ultimately occur. Active adjustment assistance encourages constant marginal adjustment of change for persons on the margin of decision (e.g., often younger persons) in such areas as mobility, occupation choices and human capital formation decisions. Passive income maintenance, in contrast, discourages such adjustment, often leading to costly infra-marginal adjustments in such forms as mass layoffs and plant closings, which can affect whole families and communities.

Labour standards do not fit neatly into either category of active adjustment assistance or passive income maintenance. They can have elements of active adjustment to the extent that they foster adjustment in the direction of basic market forces. This can occur, for example, if minimum wage legislation spurs employers to shed low-wage, low-productivity jobs for jobs of higher value added, or to substitute technology for minimum wage workers. The same can apply to equal pay laws.

In general, however, labour standards are closer to passive income maintenance programs in that they encourage the "stay" option by fostering improvements in the existing jobs. This is, of course, their intended purpose. But an unintended consequence is that it may foster people remaining in such jobs. This is not likely to be substantial, however, for most aspects of labour standards since the protections are generally sufficiently minimal that they are not likely to substantially deter mobility out of such jobs.

Kevin Banks, "Workplace Law Without the State?" in S Archer, D Drache, & P Zumbansen, eds, *The Daunting Enterprise of Law: Essays in Honour of Harry W Arthurs* (Montreal; Kingston: McGill-Queen's University Press, 2017) 233 at 234–36 and 238–39

Fears that globalization would lead to a "race to the bottom" or, more modestly, to a policy convergence on low labour standards have influenced public policy debate in industrialized countries since the mid-nineteenth century. They rest fundamentally on four propositions: (1) that unit labour costs matter in international competition for jobs and investment; (2) that jobs and investment can and do move towards jurisdictions with low unit labour costs; (3) that labour and employment laws increase unit labour costs enough to matter in this competition; and (4) as a result, international economic integration will drive a global market in workplace regulation. For this logic to operate, at least two conditions must be met. First, the labour and employment laws in question must actually raise unit labour costs. This means that they are enforced, and raise employer costs in a way that is not charged back to workers or offset by productivity gains. Second, the unit labour cost increases attributable to workplace laws must be significant in relation to other factors affecting decisions to locate jobs and investment.

There have been times and still are places within the modern global economy in which these conditions have held or now hold, and, as a result, the development of protective workplace laws has been checked, or levels of workplace legal protection have declined. Yet, for the most part, there is little evidence of this in the industrialized world. The reasons for this are many. Workplace laws often do not raise unit labour costs. Sometimes, the costs of legal compliance are simply charged back to workers in the form of lower wages (which may, nonetheless, leave workers better off if legislation is providing higher value goods that cannot be contracted for individually, such as health and safety protection). More often than contemporary economic discourse tends to suggest, well-designed laws can improve productivity. Even where legislation raises unit costs, as it no doubt sometimes does, other factors tend to matter much more to international competitiveness. These include access to large markets, resource and technical endowments, good infrastructure, a skilled workforce, political stability and the rule of law. Moreover, labour costs are often a relatively small fraction of overall cost structures in the leading export industries of industrialized countries, which tend to be capital-intensive. Some of the most competitive countries in the world, according to the World Economic Forum, rely on good government, the quality of their education and health systems, and a sound financial sector as competitive advantages, while maintaining labour and employment laws that employers find onerous by international standards.

There is, in fact, no evidence that Canadian governments have been required to change their laws to compete internationally. My own review of changes to labour and employment legislation across Canada between 2001 and 2011 found that, in quantitative terms, reforms tilted heavily towards adding—rather than removing—employee protections. Laws have responded, albeit cautiously, to the issues of the day, including work-life conflict, the erosion of the value of the minimum wage, and the effects of bullying in the workplace. Even in areas of the law that tend unequivocally to raise costs, such as collective-bargaining protection or rights to overtime pay, one finds no pattern of change attributable to economic integration. Instead, what one observes in the laws affecting traded sectors is that reforms move in different directions corresponding to the political stripe of governments....

[T]he profile, prestige and enforcement budgets of labour ministries in Canada have suffered in recent decades. But in the light of the foregoing analysis, there seems to be no reason to attribute this decline to matters of economic necessity. To the extent that globalization matters to the capacity of the state to regulate the workplace, its effects would seem to be derived from how it is understood in the policy discourse of technocrats, politicians and the general public, rather than from its economic logic....

But it does appear that, increasingly, the strongest dynamics responsible for the growing inequality in the industrialized world are far removed from the workplace, as are the major corresponding policy levers and debates. Executive compensation is as much or more a matter of corporate governance than it is of employment contract. Equal opportunity and equitable income distribution in the labour market have come to depend more heavily than ever on equality of access to higher education, access to affordable child care, and publicly supported pension and benefit programmes. Countering the erosion of labour's share in national income may depend more on tax policy or financial sector regulation than on law in the workplace. Workplace bargaining, once able to deliver equality of opportunity and income re-distribution to a very significant fraction of the workforce, now finds these goals increasingly out of reach....

[T]his presents labour law with a crisis of purpose. It is a crisis which raises profound questions for workplace law more generally, with the potential to land difficult public policy problems in the lap of the state. Labour law can continue to enable workers to organize, bargain collectively and thereby gain access to a measure of procedural justice, voice, and enhancements in pay and benefits. But it is impaired as a means of enabling workers to obtain a fair share—however defined—of the prosperity generated by a modern economy, a purpose long underpinning labour law's claims to centrality in bringing social justice to modern capitalist democracies. The effects of the new economy on labour law may thus call for both a re-thinking of both workplace law and social policy—of what constitutes a just bargain in the workplace, of what constitutes social justice for working people, and of which institutions inside and outside the workplace might implement it.

This is not an impossible task, and, indeed, scholarship and research have already made significant contributions towards accomplishing it. Some have located significant parts of workplace law within the landscape of human rights. Others have turned towards notions of human dignity or decency at work. Some have extended these inquiries, asking what capabilities individuals should carry into the workplace in order to have full opportunities to develop as human beings. While much work remains to be done, it is probably fair to say that such intellectual foundations will prove capable of justifying both the facilitation of collective bargaining, and the continued and evolving direct regulation of the employment relationship.

The more difficult questions may lie in the re-ordering of implementing institutions. It is important to ask what responsibilities employers should bear and which ones should be socialized in the light of the increased competitiveness and volatility of product and service markets. We should consider whether new or changed models of union representation might provide more workers with access to voice in the workplace than is available under the current North American dispensation, in which de-centralized union strength interacts very uneasily with the employer incentives generated by integrated product and service markets. It is imperative to ask how workplace rules can be set, modified where appropriate, and effectively enforced, particularly in the absence of union representation.

[Reprinted by permission of the author.]

1:442 Beyond Regulating Employment

There are several reasons why the category of employment is increasingly insufficient to define the scope of workplace law. First, many workers who are arguably in need of protection do not fall neatly into the category of employee. This is despite the fact that, as we will see in subsequent chapters, tribunals have expanded that category using purposive interpretations, and some legislatures have expanded it for the purposes of labour relations law by including dependent contractors within the ambit of employment. Tribunals have struggled, for example, with whether "platform workers" such as Uber drivers fall within the scope of employment. Policy makers are thus faced with the issue of whether a new category of working relationship needs to be regulated, and if so, how. Second, in many fissured production networks, employers are not solely or even principally responsible for decisions that result in the setting or violation of terms and conditions of employment. As Weil explained above, such decisions are often made at higher levels of supply chains, or in the structuring of relationships between franchisors and franchisees. Third, given its increasing precariousness, and the volatility of capital markets, the employment platform is no longer able to deliver important benefits that require long-term commitments such as pensions. Fourth, the accommodation of a diverse workforce increasingly calls upon employers to deliver important public goods at some cost, raising the question of whether some public support for accommodation would advance policy goals and provide a fairer distribution of burdens. Finally, experience makes evident that workplace equity and equality goals are increasingly bound up with wider social policies ranging from those embedded in the creditor priorities in bankruptcy and insolvency laws to workplace inclusion of persons (more often women) with family caregiving responsibilities.

David Weil, *The Fissured Workplace: Why Work Became So Bad for So Many and What Can Be Done to Improve It* (Cambridge, MA: Harvard University Press, 2014) at 20–22

> An examination of fissured employment puts the question of the boundaries of employment responsibility center stage. Most employment laws in the United States at the state and federal level define "employee" according to stated objectives of the individual statute. This has led to varied—and highly contested—debates on who is or is not an employee. Common law defines an employer as a party who has the right to "direct and control" the performance of an employee as he or she undertakes a set of compensated activities. Courts apply a long list of factors used to determine if such control exists in a given situation, such as control of the work product, determination of the time and place of work, and the provision of tools and materials....
>
> The definition of "employee" has become a hotly contested issue in recent years, particularly in regard to the reclassification of employees as independent contractors. Since independent contractors are viewed under law as business entities in their own right, they are exempted from minimum wage and overtime requirements of the Fair Labor Standards Act, workers' compensation, unemployment insurance, Occupational Safety and Health Administration (OSHA) regulations, the National Labor Relations Act, and Social Security.
>
> But as the vignettes opening Part I also make clear, fissured employment further muddies these already murky waters. Although most laws look to the owner of the

enterprise as the party ultimately responsible, in many cases the owners are only nominally involved in the setting of employment policies or their implementation. In hotels, for example, the pace and nuances of work are set by the brand (for example, Hilton); day-to-day human resource functions and oversight of the workforce are handled by an independent hotel operating company (for example, Tharaldson Lodging); and the employee may receive her paycheck from a staffing company hired by the hotel operator, rendering the owners of the property little more than the ultimate wallet from which pay is dispensed. Employment therefore bears little resemblance to the dyadic relationship often assumed in how we think about and administer our core workplace regulations.

Efforts to address conditions in the workplace arising from fissured employment structures cannot ignore the relationship between organizations at the top and bottom of those industries....

The emergence of fissuring further heightens the need to think differently about how government agencies, as well as labor unions and other worker advocates, address the problems of precarious employment. An economy dominated by large business organizations with concentrations of employees operating within their boundaries is difficult to police. An economy where much of that employment—particularly for workers with lower skills and market leverage—has been shifted outside of the boundaries of those companies poses even graver questions about the efficacy of the traditional approach to workplace regulation.

[THE FISSURED WORKPLACE: WHY WORK BECAME SO BAD FOR SO MANY AND WHAT CAN BE DONE TO IMPROVE IT by David Weil, Cambridge, Mass.: Harvard University Press, Copyright © 2014 by the President and Fellows of Harvard College.]

Elizabeth Shilton, *Empty Promises: Why Workplace Pension Law Doesn't Deliver Pensions* (Montreal and Kingston: McGill-Queen's University Press, 2016) at 5–7 and 170–71

[I]t is useful to drill down on how well ... [the workplace pension system] has done to date at delivering retirement income. Its most obvious shortcoming is that it does not include most Canadian workers. At its finest flowering in the late 1970s, the system covered no more than 46 per cent of Canadian employees. Coverage has been in slow but steady decline since then; by 2013, only about 38 per cent of employees belonged to plans. That percentage shrinks to 32 per cent when we look at the labour force as a whole, which includes the self-employed. Of the working-age adult population as a whole—all of whom will one day need retirement income—only one in four is covered by a workplace pension plan.

That lucky one-in-four is very likely among those Canadians who are already winners in the income-distribution sweepstakes. Pension wealth is highly concentrated in Canada. Government researchers examining the distribution of pension coverage in the mid-1990s concluded that "[t]he most financially insecure workers today (the non-permanent, part-time, non-unionized, short-tenured, low-wage earners working in small firms) are *much* less likely to have [work place pension] coverage than those who have been working in a permanent, full-time, unionized, high-wage position in a large firm for many years." Available data on aboriginal status, disability, and racialization suggest that Canadians with characteristics typically associated with economic disadvantage are less likely to belong to and benefit from pension plans. In a significant departure from historical patterns, Canadian women are now *more* likely than men to belong to pension plans. Despite this increase in coverage, however, women continue to receive only 60 per cent of the benefits received by male plan members, *down* from highs of 65 to 69 per cent in the early 1980s.

This coverage data is discouraging enough, but when we delve down further into the plans that do exist, the picture becomes even bleaker. Not all pension promises are of equal value, and mere coverage offers no guarantee that plans will deliver good pensions. Plans vary greatly in both the level and type of benefits they pay. Both these factors affect the adequacy, reliability, and security of the retirement income stream they can generate. For many years, the norm for Canadian pension plans was—and still is—the defined benefit (DB) plan, which calculates individual retirement benefits in accordance with a pre-determined formula and pays out a specific and consistent income stream to employees after retirement. In recent years, however, there has been a distinct trend away from plans that pay guaranteed benefits, towards capital accumulation (CAP) plans, such as defined contribution (DC) plans, group registered retirement savings plans (RRSPs), and more recently pooled retirement pension plans (PRPPs). In CAP plans, retirement income is neither guaranteed nor predictable, because it depends on the overall capital amount an individual worker is able to accumulate over a working life, and on conditions in the financial markets when that worker retires. To complicate the picture, benefit formulae have now evolved beyond the simple binaries of DB and CAP/DC, into hybrid categories that improve on DC plans, but are nevertheless not as secure and predictable for retirees as DB plans. Forms of "target benefit" plans—plans that aspire to pay a particular level of benefit but do not promise to do so if the pension fund shrinks below expectations—are now rapidly taking over, even in public sector pension plans, still the gold standard for pension security.

And finally, despite a stable and relatively efficient regulatory system, even plans that promise high quality, guaranteed benefits do not always keep that promise if they become underfunded and the companies that sponsor them become insolvent. Recent years have seen several high-profile fund failures and near-failures in Canada. Struggling companies with poor pension track records are frequently given increased time to meet their statutory obligation to fund deficits, a policy strategy that postpones the day of reckoning for these plans but may not resolve their underlying problems.

Three-quarters of Canadian adults are not covered by workplace pension plans, and the quarter who are covered may find that their plans do not deliver the pensions they expect. This is a significant problem for Canadians, because Canada is unusually dependent, by international standards, on the workplace pension system as a mechanism for delivering retirement income. This dependence has its roots in a series of policy decisions made in the early 1960s. At that time, Canadian governments agreed that Canada, like most other developed countries of that era, should build a "three-pillar" (or "three-tier") retirement income system. The first pillar—Old Age Security (OAS)—would be a basic universal poverty-relief benefit. This basic benefit would be supplemented by a second pillar, consisting of a public contributory pension plan: the Canada Pension Plan (CPP). In designing this second pillar, Canadian governments chose to peg the benefit at a level yielding a significantly lower pension than many of their international models.

CHAPTER 1: INTRODUCTION

It is conventionally estimated that, to maintain pre-retirement standards of living, retirees must replace about 70 per cent of pre-retirement income. It is not uncommon for European states to meet this target for a large proportion of their citizenry entirely from public (or mandatory) pension sources. Canada set much lower targets for public provision—closer to 40 per cent for average-income earners, and considerably less for higher-income earners. The reasoning behind this decision was that income from public sources would be supplemented by voluntary private thirdpillar instruments. Workplace pension plans were expected to be the key component of this third pillar, filling the gap between public pension provision and individual retirement income needs....

In twenty-first-century Canada, pension promises are enforceable, and plans must be managed according to modern fiduciary and solvency standards. Yet fewer and fewer workers have good pensions. This is not a coincidence. On the contrary, it is the foreseeable consequence of a voluntary, employment-based system. The legal transformation of pension rights has also transformed the employer cost-benefit equation, the practical driver of the system. The creation and strengthening of pension rights has made pensions more expensive and less useful for employers, making it much less likely that employers will voluntarily establish and maintain good plans.

This is *not* an argument that over-regulation is killing an otherwise functional system. Prior to the transformation of workplace pensions from gifts to rights, pension promises were empty promises even for members of workplace pension plans. The creation and strengthening of employee pension rights and pension funding rules was not a policy error; it was a necessary step to giving pension promises substantive content. But while regulation was a necessary step, it was not a sufficient step. The policy error was assuming that regulation would be effective even though pension promises remained embedded within a voluntary system resting on the platform of the employment relationship. Within that relationship, employers make pension decisions in their own business interests. Neither employment law nor pension law gives workers effective tools to challenge those decisions when they do not meet employee needs. In consequence, pension promises do not translate into promises of adequate, predictable, and secure retirement income. For most Canadian workers, pension promises remain empty promises.

A voluntary employment-based system works only if employers decide to create plans that yield good pensions for their employees. Some employers made that decision, and in the 1960s law-makers believed—or hoped—that more would follow. Even then, governments knew there were problems with the pension plans that employers created. But they believed—or hoped—that those problems could be fixed through regulation, and that employers would continue to provide pensions on the new regulated pension model, even though they were not compelled to do so. The basis for those hopes and beliefs was never articulated. While the trend towards pension provision still had momentum in the 1960s, it was predictable that regulatory interventions enhancing employee pension rights would increase employer pension costs. It was equally predictable that, as pension costs increased, employers would recalculate the ratio of costs to benefits, and respond either by reducing pension quality or abandoning pension provision altogether. This is the central contradiction of the voluntary workplace pension system—the legal rules that make pensions a valuable benefit for employees also make them a benefit that employers are less and less willing to provide.

While workplace pension plans are responsive to the legal environment, they also respond to broader socio-economic conditions—demographics, conditions on capital markets, the structure of workplaces, and the organization of work. Factors like these were initially favourable to workplace pensions, encouraging employers to establish and maintain plans. They might have continued to evolve in ways that offset the higher cost of rights-based pensions, at least for a time. Unfortunately, the opposite has occurred. Increasing longevity means that workplace pension plans must pay out pensions longer. The volatility of global capital markets in recent years has caused the value of pension assets to fluctuate severely and unpredictably, requiring employers to top up their pension funds based on factors unrelated either to firm profitability or worker productivity. Unionized jobs in large firms that provide full-time work and long-term permanent status—the kinds of jobs historically associated with good pension coverage—are disappearing from the modern workplace.

[Shilton, Elizabeth J. "What's Wrong with Workplace Pension Plans?" & "Lessons from History and the Road Ahead" Empty Promises. Montreal: MQUP, 2016. Print.]

K Banks, R Chaykowski, & G Slotsve, "The Accommodation Gap in Canadian Workplaces: What Does It Mean for Law, Policy and an Aging Population?" (2013) 17 *Canadian Labour and Employment Law Journal* 295

[T]he only measure universally available to Canadian employees with disabilities is the employer duty to accommodate under human rights law. Human rights codes across the country prohibit disability discrimination in employment. The Ontario *Human Rights Code*, for example, gives every person "a right to equal treatment with respect to employment without discrimination" on the basis of various prohibited grounds, including physical or mental disability. This right protects not only against direct or intentional discrimination, but also against indirect discrimination, i.e. an adverse impact resulting from a facially neutral practice or standard unless the standard is a *bona fide* occupational requirement or BFOR. A BFOR is a requirement which the employer has adopted for a purpose rationally connected to the performance of the job, and which is honestly believed to be (and in fact is) reasonably necessary to that purpose. The employer must demonstrate that it would be impossible, without incurring undue hardship, to accommodate individual employees sharing the claimant's characteristics. The duty to accommodate flows directly from the right to equal treatment without discrimination, and ends at the point of the imposition of undue hardship on the employer.

There are good reasons to believe that human rights law's reach is insufficient to ensure that Canadians with disabilities receive needed accommodation at work. Determining whether a human rights statute has been violated can be very complex and therefore time-consuming and expensive. Relatively few workers are likely to have the financial and emotional resources to pursue a complaint, particularly where discrimination occurs at the point of hire, as the hiring and pay gap studies reviewed below suggest it often does. Relatively few non-unionized employees are willing to challenge their employer by bringing a complaint during the life of the employment relationship, for fear of reprisals of various types.

Two major public reviews of human rights enforcement, in Ontario in 1992 and in the federal jurisdiction in 2001, concluded that the complaint-driven model was an outdated and ineffective way of addressing forms of discrimination that are systemic—that is, embedded in pervasive economic incentives, or in cultural stereotypes or workplace norms, rather than being individual acts of prejudice. As will be shown in Part 4 below, this conclusion is particularly apt in the case of disability discrimination at work. Both of those reports went on to recommend other options (most of which were not implemented), as did the OECD in a recent report on Canada's approach to integrating [persons with disabilities or] PWD into the workforce.

Our analysis indicates that about 35% of employed PWD in Canada do not receive needed accommodations, that the causes of the problem are often systemic, and that population aging stands to aggravate it. Yet those causes are quite likely preventable. Lack of information can be cured; stereotyping can be discouraged; rules and norms that unnecessarily disadvantage PWD can be modified; and the allocation of accommodation costs to private employers could be altered by public programs, if policy-makers were to value the public benefits highly enough....

There are unfortunately no systematic empirical studies that can help with these questions, but we do believe that a significant share of the accommodation gap is due to employer non-compliance with the duty. There are evident tensions between the widespread employer incentives and motivations documented in the literature ... and what the law requires....

[W]ith a view to fostering workplace accommodation of PWD, there is a need to look beyond the current Canadian approach. We will now outline three categories of options, with a view to illustrating the need for close policy analysis rather than endorsing any particular approach.

(a) Enhanced Compliance Programs
First, to improve the effect of complaint-driven enforcement, policy-makers might seek to enhance the deterrent and reputational effects of remedies under human rights statutes, and the capacity of employees to frame and pursue complaints under those statutes. The latter objective could be served by providing free or low-cost legal advice and representation to complainants. Deterrence might be strengthened by awarding exemplary damages in cases of deliberate non-compliance, by making more use of regulatory fines and by publishing the names of employers found to be in breach. Human rights commissions could be empowered to bring strategic litigation addressing systemic problems on the part of large employers or in problematic industry sectors.

However, given the difficulties of regulating hiring decisions, there is a serious risk that tougher complaint-driven enforcement might have unintended adverse consequences for PWD, in the form of reduced employment opportunities. There is some evidence that this is already happening, even under current enforcement strategies. Alternatives to complaint-driven enforcement should therefore be considered. One such alternative would require employers to take positive steps to reduce the risk that employees will be denied accommodations to which they are entitled. Such proactive risk management systems are required by legislation on bullying, harassment, and occupational health and safety. Another model is provided by the Integrated Accessibility Standards regulation under the *Accessibility for Ontarians with Disabilities Act 2005*. When this regulation takes effect, it will require employers to develop policies for accommodating PWD, to inform employees of those policies, to communicate the policies and the availability of accommodation to applicants for jobs or promotions, and to develop procedures for creating individual accommodation plans with the involvement of the employee and his or her representative.

Looking beyond the duty to accommodate, legislators could mandate employment equity plans under which employers would seek systematically to hire and retain a workforce that is representative of the relevant labour market. Long experience with federal employment equity legislation offers some evidence that it can help to improve opportunities for PWD. As the Canadian Human Rights Act Review Panel proposed more than a decade ago, such proactive approaches might be supported by internal responsibility systems in the form of joint employer-employee accommodation committees.

(b) Supports to Employers

A second category of options includes measures to support employers by disseminating information which includes practical advice and business case analysis, or by reducing the cost of employing disabled workers through carefully targeted wage or accommodation subsidies. As noted above, many Canadian employers express interest in programs that would provide them with information on accommodation costs and benefits. Such programs could also provide access to disability management consultants and mentoring services. Their potential value is indicated by the disjuncture between the often positive experience of employers who hire PWD and the widespread overestimation of the costs and risks of accommodation. Governments might also increase support to employment services agencies, while requiring that such agencies meet appropriate standards. These supports might conceivably be extended to make available, at the joint request of the employer and employee, case management services like those provided under workers' compensation systems.

It should be recognized, however, that none of these forms of support is likely to be effective in cases where an accommodation really would impose high costs or high risks on an employer. To deal with those situations, given the importance of the public goods at stake, policy-makers might consider an accommodation subsidy program.

(c) Supports to Workers

A third approach would support workers outside of the human rights litigation process. Such support might include informational and awareness-raising resources that would explain the legal concepts of disability and the duty to accommodate, and would offer help in resolving accommodation problems prior to litigation.

[Originally published in (2013) 17:2 CLEJ 295. Reproduced with the permission of Lancaster House.]

CHAPTER 1: INTRODUCTION

Joanne Conaghan & Kerry Rittich, "Introduction: Interrogating the Work/Family Divide" in Joanne Conaghan & Kerry Rittich, eds, *Labour Law, Work, and Family* (Oxford: Oxford University Press, 2005) 1 at 6–8 and 11–16

While it is an acknowledged tendency of labour law scholarship to equate considerations of work and family with the concerns of women workers, it has not yet fully been recognized how analysis of the work/family nexus may inform many of the wider issues relating to the regulation of work, such as what constitutes work and who is a worker. Nor is there a sophisticated and nuanced appreciation of the way in which these conceptions operate within other fields of law in relation to work, particularly welfare, tax, immigration, and citizenship law. Moreover, work/family issues are also intimately bound up with crucial debates around the transformation in state and economic forms and discourses and strategies of privatization, deregulation, and decentralization. They inform in particular debates concerning labour market flexibility, the regulation of working time, and broader work/life considerations. They are also of significance in the context of debates about different modes of labour regulation, such as the viability and desirability of individual rights versus collective strategies for workers, the uses and limits of voluntary forms of regulation, the interaction of national or supra-national regulatory levels, and the merits of 'soft' versus 'hard' regulation in the context of work issues. Work/family considerations are also of crucial importance in the context of normative or distributive questions arising from the regulation of work. This is true not just (and most obviously) around sex equality concerns, but also with regard to strategies of social inclusion and debates around distributive justice between the north and the south in the context of global economic integration.

[T]he work/family nexus and the issues it engages are fundamental to the reconstruction of the sphere of work broadly understood and any failure fully to recognize this is destined to limit the value of analyses of the changes currently taking place in that sphere....

One of the most powerful and pervasive themes emerging from scholarly scrutiny of the intersection of work and family is the presence and operative effects of an idealized worker whose experience in the labour market and encounters with paid work are unencumbered by considerations derived from their caregiving responsibilities in a family context. A related concern is the reliance upon a particular conception of paid work and the privileging of the paid work relationship as synonymous with 'work' for purposes of debate about labour regulation and policy-making... legal rules and institutions... which govern work and labour markets not only reflect deeply problematic ideas about work and workers, they help to constitute or reinforce some of the very problems scholars and policymakers are now attempting to address....

When issues of work and family surface in labour law discourse it is almost invariably in the context of 'family-friendly' policies or the 'work/life balance.' However, the primary concern is usually to increase the labour market participation of women and the primary focus has become the development of mechanisms, both legal and extra-legal, which allow women workers to effect a better reconciliation of their competing market and family demands. In many ways, developments in labour law have simply mirrored wider reform proposals to increase the number of women workers in order to relieve the wage pressure on employers and reduce the fiscal burden that 'non-productive,' 'dependent' citizens impose on states. In view of the underlying concerns, it is not surprising that the resulting reforms typically still compel women to pay a price in terms of leisure time, income, and/or work opportunities. The failure to move beyond the goal of reconciliation and consider reforms that would challenge and subvert either the gender division of labour at home or the presumption of the unencumbered worker at work raises serious questions about whether 'family-friendly' equates with 'women-friendly' and whether there is anything of substance to be gained—for women and for workers generally—from family-friendly initiatives.

[T}he emergence of work/family issues within the discipline of labour law and on the radar of policymakers has not yet led to reforms that challenge the structural causes of gender inequality arising from the conflicting demands of the market and household. Rather, a distinct cleavage seems to be emerging between reforms that merely manage the tension between work and family so as to relieve some of the pressure on women workers on the one hand and proposals that seek more profound distributive change and have as their aim substantive equality for women both at home and at work on the other. Whether more promising outcomes from the standpoint of gender equality lie in the future will depend on the acceptance of a much wider definition of the concept of work and a willingness to mount fundamental challenges to work norms and practices, both established and emerging, at home and in the labour market.

[Reprinted by permission of Oxford University Press.]

1:443 The Changing Role of the State

The above considerations tend to call for a renewed role for the state in the regulation of workplace relations. However, many seasoned observers have long contended that the changing social and political environment in industrialized economies militates against such a role. Consider the following argument, taken from a seminal article published in 1995. To what extent have conditions changed over the last two decades?

Harry Arthurs, "Labour Law Without the State" (1996) 46 *University of Toronto Law Journal* **1 at 7–11**

In the view of some observers, the present period is one in which we are experiencing a 'hollowing out of the state.' This arresting phrase is meant to call attention to the repeated and often successful attacks on the state's role in providing economic stimulus, regulation, and a social safety net. At a minimum, the existing repertoire of such benign and purposeful state interventions is more likely to contract than to expand.

Others resist the conclusion that the state is being 'hollowed out.' They rightly point to the fact that much of the new economy has been made possible not by the retreat of the state, but by its realignment with social forces hostile to the 'fordist' policies promulgated by liberal capitalist, centrist, and social democratic governments during the postwar period. The decision to abandon the Bretton Woods international financial system; to establish global and regional versions of 'free' trade; to open financial and currency markets, to implement monetarist policies in the realm of public finance; to suppress government funding of culture, welfare, public services, and infrastructure; to restrict flows of immigrants and refugees; to impose more stringent forms of social discipline through the criminal law: all of these suggest that the state is still very much intact, although its powers are being mobilized for different purposes.

Not much is gained by debating whether the state has been hollowed out, or merely captured by a particular coalition of powerful interests. It does seem clear, however, that the growing disjuncture of political, juridical, and economic spaces amounts to a structural change in the nature of the state—at least in industrialized western democracies—and that this structural change has considerable salience for labour market institutions. Moreover, this structural change can be distinguished causally and analytically from cyclical changes in the domestic political alignments of particular states, which are also highly relevant to the future of labour law.

We are living in a period of widespread cynicism about politics and public life, and of deep alienation from the political process. This is not to romanticize the past: there may never have been a true 'golden age' of democratic politics. However, whether because of the misdeeds of parties and politicians, the relentless trivialization of public affairs by the media, or exogenous events such as demographic change, it does seem that most western democracies are experiencing something of a crisis of political culture and institutions.

One manifestation is declining citizen participation in, even attention to, the electoral process. Another is the emergence of species of atavistic populism in which the views of political elites, experts, and informed observers are reflexively rejected by 'ordinary people' tantalized by the possibility that for every complex problem there must surely be a simple or common-sense solution. These developments, in turn, have magnified the political power of determined and well-financed single-issue constituencies which believe—sometimes justifiably—that conventional parties and parliamentary governments have been unwilling or unable to respond to their particular concerns. Perceiving themselves to have been spurned by the state and those who control its political processes, they in turn reject consensus, coalition-building and compromise—the traditional approach of conventional political movements in most western democracies. Instead they opt for zero-sum strategies which they can directly control, in order to gain leverage for the changes they favour, without the necessity of winning parliamentary elections or enacting legislation. These strategies include Charter litigation, plebiscites and referendums, campaigns to change public attitudes, popular culture and intellectual discourse, confrontational action against their opponents, and projects of self-help and mutual support. If such strategies succeed, they reinforce the conviction that parliamentary structures do not matter; if not, they reinforce disillusion with politics in general.

Paralleling, often reinforcing, this disparagement of public life, politics, and state action has been an active and successful campaign against what are perceived to be excessive levels of taxation. On the one hand, opposition to taxation has sometimes been promoted by the rich and privileged who, in effect, threaten a strike of capital if they are not relieved of tax burdens they deem unacceptable. On the other, tax revolts also seem to have considerable appeal for middle-class and working-class taxpayers anxious to protect their standard of living, and reluctant to support many of the state activities for which public funds are being spent. Nor are all public programs so obviously worthy that their support by taxpayers ought to be regarded as axiomatic. Depending on one's point of view, it is quite understandable that taxpayers should not wish to meet the cost of debt servicing, wasteful military expenditures, unproductive industrial subsidies, or failed social experiments. The result, in any event, has been a crisis in public finance, partly real and partly manufactured. All proposals to increase public expenditure are suspect. The only question on the agenda worth talking about anywhere in the public sector seems to be how best to manage retrenchment.

And finally, leftist and liberal political movements committed to the benign use of state power have suffered a serious erosion of confidence and credibility. Perhaps they have been unfairly associated with the patent failures of communism; perhaps they are fairly charged with their own failures of performance; perhaps their worst failure has been that they have neglected to renew themselves intellectually over the past twenty or thirty years.

What has all this to do with labour law?

The Canadian labour law system succeeded to the extent that it did during the postwar period—how well is a matter of debate—because it was lodged in a complex system of public policies, institutional arrangements, and implicit and explicit understandings involving employers, unions, and governments. We know this system by various names—fordism, corporatism, industrial pluralism—each of which emphasizes different causes and effects as distinguishing characteristics. However, as the system unravels, it becomes less important to debate or distinguish these than it is to point to the implications of their disappearance for the future of labour law as we have known it.

The most salient point is that however inclusive the consensus supporting the postwar system may have been, it has suffered important defections. Intellectuals and technocrats have become increasingly alienated from state-centred politics, after an attraction lasting three or four generations. Consequently, they are much less likely to argue for such important features of the labour law system as the efficacy of regulatory intervention, regional equalization, progressive taxation, public expenditure to offset the business cycle, or even the possibility that class differences can be mediated through state-sponsored collective bargaining.

The working class—a concept whose descriptive power always exceeded its emotive appeal—is divided within itself. Workers seem increasingly apathetic—even antipathetic—to labour organizations and labour parties; unions have failed to preserve old alliances with ethnic communities or to forge new ones with visible minority groups; and genders and generations seem to regard each other as opponents in a zero-sum competition for whatever is left of a depleting resource: regular employment. At the institutional level, unions are dismissive of the few vestigial traces of corporate *noblesse oblige*, corporations increasingly reject any conception of their own role which does not compute on next quarter's bottom line; and both mistrust government attempts to manage the economy, while seeking specific interventions favourable to their own interests or ideological beliefs....

In short, the Canadian version of the new economy is characterized by fissiparous tendencies in politics and social life. These have created an environment hostile to the survival of the postwar labour law system and make its reform or renovation very difficult. Indeed, the fault lines in that system run right to its core: the nature and organization of paid work which labour law is meant to regulate.

[Reprinted with permission from University of Toronto Press Incorporated (www.utpjournals.com).]

1:500 THE CONSTITUTIONAL DIVISION OF POWERS

Constitutional issues first emerged early in the twentieth century when both the federal and provincial governments were led to regulate some aspects of labour relations and bargaining strikes through legislative action. The courts were soon asked to determine whether the Parliament of Canada or provincial legislatures had jurisdiction over labour relations and working conditions. In response, they formulated many of the key constitutional principles on the division of powers as set forth in sections 91 and 92 of the *British North America Act, 1867* (1867, c 3 (UK)) (now the *Constitution Act, 1867*). These are examined in more detail below in this section.

A second set of constitutional issues is referred to as "Section 96" issues. They relate to sections 96 to 100 of the *Constitution Act, 1867*, which provide that judges of the courts of superior jurisdiction in each province must be appointed by the federal government, and give those judges security of tenure to protect their independence. When modern provincial labour and social welfare legislation came onto the scene after World War II, it was interpreted and applied by specially created provincial administrative bodies—including quasi-judicial administrative tribunals with specialized expertise. The members of those tribunals did not enjoy the protections of sections 96 to 100, and it was therefore argued that they had no authority to enforce rights and grant remedies which resembled the rights and remedies traditionally enforced and granted by the superior courts. The leading case in this area is *Labour Relations Board of Saskatchewan v John East Iron Works Ltd*, [1949] AC 134 (JCPC).

On its face, this debate was about the independence of adjudicators. On another level, it was about the authority of the legislative branch of government to decide that its social legislation would be administered not by the courts but by specialized tribunals which were expected to be more sympathetic to the redistributive objectives that often characterized social legislation. Because the section 96 debate involved the interface between legislative and judicial authority, it was quite closely related to the long-standing debate over the proper scope of judicial review of administrative decision-making—a debate that is at the heart of the field of administrative law.

Almost forty years ago, the section 96 issue abated as the result of a compromise of sorts. On the one hand, the Supreme Court of Canada allowed the provinces (and the federal government) to give administrative tribunals strong powers to interpret and enforce social legislation. On the other hand, the Supreme Court insisted that no legislature could exempt any tribunal from judicial review, in order to ensure that every tribunal would stay within what the courts saw as the limits of its substantive and procedural jurisdiction. See *Crevier v Attorney-General of Quebec*, [1981] 2 SCR 220. At a few points in this book, we will touch upon the lively administrative law issue of the appropriate standard of judicial review, significantly revisited by the Supreme Court of Canada in the landmark case of *Dunsmuir v New Brunswick*, [2008] 1 SCR 190. However, we will make no further direct mention of the section 96 issue.

1:510 The Division of Powers Between the Federal and Provincial Governments

Sections 91 and 92 of the *British North America Act, 1867* (1867, c 3 (UK)) (now the *Constitution Act, 1867*) do not explicitly delegate jurisdiction over labour relations and working conditions to either the federal or provincial government. This gave rise to an important judicial debate that emerged in the 1920s following the first attempts to adopt legislative standards and frameworks in labour and employment law, including the early ratification of conventions of the International Labour Organization by the federal government. See *AG (Canada) v AG (Ontario)*, [1937] AC 236.

Courts have decided that, as a general principle, labour relations and working conditions fall within the exclusive jurisdiction of the provinces, as these matters are included in the broad provincial head of power over "Property and Civil Rights" (s 92(13) of the *Constitution Act, 1867*). Parliament however retains exclusive authority over labour relations and working conditions in the federal undertakings covered by sections 91(29) and 92(10)(a), (b), and (c) of the *Constitution Act, 1867*.

Federal Labour Standards Review Commission, *Fairness at Work: Federal Labour Standards for the 21st Century* **(Ottawa: HRSDC, 2006) (Arthurs Report) at 7–9**

> In enacting ... the *Canada Labour Code*, the federal government has exercised its constitutional jurisdiction to establish labour standards for workers in federally regulated private sector industries, and in First Nations governments. Federally regulated industries include several in which enterprises typically operate across the country, such as banks, broadcasting and telecommunications companies, interprovincial and international transportation firms, and Crown corporations such as Canada Post; and a number of others as well, such as sea ports, airports, nuclear facilities and grain elevators. The federal government, however, lacks jurisdiction, except in unusual circumstances, to regulate labour standards in most ordinary enterprises—manufacturing firms, restaurants and retail stores, timber or mining companies—all of which come under provincial jurisdiction.
>
> ... The constitutional parameters of labour jurisdiction have resulted in a constituency of federally regulated employers and workers whose profile differs in many significant ways from that of its provincially regulated counterparts. This profile suggests that labour standards in the federal legislation may have to be designed to operate in a context that is very different from that of other jurisdictions.
>
> The 2005 Statistics Canada Federal Jurisdiction Workplace (FJW) Survey—the first-ever survey of federal employers—provides much valuable information. An estimated 1.132 million workers—about 8.4% of the Canadian workforce—are employed by employers subject to federal jurisdiction. Of these, some 840,000 are subject to the Part III labour standards. These workers mostly work for banks (30%), telecommunications or broadcast firms (18%), postal service and pipeline companies (14%), airlines (12%), or road transportation firms (12%).
>
> The first thing that is notable about this population is that employment is highly concentrated in large enterprises in most federally regulated sectors, with 86% of employees working for employers with 100 or more employees. To look at it another way, although federal jurisdiction employers covered by Part III account for about 6%

of employment in Canada, they comprise only about 1% of Canada's employers. Exceptions to this concentration of employment in large enterprises are found in the road transportation sector (where enterprises with fewer than 100 employees accounted for 55% of employment), the maritime transport sector (50%), and the feed, flour, seed and grain sector (48%). However, of these sectors, only road transportation accounted for a significant proportion of federal jurisdiction employment.

Second, as a group, workers in enterprises covered by Part III are more likely than other Canadian workers to enjoy working conditions above the national norm. In 2004 more than half (52%) of them were paid more than $20 per hour, versus 37% of all workers in Canada, while only 2% were paid less than $10 per hour, versus 16% nationally. Among Part III employers with 100 or more employees, 83% report offering some form of pension plan to their staff. Overall, 28% of Part III employers reported offering a pension plan to their employees, compared with 19% for the wider Canadian labour market. Similar trends can be observed with respect to insurance benefits, paid leave and personal support programs. Outside of the banking sector (which is only 1% unionized), rates of unionization in the federal jurisdiction tend to be higher than the national average for the private sector, which is approximately 19%; by sector, unionization ranges from 23% in road transportation to 81% in rail transportation, with an overall rate of 32% that rises to 46% if banking is excluded.

Third, the demographic profile of workers covered by Part III differs somewhat from the Canadian norm. They tend to be somewhat older, with fewer workers aged under 25 (8% versus 17%) and more aged 45 to 54 (29% versus 23%). This is particularly notable in rail transportation, road transportation, maritime transportation, and postal services and pipelines, where the percentage of the workforce aged 45 years or more ranges from 44 to 56%, compared with the national average of 34%. Except in banking (which is 72% female), federal jurisdiction industries also tend to be male dominated to varying degrees (ranging from 60% in postal services and pipelines to 92% in rail transportation), with the overall result that a greater percentage of the federal workforce are men than is the case for the Canadian workforce as a whole (57% versus 51%)....

To sum up, the domain of federal labour standards is configured as much by constitutional and legal doctrine as by economic or policy logic. As a result, the demographics of workers and employers in the federal domain differ from those of workers and employers covered by similar legislation elsewhere.

* * * * *

Although the general rules relating to the division of powers over labour relations and working conditions have been well settled since the middle of the twentieth century, questions still arise today in light of the impact of economic restructuring and the growing complexity of the operations of what are often called "global" firms.

Tessier Ltée v Quebec (Commission de la santé et de la sécurité du travail), 2012 SCC 23, [2012] 2 SCR 3

> ABELLA J [McLachlin CJ and LeBel, Deschamps, Fish, Rothstein, Cromwell, Moldaver and Karakatsanis JJ concurring]:

[1] Tessier Ltée is a heavy equipment rental company that rents out cranes for a variety of purposes and provides technical, operational, supervisory and consulting services in connection with its crane leasing. It is also engaged in other activities, including intra-provincial road transportation and maintenance and repair of equipment.

[2] In 2005-2006, Tessier had 25 cranes which were used in construction work and industrial maintenance. Some were also used for the loading and unloading of ships, an activity known as long-shoring or stevedoring. All of its activities took place within the province of Quebec.

[3] Stevedoring represented 14 percent of Tessier's overall revenue and 20 percent of the salaries paid to employees. Tessier's employees worked across the different sectors of the organization—an employee who operates a crane at a port one day may be involved in operating it at a construction site, or driving a truck, the next.

[4] The issue in this appeal is whether Tessier's employees are governed by federal or provincial occupational health and safety legislation. . . .

[11] Jurisdiction over labour relations and working conditions is not delegated to either the provincial or federal governments under s. 91 or s. 92 of the *Constitution Act, 1867*. But since *Toronto Electric Commissioners v. Snider*, [1925] A.C. 396 (P.C.), courts have accepted that legislation respecting labour relations is presumptively a provincial matter since it engages the provinces' authority over property and civil rights under s. 92(13) of the *Constitution Act, 1867*: *NIL/TUO Child and Family Services Society v. B.C. Government and Service Employees' Union*, 2010 SCC 45, [2010] 2 S.C.R. 696, at para. 11.

[12] Despite the provinces' presumptive interest in the regulation of labour relations, there is still a federal presence in this area. As a result of the *Snider* decision, the federal government amended the predecessor to the *Canada Labour Code*, R.S.C. 1985, c. L-2, that had been at issue in that case, restricting its application to operations which were within federal legislative authority.

[13] The constitutional validity of this narrower statute was considered in *Reference re Industrial Relations and Disputes Investigation Act*, [1955] S.C.R. 529 (the *Stevedores Reference*), where this Court answered two reference questions: whether this restricted federal labour legislation was *intra vires* Parliament; and whether it applied to the Toronto employees of a particular stevedoring company which engaged exclusively in stevedoring and did all the loading and unloading for seven companies engaged in extra-provincial shipping.

[14] This Court, in nine separate sets of reasons, answered the first question by unanimously upholding the federal statute, and concluding that notwithstanding *Snider*, Parliament was entitled to regulate labour relations when jurisdiction over the undertakings were an integral part of Parliament's competence under a federal head of power. As Abbott J. wrote:

> . . . the determination of such matters as hours of work, rates of wages, working conditions and the like, is in my opinion a vital part of the management and operation of any commercial or industrial undertaking. This being so, the power to regulate such matters, in the case of undertakings which fall within the legislative authority of Parliament lies with Parliament and not with the Provincial Legislatures. [Emphasis added; p. 592.]

[15] This Court has repeatedly confirmed Justice Abbott's conclusion that a level of government cannot have exclusive authority to manage a work or undertaking without having the analogous power to regulate its labour relations: *Commission du salaire minimum v. Bell Telephone Co. of Canada*, [1966] S.C.R. 767, at pp. 771–72; *Bell Canada v. Quebec (Commission de la santé et de la sécurité du travail)*, at pp. 816-17, 825-26 and 833; *Ontario Hydro v. Ontario (Labour Relations Board)*, [1993] 3 S.C.R. 327, at pp. 363–64 and 368–69. See also H. Brun, G. Tremblay and E. Brouillet, *Droit constitutionnel* (5th ed. 2008), at pp. 533 and 535.

[16] As to the second question in the *Stevedores Reference* asking which level of government had authority over the particular stevedoring company's labour relations, eight of nine judges concluded in separate reasons that the federal labour statute applied to the employees in question because the work they did was integral to the federal shipping companies that used them. Based on extensive evidence regarding the services that the stevedores provided to the shipping companies, the majority concluded that the employees devoted all of their time to the federally regulated companies, who relied on them exclusively for the loading and unloading of their cargo.

[17] In the *Stevedores Reference*, this Court therefore established that the federal government has jurisdiction to regulate employment in two circumstances: when the employment relates to a work, undertaking, or business within the legislative authority of Parliament; or when it is an integral part of a federally regulated undertaking, sometimes referred to as derivative jurisdiction. Dickson C.J. described these two forms of federal jurisdiction over labour relations as distinct but related in *United Transportation Union v. Central Western Railway Corp.*, [1990] 3 S.C.R. 1112, at pp. 1124–25.

[18] In the case of direct federal labour jurisdiction, we assess whether the work, business or undertaking's essential operational nature brings it within a federal head of power. In the case of derivative jurisdiction, we assess whether that essential operational nature renders the work integral to a federal undertaking. In either case, we determine which level of government has labour relations authority by assessing the work's essential operational nature.

[19] In this functional inquiry, the court analyzes the enterprise as a going concern and considers only its ongoing character: *Commission du salaire minimum v. Bell Telephone Co. of Canada*. The exceptional aspects of an enterprise do not determine its essential operational nature. A small number of exceptional extra-provincial voyages which are not part of the local transportation company's regular operations, for example, do not determine the nature of a maritime transportation operation (*Agence Maritime Inc. v. Conseil canadien des relations ouvrières*, [1969] S.C.R. 851), nor does one contract determine the nature of a construction undertaking (*Construction Montcalm Inc. v. Minimum Wage Commission*, [1979] 1 S.C.R. 754). Nor will a small amount of local activity overwhelm the nature of an undertaking that is otherwise an integral part of the postal service (*Letter Carriers' Union of Canada v. Canadian Union of Postal Workers*, [1975] 1 S.C.R. 178)....

[20] Tessier's claim that it is a federal undertaking is based on its involvement with activities related to the shipping industry. Specifically, Tessier argued that this Court concluded in the *Stevedores Reference* that stevedoring is an essential part either of "[n]avigation and [s]hipping" under s. 91(10) of the *Constitution Act, 1867* or "[l]ines of [s]team or other

[s]hips" under s. 92(10)(a) and (b) and is therefore subject to federal regulation. According to Tessier, any company whose employees are engaged in stevedoring is a company whose employees should be federally regulated for purposes of labour relations. Tessier therefore argued its case as one of direct jurisdiction. With respect, I do not share Tessier's interpretation either of the *Constitution Act* or the *Stevedores Reference*....

[34] The effect of the *Stevedores Reference* as interpreted over time, then, is that stevedoring is not an activity that brings an undertaking directly within a federal head of power, at least for purposes of labour relations regulation. Rather, Parliament will only be justified in regulating these labour relations if the stevedoring activities at issue are an integral part of the extra-provincial transportation by ship contemplated under s. 92(10)(a) and (b). This result is consistent with the understanding of the division of powers over shipping under ss. 91(10) and 92(10) and its exceptions reviewed above.

[35] What, then, is the analytical framework for assessing whether a related undertaking is integral to a federal undertaking? ...

[46] So this Court has consistently considered the relationship from the perspective both of the federal undertaking and of the work said to be integrally related, assessing the extent to which the effective performance of the federal undertaking was dependent on the services provided by the related operation, and how important those services were to the related work itself.

[47] Applying these principles to the facts of this case, can it be said that Tessier's stevedoring activities are integral to a federal undertaking in a way that justifies imposing exceptional federal jurisdiction for purposes of labour relations?

[48] To date, this Court has applied the derivative jurisdiction test for labour relations in two contexts. First, it has confirmed that federal labour regulation may be justified when the services provided to the federal undertaking form the exclusive or principal part of the related work's activities (*Stevedores Reference*; *Letter Carriers' Union of Canada*).

[49] Second, this Court has recognized that federal labour regulation may be justified when the services provided to the federal undertaking are performed by employees who form a functionally discrete unit that can be constitutionally characterized separately from the rest of the related operation....

[50] This appeal is the first time this Court has had the opportunity to assess the constitutional consequences when the employees performing the work do not form a discrete unit and are fully integrated into the related operation. It seems to me that even if the work of those employees is vital to the functioning of a federal undertaking, it will not render federal an operation that is otherwise local if the work represents an insignificant part of the employees' time or is a minor aspect of the essential ongoing nature of the operation: *Consumers' Gas Co. v. National Energy Board* (1996), 195 N.R. 150 (C.A.); *R. v. Blenkhorn-Sayers Structural Steel Corp.*, 2008 ONCA 789, 304 D.L.R. (4th) 498; and *International Brotherhood of Electrical Workers, Local 348 v. Labour Relations Board* (1995), 168 A.R. 204 (Q.B.). See also *General Teamsters, Local Union No. 362 v. MacCosham Van Lines Ltd.*, [1979] 1 C.L.R.B.R. 498; M. Patenaude, "L'entreprise qui fait partie intégrante de l'entreprise fédérale" (1991), 32 *C. de D.* 763, at pp. 791–99; and Brun, Tremblay and Brouillet, at p. 544.

[51] In this sense, Tessier's acknowledgment that it operates an indivisible undertaking works against its position that its stevedoring employees render the whole company

subject to federal regulation. If Tessier *itself* was an inter-provincial transportation undertaking, it would be justified in assuming that the percentage of its activities devoted to local versus extra-provincial transportation would not be relevant: *Attorney-General for Ontario v. Winner*, [1954] A.C. 541. But since Tessier can only qualify derivatively as a federal undertaking, federal jurisdiction is only justified if the federal activity is a significant part of its operation....

[55] In short, if there is an indivisible, integrated operation, it should not be artificially divided for purposes of constitutional classification. Only if its dominant character is integral to a federal undertaking will a local work or undertaking be federally regulated; otherwise, jurisdiction remains with the province....

[56] As noted, at the relevant time, Tessier devoted the majority of its efforts to non-shipping activities, including renting cranes for construction work and industrial maintenance, renting heavy equipment other than cranes, and intra-provincial transportation. Its stevedoring activities accounted for 14 percent of Tessier's overall revenue and 20 percent of the salaries paid to employees. Tessier's employees were fully integrated, and worked across the different sectors of the organization....

[58] What emerges from this factual review is that Tessier's stevedoring services were not performed by a discrete unit and represented only a small part of its overall operation. Tessier's employees are an indivisible workforce who work interchangeably in various tasks throughout the company. To the extent that any of Tessier's employees perform stevedoring activities, they do so only occasionally. Crane operators who work at a construction site one day might assist in unloading ships the next day.

[59] In short, Tessier's essential operational nature is local, and its stevedoring activities, which are integrated with its overall operations, form a relatively minor part of Tessier's overall operation. Not to retain provincial hegemony over these employees would subject them to federal regulation based on intermittent stevedoring, notwithstanding that the major part of Tessier's work consists of provincially regulated activities.

[60] Though it is no longer of relevance in light of this conclusion, it is worth noting that we have, in any event, little evidence that Tessier's stevedoring services were integral to the federal shipping companies it serviced. Tessier focused its argument on establishing that it was a federal shipping company directly under s. 91(10) or s. 92(10) and did not lead any evidence to show any derivative link to federal shipping undertakings. As a result, while we know that Tessier provided some shipping companies with cranes and operators to assist with the loading and unloading of their ships, we do not know much else.

[61] To be relevant at all, a federal undertaking's dependency on a related operation must be ongoing. Yet we have no information about the corporate relationship between Tessier and the shipping companies, whether Tessier's stevedoring activities were the result of long-term or short-term contracts, or whether those contracts could be terminated on short notice. There is nothing, in short, to demonstrate the extent to which the shipping companies were dependent on Tessier's employees. As a result, as in the Court of Appeal, no conclusions could even have been drawn about whether those of Tessier's employees who occasionally performed stevedoring activities were integral to federal shipping undertakings. This too argues against imposing exceptional federal jurisdiction.

1:520 Aboriginal Self-Government

Finally, another emerging set of constitutional issues concerns the impact of aboriginal self-government claims on labour and employment law. The *Constitution Act, 1982*, s 35 recognizes and reaffirms "the existing aboriginal and treaty rights of the aboriginal people in Canada." The Supreme Court of Canada has taken the lead, notably in *R v Van der Peet*, [1996] 2 SCR 507, in recognizing and defining the scope of the inherent right of aboriginal peoples to maintain their traditional and customary practices adapted to contemporary Canadian society.

The Ontario Court of Appeal grappled with these constitutional issues in *Mississaugas of Scugog Island First Nation v AG Canada & AG Ontario*, 2007 ONCA 814, leave to appeal to the Supreme Court of Canada refused, 2008 CanLII 18945 (SCC)) in which a band claimed a legal right to enact its own code of labour law to govern collective bargaining in relation to a commercial undertaking (a casino) that operated on reserve lands. The Ontario Labour Relations Board rejected the claims, characterizing the right not as one to control access to aboriginal lands, but rather as a right to regulate labour relations on the reserve. It found that there was no ancestral practice, custom, or tradition capable of supporting that right, nor was there any established treaty right that would lead to a right to regulate labour relations, nor did it find a broader right to self-government. The Court of Appeal applied the *Van der Peet* decision, affirmed that aboriginal rights must be understood in the specific circumstances of each case, but agreed with the OLRB that there was no evidence to support the claim. The conclusion was explained as follows, at para 19:

> The appellant's only witness as to aboriginal custom and practice was Professor Mark Walters. His affidavit and cross-examination indicate that the hallmarks of pre-contact Ojibway society were its family or clan base, its non-hierarchical structure and its consensual and non-adversarial dispute resolution process. These defining features are fundamentally at odds with the appellant's Code which is market-based, is hierarchical in structure and establishes an adversarial dispute resolution processes [sic] before the Dbaaknigewin, a quasi-judicial board that has no demonstrated connection with aboriginal tradition and exercises coercive powers.

The Court of Appeal further held as follows, at para 39:

> even if we were to accept the appellant's characterization of the right as an aboriginal practice to regulate work activities and access to aboriginal lands, such a practice could not be said to be integral to the distinctive culture of the appellants.... The evidence led as to the traditional regulation of work activity bears no relation to modern collective bargaining. The appellant cannot escape this deficiency by relying on the fact that the aboriginal society organized the work activities of its members: the organization of work at that level of generality is a feature of every human society.

Although the Court of Appeal recognized that aboriginal rights are "not frozen, but are capable of evolving into modern form provided there is continuity linking the present exercise of the aboriginal claim to the distinctive character and nature of the right in its original form," the court held (at paras 40–41) that the band's labour law code had no meaningful relationship with pre-contact communal practices "inspired by values of family, clan and connection to the land.... Its roots are entirely post-contact and derived from modern law dealing with contractual relationships between employers and employees in a post-industrialist capitalist economy."

The Court of Appeal made barely any mention of the fact that the code in question was passed at an informal band meeting a few days after the OLRB certified the Canadian Auto Workers (CAW), under the Ontario *Labour Relations Act*, to represent approximately 1,000 workers (less than 1 percent of whom were band members) at the casino. The band meeting was held with no notice to the public, the OLRB, the casino operator, or the CAW, and no minutes were kept. The code was closely modelled on the *Canada Labour Code*, except that strikes and lockouts were banned, a union had to pay a fee of $3,000 and obtain permission from the band's labour relations tribunal to speak to workers on the reserve, and workers had to pay a fee of $12,000 to file an unfair labour practice complaint.

Chapter 2: International and Transnational Labour Law

2:100 CONNECTING LABOUR AND EMPLOYMENT LAW AT HOME AND ABROAD

Chapter 1 has outlined the massive transformation underway in the world of work that workers in Canada are now experiencing. This transformation is one that spills over national borders; one that implicates work and workers all over the world; and one that engages questions about the nature, content, and adequacy of labour and employment law across governance levels.

More than twenty years ago, Ethan Kapstein, in "Workers and the World Economy," made the following observations about the fate of workers under conditions of globalization:

> The global economy is leaving millions of disaffected workers in its train. Inequality, unemployment, and endemic poverty have become its handmaidens. Rapid technological change and heightening international competition are fraying the job markets of the major industrialized countries. At the same time systemic pressures are curtailing every government's ability to respond with new spending. Just when working people most need the nation-state as a buffer from the world economy, it is abandoning them. This is not how things were supposed to work. The failure of today's advanced global capitalism to keep spreading the wealth poses a challenge not just to policymakers but to modern economic "science" as well. For generations, students were taught that increasing trade and investment, coupled with technological change, would drive national productivity and create wealth. Yet over the past decade, despite a continuing boom in international trade and finance, productivity has faltered, and inequality in the United States and unemployment in Europe have worsened.... It is hardly sensationalist to claim that in the absence of broad-based policies and programs designed to help working people, the political debate in the United States and many other countries will soon turn sour. Populists and demagogues of various stripes will find "solutions" to contemporary economic problems in protectionism and xenophobia. Indeed, in every industrialized nation, such figures are on the campaign trail. Growing income inequality, job insecurity, and unemployment are widely seen as the flipside of globalization. That perception must be changed if Western leaders wish to maintain the international system their predecessors created. After all, the fate of the global economy ultimately rests on domestic politics in its constituent states.... The world may be moving inexorably toward one of those tragic moments that will lead future historians to ask, why was nothing done in time? Were the economic and policy elites unaware of the profound disruption that economic and technological change

were causing working men and women? What prevented them from taking the steps necessary to prevent a global social crisis?

[Republished with permission of the Council on Foreign Relations, from Ethan Kapstein, "Workers and the World Economy" (1996) 75:3 *Foreign Affairs* 16; permission conveyed through Copyright Clearance Center, Inc.]

A premise of this chapter is that changes in the world of work and the challenges to labour and employment law are interconnected on multiple levels. Decisions about work and the law of work in one jurisdiction may well have profound effects in others.

Kerry Rittich & Guy Mundlak, "The Challenge to Comparative Labor Law in a Globalized Era" in Matthew W Finkin & G Mundlak, eds, *Comparative Labor Law* (Cheltenham, UK: Edward Elgar Publishing, 2015) 80 at 81–82

Labor law, both in general and as a subject of comparison, is traditionally situated within the confines of the nation state. Scholars of labor law typically begin with the premise that markets and production are socially and politically embedded, that regulation is centrally co-ordinated by the state or by territorial entities within it, and that collective bargaining is conducted according to rules prescribed by the state that cover the spectrum of domains from the enterprise to the national level. Where the borders of the state are drawn, however, the system of labor law reaches its limits. It is the premises of the Westphalian state system that have made it possible to compare the different legal solutions that have been devised *within* nation states to deal with problems such as the 'fissuring' or 'vertical disintegration' of enterprises and their consequences for workers' rights and power. However, it is precisely these premises that are now eroded and unstable.

When globalization is integrated into the story, framing the interaction between law and social-economic forces engages new difficulties of scale, causality and scope. The vertical disintegration of production permits employers to exploit the possibilities of lower labor costs in other jurisdictions, including those that come about because of differences in regulatory standards. But it also produces new regulatory conundrums. To the extent that vertical disintegration results in supply chains and production that cross borders, it may no longer be clear which national laws govern the workplace. Once production crosses borders ('off-shoring'), national regulatory solutions often become elusive and inadequate, and responses to the problematics of networked production may well extend beyond labor law as we have known it. Similarly, increased 'in-shoring' of, or reliance on, migrant labor often implicates fields such as citizenship and immigration law that lie beyond the traditional scope of labor and employment law. The globalization of production also imports new actors and activities into the norm generation process. Along with traditional efforts to influence the shape and content of both local and national law, employers may engage in law-shopping and regulatory arbitrage, seeking at once to identify and rely on, and, along with NGOs, to influence the laws governing their activities in ways that are congenial to their interests and objectives. The effects of these interventions, moreover, can sometimes be identified in territories that are remote from where regulatory decisions are actually made. Thus, there may be little or no overlap between the labor market or community of workers and employers affected by legal and labor market norms, the actors and

institutions that author such norms, and the location where their broader social effects are experienced. Under these circumstances, it is hardly surprising that it is now more difficult for the agents of labor to influence the shape and content of the law of the workplace.
[Reproduced with permission of the Licensor through PLSclear.]

Some problems at work may be best addressed by international and/or transnational regulatory solutions. As you will see, some initiatives may implicate private actors, such as firms or industry groups or involve public and private action jointly. And workers may be profoundly affected by trade agreements as well as decisions about monetary and fiscal policy. It becomes necessary to study labour law with an eye to the transnational, understood at least "to include all law which regulates actions or events that transcend national frontiers": Philip C Jessup, *Transnational Law (Storr's Lectures on Jurisprudence)* (New Haven: Yale University Press, 1956) at 2.

Adelle Blackett & Anne Trebilcock, "Conceptualizing Transnational Labour Law" in Adelle Blackett & Anne Trebilcock, eds, *Research Handbook on Transnational Labour Law* **(Cheltenham, UK: Edward Elgar Publishing, 2016) 1**

Some relevant changes include heightened global interdependency, technological innovation, labour migration, increasing informalization of work, and the persistence of poverty, discrimination and inequality along fault lines of historical marginalization. Today, thick webs of contractors structure global production chains, constructing yet obscuring links between workers in the global South who produce products they cannot afford to buy, and workers in the global North who both market and consume goods they no longer produce. The transnational enterprises through which markets operate are able to control the means of production, transform that control into power, and exercise it transnationally to compel workers to live and produce by their norms. Similarly complex networks of labour brokers recruit workers from an intricate range of regional peripheries, to provide a host of activities recharacterized as services. They may work in actively informalized agricultural production, building construction or care reproduction servicing global cities, shaped in the light of—rather than in opposition to—a global and regional architecture structuring the provision of services transnationally. Such phenomena reflect and adapt a Westphalian notion of state sovereignty, and the highly differentiated rules governing the conditions of movement of products, services and capital.

[Transnational labour law (TLL)] builds on a recognition that liberal states have made the global era possible: what was conceived as national becomes denationalized in a process propelled by actors and sources of authority that proliferate in territory beyond the decentred state. The changes afoot have led to substantive rethinking of the spatial and temporal configuration of the global regulation of work. They challenge deeply rooted assumptions about law, labour and the transnational. And they shift the focus to alternate actors. Workers in particular, as principal actors seeking to refocus global governance's direction, are required to reimagine if not the nature then certainly the focus of their justice claim. TLL therefore does not reflect a rigid reclassification of the field of labour law, or international (labour) law. TLL rather reflects a recognition, captured by Trubek, that: there is a missing pillar in the architecture of global governance.
[Reproduced with permission of the Licensor through PLSclear.]

CHAPTER 2: INTERNATIONAL AND TRANSNATIONAL LABOUR LAW

This chapter sketches the current global landscape of work, suggesting how and why old forms of labour market regulation are now under pressure while new ones are emerging. Our discussion covers four distinct periods, all of which are relevant to understanding both positive and normative claims around the law of work: where domestic and international labour and employment law came from; why it has taken the form that it has; what trends and developments have placed current rules and regimes under pressure; and where those rules and regimes appear to be going in the future. It is anchored around a series of vignettes, which underscore both the relationship between home and abroad, and the importance of engaging with transnational approaches to labour law.

2:200 UNDERSTANDING WORK, SOCIAL WELFARE, GLOBALIZATION, AND INTERNATIONAL LAW: FOUR PERIODS

2:210 Period I: Globalization, Work, and the Origins of the ILO

The current era of globalization is by no means the first. Increasingly, legal scholars are challenging how we start narratives about labour law's origins, by drawing attention to the often overlooked coexistence of settler colonialism, global migration, the transatlantic slave trade, indentured labour regimes, and waged labour. At the end of the nineteenth century, from roughly 1870 to World War I, a feature of the first globalization—one that is distinct from the present era—is that labour, as well as capital, from the global North was for the most part free to migrate. Many workers did move in search of work and better economic futures. This migration did not only exist alongside colonial divisions (metropolitan and peripheral territories) of the world, but was also enabled by them. The literature on racial capitalism helps us to understand how these seemingly paradoxical divisions could not only be sustained, but were perpetuated throughout the four periods chronicled in this chapter. Some sources for further reference include Adelle Blackett, "Emancipation in the Idea of Labour Law" in Guy Davidov & Brian Langille, eds, *The Idea of Labour Law* (New York: Oxford University Press, 2010) 420; Frédéric Mégret, "Transnational Mobility, the International Law of Aliens and the Origins of Global Migration Law" (2017) 111 *American Journal of International Law Unbound* 13; and E Tendayi Achiume, "Reimagining International Law for Global Migration: Migration as Decolonization?" (2017) 111 *American Journal of International Law Unbound* 142.

The first globalization was also the period that gave birth to the first institution devoted to establishing and securing international labour standards, the International Labour Organization (ILO). As the second extract discusses, Canada is a founding ILO member, and has played a pivotal role throughout its history.

Werner Sengenberger, "Restructuring at the Global Level: The Role of International Labour Standards" in Werner Sengenberger & Duncan Campbell, eds, *Creating Economic Opportunities: The Role of Labour Standards in Industrial Restructuring* (Geneva: International Institute for Labour Studies, 1994) 394 at 403

INTERNATIONAL LABOUR STANDARDS AND THE ILO

The need for providing standards at the international level was increasingly felt as the opportunity of competing through wages and working conditions expanded with increasing cross-border competition in Europe in the late nineteenth and early twentieth centuries. In the international debate which culminated in the foundation of the International Labour Organization (ILO) under Article 19 of the Treaty of Versailles in 1919, labour standards at the international level were opposed by some countries on the grounds that they would handicap them on the international market by increasing their costs relative to other countries not covered by the common rule. For example, the ratification of the Hours of Work Convention, which was the first Convention adopted by the ILO in 1919, was slowed down by this consideration. Others, on the contrary, argued that international agreements to set standards would ensure that competition was not at the workers' expense and would in fact amount to a code of fair competition between employers and between countries. This argument was in fact embodied in the Preamble of the Constitution of the ILO which states that 'the failure of any nation to adopt humane conditions of labour is an obstacle in the way of other nations which desire to improve the conditions in their own countries.'

It was perhaps not by accident that the ILO was created as an autonomous body at the end of the First World War, when nations had just passed through a period of political and social disaster. At this time there existed—as was the case later after the Second World War—the 'community of suffering' which can give rise to sufficient consensus capable of generating international order. There was agreement in the industrialized countries in 1919 to seek to create an organization apt to set international labour standards in order to relieve the social effects of international economic competition, and, more generally, advance justice in relation to the social conditions aggravated by the ravages of industrialization and the appalling working environment caused by it. The principles that 'universal and lasting peace can be established only if it is based on social justice' and 'labour is not a commodity' form cornerstones of ILO philosophy.

The following more specific objectives of the ILO are stated in its Constitution:

(a) regulation of working hours, including the establishment of a maximum working day and week;
(b) regulation of the labour supply;
(c) prevention of unemployment;
(d) provision of an adequate living wage;
(e) protection of the worker against sickness, disease and injury arising out of employment;
(f) protection of children, young persons, and women;
(g) provision for old age and injury;
(h) protection of the interests of those working in countries other than their own;
(i) equal remuneration for work of equal value;
(j) recognition of the freedom of association;
(k) organization of vocational and technical education.

From the beginning, the ILO was heavily involved in normative work and the setting of international labour standards has been its core activity. The ILO ... has a unique tripartite structure which enables national governments and workers' and employers' organizations to share power in its decision-making bodies, of which the Governing Body is the executive organ, and the International Labour Conference elaborates and adopts international labour standards. Once standards are adopted by the Conference, member States must submit them within a year to their parliaments or other legislative authorities for the enactment of national legislation or action. These authorities remain free to decide whether or not they put them into effect, but they are in any case obliged to inform the Director-General of the ILO of the action taken.

... Once ratified by the competent national authority, they involve binding international commitments. Appropriate documentation has to be supplied by the country's government about how the Convention will function. The ILO Constitution also requires non-ratifying member countries to report periodically on the extent to which their laws and practices implement the provisions of unratified Conventions. They must indicate what is preventing or delaying the ratification. Recommendations do not create any international obligation but are designed to provide guidance to governments in formulating their social policies. They have been found most suitable or appropriate whenever a subject is not yet ripe for the adoption of a Convention, or to supplement a Convention, or where it seems desirable to leave a wide latitude to states as to which action should be taken.

The application of ratified Conventions is closely monitored through ILO's reporting and review machinery, involving the International Labour Office as the secretariat of the ILO, as well as tripartite committees of the Conference, and independent experts. Reports are scrutinized with a view to helping governments to overcome difficulties which they may have in making standards effective. As concerns compliance, any member has the right to file a formal complaint with the International Labour Office if it is not satisfied that any other member is securing the effective observance of a Convention which both have ratified. The matter is then made subject to inquiry, and eventually recommendations are made as to the necessary steps to be taken to meet the complaint. The governments in question then have to either accept the recommendations or refer the complaint to the International Court of Justice, whose decision is final.

It is recognized as a problem that the record of ratification varies vastly across countries. With some notable exceptions, most ratifications are made by the industrialized or near-industrialized countries, while the developing countries have ratified far fewer Conventions. It has been debated at great length, both inside and outside the ILO, whether the developing countries can even afford to apply the minimum standards laid down in the International Labour Code. The ILO itself has responded to this question by providing some flexibility in introducing standards to take account of the widely varying economic and social conditions and legal and political systems. In view of such variety, two extremes are to be avoided. One is to set standards which can be accepted at once by the greatest possible number of countries, with the risk that the common denominator is apt to result in a standard too low to produce any significant progress. The other would be to aim at too high a standard which would not be immediately practicable in most countries.

Many standards are formulated in fairly general language, thus giving governments latitude either in the scope of setting the standard or in the methods of application.

It is generally held that the standards promulgating fundamental human rights mentioned above should apply independently of the state of a country's development. For example, no matter how rich or poor a country is, it cannot be accepted that trade union leaders be harassed, jailed, disappear, or be murdered. Substantive standards, on the other hand, usually contain flexible formulas of one kind or another. For example, with regard to minimum wages, Convention No. 131 (1970) specifies that a country should have a system of minimum wages in one form or another, but it does not stipulate the minimum wage required. It would be unrealistic to set a substantive rule, given the enormous wage differentials across member States. (In the United States, for example, the average wage per hour is about the same as that for a full working day in adjacent Mexico. In Finland, a carpenter's wage on one day is nowadays equivalent to a worker's wage for one month in neighbouring Russia.) Even so, it is the ambition of the ILO to adhere to the principle of universality in setting and enforcing standards, and not admit regional standards for groupings of countries of different degrees of development. Regional standards would accentuate rather than reduce differences in development, and would mean that in certain regions there would be 'substandards' for 'sub-human people.' ...

The other way in which the ILO, together with other specialized United Nations agencies, has attempted to deal with the wide differential in national labour conditions, has been through *technical cooperation*. This includes education, consultation and technical assistance, and is given primarily to the countries of the South to assist them in their development process, e.g. through public works projects, setting up vocational training and rehabilitation centres, promoting full employment, forming rural cooperatives, building safety and health systems, and establishing systems of social security. The setting and application of labour standards and technical cooperation are seen to complement and strengthen each other. Technical cooperation is to be designed with the aim of achieving progress towards the ratification of and compliance with international labour standards. [Copyright © International Labour Organization 2014.]

Adelle Blackett, "'This is Hallowed Ground': Canada and International Labour Law" in *Canada in International Law at 150 and Beyond,* Paper No 22 (2018)

A visitor to the palatial World Trade Organization (WTO) building in Geneva, Switzerland, would be greeted by a plaque on the founding stone of the tranquil palace that the permanent secretariat of the International Labour Organization (ILO) initially occupied. Laid by the ILO's first director general, Albert Thomas, the plaque proclaims that "if you seek peace, cultivate justice." A specialized agency of the United Nations that predates both the United Nations and the establishment of the Bretton Woods institutions, the ILO was founded at the Paris Peace Conference on April 11, 1919, and was part of the Treaty of Versailles.

Although Canada was not part of the initial Commission on International Labour Legislation of the Peace Conference that was "called upon ... to draft plans for an organization which had no parallel in the history of politics," Canada gained "international recognition of her national maturity by her admission to the League of Nations and the International

Labour Organization as an original Member." Canada also became the first ILO member to send a woman—Violet Markham—to participate in the governing body, in 1923. But Canada's most unique contribution remains that it provided a wartime home for the ILO, at McGill University; the ILO held its 1946 International Labour Conference at the Université de Montréal. In Canada, the ILO prepared its postwar policy, including its approach to decolonization, and readied itself for a more outward-looking approach as part of a soon-to-emerge UN system. During that same time, the ILO reaffirmed the "truth" of its 1919 constitutional affirmation that "lasting peace can be established only if it is based on social justice" in the historic 1944 constitutional annex adopted at the International Labour Conference in Philadelphia (the Declaration of Philadelphia). A renowned international labour official and subsequent director-general of the ILO, C. Wilfred Jenks, delivered these words as part of a thank-you speech to the Canadian government: "This is hallowed ground in the history of the ILO. Here we kept alive in a world at war the ideal and practice of international collaboration in pursuit of social justice in a world of freedom...."

The ILO was at the heart of the harmonization of [International Labour Legislation, or] ILL over time into national labour legislation—at least in industrialized, metropolitan territories that currently comprise the global North—a process that was actively supervised by the ILO's regular supervisory mechanisms in the Committee of Experts on the Application of Conventions and Recommendations and the International Labour Conference Committee on the Application of Conventions and Recommendations. In the process, Thomas himself said he "taught the world to speak something like the same language on social questions." But the paradoxical, if predictable, result was that the institution, itself, became less visibly important as—through its at once stubborn and subtle exercise of persuasion—its principles were largely normalized.

Keen observers of the ILO then and now are lucid about the ILO's standard-setting limits. Shotwell noted as early as 1934 that although the ILO had already garnered 600 ratifications of its international labour conventions, "only a fraction of these deal with major issues." Moreover, the period of rapid standard production overtook the period of rapid ratification, which was characterized as cafeteria style.

[Reproduced by permission of the publisher, © 2018 by the Centre for International Governance Innovation.]

2:220 Period II: Embedded Liberalism and the Keynesian Welfare State

The design of labour and employment law in Canada, along with many of the general and specific rules and standards that govern work, are largely the products of the post-World War II era. For example, the *Wagner Act* [*National Labor Relations Act*, 29 USC §§ 151-169 (1935)] labour relations regime upon which most of Canadian labour law is modelled was imported into Canada from the United States at that time. As the world of work changes and as deep economic integration places increasing pressure on domestic rules and standards, it is useful to reflect on the fundamental purposes of labour and employment law and how their connection to the broader economic order was originally imagined.

As the following excerpts describe, in the postwar international order, security and political stability were understood to be dependent upon avoiding economic injustice and instability, while international trade rules were deeply interlinked with the welfare state. Indeed, the case for liberalized trade was itself premised on "embedded liberalism": the availability of domestic social policies to redress the inequities between the winners and losers.

Robert Howse, "From Politics to Technocracy—and Back Again: The Fate of the Multilateral Trading Regime" (2002) 96:1 *American Journal of International Law* 94 at 94–95, 97–98

> When we turn to the regime of international trade *law*, as it has emerged in the post–Second World War era, we find an intellectual or conceptual foundation that, to be sure, assumes and assimilates the classic insights about the gains to wealth and welfare from free trade but is fundamentally concerned with the *interdependency* of different states' trade and other economic policies—i.e., managing or constraining the external costs that states impose on other states by virtue of their policies....
>
> The postwar trade and financial order was therefore mainly designed to enable states to manage their domestic economies, in a manner consistent with political and social stability and justice, without the risk of setting off a protectionist race to the bottom....
>
> This is the first and original sense in which the postwar trading order addressed itself in its very conception and structure to "trade and ..."—the system sought to structure the way domestic pressures would be addressed through trade and nontrade alternative measures. A key assumption or expectation was this: one should be able to protect domestic social and political stability, using means that avoid exporting domestic social economic difficulties and threatening global stability—in other words, to avoid destructive forms of *interdependent* behavior....
>
> This was the miracle of "embedded liberalism"—trade liberalization was embedded within a *political* commitment, broadly shared among the major players in the trading system of that era, to the progressive, interventionist welfare state; in other words, to a *particular* political and social vision, including at the same time respect for diverse ways of implementing this vision—with greater use of microeconomic intervention, such as indicative planning and public enterprise in Europe and Japan, while tax-and-transfer approaches were more typical of North America, and certainly the United States. Following an insight of Kalypso Nicolaidis, one could even say that it was the trust that emerged from this basically shared vision that produced acceptance of the differences in approach to the mixed economy and welfare state as between the United States, Europe, and Japan. The success or at least viability of the embedded liberalism bargain is reflected in the fact that high social spending and openness to trade have traditionally been positively correlated.

Consider the vision of the relationship between trade and labour contained in the text of the projected International Trade Organization, negotiated in Havana from 21 November 1947 to 24 March 1948, and set out immediately below. Ultimately, this document, the *Final Act of the United Nations Conference on Trade and Employment* (London: HM Stationary Office, 1948)—known as the *Havana Charter*—was not ratified; instead the General Agreement on Tariffs and Trade was largely extracted from Chapter IV on Commercial Policy, without the institutional framework, and without the chapter on employment and economic activity that included Article 7 on fair labour standards.

CHAPTER I
PURPOSE AND OBJECTIVES

Article 1

RECOGNIZING the determination of the United Nations to create conditions of stability and well-being which are necessary for peaceful and friendly relations among nations,

THE PARTIES to this Charter undertake in the fields of trade and employment to cooperate with one another and with the United Nations

For the Purpose of

REALIZING the aims set forth in the Charter of the United Nations, particularly the attainment of the higher standards of living, full employment and conditions of economic and social progress and development, envisaged in Article 55 of that Charter.

TO THIS END they pledge themselves, individually and collectively, to promote national and international action designed to attain the following objectives:

1. To assure a large and steadily growing volume of real income and effective demand, to increase the production, consumption and exchange of goods, and thus to contribute to a balanced and expanding world economy.
2. To foster and assist industrial and general economic development, particularly of those countries which are still in the early stages of industrial development, and to encourage the international flow of capital for productive investment.
3. To further the enjoyment by all countries, on equal terms, of access to the markets, products and productive facilities which are needed for their economic prosperity and development. ...
4. To promote on a reciprocal and mutually advantageous basis the reduction of tariffs and other barriers to trade and the elimination of discriminatory treatment in international commerce.
5. To enable countries, by increasing the opportunities for their trade and economic development, to abstain from measures which would disrupt world commerce, reduce productive employment or retard economic progress.
6. To facilitate through the promotion of mutual understanding, consultation and co-operation the solution of problems relating to international trade in the fields of employment, economic development, commercial policy, business practices and commodity policy. ACCORDINGLY they hereby establish the INTERNATIONAL TRADE ORGANIZATION through which they shall co-operate an Members to achieve the purpose and the objectives set forth in this Article.

CHAPTER II
EMPLOYMENT AND ECONOMIC ACTIVITY

Article 2

Importance of Employment, Production and Demand in relation to the Purpose of this Charter
1. The Members recognize that the avoidance of unemployment or underemployment, through the achievement and maintenance in each country of useful employment

opportunities for those able and willing to work and of a large and steadily growing volume of production and effective demand for goods and services, is not of domestic concern alone, but is also a necessary condition for the achievement of the general purpose and the objectives set forth in Article 1, including the expansion of international trade, and thus for the well-being of all other countries.

2. The Members recognize that, while the avoidance of unemployment or underemployment must depend primarily on internal measures taken by individual countries, such measures should be supplemented by concerted action under the sponsorship of the Economic and Social Council of the United Nations in collaboration with the appropriate inter-governmental organizations, each of these bodies acting within its respective sphere and consistently with the terms and purposes of its basic instrument....

Article 3

Maintenance of Domestic Employment
1. Each Member shall take action designed to achieve and maintain full and productive employment and large and steadily growing demand within its own territory through measures appropriate to its political, economic and social institutions.

2. Measures to sustain employment, production and demand shall be consistent with the other objectives and provisions of this Charter. Members shall seek to avoid measures which would have the effect of creating balance-of-payments difficulties for other countries....

Article 7

Fair Labour Standards
1. The Members recognize that measures relating to employment must take fully into account the rights of workers under inter-governmental declarations, conventions and agreements. They recognize that all countries have a common interest in the achievement and maintenance of fair labour standards related to productivity, and thus in the improvement of wages and working conditions as productivity may permit. The Members recognize that unfair labour conditions, particularly in production for export, create difficulties in international trade, and, accordingly, each Member shall take whatever action may be appropriate and feasible to eliminate such conditions within its territory.

2. Members which are also members of the International Labour Organisation shall cooperate with that organization in giving effect to this undertaking.

3. In all matters relating to labour standards that may be referred to the Organization in accordance with the provisions of Articles 94 or 95, it shall consult and co-operate with the International Labour Organisation....

As the *Havana Charter* reveals, labour law and employment standards were an important part of the embedded liberal bargain; see Harry Arthurs, "Labour Law Without the State" (in Chapter 1, Section 1:443). Those rules and standards never extended to all workers. As will be seen in the following chapters, there were important exclusions and exceptions—for example, concerning agricultural and domestic workers—which resulted in either lesser or no protection to workers outside the standard employment relationship (SER) (see Chapter 1, Section 1:431). Nonetheless, the SER provided a set of norms and benchmarks for "normal" work, as well as a set of rules and institutions to redress the imbalance in bargaining power between workers and employers.

Kerry Rittich, "The Right to Work and Labour Market Flexibility: Labour Market Governance Norms in the International Order" in V Mantouvalou, ed, *The Right to Work: Legal and Philosophical Perspectives* (Oxford and Portland, OR: Hart Publishing, 2015) 315

> [Rights at] work reflect the understanding, grounded in both theory and historical experience, that market processes do not automatically produce good, or even any, work. To the contrary, bargaining asymmetries, resource disparities and what we now identify as market failures and collective action problems are structural features of labour markets that routinely produce employment contracts with terms and conditions of work that are disadvantageous for workers. It has long been understood that the labour contract is subject to a systemic imbalance in bargaining power of a particularly marked sort. Rather than the product of negotiation among equals that reflect mutual input, interest, assent and benefit, the terms of the employment contract are typically established unilaterally by the employer; the absence of real alternatives often means that they are effectively imposed by the employer as well. For this reason, enabling or actively promoting the construction of a countervailing source of power through collective action on the part of workers has been the heart of the enterprise of labour law.
>
> In the post-war era, the objectives of access to work and better terms and conditions of work were reflected in the recognition of a series of rights at work, realized through a complex of legal entitlements as well as social and economic policies. Although the legal regimes in which rights at work manifested took a variety of forms, the general objectives were widely shared. A measure of job and income security was secured for many workers through the labour law systems operating within the different models of welfare state capitalism. Better terms and conditions of work were buttressed by minimum employment standards, whether legislated or determined through collective bargaining. Employment insurance, income transfers and other forms of social protection bridged periods of unemployment and ensured that where work itself could not be provided, the worst economic consequences of the shortfall in jobs—namely, lack of income—could be mitigated.
>
> But access to work was also supported by fiscal and monetary policy that, in the initial years and for a substantial period afterwards, was informed by Keynesian macroeconomic theory and a broadly shared belief in its utility in managing the adverse consequences of cyclical downturns in the economy. Workers' effective or social wage was a function of public services and income transfers supported by steeply progressive taxation rates, as well as income garnered in the labour market. Falling demand for jobs in the private sector, for example, was routinely met by increased demand in the public sector and/or mitigated through increased access to unemployment benefits and other social transfers.
>
> [Used by kind permission of Bloomsbury Publishing Plc.]

The ILO's former legal adviser discusses the impact of international labour standards during this period in Francis Maupain, "Revisiting the Future" (2015) 154:1 *International Labour Review* 105:

> In this context of ideological competition between two rival models of social justice, less attention was paid to whether States had ratified, or would ratify, standards than had been the case before the Second World War. The reason is that, in the context of the cold war, standard setting fulfilled a different "magisterial" function, which made ratification a less relevant test of the value and efficacy of the standards.
>
> However, as soon as the Iron Curtain came down and—thanks to the digital revolution and the free movement of capital—financial "supercapitalism" took over from industrial capitalism, the demand for the regulatory function returned with a vengeance, at least among workers in industrialized countries. The poor ratification record of ILO standards, however, called into question the Organization's ability to meet this renewed regulatory challenge.

2:230 Period III—Globalization, Rise of the Washington Consensus, and Labour Responses

2:231 Globalization

Beginning in the 1980s, trade and financial liberalization, and innovations in technology and transportation enabled new ways to order productive relations, including work and employment, a process widely described as "globalization."

Kerry Rittich & Guy Mundlak, "The Challenge to Comparative Labor Law in a Globalized Era" in Matthew W Finkin & G Mundlak, eds, *Comparative Labor Law* (Cheltenham, UK: Edward Elgar Publishing, 2015) 80 at 83–84

> At the most basic level, globalization refers to the processes of economic, cultural and social contact, inter-mixing, and integration that are such a salient condition of our time, much of which is produced by the intensified movement of capital, labor, commodities, and culture across borders. Although nations and territory remain deeply significant to the organization of economic activity, production and service provision increasingly traverse borders; as a result, both nations and enterprises face new competitive pressures from which they were, for the most part, formerly isolated. Workers—white collar as well as blue—who once enjoyed secure employment within national or regional territories now frequently find themselves in competition for jobs with workers in other states and regions. Those at the middle and lower ends of the labor market have declining bargaining power and, in consequence, are experiencing flat or falling real wages. High-skilled workers and workers in occupations for which there is high demand, by contrast, are often courted by national migration regimes, sometimes without regard for whether local supply is short or not, and typically experience increased bargaining power as a result, although some of these workers, too, face the upheaval of continuous transitions between jobs. The mobile and transitional character of the workforce fostered by these transnational forces and flows contributes to declining solidarity and

CHAPTER 2: INTERNATIONAL AND TRANSNATIONAL LABOUR LAW

growing inequality within national workforces, as well as to the maintenance of differences between workers of different countries.

[Reproduced with permission of the Licensor through PLSclear.]

On the one hand, globalization may open up opportunities, particularly in the developing world, for workers and employers to participate in an advanced industrial economic system. On the other hand, as the following excerpt explains, it may accentuate rather than overcome existing divisions of labour and inequalities of development.

David Harvey, *Spaces of Global Capitalism: Towards a Theory of Uneven Geographical Development* (London: Verso, 2006) at 100–1

> The reduction in the cost and time of movement of commodities, people (labor power), money and information through what Marx called 'the annihilation of space through time' is a basic law of capital accumulation. It has a notable presence within the historical geography of capitalism and underpins the production of uneven geographical development in many ways [including] the systematic reduction over time of the element of monopolistic competition in space fixed by transportation and communications costs. Any spatial arrangement achieved under one set of transport and communications relations (e.g. railroads and telegraph) will have to be changed to meet the conditions of any new set (e.g. air transport and the internet). Also, we must take account of the differential geographical mobilities of capital (as money, as commodities, as production activities) and of labor. The easier movement of money capital, for example, may create difficulties particularly for types of production that find it hard to move.
>
> The general diminution in transport costs in no way disrupts the significance of territorial divisions and specialization of labor. Indeed, it makes for more fine-grained territorial divisions since small differences in production costs (due to raw materials, labor conditions, intermediate inputs, consumer markets, infrastructural or taxation arrangements) are more easily exploitable by highly mobile capital. Reducing the friction of distance, in short, makes capital more rather than less sensitive to local geographical variations. The combined effect of freer trade and reduced transport costs is not greater equality of power through the evolving territorial division of labor, but growing geographical inequalities.

The globalization of product and capital markets, facilitated by international trade law and policy, has been accompanied by increases in international migration, for the most part not facilitated by international law or coordination.

World Bank, *World Development Report 2013: Jobs* (Washington, DC: World Bank, 2013) at 232

> Precise figures on the global number of international migrants are not available, an unsurprising fact given that a number of them cross borders illegally or do not return once their visas and permits expire. That is why estimates tend to rely on population censuses and household surveys. Even then, differences across countries in the way that data are gathered, and in the way legislation defines nationality and migratory status, make accurate counts difficult. The orders of magnitude are relatively uncontroversial, however. There are more than 200 million migrants worldwide, and 90 million of them are workers.

Migrants represent between 2.5 and 3 percent of the world's population and the global labor force. Many are temporary or seasonal workers and return to their home country.

Global patterns of migration

Global figures hide important differences across countries. Some countries are mainly recipients, while others are sources, and yet others neither host nor send significant numbers of migrants. In a few relatively small recipient countries, the foreign-born population makes up more than 40 percent of the total population....

The most direct impact of international migration is on living standards. Through their work in receiving countries, and through remittances to sending countries, migrants increase their incomes and those of their families. Migrants also contribute to global output if their productivity abroad is higher than it was at home, which may often be the case. They can even contribute to output in the sending country, as networks of migrants and returnees serve as channels for investment, innovation, and expertise. Social effects are mixed, however. On the positive side, migration connects people from different cultures in ways bound to widen their horizons. On the negative side, separation from family and friends can be a source of distress and isolation in the recipient country. Large numbers of immigrants can also exacerbate frustration among vulnerable groups in recipient countries, if foreigners are seen as competitors for jobs and public services.

[World Bank. 2012. World Development Report 2013: Jobs. World Development Report. Washington, DC. © World Bank. https://openknowledge.worldbank.org/handle/10986/11843 License: CC BY 3.0 IGO.]

2:232   The Rise of the Washington Consensus

Along with globalization, a new policy and regulatory consensus described by economist Joseph Stiglitz as "market fundamentalism" displaced the embedded liberal bargain and began to prevail in leading industrial economies and within the international financial and economic institutions. This consensus placed enhanced private sector activity—rather than the state—at the centre of national welfare gains and, accordingly, sought to enhance the conditions under which capital could securely invest, produce, and trade across borders.

Although frequently described in the language of "neoliberalism," the contours of this market fundamentalism were framed through what came to be known as the *Washington Consensus*, which was a series of policy prescriptions first presented in 1989 by John Williamson, an economist from an international economic think tank based in Washington, DC. Elements of this "consensus" can have significant effects on workers and labour markets because, for example, they affect the allocation of public expenditures, unemployment rates, wage levels, and/or the "social" wage. Note how Williamson qualifies that consensus when reflecting on it fifteen years later:

John Williamson, "A Short History of the Washington Consensus" (Paper commissioned by Barcelona Centre for International Affairs, for the conference "From the Washington Consensus Towards a New Global Governance" 24–25 September 2004) (2009) 15 *Law and Business Review of the Americas* 7

The ten reforms that constituted my list were as follows.

1. Fiscal Discipline. This was in the context of a region where almost all countries had run large deficits that led to balance of payments crises and high inflation that hit mainly the poor because the rich could park their money abroad.
2. Reordering Public Expenditure Priorities. This suggested switching expenditure in a pro-growth and pro-poor way, from things like non-merit subsidies to basic health and education and infrastructure. It did not call for all the burden of achieving fiscal discipline to be placed on expenditure cuts; on the contrary, the intention was to be strictly neutral about the desirable size of the public sector, an issue on which even a hopeless consensus-seeker like me did not imagine that the battle had been resolved with the end of history that was being promulgated at the time.
3. Tax Reform. The aim was a tax system that would combine a broad tax base with moderate marginal tax rates.
4. Liberalizing Interest Rates. In retrospect I wish I had formulated this in a broader way as financial liberalization, stressed that views differed on how fast it should be achieved, and—especially—recognized the importance of accompanying financial liberalization with prudential supervision.
5. A Competitive Exchange Rate. I fear I indulged in wishful thinking in asserting that there was a consensus in favor of ensuring that the exchange rate would be competitive, which pretty much implies an intermediate regime; in fact Washington was already beginning to edge toward the two-corner doctrine which holds that a country must either fix firmly or else it must float "cleanly".
6. Trade Liberalization. I acknowledged that there was a difference of view about how fast trade should be liberalized, but everyone agreed that was the appropriate direction in which to move.
7. Liberalization of Inward Foreign Direct Investment. I specifically did not include comprehensive capital account liberalization, because I did not believe that did or should command a consensus in Washington.
8. Privatization. As noted already, this was the one area in which what originated as a neoliberal idea had won broad acceptance. We have since been made very conscious that it matters a lot how privatization is done: it can be a highly corrupt process that transfers assets to a privileged elite for a fraction of their true value, but the evidence is that it brings benefits (especially in terms of improved service coverage) when done properly, and the privatized enterprise either sells into a competitive market or is properly regulated.
9. Deregulation. This focused specifically on easing barriers to entry and exit, not on abolishing regulations designed for safety or environmental reasons, or to govern prices in a non-competitive industry.
10. Property Rights. This was primarily about providing the informal sector with the ability to gain property rights at acceptable cost (inspired by Hernando de Soto's analysis).

These policy prescriptions, though not on their face necessarily redistributive in any particular direction, were often interpreted and applied in ways that redistributed income and opportunity, in relation to how things had been under embedded liberalism, from the lower and middle reaches of the income distribution towards the top of it.

David Harvey, *Spaces of Global Capitalism: Towards a Theory of Uneven Geographical Development* **(London: Verso, 2006) at 48**

> The state, once transformed into a neo-liberal set of institutions, becomes a prime agent of redistributive policies, reversing the flow from upper to lower classes that had occurred during the era of social democratic hegemony. It does this in the first instance through pursuit of privatization schemes and cut-backs in those state expenditures that support the social wage. Even when privatization appears as beneficial to the lower classes, the long-term effects can be negative.... The neo-liberal state also seeks redistributions through a variety of other means such as revisions in the tax code to benefit returns on investment rather than incomes and wages.

* * * * *

The global shift to *Washington Consensus* policies was accompanied by the replacement of embedded liberalism in international trade law and policy with the prioritization of ensuring secure market access in order to enhance the mobility of goods, services, and capital.

Robert Howse, "From Politics to Technocracy—and Back Again: The Fate of the Multilateral Trading Regime" (2002) 96:1 *American Journal of International Law* **94 at 98–99**

> The very success of the embedded liberalism bargain, along with other phenomena, led to forgetfulness or amnesia concerning the political foundation of the postwar trading regime, its character as a specific and contingent bargain about the interaction between freer trade and the welfare state....
>
> At the hands of this trade policy elite, "embedded liberalism" came to be recast as economics, and economics became ideology, the ideology of free trade. The central notion that governed the conception of the relationship of trade policy to domestic policy generally was that wherever trade barriers such as tariffs had direct price-distorting effects in the market of the importing country, removal of those barriers enhanced aggregate domestic welfare in that the total gains to consumers could be shown always to exceed the total losses to producers/workers. Put in this crude way, the case for trade liberalization appeared to be totally indifferent to any notion of a just distribution of benefits and burdens from the removal of trade restrictions. But from the perspective of a liberal democratic understanding of justice, of course, there may be good reasons of principle and/or policy to place a higher value on the avoidance of catastrophic losses to a small vulnerable group (for example, textile workers in Quebec) than on gains dispersed among millions of consumers (slightly lower prices for shirts and blouses).
>
> How then, was the insider network able to turn a blind eye to these issues of distributive justice? Above all, through the notion that gains to the winners should allow us to fully compensate the losers from removal of trade restrictions, while still netting an aggregate welfare gain. According to this conception, based on what is known in the

economics and related literatures as Kaldor-Hicks efficiency, in the end no one need be worse off as a result of trade liberalization. What was presumed, or taken for granted here, was the existence of a regulatory and social welfare state to take care of the interests of the losers (however legitimate) through the use of nontrade policy instruments (worker retraining, etc.) that are less costly to domestic welfare than trade restrictions.

If we can thus imagine that many will benefit, and no one has to lose (assuming appropriate "compensation"), from a policy move, then the question of its effect on just deserts or a just allocation of goods might seem to disappear. Who could fairly complain about having been made better off?

2:233 Labour Responses

Some have argued that economic growth under conditions of liberalized trade would itself lead to better working conditions; see for example, Robert J Flanagan, *Globalization and Labor Conditions: Working Conditions and Worker Rights in a Global Economy* (New York: Oxford University Press, 2006) at 177. It has been recognized at least since the 1995 UN Social Summit, however, that there remains a social deficit at the heart of globalization and that neglect of workers' rights and declines in workers' position and bargaining power are central to that social deficit. Some of these changes are attributable to the challenges of regulating work in transnational labour markets.

A joint study by the ILO and the WTO laid out the basic issues for work and workers. A portion of the executive summary featured in the report is excerpted below.

Marion Jansen & Eddy Lee, *Trade and Employment: Challenges for Policy* (International Labour Organization & World Trade Organization, 2007) online at: www.wto.org/english/res_e/booksp_e/ilo_e.pdf

Basic issues

Economists have long recognized that trade would lead to a division of labour advantageous to everybody involved. Indeed, by reshuffling resources in accordance with the principles of comparative advantage, they can be used more appropriately and effectively for production, thus creating the so-called gains from trade. Highly productive producers will be able to expand as they start selling their goods or services abroad. Producers and consumers will be able to take advantage of cheaper imports and of a larger product and quality choice. The latter, however, implies that some domestic production will be replaced by imports.

In other words, trade liberalization is expected to trigger a restructuring of economic activity that takes the form of company closures and job losses in some parts of the economy and start-ups of new firms, investment in increased production and vacancy announcements in other parts of the economy. Trade liberalization is therefore associated with both job destruction and job creation. In the short run the resulting net employment effects may be positive or negative depending on country specific factors such as the functioning of the labour and product markets. In the long run, however, the efficiency gains caused by trade liberalization are expected to lead to positive overall employment effects, in terms of quantity of jobs, wages earned or a combination of both. Average wage increases may, however, hide distributional changes that affect some workers negatively.

Where trade liberalization affects parts of the labour force negatively, labour and social policies are required in order to redistribute some of the gains from trade from winners to losers. This study tries to identify situations in which such government intervention may be helpful, and individuals and groups that should be targeted. It also discusses the possible effects of different types of labour and social policies in the relevant situations. In this discussion it is pointed out that labour and social policies may have unintended efficiency effects. Indeed, to the extent that such policies may have a negative effect on the above-mentioned "reshuffling" process that is necessary in order to reap the benefits from trade, policy-makers may be confronted with a trade-off, although not necessarily a very steep one.

Recent developments

Traditionally, economists expected that the reshuffling process triggered by trade liberalization would take place across sectors. Roughly speaking, it was expected that labour-intensive industries would shrink in developed countries, while skill and/or capital intensive industries would expand. The opposite phenomenon was expected to happen in developing countries. In developed countries jobs would therefore be destroyed in labour-intensive industries and capital employed in those industries would have to be re-employed. The long-run distributional consequences of trade would imply increased inequality between capital and labour or between skilled and unskilled labour in the developed world. In contrast, inequality was expected to decrease in the developing world.

Empirical evidence initially appeared to confirm these predictions. In particular, decreases in inequality were observed in a number of East Asian economies that liberalized trade. At the same time, increases in the wage differential between high-skilled and low-skilled labour — the so-called skill premium — were observed in a number of developed countries. In other developed countries where labour market policies, such as minimum wages, limited the extent of wage adjustments, increases in low-skilled unemployment were observed.

But three important phenomena emerged that were not in line with traditional trade theory, and a large body of theoretical and empirical literature has tried to respond to this discrepancy between traditional predictions and observed realities.

1. First, most industrialized countries trade above all with other industrialized countries. Traditional trade theory was only of very limited use in predicting employment effects resulting from this type of trade. Recent contributions to the theoretical trade literature have therefore looked at the question of whether trade among similar countries, i.e. intra-industry trade, may have an impact on the demand for high-skilled and low-skilled labour and some of these studies have combined trade with technological change. This literature comes to the conclusion that trade among similar countries can raise wage inequality within countries and also within sectors.

Another branch of literature has examined the relationship between openness and the sensitivity of labour demand to wage changes. In this context it has been argued that in an open economy employers would be more likely to threaten to lay off workers when they demand higher wages than in a closed economy, for instance, because they face stiffer price competition than before. Economists refer to this increased sensitiveness as an increase in the price elasticity of labour demand. This line of argumentation has two important implications. First, trade between industrialized and developing countries will affect the elasticity of labour, but the same is true for trade among industrialized countries. Second, the price elasticity of demand can be affected by the mere possibility of trade. For instance, the mere threat of sourcing inputs from another country or of delocalization may weaken workers' resistance to wage reductions.

This literature may explain why surveys in industrialized countries have revealed that workers in very different types of industries report greater perceived job insecurity as countries liberalize. The theoretical literature confirms that trade, in particular if combined with Foreign Direct Investment (FDI), has the potential to increase volatility in labour markets. Surprisingly, though, statistics on labour market reallocation do not reveal a systematic pattern of increased labour market volatility. Work on how to reconcile the conflicting evidence on workers' perceptions of insecurity on the one hand, and labour market statistics on the other, is ongoing in the research community.

2. Second, in contrast to expectations, increases in the skill premium were also observed in developing economies during periods of trade liberalization, notably in a number of Latin-American economies. A large body of empirical literature has tried to explain this phenomenon and finds that the timing of trade liberalization, the tariff schedules in place before liberalization, and technological change are some of the elements that explain why certain developing countries have experienced increases in the skill premium after trade liberalization. The relevant theoretical literature has focused on the interaction between trade, FDI and technological change in order to explain changes in wage inequality in developing countries. The increasing importance of FDI has also led to renewed interest in the functional distribution of income between capital and labour—as opposed to the ratio between wages of high-skilled and low-skilled workers—and in income inequality more generally.

3. Third, a lot of employment reshuffling was observed to take place within sectors rather than across sectors as traditional trade theory would predict. In response, a new generation of trade models was developed that describes mechanisms according to which trade liberalization encourages the expansion of the most productive suppliers in all sectors, i.e. in sectors in which countries are net exporters and in sectors in which they are net importers. As a result, these models predict that in all sectors jobs are created by those suppliers who are able to compete at the international level and destroyed by those suppliers who are unable to compete. For policy-makers this may be good news, as it is generally expected that it is easier for workers to change firms within the same sector than to find work in a different sector. Within-sector reallocation may, for instance, imply lower retraining costs for workers and shorter search periods. On the other hand, these new trade models imply that jobs are at risk in all sectors. While traditional trade models would suggest that policy-makers who wish to assist workers should focus on import-competing sectors, more recent research suggests that such

targeted intervention is not justified. Indeed, recent literature emphasizes that it will be increasingly difficult for policy-makers to predict which will be the jobs at risk and which will be the jobs in demand in the near future.

A rich empirical literature has emerged from the analysis of these different phenomena. One major difficulty that empirical studies on the impact of trade on employment face is in distinguishing the different possible causes of employment changes. Some of these causes have a global character, like technological change, others are country specific. Labour market policies, macroeconomic policies or movements along the business cycle are only a few examples of country specific factors that may affect an economy's employment level and structure. They may also affect the reaction of the labour market to changes in trade policy. Not surprisingly, therefore, one of the general conclusions that can be drawn from the literature is that the employment effects of trade have differed significantly across countries.

Rather than acting as a substitute for migration, trade liberalization appears often to have increased the economic and social pressures that lead to international migration:

Chantal Thomas, "Labour Migration as an Unintended Consequence of Globalization in Mexico, 1980–2000" in Adelle Blackett & Christian Lévesque, eds, *Social Regionalism in the Global Economy* (New York: Routledge, 2011) at 273

Increased labour migration from Mexico to the United States between 1980 and 2000 stemmed in large part from macro-economic policy reforms, implemented at the domestic and international levels, that we now associate with economic 'globalization'....

For Mexico, the adoption of NAFTA played a central role in effecting market liberalization and setting the stage for labour migration. Far from being the sole factor, however, NAFTA interacted with a host of other important reforms in Mexico's investment, fiscal and exchange rate regimes. And while conventional economic theory might have predicted that market liberalization would substitute for migration, events as they actually unfolded proved migration and liberalization to be complements rather than substitutes....

This economic dislocation displaced workers in Mexico and caused flows of surplus labour into Mexican cities, maquiladoras and ultimately the United States. This sudden increase in the labour supply had practical implications for labour practices in both Mexico and the U.S., creating additional supply, and reducing bargaining power among workers in both countries. Moreover, the relative weakness of both national and international labour protection regimes, in terms of the enforcement of labour standards and provision for labour 'adjustment,' further exacerbated the vulnerability of this excess labour supply.

These changes took place under practical and legal circumstances that bode ill for the implementation of labour standards.

The interplay between migration status and the persistence of racial divisions that enable capitalist development throughout the periods of globalization is illustrated in the following case:

Québec (Commission des droits de la personne et des droits de la jeunesse) c Centre maraîcher Eugène Guinois JR inc, 2005 CanLII 11754 (TDPQ)

[1] The events you are going to read about occurred here, in Québec, in 2000 and 2001.

The facts

[2] The Commission des droits de la personne et des droits de la jeunesse (the Commission) is exercising this recourse with the consent of complainants Ronald Champagne, Célissa Michel, Célianne Michel and Cupidon Lumène.

[3] All four are of Haitian origin and worked for the Centre Maraîcher Eugène Guinois Jr Inc. (hereinafter the "Centre Maraîcher"), among other employers, in 2000 and 2001.

[4] The Centre Maraîcher, located in Sainte-Clotilde-de-Châteauguay, is a family business specializing in the growing of lettuce and carrots. It has greatly expanded over the years and operates mainly from April to December. It hires up to 250 day labourers, the number varying according to the operations required, such as the weeding and transplanting of lettuce, and harvesting.

[5] Since there was not enough local labour due to the expansion, the Centre Maraîcher had to use the services of the U.P.A. (the Union des producteurs agricoles du Québec) the past few years.

[6] The U.P.A. is, among other things, a recruitment and placement agency for workers in the horticulture sector (especially in the western Montérégie region). Through the Agrijob Centre in Montréal, people who want to work register and are given a boarding pass in order to take chartered buses in Longueuil every day that drop them off at various farms where they work. They are also taken back to their departure point in Longueuil in the evening.

[7] At the busiest time of the season, namely, in the summer of 2000 and 2001, the Centre Maraîcher asked the U.P.A. to provide it daily with about 96 workers, who were transported in two buses of 48 passengers each. Those participating in the program were seasonal workers.

[8] For the most part, the U.P.A. workers, who were also called the [TRANSLATION] "Longueuil workers", were Haitian in origin. The Centre Maraîcher also hired foreign workers of Mexican origin, who lived in buildings separate from all the others.

[9] The workers at Centre Maraîcher were divided into three categories.

[10] Permanent employees, composed only of members of the owners' family.

[11] Then there were the regular employees and day labourers.

[12] The regular employees were paid on a weekly basis. In general, they were mechanics, sales clerks, people assigned to the bookkeeping department and carrot packers.

[13] The day labourers were those from the U.P.A. They worked in the fields and were paid on a daily basis, with no deductions at source. The great majority were Black workers of Haitian origin.

[14] As we will see further on, a few day labourers sometimes worked with the regular employees, mainly in packing carrots. These day labourers received weekly pay. Hence, they had unemployment insurance benefits in winter. The complainants, among others, were in that group of people. Their average weekly salary in 2000 and 2001 was about $350.

[15] Eugène Guinois, the father, still runs the Centre Maraîcher. His son, Daniel Guinois, is the vice-president of the company.

[16] Denise Guinois is Eugène's spouse and Daniel's mother. She is the secretary-treasurer of the business and the third shareholder. She still works in the fields.

[17] The other members of the family are the daughters, namely, Jocelyne, who handles the accounts receivable and is in charge of the business's human resources, although she has no diploma in that field; Nicole, her sister; and Sylvie.

[18] The daughters are not shareholders of the company.

[19] Described as thriving, the business has a sales figure of about $8 million a year. ...

Working conditions

[38] The claimants described the working conditions at the Centre Maraîcher as follows:

The premises: the cafeteria/the green shack

[39] Mr. Champagne explained that "the Whites" had a cafeteria reserved exclusively for their use. Located on the premises of the business itself, the cafeteria was very clean, since, according to him, Danielle Lavigne was assigned to clean it every day.

[40] The cafeteria had three microwave ovens, a refrigerator and two vending machines, one for soft drinks and one for snacks such as chocolate and chips. All the machines were in good working order and very clean.

[41] Célissa Michel added that the cafeteria was heated and it had a coffee machine.

[42] The U.P.A. workers, i.e. about 96 people, had access to a building called the [TRANSLATION] "green shack", located away from the other administration buildings and the Centre Maraîcher.

[43] All the claimants said in their testimony that it was very small and extremely dirty. Danielle Lavigne was supposed to clean it but it was never cleaned. Mr. Champagne said that sometimes the workers themselves removed the soil accumulated on the floor, picking it up with pieces of cardboard.

[44] The U.P.A. workers used the green shack to store their street clothes and change into their work clothes. There was no changing room; nor, according to Mr. Champagne's testimony, were there any hooks from which to hang their clothing.

[45] Cupidon Lumène said that, at the back of the green shack was a small room where the women could change, but it did not lock. She said the workers had to change because the work in the fields was very dirty.

[46] According to the testimony of Mr. Champagne and Cupidon Lumène, the green shack had three microwave ovens in it, but they were very dirty and only one worked. The two refrigerators were extremely dirty and did not work.

[47] The place had no running water or toilets. There was a sink, but it was unusable. To drink or wash, the workers had to use cold water hoses wound around trees outside. According to Mr. Champagne, the water in the hoses was often red and had a bad smell. There were no showers, soap or hot water for the workers.

[48] The green shack had only one table, which was clearly insufficient if it rained; then the workers had to sit on the floor or in the buses. When the weather was nice, they ate outside on picnic tables behind the shack. There was no heating and it was often very cold in October and November.

[49] Célianne Michel never took her break in the green shack. She preferred to stay outside. She said the shack was dirty and smelled bad because of the work clothes left on the floor.

[50] She never changed in the green shack because there was no privacy.

[51] Since there was no running water in the green shack, there were no toilets. The workers had to use the three chemical toilets located outside. According to Mr. Champagne, he at times saw them [TRANSLATION] "filled to the top". The other complainants added that the toilets were not cleaned every day and were very dirty. Cupidon Lumène said: [TRANSLATION] "Mondays, they were clean, but by Friday, they were disgustingly dirty".

[52] In 2000 and on his first day at work, Mr. Champagne had to eat his lunch cold since the microwave oven was too dirty to heat his food in it. Subsequently, to solve the problem, like the other complainants, he got two thermoses, one for juice and one for food.

[53] Also during the summer of 2000, Mr. Champagne was warned, without it being stipulated by whom, that he did not have the right to enter the [TRANSLATION] "cafeteria for Whites" and that, if he wanted to buy something, he could use the vending machine located outside that cafeteria. He never tried to enter the cafeteria in 2000.

[54] However, he explained that, in 2001, when he acquired the status of regular worker, he tried on two occasions to enter the "cafeteria for Whites" in order to heat his food in a microwave. [TRANSLATION] "He was thrown out". The second time, Maurice Poupart, a foreman, threatened to throw him out as well. Mr. Poupart reportedly told him: [TRANSLATION] "You have your own place". He pushed him. Mr. Champagne then went to see Louis-Marc Célestin, who was in charge of the Black workers in the fields, to complain about the situation, but Mr. Célestin responded that the cafeteria was reserved for Whites. . . .

[62] The day labourers usually did not work on Saturday or Sunday. But they did occasionally, in order to make up for a day off during the week. Mr. Champagne, as well as Célissa Michel, his daughter Célianne Michel and Cupidon Lumène thus came to work on a Saturday in 2001. Denise Guinois and Danielle Lavigne were busy moving the picnic tables. They placed them near the chemical toilets. Ms. Guinois reportedly then said: [TRANSLATION] "You Blacks are pigs, you go there". Mr. Champagne felt insulted, scorned and ill-treated. Monday morning, the tables were back in the right place.

The sign

[63] According to the testimony of the four complainants, in 2000, a sign appeared on the door of the green shack, and inside, on the refrigerator door. The sign, which was submitted as evidence, showed five smiling Black people dressed in suits and ties. The sign also bore the contact information and logo of the Centre Maraîcher. It said the following:

[TRANSLATION]

TO ALL WORKERS FROM LONGUEUIL

You have your place (cafeteria) for lunchtime. Please respect this agreement and do not go to the room for regular workers.

Thank you and keep your cafeteria clean at all times.

[64] It was signed: [TRANSLATION] "The Management". A version in Creole was also posted. In fact, the defendant admitted posting the notices and the Tribunal will recount the circumstances in which the defendant prepared them. ...

[116] Throughout his testimony, Daniel Guinois indicated that he used the services of the Union des producteurs agricoles in order to recruit day labourers for agricultural production. The season begins in mid-April and ends around November. The duties are performed mainly in the fields or in the packing room. He admitted that the work was manual and very difficult for some people. ...

[183] From the analysis of the exhibits and the testimony heard, the Tribunal is in no way reluctant to conclude that it has been shown preponderantly that all the complainants were victims of discrimination, or even harassment, in the course of their employment.

The Quebec Human Rights Tribunal awarded material, moral and punitive damages to the complainants. It is reported that the farm subsequently mechanized the work. See Adelle Blackett, "Situated Reflections on International Labour Law, Capabilities, and Decent Work: The Case of *Centre Maraîcher Eugène Guinois*" (2007) *Revue québécoise de droit international* 223.

2:240 Period IV: The Financial Crisis and its Aftermath

A key feature of the most current phase of globalization, observable within as well as across countries, is increased income inequality; as noted in Chapter 1 (Section 1:433), income inequality has spiked sharply higher in the past generation along with the rise in precarious work.

Since the global financial crisis of 2007, the conjoined problems of economic inequality and precarious work have become more central to global policy debates.

Goran Therborn, "Dynamics of Inequality" (2017) 103 *New Left Review* 67

Milanovic's latest book, *Global Inequality,* now offers a striking set of theses about the patterning and dynamics of inequality at a planetary level, with speculations on its future trends and political implications. Drawing on his analysis of international household-survey data from 1988 to 2011—the era of high globalization, the fall of the Soviet bloc, the rise of China and the financial crisis—Milanovic offers a remarkable illustration of how the world's income has been redistributed across the planet. ... There are two main winners. The largest, group A, represents those between the 50th and 60th global percentiles, the 'emerging middle class' of China, India, Thailand, Vietnam and Indonesia. Their income has increased by 70 per cent or more since the late 1980s—though as Milanovic notes, 'because they are still relatively poor compared with the Western middle classes, one should not assign to the term the same middle-class status (in terms of income and education) that we tend to associate with the middle classes in rich countries'. The other winners, group C, are the top 1 per cent, whose incomes have risen by some 65 per cent; half of these are Americans—indeed, the top 12 per cent of Americans are all in the world's top 1 per cent—and most of the rest are from Western Europe, Japan and Oceania. The big losers, group B, are at the 80th percentile of the global population, richer than the emerging Asian middle class; they are working-class and lower middle-class Americans, Europeans and Japanese.

CHAPTER 2: INTERNATIONAL AND TRANSNATIONAL LABOUR LAW

The following extract analyzing inequality in the United States turns attention to the relationship between inequality and racialization.

Peter Temin, *The Vanishing Middle Class: Prejudice and Power in a Dual Economy* (Cambridge, MA: MIT Press, 2017) at 4–7, 9–10, 12–13

> The decline in the growth of workers' compensation has been cited as a cause of the 2008 financial crisis as workers borrowed on the security of their houses to sustain their rising consumption that rising incomes had supported before 1980. And the growth of high incomes has been the stuff of recent political discussions as fundraising looms ever more important in American politics.
>
> I argue here that ... we should think of a *dual economy* in the United States.... The modern richer sector is the FTE (finance, technology and electronics) sector, containing twenty percent of the population whose incomes have risen rapidly since 1970.... Their fortunes have separated from the rest of the county; the low-wage sector contains the remaining 80 percent whose income is not growing.... The middle class is vanishing, and the American distribution of income looks like a two-humped camel. Transition from the low-wage sector is by education, which the FTE sector makes increasingly difficult by reducing funding for public schools and universities.... I analyze this disparity using this simple theory, and I examine the important role that race plays in political choices that affect public policies in this dual economy.
>
> W. Arthur Lewis, a professor at the University of Manchester in England, proposed a theory of economic development in a paper published in 1954. He noted that development did not progress only country by country, but also by parts of countries. Economic progress was not uniform, but spotty....
>
> Lewis assumed that developing countries often have what has come to be called a dual economy. He termed the two sectors, "capitalist" and "subsistence" sectors. The capitalist sector was the home of modern production using both capital and labor. Its development was limited by the amount of capital in the economy. The subsistence sector was composed of poor farmers where the population was so large relative to the amount of land or natural resources that the productivity of the last worker put to work—called the "marginal product" by economists—was close to zero. The addition of another farmer would not add to the total production. The new worker would be like a fifth wheel on your car....
>
> Lewis noted that wages in the capitalist sector were higher than in the subsistence sector because work in the port or factory was aided by capital and required more skills than farming. In addition, capitalists constantly were seeking to hire more workers to expand production. He argued that wages in the capitalist sector were linked to the farmers' earnings because capitalists needed to attract workers to their sector by offering a premium over farming wages to induce farmers and farmworkers to leave their familiar homes and activities.
>
> Lewis argued that this linkage gave capitalists an incentive to keep down the wages of subsistence workers. Business leaders in the capitalist sector want to keep their labor costs low. The wages they need to offer are the sum of the basic low wage plus the premium offered to attract low-wage workers to their sector. The business leaders cannot influence the premium, but they can work to keep wages in the subsistence sector low....

This model received a lot of attention when it was published, and Lewis was honored with a Nobel Prize in Economics for it in 1979 ...

[...]

[T]he FTE sector is largely white, with few representatives from other groups. The low-wage sector is more varied, with a mix of whites, blacks, and Latinos ("browns"). The low-wage sector is about 50 percent white, with the other half composed more or less equally of African Americans and Latino immigrants....

The rising inequality of income has led to an increase in the inequality of wealth in America. People with high incomes save more of their income than poorer people, and high earned income resulted in high capital growth. The wealth share of the top tenth of the top 1 percent has tripled since 1978 and now is near 1916 and 1929 levels. The share of the middle class fell from 35 percent of national wealth to 23 percent in 2012. The middle-class share of wealth is lower than the middle-class share of income ..., and it suffered a similar fall.

The link between the two parts of the modern dual economy is education, which provides a possible path that the children of low-wage workers can take to move into the FTE sector. This path is difficult, however, and strewn with obstacles that keep the numbers of children who make this transition small.... The result is that education, which long ago was a force for improvement of the entire labor force, has become a barrier reinforcing the dual economy.

[Temin, Peter, *The Vanishing Middle Class: Prejudice and Power in a Dual Economy*, 782 word excerpt from pages 4–7, 9–10, 12–13 © 2017 Massachusetts Institute of Technology, by permission of The MIT Press.]

The growth of inequality in Canada, trends in inequality since the financial crisis, and their relationships to gender and racialization in Canada are discussed in Chapter 1, Sections 1:432 and 1:433.

As the following excerpt describes, workers' employment prospects may be tied to developments in labour markets and production arrangements overseas, particularly in large economies such as China.

Cynthia Estlund, *A New Deal for China's Workers?* (Cambridge, MA: Harvard University Press, 2017) at 1–3

If the workers of the world are united in anything, it may be in the degree to which their working lives and their futures are being shaped by China. This is no surprise to American workers and the politicians who court them. China's deep pool of "cheap labor" has been a recurring motif in modern American politics, most recently in the 2016 presidential campaign. But China's workers are increasingly speaking up for themselves, and we should all be listening.

In the first decade or two after China opened its doors to the world and began to churn out much of the clothing, shoes, toys, and other mass consumer goods sold in Western stores, the prevailing Western image of Chinese workers—if there was one—was of an endless, faceless, voiceless mass. The millions of poor rural migrants flowing into the grim factories in China's coastal areas seemed to tolerate the intolerable—working for pennies an hour at a brutal pace for unimaginably long days and weeks. Behind them, and ready to replace those who were chewed up and spit out, were the hundreds of millions who remained in the impoverished rural villages of the interior. That seemingly bottomless supply of cheap labor gave a geographic location if not a human face to the "race to the bottom" that for many Western observers was shaping the bleak future of workers, their unions, and their families in the developed economies of the world.

One does not have to be a close China watcher to know that things have changed. To begin with, China has become an economic powerhouse—the world's second-largest national economy, home to a sizable share of global manufacturing and to a large and growing fraction of the world's middle income consumers. Since 1981, as many as six hundred million people in China have climbed out of poverty, partly through the wrenching process of migration out of destitute rural areas and into China's vast and countless factories. That process has transformed product markets, labor markets, and workers' lives both within and beyond its borders.

The rise from destitution has brought rising expectations. China's workers may still be a faceless mass to many Westerners, but they are no longer voiceless, and they are increasingly unwilling to tolerate the intolerable. That is most vividly true in the factories of the newly-industrialized coastal areas, with their mostly migrant workforces, which churn out much of the world's consumer goods. After years of widespread submission to miserable wages and working conditions, punctuated by occasional outbursts of wrath, Chinese workers are increasingly resorting to both "exit" and "voice" in response to their discontentment. They are exercising their market freedom to quit and seek better conditions elsewhere, and they are protesting, loudly and in larger numbers, against abuse and low wages.

An important spur to both "exit" and "voice" lies in the surprising appearance of labor shortages starting in the mid-2000s. The supply of new migrant workers, and especially of the skilled workers needed in the more advanced product sectors now growing up in China, began to slow as the smaller "one-child generation," born starting in 1980, entered the industrial workforce. In the meantime, enough capital had trickled into the interior to create factory jobs closer to home, so that a teenager's decision to leave home for a brutally demanding, poorly paid, and faraway factory job became more of a choice and less of a dire necessity. A tighter labor market changed the labor market calculus in the more developed coastal regions, and it emboldened many of China's workers to join together to protest against injustice, to demand a bigger share of the growing economic pie and a greater voice in their working lives. More recently, an economic slump has brought layoffs and factory closings in some areas; but those events, too, have triggered strikes, for China's migrant workers have become increasingly willing and able to mount a collective response to their grievances....

An American observer might imagine ... that China's workers had arrived at the cusp of their own "New Deal moment"—a moment when workers' political and economic power and mobilization converge to produce major industrial relations reforms and redistributive policies. Even without the ability to vote for candidates promising labor reform, labor protest and the threat of serious unrest undoubtedly put political pressure on an authoritarian regime, and China's leaders had already responded with some pro-worker reforms. Indeed, those leaders might well take note that it is not only workers who might have something to gain from a "New Deal with Chinese characteristics," for the American New Deal was both transformative and conservative. It dramatically enhanced some workers' ability to shape their own working lives and livelihoods through unionization and collective bargaining, and at the same time it helped to deflect and defuse demands for more radical political and economic change and to bolster the political legitimacy of the established order among the working classes.

In short, China is both changing the world, and is itself changing, in ways that we cannot afford to ignore. It is worth watching closely as the most populous nation in the history of the world grapples before our twenty-first-century eyes (albeit often behind closed doors) with the question of how to redefine the rights and entitlements of workers and the governance of labor relations in an increasingly advanced industrial economy. That big question may seem remote from a bigger question that has gripped many Western observers since the 1970s: is economic liberalization and growth leading, inevitably or otherwise, to political liberalization and democratization? But the two questions are linked. China's workers are demanding not only higher wages but a greater voice in their working lives. China's response to those demands will both reflect and potentially reshape the structure of governance and the prospects for broader political reform in China.

[Copyright © 2017 by Cynthia Estlund.]

Migration remains an important feature of the current period of globalization, but its character remains in flux. Largely it has entailed temporary, "managed" migration.

Fay Faraday, "Made in Canada: How the Law Constructs Migrant Workers' Insecurity" (Toronto: George Cedric Metcalf Charitable foundation, 2012) at 3, 11, 14, online: https://metcalffoundation.com/wp-content/uploads/2012/09/Made-in-Canada-Full-Report.pdf

In the past decade, Canada's labour market has undergone a significant shift to rely increasingly on migrant workers who come to Canada from around the globe on time-limited work permits to provide labour in an expanding range of industries. Since 2000, the number of temporary foreign workers employed in Canada has more than tripled. In 2006, for the first time, the number of temporary foreign workers entering Canada exceeded the number of economic immigrants who were granted permanent resident status and this trend has continued since then. The greatest proportionate growth over the past decade has been among low-skill, low-wage workers in sectors such as caregiving, agriculture, hospitality, food services, construction and tourism....

The rapid growth of the temporary labour migration programs has been employer-driven. The program has expanded over the past decade with relatively little public debate. While the work itself persists, the workers are legally constructed as "temporary." These "low-skill" migrant workers have fewer effective legal protections than Canadian workers. They are vulnerable to abuse by recruiters, consultants and employers. Because of their legally, economically and socially marginalized position, they face tremendous difficulty enforcing the rights they do have....

The dominant narrative in policy discourse depicts temporary labour migration in terms of a win-win-win scenario for participants: (i) as the receiving country, Canada benefits from enabling employers to access a flexible labour force that can respond to domestic labour shortages; (ii) countries that export labour benefit from remittances that workers send to their families and from the transfer of skills/knowledge acquired by workers in Canadian workplaces; and (iii) individual migrant workers benefit from accessing greater incomes than would be available in their home countries to support or improve their families' standard of living. In addition, this discourse is bolstered by a narrative that assumes that Canada's shortage of low-skilled labour is a temporary phenomenon and that there is no present or long-term need to recruit permanent economic immigrants to work in occupations requiring lower levels of formal training. Finally, it is supported by a narrative that migrant workers have the same workplace rights as Canadian workers.

These narratives are, however, incomplete and highly contested. Community organizations, unions, academic research, policy papers and media coverage are increasingly shining a light on the precarious conditions under which migrant workers labour. They are pointedly assessing the human cost of temporary labour migration asking who benefits, in what ways, and at what costs in these relationships. At the same time, a rights-based framework for analysis is emerging which focuses on the quality of migrant workers' experience of economic and social security, including a critical examination of the degree to which migrant workers are able to effectively access and enforce formal rights, exercise fundamental human freedoms, and experience social inclusion....

A significant challenge arises because the regulation of migrant workers lies at the intersection of employment and immigration laws. While the entry of migrant workers and their right to remain in Canada are governed by federal immigration law and policy, their employment and social rights are governed primarily by provincial laws and policy. As a result, enforcing rights involves advocating at a range of administrative tribunals and courts in both federal and provincial jurisdictions, giving rise to disputes about which level of government has responsibility or accountability for which dimensions of the relationship. A further challenge is presented by the fact that there are distinct communities of migrant workers. Each of Canada's temporary labour migration programs (low-skill migrant workers, live-in caregivers and seasonal agricultural workers) has its own distinct legal and policy regime that structures the migrant workers' experience of life and rights in Canada. Each program draws workers from different parts of the world raising logistical challenges to developing communication and collective action among and across communities of workers. [Courtesy of The George Cedric Metcalf Charitable Foundation.]

In, OECD, *International Migration Outlook 2017* (Paris: OECD Publishing, 2017), the Organisation for Economic Co-operation and Development reports that in Canada, temporary or seasonal migration has grown steadily but moderately since 2010. It reports that 30,000 workers were admitted in 2015. While there has been a recent upward trend in permanent migration, this is due to the humanitarian crisis in Syria and broader global instability. This has been reflected in a 7 percent increase in permanent migration in OECD countries, and is particularly pronounced in Germany. The OECD has been an early proponent of "managed" temporary migration schemes. It takes the following position in its 2017 report:

> There is clearly positive momentum for further reforms at national level regarding migrant integration, focussing on all migrants, not just refugees.

Integration is not only a domestic question. There is a strong case for international co-operation in this area:

- The economic, political and social costs associated with the lack of integration in one country may have negative spill-overs for others.
- In a context of increasing diversity, the development of inclusive, cohesive and harmonious societies will have a positive impact on international relations.
- Better integration outcomes are essential for the migration-development nexus — unless migrants' skills are well used in their host countries, they will not be able to contribute to the development of their origin countries.

* * * * *

Financial crises often precipitate extensive social policy reforms as part of austerity packages adopted at the behest of international lenders, as conditions for loans and other assistance to states facing rapidly deteriorating monetary and fiscal situations. The reforms initiatives have altered labour and employment laws to align them more closely with neoliberal policy thought:

Aristea Koukiadaki & Damian Grimshaw, *Evaluating the Effects of the Structural Labour Market Reforms on Collective Bargaining in Greece* **(Geneva: International Labour Organization, 2016) at 24–25, online at: www.ilo.org/wcmsp5/groups/public/---ed_protect/---protrav/---travail/documents/publication/wcms_538161.pdf**

> In terms of the processes guiding the implementation of reforms [to collective bargaining, in particular], social dialogue between the government and the social partners was almost absent. While this confirmed the strong tradition of a culture in Greece of state unilateralism in policy-decision making, it was also broadly in line with the *de facto* departure from a 'political economy' crisis response approach, where industrial relations institutions play a role, towards a 'financial market driven' approach where public policy responses are dependent on the situation in the financial market. The 2011 ILO Report of the High Mission to Greece illustrates the latter point, when it states that the issue of employment was rarely discussed during the consultation between the Greek government and the institutions representing Greece's official creditors. The lack of any influence of the social partners not only provides evidence for the unilateral character of the changes but also deprived policymakers of all the information necessary for effective policy design at a time most crucially needed, and could hinder the chances of maintaining balance in such policies by mitigating their adverse effects on the most vulnerable groups.
>
> In terms of the substance of the 'structural labour market reforms', the extent to which the relevant regulatory framework departed from the pre-crisis legal/institutional model of collective bargaining was particularly pronounced and had the potential to lead the Greek system of collective bargaining onto a different institutional trajectory, one that is possibly closer to the model of absent or single-employer bargaining of the UK and the majority of Central and Eastern European countries. In this context, the

changing pattern of legal/institutional incentives that enable or hinder the capacities of social partners to achieve consensus via collective bargaining becomes crucial. Further, the widespread absence of union organisation at company level and associated low incidence of company-level bargaining could become crucial 'data', once the institutions representing Greece's official creditors (EC, IMF and ECB and the ESM) pressed for more flexible, decentralised bargaining.
[Copyright © International Labour Organization 2016.]

* * * * *

In the current period, affirmations about the potential benefits of a range of globalizing policies and institutions (including trade) have become muddled, as mainstream trade economist Dani Rodrik affirms:

Dani Rodrik, *Straight Talk on Trade: Ideas for a Sane World Economy* (Princeton, NJ: Princeton University Press, 2017) at 211

> From a comparative advantage vantage point, trade agreements do not create jobs; they simply reallocate them across industries. From the mercantilist vantage point, they can create jobs, but only to the extent that they destroy jobs in other countries. Therefore, it is inconsistent to claim, as the US and European governments were prone to do, that these agreements would simultaneously create jobs and be mutually beneficial.

Populist politicking in many parts of the global North and the global South have become part of the mix, further complicating arguments in favour of reconciling open markets with strengthened labour and employment laws and deepened social redistributions:

Judith Butler, "Trump Is Emancipating Unbridled Hatred" *Zeit Online* (28 October 2016), online: www.zeit.de/kultur/2016-10/judith-butler-donald-trump-populism-interview

> ZEIT ONLINE: Is there greater precarity now?
>
> BUTLER: I think precarity has become a more important political concept. The scholar Isabel Lorey suggests that it is an economic and political condition that actually belongs to our present moment. The proletariat, those are workers who are not getting paid enough to eat or live well, but the precariat is a different category. The precariat may not have jobs at all. They may have a job and lose a job in quick succession. They may be transient labourers. They may have shelter and lose it the next day. The future is radically unpredictable.
>
> ZEIT ONLINE: Why is that?
>
> BUTLER: I think as labour is becoming increasingly temporary and precarious so that markets can expand without impediment, public obligations towards working people and a liveable wage become increasingly threatened. So we do see more and more people who are abandoned and dispossessed, in a certain way. Post World War I, post World War II we saw tremendous numbers of people dispossessed, but dispossession

was of a different kind. Dispossession today is also happening through war, but also through fiscal policies, Neoliberalism, and its effect on working conditions and housing, on housing market and housing possibilities, but also on food. I don't think we have to go very far, to see that many populations are suffering with very basic questions....

The problem is, neoliberal economics produces precarity throughout the population without discriminating between right and left. So there are some right-wing people, or people who have become more right-wing, because they are blaming the migrants for taking their position, but they are not identifying the root of their problem, which is an expanding precarity that cuts across economic class, though the very rich continue to profit. They have decided to blame the migrant rather than to look more carefully at some fiscal and financial policies that are actually jeopardizing the well-being of increasing numbers of people.

2:300 LABOUR LAW FROM REACTION TO RESPONSE

As discussed in Section 2:210 above, international labour law was created in response to the first wave of globalization and the conditions of crisis following World War I. Its sources lie in the institutions whose authority is delegated by ILO member states, and its legal force derives from the consent of those states. The primary sources of international labour law are outlined in Chapter 1, Section 1:250.

In the current wave of globalization additional, transnational labour regulation has emerged. This cuts across the traditional divisions between public and private international law, and between domestic and international law. It includes private sector codes of conduct and multi-stakeholder initiatives that often build upon the normative foundations of international law, seeking to extend their reach. This section first considers the development of international labour law in response to globalization, and next the roles, actual and potential, of transnational labour law in the current global economic and legal system.

2:310 Attempts to Renew International Labour Law

By the early 1990s, the second wave of globalization had generated strong public resistance and calls for a strengthening of international labour law, first and foremost by linking it to international trade law, embedding labour standards in an international regulatory system widely perceived to be enforceable, and thus to have "teeth."

2:311 Labour Standards and the Multilateral Trading System

OECD, *Trade, Employment and Labour Standards* (Paris: OECD, 1996) at 169–70

> Labour standards and WTO disciplines
>
> Introduction
> The debate about linkages between trade disciplines and labour standards is not new. Indeed, Article 7 of the *Havana Charter for an International Trade Organization*, UN

Conference on Trade and Employment, 1948, E/CONF.2/78, which was meant to establish an International Trade Organization (ITO), referred to the importance of satisfactory social conditions for the smooth operation of the trading system and invited Members to work for the establishment of such conditions within their territory. However, this article was among the provisions of the Charter that never entered into force.

Suggestions have been made recently to establish closer links between trade and core labour standards, in particular as regards the operation of the GATT/WTO system of multilateral rules and disciplines for international trade. For instance, in 1983, the European Parliament called for the negotiation of a GATT provision on labour standards engaging all GATT Members to respect ILO Conventions on freedom of association, collective bargaining, forced labour and non-discrimination. In 1986 and in 1994, the United States suggested, without success, to add worker's rights to the Uruguay Round and to the WTO agenda. In 1994, the European Parliament further suggested that GATT Article XX(e) on prison labour be amended to include forced and child labour, as well as violations of the principle of freedom of association and collective bargaining. Some have suggested making use of the WTO Trade Policy Review Mechanism (TPRM). There have been other proposals (e.g. by TUAC [the Trade Union Advisory Committee to the OECD]) for the introduction of a "social clause" into the WTO, with the aim in particular of strengthening the enforcement of "basic" labour standards.

Discussions have also taken place within the ILO. The objective was to ensure that the gradual liberalisation of markets be accompanied by improvements in conditions of work, or at least by the elimination of the most flagrant abuses and forms of exploitation. The ILO Secretariat discussed the applicability of using anti-dumping and countervailing duties provisions, general exceptions provisions, or nullification and impairment provisions for that purpose.

Subsequent debate on these ideas within the ILO Working Party on the Social Dimension of the Liberalisation of World Trade underlined their controversial nature. Many participants, in particular among the employers and the developing countries, were opposed to the implementation of a "social clause" in the WTO. In fact, the consensus that emerged at an important session of the ILO Working Party was that it "should not pursue the question of trade sanctions and that any discussion of the link between international trade and social standards, through a sanction-based social clause, should be suspended" .... Instead, the Working Party will look at ways to promote core labour standards through encouragement, support and assistance and at the means to strengthen ILO's effectiveness in achieving this task.

[© OECD, 1996, *Trade, Employment and Labour Standards: A Study of Core Workers' Rights and International Trade*. Reproduced with permission of the OECD.]

WTO, *Singapore Ministerial Declaration*, WTO Doc WT/MIN(96)/DEC, online: www.wto.org/english/thewto_e/minist_e/min96_e/singapore_declaration96_e.pdf

Trade and Economic Growth

2. For nearly 50 years Members have sought to fulfill, first in the GATT and now in the WTO, the objectives reflected in the preamble to the WTO Agreement of conducting

our trade relations with a view to raising standards of living worldwide. The rise in global trade facilitated by trade liberalization within the rules-based system has created more and better-paid jobs in many countries. The achievements of the WTO during its first two years bear witness to our desire to work together to make the most of the possibilities that the multilateral system provides to promote sustainable growth and development while contributing to a more stable and secure climate in international relations.

Integration of Economies; Opportunities and Challenges

3. We believe that the scope and pace of change in the international economy, including the growth in trade in services and direct investment, and the increasing integration of economies offer unprecedented opportunities for improved growth, job creation, and development. These developments require adjustment by economies and societies. They also pose challenges to the trading system. We commit ourselves to address these challenges.

Core Labour Standards

4. We renew our commitment to the observance of internationally recognized core labour standards. The International Labour Organization (ILO) is the competent body to set and deal with these standards, and we affirm our support for its work in promoting them. We believe that economic growth and development fostered by increased trade and further trade liberalization contribute to the promotion of these standards. We reject the use of labour standards for protectionist purposes, and agree that the comparative advantage of countries, particularly low-wage developing countries, must in no way be put into question. In this regard, we note that the WTO and ILO Secretariats will continue their existing collaboration.

Marginalization

5. We commit ourselves to address the problem of marginalization for least-developed countries, and the risk of it for certain developing countries. We will also continue to work for greater coherence in international economic policy-making and for improved coordination between the WTO and other agencies in providing technical assistance.

2:312   The ILO Declaration on Fundamental Principles and Rights at Work

The refusal of trade ministers to address labour standards within the WTO system and their recognition of the ILO as the competent body to deal with labour standards in the global economy required a response from the ILO. That response, the ILO's *Declaration on Fundamental Principles and Rights at Work*, 18 June 1998, 37 ILM 1233 (1998), CIT/1998/PR20A, achieved a global consensus, the contents and limitations of which remain controversial.

Hilary Kellerson, "The ILO Declaration of 1998 on Fundamental Principles and Rights: A Challenge for the Future" (1998) 137:2 *International Labour Review* 223 at 223–26

> After several years of discussion and intense negotiations, on 18 June 1998 the International Labour Conference adopted a Declaration on fundamental principles and rights at work and its follow-up to promote the implementation of these principles and rights.

The principles thus given expression are those concerning the fundamental rights of (a) freedom of association and the effective recognition of the right to collective bargaining; (b) the elimination of all forms of forced or compulsory labour; (c) the effective abolition of child labour; and (d) the elimination of discrimination in respect of employment and occupation (Article 2).

This Declaration is the culmination of a process which, within the ILO, has its origins in proposals for establishing a procedure similar to that of the Committee on Freedom of Association for the other rights recognized as fundamental. The freedom of association procedure, like the Declaration, is based on the principles laid down in the ILO Constitution but, unlike the Declaration's follow-up, is a complaints-based procedure and thus will continue to operate in parallel with the Declaration....

THE CONTENT OF THE DECLARATION

The first element in the Declaration is the reaffirmation of the obligation of Members of the Organization to respect the principles concerning fundamental rights.... [T]he Declaration does not seek to impose any new obligations on member States. It is based on the fact that, in voluntarily joining the ILO, each Member has endorsed the principles and rights set out in its Constitution and in the Declaration of Philadelphia which expressly, or implicitly in the case of the abolition of forced labour, recognize the rights enshrined in the 1998 Declaration (Article 1). Thus, while these principles and rights have been expressed and developed in the fundamental ILO Conventions, member States, even if they have not ratified these Conventions, have an obligation, as Members, to respect, to promote and to realise the principles concerning these fundamental rights (Article 2). Their recognition moreover confirms the status of the Conventions embodying them as core labour standards.

The reason why these principles and rights are regarded as fundamental is spelled out in the Preamble, which affirms that "in seeking to maintain the link between social progress and economic growth, the guarantee of fundamental principles and rights at work is of particular significance in that it enables the persons concerned to claim freely and on the basis of equality of opportunity their fair share of the wealth which they have helped to generate, and to achieve fully their human potential." They are thus an essential cornerstone in a world of growing economic interdependence, in which economic growth is essential but not sufficient to ensure equity, social progress and the eradication of poverty....

It was repeatedly emphasized during the discussions that the Declaration should not be seen as creating a link between labour standards and international trade or as providing a pretext for protectionist measures. On this issue the Declaration, echoing the Singapore Ministerial Declaration of the WTO, "stresses that labour standards should not be used for protectionist trade purposes, and that nothing in this Declaration and its follow-up shall be invoked or otherwise used for such purposes; in addition, the comparative advantage of any country should in no way be called into question by this Declaration or its follow-up" (Article 5).

The second major element of the Declaration is its promotional character. This finds expression in the recognition of the obligation of the ILO to assist its Members to attain the objectives of the Declaration, by offering technical cooperation and advisory services to promote ratification and implementation of the fundamental Conventions, by assisting Members' efforts to realize the principles concerning the fundamental rights which are the subject of the fundamental Conventions, and by helping Members create a climate for economic and social development. It obliges the ILO to make full use of its constitutional, operational and budgetary resources for this purpose and encourages other organizations to support these efforts (Article 3). The broad context of this promotional effort is expressed in the Preamble "confirming the need for the ILO to promote strong social policies, justice and democratic institutions."

The Declaration thus envisages a new emphasis in the use of ILO resources—constitutional, operational and budgetary as well as external—on promoting respect for the principles and rights reaffirmed in the Declaration.

THE FOLLOW-UP

There was agreement from the outset that the Declaration should be accompanied by a meaningful and effective follow-up, which would be strictly promotional in nature and not involve any punitive aspect, duplication of existing procedures or new obligations. Its aim is to encourage member States to promote the fundamental principles and rights reaffirmed in the Declaration, and for this purpose to allow the identification of areas in which the ILO's technical cooperation may be useful in supporting the efforts of member States....

The first element is an annual follow-up in which States will be asked to provide reports every year on each of the fundamental Conventions which they have not ratified. The purpose of these reports is to provide an opportunity to review, every year, the efforts made in the four areas of fundamental rights and principles specified in the Declaration by States which have not ratified the relevant Conventions....

The second element is a global report which will cover, each year, one of the four categories of fundamental principles and rights in turn, and review developments during the preceding four-year period. Its purpose will be, firstly, to provide a general overview of the situation in all member States (since ratification does not necessarily imply full implementation, and non-ratifying States do not necessarily fail to respect the fundamental principles) and establish the major trends and developments. Secondly, it will serve to assess the effectiveness of assistance provided by the ILO for the furtherance of the implementation of this Declaration in the period covered and determine priorities for technical cooperation in the following period....
[Reprinted by permission.]

Brian Langille, "The ILO and the New Economy: Recent Developments" (1999) 15 *International Journal of Comparative Labour Law and Industrial Relations* at 230–56

The adoption of this Declaration was regarded by many within and outside the ILO as an absolute priority—it was necessary for the ILO to do something in order to reassert itself and its mandate in what may be referred to as the 'new global economy.' ... In fact, the ILO regarded itself as having to respond to a de facto invitation issued by other international institutions, especially the WTO at its December 1996 Ministerial Meeting in Singapore, to reassert its institutional priority in connection with its traditional set of concerns....

For the sceptics, the Declaration does not mark a new beginning, but a kind of collective evasion, or worse—a consensus in favour of (continued) irrelevance and marginalization for the ILO. From this perspective the ILO has been historically powerless. It has no real world 'bite,' no sanctions or real incentives with which to affect behaviour in the world. It is a debating society which has been pushed to the sidelines by the overpowering nature of private global market forces and by the other public international institutions constructing the rules for the international marketplace—the WTO, the IMF, the World Bank, the OECD, etc. On the sceptical view, these are the only institutions with real clout, i.e. real incentives (access to WTO membership, IMF packages, World Bank loans) and sanctions, capable of guiding behaviour in the real world, even if only at the margins....

Nevertheless, a realistic appraisal of recent events must treat this package of views as too simplistic as well....

The options facing the ILO after Singapore were not altogether attractive. An obvious option was to accept the official WTO text at face value and carry on, as before, but also deeply aware of the risk of compromise this involved—that of continuity, but of continued marginalization and the relegation to a role of keeping labour issues on a very distant back burner.

The option actually taken, and appropriately so in my view, was to attempt to use the official text, and the overwhelming reaffirmation of faith in the ILO, as a vehicle to animate change within the ILO....

However, the concrete manifestation of this strategy—to make the most out of a difficult situation—was revealed by the Director General's 1997 report to the June Conference entitled *The ILO, Standard Setting and Globalization*. Of the proposals for institutional renewal suggested by the Director-General in his 1997 Report two are of interest here: (1) the idea of a 'Declaration' on fundamental rights; and (2) the idea of 'social labelling.' While these ideas share much in common, only the declaration proposal made it out of the starting blocks. The social labelling idea was 'shot down' immediately....

No one believed that there had been a mass conversion at Singapore. On the other hand, the risk in the strategy pursued by the ILO was that in taking up the public words of Singapore as an invitation and as a spur to renewal, it might simply fail. This would result in the worst of all possible worlds—a very public demonstration of inability, internally, to deliver on announced reform agendas, and therefore of irrelevancy....

The idea of a Declaration is both evocative and evasive in the ILO context. The ILO Constitution does not mention 'Declarations'—nor for that matter, does the constitution of any other international organization. Yet Declarations are a familiar part of the institutional vocabulary or grammar of many international organizations—the Universal Declaration of Human Rights being the most obvious example....

On the other hand, the ILO is clearly empowered to act, and has acted in a more direct manner, through the creation and adoption of Conventions which are, when ratified, binding international treaties with attached monitoring and complaint processes (although no 'hard' sanctions at the end of the day). The ILO is also expressly empowered to adopt non-binding recommendations aimed at guiding policies within member states. What then is the point of a 'Declaration' of general principle concerning core labour rights? Is there not a risk of detracting from the seven concrete Conventions dealing with the four core rights? This was an obvious concern to worker representatives at the ILO—that a Declaration of principle would be a vehicle for diluting concrete and detailed obligations contained in the relevant Conventions. On the other hand, from the perspective of governments and employers, Conventions concerning the core rights often remained unratified because of concrete problems in reconciling the details of domestic legislation with the specific demands of the conventions....

As we have seen, part of its normative, as well as its rhetorical power, is that the core rights agenda transcends the traditional divide between the language of human rights and the language of economics.

Yet it seems clear that, in spite of their universal character and cross-disciplinary appeal, the core rights agenda is at once controversial and contested when any effort is made to establish a link between those core standards and access to the global marketplace—whether in terms of trade in goods or in terms of investment, and whether couched in market friendly terms such as labelling. Any effort to move the ILO, and its international labour code, beyond its current 'sanctionless' modes of monitoring and review is, it seems, politically impossible even if such proposals are limited to providing market incentives to respect core standards. In fact, it seems that efforts to gain universal acceptance of the core rights, even in a sanctionless environment, has led to a Declaration in which members of the ILO could only agree on language which fails to take the core rights as seriously as they should be taken....

[O]ne of the basic features of the debates and discussions about the ILO and international labour standards is the seemingly unrelenting focus upon one aspect of the ILO—the standard setting and monitoring process. The focus is upon the legislative and enforcement process, that is, the 'legal machinery' of the ILO. This focus is centred upon Geneva and upon the Conventions. Perhaps this is an entirely natural focus of attention at this stage of our debates about globalization and its discontents. However, the fact is that the legislative and monitoring functions of the ILO—that is, the official legal function—is only one face of the organization and, in spite of its high profile, this legal aspect of the ILO in fact represents substantially less than 50 percent of ILO functions, as calculated in budgetary terms.

The ILO is much more than a Convention producing and monitoring machine. The ILO has in fact three dimensions, only one of which is the legal function. The other two may be described as being the world's centre of excellence for research and understanding of labour related issues, and second, a programme delivery organization actually delivering results through global, regional, and member state based programme initiatives, such as the *International Program on the Elimination of Child Labour* (IPEC).

A grasp of these fundamental points provokes the following thought. We have noticed that ILO member states were deeply resistant to, and suspicious of, any obligations or restrictions which the new Declaration would impose upon them, so much so that they included the extraordinary paragraph 5 ... in the text of the Declaration. However, a reading of the Declaration reveals that it is not only a Declaration about the obligations of member states, it is also a Declaration concerning the obligations of the organization itself....

Viewed against the backdrop of the sprawling ILO mandate and range of activities, the Declaration's legacy may indeed lie in its potential as a disciplining and focussing device for the activities of the organization itself. In so doing, the focus would not be upon imposing obligations upon the members, or upon the market-based incentives inherent in the labelling idea, but upon the use of direct aid and assistance in the form of institutional expertise, resources, 'technical cooperation' etc. to 'promote' the core values. Having rejected any notion of a 'social clause,' or trade sanctions, or other disciplining devices, no matter how market friendly, the essence of the Declaration's achievement is to focus the organization in its programme delivery, at least within one of its fundamental substantive provisions—promoting basic rights.

[Copyright © 1999. Reprinted with permission from Kluwer Law International.]

The 1998 Declaration has served to orient the ILO's technical assistance activity, and has grounded a successful campaign to increase the number of ratifications of the core ILO Conventions. As of May 2018, between 154 and 181 of the 183 ILO member states had ratified each of those Conventions.

Critics continue, however, to argue that the ILO is not effectively addressing the problems that face international labour law in the new era of globalization. Some maintain that, unlike the WTO, the ILO cannot use economic sanctions. In response, the ILO points to article 33 of the *International Labour Organization Constitution*, April 1919, 15 UNTS 40, which empowers its governing body to "recommend to the [International Labour] Conference such actions as it may deem wise and expedient to secure compliance...." This is understood by many to include economic sanctions.

The ILO has used article 33 only once, in 2000, in response to the gross and well-documented violations of the ILO's *Convention (No 105) concerning the abolition of forced labour*, 28 June 1930, 320 UNTS 291 (entered into force 17 January 1959), by the state of Myanmar (formerly Burma). However, this move did not lead to any new pressure against the military regime in that country, as the United States and the European Union had already applied economic sanctions, and Myanmar's Asian trading partners, including China and Japan, have generally opposed economic sanctions. See James Atleson et al, *International Labour Law, Cases and Materials on Worker Rights in the Global Economy* (St Paul, MN: Thomson West, 2008) at 92–93.

Other critics argue, in contrast, that the ILO should focus not on enforcement but on helping states accept and act on the idea that raising labour standards will support their economic development and is therefore in their own long-term interest. See Brian Langille, "What Is International Labour Law For?" (2009) 3:1 *Law & Ethics of Human Rights* 48.

2:313 Regional and Bilateral Trade and Labour Agreements

The failure of efforts to link labour standards to the multilateral trading system led states such as Canada and the United States to seek labour clauses and agreements in tandem with regional and bilateral trade agreements. The following passages and excerpts chart the development of trade-related labour standards.

Canada has negotiated a series of trade agreements which are accompanied by international labour obligations. The first was the *North American Agreement on Labor Cooperation Between the Government of Canada, the Government of the United Mexican States and the Government of the United States of America*, Can TS 1994 No 4 (entered into force January 1994)

(NAALC), with the United States and Mexico, which came into force in 1994 alongside the *North American Free Trade Agreement Between the Government of Canada, the Government of Mexico and the Government of the United States*, 17 December 1992, CAN TS 1994 No 2 (entered into force 1 January 1994) (NAFTA). Currently, five provinces (Alberta, Manitoba, Nova Scotia, Prince Edward Island, and Quebec) are signatories to the NAALC, through the *Canadian Intergovernmental Agreement Regarding the Implementation of International Labour Cooperation Agreements*. The full text of NAALC can be found at www.naalc.org/english/agreement.shtml.

Since then, Canada has continued to negotiate generations of labour side agreements or labour chapters, in tandem with its free trade agreements. Canada now has labour side agreements with Chile, Costa Rica, Peru, Colombia, Jordan, Panama, and Honduras. It has labour chapters with Korea and Ukraine, and most recently with the *Canada European Comprehensive Economic and Trade Agreement (CETA) between Canada and the European Union and its Member States*, 30 October 2016, OJ, L 11 (not yet entered into force), (CETA) and the *Comprehensive and Progressive Agreement for Trans-Pacific Partnership (CPTPP)*, 8 March 2018 (not yet entered into force), (CPTPP). The full text of the agreements, alongside the various submissions can be found at www.canada.ca/en/employment-social-development/services/labour-relations/international/agreements.html.

While NAALC has remained one of the most important of Canada's regional and bilateral agreements, in terms of the economic significance of the trading relationships to which it applies, the CPTPP stand to eclipse it. The chapter on labour in the CPTPP includes many of the features that social movements have asked for to improve on the first-generation NAALC model. It will likely be the text upon which NAFTA renegotiations will focus. And yet, there remains the concern that there has been a significant mismatch between the labour chapter and the concerns over the relationship between trade and labour.

North American Agreement on Labor Co-operation Between the Government of the United States of America, the Government of Canada and the Government of the United Mexican States, 13 September 1993

PART TWO: OBLIGATIONS

Article 2: Levels of Protection

Affirming full respect for each Party's constitution, and recognizing the right of each Party to establish its own domestic labor standards, and to adopt or modify accordingly its labor laws and regulations, each Party shall ensure that its labor laws and regulations provide for high labor standards, consistent with high quality and productivity workplaces, and shall continue to strive to improve those standards in that light.

Article 3: Government Enforcement Action

1. Each Party shall promote compliance with and effectively enforce its labor law through appropriate government action.

2. Each Party shall ensure that its competent authorities give due consideration in accordance with its law to any request by an employer, employee or their representatives, or other interested person, for an investigation of an alleged violation of the Party's labor law.

159

Article 4: Private Action

1. Each Party shall ensure that persons with a legally recognized interest under its law in a particular matter have appropriate access to administrative, quasi-judicial, judicial or labor tribunals for the enforcement of the Party's labor law.

    2. Each Party's law shall ensure that such persons may have recourse to, as appropriate, procedures by which rights arising under:

a. its labor law, including in respect of occupational safety and health, employment standards, industrial relations and migrant workers, and
b. collective agreements, can be enforced.

Article 5: Procedural Guarantees

1. Each Party shall ensure that its administrative, quasi-judicial, judicial and labor tribunal proceedings for the enforcement of its labor law are fair, equitable and transparent... [Published by the Secretariat of the Commission for Labour Co-operation. Reprinted by permission.]

Parts 4 and 5 of NAALC (articles 20 to 41) set out an elaborate process for handling complaints. That process is outlined in the following excerpt.

OECD, *Trade, Employment and Labour Standards* (Paris: OECD, 1996) at 178–79

The North American Agreement on Labour Cooperation

The North American Agreement on Labour Cooperation (NAALC)—more commonly known as the labour supplemental agreement to the NAFTA—links each of the North American countries' labour laws to the regional trade agreement. Both agreements entered into force on January 1st, 1994. The NAALC promotes mutually recognised labour principles including core labour standards and other standards such as the occupational health and safety of workers and the protection of migrant workers....

    The main objective of the NAALC is to improve working conditions and living standards in the United States, Mexico and Canada. The emphasis of the agreement is to encourage transparent and effective enforcement of the existing labour laws in each country through cooperation and the exchange of information. The agreement also provides for consultations between the National Administrative Offices (NAO) or at the Ministerial level, as well as comparative assessments among the three countries. Should these steps fail to solve a matter in dispute, a dispute resolution process can be invoked. This process may ultimately result in fines (monetary enforcement assessments) backed by trade sanctions in the event Mexico or the United States does not observe and enforce its own labour laws, but it must be noted that trade sanctions are not available against Canada [NAALC, Part 4 and Part 5]. Complaints or petitions can be submitted by any person with a legally recognized interest under the law of any party to the NAALC. However, the dispute settlement procedure can be quite lengthy: over two years may elapse before measures such as the imposition of action plans, or fines or trade sanctions can be enforced. In addition, trade sanctions are only possible in the areas of child labour, minimum wages and occupational safety and

health, but not in cases relating to freedom of association, right to bargain collectively, and forced labour.... Furthermore, it must be noted that the NAALC does not refer to internationally-agreed minimum labour standards as the European GSP system ... , but to standards defined under the national legislation of the parties. In particular, complaints must be both trade-related and covered by mutually recognized labour laws, and there must have been a persistent pattern of non-enforcement of the relevant labour legislation....
[© OECD, 1996, *Trade, Employment and Labour Standards: A Study of Core Workers' Rights and International Trade*. Reproduced with permission of the OECD.]

* * * * *

In some instances, obligations constituted under trade agreements may provide recourse for violations of workers' rights and labour standards where domestic remedies are unavailable. The NAALC, for example, permits the submission of complaints about violations of labour standards to the NAALC National Administrative Office (NAO) of a country other than where the violation occurred:

Stage	Labour Principle	NAALC in Practice
Stage 1— Article 21: Consultations between NAOs, Article 22: Ministerial Consultations	Freedom of association & protection of the right to organize (1), The right to bargain collectively (2), The right to strike (3)	39 submissions have been filed with NAO (only 7 in the past 12 years) Mexican NAO—10 submissions, 10 reports, 5 Ministerial Agreements US NAO—23 submissions, 11 reports, 8 Ministerial Agreements Canadian NAO—6 submissions, 2 reports, 2 ministerial consultations with one Ministerial Agreement signed
Stage 2— Stage 1 plus Article 23: Evaluation Committee of Experts	Prohibition of forced labor (4), Elimination of employment discrimination (7), Equal pay for women and men (8), Compensation in cases of occupational injuries and illnesses (10), Protection of migrant workers (11)	Never reached
Stage 3— Stages 1 & 2 plus Article 27: Consultations, Article 29: Request for an Arbitral Panel	Labor protections for children and young persons (5), Minimum employment standards (6), Prevention of occupational injuries and illnesses (9)	Never reached

As the table above demonstrates, the full NAALC dispute settlement process has yet to be reached in any of the thirty-nine complaints brought to date with respect to the alleged failures by any of the three signatory countries to enforce the provisions of its own labour legislation. This fact, among others, has led some observers to conclude that NAALC is largely ineffectual, generally having had little impact on difficult labour issues that it has been called upon to address. See Robert Finbow, *The Limits of Regionalism — NAFTA's Labour Accord* (Burlington, VT: Ashgate, 2006); Jonathan Graubart, *Legalizing Transnational Activism—The Struggle to Gain Social Change From NAFTA's Citizen Petitions* (University Park, PA: Penn State University Press, 2008); and Kevin Banks, "Trade, Labor and International Governance: An Inquiry into the Potential Effectiveness of the New International Labor Law" (2011) 32 *Berkeley Journal of Employment & Labor Law* 45 at 88–91. Critics have focused on the following features of NAALC as evidence of its weakness: a lack of detailed substantive obligations that could fill gaps in national laws; inconsistent interpretation and application of the obligations that it does set out; the unclear meaning of "effective enforcement"; the explicit unenforceability of standards other than those on minimum wages, child labour, and occupational health and safety; inherent delays and excessive political discretion in enforcement processes; and the lack of political will to use those processes. See Marley Weiss, "Two Steps Forward and One Step Back—Or Vice Versa: Labor Rights in Free Trade Agreements from NAFTA, through Jordan, via Chile, to Latin America and Beyond" (2003) 37:3 *University of San Francisco Law Review* 689.

The following early experimentation with NAALC to deal with labour law issues in Canada both reinforces and nuances those critiques. The NAALC procedure was called upon to surprising effect in Quebec. The International Brotherhood of Teamsters, Teamsters Canada, the Quebec Federation of Labour, Teamsters Local 973 (Montreal), and the International Labor Rights Fund filed a submission with US NAO on 19 October 1998:

International Brotherhood of Teamsters et al, "Violations of NAALC Labor Principles and Obligations in the Case of the St-Hubert McDonald's Restaurant," Submission under the North American Agreement on Labor Cooperation (NAALC) (1998) US NAO 9803, online: www.dol.gov/ilab/submissions/pdf/US_98-03_McDonalds_submission.pdf

> This submission raises questions regarding the absence of recourses under Quebec law for anti-union motivated plant closures, as well as unwarranted delays in the certification process. It also raises the issue of access to certification by sector in order to address problems in the certification process related to multiple employers or multiple facilities systems of corporate structures....
>
> In February 1998, a franchisee of the multinational enterprise McDonald's Corp. violated workers' rights to organize and bargin collectively when it closed its St-Hubert, Quebec, restaurant during union certification proceedings. The closure took place when certification appeared imminent, in circumstances similar to Case No. 9501 NAOMEX (the Sprint case)....
>
> A. Anti-Union Motivated Plant Closing
>
> With the possibility of using legal tactics nearing an end, the employer, with McDonald's assent, used the ultimate anti-union weapon: closing the workplace entirely. This left the union, and the individual workers, without any recourse.

Indeed, Quebec is the only Canadian jurisdiction having ratified the NAALC which maintains a legal doctrine permitting an employer to close a facility for anti-union motivation with impunity.

In Quebec, plant closure in the context of labour organizing never gave rise to an unfair labour practice as in other provinces of Canada or in the U.S. What has been the subject of litigation, is whether a lay-off resulting from an anti-union plant closing could give rise to a complaint for unjust dismissal based on union activities....

Every case involving a plant closure in Quebec has been tried under these sections.... The leading case on the subject is City Buick Pontiac (Montreal) Inc. in which the Quebec Labour Court held that as long as the closure was permanent and complete, the employer could go out of business with impunity, despite the presence of anti-union motives, as nothing in the law could be constructed as precluding it. The Court held that closing or discontinuing operations constituted just cause for termination, and that the Court could not question the motives behind the decision of the employer as long as this decision to close was real....

In the St-Hubert McDonald's case, the closure of one restaurant in a group of six should be seen as a partial closure motivated, in part, by an aim to discourage unionization in other facilities of the employer—to "send them a message" about the consequences of organizing. Under U.S. law, this is an unfair labor practice which can be remedied by an order to reopen the closed facility, or to offer reinstatement to employees at another company facility.

This remedy was not available to employees of the McDonald's St-Hubert facility.

The closing in the St-Hubert McDonald's case is a good example to illustrate how inappropriate Quebec law can be with respect to plant closings.

It is common knowledge that the fear of losing employment, especially now at McDonald's, is probably the most important reason why workers do not want to get involved with a union. This is why threats to close or threats of layoff during union organizing drives have generally been held to be an unfair labor practice.

In other words, an employer cannot make an idle threat to close a plant, but he can close down for anti-union reasons. Therefore, union organizers in Quebec can tell workers that the employer who just threatened to close the plant did not have the right to do so. However, no one can tell workers that the employer does not have the right to close. How effective is the legislation in this context?

The existence of the *City Buick Pontiac* doctrine and the failure of authorities to respond to it amounts to a violation of a number of obligations under the NAALC:

Generally, it is a failure to maintain high labor standards as contemplated by Article 2 of the NAALC ...

Also, it is a failure for Quebec to enforce its labor law. Indeed, the right of association is fully recognized by the Quebec Labour Code, but is it enforced when an employer closes a plant for anti-union motives with impunity? ...

Furthermore, in situations such as the St-Hubert McDonald's case, individual workers who have lost employment because of the exercise of a right recognized under the Quebec Labour Code have no recourse available to them by reason of the *City Buick Pontiac* doctrine. This constitutes a violation of Article 4(2) of the NAALC ...

The failure of authorities to respond to the problems raised by the *City Buick Pontiac* doctrine encourages anti-union gestures by employers. Worker's rights to associate and bargain collectively may be violated with impunity, with the assent of governmental authorities.

The US NAO accepted the submission on 18 December 1998. However, the NAO ended its review on 21 April 1999 after consultations with the Canadian NAO and the government of Quebec in which the labour organizations reached an agreement with the government of Quebec to have the issues of sudden and anti-union motivated plant closings raised in the submission studied by a provincial council. While legislative reform addressed many of the concerns about lengthy proceedings, the *City Buick Pontiac* doctrine went on to have a significant influence on decisions of the Supreme Court of Canada, in *IATSE, Stage Local 56 v Société de la Place des Arts de Montréal*, 2004 SCC 2, *Plourde v Wal-Mart Canada Corp*, 2009 SCC 54 and *United Food and Commercial Workers, Local 503 v Wal-Mart Canada Corp*, 2014 SCC 45.

The NAALC and subsequent agreements have created opportunities for the development of transnational advocacy networks:

Lance Compa, "NAFTA's Labor Side Agreement and International Labor Solidarity" (2001) 33:3 *Antipode* 451 at 459–60 and 465

A TRANSNATIONAL ADVOCACY PERSPECTIVE

[…]

Before the NAALC was created, cross-border trade union relationships mostly consisted of thin contacts at two levels. One was between high-level union leaders who attended conferences and conventions and agreed on resolutions of support without much follow-up. The other consisted of sporadic local-union-to-local-union contacts and occasional worker-to-worker delegations that usually were aimed at helping the poor Mexicans. These links paled in comparison with the business-to-business contacts and boss-to-boss delegations that occur every day in North American commerce.

The new NAALC platforms allow transnational social actors to demand investigations, public hearings and government consultations on workers' rights violations. Advocates now have the opportunity to strategize and plan together in a sustained fashion, gathering evidence for drafting a complaint, crafting its elements, setting priorities, defining demands, launching media campaigns, meeting with government officials to set the agenda for a hearing and to press them for thorough reviews and follow-up, preparing to testify in public hearings, engaging technical experts to buttress a case with scientific elements (a health and safety case, for example), influencing the composition of independent experts' panels and the terms of reference of their investigation, and other concrete tasks that go far beyond adopting resolutions or arranging serial worker-to-worker meetings....

The … instruments and institutions of international labor rights advocacy reflected in the NAALC are flawed. Nonetheless, they create spaces, terrains, platforms and other metaphorical foundations where advocates can unite across frontiers and plant their feet to promote new norms, mobilize actors, call to account governments and corporations,

disseminate research findings, launch media campaigns, educate each other and the public, challenge traditional notions of sovereignty, give legitimacy to their cause by invoking human rights and labour rights principles—in sum, to redefine debates and discourse by breaking up old frameworks and shaping new ones.
[Reprinted by permission of Blackwell Publishing.]

* * * * *

The more recent agreements illustrate the kind of evolution that has occurred in the drafting of side agreements or labour chapters, both in the crafting of obligations and the refinement of the approach to enforcement. Timelines for dispute resolution have been shortened, mechanisms have been streamlined, and monetary assessments have been added as potential sanctions. The 2008 *Canada-Colombia Free Trade Agreement* contains a labour chapter within the text of the agreement, but indicates that the parties' mutual obligations are in a separate Labour Cooperation Agreement, known as the LCA:

Article 1604: Obligations
In order to further the foregoing objectives, the Parties' mutual obligations are set out in the *Labour Cooperation Agreement between Canada and the Republic of Colombia* (LCA) that addresses, *inter alia*:

(a) general commitments concerning the internationally recognized labour principles and rights that are to be embodied in each Party's labour laws;
(b) a commitment not to derogate from domestic labour laws in order to encourage trade or investment;
(c) effective enforcement of labour laws through appropriate government action, private rights of action, procedural guarantees, public information and awareness;
(d) institutional mechanisms to oversee the implementation of the LCA, such as a Ministerial Council and national Points of Contact to receive and review public communications on specified labour law matters and to enable cooperative activities to further the objectives of the LCA;
(e) general and ministerial consultations regarding the implementation of the LCA and its obligations; and
(f) independent review panels to hold hearings and make determinations regarding alleged non-compliance with the terms of the LCA and, if requested, monetary assessments.

A recent report of the government of Canada under the LCA regarding Colombia offers a ready indication of the severity of the submissions that have been coming forward, and the extent of the engagement by the Canadian NAO with the state of Colombian law. However, ultimately there persists a limited use and impact of available mechanisms. Colombia—an ILO member since its founding in 1919—has twenty-eight current freedom of association cases before the ILO, twenty-one pending follow up, and 160 that have been closed, many of which involved the assassination of trade unionists. Consider whether the trade-labour side agreement/labour chapter approach is mismatched to the tasks that confront it in Colombia.

CHAPTER 2: INTERNATIONAL AND TRANSNATIONAL LABOUR LAW

Employment and Social Development Canada, *Review of Public Communication CAN 2016-1— Report issued pursuant to the Canada-Colombia Agreement on Labour Cooperation* (Ottawa: ESDC, 2017), online: www.canada.ca/en/employment-social-development/services/labour-relations/ international/agreements/2016-1-review.html#section1

> This report responds to Public Communication CAN 2016-1 (Colombia) submitted to the Canadian National Administrative Office (NAO) by the Canadian Labour Congress and five Colombian labour organizations pursuant to Article 10 and Annex 2 of the Canada-Colombia Agreement on Labour Cooperation (CCOALC)....
>
> Despite the progress achieved to date and the Colombian Government's commitment to urgent action, further action is required to guarantee and promote workers' fundamental rights. In particular, the Colombian government's profession of urgency must now translate into concrete and ambitious actions to: (a) ensure that Colombian labour law embodies and provides protection for internationally recognized labour rights, and that such law is effectively enforced, as required by Articles 1 and 3 of the CCOALC; and (b) ensure that Colombian workers have appropriate access to fair, equitable and transparent proceedings before a tribunal to seek appropriate sanctions or remedies for violations of labour law, in line with the obligations under Articles 4 and 5 of the CCOALC. Furthermore, attention is required to ensure that the Colombian Government does not waive or derogate from its labour law as an encouragement for trade or investment in contravention of Article 2 of the CCOALC.
>
> The two cases presented in the Public Communication, as well as the analysis of additional informational resources, illustrate the ongoing, serious and systemic precarious labour conditions for Colombian workers. The available evidence suggests that:
>
> a) unfair and discriminatory labour practices persist;
> b) the ability of workers to defend their rights to associate and bargain collectively is undermined by distorted subcontracting practices;
> c) many employers are able to engage in unethical practices by exploiting weaknesses and loopholes in the law;
> d) industrial relations are affected by the prevalent stigma surrounding trade unions and their activities;
> e) the long delays in administrative and judicial proceedings increase the sentiment of injustice among workers whose rights are violated; and
> f) measures to reduce threats, impunity and violence are only partially effective.
>
> The Canadian NAO is, however of the view that Colombia can build on recent reforms to bring its labour law into compliance with the obligations of the CCOALC for the protection of basic workers' rights, in particular the right to freedom of association and collective bargaining. The preferred approach to labour relations should be based on collaboration, respect and engagement. A system of collective bargaining, guided by core labour principles, serves the interest of both employers and workers.
>
> Against this background, the Canadian NAO offers, in the spirit of cooperative discussions, the following recommendations to the Government of Colombia aimed at addressing the issues and concerns identified during the review process:

1. In order to protect workers' fundamental rights to freedom of association and collective bargaining, remove legal vehicles used to undermine these rights by making the following changes:
   - Eliminate union contracts. These contracts have become a platform for abusive labour practices and bad faith bargaining. The use of these contracts has also had significant negative impact on the independence of trade unions and their ability to fulfill their primary purpose;
   - Eliminate collective pacts. These pacts undermine the ability of independent trade unions to organize and negotiate authentic collective agreements thereby unduly interfering with the balance of power in labour relations;
   - Eliminate the misuse of short-term contracts. Repeatedly renewed short-term contracts are being used to disguise permanent employment relationships and thereby denying workers legal protection. The resulting high degree of job insecurity significantly impedes the ability of trade unions to organize and operate;
   - Implement measures to reduce the widespread and systematic practices of illegal labour intermediation and subcontracting including:
     ◊ Repealing Decree 583 (which has, in practice, enabled the subcontracting of permanent core business functions) and replacing it with a legal instrument that unambiguously empowers labour inspectors to combat the misuse of intermediation and subcontracting;
     ◊ ensuring that labour inspectors are empowered to identify and address situations where intermediation or subcontracting is being used to disguise a direct employment relationship regardless of the formalities associated with the relationship;
     ◊ developing guidelines for labour inspectors that identify permanent core business functions in specific economic sectors;
     ◊ directing enforcement resources at ensuring that civil law contracts (e.g. SAS, associated work cooperatives) are not used to deny workers social and labour protections provided under the law;
   - Consider the creation of a specialized quasi-judicial regulatory body to make decisions on union registration and dissolution and to hear complaints of unfair labour practices and discrimination by unions and employers. This body would be independent of the government and tripartite with appointees representing employers, unions and neutrals with specialized knowledge of law and labour standards.
2. Strengthen compliance with and enforcement of labour law through a labour inspectorate that focuses on preventive measures, provides effective advice, and establishes and efficiently collects penalties by:
   - ensuring that workers have timely access to justice in a manner that workers can claim labour rights, such as reinstatement or severance for dismissals, in the ordinary judicial process;
   - streamlining the administrative process for more effective imposition of fines, including considering the harmonization of existing sanctions in both the Substantive Labour Code and other labour law;
   - ensuring that Colombia's public collector (CISA) effectively collects the fines and

makes the achieved results known in the short and medium term, including an analysis of whether the fines imposed have a sufficient deterrent effect;
- providing labour inspectors the appropriate training and resources to perform effectively their duties, including preventive and proactive labour inspections;
- investigating multiple complaints filed against a particular employer under a single process;
- increasing the supervision and monitoring of labour formalization agreements negotiated with companies that obtained a reduction or remission of a fine for illegal labour intermediation or subcontracting to ensure that these companies offer permanent contracts rather than fixed-term contracts to workers through the implementation of these agreements.

2. Strengthen efforts to fight impunity and violence in the country by bringing those responsible to justice by:
   - evaluating the effectiveness of the mandatory conciliation phase (a precondition for the investigation to start) as required by the criminal proceedings for Article 200 of the Criminal Code and ensuring that existing procedures do not curtail the timeliness and efficiency of the administration of justice;
   - reviewing active files for violations under Article 200 of the Criminal Code, in particular those that may not be pursued due to timelines and for which immediate measures would be required;
   - providing the National Protection Unit sufficient and permanent financial resources to operate effectively;
   - ensuring that inter-institutional coordination mechanisms (between the Ministry of Labour and the Office of the Attorney General) are in place for the exchange of information and sharing of relevant evidence;
   - critically and independently examining the role of the ESMAD, whose actions and interventions have been strongly criticised by Colombian and international stakeholders for excessive use of force;
   - effectively advancing the investigation of violations under Article 347 of the Criminal Code, including by ensuring that guilty parties are brought to trial when warranted; and
   - ensuring that reassignments of files are done in accordance with proper investigative practices to avoid unreasonable delays; and

3. Evaluate and report on efforts to promote freedom of association and free collective bargaining in the country....

In conclusion, and pursuant to Article 12 of the CCOALC which provides that a Party may request in writing consultations with the other Party at the ministerial level regarding any obligation under the Agreement, the Canadian NAO recommends that the Minister of Employment, Workforce Development and Labour seeks consultations with the Minister of Labour of Colombia related to the above-mentioned recommendations.

The report and recommendations name serious freedom of association challenges and provide vehicles for exchange and collaboration. But do they address the deeper structural challenges to the regulation of labour standards at the international level—challenges which arguably call for a different way of governing international economic relations? Have they led to significant reform? Do they—can they—address distributive justice concerns caused by trade dislocations?

* * * * *

Most recent trade agreements, including those negotiated and signed by Canada, now contain clauses on labour protections. To an increasing degree, such agreements also share common provisions and themes. A standard commitment, contained in the *Comprehensive Economic and Trade Agreement* (CETA) between Canada and the European Union and its member states and the *Comprehensive and Progressive Agreement for Trans-Pacific Partnership* (CPTPP), is to uphold core labour standards contained in the *ILO Declaration of 1998*; another is to refrain from encouraging trade or investment by weakening protections under labour laws and standards. In the CPTPP, state parties commit to the exchange of "information on best practices on issues of common interest" and to "cooperation in international fora that deal with issues relevant for trade and labour, including in particular the WTO and the ILO" (art 23.7). In the CPTPP, state parties also agree to potential collaboration in a wide range of areas such as job creation, promotion of sustainable enterprises and entrepreneurship, work-life balance, social protection, pension systems, workers' compensation, and "best practices" for labour relations (Chapter 22). But how feasible it is to "cooperate" on such issues, given the diversity of domestic labour and social protection regimes across states and the complex socioeconomic and labour histories in which they are embedded? For a consideration of these questions, and whether enforcement of labour chapters/agreements provides a viable alternative, see Kevin Banks, "Trade, Labor and International Governance: An Inquiry into the Potential Effectiveness of the New International Labor Law" 32:1 *Berkeley Journal of Employment & Labor Law* 35 (2011).

Comprehensive Economic and Trade Agreement (CETA) between Canada and the European Union and its Member States, 30 October 2016, OJ, L 11 (provisional entry into force 21 September, 2017; full entry into force pending ratification by all EU member states), online: www.international.gc.ca/trade-commerce/trade-agreements-accords-commerciaux/agr-acc/ceta-aecg/text-texte/toc-tdm.aspx?lang=eng

Article 23.2—Right to regulate and levels of protection

Recognising the right of each Party to set its labour priorities, to establish its levels of labour protection and to adopt or modify its laws and policies accordingly in a manner consistent with its international labour commitments, including those in this Chapter, each Party shall seek to ensure those laws and policies provide for and encourage high levels of labour protection and shall strive to continue to improve such laws and policies with the goal of providing high levels of labour protection.

Article 23.3—Multilateral labour standards and agreements

1. Each Party shall ensure that its labour law and practices embody and provide protection for the fundamental principles and rights at work which are listed below. The Parties affirm their commitment to respect, promote and realise those principles and rights

in accordance with the obligations of the members of the International Labour Organization (the "ILO") and the commitments under the ILO Declaration on Fundamental Principles and Rights at Work and its Follow-up of 1998 adopted by the International Labour Conference at its 86th Session:
(a) freedom of association and the effective recognition of the right to collective bargaining;
(b) the elimination of all forms of forced or compulsory labour;
(c) the effective abolition of child labour; and
(d) the elimination of discrimination in respect of employment and occupation.

2. Each Party shall ensure that its labour law and practices promote the following objectives included in the ILO Decent Work Agenda, and in accordance with the ILO Declaration on Social Justice for a Fair Globalization of 2008 adopted by the International Labour Conference at its 97th Session, and other international commitments:
(a) health and safety at work, including the prevention of occupational injury or illness and compensation in cases of such injury or illness;
(b) establishment of acceptable minimum employment standards for wage earners, including those not covered by a collective agreement; and,
(c) non-discrimination in respect of working conditions, including for migrant workers.

[...]

Article 23.4—Upholding levels of protection

1. The Parties recognise that it is inappropriate to encourage trade or investment by weakening or reducing the levels of protection afforded in their labour law and standards.
[...]

Article 23.5—Enforcement procedures, administrative proceedings and review of administrative action

1. Pursuant to Article 23.4, each Party shall promote compliance with and shall effectively enforce its labour law, including by:
(a) maintaining a system of labour inspection in accordance with its international commitments aimed at securing the enforcement of legal provisions relating to working conditions and the protection of workers which are enforceable by labour inspectors; and
(b) ensuring that administrative and judicial proceedings are available to persons with a legally recognised interest in a particular matter who maintain that a right is infringed under its law, in order to permit effective action against infringements of its labour law, including appropriate remedies for violations of such law.

Comprehensive and Progressive Agreement for Trans-Pacific Partnership (CPTPP), 8 March 2018 (not yet entered into force), online: https://international.gc.ca/trade-commerce/trade-agreements-accords-commerciaux/agr-acc/cptpp-ptpgp/index.aspx?lang=eng

CHAPTER 19—LABOUR

[...]

Article 19.2: Statement of Shared Commitment
1. The Parties affirm their obligations as members of the ILO, including those stated in the ILO Declaration, regarding labour rights within their territories.
    2. The Parties recognise that, as stated in paragraph 5 of the ILO Declaration, labour standards should not be used for protectionist trade purposes.

Article 19.3: Labour Rights
1. Each Party shall adopt and maintain in its statutes and regulations, and practices thereunder, the following rights as stated in the ILO Declaration:
(a) freedom of association and the effective recognition of the right to collective bargaining;
(b) the elimination of all forms of forced or compulsory labour;
(c) the effective abolition of child labour and, for the purposes of this Agreement, a prohibition on the worst forms of child labour; and
(d) the elimination of discrimination in respect of employment and occupation.

    2. Each Party shall adopt and maintain statutes and regulations, and practices thereunder, governing acceptable conditions of work with respect to minimum wages, hours of work, and occupational safety and health.

Article 19.4: Non Derogation
The Parties recognise that it is inappropriate to encourage trade or investment by weakening or reducing the protections afforded in each Party's labour laws. Accordingly, no Party shall waive or otherwise derogate from, or offer to waive or otherwise derogate from, its statutes or regulations. ...

Article 19.5: Enforcement of Labour Laws
1. No Party shall fail to effectively enforce its labour laws through a sustained or recurring course of action or inaction in a manner affecting trade or investment between the Parties after the date of entry into force of this Agreement.
    [...]
    3. Nothing in this Chapter shall be construed to empower a Party's authorities to undertake labour law enforcement activities in the territory of another Party.

Article 19.7: Corporate Social Responsibility
Each Party shall endeavour to encourage enterprises to voluntarily adopt corporate social responsibility initiatives on labour issues that have been endorsed or are supported by that Party.

Franz Christian Ebert, "The Comprehensive Economic and Trade Agreement (CETA): Are Existing Arrangements Sufficient to Prevent Adverse Effects on Labour Standards?" (2017) 33:2 *International Journal of Comparative Labour Law and Industrial Relations* 295 at 297 and 301–7

> CETA has ... turned into a crystallization point for the debate on possible adverse social effects of trade and investment agreements and the strategies to counter them. A major issue in this regard relates to CETA's implications for labour standards. A number of civil society actors have voiced concerns that CETA may result in adverse effects on the labour standards of the parties to the Agreement. The potential downward pressure due

to increased competition without appropriate social safeguards and the risk that companies may use certain provisions of CETA to legally challenge labour laws have been highlighted among other risks. These concerns remain alive also after the signing of CETA and the adoption of the Joint Interpretative Instrument, all the more so since the European Parliament's Committee on Employment and Social Affairs advised against the adoption of CETA, due to its perceived negative social effects and insufficient safeguards for labour standards, among others....

[A] risk is apparent that CETA's investment chapter may be used to challenge domestic legislation, including on labour issues. In some cases, investors have brought legal action against states that were seeking to improve labour standards. For example, in a case against Egypt, still pending at the time of writing, an investor who had been contracted to perform waste disposal services alleged a breach of the France-Egypt Bilateral Investment Treaty (BIT) due to an increase in the statutory minimum wage, among others. In another case, an investor unsuccessfully alleged a breach of the US-Romania BIT due to increased business expenses as a result of worker protests. Importantly, awards are typically susceptible to enforcement before domestic courts and have involved damages that have on occasions amounted to several billion USD, while the specific arrangements concerning the damages to be accorded are typically left to be decided by the tribunal. Concerns have also been voiced about the independence of the tribunals, alleging a pro-investor bias of many arbitrators, a high risk of conflicts of interests as well as a lack of transparency and related procedural safeguards, among other factors. In this regard, commentators have observed a risk of a regulatory chill in relation to labour standards: even investor claims with limited prospects of success can put pressure on host states to refrain from a regulatory project, also due to the risk of substantial damages involved. While much of the criticism in the literature relates to earlier international investment agreements, a number of these concerns have also been put forward with regard to CETA, including those concerning the vagueness of key concepts of the substantive provisions.

In a similar vein, it has been argued that the CETA rules dealing with public procurement could be used to challenge clauses requiring contractors to abide by certain statutory labour standards or collective agreements. Unlike relevant EU law, CETA does not expressly refer to social standards in the context of public procurement. Among other factors, this has given rise to concerns that provisions of the CETA procurement chapter could be relied upon to argue that such requirements are in contravention of the Agreement.

Furthermore, the risk of negative indirect effects on labour standards has been emphasized. In contrast to the official economic impact assessment on CETA, a recent study by scholars from Tufts University finds that 'cost-cutting and competitiveness enhancing measures induced by CETA [would] have negative long-term effects'. It anticipates outcomes such as a loss in employment, a slowdown in wage increases, and a decline of the labour share in the parties' territories alongside with broader welfare and productivity losses. In a similar vein, commentators have pointed out risks for labour standards emanating from the CETA chapters on trade in services. Among others, the concern has been voiced that the extensive liberalization of services provided for by

CETA might result in downward pressure on working conditions. Finally, some scholars point to the risk that the CETA chapter on regulatory cooperation will strengthen the position of business lobbyists at the expense of civil society representatives, and weaken the role of parliaments in policy-making. Critics have submitted, in particular, that these provisions may give rise to regulatory dynamics on the margins of parliamentary control which may curtail labour law making at the domestic level, among other effects.

In light of the above, it is apparent that while CETA's text does not expressly conflict with labour standards, it entails several risks for the protection of labour standards at the domestic level. ...

The labour provisions contained in CETA reflect a mélange of the approaches to labour provisions that the EU and Canada, respectively, have developed over time. This is already apparent from the position of the labour provisions in the text of the agreement. Canada has included such provisions mostly into side agreements accompanying the trade agreement. Meanwhile, the EU's recent practice has been to incorporate such provisions into chapters dealing with 'Trade and Sustainable Development' in the trade agreement proper, which also deal with environmental issues. The compromise between these two approaches that was reached for CETA was to insert relevant labour provisions into a specific CETA chapter on 'Trade and Labour'. An additional chapter on 'Trade and Sustainable Development' addresses certain general issues, including dialogue with civil society actors under the agreement.

Apart from a commitment to 'high levels of labour protection' of a rather hortatory character, CETA refers to and in part incorporates several international standards. In contrast with most of the EU's recent trade agreements, these requirements do not primarily concern the ILO's Fundamental Conventions. Rather, reference is made to the ILO's 1998 Declaration on Fundamental Principles and Rights at Work (1998 Declaration). This can be explained by the fact that, unlike the EU Member States, at the time of writing Canada has not ratified all the ILO Fundamental Conventions and has, in its earlier agreements, favoured references to the 1998 Declaration. In addition, CETA includes a reaffirmation of the parties' commitment to implement the ILO Fundamental Conventions that the parties have ratified and requires them to 'make continued and sustained efforts' towards the ratification of the remaining ones. The question of whether the labour provisions refer to the ILO's 1998 Declaration or to the ILO's Fundamental Conventions is of practical relevance although those instruments address the same set of labour standards. The ILO Declaration's commitments are not only less specific than those under the relevant Conventions: it is—unlike ILO conventions—also not directly subject to the ILO supervisory mechanisms that can clarify the instruments' legal meaning. Labour provisions referring to and incorporating the content of the ILO's 1998 Declaration therefore give rise to more legal uncertainty than those referring to the relevant ILO Conventions, which may also lead to difficulties in the event of a dispute between the parties on their application.

Additional obligations pertain to the ILO's Declaration on Social Justice for a Fair Globalization of 2008. Parties commit, more specifically, to 'promot[ing]' requirements relating to 'acceptable minimum employment standards', nondiscrimination in terms of conditions of work, and occupational safety and health, in line with this Declaration. The latter requirement is accompanied by detailed obligations the parties have to fulfil.

Comprehensive requirements are furthermore set out with regard to 'public information and awareness' on labour law matters as well as on the domestic labour inspection and judiciary, which are obligations common in Canada's labour side agreements.

The CETA labour chapter also contains some obligations dealing with the nexus between labour standards, on the one hand, and trade and investment, on the other. In particular, the Agreement states that it is 'inappropriate to encourage trade or investment by weakening or reducing the levels of protection afforded in their labour law and standards', a formulation that builds on earlier EU trade agreements. Further, the parties are obligated not to offer or actually proceed to 'waive or otherwise derogate from' domestic labour laws with a view to encouraging trade or investment. Finally, the Parties are precluded from failing to enforce their labour laws for such a purpose. However, the particular wording of these provisions reduces their practical relevance....

The labour chapter's dispute settlement procedure largely reflects the approach taken in the EU's recent trade agreements: This includes arrangements for amicable consultations as well as a possible review of the dispute by a 'Panel of Experts'. Breaches of the labour chapter's provisions, as established in the Panel's final report, are to be addressed through 'discussions' between the parties and are to be monitored by the TSD Committee. The parties to the dispute are furthermore required to inform their respective advisory groups about any measures taken in this regard. Trade or other sanctions are not foreseen and access to CETA's regular dispute settlement mechanism, which does allow for the imposition of sanctions, is expressly excluded. As a result, compliance with any panel findings is de facto largely left to the discretion of the party concerned.

In this light, the statement contained in the agreement that '[t]he parties understand that the obligations [in] this Chapter are binding and enforceable through the [aforesaid] procedures' is at best confusing...

In the context of CETA, neither the EU nor Canada is likely to push for significant improvements in terms of domestic labour legislation in the other party's territory. However, it appears that the CETA negotiations with the EU may have had a role in accelerating Canada's ratification of certain ILO conventions. This includes the ILO Minimum Age Convention No 138 which was ratified in 2016, and the ILO Right to Organise and Collective Bargaining Convention No 98 [ratified on 14 June 2017]..... In contrast, the effects of the labour-related cooperative mechanisms under CETA on labour standards within the parties' territories are likely to be limited. By and large, the experience with existing agreements suggest that the relevant labour provisions will mainly be used for occasional dialogue on labour related issues without contributing much to the improvement of labour standards in the parties' territories.

Labour organizations have increasingly engaged not only with concerns about a lack of transparency in the negotiating process, but also with a critical assessment of the full content of the trade agreements, recognizing that the trade effects for labour extend far beyond the labour chapters. See, for example, the AFL-CIO, *Report on the Impacts of the TPP*, (2015), online: https://aflcio.org/reports/report-impacts-tpp.

2:320 The Emergence and Roles of Transnational Labour Regulation

Adelle Blackett & Anne Trebilcock, "Conceptualizing Transnational Labour Law" in Adelle Blackett & Anne Trebilcock, eds, *Research Handbook on Transnational Labour Law* (Cheltenham, UK: Edward Elgar Publishing, 2016) at 3

> A fragmentary [transnational labor law] TLL has emerged to problematize and resist the direction of social regulation under globalization. Recognizing globalization's asymmetries, and identifying spaces for action, TLL operates within, between and beyond states to construct counter-hegemonic alternatives. The field critically encompasses actions beyond the state, to take into account the actions of transnational enterprises, labour federations, civil society and other actors. Moreover, TLL does not stop where national labour law begins: the two are deeply intertwined, and challenge each other. TLL is a form of multi-level governance, including the international, the regional, the national, and the shop floor: its ability to address challenges of economic interdependency is similarly enmeshed with its ability to acknowledge and deal with complexity, diversity and asymmetries across time and space—amongst states, across uneven regional development, amongst vastly differently empowered institutions and actors. TLL holds no monopoly on either the rise of legal centrism through the prevalence of 'rule of law' doctrines, or the expansion of pluralist, reflexive new governance methods. Its distinctiveness lies in its capacity to be counter-hegemonic, and promote social justice. We contend that it is the early International Labour Organization (ILO) constitutional *acquis*, rooted in labour history's recognition that law's normative character is indeterminate and must be the basis of continuous struggle for social justice, that is at the core of TLL's emergence. That centering of social justice—which includes but extends beyond 'bringing redistribution out of the closet' goes a long way to explaining why TLL is also such a contested terrain.

Bob Hepple, *Labour Laws and Global Trade* (Oxford and Portland, OR: Hart Publishing, 2004) at 256–57, 268–69, and 275

> While the economic models set the parameters of comparative institutional advantage, it is political choices that determine the outcomes. One of the best ways to understand the regulatory responses to economic globalisation at national level is in terms of four 'ideal types' or deductive models: (1) the liberal state; (2) the social democratic welfare state; (3) the neo-liberal state; and (4) the rights-based model. Models of this kind, freed from specific national features, help to illuminate the common tendencies and divergences in different countries, but they are not a substitute for close analysis of the actual circumstances in each country or locality at a particular time. Labour laws have not developed as a series of evolutionary stages, or as a 'necessary' or 'natural' response to globalisation. The laws in each country have been the outcome of complex, protracted and sometimes bitterly contested struggles. The comparativist has to examine the specific features of historical change in each country in order to explain differences in the laws which have shaped labour markets. For example why was the work-book or 'pass' system a feature of labour markets in some countries but not others? Why was the 8-hour day achieved in some places by collective bargaining and in others by national legislation? Why is 'protection' treated as a gift from the state in some periods and as a 'right' in others?

In seeking answers to questions such as these one has to examine how particular rights came to be introduced into each country. Labour laws are the outcome of struggle between different social groups—monarchy, aristocracy, bureaucracy, middle class, workers and peasants—and of competing ideologies of conservatives, liberals, social democrats and socialists. The rights which any particular group gets 'is not just a matter of what they choose but what they can force or persuade other groups to let them have. The crucial element in the making of labour laws is power. Many of the demands by labour movements and reformers were unsuccessful because they were unacceptable to those with greater economic and political power. It is in power relationships, which are rooted in social structure, that we may find a key to the achievement and denial of rights at work....

The question that globalization raises for all those political models is whether the employment relationships remain governable within a political system whose central unit is the nation-state.

Those—particularly public choice theorists—who give priority to the economic functions of labour laws tend to argue that that economic globalisation is leading to 'law without the state' because the state is a fetter on the free play of global market forces. On the other hand, those who continue to see the state as essential to social cohesion and consensus stress the importance of state intervention to establish a normative order for labour relations. An intermediate group of social theorists have emphasised the 'pluralism' of legal orders. The state recognises or tolerates the autonomy of these orders. This is particularly relevant in the labour field, where 'law' is not necessarily coterminous with the state. A variety of actors make rules, enforced through non-state mechanisms or customs, within the workshop or office, enterprise or industry, and these rules may be even more important in practice than state-made laws. There are also transnational rules made by TNCs as well as international and regional institutions.

The pluralist perspective sees regulatory diversity and competition not so much as a conflict between state systems of labour law, but as a strategic or political process between different legal orders both within and beyond the state. Stone argues that globalisation 'not only breeds a desire for localisation, it also breeds the means to achieve it. She points to the agglomeration of TNCs in particular places, such as the computer industry in Silicon Valley, partly because of the skills and knowledge of the locality's workforce and the networks they can establish. The attractions of such regions dissuades TNCs from moving offshore to avoid high labour costs, increases the leverage of local work and community groups, and the opportunities for local investment in human capital. If the centralised state is not able to provide the redistributive functions of labour laws, then struggles for social protection will become increasingly localised. This leads to some important conclusions. One is that local unions and community groups can act together to put pressure on TNCs to adopt best practices; another is that divisions between different employment statuses at local level (employees, contingent or atypical, and self- employed), and between working life and family life can be reduced; and a third is that solidarities can be developed with local groups employed by the same TNC in other countries.

The 'glocalisation' thesis can be criticised on the ground that it simply reinforces and aggravates inequalities between regions, those that are naturally endowed or have the appropriate workforces to attract transnational capital, and those that lack these factors of production. More generally, in the absence of supranational regulation, it is unlikely that local actors will succeed at the sharp end of regulation aimed at redistribution. This is because redistributive rules attempt to change the balance of economic and political power among different interest groups....

The conclusion to which one is led is that legal convergence is not the likely outcome of globalisation. Differences between the labour laws of countries and localities will remain and may even increase. How far, then, can the adverse effects of regulatory competition be met by transnational labour regulation?

One of the most important consequences of modern globalisation is that there are multiple, overlapping layers of norm-creation and norm-application. This is familiar in federal systems, and is a feature of the EU legal order. Corporate codes of conduct operate within systems of corporate governance and are influenced by transnational guidelines, such as those of the OECD and the ILO. None of this is surprising to labour lawyers who are familiar with the legal pluralism of employer regulation, collective bargaining, union rules and national laws. Labour lawyers are also aware that the boundaries between these orders can be vague, and that the prevalence of particular norms depends upon complex power relations that can change, sometimes rapidly.

It is within this dynamic relationship between multivalent legal orders that the ability of labour law to contribute to social justice within the global market will be determined. The supra-nationalising of labour law, through ILO standards, regional treaties and the codes of TNCs, gives trade unions, NGOs and national governments opportunities to emancipate themselves from the confines of national or local laws.

[© Bob Hepple, 2004, *Labour Laws and Global Trade*, Hart Publishing, an imprint of Bloomsbury Publishing Plc.]

Alan Hyde, "Game Theory and Labour Standards" in John DR Craig & S Michael Lynk, eds, *Globalization and the Future of Labour Law* (Cambridge: Cambridge University Press, 2006) at 146–50

I shall argue that transnational labour standards ... arise to solve coordination problems in which countries will gain by cooperation but will be disadvantaged if their trading rivals defect....

A Stag Hunt is a game in which players can gain by cooperating, but only if everyone else does.... The point is that a stag makes a much better dinner than a hare, but can only be hunted in a group in which everyone cooperates, while hare may be hunted individually. If you think that everyone will cooperate, you are better off hunting a stag. But if you expect that even one person will go off to hunt a hare, then you had better hunt hare yourself. ...

This game has two Nash equilibria: either everyone hunts stag, or everyone hunts hare. Hunting stag is "payoff dominant" (or Pareto optimal) but risky since one can easily be left with nothing. Hunting hare is "risk dominant," "secure," or "maximin," since it has the highest guaranteed payoff. Thus there is one Nash equilibrium (each hunts hare) that is not Pareto optimal. There is no strategy that is dominant in the sense of being the best regardless of what others do. The best strategy depends directly on what others do, specifically, whether they will cooperate or not. The n-player Stag Hunt is similar, except that it has a n number of Nash equilibria, each short of the Pareto-optimal solution in which everyone cooperates to hunt stag. ...

We model the adoption of transnational labour standards as solutions to Stag Hunts, in which everyone is better off if all cooperate (hunt stag), but there is a risk that any individual actor might pursue short-term advantage by defecting (hunting hare and leaving the others with only the gains from hare hunting). Actors are countries that choose whether or not to adopt and enforce labour standards. They are assumed to be rational in the sense of favouring Pareto-optimal actions that improve living standards in their population at least where this can be accomplished without taking away from any.

Consider the following highly stylized statement of the problem. It is clearly in the long-term interest of India, Bangladesh and Pakistan that all their children go to school and do not work in factories. Going to school builds human capital, attracts more and better foreign investment, and generally results in a richer society for all. However, if India and Pakistan actually succeeded in getting all their children out of workshops and into schools, there are certain specific foreign investments that would flow to Bangladesh to take advantage of its child labour, and this would be true even if (as we suppose) Bangladesh knows that it is in its long-term interest that children learn instead of work. This is a classic Stag Hunt. If all countries cooperate in ending child labour, all will be better off. Jobs will be taken by unemployed adults, and children will go to school. But if even one country defects by letting children work, it will capture a certain stream of foreign direct investment that others will not. So, if you think one of your rivals will be selfish, it is rational for you to be selfish, too. There are thus two Nash equilibria: one that is Pareto optimal (no children work), the other that is Pareto suboptimal (children work).

So stated, this is not exactly a new insight, nor one that can only be appreciated through the application of formal game theory. Child labour, noted John Stuart Mill in 1832, is a case "in which it would be highly for the advantage of every body, if every body were to act in a certain manner, but in which it is not the interest of any *individual* to adopt the rule for the guidance of his own conduct, unless he has some security that others will do so too." The value of turning toward game theory is the illumination that it offers, particularly in its behavioural version, to the legal scholars' questions of regulatory multiplicity, choosing between unilateral and multilateral norms, and sanctions. [Reprinted with the permission of Cambridge University Press.]

2:330 Transnational Uses of International Labour Law

2:331 Vignette — International Labour Law in Canadian Jurisprudence

The soft law 1998 Declaration on Fundamental Principles and Rights at Work has served to orient the ILO's technical assistance activities, and has grounded a successful campaign to increase the number of ratifications of the core ILO Conventions on the freedom of association and right to bargain collectively. Canada ratified Convention No 98 in 2017. Canada had earlier ratified Convention 87, in 1972. This section will consider what influence ILO law now has in Canada, and how ILO law came to exert that influence.

Convention (No 87) Concerning Freedom of Association and Protection of the Right to Organize, ILO, 9 July 1948, 68 UNTS 17 (entered into force 4 July 1950)

Article 2

Workers and employers, without distinction whatsoever, shall have the right to establish and, subject only to the rules of the organisation concerned, to join organisations of their own choosing without previous authorisation.

Article 3

1. Workers' and employers' organisations shall have the right to draw up their constitutions and rules, to elect their representatives in full freedom, to organise their administration and activities and to formulate their programmes.

   2. The public authorities shall refrain from any interference which would restrict this right or impede the lawful exercise thereof.

Article 4

Workers' and employers' organisations shall not be liable to be dissolved or suspended by administrative authority.

Article 5

Workers' and employers' organisations shall have the right to establish and join federations and confederations and any such organisation, federation or confederation shall have the right to affiliate with international organisations of workers and employers.

   [...]

Article 8

[...]

   2. The law of the land shall not be such as to impair, nor shall it be so applied as to impair, the guarantees provided for in this Convention.

   [...]

Article 11

Each Member of the International Labour Organisation for which this Convention is in force undertakes to take all necessary and appropriate measures to ensure that workers and employers may exercise freely the right to organise.

Convention (No 98) Concerning the Application of the Principles of the Right to Organize and to Bargain Collectively, 1961, ILO, 1 July 1949, 96 UNTS 257 (entered into force 18 July 1951)

Article 1

1. Workers shall enjoy adequate protection against acts of anti-union discrimination in respect of their employment.

   2. Such protection shall apply more particularly in respect of acts calculated to—

a. make the employment of a worker subject to the condition that he shall not join a union or shall relinquish trade union membership;
b. cause the dismissal of or otherwise prejudice a worker by reason of union membership or because of participation in union activities outside working hours or, with the consent of the employer, within working hours.

Article 2
1. Workers' and employers' organisations shall enjoy adequate protection against any acts of interference by each other or each other's agents or members in their establishment, functioning or administration.

2. In particular, acts which are designed to promote the establishment of workers' organisations under the domination of employers or employers' organisations, or to support workers' organisations by financial or other means, with the object of placing such organisations under the control of employers or employers' organisations, shall be deemed to constitute acts of interference within the meaning of this Article.

Article 3
Machinery appropriate to national conditions shall be established, where necessary, for the purpose of ensuring respect for the right to organise as defined in the preceding Articles.

Article 4
Measures appropriate to national conditions shall be taken, where necessary, to encourage and promote the full development and utilisation of machinery for voluntary negotiation between employers or employers' organisations and workers' organisations, with a view to the regulation of terms and conditions of employment by means of collective agreements.

[...]

Article 6
This Convention does not deal with the position of public servants engaged in the administration of the State, nor shall it be construed as prejudicing their rights or status in any way.

Adelle Blackett, "'This is Hallowed Ground': Canada and International Labour Law" in *Canada in International Law at 150 and Beyond*, Paper No 22 (2018) at 1 and 3–4

Many Canadian law students learn about the labour conventions reference to the Judicial Committee of the Privy Council in their first-year constitutional law studies, but the ILO is decidedly peripheral to law students' nuanced study of the federal-provincial division of powers. Difficulties in the interpretation of the division of powers are a significant part of the reason why the ILO's first international labour convention, Convention No. 1 was only ratified by Canada on March 21, 1935, along with the Weekly Rest (Industry) Convention, 1921 (No. 14), followed swiftly by the Minimum Wage-Fixing Machinery Convention, 1928 (No. 26) on April 25, 1935....

The union movement—through the Trades and Labour Congress of Canada—prioritized ILO standards implementation, but was met with deep opposition from Canadian businesses. The Canadian Manufacturers' Association warned that "disastrous consequences" would follow should an "undeveloped country," such as Canada, that needed to attract capital enacted such legislation, unless the United States passed similar legislation first. Canada did not ratify the conventions immediately. Instead, it held dominion-provincial meetings in 1922 and 1923 to discuss the question of jurisdiction....

In the first labour conventions reference [to the Supreme Court of Canada], ... Justice Duff's decision acknowledged that the subject matter of hours of labour was "generally within the competence of the legislatures of the provinces," while recognizing exclusive federal legislative authority in "those parts of Canada not within the boundaries of any province, and also upon the subjects dealt with in the draft convention in relation to the servants of the Dominion Government." Following that decision, on March 31, 1926, Canada ... ratified conventions that were resolutely within federal jurisdiction: the Minimum Age (Sea) Convention, 1920 (No. 7); the Unemployment Indemnity (Shipwreck) Convention, 1920 (No. 8); the Minimum Age (Trimmers and Stokers) Convention, 1921 (No. 15); and the Medical Examination of Young Persons (Sea) Convention, 1921 (No. 16).

Canada's slow rate of ratification did not go unnoticed. In 1934 and 1935, Jenks wrote scholarly companion articles addressing Canada's "relative backwardness" on ratification. Jenks was critical of Canada's less than fruitful process of proceeding by federal-provincial meetings, reviewed the jurisprudence to that point and argued that the constitutional question had to be resolved in favour of the federal authority to legislate, emphasizing the obligations under article 405 of Part XIII of the Treaty of Versailles, as well as section 132 of the Constitution Act, 1867. Jenks even suggested that the ILO might play an active role in assisting domestic courts to decide questions that relate to the interpretation of ILL....

Canada's 1935 ratifications of three international labour conventions on hours of work, minimum weekly rest and minimum wages followed the introduction of three pieces of related labour legislation said to reflect Canada's own New Deal response to the Great Depression.... These acts yielded the second reference to the SCC, which resulted in a 3–3 split decision. On appeal, the Judicial Committee of the Privy Council issued its decision, penned by Lord Atkin, and found that the implementing legislation was ultra vires the Parliament of Canada. Framing the "complex" problem through the lens of the dualist system in the British Empire, whereby "the making of a treaty is an executive act, while the performance of its obligations, if they entail alteration of the existing domestic law, requires legislative action," the Privy Council considered that neither section 132 nor POGG could apply, and that the exercise of that legislative authority of the provinces under section 92 could not be encroached upon simply because the federal government had made promises to foreign countries by treaty. Although the Privy Council refuted the implication that Canada is "incompetent to legislate in performance of treaty obligations," since the federal government can act together with the provinces without encroaching on provincial powers, Canada was essentially placed in default of its ILO obligations. The negative impact on future ratifications of any instruments not readily within federal jurisdiction can be gleaned from the relatively slim list of Canadian ratifications, despite Canada's leadership role both as a wartime refuge and as an active, often pivotal, actor in ILO affairs.

While this might have mattered less during the period of sustained growth and relative prosperity that ensued in Canada, by the early 1980s, inflation and high unemployment were met with a series of liberalizing measures that challenged labour's gains and exposed the precarity of preexisting categories of workers, who had always been excluded from labour law's mainstream. International labour conventions and their ratification began to look less like accessories to robust domestic labour legislation and more like a vanguard through which to safeguard labour and broader social rights—including human rights—in the face of concerted policy attack.

This moment coincided with the early days of the Canadian Charter of Rights and Freedoms (the Charter). Chief Justice Brian Dickson of the SCC offered fulsome readings of international and comparative law, including ILL, to guide the interpretation of the scope of the freedom of association under section 2(d) of the Charter. The spirit was decidedly cosmopolitan, reflecting a vision of Canada grappling with comparable, pressing concerns in a broader world. It attentively honed an independent interpretive approach that was at once rigorous, contextual and alive. Chief Justice Dickson's reliance on ILL in his dissent in *Re Public Service Employee Relations Act* remains highly influential on the contemporary decision making on section 2(d)....

In *Health Services and Support-Facilities Subsector Bargaining Association v British Columbia (BC Health Services)*, Chief Justice Beverley McLachlin and Justice Louis LeBel, writing for the majority (Justice Marie Deschamps wrote a partial dissent) drew assistance from ILL—and, in particular, the Freedom of Association and Protection of the Right to Organize Convention, 1948 (No. 87)—to interpret the freedom of association protections in section 2(d) of the Charter as including the right to bargain collectively. Drawing on past jurisprudence for the appropriate interpretative approach to be given to ratified international instruments, the SCC majority held that the Charter provides "at least as great a level of protection as is found in the international human rights documents that Canada has ratified."

The SCC refined its reliance on ILL in the cases that followed.... In the 2015 section 2(d) labour cases, an ILL methodology that carefully articulates the core functions of freedom of association, which affirms (without being wed to) a particular industrial relations tradition, is most readily exemplified. In *Mounted Police Association of Ontario v Canada (Attorney General)*, the SCC hinted at the space that it was leaving open in BC Health Services for the articulation and recognition of alternative, meaningfully enabling systems of collective autonomy over time by confirming that "Parliament's decision to use a collaborative scheme for labour relations within the RCMP is consistent with international instruments regarding freedom of association" and referencing Convention No. 87 alongside the UN International Covenant on Civil and Political Rights (article 22) and the UN International Covenant on Economic, Social and Cultural Rights (article 8).

The evolution is most readily seen in *Saskatchewan Federation of Labour v Saskatchewan*. In her section 2(d) analysis of the right to strike, Justice Rosalie Abella listed a significant number of international sources, alongside comparative law examples indicative of emerging directions worldwide. In so doing, the court sought guidance, as in other cases, on "the norm which best informs the content of the principles" in the Charter. Ultimately, though, the distinctive use of ILL is witnessed in Justice Abella's interpretation of the section 1 limits. Justice Abella argued that "the need for demarcated limits on both the right of essential services employees to strike and, concomitantly, on the extent to which services may justifiably be limited as 'essential,' is reflected too in international law." In other words, ILL is drawn upon not only to ascertain the scope of the substantive right, but to consider how it may assist, substantively, in articulating reasonable limits in a free and democratic society.

Case law developments under the freedom of association have broader implications for nuanced understandings of the dualist tradition in a Canada that has a constitutionalized

Charter. Patrick Macklem argues that there has been a "fundamental transformation" of Canada's dualist tradition, so central to the labour conventions references. For Macklem, the SCC has developed a more "relational understanding of the boundary between the international and national legal spheres." The Privy Council in the second Labour Conventions case expressly focused on implementation by the federal or provincial legislatures; however, the landscape has changed with the constitutionalization of Charter principles, including the freedom of association. Simply put, "[i]f legislatures fail to implement international labour law, they risk running afoul of the Charter." The emerging cases validate an approach embodied by the life's work of the late pioneering Quebec labour law scholar Pierre Verge: international law has a central role to play in the reconstruction of labour law, domestically. To paraphrase Guylaine Vallée in her beautiful overview of Verge's lifetime contribution: Verge was inspired by international law's capacity to affirm core principles that could bind a diversity of formal sources that might be seen as conflicting.

BC Health Services and the cases that followed it have consolidated a growing understanding by the SCC of its own role while faced with the challenge of economic restructuring to the labour law frameworks that guarantee fundamental rights and freedoms at work. Rather than assuming that the SCC is a "neutral force" in labour law, the court seems prepared to recognize that the Charter can also help to preserve spaces of collective autonomy that enable meaningful participation in debates on the direction of the world of work, and more generally of Canadian society.

With these jurisprudential developments, Canada's most recent decision ultimately to ratify the Right to Organise and Collective Bargaining Convention, 1949 (No. 98) on June 14, 2017, no longer seems surprising. It may be understood as the culmination of what has become a jurisprudential readying of Canadian law to embrace this fundamental international labour convention that embodies Canada's "reaffirm[ation of] the immutable nature of the fundamental principles and rights embodied in the Constitution of the Organization," with a view to promoting the universal application of the ILO's eight fundamental conventions. Canada has now ratified them all. As the Freedom of Association Committee recalled in its report regarding BC Health Services, "when a State decides to become a Member of the ILO, it accepts the fundamental principles embodied in the Constitution and the Declaration of Philadelphia, including the principles of freedom of association." [Reproduced by permission of the publisher, © 2018 by the Centre for International Governance Innovation.]

Saskatchewan Federation of Labour v Saskatchewan, 2015 SCC 4

[67] [O]ther sources tend to confirm the protection of the right to strike recognized in international law. Canada is a party to the International Labour Organization (ILO) *Convention (No. 87) concerning freedom of association and protection of the right to organize*, ratified in 1972. Although *Convention No. 87* does not explicitly refer to the right to strike, the ILO supervisory bodies, including the Committee on Freedom of Association and the Committee of Experts on the Application of Conventions and Recommendations, have recognized the right to strike as an indissociable corollary of the right of trade union association that is protected in that convention.... Striking, according to the Committee

of Experts, is "one of the essential means available to workers and their organizations for the promotion and protection of their economic and social interests".

[68] Under the *International Covenant on Economic, Social and Cultural Rights* signatory states are not permitted to take "legislative measures which would prejudice, or apply the law in such a manner as would prejudice, the guarantees provided for in [*Convention No. 87*]": Article 8(3) of the *ICESCR*. The principles relating to the right to strike were summarized by the Committee on Freedom of Association as follows:

> 521. The Committee has always recognized the right to strike by workers and their organizations as a legitimate means of defending their economic and social interests....
>
> 523. The right to strike is an intrinsic corollary to the right to organize protected by Convention No. 87....
>
> 526. The occupational and economic interests which workers defend through the exercise of the right to strike do not only concern better working conditions or collective claims of an occupational nature, but also the seeking of solutions to economic and social policy questions and problems facing the undertaking which are of direct concern to the workers.

[69] Though not strictly binding, the decisions of the Committee on Freedom of Association have considerable persuasive weight and have been favourably cited and widely adopted by courts, tribunals and other adjudicative boards around the world, including our Court....

[70] Canada is also a party to the *International Covenant on Civil and Political Rights*, 999 U.N.T.S. 171 (*ICCPR*), which incorporates *Convention No. 87* and the obligations it sets out: see Article 22(3)....

[71] Additionally, there is an emerging international consensus that, if it is to be meaningful, collective bargaining requires a right to strike. The European Court of Human Rights now shares this view ... that a right to strike is part of what ensures the effective exercise of a right to collective bargaining.

The Court went on to note that in restricting the right to strike, it was important that "essential services," a common basis for such restrictions, be properly interpreted, noting that the decisions of the Freedom of Association Committee of the ILO have consistently defined an essential service as a service "whose interruption would endanger the life, personal safety or health of the whole or part of the population."

* * * * *

The ILO's Committee of Experts and Freedom of Association Committee have repeatedly addressed the issue of legislative exclusions of agricultural workers from the right to organize and bargain collectively. Their exchanges have been analyzed as a dialogue between the ILO's supervisory bodies—which do not require parties to exhaust domestic remedies before they are solicited—and Canadian Courts. See Maude Choko, "The Dialogue between Canada and the ILO on Freedom of Association: What Remains after Fraser?" (2012) 28:4 Intl J Comp Lab L & Ind Rel 397.

Report of the Committee of Experts on the Application of Conventions and Recommendations, ILO, 92nd Sess, Report III (Part 1A) (2004) at 53–54

> In its previous comments, the Committee had noted that workers in agriculture and horticulture in the Provinces of Alberta, Ontario and New Brunswick were excluded from the coverage of labour relations legislation and thereby deprived of protection concerning the right to organize and collective bargaining. The Committee had also noted with regret that other categories of workers (domestic workers, architects, dentists, land surveyors, lawyers and doctors) were excluded in Ontario, under section 13(a) of the Amended Labour Relations Act, 1995.
>
> Furthermore, the Committee had noted that the Supreme Court of Canada held in December 2001 (in the Dunmore case, originating from Ontario) that the exclusion of agricultural workers was unconstitutional and gave the Government of Ontario 18 months to amend the impugned legislation. The Committee had noted that the Government of Ontario had introduced Bill No. 187 in October 2002 (Agricultural Employees Protection Act), which gives agricultural employees the right to form or join an employees' association. It appears, however, that this legislation does not give agricultural workers the right to establish and join trade unions and to bargain collectively....
>
> As concerns the Province of Alberta, the Committee notes with regret that the Government of Alberta has indicated that further review of the organization of agricultural workers will not be done at this time, considering the current challenges in the agricultural sectors. As concerns the Province of New Brunswick, the Committee notes with regret that no legislative changes are being considered to the Industrial Relations Act at this time. The Committee recalls once again that all workers, with the sole possible exception of the armed forces and the police, have the right to organize under the Convention. It requests the Governments of Alberta and New Brunswick to amend their legislation accordingly and to inform it of developments in this respect in their next reports.
> [Copyright © International Labour Organization 2004.]

It bears noting that Canada has been called to account in many cases (one active, two pending follow up, and 107 closed cases before the freedom of association committee), often for back-to-work legislation and underinclusive labour laws.

2:332   Vignette—The ILO and Maritime Labour in Canada

The maritime industry has been considered one of the first global industries. The regulation of maritime labour raises many transnational labour law issues, including the movement of persons. Maritime labour has been the subject of significant standard setting at the ILO and early ratifications by Canada. The ILO innovated in 2006, when it adopted a comprehensive, consolidated Maritime Labour Convention (MLC). In 2010, Canada ratified the ILO Maritime Labour Convention, 2006, after ensuring itself that the matter was wholly within federal jurisdiction, and after assessing the conformity of Canadian laws and practices with the MLC, 2006:

Canada, Employment and Social Development Canada, *Canadian Position with Respect to the Maritime Labour Convention, 2006* (Gatineau, QC: Human Resources and Social Development

Canada, 2006) 2 and 5, online: www.canada.ca/content/dam/esdc-edsc/migration/documents/eng/relations/international/forums/reports/docs/ilo_2006.pdf

> The MLC, 2006 is a comprehensive new labour standard for the world's maritime sector that was adopted at the 10th Maritime Session of the ILC, held in Geneva, Switzerland in February 2006. It sets out seafarers' rights to decent working conditions and helps to create conditions for fair competition for shipowners....
>
> The decision by the ILO to develop this major new maritime labour Convention was the result of a joint resolution in 2001 by international seafarers' and shipowners' organizations, later supported by governments.
>
> The industry partners called on the ILO to develop, as a matter of priority, *"an instrument which brings together into a consolidated text as much of the existing body of ILO instruments as it proves possible to achieve in order to improve the relevance of those standards to the needs of all the stakeholders of the maritime sector."*
>
> Many of the existing 68 maritime labour instruments (37 Conventions and 31 Recommendations) adopted by the ILO since 1920 were outdated and did not reflect contemporary working conditions on board ships. In addition, excessive detail in many existing maritime labour Conventions constituted a major obstacle to their broad ratification.
>
> The new Convention brings most of the existing maritime labour instruments together in a single Convention with a new format and updated language that better reflects modern working conditions in the industry. To facilitate broad ratification, the Convention takes an approach that is *"firm on rights and flexible on implementation."*
>
> The new Convention also responds to the need for a more effective enforcement and compliance system that would help eliminate substandard working conditions on ships and would work within the well established international system for enforcement of the international standards for ships safety and security and environmental protection adopted by the International Maritime Organization (IMO)....
>
> There is a high degree of conformity of Canadian laws and practices with the MLC, 2006. Most of its provisions are implemented through the *Canada Labour Code* and the *Marine Occupational Safety and Health Regulations* and the *Canada Shipping Act, 2001* (CSA, 2001) and its regulations, or through collective agreements between Canadian shipowners and unions representing seafarers.
>
> Effective July 1, 2007, the MLC, 2006 has been added to Schedule 1 of the CSA 2001. This will enable Transport Canada to implement provisions of the MLC, 2006 through its new *Marine Personnel Regulations*, which were developed in consultation with the marine community, including representatives of Canadian shipowners and seafarers, under the umbrella of the Canadian Marine Advisory Council.
>
> A review of the *Canada Labour Code's Marine Occupational Safety and Health Regulations* is ongoing with a view to ensuring compliance with relevant provisions of the MLC, 2006. In addition, new *Shipbuilding and Accommodation Regulations* are being developed under the CSA 2001.

Moira L McConnell, "The Maritime Labour Convention, 2006—Reflections on Challenges for Flag State Implementation" (2011) 10:2 *WMU Journal of Maritime Affairs* 127 at 137–38

> While there are some countries where the labour department and labour inspectors will play a central role, in many countries, implementation has occurred through cooperative arrangements between the relevant departments. This is especially important since some topics may be matters on which the maritime administration cannot develop legislation. To use the example of Canada, the majority of the MLC, 2006 provisions are addressed in a regulation under the *Canada Shipping Act, 2001*, a statute dealt with by Transport Canada. However, some elements dealing with maritime occupational safety and health (MOSH) and seafarers' accommodation on board ship are set out in a regulation under the *Canada Labour Code*, a statute under the purview of Human Resources and Skills Canada. These institutional and legal issues are complex to work out, particularly in countries where departments have not previously worked together to develop MOUs or other cooperative arrangements to address issues and legislation that straddles departmental boundaries. The MLC, 2006 requires an integrated approach in order to achieve implementation.
>
> Aside from ship inspection questions, the comprehensive coverage under the Convention also provides a challenge because the subject matter may span more than these two departments or in some cases even levels of governments (e.g. in federations). For example, the provision of social security to seafarers "ordinarily resident" in the country or access to onshore medical services may require discussion between a number of departments or levels of government, in some cases. This means that other ministries, particularly where financial or border security matters may be involved, need also to understand and support the Convention. These are all matters that can be difficult and take time to negotiate.

The relationship between maritime labour and the regulation of labour migration can be readily witnessed in the following statement about the settlement of recent lawsuits:

"Government of Canada Settles SIUC Lawsuits" *Seafarers' International Union of Canada* (15 February 2017), online: www.seafarers.ca/government-of-canada-settles-siuc-lawsuits

> The applications for judicial review filed with the Federal Court sought to quash the 44 work permits issued to the foreign crew of two flag of convenience oil tankers, the Sparto and the Amalthea.
>
> The Coasting Trade Act restricts the transportation of passengers or goods between Canadian ports ("cabotage") to Canadian registered ships. However, a Coasting Trade License ("CTL") may be issued by the Canadian Transportation Agency to allow a foreign-flagged vessel to engage in cabotage in Canada if no Canadian vessel is available. Since 2010, over 650 CTLs have been issued to foreign ships to engage in cabotage in Canada. The fact that a ship is able to operate in Canada does not provide a legal right for the crew to work in Canada. Like all non-permanent residents or non-Canadian citizens, foreign crews must first be granted Labour Market Impact Assessments ("LMIAs") and issued work permits before they can work in Canada.
>
> Since 2015, the SIU brought 55 applications for judicial review alleging that Employment and Social Development Canada ("ESDC") was routinely issuing work permits to

foreign crew without first determining, as required by law, whether there were qualified and available Canadians to perform the work. In addition, the SIU alleged that ESDC failed to ensure that foreign crew working in Canada were paid the prevailing wage in the Canadian maritime industry. The SIU uncovered evidence that some foreign crew members were paid as little as $2.41 per hour while working in Canada.

According to the federal government, "the Temporary Foreign Worker Program (TFWP) was created as a last and limited resort to allow employers to bring foreign workers to Canada on a temporary basis to fill jobs for which qualified Canadians are not available." The SIU alleged that, when it comes to cabotage, the federal government was not following its own laws and policies, but, instead, was issuing work permits to virtually all crews on all foreign ships engaged in cabotage.

In July 2016, the Government of Canada admitted that it improperly issued work permits to 11 foreign crew members of the New England, a Marshall Islands flag of convenience oil tanker that engaged in cabotage in Canada in July 2015. As a result, the Government consented to an order of the Federal Court of Canada granting judicial review in all 11 applications made by the SIU and further agreed to an order of the court setting aside the work permits. That represented the first time that a union in Canada has succeeded in receiving an order of the Federal Court granting judicial review in connection with work permits issued to foreign workers and a further order setting aside those work permits.
[Printed with the permission of the Seafarers' International Union of Canada.]

2:333 Vignette—Decent Work for Domestic Workers

Unlike maritime labour standards, standard setting on decent work for domestic workers was late in coming, and the historic 2011 convention and recommendation adopted by the International Labour Conference at its hundredth session was also a first. Yet while maritime labour standards affect over a million seafarers worldwide—mostly men—a labour standard on domestic workers is estimated to affect over 67.1 million people—mostly women. Both categories of workers travel the world under arduous conditions.

As the extract from the ILO Decent Work for Domestic Workers Convention, 2011 suggests, the convention and its accompanying, non-binding recommendation, do not use the language of slavery or trafficking. However, much of the advocacy and even court litigation tends to employ this language.

Convention (No 189) Concerning Decent Work for Domestic Workers, ILO, 16 June 2011, 2955 UNTS 1 (entered into force 5 September 2013)

> *Recognizing the significant contribution of domestic workers to the global economy, which includes increasing paid job opportunities for women and men workers with family responsibilities, greater scope for caring for ageing populations, children and persons with a disability, and substantial income transfers within and between countries, and*
>
> *Considering that domestic work continues to be undervalued and invisible and is mainly carried out by women and girls, many of whom are migrants or members of disadvantaged communities and who are particularly vulnerable to discrimination in respect of conditions of employment and of work, and to other abuses of human rights, and . . .*

Recalling that international labour Conventions and Recommendations apply to all workers, including domestic workers, unless otherwise provided . . .

Article 3

1. Each Member shall take measures to ensure the effective promotion and protection of the human rights of all domestic workers, as set out in this Convention.

2. Each Member shall, in relation to domestic workers, take the measures set out in this Convention to respect, promote and realize the fundamental principles and rights at work, namely:
(a) freedom of association and the effective recognition of the right to collective bargaining;
(b) the elimination of all forms of forced or compulsory labour;
(c) the effective abolition of child labour; and
(d) the elimination of discrimination in respect of employment and occupation.

3. In taking measures to ensure that domestic workers and employers of domestic workers enjoy freedom of association and the effective recognition of the right to collective bargaining, Members shall protect the right of domestic workers and employers of domestic workers to establish and, subject to the rules of the organization concerned, to join organizations, federations and confederations of their own choosing.
[…]

Article 5

Each Member shall take measures to ensure that domestic workers enjoy effective protection against all forms of abuse, harassment and violence.

Article 6

Each Member shall take measures to ensure that domestic workers, like workers generally, enjoy fair terms of employment as well as decent working conditions and, if they reside in the household, decent living conditions that respect their privacy.
[…]

Article 9

Each Member shall take measures to ensure that domestic workers:
(a) are free to reach agreement with their employer or potential employer on whether to reside in the household;
(b) who reside in the household are not obliged to remain in the household or with household members during periods of daily and weekly rest or annual leave; and
(c) are entitled to keep in their possession their travel and identity documents.

CN v The United Kingdom, No 4239/08 (2013), 56 EHRR 24

9. In early 2003 the applicant began to work as a live-in carer for an elderly Iraqi couple ("Mr and Mrs K"). She found the role physically and emotionally demanding as Mr K. suffered from Parkinson's disease and she was required to change his clothing, feed him, clean him and lift him as necessary. As a result, she was permanently on-call during the day and night. On one Sunday every month she was given a couple of hours leave

but on these occasions she would usually be collected by Mohammed and driven to P.S.'s house for the afternoon. She accepted that after a couple of years she was permitted to take public transport but said she was warned that it was not safe and that she should not speak with anyone.

10. The applicant claimed that the GBP 1,600 Mr and Mrs K. paid every month for her services was sent directly to Mohammed [a live-in caregiver business owner] by cheque. A percentage of that money was passed by Mohammed to P.S. on the apparent understanding that it would be paid to her. However, she received no significant payment for her labour....

42. The applicant complained that at the time of her ill-treatment the Government were in breach of their positive obligations under Article 4 of the Convention to have in place criminal laws penalising forced labour and servitude. Article 4 of the Convention provides as follows:

"1. No one shall be held in slavery or servitude.
2. No one shall be required to perform forced or compulsory labour.
3. For the purpose of this article the term 'forced or compulsory labour' shall not include:
   (a) any work required to be done in the ordinary course of detention imposed according to the provisions of Article 5 of [the] Convention or during conditional release from such detention;
   (b) any service of a military character or, in case of conscientious objectors in countries where they are recognised, service exacted instead of compulsory military service;
   (c) any service exacted in case of an emergency or calamity threatening the life or well-being of the community;
   (d) any work or service which forms part of normal civic obligations."

[...]

47. The applicant submitted that the Government were under a positive obligation to enact domestic law provisions specifically criminalising the conduct prohibited by Article 4; they failed to enact such provisions until 2009; and, as she had made a credible allegation of ill-treatment contrary to Article 4 in 2006, any investigation into her complaints was ineffective as it was not directed at determining whether or not she had been a victim of treatment contrary to Article 4 and could not therefore result in a prosecution....

70. In the present case the applicant alleges that there was a failure properly to investigate her complaints and that this failure was at least in part rooted in defective legislation which did not effectively criminalise treatment falling within the scope of Article 4 of the Convention.

71. The Court observes that in *Rantsev*, in the context of trafficking, it held that in order for an obligation to investigate to have arisen, the circumstances must have given rise to a "credible suspicion" that the applicant had been trafficked. Likewise, it considers that for an obligation to have arisen in the present case, it must be satisfied that the applicant's complaints to the domestic authorities gave rise to a credible suspicion that she had been held in domestic servitude.

72. The Court notes that the authorities were first made aware of the applicant's claim to have been kept in conditions amounting to domestic servitude after she collapsed at

the HSBC bank in Kilburn in August 2006. On 21 September 2006 she made an application for asylum, in the course of which she complained, *inter alia*, that she had been forced to work for the K family without remuneration. Furthermore, in April 2007 the applicant's solicitor wrote to the police and asked that they investigate her case. She was interviewed by the Human Trafficking Team on 21 June 2007 and gave a detailed statement in which she set out her domestic servitude complaints. The Court does not consider that the applicant's complaints concerning her treatment by P.S. and Mohammed were inherently implausible. Indeed, it notes that the circumstances which she described were remarkably similar to the facts of the *Siliadin* case, the only notable differences being that the applicant was older than the applicant in *Siliadin* and that it was an agent—and not her "employers"—who she claimed were responsible for the treatment contrary to Article 4 of the Convention. Although the Government have [*sic*] submitted that the applicant's account was not in fact credible, the Court observes that this was a conclusion reached following further investigation of her complaints. Indeed, the fact that the domestic authorities conducted any investigation into the applicant's complaints strongly indicates that, at least on their face, they were not inherently implausible. Consequently, the Court considers that the applicant's complaints did give rise to a credible suspicion that she had been held in conditions of domestic servitude, which in turn placed the domestic authorities under an obligation to investigate those complaints....

80. ... In the present case, the Court considers that due to the absence of a specific offence of domestic servitude, the domestic authorities were unable to give due weight to these factors. In particular, the Court is concerned by the fact that during the course of the investigation into the applicant's complaints, no attempt appears to have been made to interview P.S. despite the gravity of the offence he was alleged to have committed (see, by way of comparison, *M. and Others v. Italy and Bulgaria*, no. 40020/03, §§ 104 - 107, 31 July 2012). For the Court, the lacuna in domestic law at the time may explain this omission, together with the fact that no apparent weight was attributed to the applicant's allegations that her passport had been taken from her, that P.S. had not kept her wages for her as agreed, and that she was explicitly and implicitly threatened with denunciation to the immigration authorities, even though these factors were among those identified by the ILO as indicators of forced labour.

81. Consequently, the Court finds that the investigation into the applicant's complaints of domestic servitude was ineffective due to the absence of specific legislation criminalising such treatment.

82. Accordingly, there has been a violation of Article 4 of the Convention.

2:340 Self-Regulatory Initiatives

Self-regulation has emerged in the transnational economy as a response to a characteristic set of regulatory challenges and opportunities presented most directly and extensively in global supply chain production. These are outlined in the following excerpt.

CHAPTER 2: INTERNATIONAL AND TRANSNATIONAL LABOUR LAW

Kevin Kolben, "Transnational Private Labour Regulation, Consumer-Citizenship and the Consumer Imaginary" in Adelle Blackett & Anne Trebilcock, eds, *Research Handbook on Transnational Labour Law* (Cheltenham, UK: Edward Elgar Publishing, 2016) at 362–66

The effective management of global supply chains has become an important source of competitive advantage for today's corporation. Logistics and procurement, once considered to be secondary functions, have become core business activities upon which businesses succeed or fail. Prominent retailers such as Wal-Mart have come to dominate the market in no small part due to their incredible supply chain efficiency and power, becoming price-makers that can make or break their suppliers. Brands such as Nike and Apple manufacture nothing themselves—they are primarily design, retail, and marketing companies that rely on a far-flung and complex network of suppliers to manufacture and deliver its products. Boeing outsourced about 70 per cent of the manufacturing and even design for its latest 787 airplane, which constituted a significant increase from its previous planes, effectively turning the manufacture and design of its blockbuster new airplane into a highly complex, and in the end unsuccessful, supply chain management project. The list of companies that live and die by their supply chain could continue ad-infinitum. But what is key is that many corporations solely operate as primary contractors (Primaries), that contract out manufacturing and services to secondary contractors (Secondaries). The Secondaries are 'upstream' in the supply chain, and send the goods 'downstream' to the retailers and, finally, the consumers.

The rise of outsourced manufacturing has important implications for labour law, and particularly for transnational labour regulation. In this model, the entity with whom the consumer interacts and has a market relationship is no longer the direct employer of the labour that manufactures the consumed product. This contractual arrangement has clear benefits for the Primary, including protection from any legal responsibility or liability for the employees in the supply chain because human resource management, wages, and labour law compliance become the legal and economic responsibility of the supplier, rather than the primary contractor.

But while the globalization of the supply chain might seem to be in this way advantageous for the Primary, there are there are also risks associated with this strategy. Consumers and civil society have in recent decades increasingly targeted corporations that utilize upstream contractors that are found to have abusive labour conditions in their supply chains. Often, Secondaries are located in countries and jurisdictions whose labour laws are either *de jure* or *de facto* weaker than the jurisdiction of the Primary; and more importantly, those laws may substantially diverge from the normative expectations of civil society and consumers in that jurisdiction.

Out of this tension has emerged the new form of regulation [transnational private labor regulation, or] TPLR. TPLR consists of various forms of non-state, privately generated labour law rules and enforcement systems that are utilized to address labour conditions that do not meet the normative expectations of the Primary or of its stakeholders. Examples of these various private regimes include wholly self-contained corporate supply chain compliance regimes; multi-stakeholder initiatives that include various members of civil society, as well as sometimes corporations; in addition to more hybrid regimes that to some extent include governments.

The political and economic drivers of public regulation are fairly self-evident—upward pressure from labour and other constituencies on the State on one hand, and the desire of employers and the State to maintain industrial peace on the other. The underlying drivers of TPLR regimes, however are different. In TPLR, a key driver has been transnational labour activist networks (TLANs) that have developed in response to labour conditions in global supply chains, and the limited opportunities to remedy them through traditional labour regulation.

TLANs function in the following way. Poor labour conditions and abuses occur in a workplace that manufactures or provides services for export to a given multi-national consumer or contractor. Workers in that workplace, their unions, or other interested civil society organizations that are situated in that State contact, or are contacted by, the affected workers. In a well-functioning democratic regime, the State would be responsive to the demands of domestic constituents and would theoretically respond to such pressure. But in many countries that have jurisdictional authority over Secondaries in global supply chains, the State is often not responsive to such groups.

There are several reasons why this might be the case. One reason is political: That is in producing countries, capital is usually substantially more powerful than are workers and unions, and members of the political class are also often the owners of capital. A second reason is economic: The State might believe that if workers' demands and rights are respected, that the costs of doing business in the country will be too high and will drive away investment. A third reason is technical: States might not have the capacity to enforce their own labour laws.

As a result of state recalcitrance or inability to enforce labour rights domestically, domestic activists will network with NGOs and unions in the home country of the primary contractor, and sometimes directly with consumers, to form TLANs. TLANs deploy a variety of means to compel Primaries to pressure the rights-violating Secondary to alter its behaviour; or even in some rare situations to directly compensate the workers involved if the Secondary is unable or unwilling to do so.

Because of the success of these campaigns over time, the large majority of companies that source globally have instituted compliance programs in their supply chains to try and reduce the number of campaigns directed at them. Often, they create and join industry groups to combine efforts, establishing common codes of conduct for suppliers, and either coordinating or sharing compliance and enforcement systems. Especially for the most vulnerable companies that function in the highly targeted area of garments and apparel, they will join and create multi-stakeholder initiatives that bring together several different stakeholder groups, such as universities, NGOs, and governments to collaborate on compliance in the global supply chain. Private mechanisms of supply chain labour governance are now ubiquitous among companies with extensive supply chain networks, and many companies have sought to mainstream supply chain labour compliance programs into their management structures.

[Reproduced with permission of the Licensor through PLSclear.]

At the 105th Session of the International Labour Conference in 2006, the ILO adopted the resolution concerning decent work in global supply chains, which considered the prospect of standard setting:

Resolution Concerning Decent Work in Global Supply Chains, ILO, 105 Sess, ILC105-PR14-1 (2016), online: www.ilo.org/wcmsp5/groups/public/---ed_norm/---relconf/documents/meetingdocument/wcms_497555.pdf

> The General Conference of the International Labour Organization, having met at Geneva in its 105th Session, 2016,
> Having undertaken a general discussion on the basis of Report IV, Decent work in global supply chains, 1. Adopts the following conclusions ...
>
> *Conclusions concerning decent work in global supply chains*
> [...]
> 25. There is concern that current ILO standards may not be fit for purpose to achieve decent work in global supply chains. Therefore, the ILO should review this issue and convene, as soon as appropriate, by decision of the Governing Body, a technical tripartite meeting or a meeting of experts to: (a) Assess the failures which lead to decent work deficits in global supply chains. (b) Identify the salient challenges of governance to achieving decent work in global supply chains. (c) Consider what guidance, programmes, measures, initiatives or standards are needed to promote decent work and/or facilitate reducing decent work deficits in global supply chains.

While the ILO Committee of Experts met in November 2017 and identified avenues for multilateral cooperation, standard setting has not been recommended on this topic.

*****

Even if it is accepted that public transnational institutions are needed to regulate the labour market, and especially the behaviour of multinational companies, we are a long way from having such institutions—even in Europe, where the most progress is thought to have been made. A wide range of organizations that operate transnationally have built capacity to regulate corporate behaviour, local labour standards, and/or workers' rights. The results of their efforts are not neutral, nor is their emergence coincidental. Rather, they are a reminder of globalization's fundamentally asymmetrical nature.

Adelle Blackett, "Global Governance, Legal Pluralism and the Decentered State: A Labor Law Critique of Codes of Corporate Conduct" (2001) 8 *Indiana Journal of Global Legal Studies* 401 at 403–6

> [C]orporate self-regulatory initiatives tend to apply where certain governmental regulations—notably in the labor field, and often concerning freedom of association—legally do not apply, or systematically are not enforced: in EPZs [export processing zones]....
> ... The periphery is a key element of globalization's asymmetries.
> Host countries create EPZs through special re-regulatory laws in order to attract MNEs [multinational enterprises], whose activities are expected to spur economic development. A tangible contribution of the MNEs, which often boast annual revenues that exceed the GNP of the countries in which they do business, is the foreign investment that they provide. However, the contribution via taxation is often reduced through fiscal incentives to attract foreign direct investment. In addition, MNEs may create backward and forward linkages with local industry, particularly to the extent that they draw

on locally-produced goods in their production processes. There may also be some transfer of technology and expertise. Essentially, however, the contribution flows through the workers. The workers are often young women who have migrated from rural areas to find opportunities in the wage economy. They invariably redistribute their wages to family members throughout the country. Ultimately, the contribution to the host company is not the product itself, as the product is meant for export.

Although they travel across national borders to territories within the host country's legal jurisdiction, MNEs generally concentrate their offshore activities in zones that are specifically created in developing or transition economies to facilitate the export of the MNEs' products. Workers in EPZs are thrust into the post-modern system of just-in-time flexible accumulation as they enter the deterritorialized legal order of the MNEs, living and producing by their norms. Yet, they do so in particular places that may harken back to the Dickensian conditions of nineteenth-century industrialization.

Corporate self-regulatory schemes perfectly fit the EPZ model. Logically, an enterprise that establishes itself in an EPZ would seek to avoid entangling itself in a web of local regulation and enforcement. Indeed, the simplified, "deregulated" nature of these zones is meant to attract MNEs. This is not to suggest that all host countries explicitly exclude EPZs from the scope of all national labor legislation, although the tendency certainly has been noted. But the poor enforcement that may prevail throughout the host country is non-existent within EPZs. EPZs are generally operated by EPZ Authorities housed in Ministries of Trade or Foreign Affairs, outside of the purview of comparatively weak Ministries of Labor. Physical access to EPZs is also frequently restricted, prohibiting access not only to trade unions, but also to Labor Ministry officials, including their labor inspectors. In a report to the ILO, a Turkish workers' organization captured the EPZ experience as "another country in the country".

The cumulative result of MNEs in many EPZs is the de facto deregulation of labor relations in these zones. In its place, a new form of legality—corporate self-regulation via the product—is proffered. In this regard, EPZs crystallize the product/production process dichotomy so typical of the new international division of labor, and are intimately linked to the development of transnational consumerism through trade, which is at the core of corporate self-regulatory schemes.

[Copyright © 2001, Indiana Journal of Global Legal Studies. Reprinted with permission of Indiana University Press.]

As the above excerpts indicate, self-regulatory initiatives are not purely voluntary. Most are a response to pressures from consumer, worker, and other organizations that pose risks to brand value and sales revenue. It is probably fair to say that the greater such risks, the more extensive the self-regulatory response. There are a variety of self-regulatory initiatives in the transnational economy, ranging from generally worded unilateral corporate codes without monitoring or enforcement mechanisms, to multi-stakeholder initiatives providing for detailed monitoring, reporting, and problem-solving institutions. For an overview of the range of initiatives and a theory of the incentives and pressures leading to their adoption, see Kevin Banks and Elizabeth Shilton, "Corporate Commitments to Freedom of Association: Is There a Role for Enforcement Under Canadian Law?" (2012) 33:4 *Comparative Labor Law & Policy Journal* 495 at 503–9 and 537–43.

The following vignette takes a look at an extensive multi-stakeholder response to a disastrous and tragic regulatory failure in Bangladesh. Consider whether even such initiatives can be fully effective in the face of economic and political forces compromising the willingness and ability of the state to regulate.

2:341   Vignette—Rana Plaza

Juliane Reinecke & Jimmy Donaghey, "After Rana Plaza: Building Coalitional Power for Labour Rights between Unions and (Consumption-Based) Social Movement Organisations" (2015) 22:5 *Organization* 720 at 720–21, 724–25, and 736–37

> On 24th April 2013, in the Savar suburb of Dhaka, a building complex which housed several garment factories collapsed leaving 1129 garment workers dead and a further 2500 injured. The building had seen four floors added without planning permission and was originally built as a shopping complex and office block, not a number of factories housing over 3000 mainly female workers and their machines. After the collapse, it quickly emerged that factories based in the complex produced for a checklist of household brands in developed countries including Primark and Walmart to name a few. While these multinational corporations had no legal duty of care to these workers, pressure grew on them to take responsibility for the incident. Within weeks of the disaster, a host of leading clothing brands had signed up to the "Accord for Fire and Building Safety in Bangladesh" (Hereon "The Accord"), which is unprecedented in its scope and legally binding nature. However the story is more complex than simply following a horrific human tragedy, a group of leading brands devised and signed up to the Accord to improve building safety in Bangladesh.
>
> [...]
>
> ### Global supply chains and the regulation of labour
>
> A consistent theme of the employment relations literature over the past two decades has been that the traditional system of national labour regulation, in which trade unions were the driving force of labour governance, is under strain in the globalized economy. An area of growing focus has been upon the shift in the regulation of labour from the national level to the global level (Meardi and Marginson, 2014) where production is distributed across global supply chains (Gereffi, et al, 2004). Global supply chains pose a particular challenge to traditional forms of regulating labour in that they are often used explicitly to avoid regulation. Amidst growing debate on new forms of private, transnational governance, scholars have focused both on the shifting role of "traditional" actors within global labour governance, such as organized labour, as well as the role of "new" actors, such as consumers and collective actors who attempt to mobilise consumption power (Fransen and Burgoon, 2013). As a fragmented and polycentric patchwork of regulatory initiatives and hybrid forms of governance emerge, it has remained unclear what roles different actors play, how they can assert power in supply chain actors and how they can meaningfully cooperate.
>
> [...]

The Accord for Fire and Building Safety in Bangladesh

The Accord which emerged in response to Rana Plaza is a prime example of the complementarity of consumption and production-based actors coming together to facilitate the creation of innovative governance mechanisms. The Accord reflects the mobilization of consumption power at the downstream end of buyer-led supply chains, as brands were pressured to protect their brand image vis-à-vis the critical scrutiny of their consumers. For instance, the Workers' Rights Consortium mobilized students as consumers of university-licenced apparel in the United States and Canada to include the Accord into university licence agreements. The Clean Clothes Campaign educated consumers about the brands sourcing from Rana Plaza and mobilised them to put pressure on brands to sign the Accord. But the Accord also reflects the mobilization of production power, as global unions pushed for going beyond surface-level changes towards a more substantive agreement. The result is an unprecedented, legally binding agreement between global union federations, IndustriALL and UNI Global Union, Bangladeshi trade unions, and over 190 ready-made garment retailers and brands from 20 countries in Europe, North America, Asia and Australia, with four social movement organisations as "Witness Signatories" (Clean Clothes Campaign, Workers Rights Consortium, International Labor Rights Forum, Maquila Solidarity Network). Signatories agree to implement:

- Independent safety inspections by qualified engineering experts
- Support for factory remediation to ensure compliance with building, fire and electrical safety standards while maintaining employment for workers
- Worker participation in Occupational Health & Safety Committees and training
- Provision of worker complaints mechanisms & right to refuse unsafe work
- Transparent disclosure of all ready-made garment suppliers and sub-contractors, inspection reports and quarterly progress reports.

There is a complaints procedure which has a binding arbitration system where all signatories agree that awards and enforcement of fees may be pursued in their respective national legal systems. To ensure a solid commitment to the Accord, companies agree to a long-term sourcing relationship with Bangladesh, maintaining purchasing volumes for five years, thus providing an incentive for suppliers to invest in safety improvement. Brands commit to ensure that factories have the financial capacity to maintain safe workplaces and comply with remediation requirements through providing loans, accessing donor or government support or through offering other business incentives. Signatory firms agree to terminate contracts with factories that fail safety inspections. Companies assume responsibility for funding the activities of the Steering Committee, Safety Inspectors and Training Coordinators based on their annual volumes of garment purchases from Bangladesh on a sliding, pro-rata scale up to $500,000 per annum. The training foresees a central role for workers and worker representatives, including direct trade union participation in factory training and factory inspections. Demonstrating a commitment to transparency, all supplier factories and inspection reports as well as corrective action plans are made publically available on the Accord's website. The Accord specializes in three types of inspection—fire, electrical and structural—for which specialist engineers are contracted in contrast to social auditors who are ill-qualified to assess many of the crucial safety aspects....

The Accord is a unique governance mechanism. Understanding the conditions that enabled it to emerge offers potentially important lessons for the development of meaningful global governance institutions in other contexts....

The Accord and, in particular, the complementary capacities developed in its Labour Caucus does carry important lessons for future research. Based on our analysis of how campaign groups and trade unions coordinated a unified response to the 2013 Rana Plaza disaster, we argue that the intersection of production and consumption power, which has received little attention to date, is a potent mechanism that can foster labour rights in global supply chains. This research complements that of industrial relations scholars and social movement scholars by offering understanding of how distinctive leverage points of different governance actors can interact in complementary ways to create coalitional power. The consumer-driven and market-based logic of corporate social responsibility and the collective bargaining-based logic of industrial relations are not necessarily mutually exclusive. The interface of these logics may provide a fruitful avenue for scholarly engagement.

[© 2015 by Organization. Reprinted by Permission of SAGE Publications, Ltd.]

Janelle Diller, "Pluralism and Privatization in Transnational Labour Regulation: Experience of the International Labour Organization" in Adelle Blackett & Anne Trebilcock, eds, *Research Handbook on Transnational Labour Law* (Cheltenham, UK: Edward Elgar Publishing, 2015) at 334–40

Based on its long history of convening sectoral industry dialogues at international level, ILO cooperation in countries active in the textile and garment sector has focused on improving working conditions and competitiveness, and providing for protection of workers' interests including through employment injury benefits. The ILO country projects bring together national tripartite constituents with transnational corporations, global union federations, and non- governmental organizations. The aim, governance, functioning and results of three such models are compared below.

Better Work Program

Drawing on a model piloted in Cambodia, the Better Work program evolved in 2009 as a partnership between the ILO and the International Finance Corporation, a member of the World Bank Group with a mandate for private sector development. The program, now operating in seven countries, covers almost 1000 factories and over 1 million workers and aims to help 3 million workers by 2017. Buyers in the apparel industry sign up to ILO-monitored inspections of their factories in selected countries, and agree to public reporting of results. Although assessment of workplace compliance is the most visible output, Better Work conducts training and provides advice to employers' and workers' organizations to promote workplace social dialogue and improved management practices. Financing is donated primarily by public development agencies, and by direct revenue from charges for services to factories and global buyers enrolled in the programme.

Better Work is governed at international level by a Management Group comprised of ILO and IFC [International Finance Corporation] officials, and is guided by an Advisory

Committee of representatives of donor governments, international employers and workers organizations, buyers and independent experts. At country level, national tripartite Project Advisory Committees, chaired by the government and including the social partners, approve national compliance assessment tools, and advise on national and sectoral priorities and engagement with national institutions.

The ILO reports steady improvements in workplace compliance with national labour law and international labour standards in Better Work countries. The improvements have positive impact on worker health and well-being and countries' social and economic development. The factories involved independently report productivity and thus increased sales, production capacity and expanded employment. For the ILO, closer engagement with labour administrations and employers' and workers' organizations is seen as essential to growing "synergies and accountability between the efforts of the international supply chain and national constituents." Such complementarity serves to strengthen rather than duplicate or replace national regulation. As improvements occur in the textiles and garment sector, the program may serve as a catalyst to progress beyond the sector by strengthening national institutional capacity and correcting structural weaknesses in labour laws and their enforcement and in industrial relations.

Bangladesh Accord on Fire and Building Safety
The Bangladesh Accord on Fire and Building Safety is a five-year program (2013-2018) to build safe workplaces in Bangladesh. The agreement built upon a National Tripartite Action Plan agreed by the government of Bangladesh with employers' and workers' organizations to enhance factory building safety. The Accord was initiated by two global union federations (GUFs) in the textile and garment sector and eventually signed by more than 170 apparel companies as well as Bangladeshi unions and four international NGO witnesses. Each company commits to independent safety inspections at Bangladesh factories in their supply chain and public reporting of results, and to continue sourcing from Bangladesh for a five-year term subject to commercial viability and to factory compliance with contractual terms agreed. Remediation, prevention and redress are the primary aims of the Accord.

The Accord is governed by a Steering Committee appointed by the signatories with equal representation from trade unions and companies. The ILO serves as neutral chair. An NGO set up by the Accord parties oversees the inspection system financed by the signatory companies. The Government and local industry are not parties, but are to be consulted in administration and management of the program. While the Government's inspection standards apply in principle, the ILO helps to coordinate their application in practice among the actors involved and advises on relevant international labour standards.

Where an inspection discovers corrective action is necessary, signatory companies are to require the factory to undertake time-bound renovations. If closure of the factory is required, the companies are to help their suppliers maintain workers' employment relationships and regular income up to six months and thereafter take reasonable efforts to offer employment with safe suppliers. Signatory companies must also require their supplier factories, in line with ILO standards, to respect the right of a worker to refuse work that is unsafe, without discrimination or loss of pay in reprisal. A worker complaint process permits access by workers to the Safety Inspector. Complaints by local trade unions involving particular factories or workers are decided by the Steering Committee and, if resolution is unsatisfactory, the trade unions as Accord parties may invoke arbitration, with enforcement of awards in home courts of signatories.

The ILO offers its constituents and the Accord parties a means to coordinate and facilitate local and transnational effort to strengthen the labour inspectorate and workplace health and safety mechanisms in Bangladesh. The aim is to eventually replicate the methods used in the apparel sector model for inspection and safety in other workplaces in the country....

The ILO's relationship to pluralistic and privatized transnational labour initiatives may be assessed through the following early observations and conclusions that emerge from this review of the developing patterns of ILO standard-setting and cooperation described above.

The ILO's innovations in exercising standard-setting authority have the potential to strengthen national capacity to regulate transnational labour activities through innovations by focusing its content, design, and enforcement methods on national regulatory mandates over work relations affected by transnational activity. The scope of recent ILS extends to workers formerly unrecognized or excluded from legal protection, and mobilizes Members' collaboration with each other as they undertake national measures and action that address transnational forces and arenas of industrial relations. The enforcement model of the Maritime Labour Convention builds shared responsibility among countries and effective remedies for labour conditions arising in a highly globalized sector. Based on an agreed set of standards implemented through complementary public and private effort, the MLC offers a remarkably cohesive model for other transnational labour situations.

In international cooperation methods, ILO's exercise of international public authority builds on its legitimacy as the global standards authority in the world of work including in the field of labour inspection. Using this institutional convening base, the ILO programs aim to increase collaboration and accountability between national tripartite constituents and transnational actors. As a matter of international institutional law, ILO's in-country models are based on constitutionally its attributed powers and functions. The use by Bangladesh of an ILO Convention that it has not ratified in the context of mass claims settlement suggests a novel means for invoking legitimacy to strengthen a weak domestic legal regime in the face of dominant TNC operations. As a powerful tool, Better Work offers its Members demonstrated socio-economic benefits from compliance with ILS and, as such, calls for equality of access as between similarly situated countries seeking its services. [Reproduced with permission of the Licensor through PLSclear.]

Aruna Kashyap, "The April 24 Ritual—Rana Plaza's Unfinished Legacy" (24 April 2018), *Human Rights Watch,* **online: www.hrw.org/news/2018/04/24/april-24-ritual-rana-plazas-unfinished-legacy**

Within five years of the building collapse, one of two large private fire and building safety initiatives in Bangladesh—the Alliance on Bangladesh Worker Safety (Alliance), a safety effort mostly led by North American brands—announced that it is preparing to wrap up and hand over operations to an "independent, credible, locally-led organization," developed in partnership with the Bangladesh government and the Bangladesh Garment Manufacturers and Exporters Association (BGMEA).

The other private initiative—the Bangladesh Accord on Fire and Building Safety (Accord), led mostly by European brands has extended its work till 2021, saying its operations would continue "beyond May 2018 as all parties recognize, substantial additional capacity-building is necessary before responsibility to protect workers in factories producing for Accord signatory brands can be responsibly handed over to a national regulatory body." The extended Accord includes small yet concrete improvements that give protections for workers' freedom of association more teeth.

These two initiatives, both led by reputed brands, came to very different conclusions about what has changed in the past five years, which raises the question—why?

Could it be that having workers centrally involved in designing and contributing to the administration of an initiative offers a worker perspective that can better inform decisions about whether to "transition" or stay? To be clear—workers are not just "any" stakeholder in such decisions. They stand on a different footing from other "stakeholders" because they risk paying with their lives and limb.

Worker participation in such initiatives should not be a box checking exercise. When it comes to initiatives that can save workers from dying, participation within an enforceable framework agreement—as is the case with the Accord—allows worker representatives to negotiate protection until they are satisfied that the outcomes contain meaningful procedures to enhance workplace safety. . . .

Brand representatives should look for transparent and detailed reporting by local authorities regarding measures taken to remediate or shut down unsafe factories, including those terminated from the Accord and Alliance. Until now, there has been no such information. Such reporting would indicate the preparedness of the Bangladesh government to adopt and replicate one of the strongest features of the Alliance and the Accord—transparent and periodic reporting of progress—an important check against backsliding and corruption.

Second, a credible complaints process is one of the most important value-added of the private initiatives. The track record of the Bangladesh government when it comes to complaints resolution is especially poor—and brands should be looking more closely at not just numbers but how these complaints are resolved. In the past, the International Labor Organization has repeatedly criticized the Bangladesh authorities' dismal record of resolving complaints concerning unfair labor practices by factories.

Similarly, watching how the Bangladesh government and industry respect factory unions and facilitate mature industry relations is an important indicator of whether transition can work. The Bangladesh government's approach to industrial relations needs to fundamentally shift course. There are key indicators to assess this course correction. Its medieval and brutal tactics of forcibly disappearing workers and union organizers, or arresting journalists who simply write about labor rights needs to end.

In 2012, a union organizer from the Bangladesh Center for Worker Solidarity named Aminul Islam disappeared. Days later, his dead body surfaced. It was widely believed that Bangladesh's security forces were involved in his abduction and murder. But security forces responsible were never held accountable and only a former garment worker who was last known to have called Aminul Islam away from his office before he disappeared was convicted earlier this month.

Similarly, in December 2016, brands threatened to boycott an apparel industry event in Dhaka to get the Bangladesh government to back down from its arbitrary arrests and false criminal cases against union organizers and labor activists following the Ashulia wage protests in the outskirts of Dhaka.

Brands that are serious about transitioning to a credible locally-led system will watch closely how well their supplier factories respect and promote freedom of association, and whether the Bangladesh government abandons its course of misusing criminal laws to muzzle union organizers and leaders.

Third, while the Accord is a much-needed human rights risk prevention, mitigation, and remediation program for workers, it also affords legal risk mitigation for apparel companies who are sourcing from Bangladesh with its credible inspections, monitoring and complaints mechanism for workers, and transparent reporting of progress. According to early April data, 140 apparel companies from amongst the more than 220 original signatories signed the extended Accord, covering 1332 factories.

Committee on Economic, Social and Cultural Rights, *Concluding observations on the initial report of Bangladesh,* **ECOSOC, UN Doc E/C.12/BDG/CO/1 (2018)**

3. The Committee acknowledges the progress that the State party has made since its accession to the Covenant in many areas relating to the rights enshrined therein, particularly regarding poverty reduction. Between 2006 and 2016, the poverty rate was reduced from 38.4 per cent down to 24.3 per cent, per capita income has increased substantially and life expectancy has increased to 71.6 years. The Committee notes the State party's forthcoming graduation from the category of least-developed country....

36. The Committee is concerned that, despite the progress made since the Rana Plaza and Tazreen Fashions factory accidents in 2013, including the adoption of a national occupational health and safety policy, the incidence of deadly occupational accidents remains high in the textile, ship-breaking, stone-crushing and other industries. It is also concerned about the lack of adequate compensation for victims of occupational accidents and for their families, and the delay in the adoption of a national employment injury insurance scheme (arts. 7, 11 and 12).

37. The Committee recommends that the State party redouble its efforts to reduce and prevent occupational accidents, in particular by:

(a) Intensifying labour inspections, particularly in accident-prone industries;
(b) Strengthening the sanctions on employers who fail to comply with regulations;
(c) Fully implementing the national occupational health and safety policy adopted in 2013;
(d) Expediting the adoption of a national employment injury insurance scheme;
(e) Ensuring that all victims of occupational accidents, and their families, are provided with adequate compensation, which should include, as a minimum, the medical treatment necessary for their physical injuries and psychological trauma

* * * * *

2:342 Vignette—The Guiding Principles on Business and Human Rights and Global Supply Chains

In a 2008 report to the UN Human Rights Council, then UN special representative for business and human rights, John Ruggie, presented a framework for addressing the relationship between businesses and human rights, transnational as well as domestic. The framework—"Protect, Respect and Remedy"—rested on three pillars: "the state duty to protect against human rights abuses by third parties, including business, through appropriate policies, regulation, and adjudication; the corporate responsibility to respect human rights, which means to act with due diligence to avoid infringing on the rights of others and to address adverse impacts that occur; and greater access by victims to effective remedy, both judicial and non-judicial." Professor Ruggie presented a set of guiding principles on business and human rights, along with extensive commentary delineating their scope, content, and application, to the UN Human Rights Council in March 2011. Sections of the guiding principles are excerpted below.

John Ruggie, *Guiding Principles on Business and Human Rights: Implementing the United Nations "Protect, Respect and Remedy" Framework*, OHCHR, UN Doc A/HRC/17/31 (2011)

1. States must protect against human rights abuse within their territory and/or jurisdiction by third parties, including business enterprises. This requires taking appropriate steps to prevent, investigate, punish and redress such abuse through effective policies, legislation, regulations and adjudication.

2. States should set out clearly the expectation that all business enterprises domiciled in their territory and/or jurisdiction respect human rights throughout their operations.

3. In meeting their duty to protect, States should:

(a) Enforce laws that are aimed at, or have the effect of, requiring business enterprises to respect human rights, and periodically to assess the adequacy of such laws and address any gaps;

(b) Ensure that other laws and policies governing the creation and ongoing operation of business enterprises, such as corporate law, do not constrain but enable business respect for human rights;

(c) Provide effective guidance to business enterprises on how to respect human rights throughout their operations;

(d) Encourage, and where appropriate require, business enterprises to communicate how they address their human rights impacts.

[...]

10. States, when acting as members of multilateral institutions that deal with business-related issues, should:

(a) Seek to ensure that those institutions neither restrain the ability of their member States to meet their duty to protect nor hinder business enterprises from respecting human rights; ...

11. Business enterprises should respect human rights. This means that they should avoid infringing on the human rights of others and should address adverse human rights impacts with which they are involved.

12. The responsibility of business enterprises to respect human rights refers to internationally recognized human rights—understood, at a minimum, as those expressed in the International Bill of Human Rights and the principles concerning fundamental rights set out in the International Labour Organization's Declaration on Fundamental Principles and Rights at Work....

13. The responsibility to respect human rights requires that business enterprises:

(a) Avoid causing or contributing to adverse human rights impacts through their own activities, and address such impacts when they occur;
(b) Seek to prevent or mitigate adverse human rights impacts that are directly linked to their operations, products or services by their business relationships, even if they have not contributed to those impacts.

14. The responsibility of business enterprises to respect human rights applies to all enterprises regardless of their size, sector, operational context, ownership and structure....

17. In order to identify, prevent, mitigate and account for how they address their adverse human rights impacts, business enterprises should carry out human rights due diligence. The process should include assessing actual and potential human rights impacts, integrating and acting upon the findings, tracking responses, and communicating how impacts are addressed....

22. Where business enterprises identify that they have caused or contributed to adverse impacts, they should provide for or cooperate in their remediation through legitimate processes....

25. As part of their duty to protect against business-related human rights abuse, States must take appropriate steps to ensure, through judicial, administrative, legislative or other appropriate means, that when such abuses occur within their territory and/or jurisdiction those affected have access to effective remedy.

[From *Guiding Principles on Business and Human Rights: Implementing the United Nations "Protect, Respect and Remedy" Framework*, by John Ruggie, ©2011 United Nations. Reprinted with the permission of the United Nations.]

The UN Human Rights Council is now negotiating a legally binding international instrument to regulate the activities of transnational corporations and other businesses; see Human Rights Council, *Elaboration of an International Legally Binding Instrument on Transnational Corporations and Other Business Enterprises with Respect to Human Rights*, UN Doc A/HRC/RES/26/9 (2014). The instrument will build from the *Guiding Principles on Business and Human Rights* as well as other international human rights instruments.

In some sectors, such as the extractive industries, Canadian firms have been directly linked to labour standards and human rights violations abroad. Using the Ruggie principles as a benchmark, the excerpts below detail the legal challenges and complexities in holding such firms accountable.

Penelope Simons & Audrey Macklin, *The Governance Gap: Extractive Industries, Human Rights and the Home State Advantage* (New York: Routledge, 2014) at 1–2, 4–7, 17

At the time, the Canadian government contended that it had no legal means to prevent or sanction Canadian corporations, such as Talisman, operating in these types of zones of weak governance. The Canadian government further claimed to have no means of holding such corporations accountable in situations where, as Talisman had been, they were implicated in grave violations of human rights. NGO campaigns and private litigation in US courts against the company failed, ultimately, although Talisman did eventually withdraw from Sudan. In the end, Talisman sold its interest in the Sudanese oil fields for a profit. As for the victims of the terrible abuses committed by security forces for the purpose of protecting the profitable business assets, there was no recompense....

[T]he UN Human Rights Commission created a new expert mandate, the United Nations Special Representative of the Secretary-General on the Issue of Human Rights and Transnational Corporations and other Business Enterprises (SRSG) and appointed an international relations scholar, Professor John G. Ruggie, to the position. Ruggie genuflected briefly before he pushed back against calls to develop binding international legal obligations for corporate actors. Early in his first mandate, he strongly criticized the draft UN Norms and dismissed them as a basis for moving forward. He argued that the responsibility of governance over transnational corporate behaviour should lie with states, and that any global strategy for regulating such entities should focus first on reinforcing and building on state capacity to regulate the activities of business actors within their territories. Ruggie produced a policy framework and a set of Guiding Principles on Business and Human Rights which were directed at both states and business enterprises. The Framework and the Guiding Principles envisage a polycentric governance framework, which includes both binding and non-binding norms for states and non-binding 'responsibilities' for corporate actors. Thus, beyond voluntary observance by corporate actors and except where their activities violate domestic law, compliance with such human rights responsibilities is to be monitored and enforced by the 'courts of public opinion'. As Ruggie himself concedes, the normative contribution of the Guiding Principles 'lies not in the creation of new international law obligations but in elaborating the implications of existing standards and practices for States and businesses; integrating them within a single, logically coherent and comprehensive template'.

The Human Rights Council adopted the policy framework in June 2008 and three years later unanimously endorsed the Guiding Principles. It also established a Working Group on Human Rights and Transnational Corporations and Other Business Enterprises with a three-year mandate to promote dissemination and implementation of the Guiding Principles, but with no capacity to receive complaints or the power to assess the implementation and efficacy of those principles. Thus, with the exception of the obligation on all non-state actors to comply with international criminal law, there remain no international legal obligations on business actors to respect human rights and no universal grievance mechanisms to which victims can appeal for failures by corporations to comply with the Guiding Principles.

As for states, international human rights law imposes obligations on states to respect, protect and fulfil human rights. The 'obligation to respect' requires states to refrain from action that would violate human rights. Pursuant to the 'obligation to fulfil' states must take positive action through legislative and other measures to fulfil the human rights of individuals. The obligation *to protect* human rights is an obligation to exercise due diligence to ensure that private actors, including corporations, do not violate the rights of individuals who are within a state's territory or otherwise subject to its jurisdiction. Accordingly, states must, through legislation and administrative measures, control, regulate, investigate and prosecute private actors who act or may act in a manner that violates human rights. That said, the protection of individuals from violations of human rights committed by, or with the complicity of foreign corporate actors is complicated by the state-based structure of the international human rights system.

There is disagreement as to the scope of the extraterritorial dimension of the obligation to protect and thus whether there exists a legal duty on home states to exercise due diligence in relation to the extraterritorial human rights impacts of their corporate nationals. It is clear from the jurisprudence of both judicial and quasi-judicial international human rights tribunals and the International Court of Justice that states' obligations under international human rights law are not territorially confined. Rather, states are obliged to protect the human rights of individuals outside of their territory in certain narrowly defined circumstances, that is to say where individuals are subject to the home state's jurisdiction. International human rights tribunals have interpreted the concept of jurisdiction broadly. Thus,

> [a] state can be found to be in violation of its obligations under international human rights treaties for actions taken by it extraterritorially, in relation to anyone within the power, effective control or authority of that state, as well as within an area over which that state exercises effective overall control....

Both general international law and international human rights law presume that the host state will exercise regulatory oversight over transnational corporations and ensure that the activities of such entities do not violate the human rights of individuals and communities subject to the host state's jurisdiction. But, as Susan Marks points out, 'even the most powerful [states] face growing difficulty in controlling the activities of business'....

Talisman's operations in Sudan represent an extreme but in some ways paradigmatic study of the human rights implications of extractive industry investment in zones of weak governance. It is paradigmatic in so far as it replays the narrative of a transnational entity headquartered in a governance-rich state (Canada) that operates through a matrix of subsidiaries and joint ventures in a resource-rich and governance-poor region. As in most cases, the alleged wrongdoing by the company resided less in direct perpetration of harm than in wilful blindness and complicity in the violations committed by the principal state actors. The emergent role of civil society in applying political pressure on home state governments and on market actors was also a prominent feature of the Talisman episode and of many subsequent campaigns....
[Reproduced by permission of Taylor & Francis Books UK.]

2:350 The Jurisdiction of Canadian Courts in Transnational Litigation

Human rights and labour standards violations abroad by firms or enterprises abroad that are affiliated in some way with Canada may raise questions about the extraterritorial reach of domestic law; they may also engage private international law concerns, such as whether Canadian courts are the appropriate forum in which to hear disputes involving foreign actors, foreign law, or both.

Canadian courts have begun to address their jurisdiction to hold Canadian corporations liable for wrongs committed abroad by the corporation or its subsidiaries. They are also grappling the implications of doctrines such as *forum non conveniens*. Determinations on these issues are directly relevant to the litigation of workers' rights and labour standards. In a number of cases, courts have determined that they do have jurisdiction to hear such claims; as a result, there are likely to be cases in the near future where courts address the issues on their merits.

Garcia v Tahoe Resources Inc, 2017 BCCA 39

[1] On April 27, 2013, private security personnel employed at a Canadian-owned mine in Guatemala allegedly shot and injured Adolfo Agustin Garcia as well as six other Guatemalan individuals during a protest outside the Escobal mine. The mine is owned by the respondent, Tahoe Resources Inc., through its wholly owned subsidiaries. The seven plaintiffs commenced an action for damages against Tahoe in the Supreme Court of British Columbia. Tahoe, a British Columbia company, conceded that the Court had jurisdiction over the claim but applied for an order that the court exercise its discretion to decline jurisdiction on the grounds that Guatemala was the more appropriate forum for adjudicating the plaintiffs' claims. Madam Justice Gerow granted the *forum non conveniens* application sought by Tahoe and stayed the British Columbia action.

[2] The application primarily turned on the judge's assessment of the plaintiffs' ability to obtain a fair trial in Guatemala. The judge concluded that they could. The plaintiffs appeal from the judge's order....

[3] On this appeal, the appellants contend that the judge erred in law in imposing on them the burden of proving that justice could never be done in Guatemala; they say that the correct test is "whether the evidence discloses a real risk of an unfair trial process in the foreign court". Tahoe says that the appellants' arguments demonstrate a "parochial attitude towards countries that follow the civil law procedural tradition". It says that the judge properly concluded that the appellants' evidence did not meet the necessary standard of proof to justify a refusal to decline jurisdiction....

[123] In my view, the judge erred in considering the issue of corruption and injustice in the Guatemalan judiciary as a secondary stage in the analysis with the burden on the appellants to rebut her *prima facie* determination that Guatemala was the more appropriate forum. In addition, the judge erred in defining the question as whether Guatemalan courts were "capable" of providing justice....

[126] In my view, the judge erred by considering the risk of unfairness as a secondary stage in the *forum non conveniens* analysis and by defining the question as whether Guatemala was "capable" of providing justice. As a result, she gave insufficient weight to the evidence of weakness and lack of independence in the Guatemalan justice system in her discretionary weighing of the factors, particularly given the context in which the alleged shooting occurred. The evidence of weakness in the Guatemalan justice system ought not to be ignored....

V. Conclusion Regarding Stand-alone Civil Suit

[127] As LeBel J. said in *Breeden*, the *forum non conveniens* analysis does not require that all factors point to the defendant's proposed alternate forum, but it does require that the

defendant establish that the alternate forum is *clearly* more appropriate. In this case, the judge found that Tahoe had established that Guatemala was clearly the more appropriate forum. However, in my view, ... three factors discussed ... weigh against such a finding with regards to the stand-alone civil suit. The judge erred in finding that these three factors did not weigh against the suitability of Guatemala. The first factor is the limited discovery procedures available to the appellants in Guatemala; the second is the marked uncertainty as to how the expiration of the limitation period will be treated by Guatemalan courts; and the third is the real risk that the appellants will not obtain justice in Guatemala given the context of the dispute and the evidence of endemic corruption in the Guatemalan judiciary.

[128] I conclude that the judge did not give adequate consideration to the difficulties the appellants will face in bringing suit against Tahoe given the limited discovery procedures available in Guatemala. This factor weighs against a finding that Guatemala is the more appropriate forum.

[129] I find that the judge erred by concluding that the expiration of the limitation period for bringing a civil suit in Guatemala would not affect the appellants' claim. The expert evidence does not support such a conclusion. In my view, the uncertainty occasioned by the expiration of the limitation period is a juridical advantage factor that weighs heavily against a conclusion that Guatemala is the more appropriate forum. This is a significant factor because it casts doubt on whether the appellants will be able to advance a claim against Tahoe in Guatemala at all.

[130] I conclude that the judge erred by ignoring the context of this dispute and placing insufficient weight on the risk that the appellants will not receive a fair trial in Guatemala. That risk should not be ignored. In reaching this conclusion, I make no general pronouncement on Guatemala's legal system. Rather, I simply conclude that there is some measurable risk that the appellants will encounter difficulty in receiving a fair trial against a powerful international company whose mining interests in Guatemala align with the political interests of the Guatemalan state. This factor points away from Guatemala as the more appropriate forum.

[131] In the result, I conclude the judge erred in finding that Tahoe had established that Guatemala was clearly a more appropriate forum than British Columbia for adjudication of the appellants' claims.

Chevron Corp v Yaiguaje, 2015 SCC 42

[1] In a world in which businesses, assets, and people cross borders with ease, courts are increasingly called upon to recognize and enforce judgments from other jurisdictions. Sometimes, successful recognition and enforcement in another forum is the only means by which a foreign judgment creditor can obtain its due. Normally, a judgment creditor will choose to commence recognition and enforcement proceedings in a forum where the judgment debtor has assets. In this case, however, the Court is asked to determine whether the Ontario courts have jurisdiction to recognize and enforce an Ecuadorian judgment where the foreign judgment debtor, Chevron Corporation ("Chevron"), claims to have no connection with the province, whether through assets or otherwise. The Court is also asked to determine whether the Ontario courts have jurisdiction over a

Canadian subsidiary of Chevron, Chevron Canada Limited ("Chevron Canada"), a stranger to the foreign judgment for which recognition and enforcement is being sought.

[2] The courts below found that jurisdiction existed over Chevron. They held that the only connection that must be proven for recognition and enforcement to proceed is one between the foreign court and the original action on the merits; there is no preliminary need to prove a connection with Ontario for jurisdiction to exist in recognition and enforcement proceedings. They also found there to be an independent jurisdictional basis for proceeding against Chevron Canada due to the place of business it operates in the province, and at which it had been duly served.

[3] I agree with the outcomes reached by the courts below with respect to both Chevron and Chevron Canada and I would dismiss the appeal. In an action to recognize and enforce a foreign judgment where the foreign court validly assumed jurisdiction, there is no need to prove that a real and substantial connection exists between the enforcing forum and either the judgment debtor or the dispute. It makes little sense to compel such a connection when, owing to the nature of the action itself, it will frequently be lacking. Nor is it necessary, in order for the action to proceed, that the foreign debtor contemporaneously possess assets in the enforcing forum. Jurisdiction to recognize and enforce a foreign judgment within Ontario exists by virtue of the debtor being served on the basis of the outstanding debt resulting from the judgment. This is the case for Chevron. Jurisdiction also exists here with respect to Chevron Canada because it was validly served at a place of business it operates in the province. On the traditional jurisdictional grounds, this is sufficient to find jurisdiction.

II. Backgrounds and Facts

[4] The dispute underlying the appeal originated in the Lago Agrio region of Ecuador. The oil-rich area has long attracted the exploration and extraction activities of global oil companies, including Texaco, Inc. ("Texaco"). As a result of those activities, the region is said to have suffered extensive environmental pollution that has, in turn, disrupted the lives and jeopardized the futures of its residents. The 47 respondents ("plaintiffs") represent approximately 30,000 indigenous Ecuadorian villagers. For over 20 years, they have been seeking legal accountability as well as financial and environmental reparation for harms they allegedly have suffered due to Texaco's former operations in the region. Texaco has since merged with Chevron.

[5] In 1993, the plaintiffs filed suit against Texaco in the United States District Court for the Southern District of New York. In 2001, after lengthy interim proceedings, the District Court dismissed their suit on the grounds of international comity and *forum non conveniens*. The following year, the United States Court of Appeals for the Second Circuit upheld that judgment, relying in part on a commitment by Texaco to submit to the jurisdiction of the Ecuadorian courts should its motion to dismiss succeed: *Aguinda v. Texaco, Inc.*, 303 F.3d 470 (2d Cir. 2002).

[6] In 2003, the plaintiffs filed suit against Chevron in the Provincial Court of Justice of Sucumbíos. Several years of litigation ensued. In 2011, Judge Zambrano ruled in the plaintiffs' favour, and ordered Chevron to pay US$8.6 billion in environmental damages, as well as US$8.6 billion in punitive damages that were to be awarded unless Chevron

apologized within 14 days of the judgment. As Chevron did not apologize, the punitive damages award remained intact. In January 2012, the Appellate Division of the Provincial Court of Justice of Sucumbíos affirmed the trial judgment. In November 2013, Ecuador's Court of Cassation upheld the Appellate Division's judgment, except on the issue of punitive damages. In the end, the total amount owed was reduced to US$9.51 billion.

[7] Meanwhile, Chevron instituted further U.S. proceedings against the plaintiffs' American lawyer, Steven Donziger, and two of his Ecuadorian clients, seeking equitable relief. Chevron alleged that Mr. Donziger and his team had corrupted the Ecuadorian proceedings by, among other things, ghost-writing the trial judgment and paying Judge Zambrano US$500,000 to release it as his own. In 2011, Judge Kaplan of the United States District Court for the Southern District of New York granted preliminary relief in the form of a global anti-enforcement injunction with respect to the Ecuadorian judgment: *Chevron Corp. v. Donziger*, 768 F.Supp.2d 581 (S.D.N.Y. 2011). The United States Court of Appeals for the Second Circuit overturned this injunction in 2012, stressing that "[t]he [plaintiffs] hold a judgment from an Ecuadorian court. They may seek to enforce that judgment in any country in the world where Chevron has assets": *Chevron Corp. v. Naranjo*, 667 F.3d 232 (2d Cir. 2012), at pp. 245-46. In 2014, Judge Kaplan of the District Court held that the Ecuadorian judgment had resulted from fraud committed by Mr. Donziger and others on the Ecuadorian courts: *Chevron Corp. v. Donziger*, 974 F.Supp.2d 362 (S.D.N.Y. 2014). That decision and the underlying allegations of fraud are not before this Court.

[8] Since the initial judgment, Chevron has refused to acknowledge or pay the debt that the trial court said it owed, and it does not hold any Ecuadorian assets. Faced with this situation, the plaintiffs have turned to the Canadian courts for assistance in enforcing the Ecuadorian judgment, and obtaining their financial due. On May 30, 2012, after the Appellate Division's decision but prior to the release of the 2013 judgment of the Court of Cassation, they commenced an action for recognition and enforcement of the Ecuadorian judgment against Chevron, Chevron Canada and Chevron Canada Finance Limited in the Ontario Superior Court of Justice. The action against the latter has since been discontinued....

Conclusion

[94] Chevron Canada was served *in juris*, in accordance with rule 16.02(1)(c), at a place of business it operates in Mississauga, Ontario. Traditional, presence-based jurisdiction is satisfied. Jurisdiction is thus established with respect to it. As indicated for Chevron, the establishment of jurisdiction does not mean that the plaintiffs will necessarily succeed in having the Ecuadorian judgment recognized and enforced against Chevron Canada. A finding of jurisdiction does nothing more than afford the plaintiffs the opportunity to seek recognition and enforcement of the Ecuadorian judgment. Once past the jurisdictional stage, Chevron Canada, like Chevron, can use the available procedural tools to try to dispose of the plaintiffs' allegations. This possibility is foreign to and remote from the questions that must be resolved on this appeal.

[95] Further, my conclusion that the Ontario courts have jurisdiction in this case should not be understood to prejudice future arguments with respect to the distinct corporate personalities of Chevron and Chevron Canada. I take no position on whether Chevron Canada can properly be considered a judgment-debtor to the Ecuadorian

judgment. Similarly, should the judgment be recognized and enforced against Chevron, it does not automatically follow that Chevron Canada's shares or assets will be available to satisfy Chevron's debt.

2:400 MIGRANT LABOUR: LEGAL REGULATION AND CONSTRUCTION OF VULNERABILITY

As discussed above in Section 2:230, the international migration of workers is a growing feature of today's globalized economic system. It is also one the least regulated, as there are few effective multilateral international norms governing the migration of workers. The ILO Conventions mentioned below remain only lightly ratified. The regulation of migration thus most often falls to the discretion of so-called sending and receiving states.

Few states effectively regulate private recruitment practices, creating potential for abuses, discussed below. Further, many receiving states simply have no laws providing legal resident status to international migrants. Those that do, like Canada, often restrict worker rights to remain in residence, tying them to particular jobs and making them temporary. The restrictions can place workers in vulnerable positions in the labour market, even as labour and employment laws seek to protect against the consequences of such vulnerability. The result is complex interplay between legal regimes, one which first constructs and then seeks to counter worker vulnerability. The following passages introduce some key issues.

Fay Faraday, *Profiting From the Precarious: How Recruitment Practices Exploit Migrant Workers* (Toronto: George Cedric Metcalf Foundation, 2014) at 5–9 and 11–12, online: https://metcalffoundation.com/wp-content/uploads/2014/04/Profiting-from-the-Precarious.pdf

> Over the past decade, Canadian employers have increasingly demanded access to a "flexible" workforce of transnational migrant workers. In response, Canadian laws and policies have been created or expanded to bring workers to Canada with precarious temporary immigration status. As temporary labour migration has exploded, an industry of third-party, for-profit labour recruiters has emerged to match migrant workers with employers in Canada and facilitate workers' movement across national borders.
>
> It is true that "reputable recruiters [can] provide a valuable service helping to place foreign workers with companies, legitimately earning their fee from the employers." However, widespread abuse of migrant workers by disreputable recruiters who charge workers oppressive "recruitment fees" for jobs—including fees for non-existent jobs and jobs significantly different than promised—has been documented by academic and community-based researchers for years. These abuses continue to be documented on an ongoing basis. Government reports have similarly raised the alarm about exploitation by recruiters. Yet, Canadian governments have only recently begun to develop laws to target this problem. As abusive practices persist in the face of the law, it is important to ask why the legal response is falling short and what can be done to build meaningful protection for migrant workers....
>
> There is real urgency in examining how the law regulates recruiters of transnational migrant workers because these "merchants of labour" hold an imbalance of information and power that leaves migrant workers exposed to predatory practices. Recruiters

control access to jobs and help navigate the complex procedures of moving across borders for authorized work. As a result, they are uniquely placed to exert disproportionate influence over migrant workers' experience of life and work in Canada.

What information are workers given? What terms of work and expectations of citizenship are they promised? What must workers do—and pay—to secure work in Canada? What happens after workers arrive? How recruiters handle these initial stages of the labour migration cycle can determine whether workers are brought into Ontario on terms that offend fundamental human rights and labour standards, or on terms that allow them to experience and enforce their legal rights to decent work....

In 2009, a high-profile Toronto Star investigative series reported widespread exploitation of live-in caregivers by recruiters in the province. In response, the Ontario government enacted the Employment Protection for Foreign Nationals Act (EPFNA or Bill 210). The law applies only to live-in caregivers. It prohibits recruiters from charging fees to workers, prohibits employers from recouping recruitment costs from workers, and prohibits recruiters or employers from holding workers' passports or other personal documents.

... Migrant workers continue on a routine and systemic basis to be charged thousands of dollars in "recruitment fees"—fees that can equal as much as two years' wages in their home currency. In order to pay their recruitment fees, migrant workers continue to borrow money from recruiters and informal money lenders, they continue to sign over the deeds to their homes to secure these loans, and they continue to be charged oppressive interest rates on these loans. These actions effectively place them in debt bondage to their recruiters and employers. Migrant workers continue to be recruited to Ontario only to discover that the jobs they were promised do not exist and to be forced to work without status to pay off the debts they incurred to arrive here. And migrant workers continue to have their passports and travel documents seized, trapping them in abusive employment relationships....

In documents obtained in October 2013 in response to a request under the Freedom of Information and Protection of Privacy Act, the Ontario Ministry of Labour reported that since EPFNA took effect in March 2010, only $12,100 in illegal fees has been recovered from recruiters and there are only eight investigations ongoing. Yet ... since the law was enacted, two-thirds of its members have been charged illegal recruitment fees. We also know that recruitment fees extracted from migrant workers continue to rise....

The criminal law may provide tools to combat particularly abusive practices in some cases. However, using human trafficking as the analytical frame—and thinking about this as an exclusively criminal-law problem—obscures the extent to which these practices are not aberrant but are in fact core to the business model that some recruiters adopt while operating within legal migration streams....

Migrant workers' vulnerability and precariousness are not conditions that are inherent or inevitable. Their disempowerment and marginalization are the products of active choices governments have made in building the laws and policies that govern transnational labour migration.

[Courtesy of The George Cedric Metcalf Charitable Foundation.]

Fay Faraday, *Made in Canada: How the Law Constructs Migrant Workers' Insecurity* (Toronto: George Cedric Metcalf Charitable Foundation, 2012) at 52–53 and 105–06, online: https://metcalf foundation.com/wp-content/uploads/2012/09/Made-in-Canada-Full-Report.pdf

> [T]here are many international law instruments that can inform a rights-based assessment of the treatment of migrant workers.
>
> ... The objective of the Decent Work Agenda is not just to create income-producing employment, but to ensure that all workers have access to jobs of acceptable quality characterized by "conditions of freedom, equity, security and human dignity." To this end, "the ILO's Decent Work Agenda promotes access for all to freely chosen employment, the recognition of fundamental rights at work, an income to enable people to meet their basic economic, social and family needs and responsibilities, and an adequate level of social protection for the workers and family members." This goal is advanced through setting standards and developing programs and policies that promote substantive rights at work, employment, social protection and social dialogue. The substantive rights and values that are set out in the ILO's various standard-setting conventions give important insight into what constitutes "decent work." ...
>
> The detailed guidelines provided in the UN Migrant Workers Convention, the numerous ILO Conventions and the ILO *Multilateral Framework on Labour Migration* also all speak to the multitude of ways in which the legal regulation of the work relationship can either create conditions of security and decent work, or alternatively, insecurity and exploitation.
>
> To the extent that laws construct particular work and workers as "temporary" and "unskilled," this obscures the ways in which the work itself is integral to the functioning of our communities and creates a normative framework in which the work is devalued. To the extent that laws construct workers as "temporary," "foreign" and "unskilled," they likewise devalue the real contributions of these workers to the functioning of our economy and communities and construct the workers as "other," as "not us," as persons outside the community to whom we need not be accountable. To the extent that laws fail to respond to known practices which systemically marginalize and disempower migrant workers, they sustain those conditions and practices which produce insecurity and undermine the possibility of decent work.
>
> [Courtesy of The George Cedric Metcalf Charitable Foundation.]

* * * * *

The following is a summary of *Travailleurs et travailleuses unis de l'alimentation et du commerce, section locale 501 (TUAC-FTQ) et Savoura*, 2014 CanLII 76230 (QC SAT):

> [The *Savoura* case concerns two Guatemalan migrant workers who worked in Quebec from April 2008, until they were terminated by Savoura in August and December of 2008. The two workers had been hired as temporary farm workers through the FERME recruitment service along with a dozen other workers, each with eleven-month worker's visas. The workers were party to a collective agreement and represented by the United Food and Commercial Workers union.
>
> It was alleged that one of the two workers had made death threats toward two of his co-workers, and the other had allegedly been "aggressive" and threatening during a

dispute with the employer. After each alleged incident, a human resources staff person at Savoura called the Guatemalan consulate, which repatriated each worker. Neither of the workers spoke French, and neither were given an opportunity to present their case, nor was an investigation conducted by the company, nor was there the existence of any police report to rely on.

Savoura claimed that it did not terminate the employees, but that the end of their employment was simply an administrative decision that resulted from their absence from work due to repatriation.

The union argued, however, that the employer had the responsibility to exercise its powers as manager in accordance with the collective agreement, and that it failed to do so in delegating its authority to the consulate. It further argued that in doing so, Savoura's actions constituted discrimination.

The arbitrator sided with the employees, writing that it was unlikely that they were repatriated without first having been terminated by Savoura. Moreover, the arbitrator finds that Savoura had no just and sufficient cause to terminate the employees as none of the allegations against them were verifiable.

Finally, the arbitrator dealt with the allegations of discrimination by the employees, finding that Savoura violated articles 10 and 16 of Quebec's *Charter of Human Rights and Freedoms*, having treated the employees differently from other employees on the basis of their ethnicity, nationality, culture and language. Migrant agricultural workers, the arbitrator wrote, are particularly vulnerable and dependent on the employer, which offered less advantageous working conditions than for workers of Canadian origin. Whether intentionally or not, that constitutes discrimination per article 10 of the *Charter*. The arbitrator found that the employer acted arbitrarily, and based on ethnic prejudices. Furthermore, in acting so expeditiously, the employer denied the employees any chance to seek union representation and protection of their collective agreement. These acts exploited the vulnerabilities of the workers.

Ultimately, the arbitrator explained that the existence of the temporary foreign worker programme does not justify any discriminatory treatment of migrant workers. These programmes exist on the basis that such workers should be treated in the same way as workers of Canadian origin.]

PN v FR & MR and another (No 2), 2015 BCHRT 60

[1] PN has complained that both of the respondents, FR and MR, have discriminated against her on the basis of her sex, family status, age, race, ancestry, colour and place of origin, contrary to section 13 of the *BC Human Rights Code*.

[2] PN is a mother from the Philippines. She was hired through an agency to work in the respondents' home in Hong Kong as a housekeeper and caregiver to the respondents' two children. She worked for the respondents in Hong Kong for about one year. She came with the respondents when they moved to Canada and worked for them here. She was here for about six weeks when she fled their home, which was a two-bedroom suite in a hotel. She says that, for much of her employment, she was the victim of ongoing sexual assault by FR and harassment, including assault, by MR.

[3] Once she left the respondents' hotel, PN stayed at a secure women's shelter for victims of human trafficking. PN was without resources as she had no visa for work in Canada and she could not qualify for income assistance. FR made a number of efforts to have her returned either to Hong Kong or to the Philippines.

[4] The respondents say in their response that they did not discriminate against PN on any of the alleged grounds. The respondents sought to dismiss the complaint under s. 27(1) of the *Code*. The application was only partially successful. See: *PN v. FR and another*, 2015 BCHRT 4 (CanLII). Those aspects of the complaint that occurred outside of Canada are outside the jurisdiction of the Tribunal and are not part of the complaint. In addition, the parties' names have been anonymized.

[5] The original complaint was joined with a complaint under s. 43 of the *Code* that the respondents had retaliated against PN for filing the complaint by sending a letter threatening legal action in Hong Kong and demanding payment of damages. Copies of the letter were sent to a number of other recipients. . . .

[74] The stereotypes or prejudices relate to factors like sex, race, place of origin, and age especially when it comes to domestic work. In terms of their gender, or sex, the stereotypes and prejudices that govern how Filipino domestic workers are perceived often relate to them being women. As Filipino women, they are perceived to be "naturally inclined" to perform this kind of domestic care work, even as they are "naturally" or "culturally" inclined to exhibit morally suspect behaviours.

[75] These views of Hong Kong employers, makes Filipino domestic workers "ideal," highly sought-after, or employable workers, even as they are simultaneously perceived as a threat to the Hong Kong moral order and social hierarchy.

[76] Race and place of origin also have bearing on how these stereotypes play out in the lives of domestic workers. Filipino women are perceived to come from a poor nation that is unable to provide any viable employment and has created a class of workers who are desperately trying to leave their country. Relatedly, the preference for Filipinos as care workers/domestic workers is often guided by the perception that workers from the Philippines possess a work ethic and values related to family, loyalty, and authority that translate to their docility in the workplace. These characteristics are pitched as cultural (if not biological), and therefore, unique to the racial make-up of Filipinos. This is in addition to the racialization of Filipino workers as coming from a country with the linguistic advantage of English language proficiency.

[77] Age also impacts the racialization and gendering of the stereotypes that construct Filipino women as ideal domestic workers. Foreign employers often correlate age to be a reflection of strength, health, docility, and efficiency and therefore prefer to hire domestic workers under the age of 35, with a preference for workers in their 20s. Live-in domestic workers typically work anywhere from 14-18 hour work days and get one day off. The daily work schedule is fairly regimented with specific tasks and deadlines that require a certain kind of efficiency. Domestic workers' résumés, in the form of so-called "biodata" that is collected at the time of their recruitment, includes questions about age, height, and weight and is accompanied by a full body photograph. PN's application form contained much of this information. . . .

[101] PN was a virtual slave. She could not go anywhere or do anything without permission. She could not go out on her own or speak to people in her own language, even though there were people around the hotel with whom she could have struck up such a friendship. While she was allowed to sleep, it was in between the respondents' bedrooms so she was virtually on call 24/7. She was frequently humiliated and demeaned by MR who threatened her, called her names and threatened to deduct wages were she to sit down while at work.

[102] Based both on the evidence of FR and the opinion of Dr. Guevarra, I find that the protected characteristics of PN were factors in her treatment by the respondents. Certainly, the repeated sexual assaults were because PN is a woman. The threats that worked to keep her quiet were due to her family status.

[103] Many of the conditions PN was forced to endure in Canada amount to adverse impact based on the protected characteristics identified in the complaint. These characteristics were a key factor in many aspects of her employment....

[107] I find that the respondents breached s. 13 of the *Code* with their treatment of PN for the almost six weeks that she was in Canada as their employee. Virtually every aspect of her employment, including the contract, was exploitation that amounts to discrimination....

[120] PN claims damages for wages she earned while she was working for the respondents in Canada as well as prospective wages that she would have earned had the discriminatory treatment not caused her to flee from the respondents' hotel room.

[121] Given my conclusion that the contract itself was exploitation amounting to discrimination, I cannot construe this part of my decision as enforcing the contract of employment. However, as the respondents received the benefit of work from PN while they were exploiting her, I am persuaded that it is appropriate to award her compensation for wages that would have been paid absent discrimination, that is, meeting minimum standards.

2:410 Human Trafficking for Work

Prabha Kotiswaran, "From Sex Panic to Extreme Exploitation: Revisiting the Law and Governance of Human Trafficking" in Prabha Kotiswaran, ed, *Revisiting the Law and Governance of Trafficking, Forced Labor and Modern Slavery* (Cambridge University Press, 2017) 1, 2, 3, 6, 9, 10, 11, & 12

[A]nti-slavery groups remind us that we hardly need to look to faraway places like Brazil or Lebanon; literally everything that we consume on a day-to-day basis is tainted by "slave" labor. These include basic commodities like tea, sugar, coffee, prawns, chicken, eggs, onions, mushrooms, "slave chocolate" from Cote D'Ivoire and cotton from Uzbekistan. Exploitation is also rife in wartime captivity in Nigeria, bonded labor in Pakistan, fishing boats in Thailand, households employing overseas migrant domestic workers, Qatari construction sites with Nepali workers, the brick kiln industry in India, Brazilian garment factories employing Bolivian workers, in Unilever's supply chain in Vietnam and in Kenyan flower and green bean cultivation. This — anti-slavery groups claim — is "modern slavery" brought home. Drafters of the 2000 UN Protocol to Prevent, Suppress and Punish Trafficking in Persons, Especially Women and Children supplementing the UN Convention against Transnational Organized Crime 2000 could not have imagined the above interpretations of trafficking in their wildest dreams when they sat down in the late 1990s to negotiate the Trafficking Protocol. Although international law had historically targeted the "traffic" in women and children across borders particularly for prostitution, in the 1990s, this traditional concern converged with several developed states' interests in stemming illegal international labor migration to create a criminal law regime against trafficking." Consequently, under the Trafficking Protocol and the Protocol on Migrant Smuggling which supplemented the UN Convention, participating states promised to criminally sanction anyone assisting another to migrate illegally (migrant smuggling) as well as recruiting, harboring or transporting a person through means of coercion, force and deception for purposes of exploitation (trafficking). Under the Trafficking Protocol, the trafficked person cannot be criminally punished in the receiving country for being trafficked, may be able to obtain a visa to stay there, but is most likely to be repatriated. Negotiated within two years "at lightning speed on the UN clock", the Trafficking Protocol was adopted in 2000, came into force in 2003 and has been exceptionally well ratified by 170 countries to date....

A chronic challenge for anti-trafficking activists is the sheer ineffectiveness of anti-trafficking law. Despite the spectacular figures of modern slaves already mentioned, only 44,758 trafficked persons around the world have been identified resulting in 5776 convictions. Conviction rates have remained "stubbornly low" since 2003; 41 percent of countries have not had any convictions or recorded less than ten convictions between 2010 and 2012. The yawning gap between the intellectual energy and material resources expended on trafficking and the meager outcomes fundamentally problematize our continuing urgent prioritization of this issue. However, this is not simply a problem of the gap between the "law in the books" and "law in action." Although the weak enforcement of anti-trafficking criminal law is a serious matter, there is much more at stake. The very terms of the political debate, the incorporation of the Trafficking Protocol into domestic law, the interpretations of the various aspects of the definition of trafficking, the jurisdiction and suitability of institutional machineries to deal with trafficking, the nature of anti-trafficking discourse and the affective economies that accompany these are all up for grabs....

Over the past two decades, trafficking has been discussed predominantly in the key of international law. Under international criminal law, itself a relatively new field emerging in the 1990s, individuals are held criminally responsible by a supranational court for crimes such as genocide and crimes against humanity and the violation of *jus cogens* norms. The Trafficking Protocol is however better understood as an instance of "transnational criminal law" or "the indirect suppression by international law through domestic penal law of criminal activities that have actual or potential trans-border effects". In other words, the core component of transnational criminal law is a crime suppression treaty, whether agreed bilaterally, regionally or through a large UN-backed multilateral convention directed at suppressing conduct that is subsequently criminalized through domestic law....

Article 3 of the Trafficking Protocol defines trafficking as follows:

> Art. 3.(a): "Trafficking in persons" shall mean the recruitment, transportation, transfer, harbouring or receipt of persons, by means of the threat or use of force or other forms of coercion, of abduction, of fraud, of deception, of the abuse of power or of a position of vulnerability or of the giving or receiving of payments or benefits to achieve the consent of

a person having control over another person, for the purpose of exploitation. Exploitation shall include, at a minimum, the exploitation of the prostitution of others or other forms of sexual exploitation, forced labour or services, slavery or practices similar to slavery, servitude or the removal of organs; (b): The consent of a victim of trafficking in persons to the intended exploitation set forth in subparagraph (a) of this article shall be irrelevant where any of the means set forth in subparagraph (a) have been used. . . .

The Trafficking Protocol offers an expansive understanding of both the means of trafficking as well as the purpose for which one is trafficked, namely, exploitation. The concepts of coercion and exploitation are central to the Trafficking Protocol. Yet it does not define them and their meaning under international law is far from definitive even when clear. According to the ILO, discussions amongst jurists and lawmakers on the definitional aspects of trafficking continue without clear resolution. A survey of the laws relating to trafficking in twelve jurisdictions found a widespread lack of clarity on the definition of trafficking. The UNODC further admits that this lack of clarity over the parameters of trafficking hinders detection of trafficked victims and overall enforcement efforts.

Each of the two central legal concepts in the law of trafficking, namely, the means and purpose, both span a continuum of possibilities. The means of coercion can range from legally recognizable and fairly narrowly construed notions of coercion, deception, fraud and abduction (termed as "strong coercion" for ease of reference) to the capacious, outlier concept of the abuse of a position of vulnerability ("weak coercion"). Similarly, while Art. 3 points to specific labor conditions that constitute exploitation and are recognized and understood under international law ("strong exploitation"), this list of labor conditions is not exhaustive and could well include a range of working conditions that are best described as precarious, exploitative and normatively reprehensible or as "contradictory to human dignity" as described in court rulings of some European countries ("weak exploitation").

A narrow construction of the offence of trafficking might entail coercive means of entry including violence, deception or fraud (strong coercion) resulting in a slavery-like situation (strong exploitation). A paradigmatic example of the trafficking episode iterated *ad nauseam* by the media is of the young woman who is offered a well-paying job as a nanny but is duped into doing sex work in a foreign country against her will and under threat of physical and sexual violence for no pay. In contrast, a broader construction of the offence of trafficking may penalize the recruitment of a victim by abuse of a position of vulnerability (weak coercion) resulting in precarious work with less than minimum-wage pay (weak exploitation).

The author then discusses the many different approaches states may take to the interpretation of the elements of the offence of trafficking. Many work situations involve some, but not all, elements; for example, "coerced entry into a labor sector can exist without exploitation, while exploitation can exist without coerced entry." Because states tend to focus on border restrictions, the application of trafficking laws is highly uneven and leaves many workers unprotected in coerced, exploitative conditions.

Chapter 3: The Contract of Employment

3:100   INTRODUCTION

The contract of employment has been described as the cornerstone of the employment relationship. That undoubtedly remains true in the non-unionized sector, which accounts for an increasing majority of the Canadian workforce. Legally speaking, no one can become the employee of another without making a contract with that person or corporate entity. As we will see in later chapters, the role of the individual contract of employment has been greatly diminished in the unionized sector, but even there, a worker must enter into such a contract in order to be covered by collective bargaining and a collective agreement.

However important the contract of employment may be as a legal phenomenon, the body of law that interprets and applies it has not been very successful at delivering the benefits of industrial citizenship to workers in lower- to mid-income jobs. In part, this is because of the limited nature of the substantive and procedural rights which the courts have accorded to employees vis-à-vis their employers at common and civil law. From a practical standpoint, it is probably even more attributable to the fact that the civil litigation process, which is the main forum for the enforcement of the employment contract, is bedevilled by high costs and long delays and provides a relatively restricted range of remedies. Generally speaking, only higher-income managers and professionals can afford to enforce their rights in court. Even highly paid employees can typically only enforce those rights after leaving employment, as the law is primarily available after relationship breakdown, rather than providing legal mechanisms to help the parties navigate the relationship while it is underway. For a realistic protection of their workplace rights and interests, most other workers must look to employment standards legislation (which we deal with in Chapter 13) or to unionization and collective bargaining (which we deal with in Chapters 4 to 12). Indeed, it is largely the failure of the common law employment contract to deliver workplace justice that has made unionization and employment standards legislation necessary.

As a relationship of contract, with some exceptions, the employment relationship is treated at common law as any other contract and governed by general contract law principles. Those principles assume that a contract—whether it deals with a commercial transaction or with an employment relationship—is a product of relatively free bargaining between parties with relatively equal power who will negotiate terms of mutual benefit. For most workers, however, this assumption will likely not be true; their employer may have the power to dictate the terms of employment on a "take it or leave it" basis. Contract law speaks in the attractive language of freedom of choice and consensus *ad idem*, but the reality is that that the position of employees may be one of subordination, both before and after the making of the contract.

CHAPTER 3: THE CONTRACT OF EMPLOYMENT

The principles of contract law assume that the terms of the parties' bargain will reflect their actual intentions, express or implied. The role of the courts is traditionally limited to enforcing the terms of the bargain; that role does not extend to imposing on the parties obligations of the courts' own making. In the employment context, however, judges have fashioned a series of obligations implied by *law* to give content to the employment contract. Those obligations reflect judges' views of what a fair employment relationship involves and have changed over time, having regard to what they see as the "natural" content of the employment relationship and the dictates of prevailing social values, whether those be fairness between the parties or the requirements of efficient human resource management.

At the core of the employment relationship is the managerial prerogative—the employer's right to control the day-to-day functioning of the workplace. To give effect to this managerial right, the courts deploy a series of implied rights to impose substantive obligations on employees to respect and obey their employers, many of which are holdovers from feudal employment regulation systems. In this sense, it can be argued that the courts have infused a "status" element into the employment relationship, despite the predominantly contractual basis of that relationship. On the other hand, it can also be argued that, in recent years, Canadian courts have made an effort to gradually move the common law of the contract of employment in a direction that is more mindful of employee rights and interests, and have crafted new implied terms to do so.

If the managerial prerogative is at the core of the employers' rights, the right to reasonable notice of dismissal, absent cause, is the primary measure of job security for employees. In other words, at common law, an employee holds no contractual right to their job, but only a right to be dismissed with reasonable notice, which they lose if they engage in misconduct constituting cause. The common law model of dismissal is therefore a "reasonable notice" model. As will be explored in Chapter 13, some Canadian jurisdictions have also developed statutory "just cause" models of dismissal. A "just cause" model of dismissal offers higher job security and dismissal protections to employees. Conversely, such a model decreases employers' flexibility, because it is more difficult to terminate employees and shift the composition of the workforce. The "just cause" model is the predominant model of dismissal in the United Kingdom. The United States operates under the most flexible or employer-friendly model of dismissal, which is referred to as "at-will employment." Under this model, employees are hired at will, and, with some exceptions, either party may terminate the relationship at any time and for any reason.

The employment relationship is therefore understood at common law as a creature of contract, although one with some special features. For some, the employment contract is viewed as a relationship of freedom, because its creation and content is based on the individual choice and agreement of the parties. Even if employees enjoy less bargaining power than their employers, they are not obligated to enter into any particular employment relationship—they can choose between employers, and therefore still enjoy freedom over their work choices. Others take a different view, and understand the employment contract as creating a relationship of subordination, pointing to the illusory nature of "choice" in the context of economic scarcity, high unemployment, and bargaining power imbalance. For an overview of these two positions, see Claire Mummé, "Property in Labour and the Limits of Contract" in Ugo Mattei & John Haskell, eds, *Research Handbook on Political Economy and the Law* (Cheltenham, UK: Edward Elgar Publishing, 2016) 400–21.

The following texts examine the nature of the employment relationship and the consequences of casting it as a contract.

Otto Kahn-Freund, "A Note on Status and Contract in British Labour Law" (1967) 30 *Modern Law Review* 635 at 635 and 640–41

The labour law of Great Britain shares with that of the other nations in our orbit of civilisation two essential jurisprudential features: it is based on the contractual foundation of the obligation to work and of the obligation to pay wages, and it is at the same time permeated by a tendency to formulate and to enforce an ever-growing number of imperative norms for the protection of the worker, norms which the parties to the contract cannot validly set aside to the detriment of the economically weaker party. This dual insistence on agreement as the legal basis of at least some of the essential rights and obligations and on mandatory regulation as the source of the content of the relationship has given rise to a jurisprudential dilemma which has so far not been clearly faced in the literature on the subject.

The dilemma arises from the ambiguity of the term 'status' in general jurisprudence. Contemporary writers are fond of reiterating that, under the impact of modern developments, Western society is moving from 'contract' to 'status.' This observation which has been repeated almost mechanically on countless occasions is intended to signify that our society and our law have taken a course in a direction opposite to that traced more than a century ago by Sir Henry Sumner Maine, whose celebrated dictum about the displacement of 'status' by 'contract' is often quoted, but seldom in full. Not infrequently one can sense in the statement that the tendency diagnosed by Maine has been reversed, a conscious or unconscious condemnation of a retrograde evolution. Did not Maine link his famous remark with the analysis of what he called 'progressive societies'? Does not the movement, or rather the alleged movement, from 'contract' to 'status' constitute a 'regression,' a regression from the 'liberal,' 'progressive' environment of the nineteenth century to more primitive forms of social organisation such as those described by Maine in his work? ...

How can we explain the conceptual confusion between two legal phenomena as different as the imposition of rights and duties irrespective of the volition of the person concerned, and the shaping of a contractual relation into which he has freely entered? Let us admit that in terms of legal policy there may but need not be a common factor. This is the desire to protect persons who, not only, as Maine thought, owing to lack of 'faculty of forming a judgment in their own interests,' but also owing to inferior bargaining power, are liable to be exploited by others. This policy underlies some of the legal provisions or principles which, in Maine's sense, belong to the area of 'status.' They do underlie the law of infants, but certainly not that of aliens. But they also underlie those rules which shape the content of contracts. Yet the legal techniques employed by the two types of legal norms are so fundamentally different that their confusion needs to be explained. Why, then, do English lawyers see a reversion to 'status' in rules which leave the parties free to contract or not to contract, but restrict their freedom to contract except on certain minimum terms?

[Reprinted by permission of Blackwell Publishers.]

CHAPTER 3: THE CONTRACT OF EMPLOYMENT

Alan Fox, *Beyond Contract: Work, Power and Trust Relations* (London: Faber and Faber, 1974) at 181–84

THE EMPLOYMENT CONTRACT: WAS IT A CONTRACT?

Before we pursue more fully the implications of collective bargaining for our analysis, other questions must be answered if we are to assimilate into that analysis what has been noted so far about the employment relation under industrialization. One of the master symbols of the emergent social order has been seen to be contract. Voluntary agreement forged through bargaining over specific terms, the essence of economic exchange, was seen as the mechanism which articulated atomistic, self-regarding individuals into the collaborative aggregates and linked processes necessary for civil society. How did the employment relation fit into this contractual society and into the ideologies prevalent within it? Can the contract of employment be seen as simply another manifestation of this increasingly pervasive form of exchange?

Certainly one would expect to find a strong ideological drive asserting it to be so. If mediæval ideology, nourished and sustained by powerful interests, idealized the personalized bonds and commitments of feudal social structure as an equal balance of reciprocal diffuseness, the dominant ideology of newly emergent industrial society might be expected to idealize the employment contract, like all other contracts, in terms of an equal balance of reciprocal specificity. And evidence does indeed suggest a strain in this direction. Laski points to 'a growing sense, both in parliament and in the courts of law, that the nexus between a master and man is purely economic, a relation, not a partnership implying reciprocal social duties.' And did not the evolving law of employment come increasingly during the nineteenth century to emphasize 'the personal and voluntary exchange of freely-bargained promises between two parties equally protected by the civil law alone'? Capitalism indeed 'provides a legitimation of domination which is no longer called down from the lofty heights of cultural tradition but instead summoned up from the base of social labour. The institution of the market, in which private property owners exchange commodities—including the market in which propertyless private individuals exchange their labor power as their only commodity—promises that exchange relations will be and are just owing to equivalence.'

But the impersonal, calculating, low-trust attitudes of economic exchange were never universally accepted by employers, either in practice or in theory. Undoubtedly the general trend throughout the century was towards an 'impersonal management of labor which depended upon the formulation of the conditions of employment and upon elaborate controls which verified the workers' compliance with these conditions.' But persistently in some industries 'management depended upon a personal relationship between an employer and his workers, and hence upon the accidents of personal knowledge as well as upon the well-understood but unformulated relationship of trust which existed traditionally between master and his men.' This persistence might have its roots not only in cultural isolation or inertia but also in a social philosophy which stressed the coincidence of business success with high moral practice and with the principle of the master conducting himself as trustee of his men's 'true best interests.' This philosophy recommending *social* exchange in master-man relations, so far from becoming extinct, was to enjoy a minor revival in circumstances to be examined later.

We must also note the coexistence of ideology celebrating the employment contract as 'the personal and voluntary exchange of freely-bargained promises' with practical attitudes expressing a clear determination that it should be nothing of the kind. Such was the inequality of power between the employer and the individual employee that to describe 'agreements' between them as 'freely-bargained promises' obscured the high probability that for much of the time the latter felt virtually coerced by the former into settling for whatever he could get—a picture hardly consonant with the glories of contract as celebrated by, for example, Spencer. Few of those who lauded the new industrial order were prepared explicitly to emphasize, as did Adam Smith a century before Spencer was writing, that 'it is not ... difficult to foresee which of the two parties must, upon all ordinary occasions, have the advantage in the dispute, and force the other into a compliance with their terms.... In all such disputes the masters can hold out much longer. A landlord, a farmer, a master manufacturer, or merchant, though they did not employ a single workman could generally live a year or two upon the stocks which they have already acquired. Many workmen could not subsist a week, few could subsist a month, and scarce any a year without employment. In the long-run the workman may be as necessary to his master as his master is to him; but the necessity is not so immediate.'

But it was not only that the brute facts of power made the employment contract something a good deal less than contract. Had this been the case we should simply be confronting the commonplace situation of a definition diverging from reality. There was, however, a further ambivalence relating to definition. The legal construction which was put upon the contract of employment left it virtually unrecognizable as contract. To appreciate the reason for this the starting point must be that, for employers and their sympathizers, the application of pure contract doctrine to the employment relation, had this ever happened, would have borne a damaging double edge. Certainly there seemed to be a strong legitimizing principle available to hand in the idea, betrayed in practice though it might usually be, of free and equal agents negotiating contractual arrangements on the basis of each seeking to maximize his utilities in competitive markets. The legitimizing strength of this idea could surely be brought to include within its persuasiveness those who contracted to participate as employees in collaborative associations for the production of goods and service, and thereby help to integrate and stabilize the productive system? But application of the contract system proper to the employment relation would have suggested implications alarming to property owners. Since no employment contract could anticipate all relevant contingencies arising in work relations, many issues had to be settled during the everyday conduct of business. How hard was the employee to work? Under what material, social, and psychological conditions? With what tools, machines, and materials? Within what framework of rules, discipline, and sanctions? With what rights to demur against specific instructions, managerial policies, and proposals for change? These constituted the reality of life under an employment contract. But who was to settle them? How were the empty boxes of the contract clauses to be given the necessary content? The damaging implication of pure contract doctrine for the employer would have been that it could not allow him to be the sole judge of whether his rules were arbitrary or exceeded the scope of his authority. Certainly even under contract doctrine he might be granted—by the contract—the right to make rules, but he would not have the unrestricted right to decide whether the rules he had made or proposed to make were consistent with the contract .... For, as noted earlier, contract theory included the notion of appeal by either party to some outside adjudicating body in the event of behaviour claimed to be inconsistent with the contract. This incipient threat to so integral a part of everyday control as their wide discretionary powers over the labour force would have been intolerable. It followed that contract as the pure doctrine defined it could not be seen by the property-owning classes as an adequate foundation for governing the employment relation. Their needs were met by infusing the employment contract with the traditional law of master and servant, thereby granting them a legal basis for the prerogative they demanded. What resulted was a form of contract almost as far removed from the pure doctrinal form as the status relationship which had preceded it.

[Reprinted by permission of Faber and Faber Ltd.]

Christie v York Corp, [1940] SCR 139 at 141–46

RINFRET J.: The appellant, who is a negro, entered a tavern owned and operated by the respondent, in the City of Montreal, and asked to be served a glass of beer; but the waiters refused him for the sole reason that they had been instructed not to serve coloured persons. He claimed the sum of $200 for the humiliation he suffered.

The respondent alleged that in giving such instructions to its employees and in so refusing to serve the appellant it was well within its rights; that its business is a private enterprise for gain; and that, in acting as it did, the respondent was merely protecting its business interests....

In considering this case, we ought to start from the proposition that the general principle of the law of Quebec is that of complete freedom of commerce. Any merchant is free to deal as he may choose with any individual member of the public. It is not a question of motives or reasons for deciding to deal or not to deal; he is free to do either. The only restriction to this general principle would be the existence of a specific law, or, in the carrying out of the principle, the adoption of a rule contrary to good morals or public order....

As the case is not governed by any specific law or more particularly by s. 33 of the *Quebec License Act*, it falls under the general principle of the freedom of commerce; and it must follow that, when refusing to serve the appellant, the respondent was strictly within its rights....

The Quebec *Civil Code* contains a chapter on the contract of employment, composed of thirteen sections (sections 2085–2097), the first of which contains a definition, followed by provisions on the duties of both employers and employees during the life of the contract and upon its termination. The Preamble of the *Civil Code* states that the *Code* "comprises a body of rules which, in all matters within the letter, spirit or object of its provisions, lays down the *jus commune*, expressly or by implication. In these matters, the Code is the foundation of all other laws, although other laws may complement the Code or make exceptions to it." A series of statutory laws of public order (see, for example, Chapters 13 and 14) therefore complete the regulation of the employment relationship.

Pierre Verge, "Le contract de travail selon le *Code civil du Québec*: pertinence ou impertinence?" (1993) 24 *Revue générale de droit* 237–53. Footnotes and citations omitted.

A. THE DISSOCIATION OF LABOUR FROM THE PERSON OF THE EMPLOYEE

The employment relationship has been understood as a contract since the Civil Code of Lower Canada, and remains so in the Civil Code of Quebec which replaced it.

1. In the Civil Code of Lower Canada

From a historical perspective, the "lease or hire of personal service" in the 1866 Code (CCLB, arts 1667–671) marked a change from a status-based, or domestic, conception of work done for another person, to one based on a liberal ideology. This change applied as much to "domestics," who continued to remain close to the family, as to "workmen" and, more generally, to "others." Freedom of contract thus governed employment, which was consistent with the industrialization of society in 1866. "Hiring or leasing" for an unlimited term was, moreover, not possible. The law of Lower Canada thus continued the move from status to contract in employment matters, which was already underway in the society that the Code governed, and more broadly, in with the European tradition.

The contract assured the employer the labour of an employee for an agreed period, limited or indeterminate. It represented the commodification of this labour, dissociated legally and intellectually from the person of the employee. [...]

2. In the Civil Code of Quebec

At least the name given to the contract was changed: the 1991 Code includes a seventh chapter on the "contract of employment" in the section on named contracts. Leaving the content of the chapter's provisions for discussion below, the 1991 Code continues to regulate the same relationship known under the former Code as the "contract of lease or hire of personal service":

> Art. 2085 A contract of employment is a contract by which a person, the employee, undertakes, for a limited time and for remuneration, to do work under the direction or control of another person, the employer.

The contract of employment is clearly distinguished from the "contract of enterprise or for services," dealt with in a separate chapter, in which "no relationship of subordination exists between the contractor or the provider of services and the client" (art 2099). The scope of the contract of employment, by contrast, [...] corresponds to that which had already been defined by the case law; it includes all subordinated work, be it physical or intellectual, performed under the control or direction of another person. Over the years, based on, and no doubt influenced by, the application of the principles of labour law, the civil law seems to have relaxed the criterion of subordination. Here as well, the employee's integration within an organization has become the distinctive criterion. "Technical control of the activity," a criterion used to determine an employer's vicarious liability, has been replaced by the more general criterion of the worker's integration into an enterprise. The recognition of the authority exercised by an employer within the enterprise, and all that this implies, is the manifestation of the subordination inherent in the employment relationship and its contractual form. Thus, what it is now called "the contract of employment" is, in its essence, still as much a type of lease as the previous concept of a "lease of service"—the rental of labour power—which demonstrates the employee's subordination to their employer....

This new chapter in the Civil Code of Quebec on the contract of employment certainly does not prevent the application of existing labour and employment legislation. The essential difficulty remains a lack of correspondence between the legal regimes applicable to the employment relationship: given the general evolution of contemporary law, in most situations the conception of the work relationship set out by the Code is only acceptable because it is overshadowed and, in practice, superimposed by labour and employment legislation....
[Permission to translate and publish this article was given by the *Revue générale de droit*.]

3:200 EMPLOYMENT STATUS: WHO IS AN EMPLOYEE AND WHO IS AN EMPLOYER?

Since the modern inception of work regulation in the nineteenth century, the application of labour and employment statutes has relied on a distinction between "independent contractors" and "employees." As Geoffrey England explains, the former operates in an "economic zone in which business entrepreneurs are expected to compete," while the latter are "afforded the relatively substantial protections of the labour standards and the common law."[1] As will be further discussed in Chapters 4 and 13, defining the boundaries between these two concepts has been one of the most vexing problems of labour and employment law, and continues to challenge decision makers as work practices continue to change.

Up until recently, however, it was not especially difficult to determine who was an employee's *employer*. In most situations, there was one corporate entity that exercised all the tasks associated with the managerial prerogative. But the vertical disintegration of corporate organization since the 1980s, and the increase in subcontracted supply chain production, has made it more and more common for employing functions to be split up among several entities, making it difficult to identify any single employer and to determine which entity ought to hold legal responsibilities under labour and employment laws.

The following extract describes a series of typical work arrangements currently characterizing the labour market, raising difficult legal questions about who is an employee, who is an employer, and how the burden of obligations, risks, and rewards should be apportioned between them. The scenarios are taken from the United States, but similar work relationships characterize the Canadian labour market.

David Weil, *The Fissured Workplace* (Cambridge, MA: Harvard University Press, 2014) 1–5

A maid works at the San Francisco Marriott on Fisherman's Wharf. The hotel property is owned by Host Hotels and Resorts Inc., a lodging real estate company. The maid,

---

1   Geoffrey England, Innis Christie, & Merran Christie, *Employment Law in Canada*, 3d ed (Markham, ON: Butterworths, 1998) vol 1 at 21.

however, is evaluated and supervised daily and her hours and payroll managed by Crestline Hotels and Resorts Inc., a national third-party hotel management company. Yet she follows daily procedures (and risks losing her job for failure to accomplish them) regarding cleaning, room set-up, overall pace, and quality standards established by Marriott, whose name the property bears.

A cable installer in Dayton, Ohio, works as an independent contractor (in essence a self-employed business provider), paid on a job-by-job basis by Cascom Inc., a cable installation company. Cascom's primary client is the international media giant Time Warner, which owns cable systems across the United States. The cable installer is paid solely on the basis of the job completed and is entitled to no protections typically afforded employees. Yet all installation contracts are supplied by Cascom, which also sets the price for jobs and collects payment for them. The installer must wear a shirt with the Cascom logo and can be removed as a contractor at will for not meeting minimum quotas or quality standards, or at the will of the company....

A member of a loading dock crew working in Southern California is paid by Premier Warehousing Ventures LLC (PWV) — a company providing temporary workers to other businesses — based on the total time it takes him and members of his crew to load a truck. PWV, in turn, is compensated for the number of trucks loaded by Schneider Logistics, a national logistics and trucking company that manages distribution centers for Walmart. Walmart sets the price, time requirements, and performance standards that are followed by Schneider. Schneider, in turn, structures its contracts with PWV and other labor brokers it uses to provide workers based on those prices and standards and its own profit objectives....

In an earlier era, Marriott, Time Warner, Bank of America, Walmart and Hershey, as well as other large employers that produce well-known products and services, would likely have directly employed the workers in the above vignettes. Not now so. As major companies have consciously invested in building brands and devoted customers as the cornerstone of their business strategy, they have also shed their role as the direct employer of the people responsible for providing those products and services....

The vignettes reveal a transformation in how business organizes work in ways that are invisible to most of us as consumers. We walk into a Marriott and assume that the people who greet us at the front desk or who clear our rooms each day are employees of that venerable brand (as their uniforms imply). We greet the technicians sent to our home to fix our cable, not even questioning whether they work for the media company to whom we pay our bills. In short, we assume that the companies who invest millions of dollars to convince us of the benefits of buying products under their retail nameplate or to purchase the unique services they offer also undertake the operations needed to produce them — including acting as the employer of all the interconnected people who make their businesses possible.

Those assumptions are increasingly wrong.... By shedding direct employment, lead business enterprises select from among multiple providers of those activities and services formerly done inside the organization, thereby substantially reducing costs and dispatching the many responsibilities connected to being the employer of record.... In essence, private strategies and public policies allow major companies to simultaneously profit from the core activities that create value in the eyes of customers and the capital

markets and shed the actual production of goods and services. In so doing, they have their cake and eat it too.
[THE FISSURED WORKPLACE: WHY WORK BECAME SO BAD FOR SO MANY AND WHAT CAN BE DONE TO IMPROVE IT by David Weil, Cambridge, Mass.: Harvard University Press, Copyright © 2014 by the President and Fellows of Harvard College.]

3:210   Who Is an Employee?

Not every exchange of labour for money constitutes an employment relationship in law. For example, when you have your hair cut, your barber or hairdresser is not your employee but is an independent contractor who runs their own business, or is perhaps an employee of the independent contractor who owns the hairdressing shop. The law draws a distinction between employees in the strict sense of the term, to whom the law of the employment contract applies, and independent contractors who are engaged in entrepreneurial activity, to whom the principles of commercial contract law apply. The idea behind the distinction is that independent contractors are business people, and thus do not suffer from the same bargaining power differential that employees do in negotiating with an employer.

As noted above, determining who is an employee and who is an independent contractor has been one of the most vexing issues of modern labour and employment law, and continues to challenge to this day. In the current era, the difficulty arises because an increasingly large number of workers are employed in positions which exhibit the characteristics of both independent contract work and employment.

Otto Kahn-Freund, "Servants and Independent Contractors" (1951) 14 *Modern Law Review* **504 at 505–8**

> The traditional test was that a person working for another was regarded as a servant if he was 'subject to the command of the master as to the manner in which he shall do his work,' but if the so-called 'master' was only in a position to determine the 'what' and not the 'how' of the services, the substance of the obligation but not the manner of its performance, then the person doing the work was said to be not a servant but an independent contractor, and his contract one for work and labour and not of employment. This distinction was based upon the social conditions of an earlier age: it assumed that the employer of labour was able to direct and instruct the labourer as to the technical methods he should use in performing his work. In a mainly agricultural society and even in the earlier stages of the Industrial Revolution the master could be expected to be superior to the servant in the knowledge, skill and experience which had to be brought to bear upon the choice and handling of the tools. The control test was well suited to govern relationships like those between a farmer and an agricultural labourer (prior to agricultural mechanisation), a craftsman and a journeyman, a householder and a domestic servant, and even a factory owner and an unskilled 'hand.' It reflects a state of society in which the ownership of the means of production coincided with the possession of technical knowledge and skill and in which that knowledge and skill was largely acquired by being handed down from one generation to the next by oral tradition and not by being systematically imparted in institutions of learning from universities down

to technical schools. The control test postulates a combination of managerial and technical functions in the person of the employer, *i.e.*, what to modern eyes appears as an imperfect division of labour. The technical and economic developments of all industrial societies have nullified these assumptions.... To say of the captain of a ship, the pilot of an aeroplane, the driver of a railway engine, of a motor vehicle, or of a crane that the employer 'controls' the performance of his work is unrealistic and almost grotesque. But one need not think of situations in which the employee is physically removed from his employer's premises: a skilled engineer or toolmaker, draftsman or accountant may as often as not have been engaged just because he possesses that technical knowledge which the employer lacks.... No wonder that the Courts found it increasingly difficult to cope with the cases before them by using a legal rule which, as legal rules so often do, had survived the social conditions from which it had been an abstraction....

The control test had to be transformed if it was to remain a working rule and to be more than a mere verbal incantation ... the development is in the direction of something like an 'organisation' in preference to a 'control' test. In future the question may perhaps be: 'did the alleged servant form part of the alleged master's organisation?' rather than 'was he subject to his orders in the actual doing of his work?' ... in this respect, English law is coming much closer to some of the Continental systems.
[Reprinted by permission of Blackwell Publishers.]

Brian A Langille & Guy Davidov, "Beyond Employees and Independent Contractors: A View from Canada" (1999) 21 *Comparative Labor Law & Policy Journal* **7**

III. OUR "TRADITIONAL" PROBLEM

A. The Significance of the Distinction

[T]he concept of "employee" is the "gateway to most (but not all) employment protections at common law and under employment-related legislation." Thus, for example, employment standards acts which regulate the maximum hours of work, overtime, minimum wages, paid vacations, equal pay for equal work, parental leave and more, apply only to "employees." Labor relations acts, which regulate collective bargaining, similarly apply only to "employees." Common-law rights (such as reasonable notice before termination) and obligations (like restriction on competition) generally apply only to employees.

Statutory definitions of "employee" and "employer," if at all existent, are generally not very helpful; they are either vacuous or circular and are often limited to stating exceptions or extensions. Courts were thus intentionally left with the task of inserting content into these concepts and, in effect, determining the boundaries of each regulation's scope of application. Significantly, additional concepts now appear in some pieces of legislation to better define the category of people that should be included within their scope. Terms like "workers" or "dependent contractors"—designed for inclusion of more people within the scope of some protective regulations—can be understood as a response to judges' failure in standing up to their task. Alternatively, they can be seen as providing the courts with better tools for performing this task. It is important to note, however, that even with these statutory additions, the basic distinction between employees and independent contractors—and the courts' task of giving it content—are still fundamental to Canadian labor and employment law and still crucially important.

The employee/independent contractor distinction is becoming significant to more and more workers with the shift from manufacturing to services and with the current changes in the organization of work. If in the past, almost every worker was an indisputable "employee," today the number of cases in doubt is significant and rising. In 1998, out of 14,326,400 employed Canadians, 17.6% were considered self-employed, of which 5.9% were classified as employers and the remaining 11.7% as own-account workers. In addition, at least 28% of the total employment in Canada (approximately four million employees) are in contingent relationships. That includes 9.7% temporary employees, 11% part-time, 5.5% with job tenure of six months or less, and 1.9% multiple job holders. To be clear, in principle, being a temporary, part-time, casual, multiple job holder, or a home-worker does not in itself affect an employee's status; the regular tests as described below apply. But such relationships often put the workers in a position of susceptibility to employers' manipulation and evasion as regards their rights. This includes attempts to exclude the whole relationship from the employment apparatus.

B. PURPOSIVE INTERPRETATION

It is a basic rule in statutory interpretation—and as we have noted, a truism about language in general—that the meaning of words be determined with regard to the context and purpose in which and for which they are used. Since the term "employee" appears in different statutes and common-law rules, it may very well have a different meaning in each of these contexts. For example, one can be an employee for purposes of employment standards, but an independent contractor as far as vicarious liability is concerned....

The employee/independent contractor distinction is found in tort law, tax law and other fields, each with very different goals behind it. However, as far as most labor and employment law regulations are concerned, there seems to be one common idea that sheds light on them all—the protection of workers. The accompanying assumption is the existence of an employer that can and should take responsibility for these workers (now "employees"). The basic purpose of the employee/independent contractor distinction in labor and employment law can thus be understood as distinguishing those workers who are in need of a particular sort of protection (and have an identifiable employer) from those who are in a position to protect themselves in the particular regard at issue. There are, of course, specific goals to specific regulations and these should also be taken into account. But the basic purpose of protecting workers that are in need of and are entitled to certain forms of protection *vis-à-vis* their employers unites them all. We will have more to say on that at the concluding part of this essay.

C. THE "FOURFOLD" TEST AND OTHER SYNTHESES

The formulation most frequently used by Canadian courts to determine the existence of employment relationships is that articulated by Lord Wright in a 1947 decision [*Montreal v. Montreal Locomotive Works*]:

In earlier cases a single test, such as the presence or absence of control, was often relied on to determine whether the case was one of master and servant, mostly in order to decide issues of tortious liability on the part of the master or superior. In the more complex conditions of modern industry, more complicated tests have often been applied. It has been suggested that a fourfold test would in some cases be more appropriate, a complex involving (1) control; (2) ownership of the tools; (3) chance of profit; (4) risk of loss. Control in itself is not always conclusive.... In many cases the question can only be settled by examining the whole of the various elements which constitute the relationship between the parties.

These four indicia, in fact, boil down to two questions: (1) whether the worker is controlled by the employer/client; and (2) whether the worker is economically independent, that is, has the characteristics of an independent businessperson (with particular attention given to the chance of profit and risk of loss to this effect). Ownership of expensive tools is simply one indicator of economic independence—creating, to some extent, risk of loss and chance of profit or an ability to take the tools and work elsewhere.

Much attention is still given in the caselaw to the age-old criterion of control. However, the application of this test has changed dramatically over the years. Today, Canadian courts hardly ever settle for the examination of direct control over the worker's activities. It is widely recognized that employment relations often exist without such direction whether because the employee is a specialized professional, because the work requires the use of discretion or simply because it is performed outside of the employer's premises. Instead of direct control, courts have shifted attention to the existence of what may be called "bureaucratic" or "administrative" control. The power to discipline the worker, for example, or to promote her, to give a contrary example, are illustrative of this overall control within the relationship.

Similar developments occurred in Quebec, which follow the civil-law tradition. The main criterion for the existence of [the] employer-employee relationship in Quebec is the existence of "legal subordination" of the employee to the employer. Originally, "legal subordination" encompassed the notion of direction and actual control by a party over the employee's day-to-day work. More recently, however, attention has shifted from control over how the work is done to more general control over the agreed regularity with which it is done and its quality. In practice, this is much like the "bureaucratic" or "administrative" control mentioned above. But the concept of "subordination"—the shift to the worker's point of view—serves to focus attention on why this criterion is relevant to the identification of workers in need of a particular sort of protection. The subordination of some workers means that they are unable to freely and fully pursue their goals and realize themselves to make (or at least take part in) the decisions that directly affect their lives.

The second question mentioned above—whether the worker is economically independent and, in particular, whether he assumes the risk of loss and chance of profit—has gained increased attention alongside control. It is, in fact, designed to examine the degree of dependence of the worker *vis-à-vis* the employer, as a matter of economic reality, on the assumption that dependence puts the worker (now employee) in need of protection. In some cases, the chance of loss or profit has been the decisive criterion; for example, a postmistress in a small community was held to be an independent contractor because she was paid on a commission basis, and "therefore, the more efficient she is, the more money she makes." This can be problematic since the allocation of risks is open to employers' manipulation and the shifting of risks to the worker, by an employer attempting to avoid employment responsibilities, usually leaves the worker with the same need of protection (if not more).

With this problem in mind, it is perhaps better to understand the loss/profit criterion more generally as part of an inquiry into the existence of economic dependency. If this is the ultimate question, courts can more easily bypass employers' manipulation and focus on the economic reality of the relationship. Indeed, in some of the cases, courts have shown willingness to find employment relationships even when the worker assumed most of the risks, but was in fact still in a position of economic dependency.

In short, it seems fair to conclude that the determination of "employee" status in Canada generally rests on two grounds: control and economic dependency. Indeed, it is interesting to note that another test which is sometimes mentioned in the caselaw, the "business integration" or "organization" test, leads in fact to the same two bases. The organization test finds its origins in Lord Denning's statement that,

> under a contract of service, a man is employed as part of the business, and his work is done as an integral part of the business; whereas, under a contract for services, his work, although done for the business, is not integrated into it, but is only accessory to it.
>
> [...]

We have seen that both control/subordination and economic dependency are reasonably related to the basic purpose of identifying workers in need of certain forms of protection (with an identifiable employer). Unfortunately, judges sometimes seem to forget this basic goal and in such cases, the application of the tests tends to be rigid and formalistic, with the risk of excluding some workers without real reasoning.

IV. OUR "NEW" PROBLEMS

We have seen that the concept of "employee" has been used to distinguish workers who are in need of certain sorts of protection. The accompanying assumption has always been that there is an identifiable and specific "employer."

This framework indeed fits most of the relationships between workers and their employers/clients. Yet a growing number of workers is left outside of this framework. These are the independent contractors who are in need of similar protection. They are independent, in the sense that they serve different clients and can hardly be seen as dependent on any of them, and yet their position *vis-à-vis* these clients is not one that seems distinguishable from an employee with a single employer. Although independent—and hence considered independent contractors by current definitions—they are in need of protection much like employees. Unlike other independent contractors who are self-dependent entrepreneurs, these workers have such a weak market stance that, like employees, they cannot be said to be self-dependent.

The existence of these non-self-dependent contractors is not entirely new. In the media industry, for example, "freelance" reporters and photographers with very little bargaining power (or any other ability to protect themselves, for that matter) have been quite a common phenomenon for many years, in Canada as elsewhere. But the New Economy has brought a significant rise in such cases, a trend that can be expected to continue and intensify. The plight of the non-self-dependent contractors must now move to the forefront.

A. The New Economy and the Organization of Work

The last two decades of the 20th century have seen dramatic changes in the organization of work. Prominent scholars have already told the story of these changes from a variety of different angles. There is now a proliferation of part-time, casual and temporary (or otherwise short-term) arrangements, more multiple job holders, and more people who work at home. There is much less employment security; in fact, the tacit commitment to long-term relations, which was so central to the industrial order in the post-war era, is said to be an endangered species. Employees who made significant job-specific investments now face a constant risk of losing their job, even in good times. Once they lose their job, they often have no choice but to take a "bad" job based on a contingent relationship and offering less pay, no benefits and no prospects.

More generally, globalization brings with it pressures towards outsourcing and subcontracting. Businesses prefer to focus on core competencies and contract out as much as possible to others. This is beneficial for them for a number of reasons. First, subcontractors sometimes specialize in the specific field and achieve efficiencies that the ordering firm cannot. Second, they can often cut labor costs more easily thanks to their location, a non-unionized labor force and by taking the risks of ignoring labor laws (something which a large, established firm presumably cannot do). And third, due to disparities in bargaining power, subcontractors will often take some of the risks off the ordering firm's back. In most cases, work is subcontracted to firms, and performed by employees of those firms. But sometimes, the subcontractors are merely self-employed workers.

It is in this general context—less security, more contingent relations and [a] tendency towards contracting out work—that some workers find themselves self-employed, many of them involuntarily. To be sure, some of these cases are within the "traditional" problem. When employers misclassify employees as independent contractors to avoid employment responsibilities and achieve better flexibility, the regular distinctions are sufficient (assuming they are applied sensibly and purposively). Such workers should simply be considered employees. When workers are economically dependent upon a specific employer, they should be protected rather than left alone in the "free" market. Indeed, in Canada, such dependent workers enjoy access to collective bargaining and, as we have argued above, should generally enjoy the protection of employment standards legislation as well (at least in part).

Others, however—the non-self-dependent contractors—are not dependent upon any identifiable employer. Our interest here lies with this specific group of workers.

B. Non-Self-Dependent Contractors

It is difficult to come up with data about the number of non-self-dependent contractors. While it is clear that the proportion of own-account self-employed in Canada is rising, we currently lack the critical information that might tell us how many of them are not sufficiently capable of protecting themselves—how many of them are in need of collective bargaining, and perhaps mandatory employment standards, just like employees. A couple of specific examples, while anecdotal, might shed some light on the intensification of this problem.

First, consider the media and entertainment industries. As already noted, the existence of "freelancing" arrangements for photographers and reporters is not new. But it is certainly proliferating; a recent survey of the International Federation of Journalists covering 98 countries found that "the freelance sector was continuing to grow as a proportion of the total journalistic community," with approximately a third now working in freelance capacity....

Similarly, a study of the British book publishing industry revealed that publishing houses increasingly externalize jobs that have low task interdependency, use relatively inexpensive equipment and are cerebral rather than manual in nature. Proofreaders and editors have been externalized—usually involuntarily—and are now likely to work from home as self-employed. The study shows that these workers are typically heavily reliant upon a single client, sometimes their former employer, for over half their work, and upon two clients for over 80% of their work. Their hourly pay is low, and of course they have no holidays, sick leave or pension rights. These proofreaders and editors have lost their constant income-flow and they now find it difficult to deal with uneven "feast or famine" flows of work. The prevalence of such arrangements is expected to continue to grow together with continued restructuring in the industry.

A second example concerns truck owner-operators. While some of them are considered "dependent contractors" in Canada, and hence "employees" for collective bargaining purposes, others have a number of different clients and are accordingly treated as independent contractors. These workers, however, usually lack the bargaining power necessary to reach fair wages and working conditions. Although the demand for truckers is rising—the trucking industry in Canada expanded by 5% annually from 1990 to 1998, compared with 1% for airlines and railways and a drop of 1% for marine shipping—owner-operators were not able to translate this demand into better contracts. This problem received public attention in Canada during the early months of February 2000, when protests of independent owner-operators erupted across the country as a result of significant rises in fuel prices.
[Reprinted by permission.]

For a somewhat different approach to the problem, see Judy Fudge, Eric Tucker, & Leah Vosko, "Employee or Independent Contractor? Charting the Legal Significance of the Distinction in Canada" (2003) 10 *Canadian Labour and Employment Law Journal* 193.

Although central to the scope and coverage of labour and employment-related statutes in Canada, the distinction between independent contractors and employees has not been as contentious at common law. Indeed, the Canadian common law courts have recognized an intermediate position between independent contractor and employee since the early twentieth century, and have afforded such intermediary workers an entitlement to reasonable notice of dismissal long before these workers received protections under labour and employment statutes. The following cases examine the common law approach to determining employment status.

Carter v Bell & Sons (Canada) Ltd, [1936] OJ No 203, [1936] OR 290 (CA) at paras 7–13

> The plaintiff's hiring was originally in October, 1933, and undoubtedly was as a mercantile agent, plaintiff's remuneration being entirely by payment of commission upon orders sent in and accepted. In September, 1934, the defendant, whose headquarters are in England, decided to attempt to introduce its product into the Western Provinces of Canada and appointed the plaintiff superintendent of agencies for Manitoba and Saskatchewan. The plaintiff, who had theretofore been employed in Ontario, went to Winnipeg, taking his wife and children with him. His business was to select and train men to hold the position of agents for the retail sale of the defendant's product. They were to be paid a commission by the defendant, but the plaintiff was to be entitled to an overriding commission of five per cent. on all orders placed through these agents. He was to be entitled to make such sales as he could by his own effort and to be paid the entire commission upon such sales. He had not the authority to appoint agents but he would select them to be appointed and would train them and report to the defendant upon their ability and industry, when the defendant itself would appoint. The plaintiff would have the supervision of these agents after appointment.
>
> The agreement between the parties was not embodied in any written contract, but its terms are referred to in detail in a letter written by the defendant. In this letter there is nothing referring to the dissolution of the contract and the plaintiff swears that this was not discussed.... The plaintiff relies upon the contract as establishing the relationship of master and servant and so to imply an obligation to give reasonable notice when terminating the arrangement. The plaintiff was to do pretty much as he pleased so long as he rendered faithful service to the defendant. The defendant had not the right to say what he should do from day to day, nor how it should be done. In their letters to him they only undertook to advise him as to his course in searching for satisfactory agents and making inquiries. The situation was clearly not that of master and servant simpliciter.
>
> In the case of master and servant there is implied in the contract of hiring an obligation to give reasonable notice of an intention to terminate the arrangement.... This is a peculiar incident of the relationship of master and servant based largely upon custom. The master and the servant, when nothing is said, are presumed to contract with reference to this usage and so a stipulation as to notice is implied. Where a contract is made falling outside of the technical relationship of master and servant, there is not necessarily this implication and the terms of the contract must be looked at to ascertain the intention of the parties. If the contract contains an express provision it will govern. If it contains no express provision, within certain fairly well defined limits, there may be an implied provision.

On the other hand there are cases of an agreement for the sale of goods upon commission, where the so-called mercantile agent does not devote himself solely to the work of the agency, but relies upon his commission for his remuneration, and where the employer exercises no immediate control over the agent but leaves him to be his own master. In such cases it has always been held that the relationship of master and servant does not exist and the contract may be terminated by either party at will.

There are many cases of an intermediate nature where the relationship of master and servant does not exist but where an agreement to terminate the arrangement upon reasonable notice may be implied. This is, I think, such a case. The mode of remuneration points to a mercantile agency pure and simple, but the duties to be performed indicate a relationship of a more permanent character. The choice of sub-agents and their training, the recommendation of them to the company for appointment, the supervision of these men when appointed, all point to this more permanent relationship. The fact that the plaintiff was entering a new territory as representative of the defendant and was endeavouring to create a market for the defendant's products and that to their knowledge he was taking his wife and children with him to the West indicate a relationship that could not be terminated at will by either party.

The test often applied in cases in which it is sought to make a master liable for the acts of the servant is not applicable here. The question is not the same. In the one case the inquiry is as to the liability of the master for the servant's acts. In the other the inquiry is as to the existence of an implied contract to terminate the relationship only upon reasonable notice. Here there was no such contract as would make the employer liable for the agent's acts, but I think this is by no means conclusive as against the plaintiff. The contract was one which I think could only be terminated upon reasonable notice, and reasonable notice would I think, under all the circumstances, be three months.

I would award the plaintiff damages amounting in all to $750.00 and give him the costs of the action and the appeal.

McKee v Reid's Heritage Homes Ltd, 2009 ONCA 916 at paras 3–11

MacPherson JA: The principal issue on the appeal is whether McKee was an employee of RHH or a dependent contractor.

On January 8, 1987, Orin Reid, the owner and directing mind of RHH, and McKee both signed an agreement that Reid wrote by hand entitled "Sales + Advertising Agreement". McKee signed it on behalf of her business style, Nu Home Consultant Services ("Nu Home"). The Agreement provided that RHH supply approximately 69 homes in Guelph for McKee to advertise and sell, for which McKee would charge a fee of $2,500 for each home that she sold. The Agreement included something of an exclusivity clause, providing that "RHH will have sole use of [Nu Home] services unless RHH agrees to allow [Nu Home] the right to sell for another company that is controlled by Orin Reid" and it then listed two other companies under Orin Reid's control, but also added "or a company that could be formed in the future." Finally, McKee requested, and the Agreement included, a termination provision: "Either party can terminate this agreement for any reason with giving the other party 30 days notice." . . .

After the first 69, RHH continued to provide homes for McKee to sell, but RHH hired someone else to handle the advertising aspect and paid McKee $1,500 per home sold instead. Around the same time, RHH also began supplying the necessary stationery and forms for selling homes to McKee and RHH gave her the title "Sales Manager", though RHH paid her through her corporation, whose name changed to Bribet Holdings Inc. ("Bribet") in 1988. McKee became very busy with work for RHH and over time she hired, trained, and managed her own subagents with whom she split her commissions on their sales, without intervention, direction, or interference from RHH. At all times, McKee both invoiced RHH and paid her subagents through Bribet. McKee testified that Reid "pretty well left me on my own to do what I was supposed to do."

The working relationship continued in this way. In 2000, Reid died and his son-in-law, Tim Blevins, succeeded him, but the relationship continued. However, in 2004, Blevins hired Doug Sider as Corporate Sales Manager and decided to restructure RHH's entire sales force—which at that time consisted of a number of different contracted real estate agents, dependent contractors, and in-house employees—so that each commissioned agent would report directly to Sider.

Blevins told McKee on January 10, 2005, that she and her subagents would have to work for RHH as "direct employees". [The parties were unable to come to terms regarding the restructuring of the relationship, and McKee sued for constructive dismissal.] The main issue on appeal is whether the trial judge erred by determining that McKee was an employee, not a dependent contractor.

ANALYSIS

[...]

The caselaw's evolution demonstrates the existence of an intermediate category, defined by economic dependency in the work relationship, requiring, *inter alia*, some reasonable notice for termination. [...] In 1936, this court recognized the existence of an "intermediate" position "where the relationship of master and servant does not exist but where an agreement to terminate the arrangement upon reasonable notice may be implied": *Carter v. Bell & Sons (Canada) Ltd.*, 1936 CanLII 75 (ON CA), [1936] O.R. 290, at p. 297. *Carter* emphasized the permanency of the working relationship between the parties as a determinant in delineating this intermediate category: see *Carter* at pp. 297–98.

A number of courts in several Canadian jurisdictions have since found such intermediate workers in a number of reasonable notice cases, particularly where the worker is economically dependent on the defendant, generally due to complete exclusivity or a high-level of exclusivity in their work [...]. [Ontario decisions have applied] the intermediate category analysis beyond merely sales or distributorship relationships.

Recently, this court again impliedly recognized the intermediate category where the case required the court to determine the status of a commissioned salesperson [in *Braiden v. La-Z-Boy Canada Ltd.* (2008), 2008 ONCA 464 (CanLII), 294 D.L.R. (4th) 172, at para. 24].... I conclude that an intermediate category exists, which consists, at least, of those non-employment work relationships that exhibit a certain minimum economic dependency, which may be demonstrated by complete or near-complete exclusivity. Workers in this category are known as "dependent contractors" and they are owed reasonable notice upon termination....

Having concluded that there is an intermediate category between independent contractor and employee, namely "dependent contractor", I also conclude that the legal principles applicable to distinguishing between employee and independent contractors apply equally to the distinction between employees and dependent contractors. In this way, the dependent contractor category arises as a "carve-out" from the non-employment category and does not affect the range of the employment category.

[T]he proper initial step is to determine whether a worker is a contractor or an employee, for which the *Sagaz/Belton* analysis, described in the next section, controls. Under that analysis, the exclusivity of the worker is listed as a *factor* weighing in favour of the employee category (*Belton*'s first principle). The next step, required only if the first step results in a contractor conclusion, determines whether the contractor is independent or dependent, for which a worker's exclusivity is *determinative*, as it demonstrates economic dependence. Therefore, exclusivity might be a "hallmark" of the dependent contractor category vis-à-vis the broader category of contractors. However, it continues also as a factor in determining whether the worker is not a contractor at all, but rather an employee, in the first-step analysis.

This process of analysis serves the policy purposes that underlie the jurisprudence. In summarizing the caselaw, Geoffrey England, Roderick Wood & Innis Christie, *Employment Law in Canada*, 4th ed. (Markham, Ont.: LexisNexis Canada) vol. 1, at s. 2.33, describes the frequently stated policy reasons for recognizing an intermediate category:

> These decisions have frequently acknowledged the policy justification for using the "intermediate" status doctrine in order to extend the safeguards of the employment contract to self-employed workers who are subject to relatively high levels of subordination and/or economic dependency, but who, technically, do not qualify as "employees" *strict sensu*.

Given this concern to safeguard workers who are formally "contractors" but who are in a position of economic vulnerability, it only makes sense to carve the dependent contractor category out of the broader existing contractor category and leave the range of the employee category intact. Therefore the appropriate analysis for distinguishing employees from "contractors" generally is the existing analysis for distinguishing employees from independent contractors....

As the Supreme Court of Canada has recognized, "there is no one conclusive test which can be universally applied": *671122 Ontario Ltd. v. Sagaz Industries Canada Inc.*, 2001 SCC 59 (CanLII), [2001] 2 S.C.R. 983, at para. 46. Instead, Major J. stated, at para. 45, that "what must always occur is a search for the total relationship of the parties." He then approvingly quoted MacGuigan J.A. in *Wiebe Door Services Ltd. v. M.N.R.*, [1986] 3 F.C. 553, at p. 563:

> The most that can profitably be done is to examine all the possible factors which have been referred to in these cases as bearing on the nature of the relationship between the parties concerned.... [N]o magic formula can be propounded for determining which factors should, in any given case, be treated as the determining ones.

In my opinion, this language endorses a case-specific, discretionary analysis. Such analyses are best left to the trier of fact, who is closest to the facts of the case and has the best handle on the true nature of the work relationship. More specifically, the trier of fact is best equipped to settle the "central question" based on the balance of factors put forth in *Sagaz* at para. 47:

> The central question is whether the person who has been engaged to perform the services is performing them as a person in business on his own account. In making this determination, the level of control the employer has over the worker's activities will always be a factor. However, other factors to consider include whether the worker provides his or her own equipment, whether the worker hires his or her own helpers, the degree of financial risk taken by the worker, the degree of responsibility for investment and management held by the worker, and the worker's opportunity for profit in the performance of his or her tasks.

In *Belton*, Juriansz J.A., writing on behalf of the court, upheld the use of the following five principles, modelled on the *Sagaz* factors, at paras. 11, 15:

1. Whether or not the agent was limited exclusively to the service of the principal;
2. Whether or not the agent is subject to the control of the principal, not only as to the product sold, but also as to when, where and how it is sold;
3. Whether or not the agent has an investment or interest in what are characterized as the "tools" relating to his service;
4. Whether or not the agent has undertaken any risk in the business sense or, alternatively, has any expectation of profit associated with the delivery of his service as distinct from a fixed commission;
5. Whether or not the activity of the agent is part of the business organization of the principal for which he works. In other words, whose business is it?

In the present case, the trial judge reviewed the *Sagaz* balancing inquiry. Although he did not explicitly reference the five *Belton* principles, his description of the "established practice" between McKee and RHH was clearly patterned on them:

> [Principle 1:] [T]here was a tacit agreement, carried out in practice for almost twenty years, that the plaintiff would sell "exclusively" for the defendant. [Principle 2:] The defendant assigned particular subdivisions to the plaintiff, built model homes and told her which lots she could sell. The defendant told her [when she] could sell, and maintained control over how the lots were sold. The defendant set the prices and conditions of sale, and retained the right to set the hours that the model homes were open.... [Principle 3:] [T]he principle tool was the model home—provided by [RHH]. [Principle 4:] The plaintiff here had no risk in the business and was paid on a strictly commission basis. [Principle 5:] Finally, the plaintiff's activity in the present case is part of the business of the defendant. Selling the homes is the most integral part of the defendant's business. It is the defendant's business in which the plaintiff is engaged.

Based on this review of the practice, the trial judge held: "I am satisfied that the plaintiff was an 'employee' of the defendant when she was terminated in 2005." ... In my opinion, the trial judge's decision is defensible under the legal principles defining work relationships and the employee category.

CHAPTER 3: THE CONTRACT OF EMPLOYMENT

* * * * *

The emergence of the so-called gig, crowdsourced, or sharing economy has recently brought the scope of labour and employment laws to public attention. The most litigated legal question to date is whether workers in the gig economy are "employees" for the purposes of different labour and employment law regimes, with a spate of lawsuits against the sharing economy giant—Uber, in particular. The legal difficulty in determining employment status is that many workers in the gig economy work under arrangements that hold characteristics traditionally associated with independent contracting, such as ownership of the tools, but also contract with very little bargaining power and high levels of economic dependency.

The following articles discusses in more depth the nature of crowdwork and some of the labour and employment law issues it provokes.

Jeremias Prassl & Martin Risak, "Uber, Taskrabbit, And Co.: Platforms as Employers? Rethinking the Legal Analysis of Crowdwork" (2015–2016) 37 *Comparative Labor Law & Policy Journal* 619 at 622-27 [notes omitted]

II. WORKING IN THE DIGITAL CROWD

As Antonio Aloisi and Valerio De Stefano note in their contributions to this special issue, developments in information and communication technology ("ICT") have led not only to fundamental changes in traditional working relationships, but also to the emergence of new forms of employment located in the grey and often unchartered territory between employment contracts and freelance work; a difficult fit for the existing binary legal categories of dependent labor and self-employment.

A particularly salient instantiation of this phenomenon is crowdwork, a relatively recent model also known as crowdsourcing of labor or crowd employment. These notions describe an ICT-based form of organizing the outsourcing of tasks to a large pool of workers. The work (ranging from transportation services and cleaning to digital transcription or programming tasks) is referred to in a variety of ways, including "gigs," "rides," or "tasks," and is offered to a large number of people (the "crowd") by means of an internet-based "crowdsourcing platform. This organizational model forms part of a larger set of processes known as "crowdsourcing"; with customers (or indeed employers) referred to as "crowdsourcers." As detailed in *Figure 1* [omitted], the resulting contractual relationships are manifold and complex: whilst the work is usually managed through an intermediary (the crowdsourcing platform), some will insist on direct contractual relationships between crowdsourcer clients and crowd workers, whereas others will opt for tripartite contractual structures, akin to traditional models of agency work and labor outsourcing.

A. *Characterizing Crowdwork Platforms*

We have already alluded to the nearly unlimited factual variety that characterizes the emergence of online platforms, both in terms of crowdsourcing in general (including crowdfunding, or the allocation of non-labor resources such as accommodation), and crowdsourcing of labor, or crowdwork, in particular. It is therefore not useful, or indeed feasible, to construct an overall taxonomy of crowdsourcing platforms. For present purposes, however, a few fundamental distinctions may be drawn.

Crowdsourcing, first, can take place internally or externally, depending on whether the crowd comprises a company's internal workforce or simply any number of individuals on a given platform. With external crowdsourcing, the crowdsourcer generally uses crowdsourcing platforms that already have an active crowd of registered workers. In this Article, we look solely at external crowdsourcing, as internal crowdsourcing is generally arranged within the context of existing employment relationships, and therefore poses fewer fundamental legal problems, regardless of whether the platform is operated by an independent enterprise or by the company itself.

Work crowdsourced to an external crowd, on the other hand, can be seen as clustered along a spectrum of services and arrangements. On the one end, we find physical services to be undertaken in the "real" (offline) world, where the crowdworker comes into direct contact with the customer. Examples include transportation delivered via apps such as Uber, domestic services (cleaning, repair work, etc.) delivered via platforms such as Helpling and clerical work (e.g., customer service or accounting) provided by platforms like UpWork. Uber customers, for example, use an app on their smartphones to request rides from a specific location, information that is instantly broadcast to drivers in the area. Once the request has been accepted by a driver, she is directed to the passenger and onwards to the required destination, through her version of the Uber app. Payment is taken automatically from the customer by the platform, and after the taking of a commission between 20 and 30%, passed on to the driver. Customers and drivers rate each other anonymously following each journey; the resulting scores are displayed to passengers and operators respectively before the next trip commences. Helpling operates in a similar way, even though the physical work takes place in the client's home or business premises—customers login on a platform or app, type in their postcode, and indicate when cleaning is required. They are then offered profiles of workers available in their vicinity, with further information about each individual, and an online facility to complete bookings. Payment is processed via the platform, and after completion of a task, workers are rated by their customers, with the resulting score displayed online in order to inform future customers.

On the other end of the spectrum, there is digital work delivered in the virtual world, usually via an interface provided by the platform. The tasks involved here are often comparatively simple, repetitive activities involving low pay and highly standardized or automated processes. These "microtasks" include digital labeling and the creation of image descriptions, categorizing data and products, and the translation or proofreading of short texts; with larger tasks often broken down into smaller subtasks to be worked on independently. These microtasks are then posted on platforms, where crowdworkers can find and complete them. The leading platforms for this kind of "cognitive piece work" or "Neo-Taylorism" include Amazon's Mechanical Turk and Clickworker. Survey research has shown that 25% of the tasks offered on Amazon *Mechanical Turk* are valued at $0.01, 70% offer $0.05 or less, and 90% pay less than $0.10 per completed task; thus equaling an average wage of about $2 per hour.

B. Working in the Crowd

Historically, the main advantage of hierarchical employment relationships over contracts with independent contractors was understood to be the entrepreneur's degree of control, and the resulting decrease in transaction cost, whether in the search, selection and training of workers, or the employer's tight control over the production process. An increasing desire for labor flexibility, on the other hand, was the driver behind the more recent creation of different forms of atypical work, including agency work, part-time work, and fixed-term employment.

Crowdwork is a novel combination of these factors, in so far as platforms attempt to increase flexibility for the employer or customer and to reduce the cost of "empty" or unproductive moments, whilst at the same time maintaining full control over the production process in order to keep transaction costs at a minimum. In order to meet these seemingly contradictory goals, two preconditions must be met: first, the crowd has to be large enough in order always to have individuals available when needed, and to maintain enough competition between crowdworkers to keep prices low. This is usually achieved through platforms' large and active crowds, with different platforms specializing in different segments of the crowdsourcing market.

Second, instead of the command-and-control systems inherent in "traditional" employment relationships, crowdsourcers and platforms rely on "digital reputation" mechanisms to guide the selection of crowdworkers and to ensure efficient performance control. Individual models vary, but the fundamental approach is consistent: crowdworkers are awarded points, stars or other symbols of status by the crowdsourcer or customer after completing a task. Quality control itself can thus be crowdsourced by the platform to its customers or other crowdsourcers, tapping the "wisdom of the crowd" in order to determine the performance levels of each single crowdworker.

The potential upsides of this emerging model for firms and workers alike should not be underestimated. Through the use of platforms, businesses ranging from restaurants to IT service providers can draw on a large crowd of flexible workers to reduce or even eliminate the cost of unproductive time at work, and rely on reputation mechanisms to maintain full control over the production process or service delivery. The resulting competition between crowdworkers will ensure that quality remains high whilst wages are low. As Thomas Biewald, the CEO of the platform Crowdflower, put it bluntly in 2010:

> Before the Internet, it would be really difficult to find someone, sit them down for ten minutes and get them to work for you, and then fire them after those ten minutes. But with technology, you can actually find them, pay them the tiny amount of money, and then get rid of them when you don't need them anymore.

Crowdwork similarly offers significant potential upside for (at least some of) its workers: first and foremost, in terms of flexibility, as crowdworkers can decide when to work, where to work, and what kind of tasks to accept. Platform work might, therefore, be more compatible with other duties, such as childcare. The flexibility and potentially limited nature of individual engagements can also help the underemployed, providing additional income to their regular earnings, and (at least through purely virtual crowdwork) allow those excluded from regular labor markets due to disabilities or other factors to find opportunities for gainful employment. Finally, there is an increasing number of genuinely successful small entrepreneurs, focused on particular niches or offering special skills, for whom crowdwork has become a very profitable source of new business.

At the same time, however, it is important to note that working conditions for the vast majority of crowdworkers appear to be poor, irrespective of the work being delivered. A lack of union representation and organizing power, the oligopoly of but a few platforms offering certain kinds of tasks, and constant economic and legal insecurity result in a considerable imbalance of bargaining power, as evident primarily from low wage-rates and heavily slanted terms and conditions in platform use agreements. In the case of virtual crowdwork, global competition and dislocated physical workplaces further aggravate these problems, as a lack of regulation leads to "digital slaves" working away in their "virtual sweatshops."

Two problems in particular are repeatedly highlighted: low wages and workers' dependence of their ratings with a particular platform. With regard to the former problem, for example, some reports suggest that the average wage on Amazon's Mechanical Turk is less than $2 per hour, considerably below the U.S. minimum wage. A related aspect is insecurity with regard to payment: in accordance with the general terms and conditions of microtasking-platforms, crowdsourcers have the right to reject work without having to give a reason or providing payment, whilst still receiving the fruits of a worker's labor.

Various systems of "digital reputation," or rating mechanisms, which form one of the core elements of platform works, raise a second set of difficult issues: a customer-input based system of stars or points not only puts crowdworkers in a permanent state of probation, but also infringes their mobility as it ties them to particular platforms. As more attractive and better paid tasks are only offered and assigned to those with the best reputation, a change of platforms will be difficult because digital reputation is not transferable between individual platforms — a fact that also further impairs the bargaining situation of crowdworkers.

[Reprinted with permission.]

3:220 Who Is an Employer?

As noted, decision makers have long struggled to determine who is an employee for the purpose of labour and employment statutes. But until recently it has been relatively simple to determine who was the employer. Most employees had a single employing individual or entity: one employer that hired them, that paid their wages, and that held the right to direct their work. The contract of employment, after all, envisages a bilateral relationship between only two parties. But as subcontracting has become a more prevalent feature of the labour market, it is increasingly common for managerial functions to be divided up among several entities, either as between a group of related companies, or split up along a supply chain of production. In this context, identifying a single employing entity is increasingly complex. The following case describes the common law approach to determining who is the employer through the doctrine of the "common employer."

CHAPTER 3: THE CONTRACT OF EMPLOYMENT

Downtown Eatery (1993) Ltd v Her Majesty the Queen in Right of Ontario (2001), 54 OR (3d) 161 at para 1ff (CA)

INTRODUCTION

In his valuable text, *Canadian Employment Law* (Aurora: Canada Law Book, 1999), Stacey Ball states, at p. 4-1:

> The courts now recognize that, for purposes of determining the contractual and fiduciary obligations which are owed by employers and employees, an individual can have more than one employer. The courts now regard the employment relationship as more than a matter of form and technical corporate structure. Consequently, the present law states that an individual may be employed by a number of different companies at the same time.

The mechanism whereby the law concludes that an employee may be employed by more than one company at the same time is the common employer doctrine. The doctrine has a well- recognized statutory pedigree in most jurisdictions. For example, in Ontario, s. 12(1) of the *Employment Standards Act*, R.S.O. 1990, c. E.14, deems associated or related businesses to be "one employer" for the purpose of protecting the benefits to which employees are entitled under the Act.

A major issue in this appeal is the definition and application of the common employer doctrine in a common law context. A dismissed employee sued his employer for wrongful dismissal. Following a trial, he was awarded substantial damages. Unfortunately, the employer company had no assets and consequently the employee was unable to enforce his judgment. In a subsequent action, the employee sued related companies and the two main principals of all the companies in an attempt to widen its net of potential sources of recovery. His principal legal submission in support of his attempt was, and is on this appeal, the common employer doctrine. In *Canadian Employment Law*, Mr. Ball states that "[t]he finding that more than one corporation is the employer may be a benefit when parts of the corporate group are more solvent than others ..." (p. 4-1). That is precisely the benefit the dismissed employee seeks to achieve in this litigation. ...

FACTS

(1) The parties and the events

In 1992, the respondents Herman Grad ("Grad") and Ben Grosman ("Grosman") were in the nightclub business in Toronto. They owned and operated two nightclubs, The Landing Strip at 191 Carlingview Drive and For Your Eyes Only at 557/563 King Street West. ...

In December 1992, Grad offered Alouche a position as manager of the nightclub For Your Eyes Only. The only entity specifically identified in the written employment contract was For Your Eyes Only. However, the contract also provided that Alouche would receive the health care and insurance benefits available "in our sister organization", which was not identified by name.

Alouche commenced work on December 29, 1992. During the next few months, he received his pay cheques from Best Beaver Management Inc. ("Best Beaver"), a company controlled by Grad and Grosman. In May 1993, Alouche was sent a formal Notice of Discipline on the letterhead of For Your Eyes Only for committing several infractions, including:

- the employee, while soliciting in excess of $1,000.00 gratuity only generated sales of $250.00 for the employer.
- the employee allowed numerous waitresses to abandon their assigned sections to solicit gratuities in the amount of $2,800.00.

On June 15, 1993, Alouche was dismissed. On October 13, 1993, he commenced an action against Best Beaver. In subsequent proceedings which form the basis for this appeal, Alouche explained the choice of Best Beaver as the defendant in the first action: "I sued Best Beaver ... because the paycheque that they gave me in For Your Eyes Only, it says Best Beaver Management Inc."

In the spring of 1996, there was a major reorganization of the Grad-Grosman companies. Best Beaver ceased to do business.... Shortly before the start of the trial in his wrongful dismissal action in August 1996, Alouche, worried about recovery if successful in the action, moved to add Grad and Grosman as co-defendants to his claim against Best Beaver. Faced with a potential adjournment of the trial to permit Grad and Grosman to retain counsel, Alouche withdrew the motion.

The trial proceeded with Best Beaver as the only defendant. Grad, a director of Best Beaver, represented it throughout the trial. The trial judge, Festeryga J., found in favour of Alouche. He awarded Alouche damages of $59,906.76, plus pre-judgment interest of $8,608.36 and costs of $15,387.79.

Best Beaver paid Alouche nothing pursuant to the judgment. Two sheriffs, in purported execution of the judgment, attended at the premises of For Your Eyes Only and seized $1,855 in cash. This provoked Downtown Eatery (1993) Ltd., which claimed that the money belonged to it, to commence an action against Alouche.... Alouche defended the action and counterclaimed against all of the companies controlled by Grad and Grosman and against Grad and Grosman personally. In December 1997, Kiteley J. ordered that the $1,855 seized by the sheriffs be paid into court to the credit of the action....

ANALYSIS

(1) The common employer issue

The trial judge decided this issue against Alouche for two reasons: (1) Alouche was estopped from raising the issue in his counterclaim action to enforce his previous judgment because he had not raised it in his original wrongful dismissal action; and (2) Alouche had not established the prerequisites necessary to identify any of the respondents as a common employer, along with Best Beaver.

(a) Res judicata/estoppel
[...]

In this appeal, the balance between finality of litigation and achieving justice between litigants should be struck in favour of the latter. The common employer issue relating to the corporate respondents should be determined on the merits.

(b) The merits

The common employer doctrine, in its common law context, has been considered by several Canadian courts in recent years. The leading case is probably Sinclair v. Dover Engineering Services Ltd. (1987), 1987 CanLII 2692 (BC SC), affd 49 D.L.R. (4th) 297 (B.C.C.A.) ("Sinclair"). In that case, Sinclair, a professional engineer, held himself out to the public as an employee of Dover Engineering Services Ltd. ("Dover"). He was paid by Cyril Management Limited ("Cyril"). When Sinclair was dismissed, he sued both corporations. Wood J. held that both companies were jointly and severally liable for damages for wrongful dismissal. In reasoning that we find particularly persuasive, he said, at p. 181 B.C.L.R.:

> Recognizing the situation for what it was, I see no reason, in fact or in law, why both Dover and Cyril should not be regarded jointly as the plaintiff's employer. The old-fashioned notion that no man can serve two masters fails to recognize the realities of modern-day business, accounting and tax considerations.
>
> There is nothing sinister or irregular about the apparently complex intercorporate relationship existing between Cyril and Dover. It is, in fact, a perfectly normal arrangement frequently encountered in the business world in one form or another. Similar arrangements may result from corporate take- overs, from tax planning considerations, or from other legitimate business motives too numerous to catalogue.
>
> As long as there exists a sufficient degree of relationship between the different legal entities who apparently compete for the role of employer, there is no reason in law or in equity why they ought not all to be regarded as one for the purpose of determining liability for obligations owed to those employees who, in effect, have served all without regard for any precise notion of to whom they were bound in contract. What will constitute a sufficient degree of relationship will depend, in each case, on the details of such relationship, including such factors as individual shareholdings, corporate shareholdings, and interlocking directorships. The essence of that relationship will be the element of common control.

[In many of the previous cases the issue was] a "paymaster" company closely connected with another corporate entity, with both being controlled by the same principals.... Similarly, in the present appeal, Best Beaver served only as a paymaster for the employees of the nightclubs owned and operated by other Grad and Grosman companies. Accordingly, the question becomes, in Adams J.'s language in *Jones*, "where effective control over the employee resides".

In our view, in June 1993, when Alouche was dismissed, there was a highly integrated or seamless group of companies which together operated all aspects of the For Your Eyes Only nightclub. Twin Peaks owned the nightclub premises and leased them to The Landing Strip which owned the trademark for For Your Eyes Only and, significantly for a nightclub, held the liquor and entertainment licences. Downtown Eatery operated the nightclub under a licence from The Landing Strip and owned the chattels and equipment at the nightclub. Best Beaver served as paymaster for the nightclub employees. Controlling all of these corporations were Grad and Grosman and their family holding companies, Harrad Corp. and Bengro Corp. Grad and Grosman could easily have operated the nightclub through a single company. They chose not to. There is nothing unlawful or suspicious about their choice. As Wood J. said in Sinclair, "it is a perfectly normal arrangement frequently encountered in the business world."

However, although an employer is entitled to establish complex corporate structures and relationships, the law should be vigilant to ensure that permissible complexity in corporate arrangements does not work an injustice in the realm of employment law. At the end of the day, Alouche's situation is a simple, common and important one—he is a man who had a job, with a salary, benefits and duties. He was fired—wrongfully. His employer must meet its legal responsibility to compensate him for its unlawful conduct. The definition of "employer" in this simple and common scenario should be one that recognizes the complexity of modern corporate structures, but does not permit that complexity to defeat the legitimate entitlements of wrongfully dismissed employees. . . .

In these circumstances, when he was wrongfully dismissed, Alouche did his best—he sued the company which had paid him. Later, it turned out that that company had no assets. Yet the nightclub continued in business, various companies continued to operate it and, presumably, Grad and Grosman continued to make money. In these circumstances, Alouche decided to try to collect the money to which [the] Superior Court of Justice had determined he was entitled. In our view, the common employer doctrine provides support for his attempt.

In conclusion, Alouche's true employer in 1993 was the consortium of Grad and Grosman companies which operated For Your Eyes Only. The contract of employment was between Alouche and For Your Eyes Only which was not a legal entity. Yet the contract specified that Alouche would be "entitled to the entire package of medical extended health care and insurance benefits as available in our sister organization". The sister organization was not identified. In these circumstances, and bearing in mind the important roles played by several companies in the operation of the nightclub, we conclude that Alouche's employer in June 1993 when he was wrongfully dismissed was all of Twin Peaks, The Landing Strip, Downtown Eatery and Best Beaver. This group of companies functioned as a single, integrated unit in relation to the operation of For Your Eyes Only.

* * * * *

The question of who is the employer is of increasing relevance, not only for situations of affiliated companies as in *Downtown Eatery*, but also in regard to temp worker employment, in franchises, and in supply chain work. Think back to the vignettes set out in Weil's piece, in Section 3:200 above. Who among the relevant enterprises would be considered the employer of the workers, based on the analysis in *Downtown Eatery*?

3:300 THE TERMS OF THE CONTRACT OF EMPLOYMENT

It is unusual for employment contracts to have comprehensive express provisions setting out all the terms and conditions of their employment. Top executives, professionals, elite athletes, and entertainers often have detailed employment contracts and, increasingly, so do quite precarious workers, like temp agency employees. But for many employees, the terms of their employment contracts arise from a mixture of express oral terms, from implied terms, and from a variety of human resource manuals or other such documents that are intended to be observed in the workplace. How then to determine the content of an employment contract, particularly where the employment relationship changes over time?

3:310 Express Terms

3:311 Interpretational Approach

Because the employment relationship is understood as a relationship of contract, it is subject to general contractual principles of construction. However, some principles of contract interpretation play a more central role in interpreting employment contracts than they might in other types of contractual relationships. One example is the *contra proferentem* rule, which specifies that ambiguities in the written terms of a contract are to be strictly interpreted against the interests of the drafter. In the employment context, this is typically the employer. The courts are also often sensitive to the idea that a written contract may not represent the true, or complete, intentions of the parties to an employment relationship, given the asymmetry of power between them.

Ceccol v Ontario Gymnastic Federation (2001), 55 OR (3d) 614 at para 1ff (CA)

> MacPherson JA (for the court):
>
> In the domain of employment law, a fundamental common law principle is that "a contract of employment for an indefinite period is terminable only if reasonable notice is given": see *Machtinger v. HOJ Industries Ltd.*, ... The principle is not an absolute one; in *Machtinger*, Iacobucci J. described it as a "presumption, rebuttable if the contract of employment clearly specifies some other period of notice, whether expressly or impliedly." (p. 998). Moreover, as Iacobucci J.'s statement of the general principle clearly indicates, it applies only to employees engaged for an indefinite period. The principle does not apply to fixed term contracts. An employee whose contract is not renewed at the conclusion of a fixed term is not dismissed or terminated; rather her employment simply ceases in accordance with the terms of the contract: see *Chambly (City) v. Gagnon*. ...
>
> The present appeal requires consideration of both the line between fixed and indefinite term employment contracts and the requirements for successfully rebutting the common law presumption of reasonable notice. These issues arise in the context of a 16 year employment relationship between a non-profit athletic association and one of its senior managers which the association terminated, it concedes, without cause. ...
>
> The respondent, Diana Ceccol, ... was the salaried Administrative Director of the Federation from September 1, 1981 to May 9, 1997. She was essentially the number two person in a 14-person office. ...
>
> In July 1981, Ceccol accepted the position of Administrative Director with the Federation, and she commenced employment on September 1, 1981. For the next 15 years and 8 months, Ceccol's employment was governed by a series of one-year contracts. The terms of these contracts were very similar. For convenience, I will refer to the 1996–7

contract which was in force when Ceccol's employment ceased. The crucial provisions of that contract were:

1. TERM

1.1 The Federation hereby hires the Employee and the Employee hereby agrees to serve as the Administrative Director of the Federation for a period of 12 months, commencing July 1, 1996 and terminating on June 30, 1997, unless sooner terminated or extended as hereinafter provided.

1.2 Subject to acceptable performance reviews, this Agreement is subject to renewal, upon the consent of both parties as to terms and conditions.

[...]

5. TERMINATION OF EMPLOYMENT

5.1 The Federation may terminate this Agreement at any time according to the current Employment Standards Act by reason of the Employee's dissipation, violation of reasonable instructions or policies/procedures of the Federation, failure to comply with provisions of this Agreement as herein set out or for other cause....

5.3 The Employee shall have the right to terminate this Agreement at any time by giving reasonable written notice (a minimum of 2 weeks) to the Federation....

5.4 The Federation and the Employee agree to abide by the Ontario Employment Standards Act and regulations concerning notice of termination of employment.

In the late fall of 1996, there were 14 employees at the Federation's head office. On December 3, a staff meeting was called and Harold Sanin, the Vice-President (Administration), presented all of the employees with a written notice [that their employment would end on June 30, 1997] ...

In the spring of 1997, most of the senior managers were informed that the Federation would not renew their contracts after June 30. For Ceccol (and for Joe Rabel, the Executive Director), the axe fell on May 9, 1997.... The Federation paid Ceccol her salary and relevant benefits until June 30, 1997. It also offered her *ex gratia* severance payments potentially totalling three months salary if she signed a release. Ceccol declined this offer and commenced a wrongful dismissal action.

The Litigation

[T]he trial judge held that Ceccol was an indefinite term, not a fixed term, employee and that she was entitled to reasonable notice, not the statutory notice in the *Employment Standards Act*, R.S.O. 1990, c. E.14 ("*ESA*"). He fixed the reasonable notice at 16 months but reduced it by four months because of Ceccol's failure to properly mitigate her damages....

The issues on the appeal and cross-appeal are:

1) Did the trial judge err by concluding that Ceccol was an indefinite term employee?
2) Did the trial judge err by concluding that Ceccol was entitled to reasonable notice rather than to the notice provided in the *ESA*?

[...]

The Federation's Appeal

(a) Duration of Ceccol's employment

The Federation and Ceccol entered into 15 annual contracts. Each contract contained, in article 1.1, a specific final date, June 30 from 1992 onwards. However, the trial judge concluded that Ceccol was not a fixed term employee:

> I find as fact that the plaintiff and all her immediate superiors prior to Sanin, who came on the scene in 1996, believed and acted as if the plaintiff were, what the plaintiff and her witnesses described as a "full-time" permanent employee.

The trial judge gave effect to this shared perception because, in his words, "[i]n the final analysis, in these cases the decision to be made is what are the reasonable expectations of the parties."

I agree with the trial judge's conclusion. His observation about the importance of the parties' reasonable expectations is a faithful application of one of the leading decisions of the Supreme Court of Canada in the contract law domain. In *Consolidated Bathurst Export Ltd. v. Mutual Boiler and Machinery Insurance Co.*, ... Estey J. said:

> [T]he normal rules of construction lead a court to search for an interpretation which, from the whole of the contract, would appear to promote or advance the true intent of the parties at the time of entry into the contract. Consequently, literal meaning should not be applied where to do so would bring about an unrealistic result or a result which would not be contemplated in the commercial atmosphere in which the insurance was contracted. Where words may bear two constructions, the more reasonable one, that which produces a fair result, must certainly be taken as the interpretation which would promote the intention of the parties.

In this passage, Estey J. linked the factors of the parties' intention and unrealistic or fair results with contractual words that "bear two constructions." Is it fair to conclude that article 1.1 of the Federation-Ceccol contract admits of more than one construction? In my view, it is. ...

In summary, in my view the relationship between articles 1.1 and 1.2 in the contract is not entirely clear. In particular, the words "subject to renewal" in article 1.2 are not self-defining and cast doubt on the Federation's argument that article 1.1 is effective in creating a clear fixed term contract.

This ambiguity surrounding the extension of the contract (it is worth noting that the contract was in fact renewed 15 times) justified the trial judge's decision to hear, and ultimately to rely on, evidence about the parties' intentions and conduct relating to the contract. That evidence was, as the trial judge found, overwhelming in support of Ceccol's contention that she was hired, and performed for almost 16 years, as an indefinite term employee. ...

I conclude with this observation. Fixed term contracts of employment are, of course, legal. If their terms are clear, they will be enforced. ...

However, the consequences for an employee of finding that an employment contract is for a fixed term are serious: the protections of the *ESA* and of the common law principle of reasonable notice do not apply when the fixed term expires. That is why, as Professor Geoffrey England points out ..., "the courts require unequivocal and explicit language to establish such a contract, and will interpret any ambiguities strictly against the employer's interests."

It seems to me that a court should be particularly vigilant when an employee works for several years under a series of allegedly fixed term contracts. Employers should not be able to evade the traditional protections of the *ESA* and the common law by resorting to the label of 'fixed term contract' when the underlying reality of the employment relationship is something quite different, namely, continuous service by the employee for many years coupled with verbal representations and conduct on the part of the employer that clearly signal an indefinite term relationship.

In the present case, Ceccol served the Federation loyally, professionally and continuously for almost 16 years. The Federation does not say otherwise. I cannot say that the contract which governed their relationship contains the "unequivocal and explicit language" necessary to establish a fixed term contract. I conclude that the employment contract was for an indefinite term, subject to renewal and termination in accordance with other provisions in the contract.

(b) Reasonable notice or not?

The conclusion that a contract is for an indefinite term has as a corollary that, in normal circumstances, the employer can terminate the contract only by providing reasonable notice. This principle is not, however, an absolute one. There is an important exception, set out succinctly by Iacobucci J. in *Machtinger*, at p. 998:

> I would characterize the common law principle of termination only on reasonable notice as a presumption, rebuttable if the contract of employment clearly specifies some other period of notice, whether expressly or impliedly.

The Federation relies on this exception. It submits that article 5.4 expressly specifies some other period of notice. For convenience, I set out article 5.4 again:

> 5.4 *The Federation and the Employee agree to abide by the Ontario* Employment Standards Act *and regulations concerning notice of termination of employment.*

[Justice MacPherson then set out section 57(1)(h) of the *Employment Standards Act*, which provides for eight weeks termination notice for an employee with eight or more years of service with the employer.]

The Federation submits that, reading article 5.4 of the contract and s. 57(1)(h) of the *ESA* together, the result is clear: Ceccol is entitled to eight weeks of statutory/contractual notice, and not reasonable notice under the common law....

I say, candidly, that the Federation's submission on this issue is a plausible one. However, in the end, I am not persuaded by it.... In my view, the absence of "may terminate" wording in article 5.4 which, I underline, is the provision on which the Federation relies, leads to a second plausible interpretation. The interpretation is this: the Federation-Ceccol contract permits only three types of termination—by the employer for cause (article 5.1), by the employer of probationary employees (article 5.2) and by the employee (article 5.3). The contract does not deal with terminations without cause....

The question then arises: if article 5.4 is not a provision dealing with terminations without cause, what roles does it play? My answer—and I do not claim it is the only possible answer—is that article 5.4, with its "abide by the [*ESA*] ... concerning notice of termination" wording, qualifies the three termination scenarios dealt with in articles 5.1–5.3. Article 5.4 says to the parties: if you invoke the right to terminate the employment relationship pursuant to any of articles 5.1–5.3, you must do so in accordance with the *ESA*. ...

Which of the two plausible interpretations of article 5.4 should govern the Federation-Ceccol employment contract? *Machtinger* instructs that the presumption of reasonable notice can be rebutted only if the employment contract "clearly specifies some other period of notice" (p. 998). I do not think that article 5.4 achieves that high level of clarity.

Moreover, I think it is important to acknowledge what is at stake in the conflicting interpretations put forward by the parties. Ceccol worked loyally and professionally for the Federation for almost 16 years. Her final salary was $50,000. If she is entitled to only the eight week payment established by the *ESA*, she will receive approximately $7700. If she is entitled to reasonable notice, which the Federation is content to accept is 16 months, she will receive approximately $66,700.

In an important line of cases in recent years, the Supreme Court of Canada has discussed, often with genuine eloquence, the role work plays in a person's life, the imbalance in many employer-employee relationships and the desirability of interpreting legislation and the common law to provide a measure of protection to vulnerable employees. ...

These factors have clearly influenced the interpretation of employment contracts. ...

In the present appeal, there are, as I have tried to demonstrate, two plausible interpretations of article 5.4 of the employment contract. One interpretation would remove the common law entitlement to reasonable notice; the other would preserve it. One interpretation would result in a termination provision which the trial judge described as "especially stringent and onerous"; the other would provide an employee with notice which at common law, both parties accept, is reasonable. One interpretation would provide a loyal and professional 16-year senior employee with $7700 in termination pay; the other would provide her with $66,700. In my view, in each instance the second interpretation is preferable. It is also, in my view, consistent with the leading decisions of the Supreme Court of Canada in the employment law domain. ...

I would dismiss the appeal ... with costs.

* * * * *

One of the court's concerns in *Ceccol* was that there was a difference in the strict terms of the written employment contract, which stipulated that Ms Ceccol was a fixed-term employee, and the long-term nature of her employment, which suggested she was an indefinite duration employee. Whether or not Ceccol was a fixed-term employee matters, because remedies and mitigation obligations for wrongful dismissal of employees under fixed-term contracts are slightly different than those of indefinite duration employees. In particular, fixed-term employees are not entitled to reasonable notice of dismissal, and instead are owed the compensation that remains outstanding over the balance of the contract unless contractually specified otherwise or the employee is dismissed with cause. See *Howard v Benson Group Inc (The Benson Group Inc)*, 2016 ONCA 256; *Karmel v Calgary Jewish Academy*, 2015 ABQB 731; *Bowes v Goss Power Products Ltd*, 2012 ONCA 425.

To determine the nature of Ceccol's employment contract, the court used principles of contract interpretation to hold that there were ambiguities in the written contract, and that it was appropriate to resolve "ambiguities strictly against the employer's interest." Without expressly saying so, the court applied the *contra proferentem* principle of contractual interpretation in this instance.

In Ceccol's case there was a mismatch between the realities of her job and the formal legal status she was provided by contract. In other cases, the issue is that the job changes over time. Often employees receive a written employment contract at first hire, but do not receive new contracts as they advance and are promoted. Should the written terms of a contract received at initial hire, geared towards the work of a junior employee, determine the rights of the parties if the employee is dismissed many years later? The "changed substratum" doctrine addresses such situations. In *MacGregor v National Home Services*, 2012 ONSC 2042 (at para 11), the doctrine was explained in the following terms:

> The changed substratum doctrine is a part of employment law. The doctrine provides that if an employee enters into an employment contract that specifies the notice period for a dismissal, the contractual notice period is not enforceable if over the course of employment, the important terms of the agreement concerning the employee's responsibilities and status has significantly changed.... The idea behind the changed substratum doctrine is that with promotions and greater attendant responsibilities, the substratum of the original employment contract has changed, and the notice provisions in the original employment contract should be nullified.

3:312 Incorporating Terms

As noted, the terms of most employment contracts are composed of a mixture of express oral, written, and implied terms. But they may also arise from a variety of human resource manuals or policies that contain certain terms that are intended to be observed in the workplace. When a dispute arises, a party may argue that those terms have been incorporated into the employment contract. This can give rise to many legal difficulties.

Ellison v Burnaby Hospital Society (1992), 42 CCEL 239 at 241 (BCSC)

> The plaintiff was initially hired by the defendant as a general duty registered nurse in March 1967. She was gradually promoted within the hospital until she was appointed director of nursing, long term care, in 1989. She remained in that position until she was dismissed on December 10, 1991 following a structural reorganization of nursing administration at the hospital. At the time of her dismissal the plaintiff was 59 years of age and had served the defendant for almost 25 years....
>
> The first question to be resolved in this case is whether the defendant's benefits policy forms part of the contract of employment between the plaintiff and the defendant. The benefits policy was introduced by the defendant in 1988, some 21 years after the plaintiff commenced her employment with the defendant and one year before she was promoted to the position of director of nursing. The plaintiff acknowledges that she received a copy of that document in 1988. She has no recollection of reading it, although she says that she may have glanced at some parts of it. She says that she put it in a folder

in a drawer together with other documents related to her employment, such as pay stubs and information on superannuation. She specifically states that she did not know that the benefits policy provided for termination and severance.

The defendant relies on the evidence of Mr. Waldron, vice-president of hospital services for the defendant, who says that the benefits policy forms part of the plaintiff's contract of employment with the defendant. No evidence is given in support of that bald statement. Mr. Waldron also states that he thought he noticed the plaintiff's husband carrying a copy of the benefits policy at a meeting Mr. Waldron attended with the plaintiff on December 2, 1991. Assuming that this is so, and it is not clear that it is, there is no suggestion that either the plaintiff or Mr. Waldron referred to the benefits policy as being part of the contract of employment at that meeting or at any other time prior to the plaintiff's dismissal.

The defendant submits that a person in the plaintiff's position of responsibility must have been aware of the terms of the benefits policy. The defendant points to the fact that the plaintiff was aware that certain of her health benefits were set out in a separate document which she received from the defendant, and that it is reasonable to assume that she was equally aware of the benefits set out in this policy. The defendant says that by claiming some of the benefits which are referred to in the benefits policy the plaintiff must be taken to have accepted the entire policy as part of her contract of employment.

The benefits policy itself does not state that it forms part of the contract of employment between the defendant and any [of] its managerial or non-contract personnel. The policy is divided into 23 parts beginning with an introduction which provides, in part, as follows:

> Welcome to Burnaby Hospital. This booklet, along with the Burnaby Hospital Personnel Information Brochure, has been prepared to describe the complete benefit packages available to all managerial and non-contract personnel along with pertinent information which will make you aware of the current practices of our Hospital.

The policy goes on to describe various benefits provided by the defendant, and it makes several references to other sources of information relating to benefits, including brochures and the employee resources department. The policy is put together as just that—a statement of policy and information. It is not put together with the precision or certainty of terms which one would expect of a document which is intended to create a contractual relationship.

The relevant law with respect to this issue is set out in the case of *Starcevich v. Woodward's Ltd.*.... The headnote of that case, which accurately reflects the judgment, provides as follows:

> Before a 'policy' can form part of a contract of employment, there must be evidence that the policy was accepted by both the employer and the employee as a term of the employment contract, and the onus in this respect rests on the party seeking to rely on the policy as a term of the contract. One party cannot unilaterally impose a contractual term on the other. The fact that the plaintiff was aware of the policy, and in fact applied it to others in

the course of his employment, did not establish that he accepted the policy as a term of his own employment contract.

Similar statements are found in other cases.... [In] *Rahemtulla v. Vanfred Credit Union* ..., the court stated that the fact that the employee had continued to work after learning of the policy did not lead to the conclusion that the employee had accepted the terms of the policy as part of her contract of employment. The court also stated that there was no evidence that the parties intended the policy to constitute a binding contractual relationship between them.

The defendant submits that the cases referred to by the plaintiff are distinguishable, and it relies on the case of *Greene v. Chrysler Canada Ltd.*... which was upheld in the B.C. Court of Appeal for the reasons given by the trial judge.... In *Greene* the trial judge found that a notice of lay-off given by the defendant did not amount to a dismissal, apparently because the plaintiff had been provided with two booklets dealing with compensation and benefits which specifically provided for lay-offs, and which the court concluded formed part of the contract of employment. The Court of Appeal concluded that such a finding was justified.

There is no question that a policy or benefits package of an employer can form part of the contract of employment if it is clear that the employer and employee intended it to do so. In this case, however, I am not persuaded that the policy formed part of the contract of employment between the plaintiff and the defendant. The policy was instituted long after the plaintiff was originally hired by the defendant, albeit before she received her last promotion. The policy was simply given to the plaintiff without any request that she read it, or any other indication that the defendant was relying on it as forming part of the contract of employment. The plaintiff glanced at the policy, but did not in any way communicate to the defendant that she accepted the statements set out in the policy as terms of her employment. The language of the policy is not reflective of a contractual document, but rather of an information package.

Since the benefits policy did not form part of the contract of employment between the plaintiff and the defendant, the court must look to the common law to determine the reasonable period of notice which the plaintiff was entitled.

* * * * *

Unless the content of a human resource policy is expressly included at the time of contract, the question of policy incorporation is one of contractual variation. As *Ellison* makes clear, both parties must consent to the variation or incorporation for it to be enforceable. But in addition to party consent, changing the terms of a contract requires fresh consideration, as with any contractual variation. Some cases suggest that an employer provides fresh consideration simply by not terminating an employee who accepts a variation. The current consensus, however, appears to be that "mere continuation of employment" is not adequate consideration, but an express or implied promise by the employer not to dismiss for a reasonable period of time may be sufficient. For a discussion of this issue, see *Techform Products v Wolda* (2001), 56 OR (3d) 1 (CA) and *Watson v Moore Corp* (1996), 134 DLR (4th) 252 (BCCA).

3:314 Restrictive Covenants

Some employment contracts contain terms referred to as restrictive covenants. These are express contractual terms which purport to limit an employee's right to compete with their former employer after leaving their employment (non-competition clauses), or to solicit the clients of their former employer (non-solicitation clauses). Employers may wish to include such clauses because post-employment competition is otherwise permitted at common law. Restrictive covenants present interesting policy challenges for the courts, however, because they pit two cherished liberal values against each other—freedom of trade and freedom of contract. They also suggest two different ideas about how economic prosperity is best achieved in a community, that is, whether an economy flourishes most when ideas can freely circulate, or when the costs of research and innovation are protected.

The following case is the leading authority on the enforceability of restrictive covenants in employment.

Elsley v JG Collins Ins Agencies, [1978] 2 SCR 916 at 918–29

> DICKSON J.—The question for decision in this case is whether a restrictive covenant contained in a certain contract of employment, to which I will shortly refer, is valid.
>
> The facts are, to all intents, undisputed. On April 24, 1956, an agreement was entered into for the purchase by the Collins Company of the general insurance business of a competitor, D.C. Elsley Limited. The price was $46,137. The life insurance business and the real estate business conducted by the Elsley Company were not included. The agreement contained a covenant on the part of the vendor that it would not, for a period of ten years, carry on or be engaged in the business of a general insurance agency within the City of Niagara Falls, the Township of Stamford and the Village of Chippawa, all in the County of Welland, and that the vendor would pay the purchaser $1,000 for each and every breach. [The parties later entered into an interim agreement.] [The interim agreement] was replaced by an agreement of May 30, 1956 by which Elsley undertook to serve as manager of the Collins Company's general insurance business in the greater Niagara Falls area, devoting all necessary time and attention to such employment, subject to the proviso that he might supervise the Elsley Company in its real estate and life insurance business. The agreement commenced June 1, 1956 and was stated to continue in force from year to year until terminated by either party upon three months' notice. As things developed, it continued until May, 1973.
>
> Clause 3 of the management agreement contains the covenant which gave rise to the present proceedings. It reads:
>
>> 3. Subject to the restrictive covenants contained in the Agreement made between the Parties dated May 1, 1956, in consideration of the employment, the Manager shall not, while in the employ of the Company or of its successors and assigns, whether in the capacity in which he is now or in any other capacity, or during the period of five years next after he shall, whether by reason of dismissal, retirement or otherwise, have ceased to be so employed, directly or indirectly, and whether as principal, agent, director of a company, traveller, servant or otherwise, carry on or be engaged or concerned or take part in the business of a general insurance agent within the corporate limits of the City of Niagara.

Falls, the Township of Stamford and the Village of Chippawa, all in the County of Welland; and in the event of his failing to observe or perform the said agreement, he shall pay to the said Company, its successors or assigns, or other the person or persons entitled for the time being to the benefit of the said agreement, the sum of One Thousand Dollars ($1,000.00) as and for liquidated damages, and the said Mrs. Elsley, wife of the Manager, by her signature hereto, agrees to observe and be bound by the aforesaid covenant.

[...]

Elsley managed the combined general insurance businesses for seventeen years, from June 1, 1956 until May 31, 1973, at which time he gave proper notice of termination of employment.

During the seventeen-year period Elsley dealt with the customers of the agency to the almost total exclusion of Collins. To them Elsley was the business, Collins little more than a name. Elsley met the customers, telephoned them frequently, placed their insurance policies and answered their queries. Such were the findings of the trial judge. People became accustomed to doing business with him on a personal basis and he looked after their insurance needs. He served not only customers of the business he formerly owned, but also Collins' customers.

From 1956 to 1973 the business bore the name "Collins & Elsley Insurance Agencies." During that period, as a convenience, many policyholders paid their premiums at the office of D.C. Elsley Limited, the real estate office of Elsley, because a large part of the business purchased by Collins from Elsley came from the area in which this office was located. As general manager of the combined businesses, Elsley, of course, had access to all policyholder records; he was familiar with the nature and extent of coverage and the premium paid by each policyholder. He had knowledge of the insurable assets, financial credit, likes and dislikes and idiosyncrasies of each customer, in a recurring and confidential relationship not unlike that of lawyer/client or doctor/patient. It was only natural that policyholders would follow him if he made a change.

|

Following termination of his employment with Collins, Elsley commenced his own general insurance business under D.C. Elsley Limited. He took with him two insurance salesmen and an insurance clerk formerly employed by the Collins and Elsley agency. A large number of former clients of the agency transferred their business. Exhibit 10 comprised a list of approximately two hundred former clients who had advised Collins they were transferring their insurance business to Elsley. The only factual dispute in the entire case is as to whether Elsley solicited the business of former clients. He denied having done so. Collins could not say that Elsley himself had solicited former clients, but said that Elsley's employees had done so. When asked as to how many former clients he had had dealings with after leaving the employ of Collins, Elsley replied that he had never "stopped to add them up." There is evidence he advertised for general insurance business and that some advertisements referred to him as being "formerly of Collins and Elsley Insurance Agencies." In the Ontario Court of Appeal, Mr. Justice Evans (with whom Mr. Justice MacKinnon agreed) found that Elsley had actively solicited former clients. Mr. Justice Jessup took a contrary view. Both courts below considered Collins and Elsley to be successful businessmen, competent and experienced.

At trial, Mr. Justice Stark ordered Elsley restrained until September 1, 1978 from carrying on the business of general insurance agent within the defined area.... The majority of the Court of Appeal affirmed the judgment at trial, with one variation.... Mr. Justice Jessup dissented.

The point taken by Mr. Justice Jessup is central to the case. It is this. The restrictive covenant, it is contended, does not merely restrain the solicitation by Elsley of clients of the Collins & Elsley agency, it prevents Elsley engaging at all in the general insurance business in a large area and operates, therefore, to eliminate competition *per se* without regard for the public interest and beyond necessary protection of Collins' interest. The argument, in short, is that the covenant would have been valid if it had precluded Elsley from soliciting clients of his former employer but, drawn in more sweeping terms, it is unenforceable as being in restraint of trade and an interference with individual liberty of action.

II

The principles to be applied in considering restrictive covenants of employment are well established.... A covenant in restraint of trade is enforceable only if it is reasonable between the parties and with reference to the public interest. As in many of the cases which come before the courts, competing demands must be weighed. There is an important public interest in discouraging restraints on trade, and maintaining free and open competition unencumbered by the fetters of restrictive covenants. On the other hand, the courts have been disinclined to restrict the right to contract, particularly when that right has been exercised by knowledgeable persons of equal bargaining power. In assessing the opposing interests the word one finds repeated throughout the cases is the word "reasonable." The test of reasonableness can be applied, however, only in the peculiar circumstances of the particular case. Circumstances are of infinite variety. Other cases may help in enunciating broad general principles but are otherwise of little assistance....

The distinction made in the cases between a restrictive covenant contained in an agreement for the sale of a business and one contained in a contract of employment is well-conceived and responsive to practical considerations. A person seeking to sell his business might find himself with an unsaleable commodity if denied the right to assure the purchaser that he, the vendor, would not later enter into competition. Difficulty lies in definition of the time during which, and the area within which, the non-competitive covenant is to operate, but if these are reasonable, the courts will normally give effect to the covenant.

A different situation, at least in theory, obtains in the negotiation of a contract of employment where an imbalance of bargaining power may lead to oppression and a denial of the right of the employee to exploit, following termination of employment, in the public interest and in his own interest, knowledge and skills obtained during employment. Again, a distinction is made. Although blanket restraints on freedom to compete are generally held unenforceable, the courts have recognized and afforded reasonable protection to trade secrets, confidential information, and trade connections of the employer.

III

The critical question, as I have indicated, is whether the employer, in seeking to protect his trade connection, overreached in the formulation of clause 3 of the agreement of May 30, 1956.

In assessing the reasonableness of the clause with reference to the interests of the parties, several questions must be asked. First, did Collins have a proprietary interest entitled to protection? The answer to this question must surely be in the affirmative. Shortly before the agreement for the employment of Elsley, Collins had paid Elsley some $46,000 for the general insurance trade connection of Elsley. By the agreement Elsley was placed in control, not only of that trade connection, but also the trade connection which Collins enjoyed prior to that time. Second, were the temporal or spatial features of the clause too broad? Some argument was directed to the Court as to those aspects, but I am in entire agreement with the courts below that they are not open to successful challenge. The next and crucial question is whether the covenant is unenforceable as being against competition generally, and not limited to proscribing solicitation of clients of the former employer. In a conventional employer/employee situation the clause might well be held invalid for that reason. The fact that it could have been drafted in narrower terms would not have saved it, for as Viscount Haldane said in *Mason v. Provident Clothing and Supply Co., supra*, p. 732, "... the question is not whether they could have made a valid agreement but whether the agreement actually made was valid." Whether a restriction is reasonably required for the protection of the covenantee can only be decided by considering the nature of the covenantee's business and the nature and character of the employment. Admittedly, an employer could not have a proprietary interest in people who were not actual or potential customers. Nevertheless, in exceptional cases, of which I think this is one, the nature of the employment may justify a covenant prohibiting an employee not only from soliciting customers, but also from establishing his own business or working for others so as to be likely to appropriate the employer's trade connection through his acquaintance with the employer's customers. This may indeed be the only effective covenant to protect the proprietary interest of the employer. A simple non-solicitation clause would not suffice....

In the leading case of *Morris v. Saxelby, supra*, Lord Parker enunciated with clarity the circumstances in which a covenant taken by an employer from an employee or apprentice will be enforceable. He said [...]: "Wherever such covenants have been upheld it has been on the ground, not that the servant or apprentice would, by reason of his employment or training, obtain the skill and knowledge necessary to equip him as a possible competitor in the trade, but that he might obtain such personal knowledge of and influence over the customers of his employer, or such an acquaintance with his employer's trade secrets as would enable him, if competition were allowed, to take advantage of his employer's trade connection or utilize information confidentially obtained".

It is difficult to envisage a factual situation in which an employee would be in a better position than that of Elsley in the present case, to obtain "personal knowledge of and influence over the customers of his employer." Later in his speech, Lord Parker made the point that it is of importance: whether "the defendant ever came into personal contact with the plaintiff's customers." The same point is made in the following passage from Cheshire & Fifoot, *The Law of Contract* (8th ed.), at p. 369:

> A restraint is not valid unless the nature of employment is such that customers will either learn to rely upon the skill or judgment of the servant or will deal with him directly and personally to the virtual exclusion of the master, with the result that he will probably gain their custom if he sets up business on his own account.

In the view which I take of this case a covenant against solicitation would not have been adequate to protect the proprietary interest entitled to protection. Exhibit 10 is telling support of that view. Elsley testified that he did not solicit former clients; notwithstanding, two hundred clients switched their custom to him. That is a vivid illustration of what Lord Parker had in mind in speaking of the influence of an employee over the customers of his employer. And it is not suggested that Exhibit 10 was a complete list of all those who took action. It was filed as representative only. Collins estimated that Elsley had taken close to one-half of the business on the books when Elsley left. As Salter J. said in the case of *Putsman v. Taylor* [...] at p. 642, a covenant against solicitation "is difficult to enforce; it is difficult to show breach and difficult to frame an injunction." The difficulty is demonstrated in this case. Does an advertisement which comes to the attention of former clients amount to solicitation? Was there solicitation by Elsley? I need not attempt to answer those questions. The point is that a non-solicitation covenant, in the circumstances here found, would have been meaningless....

For the foregoing reasons, in my view the impugned covenant is no wider than reasonably required in order to afford adequate protection to Collins.

After the party relying on a restrictive covenant has established its reasonableness as between the parties, the onus of proving that it is contrary to the public interest lies on the party attacking it: *Morris v. Saxelby (supra)*. Since in my opinion the respondent has established what is required of him, the matter of the public interest must now be considered.

Unless it can be said that any and every restraint upon competition is bad, I do not think that enforcement of the clause could be considered inimical to the public interest. There were twenty to twenty-two general agents in Niagara Falls according to the evidence as of the date of trial, employing eighty to ninety employees. There was nothing to suggest that the people of Niagara Falls would suffer through the loss, for a limited period, of the services of Elsley in the general insurance business.

I am of opinion that the clause in contention is valid, and enforceable in accordance with its terms.

* * * * *

Relying on the Supreme Court's decision in *Elsley*, the Ontario Court of Appeal in *Lyons v Multari* (2000), 50 OR (3d) 526 (CA) refused to enforce a non-competition clause, on the basis that a non-solicitation clause would have been sufficient to protect the former employer's legitimate proprietary interests. A restrictive covenant is also not enforceable against an employee where the employee is wrongfully dismissed. See, for example, *Globex Foreign Exchange Corporation v Kelcher*, 2005 ABCA 419.

Until recently, non-competition clauses were typically only included in the employment contracts of employees whose positions required active involvement with a company's intellectual property through trade secrets, research and development, or confidential business information. But there seems to be an increasing trend to use non-competes in lower-paying customer service jobs as well.

In Quebec, the *Civil Code* sets the criteria for the validity of non-competition clauses (sections 2089 and 2095). In addition to the requirement that they be in writing, the temporal and geographic boundaries must be explicitly mentioned, as well as the type of work that cannot be performed. The limits imposed on the employee must also be restricted to what is necessary to protect the employer's legitimate interests. The onus of proving the validity of the clause lies with the employer. Finally, an employer cannot invoke a non-competition clause if it has terminated the employment contract for no serious cause, or if it has given the employee serious cause to terminate the contract.

3:320 Common Law Implied Terms

The courts sometimes make use of the device of "implied terms" where the parties' intentions do not appear to be fully represented by the written terms of a contract. There are three types of terms that may be implied into a contract: terms implied in fact, terms implied by custom or usage, and terms implied by law (*see Machtinger v HOJ Industries*, [1992] 1 SCR 986). The terms discussed here are terms implied by law. The mechanism of the implied term is used perhaps more frequently in the employment context than in any other type of contractual relationship. Hugh Collins describes the role of terms implied by law in the following way:

> This kind of implied term provides a default rule that will be inserted into contracts of a particular type such as a sale of goods or a contract of employment. These implied terms are default rules in the sense that they apply in the absence of contrary express agreement. The practice of supplying default rules is particularly evident in relation to the contract of employment. These implied terms serve as a regulatory framework that normally applies to and shapes the employment relationship. These terms "implied by law" provide a legal expression of elements of the structural principles that shape the normative core of the legal institution of the contract of employment.[2]

It has often been suggested that the courts use implied terms to facilitate the prevailing system of work organization and human resources management, and to reflect society's vision of how work relations ought to be conducted. For example, over the years, the courts have read into employment contracts a standardized set of implied rights and duties that have reflected the judges' prevailing conception of an ideal employment relationship. The content of those implied terms is not static, but is continually refashioned to reflect changing conditions in the workplace and in society at large. In theory, the parties are perfectly free to modify such implied terms by negotiating other provisions. In practice, however, they do not often

---

[2] Hugh Collins, "Implied Terms in the Contract of Employment" in Mark Freedland et al, eds, *The Contract of Employment* (Oxford, UK: Oxford University Press, 2016) at 472.

modify standard implied terms, especially those favouring the employer. This code of implied terms continues to give a strong "status" flavour to modern employment contract law.

Amongst implied duties owed by employees to their employers are the duty to obey lawful orders, the duty of fidelity, loyalty, and confidence, the duty to not compete with the employer during the life of the agreement, and the duty to perform work competently and non-negligently. An employee's breach of an implied term is a breach of an employment contract, just as it is with a written express term. Such a breach provides an employer with cause to dismiss an employee without reasonable notice, provided of course that the employer meets the requirements set out in *McKinley vs BC Tel*, discussed further in Section 3:420, below.

The primary implied obligation that employers hold is the implied duty to provide reasonable notice of dismissal, absent cause, discussed in Section 3:520, below. Breach of this implied duty gives rise to an employee's claim for wrongful dismissal.

The next section introduces some of the terms implied by law into employment contracts.

3:321 The Employer's Managerial Prerogative and the Employee's Duty of Fidelity

At the core the of contract of employment are the correlated common law managerial prerogative and the employee's implied duty of fidelity. The managerial prerogative provides the employer with a right of control over the direction of work and management of labour processes in its workplace. The prerogative is given effect in law through the employee's implied obligation to serve her employer faithfully, along with a number of additional implied duties, such as duties of obedience, loyalty, good faith, confidence, etc. Many of these implied terms have their origins in the status-based law of master and servant that pre-dated the Industrial Revolution. At that time, work relations were highly paternalistic. The master, who often shared his home with his workers in the cottage industries, could expect the highest standards of obedience and loyalty. The courts entrenched this expectation in the extensive common law duty of obedience, which was implied into employment contracts during and after the Industrial Revolution. That duty gave employers considerable control over workers, especially in the context of the mass production methods that dominated the factory system in the late-nineteenth century and most of the twentieth century.

Today, the duty of fidelity remains the cornerstone of employer control over the worker. In the leading English case of *Secretary of State for Employment v Associated Society of Locomotive Engineers and Firemen and Others (No 2)*, [1972] 2 All ER 949 (CA), railway workers sought to put pressure on their employer by "working to rule"—that is, by applying existing work rules very meticulously, and thereby doing their jobs more slowly than usual. Under the labour relations legislation in force in England at the time, the legal issue was whether this conduct constituted a breach of the workers' common law contracts of employment. Lord Justice Buckley said, at 972:

> Assuming in the [union's] favour that the direction to work to rule avoided any specific direction to commit a breach of any express term of the contract, the instruction was, nevertheless, directed, and is acknowledged to have been directed, to rendering it impossible, or contributing to the impossibility, to carry on the [employer's] commercial activity upon a sound commercial basis, if at all. The object of the instruction was to frustrate the very commercial object for which the contracts of employment were made.

It struck at the foundation of the consensual intentions of the parties to those contracts, and amounted, in my judgment, to an instruction to commit what were clearly breaches or abrogations of those contracts. These are or would be, in my judgment, breaches of an implied term to serve the employer faithfully within the requirements of the contract. It does not mean that the employer could require a man to do anything which lay outside his obligations under the contract, such as to work excess hours of work or to work an unsafe system of work or anything of that kind, but it does mean that within the terms of the contract the employee must serve the employer faithfully with a view to promoting those commercial interests for which he is employed. The contrary view is, in my opinion, one which proceeds upon much too narrow and formalistic an approach to the legal relations of employer and employee and is an approach which, I may perhaps add, seems to me to be unlikely to promote goodwill or confidence between the parties.

The employee's duty of fidelity remains a bulwark of modern Canadian employment law. In *Stein v British Columbia (Housing Management Commission)* (1992), 65 BCLR (2d) 181 at 185 (CA), Hutcheon JA said:

[A]n employer has a right to determine how his business shall be conducted. He may lay down any procedures he thinks advisable so long as they are neither contrary to law, nor dishonest nor dangerous to the health of the employees and are within the ambit of the job for which any particular employee was hired. It is not for the employee nor for the court to consider the wisdom of the procedures. The employer is the boss and it is an essential implied term of every employment contract that, subject to the limitations I have expressed, the employee must obey the orders given to him.

As noted above, there are a number of additional implied obligations that employees owe to their employers. Among other implied duties that employees owe their employers are the duty of obedience; the duty of honesty; the duty not to compete and/or make a secret profit; the duty of confidentiality; and the duty to perform competently and non-negligently. These implied terms are sometimes presented as emanations of a general duty of fidelity, but at other times they are presented as self-standing obligations.[3]

3:322 Reasonable Notice of Termination

On the other side of the coin, employers also hold implied obligations. Before the Industrial Revolution, the common law of master and servant imposed on employers a relatively extensive duty to secure their servants' well-being, as befitted the paternalistic nature of the employment relationship in that quasi-feudal era. After the Industrial Revolution, the courts continued to apply the servant's duty of fidelity to the employment relationship with full rigour, but many of the employer's implied obligations went by the board. Nineteenth-century courts did not want the trappings of *noblesse oblige* from a bygone age to trammel the employer's freedom to pursue profitability in a different economy.

---

3 See Innis Christie, Geoffrey England, & Brent Cotter, *Employment Law in Canada*, 2nd ed (Markham, ON: Butterworths, 1993) 484–86, for a general description of the implied duties in Canada.

In the current era, the primary implied duty that the employer holds is the obligation to dismiss employees with the provision of reasonable notice, absent cause. In *Carter v Bell & Sons (Canada) Ltd*, [1936] OR 290 (CA), the court explained that:

> In the case of master and servant there is implied in the contract of hiring an obligation to give reasonable notice of an intention to terminate the arrangement.... This is a peculiar incident of the relationship of master and servant based largely upon custom. The master and the servant, when nothing is said, are presumed to contract with reference to this usage and so a stipulation as to notice is implied. Where a contract is made falling outside of the technical relationship of master and servant, there is not necessarily this implication and the terms of the contract must be looked at to ascertain the intention of the parties.

The implied right to reasonable notice of termination, absent cause, is the primary job security mechanism provided to employees at common law. Employees do not, therefore, hold a contractual right to their job—rather, they hold the right to receive notice of termination, absent cause. As the Ontario Court of Appeal held in *Brown v Waterloo Regional Board of Commissioners of Police* (1983), 43 OR (2d) 113: "It is trite law that an employer is entitled to terminate his employee's contract of employment either on reasonable notice or by giving compensation in lieu of notice. If he fails to give reasonable notice, the wrong he does is not the termination of the contract, but the failure to give reasonable notice." The breach in a wrongful dismissal claim, therefore, is breach of the obligation to provide reasonable notice, absent cause—it is not the dismissal itself. Reasonable notice of termination is both the legal entitlement, and the measure of damages owed for the breach in a wrongful dismissal claim. The method by which such damages are assessed are discussed in Section 3:520, below.

3:323 The Duty of Honesty in Contractual Performance

Although employees have long held an obligation of fidelity and good faith towards their employers, employers did not always hold a corresponding duty of good faith towards their employees. In the 1990s, the Canadian Supreme Court moved to impose a duty to dismiss in a good faith manner in *Wallace v United Grain Growers Ltd*, discussed in Section 3:530, below. This obligation applies only to the manner in which termination is effectuated, not to employer decisions during the life of the agreement, and not to the decision to terminate itself.

The common law Canadian courts have until recently been reticent to impose a generalized good faith obligation on employers, outside of the duty to dismiss in a good faith manner. This is in contrast to Quebec, where the *Civil Code* (in sections 6, 7, and 1375) explicitly recognizes the general duty of good faith that applies to the formation, the performance, and the termination of the employment contract. Still, as Kevin Banks argues, the courts, over the 1990s and 2000s, did quietly develop several discrete doctrines that could be used to limit employers' exercise of discretion. Addressing the situation prior to the decision in *Bhasin v Hrynew*, 2014 SCC 71, Banks explains that:

> The Supreme Court has avoided the issue of whether the scope of the duty [of good faith] should extend into the life of the employment relationship, and very few lower courts have taken that step. The concept of required good faith nonetheless finds expression

in the guise of a series of other restraints and duties placed upon employers by the common law. Taken together, these common law rules occupy much of the terrain that would be occupied by a more general duty of good faith and fair dealing.[4]

In 2014, the Supreme Court in *Bhasin v Hrynew* decided that it was time that the Canadian common law take the incremental step of recognizing that good faith is a general organizing principle of contract law, as well as crafting a new independent obligation of honesty in contractual performance. *Bhasin* was not an employment case, but the decision is likely to impact the development of existing employment law doctrines, and has the potential to open new avenues of compensation for employees as well. Reading through the decision, it is important to note that the Court holds that the duty of honest contractual performance is not in the nature of an implied term. What, then, is its legal status, and what is at stake in how it is characterized?

Bhasin v Hrynew, 2014 SCC 71 at para 32ff

> The notion of good faith has deep roots in contract law and permeates many of its rules. Nonetheless, Anglo-Canadian common law has resisted acknowledging any generalized and independent doctrine of good faith performance of contracts. The result is an "unsettled and incoherent body of law" that has developed "piecemeal" and which is "difficult to analyze": Ontario Law Reform Commission ("OLRC"), *Report on Amendment of the Law of Contract* (1987), at p. 169. This approach is out of step with the civil law of Quebec and most jurisdictions in the United States and produces results that are not consistent with the reasonable expectations of commercial parties.
>
> In my view, it is time to take two incremental steps in order to make the common law less unsettled and piecemeal, more coherent and more just. The first step is to acknowledge that good faith contractual performance is a general organizing principle of the common law of contract which underpins and informs the various rules in which the common law, in various situations and types of relationships, recognizes obligations of good faith contractual performance. The second is to recognize, as a further manifestation of this organizing principle of good faith, that there is a common law duty which applies to all contracts to act honestly in the performance of contractual obligations....
>
> *(iii) The Way Forward*
> [...]
> Commercial parties reasonably expect a basic level of honesty and good faith in contractual dealings. While they remain at arm's length and are not subject to the duties of a fiduciary, a basic level of honest conduct is necessary to the proper functioning of commerce. The growth of longer term, relational contracts that depend on an element of trust and cooperation clearly call for a basic element of honesty in performance, but, even in transactional exchanges, misleading or deceitful conduct will fly in the face of the expectations of the parties: see Swan and Adamski, at §1.24....

---

4   Kevin Banks, "Progress and Paradox: The Remarkable Yet Limited Advance of Employer Good Faith Duties in Canadian Common Law" (2010–2011) 32 *Comparative Labour Law & Policy Journal* 547 at 547–48.

It is, to say the least, counterintuitive to think that reasonable commercial parties would accept a contract which contained a provision to the effect that they were not obliged to act honestly in performing their contractual obligations.

I conclude from this review that enunciating a general organizing principle of good faith and recognizing a duty to perform contracts honestly will help bring certainty and coherence to this area of the law in a way that is consistent with reasonable commercial expectations.

(iv) Towards an Organizing Principle of Good Faith

The first step is to recognize that there is an organizing principle of good faith that underlies and manifests itself in various more specific doctrines governing contractual performance. That organizing principle is simply that parties generally must perform their contractual duties honestly and reasonably and not capriciously or arbitrarily.

As the Court has recognized, an organizing principle states in general terms a requirement of justice from which more specific legal doctrines may be derived. An organizing principle therefore is not a free-standing rule, but rather a standard that underpins and is manifested in more specific legal doctrines and may be given different weight in different situations.... It is a standard that helps to understand and develop the law in a coherent and principled way.

[T]he organizing principle of good faith exemplifies the notion that, in carrying out his or her own performance of the contract, a contracting party should have appropriate regard to the legitimate contractual interests of the contracting partner. While "appropriate regard" for the other party's interests will vary depending on the context of the contractual relationship, it does not require acting to serve those interests in all cases. It merely requires that a party not seek to undermine those interests in bad faith. This general principle has strong conceptual differences from the much higher obligations of a fiduciary. Unlike fiduciary duties, good faith performance does not engage duties of loyalty to the other contracting party or a duty to put the interests of the other contracting party first.

This organizing principle of good faith manifests itself through the existing doctrines about the types of situations and relationships in which the law requires, in certain respects, honest, candid, forthright or reasonable contractual performance. Generally, claims of good faith will not succeed if they do not fall within these existing doctrines. But we should also recognize that this list is not closed. The application of the organizing principle of good faith to particular situations should be developed where the existing law is found to be wanting and where the development may occur incrementally in a way that is consistent with the structure of the common law of contract and gives due weight to the importance of private ordering and certainty in commercial affairs....

(v) Should There Be a New Duty?

[...]

The key question before the Court, therefore, is whether we ought to create a new common law duty under the broad umbrella of the organizing principle of good faith performance of contracts. In my view, we should. I would hold that there is a general duty of honesty in contractual performance. This means simply that parties must not lie or otherwise knowingly mislead each other about matters directly linked to the performance of the contract. This does not impose a duty of loyalty or of disclosure or require a party to forego advantages flowing from the contract; it is a simple requirement not to lie or mislead the other party about one's contractual performance. Recognizing a duty of honest performance flowing directly from the common law organizing principle of good faith is a modest, incremental step. The requirement to act honestly is one of the most widely recognized aspects of the organizing principle of good faith ... For example, the duty of honesty was a key component of the good faith requirements which have been recognized in relation to termination of employment contracts: *Wallace*, at para. 98; *Honda Canada*, at para. 58.

There is a longstanding debate about whether the duty of good faith arises as a term implied as a matter of fact or a term implied by law: see *Mesa Operating*, at paras. 15-19. I do not have to resolve this debate fully, which, as I reviewed earlier, casts a shadow of uncertainty over a good deal of the jurisprudence. I am at this point concerned only with a new duty of honest performance and, as I see it, this should not be thought of as an implied term, but a general doctrine of contract law that imposes as a contractual duty a minimum standard of honest contractual performance. It operates irrespective of the intentions of the parties, and is to this extent analogous to equitable doctrines which impose limits on the freedom of contract, such as the doctrine of unconscionability....

That said, I would not rule out any role for the agreement of the parties in influencing the scope of honest performance in a particular context. The precise content of honest performance will vary with context and the parties should be free in some contexts to relax the requirements of the doctrine so long as they respect its minimum core requirements....

Certainly, any modification of the duty of honest performance would need to be in express terms....

The duty of honest performance that I propose should not be confused with a duty of disclosure or of fiduciary loyalty. A party to a contract has no general duty to subordinate his or her interest to that of the other party. However, contracting parties must be able to rely on a minimum standard of honesty from their contracting partner in relation to performing the contract as a reassurance that if the contract does not work out, they will have a fair opportunity to protect their interests. That said, a dealership agreement is not a contract of utmost good faith (*uberrimae fidei*) such as an insurance contract, which among other things obliges the parties to disclose material facts: *Whiten*. But a clear distinction can be drawn between a failure to disclose a material fact, even a firm intention to end the contractual arrangement, and active dishonesty....

I conclude that at this point in the development of Canadian common law, adding a general duty of honest contractual performance is an appropriate incremental step, recognizing that the implications of the broader, organizing principle of good faith must be allowed to evolve according to the same incremental judicial approach.

* * * * *

Shortly after the decision in *Bhasin*, the Supreme Court applied the organizing principle of good faith to a constructive dismissal case in *Potter New Brunswick v Legal Aid Services Commission*, [2015] 1 SCR 500. (See Section 3:430, below.) *Bhasin* has been pleaded and cited in many employment cases since it was decided, but its full significance has not yet been developed. At least one decision has used it to hold that employers owe a duty of good faith during the life of an employment contract, not only in dismissal: see *Karmel v Calgary Jewish Academy*, 2015 ABQB 731.

There are other doctrines that serve to promote an employer's good faith in the employment relationship; they are mostly concerned with controlling employee mistreatment by the employer. One is the employer's duty to dismiss in a good faith manner, discussed in Section 3:530, below. Another is the doctrine of constructive dismissal, which permits employees to leave their employment and sue for constructive dismissal (discussed in Section 3:430, below), where mistreatment demonstrates the employer's intention to be no longer bound to the contract. The tort of intentional infliction of mental distress is also available (*Prinzo v Baycrest Centre for Geriatric Care*, 60 OR (3d) 474 (CA), although, in Ontario and Nova Scotia at least, negligent infliction of mental distress is not (*Piresferreira v Ayotte*, 2010 ONCA 384; *Sanford v Carleton Road Industries Association* 2014 NSSC 187). Finally, there are a variety of statutory provisions designed to prevent and compensate for employer harassment (see Chapters 13 and 14). In theory, general contract doctrines that are concerned with fairness are available in the employment context, but the courts are generally wary of using them to render unenforceable employment contract terms. Instead, courts have preferred to use principles of contract interpretation to address potential unfairness in the employment contract, as discussed above in Section 3:310.

3:324 Fiduciary Employees

All employees owe their employers a duty of fidelity. For most employees, however, the duty of fidelity, as with the other implied duties, ends when the employment relationship ends. Some employees however, are fiduciaries. Fiduciaries owe duties to their employers that subsist after the relationship is finished.

Until recently, fiduciaries were typically confined to the senior ranks of an employing entity—to employees who could be said to be within the controlling mind of the company. But in the last few years there has been an increasing expansion of fiduciary duties, as courts have imposed fiduciary duties on employees with little formal authority within their employer's organization.

GasTOPS Ltd v Forsyth, [2009] OJ No 3969 at paras 75–88 (SCJ)

> Action by the employer, GasTOPS Limited, against the defendants, Forsyth, Brouse, Cass, Vandenberg and MxI Technologies, for damages and injunctive relief for breach of fiduciary duty and breach of contract in connection with their employment with the plaintiff. The plaintiff was involved with maintenance of marine and aviation gas turbine engines. It also provided engineering consulting services and developed related computer software programs. In October 1996, the individual defendants resigned from their senior management positions with the plaintiff. One week later, Forsyth and Brouse incorporated MxI. Cass and Vandenberg immediately commenced employment with MxI. An attempt at negotiating a cooperation and subcontracting agreement between the companies fell through. The plaintiff alleged that the personal defendants failed to give reasonable notice of their intention to resign. The plaintiff alleged that they breached their fiduciary duties and implied contractual obligations through misappropriation of confidential information, trade secrets and corporate opportunities. The defendants denied

competing with the plaintiff or soliciting its customers. They denied any misappropriation of technology or programs developed by the plaintiff. The defendants contended that MxI utilized fundamentally different software and related technology....

III. INDIVIDUAL DEFENDANTS' ROLES AT AND DUTIES OWING TO GASTOPS

The individual defendants' roles at GasTOPS are important in considering the duties (fiduciary and otherwise) they owed GasTOPS, including the implied period of notice they were required to give to GasTOPS upon resignation.

The Law

As I describe the individual Defendants' roles at GasTOPS in this section, I will be making findings about the fiduciary and other duties they owed to GasTOPS. To ground those findings, I will first outline the relevant legal principles.

Existence and Duration of a Fiduciary Duty
All employees owe their employer a general duty of good faith and fidelity, even if they are not fiduciaries (*57134 Manitoba Ltd. v. Palmer* (1989), 37 B.C.L.R. (2d) 50 (C.A.) at 5). It is an implied term of every contract of employment that an employee must, at all times during the employment relationship, protect the employer's interest. In *CRC-Evans Canada Ltd. v. Pettifer*, [1997] A.J. No. 20, Sanderman J. described the common law duty of an employee to an employer at para. 45:

> It has long been accepted that there is a fundamental term implied in every contract of employment. The employee is expected to serve his employer honestly and faithfully during the term of his employment. This duty of fidelity permeates the entire relationship between employer and employee. It is a flexible concept that is paramount to the basic relationship. There is an implied obligation placed upon the employee to act in the best interests of his employer at all times. The employee shall not follow a course of action that harms or places at risk the interests of the employer.

A fiduciary duty elevates this common law duty, but it is grounded in the same policy. In *Canadian Aero Service Ltd. v. O'Malley*, [1974] S.C.R. 592 [*CanAero*], Justice Laskin in reviewing the policy behind the Court's approach to fiduciary obligation in the corporate context stated:

> What these decisions indicate is an updating of the equitable principle whose roots lie in the general standards that I have already mentioned, namely, loyalty, good faith and avoidance of a conflict of duty and self-interest. Strict application against directors and senior management officials is simply recognition of the degree of control which their positions give them in corporate operations, a control which rises above day-to-day accountability to owning shareholders and which comes under some scrutiny only at annual general or at special meetings.

The Courts have provided some guidelines for determining whether a fiduciary relationship exists but stopped short of defining a strict test. Instead, the courts have stated that "the categories of fiduciary, like those of negligence, should not be considered closed" (*Guerin v. The Queen*, [1984] 2 S.C.R. 335 at 384) and that the determination of a fiduciary duty must be based on the facts of each particular case.

The seminal case on fiduciary duty is the Supreme Court of Canada decision of *CanAero*. There it was held that for a fiduciary obligation to attach to an employee, the employee must be in a position to exert or exercise some independent power or discretion over the employer's business. As such, fiduciary duty demands the general responsibilities of loyalty, good faith, and avoidance of a conflict of duty and self-interest. In *Frame v. Smith* (1987), 42 D.L.R. (4th) 81, the Supreme Court provided three defining characteristics of a fiduciary employee:

1. the fiduciary has scope for the exercise of some discretion or power;
2. the fiduciary can unilaterally exercise that power or discretion so as to affect the beneficiary's legal or practical interests;
3. the beneficiary is peculiarly vulnerable to or at the mercy of the fiduciary holding the discretion or power.

And according to the Supreme Court in *Hodgkinson v. Simms* (1994), 117 D.L.R. (4th) 161, to find a fiduciary relationship requires finding "evidence of a mutual understanding that one party has relinquished its own self-interest and agreed to act solely on behalf of the other party" (176–77).

In determining whether an individual is a fiduciary, the court must look at the nature of the relationship between the parties, the job function and the responsibilities being performed, as being more determinate of the issue, than the title held by the employee. The varying degrees of trust, confidence and reliance given to the employee and the corresponding vulnerability or dependency of the employer to competition when the person leaves, are the most pertinent factors in determining whether a fiduciary duty exists.

Although in most cases fiduciary duties or obligations have been limited to senior officials or management of a company, on occasion, the Courts have extended fiduciary obligations to lower level employees, including those with technical rather than administrative duties, when an individual is found to be a key employee (*Wilcox v. G.W.G. Ltd.* (1984), 4 C.C.E.L. 125 (Alta. Q.B.)). A key employee is one whose position and responsibilities are essential to the employer's business, making the employer particularly vulnerable to competition upon that employee's departure.

M.E.P. Environmental Products Ltd. v. Hi Performance Coatings Co., [2006] M.J. No. 211 (M.B.Q.B.), aff'd 2007 M.B.C.A. 71 [*M.E.P. Environmental*], enumerates more specific indicia that can be used to determine whether a former employee could be classified as "key":

> The *indicia* to be considered on the issue of whether a former employee was a "key employee", such that he or she owed a fiduciary duty to their former employer and not to solicit former employer's customers may be summarized as follows:
>
> i. What were the employee's job duties with the former employer?
> ii. What was the extent or frequency of the contact between the employee and the former employer's customers and/or suppliers?
> iii. Was the employee the primary contact with the customers and (or) suppliers?
> iv. To what extent was the employee responsible for sales or revenue?

v. To what extent did the employee have access to and make use of, or otherwise have knowledge of, the former employer's customers, their accounts, the former employer's pricing practices, and the pricing of products and services?

vi. To what extent was the former employee's information as regards customers, suppliers, pricing, etc., confidential?

After identifying an employee as "key", further determining whether that employee is a "fiduciary" is a difficult endeavour. According to James D'Andrea, "generally, a fiduciary is one who is empowered to act on behalf of and for the benefit of another with the ability to affect that other's interest through the use of discretion" (*Employment Obligations in Canada*, looseleaf (Aurora Ont.; Canada Law Book 2006))

The jurisprudence has imposed fiduciary obligations on employees in a number of different factual circumstances and in so doing have considered:

(a) whether the employee has scope for the exercise of some discretion or power, the employee can unilaterally exercise that power or discretion so as to effect the beneficiary is legal or practical interest and whether the beneficiary is vulnerable to or at the mercy of the fiduciary holding the discretion or power;

(b) knowledge of customer contact information, needs and preferences, and therefore, an ability to influence customers. An employee may be held to be a fiduciary if they are found to have "encyclopedic knowledge" of their employer's customers, unrestricted access to all customer lists and information concerning customers, privy to policy issues and personal contact with, and responsibility for, a large portion of customers: see *Smyth v. UndercoverWear Ltd.*, [1993] O.J. No. 2180 at para. 32 citing *Hudson's Bay Company v. McClocklin*, [1986] 5 W.W.R. 29;

(c) knowledge of the business and market opportunity of the employer or playing a role in the employer's strategic market development is a consideration in determining if the employees owed a fiduciary duty to the former employer....

(d) knowledge of and access to confidential information. It is not necessary for an employee to have access to corporate financial information to be found to be a fiduciary. It is the employee's access to information of which disclosure would make the employer vulnerable. In a sales environment, customer information is critical or in a technological environment, product specifications are critical....

(e) direct and trusted relationships with existing and potential customers, particularly where there is a "unique relationship with the clients personnel contacts and [the defendants] had direct access to confidential information as to the clients' needs, preferences and accepted rates": see *Quantum Management Services Ltd. v. Hann et al.*, 1996 CanLII 11785 (ON SC), [1996] O.J. No. 5382;

(f) whether or not the employee's functions are essential to the employer's business, therefore rendering the employer vulnerable to the employee's departure: see J. Thorburn and K. Fairbairn, *Law of Confidential Business Information*, looseleaf, (Aurora, Ontario: Canada Law Book, 1998) at 4:5200 at 4-26.

Any one of these factors, or a combination of them, could result in a finding that an individual owes a fiduciary obligation to his employer.

The content of the duty is threefold. As D'Andrea notes, whether one determines the existence of a fiduciary duty through 'vulnerability' or through 'dependence of beneficiaries', courts demand fiduciaries:

1. avoid all conflict of interest;
2. act only in the best interest of the trust of beneficiary; and
3. do not profit as a result of their position.

[...]

CanAero stands for the proposition that if an employee is a fiduciary, that employee is further held to those responsibilities post-employment. At a minimum, beyond the duties of loyalty and good faith owed by all employees to their employers, fiduciary employees are limited in their ability to compete with their former employer and a departing fiduciary cannot take advantage of a corporate opportunity that ripened during the course of his or her fiduciary employment.

Although *CanAero* did not provide for how long fiduciary obligations should last post-employment, there have been a number of decisions that have suggested it ought to last for a "reasonable" period of time (see *Cline v. Don Watt & Associates Communications Inc.* (1986), 15 C.C.E.L. 181 (Ont. Dist. Ct.) at 206; *Genesta Manufacturing Ltd. v. Babey* (1984), 6 C.C.E.L. 291 at 311; *Wallace Welding Supplies Ltd. v. Wallace* (1986), 11 C.C.E.L. 108 (Ont. H.C.J.)).

[The court went on to conclude that the individual defendants were fiduciaries, and fleshed out the content of the duties they thereby owed their former employer.]

* * * * *

There is an active debate in the caselaw as to the scope of fiduciary employment in Canada. While the court in *GasTOPS* refers to the term "key employee" as the defining concept, there are in fact two approaches visible in the caselaw. One approach is to impose fiduciary duties only on those employees who are "key employees" within an employer's organization. As traditionally defined, the "key employees" approach remains closely bound to the Supreme Court's decision in *CanAero v O'Malley*, [1974] SCR 592. According to the New Brunswick Court of Appeal in *Imperial Sheet Metal v Landry*, 2007 NBCA 51, a key employee is someone who "exercises control over the daily operations of the employer or is integrally involved in the decision-making process." A second, broader approach is the "vulnerabilities" approach, which adopts a broader definition of what constitutes a "key employee." This approach extends fiduciary responsibilities where, by virtue of the nature of a business, the employer is particularly vulnerable to the employee's actions. This situation typically occurs where client relations are a significant portion of the business's value and the employee in question held significant responsibilities over the cultivation and maintenance of those relationships. Although the court in *GasTOPS* says it is adopting the "key employee" approach, it in fact relies on *MEP Environmental Products Ltd v Hi Performance Coatings Company Limited et al*, [2006] MJ No 211 (MBQB), aff'd 2007 MBCA 71, whose criteria are typically associated with the "vulnerabilities" approach.

There is currently no unanimity as to which approach should prevail, and both have been used by different courts. In *Imperial Sheet Metal*, above, Robertson J for the NBCA (at para 58) explained what he viewed as the problems with the "vulnerabilities" approach:

In my view, the key employee test or approach is the only one that is consistent with the Supreme Court's decision in *Canaero*. Indeed, if one were to adopt and apply the vulnerability test, in the manner reflected in the jurisprudence, it is conceivable that every lorry driver in this country would owe the same post-employment obligations encumbering the executives of our largest corporations. But I have other more basic or fundamental objections to the so-called broader approach to qualifying former employees as fiduciaries. The broader approach amounts to a reformation of the common law principles and an implicit recognition of a duty restricting former employees from pursuing their own self-interests at the expense of their former employers. Moreover, the broader approach is an implicit recognition of the belief that former employers possess exclusive rights of access to their customers when it comes to competition from former employees. Finally, the broader approach can be rightly criticized for dispensing with the need of employers to require their employees to sign confidentiality and non-competition clauses. Why bother having a contractual provision that is subject to judicially imposed restrictions when more may be obtained by having the employee declared a fiduciary? I recognize that the vulnerability argument is valid to the extent that the former employee possesses trade secrets or confidential information that if disclosed to a competitor will provide an unfair competitive advantage. However, that type of vulnerability does not lead to the conclusion that a fiduciary relationship should be recognized. As Justice Sopinka stated in *Lac Minerals*, at page 596, fiduciary duties must be "reserved for situations that are truly in need of the special protection that equity affords."

3:400 TERMINATING THE CONTRACT OF EMPLOYMENT

3:410 Wrongful Dismissal

Dismissal is "wrongful" at common law where: (a) the employer dismisses the employee without alleging cause and without giving notice or wages in lieu of notice, as required by the express or implied terms of the employment contract (see Section 3:521, below, for the assessment of what constitutes reasonable notice); or (b) the employer summarily dismisses the employee, alleging cause that is not proven; or (c) the employee quits in response to repudiatory breach of the employment contract by the employer, sues for damages, and the employer cannot demonstrate cause (constructive dismissal); or (d) the employee is dismissed in breach of a statutory rule governing the employment relationship. Dismissal is not, in itself, wrongful and/or a breach of contract.

3:420 Cause for Dismissal

The legal theory of summary dismissal at common law is couched in terms of traditional contract law principles. If an employee commits a breach that is severe enough to constitute a repudiation of the employment contract, the employer has cause for dismissal. That breach can come from the violation of an express term of the employment contract, but it can also arise from breach of the employee's implied obligation, or from general conduct demonstrating the employee's intention to no longer be bound to the contract. Faced with a

CHAPTER 3: THE CONTRACT OF EMPLOYMENT

repudiatory breach, the employer is entitled to treat the contract as terminated, and to dismiss the employee without reasonable notice or pay in lieu of notice. The employer can also sue for damages for losses caused by the employee's dereliction of duty, but this is seldom done.

Courts have given extensive consideration to what sorts of employee conduct are serious enough to provide cause for dismissal. The Supreme Court of Canada addressed this matter in the following case.

McKinley v BC Tel, [2001] 2 SCR 161 at para 1ff

IACOBUCCI J.—

I. INTRODUCTION

This appeal arises out of a wrongful dismissal action. It calls upon the Court to elaborate the circumstances in which an employer would be justified in summarily dismissing an employee as a result of the latter's dishonest conduct. More specifically, the question is whether any dishonesty, in and of itself, suffices to warrant an employee's termination, or whether the nature and context of such dishonesty must be considered in assessing whether just cause for dismissal exists.

The appeal also raises ancillary questions relating to the propriety of the trial judge's decision to put to the jury questions related to awards for an extended notice period, aggravated damages, and punitive damages. In addition, the parties sought a review of the reasonableness of the jury verdict on various matters decided at trial. A cross-appeal also has been brought, wherein the respondents submitted that, if the Court dismissed the appeal, it ought to dismiss the appellant's wrongful dismissal action outright rather than order a new trial.

For the reasons that follow, I am of the view that this appeal should be allowed and that the jury's verdict should be restored on all questions except that related to aggravated damages. As I would allow the appeal, the cross-appeal must perforce be dismissed.

II. FACTUAL BACKGROUND

The appellant, Martin Richard McKinley, is a chartered accountant who was employed by the respondents, the BC Tel group of companies ("BC Tel"). While working for BC Tel, he held various positions, earned promotions, and received salary increases. In 1991, he became Controller, Treasurer and Assistant Secretary to certain BC Tel companies. But in 1993, the appellant began to experience high blood pressure as a result of hypertension. Initially, this condition was brought under control through medication, and by taking some time away from work. However, by May of 1994, the appellant's health took a turn for the worse. His blood pressure had begun to rise again, and by June of that year, it was rising on a daily basis. Following his physician's advice, the appellant took a leave of absence from work.

By July 1994, the appellant's superior, Ian Mansfield ("Mansfield"), raised the issue of the appellant's termination from his employment. During discussions with his employer, the appellant indicated that he wished to return to work, but in a position that carried less responsibility. He was advised that BC Tel would attempt to find another suitable position for him within its corporate structure. However, alternative employment was never offered to the appellant. Although at least two positions for which the appellant qualified opened during the period in question, these were filled by other employees.

While the appellant was still on leave from work owing to his health condition, Mansfield telephoned him and instructed him to report to the respondents' offices on August 31, 1994. The appellant complied, and on that day, the respondents terminated his employment. By that time, the appellant had worked for BC Tel for almost 17 years and was 48 years of age.

Although the respondents made the appellant a severance offer, this was rejected. According to the appellant, his employment was terminated without just cause and without reasonable notice or pay in lieu of reasonable notice. He thus brought a wrongful dismissal action in the Supreme Court of British Columbia, arguing that his termination was an arbitrary and wilful breach of his employment contract, which was conducted in a high-handed and flagrant manner. The appellant maintained that the respondents' actions amounted to an intentional infliction of mental suffering. He alleged that, as a result of the wrongful dismissal, he lost his employment income and benefits, as well as the short-term disability benefits he was then receiving. He also argued that the dismissal prevented him from qualifying for, or receiving, any long-term disability benefits, and caused him to lose his future pension benefits. As such, the appellant sought an order for general compensatory damages, special damages for the expenses incurred in attempting to find new employment, aggravated damages, and damages for mental distress and the intentional infliction of mental suffering, as well as punitive damages.

Aside from his wrongful dismissal action, the appellant filed an information with the Canadian Human Rights Commission, based on the same allegations of fact. He argued that his dismissal contravened the *Canadian Human Rights Act*, R.S.C., 1985, c. H-6. At the time of trial, he had not yet filed a formal complaint.

The respondents admitted to having terminated the appellant's employment on August 31, 1994....

They ... argued that just cause for the appellant's summary dismissal existed. Specifically, the respondents alleged that the appellant had been dishonest about his medical condition, and the treatments available for it. This argument was based on the respondents' recent discovery of a letter (dated December 12, 1994) written by the appellant to Dr. Peter Graff, an internal medicine and cardiac specialist, who was one of the appellant's attending physicians. In this letter, the appellant wrote to Dr. Graff acknowledging that, during a previous medical appointment, Dr. Graff had recommended a certain medication—the "beta blocker"—as the next method of treatment for the appellant's hypertension. Although beta blockers were not prescribed at that time, the letter indicated that Dr. Graff had advised the appellant that such treatment should begin upon the latter's return to work, if his blood pressure remained high.

The respondents claimed that the appellant deliberately withheld the truth as to Dr. Graff's recommendations regarding the use of beta blockers and their ability to enable him to return to his job without incurring any health risks. However, the appellant's evidence at trial revealed that, insofar as he was concerned, he had not lied to the respondents.

At trial, the appellant's wrongful dismissal action was heard before a judge and jury. Paris J. held that there was sufficient evidence to put the question of just cause for dismissal to the jury. In instructing the jury on this point, Paris J. stated that, in order for just cause to exist, it must find (a) that the appellant's conduct was dishonest in fact, and (b) that "the dishonesty was of a degree that was incompatible with the employment relationship." Paris J. also held that the jury could consider whether aggravated damages, as well as damages for bad faith in the conduct or manner of the dismissal were warranted. On the other hand, he held that there was no evidence upon which a claim for punitive damages could be based, and thus, this question was not put to the jury.

The jury found in favour of the appellant, awarding him the following amounts: $108,793 in general damages; $1,233 in special damages; $100,000 in aggravated damages; $6,091 in pension contributions; prejudgment interest; and costs. Paris J. refused to make an order for special costs, and for increased costs.

The Court of Appeal for British Columbia set the jury award aside and ordered a new trial. The appellant's cross-appeal on the question of punitive damages was dismissed. According to the Court of Appeal, dishonesty is always cause for dismissal.

III. JUDICIAL HISTORY

A. Supreme Court of British Columbia (Paris J.)

[...]
In charging the jury on the issue of dismissal for just cause on the basis of an employee's dishonesty, Paris J.'s instructions were as follows:

> Now what constitutes just cause for dismissal may vary depending upon the circumstances of the case which must be assessed by you the jury. Generally speaking, however, examples of just cause would be an employee's serious misconduct, habitual neglect of duty, incompetence, repeated willful [sic] disobedience, or *dishonesty of a degree incompatible with the employment relationship. The conduct must be such as to undermine or seriously impair the trust and confidence the employer is entitled to place in the employee in the circumstances of their particular relationship. Something less than that is not sufficient cause for dismissal without reasonable notice.* [Emphasis added.]

The question put to the jury on this point asked simply:

> Have the Defendants proven that (unknown to them at the time), cause for dismissal existed when they terminated the Plaintiff on August 31, 1994?

The jury responded to this question in the negative.

B. Court of Appeal for British Columbia

[...]
The Court of Appeal held that the dishonesty asserted by the respondents was not as clear as in *McPhillips*, where an employee billed his employer for unauthorized personal expenses. However, it found that Paris J. invited the jury to consider the extent of the

dishonesty alleged, and to determine whether this "was of a degree that was incompatible with the employment relationship," and thus "sufficient to warrant dismissal." According to the Court of Appeal, such instructions were incorrect as a matter of law. In this regard, Hollinrake J.A. stated at para. 25:

> Dishonesty within the contract of employment, as is the case alleged here, is cause and that cause is not founded on the basis of the "degree" of the dishonesty.

IV. ISSUES

This appeal raises the following issues:

A. Did the trial judge err by instructing the jury that, to find just cause for dismissal, it would have to find not only that the plaintiff was deceitful, but that the dishonesty was "of a degree that was incompatible with the employment relationship"?
B. Based on the evidence before it, could the jury, acting judicially, have reasonably found that the appellant's conduct was not dishonest and thus, that just cause for summary dismissal did not exist?

[...]

V. ANALYSIS

A. The Standard for Dishonest Conduct in the Employment Relationship

Although this Court has yet to consider the question of whether an employee's dishonesty, in and of itself, necessarily gives rise to just cause for summary dismissal, this issue has been examined by the English courts, as well as appellate and lower courts in Canada. From an analysis of this jurisprudence, no clear principle or standard emerges. Rather, while one line of authority suggests that the nature of the dishonesty and the circumstances surrounding its occurrence must be considered, another seems to indicate that dishonest conduct alone—regardless of its degree—creates just cause for dismissal. A brief review of these two strands of jurisprudence would be useful before determining which should guide this Court's analysis in the present case.

1. Authority Indicating that *Context* Must Be Considered when Assessing Whether Dishonesty Amounts to Just Cause for Dismissal

When examining whether an employee's misconduct—including dishonest misconduct—justifies his or her dismissal, courts have often considered the context of the alleged insubordination. Within this analysis, a finding of misconduct does not, by itself, give rise to just cause. Rather, the question to be addressed is whether, in the circumstances, the behaviour was such that the employment relationship could no longer viably subsist.

The Privy Council's decision in *Clouston & Co. v. Corry* ... adopted this analytical framework. The question arising in that case was whether an employee's public drunkenness and disobedient conduct warranted his dismissal. The Privy Council's ruling spoke generally to the concept of "misconduct" and held that there was no fixed rule of law to define when termination would be warranted. The question is one of degree. The trial judge must first determine whether there is any evidence to submit to the jury in support of the allegation of justifiable dismissal. He or she also may direct jurors by informing them of the nature of the acts which, as a matter of law, will justify dismissal. However, the ultimate question of whether just cause for such dismissal exists is one of fact that the jury must decide. Thus, the Privy Council indicated that it is not sufficient that the jury find misconduct alone, since this will not necessarily provide a basis for dismissal. Rather, the jury must determine that the misconduct is impossible to reconcile with the employee's obligations under the employment contract. ...

A similar analysis was undertaken in subsequent decisions dealing with this issue. For instance, in *Laws v. London Chronicle, Ltd.*, ... the English Court of Appeal stated the following. ...

> [S]ince a contract of service is but an example of contracts in general, so that the general law of contract will be applicable, it follows that, if summary dismissal is claimed to be justifiable, *the question must be whether the conduct complained of is such as to show the servant to have disregarded the essential conditions of the contract of service.* [Emphasis added.]

As such, Lord Evershed, M.R. held that a single act of disobedience justified dismissal only if it demonstrated that the servant had repudiated the contract or one of its essential conditions. In this way, the ruling in *Laws* indicated that an analysis of whether an employee's misconduct warrants dismissal requires an assessment of its degree and surrounding circumstances.

This contextual approach also has been adopted in several decisions by Canadian appellate courts. ...

[A]ccording to this reasoning, an employee's misconduct does not inherently justify dismissal without notice unless it is "so grievous" that it intimates the employee's abandonment of the intention to remain part of the employment relationship. ...

The jurisprudence also reveals that an application of a contextual approach—which examines both the circumstances surrounding the conduct as well as its nature or degree—leaves the trier of fact with discretion as to whether a dishonest act gives rise to just cause. For example, in *Jewitt v. Prism Resources Ltd.* ... Taggart J.A. held that an analysis of the employee's misconduct "in the circumstances" of that case did constitute cause for dismissal. *Jewitt* involved an employee who allowed a co-director's signature to be traced on a balance sheet. In contrast, an examination of the surrounding circumstances in *Hill v. Dow Chemical Canada Inc.* ... led the Alberta Court of Queen's Bench to conclude that the misconduct in question merely reflected a single incident of "poor judgment." This finding, along with the conclusion that the employee lacked an intention to deceive, caused the court to conclude that the impugned behaviour did not warrant summary dismissal. At issue in *Hill* was an employee's unauthorized donation of bandages and ice packs owned by his employer to a local hockey team, in breach of company procedure. ...

Cases in which courts have explicitly ruled that the issue of just cause is one of fact to be put to a jury lend further support to an approach that considers the particular circumstances surrounding the alleged employee misconduct. Rather than viewing cause for dismissal as a legal conclusion that must be drawn in any case where disobedience (including dishonesty) is proven, these cases indicate that just cause can only be determined through an inquiry by the trier of fact into (a) whether the evidence demonstrated employee misconduct and (b) whether, in the circumstances, such misconduct sufficed to justify the employee's termination without notice....

To summarize, this first line of case law establishes that the question whether dishonesty provides just cause for summary dismissal is a matter to be decided by the trier of fact, and to be addressed through an analysis of the particular circumstances surrounding the employee's behaviour. In this respect, courts have held that factors such as the nature and degree of the misconduct, and whether it violates the "essential conditions" of the employment contract or breaches an employer's faith in an employee, must be considered in drawing factual conclusions as to the existence of just cause....

2. Authority Indicating that Dishonesty *In and Of Itself* Warrants *Dismissal Without Notice*

The broad language used in a second line of decisions indicates that dishonesty, in and of itself, provides just cause, irrespective of the factors and circumstances surrounding the conduct, the nature or degree of such dishonesty, or whether it breached the essential conditions of the employment relationship.

This approach was articulated by the English Court of Appeal in *Boston Deep Sea Fishing and Ice Co. v. Ansell* ... In that case, an agent had been instructed to arrange for several fishing boats to be built for his employer. The agent then received a secret commission from the boat builder, which the company learned of approximately one year later. The employee's conduct was found to be fraudulent, and this was held to provide ample justification for dismissal without notice. In reaching this conclusion, Bowen L.J. discussed the standard applicable for determining when dishonesty suffices as cause for terminating the employment relationship. At p. 363 he stated:

> [I]n cases where the character of the isolated act is such as of itself to be beyond all dispute a violation of the confidential relation, and a breach of faith towards the master, the rights of the master do not depend on the caprice of the jury, or of the tribunal which tries the question. Once the tribunal has found the fact—has found that there is a fraud and breach of faith—then the rights of the master to determine the contract follow as matter of law.

This passage indicates that once the confidence inherent to the master-servant relationship is breached, just cause for dismissal—*as a matter of law*—is automatically triggered, and must not depend on whether the trier of fact finds that such cause exists. Although Bowen L.J. spoke primarily to fraud, he also indicated that "breach of faith" in general may warrant dismissal. Such broad language suggests that any dishonest conduct which ruptures the trust inherent to the employer-employee relationship provides just cause....

The strict approach ... resonates in several ... decisions rendered by Canadian courts, which have held that a finding of dishonesty, in and of itself, creates just cause for summary dismissal. In each of these cases, however, the courts dealt with forms of dishonesty that ... bordered on theft, misappropriation, forgery or a fraudulent sham. In that connection, the courts drew parallels between dishonesty and fraud, either by noting their common ingredients.... In this vein, courts also emphasized that, for dishonesty to amount to cause, the employer must prove intent on the employee's part to engage in deceitful conduct....

This line of jurisprudence seems to indicate that a finding of dishonesty gives rise to just cause as a matter of law. However, I am struck by the fact that, in all of the cases considered here, where cause was found to exist, courts were confronted with very serious forms of employee dishonesty. This point is instructive for determining the proper analytical approach to be adopted in the case at bar.

3. Applicable Standard for Assessing Whether and in What Circumstances Dishonesty Provides Just Cause

In light of the foregoing analysis, I am of the view that whether an employer is justified in dismissing an employee on the grounds of dishonesty is a question that requires an assessment of the context of the alleged misconduct. More specifically, the test is whether the employee's dishonesty gave rise to a breakdown in the employment relationship. This test can be expressed in different ways. One could say, for example, that just cause for dismissal exists where the dishonesty violates an essential condition of the employment contract, breaches the faith inherent to the work relationship, or is fundamentally or directly inconsistent with the employee's obligations to his or her employer.

In accordance with this test, a trial judge must instruct the jury to determine: (1) whether the evidence established the employee's deceitful conduct on a balance of probabilities; and (2) if so, whether the nature and degree of the dishonesty warranted dismissal. In my view, the second branch of this test does not blend questions of fact and law. Rather, assessing the seriousness of the misconduct requires the facts established at trial to be carefully considered and balanced. As such, it is a factual inquiry for the jury to undertake....

I conclude that a contextual approach to assessing whether an employee's dishonesty provides just cause for dismissal emerges from the case law on point. In certain contexts, applying this approach might lead to a strict outcome. Where theft, misappropriation or serious fraud is found, the decisions considered here establish that cause for termination exists. This is consistent with this Court's reasoning in *Lake Ontario Portland Cement Co. v. Groner*, ... where this Court found that cause for dismissal on the basis of dishonesty exists where an employee acts *fraudulently* with respect to his employer. This principle necessarily rests on an examination of the nature and circumstances of the misconduct. Absent such an analysis, it would be impossible for a court to conclude that the dishonesty was severely fraudulent in nature and thus, that it sufficed to justify dismissal without notice.

This is not to say that there cannot be lesser sanctions for less serious types of misconduct. For example, an employer may be justified in docking an employee's pay for any loss incurred by a minor misuse of company property. This is one of several disciplinary measures an employer may take in these circumstances.

Underlying the approach I propose is the principle of proportionality. An effective balance must be struck between the severity of an employee's misconduct and the sanction imposed. The importance of this balance is better understood by considering the sense of identity and self-worth individuals frequently derive from their employment, a concept that was explored in *Reference Re Public Service Employee Relations Act (Alta.)*, ... where Dickson C.J. (writing in dissent) stated at p. 368:

> Work is one of the most fundamental aspects in a person's life, providing the individual with a means of financial support and, as importantly, a contributory role in society. A

person's employment is an essential component of his or her sense of identity, self-worth and emotional well-being.

This passage was subsequently cited with approval by this Court in *Machtinger v. HOJ Industries Ltd.*, ... and in *Wallace, supra*, at para. 95. In *Wallace*, the majority added to this notion by stating that not only is work itself fundamental to an individual's identity, but "the manner in which employment can be terminated is equally important."

Given this recognition of the integral nature of work to the lives and identities of individuals in our society, care must be taken in fashioning rules and principles of law which would enable the employment relationship to be terminated without notice. The importance of this is underscored by the power imbalance that this Court has recognized as ingrained in most facets of the employment relationship....

In light of these considerations, I have serious difficulty with the absolute, unqualified rule that the Court of Appeal endorsed in this case....

I favour an analytical framework that examines each case on its own particular facts and circumstances, and considers the nature and seriousness of the dishonesty in order to assess whether it is reconcilable with sustaining the employment relationship.

4. Application to Paris J.'s Jury Instructions

Applying the foregoing analysis to this case, unlike the Court of Appeal, I see no reason to interfere with the trial decision on the basis of Paris J.'s instructions to the jury.... Paris J.'s instructions therefore were entirely consistent with the contextual approach discussed above, and thus do not serve as a basis for setting the jury verdict aside.

B. Reasonableness of the Jury Verdict

[...]

In the present case, given the variance in the evidence before the jury, I must conclude that it could have reasonably and judicially found that the appellant did not engage in dishonest conduct of a degree incompatible with his employment relationship. Therefore, the requisite standard for setting aside the verdict was not met, as I now will discuss.

The December 12, 1994 letter from the appellant to Dr. Graff, an internal medicine and cardiac specialist and one of his treating physicians, provides an instructive starting point for the analysis of this issue. In this letter, the appellant requested that Dr. Graff clarify his recollection of the treatment recommended during a medical appointment that had taken place on July 20, 1994. The most relevant passage of this letter for the purposes of the present appeal states the following:

> The only issue that concerns me is that while I agree that you recommended a "beta blocker" as the next method of treatment on July 20, 1994, it is my understanding that you did not want me to start treatment until I returned to work. I remember telling you that BC TEL did not want me back at work until my blood pressure was fully controlled — a concept that bothered you at the time.... My recollection is that you said that if I was not returning to the stressfull [sic] job that causing [sic] my elevated blood pressure, then I should remain on Adalat until I was in my new job. If my blood pressure remained

elevated in my new job, I was to return to see you to begin a "beta blocker" treatment. You did not issue me a prescription or give me any "beta blocker" samples on July 20....

It does not make sense to me that I would refuse to try "beta blockers" as it also does not make sense that you would prescibe [sic] medication where the apparent cause or trigger was removed!

According to the respondents, this letter revealed the appellant's knowledge of the availability of a medication, namely, the beta blocker, which one of his physicians believed could effectively enable him to return to his former position without any risk to his health. Moreover, the respondents pointed out that, on cross-examination, the appellant testified that Dr. Graff did not discuss any of the adverse side effects of this medication with him. The appellant further testified that Dr. Graff was of the view that, while this medication should not be prescribed at that time, if the appellant returned to work in his former position and his blood pressure continued to rise, there would be a reason to consider administering the beta blockers.

The respondents also argued that this letter indicated that Dr. Graff had implied during the July 20, 1994 appointment that the appellant could return to work, in which case beta blockers might eventually become necessary. However, in voice mail messages left for his immediate superior just after that appointment (on July 20th and 27th, 1994), the appellant stressed that both his family doctor and Dr. Graff were of the view that "a new job, a new change of environment" was what he truly needed. While the appellant alluded to the possibility of trying a "new medication," he indicated that Dr. Graff was of the view that it should not be attempted—given its adverse side effects—if his health could be improved by "a job change in a different kind of environment."

From this evidence, a certain degree of inconsistency can be identified between what the appellant appears to have been told by Dr. Graff, and the information he subsequently conveyed to his employers. The evidence suggests that Dr. Graff believed that the appellant could return to work, even in his former position as Controller, and, if his hypertension became more acute at that point, it could be controlled through the use of beta blockers. However, the voice mail messages of July 20th and July 27th indicate that the appellant did not put this information forward as fully and clearly as he might have. Rather than mention the possibility of returning to his former position if beta blockers were administered, he instead stressed that his physicians were of the view that a change in jobs would in fact be the most beneficial form of "treatment." At trial, however, the appellant admitted on cross-examination that this advice had not in fact been given by his specialist.

This contradiction could raise some suspicion in the minds of jurors as to the trustworthiness of the appellant's character. But, does the evidence lead unquestionably and unequivocally to the conclusion that the appellant's conduct was sufficiently dishonest to provide just cause for summary dismissal? A review of the evidence in its entirety leads me to answer this question in the negative. To my mind, the material in the record provides a sufficient basis for a jury to conclude that the appellant reasonably and truly believed that his physicians, including Dr. Graff, were of the view that beta blockers should be considered only as a "last resort" treatment, and that they were not yet required at that point in time....

The respondents claimed in oral argument that the appellant's falsehood lay in giving Dr. Graff's imprimatur to the notion that beta blockers carried adverse side effects. . . .

Thus, while there may not have been a full disclosure of all material facts by the appellant, this was not required of him. Rather, the question is whether he engaged in dishonesty in a manner that undermined, or was incompatible with his employment relationship. An analysis of the record as a whole leads me to conclude that the jury, acting judicially, could have reasonably found that this was not the case. For this reason, there is no basis upon which to interfere with the jury's verdict that the respondents had not proven just cause warranting dismissal.

VI. DISPOSITION

For the foregoing reasons, the appeal is allowed, the judgment of the British Columbia Court of Appeal is set aside, and the order of Paris J. is restored, with the exception of the award for aggravated damages, which is struck.

* * * * *

Quebec civil law is similar to the Canadian common law on the question of what constitutes cause for dismissal. Section 2094 of the Quebec *Civil Code* states: "One of the parties may, for a serious reason, unilaterally resiliate the contract of employment without prior notice."

In *McKinley*, the primary ground of cause for dismissal was dishonesty. Other common types of cause asserted are: disobedience and insubordination (violation of the duty of obedience); competition and disclosure of confidential information (violation of the duty of fidelity); cause for negligent/incompetent work (violation of the duty to perform competently); off-duty misconduct; and so on. *McKinley*'s proportionality analysis has been interpreted, in both common and civil law jurisdictions, to require that the employer apply a graduated scale of disciplinary measures prior to dismissal in all but the most serious cases.

3:430 Constructive Dismissal

Strict contractual principles dictate that if the employer commits a repudiatory breach of the express or implied terms of the employment contract, the employee may treat themselves as dismissed, elect to terminate the contract, and sue for damages. In this situation, although the employer has not expressly dismissed the employee, the employer's actions have the effect of bringing the employment relationship to an end and entitling the employee to reasonable notice damages. This is referred to as the doctrine of constructive dismissal.

There are two types of constructive dismissal or employer repudiatory breaches. The first is the unilateral alteration of an essential term of the employment contract. This often arises where the employer demotes, transfers, varies salary, and so on. The second arises from mistreatment that demonstrates that the employer no longer views itself as bound to the employment contract.

The first case in this section provides an overview of the law of constructive dismissal. The second case examines the situation of constructive dismissal through unilateral alteration. The third is an example of constructive dismissal through employer mistreatment.

Potter v New Brunswick Legal Aid Services, [2015] 1 SCR 500 at para 2ff

Background

Mr. Potter is a lawyer who was admitted to the Law Society of New Brunswick in 1977. After serving in various positions primarily with the Province of New Brunswick, Mr. Potter became the Province's interim Director of Legal Aid in 1993. He remained in that position until 2005, when the *Legal Aid Act*, R.S.N.B. 1973, c. L-2, was amended to create a new scheme under which staff lawyers would represent litigants (S.N.B. 2005, c. 8). Under the former system, lawyers in private practice had been paid for performing legal aid work. The amendments also created the position of Executive Director of Legal Aid ("Executive Director").

On December 12, 2005, the day the amendments were proclaimed, the Board of Directors ("Board") of the newly created Commission nominated Mr. Potter for appointment as the Executive Director. The Lieutenant-Governor in Council formally appointed him to that office on March 16, 2006, by means of Order-in-Council 2006-85. The appointment was for a seven-year term that was to expire on December 12, 2012.

Mr. Potter's appointment as the Executive Director was governed by s. 39 of the *Legal Aid Act* ...

The Board had also established the terms and conditions of Mr. Potter's appointment, as required by s. 39(2), in a resolution dated December 12, 2005 that included provisions on remuneration, insurance benefits, pension benefits, vacation and sick leave, and a vehicle allowance. Section 39(6) provides that certain powers and duties are attributed to the Executive Director by the *Legal Aid Act* itself, by the regulations or by the Board....

In October 2009, after Mr. Potter had completed nearly four years of his seven-year contract, his physician advised him to take time off for medical reasons. Although initially one month, the period of his medical leave was subsequently extended, first to January 4, 2010, and then to January 18, 2010. The second extension was accompanied by a note in which Mr. Potter's physician observed that he "needs to be reassessed before [going] back" (Court of Appeal reasons, at para. 31). In his absence, Mr. Potter delegated his powers and duties to Peter Corey, the Commission's Director of Criminal Operations.

Before then, in the spring of 2009, Mr. Potter and the Board had begun to negotiate a buyout of his contract. If successful, that process would have culminated in Mr. Potter's resignation in exchange for an agreed-upon compensation package.

On January 5, 2010, the Board decided—without alerting Mr. Potter—that if the buyout negotiations were not resolved before January 11, it would request that the Lieutenant-Governor in Council revoke Mr. Potter's appointment for cause pursuant to s. 39(4) of the *Legal Aid Act*....

On January 11, unbeknownst to Mr. Potter, the Chairperson of the Board sent a letter to the Minister of Justice recommending that Mr. Potter be dismissed for cause and outlining in general terms the grounds for dismissal.

Also on January 11, counsel for the Commission sent a letter to counsel for Mr. Potter advising him that Mr. Potter was not to return to work "until further direction" ...

On January 12, counsel for Mr. Potter replied, acknowledging receipt of that letter and requesting clarification of the Commission's instructions:

I have received your letter dated January 11, 2010. I note the use of the phrase that "Mr. Potter *ought not to return* to the work place . . ." The phrasing could be interpreted as advisory as opposed to directive.

Given that Mr. Potter occupies a position which sets out a statutory obligation to perform the duties of his position, can you confirm whether the Board has suspended Mr. Potter[?] [Emphasis in original.]

On January 13, counsel for the Commission confirmed that the statement was directive: "I am surprised that you and your client are confused. He is not to return to work until further notice."

Mr. Potter was not aware of the Board's letter recommending that he be dismissed for cause, and there is no evidence that the Lieutenant-Governor in Council took any steps towards acting on the recommendation. Mr. Potter's sick leave was due to expire on January 18, 2010, but having received the instruction of January 11, as clarified in the letter of January 13, he did not return to work. The Board delegated the powers and duties of the Executive Director to Mr. Corey, to whom Mr. Potter had previously delegated them.

On March 9, 2010 — eight weeks after the Board's instruction to stay away from the workplace, and seven weeks after Mr. Potter had been scheduled to return from sick leave — Mr. Potter commenced an action for constructive dismissal. . . .

In response, the Board stopped Mr. Potter's salary and benefits. . . .

Analysis

Was Mr. Potter Constructively Dismissed?
When an employer's conduct evinces an intention no longer to be bound by the employment contract, the employee has the choice of either accepting that conduct or changes made by the employer, or treating the conduct or changes as a repudiation of the contract by the employer and suing for wrongful dismissal. This was clearly stated in *Farber*, at para. 33, the leading case on the law of constructive dismissal in Canada. See also *In re Rubel Bronze and Metal Co. and Vos*, [1918] 1 K.B. 315, at p. 322. Since the employee has not been formally dismissed, the employer's act is referred to as "constructive dismissal". The word "constructive" indicates that the dismissal is a legal construct: the employer's act is treated as a dismissal because of the way it is characterized by the law (J. A. Yogis and C. Cotter, *Barron's Canadian Law Dictionary* (6th ed. 2009), at p. 61; B. A. Garner, ed., *Black's Law Dictionary* (10th ed. 2014), at p. 380).

The burden rests on the employee to establish that he or she has been constructively dismissed. If the employee is successful, he or she is then entitled to damages in lieu of reasonable notice of termination. In *Farber*, the Court surveyed both the common law and the civil law jurisprudence in this regard. The solutions adopted and principles applied in the two legal systems are very similar. In both, the purpose of the inquiry is to determine whether the employer's act evinced an intention no longer to be bound by the contract.

Given that employment contracts are dynamic in comparison with commercial contracts, courts have properly taken a flexible approach in determining whether the employer's conduct evinced an intention no longer to be bound by the contract. There are two branches of the test that have emerged. Most often, the court must first identify an express or implied contract term that has been breached, and then determine whether that breach was sufficiently serious to constitute constructive dismissal ... Typically, the breach in question involves changes to the employee's compensation, work assignments or place of work that are both unilateral and substantial ... In the words of McCardie J. in *Rubel Bronze*, at p. 323, "The question is ever one of degree."

However, an employer's conduct will also constitute constructive dismissal if it more generally shows that the employer intended not to be bound by the contract. In applying *Farber*, courts have held that an employee can be found to have been constructively dismissed without identifying a specific term that was breached if the employer's treatment of the employee made continued employment intolerable: see, e.g., *Shah v. Xerox Canada Ltd.* (2000), 131 O.A.C. 44; *Whiting v. Winnipeg River Brokenhead Community Futures Development Corp.* (1998), 159 D.L.R. (4th) 18 (Man. C.A.). This approach is necessarily retrospective, as it requires consideration of the cumulative effect of past acts by the employer and the determination of whether those acts evinced an intention no longer to be bound by the contract.

The first branch of the test for constructive dismissal, the one that requires a review of specific terms of the contract, has two steps: first, the employer's unilateral change must be found to constitute a breach of the employment contract and, second, if it does constitute such a breach, it must be found to substantially alter an essential term of the contract (see Sproat, at p. 5-5). Often, the first step of the test will require little analysis, as the breach will be obvious. Where the breach is less obvious, however, as is often the case with suspensions, a more careful analysis may be required. ...

The two-step approach to the first branch of the test for constructive dismissal is not a departure from the approach adopted in *Farber*. Rather, the situation in *Farber* was one in which the identification of a breach required only a cursory analysis. The emphasis in *Farber* was on the second step of this branch, as the evidentiary foundation for the perceived magnitude of the breach was the key issue in that case. However, the identification of a unilateral act that amounted to a breach of the contract was implicit in the Court's reasoning. In many cases, this will be sufficient. The case at bar, however, is one in which the claim can be properly resolved only after both steps of the analysis have been completed.

At the first step of the analysis, the court must determine objectively whether a breach has occurred. To do so, it must ascertain whether the employer has unilaterally changed the contract. If an express or an implied term gives the employer the authority to make the change, or if the employee consents to or acquiesces in it, the change is not a unilateral act and therefore will not constitute a breach. If so, it does not amount to constructive dismissal. Moreover, to qualify as a breach, the change must be detrimental to the employee.

This first step of the analysis involves a distinct inquiry from the one that must be carried out to determine whether the breach is substantial, although the two have often been conflated by courts in the constructive dismissal context. Gonthier J. conducted this inquiry in *Farber*, in which an employee had been offered a new position that was found to constitute a demotion. He stated that "the issue of whether there has been a demotion must be determined objectively by comparing the positions in question and their attributes": *Farber*, at para. 46.

Once it has been objectively established that a breach has occurred, the court must turn to the second step of the analysis and ask whether, "at the time the [breach occurred], a reasonable person in the same situation as the employee would have felt that the essential terms of the employment contract were being substantially changed" (*Farber*, at para. 26). A breach that is minor in that it could not be perceived as having substantially changed an essential term of the contract does not amount to constructive dismissal.

The kinds of changes that meet these criteria will depend on the facts of the case being considered, so "one cannot generalize": Sproat, at p. 5-6.5. In each case, determining whether an employee has been constructively dismissed is a "highly fact-driven exercise" in which the court must determine whether the changes are reasonable and whether they are within the scope of the employee's job description or employment contract: R. S. Echlin and J. M. Fantini, *Quitting for Good Reason: The Law of Constructive Dismissal in Canada* (2001), at pp. 4-5. Although the test for constructive dismissal does not vary depending on the nature of the alleged breach, how it is applied will nevertheless reflect the distinct factual circumstances of each claim.

The uniqueness of the application of this first branch of the test is evident in cases involving administrative suspensions. In all cases, the primary burden will be on the employee to establish constructive dismissal, but where an administrative suspension is at issue, the burden will necessarily shift to the employer, which must then show that the suspension is justified. If the employer cannot do so, a breach will have been established, and the burden will shift back to the employee at the second step of the analysis.

The second branch of the test for constructive dismissal necessarily requires a different approach. In cases in which this branch of the test applies, constructive dismissal consists of conduct that, when viewed in the light of all the circumstances, would lead a reasonable person to conclude that the employer no longer intended to be bound by the terms of the contract. The employee is not required to point to an actual specific substantial change in compensation, work assignments, or so on, that on its own constitutes a substantial breach. The focus is on whether a course of conduct pursued by the employer "evince[s] an intention no longer to be bound by the contract": *Rubel Bronze*, at p. 322. A course of conduct that does evince such an intention amounts cumulatively to an actual breach. . . .

Thus, constructive dismissal can take two forms: that of a single unilateral act that breaches an essential term of the contract, or that of a series of acts that, taken together, show that the employer no longer intended to be bound by the contract. The distinction between these two forms of constructive dismissal was clearly expressed by Lord Denning M.R. in a leading English case, *Western Excavating (ECC) Ltd. v. Sharp*, [1978] 1 All E.R. 713 (C.A.). First of all, an employer's conduct may amount to constructive dismissal if it "shows that [he] no longer intends to be bound by one or more of the essential terms of the contract": p. 717. But the employer's conduct may also amount to constructive dismissal if it constitutes "a significant breach going to the root of the contract of employment": *ibid*. In either case, the employer's perceived intention no longer to be bound by the contract is taken to give rise to a breach.

In applying the first branch of the test for constructive dismissal to the facts of the case at bar, this Court must ask, first, whether the Board's suspension of Mr. Potter amounted to a breach of the employment contract. For this, it must determine whether the suspension was a unilateral act. On its face, the Board's decision to suspend Mr. Potter was clearly unilateral, since he did not consent to the suspension. But the Commission counters that the suspension does not evince an intention no longer to be bound by the contract, as it was authorized by an express or an implied term of the contract, which is a way of saying that Mr. Potter consented to such a change by signing the contract. I agree that the question whether the suspension amounted to constructive dismissal turns in part on whether it was authorized by the contract. If there was an express or an implied term that authorized the Board to suspend Mr. Potter as it did, then there was no unilateral act and, therefore, no breach of the contract—let alone a substantial change to the essential terms of the contract—and the constructive dismissal claim must fail.

If, however, the suspension was not authorized by the contract, then it satisfies the requirements of the first step of this branch of the test, that is, it constitutes a unilateral change that amounts to a breach of the contract. It would then be necessary to turn to the second step and ask whether the Board's unilateral decision to suspend Mr. Potter could reasonably be perceived as having *substantially changed the essential terms of the contract*. It is clear that a suspension can amount to constructive dismissal: *Cabiakman*, at paras. 71-72. In determining whether the unauthorized suspension constituted a substantial breach, the Court must consider whether a reasonable person in the employee's circumstances would have perceived, *inter alia*, that the employer was acting in good faith to protect a legitimate business interest, and that the employer's act had a minimal impact on him or her in terms of the duration of the suspension. With respect, the trial judge erred in failing to consider the two steps of the inquiry independently.

Applying the principles discussed above to the facts of the instant case, I find that Mr. Potter was constructively dismissed by the Board. In light of the indefinite duration of the suspension, of the fact that the Commission failed to act in good faith insofar as it withheld valid business reasons from Mr. Potter, and of the Commission's concealed intention to have Mr. Potter terminated, I respectfully find that the trial judge erred in concluding that the suspension was authorized by the contract of employment. Moreover, for the reasons set out below, I find that this breach of the contract amounted to a substantial change to the essential terms of the contract that was imposed unilaterally by the employer.

[The majority reached this conclusion based on its decision in *Cabiakman v Industrial Alliance Life Insurance Co*, 2004 SCC 55. There the Court held, in interpreting the requirements of the Quebec *Civil Code*, that an employer could not suspend an employee, with or without pay, unless it had legitimate business reasons, the suspension was issued in good faith, and the duration of the suspension was reasonable. An unjustified suspension, like the one that occurred here, is a breach of the employment contract.]

* * * * *

Constructive Dismissal Through a Unilateral Contractual Alteration
The doctrine of constructive dismissal holds that the employer may not unilaterally alter an essential term of the employment contract without the employee's consent. From the employer's perspective, the constructive dismissal doctrine may severely limit flexibility in modifying terms and conditions of employment, because a significant change of terms may constitute a repudiatory breach of the express or implied terms of the employment contract. Today, competitive pressures are pushing Canadian employers to demand a more flexible approach with regard to hours of work, economic benefits, and job duties. Technological

advances are constantly challenging old production techniques. The clash between the employer's need for flexibility and the employee's need for security is nowhere more manifest than in the context of constructive dismissal.

In most instances, as in *Potter*, a unilateral alteration by an employer will force an employee's hand, who will either accept the change or sue for constructive dismissal (or lump it). The claimant in *Potter*, for instance, was suspended and could not, therefore, continue to work in his position. But in some cases, an employee may refuse consent to a proposed variation of the contract terms, but be able to continue to work in their position. What is the employee's legal situation when this occurs? The following seminal employment law case discusses this issue.

Hill v Peter Gorman Ltd (1957), 9 DLR (2d) 124 at 125ff (Ont CA)

> Laidlaw J.A: The plaintiff was employed by the defendant as a salesman for various periods of time commencing in January 1950 and ending in April 1953. He was re-employed by the defendant by an oral agreement, to commence a new period of employment on November 4th, 1953. It was a term of that oral agreement that the plaintiff would receive 2% on the sales made by him of tobacco, 2 1/2% on confectionery and 3% on sundries. There was no definite term of employment.
>
> Subsequent to the oral agreement made between the parties an agreement in writing was made between them under date 11th day of December, 1953.... There is no right of the appellant expressed therein, nor was there any such right in the oral agreement, between the parties to make any deductions from the amount of commission payable to the respondent for any purpose or reason whatsoever ... there is no provision therein and it was not a term or condition of the oral agreement between the parties, that the respondent would assume any responsibility or liability for any account or amount not paid by a customer to the appellant for goods sold to him by the respondent.
>
> During the year 1954, Mr. Peter Gorman, President of the appellant Company, was concerned about the state of customers' delinquent accounts. He brought that matter to the attention of the salesmen from time to time at weekly meetings. In the last of such meetings for the month of August, 1954, he notified the salesmen, including the respondent, that he was setting up a reserve for bad debts and that 10% would be deducted from their commissions....
>
> The learned trial Judge made basic findings of fact upon which the rights of the parties depend. I quote the all important finding made in these words — "I am satisfied that the plaintiff Hill did not at anytime accept the procedure adopted by the employer for a deduction of 10% to set up a reserve for bad debts. The parties were never together in this regard"....
>
> There is ample evidence to support the findings of fact made by the learned trial Judge....
>
> It follows from the finding of fact made by the learned trial Judge that the plaintiff was entitled to recover from the defendant the amount of money withheld and retained by the defendant from the commissions payable to the plaintiff. Therefore, in my opinion, this appeal should be dismissed with costs.
>
> J.K. MACKAY J.A.: I am respectfully of opinion that it cannot be said, as a matter of law, that an employee accepts an attempted variation simply by the fact alone of continuing

in his employment. Where an employer attempts to vary the contractual terms, the position of the employee is this: He may accept the variation expressly or impliedly in which case there is a new contract. He may refuse to accept it and if the employer persists in the attempted variation the employee may treat this persistence as a breach of contract and sue the employer for damages, or while refusing to accept it he may continue in his employment and if the employer permits him to discharge his obligations and the employee makes it plain that he is not accepting the variation, then the employee is entitled to insist on the original terms.

I cannot agree that an employer has any unilateral right to change a contract or that by attempting to make such a change he can force an employee to either accept it or quit.

If the plaintiff made it clear to Gorman that he did not agree to the change made in September, 1954, the proper course for the defendant to pursue was to terminate the contract by proper notice and to offer employment on the new terms. Until it was so terminated, the plaintiff was entitled to insist on performance of the original contract.

Constructive Dismissal Through General Employer Repudiation

As noted, a second species of constructive dismissal cases arises where the employer generally demonstrates an intent no longer to be bound to the contract. This type of employer repudiation usually, although not exclusively, occurs where the employer mistreats an employee in a significant way. Were it not for the constructive dismissal doctrine, an employer could make life so miserable for an employee that she would be driven from the job without legal recourse.

Lloyd v Imperial Parking Ltd, [1997] 3 WWR 697, 46 Alta LR (3d) 220 at para 1ff (QB)

SANDERMAN J.: Mr. Lloyd claims that he was constructively dismissed from his employment with Imperial Parking Limited (hereinafter "Imperial Parking") on October 6, 1993. He seeks a declaration that he was constructively dismissed and asks for damages as a result of the actions of his former employer....

The Defendant still claimed an after-acquired right to dismiss the Plaintiff on the basis of his authorization of full payment of the insurance premium for his automobile when this was not proper....

Certain facts are not in dispute. Mr. Lloyd took a position with Imperial Parking in Calgary, Alberta on July 1, 1992.... The position filled by Mr. Lloyd was City Manager of the operation in Calgary. Mr. Noiles was the Regional Manager of Imperial Parking. He was responsible for the company's operations in Alberta and Saskatchewan. During the course of Mr. Lloyd's employment, Mr. Noiles was promoted to the position of Vice-President of Imperial Parking.

Mr. Lloyd had no experience in the parking industry. Although he had some property management experience, it did not relate to the type of work that he would be doing with Imperial Parking. This was the best job that Mr. Lloyd ever had. He entered into a contract with Imperial Parking. He was to be paid $46,000.00 per year. He was to have a vehicle allowance in the sum of $350.00 per month. Within a few months, his salary was increased to $50,000.00 per annum. The vehicle allowance was raised to $400.00 a month. In addition to this, his employer paid for his Alberta Health Care benefits and for group benefits through an insurance plan. His employment contract also provided for three weeks vacation for his first year of employment....

In addition to the vehicle allowance that Mr. Lloyd received, Imperial Parking was to pay his vehicle insurance and gasoline expenses. Mr. Lloyd had a bad driving record. Because of this, his insurance rates were high. He brought this to the attention of Imperial Parking. He notified them that he thought it would be inappropriate for Imperial Parking to have to pay the entire insurance premium. An arrangement was worked out between Imperial Parking and Mr. Lloyd. Quotes were obtained from insurance agencies as to what a person in Mr. Lloyd's position, driving the car he was, would pay, absent the bad driving record. Imperial Parking was prepared to pay up to that amount. Anything beyond that amount would be the responsibility of Mr. Lloyd. In September of 1992, Mr. Lloyd's insurance premium was $2,544.00. Imperial Parking paid $1,200.00 of that amount. Mr. Lloyd paid $1,344.00.

When this insurance coverage had to be renewed, Mr. Lloyd authorized Imperial Parking to pay the entire insurance premium of $2,581.00. Imperial Parking was prepared to pay $1,200.00 of this amount, but not the additional $1,381.00. Mr. Lloyd did not seek the approval or authorization of Mr. Noiles in order to pay the full insurance premium.

As Mr. Lloyd had no experience in the parking business, it was necessary for him to work closely with Mr. Noiles during the initial stages of his employment. Mr. Noiles preferred a team approach through this period. He wanted to ensure that Mr. Lloyd had a firm foundation in the parking industry before he was prepared to allow him to make autonomous decisions. The relationship between Mr. Noiles and Mr. Lloyd was a positive one during the first eight or nine months of Mr. Lloyd's employment. It was a busy time. He was working long hours. Although he had a significant workload and was under pressure to learn and perform, he was content and was making progress in the parking industry. Not only was this the best job that he ever had, but it was one that he hoped to make into a career....

Mr. Noiles is an aggressive type of manager whose eye is always on the bottom line. He is concerned about the profitability of those operations under his control. He attempts to get the best performance possible from every employee under his direction for the benefit of his employer. His approach is geared towards making the operation as profitable as possible.

Within eight or nine months of Mr. Lloyd's starting date, the relationship between he and Mr. Noiles had deteriorated considerably.... This conflict culminated in Mr. Lloyd phoning in sick on October 3, 1993. He did not show up for work on Monday or Tuesday of that week. On October 6, 1993, Imperial Parking was notified by facsimile transmission that he considered that he had been constructively dismissed from his employment effective that date. He attributed this to the conduct of Mr. Noiles. He claimed that Mr. Noiles had been continually rude and abusive towards him and had been intimidating through his constant threats to terminate his employment. There is no issue taken by the parties in relation to the facts set out above.

The Plaintiff called evidence in order to attempt to establish an atmosphere of oppression and intimidation being directed toward Mr. Lloyd by Mr. Noiles. The Plaintiff put forward the theory that Mr. Noiles made it impossible for Mr. Lloyd to carry out his functions at work because of his mean-spirited and unwarranted attacks upon him....

The position of the Defendant is that Mr. Lloyd had not been able to master the requirements of his job to a level that would allow him to operate without supervision from Mr. Noiles. This inability on his part to carry out his functions as expected, coupled with the difficult times that the company was experiencing in Calgary during 1993, led to many arguments between Mr. Noiles and Mr. Lloyd.... The Defendant put forward the position that the relationship in existence between Mr. Noiles and Mr. Lloyd became more adversarial and confrontational as time passed. The Defendant suggests that this approach was one that was embraced by Mr. Lloyd. Mr. Noiles was only reacting to an untenable situation created by Mr. Lloyd's inability to grow into the requirements of his position. In essence, the Defendant strenuously disputes the scenario put forward by the Plaintiff. The Defendant denies any form of abusive treatment directed towards Mr. Lloyd by Mr. Noiles....

After assessing the credibility of the various witnesses who testified and examining their evidence closely, the findings of fact in relation to the dealings between Mr. Noiles and Mr. Lloyd during the late spring and early summer of 1993 can be summarized as follows. Over the last four or five months of Mr. Lloyd's employment, friction was increasing between he and Mr. Noiles. This friction came about because of the displeasure Mr. Noiles felt with Mr. Lloyd's inability to grasp his job function as quickly as possible. Mr. Noiles expected more from him. He showed his displeasure by the abusive manner in which he treated Mr. Lloyd. During the latter months of Mr. Lloyd's employment, Mr. Noiles frequently yelled at him in a demeaning fashion. The yelling and shouting took place on a regular basis. At times, it appeared as if this was the only way in which Mr. Noiles communicated with Mr. Lloyd. Although there was no set pattern to the incidents of yelling, they were numerous and had an adverse effect upon Mr. Lloyd. On occasion, the incidents of yelling were prolonged. This type of behaviour was far from inconsequential.

In addition to this, Mr. Noiles made Mr. Lloyd feel very insecure about his continued employment. He threatened to fire or terminate Mr. Lloyd's employment between 50 and 100 times during this period. The verbal abuse also took the form of Mr. Noiles calling Mr. Lloyd vulgar names. This behaviour was not frequent. It only happened three times. Still, Mr. Lloyd was shocked by the viciousness of the name calling. Further examples of the oppressive behaviour directed towards Mr. Lloyd by Mr. Noiles include Mr. Noiles' refusal to allow Mr. Lloyd to take the vacation time that he was entitled to pursuant to the employment contract and Mr. Noiles' improper suggestions that Mr. Lloyd was engaging in sexual activity with female subordinate workers.

After reviewing the evidence of Mr. Lloyd and Ms. Meechan closely, it is apparent that during the late spring and summer of 1993 Mr. Noiles was treating Mr. Lloyd in an abusive fashion on a regular basis. Although there was no set pattern to it, it occurred frequently. One cannot but come to the conclusion that it was intentional. The purpose of it seems to have been to make the workplace so uncomfortable for Mr. Lloyd that he would want to leave. To this end, it was successful.

The evidence that has been accepted by the Court shows that the abuse was one-sided. There is no credible evidence before the Court that would lead me to believe that

Mr. Lloyd responded to the abuse in kind. Quite to the contrary, it appears as if he did not challenge Mr. Noiles in any meaningful fashion. It appears as if he was cowed and intimidated by his superior.... The interaction between Mr. Noiles and Mr. Lloyd during the last four or five months of Mr. Lloyd's employment was not merely the byproduct of a personality clash. It was a calculated pattern of behaviour employed by Mr. Noiles.

Does this persistent conduct, which led Mr. Lloyd to leave his employment, constitute a constructive dismissal? The answer is yes. The vulgar name calling, the failure to schedule holidays and the suggestions of inappropriate sexual conduct with female subordinate workers would not support this conclusion by themselves. It is the repeated and continuous incidents of yelling and screaming at Mr. Lloyd by Mr. Noiles in the workplace and the repeated threats to terminate his employment that support this finding. These two separate but interrelated patterns of behaviour form the basis of the case made out by the Plaintiff. The other types of behaviour add to the overall strength of the Plaintiff's case but it is not dependent upon them.

It is well-recognized that in the absence of cause, any fundamental breach by the employer of a major term of the employment relationship allows the employee to take the position that a constructive dismissal has occurred. In order for a constructive dismissal to exist, the breach must be in relation to a fundamental term of the employment relationship rather than just a minor or incidental term. There must be a fundamental breach of a fundamental term of employment before one can claim to be constructively dismissed.

A fundamental implied term of any employment relationship is that the employer will treat the employee with civility, decency, respect, and dignity. The standard that has to be adhered to by the employer is dependent upon the particular work environment. This appears to be part of the trend to establish a duty upon an employer to treat employees "reasonably" in all aspects of the labour process....

In this case, a fundamental implied term of the employer/employee relationship has been breached. Mr. Noiles, Mr. Lloyd's superior, did not treat Mr. Lloyd with the civility, decency, respect, and dignity to which he was entitled. The abusive pattern of behaviour during 1993 was in contravention of this requirement.

Imperial Parking argued that the concept of after acquired cause is applicable to this case. This argument is founded on Mr. Lloyd's authorization of full payment of his car insurance premium when the time for renewal came in 1993. Although he had the authority to issue the cheque to make the payment, this contravened the understanding that he had with his employer. The employer was only prepared to pay for an amount that reflected the rate that would have been charged a person in Mr. Lloyd's position with a good driving record. Anything in excess of this basic amount would not have been paid by Imperial Parking.

Imperial Parking characterizes this act as one of gross dishonesty that rescues the Defendant from this lawsuit. It is argued on behalf of the Defendant that the discovery of this dishonest behaviour is just cause for dismissal even if it came to light after the employee has ended his employment with the employer.... The principle is one recognized by the Court.

In this case, it is not applicable. The evidence of Mr. Lloyd is accepted in this regard. I do not find that this was an intentional act of dishonesty on his part. At the time the insurance had to be renewed, his relationship with Mr. Noiles had deteriorated to such an extent that Mr. Lloyd avoided having unnecessary contact with Mr. Noiles. He did not seek him out. Certainly, Mr. Lloyd exhibited a weakness in character in behaving in this fashion, but it is understandable when the relationship between these two men is closely examined. I find that Mr. Lloyd did not deal with this matter in a proper fashion because of his disinclination to give Mr. Noiles' another opportunity to yell at him. In this case, the evidentiary basis for the notion of after acquired cause is absent. The wrongdoing pointed to does not support this contention.

Although I have found that the notion of after-acquired cause does not play a role in this lawsuit, the behaviour of Mr. Lloyd in relation to the payment of the insurance premium is something that can be considered in relation to the damages that flow from the wrongdoing of Imperial Parking. . . .

As Mr. Lloyd concedes that he received a benefit in the sum of $1,381.00 from Imperial Parking when he arranged to have his entire insurance premium paid by his employer, that amount must be set off against the total judgment. Consequently, the total judgment of $29,274.85 is reduced by $1,381.00. There will be judgment for the Plaintiff in the amount of $27,893.85.

There will be interest payable on this amount pursuant to the *Judgment Interest Act*.

* * * * *

Constructive dismissal is understood as a repudiatory breach by an employer of the employment contract. Where an employer mistreats an employee, however, it is not always easy to locate a particular contractual term that has been breached. In *Imperial Parking* this was addressed by holding that employers have an implied duty to treat employees "with civility, decency, respect, and dignity," violation of which may constitute a repudiatory breach by the employer and thus constructive dismissal. A second approach was also developed in the Ontario decision of *Shah v Xerox Canada Ltd* (2000), 131 OAC 44 (CA), which was upheld by the majority of the SCC in *Potter*. In *Potter*, discussed in Section 3:430, above, the majority explained (at para 33) that:

> [A]n employer's conduct will also constitute constructive dismissal if it more generally shows that the employer intended not to be bound by the contract. In applying *Farber*, courts have held that an employee can be found to have been constructively dismissed without identifying a specific term that was breached if the employer's treatment of the employee made continued employment intolerable.

For a discussion of what is at stake as between these two approaches, see David Doorey, "Employer Bullying: Implied Duties of Fair Dealing in Canadian Employment Contracts" (2005) 30 *Queen's Law Journal* 500.

In *Imperial Parking*, the employer argued that it had after-acquired cause that obviated its need to provide reasonable notice for constructive dismissal. The doctrine of after-acquired cause specifies that an employer may not be liable for reasonable notice damages if cause existed at the time of dismissal, even if the employer only became aware of it after termination. However, as explained by the Ontario Court of Appeal in *McIntyre v Hockin* (1889), 16

OAR 498, a "plea of after acquired cause could be defeated in cases where the employer had knowledge of the prior misconduct and did nothing to address the situation"; in other words, it condoned the misconduct.

3:500 REMEDIES FOR WRONGFUL DISMISSAL

It is often said that the effectiveness of an area of law is best judged by the effectiveness of the remedies that are available when the law has been breached. The rest of this chapter will look at the remedies granted to wrongfully dismissed workers at common law.

Later chapters of this book will shed light on remedies available to unionized workers under collective agreements (see Chapter 9, Section 9:400); with those available to non-unionized workers in a few Canadian jurisdictions under statutory systems of adjudication such as that in sections 240–46 of the *Canada Labour Code*, sections 124–28 of the Quebec *Labour Standards Act*, and section 71 of the *Nova Scotia Employments Code* (see Chapter 13, Section 13:400), and with those available to workers (whether unionized or not) who are dismissed in breach of human rights statutes (see Chapter 14). In contrast to those regimes, the common law of wrongful dismissal makes virtually no provision for a remedy of reinstatement. Only money damages are available at common law, and the courts have been reluctant to take a make-whole approach to the calculation of those damages.

3:510 Reinstatement

Geoffrey England, "Recent Developments in the Law of the Employment Contract: Continuing Tension Between the Rights Paradigm and the Efficiency Paradigm" (1995) 20 *Queen's Law Journal* 557 at 605–9

> The future of the remedy of compulsory reinstatement will be a useful gauge of the shifting balance between the two paradigms [the rights paradigm and the efficiency paradigm]. Courts have traditionally refused equitable or other discretionary remedies that would have the effect of specifically enforcing an employment contract, except where a public officeholder is dismissed in violation of a statutory procedure or the administrative law duty of fairness. This has been justified in part by the principle of mutuality. The courts will not endorse slavery by forcing an unwilling employee to work for an employer, and this has been taken to preclude forcing an unwilling employer to take back a wrongfully dismissed employee. In reality, however, the two situations are not on a par, as it is not tantamount to slavery to reinstate an employee who requests that remedy.
>
> While the practical difficulty of enforcing reinstatement orders has unquestionably contributed to the courts' policy against granting such orders, the main rationale appears to be a reluctance to question the employer's judgment of what is best for the enterprise. The assumption is that mutual trust and confidence have been irretrievably destroyed by the dismissal, or that the production process would otherwise suffer if the employee were reinstated. This is the quintessence of the efficiency paradigm.

In contrast, the rights paradigm envisages some circumstances when reinstatement would be justifiable. One such situation, referred to above, arises where the contract contains an express procedure which the employer has violated in dismissing the employee. In that situation, reinstatement may be ordered pending compliance with the proper procedures, as damages alone cannot fully compensate for the employee's loss of the opportunity to persuade the employer to change its mind before carrying out the dismissal. Mutual trust and confidence would hardly be undermined by requiring the employer to honour obligations of its own making.

Similarly, where the employer fires a worker for an alleged criminal offence, but promises reinstatement if the worker is found not guilty, it seems unfair to allow the employer to renege on the promise. A recent Nova Scotia trial judgment hinted that reinstatement might be appropriate in these circumstances, at least where the worker does not occupy a managerial position.

Second, some workers derive a unique personal benefit from actually doing the job, which money cannot adequately replace. Doctors and university professors develop professional skills and derive vocational satisfaction, as do nurses, pastors, and teachers. Under the rights paradigm, courts have begun to protect this largely psychological benefit by what amounts to a reinstatement order. Thus, an English court has granted an injunction preventing an employer from unilaterally transferring a social worker from a research team on child abuse to less professionally satisfying duties. The Ontario Court of Appeal has granted a declaration that the removal of a clergyman from the rolls of the United Church was void because of failure to comply with the procedures in the Church's constitution. The Court distinguished this situation from the normal employment relationship, but the declaration nonetheless reinstated the plaintiff indirectly. In a Québec case where there was a misunderstanding on whether an orchestra conductor's term contract had been renewed, the court granted an interlocutory injunction reinstating him, pending resolution of the issue at trial. The crucial factor in that case was the unique benefit of remaining in the job, as the conductor did not want to miss a major upcoming performance. However, the Court condemned as outdated the general policy against ordering reinstatement. The principle that an equitable remedy will be granted where damages cannot adequately make up for such vocational losses is plainly applicable to many mainstream employment relationships.

Third, a strong rights argument can be made for reinstatement in order to achieve parity between the common law and other labour law regimes. Reinstatement is the normal remedy for unionized workers under the unjust discharge provisions of collective agreements. It is available, although it is granted more sparingly to non-unionized workers under statutory unjust dismissal provisions in the few Canadian jurisdictions which have such provisions. It is available to all workers, unionized or not, who are dismissed in violation of human rights, health and safety, and labour relations legislation. It is mandated by international labour law conventions which Canada has ratified. Furthermore, increasingly sophisticated personnel management techniques should make it easier, at least for large employers, to reintegrate wrongfully dismissed employees into the workplace. In exceptional circumstances, where the work environment has been irredeemably soured, reinstatement could be denied, as is the practice in arbitration and statutory adjudication.

Recent empirical evidence confirms the limited effectiveness of reinstatement orders in the non-unionized workplace, where there is no employee representation machinery to police how the reinstated employee is treated. One possible solution is to award a sizeable amount of punitive damages in conjunction with the reinstatement order, but the souring effect of such an award could make reinstatement even more precarious. Another possibility is to vest authority for supervising such orders in joint labour-management health and safety committees, or health and safety representatives in smaller firms, but these bodies have not been particularly successful even in their primary function of enforcing health and safety legislation. For the time being, in any event, the chances are that, if reinstatement is adopted at all, it will be limited to situations where the court is enforcing agreed-upon procedural machinery which the employer has chosen to disregard.

[Reprinted by permission.]

3:520 Extent of Financial Compensation

3:521 The Assessment of Reasonable Notice Damages

The measure of damages for wrongful dismissal is determined by the amount of reasonable notice to which the employee is entitled, because what makes dismissal unlawful at common law is the employer's failure to give such notice. If, therefore, an employment contract contains an express notice term, the amount stipulated in the contract is the amount to which the employee will be entitled, so long as it does not fall beneath the requirements of the relevant employment standards statute. As the Supreme Court held in *Machtinger v HOJ Industries*, however, where an employment contract is silent on the question of notice, an employee under an indefinite duration contract is entitled to common law reasonable notice. At common law, damages for wrongful dismissal amount to the wages and benefits to which the employee would have been entitled during the notice period.

The seminal case on the assessment of reasonable notice damages is *Bardal v Globe & Mail Ltd* (1960), 24 DLR (2d) 140 (Ont SCJ) at para 21. There McRuer J explained the principles as such:

> There can be no catalogue laid down as to what is reasonable notice in particular classes of cases. The reasonableness of the notice must be decided with reference to each particular case, having regard to the character of the employment, the length of service of the servant, the age of the servant and the availability of similar employment, having regard to the experience, training and qualifications of the servant.

This approach was cited with approval by the Supreme Court in *Machtinger v HOJ Industries*, [1992] 1 SCR 986, and remains the foundation for the reasonable notice assessment at common law.

Over the years, two sources of controversy have repeatedly arisen in regard to the *Bardal* factors. The first is whether the factor of "character of employment" ought still to be understood as providing longer notice to higher-income employees, on the assumption that there are fewer higher-status jobs available on the labour market. The second issue is what role, if any, the general economic climate and the financial situation of the particular employer should play in the assessment of reasonable notice damages.

Cronk v Canadian General Insurance Co (1994), 19 OR (3d) 515 (Gen Div), rev'd (1995), 128 DLR (4th) 147 (Ont CA)

[In 1993, Edna Cronk was dismissed from her position as a clerk-stenographer as a result of internal restructuring. She was 55 years old and had been employed by the company since 1958, save for six years spent raising her children. She sued for damages for wrongful dismissal, and argued that twenty months would have been a reasonable period of notice in the circumstances.]

MACPHERSON J.: Every year in Ontario good and loyal workers lose their jobs through no fault of their own. Companies die or get smaller or make changes. Almost inevitably, the waves that wash over a company and bring these changes are accompanied by a powerful undertow that drags down some of the employees of the company.

In 1993 Edna Cronk got caught in the undertow. She lost her job at a major Canadian insurance company when it made substantial organizational changes. Edna Cronk did nothing to cause the termination of her employment; she was simply dismissed after long years of service. In her world she joined the long ranks of the unemployed. In the legal world she joined the long ranks of plaintiffs in cases bearing the bland rubric 'Wrongful Dismissal.'

In many ways, as will be seen, Edna Cronk's case is similar to the hundreds of other wrongful dismissal claims that arise in Ontario each year. She seeks compensation from her former employer for the loss of her job. The employer acknowledges that some compensation must be paid. But the employer and employee disagree on the question of what amount would constitute fair compensation. The result is a lawsuit which requires this court to set a proper amount.

However, in one important respect this lawsuit is different from many other wrongful dismissal cases. Edna Cronk seeks the equivalent of 20 months' salary as compensation for her dismissal. In a good many cases the Ontario courts have awarded long-serving employees 20 or 21 or 22 months' salary. In all of these cases the dismissed employee was 45 years of age or older, had worked for the company for 20 years or more, and was employed in a reasonably senior management position at the time of dismissal.

Edna Cronk was older than 45 when she was dismissed. She had worked for her company for more than 20 years. But she was not a senior manager, she was essentially a clerical employee with some minor administrative duties.

The pivotal question which this case raises is whether an employee's position in the hierarchy of a company is a major factor in setting the period of compensation to which the employee is entitled when she is dismissed without cause.

This question can be illustrated quite graphically by comparing Edna Cronk's situation to that of the plaintiff in one of the leading Ontario cases in the dismissal domain. Geoffrey Stevens was a renowned journalist and senior manager for the Globe and Mail newspaper for 24 years. When he was fired he was 46 years of age. He was awarded compensation of 21 months' salary by a judge of this court in 1992.

Edna Cronk had been employed by the defendant insurance company for 29 years when she was fired. She was 55 years of age. However, unlike Geoffrey Stevens, she was not a highly visible and renowned employee occupying a senior management position.

Viewed from an external perspective, she was in fact an invisible, unknown and junior employee—a small cog in a large corporate enterprise.

The question which this case poses squarely is whether the law of Ontario provides as much protection to Edna Cronk for the loss of her job as it did to Geoffrey Stevens when he lost his job.... The plaintiff requests damages in lieu of notice equivalent to 20 months' salary less proper credit for amounts equal to 24 weeks previously paid. The defendant contends that its original offer of nine months' salary was, and still is, reasonable.

The factors to be considered in determining reasonable notice have remained more or less constant for over 30 years. They were enunciated by McRuer C.J.H.C. in *Bardal v. Globe and Mail Ltd.*...:

> There could be no catalogue laid down as to what was reasonable notice in particular classes of cases. The reasonableness of the notice must be decided with reference to each particular case, having regard to the character of the employment, the length of service of the servant, the age of the servant and the availability of similar employment, having regard to the experience, training and qualifications of the servant.

These two sentences constitute the most often cited passage in wrongful dismissal cases, not only in Ontario but throughout Canada....

Several of these factors clearly tell in favour of a generous notice period for Ms Cronk. First, she was 55 years old when she was fired. That is, in my view, a particularly vulnerable age for an employee. She is probably too old to embark upon a lengthy or strenuous retraining programme. Yet she may well be too young to contemplate retirement. The London Life Freedom 55 television commercial paints an attractive picture of the 55-year-old professional woman chucking it all and retreating, with Mustang convertible and surfboard in the rear, to a tropical paradise for a long and deserved retirement. Alas, for most women this commercial is a fantasy. The statistically average Canadian woman struggles to find a job, she receives about 60–70 per cent of the wages received by men doing the same work, she strives to balance family and career, she worries about losing her job, and if she does lose it she desperately seeks to obtain a new job. Edna Cronk was 55 years old when she was fired. But after long years of clerical work at a very modest salary, it is almost certain that she was not able to contemplate the Freedom 55 Mustang convertible and surfboard. She needs another job.

Second, with respect to McRuer C.J.H.C.'s statement regarding the 'availability of similar employment, having regard to the experience, training and qualifications' of the employee, Ms Cronk's position can be described as follows: she has a Grade 12 education; for parts of five decades (1950s to 1990s) her only training has been in the clerical duties domain of an insurance company; she has no qualifications for any other job; she lives in Hamilton and does not have a driver's licence; and her Hamilton employer has fired her because it does not have a job for her. This is not a description that suggests a quick and painless re-entry by Ms Cronk into the work force.

Third, Ms Cronk has worked for a long period of time—29 years—for the defendant. She has devoted virtually her entire career to the defendant. The case law, throughout Canada, quite properly attaches great significance to what I would call the long and loyal service factor....

Taken together, these three factors would seem to suggest that Ms Cronk should receive a reasonably long notice period. The case law establishes an upper limit of about twenty-four months. It would appear that, applying the *Bardal* factors, Ms Cronk would be entitled to something near this upper limit. And that is in fact what she asks for — 20 months.

Why then does the defendant contend that nine months is the appropriate notice period? There are really two reasons: first, an argument that Ms Cronk's term of employment with the defendant was not, for purposes of compensation in a wrongful dismissal context, 29 years; and second, that the upper limits of reasonable notice periods are reserved for quite senior employees with high salaries and major responsibilities. I will deal with each of these arguments in turn.

(a) Calculation of length of service

Ms Cronk worked for the defendant and its predecessor from 1958–1971 and 1977–1993, a period of 29 years. There is a gap of six years between these two periods of employment. The defendant contends that the gap has legal significance....

I disagree with this argument for several reasons. First, it needs to be recorded that the plaintiff is not asserting that the length of her employment should run 'continuously through the interruptions.' In fact Ms Cronk makes no claim for the six-year interruption in her periods of full-time employment with the defendant....

Second, most of the decided cases do not hold that an interruption in employment wipes out the first period for purposes of calculating reasonable notice entitlements....

Third, in the decided cases there are two rationales for not counting an interruption between two periods of employment against the employee: first, if the employee was accorded any seniority or other rights upon rehire in recognition of his or her earlier period of employment; and second, whether the employer actively sought to rehire the employee. There is no evidence either way on the first of these factors in the record in this case. However, there is uncontradicted evidence that the defendant did approach the plaintiff to resume her employment in 1977....

Fourth, Ms Cronk had a very good reason for interrupting her career in 1971. She was about to give birth to a second child and wanted to stay home to raise her children. It would be unconscionable, in my view, for the law to protect employees who interrupt their careers with one employer to take a position with another employer only to return later to the first employer (the situation in cases like *Stevens*, *Roscoe* and *Wilson*) and not to afford similar protection to a woman who interrupts her career with one employer to stay home and raise a family.

Fifth, the interruption in Ms Cronk's employment with the defendant was not a complete one. She worked on a part-time basis for the defendant during the 1971–1978 period. Admittedly, she was not a formal part-time employee of the defendant; she worked through the intermediary of a secretarial services company. But that was not Ms Cronk's decision; it resulted from the defendant's policy at the time of not hiring its own part-time employees.

For all of these reasons, I have no hesitation concluding that Ms Cronk is entitled to be compensated for the full period of her employment with the defendant. That period was 29 years, a very very substantial period indeed.

(b) Relationship between type of employment and reasonable notice periods

The defendant's principal argument against a long notice period was the nature of the plaintiff's work which, the plaintiff and defendant agree, was essentially clerical in nature. The defendant argued that senior management or specialized employees with higher educational training should be awarded longer notice periods than non-managerial employees with little or no higher education or specialized training. The reason offered for this distinction is that the higher an employee's rank or the more specialized the position, the smaller are the number of other similar positions available. Unspecialized workers, such as clerical workers, on the other hand, were said to have a larger range of similar jobs available. Therefore, they would need less time to find reasonable equivalent employment. Furthermore, the defendant contends that there is a greater stigma attached to a senior manager being fired than there is with respect to the dismissal of a clerical worker. The greater stigma purportedly makes it more difficult for a senior manager to find equivalent employment.

The stigma component of the defendant's argument can be dealt with quite briefly. I simply do not see how the stigma that a dismissed employee may personally feel, or that may be created in the minds of others, is dependent on the employee's level of employment. A job is a job. It is one of the most important components of the lives of the vast majority of adult Canadians. The loss of a job is almost always a devastating experience, financially and emotionally, for any employee. A secretary or cafeteria worker in a company who is fired will probably feel just as terrible as would the president of the same company if he or she were fired. And if outsiders attach a stigma to dismissal, it results from the fact of dismissal, not the level of the job from which the employee has been dismissed.

I turn then to the defendant's heavy reliance on the managerial/clerical distinction in the wrongful dismissal domain. The defendant contends that the case law supports the proposition that the higher notice periods are reserved for dismissed senior managers and professionals and are not available to a clerical employee like Ms Cronk.

There is some support for this proposition. Ellen Mole has provided a useful summary of the wrongful dismissal decisions throughout Canada in the 1980–1994 period in her book *Wrongful Dismissal Practice Manual* (1984, with regular loose leaf updates to February 1994). Based on her analysis of the cases she has written ...:

> Generally, a senior, high-level or management employee, or one in a highly skilled, technically demanding position, will be entitled to a longer notice period than a junior, semi-skilled or non-managerial employee. This is sometimes expressed by asking whether or not the employee held a key position with the employer.

I have reviewed the Ontario cases collected and summarized in Ms Mole's book. It will be recalled that Ms Cronk is requesting a notice period of 20 months. I have accordingly concentrated on the decided cases in which the Ontario courts have awarded 19-, 20- and 21-month notice periods. I believe that in the 1980–1994 period there were six cases in this category in which all five of the following factors emerge from the judgments: age when fired, position, length of service, length of period of unemployment following dismissal, and judicially determined period of notice....

It is clear that all of these employees held reasonably senior positions. And they all received generous notice periods. The defendant contends that the reason for the 20- and 21-month notice periods—and the factor that separates the six recipients from Ms Cronk—is the greater difficulty these senior, specialized employees will have in securing new employment.

I have great difficulty accepting this argument, for three reasons. First, the defendant has offered no evidence to support its argument....

Second, a close examination of the table above dealing with the six Ontario employees who have been awarded 20- and 21-month notice periods contradicts the defendant's argument at its crucial point. It will be recalled that the defendant asserts that the principal rationale for the long notice periods is the great difficulty these senior employees will have in securing new employment. Yet the average period of post-dismissal unemployment for these six employees was 9 1/3 months. Ms Cronk was unemployed for almost eight months when this motion was heard, and her unemployment [sic] prospects were very bleak indeed. It is difficult to see how her employment prospects are better than the senior managers in the decided cases.

Third, the reality is—as we are all told by our parents at a young age—that education and training are directly related to employment. The senior manager and the professional person are better, not worse, positioned to obtain employment, both initially and later in a post-dismissal context. Higher education and specialized training correlate directly with *increased* access to employment.

This conclusion is supported by many public documents. One example is the recent study published by the Council of Ontario Universities entitled *The Financial Position of Universities in Ontario: 1994*. The study examined many aspects of the relationship between education and employment. One of those aspects was the unemployment rates in Canada from 1977 to 1992. During that period, the unemployment rate for high school graduates ranged from a low of 7.8 per cent to a high of 14.8 per cent. For people with a university degree, the range was 2.4–5.0 per cent—i.e. three times lower.

Not surprisingly, the picture in Ontario is quite similar to the national picture. In another study published by the Council of Ontario Universities, *Facts and Figures: A Compendium of Statistics on Ontario Universities* (1994), the authors review the same education/employment relationship, but this time in an Ontario-specific context and in a slightly different time frame, namely 1984–1993. In that ten-year period the unemployment rate for high school graduates in Ontario ranged from 5.7 to 12.5 per cent. For university graduates, the range was 1.6–5.1 per cent. And in Ontario in 1993—and it was in Ontario in 1993 that Ms Cronk was fired—the unemployment rate for university graduates was 4.2 per cent whereas for high school graduates, like Ms Cronk, it was 12.5 per cent, the highest it had been in the entire decade and almost exactly triple the figure for university graduates....

My conclusion, based on the above data is that it is wrong to contend, as the defendant has, that clerical workers like Ms Cronk or other employees in low level positions should receive a shorter notice period than managers or professionals because the former are likely to obtain new positions more quickly than the latter. Indeed, the data support the opposite conclusion. Statistically speaking, in Ontario in 1993 a fired clerical employee was in a terrible situation with respect to finding employment.

For these three reasons, I do not accept the defendant's argument based on a managerial/clerical distinction. In the six Ontario cases discussed earlier, including the well-known *Stevens* case, the average age of the six dismissed men was 54 years. Edna Cronk was 55 when she was fired. The average length of service of the six men was 22 years. Ms Cronk was employed by the defendant for 29 years. The average post-dismissal period of unemployment of the six men was 9 1/3 months. Ms Cronk had been unemployed for almost eight months when the hearing of this motion took place and her employment prospects continued to be bleak.

The six men all received notice periods, as determined by the Ontario courts, of 20 or 21 months. There is, in my view, no reason for according Ms Cronk a shorter notice period. The reality is that she is older, has worked for her employer longer, and is less likely to find a new job than most of the six men who have received the 20- and 21-month periods. Accordingly, I award her what she has requested, namely damages in lieu of her notice equivalent to 20 months salary less proper credit for amounts previously paid, plus eight percent for vacation pay....

The judgment of Macpherson J was reversed by the Ontario Court of Appeal, in the following judgment.

LACOURCIÈRE J.A.: In my opinion, the learned motions court judge's reasons do not justify departing from the widely accepted principle. He erred in doing so on the basis of his own sociological research without providing counsel an opportunity to challenge or respond to the results of the two studies relied upon....

Before taking new matters into account based on statistics which have not been considered in the judgment under appeal, the adversarial process requires that the court ensure that the parties are given an opportunity to deal with the new information by making further submissions, oral or written, and allowing, if requested, fresh material in response.

The result arrived at has the potential of disrupting the practices of the commercial and industrial world, wherein employers have to predict with reasonable certainty the cost of downsizing or increasing their operations, particularly in difficult economic times. As well, legal practitioners specializing in employment law and the legal profession generally have to give advice to employers and employees in respect of termination of employment with reasonable certainty. Adherence to the doctrine of *stare decisis* plays an important role in that respect....

In my opinion, the character of the employment of the respondent does not entitle her to a lengthy period of notice. As pointed out by Saunders J. in *Bohemier v. Storwal International Inc.,* ...:

> It seems to me that the character of the employment of the plaintiff with Storwal does not entitle him to a lengthy period of notice on the basis of decided cases and the reasons I have stated. If the issue had been addressed at the time he was first employed, it would not have been reasonable for his employer to have agreed to a notice period sufficient to enable him to find work in difficult economic times. In saying this, I hope that it is not thought that I am unsympathetic to the plight of the plaintiff. His claim, however, is based on contract and it is not reasonable to expect that his employer would or could have agreed

to assure that his notice of termination would be sufficient to guarantee that he would obtain alternative employment within the notice period.

In calculating the period of notice for this respondent it is necessary to balance the traditional factors enumerated in *Bardal, supra*, which the motions court judgment appears to have improperly collapsed into the re-employability factor. While the character of the respondent's employment will restrict her to the level of a clerical, non-managerial employee, the respondent's age and lengthy faithful service for the appellant properly qualify her for the maximum notice in her category.

For these reasons, I would vary the judgment of MacPherson J. so that the plaintiff respondent will recover damages based on a salary calculation covering 12 months from September 9, 1993, including vacation pay for the amount accrued at the date of termination plus the statutory entitlement, less appropriate deductions and after allowing credit for amounts previously paid....

[Justice Weiler dissented in part, and would have remitted the case to the lower court for a full inquiry into the empirical validity of the idea that higher status workers face increased difficulties in finding replacement work. She noted that principle that high occupational status automatically attracts a notice premium was "troubling." In her words, "Our notion of justice is bound up with equality."]

* * * * *

The debate over the significance of job status has continued over the years. In 2011, it was again before the Ontario Court of Appeal, when a non-managerial employee of thirty-three years sued for wrongful dismissal in *Di Tomaso v Crown Metal Packaging Canada LP*, 2011 ONCA 469. Justice MacPherson, now sitting on the Court of Appeal, wrote for the court and reiterated that there is no empirical evidence to support a presumption that higher status employees face greater difficulties finding new employment. He stated that the factor of employee status was of "declining significance." This statement has been repeated several times since *Di Tomaso*. While non-managerial status appears to reduce the length of notice with declining frequency, the fact of higher job status is still used to lengthen the notice assessment, as visible in *Love v Acuity Investment Management Inc*, 2011 ONCA 130.

Another issue that has arisen is the extent to which general economic conditions, and the financial health of the employer, ought to factor into the assessment of the length of reasonable notice.

Bartlam v Saskatchewan Crop Insurance Corp (1993), 49 CCEL 141 at 148–51 and 155–58 (Sask QB)

[The plaintiff was a senior manager who supervised 650 employees and was 62 years old. He had eighteen years of service with the employer, but the first nine were part-time and he was appointed to the senior position only two years before his dismissal. The court had to decide whether the reasonable notice period should be based on the parties' factual intentions or on broader public policy grounds.]

KLEBUC J.:

[...]

Theoretical Approach to Assessment

While the principle of reasonable notice is well understood, there is a divergence of opinion as to what theoretical approach or test should be followed in determining a reasonable notice period for a specific employment contract. On the one hand is a series of decisions suggesting that reasonable notice is to be determined by the court as of the date an employment contract was terminated. These decisions do not require the court to consider what the parties would have negotiated at the time they entered into their contract had they directed their minds to such issue or to other matters such as: whether the employee, if he were to leave his or her employment, would be prepared to give the employer the same notice period the court considers reasonable to require the employer to provide the employee. This approach, which for ease of reference I shall refer to as the 'Bardal Approach,' is based on the decision of McRuer C.J.H.C. in *Bardal v. Globe & Mail* ... where ... he stated:

> There could be no catalogue laid down as to what was reasonable notice in particular classes of cases. The reasonableness of the notice must be decided with reference to each particular case, having regard to the character of the employment, the length of service of the servant, the age of the servant and the availability of similar employment, having regard to the experience, training and qualifications of the servant.

On the other hand is a series of decisions suggesting that a period of reasonable notice should be determined as of the time the parties entered into their employment contract with the length of the notice to be implied by the court being the same whether the employer or the employee is terminating the employment contract. These decisions direct the court to look at all relevant factors existing at the time the employment contract was entered into and then imply a notice provision of the kind the parties would have agreed to had they considered the same. This approach, which for ease of reference I shall refer to as the 'Lazarowicz Approach,' is based on the decision of Roach J.A. in *Lazarowicz v. Orenda Engines Ltd.* .... where ... he said:

> Opinions might differ as to what was reasonable, but in reaching an opinion a reasonable test would be to propound the question, namely, if the employer and the employee at the time of the hiring had addressed themselves to the question as to the notice that the employer would give in the event of him terminating the employment, or the notice that the employee would give on quitting, what would their respective answers have been? ...

The Manitoba Court of Appeal in *Yosyk v. Westfair Foods Ltd.* .... approved the approach of Roach J.A. in *Lazarowicz* and refined it. Twaddle J.A. for the court ... noted:

> The relationship between an employer and an employee is contractual. Save to the extent that statute law imposes a minimum standard, the notice required to terminate employment of indefinite duration is that agreed to by the parties. In many cases, the length of notice will be fixed by express agreement, trade custom or a practice established by the employer. In other cases the implied term is that reasonable notice must be given.
>
> The length of notice which is reasonable is not a matter for subjective judgment. It must be determined having regard to the intention of the parties. The test was stated by

> Roach J.A., delivering the judgment of the Court of Appeal of Ontario, in *Lazarowicz v. Orenda Engines Ltd.*. . . .
>
> In my opinion, it is the proper test in all cases, save for one refinement. The relationship between an employer and an employee is not a static one. During it, the contract is often amended by agreement on such fundamental terms as remuneration and the responsibilities of the employee. In a similar manner, the intention of the parties as to the length of notice required to end their relationship may change. The relevant intent is that which the parties had when the conduct was last changed prior to the events leading to its termination. . . .

In my opinion the Bardal Approach and the Lazarowicz Approach are irreconcilable and when applied to the same facts may lead to substantially different conclusions. . . .

What theoretical approach or test should be applied in Saskatchewan? In considering which of the two noted approaches is the more appropriate for Saskatchewan, attention must be given to the complexity and dynamics of Canada's social and economic environment. Failure to do so could lead to circumstances where the principles of law applied are out of step with the community it is intended to serve. In my opinion, consideration must be given to the dramatic changes that have taken place since the late 1950s and early 1960s. Rapid advances in technology, coupled with enormous gains in scientific knowledge, have increased the speed of change, particularly in the area of commerce and trade. Many established ventures have or will shortly become obsolescent. 'Rust Belts' have become commonplace. Many ventures that did not exist 25 years ago have become a driving force in our economy. Of these new economic activities, many will have a short lifespan.

The community at large generally recognizes that the average employee will have to change jobs or employers, or both four to five times during his or her lifetime. No longer is the concept of a 'job for life,' which was predominantly held in the 1950s and 60s, realistic. While there remain many established corporations with enormous pools of capital, a substantial portion of Canada's economy and new employment opportunities are being created by small corporations, sole proprietorships and partnerships who often have very little capital but many employees. The equity owner is usually personally involved in the day-to-day operation of the venture and may earn little more than his or her employees. These and other factors must be considered in the context of expanded world trade which exposes both employers and employees to the benefits and disadvantages of international competition.

Any approach adopted to imply a period of reasonable notice in an employment contract must be able to effectively and equitably address the economic realities of Saskatchewan's diverse social and economic environment. In my opinion, the Bardal Approach, narrowly applied, is incapable of fulfilling such role. It requires the court to imply a reasonable notice period having regard only to limited criteria. Hence, the court's decision will be a subjective one based on what the judge perceives to be reasonable at the time the employment contract was breached. Such decision may be substantially different than what the parties, and the economic community in which they function, consider appropriate having regard to all relevant factors. . . .

In addition to the degree of capitalization and employee-to-earnings ratio, any theoretical approach adopted must be able to take into account other factors, such as whether the activity involved is gradually becoming redundant or of lesser significance but still capable of providing meaningful employment opportunities in the short run. In these circumstances both the employees, particularly those in management positions, and the employer will be aware of the long term prospects of the activity they are involved in and would have agreed to shorter notice periods had their minds been directed to the subject. In my opinion, a court dealing with such circumstances should be able to imply a shorter notice period even though the employee may have been employed by the employer for a period of 26 years.

There is very little evidence confirming that the Bardal Approach is capable of adequately dealing with complex issues that may arise in diverse circumstances. In fact, the Saskatchewan decisions that I reviewed support my conclusion. In these decisions, there is no in depth discussion of the nature of the activity the employer and employee are involved in, no expert evidence led as to what the 'industry' or 'employment activity' in which the employer and employee are involved in considers to be reasonable notice, or what the parties to the employment contract may have contemplated at the time of entering into the employment contract. In these cases, the evidence appears to have been focused almost exclusively on the nature of the employee's duties, the age of the employee and employment opportunities available, all viewed from the employee's perspective. Counsel in these cases cited authorities, sometime in the form of a matrix, setting out only the duties of the employee, the number of years of employment, the age of the employee and the notice period judicially determined.

The case at bar reflects what commonly occurs when the Bardal Approach is exclusively adopted. Bartlam provided evidence as to his age, level of education, years of employment, and the nature of his duties with his employer, but led no evidence regarding: (a) what he believed the notice period was to be at the time he accepted full-time employment with the Corporation or what he thought the notice period was to be when he accepted his last promotion in 1990; (b) the nature of his employer's business; (c) any policy adopted by the Corporation with respect to notice periods; or (d) what notice periods are generally considered to be reasonable in the industry in which he and the Corporation were involved. Given that Bartlam considered himself to be part of senior management and was responsible for 650 people who reported directly or indirectly to him, he surely had some understanding as to what the Corporation and other employees considered to be reasonable notice for employment contracts similar to his.

The Corporation led no evidence regarding its capitalization, employee-to-earnings ratio or other factors such as organizational changes undertaken due to economic and other events affecting it. Further, its counsel did not vigorously cross-examine the employee on any of the aforementioned points. I am not critical of counsel for either party for they both relied on *Bardal* and were induced by it to limit the scope of their evidence. They put forward very basic evidence and then left it to this court to imply a reasonable notice period based on such evidence.

If the Bardal Approach is to be applied in the future, I am of the opinion from a policy point of view it must be amended to take into account additional criteria. The criteria set out in *Bardal* may have been adequate for the 1950s and early 1960s, but such criteria certainly is inadequate today.

In my opinion, the Lazarowicz Approach, particularly as refined in *Yosyk*, is the better approach for Saskatchewan because it is capable of addressing all relevant criteria when a term of reasonable notice is to be implied, including most of the criteria suggested in *Bardal*, but always in the context of what the employer and the employee would have agreed to having regard to the nature of their employment activity and economic and other factors associated therewith. It facilitates the creation of general understandings and customs in specific industries and activities of the kind which will enable employers and employees to function with a degree of certainty as to what their respective rights and obligations are regarding the giving of notice.

[The court held that the plaintiff was entitled to twelve months' notice.]

* * * * *

Other cases have taken a different view of the relevance of the financial situation of the employer, and of the general economic climate.

Anderson v Haakon Industries (Canada) Ltd (1987), 48 DLR (4th) 235, [1987] BCJ No 2721 at para 2ff (CA)

LAMBERT JA: Mr. Anderson in 1973 was Alberta branch manager of an engineering company. He was approached with an offer of employment by Mr. Jim Hole, one of the owners of Lockerbie and Hole Co. Ltd., which was a large mechanical contracting company with its head office and principal operations in Alberta.

After negotiations, Mr. Anderson left his employment with the engineering company in Alberta and became the general manager, in effect, whether or not that was his title, of a new company called Haakon Industries (Canada) Ltd., which had its centre of operations in British Columbia. The operations at Haakon were to consist of subcontracting work on general heating and sheet metal business. It took over a number of unremunerative subcontracts on which Lockerbie and Hole was the main contractor and it started off competing for new work. The number of employees varied from twenty to sixty.

Not surprisingly, having regard to the unremunerative contracts with which Haakon started, it made losses in the first few years of operations. But it was in a close relationship with Lockerbie and Hole and Mr. Anderson's salary was paid by Lockerbie and Hole and it may be that there were other corporate goals of Lockerbie and Hole that were being fulfilled by the existence of Haakon and the way it was carrying on business. The evidence is fragmentary at best about the full business relationship between the parent company, Lockerbie and Hole, and the effective British Columbia subsidiary, Haakon Industries (Canada) Ltd.

Mr. Anderson's employment with Haakon in British Columbia started in 1973. He was told by Mr. Jim Hole that he should carry on in relation to Haakon as if the company was his own.

In 1981 Mr. Robert Hole, a nephew of Mr. Jim Hole, became an employee of Haakon. Mr. Robert Hole bought the beneficial interest in the shares of Haakon in early 1982. The relationship between Mr. Anderson and Mr. Robert Hole seems to have varied a little from a cordial and sensible working relationship to something less satisfactory than that. Eventually, in November, 1983, about ten years after he started working for Haakon, Mr. Anderson's employment terminated.

In the financial period ending at the end of August, 1974, Haakon sustained an actual loss of about $11,000.00. The following year it was $77,000.00. In the year ending February, 1976 it was $4,000.00, and at the end of the year ending February 1977 it was $6,000.00. In the year ending February, 1978, there was a profit of $117,000.00, and that was followed by two years of losses, the loss in each case being less than $100,000.00.

When Mr. Hole joined the company he reconsidered the accounting basis that had been used and he made a significant change. In the year ending February, 1982 there was an actual loss of about $550,000.00. There was a loss in the year ending February, 1983 of about $170,000.00. The two losses taken together produced a deficit at the end of the February 1983 year of about $660,000.00. The following year there was a profit of about $240,000.00 which had the effect of reducing the deficit to about $420,000.00. That was the position at the end of February, 1984. By then Mr. Anderson's termination had occurred three months earlier. . . .

Mr. Anderson brought an action for what is usually called wrongful dismissal. The action came on for trial before Mr. Justice Hinds at the end of 1985. . . .

This appeal is brought by the defendant Haakon. There is only one issue in the appeal. It is put this way in the appellant's factum:

> "The learned trial judge erred in failing to take into account the financial position of Haakon at the time of termination, which financial position Anderson directly contributed to in his position of general manager and running the company as if it were his own."

[T]he appellant's argument was that the economic circumstances in the industry in question, and particularly the economic circumstances of the employer itself, when those economic circumstances are in significant measure under the control of the employee being considered, are a major factor, which should be taken with the other major factors enumerated by Mr. Justice Hinds in this case, in determining the notice period. . . .

Counsel for the appellant also relied on the decision of Mr. Justice Saunders in the Ontario High Court in *Bohemier v. Storwal International Inc.* (1982) 142 D.L.R. (3d) 8, and the decision of the Ontario Court of Appeal, upholding Mr. Justice Saunders' reasons, but varying his decision. In particular, the appellant relied on these two passages from the reasons of Mr. Justice Saunders, at p. 13:

> "What may be a reasonable period to allow a discharged employee to find new employment may be more than an employer should be asked to pay. An employer may dismiss for cause without notice but the economic requirements of the business or even the incompetence or negligence of the employee do not constitute cause. If the period of notice is extended too far, the ability to dismiss an employee for economic or other reasons may be seriously impaired or rendered illusory." . . .

> "In my view there is a need to preserve the ability of the employer to function in an unfavourable economic climate. He must, if he finds it necessary, be able to reduce his work force at a reasonable cost. If he cannot do so, the alternative may be bankruptcy

or receivership. It seems to me that when employment is unavailable due to general economic conditions, there has to be some limit on the period of notice to be given to discharged employees even if they are unable to secure similar employment within the notice period." ...

The economic circumstances must certainly form a part of the background in which the business and employment relationship is assessed, but the appellant's argument goes much farther than that. It is to the effect that the economic circumstances of the company constitute a major factor which must be taken into account in determining the correct notice period and that to fail to do so constitutes an error in law.

In my opinion that argument is not a correct one. In a case based on an allegation of wrongful dismissal, the true analysis is no different from any other case of breach of contract. The breach must be proved, and, once proved, the damages must be assessed on the basis of the determination of the plaintiff's loss. But since proper notice could have been given in such cases, the loss cannot be greater than the length of the proper notice period, and the loss might be less if there was actual mitigation or a contingency of mitigation. In setting the notice period, the courts are using that as an indicator of the loss suffered by the plaintiff in order to assess his damages for the breach of contract which occurred at the time of the wrongful termination. It is very hard to see how the plaintiff's loss is affected by the financial performance of the company. Certainly an assessment of the plaintiff's own contribution, if any, to the financial performance of the company would be likely to run contrary to the decision of this court in *Steinicke v. Manning Press Ltd.*

In this case there is nothing in the evidence to which we have been referred to persuade me that economic circumstances, generally, or the economic performance of this company, or any alleged contribution by Mr. Anderson to the economic performance of this company, are factors which ought to be added to the four major factors considered by Mr. Justice Hinds. I consider that they are not; that the four factors considered by Mr. Justice Hinds were the four proper factors to be considered; and that there is no basis on which this court could find error in Mr. Justice Hinds' decision that the proper notice period was sixteen months.

I would like to say a word about the passage that I have quoted from my own reasons for judgment in *Lesiuk v. British Columbia Forest Products Limited*. The point that was being considered in that case was whether the notice period should be extended because economic circumstances generally had made the employment market such that the plaintiff was unlikely to be able, to obtain employment at all readily. A similar issue was under consideration in the Hunter case. I continue to be of the view that a poor general employment environment may work to extend the period of reasonable notice, because it works to extend or increase the loss actually suffered by an employee from the breach of his employment contract. That was the point that I was addressing when I said the economic circumstances may alter the period of reasonable notice. But, as I have indicated in this judgment, the economic performance of an employer would not serve to reduce the period of reasonable notice unless it were demonstrated that those economic circumstances actually reduced the amount of the loss suffered by the employee for the breach of his contract of employment. For those reasons I would dismiss the appeal.

[Separate and concurring reasons for judgment delivered by Wallace and Locke JJA, dismissing the appeal.]

* * * * *

Despite the debates discussed in the previous cases, the factors from *Bardal* continue to guide the reasonable notice analysis. Two additional factors were added by the Supreme Court in the *Wallace* decision, reproduced below. These are whether the employee was induced to leave secure employment, and whether the employee was given a promise of job security at the time of hire.

As in the common law provinces, Quebec civil law allows either party to terminate an employment contract of indefinite duration without cause by giving notice to the other party. Section 2091 of the Quebec *Civil Code* states that such notice "shall be given in reasonable time, taking into account, in particular, the nature of employment, the special circumstances in which it is carried on and the duration of the period of work." The *Code* also prohibits the employee from waiving the right to be indemnified if insufficient notice of termination is given or if the termination was done in an abusive manner (CCQ s 2092). As in the rest of Canada, there is extensive caselaw on the meaning of reasonable notice. See, particularly, *Quebec (Commission des normes du travail) v Asphalte Desjardins Inc*, [2014] 2 SCR 514. While all common law provinces operate on a reasonable notice model of dismissal, some jurisdiction, such as Quebec, Nova Scotia, and in the federal jurisdiction, have also implemented statutory just cause dismissal protections. See Chapter 13, Section 13:400.

3:522 Mitigation

As outlined in *Ceccol v Ontario Gymnastic Federation* (2001), 55 OR (3d) 614 (CA), and set out in Section 3:311, the general private law obligation to mitigate one's damages applies to the wrongful dismissal claim. A wrongfully dismissed employee is under an obligation to mitigate the financial loss resulting from the dismissal by making reasonable efforts to obtain comparable employment. If the employee fails to meet the duty to mitigate, the damages awarded will be reduced according to their degree of inactivity. In *Red Deer College v Michaels*, [1976] 2 SCR 324, the Court at page 128 explained that:

> The principle of mitigation is a necessary corollary of the basis of damages, namely, that they have arisen in a legal sense from a violation of a right. Underlying this is the assumption that a person must concern himself with his own interest if he would seek from the law the vindication of his civil engagements. In a contract of employment, the remuneration is either for work done or for the commitment to work. Upon a dismissal which is a repudiation of the obligation to accept the one or the other, as the remedy of specific performance is not available, the employee's capacity to work is now released to him to be used as he sees fit. He may decide to waste it or he may demand that the employer make good its full utility. In that event, he must act reasonably in seeking to employ it as he would or might have had the particular engagement not been made. It is the loss of earnings resulting from a denial of a right to use or commit his working capacity profitably that is the substance of his claim, and as he must prove his damages, it must appear that they arose from the breach of contract.

CHAPTER 3: THE CONTRACT OF EMPLOYMENT

Caselaw developed in the late 1980s held that constructively dismissed employees could, in some circumstances, be obliged to accept an offer of re-employment from their dismissing employer in mitigation of their loss (see *Mifsud v MacMillan Bathurst Inc* (1989), 70 OR (2d) 701 (CA)). This approach was not, however, required of wrongfully dismissed employees, until the Supreme Court's ruling in the following decision.

Evans v Teamsters Local Union No 31, [2008] 1 SCR 661, 2008 SCC 20 at para 1ff

Bastarache J. for the majority (Abella J. dissenting)—This appeal concerns an employee's duty to mitigate damages for wrongful dismissal. In particular, the Court is asked to determine whether an employee who has been wrongfully dismissed is required to mitigate damages by returning to work for the same employer who terminated the employment contract.

Facts

The appellant, Donald Evans, was employed for over 23 years as a business agent in the respondent union's Whitehorse office. He was one of two employees in this office; the other was his wife, Ms. Barbara Evans. Mr. Evans was dismissed on January 2, 2003 after the election of a new union executive. During the election campaign, held in December 2002, Mr. Evans supported the incumbent president, who was defeated.

Prior to taking office on January 1, 2003, the incoming president, Mr. Hennessy, asked the union's legal counsel, Mr. McGrady, for an opinion regarding the termination of six employees, including Mr. Evans and three other business agents located in other cities. In a letter dated December 31, 2002, counsel suggested that a court would find that Mr. Evans was an "indefinite term employee" and that the union's severance pay plan was "not a substitute for the Local's obligation to provide working notice or pay in lieu of notice". He also suggested the wording of a letter to be sent to the four business agents.

On January 2, 2003, Mr. Hennessy faxed a letter to Mr. Evans. This letter was almost entirely in the form suggested by counsel, but did not include the clause regarding working notice. The letter could not have come as a surprise to Mr. Evans because earlier that day he had received a copy of Mr. McGrady's opinion letter, "leaked" by somebody at the union's main office in Delta. As promised in his letter, Mr. Hennessy telephoned Mr. Evans later that same day to "commence ... discussions". This conversation was surreptitiously tape recorded by Mr. Evans.

Mr. Evans' legal counsel, Mr. Macdonald, wrote a letter to Mr. Hennessy on January 3, 2003. He submitted that Mr. Evans was entitled to reasonable notice of the termination of his employment. He said that Mr. Evans was prepared to accept 24 months' notice of termination and suggested that this could be granted through 12 months of continued employment followed by a payment of 12 months of salary in lieu of notice.

Subsequent to this proposal there was a continuing exchange of correspondence between the lawyers, but no resolution was reached. Mr. McGrady insisted that the original letter of January 2, 2003 "was not intended as a termination without notice", while Mr. Macdonald questioned that position, but pushed for negotiations. In the meantime, the union continued to pay Mr. Evans his salary and benefits, a fact which added a wrinkle to the ongoing discussions. Further, Mr. Evans stated during this period that he wanted a settlement which would see him retire and his wife replace him as the union's business agent.

Mr. McGrady stated the following in a letter dated May 23, 2003:

> I am replying to your letter of May 12, 2003. My client is unable to agree to Ms. Evans' demands, for reasons that are too extensive to enumerate. There appears to be no basis for further negotiations.
>
> On behalf of the Local, we request that Mr. Evans return to his employment no later than June 1, 2003, to serve out the balance of his notice period of 24 months. To be clear, the total notice period is the 24 months from January 1, 2003 until and including December 31, 2004.
>
> If Mr. Evans refuses to return no later than June 1, 2003, my client will treat that refusal as just cause, and formally terminate him without notice.
>
> We will also amend the Statement of [Defence] adding a claim, amongst others, that he has failed to mitigate his loss by rejecting this return to work.

Mr. Macdonald, in a letter also dated May 23, 2003, asked to be provided with documentation "evidencing that Mr. Evans was ever given 24 months notice of termination of his employment"....

Mr. McGrady replied on May 27, 2003 that the union had "no plans to suspend, discipline or lay off Ms. Evans", but that it was not prepared to negotiate any special arrangements with her.... In a second letter of the same date, Mr. McGrady informed Mr. Macdonald that the union was requesting that Mr. Evans return to work on June 1, 2003 and that in doing so he would "be working through the 24-month notice period from January 1, 2003 through to December 31, 2004".

Mr. Macdonald responded on May 30, 2003, stating that Mr. Evans would return to work provided the union "immediately rescinds and withdraws" its termination letter of January 2, 2003. Mr. McGrady replied that the union was not prepared to withdraw its notice of termination. Mr. Macdonald then declared that Mr. Evans had never "received 24 months notice of the termination of his employment", and therefore "he cannot rationally be expected to respond positively to your client's directive to return to work".

The exchange of correspondence ended with a letter from Mr. McGrady to Mr. Macdonald dated June 2, 2003 in which he stated that the union would be pleading that Mr. Evans had failed to mitigate his loss by declining to return to work....

Analysis

On appeal to this Court, the appellant argues that cases requiring that an employee mitigate damages by returning to the same employer deal primarily with individuals who have been constructively dismissed. He says that the trial judge was correct in finding that those cases must be distinguished from others in which the employee has been wrongfully dismissed. In support of this position, the appellant cites a judgment by the Alberta Court of Appeal in which it was held that in wrongful dismissal cases "the plaintiff need not mitigate damages by ... going back to the employer who fired him or her" (*Christianson v. North Hill News Inc.* (1993), 106 D.L.R. (4th) 747, at p. 750). The British Columbia Court of Appeal appeared to make a similar finding in *Farquhar v.*

Butler Brothers Supplies Ltd. (1988), 23 B.C.L.R. (2d) 89, at p. 93, stating that although a constructively dismissed employee may at times be required to mitigate by returning to the same employer, there is "normally no question" that an employee will be required to do so where there has been a wrongful dismissal.

Ten years after *Farquhar*, however, the British Columbia Court of Appeal accepted that even a wrongfully dismissed employee could be required to mitigate by accepting re-employment with his or her former employer on a temporary basis. While the court in *Cox* held that on the facts before it a dismissed dental assistant did not need to return to work for the same dentist, its decision clearly contemplated that such mitigation may in some circumstances be required of wrongfully dismissed employees. In that case, the court applied the same principles it articulated in *Farquhar*, notwithstanding the fact that the earlier case dealt with a constructive dismissal while the facts before it concerned a wrongful dismissal.

In my view, the British Columbia Court of Appeal was correct to apply the same principles to both constructively dismissed and wrongfully dismissed employees. The key element is that in both situations the employer has ended the employment contract without notice. Indeed the very purpose behind recognizing constructive dismissal is to acknowledge that where an employer unilaterally imposes substantive changes to an employment contract, the employee has the right to treat the imposition of those changes as termination. This termination is every bit as "real" as if the employee were actually told of the dismissal and is, accordingly, accompanied by the same right to claim for damages in lieu of notice....

Given that both wrongful dismissal and constructive dismissal are characterized by employer-imposed termination of the employment contract (without cause), there is no principled reason to distinguish between them when evaluating the need to mitigate. Although it may be true that in some instances the relationship between the employee and the employer will be less damaged where constructive rather than wrongful dismissal has occurred, it is impossible to say with certainty that this will always be the case. Accordingly, this relationship is best considered on a case-by-case basis when the reasonableness of the employee's mitigation efforts is being evaluated, and not as a basis for creating a different approach for each type of dismissal.

In my view, the courts have correctly determined that in some circumstances it will be necessary for a dismissed employee to mitigate his or her damages by returning to work for the same employer. Assuming there are no barriers to re-employment (potential barriers to be discussed below), requiring an employee to mitigate by taking temporary work with the dismissing employer is consistent with the notion that damages are meant to compensate for lack of notice, and *not* to penalize the employer for the dismissal itself. The notice period is meant to provide employees with sufficient opportunity to seek new employment and arrange their personal affairs, and employers who provide sufficient working notice are not required to pay an employee just because they have chosen to terminate the contract. Where notice is not given, the employer is required to pay damages in lieu of notice, but that requirement is subject to the employee making a reasonable effort to mitigate the damages by seeking an alternate source of income.

There appears to be very little practical difference between informing an employee that his or her contract will be terminated in 12 months' time (i.e. giving 12 months of working notice) and terminating the contract immediately but offering the employee a new employment opportunity for a period of up to 12 months. In both situations, it is expected that the employee will be aware that the employment relationship is finite, and that he or she will be seeking alternate work during the 12-month period. It can also be expected that in both situations the employee will find that continuing to work may be difficult. Nonetheless, it is an accepted principle of employment law that employers are entitled (indeed encouraged) to give employees working notice and that, absent bad faith or other extenuating circumstances, they are not required to financially compensate an employee simply because they have terminated the employment contract. It is likewise appropriate to assume that in the absence of conditions rendering the return to work unreasonable, on an objective basis, an employee can be expected to mitigate damages by returning to work for the dismissing employer. Finding otherwise would create an artificial distinction between an employer who terminates and offers re-employment and one who gives notice of termination and offers working notice. In either case, the employee has an opportunity to continue working for the employer while he or she arranges other employment, and I believe it nonsensical to say that when this ongoing relationship is termed "working notice" it is acceptable but when it is termed "mitigation" it is not.

I do not mean to suggest with the above analysis that an employee should always be required to return to work for the dismissing employer and my qualification that this should only occur where there are no barriers to re-employment is significant. This Court has held that the employer bears the onus of demonstrating both that an employee has failed to make reasonable efforts to find work and that work could have been found (*Red Deer College v. Michaels*, [1976] 2 S.C.R. 324). Where the employer offers the employee a chance to mitigate damages by returning to work for him or her, the central issue is whether a reasonable person would accept such an opportunity. In 1989, the Ontario Court of Appeal held that a reasonable person should be expected to do so "[w]here the salary offered is the same, where the working conditions are not substantially different or the work demeaning, and where the personal relationships involved are not acrimonious" (*Mifsud v. MacMillan Bathurst Inc.* (1989), 70 O.R. (2d) 701, at p. 710). In *Cox*, the British Columbia Court of Appeal held that other relevant factors include the history and nature of the employment, whether or not the employee has commenced litigation, and whether the offer of re-employment was made while the employee was still working for the employer or only after he or she had already left (paras. 12–18). In my view, the foregoing elements all underline the importance of a multi-factored and contextual analysis. The critical element is that an employee "not [be] obliged to mitigate by working in an atmosphere of hostility, embarrassment or humiliation" (*Farquhar*, at p. 94), and it is that factor which must be at the forefront of the inquiry into what is reasonable. Thus, although an objective standard must be used to evaluate whether a reasonable person in the employee's position would have accepted the employer's offer (*Reibl v. Hughes*, [1980] 2 S.C.R. 880), it is extremely important that the non-tangible elements of the situation—including work atmosphere, stigma and loss of dignity, as well as nature and conditions of employment, the tangible elements—be included in the evaluation.

I note that the nature of this inquiry increases the likelihood that individuals who are dismissed as a result of a change to their position (motivated, for example, by legitimate business needs rather than by concerns about performance) will be required to mitigate by returning to the same employer more often than those employees who are terminated for some other reason. This is not, however, because these individuals have been constructively dismissed rather than wrongfully dismissed, but rather because the circumstances surrounding the termination of their contract may be far less personal than when dismissal relates more directly to the individuals themselves. This point is illustrated by *Michaud* in which a bank executive was constructively dismissed as a result of an organizational restructuring. The evidence showed that the bank offered the employee another executive position and was anxious to have him continue working for them. Importantly, there was no evidence that the relationship between the employee and the bank was acrimonious or that he would suffer any humiliation or loss of dignity by returning to work while he looked for new employment. As a result, mitigation was required. . . .

In sum, I believe that although both constructively dismissed and wrongfully dismissed employees may be required to mitigate their damages by returning to work for the dismissing employer, they are only required to do so where the conditions discussed in para. 30 above are met and the factors mentioned in *Cox* are considered. This kind of mitigation requires "a situation of mutual understanding and respect, and a situation where neither the employer nor the employee is likely to put the other's interests in jeopardy" (*Farquhar*, at p. 95). Further, the reasonableness of an employee's decision not to mitigate will be assessed on an objective standard. . . .

Accepting that it is for the union to prove that Mr. Evans has failed in his duty to mitigate his damages (*Red Deer College*, at p. 332), it is instructive, I believe, to consider the reasons the appellant says the prospect of returning to work for the union made him apprehensive. He mentions in his factum:

(a) he was terminated without cause;
(b) the termination was planned and deliberate;
(c) he was "treated like a dog" in the telephone conversation of January 2;
(d) no mention was made of working notice or payment in lieu of notice in the telephone conversation with Mr. Hennessy;
(e) an audit of the Whitehorse office was commissioned in March 2003 under the guise of assessing property management issues;
(f) he was being treated differently than other business agents who were terminated on the same day;
(g) he had lost the respect of employers as the termination by the union was well known in Whitehorse;
(h) he felt ostracized because he had supported the outgoing president.

And later adds the fact of pending litigation and apprehended difficulty in working with the new executive.

The first two of these reasons are, in my view, entirely irrelevant. The trial judge concluded that there was no bad faith in the termination, and that finding is not under appeal—the issue is solely that of mitigation. In evaluating the mitigation requirement, the trial judge had to consider the other reasons listed above by taking into account all of the evidence and the entire context in which the termination occurred. It is therefore important to note that the written notice of termination was followed immediately by a telephone call whose object was to engage Mr. Evans in negotiations about a possible rehiring.

The trial judge did not find that there was any acrimony between Mr. Hennessy and Mr. Evans, or, for that matter, between Mr. Evans and anyone else at the union. On the contrary, he said there was no bad faith on the part of the union in the negotiations. The evidence was that the tone of the conversation of January 2, 2003 was respectful and friendly (A.R., at p. 401). There is certainly no support for the allegation that Mr. Evans was "treated like a dog". This claim had to be addressed on an objective basis....

Other evidence of the work situation also had to be considered — Mr. Evans affirmed in his examination for discovery of June 2, 2005, for example, that his work environment had not changed in May of 2003 (R.R., at p. 103). This is relevant to the reasonableness of his feelings of ostracization and claims that he would find it difficult to work with the new executive. It appears that the feelings of ostracization related more to the fact that Mr. Evans had spoken to other dismissed employees who felt ostracized than to his own experiences with the union.... The trial judge apparently ignored the fact that there seemed to be no difficulty in the relationship of other dismissed employees with the new union executive, such as Mr. Owens, Mr. Ellis, Mr. Kelava and Mr. Cooper (R.R., at pp. 41–43, 80–81, 83–85, 95 and 98).

Mr. Evans' belief that he would no longer have the respect of employers and would be unable to perform effectively as a business agent in Whitehorse would also seem to be an entirely subjective concern since there is no evidence in the record to demonstrate that there was a reasonable basis for this belief. Furthermore, Mr. Evans operated in a highly independent way and offered to go back to work without mentioning this difficulty, under conditions he had set himself.

With regard to the fact that Mr. Evans had started legal proceedings, I would note that this course of action can have an effect on the relationship between the parties and that this should be taken into account in each case, but that starting an action does not by itself relieve the employee from the duty to mitigate his or her damages. Again, I reiterate that it is the entirety of the situation that must be evaluated in every case (see *Cox*, at paras. 13–18).

I recognize that it is not for the Court of Appeal to substitute its opinion for that of the trial judge on findings of fact. In this case, however, the Court of Appeal found that the trial judge applied a purely subjective test (at paras. 47, 54–55) and that he failed to consider relevant evidence (at para. 56), both of which are errors of law. I agree with those conclusions....

I agree with the Court of Appeal that on an objective test, a reasonable person would have viewed the union's May 23, 2003 letter as a *bona fide* employment opportunity. Although the request to return to work should have been drafted differently, Mr. Evans clearly understood that this was a unique position and that he had no work alternative if he were to remain in Whitehorse. The request fulfilled the 24 months' notice that Mr. Evans had offered on January 3, 2003. He had been paid full salary and benefits for 5 months and the duration of his employment with the union would be for an additional 19 months. The trial judge had found that during the January 2, 2003 telephone conversation, Mr. Hennessy was attempting to negotiate an alternative to the immediate cessation of employment. The union had then and there demonstrated that it wanted Mr. Evans to continue his work with the organization....

In my view, this evidence makes it clear that the relationship between Mr. Evans and the union was not seriously damaged and, given that the terms of employment were the same, it was not objectively unreasonable for him to return to work to mitigate his damages.

For the above reasons, I would dismiss the appeal with costs.

* * * * *

3:530 Other Damages

As discussed, reasonable notice is the primary measure of damages for wrongful dismissal. Since the 1980s, however, there has been ongoing debate as to whether any other type of loss is compensable in the employment context, and whether any other types of damages are available.

Since the 1980s, the Canadian common law courts have consistently relied on the seminal English case of *Addis v Gramophone Co Ltd*, [1909] AC 488 (HL) to hold that because an employment contract may always be terminated with the provision of reasonable notice, no damages lie for the fact of dismissal alone, nor for the loss of reputation that dismissal may entail. Where there have been recent developments, however, is in regard to damages for mental distress and punitive damages for losses arising from the manner of dismissal. For analysis of the significance of the *Wallace* decision, see Judy Fudge, "The Limits of Good Faith in the Contract of Employment: From *Addis* to *Vorvis* to *Wallace* and Back Again?" (2007) 32 *Queen's Law Journal* 529.

Wallace v United Grain Growers Ltd, [1997] 3 SCR 701 at para 2ff

IACOBUCCI J (LAMER CJC, SOPINKA, GONTHIER, CORY, and MAJOR JJ concurring): —

1. FACTS

In 1972, Public Press, a wholly owned subsidiary of the respondent, United Grain Growers Ltd. ("UGG"), decided to update its operations and seek a larger volume of commercial printing work. Don Logan was the marketing manager of the company's publishing and printing divisions at that time. For Logan, the key to achieving this increase in volume was to hire someone with an existing record of sales on a specialized piece of equipment known as a "Web" press.

In April 1972, the appellant, Jack Wallace, met Logan to discuss the possibility of employment. Wallace had the type of experience that Logan sought, having worked approximately 25 years for a competitor that used the "Web" press. Wallace had become concerned over the unfair manner in which he and others were being treated by their employer. However, he expressed some reservation about jeopardizing his secure position at the company. Wallace explained to Logan that as he was 45 years of age, if he were to leave his current employer he would require a guarantee of job security. He also sought several assurances from Logan regarding fair treatment and remuneration. He received such assurances and was told by Logan that if he performed as expected, he could continue to work for Public Press until retirement.

Wallace commenced employment with Public Press in June of 1972. He enjoyed great success at the company and was the top salesperson for each of the years he spent in its employ.

On August 22, 1986, Wallace was summarily discharged by Public Press' sales manager Leonard Domerecki. Domerecki offered no explanation for his actions. In the days before the dismissal both Domerecki and UGG's general manager had complimented Wallace on his work.

By letter of August 29, 1986, Domerecki advised Wallace that the main reason for his termination was his inability to perform his duties satisfactorily. Wallace's statement of claim alleging wrongful dismissal was issued on October 23, 1986. In its statement of defence, the respondent alleged that Wallace had been dismissed for cause. This allegation was maintained for over two years and was only withdrawn when the trial commenced on December 12, 1988.

At the time of his dismissal Wallace was almost 59 years old. He had been employed by Public Press for 14 years. The termination of his employment and the allegations of cause created emotional difficulties for Wallace and he was forced to seek psychiatric help. His attempts to find similar employment were largely unsuccessful.

On September 26, 1985, Wallace made a voluntary assignment into personal bankruptcy. When he commenced his action against the respondent, Wallace remained an undischarged bankrupt. After Wallace had completed his case at trial, UGG moved to amend its statement of defence to assert that as an undischarged bankrupt, Wallace lacked the capacity to commence or continue the proceedings. UGG requested that Wallace's claim for damages for failure to provide reasonable notice of termination be struck out.

The trial judge granted leave to amend the statement of defence and then struck out Wallace's claim for damages for breach of contract. He held that the action in that regard was a nullity from the outset. Wallace's attempt to appeal that ruling was stayed by the Manitoba Court of Appeal pending completion of the trial. The trial resumed and subject to the outcome of the appeal on the bankruptcy issue, Wallace was awarded damages for wrongful dismissal based on a 24-month notice period and aggravated damages.

The Manitoba Court of Appeal reversed the findings of the trial judge with respect to the appellant's capacity to maintain an action for breach of contract. It also allowed the respondent's cross-appeal, substituting a judgment in favour of the appellant based on a 15-month reasonable notice period, and overturned the award of aggravated damages....

[The parts of the judgment dealing with the bankruptcy issue have been omitted.]

The appeal raises five issues:

a. Was there a fixed-term contract?
b. Did the Court of Appeal err in overturning the trial judge's award for aggravated damages resulting from mental distress?
c. Can the appellant sue in either contract or tort for 'bad faith discharge'?
d. Is the appellant entitled to punitive damages?

e. Did the Court of Appeal err in reducing the appellant's reasonable notice damages from 24 to 15 months?

[...]

B. Fixed-Term Contract

The appellant submitted that the courts below erred in rejecting his claim that he had a fixed-term contract for employment until retirement. The learned trial judge exhaustively reviewed all of the circumstances surrounding Wallace's hiring and concluded that there was insufficient evidence to support this claim. The Court of Appeal accepted the facts as they were found by the trial judge and agreed with his conclusion. In light of these concurrent findings of fact, I see no palpable error or other reason to interfere with the conclusion of the courts below.

C. Damages for Mental Distress

Relying upon the principles enunciated in [*Vorvis v. Insurance Corporation of British Columbia*], ... the Court of Appeal held that any award of damages beyond compensation for breach of contract for failure to give reasonable notice of termination 'must be founded on a separately actionable course of conduct.' Although there has been criticism of *Vorvis*, ... this is an accurate statement of the law. The Court of Appeal also noted that this requirement necessarily negates the trial judge's reliance on concepts of foreseeability and matters in the contemplation of the parties. An employment contract is not one in which peace of mind is the very matter contracted for ... and so, absent an independently actionable wrong, the foreseeability of mental distress or the fact that the parties contemplated its occurrence is of no consequence, subject to what I say on employer conduct below.

The Court of Appeal concluded that there was insufficient evidence to support a finding that the actions of UGG constituted a separate actionable wrong either in tort or in contract. I agree with these findings and see no reason to disturb them. I note, however, that in circumstances where the manner of dismissal has caused mental distress but falls short of an independent actionable wrong, the employee is not without recourse. Rather, the trial judge has discretion in these circumstances to extend the period of reasonable notice to which an employee is entitled. Thus, although recovery for mental distress might not be available under a separate head of damages, the possibility of recovery still remains. I will be returning to this point in my discussion of reasonable notice below.

D. Bad Faith Discharge

The appellant urged this Court to find that he could sue UGG either in contract or in tort for 'bad faith discharge.' With respect to the action in contract, he submitted that the Court should imply into the employment contract a term that the employee would not be fired except for cause or legitimate business reasons. I cannot accede to this submission. The law has long recognized the mutual right of both employers and employees to terminate an employment contract at any time provided there are no express provisions to the contrary. In *Farber v. Royal Trust Co.*.... Gonthier J., speaking for the Court, summarized the general contractual principles applicable to contracts of employment as follows ...:

> In the context of an indeterminate employment contract, one party can resiliate the contract unilaterally. The resiliation is considered a dismissal if it originates with the employer and a resignation if it originates with the employee. If an employer dismisses an employee without cause, the employer must give the employee reasonable notice that the contract is about to be terminated or compensation in lieu thereof.

A requirement of 'good faith' reasons for dismissal would, in effect, contravene these principles and deprive employers of the ability to determine the composition of their workforce. In the context of the accepted theories on the employment relationship, such a law would, in my opinion, be overly intrusive and inconsistent with established principles of employment law, and more appropriately, should be left to legislative enactment rather than judicial pronouncement.

I must also reject the appellant's claim that he can sue in tort for breach of a good faith and fair dealing obligation with regard to dismissals. The Court of Appeal noted the absence of persuasive authority on this point and concluded that such a tort has not yet been recognized by Canadian courts. I agree with these findings. To create such a tort in this case would therefore constitute a radical shift in the law, again a step better left to be taken by the legislatures.

For these reasons I conclude that the appellant is unable to sue in either tort or contract for 'bad faith discharge.' However, I will be returning to the subject of good faith and fair dealing in my discussion of reasonable notice below.

E. Punitive Damages

Punitive damages are an exception to the general rule that damages are meant to compensate the plaintiff. The purpose of such an award is the punishment of the defendant ... The appellant argued that the trial judge and the Court of Appeal erred in refusing to award punitive damages. I do not agree. Relying on *Vorvis*, ... Lockwood J. found that UGG did not engage in sufficiently 'harsh, vindictive, reprehensible and malicious' conduct to merit condemnation by such an award. He also noted the absence of an actionable wrong. The Court of Appeal concurred. Again, there is no reason to interfere with these findings. Consequently, I agree with the courts below that there is no foundation for an award of punitive damages.

F. Reasonable Notice

The Court of Appeal upheld the trial judge's findings of fact and agreed that in the circumstances of this case damages for failure to give notice ought to be at the high end of the scale. However, the court found the trial judge's award of 24 months' salary in lieu of notice to be excessive and reflective of an element of aggravated damages having crept into his determination. It overturned his award and substituted the equivalent of 15 months' salary. For the reasons which follow, I would restore the trial judge's award of damages in the amount of 24 months' salary in lieu of notice.

In determining what constitutes reasonable notice of termination, the courts have generally applied the principles articulated by McRuer C.J.H.C. in *Bardal v. Globe & Mail Ltd.* ... :

> There can be no catalogue laid down as to what is reasonable notice in particular classes of cases. The reasonableness of the notice must be decided with reference to each particular case, having regard to the character of the employment, the length of service of the servant, the age of the servant and the availability of similar employment, having regard to the experience, training and qualifications of the servant.

[...]

Applying these factors in the instant case, I concur with the trial judge's finding that in light of the appellant's advanced age, his 14-year tenure as the company's top salesman and his limited prospects for re-employment, a lengthy period of notice is warranted. I note, however, that *Bardal, supra*, does not state, nor has it been interpreted to imply, that the factors it enumerated were exhaustive. ... Canadian courts have added several additional factors to the *Bardal* list. The application of these factors to the assessment of a dismissed employee's notice period will depend upon the particular circumstances of the case.

One such factor that has often been considered is whether the dismissed employee had been induced to leave previous secure employment.... According to one authority, many courts have sought to compensate the reliance and expectation interests of terminated employees by increasing the period of reasonable notice where the employer has induced the employee to 'quit a secure, well-paying job ... on the strength of promises of career advancement and greater responsibility, security and compensation with the new organization' ...

In my opinion, such inducements are properly included among the considerations which tend to lengthen the amount of notice required. I concur with the comments of Christie *et al., supra*, and recognize that there is a need to safeguard the employee's reliance and expectation interests in inducement situations. I note, however, that not all inducements will carry equal weight when determining the appropriate period of notice. The significance of the inducement in question will vary with the circumstances of the particular case and its effect, if any, on the notice period is a matter best left to the discretion of the trial judge.

In the instant case, the trial judge found that UGG went to great lengths to relieve Wallace's fears about jeopardizing his existing secure employment and to entice him into joining their company....

In addition to the promise that he could continue to work for the company until retirement, UGG also offered several assurances with respect to fair treatment.... Although the trial judge did not make specific reference to the inducement factor in his analysis of reasonable notice, I believe that, in the circumstances of this case, these inducements, in particular the guarantee of job security, are factors which support his decision to award damages at the high end of the scale.

The appellant urged this Court to recognize the ability of a dismissed employee to sue in contract or alternatively in tort for 'bad faith discharge.' Although I have rejected both as avenues for recovery, by no means do I condone the behaviour of employers who subject employees to callous and insensitive treatment in their dismissal, showing no regard for their welfare. Rather, I believe that such bad faith conduct in the manner of dismissal is another factor that is properly compensated for by an addition to the notice period.

In *Lojstrup v. British Columbia Buildings Corp.* . . . the British Columbia Court of Appeal found that *Addis v. Gramophone Co.* . . . *Ansari v. British Columbia Hydro and Power Authority* . . . and *Wadden v. Guaranty Trust Co. of Canada* . . . preclude extending the notice period to account for manner of dismissal. Generally speaking, these cases have found that claims relating to the manner in which the discharge took place are not properly considered in an action for damages for breach of contract. Rather, it is said, damages are limited to injuries that flow from the breach itself, which in the employment context is the failure to give reasonable notice. The manner of dismissal was found not to affect these damages.

Although these decisions are grounded in general principles of contract law, I believe, with respect, that they have all failed to take into account the unique characteristics of the particular type of contract with which they were concerned, namely, a contract of employment. Similarly, there was not an appropriate recognition of the special relationship which these contracts govern. In my view, both are relevant considerations.

The contract of employment has many characteristics that set it apart from the ordinary commercial contract. Some of the views on this subject that have already been approved of in previous decisions of this Court (see e.g. *Machtinger, supra*) bear repeating. As K. Swinton noted in 'Contract Law and the Employment Relationship: The Proper Forum for Reform' in B.J. Reiter and J. Swan, eds., *Studies in Contract Law* . . . :

> the terms of the employment contract rarely result from an exercise of free bargaining power in the way that the paradigm commercial exchange between two traders does. Individual employees on the whole lack both the bargaining power and the information necessary to achieve more favourable contract provisions than those offered by the employer, particularly with regard to tenure.

This power imbalance is not limited to the employment contract itself. Rather, it informs virtually all facets of the employment relationship. In *Slaight Communications Inc. v. Davidson* . . . Dickson C.J., writing for the majority of the Court, had occasion to comment on the nature of this relationship. . . . [H]e quoted with approval from P. Davies and M. Freedland, Kahn-Freund's *Labour and the Law* . . . :

> [T]he relation between an employer and an isolated employee or worker is typically a relation between a bearer of power and one who is not a bearer of power. In its inception it is an act of submission, in its operation it is a condition of subordination. . . .

The vulnerability of employees is underscored by the level of importance which our society attaches to employment. . . .

[F]or most people, work is one of the defining features of their lives. Accordingly, any change in a person's employment status is bound to have far-reaching repercussions. In 'Aggravated Damages and the Employment Contract,' . . . Schai noted . . . that, '[w]hen this change is involuntary, the extent of our "personal dislocation" is even greater.'

The point at which the employment relationship ruptures is the time when the employee is most vulnerable and hence, most in need of protection. In recognition of this need, the law ought to encourage conduct that minimizes the damage and dislocation (both economic and personal) that result from dismissal. In *Machtinger* [*v. HOJ Industries Ltd.*], ... it was noted that the manner in which employment can be terminated is equally important to an individual's identity as the work itself (at p. 1002). By way of expanding upon this statement, I note that the loss of one's job is always a traumatic event. However, when termination is accompanied by acts of bad faith in the manner of discharge, the results can be especially devastating. In my opinion, to ensure that employees receive adequate protection, employers ought to be held to an obligation of good faith and fair dealing in the manner of dismissal, the breach of which will be compensated for by adding to the length of the notice period....

The obligation of good faith and fair dealing is incapable of precise definition. However, at a minimum, I believe that in the course of dismissal employers ought to be candid, reasonable, honest and forthright with their employees and should refrain from engaging in conduct that is unfair or is in bad faith by being, for example, untruthful, misleading or unduly insensitive. In order to illustrate possible breaches of this obligation, I refer now to some examples of the conduct over which the courts expressed their disapproval in the cases cited above.

In [*Trask v. Terra Nova Motors Ltd.*] ... an employer maintained a wrongful accusation of involvement in a theft and communicated this accusation to other potential employers of the dismissed employee. *Jivrag* [*v. City of Calgary*] ... involved similar unfounded accusations of theft combined with a refusal to provide a letter of reference after the termination. In *Dunning* [*v. Royal Bank*], ... bad faith conduct was clearly present. Although the plaintiff's position had been eliminated, he was told by several senior executives that another position would probably be found for him and that the new assignment would necessitate a transfer. However, at the same time that the plaintiff was being reassured about his future, a senior representative of the company was contemplating his termination. When a position could not be found, the decision was made to terminate the plaintiff. This decision was not communicated to the plaintiff for over a month despite the fact that his employers knew he was in the process of selling his home in anticipation of the transfer. News of his termination was communicated to the plaintiff abruptly following the sale of his home.

In *Corbin* [*v. Standard Life Assurance Co.*], ... the New Brunswick Court of Appeal expressed its displeasure over the conduct of an employer who made the decision to fire the employee when he was on disability leave, suffering from a major depression. The employee advised the manager as to when he would be returning to duty and informed him that he was taking a two-week vacation. He was fired immediately upon his return to work. The facts in *MacDonald* [*v. Royal Canadian Legion*] ... are also illustrative of bad faith conduct. In that case, the defendant employer closed its bar for three months and laid off the plaintiff bartender. While the bar was closed, the executive committee was replaced and the new officers decided to implement a different salary structure for bartenders when the bar reopened. The employer advertised for a bartender at a rate of almost half of the plaintiff's hourly rate. The plaintiff was unaware of any change in his status, and it was only when he saw the advertisement in the newspaper that he learned that he had been dismissed and was not to be offered reinstatement.

These examples by no means exhaust the list of possible types of bad faith or unfair dealing in the manner of dismissal. However, all are indicative of the type of conduct that ought to merit compensation by way of an addition to the notice period. I note that, depending upon the circumstances of the individual case, not all acts of bad faith or unfair dealing will be equally injurious and thus, the amount by which the notice period is extended will vary. Furthermore, I do not intend to advocate anything akin to an automatic claim for damages under this heading in every case of dismissal. In each case, the trial judge must examine the nature of the bad faith conduct and its impact in the circumstances.

The Court of Appeal in the instant case recognized the relevance of manner of dismissal in the determination of the appropriate period of reasonable notice. However, ... the court found that this factor could only be considered 'where it impacts on the future employment prospects of the dismissed employee' (p. 180). With respect, I believe that this is an overly restrictive view. In my opinion, the law must recognize a more expansive list of injuries which may flow from unfair treatment or bad faith in the manner of dismissal.

It has long been accepted that a dismissed employee is not entitled to compensation for injuries flowing from the fact of the dismissal itself.... Thus, although the loss of a job is very often the cause of injured feelings and emotional upset, the law does not recognize these as compensable losses. However, where an employee can establish that an employer engaged in bad faith conduct or unfair dealing in the course of dismissal, injuries such as humiliation, embarrassment and damage to one's sense of self-worth and self-esteem might all be worthy of compensation depending upon the circumstances of the case. In these situations, compensation does not flow from the fact of dismissal itself, but rather from the manner in which the dismissal was effected by the employer.

Often the intangible injuries caused by bad faith conduct or unfair dealing on dismissal will lead to difficulties in finding alternative employment, a tangible loss which the Court of Appeal rightly recognized as warranting an addition to the notice period. It is likely that the more unfair or in bad faith the manner of dismissal is the more this will have an effect on the ability of the dismissed employee to find new employment. However, in my view the intangible injuries are sufficient to merit compensation in and of themselves. I recognize that bad faith conduct which affects employment prospects may be worthy of considerably more compensation than that which does not, but in both cases damage has resulted that should be compensable....

I note that there may be those who would say that this approach imposes an onerous obligation on employers. I would respond simply by saying that I fail to see how it can be onerous to treat people fairly, reasonably, and decently at a time of trauma and despair. In my view, the reasonable person would expect such treatment. So should the law.

In the case before this Court, the trial judge documented several examples of bad faith conduct on the part of UGG. He noted the abrupt manner in which Wallace was dismissed despite having received compliments on his work from his superiors only days before. He found that UGG made a conscious decision to 'play hardball' with Wallace and maintained unfounded allegations of cause until the day the trial began. Further, as a result of UGG's persistence in maintaining these allegations, '[w]ord got around, and it was rumoured in the trade that he had been involved in some wrongdoing' (p. 173). Finally, he found that the dismissal and subsequent events were largely responsible for causing Wallace's depression....

I agree with the trial judge's conclusion that the actions of UGG seriously diminished Wallace's prospects of finding similar employment. In light of this fact, and the other circumstances of this case, I am not persuaded that the trial judge erred in awarding the equivalent of 24 months' salary in lieu of notice. It may be that such an award is at the high end of the scale; however, taking into account all of the relevant factors, this award is not unreasonable and accordingly, I can see no reason to interfere. Therefore, for the reasons above, I would restore the order of the trial judge with respect to the appropriate period of reasonable notice and allow the appeal on this ground....

[Justice McLachlin, with La Forest and L'Heureux JJ concurring, dissented in part.]

Honda Canada Inc v Keays, 2008 SCC 39 at para 1ff

BASTARACHE J (McLachlin CJ and Binnie, Deschamps, Abella, Charron, and Rothstein JJ concurring):

On March 29, 2000, after 14 years of employment, the respondent, Kevin Keays, was terminated from his employment at Honda Canada Inc. ("Honda"). Keays sued for wrongful dismissal. The trial judge found that Keays was entitled to a notice period of 15 months. He then considered additional damages dependent on the manner of dismissal (the so-called "Wallace damages") and increased the notice period to 24 months. In addition, the trial judge awarded punitive damages against Honda in the amount of $500,000, plus costs on a substantial indemnity scale with a 25 percent premium. The Court of Appeal unanimously upheld the finding of wrongful termination as well as the regular damages and the damages for manner of dismissal (Wallace damages). It also ordered that the costs premium be reduced. A majority (Goudge J.A. dissenting) ordered that the quantum of punitive damages be reduced from $500,000 to $100,000.

I would allow the appeal in part. The regular damages award should be maintained. The Court of Appeal erred however in maintaining the damages for manner of dismissal (Wallace damages) and simply reducing the quantum of punitive damages. These awards, as well as the costs premium, must thus be set aside. I would deny the cross-appeal dealing with the reduction of the award of punitive damages.

Keays started working for Honda in 1986, first on the assembly line and later in data entry. In 1997, his diagnosis of chronic fatigue syndrome ("CFS") was confirmed by a doctor from the Sleep Disorder Clinic in Toronto, Dr. Moldofsky. He ceased work and received disability insurance benefits through an independent insurance provider, London Life Insurance Co., until 1998 when his benefits were discontinued based on the insurer's evaluation that Keays could return to work full-time. Keays' appeal to the insurer on this evaluation was denied. Honda had no part in the decision to terminate Keays' benefits.

Although London Life's decision was based on medical opinion that Keays could return to work without restrictions, Keays continued to absent himself. He was placed in the Honda Disability Program, which permits disabled employees to take absences without the invocation of Honda's attendance policy by confirming that the absence from work is related to the disability. However, Keays missed more work than his diagnosing physician, Dr. Morris, had predicted, and the notes he offered to explain his absences changed in tone leaving the employer to believe that the doctor did not independently evaluate whether he missed work due to disability.

In late 1999, Honda's administrative coordinator, Susan Selby arranged for Keays to see Dr. Lester Affoo, an independent physician hired by Honda, because of the increasing frequency of absences. In January and February 2000, Keays again experienced increased absences (14 days in total). This prompted Betty Magill, Keays' manager, to raise the issue with Selby. They met on March 3 and decided to ask Keays to meet with Dr. Brennan, an occupational medicine specialist, in order to determine how his disability could be accommodated. After this meeting, but before Honda had a chance to meet with Keays, Keays decided to retain counsel to attempt to mediate his concern that he would ultimately be terminated. On March 17, Honda received a letter from Keays' counsel outlining his concerns and offering to work towards a resolution. Honda did not respond.

On March 21, Magill and Selby met with Keays to explain their concerns about the deficiencies in the doctors' notes, described as "cryptic" by Dr. Reinders, and asked him to meet with Dr. Brennan to determine what could be done to support him at his work. They also discussed the letter they had received from Keays' lawyer a few days earlier and explained that they had not responded to the lawyer because they had a practice of dealing with associates directly, not with third party advocates. At this meeting, Keays agreed to meet with Dr. Brennan. However, the next day he told Honda that, on the advice of counsel, he would not meet with Dr. Brennan without explanation of the purpose, methodology and parameters of the consultation. Keays did not come to work for a week following this incident. Upon his return to work, on March 28, 2000, Selby gave Keays a letter ("March 28 letter") [stating, in part]:

> Our position remains as we explained it to you on March 21, 2000. Kevin, we do not accept the need for your recent absence nor do we intend to elaborate further on the purpose of your meeting with Dr. Brennan. This was all explained to you carefully on March 21, 2000. Our position remains the same. We expect you to meet with Dr. Brennan and, we expect you to come to work.
>
> Kevin, we sincerely hope that you will co-operate with our efforts. As you have admitted, your condition has not improved over the past three years and you would do anything to get better and come to work on a regular basis. We are committed to supporting you in a full return to work. We sincerely hope that you will co-operate with us.
>
> Kevin, you must understand that the current situation is unacceptable. If you do not agree to meet with Dr. Brennan, we will have no alternative but to terminate your employment.

Later the same day, Selby telephoned Keays to urge him to reread the letter and re-consider. Keays remained unwilling to meet Dr. Brennan. In accordance with its warning, Honda terminated his employment.

The trial judge's decision in this case highlights the problems we face in dealing with damages for conduct in the context of termination of employment. In particular, it raises questions about the propriety of damages for manner of dismissal, whereby damages are awarded by extending the notice period (Wallace damages). This re-evaluation is mandated particularly by this Court's recent decision in *Fidler v. Sun Life Assurance Co. of Canada*, [2006] 2 S.C.R. 3, 2006 SCC 30.

Current State of the Law

An action for wrongful dismissal is based on an implied obligation in the employment contract to give reasonable notice of an intention to terminate the relationship in the absence of just cause. Thus, if an employer fails to provide reasonable notice of termination, the employee can bring an action for breach of the implied term (*Wallace*, at para. 115). The general rule, which stems from the British case of *Addis v. Gramophone Co.*, [1909] A.C. 488 (H.L.), is that damages allocated in such actions are confined to the loss suffered as a result of the employer's failure to give proper notice and that no damages are available to the employee for the actual loss of his or her job and/or pain and distress that may have been suffered as a consequence of being terminated. This Court affirmed this rule in *Peso Silver Mines Ltd. (N.P.L.) v. Cropper*, [1966] S.C.R. 673, at p. 684:

> the damages cannot be increased by reason of the circumstances of dismissal whether in respect of the [employee's] wounded feelings or the prejudicial effect upon his reputation and chances of finding other employment.

Later in *Vorvis v. Insurance Corp. of British Columbia*, [1989] 1 S.C.R. 1085, McIntyre J. stated at p. 1103:

> I would conclude that while aggravated damages may be awarded in actions for breach of contract in appropriate cases, this is not a case where they should be given. The rule long established in the *Addis* and [page 388] *Peso Silver Mines* cases has generally been applied to deny such damages, and the employer/employee relationship (in the absence of collective agreements which involve consideration of the modern labour law régime) has always been one where either party could terminate the contract of employment by due notice, and therefore the only damage which could arise would result from a failure to give such notice.

The Court in *Vorvis* nevertheless left open the possibility of allocating aggravated damages in wrongful dismissal cases where the acts complained of were also independently actionable. McIntyre J. stated at p. 1103:

> I would not wish to be taken as saying that aggravated damages could never be awarded in a case of wrongful dismissal, particularly where the acts complained of were also independently actionable, a factor not present here.

In *Wallace*, Iacobucci J. endorsed a strict interpretation of the *Vorvis* "independently actionable wrong" approach, rejecting both an implied contractual duty of good faith and a tort of bad faith discharge. At para. 73, he said:

> Relying upon the principles enunciated in *Vorvis*, supra, the Court of Appeal held that any award of damages beyond compensation for breach of contract for failure to give reasonable notice of termination "must be founded on a separately actionable course of conduct" (p. 184). Although there has been criticism of *Vorvis* ... this is an accurate statement of

the law.... An employment contract is not one in which peace of mind is the very matter contracted for (see e.g. *Jarvis v. Swans Tours Ltd.*, [1973] 1 Q.B. 233 (C.A.)) and so, absent an independently actionable wrong, the foreseeability of mental distress or the fact that the parties contemplated its occurrence is of no consequence ...

This brings us to *Fidler*, where the Court, per McLachlin C.J. and Abella J., concluded that it was no longer necessary that there be an independent actionable wrong before damages for mental distress can be awarded for breach of contract, whether or not it is a "peace of mind" contract. It stated at para. 49:

> We conclude that the "peace of mind" class of cases should not be viewed as an exception to the general rule of the non-availability of damages for mental distress in contract law, but rather as an application of the reasonable contemplation or foreseeability principle that applies generally to determine the availability of damages for breach of contract.

This conclusion was based on the principle, articulated in *Hadley v. Baxendale* (1854), 9 Ex. 341, 156 E.R. 145, that damages are recoverable for a contractual breach if the damages are "such as may fairly and reasonably be considered either arising naturally ... from such breach of contract itself, or such as may reasonably be supposed to have been in the contemplation of both parties" (p. 151). The court in *Hadley* explained the principle of reasonable expectation as follows:

> Now, if the special circumstances under which the contract was actually made were communicated by the plaintiffs to the defendants, and thus known to both parties, the damages resulting from the breach of such a contract, which they would reasonably contemplate, would be the amount of injury which would ordinarily follow from a breach of contract under these special circumstances so known and communicated. But, on the other hand, if these special circumstances were wholly unknown to the party breaking the contract, he, at the most, could only be supposed to have had in his contemplation the amount of injury which would arise generally, and in the great multitude of cases not affected by any special circumstances, from such a breach of contract.

Thus, in cases where parties have contemplated at the time of the contract that a breach in certain circumstances would cause the plaintiff mental distress, the plaintiff is entitled to recover (*Fidler*, at para. 42; *Vorvis*, at p. 1102). This principle was reaffirmed in para. 54 of *Fidler*, where the Court recognized that the *Hadley* rule explains the extended notice period in *Wallace*:

> It follows that there is only one rule by which compensatory damages for breach of contract should be assessed: the rule in *Hadley v. Baxendale*. The *Hadley* test unites all forms of contractual damages under a single principle. It explains why damages may be awarded where an object of the contract is to secure a psychological benefit, just as they may be awarded where an object of the contract is to secure a material one. It also explains why an extended period of notice may have been awarded upon wrongful dismissal in employment law: see *Wallace v. United Grain Growers Ltd.*, [1997] 3 S.C.R. 701. In all cases, these results are based on what was in the reasonable contemplation of the parties at the time of contract formation. [Emphasis deleted.]

We must therefore begin by asking what was contemplated by the parties at the time of the formation of the contract, or, as stated in para. 44 of *Fidler*: "[W]hat did the contract promise?" The contract of employment is, by its very terms, subject to cancellation on notice or subject to payment of damages in lieu of notice without regard to the ordinary psychological impact of that decision. At the time the contract was formed, there would not ordinarily be contemplation of psychological damage resulting from the dismissal since the dismissal is a clear legal possibility. The normal distress and hurt feelings resulting from dismissal are not compensable.

Damages resulting from the manner of dismissal must then be available only if they result from the circumstances described in *Wallace*, namely where the employer engages in conduct during the course of dismissal that is "unfair or is in bad faith by being, for example, untruthful, misleading or unduly insensitive" (para. 98).

The application of *Fidler* makes it unnecessary to pursue an extended analysis of the scope of any implied duty of good faith in an employment contract. *Fidler* provides that "as long as the promise in relation to state of mind is a part of the bargain in the reasonable contemplation of the contracting parties, mental distress damages arising from its breach are recoverable" (para. 48). In *Wallace*, the Court held employers "to an obligation of good faith and fair dealing in the manner of dismissal" (para. 95) and created the expectation that, in the course of dismissal, employers would be "candid, reasonable, honest and forthright with their employees" (para. 98). At least since that time, then, there has been expectation by both parties to the contract that employers will act in good faith in the manner of dismissal. Failure to do so can lead to foreseeable, compensable damages. As aforementioned, this Court recognized as much in *Fidler* itself, where we noted that the principle in *Hadley* "explains why an extended period of notice may have been awarded upon wrongful dismissal in employment law" (para. 54).

To be perfectly clear, I will conclude this analysis of our jurisprudence by saying that there is no reason to retain the distinction between "true aggravated damages" resulting from a separate cause of action and moral damages resulting from conduct in the manner of termination. Damages attributable to conduct in the manner of dismissal are always to be awarded under the *Hadley* principle. Moreover, in cases where damages are awarded, no extension of the notice period is to be used to determine the proper amount to be paid. The amount is to be fixed according to the same principles and in the same way as in all other cases dealing with moral damages. Thus, if the employee can prove that the manner of dismissal caused mental distress that was in the contemplation of the parties, those damages will be awarded not through an arbitrary extension of the notice period, but through an award that reflects the actual damages. Examples of conduct in dismissal resulting in compensable damages are attacking the employee's reputation by declarations made at the time of dismissal, misrepresentation regarding the reason for the decision, or dismissal meant to deprive the employee of a pension benefit or other right, permanent status for instance (see also the examples in *Wallace*, at paras. 99–100).

In light of the above discussion, the confusion between damages for conduct in dismissal and punitive damages is unsurprising, given that both have to do with conduct at the time of dismissal. It is important to emphasize here that the fundamental nature of damages for conduct in dismissal must be retained. This means that the award of damages for psychological injury in this context is still intended to be compensatory. The Court must avoid the pitfall of double-compensation or double-punishment that has been exemplified by this case.

Application of the Revised Test to This Case

I have reviewed the major overriding and palpable errors which undermine the trial judge's finding that Honda acted in "bad faith" when terminating Keays. There was, in my opinion, no such breach and no justification for an award of damages for conduct in dismissal.

Punitive Damages

In *Vorvis*, McIntyre J., for the majority, held that punitive damages are recoverable provided the defendant's conduct said to give rise to the claim is itself "an actionable wrong." This position stood until 2002 when my colleague Binnie J., writing for the majority, dealt comprehensively with the issue of punitive damages in the context of the Whiten case. He specified that an "actionable wrong" within the *Vorvis* rule does not require an independent tort and that a breach of the contractual duty of good faith can qualify as an independent wrong. Binnie J. concluded, at para. 82, that "[a]n independent actionable wrong is required, but it can be found in breach of a distinct and separate contractual provision or other duty such as a fiduciary obligation." In the case at hand, the trial judge and the Court of Appeal concluded that Honda's "discriminatory conduct" amounted to an independent actionable wrong for the purposes of allocating punitive damages. This being said, there is no need to discuss the concept of "actionable wrong" [page 393] here; this was done in *Whiten*. What matters here is that there was no basis for the judge's decision on the facts. I will therefore examine the facts and determine why punitive damages were not well justified according to the criteria in *Whiten*. I will also discuss the need to avoid duplication in damage awards. Damages for conduct in the manner of dismissal are compensatory; punitive damages are restricted to advertent wrongful acts that are so malicious and outrageous that they are deserving of punishment on their own. This distinction must guide judges in their analysis.

In this case, the trial judge awarded punitive damages on the basis of discriminatory conduct by Honda. Honda argues that discrimination is precluded as an independent cause of action under *Seneca College of Applied Arts and Technology v. Bhadauria*, [1981] 2 S.C.R. 181. In that case, this Court clearly articulated that a plaintiff is precluded from pursuing a common law remedy when human rights legislation contains a comprehensive enforcement scheme for violations of its substantive terms. The reasoning behind this conclusion is that the purpose of the Ontario *Human Rights Code* is to remedy the effects of discrimination; if breaches to the Code were actionable in common law courts, it would encourage litigants to use the Code for a purpose the legislature did not intend — namely, to punish employers who discriminate against their employees. Thus, a person who alleges a breach of the provisions of the Code must seek a remedy within the statutory scheme set out in the Code itself. Moreover, the recent amendments to the Code (which would allow a plaintiff to advance a breach of the Code as a cause of action in connection with another wrong) restrict monetary compensation to loss arising out of the infringement, including any injuries to dignity, feelings and self-respect. In this respect, they confirm the Code's remedial thrust.

The Court of Appeal, relying on *McKinley*, concluded that *Bhadauria* only precludes a civil action based directly on a breach of the Code—but does not preclude finding an independent actionable wrong for the purpose of allocating punitive damages. It is my view that the Code provides a comprehensive scheme for the treatment of claims of discrimination and *Bhadauria* established that a breach of the Code cannot constitute an actionable wrong; the legal requirement is not met.

Keays argued in cross-appeal before this Court that the decision in *Bhadauria* should be set aside and that a separate tort of discrimination should be recognized. In *Bhadauria*, Laskin C.J., writing for the Court, held that the plaintiff was precluded from pursuing a common law remedy because the applicable human rights legislation (the Code) contained a comprehensive enforcement scheme for violations of its substantive terms. The subtext of the *Bhadauria* decision is a concern that the broad, unfettered tort of discrimination created by the Court of Appeal would lead to indeterminate liability. Laskin C.J. wrote, at p. 189:

> It is one thing to apply a common law duty of care to standards of behaviour under a statute; that is simply to apply the law of negligence in the recognition of so-called statutory torts. It is quite a different thing to create by judicial fiat an obligation—one in no sense analogous to a duty of care in the law of negligence—to confer an economic benefit upon certain persons, with whom the alleged obligor has no connection. . . .

The concern that a tort of discrimination does not contain an effective limiting device was raised by interveners in this appeal. Moreover, as noted by the intervener Manitoba Human Rights Commission, jurisdictions outside Ontario have human rights legislation that vests jurisdiction exclusively with the provincial/territorial human rights tribunal. Accordingly, the concern in *Bhadauria* that recognition of a tort of discrimination would be inconsistent with legislative intent is still real.

The Council of Canadians with Disabilities, another intervener, raised the concern that recognition of a tort of discrimination may undermine the statutory regime which, for many victims of discrimination, is a more accessible and effective means by which to seek redress.

This said, there is no need to reconsider the position in *Bhadauria* in this case and deal with Keays' request for recognition of a distinct tort of discrimination. There was no evidence of discrimination to support a claim under s. 5 of the Ontario *Human Rights Code*, therefore no breach of human rights legislation serving as an actionable wrong, as required by Goudge J.A. Furthermore, there was no evidence of conduct meeting the strict requirements in *Whiten*. The trial judge concluded that the accommodation provided by admission to the disability program was itself discriminatory because Keays "had to 'earn' each dispensation from being 'coached' for any absences by presenting a 'note' from his doctor like some child who is suspected of 'playing hooky' from school" (para. 53). The trial judge then added that it made little sense to have a disability program and then deter its use by asking for doctors' notes. The association of coaching and the requirement of notes made by the trial judge here is puzzling. The requirement of notes was in effect part of the accommodation because it permitted absences without the possibility of the same leading to disciplinary action for failing to meet work requirements. There was no detriment in being part of the disability program and being treated differently from persons with "mainstream illnesses." The differential treatment was meant to accommodate the particular circumstances of persons with a particular type of disability and to provide a benefit to them. It is indeed apparent from the record that the program was designed to establish a continuous relation between management and treating physicians and monitor absences in order to establish in particular an expected rate of absences which would not give rise to disciplinary action. The suggestion that the program itself was discriminatory is not supported by the facts.

Even if I were to give deference to the trial judge on this issue, this Court has stated that punitive damages should "receive the most careful consideration and the discretion to award them should be most cautiously exercised" (*Vorvis*, at pp. 1104–5). Courts should only resort to punitive damages in exceptional cases (*Whiten*, at para. 69). The independent actionable wrong requirement is but one of many factors that merit careful consideration by the courts in allocating punitive damages. Another important thing to be considered is that conduct meriting punitive damages awards must be "harsh, vindictive, reprehensible and malicious," as well as "extreme in its nature and such that by any reasonable standard it is deserving of full condemnation and punishment" (*Vorvis*, at p. 1108). The facts of this case demonstrate no such conduct. Creating a disability program such as the one under review in this case cannot be equated with a malicious intent to discriminate against persons with a particular affliction.

The majority of the Court of Appeal upheld the award of punitive damages, but reduced the quantum to $100,000. The findings supporting this decision are demonstrably wrong and, in some cases, contradict the Court of Appeal's own findings. Before delving into the factual analysis, however, it is worth mentioning that even if the facts had justified an award of punitive damages, the lower courts should have been alert to the fact that compensatory damages were already awarded, and that under the old test, they carried an element of deterrence. This stems from the important principle that courts, when allocating punitive damages, must focus on the defendant's misconduct, not on the plaintiff's loss (*Whiten*, at para. 73). In this case, the same conduct underlays the awards of damages for conduct in dismissal and punitive damages. The lower courts erred by not questioning whether the allocation of punitive damages was necessary for the purposes of denunciation, deterrence and retribution, once the damages for conduct in dismissal were awarded. Be that as it may, we now have a clearer foundation to distinguish between damages for conduct in dismissal and punitive damages.

As earlier mentioned, there was considerable duplication in the award of damages for conduct in dismissal and punitive damages in this case. The discussion of punitive damages must nevertheless begin with a consideration of the conduct attributed to Honda that justified the award.

As earlier mentioned, the main allegation was that Honda discriminated by requiring Keays to bring in a doctor's note to justify each absence when employees with "mainstream illnesses" did not have to do so. The trial judge also found that this requirement had the effect of lengthening absences, ignoring the evidence of Ms. Selby who testified that Honda did not require the employee to produce a doctor's note as a precondition to returning to work. As discussed earlier, employees outside the disability program did not require notes for absences of less than five days but were subject to discipline for excessive absences (A.R., at pp. 282–83), whereas employees in the program were allowed regular absences without discipline beyond the usual attendance requirement under a system of supervision based on regular contacts with doctors. The object of the disability program is to maintain regular contact with the family doctor in order to support treatment. It allows for disability-related absences, a form of accommodation determined in consultation with doctors. The program requires that medical notes be provided to establish that absences are in fact related to the disability. There is no stereotyping or arbitrariness here (*McGill University Health Centre (Montreal General Hospital) v. Syndicat des employés de l'Hôpital général de Montréal*, [2007] 1 S.C.R. 161, 2007 SCC 4, at para. 49). In addition, I accept that the need to monitor the absences of employees who are regularly absent from work is a *bona fide* work requirement in light of the very nature of the employment contract and responsibility of the employer for the management of its workforce.

The trial judge also found the refusal to remove the "coaching" record from Keays' file to be discriminatory, even if there was no evidence of any adverse consequences to the existence of a coaching file. The evidence was that coaching is not a disciplinary procedure and would simply permit entry into the disability program allowing absences without disciplinary consequences (A.R., at pp. 306–14).

The trial judge also based his decision on harassment; he seemed to relate this entirely to a suggestion made by Dr. Affoo that Keays consider taking a position with a light physical component (para. 55). It is certainly difficult to see a course of conduct in a single incident. Moreover, this was a single suggestion made by an independent expert, never acted upon. I have already dealt with this argument at para. 39 when discussing the damages for conduct in dismissal.

A final basis for the finding that punitive damages were justified is that Honda had "retaliated" against Keays. I have dealt with this at para. 47.

The Court of Appeal pointed to the finding that Honda knew that Keays valued his employment and was dependent upon it for disability benefits. It is no doubt true that Keays valued his job and that he was dependent upon that employment for his disability benefits. However, knowledge of this cannot justify an award of punitive damages. All employees value their jobs. What matters is Honda's conduct with regards to Keays' need for medical attention and special accommodation. In this respect, it was wrong to blame Honda for Keays' loss of disability benefits. London Life's decision to cut off Keays' long-term disability benefits had nothing to do with Honda. It was therefore erroneous to attribute the insurer's decision to Honda and allow for punitive damages on such grounds.

The Court of Appeal found that Honda knew Keays was particularly vulnerable because of his medical condition. However, according to the Court of Appeal's own findings, Honda did not know about the seriousness or true nature of Keays' medical condition because Keays would not facilitate an exchange of information about it. Honda was sceptical about Keays' disability and was taking steps to confirm it. His medical file did not disclose a definitive diagnosis of CFS and Keays refused to meet with Dr. Brennan despite repeated assurances that the meeting was only a "get to know you" session, to be followed by contacts with Keays' personal physician.

Finally, the Court of Appeal pointed to Honda's refusal to deal with Keays' counsel. There is no legal obligation on the part of any party to deal with an employee's counsel while he or she continues with his or her employer. Parties are always entitled to deal with each other directly. What was egregious was the fact that Honda told Keays that hiring outside counsel was a mistake and that it would make things worse. This was surely a way of undermining the advice of the lawyer. This conduct was ill-advised and unnecessarily harsh, but it does not provide justification for an award of punitive damages.

The evidence and the Court of Appeal's own findings lead me to conclude that Honda's conduct was not sufficiently egregious or outrageous to warrant an award of punitive damages under the Whiten criteria. The Court of Appeal's award must thus be overturned.

LeBel J. (Fish J. concurring) (dissenting in part) —

I have read the reasons of my colleague Justice Bastarache. I agree with him that there was no basis for the claim for punitive damages and that it overlaps with the award of what were formerly known as "*Wallace* damages." I also agree with him that there is a need to review the categories of damages for dismissal. But any revision must reflect the view accepted by this Court that the contract of employment is a good faith contract that is informed by the values protected by and recognized in the human rights codes and the *Canadian Charter of Rights and Freedoms*, particularly in respect of discrimination. As the Court found in *Wallace v. United Grain Growers Ltd.*, the contract of employment often reflects substantial power imbalances. As a result, it must be performed and terminated in good faith, and fairly.

With respect, I believe that on the facts of this case, the award of additional damages for manner of dismissal (formerly "*Wallace* damages") should stand. The trial judge committed no overriding errors in this respect. Although his review of the facts may not have been flawless, there was a sufficient basis for the findings of bad faith and discrimination in the manner in which the employment of the respondent, Kevin Keays, was terminated by Honda.

Chapter 4: Status Under Collective Bargaining Legislation

4:100 INTRODUCTION

Collective bargaining is an important component of Canadian labour policy. The reach of the collective bargaining regime is therefore both a hotly contested political issue and the subject of extensive litigation, with repercussions for those who are included or excluded from its ambit. Not everyone is entitled or required to bargain collectively under prevailing labour relations legislation. This chapter is about the status of those so affected: employees, unions, and employers.

The right to join a union and thereby engage in collective bargaining is reserved for "employees." The meaning of "employee" is increasingly difficult to determine, given the growing variety of contractual arrangements in the labour market, such as those that apply to operators of food franchises, people who work from their homes as consultants or contractors, workers in the so-called gig or sharing economies supplying services through online platforms, and casual workers sent by employment agencies. The problem of how to characterize workers in these developing variants of traditional employment is not restricted to collective bargaining; it also arises in assessing whether such workers are covered by legislation on such matters as employment standards (see Chapter 13), unemployment insurance, workers' compensation, pensions, and occupational health and safety.

Moreover, some people who are employees by any definition may be legally ineligible to bargain collectively. If they work for certain kinds of employers—typically those in the public and quasi-public sector—they may be barred from collective action or are required to bargain under more restrictive procedures than those set out in general labour relations legislation. If they are employed in certain occupations—predominantly the professions, agriculture, and domestic service—they may be entirely excluded from statutory collective bargaining because legislatures have concluded that it is inappropriate or unworkable for them. Even employees who work at conventional jobs that fall under ordinary labour legislation are denied the right to bargain collectively if they have significant responsibility for representing management in its relations with workers and unions, or if they have other important managerial responsibilities. The rationale for this restriction is that such employees would find themselves in a conflict of interest.

Even if a person is clearly an employee eligible for inclusion in collective bargaining, it is not always clear who her legal employer is. An entrepreneur may set up a complex and confusing corporate structure, perhaps for legitimate business reasons or perhaps to avoid obligations under labour or tax legislation. The restructuring of companies, and the growth of outsourcing and more flexible methods of production, may mean that workers who were once employed by, say, an automobile manufacturer, are now employed by a different entity that is part of that manufacturer's tightly integrated network of suppliers.

As for employee organizations, they are of many kinds, both in the workplace and outside of it — social clubs, groups based on a common ethnic or religious identity, and so on. In order to fall within the statutory definition of a trade union, and therefore be eligible to acquire the privileges and responsibilities of a bargaining agent under labour relations legislation, an organization must have been formed for purposes that include collective representation of its members vis-à-vis their employer. In addition, other questions may arise in determining whether an organization that claims union status is indeed eligible to represent workers. For example, does the organization have sufficient structure and permanence to represent workers effectively? Should it have the right to function as a collective bargaining agent if its internal decision-making processes are not democratic? These are important public policy questions, and the answers to them may affect the balance of power in the particular workplace and across the whole economy.

The advent of collective bargaining does not invariably improve the position of employees, nor does denial of access to collective bargaining always disadvantage them. For example, under some labour relations statutes, domestic and agricultural workers are denied collective bargaining rights because of what are often seen as anachronistic or disingenuous arguments about the need to protect the sanctity of the household or the family farm. However, even where those groups have been given bargaining rights, they have seldom been able to use them to much effect. Conversely, medical doctors generally are not employees by any definition and do not formally bargain collectively under conventional labour legislation, but they have been very successful in advancing their economic interests through lobbying, negotiations, public appeals, and even work stoppages. These two examples (the former involving the powerless, the latter involving the powerful) suggest that there are limits to the effectiveness of our collective bargaining laws in reducing income disparities in society.

In recent decades, fundamental changes in our economy have called into question the logic that underlies the boundaries drawn by labour relations legislation around the right to bargain collectively. That logic is based on the assumption that the legislation will be used by certain kinds of people, namely skilled and semi-skilled blue-collar workers in relatively stable employment relationships with corporate enterprises structured on a traditional hierarchical basis. This assumption may have been reasonably accurate when collective bargaining legislation was introduced during and shortly after World War II. It has become less accurate as rapid changes in technology have influenced the shape of employment and corporate organization in the new economy. Will unions be able to organize the growing number of highly skilled knowledge workers employed in organizations where managerial authority is less clearly defined?

At the other end of an increasingly polarized workforce, an even greater challenge for unions is what to do about unorganized workers in the expanding secondary labour market. These employees may often work on a part-time or casual basis and may need to hold more than one job to make ends meet. The precariousness of their employment raises the question whether, even as a collective, they could muster enough power to bargain effectively under existing labour relations legislation.

As large firms break down into much smaller production units, creating what David Weil has described as "the fissured workplace," the attachment of collective bargaining rights to the individual firm—a cornerstone of our present system—may further limit employee bargaining power. It can be argued that our present collective bargaining system only works well in large firms, where unions can collect enough revenue from dues to be able to bargain effectively and where the firm itself has the economic and political leverage to pass on the costs of collective bargaining settlements to society at large. Perhaps it is time to re-examine the assumption that access to collective bargaining should depend on a proximate relationship with a particular employer, and to look instead to the worker's attachment to a particular industry.

It may also be time to re-examine who should and should not have access to collective bargaining, and with what consequences. Very affluent "employees" such as elite professional athletes may appear to have no need for collective bargaining, but they enjoy the right to engage in it and they do so very effectively. Distinctly less advantaged "employees"—non-elite musicians and writers, for example—may well need collective bargaining, but cannot have it under ordinary labour relations legislation because they lack a specific employer with whom they can bargain in any conventional sense. Some small businesspeople, such as consultants and the owners of franchised food outlets, may be at the mercy of a single provider of supplies or work opportunities, but they still have no access to collective bargaining. Other people with small businesses—for example, doctors paid on a fee-for-service basis by government health plans, and lawyers paid by legal aid plans—also have no employer in the conventional sense, but nevertheless manage to bring collective pressure to bear on the source of their income (the government).

Each of these cases presents special problems. If the workers concerned are not covered by labour relations statutes, they may be covered by special legislation. This is the case, for example, with artists and performers who are subject to the federal *Status of the Artist Act,* SC 1992, c 33. Doctors and legal aid lawyers may operate under special bargaining and dispute resolution procedures established by statutes, regulations, agreements between the government and professional bodies, or unwritten understandings. In the absence of such arrangements, collective activities are regulated by the general law of the land. The federal *Competition Act,* RSC 1985, c C-34 (referred to briefly at the end of Section 4:200) is very important in this regard. It provides for criminal, administrative, and civil sanctions. Also important is the common law of tort (discussed in Chapter 8). It gives plaintiffs who are adversely affected by certain kinds of collective economic sanctions the right to sue for damages or injunctions.

The express exclusion from collective bargaining legislation of managerial employees and those employed in a confidential capacity relating to labour relations raises a different concern. This exclusion reflects the classic adversarial paradigm of collective bargaining, which posits a divergence of interest between workers and management and their necessary separation into opposing camps. The appropriateness of that paradigm becomes more questionable as external economic forces generate pressure for greater labour-management co-operation, even within the largest corporations. In addition, the emergence of a large group of knowledge workers, and an increasing emphasis on non-hierarchical and participatory management, suggest that the present managerial exclusion may be overly broad.

Similar concerns arise when considering what types of organizations are granted status as trade unions under collective bargaining legislation. Because of a considerable history of employer co-optation of bodies seemingly set up to encourage labour-management co-operation, unions are often wary of participating in such bodies. Collective bargaining legislation was originally designed to ensure that company-dominated employee organizations did not pre-empt the formation of genuine trade unions. Today, however, greater union participation in corporate management, and an increasing employee ownership stake in some unionized companies, raises questions about whether it is still appropriate to require an arm's-length relationship between unions and employers. That requirement must also be looked at in the context of a harsher economy, which has forced many unions and employers to adopt more flexible approaches in order to maintain the economic viability of enterprises with well-established collective bargaining relationships.

In principle, an employer can be an individual, a partnership, a corporation, a grouping of inter-related employers, or a formalized employers' organization. An employer may use multiple or complex corporate legal vehicles to conduct its business. These vehicles may obscure the nature and identity of the true employer in such a way as to hamper union efforts at certification. Labour relations statutes commonly authorize labour relations boards to resolve this type of confusion. A similar problem may arise upon the sale of a business enterprise or part of its operations. In such circumstances, the identity of the employer, and which entity is to be bound by pre-existing bargaining rights is frequently at issue. Finally, what happens if a unionized employer contracts out some of its operations, with or without an intention to avoid its collective bargaining obligations? Is the successor or contractor bound by such obligations?

The next sections explore the boundaries of employee status and union status under labour relations law. What types of workers are entitled to make use of collective bargaining statutes, and what types of employee organizations are recognized by these statutes? The chapter ends with a section on the status of employers and the remedial possibilities where the identity of the employer is at issue or where an employer is alleged to be structuring its activities to avoid its responsibilities under labour relations legislation.

4:200 WHO IS AN EMPLOYEE?

A major concern, in Canada and elsewhere, is that too broad a definition of "employee" will sweep into the sphere of collective bargaining a range of economic relationships that do not really involve the interaction between an employer and an employee but between a buyer and a seller of business services. If economic arrangements of the latter type are held to fall within collective bargaining legislation, there may be a conflict with competition policy.

Canadian public policy (as reflected in the *Competition Act*, RSC 1985, c C-34) favours the preservation of business competition and forbids businesses to enter into conspiracies that would unduly restrict such competition. Section 45(1) of the *Competition Act* makes it illegal for persons to form combinations that would unduly restrain or injure competition. It should also be noted that as a result of broad definitions contained in section 2(1) of the same Act, it forbids restraints on or injury to competition respecting "products," which include not only "articles" but also "services … of any description whether industrial, trade, professional or otherwise." Reading these two provisions literally and together, there is a risk that section 45 could be taken to prohibit certain union tactics, such as strikes and picketing, as concerted activity designed to restrain or injure competition in the supply of services. However, section 4(1)(a) of the *Competition Act* provides a general exemption for "combinations or activities of

CHAPTER 4: STATUS UNDER COLLECTIVE BARGAINING LEGISLATION

workmen or employees for their own reasonable protection as such workmen or employees," and section 4(1)(c) provides a more specific exemption for arrangements "pertaining to collective bargaining ... in respect of salary or wages and terms and conditions of employment."

Interestingly, although private parties injured by a violation of the *Competition Act* have had a right to sue for damages since 1975, no such suits have been brought against unions, nor have other proceedings been brought against them under that Act in recent years. This may signal recognition of the fact that competition policy somehow has to be squared with collective bargaining policy. The point is of particular importance in assessing the cases in the following subsection, which deal with the legislative conferral of employee status on individuals who might also be deemed to be entrepreneurs and thus subject to the restrictions of the *Competition Act*.

4:210 Dependent Contractors

Labour boards and courts have constantly struggled with the question of the distinction between an "employee" and an "independent contractor." In the absence of legislative guidance on that question, decision makers have sometimes borrowed definitions from the common law. In Canada, one such borrowing produced what is known as the "fourfold test," which is discussed in Chapter 3 (Section 3:200) and below in the *Egg Films* case. That test took into account four factors—control of the relationship, ownership of the tools, chance of profit, and risk of loss. The presence of some of these factors and not others has, however, sometimes led to confusion and to the exclusion from collective bargaining of groups of workers for whom a right to collective action may be appropriate. Consequently, some Canadian legislatures have adopted "dependent contractor" provisions, which extended the reach of the term "employee" (for collective bargaining purposes) to cover some of the most problematic and marginal parts of the universe of independent contractors. A typical statutory definition of "dependent contractor" is found in the Ontario *Labour Relations Act, 1995*, SO 1995, c 1, Schedule A, s 1(1):

> "dependent contractor" means a person, whether or not employed under a contract of employment, and whether or not furnishing tools, vehicles, equipment, machinery, material, or any other thing, or any other thing owned by the dependent contractor, who performs work or services for another person for compensation or reward on such terms and conditions that the dependent contractor is in a position of economic dependence upon, and under an obligation to perform duties for, that person more closely resembling the relationship of an employee than that of an independent contractor.

The following case applies the concept of the dependent contractor, despite the absence of statutory language, to motion picture technicians.

International Alliance of Theatrical Stage Employees, Moving Picture Technicians, Artists and Allied Crafts, Local 849 v Egg Films Inc, 2012 NSLB 120, application for judicial review denied 2013 NSSC 123 (*sub nom Egg Films Inc v Nova Scotia (Labour Board)*), aff'd 2014 NSCA 33

> 1. The International Alliance of Theatrical Stage Employees, Moving Picture Technicians, Artists and Allied Crafts of the United States, Its Territories, and Canada, Local 849 ("I.A.T.S.E., Local 849") has applied under section 23 of the *Trade Union Act* ("the Act") to become certified as the bargaining agent for certain employees of the Respondent Egg

Films Inc. doing technical work on March 5, 2011.... The Respondent says that it has no employees performing the work described in the proposed bargaining unit, but rather engages independent contractors on a sporadic basis to provide services and equipment to perform technical work of the sort described in the Union's Application....

5. ... Egg Films/Hatch Post does projects where "the filming may last only a day." The Egg/Hatch operation has about 14 full time employees and hires others as required for particular projects. Egg Films may only do 10 to 15 shooting days per year, mostly to produce commercial advertising. Some of these projects may involve small crews of 3 to 5 people who are "multi-tasking", while others may need a dozen or so specialist technicians. The project which led to this Application for Certification was a one day "shoot" of a "commercial" for the Atlantic Lotto Corporation. It occurred at a hotel in Halifax, primarily in order to have a "spa" location as a primary backdrop. This was a major project which involved the hiring of approximately 25 people, a significant number of whom were members of the Applicant Union....

(1) The Constitutional Context

42. Since the advent of the *Canadian Charter of Rights and Freedoms* as part of the constitution by virtue of Canada Act 1982 (U.K.) c.11 proclaimed in force April 17, 1982, it has been understood that joining a trade union is an exercise of one's freedom of association guaranteed by virtue of *Charter* section 2(d).... More recently, the Supreme Court of Canada, in *Heath Services and Support—Facilities Subsector Bargaining Association*, 2007 SCC 27 (CanLII), [2007] 2 S.C.R. 391 (the "B.C. Health Case"), at para. 19 has stated:

> "... We conclude that s.2(d) of the *Charter* protects the capacity of members of labour unions to engage, in association, in collective bargaining on fundamental workplace issues. This protection does not cover all aspects of 'collective bargaining' as that term is understood in the statutory labour relations regimes that are in place across the country. Nor does it ensure a particular outcome in a labour dispute, or guarantee access to any particular statutory regime. What is protected is simply the right of employees to associate in a process of collective action to achieve workplace goals. If the government substantially interferes with that right, it violates section 2(d) of the *Charter*."

More recently still, in *Ontario (Attorney General) v. Fraser*, 2011 SCC 20 (CanLII), the Supreme Court of Canada re-affirmed its views about the constitutionalization of collective bargaining.... This Board can only infer that the Supreme Court of Canada was strongly reinforcing the notion that labour relations tribunals must be careful to ensure that in interpreting their constitutive statutes, they engage in a purposive interpretational approach which is consonant with the *Charter* values of freedom of association in *Charter* section 2(d) and upholds at least the minimal core of collective bargaining rights deemed to be protected by the reasoning in *B.C. Health*....

(4) The Socio-economic Context for Interpretation.

49. There is also a broader socio-economic context within which the purposive statutory interpretation exercise occurs. There is a balance to be struck, in labour market

regulation, between promoting economic efficiency in sometimes highly competitive, globalizing markets, on the one hand, and supporting, encouraging and protecting increasingly vulnerable members of the workforce on the other. The new Preamble to the Act also speaks of determining "... good working conditions and sound labour-management relations ..." But there can be no "sound labour-management relations" if labour and employment statutes are interpreted in ways which systematically render firms non-competitive or force them out of business. If Andrew Sims' recommendation, not to include "productivity and competitiveness" as elements of the preamble to the federal Labour Code, is taken to mean that these considerations are never relevant to the purposive interpretation of the *Trade Union Act*, surely that must be wrong. In the words of the highly respected labour scholars Paul Davies and Mark Freedland, one must be concerned with both economic "efficiency" in commercial law terms and the "welfare" of vulnerable employees when interpreting labour and employment law statutes....

(5) The Film Technicians are Employees

50. On the question of whether the film technicians sought to be represented by the Applicant Union are employees or independent contractors for the purposes of the Act one must begin with the definition of employee found in section 2(1)(k). It reads as follows:

> (k) "employee" means a person employed to do skilled or unskilled manual, clerical or technical work....

Defining "employee" in significant part by saying it means "a person employed ..." is notoriously circular and unhelpful. Nor does one receive great assistance in sorting out employees from independent contractors by reading section 2(1)(l) of the Act, which says "employer" means "any person who employs more than one employee". For many years the most cited case for drawing the line on what was assumed to be a simple distinction between "employees" and "independent contractors" was the Supreme Court of Canada's *Montreal Locomotive* decision, supra, cited by the Applicant Union. It was rooted in the ancient law of "master and servant" which predated modern employment statutes and rested on a notion of "control". A "master" (i.e. employer) was thought to engage a "servant" (i.e. employee) in a "contract of service" on the understanding that the master could control and direct the actions of the unskilled servant in notionally straightforward and simple tasks. However, a person would engage an "independent contractor" in a commercial "contract for services" where hiring party desired a specific outcome from skilled tradesman, whose knowledge and abilities were, by definition, beyond the unskilled hirer's capacity to control. See Otto Kahn-Freund "Servants and Independent Contractors", (1951) 14 *Modern Law Review* 504. The *Montreal Locomotive* case purported to go beyond the older "control" test by referring to (1) control, (2) ownership of the tools, (3) chance of profit, and (4) risk of loss. However, it has been correctly observed that these four factors boil down to two questions: (1) whether the worker is controlled by the employer/client: and (2) whether the worker is economically independent (calculating profit and loss, and owning expensive tools to carry out a commercial contract, being the indicia): see Brian A. Langille and Guy Davidov "Beyond Employers and Independent Contractors: A View From Canada" (1999) 21 *Comp. Lab L. & Policy J*. 7.

51. The "control" test of yore has proved difficult to apply for decades. The definition of employer in section 2(1)(k) of the Act undermines the simple application by referring to the fact that an employee may be employed to do "*skilled* or unskilled manual labour, clerical or *technical* work" [emphasis added]. Certifications in the health and university sector provide ample and eloquent examples of persons deemed "employees", and unionized as a result, but whose skills and technical abilities are beyond the capacity of managers to "control" or even understand in any narrow or literal sense. Indeed, people in these sectors are employed, often paid by salary rather than hourly wages, precisely because the[y] have skills and can do technical things which the person who engages them cannot do and trusts them to carry out on their own. However, their particular skill, technical abilities or professional knowledge is necessary to the organization. Thus, it is not surprising that in *The City of Pointe Claire*, supra, at paragraph 48, the Supreme Court of Canada refers to "legal subordination" and "integration into the business" as relevant criteria for determining who is the "real employer" of an employee, while still referring to the question of who "exercises the greatest control over all aspects of their work". In regard to the latter concept, the Court refers to a non-exhaustive list of factors: "the selection process, hiring, training, discipline, evaluation, supervision, assignment of duties, remuneration and integration into the business" . . .

52. On the question of economic dependence or independence, this Board, like others across Canada, has been governed by substance rather than form. Just because an employer calls the relationship one of "independent contract" rather than "employment" (or the union asserts the reverse) does not determine the matter: see *Retail Wholesale and Department Store Union, Local 1015 and Sobey's Stores Limited (Warehouse)* N.S. L.R.B. No. 2276, May 10, 1976 (where truckers who owned their own trucks in a "broker" arrangement were held to be employees and not independent contractors) and *Bakery, Confectionary and Tobacco Workers International Union, Local 446 and Baxter Foods Limited*, N.S. L.R.B. No. 4321, February 7, 1996 (where truck drivers and largely self-directing merchandizers were deemed employees rather than independent contractors). These were cases under Part I of the Act, though the same issue has been arisen in the construction industry under Part II of the Act: see *United Brotherhood of Carpenters and Joiners of America, Local 83 and Fitzgerald and Snow Ltd.*, L.R.B. No. 1753C, January 13, 1997; and *United Brotherhood of Carpenters and Joiners, Local 83 and Mainland Development Limited*, L.R.B. No. 1768C, April 17, 1997 (reasons issued October 19, 1998). The Board and Panel before it have tended to cast the discussion in terms of a straight forward dichotomy between "employees" and "independent contractors". However, the reality on the ground, in the "new economy" of flexible work forms and variable employment arrangements, is far more complex. There is really a continuum of legal arrangements governing the provision of work performed personally by individuals who may do "piece work" at home (whether old fashioned sewing or new fangled tele-marketing and computer programming), engage in tasks for others in the community (taxi-drivers, "free-lance" reporters, merchandizers, sales personnel), work at another person's establishment or work site on a sporadic basis (retail sales, seasonal truck drivers, film technicians) or work in a "standard" industrial employment relationship. The legal forms governing such personal work may depend on the preferences of the people doing the hiring, or the people being

hired. Thus, an employer for its own reasons may wish to have its truck driver workforce own and maintain their own vehicles and get paid other than by an hourly wage, in contrast to the other employees. Or, someone who is doing sporadic work for one or more employers, the free-lance editor of texts for example, may wish for various reasons to do so through a corporate vehicle of which they are the sole beneficial owner. Many labour boards have recognized that such persons are often not truly "independent" contractors but rather "dependent" contractors whose activities exist for and are contracted by the hirer upon whom the performer of the work is dependent, as an employee, even if the legal relationship takes the "form" of a commercial contract arrangement. An early and influential example of this reasoning is found in *National Labor Relations Board v. Hearst Publications Inc.*, 322 U.S. 111 120 (1944) where newspaper sellers ("paper boys") were found to be unionisable employees in the face of the employer's assertion they were non-unionisable independent contractors.

53. Over the years, the confusion concerning these distinctions has been such that some jurisdictions have amended their labour relations legislation to make specific reference to the principle that "dependent contractors" are to be treated as "employees" for the purposes of certification: see *Winnipeg Free Press v. Media Union of Manitoba*, (1999) (Case No 443/97/LRA), Manitoba Labour Board. Some jurisdictions have even gone so far as to hold that trucking owner-operators who have more than one truck are employees even though they hire others who are their employees, so long as the trucking services are for the same "employer": see *Fownes Construction Company*, [1974] 1 Can. L.R.B.R. 510 (B.C.L.R.B.) and *Mackie Moving Systems Corp (Re)*, 2002, 80 C.L.R.B. R. (2d) 195 (Canada Industrial Relations Board). Dependence on the "employer" is the key concept in these circumstances, along with the extent of direction and control of the nominally "independent" truckers in the circumstances ... [T]here is a serious issue as to whether, pursuant to a purposive interpretation of the Act, and in the interests of promoting collective bargaining consistent with constitutional values of freedom of association and the Preamble to the Act, dependent personal workers who provide services as "dependent" contractors, or even "non-self-dependent workers", should be treated as employees.

54. ... The problem with much of the foregoing analysis of "dependent contractors" is that it assumes an on-going employment relationship of "dependency" on one employer (*vide*: *Fownes Construction* and *Mackie Moving Systems, Corp supra*). However, as with much precarious employment in the so-called "new economy", workers with particular skills may be unable to gain full-time or even regular part-time work with a single employer needing her or his particular skills in a given industrial context. In some industries, serial, or even concurrent employment with a number of employers, may be the norm. Thus, while these workers are not really "self employed" or "independent contractors", they are not "self-dependent" either; rather, they are dependent on a number of employers in an industry. This may be a *wide-spread* phenomenon in the "new", or at least "current", economy, but it is not a *new* phenomenon. It has been the case for generations in the construction industry. While some craft persons or trade workers in construction may be fortunate enough to have long-term and perhaps full-time, or at least regular part-time, employment, many move from project to project not with the same, but rather a series, of different employers. These people can be "obvious" employees, or may be

dependent or non-self-dependent workers whose status requires analysis going beyond mere appearances in order to determine whether they are employees for the purpose of the *Act*. Despite "sporadic" employment, when they are working for a given employer, they may, according to the particular circumstances of the case, be seen as employees of that employer for the purposes of the *Act*. Thus, "non-self-dependent" personal workers can be "employees" where the facts of a particular case so warrant.

55. This brings us to one of the Respondent's important arguments. Egg Films says that Mr. Mitchell, or any of the other technicians employed on March 5, 2011, gain only a small portion of their income from Egg Films, and may or may not have a continuing association with Egg Films in the future. It is indeed clear that Mr. Mitchell gains far more of his income as a Genny Op from firms other than Egg Films. However, it is also clear that he is dependent on firms in the film and/or commercial production industry for his livelihood. He is not self-dependent, but is rather dependent on an industry, of which Egg Films is a part, which regularly hired "Genny Ops". He is hired to do his work in the industry because of his personal skills and ability, but he is not dependent solely on Egg Films. This, of course, is exactly the same situation as skilled trades persons in the construction industry. The recognized union representing a particular trade in the construction industry can obtain certification for the relevant employees working for an employer in the construction industry if it represents the majority of the employees working on site in that trade on the day when it applies. This is the case under current Part II of the *Act* regulating construction, and was so under the previous Act which lacked such specific rules for construction or other such occupational categories. The point is that such workers who perform technical skills personally are and were deemed employees for the purposes of certification even if they were not expected to necessarily have a long-term "dependency" on the relevant employer. This is because it is assumed that the employer will wish in the relatively near future to hire or re-hire the same or similar persons with technical skills that the union represents. This is not new or radical. It is a situation which existed for decades before the current *Act*. Interpreting the *Act* in a manner which enables non-self-dependent workers in a particular industry to exercise their freedom of association and successfully achieve certification of their union, provided they represent a majority of the employer's employees in a recognized occupation in the industry, is consistent with Charter values and the purposes of the *Act* as stated in its new preamble and the Board's traditional jurisprudence (e.g. *Parkland, Empire Theatres,* etc.).

56. ... The Board thus concludes that for the purposes of the *Act*, the commercial and corporate advertising industry is a part of the film industry for purposes of the *Act*, even if it may not be so for other commercial purposes. Such an approach helps to structure the exercise of the employees' s.13 rights of freedom of association as union members in this industry, in a manner which accords with constitutional values and the purposes of the *Act*.

57. What, however, of concerns with economic efficiency, as opposed to the associational welfare of motion picture technicians, in this context? What is the potential impact of interpreting the word "employee" as including "non-self-dependent" workers on the economic efficiency of the employer as a player in the "film" industry as broadly defined above? There are a number of dimensions emerging from the evidence: wage

costs, hiring the best people, development of the workforce, and the question of benefits. Mr. Hachey's evidence was that he is competing on the basis of quality with firms in Toronto. To get the best people he said he generally pays above union rates. This, then, is unlikely to be problematic if the Applicant Union adheres to its practice of seeing wages in the collective agreement as being a minimum floor, and allowing the employer and individual technicians to bargain for rates above them. In argument, counsel for the Respondent adverted to the spectre of the Applicant Union "imposing" a "closed shop" or "hiring hall" arrangement on the Respondent, which would limit its freedom of choice in locating the best technicians available. Setting aside the Applicant Union's possibly self-serving claim that its members are the best people available, counsel for the Union observes correctly that security clauses are a matter of negotiation and, by implication, that the Union might agree for example to a union shop as opposed to a closed shop, leaving broader scope for the Respondent to select the technicians it prefers. On the matter of deployment of the workforce, Mr. Hachey is clearly concerned about flexibility and efficient multi-tasking on the set, to which Mr. Mahoney replied that the Applicant Union accepts the "principle of assistance". Finally, on the question of benefits, the Respondent's current arrangements, based on an assumption that it engages "independent contractors", avoids the burden of having to establish employer sponsored pension or other benefits plans. However, the I.A.T.S.E. contract with Furniture Productions indicates that the union carries the benefits plans in this industry, and that the employer may be expected to make contributions to them. This, of course, helps to maintain a stable and flexible workforce by having the security of benefits plans, without employers having to organize them. This seems an efficient model, familiar as well in the construction industry. All of the foregoing matters are questions for collective bargaining and beyond the regulatory jurisdiction of the Board in the context of an application for certification. However, if economic efficiency is a purposive concern in the interpretation of who is an employee for the purposes of the *Act*, the admittedly sparse evidence available on this matter does not point to ruinous consequences for the Respondent of a finding that the motion picture technician members of the Applicant Union are non-self-dependent workers and thus employees for s.2(1)(k).

58. To leave the issue of "independence" and return to the question of "control" or "subordination", the Board wished to briefly outline its findings in relation to the evidence. The Board finds that the Respondent's contentions that the technicians working on March 5 were self-directing, independent contractors exercising the skills autonomously does not comport with the evidence. Mr. Hachey, in consultation with the client, set out the vision for the project and hired the Line Producer and Director of Photography to see that this vision was made a reality in artistic terms. The technicians, while using their various skills to run their particular equipment, did so under the close direction of the Line Producer and Director of Photography, who brought the project to creative fruition. The Respondent's staff negotiated rates of pay with each of the technical workers, and it is of no moment that they were paid daily rates rather than an hourly wage. The fact that some paid HST and some did not is of interest, but not determinative, of whether they are employees for the purposes of the *Act*; rather, it relates to their own financial circumstances and the laws relating to taxation. In this arrangement, there was

no "profit or loss" calculation by the technicians, in that none made particularly onerous outlays for equipment and supplies in relation to this particular shoot. The Respondent paid many of the technicians for a previous shoot date which had been cancelled. This was a simple compensation for the loss of wages for the shoot for which day they had been hired which was cancelled. The employees did not bear that risk of loss. Egg Films rented the generator truck, for example, and gave the wardrobe designer a budget for costumes. The sound person did bring his own board, but was this not something which he apparently bought for this project and which appeared to have impacted on the wage he negotiated. The technicians on this shoot were paid for their time in the exercise of their skills in their work performance or for their opportunity costs in that regard. They were not making a profit or loss on an investment in a commercial sense. Mr. Hachey agreed that he could, and would, dismiss or send home technicians who were not performing satisfactorily. None of the people on the shoot, with the possible exception of the Line Producer in relation to the Director of Photography, hired other technicians to do the work for them in a business sense. All were hired for their own personal skills and performed them. As to the question of an "intention" to create an employer/employee relationship, the views of the parties are certainly relevant, but not determinative. Clearly, Mr. Hachey believed he was hiring independent contractors, while Mr. Mitchell viewed himself as a temporary or casual employee of Egg Films in the film industry. It is also to be noted that the local IATSE film contract with Furniture Productions contract asserts that the Union considers the category "employee" to include "dependent contractors".

59. On the foregoing assessment of the evidence, the Board concludes that the Applicant Union is correct that the "motion picture technicians" employed by Egg Films on March 5, 2011 were employees within the meaning of the *Act* and were not independent contractors. On March 5 the technicians had agreed to become integral part of the shoot directed and produced by the Respondent, and agreed to perform their work for the day under the supervision of Egg Films. While it was not a long term period of "subordination" to the Respondent's project needs, they were fully integrated into the shoot activities and integrated into the vision of the project which was not in their hands or of their making. While the technicians are far from entirely dependent on Egg Films for all their employment income, they are part of a workforce in the local film industry which is generally available for personal hire by production companies like the Respondent. The film technicians are not self-dependent, but dependent on the industry of which both they and Egg Films are a part. In accordance with the short hand phrase often used by labour boards when describing a purposive approach to the interpretation of the *Act*, it makes "good labour relations sense" to characterize those film technicians as employees in the Nova Scotia film industry.

* * * * *

If B hires C to do certain work, and C then hires D and E to do some of that work, can C still be considered an employee of B for the purposes of collective bargaining legislation? According to the British Columbia Labour Relations Board, the answer may be yes. In *Re Fownes Construction Co*, [1974] 1 CLRBR 510, 512–13 (BCLRB), that board said:

What is to be done with owner-operators who own more than one truck and thus employ other drivers to operate them? A person who owns quite a few trucks, whose main concern is renting the trucks with a driver, and who does not regularly drive a truck himself would not come within the scope of the "dependent contractor" provision because he does not "perform work or services" in a manner analogous to an employee. Another person with several trucks may drive one of these trucks regularly, but because of the total character of his business, should not be considered to be "dependent." However, we do not believe that an individual who owns perhaps two trucks, and thus employs a driver to operate one of them, is necessarily removed from the category of "dependent contractor." There is nothing illogical about finding that an individual is, at one and the same time, both an employer and an employee and it can also be true that an individual is both an employer and a dependent contractor. That always turns on a judgment about the facts of the particular case.

The more difficult question is whether an individual, having been found to be a dependent contractor, should appropriately be included in the same bargaining unit as his employee. On the surface, that would seem to produce the kind of conflict of interest which the Code tries to prevent by such provisions as the managerial exclusion from the definition of "employee." However, we are now inclined to the view that this is largely a hypothetical concern in the real world of the construction industry. The opposing problem, which we have already mentioned in the earlier decision, is the owner-operator with two or three trucks becoming a major bone of contention in negotiations between the Teamsters and [the Construction Labour Relations Association] if he must be excluded from the unit. Counsel for Fownes, after arguing that all employers should be excluded, said that "if it is of any comfort, it may be a safe assumption that owner drivers in this category would receive essentially the same treatment as those outside the category." In view of the history of this problem (as reflected in a case such as *Therien v. Teamsters*, [1960] S.C.R. 265) we are not so confident in that assumption. For this reason, we are not prepared at this stage to lay down any rule excluding all owner-operators who are also employers from the scope of the bargaining unit. Should there be challenges to the inclusion of any particular individual in the voting constituency ... we shall deal with such cases in all of their concrete detail.

Different jurisdictions take different approaches to the appropriate bargaining structure for dependent contractors. Where there is an existing bargaining unit of other employees, the British Columbia *Labour Relations Code*, RSBC 1996, c 244, s 28(1)(b), requires the Labour Board to "determine whether inclusion of the dependent contractors in the existing unit would be more appropriate for collective bargaining and, if so, require that an application be made to vary the certification." On the other hand, the Ontario *Labour Relations Act*, s 9(5), says:

> A bargaining unit consisting solely of dependent contractors shall be deemed by the Board to be a unit of employees appropriate for collective bargaining but the Board may include dependent contractors in a bargaining unit with other employees if the Board is satisfied that a majority of the dependent contractors wish to be included in the bargaining unit.

The British Columbia provision tends to bring together dependent contractors and other employees in a single bargaining unit, whereas the Ontario provision favours a more fragmented structure. This may help to explain the different approaches to whether a dependent contractor who is also an employer falls within the legislation. Including dependent contractors with other employees for collective bargaining purposes may eliminate any economic advantage to the employer of continuing the dependent contractor arrangement, while separate bargaining units may have the opposite effect. As firms increasingly contract out many of their core functions, this difference in approach becomes more significant.

In the federal jurisdiction, the Canada Industrial Relations Board has ruled that trucking owner-operators who employ drivers, and also drive themselves full-time for a trucking company employer and derive all of their revenue from this employer, are "dependent contractors" under the *Canada Labour Code, RSC 1985, c L-2*, and that both they and their drivers are "employees": *Re Mackie Moving Systems Corp*, [2002] CIRB No 156.

4:220   Near-Employees

Independent contractor and dependent contractor relationships are by no means the only ones in which services are provided outside the traditional employment relationship. Student nurses, medical residents and interns, articling law students, prison inmates, and participants in training programs and government-funded job creation programs may all supply services in return for some form of remuneration. Do they have access to collective bargaining? The answer appears to depend on how closely the particular relationship resembles traditional employment. In one case, student nurses assigned to a hospital for training were found not to be employees of the hospital. In another case, inmates working for a commercial abattoir on the premises of a correctional centre were considered to be employees of the abattoir.

Consider the case of individuals who perform services under "workfare" programs (called "community participation activities" in Ontario) as a condition of receiving welfare benefits. Ontario has specific legislative provisions which state that the Ontario *Labour Relations Act*, "does not apply with respect to participation in a community participation activity," and which go on to prohibit anyone engaged in such an activity from being covered by collective bargaining or from joining a trade union within the meaning of that Act. Those provisions were originally enacted by the provocatively named *Prevention of Unionization Act (Ontario Works), 1998*, SO 1998, c 17, and are found in the *Ontario Works Act, 1997*, SO 1997, c 25, Schedule A, section 73(1). The International Labour Organization Committee on Freedom of Association has urged the Ontario government to amend them, but to no avail: *330th Report of Committee on Freedom of Association*, UNILOOR, 286th Sess, UN Doc GB.286/11 (2003) 6 at paras 35–37.

4:300   EXCLUDED EMPLOYEES

As noted earlier, not every type of employee is given access to collective bargaining under general labour relations legislation. The statutory exclusions vary considerably from jurisdiction to jurisdiction. For example, the Ontario *Labour Relations Act* has a relatively long list of wholly or partially excluded groups: civil servants, firefighters, police officers, domestic workers, agricultural workers, and members of certain professions. Each of those groups is covered by general collective bargaining statutes in one or more of the other jurisdictions across the country: see Bernard Adell, Michel Grant, & Allen Ponak, *Strikes and Lockouts in Essential Services* (Kingston: Queen's IR Press, 2001) ch 2.

These divergences call attention to the politics of inclusion, and raise the question whether there are rational grounds for drawing the line at any particular point. They raise the question whether exclusion from legislation protecting and enabling collective bargaining interferes with the right to bargain collectively recognized as an aspect of freedom of association under the *Canadian Charter of Rights and Freedoms*, and if so, whether such interference can reasonably be justified under section 1 of the *Charter*. In recent years, this question has been dealt with in an important and controversial line of jurisprudence in the Supreme Court of Canada and other Canadian courts. That jurisprudence will be dealt with at some length in Chapter 12.

4:310 Professionals

Some Canadian jurisdictions still exclude certain groups of professional employees, such as physicians, lawyers, dentists, and architects, from the scope of collective bargaining legislation. These exclusions are now the exceptions to a general trend that has seen professional employees enthusiastically embrace collective bargaining. Nurses, engineers, teachers, and university professors have led this trend, and have had considerable success in advancing their economic and professional interests through collective action. This success raises the question whether collective bargaining is becoming the preserve of employees who already enjoy a privileged economic position, and whether it increases rather than decreases the income gap between the primary and secondary labour markets, to the further disadvantage of employees at the bottom of the economic ladder.

4:320 Public Employees

Collective bargaining in Canada has its roots in the private sector and did not spread throughout the public sector until legislative amendments encouraged it to do so from the late 1960s on. Until that time, collective bargaining legislation usually covered employees in the broader public sector, such as hospital and municipal workers, but not those employed directly by government. In many Canadian jurisdictions, civil servants were implicitly excluded from collective bargaining through the application of the canon of statutory interpretation which says that the Crown will be bound by a statute only if the statute so provides by explicit language.

Today, the rate of unionization in the public sector in Canada far exceeds that in the private sector. In most Canadian jurisdictions today, civil servants (core government employees) are covered by special public sector collective bargaining statutes, which vary considerably across the country but generally put more restrictions than private sector labour relations statutes on the subject matter of collective bargaining and on the right to strike. Employees who are not civil servants but who work in the broader public sector (for example, in hospitals, municipalities, and universities) may be covered by general collective bargaining legislation but are sometimes placed under special regimes, such as Ontario's *Hospital Labour Disputes Arbitration Act*, RSO 1990, c H.14. For a review of the collective regimes for public sector employees, see Bernard Adell, Michel Grant, & Allen Ponak, *Strikes and Lockouts in Essential Services* (Kingston: Queen's IR Press, 2001) ch 2.

It should be noted that some of the specialized public sector bargaining statutes across the country have excluded certain categories of employees from collective bargaining rights under those statutes. The validity of some of these exclusions are being challenged as a result of the constitutionalization of the right to collective bargaining in *Health Services and Support — Facilities Subsector Bargaining Assn v British Columbia*, 2007 SCC 27 [*Health Services*], dealt with in Chapter 12. In Nova Scotia, for example, part-time seasonal workers such as summer parks attendants, who may have had long-standing annual employment relationships with governments, have only recently been brought under the civil service collective bargaining regime by virtue of the long-shadow being cast by the *Health Services* case.

4:330 Managerial Employees

North American labour relations policy assumes an adversarial relationship between management and union, or at least an arm's-length relationship, with a view to avoiding conflicts of interest. Trade unions seek to exclude management personnel from interfering in their internal affairs, and employers seek assurance that the people responsible for management policies will not be deflected from their duty to the employer by loyalty to "the other side."

Accordingly, labour relations statutes have traditionally tried to draw a clear line between those who are "employees" and those who exercise "managerial functions": see, for example, the Ontario *Labour Relations Act* s 1(3)(b). "Employees" may bargain collectively under the statute, but managers may not. However, this dichotomy is easier to state than it is to apply. The line between manager and employee is not always clear, and it may vary with the approach taken by the particular labour board. Consider the following examples.

The first case provides some explanation for the exclusion:

Re Burnaby (District) and CUPE, Local 23, [1974] 1 CLRBR 1 (BCLRB)

Weiler, P., Chair

[8] The explanation for this management exemption is not hard to find. The point of the statute is to foster collective bargaining between employers and unions. True bargaining requires an arm's length relationship between the two sides, each of which is organized in a manner which will best achieve its interests. For the more efficient operation of the enterprise, the employer establishes a hierarchy in which some people at the top have the authority to direct the efforts of those nearer the bottom. To achieve countervailing power to that of the employer, employees organize themselves into unions in which the bargaining power of all is shared and exercised in the way the majority directs. Somewhere in between these competing groups are those in management—on the one hand an employee equally dependent on the enterprise for his livelihood, but on the other hand wielding substantial power over the working life of those employees under him. The British Columbia Legislature, following the path of all other labour legislation in North America, has decided that in the tug of these two competing forces, management must be assigned to the side of the employer.

[9] The rationale for that decision is obvious as far as the employer is concerned. It wants to have the undivided loyalty of its senior people who are responsible for seeing that the work gets done and the terms of the collective agreement are adhered to. Their decisions can have important effects on the economic lives of employees, e.g. individuals who may be disciplined for "cause" or passed over for promotion on the grounds of their "ability". The employer does not want management's identification with its interests diluted by participation in the activities of the employees' union.

[10] More subtly, but equally as important, the exclusion of management from bargaining units is designed for the protection of employee organizations as well. An historic and still current problem in securing effective representation for employees in the face of employer power is the effort of some employers to sponsor and dominate weak and dependent unions. The logical agent for the effort is management personnel. One way this happens is if members of management use their authority in the work place to interfere with the choice of a representative by their employees. However, the same result could happen quite innocently. A great many members of management are promoted from the ranks of employees. Those with the talents and seniority for that promotion are also the very people who will likely rise in union ranks as well. In the absence of legal controls, the leadership of a union could all be drawn from the senior management with whom they are supposed to be bargaining. If an arm's length relationship between employer and union is to be preserved for the benefit of the employees, the law has directed that a person must leave the bargaining unit when he is promoted to a position where he exercises management functions over it.

* * * * *

The following case engages in balancing the right to access collective bargaining against concern for conflicts of interest and loyalty to the employer.

Captains and Chiefs Association v Algoma Central Marine, 2010 CIRB 531

Elizabeth MacPherson, Chairperson:

I—BACKGROUND

[1] Algoma Central Corporation (ACC) owns and operates Canadian-flagged ships on the Great Lakes and the East Coast of Canada. Domestically, it has two operations: a tanker fleet operated by Algoma Tankers Limited (ATL) and a dry-bulk fleet that operates on the St. Lawrence Seaway and the Great Lakes. The commercial and operational aspects of the dry-bulk fleet are the responsibility of Seaway Marine Transport (SMT), pursuant to a bare-boat charter with ACC. However, the shipboard workforce on the bulkers, including the captains and chief engineers, are employed by Algoma.

[2] On May 1, 2009, the Board received an application for certification from the CCA pursuant to section 24 of the *Canada Labour Code (Part I—Industrial Relations)* (the *Code*), seeking the right to represent some 63 marine captains and chief engineers employed by Algoma....

[4] The issue for the Board to determine was whether captains and chief engineers fall within the definition of "employee" and are subject to the *Code*, or whether they

perform management functions and/or are employed in a confidential capacity in matters relating to industrial relations, such that they should be excluded from collective bargaining under the *Code*....

II—THE LAW

[5] Section 3 of the *Code* defines an "employee" as follows:

> "employee" means any person employed by an employer and includes a dependent contractor and a private constable, *but does not include a person who performs management functions or is employed in a confidential capacity in matters relating to industrial relations.* (emphasis added)

[6] Section 8 of the *Code* provides:

> 8.(1) Every employee is free to join the trade union of their choice and to participate in its lawful activities.
>
> (2) Every employer is free to join the employers' organization of their choice and to participate in its lawful activities.

[7] Section 27 of the *Code* provides:

> ...
>
> 27(5) *Where a trade union applies for certification as the bargaining agent for a unit comprised of or including employees whose duties include the supervision of other employees, the Board may, subject to subsection (2), determine that the unit proposed in the application is appropriate for collective bargaining.*
>
> ...
>
> (emphasis added)

[8] The rationale for the exclusion of managerial personnel from the right to collective bargaining that applies to all other employees was explained by the predecessor to this Board, the Canada Labour Relations Board (CLRB) in *Bank of Nova Scotia (Port Dover Branch)* (1977), 21 di 439 (CLRB no. 91) (application for judicial review dismissed in *Bank of Nova Scotia v. Canada (Labour Relations Board)*, [1978] 2 F.C. 807 (Fed. C.A.)), as follows:

> The basis of the exclusion of certain "management" persons from the coverage of collective bargaining is the avoidance of conflicts of interest for those persons between loyalties with the employer and the union. This avoidance of conflicts protects both the interests of the employer and the union. The conflict is pronounced when one person has authority over the employment conditions of fellow employees. It is most pronounced when the authority extends to the continuance of the employment relationship and related matters (e.g., the authority to dismiss or discipline fellow employees.) It is for this reason that certain persons are denied collective bargaining rights granted to other employees. The *Code* is clear that the mere supervision of fellow employees does not satisfy the rationale for exclusion from employee status under Part V [now Part I] (see section 125(4) [now section 27(5)])....
>
> (pages 457–458)

[9] As has been pointed out on a number of occasions, the *Code* does not contain a definition of "management functions." In its review of the *Bank of Nova Scotia* case, *supra*, the Federal Court of Appeal stated at page 813:

> ... the concept of 'management functions' must be interpreted and applied according to the circumstances of each case and, except in very extreme cases, I am inclined to the view that its precise ambit is a question of fact or opinion for the Board rather than a question of law ...

[10] Unlike some provincial labour relations boards, the CLRB and subsequently the CIRB have interpreted the managerial exclusion narrowly. The Board's approach was explained in *Cominco Ltd. (1980)*, 40 di 75 (CLRB no 240). After a lengthy review of the commitments that the Government of Canada has made to freedom of association, including that contained in the Preamble to the *Code*, the Board went on to say:

> In this context it is no longer apposite to view the conflict of interest rationale for the managerial exclusion in terms of sworn oaths of membership in unions and unswerving loyalty to the brotherhood of membership. These terms are clearly outdated. The potential conflict of interest to be considered is one between employment responsibilities and the union as an instrument for collective bargaining in a climate where there is legal protection for the individual in his relationship to the union both as bargaining agent and organization. *To say because a person is the sole supervisor present at a time or place creates a conflict because he must be the "management presence" is to think of conflicting loyalties in an outdated framework. Many employees in innumerable circumstances act alone and perform responsible tasks. The fact they also engage in collective bargaining has no impact on their loyalty to their employer or dedication to their job. Supervision by its nature has always required persons to act as the final on-the-site authority.*
>
> The fact that employees influence corporate policy or commit an enterprise to expenditures is equally not grounds for finding a conflict. These are common characteristics of the functions of professionals. They have been given collective bargaining rights. They are also common characteristics of the functions of specialists generally, whether tradesmen, technicians or other groups of employees.
>
> Similarly, *the fact a person is a supervisor and as such directs the work of others, corrects and reprimands where necessary, allocates work among men and equipment, evaluates or assesses new and longstanding employees, authorizes overtime when necessary, calls in manpower when needed, trains others, receives training to supervise, selects persons for advancement, authorizes repairs, can halt production when problems arise, schedules holidays and vacations, verifies time worked, authorizes shift changes for individuals, and requisitions supplies when needed does not create the conflict or potential conflict that disentitles him to the freedom to associate.* The loyalty and integrity of such a person is not altered by union membership or representation.

(page 90, emphasis added)

[11] In *Cominco Ltd.*, *supra*, the CLRB also remarked on the difference between it and other labour boards in the approach to the determination of management functions:

> While at least one provincial Board found masters of vessels not to be employees (*British Columbia Ferry Corporation* [1979] 1 Can LRBR 116 (BCLRB), in the federal jurisdiction,

masters of vessels have traditionally been represented by a trade union. As a second example, the weighted value ascribed to the ability to effectively recommend by the Ontario Board (*McIntyre Porcupine Mines Limited* [1975] 2 Can LRBR 234 at pp 241-2, OLRB) is not shared by this Board (see *Vancouver Wharves Ltd.*, supra, and *British Columbia Telephone Company*, 20 di 239; [1976] 1 Can LRBR 273; and 76 CLLC ¶16,015). But under Part V [now Part I] of the *Canada Labour Code*, the assessment made by the Board in 1974 stands today tested by time and the experience with several certifications issued by the Board:

> "There is no dispute, the Board believes, with the recognition that the Canadian Parliament, together with the Provincial Legislatures is committed to the fundamental policy that collective bargaining must be facilitated and enhanced for as many people as possible. Collective bargaining rights are not a privilege, not a concession, not a favour, they are a basic right which will not be withdrawn from any employee unless there are very serious reasons." (*Vancouver Wharves Ltd.*, supra, pp 52–3; p 167; and pp 966–7).

(pages 92–93)

III—THE FACTS

...

[15] While the captain is the most senior Algoma employee on board the vessel, he/she reports to a ship manager employed by SMT. Reporting to the captain are the chief engineer, the deck officers (1st, 2nd and 3rd mates) and the galley staff. The able seamen and ordinary seamen report to the mate who is on duty at any given time.

...

A—Captains/Masters

[18] The *Canada Shipping Act, 2001*, S.C. 2001, c. 26 (the *Canada Shipping Act*), defines a "master" as the person in command and charge of a vessel and assigns significant responsibilities to the person fulfilling that role (see sections 2, 82–86 and 107 of that statute). While it may be accurate to say that, at one time, the captain of a vessel was master of all he surveyed and that his word was law on board the ship, the evidence revealed that a number of developments over the years have significantly reduced the scope of a captain's decision-making power and influence. These developments include technological changes such as the availability of cellular telephones that make instant communication with shore-based management possible; increased regulation of the marine industry by government; organizational structures that have resulted in greater centralization of decision-making; and the unionization of subordinate personnel with the consequent negotiation of collective agreements establishing common terms and conditions of employment and grievance/arbitration rights. As counsel for the employer observed, the days in which a captain could impose discipline by forcing a sailor to "walk the plank" are long gone.

[19] There is no doubt that captains still have significant responsibilities. The vessels they command are worth millions of dollars, as are the cargoes carried by those vessels. The captain is responsible for all aspects of a ship's operation. Various statutes

and regulations recognize the master as the responsible authority on board ship for a number of regulatory purposes ...

[20] A master has ongoing, front-line responsibility for the safety of the crew and the protection of the environment, the vessel and its cargo. On a practical level, he/she has the necessary authority and obligation to make on-the-spot decisions with respect to safety and pollution prevention. In view of their responsibilities, masters do not have any set or standard hours of work, as they are responsible for their assigned vessel 24 hours per day, 7 days per week. Masters work a 60 day rotation and live on board the vessel during their rotation. Each vessel has a permanent captain and a relief captain (relief captains are assigned to cover 2 vessels and replace the permanent captain during the latter's time off). Masters are paid a flat rate based on 185 days of work per navigation season and no record of their hours of work is kept for payroll purposes.

[21] As noted above, captains report to an SMT Operations Manager on shore with respect to operational and technical matters. They interface with the Traffic Group or other charterers on commercial matters. Limits on the authority of masters have been established by written policies and procedures adopted by SMT. Masters are required to comply with and enforce the employer's policies and procedures and to follow the provisions of the collective agreements that apply to the vessel's officers, engineers and unlicensed crew. Although, in the past, the ship's master had an individual employment relationship with each seaman on his vessel, entered into when they signed a document known as the "Articles of Agreement," this practice is no longer in place at Algoma.

...

IV—ANALYSIS AND DECISION

[26] Individuals can be denied the right to collective bargaining under the *Code* on one of two grounds: if they perform management functions or if they are employed in a confidential capacity in matters relating to industrial relations. The *Code* expressly envisions that supervisory employees have the right to organize and bargain collectively (see section 27(5) of the *Code*). With respect to certification applications involving supervisory employees, the Board must determine, on a case by case basis, whether it is appropriate to include these employees in the same unit as those whom they supervise, or in a separate bargaining unit of their own.

[27] In the years since the *Cominco Ltd., supra*, decision was issued, Parliament has enacted the *Canadian Charter of Rights and Freedoms* and the Supreme Court of Canada has affirmed that the Charter right to freedom of association, section 2(d), protects the right to collective bargaining (*Health Services & Support-Facilities Subsector Bargaining Assn. v. British Columbia*, 2007 SCC 27, [2007] 2 S.C.R. 391 (S.C.C.)). These developments reinforce the Board's view that any decision that has the effect of removing collective bargaining rights from individual citizens, including a decision that they exercise management functions and thus are not employees entitled to the benefits and protections of the *Code*, is one that must not be taken lightly.

[28] In light of this constitutional protection, the Board begins with the presumption that individuals who wish to exercise the right to organize and bargain collectively are

entitled to such rights. The burden of proving that these individuals exercise management functions or are employed in a confidential capacity in matters related to industrial relations, and that they should therefore be excluded from collective bargaining, rests on the party arguing for such exclusion.

[29] Before excluding anyone from the right to organize and bargain collectively on the basis of either of these grounds, the Board must be persuaded that the individuals who are proposed for exclusion actually exercise the functions attributed to their position. With respect to alleged "management responsibilities," this requires evidence that the incumbent exercises functions that are more than supervisory and has real (*de facto*) independent decision-making authority. With respect to alleged "confidential" functions, regular on-going responsibilities related to labour relations matters must be demonstrated.

A—Captains/Masters

1—Management functions
[30] The traditional indicia of management responsibility are authority over the employment conditions of other employees, particularly the authority to hire, fire, promote and discipline employees.

a) Hiring
[31] The evidence before the Board was that, prior to the start of the shipping season, Algoma's H.R. department, in co-ordination with SMT, determines the assignment of crews to the various ships that will be in service during that season. The Vice-President of H.R. described this process as putting together a jigsaw puzzle. While captains may express a preference for certain crew members, there is no guarantee that their preferences will be honoured in the assignment of crews at the commencement of the season.

[32] If a vacancy arises during the season, the captain contacts H.R. to obtain a replacement. At some time in the past, captains were able to contact the appropriate union hiring hall directly to obtain replacement crew members, but this is no longer the case: orders must now be placed through the H.R. department.

[33] The H.R. department does the initial screening of those individuals referred for employment, as they wish to avoid dispatching someone to the vessel who does not have the appropriate qualifications. At that point, the Crew Co-ordinator creates a "crewing assignment" in the enterprise system, which sends the information to the "Shipboard Crewing Interface," an on-board computerized human resources management system. When the crew member reports to the vessel, the captain must verify that the individual in fact possesses the qualifications that he/she is reputed to have and reviews their discharge book, medical fitness card and union dispatch slip. The individual's paperwork will be checked by the captain or the 1st mate, and once this is complete, the captain will enter the appropriate information in the Shipboard Crewing Interface. At this point, the individual is considered "signed on" to the ship.

[34] According to the evidence provided to the Board, it appears that the captain has very little discretion to refuse a crewperson who has been referred by the hiring hall or the H.R. department. The parties agree that an individual can be refused by the captain

if he/she does not have the required credentials, as noted above, or if they report to the ship in an unfit condition (e.g., under the influence of alcohol or drugs).

[35] On the basis of the evidence provided to it, as described above, the Board concludes that the captain has no independent authority to hire employees, given the constraints imposed by company policies and practices and the collective agreements.

b) Promotion

[36] Captains are requested by the H.R. department to complete evaluations of crew members, to make recommendations regarding promotions and to assist in identifying likely candidates for advancement. However, the H.R. department is not bound to act on the captain's recommendations; examples were given to the Board of individuals who were promoted against a captain's recommendation. It is evident that H.R. considers a number of factors and the evaluations of more than one captain in reaching its decisions.

[37] Although the captains feel that their recommendations for promotion are not considered by the H.R. department, the evidence before the Board demonstrated that the H.R. department does follow up on such recommendations. In several cases cited to the Board, H.R. discovered that the individual recommended for promotion either did not have the requisite certification or did not want the promotion. It appears that the captains' perception that they are not listened to is due to H.R.'s failure to report back to them as to the reason why the promotion could not be implemented.

[38] While H.R. makes the final decisions with respect to permanent promotions, captains do have the ability to temporarily promote or demote an employee, for example during an emergency or for the balance of a voyage. However, on the basis of the evidence provided, the Board concludes that, although captains have some influence over the process, they do not have the authority to make independent decisions regarding the advancement of employees.

c) Discipline

[39] The employer has entered into a Letter of Understanding with the unions representing the deck officers, marine engineers and seamen, which establishes a common Disciplinary Code.... This Code is characterized as a "guide" to supervisors on board and sets out the penalty for various infractions. A copy is kept on board each vessel and is annexed to the collective agreements. The Code states that "Discretion, good judgement and consistency should be applied in all instances."

[40] The Code sets out offences that warrant immediate dismissal, those which warrant suspension, and those which require written warnings. Repeated commission of offences in the latter two categories may also result in dismissal. The parties agree that the captain is not the only person aboard who can issue warning letters for misconduct; such letters can also be issued by the 1st mate, the chief engineer or the 2nd engineer and examples were provided of instances in which this has happened.

[41] Captains clearly have the authority to impose discipline, be it a warning letter, suspension or removal from the ship. However, an employee who has been disciplined has the right to file a grievance under the collective agreement applicable to them. The evidence before the Board is that such grievances are dealt with by the H.R. department,

which has the power to rescind the discipline without consulting with the captain, for example when it negotiates with the union to settle a grievance.

[42] The Board finds that captains do have authority to impose discipline and regularly exercise discretion and judgement as to the severity of the punishment to be imposed. However, their decisions can and have been overridden by the H.R. department in the case of grievances. In this regard, the captain's role in discipline is no greater than that of any first line supervisor, whose decisions are subject to review and countermand by senior authorities in the company.

d) Firing

[43] The evidence before the Board was that the captain can have an employee removed from the ship for a number of reasons, which are set out in the Disciplinary Code. These include: possession, consumption or the bringing aboard of illegal drugs; acts of violence; refusal to obey lawful commands or to comply with the safety standards, rules and regulations contained in the *Canada Shipping Act* or the Company's safety regulations; theft; sabotage; absence from duty endangering the safety of the ship and/or its crew; gross incompetence or gross negligence endangering the safety of the ship and/or its crew; smuggling and desertion.

[44] The Disciplinary Code indicates that its application requires good judgement and discretion. The evidence before the Board was that captains do indeed exercise discretion, including giving a crew member a "second chance" after an offense that would otherwise have resulted in dismissal.

[45] There was significant discussion between the parties as to whether removal from the ship constituted dismissal from employment with Algoma. The Board is satisfied that dismissal from a ship in most cases does constitute termination of the individual's employment with Algoma. Although the evidence of the captains was that they had seen or heard of instances where an individual who was dismissed from a particular vessel ended up working on another Algoma ship, the nature of the industry is such that there are a limited number of persons qualified for employment. As a result, a person dismissed from one company vessel may well be assigned to another ship in the same fleet as a result of an arbitration award, the settlement of a grievance or the passage of time.

[46] The Board is satisfied that Captains do have full authority to dismiss an employee for cause and that dismissal from the ship may also constitute dismissal from the company. However, this authority is exercised within well defined limits and thus is no greater than that of any first line supervisor.

e) Supervision

[47] The captain is responsible for the safe operation of the vessel and must ensure that all laws and company policies are followed. SMT has created a comprehensive "Safety Management Manual" (the manual) containing all of the company's policies and all crew are required to follow them. The manual sets out procedures for every situation, including the notifications that must be given in the event of certain events (for example, an oil spill or other environmental hazard). Where the safety of the ship is concerned, the captain has discretion to deviate from a planned route (for example, because of weather conditions), but must advise shore based personnel of any delays.

[48] The duties of each position on a vessel are prescribed in the manual and there are standard day work orders, so that each crewperson knows what their assigned tasks are at all times. It is thus not necessary for the captain to plan or assign the work, as each crew member knows what their routine duties are and will bring any problems to the captain's attention. Overtime is rare and is discouraged by SMT policy; in most cases, there is no requirement for the captain to authorize overtime, as the tasks are standard and it is understood when overtime is required to complete them. The captain requires the permission of the shore-based ship manager to incur any expenditures, thus any special projects (projects outside of immediate operational needs) would require authorization of the SMT manager.

[49] The Board was informed that, in the present day, much of the captain's work consists of administrative tasks (for example, the preparation of customs documentation and reports). While there must be a licensed officer on the bridge at all times when the ship is underway, the deck officers (mates) perform this function on the "4 hours on/8 hours off" watch system that is traditional in the marine industry. Supervision of the crew is delegated to the mate on watch at any given time. The captain is not required to be in the wheelhouse when the vessel is in open water, but is "on-call" 24/7 and must be on the bridge when the vessel is in confined waters (e.g., in a canal or approaching a lock), as complex manoeuvring is his responsibility.

[50] The captain and the chief engineer meet each morning to discuss any concerns regarding the operation of the vessel and then the captain and the 1st mate review the activities anticipated for the remainder of the day. The captain and the 1st mate must work closely, but it is the 1st mate who has most of the dealings with the crew.

[51] Vacation scheduling is prescribed by the various collective agreements, thus leaving the captain little discretion with respect to scheduling. Although the captain signs off on the vacation schedule once it has been prepared, his approval of the vacation requests made by incumbents of certain positions (e.g., head cook, electrician and head tunnelman) can be overridden by the H.R. department based on the availability of relief (replacement) personnel. Nevertheless, vacation requests, other than for Engine Room crew, must first be submitted to the captain and cannot be sent directly to H.R. Although crew can go on shore leave if they are not scheduled to work when a vessel is in port, the captain may deny shore leave if departure is delayed due to weather conditions or mechanical issues.

[52] The captain clearly has all of the supervisory authority that is required to ensure that there is compliance with statutory requirements, company policies and procedures and the collective agreements. However, the nature of this authority is supervisory rather than managerial as it is exercised within established and commonly understood parameters.

f) Policy Development

[53] The captain's authority to supervise the crew and direct the operation of the vessel does not extend to independently developing his/her own policies regarding the manner in which the ship will be run. Operational policies are developed and prescribed by SMT. The evidence indicated that SMT is selective in its choice of the captains and chief engineers whom it consults in the development of these policies; there is no general mechanism in place that requires the captains' participation in policy development.

[54] A regular "management meeting" is held on board ship monthly, involving the captain, the chief engineer, the 1st mate and the 2nd engineer. The agenda for the meeting is prescribed by SMT. Despite the name given to this meeting, the matters discussed by the participants relate primarily to the ship's operations and the identification of any issues that may affect those operations, rather than the management of the company as a whole.

[55] SMT convenes various meetings with the captains and chief engineers during the off-season (i.e., when the St. Lawrence Seaway is closed, normally from the end of December to the end of March). For example, in 2009, the "Captains & Chief Engineers Committee" met with senior management in January. This Committee is composed of 4 captains and 4 chief engineers, although other captains or chief engineers are permitted to attend the meetings with management. A "senior management" meeting was held in February, to which all captains and chief engineers were invited. The agendas provided to the Board suggest that these meetings are primarily informational in nature; the participants are provided with information regarding the company's operations, safety issues, changes in regulations and various company initiatives. The views of the captains and chief engineers are sought on the various topics put forward by management and they are provided with an opportunity to ask questions. Although senior management may make decisions based on the information and discussions that take place at these meetings, there was no evidence to indicate that the meetings involving the captains and chief engineers are intended to be "decision making" meetings.

g) *Other Duties*

[56] Captains have no independent authority to initiate expenditures; they must seek the approval of the ship manager for any unbudgeted expenses. They also do not play a significant role in the development of the annual budget for their vessel. While the captain may submit a "wish list," approval of funding for specific items and the budget preparation and approval process is performed entirely by the shore based personnel at SMT and Algoma.

[57] Once the budget has been established, captains are expected to control crew costs, which primarily involves controlling overtime and food costs. With respect to the latter, SMT has provided a 21 day meal plan that it characterizes as a guideline. The Board was informed that the SMT ship manager would intervene in the event that it appeared a captain was authorizing excessive amounts of overtime or incurring above-average food costs.

[58] Each senior officer is responsible for training those junior to him/her, and the captains are ultimately responsible for ensuring that training is carried out in a satisfactory manner. Captains are personally responsible for making sure that deck officers receive the requisite training in navigating in confined waters. Captains are expected to provide an assessment of the skill, judgement and attitude of subordinate officers through periodic appraisals and Instructor Observation forms.

[59] As the senior person on board, the captain is called upon to make numerous decisions that are not subject to review during emergency situations. However, even in an emergency, there are a number of other authorities, both within SMT and government regulatory agencies, who must be notified. Captains are responsible for ensuring that numerous inspections, certificates and documents are properly completed and up to date.

[60] The captain is responsible for ensuring the safe loading and unloading of cargo from the vessel, and decides how much of each type of cargo the vessel can carry. The Board was informed that the Great Lakes are considered particularly challenging from a navigation perspective, given the amount of confined water. Thus a greater skill set is required for navigating in the Great Lakes than in deep sea. Monthly safety meetings involving all crew are mandatory; these are organized by the 3rd mate but the captain is responsible for ensuring that they take place.

[61] The captain has ultimate responsibility for the navigation of the ship, although the plotting of courses is delegated to the 2nd mate. Within the Great Lakes, the routes are generally standardized, although the captain does have the ability to deviate if necessary (for example, bad weather). Changes to the route must be reported to shore.

h) Conclusion Regarding Management Functions

[62] The employer argues that masters perform many managerial functions that derive from both company policy and statutes and regulations. It argues that the master is the undisputed authority on board the vessel and is one of only two management representatives on board each vessel. It argues that, if masters are not managers then for all practical purposes the employer has no management representatives on the ship, a circumstance that they argue is unimaginable.

[63] The employer also argues that masters and chief engineers are an integral part of Algoma's management team, and are motivated to save the company money and do what is in the best interest of the company. It contends that the statutory and regulatory regime applicable to the maritime industry gives managerial power and responsibility to masters, and that it flies in the face of common sense and Parliamentary intent to hold that they are not managers. The employer argues that including masters and chief engineers in a bargaining unit would deprive Algoma's vessels of their management representatives.

[64] In the Board's view, a master's position on board a vessel is to some extent analogous to the positions of airline pilots and locomotive engineers and conductors. These individuals all have command and control of extremely valuable equipment and responsibility for the safety of the crew and cargo. All of these professions are subject to extremely detailed regulation, both by the government and by their respective employers. Airline pilots, locomotive engineers and conductors are all categories of employment that have been highly unionized for many years and no evidence was led to suggest that being unionized has had any negative effect on their ability to carry out their responsibilities in a professional manner. The Board recognizes that there are some differences between ship's captains and pilots and locomotive engineers; for example, Algoma's captains are obliged to remain on board the vessel 24 hours per day for a period of 60 days until they are relieved, and their pay is based on a work year of 185 days. However, in the Board's view, these differences are not so significant as to affect its analysis of the nature of a master's responsibilities.

[65] Furthermore, the Board cannot find any merit in the employer's contention that the unionization of masters and chief engineers would create an untenable situation from a management perspective. As noted in *Cominco, supra*, in the federal jurisdiction, masters of vessels have traditionally been represented by a trade union. Accordingly, the Board

cannot give credence to the employer's predictions of a managerial vacuum on board its vessels should masters and chief engineers be granted collective bargaining rights.

[66] The Board has been unable to find the degree of independence vested in Algoma's captains that the British Columbia Labour Relations Board found existed with respect to the captains employed by the British Columbia Ferry Corporation (*British Columbia Ferry Corporation, supra*). While Algoma's captains undoubtedly have supervisory responsibilities and make numerous important decisions each day, the evidence presented did not persuade the Board that captains are possessed of and exercise the level of independent decision-making authority necessary to find that they are managers within the meaning of the *Code*....

B—Chief Engineers

1—Management Functions

...

h) Conclusion Regarding Management Functions
[91] While chief engineers undoubtedly have supervisory responsibilities and make decisions affecting the care of the ship's equipment, the evidence presented did not persuade the Board that they are possessed of and exercise the level of independent decision-making authority necessary to find that they are managers within the meaning of the *Code*....

D—The Appropriate Bargaining Unit

...

[96] Having found that the applicant represents a majority of the employees in the bargaining unit that the Board had found to be appropriate, the Board therefore issued a certification order to the Captains and Chiefs Association, pursuant to section 28 of the *Code*.

* * * * *

As noted above in *Algoma Central Marine*, there has been considerable disagreement over the scope of the managerial exclusion. Economists, management theorists, and some unionists have advocated for more participation by workers in management decisions generally, and especially in those that affect workers directly. A number of European countries have had considerable experience with both works councils of various sorts and employee directors. A few North American companies have also experimented with employee directors. If workers participate in management, the strict dichotomy between management and labour begins to break down, and this creates problems in the application of our current statutory arrangements.

Universities have been a testing ground for the permissible limits of employee participation in management. In Canada, labour boards regard university professors as employees under labour relations statutes, despite their role in the academic governance of the university—see *Mount Allison University (Re)*, [1982] 3 CLRBR 284. The US Supreme Court took a different view in *National Labor Relations Board v Yeshiva University*, 100 S Ct 856 (1980).

It held that professors in private universities exercised managerial functions because they sat on university bodies that decided on appointments and promotions, awarded tenure, and formulated curricula and teaching methods—matters that would be prerogatives of management in a private business. Not surprisingly, this holding did not meet with universal approval among academics.

* * * * *

In the following case, the Ontario Labour Relations Board concludes that certain supervisors are managerial employees. Consider whether the Canada Board in *Algoma Central Marine*, above, and the Ontario Board are placing different weights on the various principles informing the determination of whether a worker is a managerial employee.

Children's Aid Society of Ottawa-Carleton, [2001] OLRD No 1234

> [OPSEU applied to represent a unit of forty-three supervisory social workers who had traditionally been excluded from a CUPE bargaining unit containing non-supervisory social workers, counsellors, and support staff. These supervisors had nevertheless informally bargained with the employer, but now wanted to be represented by a formally certified union.]
>
> PAMELA A. CHAPMAN, Vice-Chair:
>
> [...]
>
> [¶ 10] Supervisors are the front-line of management and supervise employees in the bargaining unit directly. They in turn report to either Assistant Directors, who are also alleged by CUPE to be appropriate for inclusion in the proposed bargaining unit, or more often to Directors, who are agreed to be excluded. Directors in turn report either to the Executive Director, who heads the organization, or to the Director of Service who reports to the Executive Director.
>
> [¶ 11] The job description for supervisors emphasizes their role in supervising the daily work of employees in their area. Flynn testified about the criteria used by the agency when selecting persons for hire into these positions, which emphasizes their ability to manage employees rather than just clinical expertise. Staff who become supervisors take a three day course in "Interactive Management" which trains them in a particular framework for managing performance and discipline issues in the workplace.
>
> [¶ 12] Supervisors are required to do "supervisions" with employees at particular intervals, in order to review their caseload and the progress made. Many of these standards are imposed by the Ministry of Community and Social Services, which sets very particular requirements in terms of record-keeping, contact with clients, etc.
>
> [¶ 13] Flynn described the role the supervisors play in staffing the agency. When a vacancy occurs, the supervisor in the area affected completes a form making a request for staff, which is signed off by the Director and Executive Director.... Interview panels are generally made up of three people: two supervisors and a representative from human resources.... Both Dill and Laurin [supervisors who the employer claims are managerial employees] have been involved in such interviews, and concurred with the notion that decisions are made on a consensus basis....

[¶ 15] Human resources personnel sometimes "screen" prospective candidates without supervisors present when there is some urgency, ... but the "receiving" supervisor is consulted before a final decision is made.

[¶ 16] Gerry Laurin, as a supervisor in the Parent Model Homes programme, has had some additional involvement in the hiring of casual employees with only limited involvement by human resources personnel. Most recently, he and another supervisor interviewed a number of potential candidates for casual positions and provided the names and interview questionnaires together with his recommendations to human resources, so that they could complete reference checks and proceed with offers of employment. To avoid delay the supervisors did some of the reference checks as well.

[¶ 17] Laurin also testified that supervisors have in the past had greater independence in the hiring of new staff, with human resources playing only a "supportive" function, but that more recently a different management style has led to greater involvement by professional human resources staff.

[¶ 18] Sometimes permanent positions are filled internally without the use of a formal interview process. Recently 29 contract positions were "converted" to permanent positions, and the candidates were assessed by an evaluation method which did not include an interview, but instead gave significant weight to performance reviews completed by supervisors....

[¶ 19] When an employee earns a permanent position, they are placed on a six-month probationary period. Just prior to the end of that period, human resources forwards to the employee's supervisor a form asking for their recommendation, which is completed and signed by the supervisor and then approved by the Director and by human resources.

[¶ 20] Supervisors carry out the agency's performance review program, completing performance reviews on bargaining unit staff annually.... Supervisors review the goals set in the previous round, provide comments as to an employee's success in reaching those goals, and assign a rating. The performance review is then forwarded to the director for signature. Supervisors are permitted to meet with employees to discuss their appraisals before sending them to the Director. Flynn testified that sometimes she is asked by supervisors for advice in framing particular comments, but that there is no requirement that supervisors involve her, and that she does not provide substantive input in that she has no opportunity to assess employees. Dill testified about challenges she faced in managing a particular employee who had had difficulties meeting the reporting requirements. She discussed possible approaches with Val Flynn, and with her Director, at various points during her management of this employee. When it came time to complete the performance review, however, she did not consult with them and simply assigned a poor rating based on the problems she had observed and had discussed with the employee. If she was planning on "failing" someone, though, she would consult with human resources "because of the union."

[¶ 21] Supervisors also carry out the attendance review program, maintaining a calendar which monitors employee attendance.

[¶ 22] Discipline issues usually arise as part of the overall program for the management of employee performance, and are handled by supervisors using the principles of "interactive management" in which they are trained. This involves counselling employees ... before taking any steps which might appear to constitute conventional discipline....

[¶ 23] Katharine Dill testified that she would never impose formal discipline on an employee without consulting with her Director, and likely human resources as well, although she has issued verbal reprimands and warnings. She did not attribute this approach to any particular prohibition imposed upon her, ... but rather stated that she felt that with a union in place she would want to ensure that she was "going in the right direction"....

[¶ 26] Supervisors schedule employees, assign them cases, and approve overtime and vacation leave within the scope of the agency's policies respecting such leaves.

[¶ 27] Personnel files are maintained by the human resources department but supervisors have access to the files of employees under, or about to be under, their supervision....

[¶ 30] Flynn also described the involvement of several supervisors in decision-making about a proposed down-sizing on a panel which assessed the skills and abilities of displaced employees and matched them with available jobs.... When layoffs did occur in 1995 and 1996 Laurin sat on another committee with another supervisor and a human resources representative charged with the task of implementing the layoffs in accordance with the collective agreement, which required an assessment of the skills, abilities and experience of affected employees in order to reach decisions about layoff and/or redeployment

[¶ 31] Flynn was involved in the grievance procedure as a supervisor when an employee grieved a disciplinary letter which she had issued, attending meetings at the early stages. Dill testified that she had never attended at grievance meetings but assumed she would if a grievance matter arose....

[¶ 32] This application raises again, for the first time in several years, the question of whether or not units made up of persons who supervise employees will be permitted to bargain collectively in Ontario.

[¶ 33] The legal framework for the resolution of this issue is not in dispute. Section 1(3)(b) of the Act provides as follows:

> 1.(3) Subject to section 97, for the purposes of this Act, no person shall be deemed to be an employee,
> (b) who, in the opinion of the Board, exercises managerial functions or is employed in a confidential capacity in matters relating to labour relations.

[¶ 34] The question before me is therefore: do the supervisors at the CAS exercise managerial functions within the meaning of section 1(3)(b)?

[¶ 35] The parties placed before me several authorities dealing with the purpose of the managerial exclusion in the Act, which was the starting point for each of their arguments in the present case. The following excerpt from *The Corporation of the City of Thunder Bay* ... is perhaps the most often-cited discussion of the statutory goals represented by section 1(3)(b):

> 2. Section 1(3)(b) excludes from collective bargaining persons who in the opinion of the Board exercise managerial functions. The purpose of the section is to ensure that persons who are within a bargaining unit do not find themselves faced with a conflict of interest as between their responsibilities and obligations as managerial personnel, and their responsibilities as trade union members or employees in the bargaining unit. Collective bargaining, by its very nature, requires an arm's length relationship between the "two

sides" whose interests and objectives are often divergent. Section 1(3)(b) ensures that neither the trade union, nor its members will have "divided loyalties"....

[¶ 38] In the present case, the employer has the onus to establish that the supervisors perform managerial functions within the meaning of the Act, given that it is seeking to prevent these persons from obtaining the protections of the Act through collective bargaining. At the same time, though, the status quo, over many years of a collective bargaining relationship between OPSEU and the CAS, has been to treat the supervisors as excluded employees exercising managerial functions, which should be taken into account in considering the demand of the union that collective bargaining now be extended to the first layer of supervisors outside of the existing OPSEU unit....

[¶ 40] ... *Ford Motor Company of Canada Limited* ... reiterated ... the purposes served by the managerial exclusion "in order to protect the institutional interests of both employers and unions".... The Board reviewed many of the examples of "conflicting interests on the shop floor" which have traditionally driven the exclusion of managers from the bargaining units they supervise, but also considered whether the purposes of the managerial exclusion are engaged by a grouping of supervisors into a separate unit:

> 14. In addition to the obvious examples of conflicting interests on the shop floor, there are broader, systemic concerns which require the exclusion of "management" from participation in trade union activities. For if management personnel were treated like ordinary employees, and were free to organize or promote particular trade unions, the freedom of these *other workers* could be undermined and the independence of *their trade unions* could be jeopardized. And this problem may not be resolved merely, as here, by segregating the "supervisors" into their own bargaining unit.
>
> 15. ... if "foremen" had the same rights as other employees, what would prevent them, acting in their own interest, from trying to persuade those other workers to join, support or discard a particular union? ... Section 1(3)(b) not only defines who is *excluded* from the collective bargaining process; it also identifies who is *prevented* from using "managerial" authority to interfere with the collective bargaining rights of others.
>
> 16. This is not an academic concern either. What distinguishes "management" from ordinary "employees" is the power that managers exercise over the economic security of their fellow workers—a power which, in the Board's experience, "foremen" have sometimes used to interfere with the right of those workers to engage in collective bargaining through a trade union of *their choice*.... That is why section 1(3)(b) is but one of a constellation of statutory provisions designed to segregate "employees" from "management," and ensure that the employees and their unions are entirely independent of managerial influence.
>
> 17. ... Collective bargaining might well be a useful tool for managerial employees, just as it is for ordinary workers. However, the Legislature has determined that the process is better served if those obliged to act on behalf of the employer are completely segregated from the union institutions and the collective bargaining mechanism that employees use to promote their interests....

[¶ 43] The Board has acknowledged in numerous cases that the assessment of whether an individual performs "managerial functions" is an exercise in characterization, with factors pointing in one direction being weighed against those suggesting an opposite result. These decisions are also of course essentially fact-driven, as the particular nuances of authority and discretion vary in each case. To further complicate matters, the scope of a supervisor's ostensible authority is often affected by the unique experience, skills and disposition of a particular incumbent, meaning that two different people apparently occupying the same position may appear to fall on opposite sides of the managerial divide....

[¶ 44] ... As was said in *The Corporation of the City of Thunder Bay*, "the important question is the extent to which [first line managerial employees] make decisions which affect the economic lives of their fellow employees thereby raising a potential conflict of interest with them".... Thus, the parties generally agreed that the Board ought to focus on what have been described as the real indicia of economic power over employees: the power to hire, fire, promote, demote, grant wage increases or discipline employees....

[¶ 48] ... it is obvious that the size of an employer's operations will change the type of role played by supervisors and must be taken into account in trying to determine whether they exercise real managerial authority. This is particularly the case where the employer has a large unionized workforce. The Board put it this way in *E.B. Eddy* ... ;

> 34. In a [large] workplace ..., it is ... not surprising that the classic managerial duties have been divided up in a hierarchical way, with the lower level managers playing more of a monitoring and reporting role and significant decisions being made at a higher level. In a small workplace, all managerial tasks may be performed by a single individual; but once large numbers of employees are involved, and therefore more supervisors, it makes little sense for each and every supervisor to be engaged in all of those same tasks. Instead, the pool of managers is likely to be divided in much the way it has been at *E.B. Eddy*, with senior managers, together with human resources professionals who have no direct supervisory responsibilities, setting policies for the management of employees, monitoring the front-line supervisors, and setting working terms and conditions through the bargaining process. The management role would not be complete, however, if these tasks were to be separated from those carried out by the foremen, as the higher level of management is generally not engaged in the direct supervision of employees and would therefore have no effective way to ensure the implementation of its policies, or to obtain information critical to the monitoring of that implementation. The pool of managers must be considered as an organism, which cannot function without all of its parts.

[¶ 49] Also significant is the nature of the managerial or administrative structure adopted in the workplace. The B.C. Board in *Cowichan* contrasted hierarchical structures with many layers of managerial responsibility to the more flattened management structures which are increasingly common. In the present case we see a perfect example of the unique managerial strategies which are often adopted in settings where large numbers of professional employees are employed at both bargaining unit and managerial levels....

[¶ 50] Such professional environments sometimes create forms of supervision which appear at first instance to be managerial but in fact involve the provision of only technical or professional advice to less skilled employees, and the Board must be cautious in examining this form of supervision. On the other hand, that is not to say ... that professional or technical employees may not also exercise managerial functions. In fact, real managerial authority may be present but difficult to discern in these settings, where collegial modes of decision-making and performance management through counselling may be the norm....

[¶ 51] In the present case we are dealing with just such a large, unionized, and professional environment, and its effect on the nature of the managerial authority exercised by the supervisors is clear. The duties and responsibilities of the persons in dispute are structured in many important respects by the requirements of the collective agreement, and discretion is limited by the requirement for consistency throughout a large organization, and for compliance with the contract, which leads to the adoption of various policies and procedures for the management of staff. As well, the Ministry of Community and Social Services establishes various standards which impact on what supervisors require of employees under their direction. There are professional human resources staff who coordinate the implementation of personnel policies and advise supervisors on particular supervisory challenges. And the style of management consciously adopted by the organization is a consensual and non-confrontational one, described as "interactive management," which means that there are fewer obvious examples of the traditional mechanisms of front-line management.

[¶ 52] Does this context mean that the front-line managers, here the supervisors, do not exercise real managerial authority? In the present case, I have concluded that the supervisors about whom I heard evidence do exercise managerial functions within the meaning of the Act, despite the constraints upon their roles described above.

[¶ 53] First, the supervisors play an important role in both the hiring of casual and contract staff, and the promotion of staff to permanent positions. Supervisors regularly sit on interview panels, and I am satisfied that they have meaningful input into the selection of staff, particularly as to their ability to meet the needs of the area which requires staff, rather than their general suitability for employment with the agency. This contribution is also apparent in the role that some supervisors have played in developing questions or criteria for the interview protocols....

[¶ 54] Is the input of supervisors into hiring and promotion decisions to be discounted given that the final decisions are made by consensus, and therefore no one person has the ultimate authority? In discussing the concept of the "effective power of recommendation" the Board has emphasized that when assessing the role of a front-line manager whose decision making is not entirely independent of senior management "it is necessary to show that his recommendations are really effective, so that, in practice, and to a substantial degree, he becomes the effective decision maker in respect of matters impacting upon his fellow employees".... I am satisfied, though, that the supervisors play as important a role in the selection of the people who work under their direction as do any other managers in the organization. It is not the case, for example, that their recommendations are regularly overruled by human resources, Directors or by the Executive Director; the opposite seems true. Surely that level of involvement must meet the test of effective recommendation in a setting like this.

[¶ 55] Supervisors have essentially complete control over the formal performance review program, which has had a critical impact on the ability of contract staff to obtain permanent positions, and on the retention of probationary staff....

[¶ 56] As noted in many earlier cases, involvement in the discipline and discharge of employees is perhaps the most critical indicia of true managerial authority. It is not really in dispute that in the present case the supervisors are the "eyes and ears" of the employer; they are the only members of management who really monitor the work and conduct of employees and they are therefore the ones who are in a position to identify and express management concerns....

[¶ 57] When conduct does not improve, or very serious conduct occurs in the first instance, there is no doubt that the supervisors who testified, and likely any supervisor, would consult with their Director and/or a human resources professional about the appropriate course of action....

[¶ 59] When we consider the disciplinary style encouraged at the CAS, the entirely appropriate reliance upon human resources professionals to provide consistency of approach and professional expertise, and the participatory form of decision-making, it is not surprising that the supervisors have had only limited involvement in imposing formal and/or serious discipline on the employees they direct....

[¶ 60] Having read the decisions in *Ford* and *E.B. Eddy* closely, I am satisfied that the supervisors in the present case, despite the less traditional disciplinary style adopted at the CAS, play at least as significant a role in monitoring employee performance and initiating disciplinary responses where required as did the foremen considered in those decisions. As well, in the present case the supervisors play a significant role in performance appraisal, which has an impact on the promotion and retention of employees, and in hiring; the foremen in *Ford* and in *E.B. Eddy* had no role in hiring, and there was no formal system of performance evaluations. Also important is the fact that, as in the two earlier cases, the supervisors in the present case are engaged full-time in supervisory work and do virtually no bargaining unit work. This, more than anything else, differentiates them from the category of "team leader" as that concept has been developed in the caselaw....

[¶ 67] This leads us to the issue of the ratio of supervisors to bargaining unit employees.... The Board has regularly considered the number of front-line managers as compared to the number of employees they supervise, and also the number of higher level managers involved in the direction of the supervisors in issue, in examining the claim that the front-line is indispensable to the management structure as a whole....

[¶ 68] I have concluded that the supervisors about whom evidence was heard play a role in hiring, discipline and performance appraisal such that the mischief to which section 1(3)(b) is directed would likely be engaged should they be found to be employees within the meaning of the Act. Ought that conclusion to be modified by the fact that, by the terms of the present application for certification, they would be in a different bargaining unit than the employees they supervise, represented by a different union?

[¶ 69] The supervisors considered in the *Ford* and *E.B. Eddy* cases were found not to be employees within the meaning of the Act despite the proposal that they be placed in a separate bargaining unit. In British Columbia, the labour relations statute makes specific reference to the possibility of placing supervisors in separate units, and the labour board discusses the significance of that statutory tool in determining employee status in the *Cowichan* case:

117. ... the placement of an individual into a separate bargaining unit does not address the issue of a potential conflict of interest in dealing with the issue of undivided loyalty or commitment. As stated, the issue is one of dual loyalties between the employer and a bargaining unit.... [T]he potential conflict of interest ... is not the one which is internal to the bargaining unit (which will be dealt with under appropriateness); but rather, is directed at maintaining an arm's length relationship between supervisors and any unionized bargaining unit.

[¶ 70] Similarly, this Board in *Ford* emphasized the employer's reasonable expectation that its supervisors will be undivided in their loyalty, concluding that their duties and responsibilities assign to them "a role which inevitably puts them in the employer's camp, pitted against the employees who report to them"....

[¶ 72] The presumption that there is an inherent conflict between the interests of employers and any ability to bargain collectively by those to whom it delegates some of its authority, even in a separate bargaining unit, has been challenged by some commentators who bemoan the focus on conflict and adversity of interests which underlies our present system, but it remains a central tenet of the statute under which this application for certification has been brought. As such, I must conclude that the two employees about whom evidence was heard, Katharine Dill and Gerry Laurin, are not employees within the meaning of the Act and as such must be denied access to collective bargaining as structured and facilitated by the Act.

[¶ 73] This ruling of course does not restrict the ability of supervisors at the CAS to deal collectively with their employer as they have done in the past, through a staff association, with or without the assistance of CUPE or some other union.

Canadian labour law has recognized for some time that the managerial exclusion should be tailored to the reality of greater employee participation in the workplace. In *Ontario Public Service Employees Union v Family Services of Hamilton-Wentworth Inc*, [1980] 2 CLRBR 76, the Ontario Labour Relations Board considered whether employee-directors of a social service agency exercised the kind of independent decision-making authority which would bring them within that exclusion. The board concluded that because of the nature of the particular employer, the composition of its workforce, and its history of employee involvement, the employee-directors should not be considered managers. Quebec's *Labour Code* excludes from the definition of employee "a director or officer of a corporation, unless a person acts as such with regard to his employer after having been designated by the employees or a certified association." This provision clearly contemplates that employee-directors are not to be excluded from collective bargaining.

The *Canadian Charter of Rights and Freedoms*, with its guarantee of freedom of association, provides another basis for questioning the managerial exclusion. Recent Supreme Court of Canada decisions (see Chapter 12) have determined that freedom of association provides protection for collective bargaining and the right to strike. In a pair of decisions made by the Quebec Administrative Labour Tribunal, *Association professionnelle des cadres de premier niveau d'Hydro-Québec (APCPNHQ) et Hydro-Québec*, 2016 QCTAT 6871 and *Association des cadres de la Société des casinos du Québec et Société des casinos du Québec Inc*, 2016 QCTAT 6870, the exclusion of managerial workers from the definition of "employee" in the *Code* was found to be in violation of the *Charter*. The tribunal, in finding that the exclusion could not be justified pursuant to section 1 of the *Charter*, noted that while the goals of maintaining managerial loyalty and avoiding conflict of interest were important, the exclusion of managerial employees from collective bargaining was not rationally connected to this purpose. It held that there was no foundation for the view that unionization necessarily harms labour relations, and indeed, that respect for freedom of association may even ensure rather than compromise the existence of and the stability of good relations. The employers in the two cases are seeking judicial review.

4:340 Confidential Employees

Except in Quebec, Canadian collective bargaining legislation excludes employees who are employed in a confidential capacity in matters relating to labour relations. This exclusion, like that of managers, is based on the possibility of a conflict of interest, but labour boards are reluctant to apply it as rigorously. The following excerpt considered whether a payroll officer and financial officer employed at a school board should be excluded as a confidential employee.

Grande Prairie Roman Catholic Separate School District No 28 v CEP, Local Union No 328 (2011), 198 CLRBR (2d) 106 (Alta LRB)

> 1 The Grande Prairie Roman Catholic Separate School District No. 28 (the "Employer" or the "District") applies to have Ginette Batt and Sandy Krahn excluded from a bargaining unit represented by the Communications, Energy and Paperworkers Union of Canada, Local Union No. 328 (the "Union") ... The Employer says the individuals in question perform managerial functions and are employed in a confidential capacity in matters relating to labour relations....
>
> 4 Sandy Krahn and Ginette Batt work in the Employer's central office in Grande Prairie. Ms. Krahn is the Payroll Officer and Ms. Batt is the District Based Finance Officer. Both report to the Employer's Associate Superintendent of Business Operations, Bryan Turner. Mr. Turner reports to the Employer's Superintendant, Karl Gemann. Ed Buckle is the Deputy Superintendent....
>
> 22 The *Code's* definition of "employee" excludes persons who are "... employed in a confidential capacity in matters relating to labour relations." As noted in *Canadian Union of Public Employees, Local 38* v. *City of Calgary and Stordy*, [2009] A.L.R.B.D. No. 53, [2009] Alta. L.R.B.R. LD-043 at para. 20:
>
>> The purpose of the confidentiality exclusion is based on similar considerations to those underlying the management exclusion. The intent is to ensure the employer can rely on the undivided loyalty of those persons entrusted with confidential labour relations information and decisions. In particular, it is meant to ensure the collective bargaining interests of the employer are not adversely affected by the disclosure of this confidential information.
>
> 23 The Board applies a three-fold test to determine whether exclusion is warranted:
>
> - Do the person's duties involve labour relations activities, information handling or strategy?
> - Is the involvement with this information on a regular basis as opposed to incidental or accidental? and

- Would disclosure of the information adversely affect the employer's interests in industrial relations? [See *Stordy, supra*, at para. 21 ...]

All three parts of the test must be satisfied to justify exclusion.

24 The cases speak of a distinction between confidential matters relating to labour relations and those relating to personnel or other information. Many employees have duties that involve the handling of confidential information. But, to be excluded from the bargaining unit, the duties must be confidential in reference to labour relations: *Christenson v. County of Parkland and Central Alberta Association for Municipal & School Employees*, [1989] Alta. L.R.B.R. 155.

25 In *Canadian Association of Industrial, Mechanical and Allied Workers, Local No. 3 v. Transair et al.*, [1974] CLLC ¶16,111 at p. 911, the Canada Labour Relations Board explained:

> ... "in matters relating to industrial relations." means information relating to such matters as contract negotiations: for example, the persons that sit together to establish, on behalf of management, the range of salary increase that the bargaining team will be mandated to operate within at forthcoming negotiations; or to such matters as the proceedings before the Board like this one: for example, the persons that sit together and plan the strategy which the employer will use as well as the tactics used in the pursuance of its legitimate interests before a Labour Board; or to such matters as the disposition of grievances: for example the persons who plan or who know what compromise will be offered to a grievor. [Upheld: [1976] CLLC ¶14,024 (S.C.C.). [See also: *ATU, Local 569 v. City of Edmonton et al.*, [1990] Alta. L.R.B.R. 486.]

26 Neither individual is involved in matters relating to labour board proceedings or grievances. They do, however, have some connection to collective agreement negotiations. Each individual has provided information to the Employer for the purposes of bargaining.

27 Ms. Krahn prepares costing information for the Employer's bargaining team for both negotiations with the Union and the ATA. The information gathered relates to various options being considered by the Employer in terms of wages and benefits. The work begins prior to the start of bargaining. Ms. Krahn also assists the bargaining team during the course of bargaining by costing out proposals made by the Union and proposals being considered by the Employer in response. She is not involved in the decision-making process to determine what option the negotiating committee advances or agrees to. But, she knows what the Employer is considering before the Union does.

28 The assistance she provides extends beyond the mere gathering of information and number crunching. She has provided information to the bargaining committee regarding the pros and cons to the Employer of switching teaching assistants from being paid on an hourly to a monthly basis. She has also provided information regarding the impact to the Employer of changing the way vacation is calculated for employees in the CEP unit. The information she provides helps form the foundation for management's position in bargaining. She has done this kind of work in each round of bargaining since she started working for the Employer 12 years ago....

31 ... [T]he assistance Ms. Krahn provides before and during bargaining was neither accidental nor incidental. The reason Mr. Buckle speaks so freely around her is based

on the fact she provides critical support to the Employer before and during bargaining. She has had regular involvement in collective bargaining in the way described above for many years now in respect of the Union agreement. Ms. Krahn's knowledge of options being considered by the Employer during bargaining and before bargaining even starts makes her privy to collective bargaining strategies being considered by the Employer. We conclude she is employed in a confidential capacity in matters relating to labour relations and should be excluded from the unit.

32 Ms. Batt has not had the same involvement thus far during collective agreement negotiations. In large measure, that may be a result of her not having been in the position for long. It is also due to the fact the Employer did not seek her assistance during the last round of bargaining because it believed she was planning to become a Union steward. Since she started working in her position four years ago, she has answered two questions during bargaining. One request was made to Ms. Batt simply because the Ms. Krahn was away on the particular day in question.

33 It is Ms. Batt's involvement in the preparation and review of the Employer's budget that causes more concern. Ms. Batt assists in the creation of the District's budget by, among other things, preparing salary and benefit cost projections for support staff based on changes contemplated by the Employer. It is also a key part of Ms. Batt's duties to monitor the District's spending and report on the surpluses and shortfalls during monthly meetings with the Superintendent and Mr. Turner. At those meetings, she is integrally involved in making suggestions as to how the Employer might cut spending and spend surpluses. At the time of negotiations, she is well aware of what padding is available in the budget and is expected to provide advice on what the Employer can and cannot afford.

34 ... While it is true that the budget is made public, there are no specifics set out about the particular changes to wages and benefits contemplated by the Employer. The Union has a ballpark idea only, based on any change from the last budget. Conversely, Ms. Batt knows the specific wage and benefit changes contemplated in the budget. She is also intimately familiar with the Employer's financial circumstances at the time of negotiations. Her participation in the creation of the budget (including the confidential labour relations information forming the foundation for part of that budget) and her on-going monitoring of and support regarding the Employer's financial circumstances, place her within the confidential labour relations exception found under section 1(l) of the *Code*. She is, accordingly, excluded from the bargaining unit.

III. CONCLUSION

35 For the reasons set out above, the Employer's application under section 12(3) is allowed. Both Ginette Batt and Sandy Krahn are excluded from the bargaining unit on the basis that they are employed in a confidential capacity in matters relating to labour relations.

* * * * *

4:400 QUALIFIED TRADE UNIONS

4:410 The Union as an Organization

Section 3(1) of the *Canada Labour Code* defines a trade union as "any organization of employees, or any branch or local thereof, the purposes of which include the regulation of relations between employers and employees." Similar definitions are found in other statutes across Canada.

Although this definition does not specify that a union must have any particular constitutional structure, labour boards have held that an organization must meet certain requirements of form in order to be recognized as a trade union under labour relations legislation. It has never been entirely clear whether those requirements reflect a simple concern that unions should have a viable organizational framework, or a more ambitious and controversial concern that they should be democratic in their structure and functions.

Requiring employees to follow certain traditional procedures in setting up a union can constitute a trap for those who are unwary or inexperienced. For example, in early cases, the Ontario Labour Relations Board held that an association could not be considered a trade union if its officers were appointed before its constitution had been adopted. Today, labour boards appear to be insisting on only a minimum of formality, and to be concerned primarily with ensuring the existence of a viable organization that can function as a bargaining agent.

***Ontario Workers' Union v Humber River Regional Hospital* (2011), 195 CLRBR (2d) 286 (OLRB)**

> [The Ontario Workers' Union, newly formed, is applying to be certified. The incumbent union and the employer argue the applicant is not a trade union within the meaning of the Ontario *Labour Relations Act*. In particular, they claim that the organization had no officers because the organization's constitution did not provide for the election of founding officers and that the founding members were not employees.]
>
> 26 In our view, and subject to one caveat, the applicable principles for the determination of the issue before us were well summarized in *ABC Climate Control Systems Inc.*, [2009] OLRB Rep. Sep./Oct. 639:
>
>> 6. I find the following summary of the applicable law from *Canadian Labour Congress v. University of Toronto* [1999] OLRB Rep. July/August 742 useful:
>>
>>> 10. In applying the definition of "trade union", the Board's caselaw establishes that:
>>> 1) trade unions are, for the most part, unincorporated associations of individuals;
>>> 2) two or more such individuals must have agreed to be bound by the terms of an identifiable written agreement between them;
>>> 3) one of the purposes of the organization, usually expressed in the constitution, must include the regulation of relations between employees and employers;
>>> 4) the organization must be viable and therefore must have at least one officer, official or agent to act on its behalf.
>>>
>>> 11. The Board has also set out a "five-step" guideline for those wishing to set up a trade union. These steps are set out in Local 199, U.A.W. Building Corporation [1977] OLRB Rep. July 472, as follows:

1. a constitution should be drafted setting out, among other things, the purpose of the organization (which must include the regulation of labour relations) and the procedure for electing officers and calling meetings;
2. a constitution must be placed before a meeting of employees for approval;
3. the employees attending such a meeting should be admitted to membership;
4. the constitution should be adopted or ratified by the vote of said members;
5. officers should be elected pursuant to the constitution.

12. Difficulties, however, often arose where the steps were not followed precisely or were not followed in the right sequence. The Board therefore subsequently noted that the five steps originally laid out were meant to be facilitative rather than restrictive and that following these five steps was not the only manner in which a trade union could achieve status. For example, in Caterair Shadow Canada Limited [1994] OLRB Rep. April 365 para. [8], the Board stated:

> More generally, the Board is interested in the substantial, rather than technical, compliance with the procedural steps involved in the formation of a trade union, since the purpose of its inquiry is not so much in ensuring that the precise requirements of the constitution are followed rather than to ascertain that the organization seeking trade union status is a viable one for the purposes of carrying out its obligations under the Act.

...

28 The requirement that there be an identifiable set of rules by which the individuals have agreed to be bound arises from the fact that a trade union is "more than just an informal joining together of individuals", it is "a formal organization whose members have bound themselves together on the basis of specific terms for purposes that include the regulation of relations between employees and employers": *Kubota Metal Corporation* at paragraph 35 ... As stated by the Board in *Kubota Metal Corporation*, at paragraph 36: "it is of fundamental importance that a contractual relationship be created and maintained".

29 The need for a specific set of identifiable rules is reflected in the "first step": a constitution, or similar document, must be drafted. Further, the rules must be sufficiently clear that they are identifiable to the members, and to render the organization legally viable. In our view, however, in determining whether the document is sufficiently clear, the Board should avoid overly formalistic interpretations of the document before it. While mere intention to form a trade union is not sufficient, if the document manifests such an intention the question for the Board is whether the document can be interpreted in such a way as to give effect to that intention.

30 The process of a group of employees agreeing to be bound by the set of identifiable rules, or **as** it is sometimes put settling on the terms of that constitution and entering into the contractual relationships, is reflected in the "second step", "third step" and "fourth step": see *KUS Canada* at paragraph 64.

31 Those steps, however, are not the only means by which a group of employees can agree to be bound by a constitution and enter into the contractual relationships to which it gives rise. In *ABC Climate Control Systems*, the Board observed:

I can see no reason why a group of individuals seeking to form an unincorporated association cannot unanimously agree to bind themselves to an identifiable set of rules.

At issue in that case was the absence of a mechanism in the constitution for accepting individuals into membership. The principle, however, is one of basic contract law. At its simplest, a contract is an agreement to which all the parties have agreed to be bound. It follows that the parties to a contract can unanimously agree to waive, suspend or vary any of the provisions of the contract.

32 The "second step", "third step" and "fourth step" are simply a process, developed by the Board, which permits the Board to conclude that the necessary agreements have been reached. A meeting is called for the purpose of forming a trade union. A constitutional document meant to effect this purpose is placed before those in attendance. Some or all present will agree to the constitution, as they have amended it. In any event, it would not be surprising if only those who agree with the constitution, as amended, would then apply for and be admitted into membership. It is also common for membership applications to include an agreement to abide by the constitution. If so, upon acceptance all members will have agreed to abide by the constitution. Further, since, the members will generally be those who agreed to the document in the first place, it would not be surprising if all of them then ratified the document. Thus, while the Board does not require evidence that unanimity was achieved as these steps are followed, the process is designed to ensure that some identifiable group of employees has agreed to be bound by a constitution at one or more of the steps.

33 The requirement that the organization have at least one officer through which it can act speaks to the legal viability of the organization, and perhaps most importantly to its capacity to actually fulfill the statutorily required purpose of a trade union: "the regulation of relations between employers and employees". The organization must have the capacity to engage in activities like organizing, applying for certification, negotiation, approval and administration of collective agreements. While organizations can act only through individuals, it does not follow that actions of all individuals who are members are that of the organization. One or more individuals must be authorized to act for the organization. This is reflected in the "fifth step" that officers be elected in accordance with the constitution of the organization.

34 Observance of the election process set out in a constitution eliminates the need for unanimity with respect to who is authorized to act for the organization. The minority cannot complain about the authority of officers elected by a majority if all have agreed to be bound by a constitution which provides for this result. Equally, however, unanimity of all members eliminates the need to follow process. All members of the organization have simply agreed as to who the officers of that organization will be, regardless of written constitutional processes.

35 In this case, it is clear that the intention manifested in the Constitution is to create a trade union. It is correct, as argued by HRRH and SEIU, that the Constitution lacks a specific process for the election of the original officers of the organization and that the general process for the election of officers cannot apply because, among other things, the Constitutional requirements for quorum for the meeting were not met and none of Orbine,

Downes or Kucey met, or could have met, the Constitutional requirement for one year membership in the organization as of the time of its founding meeting. However, the fact of the matter is that Orbine, Downes and Kucey agreed to become members of the organization and then agreed that they would be the President, Vice-President/Secretary Treasurer and General Counsel respectively. As they were the only members of the organization, their agreements were unanimous agreements of all the members.

36 Indeed, it appears that the process which they followed may be precisely what the Constitution contemplated would happen. Article 4, Section 1 provides in part that:

> The officers of OWU shall be the President, Vice-President/Secretary Treasurer and General Counsel. The first three named officers shall constitute the Executive Board.

The lack of a process for the election of those officers may reflect the fact that the Constitution contemplated that the first officers would be unanimously agreed upon by the members of the organization. Certainly this appears to be consistent with what happened: Orbine, Downes and Kucey decided that the three of them would form a trade union and decided amongst themselves who the officers of that union would be. . . .

43 The remaining issue is whether the rules set out in the Constitution are sufficiently clear as to be identifiable to the members, and to render the organization legally viable.

44 It must be said that the Constitution is not a model of clarity. However, notwithstanding the fact that Article 4 appears to define the Executive Board as consisting of the three officers while Article 5 appears to define the Executive Board as consisting of the three officers "and four (4) additional Elected Executive Board members", as of the date of the application there were only the three original officers. There is no quorum specified for the Executive Board. The three officers, accordingly, were able to act as the Executive Board. Article 4, Section 1 gives the Executive Board the power to conduct "the day-to-day operations of the organization". Article 2, section 2 authorizes "all elected officers" of OWU to accept applications for membership. Thus, the OWU has an identifiable set of rules that render the organization legally viable for the purpose of the Act. Further, to the extent that the Constitution is otherwise deficient we note that Article 11, Section 1 (a) provides a mechanism for the amendment of the Constitution.

Disposition

45 For the foregoing reasons, we find that the applicant was a trade union within the meaning of the Act as of the date of filing of these applications.

*****

The statutory definitions of a trade union require that its objects include "the regulation of relations between employers and employees" (See *Canada Labour Code*, s 3(1)). In *Graham Cable TV/FM, Toronto v Cable Television Workers Association* (1986), 14 CLRBR (NS) 250, the federal board held that a particular association of employees was not a trade union within the meaning of the *Canada Labour Code*, because its true aim was not to regulate employer-employee relations, but merely to get the incumbent union out. In the alternative, the board found that there was enough employer influence to undermine the fitness of the association to represent the employees.

A more controversial question is whether union status will be reserved for organizations that are democratic in their structure and practices. The meaning of democracy in the context of internal union affairs, and the extent to which labour boards and courts will seek to enforce democratic governance within unions, will be adverted to in Chapter 11, Section 11:300. By and large, except for cases of discrimination on grounds prohibited by human rights legislation, labour boards have taken the approach that they do not have the authority to deny trade union status to an otherwise bona fide workers' organization for the reason that it fails to adhere to democratic forms and practices in its internal decision making.

Smith & Rhuland Ltd v Nova Scotia, [1953] 2 SCR 95, 53 CLLC para 15,057

RAND J.:

[1] This is an appeal from a judgment of the Supreme Court of Nova Scotia sitting *in banco* by which an order made by the Labour Relations Board of that province rejecting an application by the Industrial Union of Marine and Shipbuilding Workers of Canada, Local 18, for certification as the bargaining agent of employees in a collective unit was, on *certiorari*, set aside and a mandamus to the Board directed. The latter had found the unit to be appropriate for bargaining purposes and 'that the other 'conditions to certification had been met; but, on the ground that one Bell, the secretary-treasurer of the Union, who had organized the local body and 'as its acting secretary-treasurer had signed the application, was a communist and the dominating influence in the Union, refused the certificate. The court in appeal held the Board to have had, in the circumstances, no discretion to refuse, but that even if it had, the discretion had been improperly exercised.

. . .

[2] Before us, Mr. Robinette challenged both of these grounds. The first depends on the interpretation of the word "may" in s. 9(2)(b) of the *Trade Union Act* which reads: —

> If a vote of the employees in the unit has been taken under the direction of the Board and the Board is satisfied that not less than 60 per cent of such employees have voted and that a majority of such 60 per cent have selected the trade union to be bargaining agent on their behalf; the Board may certify the trade union as the bargaining agent of the employees in the unit.

[6] I agree, therefore, with Mr. Robinette's first contention that the word is to be interpreted as permissive and as connoting an area of discretion. The remaining question is whether the Board, in its rejection, acted within the limits of that discretion, in examining which I assume the findings made as to Bell's adherence to the doctrines of communism and the strategy and techniques by which they are propagated.

[7] The "domination" I take to mean not particularly or directly that of the local union. Bell was, by the constitution of the federated body, the provisional secretary-treasurer of every local union until it had elected its own officers, and in fact he had ceased to hold that office of the applicant before the hearing had taken place, although he did not know of it until afterwards. Nor is it to be related to the fact of his having been an or the leading actor in organizing the local: that was part of the duties of his office.

[8] The domination found was evidenced by Bell's forcefulness in the key position of general secretary-treasurer and organizer, by his acceptance of communistic teaching and by the fact that the party espousing those teaching demands of its votaries unremitting pressure, by deceit, treachery and revolution, to subvert democratic institutions and to establish dictatorship subservient to Soviet Russia. That is to say, the circumstance that an officer of a federated labour union holds to these doctrines is, per se, and apart from illegal acts or conduct, a ground upon which its local unions, so long as he remains an officer, can be denied the benefits of the *Trade Union Act*.

[9] No one can doubt the consequences of a successful propagation of such doctrines and the problem presented between toleration of those who hold them and restrictions that are repugnant to our political traditions is of a difficult nature. But there are certain facts which must be faced.

[10] There is no law in this country against holding such views nor of being a member of a group or party supporting them. This man is eligible for election or appointment to the highest political offices in the province: on what ground can it be said that the legislature of which he might be a member has empowered the Board, in effect, to exclude him from a labour union? or to exclude a labour union from the benefits of the statute because it avails itself, in legitimate activities, of his abilities? If it should be shown that the union is not intended to be an instrument of advantage and security to its members but one to destroy the very power from which it seeks privileges, a different situation is presented and one that was held to justify a revocation of the certificate by the Dominion Labour Board in *Branch Lines Limited v. Canadian Seamen's Union*.

[11] The statute deals with the rights and interests of citizens of the province generally, and, notwithstanding their private views on any subject, assumes them to be entitled to the freedoms of citizenship until it is shown that under the law they have forfeited them. It deals particularly with employees in and of that citizenry and gives to them certain benefits in joint action for their own interests. Admittedly nothing can be urged against the bona fides of the local union; it seeks the legitimate end of the welfare of those for whom it speaks. During 1951, at least two local units of this union were certified by the Board notwithstanding that Bell at the time held the same office and adhered to the same views as found against him. One local includes employees working in the Halifax shipyards. Hubley, the associate of Bell in the application to the Board, who is president of the federated body, has been found by the Department of Defence to be unobjectionable on security grounds and is the holder of a pass to the Dartmouth shipyards; and the federation is affiliated with the Canadian Congress of Labour.

[12] To treat that personal subjective taint as a ground for refusing certification is to evince a want of faith in the intelligence and loyalty of the membership of both the local and the federation. The dangers from the propagation of the communist dogmas lie essentially in the receptivity of the environment. The Canadian social order rests on the enlightened opinion and the reasonable satisfaction of the wants and desires of the people as a whole: but how can that state of things be advanced by the action of a local tribunal otherwise than on the footing of trust and confidence in those with whose interests the tribunal deals? Employees of every rank and description throughout the Dominion furnish the substance of the national life and the security of the state itself resides in their

solidarity as loyal subjects. To them, as to all citizens, we must look for the protection and defence of that security within the governmental structure, and in these days on them rests an immediate responsibility for keeping under scrutiny the motives and actions of their leaders. Those are the considerations that have shaped the legislative policy of this country to the present time and they underlie the statute before us.

[13] I am unable to agree, then, that the Board has been empowered to act upon the view that official association with an individual holding political views considered to be dangerous by the Board proscribes a labour organization. Regardless of the strength and character of the influence of such a person, there must be some evidence that, with the acquiescence of the members, it has been directed to ends destructive of the legitimate purposes of the union, before that association can justify the exclusion of employees from the rights and privileges of a statute designed primarily for their benefit.

[14] The appeal must, therefore, be dismissed with costs.

4:420 Employer Influence

Management interference with, or domination of unions is prohibited by labour relations legislation as an unfair labour practice, as we will see in Chapter 5. The policy of protecting union autonomy to ensure that unions act as the authentic voice of employees is also reflected in the denial of employee status to members of management, as we have seen in Section 4:330, and by statutory provisions preventing employer-dominated organizations from being certified as trade unions.

An example of this type of provision is section 15 of the Ontario *Labour Relations Act* which forbids certification of a union "if any employer ... has participated in its formation or administration or has contributed financial or other support to it." This prohibition posed a problem in the sort of situation that frequently occurred with the spread of unionization outside the traditional blue-collar context: the effort by an employee association which had included managers among its membership to evolve into a trade union in order to be certified as bargaining agent. For a time, the Ontario Labour Relations Board attempted a sort of compromise resolution to that problem. It held that the association's constitution must exclude from membership anyone who fell within the managerial exclusion, but that the board would not "require an organization seeking recognition as a trade union to correctly guess the [managerial or non-managerial] status ... of those it is seeking to organize, and to purge [before applying for certification] all those who *might* be managerial or risk the imposition of the [section 15] bar": *Children's Aid Society of Metropolitan Toronto*, [1977] 1 CLRBR 129 at para 16 (OLRB). In other words, if an association happened to have some people in it who were found by the labour board to be managers but who were not doing management's bidding within the association, that would not disqualify the association from certification if the association's rules made such people ineligible for membership, and if they were expelled when their managerial status became known.

Later, in *OSSTF v Toronto (City) Board of Education*, [1994] OLRB Rep August 1098, the Ontario Labour Relations Board (OLRB) went further, holding that "the fact that the constitution of the Association permits the admission of non-employees and that it in fact does so would not in itself prevent the Association from being considered a trade union within the meaning of the Act." The board stated, "the structure of the Act ... does not merely tolerate membership by non-employees, it contemplates it." The board concluded: "In short ... the composition of an organization's membership, although in certain circumstances relevant to the question of whether a trade union is *dominated* by the employer ... does not enter into the question as to whether that organization is a trade union."

* * * * *

As noted earlier in this chapter, developments in technology and the organization of work as well as the challenges of globalization have called into question the adversarial model of labour relations. Employers seeking to capitalize on the desire of their employees for increased responsibility and input into decision making have instituted a variety of employee participation programs, often giving rank-and-file workers responsibility over matters previously dealt with by lower-level management. Are employees who have this sort of role in the new economy properly excluded from trade union representation?

Along these lines, the Canada Labour Relations Board has held that an employee organization does not have to be committed to an adversarial form of collective bargaining in order to qualify as a trade union: *British Columbia Transit and Transit Management Assn* (1990), 6 CLRBR (2d) 1 (BCLRB). There are few decided cases in this area, perhaps because unions have not often been able to mount successful organizing campaigns in workplaces that use new economy management practices.

In 2007, the Canadian Auto Workers (CAW) signed a "Framework of Fairness" document with a large automobile parts manufacturer, Magna International. Magna agreed, among other things, to give the CAW unopposed access to its many Canadian plants for organizing purposes, in return for the CAW's renunciation of its right to strike. The parties also agreed to various internal dispute resolution procedures of a cooperative nature. In the United States, such arrangements have existed for some time under the label of "neutrality agreements." They are controversial in both the US and Canada. See David Doorey, "Neutrality Agreements: Bargaining for Representation Rights in the Shadow of the State" (2007) 13:1 *Canadian Labour & Employment Law Journal* 41.

4:500 THE EMPLOYER FOR PURPOSES OF COLLECTIVE BARGAINING

4:510 Identifying the Employer

C Michael Mitchell & John C Murray, *Changing Workplaces Review: Special Advisors' Interim Report* (Ontario: Ministry of Labour, July 2016) at 64–67 [footnotes omitted]

> In an increasing range of circumstances, it has become important to determine, for the purposes of the LRA:
>
> - which of two entities is the employer;
> - whether a number of entities are a related employer; or
> - whether entities are joint employers.

Increasingly, organizations do not always operate as a single employer that directly hires its workforce and controls all aspects of its business. For example, it is common for businesses to supplement, and even replace, some or all of their regular workforces by engaging workers from a temporary help agency (THA) or labour broker.

Businesses may subcontract supervision for particular parts of an operation to a contractor together with the staffing responsibility for that part of the operation. Or an enterprise may be organized in such a way that different entities have responsibility for different facets of the business. It may not be clear who the employer is. An entity with real influence and control on the terms and conditions of employment may appear not to be an employer at all.

Similarly, franchisees must comply with the franchise agreement and the requirements of a franchisor, which could affect the manner in which they manage their workforce or operate their business. Some franchisors may exert more control or less control over the business of a franchisee and over terms and conditions of employment.

Several policy questions arise in these situations, including whether a collective bargaining relationship can be effective or stable if parties who also impact the employment relationship are not at the bargaining table. Another question is how to distinguish between different situations where part of a business is contracted-out. For example, where the lead business has no involvement in highly specialized work performed by a subcontractor, then involving the lead business in bargaining with respect to the subcontractor and imposing employer obligations on the lead business would arguably be unfair and excessive. However, this may be different from situations where the lead business is closely involved or has ultimate authority on an on-going basis with the core work performed by a contractor or franchisee.

True Employer

Where there is more than one potential employer for a group of employees under the LRA, the OLRB will determine which employer is the "true employer" on a case-by-case basis, weighing various factors to determine which choice appears to be consistent with the statutory and labour relations framework.

The OLRB has wrestled with the issue of determining the true employer. The analysis has evolved over the years as the context has changed and as these triangular relationships have become common. Historically, the Board has considered numerous factors such as whether a party:

- exercises direction and control over the employees;
- has authority to dismiss employees;
- is perceived by the employees to be the employer; and
- whether there exists an intention to create an employer-employee relationship.

The Board now emphasizes that it makes a purposive and contextual analysis. There is no single factor that is determinative and no exhaustive list of factors to apply mechanically to a particular situation. The question to be asked is, "having regard to all of the facts of the specific case, which entity should the union be required to bargain with and represent the employees with so that collective bargaining can be as effective and stable as possible?"

The OLRB has considered the non-exhaustive factors in determining the true employer identified by the Supreme Court of Canada in *Pointe-Claire (City) v. Québec (Labour Court)*, including: the selection process, hiring, training, discipline, evaluation, supervision, assignment of duties, remuneration and integration into the business.

Accordingly, unlike the [Employment Standards Act], the OLRB typically does not treat assignment workers as employees of the THA. Instead, the question of who is the employer is determined on a case-by-case basis. Most often, the issue of who is the employer arises in certification applications.

If the OLRB determines that the assignment workers are employees of the client, they may be included in a proposed bargaining unit and count for the purposes of a representation vote at the client workplace, but such workers have also been excluded on occasion at the request of the union because of the difficulty in organizing them. However, if assignment workers are found to be employees of the THA and not of the client, they would be unable to unionize at the client workplace.

Although labour relations legislation technically enables THA workers to organize at the level of the THA, there are numerous challenges, and unionization at the agency level is almost non-existent in Canada.

In certification applications that involve THA workers, there is often prolonged litigation at the OLRB to determine the true employer and, most frequently, the client has been found to be the employer by the OLRB. However, in at least two certification applications, the OLRB has exercised its discretion to make a related employer declaration pursuant to section 1(4) of the LRA, and the temporary help agency and client business were both found to be the employer.

Related Employer

The OLRB has the power to treat related or associated businesses as a single employer for the purposes of the LRA, where they carry on associated or related activities under common control or direction. These activities need not be carried on simultaneously and there is no need to establish that the businesses were structured for anti-union purposes.

Pursuant to the related employer provision under the LRA, the OLRB may "pierce the corporate veil" where more than one legal entity carries out economic activity that gives rise to employment or collective bargaining relationships regulated by the LRA. The OLRB has stated that the purpose of this provision is to prevent mischief, by protecting the bargaining rights a union from being deliberately or inadvertently eroded by the commercial operations of related employers.

As indicated above, section 1(4), the related employer section, has been applied in certification applications to find that a temporary help agency and client business were carrying on associated or related activities under common control and direction. In distinguishing between those subcontracting arrangements where section 1(4) would apply and those where it would not, the OLRB has distinguished between situations where the subcontracting was legitimate and those where it was not. In general, the OLRB would be less likely to find that two entities are related in situations where the subcontracted work was not for core functions, was less permanent, and was more subject to the control of the subcontractor.

The OLRB has also been asked to treat franchisors and franchisees as related employers and, depending on the context, has done so on some occasions but not on others. [© Queen's Printer for Ontario, 2016. Reproduced with permission.]

* * * * *

In the *Changing Workplaces Review—Final Report*, Mitchell and Murray recommended no change to the law with respect to the treatment of franchisors and franchisee as related employers, with the determination to be made on the facts of each case, with no presumption in favour or against treating them as common or related employers. However, they did recommend that persons assigned by temporary help agencies to perform work for clients of the agency should be deemed to be employees of the client for purposes of the Ontario *Labour Relations Act*. They argued that such a deeming provision serves the interest of and provides access to meaningful collective bargaining for many vulnerable and precariously employed people. This recommendation has not been enacted. Consider the merits of such an approach in light of the following decision.

Pointe-Claire (City) v Quebec (Labour Court), [1997] 1 SCR 1015, 97 CLLC para 220-039.

Lamer C.J. (La Forest, Gonthier and Cory JJ. Concurring):

1. This appeal raises the question of determining the real employer in a tripartite relationship in the collective labour relations context. What must be determined in the present case is whether the Labour Court made a patently unreasonable decision when it ruled that a temporary employee of the City of Pointe-Claire (the "City") who had been hired through a personnel agency was included in the bargaining unit of the union that represented the City's permanent employees.

I. FACTS

2. Personnel Hélène Tobin inc. (hereinafter the "agency") is an agency whose business involves, *inter alia*, supplying temporary staff to businesses that are part of its clientele. The agency's staff consists of three permanent employees and at least thirty employees ("temporary employees") whose services are supplied to its clients on a temporary basis. The temporary employees are recruited and selected by the agency, which administers evaluation tests to them. The agency sees to the employees' career development by entrusting them with increasingly demanding assignments and sometimes recommending that they take courses. It agrees with the client on the rate for the temporary employees' services without regard to what the client pays its own employees in the same category. The agency pays its temporary employees an hourly wage that varies depending on the specific assignment. The wage paid by the agency is calculated on the basis of the number of hours recorded on a form filled out by the employee and countersigned by the client. The agency does not pay its temporary employees when they are not assigned to a client. The client can officially hire the employee, but the agency charges additional fees if this is done before the end of an assignment of 18 consecutive weeks. If the client is not satisfied with the quality of the temporary employee's work, it must

inform the agency, which will then take the appropriate action. The agency can change an employee's assignment if the employee is underqualified or overqualified. As well, the agency has an employer number assigned by the Commission de la santé et de la sécurité du travail ("CSST") and it withholds the necessary amounts from the employee's wages for taxes and employment-related costs (vacation pay and contributions to unemployment insurance, the CSST and the Quebec Pension Plan).

3. The City asked the agency to send it someone to serve as receptionist at city hall from November 5 to December 14, 1990. The agency assigned Ginette Lebeau to the position. At the end of this initial six-week assignment, Ms. Lebeau informed the agency that she did not want another assignment before the beginning of January 1991. She also informed the City that she would like to apply for permanent employment. The City had her complete a form and, on December 17, 1990, had her take the necessary tests. Ms. Lebeau qualified for a position as a clerk with the City with an average of 94 percent.

4. After New Year's Day, the agency offered Ms. Lebeau another work assignment with the City, this time as a clerk in the purchasing department. That second assignment lasted 18 weeks, from January 14 to May 17, 1991. On May 20, 1991, after the time allotted for the second work assignment had expired, Ms. Lebeau was hired directly by the City as a temporary employee. On June 17, 1991, she became a permanent employee at the City's Municipal Court.

5. During the two work assignments in question, which lasted 6 and 18 weeks respectively, Ms. Lebeau's wages were determined and paid by the agency. She filled out a time sheet given to her by the agency, had it signed by the City and then returned a copy to the agency. When the agency was informed of the number of hours she had worked, it paid her and submitted an invoice to the City, without informing the City what wages it had paid. Ms. Lebeau performed her work under the direction and supervision of a manager working for the City. The City also took part in her training, since it showed her how to do her work. Ms. Lebeau's general working conditions, such as hours of work, breaks and statutory holidays, were dictated by the City. If she had not been qualified or had experienced problems in adapting, the City was supposed to inform the agency, which would have found the solution necessary to remedy the situation. In practice, when Ms. Lebeau was late or absent, she notified her immediate supervisor at the City.

6. The respondent Syndicat des employées et employés professionnelles et de bureau, section locale 57 (S.E.P.B.O.P.E.I.U.C.L.C.F.T.Q.), holds the certification certificate for most of the City's employees. On January 25, 1991, the respondent union submitted a request to the office of the labour commissioner general under s. 39 of the *Labour Code*, R.S.Q., c. C27, seeking, *inter alia*, a declaration that Ms. Lebeau was included in the union's bargaining unit because she was employed by the City during her two work assignments of 6 and 18 weeks respectively.

II. RELEVANT STATUTORY PROVISIONS

7. The *Labour Code* defines "employer" and "employee" as follows:

    1. In this code, unless the context requires otherwise, the following expressions mean:

       . . .

(k) "employer—anyone, including Her Majesty, who has work done by an employee;
(l) "employee—a person who works for an employer and for remuneration, but the word does not include: [the exceptions are not applicable in this case]

...

V. ANALYSIS

26. Personnel agencies are occupying an increasing share of the labour market. These agencies might be described as intermediaries in that they supply businesses with the services of employees they recruit. That supplying of services gives rise to a triangular relationship among the parties—the agency, the client and the employee—whose legal relationship is not clearly defined by labour legislation. While it is easy to identify the employee in such a tripartite relationship, the identification of the real employer is another matter. Generally speaking, both the agency and the client have some of the traditional attributes of an employer within the meaning of the *Labour Code*. There is accordingly a certain splitting of the employer in a tripartite relationship. The agency may recruit, train, pay and discipline the employee, while the business supervises the work, imposes the employee's working conditions and bears the financial burden of the wages paid. An interesting labour law issue therefore arises, namely whether temporary employees engaged by a business through a personnel agency can in some cases be included in the bargaining unit of the union that represents the business's permanent employees, or whether they are employees of the agency. Despite the importance of this issue, in this appeal I do not have to determine how to identify the real employer in all tripartite relationships involving a personnel agency. In the present case, the only issue is whether the Labour Court made a patently unreasonable error by holding, in the context of a request under s. 39 of the *Labour Code*, that the City was Ginette Lebeau's employer during her two work assignments.

...

1. Is the Labour Court's Reasoning Patently Unreasonable?

33. The Quebec *Labour Code* and Canadian labour legislation provide few indications of how to determine the real employer in a tripartite relationship. For the purposes of such an analysis, the *Labour Code* merely defines the terms "employer" and "employee." According to s. 1(k) and (l) of the *Labour Code*, an employer is "anyone, including Her Majesty, who has work done by an employee," while an employee is "a person who works for an employer and for remuneration." On the basis of these two definitions, it has been established that the employer-employee relationship is defined by three essential elements: the performance of work, remuneration and the legal subordination of the employee to the employer ...

34. These definitions, which are terse to say the least, have had to be interpreted by specialized administrative tribunals in cases requiring them to identify the employer in a tripartite relationship. Those tribunals have made up for the gaps in the legislation by examining the various components of the employer-employee relationship and proposing certain criteria to define that relationship more clearly. I shall consider the Quebec and Canadian decisions on the subject before analysing the approach taken by the Labour Court in the present case.

(i) Quebec Cases

...

43. In summary, the majority of Labour Court decisions have held that legal subordination is an important criterion for identifying the employer in a tripartite relationship. More specifically, the Labour Court has said that it is important to determine which party exercises the most direct control over the temporary employee's day-to-day work. It is essential to point out, however, that in none of the cases cited did the Labour Court consider only the criterion of legal subordination. Each decision was based on a complete assessment of the evidence and a consideration of other factors relating to the employer-employee relationship, such as remuneration ...

...

45. In *Hôpital Royal Victoria v. Vassart*, [1990] R.J.Q. 1961, the Superior Court ... had to determine whether the Labour Court had made a patently unreasonable error in finding that temporary nurses hired by the hospital through a personnel agency were the hospital's employees for the purposes of the *Labour Code*. The Superior Court stated that it was patently unreasonable to identify the real employer by relying solely or predominantly on the legal subordination test. Grenier J. said the following, at p. 1970:

> [TRANSLATION] In a tripartite situation, the *test of actual control over work performance is much too rigid and does not take account of other fundamental aspects that are obviously important*. Any interpretation of the concept of "employee" must remain consistent with the tripartite context described above. Whether the nurses are employees of the supplier or the user of their services depends on *a series of factors, of which actual control over the work is but one*. Otherwise, the balance struck in the labour legislation enacted by the legislature would be upset ... [Emphasis added.]

...

47. I agree with the more comprehensive approach proposed by Grenier J. in *Vassart* for identifying the real employer in tripartite relationships. ...

48. According to this more comprehensive approach, the legal subordination and integration into the business criteria should not be used as exclusive criteria for identifying the real employer. In my view, in a context of collective relations governed by the *Labour Code*, it is essential that temporary employees be able to bargain with the party that exercises the greatest control over all aspects of their work—and not only over the supervision of their day-to-day work. Moreover, when there is a certain splitting of the employer's identity in the context of a tripartite relationship, the more comprehensive and more flexible approach has the advantage of allowing for a consideration of which party has the most control over all aspects of the work on the specific facts of each case. Without drawing up an exhaustive list of factors pertaining to the employer-employee relationship, I shall mention the following examples: the selection process, hiring, training, discipline, evaluation, supervision, assignment of duties, remuneration and integration into the business.

(ii) Canadian Cases

49. In applying collective labour relations legislation that is similar to that in Quebec, Canadian administrative agencies have also dealt with how to identify the real employer in a

tripartite relationship. Most of the decisions of those agencies, and specifically the Ontario Labour Relations Board ("OLRB") and the Canada Labour Relations Board ("CLRB"), have noted that the essential test for identifying an employer-employee relationship in a tripartite context is that of fundamental control over working conditions. The application of the fundamental control test leads to an analysis of which party has control over, *inter alia*, the selection, hiring, remuneration, discipline and working conditions of temporary employees and to a consideration of the factor of integration into the business. In the final analysis, the application of the fundamental control test involves an examination of a series of factors that are similar to those suggested by the comprehensive approach set out in *Infirmières & infirmiers unis Inc.* and in the Court of Appeal's decision in the instant case.

. . .

(iii) Labour Court Decision in the Instant Case

51. The issue before Judge Prud'homme was how to identify the employer, within the meaning of the *Labour Code*, in a tripartite relationship. More specifically, he had to determine whether the agency or the City should be considered Ginette Lebeau's real employer for the purposes of s. 39 of the *Labour Code*.

52. Judge Prud'homme acknowledged that the agency recruited, assigned positions to, evaluated, disciplined and paid the temporary employees. However, by focusing on the question of which party had control over the temporary employee's working conditions and the performance of her work, he concluded that the City was Ms. Lebeau's real employer. According to the evidence, Ms. Lebeau had the same working conditions as the City's permanent employees in terms of working hours, meal periods, breaks and statutory holidays. Judge Prud'homme gave predominant weight to working conditions because of the purpose of the *Labour Code*: [TRANSLATION] "[t]he Code is concerned with the realities of the 'employer-employee' relationship rather than the form in which that relationship has been established; those realities essentially relate to the working conditions that the Code seeks to ensure are set up in a certain way" (p. 13). The judge also found that there was a relationship of legal subordination between the City and Ms. Lebeau because the City's managers directed and supervised how she did her day-to-day work. According to the judge, that complete legal subordination of Ms. Lebeau to the City went to [translation] "the heart of the traditional 'employer-employee' relationship" (p. 11).

53. In addition to considering the criterion of control over Ms. Lebeau's day-to-day work and her general working conditions, the Labour Court looked at other aspects that define the employer-employee relationship, namely wages, discipline and the feeling of integration into the business.

54. With respect to wages, the judge noted that although Ms. Lebeau's wages were paid by the agency, they were entirely dependent on the number of hours she actually worked for the City. Moreover, Ms. Lebeau's wage rate varied depending on her position with the City. According to the judge, the City therefore had a role to play in determining her wages, which correspondingly lessened the impact of the agency's authority over that traditional element of the employer-employee relationship.

55. I shall add two important elements that show that the criterion of remuneration was not determinative in this case. First, according to the evidence, a temporary

employee was not paid unless he or she was assigned to work for one of the agency's clients. Thus, between her two work assignments with the City, that is, during the 1990 holiday season, Ms. Lebeau was not paid at all by the agency. Second, the definition of "employee" in the *Labour Code* does not specify who must pay the employee. The source of remuneration is therefore not conclusive in identifying the employer, because the statute does not mention it. To be covered by the *Labour Code*, the employee need only receive financial compensation in the form of wages.... In actual fact, the City bore the financial burden of Ms. Lebeau's wages even though the agency actually paid those wages to the temporary employee. Thus, both entities, the agency and the City, could be seen as the employer since the former paid Ms. Lebeau's wages directly while the latter bore the cost of those wages by fully reimbursing the agency for them on the basis of the hours she worked and paying an additional amount for the agency's services ...

It is therefore not patently unreasonable that the Labour Court did not give predominant weight to the fact that the agency paid the temporary employee's wages. Since both parties had a role to play with respect to Ms. Lebeau's wages, those wages could not be a decisive criterion for identifying the real employer.

56. With respect to discipline, Judge Prud'homme acknowledged that the City had to inform the agency if it had any grounds for complaint against Ms. Lebeau. However, the judge also noted that the only possible disciplinary action would have been for the agency to remove Ms. Lebeau from her work assignment. The agency did not have a system involving a continuum of penalties or a disciplinary system such as is normally found in businesses. Moreover, Judge Prud'homme noted that the agency would not have taken disciplinary action in a vacuum: since it had no authority over Ms. Lebeau's daytoday performance of her work, the agency would have had to be notified first by the City that there was some problem with the employee. Once again, the City was not uninvolved in this additional component of the employer-employee relationship. For these reasons, the Labour Court did not give predominant weight to the criterion of discipline.

57. Finally, although Judge Prud'homme did not explicitly state that Ms. Lebeau viewed the City as her employer, he noted that the temporary employee felt as though she worked for the City and not the agency. According to the evidence, when she was late or absent, she contacted the City directly, without informing the agency. I also note that the facts show that Ms. Lebeau worked twice for the City for relatively long periods of time, namely 6 weeks and 18 weeks. Although the judge did not specifically raise this point, the length of assignments is an important factor in assessing the feeling of integration into the business. Moreover, at the end of her first work assignment, Ms. Lebeau passed tests administered by the City in order to qualify for a possible position as a clerk. Her second work assignment with the City was in fact as a clerk.

58. In my view, the Labour Court's reasoning is not patently unreasonable. It used a comprehensive approach by not basing its decision solely on the criterion of legal subordination ...

2. Is the Result Patently Unreasonable?

59. Does the conclusion that the City was Ms. Lebeau's employer for the purposes of the *Labour Code* lead to a patently unreasonable result? I raise this question in relation

to two grounds that were argued before this Court. First, I must consider whether the application of the City's collective agreement to Ms. Lebeau would in fact have created a problem and, if so, whether it would therefore be patently unreasonable to uphold that conclusion. The City also raised the issue of inconsistency in the application of two Quebec labour statutes. According to the appellant, it is unreasonable to find that the City was Ms. Lebeau's employer under the *Labour Code* when the agency already had that role for the purposes of the *Act respecting labour standards*, R.S.Q., c. N1.1.

60. The City's collective agreement would have applied to Ms. Lebeau during the two work assignments in question. When she was assigned to the City first as a receptionist and later as a purchasing clerk, she performed her work in unionized positions. Those positions were covered by the collective agreement and specific wages applied to them. Thus, Ms. Lebeau's wages would have had to be the same as those established by the collective agreement. This conclusion is not contrary to common sense, since the working conditions established by the collective agreement applied to Ms. Lebeau. In so far as she did not receive the wages that the union had negotiated with the City for those two positions, she would have been entitled to receive the difference. The agency would then have had to adjust her wages to take account of the wage rate determined by the collective agreement for the assigned positions. Moreover, a grievance could have been filed if there had been any disagreement as to the interpretation or application of the collective agreement. The applicability of the City's collective agreement to Ms. Lebeau does not raise any major difficulties. Accordingly, I do not feel that the result of the decision is patently unreasonable.

61. The City argued that the Labour Court's decision leads to inconsistency in the application of two statutes that govern employer-employee relations in Quebec: the *Act respecting labour standards* and the *Labour Code*. By assuming the obligations set out in the *Act respecting labour standards* in respect of Ms. Lebeau, the agency acknowledged that it was her employer under that Act. The evidence showed that the agency paid an amount representing about 20 percent of Ms. Lebeau's wages to cover its employment-related costs (such as vacation pay) and that it had an employer number from the CSST. The City argued that since the definition of "employer" is practically the same in both statutes, it would be inconsistent for two separate entities to be the employer of the same employee. There is no doubt that the principle that statutes dealing with similar subjects must be presumed to be coherent means that interpretations favouring harmony among those statutes should prevail over discordant ones: P.A. Côté, *The Interpretation of Legislation in Canada* (2nd ed. 1991). However, I cannot find any inconsistency in the application of these two statutes. Each of the labour statutes has a distinct object and its provisions must be interpreted on the basis of their specific purpose. Moreover, the case at bar relates to provisions of the *Labour Code*, specifically whether the Labour Court's decision was patently unreasonable, and not to the *Act respecting labour standards*.

62. I am aware that the arrangement is not perfect. However, it must not be forgotten that the relationship in question here is not a traditional bipartite relationship but a tripartite one in which one party is the employee and the other two share the usual attributes of an employer. In such a situation, it is natural that labour legislation designed to govern bipartite situations must be adjusted in some ways . . .

63. Unfortunately, tribunals and courts must often make decisions by interpreting statutes in which there are gaps. The case at bar shows that situations involving tripartite relationships can cause problems when it comes to identifying the real employer if the labour legislation is incomplete in this regard. The tripartite relationship does not fit very easily into the classic pattern of bilateral relationships. The *Labour Code* was essentially designed for bipartite relationships involving an employee and an employer. It is not very helpful when a tripartite relationship like the one at issue here must be analysed. The traditional characteristics of an employer are shared by two separate entities—the personnel agency and its client—that both have a certain relationship with the temporary employee. When faced with such legislative gaps, tribunals have used their expertise to interpret the often terse provisions of the statute. In the final analysis, however, it is up to the legislature to remedy those gaps. The Court cannot encroach upon an area where it does not belong.

VI. Disposition

64. For these reasons, I would dismiss the appeal with costs.

4:520 Related Employers

Sometimes an employer may carry on business through two or more corporate entities sharing certain facilities and management structures. Further, an employer may sell a part of its business to another party within the meaning of the successor rights provisions (discussed in the following section) but may nevertheless keep considerable control over how that purchaser operates. The form of these arrangements may suggest the existence of more than one employer, and corporate law may indeed treat each of the entities as separate bodies. However, treating them as separate employers for labour law purposes may mean that the union which represents employees in the subordinate business is unable to bargain with the company that has real control over the entire operation. To meet this problem, many Canadian jurisdictions provide that the labour board may treat associated or related employers under common control and direction as a single employer for the purpose of bargaining unit determination and for other collective bargaining purposes. Ontario goes so far as to place on the putative employer the onus of disclosing all relevant facts relating to such determination.

The following case illustrates the operation of the "related employer" or "common employer" provisions. These provisions interface with the "successor employer" provisions discussed in the following section of this chapter.

White Spot Ltd v British Columbia (Labour Relations Board), [1997] BCJ No 1440 (SC)

MACKENZIE J.:

1. This is a petition seeking to quash decisions of the Labour Relations Board ... declaring the petitioner, White Spot Limited [which operated a chain of restaurants in British Columbia] ... and Gilley Restaurants Ltd. ... to be a common employer pursuant to s. 38 of the *Labour Relations Code*, R.S.B.C. 1996 c. 244.

2. White Spot sold to Gilley the assets and undertaking of a White Spot restaurant in Langley, B.C. The restaurant continues to be a White Spot, operated pursuant to

franchise agreements between the petitioner and Gilley. Employees of the Langley restaurant are members of the union, which has a collective agreement with White Spot covering 17 White Spot restaurants in the Lower Mainland. White Spot and Gilley both accept that Gilley is bound by the terms of the collective agreement as a successor pursuant to s. 35 of the Code.

3. A panel of the Board made the common employer declaration ... on the union's application and issued an amended certification ...

[The board had set out the following in its original decision (*White Spot Ltd v CAW-Canada, Local 3000* (1995), 95 CLLC 220-058 at para 74), as "the most significant [facts] amongst others ... which lead us to conclude that White Spot and Gilley Restaurants are under common control or direction":

1. White Spot has the substantial control over menu prices and food items despite [the fact] that the WFOA has some input and a few restaurants have different food items.
2. Gilley Restaurants is required to use the White Spot approved suppliers and delivery company. The price of food supplies is in the control of White Spot who negotiates with suppliers. Those prices impact profit by constituting 25% to 30% of total sales. This, coupled with White Spot's control over prices, leads to substantial control over the profit of the franchisee.
3. White Spot requires a marketing fee be paid which it controls for the purposes of promotions and advertising intended to bring business in to all restaurants operating under the White Spot trademark and logo.
4. White Spot requires that a franchisee have a White Spot trained general manager and requires that restaurants operate within its standards. White Spot ensures its standards are met through a comprehensive standards review and frequent quality checks....]

White Spot and Gilley then applied to the Board for reconsideration of the original decision. Another panel of the Board upheld the original panel's decision.... White Spot then commenced these proceedings to quash both decisions of the Board. Gilley supported White Spot's petition.

4. White Spot contended that the collective bargaining rights of the parties on Gilley's succession to the Langley restaurant are exclusively and automatically determined by the application of s. 35 and the Board has no jurisdiction to "override" the effect of s. 35 by a common employer declaration under s. 38. Mr. Jordan [counsel for White Spot] conceded that s. 38 might have some application if the motive for the succession was an attempt to undermine the union, but there is no such motive here. The Board has concluded that White Spot and Gilley were engaged in a bona fide arm's length transaction for commercial reasons without any ulterior collective bargaining purpose.

5. It is agreed on all sides that there has been a succession to the Langley restaurant to which s. 35 applies. Mr. Jordan, on behalf of White Spot, contended that the effect of s. 35 succession is to sever the single bargaining unit for the Langley restaurant and the other unionized restaurants owned and operated by White Spot. Two bargaining units are automatically created by the succession, with the Langley restaurant forming one of them under a collective agreement on the same terms and conditions as the original White Spot collective agreement, except that Gilley is the employer and the bargaining unit is limited to the

employees at the Langley site. The union's concern, which apparently led to its application to the Board, was that the Langley employees would lose the benefits of being part of a broader bargaining unit and the ability to deal with White Spot across the bargaining table ...

6. The issues turn on the interpretation and the interrelationship of the relevant provisions of the Code, namely, s. 38 and s. 35 as follows:

> 38 If in the board's opinion associated or related activities or businesses are carried on by or through more than one corporation, individual, firm, syndicate or association, or a combination of them under common control or direction, the board may treat them as constituting one employer for the purposes of this Code and grant such relief, by way of declaration or otherwise, as the board considers appropriate.
>
> 35 (1) If a business or a part of it is sold, leased, transferred or otherwise disposed of, the purchaser, lessee or transferee is bound by all proceedings under this Code before the date of the disposition and the proceedings must continue as if no change had occurred.
>
> (2) If a collective agreement is in force, it continues to bind the purchaser, lessee or transferee to the same extent as if it had been signed by the purchaser, lessee or transferee, as the case may be.
>
> (3) If a question arises under this section, the board, on application by any person, must determine what rights, privileges and duties have been acquired or are retained.
>
> (4) For the purposes of this section, the board may make inquiries or direct that representation votes be taken as it considers necessary or advisable.
>
> (5) The board, having made an inquiry or directed a vote under this section, may
>
> (a) determine whether the employees constitute one or more units appropriate for collective bargaining,
> (b) determine which trade union is to be the bargaining agent for the employees in each unit,
> (c) amend, to the extent it considers necessary or advisable, a certificate issued to a trade union or the description of a unit contained in a collective agreement,
> (d) modify or restrict the operation or effect of a provision of a collective agreement in order to define the seniority rights under it of employees affected by the sale, lease, transfer or other disposition, and
> (e) give directions the board considers necessary or advisable as to the interpretation and application of a collective agreement affecting the employees in a unit determined under this section to be appropriate for collective bargaining.

7. The Board relied on two decisions of the Ontario Labour Relations Board in support of its decisions, *Dominion Stores Ltd. and Willett Foods Ltd. and Penmarkay Foods Ltd. ..., and RPKC Holding Corp.* .... In both cases Dominion Stores sold retail grocery stores to the franchisors, RPKC and Penmarkay, triggering a succession invoking the Ontario equivalent of s. 35. The Ontario board granted common employer declarations. Mr. Jordan sought to distinguish those decisions on the ground that the Ontario board found a corporate motivation to weaken the union's collective bargaining position in the franchised operations and perhaps achieve decertification. The Board found no such motivation on the part of White Spot and Gilley for the succession here. ... While a labour

relations advantage may have been one factor motivating the franchise arrangements in the Ontario cases, it was not the dominant factor influencing the Ontario board's decisions. In both cases the board stressed the degree of control exercised by the franchisor under the franchise agreements and the desirability for the union to be able to bargain with the party exercising the dominant influence on the employers' side. The fact that the franchisee was a successor to a collective agreement under the Ontario equivalent of s. 35 was not seen as an obstacle to a common employer declaration.

8. The approach taken by the Board here is consistent with the Ontario jurisprudence. The Board was influenced by the single bargaining unit structure which had existed before the Langley restaurant was franchised and the union's desire to "preserve" that structure. As Mr. Jordan stressed, that structure was divided automatically by the s. 35 succession, and the union's application is more accurately characterized as one to restore a pre-existing structure rather than preserve an existing one.... Nonetheless, whether it is preservation or restoration, the Board intended a single bargaining unit structure to permit the union to bargain with White Spot as well as Gilley for the Langley employees. The Board has found that White Spot dominates the franchise relationship and that effective bargaining by the union requires that it bargain with White Spot. I do not think that simply because s. 35 created an automatic severance of the bargaining unit on succession, that fact alone precludes the Board from invoking its s. 38 jurisdiction where it considers it to be appropriate.

...

10. Counsel for White Spot and Gilley both contended that the common employer declaration drags Gilley into bargaining with White Spot for the other restaurants in the bargaining unit still owned and operated by White Spot, in which Gilley has no interest.... The form and scope of the existing certification order is a matter of remedy which the Board has the jurisdiction to vary on application by the parties.... If White Spot and Gilley wish to pursue complaints about the particulars of the s. 38 remedy granted here they should return to the Board on proper application. The Board's powers under s. 38 are to "grant such relief ... as the board considers appropriate" which allows the Board latitude to fashion a remedy which meets the exigencies of particular circumstances....

11. Gilley advanced an alternative argument that, irrespective of s. 35, the Board was incorrect in concluding that White Spot and Gilley could be under "common control or direction" as required by s. 38, because they are separately owned and managed entities dealing with each other at arm's length....

12. The Ontario board's decisions in *Penmarkay* and *RPKC*, under very similar statutory provisions, held franchisor and franchisees to be a common employer notwithstanding separate ownership and management, on the basis of the degree of control exercised by the franchisors over the franchisees' activities through the franchise arrangements. Labour relations board jurisprudence, both in British Columbia and Ontario, interprets "common control and direction" as extending to dominant control exercised by a franchisor under franchise agreements with an independently owned franchisee. In my view, the words "common control or direction," in context, are capable of bearing that interpretation. The Board's functional interdependence test is within those parameters. Once that test is met and the interpretation adopted by the Board is one that can reasonably be

supported by the wording of the section, the application of the section to any particular circumstances is a matter for the Board. Its exercise of jurisdiction within those limits can only be attacked successfully if its conclusions are patently unreasonable ...

13. The issue then becomes whether in the particular circumstances the franchisor has sufficient control to justify a declaration. The control exercised by a franchisor in a particular franchise arrangement and whether that degree of control is sufficiently dominant to be common control or direction of the franchised operations are inferences or conclusions of fact flowing from the evidence. The Gilley submission reviewed the facts in detail and argued that Gilley's authority under the franchise arrangements with respect to pricing, labour relations and other aspects of the day to day management, plus the independent financial risk for the operations assumed by Gilley on the purchase, precluded a reasonable conclusion that White Spot dominated the relationship, and the Board's declaration was patently unreasonable. The Board made an extensive inquiry into the franchise arrangements between White Spot and Gilley and reached certain conclusions as to White Spot's degree of control which prompted the declaration ... I cannot say here that the Board has so obviously misperceived the evidence before it that its factual conclusions are patently unreasonable.

14. The petition is dismissed.

4:530 Successor Employers

In the absence of any statutory provision to the contrary, the concept of the "corporate veil" means that a change in the employer's corporate identity puts an end to any statutory bargaining rights by which the "old" employer was bound, and to any collective agreement negotiated pursuant to those bargaining rights. As a result, all Canadian labour relations statutes now have detailed provisions intended to give significant protection to existing bargaining rights where a business has been sold or transferred to a new employer. Typical of this kind of legislation is section 44 of the *Canada Labour Code*, which preserves existing bargaining rights and collective agreements where a business is sold. Such provisions apply only where the labour board finds that the transaction in question does indeed constitute the sale of a business. However, the case of *Ajax (Town) v National Automobile, Aerospace and Agricultural Implement Workers Union of Canada (CAW-Canada) Local 222* (1998), 41 OR (3d) 426 (CA), aff'd 2000 SCC 23, [2000] 1 SCR 538, exemplifies the willingness of boards and courts to show some flexibility in finding a sale of a business, even in situations where there has been no apparent exchange between the predecessor and the successor. In the case, the Town of Ajax had contracted for many years with Charterways Transportation to provide it with skilled drivers and the limited number of mechanics and cleaners needed to operate the Town's transit system. The Town however, owned the buses. Charterways employees were represented in collective bargaining by the National Automobile, Aerospace and Agricultural Implement Workers Union of Canada (CAW-Canada). The Town decided that it would take back the operation of its transit system. It cancelled its contract with Charterways and hired its own employees, the vast majority of whom had been employed by Charterways. CAW-Canada was successful in arguing that there was a sale of a business from Charterways to the Town of Ajax. There was a nexus between Charterways and the Town from their long-term commercial relationship and the continuity, experience and stability of this work force was a key part of Charterways' business. The Town acquired that part of Charterways' business when it hired the Charterway employees, which the Court of Appeal characterized as the most valuable asset of Charterways' business. This constituted a transfer, and thus a sale, under the statutory successorship provision.

Nevertheless, boards have been much less willing to apply the successorship provision when a business terminates the contract of a service provider and enters into a new contract with a different provider, as exemplified in the following case.

Hospitality & Service Trades Union, Local 261 v Service Star Building Cleaning Inc, 2013 CanLII 34400 (OLRB)

BEFORE: Tanja Wacyk, ViceChair, and Board Members Richard O'Connor and Shannon McManus.

1. This is an application under section 69 of the *Labour Relations Act*, 1995, S.O. 1995, c.1, as amended (the "Act").

2. The application is brought by the Hospitality & Service Trades Union, Local 261 (the "applicant"). The applicant maintains the sale of a business occurred when Service Star Building Cleaning Inc. ("Service Star") assumed the cleaning and maintenance contract at 3500 Carling Avenue. The contract had previously been held by ARAMARK Canada Ltd. ("ARAMARK"), and the applicant held representation rights for the ARAMARK employees.

3. The applicant requests a declaration that Service Star is a successor employer to ARAMARK and therefore continues to be bound by the collective agreement between the applicant and ARAMARK.

. . .

5. Service Star, ARAMARK and the SEIU [Service Employees International Union] dispute that a sale of a business occurred between ARAMARK and Service Star. Rather, they maintain that in January 2013, Service Star simply bid for and was awarded the janitorial contract at 3500 Carling Avenue.

. . .

12. The applicant submits Service Star took over the operation as a going concern, and that all employees, including the three managerial personnel, who had been working for ARAMARK continued to work for Service Star.

. . .

14. The applicant submits Service Star has directed its staff to continue using some of the equipment that they had used when they were working for ARAMARK, although they have been issued new uniforms, mops and pails.

15. Employees of Service Star continued to use the same work methods once Service Star assumed responsibility for the Contract.

16. Service Star has continued all of the terms and conditions of employment that existed under the Collective Agreement between the applicant and ARAMARK.

17. Service Star took over the responsibility for cleaning and maintenance as a turnkey operation. It was able to do so because it was able to make use of the knowledge of key managerial staff and all existing employees at the site.

18. Because it was able to rely extensively on the knowledge and expertise of the managers, Service Star did not require a full list of "normally essential" details, such as the total area to be cleaned, in advance of assuming responsibility for the Contract.

19. The relationships built by the managers and the employees with the property owners and tenants represented the good will of the cleaning business at the site. That good will was transferred to Service Star when it assumed responsibility for the Contract.

20. The applicant maintains Service Star is a successor employer within the meaning of section 69 of the Act, as there has been a sale to Service Star of the business that was covered by the Collective Agreement.

...

48. The critical provisions of section 69 are:

69. (1) In this section,

"business" includes a part or parts thereof;

"sells" includes leases, transfers and any other manner of disposition, and "sold" and "sale" have corresponding meanings.

(2) Where an employer who is bound by or is a party to a collective agreement with a trade union or council of trade unions sells his, her or its business, the person to whom the business has been sold is, until the Board otherwise declares, bound by the collective agreement as if the person had been a party thereto and, where an employer sells his, her or its business while an application for certification or termination of bargaining rights to which the employer is a party is before the Board, the person to whom the business has been sold is, until the Board otherwise declares, the employer for the purposes of the application as if the person were named as the employer in the application.

...

51. In considering whether a sale of a business has occurred, we adopt the two step analysis set out in *Metropolitan Parking Inc., supra.*

52. Specifically, the first question to be addressed is "Has there been a "sale?" within the extended statutory definition of that term. This finding is critical as the jurisprudence is clear that bargaining rights do not attach to individual employees or even to work being performed—but rather attach to the business itself (see reference to *N.A.B.E.T. v. Radio CJYC Ltd. et al.*, in paragraph 27 above). Accordingly, it is the "sale" that creates the nexus between the two employers and attaches the bargaining rights to the business which has transferred from the predecessor to the successor.

53. As seen in the jurisprudence, the term "sale" has been broadly interpreted and can be found to apply, in this context to myriad of transactions, including exchanges, gifts, trust or a chain of transactions. However, as stated in the Board's decision in *United Steelworkers of America v. Thorco Manufacturing Ltd.* (1965), CLLC ¶ 16,052 and cited favourably at paragraph 28 in *Metropolitan Parking Inc.*:

The manner of disposition is irrelevant so long as a transfer has, in fact, taken place.

54. In this instance, we are not persuaded the applicant has pled anything that suggests there has been a sale or transfer of a business between ARAMARK and Service

Star. Rather, the applicant has relied primarily on the continued employment of the predecessor's employees, as well as the continuity of the work.

55. However, the jurisprudence set out above is clear that the continued employment of the predecessor's employees is a factor to be considered in the second step of the analysis. It follows a determination that a sale has indeed occurred, and it must then be determined whether what has been transferred or sold is a "business" as opposed to a mere transfer of assets.

56. Similarly, with regard to continuity of a business, as stated in *N.A.B.E.T. v. Radio CJYC Ltd. et al.*, and cited with approval in *Metropolitan Parking Inc.*, set out again for ease of reference:

> But continuity of the work done is not sufficient alone to satisfy section 144. There must be some nexus between two employers other than the fact that one employed persons to do certain work that the other now does or will do, before one can be declared the successor of the other. Otherwise a loss of work to a competitor employer would result in a successorship. There must be some continuity in the employing enterprise for which a union holds bargaining rights as well as continuity in the nature of the work. The two go hand in hand...

57. In this instance we have no difficulty finding the applicant has not pled any allegations that suggest the assumption of the janitorial work at 3500 Carling Avenue was anything other than a "the loss of work to a competitor". This is not a circumstance intended to be caught by section 69.

58. In making that determination, we are not persuaded the cases relied on by the applicant are applicable in the instant case.

59. For example, there was no dispute that, as the Court of Appeal held in its decision in *Town of Ajax*, in making a section 69 determination, one can consider both the commercial history of the operation, and whether or not the "new" employer inherited a trained coordinated workforce. However, in this instance, as we have indicated, the applicant has made no allegations regarding any "commercial history" between ARAMARK and Service Star that suggests anything other than that they were and remain competitors in the janitorial industry.

60. That is distinct from the facts in the *Town of Ajax*, where the Town of Ajax, in addition to owning all the assets, controlled the manner in which the work was performed from the outset. When it decided to move the work in-house, this triggered the "transfer" at issue. That is distinct from the facts in this instance where there is no nexus between ARAMARK and Service Star that can be construed as resulting in the transfer of the business ARAMARK operated to Service Star.

61. It is also apparent the Court's decision in the *Town of Ajax* focussed primarily on the Court's determination that the Board's decision was not patently unreasonable.

62. In *Thunder Bay Ambulance Services Inc.* the Board stated at paragraph 14:

> 14. *This case requires a careful analysis because of the complicating factor of third party involvement. The Ministry of Health, although neither the predecessor nor successor employer, owned the assets which were necessary to the ambulance service provided by both the alleged predecessor and successor and licensed and regulated the alleged predecessor as it does the successor.* The

Ministry is also the source of the cash flow as it provided and continues to provide funds on a monthly basis in an amount agreed between the operator of the ambulance service and itself. These funds are the only source of revenue for the operator of the ambulance service. *The integral involvement of the Ministry must be taken into account in considering the nature of the alleged predecessor's business and more importantly, in determining whether or not there has been the transfer of that "business" or the establishment of a parallel or similar business.* [emphasis added]

63. Accordingly, the Board indicated at paragraph 18 of that decision, that having regard to the transfer of the exclusive right to use the Ministry's assets, managerial skills, and to the uninterrupted continuation of the identical job functions, it concluded that the Ministry of Health "served as the necessary link" in the transfer of the predecessors' businesses to the successor.

64. What is missing in the instant case is this "necessary link" which facilitates or caused a sale of ARAMARK's business to Service Star.

65. Furthermore, we note that the decision in *Thunder Bay Ambulance Services Inc.* was issued in 1978, prior to *Metropolitan Parking Inc.* where the Board laid the foundation for the analysis that has been reflected in the jurisprudence in ensuing decades.

66. Accordingly, in the absence of allegations that could, if true, establish that a sale or transfer of ARAMARK's business to Service Star has occurred, we do not need to examine the second element of the test—i.e. whether all of ARAMARK's "business" has been transferred and continued by the Service Star or, alternatively, there has merely been a transfer of assets or other incidental elements of the business.

67. For all the reasons set out above, the Board will not inquiry further into this matter.

4:540 Contracting Out

Very commonly, companies subcontract services, such as cleaning or cafeteria services, which are auxiliary to their main business. If a company ends such a contract with one contractor, for whose employees a union has bargaining rights, and gives it to a second contractor, should the second contractor be bound by those bargaining rights? Between 1992 and 1995, the Ontario *Labour Relations Act* said yes; it dispensed with the need to demonstrate that a sale of a business had taken place if "substantially similar services are subsequently provided at the premises under the direction of another employer." The Quebec *Labour Code* has never had a provision of that sort, but in *Ivanhoe Inc v UFCW, Local 500*, 2001 SCC 47, [2001] 2 SCR 565, the Supreme Court of Canada upheld the Quebec Labour Court's position that a certification could extend to a new subcontractor, at least where the employees of the company contracting out the work had been covered by the certification before the work was originally subcontracted. The court emphasized the wide discretion of labour tribunals in determining and weighing the factors to be applied and the legal tests to be applied in deciding cases involving the transfer of an undertaking in any given industry.

In *Sept-Îles (City) v Quebec (Labour Court)* 2001 SCC 48, [2001] SCJ No 48, the Supreme Court of Canada again accepted the Quebec Labour Court's view that a subcontracting of work alone was in some circumstances enough to ground the transfer of bargaining rights. In that case, it was not an auxiliary function that was contracted out, but a central function—municipal garbage collection.

In 2003, the Quebec government responded to widespread employer objections that such restrictions on subcontracting were impairing the competitiveness of Quebec businesses. It amended article 45 of the *Labour Code*, the successor rights provision, to provide that bargaining rights do not follow "the transfer of part of the operation of an undertaking" unless what is transferred are not only "functions or the right to operate" but also "most of the elements that characterize the part of the undertaking involved": *An Act to Amend the Labour Code*, SQ 2003, c 26, s 2.

These amendments brought successor employer law in Quebec closer to that found in other Canadian jurisdictions. As the *Service Star Building Cleaning* case (see Section 4:530 immediately above) demonstrates, for the purposes of successor employer provisions, bargaining rights do not attach to employees, but rather to a business or a part of a business. Unless the transfer of a group of employees constitutes a transfer of part of a business, there is no succession of collective bargaining rights and obligations. Thus an employer can often contract out functions or operations to an external service provider without triggering the successor employer provisions of labour relations legislation.

The following case considers whether such contracting out triggers the related or common employer provisions of the *Canada Labour Code*.

Re Canada Post Corp and CUPW, 2013 CIRB 672

> [5] CPC [Canada Post Corporation] is a federal Crown corporation created in 1981 that is responsible, pursuant to the *Canada Post Corporation Act*, R.S.C. 1985, c. C-10 (the *CPC Act*), for providing services for the collection, transmission and delivery of messages, information, funds and goods both within Canada and between Canada and places outside Canada. To carry out this mandate, CPC employs more than 60,000 employees in a variety of capacities. It also enters into contracts with external service providers (contractors) for certain activities, including highway services (HS) and combined urban services (CUS), and has done so for decades....
>
> [6] The CPC network consists of mechanized plants, distribution centre facilities (DCFs) and local post offices. There are some 130 national "lanes" or routes and 1,060 regional routes through which mail is transferred between the plants, DCFs and local post offices. The transportation of mail between the plants, DCFs and local post offices is undertaken by HS contractors; there are no CPC employees who perform this work. With respect to the national contracts, the mail is loaded on and unloaded from the vehicles by CPC employees who are CUPW [Canadian Union of Postal Workers] members. However, regional HS workers load and unload their own vehicles.
>
> [7] Tenders for HS contracts are very detailed. Schedule A of each Invitation to Tender document specifies not only the exact delivery and pick up time for each stop along each route, but also the type of vehicle required, the age of the vehicle and the equipment that must be provided by the contractor. Contractors are required to obtain security clearances (criminal record checks) for any employee who has access to the mail

or CPC's property or equipment. Schedule A of the Invitation to Tender is subsequently incorporated into the final contract that CPC enters into with the successful bidder.

[8] In total, CPC contracts with some 600 to 800 different contractors to cover the HS routes. The contractors vary from large national or international trucking companies to small sole operators. The class of vehicles used depends on the requirements of the route, from 53 foot tractor trailers to small cargo vans. Depending on the contract, the contractor may be remunerated on an invoice (volume) basis or on a fixed, recurring payment basis. The contractor may incur a loss if it has underbid the contract or if expenses increase unexpectedly. Other than a formula for increases in fuel prices and ad hoc or overload runs, a contractor has no ability to pass on increased costs to CPC. The average length of an HS contract is five years and, since 2005, 70% of HS contracts have been renewed with the same contractor.

[9] CUS contracts involve the delivery of mail and parcels between local post offices and retail outlets, relay boxes and/or street letter boxes. In this regard, the work is similar, although not identical, to that performed by Mail Service Couriers (MSCs), who are Canada Post employees. MSCs are members of the bargaining unit represented by CUPW. In locations where CPC employs MSCs, there are no CUS contractors and vice versa. The CUS Invitations to Tender and final contracts are extremely detailed. CPC specifies the vehicles that are to be used, and the work schedules. The contractor trains and assigns the workers it hires, but must comply with CPC's requirement that its employees maintain dress and grooming standards, including wearing a uniform. The only equipment and training provided by CPC is a hand-held scanner (PDT) used to document the movement of letters and packages. Should the timing of their route require it, CUS workers have access to the keys to certain CPC facilities.

[10] Nationally, there are some 200 CUS contracts with approximately 108 different CUS contractors. The average length of a CUS contract is five years and, since 2005, only 58% of incumbent contractors have had their contracts renewed. In many cases, this is because the incumbent decided not to bid on the retender. In other cases, it was because another contractor made a lower bid and was successful in displacing the incumbent.

[11] RMS Pope is a family-owned, Newfoundland based company that has entered into a number of contracts with CPC to provide both CUS and HS services in the Atlantic provinces. At the time of the Board's proceedings, RMS Pope was party to 14 HS and 9 CUS contracts with CPC in Atlantic Canada; the majority of which are in Newfoundland. The largest contract RMS Pope currently holds with CPC is a CUS contract for Cape Breton that it won in 2010. The Board was advised that the Cape Breton CUS contract is one of the largest CPC contracts in Atlantic Canada, encompassing 11 routes serving Sydney, North Sydney, Glace Bay and New Waterford. In addition to its work for CPC, RMS Pope engages in property rentals, video equipment maintenance and landscaping/snow removal. Its work for CPC represents between 40 and 60% of its business. RMS Pope employees performing HS and CUS work in Newfoundland are not unionized, while those in the remaining Atlantic provinces are members of CUPW.

[12] CUPW is a national trade union. It is the certified bargaining agent for two units of operational employees of CPC, the urban operations unit and the rural and suburban mail carriers' unit. In the late 1990s, CUPW began organizing HS and CUS workers throughout Canada. It was certified to represent a unit of HS and CUS workers

employed by RMS Pope in Nova Scotia, New Brunswick and Prince Edward Island in December 2006 (Board order no. 9215-U).

[13] CUPW's application seeks to have CPC and RMS Pope declared to be a single employer for labour relations purposes, pursuant to section 35 of the *Code*.

. . .

[53] The Board has established well known criteria that must be met before it will consider making a declaration of single employer under section 35 of the *Code* (see *Murray Hill Limousine, supra*):

1. that there be two or more enterprises (businesses);
2. both under federal jurisdiction;
3. that are associated or related;
4. of which at least two, but not necessarily all, are employers; and
5. which are under common control or direction.

[54] Even when the Board finds that these five criteria have been met, it has discretion as to whether a declaration of single employer should be issued. . . .

[55] Thus, it is clear that the main purpose of section 35 is to deal with complex corporate arrangements that conceal the true relationship between a business and those who work for it. While the Board has used this provision to rationalize a bargaining unit structure in order to prevent disruption caused by inter-unit conflict (see, for example, *C.U.P.E., Airline Division v. Air Canada*, 2000 CIRB 78 (C.I.R.B.)), preventing the erosion of bargaining rights remains the primary purpose of this provision.

B—Application of the Criteria to the Facts of this Case

[56] In the instant case, the Board is satisfied that there are two or more enterprises, namely CPC and RMS Pope . . .

[57] [T]he Board finds that both CPC and RMS Pope are employers within the meaning of the *Code*.

[58] In *Canadian Press, supra*, the CLRB provided the following guidance as to the factors to be considered in determining whether two enterprises are associated or related:

> . . . To be considered is the degree of interrelationship of the operations of the various enterprises. Do they provide similar services and product? Are they part of a vertically integrated process whereby one business carries out one function, for example, mining ore, and another business, in the organization, processes it? In determining whether the companies are associated or related, the Board would also look into what extent ownership or management of the enterprises are common.
>
> (pages 45; 359; and 441)

[59] In *Muir's Cartage Ltd., supra*, the CLRB held that common ownership is not required for a finding that two enterprises are associated or related. It is sufficient if the businesses are interrelated and complementary. In that case, the CLRB found that both CPC and its contractor, Muir's Cartage Ltd., were, to different degrees, elements of a single, totally integrated postal service. In this case, the Board has found that RMS

Pope's activities under its contract with CPC are integral to the operation of CPC's postal operations network. The evidence before the Board is that RMS Pope's activities are very closely coordinated with those of CPC. As was the case with Muir's Cartage Ltd., RMS Pope's activities are an element of a single, totally integrated postal service. Accordingly, the Board finds that RMS Pope's operations are associated or related to those of CPC.

[60] The final criteria for a section 35 declaration is whether the two employers are subject to common control or direction. With respect to this criteria, the CLRB observed in *Canadian Press, supra*:

> An indication of the fact that the enterprises are related is not necessarily decisive. Two or more enterprises may have common shareholders and the ownership of the assets may be held in common. However, the companies themselves may function as distinct, autonomous units. A more decisive test is the extent of common direction or control. The Board does not require total commonality of control in that all the enterprises are controlled by the same group of individuals. There may very well be a breakdown of functions whereby different persons have different responsibilities and play different roles in each of the companies involved or possibly no role at all in one or more of the companies. If it is established however, that the policies of the various enterprises are closely co-ordinated, integrated and subject to joint direction, even though the individuals are not directly tied to all of the companies involved, this would appear to show common direction and control.

(pages 45; 359; and 441)

[61] In *Murray Hill Limousine, supra,* and *Muir's Cartage, supra,* the CLRB held that it is the activities that must be under common control or direction, and not necessarily the employers themselves. The Board has distinguished between common direction, which relates to day to day operational activities, and common control, which considers indicia of longer term integration such as ownership, financial links and/or the setting of strategic direction. For the purposes of section 35 of the *Code*, it is sufficient that either common direction or common control be found to exist. In *Muir's Cartage Ltd., supra,* the CLRB found that common direction existed in the case of a contractor that provided mail sorting and delivery services under CPC's strict supervision. However, the Board has also held that necessary co-operation does not mean that two businesses are under common control (see *P.S.A.C. Saskatoon Airport Authority,* [2005] C.I.R.B. No. 340 (C.I.R.B.)). The mere fact that the contract governing the relationship between the two employers contains detailed direction as to how and when the work is to be performed is, in and of itself, insufficient to prove common control or direction. The Board must look at the details of the actual relationship between the parties.

[62] At the time of the Board's proceedings, RMS Pope held a total of 14 HS and 9 CUS contracts with CPC. Although these contracts are very detailed, this level of detail is necessary in order to co-ordinate the activities required for efficient operation of the postal service. With respect to all matters other than those prescribed by its contracts with CPC, RMS Pope operates its business independently and without reference to any of CPC's employment policies, strategic plans or other business planning tools. As a result, the Board is unable to find that the two companies are under common control.

[63] The HS workers employed by RMS Pope operate relatively independently. They have access to the CPC facilities and perform their work without any direct supervision by RMS Pope or CPC. In the event CPC is not satisfied with an HS worker's performance, it contacts RMS Pope management, who deal with the HS worker directly. Based on the evidence provided, the Board is unable to find that there is common direction with respect to the day to day operational activities related to highway services.

[64] The parties disagree over whether the CUS workers employed by RMS Pope perform the same work as MSCs employed by CPC. The Board was provided with the job description for an MSC and extensive testimony as to the various functions performed by CUS workers and MSCs. The Board was also informed that CUS workers and MSCs never work in or from the same facilities; in other words, the necessary tasks are undertaken either by an MSC employed by CPC or, in the locations covered by its CUS contracts, by RMS Pope's employees. On the basis of this evidence, the Board is satisfied that the functions of MSCs and CUS workers are sufficiently similar to find that they are engaged in a common activity.

[65] The evidence demonstrates that RMS Pope provides very little on-site supervision of the employees who perform the CUS work. Due to the nature of that work, there is consequently daily interaction between the CUS workers and CPC supervisors. On occasion, for example when letter carrier volumes are so great that they cannot deliver the A.M. priorities, CPC supervisors may assign the work to CUS drivers. CPC supervisors complete a count of all items assigned to the CUS drivers for delivery. CPC supervisors may contact a CUS driver by cell phone during the work day to check on the timing of deliveries. In the Board's view, the totality of the evidence regarding the nature of the CUS work and the degree of interaction between CPC supervisors and the RMS Pope employees performing this work is sufficient to conclude that common direction exists.

C — Labour Relations Purpose

[66] As noted above, the primary purpose of section 35 of the *Code* is to prevent an employer from using its corporate structure to avoid its collective bargaining responsibilities, for example, by shifting work from a unionized entity to one that is non-union. Essentially, this provision of the *Code* allows the Board to lift the corporate veil in order to determine whether rights granted under the *Code* are being defeated by illegitimate employer actions. A labour relations purpose has been found to exist, for example, when an employer contracted out a portion of its unionized business through a franchising agreement while retaining significant control over the franchisee's operations (see *Coopérative des travailleurs routiers, Trans-Coop* (1996), 101 di 159 (Can. L.R.B.) (CLRB no. 1170)) and when an employer contracted out work it had previously done in-house to a contractor that was wholly dependent on the contracting entity (see *I.B. of T.C.W.& H. of A., Local 979 v. Remier Express Lines Ltd.* (1984), 56 di 83; 7 C.L.R.B.R. (N.S.) 21 (Can. L.R.B.); and (1984), 84 C.L.L.C. 16,036 (Can. L.R.B.) (CLRB no. 465)).

[67] CUPW invites the Board to expand the scope of application of section 35 beyond its historical interpretation. It points to the Board's decision in *Landtran Systems Inc., supra,* for the proposition that section 35 is not merely remedial and should be interpreted so as to promote the objectives of the *Code*. In this case, CUPW suggests that

there are two important factors supporting a finding that there is a labour relations purpose for a declaration of common employer as between CPC and RMS Pope. Firstly, it alleges that mail contractors that are unionized are less likely to obtain or retain CPC contracts and that the employees' *Charter* right to collective bargaining is thwarted when a contract is terminated. Secondly, CUPW asserts that, for bargaining to be meaningful, it needs to be able to negotiate directly with the contracting authority.

[68] In *Landtran Systems Inc., supra*, the Board was dealing with some twenty four companies who were part of, or in some way associated with, Landtran Systems Inc. (the Landtran Group). With respect to the four companies operating within the Landtran Group's domestic less-than-truckload (LTL) division, the Board held as follows:

> [38] At the end of the day, the Board was left with the conclusion that the *corporate boundaries that exist between the entities in the Canadian LTL group are artificial and virtually indistinguishable from a functional perspective.* Although the different companies may have a separate historical and geographical base—and they may well have complemented each other following the integration of the businesses after the purchase of BTL in 1990—in light of the functional restructuring, it no longer makes sense to maintain the artificial distinctions between companies within the Canadian LTL segment. And, it no longer makes practical labour relations sense to have two unions and a non-union company operating within that same segment of the business.
>
> . . .
>
> [48] Even leaving aside the issue of whether bargained or bargaining rights are—or are likely to be—jeopardized, in the circumstances of the present case, it is untenable that two trade unions should represent two separate common employers in the same division of the employer's operation. It simply does not make labour relations sense, nor does it represent a rationalization of bargaining units which would promote sound labour relations and/or which would help to prevent disruption caused by inter-unit conflicts. . . .
>
> [49] The employer's restructuring of its overall business along new functional lines has dictated the need for a rationalization of bargaining units within the now fully integrated and delineated LTL segment of the network.
>
> (emphasis added)

[69] The Board went on to deny the portion of the union's application that sought to sweep all of the other Landtran Group companies into a common employer, stating:

> [82] Even considering the broader and more expansive interpretation of the Board's discretion under section 35—and the resultant criteria of what constitutes an appropriate labour relations purpose for issuing a common employer declaration—a common employer declaration over the remaining network of companies would not serve to promote harmonious labour relations. *A common employer declaration—beyond that within each of the LTL and FTL segments—would, in these circumstances, be tantamount to expanding the unions' existing bargaining rights.*
>
> (emphasis added)

[70] In the Board's view, although *Landtran Systems Inc.*, *supra*, suggested that the exercise of its discretion under section 35 of the *Code* need not be remedial alone, the decision merely reaffirms that the promotion of harmonious labour relations, as mandated in the *Preamble* to the *Code*, remains the overarching principle informing the interpretation and application of the statute.

[71] In the instant case, the corporate boundaries between CPC and RMS Pope are not artificial or indistinguishable from a functional perspective, as was the case in *Landtran*, *supra*. The imperatives that led the Board to make a common employer declaration in that case are simply not present in the current matter. The evidence before the Board indicates that RMS Pope has had a number of contracts with CPC, beginning in at least 2000. It was successful in obtaining such contracts even after CUPW unionized part of its workforce in 2006. Between 2005 and 2012, RMS Pope was the successful bidder in 37 of 55 tenders issued by CPC in Atlantic Canada. Seventeen of these contracts were in Nova Scotia, New Brunswick or Prince Edward Island and 20 were in Newfoundland. Over the same time period, RMS Pope lost 18 of the tendered contracts for which it was the incumbent contractor. Sixteen of the 18 it lost were in Nova Scotia, New Brunswick or Prince Edward Island. CPC's evidence was that, in the cases where RMS Pope lost a contract, it was because a competitor submitted a lower bid and not because RMS Pope's employees were unionized.

[72] It is a commercial reality that non-union contractors are often able to under-bid unionized contractors. It is also a commercial reality that contracts for service that provide for a fixed price, rather than a flow-through of costs (cost plus), often result in little or no flexibility for the negotiation of improvements in employee wages, benefits and working conditions during their term. However, the legitimate retendering of contracts for service is not a circumstance that section 35 of the *Code* was designed to address. Parliament has provided an alternative solution to the problems caused by successive contracts for services in section 47.3 of the *Code*. While that provision currently only applies to contracting out for pre-board security screening services, the Governor in Council has authority to extend the application of this provision by designating other services, in other industries, by means of regulations.

[73] In this case, the Board is unable to conclude that the contracts with RMS Pope have been used by CPC to undermine CUPW's bargaining units or bargaining rights at CPC. There is no evidence that the work of unionized CPC employees has been transferred to lower paid unionized employees of RMS Pope or that CPC engages in the contracting out of its HS and CUS work in order to avoid its obligations under the *Code*. The Board is satisfied that CPC's tendering process is designed to accomplish a legitimate business purpose and does not have, as its objective or effect, the nullification of rights granted to any employees by the *Code*. The employees of RMS Pope remain entitled to organize and bargain collectively, even if their employer does not have the same financial capacity as CPC. The union has not persuaded the Board that a common employer declaration would promote harmonious labour relations, either in respect of its relationship with CPC or with RMS Pope.

[74] The Board can also find no merit in the union's argument that the guarantee of freedom of association contained in section 2(*d*) the *Canadian Charter of Rights and*

Freedoms requires the Board to provide RMS Pope's employees with enhanced bargaining power by means of a declaration of common employer. Although the Supreme Court of Canada's decision in *Plourde c. Québec (Commission des relations du travail), supra,* dealt with the interpretation of the Quebec *Labour Code,* R.S.Q., c. C-27, the observations of the majority of the Court are equally applicable to the *Code*:

> [56] The appellant's argument extends the reasoning in *Health Services* well beyond its natural limits. In that case the state was not only the legislator but the employer. Here the employer is a private corporation. Section 3 of the *Code* guarantees the right of association to workers in Quebec. Other provisions implement this general guarantee. *The legislature has crafted a balance between the rights of labour and the rights of management in a way that respects freedom of association.* No argument was raised by the appellant or any of the interveners against the constitutionality of *any* provisions of the *Code,* or claimed that in its entirety the *Code* fails to respect freedom of association. The appellant says the interpretation of the *Code* should be developed to reflect "*Charter* values", but *the entire* Code *is the embodiment and legislative vehicle to implement freedom of association in the Quebec workplace.* The *Code* must be read as a whole. It cannot be correct that the Constitution requires that every provision (including s. 17) must be interpreted to favour the union and the employees.
>
> [57] Care must be taken not only to avoid upsetting the balance the legislature has struck in the *Code* taken as a whole, but not to hand to one side (labour) a lopsided advantage because employees bargain through their union (and can thereby invoke freedom of association) whereas employers, for the most part, bargain individually.

(emphasis added)

[75] As noted above, the *Code* contains alternatives to a common employer declaration under section 35 that are intended to address the economic consequences of the contract tendering system. The Board therefore declines to extend the concept of "labour relations purpose" under section 35 of the *Code* to encompass the notion that a contractor's employees should be fully insulated from the normal consequences of contract tendering and retendering.

[76] For all of the reasons set out above, the Board finds that there is no labour relations purpose necessitating a declaration of common employer as between CPC and RMS Pope. The union's application under section 35 of the *Code* is therefore dismissed.

Chapter 5: The Right to Join a Union

5:100 INTRODUCTION

This chapter examines the legal protection given to employees in the exercise of their right to choose collective representation by a trade union. The current legal safeguards were developed against an historical backdrop of strenuous and sometimes violent resistance by employers (and at times by government as well) to union-organizing efforts—efforts which themselves were not always free of coercive elements. The following excerpt describes a violent episode in a union recognition dispute in Estevan, Saskatchewan, during the Great Depression.

Stanley Hanson, "Estevan 1931" in Irving Abella, ed., *On Strike: Six Key Labour Struggles in Canada, 1919–1949* (Toronto: James Lorimer, 1974) 33 at 43–51

> With the formation of a branch of the MWUC [Mine Workers' Union of Canada] in the Souris coal field, a crisis arose that eventually culminated in the September 8 walkout. The operators of the large mines adamantly refused to recognize the new organization as a body with constituted authority to negotiate on behalf of the miners. The miners were equally adamant in their refusal to negotiate independently of their union. When requested by the union to attend a joint meeting of all operators and miners' representatives in the Estevan Town Hall at 8:30 p.m. on September 3 for the purpose of reaching an agreement on hours of work, wages and living conditions, only the operators of six smaller mines complied. The operators of the ["Big Six"] deep-seam mines stated:
>
>> We will not meet you [Sloan, the President of the MWUC] or any representative of an organization such as yours which, by your own statement, boasts a direct connection with the 'entire Workers' Unity League and the Red Internationale of Soviet Russia.'
>
> Under these circumstances, the union decided to use its ultimate weapon and voted to cease work at midnight on September 7, 1931....
>
> When mine operators in the Souris coal field awoke on the morning of September 8, only one was in operation. Because Truax-Traer [the mining company] did not employ men underground and its employees were non-union, it was not directly affected by the work stoppage. Sloan intimated that the fifty men engaged in stripping coal and laying track there would be allowed to continue working despite the union's call for a one hundred per cent walkout. He warned, however, that there would be trouble if any attempt were made to have the men load or ship coal. The union further stated that it was prepared to permit coal to be shipped to Dominion Electric Power and the Estevan

Hospital, but would vigorously oppose shipments destined for outside markets. Provision was also made for local supply. Soon after the strike began, union officials granted the owners of several hillside mines permission to supply coal for local consumption, and to fill orders from farmers within a twenty-five mile radius of Estevan.

Despite the gestures of goodwill by the union towards those in the vicinity of the coal field who might require fuel, and despite the sympathetic response to the plight of the striking miners by workers and others elsewhere, suspicions quickly arose that the strike might not be altogether peaceful. Hence, to assist the two-man local detachment in quelling any future disturbance, a squad of four RCMP officers arrived in Estevan from Regina at noon on September 8.

As the strike progressed and tension mounted, additional reinforcements were sent to the strike zone. A dozen RCMP under the command of Detective Staff-Sergeant Mortimer arrived and began operating twenty-four-hour-a-day patrols throughout the district for the stated purpose of maintaining law and order. In addition, the Saskatchewan Coal Operators' Association engaged a private force of thirteen special constables to assist police in protecting mine property....

Despite the increasing number of law-enforcement personnel in the district, the coal operators were dissatisfied. Morfit [a consulting engineer at one of the mines], in particular believed that the RCMP were handling the situation poorly. Morfit, 'an American with extreme ideas who has had experience in the Pensylvania [sic] USA strikes,' reportedly stated that 'if this was in the States it would soon be settled ... the strikers would be mowed down with machine guns if they carried on the way they do up here.'

At the conclusion of a conference held September 18, the coal operators issued a statement charging that the absence of adequate police protection had prevented the reopening of the mines. A few days later, the operators requested that additional police be sent to the strike sector 'to insure protection to life, property and the peaceful operation of our industries.' Their plea fell on deaf ears. The acting attorney-general, the Honourable Howard McConnell, seemingly of the opinion that the Saskatchewan government was not responsible for breaking strikes, stated that the government had been and still was according the mine owners ample police protection in the Estevan district coal field.

At about the same time, M.S. Campbell, chief conciliation officer with the Canada Department of Labour, arrived in Estevan. After a brief conference with the coal operators, he obtained their assurance that if the miners agreed to return to work pending an investigation of their grievances, they would be reinstated in their former positions without discrimination. However, when it became obvious that the operators would not recognize the union, negotiations collapsed and Campbell proceeded to Regina to meet with provincial authorities. Testifying later before a royal commission, Dan Moar, a miner and officer of the MWUC local, stated that upon his arrival Campbell told the miners' committee that the royal commission, headed by Judge E.R. Wylie of Estevan, which had just been appointed to inquire into the labour dispute, could not proceed until the men resumed work. He quoted Campbell as saying that 'the government wasn't going to spend money if we wouldn't go back to work....' When told the men would not do so, Campbell allegedly said: 'If that is your attitude, I am through with you, I leave this morning.' Thus, the stalemate continued and the stage was set for violence.

On September 28, information was conveyed to Estevan Police Chief McCutcheon that the miners' intended to hold a 'nuisance parade' in Estevan the following day. The parade was to be held for the purpose of dramatizing the miners' plight in order to gain local support, and to advertise a mass meeting scheduled for the evening of the twenty-ninth in the town hall, at which time Anne Buller, a WUL [Workers' Unity League of Canada] organizer from Winnipeg, would address the assembly. As no application for a permit to hold the parade had been made, Mayor Bannatyne called a special session of the town council for the morning of the twenty-ninth to discuss it, as well as the matter of renting the hall to the strikers. After brief deliberations, council, it has been said, passed a resolution prohibiting the renting of the town hall to the miners, banning the parade and authorizing the Estevan police and the RCMP to prevent any such demonstration....

At 1:30 P.M., on the twenty-ninth, some two hundred miners, all of them evidently unaware that they would soon be confronted by the police, assembled in Bienfait [a mining town near Estevan], intent on motoring to Estevan, accompanied by their wives and children, to interview Mayor Bannatyne regarding prohibition of the public meeting scheduled that evening in the town hall. At two o'clock the group departed for Crescent Collieries, three miles distant. That mine had been chosen for a rendezvous and soon cars and lorries bearing strikers and their families arrived from various points throughout the district. Here the men boarded lorries, a few of which were draped with Union Jacks, and the women and children entered automobiles for the seventeen-mile journey. The caravan, consisting of thirty or forty vehicles, extending for a distance of a mile along the highway and moving at a speed aptly described as that of a funeral cortège, then threaded its way through the idle mining district, picking up recruits en route. As it approached Estevan, banners proclaiming 'We will not work for starvation wages,' 'We want houses, not piano boxes' and 'Down with the company stores' were unfurled.

Meanwhile, in Estevan the police were reportedly charting strategy to prevent any violation of the town council's edict forbidding any parade or demonstration. They are said to have decided that should any attempt to demonstrate occur, they would concentrate their forces at the limits of the town to prevent the striking miners from entering. Reinforcements had arrived intermittently during the strike, and by the twenty-ninth Inspector Moorhead had forty-seven RCMP under his command. The police were equipped with thirty rifles (one hundred rounds of ammunition per rifle), forty-eight revolvers, forty-eight riding crops and four machine guns capable of firing three hundred shots per minute. Rumours were prevalent that the police also were holding a stock of tear-gas bombs in readiness.

Shortly before three P.M., three to four hundred striking miners plus members of their families reached the outskirts of the town. The motorcade approached Estevan from the east on Highway 39 and proceeded west along Fourth Street, the principal thoroughfare, to Souris Avenue, where twenty-two policemen had formed a cordon across the street. Chief McCutcheon approached the lead vehicle and told the strikers: 'Now boys youse had better pull back home for we are not going to allow you to parade through town....' During the ensuing argument, McCutcheon apparently grabbed hold of [striking miner] Martin Day and attempted to pull him down off the lorry. While some of his colleagues were engaged in holding Day back, another struck McCutcheon in the face and knocked him to the ground. It was at this point that McCutcheon ordered Day's arrest and the initial struggle began. The strikers leaped from the lead truck and, led by Martin Day, who shouted: 'Come on boys, come on, give it to them,' rushed the arresting officers.

Almost simultaneously, the fire brigade was called to the scene. Their intervention, however, proved both unavailing and tragic. After a brief encounter, five miners succeeded in driving the firemen from the equipment and prevented the anticipated drenching. One striker climbed up on the engine and declared it 'captured.' He was shot dead on the spot.

Striking miners and their women, wielding clubs and throwing stones and other missiles, then launched the final assault. Hopelessly outnumbered and unable to halt the advancing crowd, the police retreated step by step, firing warning shots above the heads of the demonstrators and at their feet. It was not until the police, 'with blood streaming down their faces,' stood with their backs to the town hall that Inspector Moorhead, accompanied by a squad of about thirty RCMP, arrived on the scene from Truax-Traer. The police then took the offensive and by 4:15 P.M. the mob had been dispersed, leaving in its wake some wounded, dead and dying, and sixty thousand dollars' damage to store fronts, light standards and the fire-fighting equipment.

The grim toll of the battle consisted of three dead and twenty-three injured. Nick Nargan, a twenty-five-year-old miner from Taylorton, died instantly from a bullet in the heart; Julian Gryshko, age twenty-six, died of abdominal bullet wounds. Pete Markunas, a Bienfait miner aged twenty-seven, died in Weyburn General Hospital two days later as a result of bullet wounds to the abdomen. Eight other miners, four bystanders and one RCMP constable also suffered bullet wounds. In addition, eight RCMP personnel and Chief McCutcheon were injured by weapons wielded and thrown by the strikers.
[Reprinted by permission.]

Further accounts of the history of resistance to unionization can be found in Judy Fudge & Eric Tucker, *Labour Before the Law: The Regulation of Workers' Collective Action in Canada, 1900–1948* (Toronto: Oxford University Press, 2001).

* * * * *

Before World War II, a strike or the threat of a strike was the only way for a group of employees to compel a reluctant employer to engage in collective bargaining. Since the 1940s, however, legislation across Canada has required an employer to negotiate with a trade union that has been certified by a labour relations board to represent employees in a defined "bargaining unit." To be certified, the union usually must have the support of a majority of the employees in that unit. How a bargaining unit is defined, and how majority support is determined, will be addressed in Chapter 6. An employer's duty to bargain with a certified union is dealt with in Chapter 7. For the purposes of the present chapter, the important point is that employees no longer need to strike to obtain recognition of their chosen union. Indeed, as is discussed in Chapter 8, recognition strikes are now illegal.

Because an employer is legally obliged to recognize and bargain with a certified trade union, and because many employers prefer not to bargain collectively, management representatives have an incentive to prevent the union from obtaining or retaining the majority support on which its collective bargaining rights are based. Labour relations legislation restricts anti-union activities by an employer during an organizing campaign, and also before and after that campaign. Conduct that violates these restrictions is commonly called an unfair labour practice. The legislation also prohibits union unfair labour practices, including improper conduct in attempting to win new members. The focus of most of this chapter is on unfair labour practices during organizing campaigns. Later chapters will deal with such practices at other times.

The regulation of employer unfair labour practices during an organizing campaign rests in large part on the premise that such conduct unduly influences employee choice for or against collective bargaining, and therefore interferes with freedom of association. The following is an excerpt from a report which considered whether American labour law restrictions on employer interference in union organizing (similar in many ways to those in Canadian law) met international human rights standards on the protection of freedom of association.

Human Rights Watch, *Unfair Advantage: Workers' Freedom of Association in the United States under International Human Rights Standards,* **(2000), Part I, "Summary—Policy and Reality," online: www.hrw.org/reports/2000/uslabor**

> The NLRA [*National Labor Relations Act*] declares a national policy of "full freedom of association" and protects workers' "right to self-organization, to form, join, or assist labor organizations, to bargain collectively through representatives of their own choosing, and to engage in other concerted activities for the purpose of collective bargaining or other mutual aid or protection ..." The NLRA makes it unlawful for employers to "interfere with, restrain, or coerce" workers in the exercise of these rights. It creates the National Labor Relations Board (NLRB) to enforce the law by investigating and remedying violations. All these measures comport with international human rights norms regarding workers' freedom of association.
>
> The reality of NLRA enforcement falls far short of its goals. Many workers who try to form and join trade unions to bargain with their employers are spied on, harassed, pressured, threatened, suspended, fired, deported or otherwise victimized in reprisal for their exercise of the right to freedom of association.
>
> Private employers are the main agents of abuse. But international human rights law makes governments responsible for protecting vulnerable persons and groups from patterns of abuse by private actors. In the United States, labor law enforcement efforts often fail to deter unlawful conduct. When the law is applied, enervating delays and weak remedies invite continued violations.
>
> Any employer intent on resisting workers' self-organization can drag out legal proceedings for years, fearing little more than an order to post a written notice in the workplace promising not to repeat unlawful conduct and grant back pay to a worker fired for organizing.... Many employers have come to view remedies like back pay for workers fired because of union activity as a routine cost of doing business, well worth the price of getting rid of organizing leaders and derailing workers' organizing efforts. As a result, a culture of near-impunity has taken hold in much of U.S. labor law and practice.
>
> [© 2000 Human Rights Watch. Reprinted by permission.]

CHAPTER 5: THE RIGHT TO JOIN A UNION

However, the premise that employer interference negatively affects union organizing was questioned by an American empirical study published in 1976—*Union Representation Elections: Law and Reality*, by Julius G Getman, Stephen B Goldberg, and Jeanne B Herman (New York: Russell Sage Foundation). That study looked at a sample of certification votes conducted by the US National Labor Relations Board (NLRB), and reached the controversial conclusion that illegal employer tactics did not significantly affect the result in those votes. The following excerpt challenges the validity of that conclusion.

Paul Weiler, "Promises to Keep: Securing Workers' Rights to Self-Organization under the NLRA" (1983) 96 *Harvard Law Review* 1769 at 1782–86

> [In] *Union Representation Elections: Law and Reality* ... Getman and his co-authors concluded that even the most egregious of illegal employer tactics had no discernible impact on the results of NLRB representation elections.
>
> The authors selected a sample of thirty-one hotly contested campaigns from the period 1972–1973. In each unit, shortly after the NLRB had directed a vote, the authors interviewed the employees about whether they had signed a union card and how they intended to vote. The authors then gathered and evaluated information about the ensuing campaign, and finally, after the election, reinterviewed the employees about their impressions of the campaign and how they had actually voted. The authors concluded that the votes of more than 80% of the employees, and hence the results in twenty-nine of the thirty-one elections, could have been predicted from precampaign attitudes and intentions. The other side of the coin was that the campaign was discovered to have very little impact; the employees had scant recall of the issues, and even illegal employer coercion of the most serious kind did not affect a significant proportion of the votes. The importance Getman and his co-authors attributed to their empirical findings can be seen in the policy recommendation they made—a systematic deregulation of the representation election.
>
> On their face, the Getman findings pose a major challenge to my argument that discriminatory discharges and other forms of coercive behavior by American employers have significantly contributed to the steep decline in union success under the NLRA [National Labor Relations Act]. A closer look at the Getman study, however, reveals two critical flaws in its analysis. The first consists in the study's appraisal of the evidence of the impact of coercive campaigning by employers. The authors actually found that, among the surveyed workers who had indicated before the campaign either that they were undecided or that they favored the union, the percentage of votes against unionization was somewhat higher after an illegal employer campaign than after a clean one. The magnitude of this difference, however, was too small to pass a 99% test of statistical significance in such a limited sample. Thus, the authors asserted, one could not conclude with certainty that the observed relation was attributable to anything but chance.
>
> This sort of statistical judgment is hardly sufficient for the making of legal policy. It may be legitimate for Getman and his coauthors to conclude that their own data do not demonstrate with certainty that employer coercion affects employee voting, but it is entirely unjustified to infer from that fact alone that the contrary is true. The failure to find a statistically significant connection between employer intimidation and employee

votes in this limited sample neither proves that there is no such relationship nor provides a basis on which to argue that we may safely abandon efforts to protect employee choice. Legal policy must almost invariably be formulated in the absence of absolute certainty about the causes and effects of social phenomena. Given the inherent plausibility of the notion that employees will respond to threats to the jobs that are crucial to their lives, and given that the data in the Getman study indicate that it is more likely than not that such threats do affect employee votes, it is only prudent to take steps that will ensure freedom of choice in the workplace.

In any event, the data gathered by Getman and his co-authors have been used by another scholar, William Dickens, to calculate the actual probabilities that the employer campaigns had varying levels of impact. Dickens' best estimate was that, in the average campaign studied, unfair labor practices reduced the number of pro-union votes by 4%. The reduction was 15% when the unfair labor practices took the form of specific threats or actions against union supporters. Furthermore, when both legal and illegal practices were taken into account, it was more than 99% certain that the typical employer campaign reduced by at least 5% the probability that the average worker would vote for unionization, and it was more than 90% certain that the campaign reduced that probability by at least 10%.

Some might argue that effects of this magnitude do not warrant the kind of concern that the NLRB, the courts, and the Congress have shown for the trends of the last decade. But such a quick dismissal would be unfounded. The importance of the campaign lies in its effect on the ultimate election verdict, and a small shift in the number of workers voting for union representation may have a substantial effect on the number of union victories. This possibility points to the second crucial flaw in the analysis by Getman and his coauthors: their focus on the average voter rather than the election verdict. Their procedure was to interview each employee before and after the campaign, correlate any changes in his decision about union representation with the type of campaign to which he was exposed, and then simply aggregate these results across all the campaigns in order to determine the effect of the campaign on the average voter. The number of election results changed by employer coercion, however, depends not only on how many votes are affected in all campaigns combined, but also on how close the elections are and on how the affected voters are distributed among the different employee units.

The distribution of affected voters is unlikely to be random. Employers' efforts to influence workers' votes will probably be concentrated on swing voters in close elections; and it is in close elections, when workers believe that their votes will really make a difference, that they may pay more attention to the employer's threats about the dire consequences of a union victory. Moreover, employees are affected by peer group support and pressure. Intimidation is more likely to be effective in a unit in which enthusiasm for collective bargaining is marginal than in a unit in which the union enjoys overwhelming support.

The elections studied by Getman and his coauthors show how shifts among small numbers of critically located voters can have large effects on the overall success of union organizing efforts. The unions won just over one-fourth (eight of thirty-one) of the elections studied. To win a majority of those elections, the unions would have had to be successful in eight more campaigns. A shift of only 2% of the total votes cast in the thirty-one elections, if those 2% had been carefully allocated, would have been sufficient to provide the eight additional victories. This simple calculation demonstrates that even a slight impact from employer unfair labor practices may seriously reduce union success in a representation system based on the rule that the majority vote wins and the winner takes all.

Employing a more sophisticated methodology than my back-of-the-envelope calculation, the Dickens study tested for the multiplier effect that marginal changes in employee support had on election results. Dickens used the Getman study's background information about plant settings and employee attitudes to run computer simulations of each of the thirty-one elections. The elections were simulated once on the basis of the campaigns that were actually conducted, a second time on the assumption that illegal practices took place in all campaigns, and a third time on the assumption that all campaigns were clean.

Dickens' results suggest a starkly different conclusion from that reached by Getman and his coauthors. Dickens found that unions would have won 46% to 47% of the elections if the employer had campaigned entirely cleanly (and 53% to 75% of the elections if there had been no campaign at all), but only 3% to 10% if every employer had campaigned with the highest intensity and greatest illegality identified in the sample. Ironically, then, the raw data that Getman and his coauthors so carefully gathered point to precisely the opposite conclusion from the one they drew. A protracted representation campaign, punctuated by discriminatory discharges and other reprisals against union supporters, can have a pronounced effect on the ultimate election verdict.

[Copyright © 1983 by the Harvard Law Review Association.]

Given the conflicting interpretations of the data, how much legal restriction on employer resistance to union organizing do you think is justified in an effort to safeguard freedom of association?

5:200 NON-MOTIVE UNFAIR LABOUR PRACTICES

Although some legislative provisions concerning unfair labour practices refer to motive, others are silent on this point. See, for example, s. 94(1)(a) of the *Canada Labour Code* and s. 70 of the Ontario *Labour Relations Act, 1995*. The latter section reads as follows:

> No employer or employers' organization and no person acting on behalf of an employer or an employers' organization shall participate in or interfere with the formation, selection or administration of a trade union or the representation of employees by a trade union or contribute financial or other support to a trade union, but nothing in this section shall be deemed to deprive an employer of his freedom to express his views so long as he does not use coercion, intimidation, threats, promises or undue influence.

Canadian Paperworkers Union, Canadian Labour Congress and Its Local 305 v International Wallcoverings, a Division of International Paints (Canada) Limited, [1983] OLRB Rep 1316 at 1328–37

> [The company kept its operations going during a legal strike by using agency-supplied strikebreakers who were picked up at secret locations each morning by the agency and

driven to the plant in specially adapted vans. The strikers learned that the strikebreakers would be picked up at the Vesta Restaurant one morning, and a number of strikers showed up there at the pickup time. An altercation ensued.

The board made the following findings of fact with respect to the nine strikers whose dismissal led to this complaint. Strikers D McCarroll (local union president), Lutes (local union secretary), and Prewal kicked, punched, or otherwise assaulted strikebreakers. Striker M McCarroll (local union vice-president) attacked and slightly damaged the agency's van, but did not (as the company alleged and perhaps believed) threaten a strikebreaker with a knife. Strikers Brinston, Carrier, and Mez were at the restaurant but did not participate in the attack on the strikebreakers or the van. Strikers Blanchard and Richard were found by the board not to have been at the restaurant at all. All nine of the strikers mentioned above were dismissed by the company's labour relations manager, Clayton, as soon as he was advised of the incident and of the names of the strikers who were thought to have been present.]

ADAMS Chair: What becomes immediately apparent is the use in sections 66 and 70 [now ss 72 and 76 of the OLRA] of words suggesting a motive requirement whereas section 64 [now s 70 of the OLRA] is expressed more in terms of effect. More specifically, section 66 uses the words 'because,' 'seeks' and section 70 the word 'seek.' These words are not to be found in section 64. Instead, section 64 refers to interference. That section is also a very general one cast in terms, inter alia, of interference with the formation, selection or administration of a trade union. On the other hand, sections 66 and 70 are more particular in scope, aimed at particular kinds of improper action which impede or prevent persons from exercising rights under the Act. The result is that any conduct that violates sections 66 and 70 arguably will also offend section 64 but the opposite will not necessarily be so. For this reason, the inter-relationship and scope of these sections (principally sections 64 and 66) are absolutely critical. If section 64 does not require an 'intent' to interfere and sections 66 and 70 do, complainants would be better off filing complaints only pursuant to section 64. The result would be, however, to read sections 66 and 70 out of the Act. This would be a dubious application of legislative intent. On the other hand, interpreting section 64 always to require motive gives little or no effect to the difference in language between the sections.

This tension accounts for the somewhat different treatment accorded to section 64 in [a number of board decisions]. For example in *A.A.S. Telecommunications* ... the then Chairman of the Board ... read into the statute an exception for employer conduct 'that only incidentally affects a trade union.' In this manner the Board proposed, pursuant to section 64, to distinguish between legitimate and illegitimate management initiatives. Presumably an adverse impact on union activity would be characterized as 'incidental' where, relying on its expertise, the Board accepted the employer's action as classic business or collective bargaining activity not inconsistent with the scheme of the Act. In effect, the Board would 'balance' the conflicting interests of labour and management, honouring accepted relationships but being vigilant that intrusions on statutory entitlements have suitable justifications. In fact, labour board analysis of no-solicitation rules has tended to follow non-motive approach after an adverse effect has been established or inferred. This is particularly apparent from the touchstone American cases which have been referred to and relied upon in Canada ... However, we wish to stress that 'the balancing' has been more one of examining the record for a legitimate management interest to support the adverse impact on union activity. It has not usually involved a delicate weighing of legitimate but conflicting interests with labour boards being the final arbiters of the right policy mix. We know of no case in Canada or the United States in which a labour board has purported to balance a bona fide exercise of a managerial prerogative, for example, a layoff or subcontracting decision, against its impact on union activity. The no-solicitation cases have looked to identify the managerial interest in a sweeping no-solicitation rule over and above a simple reliance on property rights. Where such an interest is absent, there exists a significant imbalance in favour of the protected activity and this clear imbalance triggers a statutory violation. Indeed, this absence of a managerial interest is the same kind of a condition often justifying an inference of improper motive. The real balancing, in the no-solicitation cases, has been between property rights and statutory rights. Unfortunately, this point was not made in the *A.A.S.* case which in turn gave rise to a concern within the Board itself over the viability of an unrestrained balancing approach.

In *Skyline Hotels Limited* ... the Board indicated its concern about the open-ended nature of section 64 and its potential triggering by any bona fides management action having an adverse impact on trade union activity. In contrast to the *A.A.S.* decision, the *Skyline* decision proposed to avoid this possibility by implying in section 64 a motive requirement while noting that motive need not be established always by direct evidence. In this respect the decision stated ... :

> The striking aspect of this section is that on its face it makes no mention of anti-union motive or purpose. It simply uses the word 'interfere,' which, in normal parlance, could be taken to connote either intentional or unintentional conduct....
>
> But the Board has always had regard to industrial relations reality, and to the scheme of the Act as a whole, and has never interpreted the section in this manner. To do so would of course render meaningless the other specific provisions of the Act, such as section 58, which clearly require the finding of an anti-union motive. Any discharge of a union organizer, or perhaps of any employee during a campaign, for example, could be litigated successfully by a trade union under section 56, whether or not an anti-union motive could be shown under section 58. It is impossible to contemplate that section 56 creates that kind of unfair labour practice....
>
> *In the absence of an anti-union motive, in other words, it is not a violation of the section if the employer's conduct simply affects the trade union in pursuit of an unrelated business purpose.* ...
>
> As has often been noted, however, the trade union will not in every case be required to prove by affirmative evidence the existence of an anti-union motive. This is so because the effect of certain types of conduct is so clearly foreseeable that an employer may be presumed to have intended the consequences of his acts ... *Once such conduct has been established, then as a practical matter (and whether or not section 79(a) of the Act applies to the situation) the onus is upon the employer to come forward with a credible business purpose to justify the conduct.* ... It is up to the Board then, in all the circumstances, to decide what the motive of the employer really was. [Emphasis added.]

In comparing this statement to the A.A.S. approach, emphasis must be given to the *Skyline* observation that specific evidence of intent to interfere is not an indispensable element of proof. As the United States Supreme Court explained in *Radio Officers' Union v. NLRB*....

> Both the Board and the courts have recognized that proof of certain types of discrimination satisfies the intent requirement. This recognition that specific proof of intent is unnecessary where employer conduct inherently encourages or discourages union membership is but an application of the common-law rule that a man is held to intend the foreseeable consequences of his conduct.

Also relevant is the fact that improper motive need not be the dominant purpose underlying disputed conduct for the Act to be breached. It is sufficient that employer conduct only be partially motivated by anti-union considerations.... [T]he combined effect of the mixed motive approach and legal inference can result in the striking down of employer conduct where the Board is not prepared to accept tendered evidence of a bona fides business purpose as a complete answer to the adverse impact on trade union activity complained of. However, usually the Board has been reluctant to find by legal inference a partial but improper motive where direct and persuasive evidence of an acceptable business justification has been established by a respondent employer.... [W]hen direct evidence of motive is not available, the Board is often required to engage in a form of balancing of conflicting interests in deciding whether to infer an improper (and possibly partial) motive on the evidence before it. Balancing is not eliminated by requiring that motive be established and this, on occasion, has caused motive to be referred to as 'fictive formality.' In this respect, labour law is little different from those other fields of law discussed above. As the United States Supreme Court stated in *NLRB v. Erie Resistor*... the necessary intent may be:

> founded upon the inherently discriminatory or destructive nature of the conduct itself. The employer in such cases must be held to intend the very consequences which foreseeably and inescapably flow from his actions and if he fails to explain away, to justify or to characterize his actions as something different than they appear on their face, an unfair labor practice charge is made out... But, as often happens, the employer may counter by claiming that his actions were taken in the pursuit of legitimate business ends and that his dominant purpose was not to discriminate or to invade union rights but to accomplish business objectives acceptable under the Act.
>
> Nevertheless, his conduct does speak for itself—it *is* discriminatory and does discourage union membership and whatever the claimed overriding justification may be, it carries with it unavoidable consequences which the employer not only foresaw but which he must have intended. As is not uncommon in human experience, such situations present a complex of motives and *preferring one motive to another is in reality the far more delicate task, reflected in part in decisions of this Court, of weighing the interests of employees in concerted activity against the interest of the employer in operating his business in a particular manner and of balancing in the light of the Act and its policy the intended consequences upon employee rights against the business ends to be served by the employer's conduct.* This essentially is the teaching of the court's prior cases dealing with this problem and, in our view, the Board did not depart from it. [Emphasis added.]

Thus the differences between the *A.A.S.* and *Skyline* decisions are not as great as may at first appear. Both approaches involve some balancing; both take into account the scheme of the Act; and, without direct evidence of motive, both approaches in effect require a considerable imbalance of interests in favour of the protected activity before a violation will be established. Unfortunately, however, it cannot be said that the requirement of motive in all claimed applications of section 64 is a superfluous detail and that both approaches always result in the same outcome. A non-motive approach to section 64, by requiring a substantial imbalance of interests, is capable of accommodating the concern that section 66 not be read out of the Act. Usually, the same imbalance will support an inference of improper motive which should negate the superiority of section 64 in the run of the mill section 89 case. On the other hand, the universal requirement of motive for section 64 can deprive the statute of the necessary flexibility to respond to certain troublesome situations which its otherwise general wording would provide.

For example, cases arise where employer conduct has a significant impact on protected activity and, while supported by good faith, does not reflect a persuasive or worthy business purpose. The balance between employer and employee interests may therefore strongly favour the protected activity, but the absence of a motive to interfere precludes a remedy. The no-solicitation cases are one example but not the only illustration of this problem. Indeed, the no-solicitation cases could probably be preserved on a compulsory motive test by employing a legal inference of intended interference notwithstanding the longstanding and consistent application of a no-solicitation rule without discrimination. But the problem transcends the no-solicitation cases. In *NLRB v. Burnup & Sims Inc.* . . . two employees, who had been active in an attempt to organize the respondent's plant, were discharged as a result of the employer's sincere but mistaken belief that they had threatened to dynamite his plant if the organizational drive was unsuccessful. The situation was therefore somewhat analogous to the submission of the complainant in this case that, as a minimum, Blanchard and Richard were discharged because of a mistaken belief as to their presence at the restaurant. The same argument can also be made with respect to Mark McCarroll's termination to the extent it was based on his alleged threatening with Turnbull's knife. Justice Douglas for the United States Supreme Court in the *Burnup & Sims Inc.* case . . . ruled that a discharge for alleged misconduct arising out of protected activity constituted a violation . . . no matter what the employer's motive when it was shown that the misconduct never in fact occurred. . . .

Such cases can and should be considered pursuant to section 64. The only other course open to us would be to dismiss a complaint where mistake has been established and then carefully scrutinize the employer's subsequent hiring decision when the grievor reapplies for employment. It is our view that such an approach would be too indirect and would not encourage the requisite caution that an employer should exercise when administering discipline in the context of activity protected by this Act. Accordingly, we hold that the respondent violated section 64 of the Act in discharging R. Richard, R. Blanchard and M. McCarroll. They are to be immediately reinstated to their former positions. In the cases of Blanchard and Richard, they are to receive full back pay with interest in accordance with Board policy. McCarroll, however, is to be reinstated without back pay and on terms stated below having regard to the conduct it was established he engaged in. We will not condone such conduct with a back pay order. It is not, however, clear that he would have been terminated for only that misconduct having regard to the company's response to similar actions on the picket line. As for the argument that McCarroll would have been terminated simply for his presence at the restaurant our following findings are applicable.

In this case all of the grievors had been involved in picketing and strike activity which are fundamental rights under the Act. As the Board held in *Dominion Citrus and Drug Ltd*. ... lawful strike activity is protected by sections 3 and 66. Picketing, being a normal adjunct of a strike, is also protected....

The respondent, however, contends that the manner in which the grievors attended the restaurant demonstrates that their arrival there was not a simple extension of the picket line, but rather a concerted attempt to interfere unlawfully with the pick-up and the workers involved. In this respect it relies on the numbers of striking employees involved, the way in which they blocked the van with their vehicles, and the physical assault on Mr. Turnbull and Mr. McCarthy. Counsel submits that they were discharged because they were all party to the unprovoked assaults and not for any other reason. We further note that this employer has not committed any earlier unfair labour practices and the collective bargaining relationship is not a recent one involving a first contract.

Subject to our comments on section 64 above, the Board is concerned with the actual motivation of the respondent in acting as it did. The Board must look beneath the stated purposes and focus on the facts established. Like many of the difficult cases brought before this Board, there is no direct evidence that the respondent was improperly motivated. The assault on two innocent persons was unprovoked and constituted serious misconduct. It therefore cannot be said that discharge was a clearly excessive response for those who engaged in the physical assault. The respondent was also under no legal obligation to arbitrate the discharges and trade union officials who engage in misconduct have no immunity from discipline under the Act. Whether Clayton [the company's labour relations manager] knew that D. McCarroll and L. Lutes, the president and recording secretary, were the individuals along with Prewal who carried out the assault does not and cannot change the matter. These three grievors were the authors of their own misfortune and, on the evidence before us, we are not prepared to draw an inference that discharge was selected, in part, because of their official status and because they were engaged in a strike.

It is important to point out in light of the earlier discussion of principle, that even a non-motive section 64 analysis of these three discharges and refusal to arbitrate would not produce a different result to this point. We have found that, given the circumstances, the decision to discharge was not clearly excessive and by itself a hallmark of anti-union animus. The decision not to arbitrate merited no different characterization. Were we to intervene on the basis of section 64, the Board would be saying that all discipline issued during a strike must be submitted to arbitration because any potential excessiveness could deter participation in protected activity. This extreme sensitivity to protected activity might well be seen as insufficiently sensitive to improper picket-line misconduct and would not obligate trade unions to take all such issues to arbitration instead of placing them on the bargaining table. It would also be difficult to reconcile our sensitivity to any adverse impact on protected activity with the absence of a legal obligation to arbitrate arising under the

Act. A clear imbalance in favour of protected activity does not exist. In this type of situation it seems to us that a non-motive approach to section 64 should be reserved for instances of clear mistake or for discipline clearly out of all proportion to the misconduct in issue.

The discharges of Carrier, Brinston and Mez are, however, a different matter. It is clear that these employees were simply present at the restaurant. They did not engage in the assault. We have found above that their presence at the restaurant would be an aspect of protected activity (in effect an adjunct of their strike) unless their sole motivation for attending was to facilitate the assault on Turnbull and McCarthy. M. McCarroll testified that the purpose of the mission to the restaurant was to identify the strike replacements given the strategy of concealment the respondent had adopted. This rationale is a plausible one notwithstanding their manner of arrival. In any event, the respondent decided on termination before it knew of the details of the incident and at no time did it engage in an inquiry which attempted to assess the motives of Carrier, Mez and Brinston in attending. In our view, the speed and severity of the respondent's response indicated a disposition that they had 'no business' being at the restaurant whatever their purpose. On the evidence before us we are prepared to infer that in expanding the circle of discharges beyond those who actually inflicted the assault, the respondent was at least in part objecting to their presence at the restaurant regardless of their motive and seizing upon a response that would make the greatest impression on other employees for the duration of the strike. Accordingly, we find that the respondent breached section 66 in dismissing these three employees. This conclusion would also apply to the Richard and Blanchard discharges. Had the respondent demonstrated to us that it was sensitive to the protected right of striking employees to attend at the restaurant unless their intent was to assault the employees, our conclusion would have been different because these three employees did not testify to permit us to assess their actual intent. There would have been no evidence on which to find a mistaken belief and no basis for inferring an improper motive. Indeed, because these employees did not testify before the Board, we have decided to reinstate them to their former positions with no compensation. We understand that they are facing criminal trials but we are uncomfortable with their decisions not to testify. In the circumstances, our concern for what happened at the restaurant leads us to tailor a remedy for these employees which conveys that concern. No compensation is directed.

Finally, we turn to the dismissal of M. McCarroll which in many respects is the most difficult matter. We have found the respondent to have been mistaken with respect to the alleged knife threat but, on his own admission, McCarroll assaulted the van. Nevertheless, there is no evidence before us that at the time the company decided on the discharges it was directing its attention to anything other than the assaults on the two strike replacements. Moreover, the company had not issued any discipline in relation to earlier mischief on the picket lines at the plant. On the evidence then we are prepared to infer that M. McCarroll was, in part, terminated for just being present at the restaurant in the same manner as Brinston, Mez and Carrier or he was terminated in the mistaken belief that he had physically threatened one of the strike replacements. His termination therefore offends sections 66 and 64 of the Act. However, we are not about to condone the misconduct he did engage in or the incident as a whole by awarding him any back pay. We are, however, prepared to direct his reinstatement to his former position provided that he reimburses or makes arrangements to reimburse the company for the damage inflicted on the van driven by Auger.

Canadian Broadcasting Corp v Canada (Labour Relations Board), [1995] 1 SCR 157 at para 2ff

[The union filed a complaint with the Canada Labour Relations Board (now known as the Canada Industrial Relations Board), alleging that the CBC had breached sections 94(1)(a), 94(3)(a)(i), 94(3)(b), 94(3)(e), and 96 of the *Canada Labour Code*. Section 94(1)(a) is the "non-motive" section of the *Canada Labour Code*. A majority of the CLRB found that the CBC had violated section 94(1)(a), and the CBC's application for reconsideration by the CLRB was denied, and the Federal Court of Appeal dismissed the CBC's application for judicial review. The CBC appealed to the Supreme Court of Canada.]

IACOBUCCI J. (Lamer C.J., Cory J., and Major J. concurring):

I. FACTS

The membership of ACTRA is divided into three guilds: writers, journalists and performers. ACTRA, like many unions, takes official positions on various issues. For example, it supports the Canadian content rule for broadcasters. It apparently also opposes free trade. ACTRA has an official newsletter, *ACTRASCOPE*, which is distributed to its 10,000 members across Canada.

ACTRA's by-laws provide that the president of ACTRA is also to be its official spokesperson. In 1988 the president of ACTRA was a journalist, Dale Goldhawk. Goldhawk had been hired by the CBC in January 1988 to host a national weekly open-line current affairs radio program, *Cross Country Checkup*. At the time of his hiring, the CBC was aware that he was the president of ACTRA.

In the late summer of 1988, Goldhawk wrote an article in "The President Reports" column of the fall issue of *ACTRASCOPE*. Under the title "Election brings the trade debate to a boil," he took a strong position against the Free Trade Agreement then being negotiated with the United States. In the article he attacked the agreement and invited membership of ACTRA to mount a campaign in opposition. At the time of the publication of the article, the country was in the midst of an election campaign in which free trade was a central issue.

In November 1988, the existence of Goldhawk's column was made known to the general public in a newspaper article written by Charles Lynch, a journalist and long-standing member of ACTRA. Lynch's article, entitled "Free trade: foes are alive and well and working for the CBC," was published in the *Ottawa Citizen* and the *Vancouver Province*. In his article, Lynch argued that the listening public was entitled to on-air disclosure of Goldhawk's role in ACTRA and the union's position on free trade.

Lynch's article was brought to the attention of the area head of current affairs for the CBC Radio. This prompted a series of meetings between Goldhawk and representatives of the CBC to determine the appropriate course of action. At issue was whether Goldhawk's article, and his public involvement as president of ACTRA, violated the Journalistic Policy of the CBC. It was agreed that, as an interim measure, Goldhawk would cease hosting *Cross Country Checkup* until after election day. Goldhawk simultaneously withdrew from any further public involvement on behalf of ACTRA.

After the election, Goldhawk offered to relinquish his duties as ACTRA's spokesperson, while remaining its president, in order to accommodate the concerns of the CBC. This offer was rejected. The CBC told Goldhawk that he had to choose between his job as host of *Cross Country Checkup* and his role as the president of ACTRA. Goldhawk resigned as ACTRA president and resumed hosting his radio program....

III. JUDGMENTS BELOW

Canada Labour Relations Board (1990), 83 di 102

Majority (Vice-Chairman Serge Brault and Member Linda Parsons)

At the outset of their extensive reasons, the majority stated that the issue to be decided was whether the *Canada Labour Code* was violated when Goldhawk was asked to choose between his position as a radio host and his position as president of the union.

On the issue of the burden of proof, the majority noted that s. 98(4) of the Code placed the onus of proof on the employer in respect of all of the sections invoked except ss. 94(1)(a) and 96. The majority pointed out that a distinction could also be drawn between s. 94(1)(a), and the other sections invoked by the union, in respect of the issue of motive. To succeed under s. 94(1)(a), it was not necessary for a complainant to establish anti-union *animus* on the part of the employer. Rather, this provision called for an objective test which focused on the effect of the employer's actions on the legitimate rights of employees or their unions.

The majority added, however, that not every difficulty encountered by a union in its formation and administration would give rise to a finding that s. 94(1)(a) had been violated. The Board would instead apply a balancing test, which considered whether the adverse impact on union activity was counterbalanced by a "sufficient or legitimate managerial, entrepreneurial, or collective bargaining justification" (p. 128). In cases where the balance was equal, motive would be the determining factor.

In defining what amounted to a "legitimate management interest," it was clear that the detrimental effect on entrepreneurial interests had to be real and to constitute more than a minor annoyance or inconvenience to the employer. The majority summarized the test to be applied under s. 94(1)(a) in the following terms (at p. 131):

> In brief, under the Canada Labour Code, an employer's actions that actually interfere with employee solicitation on the job will indeed be subject to a balancing test and will be found illegal pursuant to section 94(1)(a) unless *compelling* and *exceptional* circumstances justify such bans. Other kinds of employer's decisions that actually interfere with the rights protected under section 94(1)(a) will be assessed on the basis that the Code takes precedence over any employer rule.

The majority considered whether Goldhawk was engaged in a lawful union activity contemplated by the Code when he signed his article in *ACTRASCOPE*. The majority recognized that s. 94(1)(a) could not serve as an umbrella for all union activities. The activity in which Goldhawk participated was the signing of an article in a union newspaper as spokesperson for that union. It was the role of the Board to decide whether ACTRA as a union and Goldhawk as a union official were entitled to statutory protection in this situation. The majority answered this question in the affirmative, and commented (at p. 133):

> In the instant case, Mr. Goldhawk's article was published in the union's newsletter and was aimed at a limited union readership. It seems reasonable to assume that under the Code a union president may at least say to his troops verbally or in writing what he can say to the public at large.

The majority noted that the *Broadcasting Act*, R.S.C., 1985, c. B-9 (as it then read), provided that Goldhawk was not a public servant. His labour relations were to be governed by the same provisions of the Code as those of persons working for private broadcasters. After reviewing numerous previous decisions of the Board, the majority (at p. 137) referred to *Canada Post Corp.* (1988), 75 di 189, where the Board set out the following guidelines on the right of a union officer to speak publicly:

> [The statement] would have to be relevant to the policies, interests and concerns of the union as such, although it would not have to be something virtually scripted by the union and followed slavishly by the officer. The protection of the Code would not extend to a union officer who used his or her position to make public comments concerning an employer in furtherance of a personal or other objective which could not be linked to the interests of the collectivity.

Statements which were malicious or recklessly untrue would lose the protection of the Code.

The majority noted that all but one of the decisions cited by the parties dealt with public statements aimed directly at the employer. They made it clear that the right of union officials to make such statements flowed from the Code, and that officials acting in good faith could expect statutory protection that was not necessarily granted to all employees. This jurisprudence, however, was of limited application in the present case, since it concerned an article published by a union official in a union newspaper in a context where he was gathering support within the union for a position it had officially adopted. The majority concluded (at pp. 144–45):

> When a union finds that a government economic policy such as free trade constitutes a threat or a benefit to its membership, an article on that subject appearing in a union publication is indeed a lawful union activity under the Code.
>
> For the majority, for a union of artists and performers who work in an often highly subsidized industry to take a position on a Free Trade Agreement is as legitimate as it is for the Teamsters Union to express their opinion on deregulation in the transportation industry.
>
> Further, the fact that Mr. Goldhawk's role as a spokesperson was determined by ACTRA in its by-laws is protected under the right of unions to adopt their own constitutions and rules protected by section 94(1)(a) of the Code.

The majority found that the choice given to Goldhawk, to resign his post with ACTRA or to lose his job with the CBC, was not tainted with anti-union *animus*, and therefore no violation of ss. 94(3)(a)(i), 94(3)(e) or 96 could be established. ACTRA does not dispute this finding.

Turning to the justification part of the s. 94(1)(a) test, the majority noted that the question was not whether the CBC's Journalistic Policy was reasonable, as arbitration boards in other situations had found, but whether it was legal to apply it to Goldhawk in the circumstances. The particular application of the Policy had to be compatible with the CBC's statutory obligations under the Code. The majority considered whether the CBC had shown compelling business reasons for its decision. They noted that if the bargaining unit represented by ACTRA had been composed solely of on-air journalists, the union would have been paralysed. In holding that a violation of s. 94(1)(a) had been established, the Board concluded (at pp. 147–48):

> Past experience within the CBC shows that other means, such as on-air disclosure, were used to ensure the public's right to impartiality. Further, we do not see how Mr. Goldhawk's forced resignation made him less identifiable with a controversial issue than before. In fact, it could be argued at least in the eyes of some, that he was sacrificed to free trade and in that sense that he is still very much identified with the issue, regardless of his resigning his union office.

The majority found that Mr. Goldhawk's article was related to the interests of the collectivity of the union and was neither reckless nor maliciously untrue. The effect of the CBC's decision was to prevent a CBC journalist from being the president of ACTRA. That alone constituted a violation of the Code. Moreover, on an application of the balancing test, it was clear that the CBC did not try to reconcile its own legitimate business interests with those of Goldhawk as a union member. It failed to show any convincing causal relationship between its image of impartiality and Goldhawk's continuing to hold office as ACTRA president. The majority found a violation of s. 94(1)(a) of the Code, and issued a declaration and accompanying cease and desist order. . . .

B. Reasonableness of the Decision

The question which this Court must address is whether the decision of the Board that the appellant had interfered with the administration of a trade union or the representation of employees by that union was patently unreasonable. . . .

To determine whether the decision of the Board in this case was patently unreasonable, it is first necessary to identify with some precision what the Board actually decided. As noted above, the contested issue in this appeal is whether the activities of the respondent ACTRA which were affected by the ultimatum given by the appellant CBC to Goldhawk, were within the scope of s. 94(1)(a). The appellant argues that the Board, in extending protection to purely political activities, committed a patently unreasonable error.

In general, the issue as defined by the Board was whether s. 94(1)(a) was violated when Goldhawk was asked to choose between his position as a radio host and his position as president of the union. This ultimatum affected two identifiable and discrete activities of the union. First, the CBC's action was specifically a response to the publication by Goldhawk of the article in *ACTRASCOPE*. In this sense the ultimatum, if left unchallenged, precluded future articles by the union president in the union news magazine on issues such as free trade, if that president belonged to the subset of ACTRA members who were CBC journalists. Second, the ultimatum affected the ability of the union members to choose an on-air journalist as their president at all. It must be remembered that the Board found that Goldhawk had offered the appellant a compromise in which he would step down as spokesperson, but would remain union president. This compromise was rejected by the appellant.

In short, both the ability of the union to choose an on-air journalist as president, and the ability of the union to have the person whom it chose as president also act as its spokesperson, were circumscribed by the actions of the appellant. The task of the Board was to determine if these two activities were part of the administration of a trade union or the representation of employees by a trade union. The task of this Court is to determine whether the conclusions of the Board in this regard were "so patently unreasonable that [they] cannot be rationally supported by the relevant legislation."

The Board considered whether the signing of the article in *ACTRASCOPE* by Goldhawk as a union spokesperson was a lawful union activity contemplated by the Code. In a more general sense, the question was whether s. 94(1)(a) protected the publication by a union and its officer of an article in a union newsletter expressing an opinion that a government economic policy constituted a threat or a benefit to its members. The Board answered this question in the affirmative.

The appellant argues that in making this decision the Board held that the purely political activities of unions were entitled to the protection of s. 94(1)(a). However, this describes the Board's finding too narrowly. The Board considered the specific act of this union in context. It recognized that s. 94(1)(a) has its limits. The existing jurisprudence of the Board had already made it clear that in order for s. 94(1)(a) to apply *prima facie*, public statements by union officials had to relate to the interests of the union as a collectivity, and not to the personal concerns of the union official. Nor could such statements be reckless or maliciously untrue.

The Board recognized that its previous jurisprudence was in a sense distinguishable, as these cases dealt with public statements aimed directly at the employer. This case concerned an article published in a union newsletter and directed at union members. This is not the same sort of public statement that was at issue in the previous cases. Moreover, the substance of the article was not aimed at the employer, but rather at gathering support from members for the union's official position. The Board held that, in this situation, the Code should also apply. In my view, given this context, the extension of the content protection was not wholly unwarranted. The distinguishing features of this fact situation must be recognized in any consideration of whether the decision was unreasonable.

The decision of the majority was arrived at in a principled manner and was not irrational. The Board set out the established analytical framework for a s. 94(1)(a) determination, considered its existing jurisprudence, recognized the differences between this case and those it had discussed, and gave rational reasons why those principles could be by analogy applied to this case. The Board was entitled to apply the law as found in existing decisions to new and analogous facts. ...

The comments of Wilson J. in *Lavigne v. Ontario Public Service Employees Union*, [1991] 2 S.C.R. 211, relating to the characterization of union participation in activities beyond the workplace are, although *obiter*, further indication that the Board's conclusion on this point is a rational one. In *Lavigne* the issue was whether the s. 2(b) and (d)

Charter rights of a union member were violated when his compulsory union dues were directed to causes which were not directly related to his employment context, such as the campaign opposing construction of the Skydome. Wilson J. (L'Heureux-Dubé and Cory JJ. concurring), while finding that neither section had been infringed, nonetheless went on to consider, in *obiter*, whether any such violations could be justified under s. 1 of the *Charter*. In dealing with whether there was a rational connection between the Rand formula mandating compulsory payment of union dues which could then be used to advance "political" matters unrelated to contract negotiation, and the government objective of the promotion of industrial peace through the encouragement of free collective bargaining, Wilson J. stated at p. 291:

> Whether collective bargaining is understood as primarily an economic endeavour or as some more expansive enterprise, it is my opinion that union participation in activities and causes beyond the particular workplace does foster collective bargaining. Through such participation unions are able to demonstrate to their constituencies that their mandate is to earnestly and sincerely advance the interests of working people, to thereby gain worker support, and to thus enable themselves to bargain on a more equal footing with employers. To my mind, the decision to allow unions to build and develop support is absolutely vital to a successful collective bargaining system.

> [...]

Additionally, even if it can be said that the decision of the Board relating to the signing of the article in the newsletter is either patently unreasonable, or a decision going to jurisdiction that is incorrect, this does not affect the result. It must be remembered that the Board identified two union activities that were affected by the actions of the appellant. In addition to the signing of the article, the Board also found that the actions of the CBC had the effect of preventing any broadcast journalist from being the president of ACTRA. This was so because the appellant refused to accept the compromise suggested by Goldhawk that he retain his position as ACTRA president while no longer serving as its spokesperson.

The Board found, and was rationally justified in finding, that this act alone amounted to a violation of the Code. On any standard of review, it is clear that the Board was entitled to find that the election of whichever person the other union members wish to have as their president is an activity that falls within the concept of "administration" of a trade union or "representation" of employees by that union. This conclusion is not in error....

It was not unreasonable for the Board in this case to conclude that included in the dominant purpose of the *Canada Labour Code*, or necessarily incidental to that purpose, was the right of the union president to communicate to union members in a union publication on issues of importance to the members in their capacity as journalists, writers and performers. The same can be said for the right of the union to choose its president from among its entire membership and not from a subset circumscribed by the employer.

The appellant also argues that it was patently unreasonable for the Board to find that, if the appellant did interfere with the administration of a trade union, it did not have a valid justification for so doing. In this regard the appellant once again points to the provisions of the *Broadcasting Act* and their interpretation in the Journalistic Policy of the

CBC. As noted above in my discussion on jurisdiction, I am of the view that there are no grounds for interfering with the Board's decision in this regard.

The Board considered the portions of the Journalistic Policy that the appellant argued were mandated by the *Broadcasting Act*, but did not find that they compelled the appellant to take the position that it did. The Board pointed out that in the past the CBC had used other methods, such as on-air disclosure, to respond to the perceived appearance of bias. The Board was also of the opinion that requiring Goldhawk to resign may well have served only to identify him more closely with the issue. Therefore, even if there were obligations relating to impartiality imposed by the Act on the CBC, they were not determinative, given the Board's finding that there was no causal connection between this requirement and the continued presidency of Goldhawk. The Board found that the CBC failed to try and reconcile its own interests with those of Goldhawk as a union member. To paraphrase the Board (at p. 151), the appellant failed to show any convincing causal relationship between its image of impartiality and Goldhawk's continuing to hold office as ACTRA president. The conclusion of the Board that the appellant had failed to show a valid and compelling business justification for its interference is not unreasonable.

Is there a real difference between proving improper employer motive and proving a lack of justifiable business reasons in non-motive cases? Should non-motive provisions be interpreted more broadly, with an emphasis on the effect of the employer conduct on protected activity rather than on the business reasons for such conduct?

In *Westinghouse Canada Ltd*, [1980] 2 CLRBR 469 (OLRB) (Burkett, alternate chair), the employer decided to close a centralized manufacturing operation and open several new plants at different locations. The old plant was unionized, and the new ones were deliberately located in areas where there was little trade union presence. Having determined that the employer was motivated by anti-union considerations, the board concluded that it had committed an unfair labour practice. The board suggested (at 497) that its conclusion might have been otherwise had the scenario unfolded in a slightly different way:

> Can an employer faced with economic difficulties caused by collective bargaining-related factors (wages, benefits, seniority, work practices etc.) act to remove himself from his collective bargaining relationship? It may well be that it is more profitable to operate without a union than with one but if an employer can react to this reality simply by moving his business the right of employees to engage in collective bargaining would be seriously undermined. What of the employer who is faced with an economic crisis caused by collective bargaining related factors, seeks relief from the union and is met with an unsympathetic or unsatisfactory response? Assuming that these factors could be established, the answer is by no means clear. The question, however, is not raised by the factors of this case. This company was not faced with an economic crisis and notwithstanding the constraints to productivity perceived by it, there is no evidence that the company ever raised its concerns with the trade union prior to making its decision to relocate.

In *Kennedy Lodge Nursing Home* (1980), 81 CLLC para 16,078 (OLRB), the employer had contracted out its housekeeping and janitorial functions and had laid off sixteen of sixty-five employees represented by the union. Testimony led by the employer indicated that the decision was made to "save money." In response to the union's argument that the situation was indistinguishable from *Westinghouse*, the board wrote (at 473):

> If the cost of doing business is too high in relation to the business revenues generated, the employer, who is motivated solely by correcting that imbalance, is not precluded by the Act from taking that action. Absent restrictions in the relevant collective agreement, business operations are not 'frozen' by the collective relationship so long as the action taken is not in any way motivated by the accomplishment of an unlawful objective.
>
> Business decisions must be made on the basis of the overall viability of an operation—one aspect of which might be the cost of labour. In the *Westinghouse* case it was found that the company's decision to relocate its operations was 'motivated in large part by anti-union considerations.' There was evidence in that case that the company had explicitly set non-union operation as a goal to be achieved. However, in the case before the Board there was no evidence that the fact that the employees had engaged in collective bargaining and were represented by a trade union played any part in the employer's decision to contract out some bargaining unit work. We accept Mr. Duncan's [an administrator for the employer] testimony on this point. *Westinghouse* makes it clear that an employer may discontinue operations for cause so long as the decision is not motivated by anti-union *animus*. A desire to save money and thereby increase profits is not equivalent to anti-union *animus* simply because the money saved would otherwise have been paid as wages to employees in the bargaining unit.

In "Equal Partnership in Canadian Labour Law" (1983) 21 *Osgoode Hall Law Journal* 496 at 531, B Langille quoted the above passage, and added:

> All one can do is note that this simply collapses the distinction between discriminatory (anti-union) and economic motives, at least in a good number of cases. What is it that the Board wishes to have as evidence of anti-union animus? The rational employer, intent on avoiding the collective bargaining process for rational reasons is protected through this test. Applying this test, it is difficult to see that *Westinghouse* itself is correctly decided. It seems clear that, absent provisions in the collective agreement empowering the employer to unilaterally make those decisions, employer action violates the act and is a most blatant unfair labour practice. Contracting out to avoid the axiomatic effects of unionization is contracting out with an anti-union animus.

The same employer subsequently entered into an arrangement with an employment agency for the supply of nursing and health aides who would displace about two-thirds of the union's bargaining unit. In the unfair labour practice proceedings that ensued, the employer was found not to have relinquished control over employees performing these "core functions" of the business. Accordingly, the board concluded that it was still the employer or, in the alternative, that the employer and the subcontractor shared control and the subcontractor was a related employer within the meaning of the legislation. After making these findings the board went on to consider the relationship between contracting out for economic reasons and unfair labour practices. The board stated that where an employer retains control, "an inference can be easily drawn that the employer has acted to replace his bargaining unit employees in order to undermine their collective bargaining rights." Accordingly, the employer was found to have engaged in an unfair labour practice. See *Kennedy Lodge Inc*, [1984] OLRB Rep 931.

* * * * *

Should the legislation governing unfair labour practices collapse the distinction between discriminatory motives and economic motives for employer conduct? What is the appropriate test for whether an employer has interfered with protected union activity? Labour boards have largely avoided grappling with these difficult questions by focusing on the extent to which important business decisions like relocation and plant closure must be negotiated under the statutory "duty to bargain in good faith," discussed in Chapter 7. Where circumstances warrant, labour boards also deal with such business decisions under the statutory freeze provisions, which are more specific in scope. These freeze provisions are examined next.

5:300 ALTERATION OF WORKING CONDITIONS: THE STATUTORY FREEZE

Collective bargaining legislation generally provides for a two-stage "statutory freeze" that prohibits the unilateral alteration of terms and conditions of employment, first during the certification process, and then during much of the bargaining process after certification. The pre-certification stage of the freeze begins when an application for certification is filed, and ends when the application is dismissed or soon after the certificate is issued—for example, under the Ontario *Labour Relations Act, 1995*, when notice to bargain is given. At that point, the bargaining stage of the freeze begins, and it continues until the parties are in a legal strike or lockout position. For convenience, both the pre-certification stage and the bargaining stage will be dealt with in this section, although the bargaining freeze will be mentioned again briefly in Chapter 7.

The freeze aims to restrain employer conduct that may have the effect of undermining the union's organizing or negotiating efforts. Anti-union motive on the employer's part is not required for a breach of the freeze provisions, so even employer action that is taken for a legitimate business purpose may be illegal during the freeze period. It is important to understand that the freeze operates in addition to the other statutory unfair labour practice provisions, and that it supplements rather than displaces those provisions.

The Supreme Court of Canada recently affirmed and clarified the purpose and objective of the section 59 Quebec *Labour Code* freeze provision in its majority opinion in the *United Food and Commercial Workers, Local 503 v Wal-Mart Canada Corp*, 2014 SCC 45 decision. In doing so, it rejected the view that the purpose of the provision was "to maintain a certain balance, or even the *status quo*, [that had existed between the parties prior to the certification application being filed] during the negotiation of a collective agreement" (para 33). The majority explained:

> 34 [T]he purpose of s. 59 in circumscribing the employer's powers is not merely to strike a balance or maintain the *status quo*, but is more precisely to facilitate certification and ensure that in negotiating the collective agreement the parties bargain in good faith....
>
> 35 The "freeze" on conditions of employment codified by this statutory provision limits the use of the primary means otherwise available to an employer to influence

its employees' choices: its power to manage during a critical period (see G. W. Adams, *Canadian Labour Law* (2nd ed. (loose-leaf)), vol. 2, at p. 10-80.3; B. W. Burkett *et al.*, eds., *Federal Labour Law and Practice* (2013), at p. 171). By circumscribing the employer's unilateral decision-making power in this way, the "freeze" limits any influence the employer might have on the association-forming process, eases the concerns of employees who actively exercise their rights, and facilitates the development of what will eventually become the labour relations framework for the business.

36 In this context, it is important to recognize that the true function of s. 59 is to foster the exercise of the right of association: (references omitted).

37 By codifying a mechanism designed to facilitate the exercise of the right of association, s. 59 thus creates more than a mere procedural guarantee. In a way, this section, by imposing a *duty* on the employer not to change how the business is managed at the time the union arrives, gives employees a substantive *right* to the maintenance of their conditions of employment during the statutory period. This being said, it is the employees, as the holders of that right, who must ensure that it is not violated....

38 I wish to note first that, since s. 59 is not directly concerned with the punishment of anti-union conduct, the prohibition for which it provides will apply regardless of whether it is proven that the employer's decision was motivated by anti-union animus [references omitted]. The essential question in applying s. 59 is whether the employer *unilaterally* changed its employees' conditions of employment *during the period of the prohibition.*

39 As a result, s. 59 requires that the union representing the employees prove that a unilateral change has been made. To discharge this burden, the union must show: (1) that a condition of employment existed on the day the petition for certification was filed or a previous collective agreement expired; (2) that the condition was changed without its consent; and (3) that the change was made between the start of the prohibition period and either the first day the right to strike or to lock out was exercised or the day an arbitration award was handed down, as the case may be....

In this decision the Supreme Court also affirmed that "[t]he 'condition of employment' concept has been given a large and liberal interpretation" and that it includes "anything having to do with the employment relationship on either an individual or a collective level" (paras 40 & 41). Specifically with respect to continuation of employment, the majority held:

43 Whether it is based on the *Civil Code*, on labour legislation or on the implicit content of a contract of employment, this right to continued employment is therefore always the basis for a condition of employment for employees (art. 1434 C.C.Q.). However, this condition is not absolute. The employer retains at all times the power to manage its business, and this includes the power to resiliate the contract of employment of one or more of its employees for "legitimate reasons" (economic, disciplinary, etc.) or upon "sufficient" notice of termination.

44 Section 59 does not change this factual and legal situation. Like any other condition of employment, maintenance of the employment relationship remains a condition but is nevertheless subject to the employer's exercise of its management power. Therefore, in the words of Deschamps J.A., as she then was, [TRANSLATION] "although dismissal is not, strictly speaking, a condition of employment, the condition of continued employment, and thus the protection against dismissal without a good and sufficient reason, can be included in the conditions of employment covered by section 59 L.C.": *Automobiles Canbec inc.*, per Deschamps J.A., at p. 13.

Further, the Court held that a change to a condition of employment does not violate the freeze provision in the following circumstances:

> 57 Thus, a change can be found to be consistent with the employer's "normal management policy" if (1) it is consistent with the employer's past management practices or, failing that, (2) it is consistent with the decision that a reasonable employer would have made in the same circumstances. In other words, a change [TRANSLATION] "that would have been handled the same way had there been no attempt to form a union or process to renew a collective agreement should not be considered a change in conditions of employment to which section 59 of the Labour Code applies": *Club coopératif de consommation d'Amos*, at p. 12.
>
> 58 In either case, whatever the nature of the circumstances relied on by the employer in making the change, the arbitrator dealing with the complaint must first be satisfied that those circumstances exist and that they are genuine. . . .

However, as the following cases suggest, the "business as before" test may often not be very helpful.

Simpsons Limited v Canadian Union of Brewery, Flour, Cereal, Soft Drink and Distillery Workers (1985), 9 CLRBR (NS) 343 at 356–60

> [The employer, a national department store chain, was in financial difficulty. The union had recently acquired bargaining rights for one of the employer's warehousing and soft goods manufacturing facilities in Toronto. Just before the union gave notice to bargain, the employer gave layoff notice to more than one-tenth of its nationwide workforce, including a substantial number in the recently certified unit. The functions of most of the laid-off employees in that unit were discontinued, but the functions of some of them (those in the drapery workroom) were contracted out. The union alleged a violation of section 79(2) (now section 86(2)) of the Ontario *Labour Relations Act*, which read:
>
>> Where a trade union has applied for certification and notice thereof from the Board has been received by the employer, the employer shall not, except with the consent of the trade union, alter the rates of wages or any other term or condition of employment or any right, privilege or duty of the employer or the employees until,
>> (a) the trade union has given notice under section 16, in which case subsection (1) applies; or
>> (b) the application for certification by the trade union is dismissed or terminated by the Board or withdrawn by the trade union.
>
> The board accepted that the layoffs were done without anti-union animus and for legitimate economic reasons. It went on as follows:]

> TACON Vice-Chair: The Board could have interpreted s. 79 so as to freeze the precise conditions extant at the time the statutory provision was triggered. The Board, though, has consistently rejected that approach as an unreasonable interpretation of the legislation.

In the Board's view, such an interpretation would effectively paralyze an employer's operations for the duration of the statutory freeze, a period which could be quite lengthy. In effect, the 'business as before' formulation in *Spar Aerospace* ... was the Board's response to too expansive a view of employee privileges. To paraphrase *Spar Aerospace*, the employer's right to manage its operation was maintained subject to the condition that the operation conform to the pattern established when the freeze was triggered.

'Business as before' is a 'slippery' concept to apply to specific fact situations. The focus of the test is the 'pattern of operations', the employer's 'practice'. Certainly, where the 'practice' is accurately embodied in an employer's policy manual, the application of 'business as before' has been relatively straightforward.... There have been other instances where a practice has been so well entrenched so as to be beyond dispute: *Spar Aerospace, supra*, with respect to annual merit and annual cost of living increases. On the other hand, the 'increased parking fee' cases illustrate the difficulty in looking for a pattern....

The freeze provisions catch two categories of events. There are those changes which can be measured against a pattern (however difficult to define) and the specific history of that employer's operation is relevant to assess the impact of the freeze. There are also first time' events and it is with respect to that category that the 'business as before' formulation is not always helpful in measuring the scope of employees' privileges. Some 'first time' events have been readily rejected by the Board, where, for example, the employer has instituted parking fees for the first time during the freeze.... On the other hand, the Board has upheld an employer's right to lay-off employees during the freeze (assuming there is no anti-union animus in the decision).... This right has been confirmed even where the first instance of layoff occurred during the freeze ... ; and where the layoffs had occurred elsewhere in the employer's operation but not at the specific location in question. The respondent in the instant case cited *Corporation of the Town of Petrolia* ... for the proposition that the employer may also contract out work for the first time during the freeze.

Instead of concentrating on 'business as before', the Board considers it appropriate to assess the privileges of employees which are frozen under the statute and thereby, delimit the otherwise unrestricted rights of the employer, by focusing on the 'reasonable expectations' of employees. The 'reasonable expectations' approach, in the Board's opinion, responds to both categories of events caught by the freeze, integrates the Board's jurisprudence and provides the appropriate balance between employer's rights and employees' privileges in the context of the legislative provisions....

The 'reasonable expectations' approach clearly incorporates the 'practice' of the employer in managing the operation. The standard is an objective one: what would a reasonable employee expect to constitute his or her privileges (or, 'benefits', to use a term often found in the jurisprudence) in the specific circumstances of that employer. The 'reasonable expectations' test, though, must not be unduly narrow or mechanical given that some types of management decision (e.g., contracting out, workforce reorganization) would not be expected to occur everyday. Thus, where a pattern of contracting out is found, it is sensible to infer that an employee would 'reasonably expect' such an occurrence during the freeze....

Finally, the 'lay-off' cases are consonant with the 'reasonable expectations' approach. Very few, if any, work forces are entirely static; fluctuations in the size of the staff complement and its composition are the norm. Employers are generally expected to respond to changing economic conditions through the hiring, termination and attrition of employees. It is in this sense that it is 'reasonable' for employees to expect an employer to respond to a significant downturn in the business with layoffs (or terminations) even where such layoffs are resorted to for the first time during the freeze. The magnitude of the layoffs, of course, must be proportional or relative to the severity of the economic circumstances. Economic justification must be proven where relied on and there must be an absence of anti-union animus. It must also be stressed that, while the expectation of layoffs does not initially depend on the specific history of the employer's operation, there might well be specific evidence with respect to that employer which would negate the otherwise usual 'reasonable expectation' of layoffs in response to an economic downturn.

The 'reasonable expectations' approach also distinguishes between layoffs and contracting out. Where there was a pattern of contracting out, of course, there would be no violation of s. 79 where work was contracted out during the freeze. However, in the Board's opinion, while an employee would reasonably expect a layoff where there was no 'demand', *i.e.*, where there was an economic downturn, an employee would not reasonably expect that the work would continue to be performed for the benefit of the employer's operation but through contracting out. This is not to say that the employer does not have the right to contract out work during non-freeze periods, except as limited by a collective agreement. During the freeze, however, and unless there is a practice of contracting out, the employer's 'right' to contract out is limited by the employees' 'privilege' of performing the work if the work is to be performed for the benefit of the employer's operation. Contracting out is merely one of the ways an employer might otherwise increase productivity or efficiency which is caught by the freeze; reducing wages, instituting parking fees, ignoring its policy manual are other means of achieving such goals which are proscribed by the statutory provision.

[The board concluded (at 360) that the employees whose functions were discontinued should reasonably have expected to be laid off, given the company's widely known economic problems, and that the company had "demonstrated that the scale of the terminations was related to the economic conditions." However, the contracting out of the drapery workroom functions was held (at 360) to be a breach of the freeze because it involved "the introduction of a new means to continue to have the work performed (which is outside the employees' reasonable expectations) ..."]

* * * * *

Does the addition of the "reasonable expectations" test to the "business as before" test weaken the statutory freeze protection for employees? Does ascertaining the "reasonable expectations" of the employees amount to anything more than a simple determination of where the balance of competing interests lies? In the following excerpt, the Ontario Labour Relations Board considered this matter, and also considered the relationship of the statutory freeze to the general labour practice provisions and to the duty to bargain, which will be dealt with in Chapter 7. The board noted that "business as before" is a problematic basis for

Ontario Public Service Employees Union v Royal Ottawa Health Care Group, [1999] OLRB Rep July/August 711 at para 27ff

> [The hospital admitted that it had reduced the level of employee benefits during the negotiation of a collective agreement—that is, during the bargaining stage of the statutory freeze. The union brought forward a complaint that the hospital's actions violated that freeze.]
>
> MacDowell, Chair:
>
> [...]
>
> The hospital maintains that it was acting *bona fide*, in response to serious budgetary pressures, and that, in the circumstances, it fairly concluded that reducing benefits was a way of realizing savings, without impairing other employee entitlements and without impinging upon patient care. In the hospital's submission, it was merely carrying on "business as usual"—making modifications to employee benefits as it had done in the past, and in accordance with its own assessment of the situation.
>
> The hospital says that it was entitled to proceed unilaterally. It needed to save money, and reducing benefits was the most appropriate way of doing so....
>
> [W]hile there may be an "overlap" between the various sections of the Act, in the sense that particular behaviour can engage several provisions at once, each section makes its own contribution to the regulatory scheme, which in turn should be considered as a whole. From that perspective, the freeze captures something that the other provisions do not: *bona fide* business behaviour that is not motivated by anti-union considerations and may not be a breach of section 17 [the duty to bargain], but is nevertheless prohibited (for a time, at least) because it undermines bargaining. The mischief to which section 86(1) is directed is an unexpected shift in the starting point or basis for bargaining, during the initial stages of that bargaining.... [L]acking a requirement for "anti-union motivation," [the freeze provisions] are more accurately viewed as a form of economic regulation, rather than a fault-based prohibition. A "pure freeze case" does not have the pejorative flavour of the traditional unfair labour practice sections. The freeze provisions ... stipulate that, for a time, even *bona fide* business decisions may be suspended while the bargaining process unfolds. In contrast to the "traditional" unfair labour practice provisions, the freeze is directed more towards facilitating bargaining, than protecting employees from "victimization" at the hands of an anti-union employer....
>
> The problem with the so-called "business as usual" "test" is not simply that it is a "slippery concept"—to use the words of the Board in *Simpsons*.... "Business as usual" has been taken as the "answer" or "end of the enquiry" rather than an "approach" or aid to interpreting difficult language in a particular context.... When the words of section 86(1) are read in conjunction with its purpose, and in conjunction with the related provisions of the Act, (especially sections 17 and 73), it is quite evident that an employer cannot carry on 'Business as before'. Once certification is granted, a new legal regime is introduced; and once notice to bargain is given, the employer must not ignore the union

or act unilaterally as it might have done in a pre-collective bargaining regime. Indeed, if the employer really does try to carry on "business as before," purportedly exercising managerial "rights" and "prerogatives" derived from the common law of master and servant, it may well collide with the requirements of the statute ... Since neither the union nor these statutory requirements were part of the pre-collective bargaining regime, it is quite misleading for an employer to look exclusively to that regime for guidelines on how it should conduct itself in the course of bargaining. ...

Nor, for the same reason, do the "reasonable expectations of employees" provide an unfailing guideline for what can or cannot be changed during the currency of the statutory phrase. The fact is, that test is just as "slippery" as "business as usual"—not least because it is not at all clear how such "employee expectations" might be ascertained. It is of necessity a Board construct, applied in particular circumstances to give expression to the competing policy considerations underlying the ambiguous language of section 86(1). It is a way of rationalizing competing interests, when the statute itself does not point unambiguously to a particular result. ...

More to the point: is this focus on "employee expectations" congruent with the language and collective bargaining purpose of section 86(1)? For having just voted in favor of trade union representation, would those same employees not reasonably expect that ... wages and benefits ... would be bargained about by their trade union? ... Or are the rights of employees in a collective bargaining regime to be determined by what employees THINK the employer might have done in other pre-collective bargaining circumstances? ...

[Chair MacDowell concluded that in the post-certification context, the existing tests must be supplemented by a third approach—one that would read the freeze provisions in light of the need to bolster the bargaining process, reinforce the status of the union as bargaining agent, and provide a firm (if temporary) starting point for collective bargaining:]

In my view, and in light of experience, these traditional views have to be augmented by another perspective that is more in tune with the precise role that section 86(1) is to play in the regulatory framework, once bargaining has begun. The language of section 86 has to be read as the Board did in *Ottawa Public Library, supra*, with these statutory purposes clearly in mind: bolstering the bargaining process; reinforcing the status of the union as the employees' bargaining agent (hence the distinction between the section 86(1) and 86(2) freezes); and providing a firm (if temporary) starting point from which bargaining will take off.

From that perspective it is necessary to pay particular attention to how the proposed change in employment conditions relates to *bargaining*. Is it the kind of thing that would typically be the subject of collective bargaining? And would changes of this kind, if implemented unilaterally in these circumstances, unduly disrupt, vitiate, or distort that bargaining process (what the freeze is designed to avoid whether or not the changes would *also* be a *breach* of section 17)? Is it the kind of thing about which the employer would normally be required to bargain by virtue of section 17? Because if the answer to these questions is "yes," it is the kind of thing that probably falls within the ambit of section 86(1) and "should" be frozen (at least for a time) while that bargaining process proceeds ("should" because while the words themselves are open to alternative interpretations, policy and purpose point in favour of that one).

It is also useful to consider whether the employer action is broadly based and treats employees *as a collectivity* (as a "collective" agreement does); or, alternatively, whether it is something intrinsic to an individual employee's situation (reclassifying an individual as opposed to introducing a new classification system; granting a promotion as opposed to creating a new process for promotions; disciplining an employee for misconduct as opposed to publishing a new scheme of workplace rules enforceable by discipline, etc.). For even in a collective bargaining regime, there is considerable scope for unilateral action impacting on employees and unaccompanied by any individual interaction that could be construed as "bargaining" with the employee(s).

If the change in question is the kind of thing that affects employees *as a collectivity*, and it is the kind of thing that the employer would be obliged to bargain about (per section 17), and it is the kind of thing that, as a matter of labour relations practice, employers typically do bargain about, then it is likely to be the kind of thing that the employer cannot implement unilaterally during the currency of the statutory freeze. In other words, it is the kind of change to employee "terms and conditions of employment rights, privileges or duties" that requires the consent of the bargaining agent.

Conversely, (and subject to section 73) there is nothing inimical to collective bargaining if an employer carries on business as before in respect of individual hiring, firing, promotions, demotions, work assignment and so on—the daily stuff of individual employer-employee interactions, that in large measure, are unrelated to the collective bargaining process, and are typically presented to employees as a *fait accompli*.

It seems to me that the answer to questions such as these, may provide a better guideline to the Board's actual interpretation of section 86(1), than asking whether the employer is carrying on "business as usual," or whether the changes are ones that employees might reasonably expect to be implemented unilaterally; because, unlike these other formulations, these questions require the Board to consider how the words of section 86(1) apply or relate to the *bargaining process*—the actual subject of regulation. At the very least, the answer to these questions helps to illuminate the purposive approach which the Board applies in respect of section 86(1), and thus fills out the picture painted by the "reasonable expectations" considerations in *Simpsons*, and the "business as usual" analysis in *Spar*.

* * * * *

Simpsons Limited and *Royal Ottawa Health Care Group*, just quoted, discussed the "reasonable expectations of employees" test, which permits employers to modify terms and conditions during a statutory freeze in certain circumstances. Note that this test is somewhat different from the statutory freeze test that has developed in Quebec labour law. As indicated in the earlier excerpt from the *UFCW, Local 503 v Wal-Mart* case, in Quebec the test is whether the change is consistent with the decision that a reasonable *employer* in the same position would have made. The former test takes the perspective of an objective *employee*. Although these two different tests will often yield the same result (as a reasonable employee would typically expect the employer to make reasonable business decisions), these tests might lead to different outcomes in some situations.

We have just discussed cases involving both stages of the freeze, and these stages have discrete time periods. The pre-certification statutory freeze applies only from the date when an application for certification is filed with the labour board. May the employer alter the terms and conditions of employment before that date? Does it matter whether the change is one that benefits the employees? Consider the perspective of a US court on NLRA freeze provisions.

National Labor Relations Board v Exchange Parts Co, 375 US 405 (1964) at 409

> HARLAN J.: The broad purpose of ss. 8(a)(1) [of the *National Labor Relations Act*] is to establish 'the right of employees to organize for mutual aid without employer interference.' ... We have no doubt that it prohibits not only intrusive threats and promises but also conduct immediately favourable to employees which is undertaken with the express purpose of impinging upon their freedom of choice for or against unionization and is reasonably calculated to have that effect. In *Medo Photo Supply Corp. v. Labor Board*. ... this Court said ...: 'The action of employees with respect to the choice of their bargaining agents may be induced by favors bestowed by the employer as well as by his threats or domination.' Although in that case there was already a designated bargaining agent and the offer of 'favors' was in response to a suggestion of the employees that they would leave the union if favors were bestowed, the principles which dictated the result there are fully applicable here. The danger inherent in well-timed increases in benefits is the suggestion of a fist inside the velvet glove. Employees are not likely to miss the inference that the source of benefits now conferred is also the source from which future benefits must flow and which may dry up if it is not obliged. The danger may be diminished, if, as in this case, the benefits are conferred permanently and unconditionally. But the absence of conditions or threats pertaining to the particular benefits conferred would be of controlling significance only if it could be presumed that no question of additional benefits or renegotiation of existing benefits would arise in the future; and, of course, no such presumption is tenable.

5:400 EMPLOYER SPEECH

During a union organizing campaign, management representatives often want to communicate with employees, with a view to persuading them not to opt for unionization. What should an employer be allowed to say in those circumstances?

In *National Labor Relations Board v Federbush Co*, 121 F 2d 954 (2d Cir 1941) at 957, Learned Hand J made these often-quoted comments:

> The privilege of "free speech," like other privileges, is not absolute; it has its seasons; a democratic society has an acute interest in its protection and cannot indeed be without it; but it is an interest measured by its purpose. That purpose is to enable others to make an informed judgement as to what concerns them, and ends so far as the utterances do not contribute to the result. Language may serve to enlighten a hearer, though it also betrays the speakers feelings and desires; but the light it sheds will be in some degree clouded, if the hearer is in his power. Arguments by an employer directed to his employees have such an ambivalent character; they are legitimate enough as such, and

pro tanto the privilege of free speech" protects them; but, so far as they also disclose his wishes, as they generally do, they have a force independent of persuasion. The [National Labor Relations] Board is vested with the power to measure these two factors against each other.... Words are not pebbles in alien juxtaposition; they have only a communal existence; and not only does the meaning of each interpenetrate the other, but all in their aggregate take their purport from the setting in which they are used, of which the relation between the speaker and the hearer is perhaps the most important part. What to an outsider will be no more than the vigorous presentation of a conviction, to an employee may be the manifestation of a determination which it is not safe to thwart. The Board must decide how far the second aspect obliterates the first.

Legislation in some Canadian jurisdictions expressly recognizes a right of employer free speech, but adds the qualification that the employer must not use threats, promises, or undue influence. The following case shows the importance of this qualification.

United Steelworkers of America v Wal-Mart Canada, [1997] OLRD No 207 at para 1ff (OLRB) (Upheld on judicial review: *Wal-Mart Canada Inc v United Steelworkers of America*, [1997] OJ No 3063 (Div Ct) leave to appeal refused, [1999] OJ No 2995 (CA)).

[An organizing drive at Wal-Mart's Windsor, Ontario, store began on 14 April 1996. By 27 April, it had collected a total of eighty-four membership cards, and between 27 April and 2 May it collected only seven more. On 26 April, an employee had told the store manager, Mr Johnston, that employees were being approached to sign union membership cards. Mr Johnston, as he had been earlier instructed to do, immediately told Mr Ratzlaff, Wal-Mart's labour relations specialist. The union filed a certification application on 2 May 1996, and provided ninety membership cards in support of the application. On 7 May, the board directed that a representation ballot be held on 9 May. A total of 205 ballots were cast; forty-three were for certification, 151 were against, and nine were segregated and not counted.

The union brought numerous allegations of unfair labour practices against Wal-Mart, resulting in thirty-five days of hearing before the OLRB.]

JOHNSTON Vice-Chair: ... While the union has asserted numerous breaches of the Act by the company, the key allegation in the union's view is that the company raised issues of economic and job security with the employees and then refused to answer questions asked on these matters. In the union's view, the company's failure to answer the question "will the store close if the union is successful" led the employees to conclude that the store would in fact close if the union was successful. Therefore, the union requests that the Board set aside the vote and certify the union pursuant to section 11 of the Act....

The store is open from 9:00 a.m. to 9:00 p.m. Monday to Saturday and from 11:00 a.m. to 5:00 p.m. on Sundays. The full-time employees generally work Monday to Friday on a day shift. Peak-time associates fill in hours whenever necessary. The management structure at this store consists of a Store Manager, Mr. Andy Johnston, and 6 assistant managers.... Above the store manager, is a District Manager, Mr. Tino Borean, who is responsible for a total of 8 stores located in London, Windsor, Sarnia, Chatham and Goderich. The company's head office or "home" office as it was referred to in this case, is located in Toronto. Mr. Jon Sims, the Regional Vice-President of Operations for Region 2 in Canada (Windsor being in Region 2), Mr. Paul Ratzlaff, Director of Associate Relations and Ms. Karen Duff, a Regional Personnel Officer, all work out of the home office....

Wal-Mart seeks to promote an atmosphere or "culture" in its stores which is positive and friendly, customer oriented and in which associates work together as a family or team.... [I]n support of its goal of regular information sharing with its employees, Wal-Mart holds daily meetings with its staff. The daily morning meeting is held at 8:45 a.m. and is attended by all associates scheduled to commence work up to 9:00 a.m. in the morning. This meeting is held at the front of the store near the courtesy desk. The meeting in this Windsor store is run by either Mr. Johnston or in his absence one of the assistant managers. At this meeting management provides financial information such as sales figures for the previous day as well as information concerning who the top performing department and individuals were on the previous day. New items of stock are discussed as well as issues around safety, shrinkage and loss prevention. An exercise to help associates limber up is also done. The Wal-Mart culture is often discussed by reference to the history of the store and its founder, Sam Walton. Associates are encouraged to participate, become involved and ask questions. The meeting normally ends just before 9:00 a.m. with the Wal-Mart cheer and then the store opens its doors to customers. An additional meeting is held every day after the store closes at 9:00 p.m. It follows the same format as the morning meeting and is an opportunity for the company to provide information to those employees who are not working in the morning and did not attend the morning meeting....

The first thing Mr. Ratzlaff did [upon learning, on April 26, that employees were being approached to sign union membership cards] was to telephone Mr. Borean to advise him of the situation. Mr. Borean then contacted Mr. Johnston and told him that he would come to the store the next day, Saturday, April 27, 1996 for the morning meeting. Mr. Borean indicated that he was planning a trip to Windsor for that day to attend the funeral of an associate who had worked in the other Windsor store. At the end of this conversation, Mr. Johnston directed one of his assistant managers to telephone all of the associates scheduled to work the next morning to tell them to ensure that they reported for work in time for the morning meeting as Tino Borean was coming to visit the store. Mr. Johnston had the employees contacted because it was the first time Mr. Borean had attended a Saturday morning meeting and he wanted to make sure that all of the scheduled associates attended the meeting and had a chance to hear what Mr. Borean had to say. It was highly unusual for the company to call employees in this fashion and Mr. Johnston was unable to think of another occasion when it had occurred.

Approximately 25 to 30 associates attended the morning meeting on April 27th. After concluding the usual routine, Mr. Johnston introduced Mr. Borean and Mr. Borean spoke. Mr. Borean indicated that he was in Windsor to attend the funeral of an associate who had worked at the other store in Windsor. There is some dispute as to what Mr. Borean said next. Mr. Johnston testified that Mr. Borean then indicated to the associates that he had heard that associates were being approached by other associates in the parking lot to sign union cards. Mr. Borean indicated that if anyone had any questions he would be there for the day to answer them, other than the couple of hours he would spend at the funeral. Ms. Mary McArthur, one of the union's inside organizers was at this meeting. She testified that Mr. Borean said that he had heard that there were people going around trying to sign union cards, that he was at the store to find out why people thought they needed a union and that he would be coming around the sales floor to talk to people about that. Ms. Debbie Kulke, a peak-time associate called by the company to give evidence about this meeting, gave another version of what was said by Mr. Borean at the meeting. She indicated that Mr. Borean stated that he knew that there was some talk about a union going on, that he would be in and out of the store, that he was going to go out and ask people if they had any questions or concerns and that he would be there if anyone had any questions or concerns. If anyone wanted to speak to him they were to feel free to do so. Ms. Norma Passador, another associate called by the company to testify indicated that Mr. Borean said that he had heard there was talk about a union. In her words, "later on he would like to go around and talk to associates and see if there was a problem and if he could handle it himself." There was no dispute that after Mr. Borean finished speaking that Ms. McArthur spoke out saying to the associates gathered that it was illegal for management to interfere or coerce or intimidate them to change their decision, that they had a right to be part of whatever was happening and that they did not have to speak to management. After the meeting concluded Mr. Borean did circulate throughout the store speaking to employees for the majority of the day. We heard no evidence as to the substance of those conversations.

Although it appears he is still employed by the company, Mr. Borean was not called upon to testify.... The employer was aware that Mr. Borean's conduct at this meeting and his individual conversations with associates thereafter was asserted by the union to be a violation of the Act ... The union urges us to prefer the testimony of Ms. McArthur regarding what Mr. Borean said and did on April 27, 1996. In the circumstances it is appropriate for us to draw an adverse inference from the company's failure to call Mr. Borean. ...

The line between legitimate employer persuasion and unlawful intimidation or undue influence must be determined on the particular facts of each case. The company contacted the associates scheduled to work on April 27th and told them to ensure that they were at work in time for the morning meeting as Mr. Borean would be attending the store. This was an unprecedented call and sent the message to employees that the meeting was important. The associates who attended this important meeting then heard from Mr. Borean that he is aware of the union and will circulate throughout the store to discuss presumably either in small groups or individually with associates, why they wanted a union or what problems or concerns they had causing them to want a union. Mr. Borean then circulated throughout the store speaking to employees. While the conduct of Mr. Borean is not a violation of the Act, it sets the tone for what is to follow. In addition, not surprisingly, the union's organizing drive began to falter shortly after Mr. Borean's visit.

On Monday, April 29, 1996, Ms. Norma Passador, an associate, approached Mr. Johnston and asked if she could speak at the morning meeting the next day. Mr. Johnston agreed. Ms. Passador did not volunteer and Mr. Johnston did not ask what she wanted to speak about. On Tuesday, April 30th, at the conclusion of the regular morning meeting, Mr. Johnston asked if any associates had any questions and Ms. Passador stated that she had something she wanted to read. She read the following speech:

I have asked to come here this morning as a concerned associate to voice my opinion against the "alleged" rumor [sic] of a union trying to be put in this store. I have worked in this building for 20 years, 18 with Woolco and the same as many of you with Wal-Mart. When Wal-Mart took over Woolco they let us keep our years of seniority for pension, vacation and rate of pay, this is something they did not have to do, but to me as a senior associate it meant a lot.

The young people in the store that have started this do not realize the consequences involved. For some of them the company is not their future when they finish their schooling they will leave and move on to better jobs in their fields, but for the rest of us this is our only income. I for one would like to know what they think they are going to receive from this action.

I believe we receive what other dept. stores have and then some. I know some of you think when we get our annual raise it should be more this is the retail business and that is how it is run. Eventually even big businesses such as the auto companies will have to accept lower wages. A union will only cause discontentment in our store and I assure you as I am standing here Wal Mart [sic] will not put up with this.

I cannot be called a company person because I complain like everyone else if not more. But I am for for [sic] what's best for me and a union is not it.

Also a word to the associates who have started this. Remember the old ruling used to be 51% and the union is in. WRONG every person MUST have a vote, because now the government steps in and posts a notice in the store when a vote will be taken and we all vote and remember as far as I am concerned the union is not your friend, it is the friend of people who don't like to work. Also please remember that there are people working in union places that do not get all the benefits we have and you all know what they are. Also if anything if anything [sic] comes of this I assure you I will be one of the first associates to cross a picket line because I need my job.

Thank you for listening to me this morning.

When Ms. Passador finished speaking there was considerable commotion. Some of the associates present applauded Ms. Passador's speech, others did not. Either Ms. McArthur or Mr. Dave Cartier (another inside organizer), or both, indicated that they wanted to respond to Ms. Passador's speech. Mr. Borean, who was in attendance at the meeting, did not allow either employee to speak and ended the meeting. He indicated that it was time to open the store as they had customers waiting. It was either 9:00 o'clock or shortly after 9:00 a.m. when the meeting ended.

Later the same day Mr. Johnston approached an associate, Jamie Campbell, while he was working. Mr. Johnston opened the conversation by telling Mr. Campbell about the morning meeting, as Mr. Campbell worked an evening shift, either 4:00 p.m. to 9:30 p.m. or 5:00 p.m. to 9:30 p.m. Mr. Johnston then asked Mr. Campbell if he knew what was going on in the store regarding the union and Mr. Campbell answered that he did. Mr. Johnston asked Mr. Campbell if he had been approached by anyone from the union about signing a union card and Mr. Campbell answered that yes he had been approached. Mr. Johnston next, in Mr. Campbell's words, "went on to say something along the lines of a union would not necessarily benefit the store because all of the benefits and everything would have to be bargained for and he also suggested that neither side would have to agree to any specific details." The benefits or details referred to are what are called stakeholder payments or the profit sharing programme. The last thing mentioned by Mr. Johnston to Mr. Campbell was that some employees had been tricked into signing union cards as they were being told they were signing the card to get more information. Mr. Johnston then advised Mr. Campbell to use his own judgement when he was making decisions....

On Saturday, May 4, 1996 Mr. Johnston ran the morning meeting. Mr. Ratzlaff, Mr. Sims, Mr. Borean and Ms. Duff were present at the meeting. Mr. Johnston read from a prepared text and told the employees present at the meeting the following:

> The Steelworkers Union applied to the labour board to get in at this store. The labour board will now check to see if the union has enough support for the board to hold a vote on the issue. Does this mean that the union is in? No! It "means the union has applied to get in. The union can not [sic] get in until it has a vote. That vote would be by secret ballot and everyone get [sic] to vote no matter if they have signed or not signed a union card.
>
> I want to be sure we get the right answers to your questions. To make that easier, I've put up a question box. You can write down your questions and put them in the box. You don't need to put your name on the question. I'll get answers and give the answers to all of you.

Mr. Johnston indicated that pursuant to Mr. Ratzlaff's instructions he had put the question and answer box up on Friday. Employees were told to put questions in the question box if they wanted to and that management would answer their questions. Mr. Johnston then introduced the three home office managers and Tino Borean to the group of employees present. He told the associates that he had been inundated with questions with regard to the union's application. The additional managers were there to answer questions and to provide information about the union's application and about the vote or anything else. Mr. Ratzlaff also spoke and then the meeting ended. This format with a few additions was followed that evening, at the meeting Sunday and at the two meetings on Monday.

After the meeting concluded, the three home office managers, Mr. Borean and Mr. Johnston began to circulate throughout the store. Mr. Ratzlaff described his approach to employees as follows. He told the Board that sometimes while he was walking around an associate would approach him if they saw him coming. However, more often he would go to an associate who was working and strike up a conversation. If the associate kept working Mr. Ratzlaff would help the person. When they stopped working to talk to him, he would introduce himself and indicate where he was from. Mr. Ratzlaff would then ask the associate if he/she had been present at the morning meeting that day. If the answer was yes then Mr. Ratzlaff would tell the person that "we" (the outside managers) were there to answer questions about the union if they had any or about anything else. Mr. Ratzlaff would indicate that if they wanted to talk about the union issue they would have to raise it with him and it was purely voluntary to do so. If the associate indicated that he/she had not attended the morning meeting then Mr. Ratzlaff would make sure that they knew about the union's application. He would ask if they had seen the notice posted in the employee lounge with regard to the application and if the person had not seen it Mr. Ratzlaff would tell them to feel free to go look at it. If the person had any questions after reviewing the notice he/she was told to approach the managers who were visiting the store or Andy Johnston as any of this group would be happy to answer questions. When he was asked whether the store would close if the union was successful Mr. Ratzlaff indicated that it was not appropriate to answer that question. On one occasion, while being confronted by an inside organizer concerning the effect that the employer's refusal to answer any questions concerning whether or not the store would close was having on employees, Mr. Ratzlaff told a group of employees that he had been given legal advice that it was not appropriate to tell employees what the company might or might not do as a result of the vote.

The approach utilized by Mr. Sims was similar to that of Mr. Ratzlaff.... Mr. Sims indicated that his goal was to talk to as many employees as possible and answer their questions on any topic. Mr. Sims recalled being asked whether the store would close if the union got in and the answer he gave was, in his words, "it would be inappropriate to comment on what might or might not happen." ...

The three home office managers, Mr. Ratzlaff, Mr. Sims and Ms. Duff plus Mr. Borean were in the store circulating amongst the employees from May 4, 1996 until the day of the vote, May 9, 1996....

The union issue came up in one way or another at every morning (and presumably every evening) meeting between May 4th and the day of the vote. After each of the morning meetings concluded, the management group present in the store would move throughout the store for the remainder of the day approaching employees to see if they had any questions. On at least two occasions, both Mr. Sims and Mr. Ratzlaff were advised by one of the union's inside organizers that the refusal of management to answer any questions concerning whether the store would close if the union was successful, was causing employees to fear for their jobs. Management never changed its approach.

On May 5, 1996 between 4 and 5 o'clock Mr. Johnston approached a peak-time associate, Mr. Walter Dinatale. Mr. Johnston asked Mr. Dinatale if he had any questions concerning the union or what was going on in the store. Mr. Dinatale told Mr. Johnston that he did not have any questions. Mr. Johnston then went on to tell Mr. Dinatale that he should not feel pressured into signing anything and that he should feel free to make up his own mind. Mr. Johnston told Mr. Dinatale that a lot of things would change if the union was successful, for example, the stakeholders' benefit would be revoked. Then Mr. Johnston told Mr. Dinatale that if he had any further questions he should speak to a member of management.

In final submissions counsel for the company acknowledged that both Mr. Campbell and Mr. Dinatale were credible witnesses. Given this concession on the part of counsel and the fact that both Mr. Campbell and Mr. Dinatale's recollection of the conversation they had with Mr. Johnston were clearer and more complete than the recollection of Mr. Johnston, we have accepted their version of the conversation. In his conversation with Mr. Dinatale Mr. Johnston made an explicit threat going to Mr. Dinatale's economic security. In threatening to take away benefits if the union was successful, Mr. Johnston breached section 70 of the Act.

At the morning meeting on May 7, 1996, the employees were given the answers to the questions which had been put into the question box. At the end of the meeting Mr. Ratzlaff indicated that all of the employee questions, with answers provided, had been set out in a written document. That written document was available for employees to pick up. The order in which the questions and answers were set out was determined by Mr. Ratzlaff. As it is lengthy we will only set out the first two questions and the answers provided by the company....

> Q. "There is an overwhelming concern that if the store unionizes, Wal-Mart will close the store. Is this true?"
> A. It would be inappropriate for your Company to comment on what it will or will not do if the store is unionized.
>
> Q. "Some people have said that if the store unionized it would be illegal for Wal-Mart to close the store. Is that true?"
> A. This statement is not factually correct. What would or would not be legal for your Company to do following the store becoming unionized depends on the factual circumstances and the application of the law against those circumstances. It would be inappropriate for your Company to comment or suggest what those factual circumstances might be.

[...]

As is obvious, the questions pertaining to whether the store would close if the union was successful were answered with the indication that the company could not answer the question. Before leaving the question and answer sheet we would point out that in response to two other questions concerning the store's lease the employer gave the same response. In response to a question concerning profit sharing and a question concerning payment for work on Sundays the company responded by indicating that this was a matter to be decided at the bargaining table. While this answer may have been interpreted as an indication that perhaps the company would not immediately close the store if the union was successful, the kind of mixed message generated by these inconsistent responses is not sufficient to counteract the fear generated by the employer's consistent failure to respond to the direct questions with regard to the store closure....

We have two concerns with Ms. Passador's speech on April 30, 1996. First of all the company, at the end of Ms. Passador's speech did not distance itself from her comments. Neither Mr. Borean nor Mr. Johnston stated that her comments were not reflective of the company's views on unions and the effect that a union would have in the store. Secondly, even though we accept that there were legitimate reasons for ending the meeting at that point, namely that it was time for the store to open to its customers, by not allowing the union supporters to speak, the associates who were present were left only with the views of Ms. Passador. What is crucial in our view, is the effect that Ms. Passador's comments may have had on employees in the store. What message would the average or reasonable associate hear upon listening to Ms. Passador's speech? ... Ms. Passador never said that the store would close if the union was successful in its attempt to organize employees. However, because of what she did say an associate listening to her would have likely concluded that she had concerns for her future job security in the event that the union was successful....

It was never suggested that management arranged for Ms. Passador to make the comments she did. We accept that the views expressed were her views. There is nothing wrong with allowing Ms. Passador to speak her mind. However, in light of the fact that the company after inviting questions or comments, did not clarify that the comments were not reflective of the company's views, allowed the spectre of job insecurity to be raised in a situation in which it is reasonable for employees to conclude that it was a legitimate concern. In the circumstances, it would not be unreasonable for some of the associates to conclude that the views of Ms. Passador were reflective of the views of the company and that the company agreed with her assessment of the situation. In allowing this message to be sent at a meeting which management directs and controls, without distancing itself from her remarks or allowing the union supporters the opportunity to balance her remarks, the company has sought to intimidate or unduly influence employees with regard to their decision on union representation contrary to section 70 of the Act. An employer simply cannot allow an employee to make a speech containing the subtle threats to job security such as those contained in Ms. Passador's speech, at a meeting run by management, fail to distance itself from the comments and then silence the union's supporters in the manner in which it did. While the company did not make any threats, it allowed threats to be made in circumstances in which they could be attributed to the company. Ms. Passador's speech had a chilling effect on the union's organizing drive.

The attendance of four outside managers in the store from May 4th to May 9th who spent the vast majority of their time approaching employees while they were working in the store and engaging them repeatedly in conversations regarding the union, was an extremely risky response for the company to have made to the union's organizing drive ...

In this case there was no surveillance or pressure being brought upon the union's inside organizers. Nor was there a series of management meetings opposing the union. However, there were daily morning meetings at which the union issue was discussed. At their conclusion the four outside managers would start circulating and continued to do so for the majority of their time until the store closed for the day. They did this for the five days leading up to the vote and on the day of the vote. In the course of these conversations they learned who the union supporters were and who were not union supporters contrary to the protection afforded by the Act. The presence of the four outside managers certainly sent the message that the union issue was a very important one to the company. The Board heard a great deal about the Wal-Mart culture and the open relationship between management, as representatives of the company, and the employees. Given this "culture" it is understandable that Mr. Ratzlaff, as the official co-ordinating the company's response, would want to ensure that resources were available to deal with employee questions. But, there is a big difference between having resources available, which employees can seek out and what occurred in this case. Mr. Ratzlaff's strategy was to have four outside managers, senior managers, constantly approaching employees over a six day period actively soliciting questions from the employees on the union issue. This conduct, four managers (and this is not counting Mr. Johnston who is doing the same thing) repeatedly engaging employees in a conversation about the union, goes beyond mere assistance to employees based on a concern that their questions be answered, and becomes an extremely effective tactic of intimidation or undue influence contrary to section 70 of the Act. As the Board has noted before, an employer cannot hide behind "open door" policies when the effect of the open communications is to put undue influence on employees concerning their selection of a trade union to represent them. This repeated and persistent personal contact initiated by the employer and not requested by the employees was clearly designed to identify the union supporters as well as communicate the message which we will next deal with.

This conduct of the employer, namely the strategy of having four managers constantly engaging employees in conversations about the union, is not the breach of the Act or the conduct in and of itself which led us to conclude that it is appropriate to certify the union pursuant section 11. The conduct of the employer which gave us the most concern, while part of the approach detailed above, was far more harmful to the free will of the employees.... We accept that there is a unique culture fostered in this company, one in which employees are encouraged to ask questions and expect to get answers. One of the key concerns of the associates in this store was whether the company would continue to operate the store if the union was successful ...

Given the Wal-Mart culture and the expectations of employees that answers to their questions would be given, what would the effect of this refusal to answer such a crucial question be on the average, reasonable associate? In assessing the effect of the refusal to answer it is also important to bear in mind that management over a six day period is continually approaching the associates and asking them if they have any questions about the union's organizing drive. The managers present in the store in the days leading up to the vote entered into dozens of daily one-on-one conversations with associates about the union and when asked, refused to answer any questions with regard to the store closure issue. The company attempted to portray the store closure issue as a union issue and pointed out that it was not raised with a great deal of frequency with the managers. In our view it is irrelevant how many times the associates asked one of the managers this question, as it would not take long for it to "get around" the store that this question was not being answered. Why ask if you knew it would not be answered? ...

The managers, knowing the effect the refusal to answer the questions of employees with regard to store closure was having, nevertheless continued to refuse to answer any questions on this issue.

In our view you cannot have it both ways. If you adopt the approach of constantly soliciting questions in an environment such as was present in this case, you have to answer them. Either you answer the questions asked or you do not circulate amongst employees in the manner in which management did in this case....

It is always difficult to place oneself in the shoes of the employees in the store to determine what effect the company's campaign would have had on them. However, in the unique circumstances of this case, and we stress that they are unique, we are of the view that the company's failure to answer the questions of associates with regard to the issue of store closure would cause the average reasonable employee to conclude that the store would close if the union got in. Given that the inside organizers told management that this was in fact happening, and management did not change its approach, we are satisfied that the company intended employees to draw this conclusion. There is no legal prohibition against answering questions with regard to store closure by saying that the company would not close and would sit down and negotiate with the union if the union was successful. Obviously, it is only illegal for the company to say that the store would close. Therefore, by not alleviating employees' concerns by answering the question, the company was intentionally fuelling employee concerns. Accordingly, we find that the conduct of the employer in circulating amongst the employees and engaging them in individual and group discussions regarding the union, in the fashion in which it did, and the company's refusal to answer any questions with regard to what the store would do if the union was successful, was a breach of section 70 of the Act.

* * * * *

In *RMH Teleservices International Inc*, [BCLRB Decision No B345/2003 (reconsidered in BCLRB Decision No B188/2005, and returned to original panel for remedies in BCLRB Decision No B280/2005)], numerous allegations were made of employer unfair labour practices during union organizing, including several involving employer speech. One complaint centred on a slide show the company ran at various times during the workday, containing anti-union messages, projected onto all four walls of the large room where the employees worked and onto a double-sided screen in the centre of the room. The show was made up of slides containing a variety of anti-union messages, and there was no audio component.

The original panel held that the slide show was not an unfair labour practice. It concluded that employees were able to go about their work without constantly reading the projected messages, and were not compelled to look at or listen to the employer's views during the course of their work.

The reconsideration panel reached a different conclusion.

> "We do not agree with the original panel that employees should have to avert their eyes from employer communications in the course of their ordinary working circumstances (thus, bulletin boards or other such locations may be different). The slide shows were so prominent, persistent, and impossible to miss that employees, while at work, would inevitably have been forced to view them or forced to consciously turn away from them. This is the type of communication where otherwise permissible views become coercive or intimidating." (at para. 66)
>
> "In terms of the Union's arguments, we conclude that the concept of "forced listening" comes closer to capturing the essence of what can make an otherwise acceptable employer expression of views during an organizing drive coercive or intimidating. Section 8 does not guarantee an audience. The right of expression under Section 8 does not entail a right to compel others to listen to those views. A reasonable employee who has no choice but to listen to an employer's views regarding unionization may feel coerced or intimidated by the very fact that they have no choice but to hear their employer's views. Whereas they can turn away from a union organizer or a co-worker and decline to listen to them on the topic of unionization, an employee is far less able to turn away from their employer. By virtue of their authority in the workplace, employers can compel their employees to listen to them. Compelled or forced listening raises serious concerns regarding employee free choice on the issue of unionization." (para. 58)
>
> [...]
>
> "The expression of views by an employer, including views about unionization, is not necessarily inconsistent with free choice. However, where an employer expresses its views on unionization in a manner that effectively forces employees to listen, this manner of communicating views may render otherwise permissible expression coercive or intimidating. In each case, both the content and the method used must be considered" (para. 61).

CHAPTER 5: THE RIGHT TO JOIN A UNION

* * * * *

In the federal jurisdiction, the Canada Industrial Relations Board imposes what has been called a "neutrality standard" for employer communications with workers during union organizing, and also takes a very strict approach to "captive audience" meetings. The CIRB explained its position in *American Airlines Incorporated* (1981), 43 di 114; [1981] 3 CLRBR 90 (CLRB no 301) at p 133:

> Any involvement by the employer in the exercise by the employee of his/her basic right to join a union puts unfair pressure on the employee. An employee joining a union must not be put in a situation of a second class citizen who is adhering to a secret society and being ashamed of it. Either the right is recognized or it is not; if it is, it must be exercised in full light and without fear.
>
> The employer's right to communicate with its employees must be strictly limited to the conduct of the business. The employer is only permitted to respond to unequivocal and identifiable, adversarial or libellous statements; by this we do not consider as being adversarial the fact that an employee wishes or does not wish to join a union. In the light of this background, employer's communications are to be permitted inasmuch as they are related to the efficient operation of the business. If they are not, then they must be viewed as a participation or interference in the representation of employees by a trade union and thus in contravention of Section 184(1)(a).

5:500 SOLICITATION ON EMPLOYER PROPERTY

The workplace is the usual location for union organizing. It is also the employer's property. How should labour legislation balance employees' rights to act collectively with the employer's right to control conduct on its premises?

Canada Post Corporation (1995), 95 CLLC para 220-042 (CIRB)

> Louise Doyon, Vice-Chair:
>
> On November 24, 1994, the Letter Carriers Union of Canada (LCUC) filed a complaint with the Board alleging that Canada Post Corporation (CPC or the Corporation) had violated sections 94(1)(a) and 94(3)(a)(i) of the Canada Labour Code.
>
> These sections read as follows:
>
>> 94.(1) No employer or person acting on behalf of an employer shall
>> (a) participate in or interfere with the formation or administration of a trade union or the representation of employees by a trade union; or ...
>>
>> (3) No employer or person acting on behalf of an employer shall
>> (a) refuse to employ or to continue to employ or suspend, transfer, lay off or otherwise discriminate against any person with respect to employment, pay or any other term or condition of employment or intimidate, threaten or otherwise discipline any person, because the person

(i) is or proposes to become, or seeks to induce any other person to become, a member, officer or representative of a trade union or participates in the promotion, formation or administration of a trade union, ...

LCUC alleged that the Corporation contravened the Code by refusing to grant access to employees from other than their own work locations. The employees wanted to canvass co-workers at other CPC premises during non-working hours and within designated lunch areas. The employees were part of LCUC's raiding campaign to replace the Canadian Union of Postal Workers (CUPW) as bargaining agent for the operational bargaining unit [one nationwide unit]. LCUC says the employer had no compelling business reasons or justification to prohibit access at any location to its employees who were not scheduled for work at their own premises. The decision, LCUC says, was aimed at prohibiting the solicitation of employees. In the result, CPC reduced the status of its employees to that of any "stranger" to the Corporation.

The complainant asked the Board to declare that CPC violated the Code by interfering with the organization and formation of a trade union. LCUC also asked the Board to order the Corporation to grant LCUC representatives, who are its employees, access to designated lunch areas, in order to canvass during rest periods and lunch breaks at any of CPC's worksites. LCUC agrees that if membership solicitation takes place on CPC's premises, it should only be carried out in the cafeterias or lunch areas during non-working hours.

The employer's position can be summarized as follows. Firstly, solicitation on the employer's premises would be allowed if it was carried out by employees employed at the worksite, outside of business hours and in non-working areas. Thus, the October 21st, 1994 memorandum signed by Mr. G. Courville, Corporate Manager, Labour Relations, stating that position, which excludes access by employees from other locations or non employees, did not unlawfully restrict organizing activity at the work place. This position reflects the employer's general policy restricting employee access to CPC facilities for any purpose other than to carry out their work, unless prior permission is obtained. Given the nature of CPC's operations, there are valid business and security reasons for this policy. The employer's main concern is security, either at the point of access, as for example in smaller postal stations and depots, or in larger plants, once the person has gone through the security check point.

Secondly, the employer relies on its obligation to act in a strictly neutral manner when two unions are competing to represent a group of its employees, as in the present case.

The employer considered that granting access to its facilities for organizing purposes, when such access is normally prohibited for other purposes, could be seen as favouring LCUC. CPC referred to a letter dated June 9, 1994 on that subject, from Mr. D.W. Tingley, CUPW's National President, requesting that the employer remain neutral vis-à-vis LCUC's efforts to displace CUPW as the certified bargaining agent for the operational unit. One of the contentious issues cited by Mr. Tingley in that letter was allowing LCUC canvassers access to CPC premises....

The employer's greatest concern is the question of security, given the nature and magnitude of CPC's operations. The Corporation has approximately 52 000 employees who work in 21 mechanized facilities and 400 depots or postal stations. It moves about

30 to 35 million pieces of mail per day, excluding advertisements. Mr. Alan Whitson, Manager, Loss Prevention and Special Projects, stated that not all employees have identification cards. Only certain letter carriers have identification cards, as the Corporation stopped issuing such cards to external workers some time ago. The identification cards that employees do have only give them access to the plant where they normally work, and this has been the practice for several years.

The Corporation's plant security guidelines, in effect since 1989, define non-employees and employees from other plants as "visitors." According to these guidelines, visitors must sign in, visibly display an ID card, and be escorted by an employee, whereas employees carry their CPC identification card at all times. Drivers of any vehicles entering the plants, must stay in certain areas and only use certain entrances and exits....

At postal stations and depots, security rules are different since occasionally, there are no managers on duty. Visitors to any of these facilities will be questioned as to the purpose of their visit when they enter. Here as well, once visitors are inside, it is unlikely that they would be challenged.

In Mr. Whitson's view, the security of a facility is essential since once CPC has given visitors access to its premises, they are rarely stopped. Despite the fact that visitors should remain where they have business, once they pass the security point, they can virtually circulate as they wish, unless challenged by someone in the plant. Even if this rarely occurs, in Mr. Whitson's experience, there is little control over visitors, and breaches of security can lead to loss of customers and CPC products....

Mr. Dale Clark, First National Vice-President, testified at CUPW's request. CUPW maintained that granting LCUC supporters access to CPC's premises would amount to assisting the LCUC raid. Access given to LCUC canvassers should be restricted to employees at their own work locations, to neutral areas, outside of business hour; and no access should be granted to any employees on leave or not scheduled to work. He said that if extensive access was given to LCUC canvassers, "there will be major disruption" in the work place....

The issues the Board must decide, since the parties agree that organizing activities would take place in cafeterias and lunch areas during non-working hours, are:

1. Was CPC's refusal to grant access for organizing purposes, to employees employed at any other CPC worksite, a violation of section 94(1)(a) of the Code?
2. Was CPC's refusal to grant employees access to their own worksite for organizing purposes if the employee was on leave or not scheduled for work, a violation of section 94(1)(a) of the Code?

To answer these questions, the Board must consider whether the employer has demonstrated any valid and compelling business reasons for restricting access....

Section 94(1))(a) provides union activities with extensive protection.... The Board has, however, recognized that not all union activities fall under that provision. In *Brazeau Transport Inc.* ..., the Board said:

> Union activities—whether those of the union's executive, its officer or its members—must be carried out within the framework recognized by the Code. The only union activities that are protected are those which are recognized by the Code. Section 184 [now 94] cannot serve

as an umbrella for all union activities regardless of their merits. A union president who speaks on behalf of his organization's members is clearly taking an action that can always be associated with the performance of union activities. This does not give him free rein to do anything whatsoever at any time because his actions fall within the framework of union activities. To say that it did would force us to recognize anarchy and chaos, which are precisely what the Code seeks to avoid by setting forth rules and a framework within which the said union activities must be carried out.

Section 95(d) of the Code explicitly restricts the exercise of union activities which are protected by section 94(1)(a). It reads as follows:

> 95. No trade union or person acting on behalf of a trade union shall
>
> ...
>
> (d) except with the consent of the employer of an employee, attempt, at an employee's place of employment during the working hours of the employee, to persuade the employee to become, to refrain from becoming or to cease to be a member of a trade union; ...

This section clearly prohibits union solicitation at the work place during working hours. However, according to the interpretation of this provision by this Board and other relations boards in Canada, section 95(d) does not prohibit organizers from signing up of members in a trade union at the work place, outside working hours....

The Ontario Labour Relations Board, in *Adams Mine, Cliffs of Canada Ltd.*...., defined as follows the words "working hours" found in section 71 of the Labour Relations Act, R.S.O. 1980, c. 228, a provision which has the same object as section 95(d) of the Code:

> Labour boards have consistently interpreted the phrase 'working hours' to refer only to the period of time during which an employee is required to undertake his duties and responsibilities. Therefore the section does not apply to those periods of time an employee is on company property before shift, during coffee break, during lunch break, or after shift. This is so even if the employee is being paid for such time, otherwise an employer could prevent the exercise of statutory activity by the simple expedient of a money payment.

In the above mentioned decision, the Ontario Board adopted and applied the interpretation provided by this Board in *Bell Canada, supra*, concerning the right to solicit outside working hours—a right that can only be restricted if the employer can demonstrate the existence of "compelling and justifiable business reasons." The Nova Scotia Labour Relations Board ... had previously adopted a similar position.

This interpretation of section 95(d), regulating the time frame within which membership solicitation can take place on the employer's premises, is not contested in the present case.

The Board must determine in this case whether employees, who work for an employer operating at several locations, have the right to solicit membership of their co-workers in the same bargaining unit during non-working hours at the company's work locations other than at their own work place. This is the first time that this specific issue is before the Board. Section 95(d) and other sections of the Code do not however define in any way who, acting on behalf of a trade union, has the right to engage or participate in such solicitation....

An absolute rule of non admittance concerning union organizing applied to employees not scheduled to work, at any time and at any of the employer's worksites, because of apprehended fears related to security and safety, is not compatible with the provisions of the Code, nor with the jurisprudence of some other labour relations boards. Over the years, labour relations boards have shed light on the meaning and scope of the conditions relating to the exercise of the right of association. We must reiterate that nothing in the Code prohibits an employee from encouraging fellow employees to join a trade union on the employer's premises outside working hours. On the other hand, membership solicitation is an integral part of the expression of the fundamental right of freedom of association provided for in the Code and, in this regard, should be allowed and protected. It should only be restricted for compelling and justifiable reasons, including safety and security concerns.

As the Board stated in *Canada Post Corporation, supra*:

> The purpose of raiding is to displace a certified bargaining agent. The only means to achieve that result is to convince a majority of employees in the bargaining unit to support the raiding union. This activity of persuading employees to become a member of a union during a raid period is essential, and not only incidental to the formation of a trade union. (page 56)

Therefore, the Board concludes that such action is not prohibited by the Code, when it is carried out by those directly affected in collectively choosing a bargaining agent whose task will be to negotiate the terms and conditions of employment of the group of employees included in the bargaining unit. The Board finds that to conclude otherwise would unduly restrict the means of exercising the right of association set out in section 8 of the Code as well as the scope of the protection provided by section 94 of the Code.

Nothing in the Code prohibits an employee who is a member of a bargaining unit from engaging in such solicitation. Therefore, the Board finds that the employer, by prohibiting bargaining unit members from other locations from meeting with fellow employees during non-working hours and in non-working locations within CPC premises, such as cafeterias and lunch areas, is prima facie in violation of section 94(1)(a).

Having said this, there is no doubt that solicitation must nevertheless comply with conditions that ensure a balance between an employer's right to productivity and sound management on the one hand, and on the other hand, the employees' right to freely exercise their right of association.

The balancing test between the parties' interests has been developed over the years by labour boards. It was first established in *Bell Canada, supra*, where it was referred to as the employer's "compelling and justifiable business reasons" to justify that its actions do not amount to interference pursuant to section 94.

In *Ottawa-Carleton Regional Transit Commission, supra*, the Board defined what it considered to be "compelling and justifiable business reasons." In that case, the Board had to determine whether prohibiting employees from wearing union insignia during an organizing campaign constituted interference in union business by the employer.

[T]he Board characterized the reasonableness of an employer's decision to restrict union activities in the following manner:

Reasonableness in the context of restricting a lawful union activity such as the wearing of a union insignia during working hours must surely include the ability to show a detrimental effect on entrepreneurial interests such as, negative customer reaction, security, safety or other business considerations. In other words, "compelling or justifiable business reasons."

In *Canada Post Corporation* ..., the Board defined "compelling and justifiable business reasons" as follows:

> For an employer to establish compelling and justifiable business reasons, it must show that its operations are being disrupted or that other legitimate business interests are being adversely affected.

In *Adams Mine, supra,* the Ontario Board recognized, as this Board and the Nova Scotia Board did, the right of employees to solicit membership from other employees on the employer's premises outside working hours. The Ontario Board expressed its concerns on the issue of protection of the employer's rights as follows:

> This, of course, does not mean an employer is deprived by the Act of maintaining productivity or discipline or of securing his property from encroachment by strangers with whom he has no relationship.

The meaning and scope of this statement has to be addressed in the present case, since CPC claimed that it had no relationship with employees who intended to solicit membership elsewhere than at their own worksite. For the Board to accept the employer's argument that those employees seeking access to CPC locations for the purpose of promoting LCUC are "strangers" because they do not work at or out of that location would restrict them from attempting to speak to their fellow bargaining unit members on this important issue and unduly limit the employees' right under section 8 in the circumstances. There is one nation-wide bargaining unit in existence in this case. The Board would effectively deprive employees of their right to participate in the formation of the trade union of their choice if it accepted the employer's and intervener's positions and concluded that an employee may only solicit fellow employees at his or her own work location. Consequently, in this case and for the purpose of this decision, it suffices to say that the Board does not consider that employees at one work location are strangers to any other work location such that they can be treated as strangers with whom the employer has no relationship....

[T]he employer did not point out any specific disruption or adverse effect on its business which could reasonably be anticipated should greater access to its premises be granted as requested by LCUC.

CPC has established a complete set of security guidelines that can be adapted and followed to ensure that LCUC supporters are identified and monitored when they legally canvass on CPC's premises....

Consequently, the Board orally issued this order at the hearing:

> Canada Post shall grant access to employees in the bargaining unit acting as LCUC representatives for the purposes of canvassing and soliciting union membership during employee rest breaks and lunch periods in the cafeterias and/or lunch areas only. Such access will be subject to CPC security guidelines currently in effect, to the extent they apply in light of this order.

CHAPTER 5: THE RIGHT TO JOIN A UNION

* * * * *

In *T Eaton Co*, [1985] OLRB Rep June 941, the workplace in question was a department store located entirely within the Toronto Eaton Centre, an enclosed shopping mall. The Ontario Labour Relations Board held that the T Eaton Co—the employer and operator of the store—had unlawfully interfered with the formation of a trade union by applying a blanket rule prohibiting the distribution of union literature on its premises at all times, including those when the store was not open to the public and when the employees concerned were not working. The board ruled that the employer could not prohibit the occasional distribution of union literature before the store opened, because that would not interfere with the employer's legitimate business interests.

The company which managed the shopping mall—Cadillac Fairview—maintained a no-solicitation policy for all areas of the mall, even those areas which were rarely used. That policy totally prohibited union organizers from soliciting employees. The OLRB held that Cadillac Fairview had unlawfully interfered with the formation of a trade union by the Eaton employees, because Cadillac Fairview's no-solicitation policy lacked a sufficient business justification.

In *Cadillac Fairview Corporation v Retail, Wholesale and Department Store Union* (1989), 71 OR (2d) 206 (CA). The Ontario Court of Appeal upheld the OLRB's decision. Speaking for the court, Robins J said:

> In my opinion, notions of absolutism have no place in the determination of issues arising under a statute designed to further harmonious labour relations and to foster the freedom of employees to join a trade union of their choice. In this area of the law, as in so many others, a balance must be struck between competing interests which endeavours to recognize the purposes underlying the interests and seeks to reconcile them in a manner consistent with the aims of the legislation ...
>
> Once Cadillac Fairview was found to have no valid business purpose that would justify its interference with the protected union activity, its property rights were required to yield, at least to the limited extent ordered by the Board, to the employees' s. 3 organizational rights.

5:600   UNION UNFAIR LABOUR PRACTICES

The law forbids trade unions from coercing employees to become members, in much the same way as management is forbidden to exert pressure in the opposite direction. Union unfair labour practice cases are much less common than employer unfair labour practice cases. What might explain that difference?

In *Milnet Mines Ltd* (1953), 53 CLLC para 17,063 (OLRB), threats of violence against organizers and supporters of an intervenor union by supporters of the applicant union led the Ontario Labour Relations Board to dismiss the application, without even holding a vote, because the board considered that such intimidation would have a continuing effect. Similarly, in *Canadian Fabricated Products Ltd* (1954), 54 CLLC para 17,090 at 1511–12 (OLRB), an application by the applicant union to replace the intervenor union as bargaining agent for the respondent company's employees was dismissed on the basis of testimony from several of those employees that the applicant's canvassers had told them that it "had collective relations with several of the companies upon whom the respondent was dependent for business and that, unless the employees of the respondent became members of the applicant, the members of the applicant employed by other companies would see to it that the respondent's goods were rejected and ultimately the witnesses would find themselves without work and would lose their jobs." The OLRB concluded (at 1512) that "[t]hreats of economic reprisals of this nature are forbidden by section 48(1) [now section 76] of the [Ontario *Labour Relations Act*] which declares that "no person shall seek by intimidation or coercion to compel any person to become ... a member of a trade union."

5:700 REMEDIES FOR INTERFERENCE WITH THE RIGHT TO ORGANIZE

A test of any legal system is the extent to which its norms are applied in practice. When private actors do not comply voluntarily, effective remedies ensure that the law is implemented. This is expressed in the Latin maxim *ubi jus ibi remedium*. In labour-management relations, remedies play a particularly important role because time is of great tactical importance in a union organizing campaign, and the parties do not normally sever their relationship when the litigation is over.

Labour relations legislation typically provides for both quasi-criminal penalties and administrative remedies. Under many of the statutes, certain unfair labour practices are treated as offences subject to prosecution. An aggrieved party may launch a prosecution only with leave from the responsible minister or labour relations board. See, for example, Ontario *Labour Relations Act, 1995*, sections 104–7 and 109. However, such penalties are rarely sought or ordered.

Administrative penalties are available from a labour relations board and are most commonly sought for unfair labour practices. Boards in most jurisdictions have a broad legislative mandate to provide remedial relief. For example, section 96(4) of the Ontario *Labour Relations Act, 1995* authorizes the OLRB to determine what should be done to redress any contravention of the legislation.

Labour boards have used this jurisdiction to develop an array of remedies to be applied individually or in combination. This includes orders to employers to provide information to employees or to give a union an opportunity to communicate with workers. That opportunity may take the form of meetings at the workplace and on working time, access to a workplace bulletin board, posting a statement or a board decision in the workplace, or mailing materials to employees. Such orders are meant to counter the discouraging effect that an employer's unfair labour practices may have on other employees, and to correct misinformation about unions or unionization. Labour boards will also commonly issue declarations that there has been a statutory violation, and where the wrongdoing is found to be ongoing or likely to recur, they will issue a cease and desist order.

* * * * *

The following comments of Lamer CJ in *Royal Oak Mines v Canada (Labour Relations Board)*, [1996] 1 SCR 369 at paras 55, 56, and 58, demonstrate the wide deference that courts have given to labour boards' remedial awards.

In examining the legislation itself it is apparent that Parliament has clearly given the Canada Labour Relations Board a wide remedial role. The wording of s. 99(2) does not place precise limits on the Board's jurisdiction. In fact, the Board may order anything that is "equitable" for a party to do or refrain from doing in order to fulfil the objectives of the Code. In my view, this was done to give the Board the flexibility necessary to address the ever changing circumstances that present themselves in the wide variety of disputes which come before it in the sensitive field of labour relations. The aims of the *Canada Labour Code* include the constructive resolution of labour disputes for the benefit of the parties and the public. The expert and experienced labour boards were set up to achieve these goals. The problem before the Board was one which Parliament intended it to resolve.

The requirement that the Board's order must remedy or counteract any consequence of a contravention or failure to comply with the Code imposes the condition that the Board's remedy must be rationally connected or related to the breach and its consequences. This requirement is also consistent with the test established in *National Bank of Canada v. Retail Clerks' International Union*, [1984] 1 S.C.R. 269, which required that there be a relation between the breach, its consequences and the remedy. Section 99 also provides that the Board may remedy breaches which are adverse to the fulfilment of the objectives of the Code. This empowers the Board to fashion remedies which are consistent with the Code's policy considerations. Therefore, if the Board imposes a remedy which is not rationally connected to the breach and its consequences or is inconsistent with the policy objectives of the statute then it will be exceeding its jurisdiction. Its decision will in those circumstances be patently unreasonable....

In my view remedies are a matter which fall directly within the specialized competence of labour boards. It is this aspect perhaps more than any other function which requires the board to call upon its expert knowledge and wide experience to fashion an appropriate remedy. No other body will have the requisite skill and experience in labour relations to construct a fair and workable solution which will enable the parties to arrive at a final resolution of their dispute. Imposing remedies comprises a significant portion of the Board's duties. Section 99(2) of the Canada Labour Code recognizes the importance of this role and accordingly, gives the Board wide latitude and discretion to fashion "equitable" remedies which it feels will best address the problem and resolve the dispute. By providing that the Board may fashion equitable remedies Parliament has given a clear indication that the Board has been entrusted with wide remedial powers. Furthermore, a broad privative clause in s. 22(1) provides that, not only are the Board's decisions final, but so too are its orders. This provision lends support to the position that the court should defer to the remedial orders of the Board which are made within its jurisdiction. That is to say there should be no judicial interference with remedial orders of the Board unless they are patently unreasonable.

* * * * *

When an employer engages in an unfair labour practice by suspending or dismissing an employee, the normal remedy is reinstatement with compensation for lost wages and benefits. Such relief reaches only the harm done to the individual employee. However, boards have recognized that the employer's actions may have discouraged other employees from supporting the union, and have fashioned a variety of remedies designed to counteract this sort of collective harm.

As is noted in Section 5:220, in *Westinghouse Canada Ltd*, [1980] 2 CLRBR 469 (OLRB), the employer closed its old plant and opened new ones in an attempt to escape a union. The OLRB directed the employer to give employees of the old plant a right of first refusal on the new jobs, with no loss of seniority or fringe benefits, and to pay a relocation allowance to those employees who chose to move. The employer was also ordered to give the union a list of those employed at the new plant, to give the union access to company bulletin boards, and to permit union representatives to address employees during working hours. In addition, the union was awarded compensation for expenses incurred in organizing the new plants. Are these orders appropriate in the circumstances? Are they sufficient?

In *United Steelworkers of America and Radio Shack*, [1980] 1 CLRBR 99, the OLRB, having found that the employer had engaged in very serious and sustained unfair labour practices, awarded a number of remedies, including a direction that the employer post, for a sixty-day period, a notice drafted by the board. This notice informed employees of their rights, stated that the employer had violated those rights, and set out a promise by the employer to comply with both the legislation and the board's orders. Is this type of posting effective?

On an application for judicial review of the board decision in *Radio Shack*, the Ontario Divisional Court (*Re Tandy Electronics and United Steelworkers of America* (1980), 115 DLR (3d) 197 (Ont Div Ct)) refused to interfere with the board's remedy. Justice Cory said (at 215):

> So long as the award of the Board is compensatory and not punitive; so long as it flows from the scope, intent and provision of the act itself, then the award of damages is within the jurisdiction of the Board. The mere fact that the award of damages is novel, that the remedy is innovative, should not be a reason for finding it unreasonable.

On occasion, monetary awards have been granted to compensate unions for legal costs or wasted organizing costs resulting from employer unfair labour practices. In *Baron Metal Industries Inc*, [2001] OLRD No 1210, at para 140, where the employer was found to have committed particularly egregious unfair labour practices, the OLRB concluded that the union had been put to unnecessary expense in its organizing campaign, and ordered the employer to compensate it for all organizing expenditures from the beginning of the campaign, to the date of the representation vote. However the board rejected the union's request for legal costs. It noted that in Ontario, such costs had only been ordered where there was no chance of an ongoing relationship between the parties, and where the employer had failed to comply with the board's remedial orders. The board went on, at para 31:

> In this case there is a reasonable prospect of a continuing relationship developing between the parties. There is a prospect of the union recovering its investment in organizing the workers of Baron Metals. Pursuit of this case may be rewarded by the union being certified eventually. If the union is successful in the forthcoming representation vote, the parties will need to endeavour to reach a collective agreement. They may be engaged with each other for years to come. Costs orders are generally not granted by the Board, in part

because it is not obvious that the Board has jurisdiction to do so, and in part because such orders tend to rankle; they cause resentment within a relationship in which the parties should expect some degree of legal contest and dispute, some litigation at arbitration. Costs orders add a punitive element to an on-going relationship. They tend to detract from a relationship which should be able to accommodate some degree of give and take.

The courts have on occasion set limits on the power of boards to remedy unfair labour practices, particularly where a remedy is seen as punitive in nature. An important example is provided by the Supreme Court of Canada's response to the following decision of the federal board.

National Bank of Canada and Retail Clerks' International Union, [1982] 3 CLRBR 1 at 16–18, 24, and 32–34

[The union was certified to represent employees at the bank's Maguire Street branch. The *Canada Labour Code* imposed a statutory freeze on the terms and conditions of employment from the date of the application for certification until thirty days after the certificate was granted. The giving of notice to bargain led to another statutory freeze, but the union did not give such notice until more than thirty days after being certified. As a result of that delay, neither freeze was in force for about three days. During that interval, senior bank officials met and changed a plan to reduce services at the Maguire Street branch to a plan to close that branch and transfer its accounts to the non-unionized Sheppard Street branch. The union complained that this was an unfair labour practice. The board concluded that the employer's decision to close the Maguire Street branch was motivated by anti-union *animus*.]

FOISY Vice-Chair: . . . .

[T]he Bank's officers saw a golden opportunity to "get rid of" the Union. The best way of achieving this, according to them, was simply to close the Maguire Street branch. If there were no longer any employees at this branch, the Bank would not have to negotiate with the Union. Moreover, it is for this reason that the Bank hurriedly informed all the employees that the branch would be closed. The Bank wanted to present the employees and the Union with a *fait accompli*: any collective bargaining would be pointless. . . . The building housing this branch was sold shortly after it was closed. In reality, every effort was made to close the books once and for all on the Maguire Street branch; they buried it posthaste.

What is the effect of the Bank's unlawful actions? The Bank wanted to show the employees that they had made a mistake by joining a union. The message was clear and unequivocal: they would have been better off without a union.

[After making the finding of anti-union *animus*, the board found that there had been a transfer of a business between the unionized and non-unionized branches and an intermingling of employees from the two branches. Without regard to the wishes of the original employees of the Sheppard Street branch, the board held that the union was the bargaining agent for employees at this branch. The board went on to grant remedies for the employer's unfair labour practice.]

[T]he Union is now bargaining agent for the employees of the Sheppard Street branch. Nevertheless, it has been seriously, perhaps fatally, injured by the unlawful closure of the Maguire Street branch.... However, according to the provisions of the Code, it must negotiate a collective agreement with the employer for its group. To do so, it will need the employees' support. It will have to begin by learning who they are and meeting with them. It will also have to be able to communicate with them. In short, owing to the employer's unlawful action, the Union is in the position where it must recruit members as if it had never been certified. Paradoxically, it must represent all the members of its unit fairly under Section 136.1. We must assist it so that, in spite of the employer's unlawful action, it can fulfill the obligations imposed on it by the Code....

From the psychological point of view, the Bank's unlawful action is particularly fraught with consequences in that it gives management employees and those likely to join a union the clear message that the prospect of access to free collective bargaining is not welcomed by the Bank. The public nature of the instant decision and its broad distribution throughout Canada can only give the employer's unlawful action greater publicity. For the objectives concerning free access to collective bargaining to be attained, it is important that employees who want to take advantage of this fundamental right perceive it as a meaningful one. If employees cannot be sure that the exercise of their right is more than an illusion, it follows that they will not want to exercise it. A right is of value only when effective remedies protect its exercise.

[The board ordered the employer to do the following:

1) Give the union lists of employees at the Sheppard Street branch.
2) Allow the union to hold meetings at that branch during working hours.
3) Allow the union to install a bulletin board in the staff area of that branch.
4) Pay all associated costs.
5) Send a letter to all employees across Canada saying that it had violated their rights under the *Code*, that it recognized that they had a right to organize, and that managers must also recognize that right.
6) Deposit $144,000 into a trust fund to be administered jointly by the union and the bank, subject to the board's approval, for the purpose of promoting the *Code*'s objectives among all of the bank's employees. The $144,000 figure was an estimate of the amount that the bank had saved by closing the branch.]

In the following decision, the Supreme Court of Canada struck down the last two of those remedies.

National Bank of Canada v Retail Clerks' International Union et al, [1984] 1 SCR 269 at 291–96

[Justice Chouinard, for the Court, looked at earlier cases where the Court had reviewed labour board remedies, then continued as follows.]

In each of the foregoing cases a relationship can be seen between the act alleged, its consequences and the thing ordered as a means of remedying it.... In the case at bar, however, and I say so with respect, this relationship between the alleged unfair labour practice and its consequences on the one hand and [the trust fund] on the other is in my opinion absent.

The order that there had been a sale within the meaning of s. 144 of the Code guaranteed the continuance of the certificate, which the Board extended to all employees in the new work location, the Sheppard Street branch.

Remedies Nos. 1 to 4, which were not disputed, are designed to ensure that the Union would be firmly established at the new branch.

However, remedy No. 6, regarding the creation of a trust fund to promote the objectives of the Code among other employees of the Bank, which in my view means promoting the unionization of those other employees, is not something intended to remedy or counteract the consequences harmful to realization of those objectives that may result from closure of Maguire Street and its incorporation in the Sheppard Street branch. The fact that a large number of the Bank's other employees are not unionized is not a consequence of closure of the Maguire Street branch, where the Union continued to exist and had its certificate extended. Thus, I consider that this remedy should be set aside.

In accordance with a practice followed by a number of labour relations boards, including the Board, the latter ordered in remedy No. 5 that a letter signed by the president and chief executive officer of the Bank be sent to all employees, including management personnel....

The Bank submitted that this was in actual fact a humiliating letter, that this order is unreasonable and vexatious and that the Board's decision was intended to be not compensatory but punitive, exemplary and humiliating, which constitutes an excess of its powers. The Bank further submitted that the letter repeats the conclusions of remedy No. 6 regarding the creation of the trust fund, which should be set aside.

In my view, this last ground suffices for remedy No. 5 to be likewise set aside. The announcement of the creation of this fund in this letter is at the very least a key feature of the letter. Since remedy No. 6 regarding the fund should be set aside, the Court should also set aside remedy No. 5, regarding the letter which puts emphasis on the fund....

Beetz J (Estey, McIntyre, Lamer, and Wilson JJ concurring):

I have had the benefit of reading the opinion of my brother Chouinard, and I concur in his findings and reasons.

Like him, I consider that remedy No. 6 is not a true remedy; but I also think that, like remedy No. 5, it is clearly punitive in nature. It was acknowledged by all counsel at the hearing that the Canada Labour Relations Board has no power to impose punitive measures....

This type of penalty is totalitarian and as such alien to the tradition of free nations like Canada, even for the repression of the most serious crimes.

Could either of the two disputed remedies in the *National Bank* case be upheld as reasonable after *Royal Oak Mines*, above?

5:710 Interim Relief

The litigation of unfair labour practices is a time-consuming process. A remedy granted after a complaint has been adjudicated on its merits may come weeks or months after the violation was committed. In the meantime, support for the union may have plummeted because of the employer's unlawful conduct. In 1992, the Ontario Labour Relations Board was authorized by statute to grant interim relief pending the final disposition of a complaint. In *Loeb Highland v United Food and Commercial Workers Union*, [1993] OLRB Rep March 197 (McCormick, Chair), an employee allegedly fired for participating in an organizing campaign was reinstated pending the adjudication of his complaint on the merits. The board's power to give interim relief was repealed in 1995, but reintroduced in 2005.

5:720 Remedial Certification

Most of the administrative remedies that seek to protect union organizing activities are process-oriented, in that they attempt to redress the harm caused by illegal employer conduct while leaving employees to choose or reject collective bargaining. Labour legislation in several jurisdictions also specifically permits boards to order a new representation vote or, in some jurisdictions, to grant remedial certification. Remedial certification (or "unfair labour practice certification," as it is sometimes called) is regarded as the most severe remedy, and is meant to counter illegal employer interference by granting employees the union representation they would likely have obtained but for the employer's misconduct. This remedy is generally only available where the labour board concludes that the employer interference was so serious that no other remedy would suffice, and that a representation vote would not likely reflect employees' true wishes on unionization.

As explained in C Michael Mitchell and John C Murray's *Changing Workplaces Review—Final Report* (Ontario: Ministry of Labour, May 2017), Ontario's remedial certification provision has undergone many changes in recent decades:

> Prior to 1993, if employer misconduct resulted in the true wishes of employees being unlikely to be ascertained in a vote, the union would be certified without a vote, provided there was adequate membership support for bargaining. Then in 1993, the requirement for adequate membership support for bargaining was eliminated. However, in 1995, the requirement for adequate membership support was reinstated. More importantly, in 1995, remedial certification was limited to situations where the Ontario Labour Relations Board (OLRB) found that no other remedy, other than a second vote, would counter the employer's misconduct. Then, in 1998, remedial certification was eliminated altogether. Finally, in 2005, remedial certification was reinstated, but the OLRB could now certify the union without a vote only if "no other remedy would be sufficient to counter the effects of the contravention." That remains the situation today. The OLRB may also now consider the results of a previous representation vote and whether the union has "adequate membership support" for collective bargaining.
>
> These changes were introduced without any independent or outside assessment and, from time to time, represented political positions and some compromises over the interests of labour and employers, with profound impact on the rights of employees (at 314).

The *Final Report* criticized the existing provisions and recommended substantial revisions:

> The current provisions of the LRA are not sufficiently responsive to the adverse impact that employer misconduct has on the rights of employees to free and independent choice (at 320)....

If employer misconduct has eroded union support prior to a first vote, or made it impossible to obtain enough support for an initial vote, it is illogical to consider the results of that vote or the absence of membership evidence, as factors in determining whether there should be a second vote. A second vote in such circumstances is not an effective response to counter unlawful conduct aimed at influencing employee choice. It is tantamount to condoning a violation of the Act.

The premise that steps can be taken to ensure a second vote is sufficient to counter the effects of employer misconduct is flawed. While there may be rare cases where a union could win a second vote following employer misconduct, in our collective experience over a lifetime of practice, like scrambled eggs, the status quo ante cannot be restored and the second vote will generally be tainted by the misconduct. Employer conduct that is designed to raise or results in employee concern about the future stability or security of their employment leaves an indelible mark. Fear of supporting the union, or the hope of reward for voting against the union, which results from illegal threats or promises, is not likely rectified by a decision of a labour board finding unlawful conduct, even if coupled with a "mea culpa" statement made by the employer to employees as a result of a board order.

The power of the employer to influence the livelihood of employees is real. Everyone who has been employed, in positions high or low, understands the power of those in authority to control employment, including allocation of duties and responsibilities, career advancement and promotion, demotion, compensation and continued employment. Employees understand the power of the employer to make decisions affecting the future of the entire enterprise such as layoffs, or moving, or closing all or part of its operations. Once employer misconduct undermines the true wishes of employees, the results of a vote are, more likely than not, unreliable (at 321).

In the *Final Report*, the Special Advisors regarded the certification process to be necessarily linked to first contract arbitration and remedial certification provisions, and that the existing provisions were "insufficient to protect the freedom of association of employees" (at 323):

> If a secret ballot vote is to be maintained as the norm in our labour relations system, then it is proper and correct policy to insist on the integrity of that process by not permitting employer misconduct and interference to undermine it. It is unreasonable to insist on the most democratic and preferred means of determining employee choice, namely the secret ballot vote, while at the same time effectively sanctioning and countenancing employer misconduct, which undermines the integrity of the voting process. A second vote, following employer misconduct, cannot rectify or eliminate the impact of employer misconduct and is an unreliable measure of free and voluntary support of the union. Once everyone knows the well is poisoned, no one will drink the water. Accordingly, if an employer unlawfully interferes with the employees' rights to freedom of association and honest independent choice, that conduct must trigger a meaningful remedy, namely certification without a vote and access to first contract arbitration (at 324, footnotes omitted)....
>
> [O]ur view is that a second vote is an inappropriate response to employer misconduct that undermines employee choice and independence and the integrity of a first vote. We also consider that the criterion of adequate support for bargaining is inappropriate as a

threshold test for remedial certification where there has been employer misconduct. This criterion is incongruous with a fair outcome because it rewards employers who violate the LRA early to prevent the union organizing campaign from getting off the ground, or who engage in illegal activity later in the campaign, which demoralizes and frightens employees, thereby destroying support for the union. Employer misconduct that warrants a conclusion by the OLRB that that the true wishes of the employees of the employer are not likely to be ascertained in a secret ballot vote should result in certification (at 325).

[© Queen's Printer for Ontario, 2016. Reproduced with permission.]

The following recommendation by the Special Advisors has been incorporated into the Ontario *Labour Relations Act*:

> We recommend that section 11 of the *Labour Relations Act, 1995* be revised to provide as follows:
>
>> Where an employer, an employers' organization, or a person acting on behalf of an employer or employer's organization contravenes this Act so that the true wishes of the employees of the employer or of a member of the employers' organization are not likely to be ascertained, the Board, shall on the application of the trade union, certify the trade union as the bargaining agent of the employees in the bargaining unit. (Recommendation 145 at 326.)

5:730 What if the Employer Closes Down the Workplace?

Labour boards across Canada have generally been hesitant to order a resumption of operations in situations where an employer has shut down or moved its operations to avoid a trade union, but boards have crafted a number of creative remedies. As mentioned in Section 5:700, in *Westinghouse*, dismissed employees received preferential access to employment at the employer's other locations and associated relocation costs; and in both *Westinghouse* and *National Bank*, the union was awarded certain advantages that would facilitate certification at other employer locations. The following excerpt, from a case already introduced in Section 5:300, deals with whether remedies are available when an employer decides to close a store during a period of statutory freeze.

United Food and Commercial Workers, Local 503 v Wal-Mart Canada Corp, 2014 SCC 45, [2014] 2 SCR 323

> [In 2004, an all-employee unit at a Wal-Mart store in Jonquière was certified to a local of the United Food and Commercial Workers union (UFCW). In February 2005, the UFCW applied for first contract arbitration under the Quebec *Labour Code*. The following week, Wal-Mart informed the Minister of Employment and Social Solidarity that it intended to close the Jonquière store, and did so in April 2005, terminating the employment of all the store employees.
>
> Among a variety of claims brought against Wal-Mart in different forums, by the UFCW as well as groups and individual employees, was a grievance filed by UFCW claiming that the terminations violated the section 59 freeze provisions of the *Code*. (While in other

jurisdictions such claims would be heard by the labour board, the *Code* explicitly gives arbitrators jurisdiction over complaints of violations of the freeze provision.) The arbitrator upheld the grievance, and this decision was affirmed by the Superior Court but overturned by the Court of Appeal. The matter was then appealed to the Supreme Court of Canada.]

64 Wal-Mart argues that the closure of its Jonquière establishment bars its employees from invoking s. 59. In the alternative, it submits that in any event, the closure constitutes a full defence that justifies the change in the employees' conditions of employment. Neither of these arguments is valid. In my opinion, the employer is (1) neither shielded by the closure of its establishment (2) nor, otherwise, relieved of the burden of proving that its decision was consistent with its normal management practices....

[The majority noted that "s. 59 contains no word or language that would support a conclusion that its applicability depends on the existence of an active business or, more simply, of a possibility of reinstatement."]

67 I would stress in passing ... that if the Quebec legislature had intended reinstatement to be the only possible remedy for violation of the right to unchanged conditions of employment, it would have "actually *said* [so] in the relevant statutory provisions": *Plourde* [*v. Wal-Mart Canada Corp.*, 2009 SCC 54 (CanLII), [2009] 3 S.C.R. 465], at para. 36. Given the absence of such an indication, there is nothing to preclude the arbitrator from ordering an alternative remedy in the form of damages....

70 Thus, in the absence of clear language excluding any form of remedy other than reinstatement, or if the claimant is not seeking such reparation "in kind", the arbitrator, who cannot of course impose the reinstatement of an employee in a establishment that has been closed, nonetheless retains the power to order reparation by equivalence. However, Wal-Mart, with which Rothstein and Wagner JJ. [dissenting] agree, counters the possibility of such an order by further submitting that the purpose and the nature of s. 59 preclude the courts from applying that section once the business has been closed. In short, Wal-Mart argues that the section's purpose is to maintain a balance between the parties, but only during the collective bargaining period, in order to preclude the employer from putting pressure on its employees. But in putting an end to collective bargaining, the closure renders s. 59 inapplicable, since, Wal-Mart alleges, there is no longer a balance to maintain, nor are there employees to protect.

71 With respect, this argument is wrong. On the one hand, it seems to me to disregard the fact that, *absent a clear indication to the contrary*, the content of a substantive right is not determined by the scope of a particular remedy. On the other hand, insofar as it presupposes that the purpose of s. 59 is to maintain the *status quo*, it is based on a flawed premise. As I mentioned above, the primary purpose of s. 59 is not, in itself, to restore the balance for a given period of time, but to facilitate certification and foster good faith in collective bargaining in order, ultimately, to enable employees to exercise their right of association. Hence, the fact that it is impossible to attain the procedural balance the legislation is designed to maintain during a bargaining period does not preclude the arbitrator from giving full effect to s. 59 by ordering that an employer that has violated its employees' *rights* remedy the resulting harm, if only by way of reparation by equivalence.

72 In other words, the termination of the process undertaken further to the petition for certification does not eliminate the employer's obligation to make reparation for a violation of s. 59. Nor can it be said that a breach of the duty defined in s. 12 of the *Code* not to interfere with employees' freedom of association cannot be sanctioned if the employer has gone out of business (*Plourde*, at paras. 26-31). By way of analogy, would a court considering a breach, as of the time the breach occurred, of the duty of good faith codified as part of the general law in art. 1375 *C.C.Q.* refuse to sanction that breach solely because at the time of the hearing, the contract between the parties had been resiliated? Of course not. In such a case, resiliation does not erase the violation of the right of the creditors, the employees in the case at bar. If an employee proves the injury, he or she can be granted compensation (arts. 1458, 1590 and 1607 *C.C.Q.*; *Automobiles Canbec inc.; Union des routiers, brasseries, liqueurs douces & ouvriers de diverses industries (Teamsters, Local 1999); Natrel inc. v. Syndicat démocratique des distributeurs (CSD)*, [2000] R.J.D.T. 670 (T.A.).

73 From this perspective, the purpose of s. 59 of the *Code* does not preclude reparation by equivalence, and neither do the section's words or its nature. As professors Verge and Roux point out, the law is not [TRANSLATION] "powerless when it comes to remedying the consequences of the closure of a business. Generally speaking, independently of any penal sanctions that might be applicable under the *Labour Code*, reparation by equivalence is always possible", P. Verge and D. Roux, "Fermer l'entreprise: un 'droit' ... absolu?", in *Développements récents en droit du travail* (2006), vol. 245, 223, at p. 259. As a result, an arbitrator considering a case involving a closure cannot refuse to apply s. 59 of the *Code* on the basis that specific performance is no longer possible. . . .

Employer's Justification: Need to Explain the Closure

79 Ten years ago, in *Place des Arts*, our late colleague Gonthier J. stressed that neither the *Code* nor Quebec law in general precludes companies "[from going] out of business, either completely or in part" (para. 28). He added, however, adopting the words of Judge Lesage from *City Buick Pontiac (Montréal) Inc. v. Roy*, [1981] T.T. 22, that the exercise of the right to do so is contingent upon the decision to go out of business being [TRANSLATION] "authentic and not a simulation" (para. 29).

80 Contrary to the view expressed by Rothstein and Wagner JJ. (at paras. 119 and 129), the application of s. 59 of the *Code* does not call this now well-established principle into question (see *Plourde*, at paras. 41 *et seq.; Boutin v. Wal-Mart Canada inc.*, 2005 QCCRT 269 (CanLII); *Société du centre Pierre-Péladeau; Syndicat des travailleuses et travailleurs du Centre d'approbation de Nordia — CSN*). Although s. 59 does not in fact deprive the employer of this power to go out of business either in part or completely, and by extension to resiliate the contracts of employment of some or all of its employees, the section does require that it exercise the power in a manner consistent with its normal management practices (see *Gravel & Fils inc.*, at p. 90; *Syndicat des employés de Télémarketing Unimédia (CSN)*, at pp. 559-60; *Société du centre Pierre-Péladeau*, at para. 74; *Syndicat des travailleuses et travailleurs du Centre d'approbation de Nordia — CSN*, at para. 429-49). As I mentioned above, the necessary principal effect of the section is to "freeze"

the employer's business environment as it existed at the time the union arrived, which includes how the employer exercised its management power.

81 In this context, if the union's evidence satisfies the arbitrator that the resiliation of the contracts was not consistent with such a practice, the employer must present evidence to prove the contrary (Royer and Lavallée, at p. 748).

82 If the employer wishes to avoid having the arbitrator accept the complaint filed under s. 59, therefore, it must show that the change in conditions of employment is not one prohibited by that section. To do so, it must prove that its decision was consistent with its normal management practices or, in other words, that it would have proceeded as it did even if there had been no petition for certification. Given that going out of business either in part or completely is not something that occurs frequently in any company, the arbitrator often has to ask whether a reasonable employer would, in the same circumstances, have closed its establishment: see *Syndicat des travailleuses et travailleurs du Centre d'approbation de Nordia—CSN*. Without suddenly becoming an expert in this regard, the arbitrator must also, therefore, above all else, be satisfied of the truthfulness of the circumstances relied on by the employer and of their significance.

83 If, after conducting this inquiry, the arbitrator is convinced that the resiliation is not consistent with the employer's normal management practices, he or she must find that the employer's decision resulted in a unilateral change in conditions of employment that is prohibited by s. 59 of the *Code*. The arbitrator will then have no choice but to sanction the violation of the right protected by that section by deciding on the appropriate remedy. Given that the employer cannot be ordered to continue operating or to reopen its business, the arbitrator can order it to compensate the employees whose rights have been violated.

[The majority allowed the appeal, and remanded the case to the arbitrator to decide the appropriate remedy in accordance with his finding that the store closure and terminations had violated the statutory freeze provision.]

This *Wal-Mart* case followed another decided by the Supreme Court of Canada, arising out of the same set of facts: *Plourde v Wal-Mart Canada Corp*, 2009 SCC 54, [2009] 3 SCR 465. *Plourde* dealt with whether a dismissed employee at the closed Jonquière store could rely on section 15 of the Quebec *Labour Code*, which allows the labour tribunal to award reinstatement in the event of a dismissal "because the employee exercises a right arising from the *Code*." The majority ruled that, on the basis of the applicable jurisprudence and specific wording of the *Code*, employees could not seek a remedy under section 15 in situations of store closure, for two reasons. First, damages are not an alternative remedy open to the tribunal under section 15, and this combined with the inability to force the store to remain open meant that there was no effective remedy available. Second, even if the commission did have such a power, on the basis of Quebec caselaw, the closure would be a "good and sufficient reason" for dismissal under section 17 of the *Code*, and would therefore constitute a complete answer for an employer facing a section 15 complaint. This is so regardless of whether the closure was motivated by anti-union animus.

A number of other jurisdictions have expressly specified *in their labour legislation* that employers have the freedom to close their operations, similar to the freedom found in the caselaw at issue in *Plourde* (see, for example, section 49(3) of Nova Scotia's *Trade Union Act* and section 121.1 of Newfoundland's *Labour Relations Act*). However, the extent to which such express provisions might shield an employer from remedies for unfair labour practices may now be limited by the reasoning in *United Food and Commercial Workers, Local 503 v Wal-Mart Canada Corp*.

5:740 Criminal Law Penalties

The criminal law is rarely invoked against employers who engage in anti-union activity. In the following case, a criminal court imposed a fine of $25,000 on the employer for the *Criminal Code* offence of conspiring to effect an unlawful purpose, that purpose being to commit unfair labour practices prohibited by provincial labour relations legislation. The Crown appealed, and argued that the fine was too light in the circumstances.

R v K-Mart Canada Ltd, [1982] OJ No 54 at para 2ff (Ont CA)

> HOWLAND CJO: Prior to 1975, the respondent [K-Mart] maintained a warehouse on Progress Avenue in Scarborough and Local Union No. 419 of the International Brotherhood of Teamsters, Chauffeurs, Warehousemen, and Helpers of America ("the Union") had been certified as the bargaining agent for the respondent's employees at that location.
>
> During 1975, the respondent opened a new distribution centre in Bramalea and some employees were moved from the Scarborough warehouse to the new operation. On April 16, 1975, an application was made to the Ontario Labour Relations Board for certification of the Union as the bargaining agent at the new distribution centre.
>
> The respondent opposed the application and a postponement of the certification vote was granted by the Ontario Labour Relations Board on the representation that the work force of the respondent at Bramalea would be quadrupled to exceed 120 shortly after the centre opened. This representation was made under the signature of Michael Clarke as Vice-President of Personnel and Employee Relations of the respondent. In fact, there was no intention to augment the respondent's work force at Bramalea to this extent.
>
> Centurion Investigation Limited ('Centurion') and Mark-Anada Associates Limited ('Mark-Anada') of which Daniel McGarry was the principal shareholder and officer, had agreements with the respondent to provide security and personnel services. While the application for certification was under consideration, a further agreement was made between Daniel McGarry and senior officials of the respondent whereby a number of employees of Centurion and Mark-Anada would be hired by the respondent to get information about the organizing efforts of the Union, to dissuade other employees from voting for certification, and to vote against certification themselves.
>
> As the number of employees at the new centre did not increase, the Ontario Labour Relations Board ordered a certification vote to take place on September 19, 1975. On September 7 a strategy meeting was held, attended by Daniel McGarry, Jenkins, who was the director of security of the respondent, and Seunik, who was directing the movement of employees to the new centre in Bramalea, together with a number of employees of Centurion. At this meeting discussions took place as to the ways and means of discrediting the Union and its leaders and defeating the certification vote.

The voters' list contained the names of sixteen Centurion employees who were not *bona fide* employees of the respondent. The certification vote took place on September 18 and 19, 1975 and resulted in a tie vote of 30 votes for and 30 votes against certification. Two of the ballots cast were segregated and were further investigated.

At a hearing of the Ontario Labour Relations Board into the circumstances surrounding the certification vote, one Centurion undercover employee gave false evidence detrimental to the Union, in the presence of Michael Clarke. At a later hearing another undercover employee stated in Mr. Clarke's presence that he was a *bona fide* employee of the respondent and that his connection with Centurion was innocuous.

During this period, a productivity flow analysis agreement, back-dated to April 1975, was prepared and signed by Daniel McGarry and Seunik on behalf of the respondent to attempt to explain the influx of undercover employees into the Bramalea distribution centre.

The Ontario Labour Relations Board then directed that a further certification vote be held on January 30, 1976. Before that vote was taken the respondent had obtained new legal advice and had discharged Centurion and Mark-Anada. The second certification vote resulted in 37 votes being cast in favour of certification, and 8 votes against.

After the Union had been certified, it was unable to negotiate a contract with the respondent. A long strike ensued and finally the Union ceased to act as the bargaining agent for the respondent's employees at the Bramalea distribution centre.

The respondent expended over $167,000 to achieve its ends in connection with the certification votes, but this sum may have included, in part, the cost of security services being provided for the respondent.

* * * * *

The Court of Appeal increased the fine from $25,000 to $100,000. Was this an adequate penalty? Should the courts impose jail sentences on company officers who engage in this sort of conduct? What are the advantages and disadvantages of using the criminal law rather than administrative proceedings in such cases?

5:800 THE PROFESSIONAL RESPONSIBILITY OF LAWYERS

Lawyers practicing in the field of labour relations are not uncommonly faced with clients who are contemplating illegal conduct—management representatives who are determined to interfere in an organizing campaign, or union representatives who believe that an untimely (and therefore unlawful) work stoppage will be to their advantage. Parallel situations of course arise in other fields of law practice, but the emotional and ideological overlay of union-employer relations may make the position of labour lawyers particularly difficult—a difficulty which is compounded by the fact that most of them act only for management or labour and never for the other side. This may promote an unusually close identification between lawyer and client—a situation that can have real dangers.

The canons of legal ethics of law societies across Canada prohibit a lawyer from knowingly helping or encouraging a client to break the law, or advising on how to do so in a way that might avoid or limit punishment. Consider what these obligations mean for a lawyer whose management client appears to have weighed the costs of being found guilty of an unfair labour practice and to have concluded that it is worth incurring those costs to keep the union out—or for a lawyer whose union client seems to have made a similar cost-benefit analysis with respect to taking illegal strike action.

The following are excerpts from a decision of the Discipline Committee of the Law Society of Upper Canada.

Law Society of Upper Canada v Rovet, [1992] LSDD No 24

In early January, 1991, A Company learned that certain of its employees were considering joining a union. The company's president, B, spoke to several lawyers who specialize in the representation of employers in labour relations matters, most of whom informed him that there was little the company could do that would be effective in blocking the unionization of the employees.

One of the lawyers with whom B spoke was the Solicitor, who was not as pessimistic about the company's prospects of blocking the unionization attempt as were most of the other lawyers with whom B spoke. B arranged to meet with the Solicitor, and they met for the first time on January 8, 1991. Another executive employed by A Company, C, was also in attendance. The Solicitor outlined the process of union certification under applicable legislation. He told B and C that the number of employees who would be included in the bargaining unit is a critical factor in the success of an organizational drive.

The Solicitor also asked B and C whether A Company had any plans to increase the size of the company's work force, as that would affect the size of the bargaining unit and might have the effect of reducing the proportion of employees who supported the union.

B informed the Solicitor that the company's business had increased significantly in the autumn of 1990 and that an expansion of the work force was justifiable. The Solicitor said that he knew of a company, D Company, which was able to provide employees who were favourably disposed to the employer's interests in an organizational drive, on a contract basis, until the union organizing campaign was over....

Two days later, on January 10, 1991, a representative of D Company met with the Solicitor and B. After preliminary discussions about how many additional employees were justifiable, the Solicitor left the meeting and A and D Company's representative negotiated an agreement in principle that day whereby A Company agreed to utilize the services of D Company and to employ a specified number of workers provided by D Company. The Solicitor was informed of the agreement in principle.

On January 17, 1991, the Solicitor met with representatives of A Company and D Company. At that time, the main terms of an agreement were worked out. The agreement called for a separate, confidential contract to be entered into between D Company and a numbered company owned by the principal shareholders of A Company. This separate contract provided for extra payments to be made to D Company. At the conclusion of the meeting the numbered company made an initial payment to D Company in the amount of $125,000. The numbered company agreed to pay that sum to D Company each week until the certification application was concluded.

Over the next few days the Solicitor drafted the two contracts. The initial drafts of the contract between A Company and D Company, whereby the former agreed to employ certain workers of the latter, were dated December 14, 1990.

On January 23, 1991, the Solicitor met with representatives of A Company and D Company to deal with certain issues which had to be resolved before the contracts could be signed. During or after the meeting, the Solicitor and the others in attendance learned that the union had filed an application for certification the previous week. One effect of the filing of the application was to settle the bargaining unit for the purpose of determining support for the union as of the date of filing. As of the date of filing, there was an agreement in principle between A Company and D Company whereby the former would hire extra workers and the number of workers had been determined and were on standby, but none of them had yet started to work for A Company. A Company nevertheless decided, with the Solicitor's concurrence, to carry into effect the agreed upon strategy of employing workers provided through D Company and to submit that they should be treated as members of the unit and eligible to vote.

On or after January 23, 1991, the Solicitor prepared the two contracts in their final form. The contract between A Company and D Company was backdated to November 23, 1990, and its commencement date was specified as being January 1, 1991.

In addition, at the request of B, correspondence between A Company and D Company was created. This correspondence purported to reflect negotiations between the two companies beginning in early October, 1990, which culminated in the November 23, 1990, contract. This correspondence was generated in draft form by a junior lawyer in the Solicitor's firm in consultation with B, to the Solicitor's knowledge. The junior lawyer gave the draft correspondence to the Solicitor, who then gave them to B and a representative of D Company, E. The letters were then typed on the letterheads of A Company and D Company, and copies were returned to the Solicitor.

In late February, 1991, B and E had a falling out, and B concluded that E would be a liability to A Company if called upon to testify. Another representative of D Company, F, was introduced to A Company. To the Solicitor's knowledge, new backdated contracts and correspondence were prepared and signed. This time F signed on behalf of D Company, as if he had been involved from the beginning.

As the certification process continued, A Company continued to make weekly payments in the amount of $125,000 to D Company.

The Solicitor made his final written submission to the labour relations board in relation to the certification application in a letter dated March 11, 1991. The submission made was voluntary and not required. The statutory reply, which was required, was accurate and was filed. No contractual documents were appended to the voluntary submission. In his letter the Solicitor made the following representations which he knew to be false:

1. That negotiations between A Company and D Company began in October, 1990. (In fact negotiations began on January 10, 1991.); and
2. That the contract was made on November 23, 1990, and that the new workers were employed beginning on January 1, 1991. (In fact there was no agreement in principle

until January 10, the terms of the contract were not agreed upon until after the date on which the certification application was filed, and the new workers were not paid for any work they did for A Company until at least January 23, 1991.)

The labour relations board granted the certification application. Shortly thereafter, representatives of A Company consulted with another lawyer, who, after consulting with other senior members of the bar, reported the matter to the Society and to the Solicitor's firm.

The Solicitor's firm thereupon reviewed the Solicitor's file. Because it appeared that several undocumented disbursements (payments to the Solicitor's American Express account) had been charged to A Company, the firm retained an accounting firm, Price Waterhouse, to review the Solicitor's fee billings from April, 1989, to April, 1991.

Price Waterhouse's examination in conjunction with a follow up review by the Society disclosed that the Solicitor charged numerous personal expenses to client files and arranged for the firm to pay these expenses....

The personal expenses which the Solicitor charged to clients as fees included such items as newspaper subscriptions, airplane tickets, automobile expenses, restaurant meals, drycleaning, hardware, baseball and theatre tickets, household items, landscaping, photographs, furniture, ski equipment, clothes, books, and art. It is not possible to determine precisely the amount of personal expenses included by the Solicitor in client fee billings over the period during which the Solicitor was a partner in Fogler, Rubinoff (a period of two years), but the amount is in the range of approximately $35,000. The Solicitor generally reduced the fee billings to accommodate the personal expenses so that he did not overcharge or double bill the client.

The Solicitor has co-operated fully in the Law Society's investigation, and voluntarily undertook not to practise pending the hearing of the complaint. He has not practised, pursuant to his undertaking, since May 11, 1991....

The Committee finds the Solicitor guilty of professional misconduct.... The Committee recommends that the Solicitor be suspended from practice for a period of six months from an effective date of June 1, 1991.

The evidence demonstrated that the Solicitor is an intelligent, experienced, wholly competent practitioner of many years experience, who enjoyed an enviable reputation within the legal community and with an apparently sound family relationship.

The character evidence led on his behalf uniformly makes these points:

(a) The Solicitor has never been known to have engaged in unethical or improper activities, other than the conduct evident in these complaints.
(b) His conduct in respect of the complaints appears to be an aberration, and the Committee is unanimously of the belief that the possibility of the conduct re-occurring is at least remote.

The Solicitor has engaged himself actively in community activities, to the obvious benefit of the public in general.

[This recommendation was considered by Convocation, the governing body of the Law Society of Upper Canada, which made the final decision. Convocation determined that the appropriate penalty was a one-year suspension running from the date of its decision.

A dissenting bencher, whose reasons are excerpted below, was of the view that the solicitor should be disbarred.]

Bencher Lax (dissenting):

Had this been a case of a serious misappropriation of client funds, even in circumstances where a lawyer had never been before the Society previously, the solicitor would have been disbarred. Indeed, Mr. MacKenzie said as much in his submissions to Convocation. However, he also said that Mr. Rovet's conduct had not been regarded in the past as the kind of case which would have attracted a penalty of disbarment. Convocation was referred to several authorities, decided in 1984 and 1985, none of which were on all fours with this case. However, even had they been, that is not to say that they were correctly decided. In any event, as Mr. MacKenzie pointed out, ethical standards imposed on lawyers change over time and if anything, should be higher today than they were in the past. In my view, a solicitor who cheats his partners, lies to an administrative tribunal, and prepares fraudulent documents for submission to the tribunal, engages in conduct which is equally reprehensible as the conduct of a solicitor who misappropriates client funds. In both kinds of cases, there is a serious violation of trust. In both kinds of cases, there is harm suffered. Although it may be easier to point to the direct harm suffered by clients when lawyers steal their money, this does not mean that the harm done in this kind of case is any less damaging. In both, the public is made vulnerable and the ethical standards of the profession and the public's confidence in it are seriously diminished.

* * * * *

Consider these questions about the above case.

1) Focus on the issue of misleading the board. What is a lawyer's duty in this respect? Not to counsel or assist a client to build a record of false facts that would defeat the right of workers to organize? Not to tender those facts in the form of an affidavit? To warn the client not to come forward with false facts? To appear before the board or to complain to the Law Society if she gets wind of the possibility that false facts will be or have been tendered to the board?
2) What explanation might Rovet have had for his actions, other than an uncharacteristic lapse of judgment? That he needed the business? That all's fair in love and labour relations? That the practice of gerrymandering the bargaining unit was widespread (witness the availability of the firm that supplied the additional workers and his knowledge of it), and that he was being penalized for what others were doing all the time? That the board was not a court, but rather a tribunal thought to be unfriendly to employers, and therefore not entitled to the same degree of deference from advocates?
3) What would have happened to a non-lawyer advocate (a union representative or a management consultant, for example) who engaged in similar behaviour? What should have been done with Company D, which supplied the additional workers? What should have been done with Company A, which attempted, with Rovet's help, to mislead the board?

Chapter 6: The Acquisition and Termination of Bargaining Rights

6:100 THE *WAGNER ACT* MODEL AND THE PRINCIPLE OF EXCLUSIVITY

Before the advent of modern collective bargaining legislation, workers and trade unions had to rely on economic sanctions to induce employers to engage in collective bargaining. Some of the most bitter strikes in North American labour history were fought more for trade union recognition than over demands for improvements in terms and conditions of employment. In fact, labour relations legislation was mainly introduced to remedy the problem of union recognition.

As has been noted in earlier chapters, the current North American system of labour law, often known as the *Wagner Act* model, was created in the 1930s in the United States and was adopted across Canada in the aftermath of World War II. In every Canadian jurisdiction, there is a statutory procedure known as certification, which allows a union, upon proving that it has majority support among a unit of employees, to become the exclusive bargaining agent for those employees and to compel their employer to bargain with it on their behalf.

These principles of majority rule and exclusivity of bargaining rights are central to the *Wagner Act* model. They are closely related; exclusivity is justified by the fact that the union has demonstrated that it has the support of a majority of the employees, as well as by the assumption that it is generally to the advantage of all parties to have one clearly identified interlocutor on the employee side.

An alternative but less common route allows a union to be "voluntarily recognized" by the employer as the exclusive bargaining agent for its employees. In either case, the union is prohibited from exercising economic sanctions in its efforts to acquire bargaining rights. And in either case, it becomes the bargaining agent for all of the employees in the unit, including the minority who did not support certification.

The *Wagner Act* model was designed to reflect the economic and industrial relations realities of what is sometimes called its golden age — from the 1940s to the 1960s. It was created with large and stable manufacturers in mind, such as Ford and General Motors, and on the assumption that once workers were unionized, they would be able to bargain on a more or less equal footing with their powerful employers. As the following extract explains, some aspects of the *Wagner Act* model are unique to North America.

Roy Adams, "Union Certification as an Instrument of Labor Policy: A Comparative Perspective" in Sheldon Friedman et al, eds, *Restoring the Promise of American Labor Law* (Ithaca: ILR Press, Cornell University, 1994) 260 at 260–65

> In comparative perspective, the North American practice of union certification is very unusual. Generally, other countries do not divide the labor force into tiny bargaining units

and do not require representatives of employee interests to win the support of the majority of employees in each microunit to acquire government support for recognition....

When the World War I period dawned, a broad consensus had emerged that all employees should be able to participate in the making of the decisions under which they labored. There was, however, no consensus on how that principle should be put into practice. The dominant position among employers was that there should be mechanisms composed entirely of representatives chosen by and from enterprise employees rather than from national unions. The justification was that 'outside unions' had no interest in the welfare of the enterprise and thus were likely to have a disruptive effect on productivity and competitiveness. The solution offered by this group to the participation imperative was the establishment voluntarily by companies of employee representation plans.

The compromise position worked out by the NWLB [National Wartime Labor Board] for the contrary stances of labor and management was acceptable to the American Federation of Labor. The AFL felt confident that under a 'true open shop' system in which employees were free to join or not join but in which employers did not discriminate against those who became active in a union, the free and independent labor organizations would be able to convince the enfranchised employees to vote for union activists and, by demonstrating their ability, attract most employees to their ranks. Employers were not so confident of maintaining control of employment relations under such a system and thus shortly made new demands. At its conference in October 1918, the National Industrial Conference Board (NICB) stated that its members would tolerate what they called 'cooperative representation' (rather than collective bargaining) only if the majority of employees entitled to vote requested such a system by voting in favor of it in an election held on company premises.... In the 1930s, when the first National Labor Board was established under the National Industrial Recovery Act, it drew upon this experience to hold elections when the majority status of a bargaining agent was in doubt.... Later, the majority principle was embedded in the Wagner Act....

For the unions, certification results in compulsory collective bargaining, backed by a government agency with powers to compel an intransigent employer to enter into negotiations with a view toward signing a written collective agreement. Since achieving recognition for the purposes of collective bargaining is extremely difficult even with the aid of a government agency with substantial enforcement powers, without the aid of such an agency it would no doubt be much more difficult. Since certification leads to legal orders requiring reluctant employers to enter into negotiations, it is generally looked on as a pro-union policy invention. As noted above, however, it was first called for by employer spokespeople and for good reason. From the point of view of the nonunion employer seeking to maintain the status quo, certification has some outstanding positive traits.

First of all, American policy as it has evolved to the present permits the employer to contest employee representation campaigns....

A second major positive aspect of certification from the position of the nonunion employer is that it has entirely dissipated the pressure that existed during the first four decades of the twentieth century for the general enfranchisement of the industrial citizenry. As it has evolved in the United States, certification legitimizes industrial autocracy. Because employees have a means to establish collective bargaining through an electoral process, noncertified employers are considered entirely justified in refusing to recognize and deal with independent unions representing a minority of their employees....

Not only are employers permitted to attempt to maintain unilateral control over the establishment of terms and conditions of employment, they are also forbidden from establishing employee representation plans voluntarily. Their alternative to collective bargaining with independent unions as a means of establishing industrial democracy has been outlawed. The unions successfully argued in the 1930s that such plans generally did not provide for genuine employee representation but instead were used by employers to avoid dealing with organizations freely chosen by the employees themselves. To remove that blockage on the road to real joint regulation of the conditions of work, the Wagner Act outlawed company unions.... Because of this development, employers have been effectively relieved of the duty resting upon them earlier in the century to address the democratic void in industry positively.

The result of this evolution is that, in the United States today, only a small and diminishing part of the labor force has in place institutions that allow employees to influence the conditions under which they work. Four out of five American employees have their conditions of employment established within a system of industrial autocracy.

[Copyright © 1994 by Cornell University. Used by permission of the publisher, Cornell University Press.]

* * * * *

In recent decades, the feasibility of the *Wagner Act* model for acquiring bargaining rights has been called into question due to various characteristics of the modern economy, such as increased globalization of the economy, and widespread organizational "fissuring." As one reads this chapter's discussion of how the Canadian variant of the *Wagner Act* model works and how it might be changed, bear in mind the following two excerpts in order to consider how globalization and organizational fissuring have each affected the distribution of power among firms, workers, unions, and governments, particularly insofar as these phenomena have occurred while a Canadian version of the *Wagner Act* model has been in effect.

Harry Arthurs, "Reinventing Labor Law for the Global Economy" (2001) *Berkeley Journal of Employment & Labor Law* 271 at 282–83

[G]lobalization has changed the effect of the law by placing groups of workers in different jurisdictions in competition with each other. Employers now have a choice—and are perceived to have a choice—between producing in their own countries using local workers and local suppliers, shifting production off-shore to foreign workers and subsidiaries, or out-sourcing production altogether to foreign suppliers and subcontractors. Indeed, thanks to technology, service functions such as data entry and call centers are even more easily moved offshore than production functions. Thus workers across the globe are effectively forced to compete for jobs: they must underbid their rivals in other countries by promising not only to be more productive, but to work harder and more cheaply and to be less assertive about their rights.

In a sense, the pressures—or temptations—for employers to shift work to jurisdictions with low labor standards resemble those which prevailed in the United States before the federal commerce power was used to establish a single system of labor law. However, today these competing groups of workers are located in jurisdictions that are sovereign nations, not stated in a federal union, and there appears to be no way to bring them all under one overarching legal regime....

[G]lobalization has helped to attenuate the connections between employers and employees and to dilute the whole notion of community of interest among workers. Whereas employees used to work for an identifiable common employer, today they occupy an often-uncertain location on a global production and distribution chain that links transnational operations, their divisions, subsidiaries and allies to a host of ephemeral local contractors, brokers, and distributors. Whereas employees of a given employer used to share many common interests and characteristics—language, culture, politics, history, legal rights, managerial supervision, and integrated work processes—workers in the global economy may share none of the above. And whereas "employees" used to be pretty much identifiable as such for statutory and social purposes, today more and more workers around the world are self-employed, are reluctant parties to the "new psychological contract" of discontinuous, serial and sometimes contingent jobs, or work under other coercive arrangements that leave their legal status unclear, their economic future uncertain, and their sense of solidarity greatly attenuated. For all of these reasons, it is increasingly difficult for workers in the global economy even to identify their common adversary, let alone to define common expectations, claim common entitlements, or implement common strategies....

[E]ven when workers occasionally transcend these perceptual and conceptual difficulties and organize across national boundaries, they confront systemic difficulties in the form of local labor laws with inconsistent legal rules. Even as between democratic countries where workers have comparable legal protections, and even within industries where operations are integrated across national boundaries, these systemic difficulties are formidable. Just imagine the problem of trying to create a bargaining unit or negotiate a collective agreement that covers all Daimler Chrysler workers in America, Canada, and Germany. Just imagine the complexity of orchestrating a strike of professional athletes that is legal on both sides of the Canada-U.S. border in, say Major League Baseball. [Reprinted by permission.]

* * * * *

David Weil, *The Fissured Workplace: Why Work Became So Bad for So Many and What Can Be Done to Improve It* (Cambridge, MA: Harvard University Press, 2014) 43, 44, 89–92

The large corporation of days of yore came with distinctive borders around its perimeter, with most employment located inside firm walls. The large business of today looks more like a small solar system, with a lead firm at its center and smaller workplaces orbiting around it. Some of those orbiting bodies have their own small moons moving about them. But as they move farther away from the lead organization, the profit margins they can achieve diminish, with consequent impacts on their workforces....

The fissured workplace reflects two interrelated changes that led companies to shed more and more employment as they faced intensifying pressure to focus on their core competencies. First, capital markets demanded it, reflective of changes in how those markets operate and the standards to which they held (and hold) businesses seeking financing. Berle's and Mean's concern that the separation of ownership from management insulated the modern corporation from scrutiny was replaced by a concern that the harsh stewardship of capital markets caused corporations to focus too strenuously on the short term. Changes in the financial sector created powerful incentives for lead firms to redraw the very boundaries of the corporation. Second, technological changes created new ways of designing and monitoring the work of other parties, inside or outside the corporation. This enabled companies to shed activities while still ensuring that subordinate businesses adhered to detailed and explicit performance standards. Over the past three decades, it has become far less expensive to contract with other organizations—or create new organizational forms—to undertake activities that are part of producing goods or providing services. That alters the calculus of what should be done inside or outside enterprise boundaries. As a result, lead companies can simultaneously focus attention on a core set of activities (and direct employment relationships) as demanded by capital markets and shed more and more of the actual work done by the enterprise....

By shifting employment to smaller organizations operating in competitive markets, a large employer creates a mechanism to pay workers closer to the additional value they create but avoids the problem of having workers with very different wages operating under one roof. In so doing, the employer captures the difference between the individual additional productivity of each worker and what would be the prevailing single wage rate if it set one.

Businesses at the top of supply chains split off employment so that they can focus their attention on more profitable activities connected to the revenue side of their income statement, leaving the manufacture of products or the provision of service to be fissured off. This has important implications for how the profitability of those companies is shared between different parties. Recall that in the former, integrated model of large employers, firms ended up sharing part of their gains with the workforce in the form of higher pay to deal with internal perceptions of fairness. That meant less to share with consumers in the form of lower prices and with investors in the form of higher returns.

With fissuring, the fairness problems are less acute and wages can be pushed downward. That means more gains to be passed on to consumers as lower prices or better returns for investors. In those fissured structures where a firm's core competency has attracted a particularly devoted customer base through branding or the ongoing introduction of cool new products, the reduced wage costs will flow particularly toward investors. Shifting work outward allows redistribution of gains upward....

The fissured workplace is not simply another term for subcontracting, out-sourcing, or off shoring. Nor does it solely arise from lead companies seeking to avoid payment of private or socially required benefits. Rather, the fissured workplace reflects a fundamental restructuring of business organizations. Employment decisions arise from a careful and ongoing balancing act by lead companies and the subsequent behaviors of the many smaller companies operating beneath them.

What makes sense from a private calculus of balancing the benefits and costs of shedding business functions and employment relationships may differ from what is socially desirable. The economic concept of an externality—the failure of private parties to fully weigh the social costs of their actions—can be usefully applied here. A major retailer or telecommunication company may decide that it can reduce its costs and exposure to liability by contracting out work to another party (who in turn breaks the task into several additional layers of contractors) and still maintain quality, technical requirements, or brand reliability through some of the mechanisms described above. But if the consequence of the decision to shed activities is to reduce the labor force's pay, protections, benefits, and access to longer-term career opportunities, the social costs of those actions are borne by others.

The integrated elements underlying the fissured workplace help explain why trends like wage stagnation have been so persistent and noncompliance with workplace laws increasingly common in many parts of the economy. They help explain why work has become so much worse for so many, even as the share of national income going to reward investors (and the very top of the income distribution) has increased.

[THE FISSURED WORKPLACE: WHY WORK BECAME SO BAD FOR SO MANY AND WHAT CAN BE DONE TO IMPROVE IT by David Weil, Cambridge, Mass.: Harvard University Press, Copyright © 2014 by the President and Fellows of Harvard College.]

6:200   THE APPROPRIATE BARGAINING UNIT

Describing the North American model as a majority rule system built on a principle of exclusivity may be accurate, but it is too abstract to explain much about the certification process. One cannot have a majority in the air; it has to be a majority of some constituency. In Canadian and American labour law, that constituency is called the "bargaining unit."

6:210   Bargaining Unit Determination: General Principles

A bargaining unit is a group of employees defined on the basis of the employer for whom they work and the positions they occupy. In some cases, it consists of all employees of the employer who are engaged in the production of a particular good or service. In other cases, it consists only of a subset of those employees who perform certain tasks. It can include workers employed at only one workplace or at several locations. Certification applications typically involve only one union and one employer—a fact which, as we will see later in this chapter, is often considered to be a serious shortcoming in our labour law system.

A bargaining unit has two distinct functions. First, it serves as an electoral constituency for the purposes of certification and decertification. Second, it serves as the basis for collective bargaining, because a collective agreement drawn up at the bargaining table normally covers all employees in the bargaining unit.

Traditionally, the most important consideration in determining an appropriate bargaining unit is whether there is a "community of interest" among the employees in question. However, for many years that has by no means been treated as the only criterion: the ideal bargaining unit was described by Paul Weiler of the British Columbia Labour Relations Board in the leading case of *Insurance Corp of British Columbia and CUPE*, [1974] 1 CLRBR 403 at 405–12 as one that is broadly drawn to include all of the employees of a single employer. The simplest reason for this view is that a broader unit can be, administratively, more efficient and can often facilitate collective bargaining for both parties. It does not impede the lateral mobility of employees and it allows for a common framework of employment conditions. It may also promote industrial peace and stability by making strikes and lockouts less likely than if there are several separate sets of negotiations.

The parameters of the unit will affect the ongoing employer-union relationship in several ways. First, there may be strong pressure toward the compression of wage differentials and toward uniformity in other terms of employment for everyone covered by the agreement. For management, this may facilitate the administration of the enterprise. Employees with special skills or other employment advantages, however, may not want to be swept into a unit with their fellow workers. The failure of an all-embracing union to meet the needs of special groups may undermine morale or make recruiting more difficult.

Second, if there is a multiplicity of units within a single enterprise, disputes may well occur over which collective agreement governs particular tasks. Inter-union "jurisdictional disputes" may arise over which of two or more unions should have the exclusive right to bargain for a particular group of employees. More often, however, jurisdictional disputes involve a dispute between the members of different unions over who should do certain work—for example, who replaces light bulbs, a janitor or a maintenance electrician?

Third, the degree of economic pressure that each party can bring to bear on the other will also be affected by the design of the bargaining unit. Economic action in support of negotiation demands is often restricted to the same unit as is covered by the collective agreement. At a certain point, workers within the unit may strike in support of their demands, or the employer may lock them out in support of its demands. In addition, a work stoppage within the unit may interrupt other processes outside it that are functionally integrated. Often these are the only economic pressures that one party can lawfully exert on the other. Strikes or lockouts involving workers outside the unit are unlawful in most jurisdictions unless those workers themselves have the right to strike or their employer has the right to lock them out. Picketing by lawfully striking bargaining unit employees that is directed at workers who are outside that unit may also be held to be illegal. Issues of this sort are considered in Chapter 8.

The size and shape of the bargaining unit can have a dramatic effect on bargaining power and on the frequency and impact of strikes. If there are many units in a particular enterprise, there is the possibility of a number of legal strikes at different times, which may be quite disruptive and therefore quite effective as a bargaining tactic. If only one unit is on strike and its members are few in number or not particularly indispensable, the employer may easily be able to continue operating despite the strike. Strategically placed employees can, however, have a tremendous amount of bargaining power, even if their numbers are small. It may make a significant difference whether such employees bargain on their own or as part of a larger group. Further, each wage settlement is strongly influenced by "coercive comparisons" to settlements for other units. As the number of bargaining units increases, *ceteris peribus*, so do opportunities for such comparisons. The tactic whereby a unit seeks to obtain a settlement better than one previously negotiated for another group is known as leapfrogging. In recent decades, however, this has become more difficult, as many unions have been put on the defensive by recessionary tendencies, labour saving technologies, employer attempts to outsource work to non-union firms, and growing international competition.

As well, where widespread organizational fissuring takes place within an economy governed by the *Wagner Act* model (and by our current legal concepts of "the employer"—see discussion in Chapter 4) this combines to generate a tendency towards yet further "decentralization" in collective bargaining. In other words, without some other measure to counter this tendency under our current legal framework, organizational fissuring tends to create pressures for potential bargaining units to be conceived and defined at lower levels within the interorganizational networks of productive activities constructed under fissuring, often tending to reduce the potential bargaining power of such bargaining units.

These observations point to the dilemma of defining an appropriate bargaining unit. The optimal unit for effective long-term collective bargaining may be larger than the group within which a union can, in the short-term, obtain the majority support necessary to get collective bargaining started at all. How should these competing considerations be weighed? And should the public interest be considered, as distinguished from the interests of the parties? If so, how should it be identified?

6:220 Voluntary Delineation of the Bargaining Unit

While the most frequent context for bargaining unit determination is during an application for certification (to be discussed in detail below), the employer and the union may be able to delineate the bargaining unit on their own, in one of two related ways. The first is through what is called voluntary recognition, and the second is through collective bargaining after certification.

First, the union may try delineation through voluntary recognition. Labour relations statutes in Canadian jurisdictions other than Quebec generally allow for an employer to voluntarily recognize a union purporting to represent its employees as the exclusive bargaining agent for those employees and to define the bargaining unit to which such recognition extends. The normal process is for such an agreement to be filed with the minister of labour or labour relations board, at which point the other provisions of the legislation take over and govern relations between the parties as if the union had been certified by the board. However, the statutes typically guard against potential abuses of this process. A voluntary recognition agreement must usually be posted in the workplace to give all affected employees notice of its existence. Voluntary recognition agreements are not valid if the union is dominated or inappropriately influenced by the employer, if it engages in discriminatory behaviour against members on prohibited human rights grounds, if it does not actually represent a majority of the employees in the relevant bargaining unit, or if another union already has acquired bargaining rights in relation to the employees in question.

Labour boards are given jurisdiction to adjudicate these latter questions in an application brought for that purpose, just as if the matter had arisen in a certification application, and the boards may declare a purported voluntary recognition to be a nullity. Furthermore, bargaining rights acquired by a union through voluntary recognition can be the subject of a revocation application (just as if they had been acquired through certification) if, after a specified time has elapsed, the union has failed to adequately fulfill its bargaining responsibilities or no longer represents a majority of the employees in the unit (see Section 6:500).

Second, the union may try delineation of the unit (or more exactly, modification of it) through collective bargaining. Standard in virtually all collective agreements is a "recognition clause," whereby the employer acknowledges the union as exclusive bargaining agent for the relevant unit of employees to which the agreement applies. This clause may in fact be the only manifestation of the "recognition agreement" described above, in which case the voluntary recognition provisions in the legislation take effect upon the filing of the whole collective agreement. In other circumstances, the voluntary recognition agreement may be a separate document filed prior to the commencement of full collective bargaining. Recognition clauses are also commonly found (and indeed, required by statute) in collective agreements negotiated after certification. Sometimes the parties will agree to alter the bargaining unit description set out in the labour relations board's certification order.

The legality of such voluntary changes to a certified bargaining unit description varies somewhat across the country. Legislation in all jurisdictions sets out a process for applying to the labour relations board to amend a bargaining unit description, particularly where the parties cannot agree on the change (See the discussion of amending the scope of the bargaining unit, post-certification, in Section 6:240). Whether the board will accept an agreed-upon change to the makeup of a certified unit description will depend on the wording of the particular statute and the extent to which the particular board accepts the idea of voluntarism. There may at times be reason to believe that the public interest, or the interests of particular individuals or groups in the workplace, is inconsistent with the terms of a private arrangement between union and employer on the parameters of the unit.

6:221 Delineation of the Bargaining Unit by a Labour Relations Board

A union seeking certification for a unit that it claims to be appropriate for collective bargaining will apply to the relevant labour relations board. The board must decide whether that unit, or some variation of it, is an appropriate one. Sometimes (most often where public sector employees are involved) the legislation may be quite specific about what constitutes an appropriate unit. In the private sector, boards usually have wide discretion to determine what is an appropriate unit.

As noted above, the two most widely accepted criteria of bargaining unit delineation are the presence of a "community of interest," consideration of which is mandatory in Nova Scotia, and the concern that the particular bargaining unit not create a significant degree of labour relations harm, a commonly cited example of which is excessive fragmentation of the workplace. These two principles can be somewhat in conflict. Community of interest may point to the creation of several units in a particular enterprise; employees who differ significantly in such matters as background, skill, type of work, method of payment, and geographical location are often placed in separate units. In recent years, however, as the following decision indicates, the criterion of community of interest has yielded somewhat to the preference for broadly based units.

Metroland Printing, Publishing and Distributing Ltd, [2003] OLRD No 514

McLEAN, Vice-Chair:

[...]

¶2 Metroland Printing, Publishing and Distributing Ltd. ("Metroland") is a large publisher of, among other things, community newspapers. The trade union applied for certification of the following "all employee" bargaining unit of the employees of Metroland in its operation in Midland:

> all employees of Metroland, Printing, Publishing and Distributing Ltd. in the Town of Midland, save and except supervisors, persons above the rank of supervisor, and those employees in bargaining units for which any trade union holds bargaining rights as of the application date (July 31, 2002).

¶3 The employer and the intervenor, Mr. Walker, asserts that the proposed bargaining unit is not appropriate....

FACTS

¶5 Metroland publishes the Midland-Penetanguishene Mirror out of its office in Midland, Ontario.... The Mirror is one of 69 community newspapers published by Metroland through various offices....

¶7 The Midland office has two departments. The sales department consists of three advertising representatives and one telemarketing representative. The sales employees are paid on a commission basis. The distribution department, as the name suggests, is engaged in activities to ensure that the paper is distributed to customers. Such activities include warehousing and the recruitment and monitoring of carriers. The employees in the distribution department are hourly paid employees. Two employees, including Mr. Walker, work in the distribution department.

¶8 From time to time the employer hires part time and temporary employees. Part time employees generally work 19 or 20 hours per week and are usually, but not always temporary. In contrast to regular full time employees who receive a full benefit package (life insurance, long term disability, dental, accidental death & dismemberment, extended health care, and access to an employee assistance program), part time and temporary employees do not get a benefit package. Part time employees can be and are sent home if there is no work to be done. Their shift schedule can change on short notice. Full time employees work regular hours on a regular schedule.

¶9 Temporary employees are hired for two purposes: to replace an employee on leave (up to a year) or to assist the company during busy periods (usually 3–4 months). The latter category of temporary employee does not do the same work as regular full time employees. Temporary employees are hired pursuant to a written contract of employment, regular full time employees are not.

¶10 The company also utilizes/trains co-operative students on occasion. They are placed with the company pursuant to a Ministry of Education program. The co-operative students sign a contract supplied by the Ministry and are not paid any salary or benefits.

They are assigned a variety of work. The Ministry of Education covers their Workplace Safety & Insurance Board coverage. The employer interviews co-operative students before they start with the company to determine if they are acceptable....

¶12 All of the company's current full time employees began with the company on a one year contract working 19 or 20 hours per week.

ARGUMENT

¶13 The employer asserts that part-time employees, temporary employees and co-operative students should be excluded from the bargaining unit. There should either be one bargaining unit for each of the part time and temporary employee groups or one combined bargaining unit for the temporary and part time employees. Students should be included with the part-time employees.

¶14 The intervenor asserts that the two employees in his department do not want to be represented by the trade union and that therefore the bargaining unit should not include the distribution department.

¶15 The employer urges the Board not to have a "knee jerk" reaction to its proposed bargaining unit(s). Prior to the Bill 40 and Bill 7 amendments to the Act the Board used to make assumptions about the appropriateness of bargaining units (for example with respect to part time and full time employees) but those assumptions have been rejected in favour of bargaining units which are designed to fit the circumstances of each workplace. In this regard community of interest is still a relevant factor when the Board determines bargaining units. In this case the full time employees simply do not have a community of interest with the part-time employees, temporary employees and co-operative students. They are paid differently, they receive different benefits and they work on different schedules.

¶16 The employer relies on the Board's decision in *Hospital for Sick Children*.... There the Board stated:

> ¶17. Given that the definition of the bargaining unit can materially affect the ability of employees to organize, and that uncertainties concerning its contours can provoke costly litigation and potentially prejudicial delay, what then is the purpose of the concept of the "appropriate bargaining unit"? Quite simply, it is an effort to inject a public policy component into the initial shaping of the collective bargaining structure, so as to encourage the practice and procedure of collective bargaining and enhance the likelihood of a more viable and harmonious collective bargaining relationship.... [T]he discretion to frame the "appropriate" bargaining unit during the initial organizing phase provides the Board with an opportunity (albeit perhaps a limited one) to avoid subsequent labour relations problems. Now, of course, this is not necessarily the same thing as minimizing administrative problems for the employer or organizing problems for the union. The structures and policies that promote a maximization of the employer's business interests are not those that will necessarily describe a viable bargaining unit, or the only viable bargaining unit—particularly since those interests may include a desire to avoid collective bargaining altogether, or limit its effectiveness. The employer's administrative structures are relevant in determining the bargaining unit, but they are not necessarily to be taken as the conclusive blue print

in deciding what is appropriate. Nor is it a matter of simply giving an applicant union what it wants. It is, as we have noted, a matter of balancing competing considerations, including such factors as: whether the employees have a community of interest having regard to the nature of the work performed, the conditions of employment, and their skills; the employee's administrative structures; the geographic circumstances; the employees' functional coherence, or interdependence or interchange with other employees; the centralization of management authority; the economic advantages to the employer of one unit versus another; the source of work; the right of employees to a measure of self-determination; the degree of employee organization and whether a proposed unit would impede such organization; any likely adverse effects to the parties and the public that might flow from a proposed unit, or from fragmentation of employees into several units, and so on.

[...]

¶17 The employer argues that, applying the *Hospital for Sick Children* test, that there are two requirements to a finding that a bargaining unit applied for by a trade union is appropriate: first the employees in the bargaining unit must have sufficient community of interest that they can bargain together and; second, the bargaining unit must not create serious labour relations problems for the employer. In this case, the employer asserts, the groups of employees have almost no community of interest in that they are paid differently, have different hours of work and shift expectations and receive different benefit packages. In addition, the part time, temporary and co-operative students have little real connection to the workplace because they are interested in short term monetary reward rather than a career with the employer.

DECISION

¶18 The starting point for the determination of a bargaining unit is the Board's decision in *Hospital for Sick Children*. I agree with the employer that there are two parts to that test: "*sufficient* community of interest" and no "serious labour relations problems for the employer." I also agree that the Board should not automatically make assumptions about community of interest.

¶19 In my view, the Board's assessment of the level of community of interest required to be sufficient to permit a single bargaining unit has evolved. As the employer rightly asserts, for example, at one time part-time employees were automatically excluded (at the employer's request) from a full time employee bargaining unit. Now the Board frequently places such employees in the same bargaining unit. It is no longer assumed that part time employees have a different community of interest than full time employees. The Board determines an appropriate bargaining unit based on the particular circumstances of each workplace.

¶20 The Board has significant experience in placing disparate groups of employees in one bargaining unit with little apparent negative effect on labour relations. It is now common for employees with quite different terms and conditions of employment and different employment aspirations, including part-time and full-time and temporary employees, to be placed in one bargaining unit. As a result, community of interest has much less influence on the determination of an appropriate bargaining unit than it once may have had.

¶21 This evolution has been recognized in the case law. In *Active Mold Plastic Products Ltd.,* ... the Board stated:

> Most recently, in *Burns International Security Services* ..., the Board addressed the utility of the concept of "community of interest." In this decision, it was noted that the term "community of interest" does not usually provide the Board with much assistance in determining whether an applied-for bargaining unit is appropriate. It was observed in this decision that the focus before the Board in bargaining unit determination cases should be upon "concrete problems rather than the sometimes nebulous concept of 'community of interest'." ...

¶23 In my view the result of the evolution in the Board's analysis of the determination of an appropriate bargaining unit is that the Board has recognized that employees share a community of interest simply by being employed by the same employer in the same workplace and that employees with quite different terms and conditions of employment can effectively bargain together. In essence, what has happened, is that the "sufficient community of interest" part of the *Hospital for Sick Children* test and the serious labour relations problems part of the test have merged. Employees of the same employer will generally be found to have sufficient community of interest to bargain together unless the placement of them in the same bargaining unit, due to lack of community of interest or otherwise, creates serious labour relations problems for the employer.

¶24 In this case, I am satisfied that the various (groups) of employees at this workplace have sufficient community of interest that they can bargain together. I also see no prospect that the inclusion of all of these categories of employees in a single bargaining unit will create serious labour relations problems for the employer. While the employees in question have different terms and conditions of employment, the differences are not so great so as to cause serious (or likely any) labour relations problems. In addition, given the fact that the majority, or perhaps all, of the current employees began with the company on a part-time contract, the group of employees are all in potentially similar career positions.

¶25 In addition, it is apparent that the employer's proposed bargaining unit would lead to inappropriate bargaining unit fragmentation at the employer's workplace. Fragmentation can itself lead to serious labour relations problems for the workplace parties. Moreover, the Board has frequently said that broader-based bargaining units are better for collective bargaining. As the Board stated in a different context in *Humber/Northwestern/York-Finch Hospital* ...,

> ¶32 This is not to say that "bigger is always better." However, labour relations boards across the country have all recognized the utility of broader-based bargaining structures, because they are more likely to: promote stability, increase administrative efficiency, enhance employee mobility, and generate a common framework for employment conditions for all employees in an enterprise. Bigger bargaining units also have more critical mass, so that they are better able to facilitate and accommodate change....
>
> ¶33 In the absence of statutory prescriptions, there is, today, a pronounced preference for broader-based bargaining units, unless that objective collides in a serious way with the employees' ability to organize themselves. Indeed, the Board has often favoured broader-based bargaining units, even in certification situations, where the shape of the unit may

well influence whether there will be any collective bargaining at all. The Board has recognized that the *structure* of collective bargaining "*matters*".... Fragmented bargaining structures can pose serious labour-relations problems. Conversely, broader based bargaining units make collective bargaining go more smoothly and successfully.

¶34 There is nothing particularly novel about these observations. Nor are they unique to Ontario, or to the Ontario Labour Relations Board. The consolidation of bargaining structures has been ongoing in other jurisdictions for many years (the Post Office, CBC, railways, and airlines come to mind); and policy considerations such as those discussed in the Ontario cases can be found in the reasons of other adjudicators in other jurisdictions. Those boards, too, have been inclined to favour more comprehensive bargaining units unless there are persuasive countervailing considerations....

¶26 In this case there are only a total of approximately 10 employees at the workplace. One of those employees is already in a separate bargaining unit. Therefore, the employer's proposals could lead to a total of three or four bargaining units for a very small workplace. This is unacceptable in such a small bargaining unit even in this industry, which has a history of fragmentation. Finally, to the extent that the students are employees at all, which I doubt, there is no reason why they cannot be included in an all employee bargaining unit.

¶27 As for the position taken by the intervenor, the preceding comments apply equally to Mr. Walker and the other employee in the advertising department. It simply makes no labour relations sense to hive off a small department of two employees into their own separate bargaining unit. Employee wishes are just one of the factors the Board may consider when determining an appropriate bargaining unit. Those wishes are balanced, among other things, against the Board's aversion to fragmentation and the viability of the bargaining unit as a whole. It is not surprising that in this application for certification, there are employees (like Mr. Walker) who do not wish to be represented by a trade union. That is the case in many of the applications for certification which come before the Board....

¶33 The Board finds that:

> all employees of Metroland, Printing, Publishing and Distributing Ltd. in the Town of Midland, save and except supervisors, persons above the rank of supervisor, and those employees in bargaining units for which any trade union holds bargaining rights as of the application date ... constitutes an appropriate bargaining unit.

6:222 Bargaining Unit Delineation and Part-Time Employees

The *Wagner Act* model, now three-quarters of a century old, was initially premised on the prevalence of full-time, blue-collar employment in an industrial (mainly manufacturing) setting. In more recent years, part-time and casual employees in those sectors, and above all in the service sector, have become subjects of prime concern for the union movement and for scholars interested in labour law reform. Part-time and casual employment has been the largest growth segment (and often the only one) in the Canadian labour market since the late 1980s. Part-time employees, defined by Statistics Canada as those who work thirty or fewer hours a week, now make up around 20 percent of the labour force, and their numbers have been growing steadily throughout the industrialized world since the 1950s. With the rise of a globalized economy, industrial economies have been shifting from manufacturing goods to producing services. Part-time employment has grown along with the growth of the service sector; in 2017 that sector accounted for 93 percent of all part-time jobs in Canada. This is especially significant given that as of 2017, service work makes up 79 percent of total Canadian employment. Most service sector firms are relatively small and face a high degree of competition. As a result, they tend to favour part-time workers, who generally receive lower wages and fewer benefits than full-time workers.

As well as being the fastest-growing segment of the workforce, part-time employees are disproportionately female. In 2017, working women represent around 47 percent of the total Canadian workforce, but 65 percent of part-timers. Some women prefer to work part-time to enable them to attend to family responsibilities.

Because part-time workers generally have less job security as well as inferior terms and conditions, they might be expected to be fertile ground for union organizers. Statistics Canada data from 2017 showed that only 24 percent of part-timers were unionized, in contrast to 31.8 percent of full-timers. Many unions traditionally opposed the hiring of part-timers, whom they saw as competitors for jobs and as exerting downward pressure on wages. Part-timers often returned this hostility.

As is indicated by the *Metroland* case excerpted above, labour relations boards have been moving toward a more flexible approach to the inclusion of part-timers in bargaining units with full-time employees. Nevertheless, debate continues in the labour law community about how best to handle the growing phenomenon of part-time work.

Casual employees are another group that presents difficult issues of bargaining unit determination. In the following case, the federal board considered whether casual employees ought to be included in a pre-existing unit comprising the full-time and part-time employees of a particular branch of a bank. The broader question of the appropriateness of single branch units in nationwide banks will be considered in the next section of this chapter.

Canadian Imperial Bank of Commerce (Powell River Branch) v British Columbia Government Employees' Union (1992), 15 CLRBR (2d) 86 at 87–89

JAMIESON, Vice-Chair:

[...]

What do we mean when we refer to 'casual employees'? Generally speaking, this term has been used to describe employees who are employed on a call-in basis. Usually these employees work very irregular hours as required. When they are called by an employer about their availability for work there is no obligation for them to accept the hours offered. Conversely, there is no obligation upon the employer to call the casuals to work. Normally casuals are paid on an hourly basis plus the minimum percentage of vacation pay. They are not usually entitled to any other benefits.

Much has been written by this Board and other boards about the advisability of including employees who do not work a regular full-time schedule with those who do. . . . What can be drawn from those decisions are several principles which will influence the Board when it is faced with the problem of including or excluding casual employees from bargaining units. Some major concerns for the Board are:

1) The possibility of casual employees preventing full-time employees from having access to collective bargaining. This situation could arise where the full-time employees are outnumbered by casuals who may not be interested in participating in collective bargaining. If the Board were to insist on the inclusion of casuals in these circumstances, the smaller group of full-time employees who may opt for collective bargaining could have their attempts to do so vetoed by the contrary wishes of the casuals.
2) There is a possible negative impact on the free collective bargaining process if casuals are included because in most cases casual employees have a different community of interest from regular full-time or regular part-time employees. Obviously, the bargaining strength of regular employees would be considerably diluted if the bargaining unit was flooded with casuals. These casuals could not be expected to support strike action over issues such as seniority or pensions which have more impact on the employment of regular employees.
3) The Board is also hesitant to confer full collective bargaining rights, including the right to halt operations by strike action, on small groups of casual employees who only have a marginal connection with a given industry.

For these reasons as well as others, the Board has shown a preference for excluding casuals from bargaining units, particularly when dealing with new applications where there are no established collective bargaining relationships.

Notwithstanding the Board's stated preference for bargaining-unit construction excluding casuals, the fact remains that casuals are 'employees' within the meaning of the Code (s. 3) and they do have the rights and protections bestowed upon employees by the statute. The Board's dilemma has been how to balance the rights of casual employees with those of regular employees and this can only be done depending upon the particular circumstances of any given case. One example of where the Board did include casuals in a bargaining unit with full and part-time employees is *Pacific Western Airlines Ltd.*, (1984) ... There the Board found it appropriate to include some 21 casuals in a bargaining unit containing 960 or so regular employees. In that instance the Board was also dealing with an application for review where there was an established collective bargaining relationship. There the Board expressed its satisfaction that the usual concerns about including casuals were alleviated in the circumstances before it, i.e., there was no opportunity for the casuals to prevent regular employees from exercising their rights under the Code as they were already organized. Also, there was little possibility of the casuals dominating the bargaining unit because of the large number of regular employees in the unit as opposed to the number of casuals being sought to be added.

In that decision the Board emphasized the importance of identifying a real community of interest between the casuals and the other employees in the bargaining unit. The Board also said that an important consideration is the continuity or the pattern of employment of the casuals notwithstanding the irregularity of the hours worked....

We concur with that view that the continuity of employment should be a telling factor. If an employer has created a regular standby pool of employees upon which it relies to do its extra production work or to fill in for its regular staff on an ongoing basis, this pool of employees should be viewed as an integral part of the employer's workforce. This is not like an employer calling office overload or the likes to fill an occasional vacancy or to deal with an unforeseen increase in the workload.

6:230 Bargaining Unit Determination and the Organizing Drive

Recall again the crucial fact that the bargaining unit performs two main functions: it serves as an electoral district for certification purposes and as the basis for collective bargaining. These two functions often conflict in cases where an employer has several outlets or branches. Although it may be easier to organize employees branch by branch, single branch bargaining units may not have enough power to engage in effective collective bargaining.

The following readings describe the history of union efforts to organize bank employees in Canada. They illustrate how labour relations boards have grappled with the tension between the bargaining unit's two main functions. Furthermore, they draw attention to the particular consequences that traditional principles of bargaining unit determination have had for women workers and bank employees.

Elizabeth Lennon, "Organizing the Unorganized: Unionization in the Chartered Banks of Canada" (1980) 18 *Osgoode Hall Law Journal* **177 at 179–84**

> There are currently ten chartered banks in Canada, functioning through a very widespread network of small branches. While some of these banks are localized, and several are small, the 'Big Five,' which control ninety-one percent of total bank assets, operate throughout Canada. Organization is highly centralized, with most important decisions emanating from the head offices in either Toronto or Montreal. Most have provincial or regional administrative subdivisions as well....
>
> Bank employment patterns are changing slowly in response to changing social and economic conditions, but in general they still reflect the policies of an earlier era. Banks employ a remarkably high percentage of women in comparison with the Canadian labour force as a whole: in 1975 the figure was seventy-two percent. These women are heavily concentrated in low-paying, routine clerical jobs. The Bank of Nova Scotia indicates that while between eighty and ninety percent of its management employees are male, ninety percent of its clerical employees are female. This profile is typical of the industry as a whole. Comparative male/female salary levels reflect this difference in functions.
>
> Working conditions in the banks are fairly typical of 'white-collar' employment.... There is a high turnover rate, which the banks estimate variously at between twenty-seven and thirty-six percent. Since turnover is confined largely to clerical (and therefore female) ranks, the figure for this class of employee would be even higher. Compensation levels for clerical employees are somewhat lower than the average for clerical work across all industries in Canada, and this is probably true for management employees as well....
>
> The chartered banks have been notoriously resistant to trade unionism, and there have been only sporadic attempts to organize them over the years. It was not until 1959 that the Canada Labour Relations Board received its first application for certification from a union seeking to represent bank employees. The Kitimat, Terrace and District

General Workers' Union, Local 1583 applied for a unit of three workers among a total staff of five in the Kitimat branch of the Bank of Nova Scotia. The bank contested the application on the grounds that the unit was not appropriate for collective bargaining, taking the position that only a national unit would be appropriate. Although the application was dismissed on the basis that the unit was not appropriate, the Board was careful to point out that it was not accepting the argument that only a national unit would be suitable: 'It may well be that units of some of the employees of a Bank, grouped together territorially or on some other basis, will prove to be appropriate, rather than a nationwide unit.' It was clear, however, that a branch was not an appropriate unit.

This decision understandably daunted the trade union movement. In 1959 the Royal Bank had 503 branches nationally and presented a truly formidable organizing task. The task became even more formidable as branches proliferated with the passage of time. Although the *Kitimat* decision hinted at some more manageable unit, none was readily apparent since the administration of bank personnel was, in fact, largely handled at the national level, as the bank had argued. The response of the trade union movement to the *Kitimat* decision was virtually to suspend organizing for about fifteen years....

Aside from a sprinkling of provincial certifications held by various unions in trust companies and credit unions, the financial sector in 1976 was still virgin territory for the labour movement....

If unions did not appear to be very interested in bank workers, at least some bank workers were interested in unions. This interest crystallized independently in two parts of the country: Ontario and British Columbia. In mid-1976 the first applications for branch certification since *Kitimat* were filed.

The history of the Service, Office and Retail Workers' Union of Canada (SORWUC) and its contact with bank workers is quite different [from the normal union experience]. This union was an outgrowth of the Vancouver women's liberation movement, and was founded in 1972 by the Working Women's Association (WWA), a feminist labour support group. Although WWA members were working women, in general they worked in unorganized workplaces. Their contacts with the trade union movement had been uniformly negative.... They felt that there was a pressing need for a union organized and controlled by women and committed to organizing places where women worked....

Although bank workers are mainly women and, thus, are part of SORWUC's natural jurisdiction, the union did not move into the banking field immediately. However, in the spring of 1976 it campaigned with leaflets in Vancouver's downtown area, inviting contact from clerical women interested in organizing. There was a strong response from bank workers and the union decided to follow up on these contacts made in the various branches.

SORWUC and its legal advisors were not at all confident that the CLRB would accept an individual bank branch as a unit appropriate for collective bargaining, although that was always a possibility....

The strategy was, then, to assemble as many applications for certification as possible and to file them in rapid succession. The first was an application for employees at the Victory Square branch of the Canadian Imperial Bank of Commerce in Vancouver, filed on August 16, 1976. Sixteen more branches of various banks applied before the end of 1976. Momentum dropped somewhat after that, but SORWUC had filed a total of twenty-two applications for certification before the first hearings were held in April of 1977.

[Reprinted by permission.]

Service, Office and Retail Workers' Union of Canada [SORWUC] v Canadian Imperial Bank of Commerce, [1977] 2 CLRBR 99 at 110, 113, and 117–25

[The applicant asked to be certified for eight bargaining units, each corresponding to a different branch of the bank. The bank claimed that the only appropriate unit was all of its branches across Canada.]

DORSEY, Vice-Chair: The Canadian Imperial Bank of Commerce is one of Canada's 12 chartered banks. It has 34,000 employees and operates a nationwide branch banking system with 1,693 branches in Canada and 114 branches outside Canada. The essence of the branch banking system is that, through the branch, all customers of the bank have access to all the banking facilities of the bank. The bank can concentrate deposits, its lifeblood, and deploy them to work for it wherever there is a profitable market. To make this system effective, each branch is supported by a central pool of resources. . . .

The branch is not a totally autonomous unit and each branch manager cannot organize his branch to suit his personal philosophy or business attitudes. The financial success of the bank depends upon the success of each branch and the ability of the system to service all its customers. Each branch has its own deposit and borrowing customers with their needs, but uniformity of systems promotes efficiency and reduces costs. To this end, several financial and administrative functions are centralized. There are at least 30 financial functions that are centralized to the extent that they require the completion or accounting to be done outside the branch. . . .

What emerges from this picture is an operation that for purposes of efficiency and ease of administration seeks to maintain standardized procedures and uniformity of employment policy. But on the employment side this centralization must not be overemphasized. The picture is well summarized by Mr. Duffield who testified that hiring, assessment, promotion, discipline and termination are usually initiated at the branch level because the bank has to rely upon its managers in its many locations. . . .

The Board is vested with the exclusive authority and responsibility to determine the appropriateness of proposed bargaining units. . . .

Why has Parliament vested this authority and responsibility in the Board? The answer to this question is obvious when the consequences of a certification order are considered.

Once a trade union is certified it is vested with the 'exclusive authority to bargain on behalf of the employees in the bargaining unit' (s. 136(1)(a)). The union acquires the right to bargain for all employees in the unit, not just those who are members of the trade union. The issuance of a certification order affects not only union members but other employees as well. They become represented by the certified trade union whether they do not wish any union representation or wish to be represented by another trade union. These employees lose their right to negotiate directly with their employer on terms and conditions of employment. That change in the employment relationship may last indefinitely and is of considerable importance to these employees.

Secondly, the issuance of a certification order has legal consequences for the employer. Once a trade union is certified it may require the employer to bargain collectively with it (s. 146). The employer is obliged to bargain in good faith and make every reasonable effort to enter into a collective agreement. It is also precluded, for a time, from unilaterally altering terms and conditions of employment (s. 148).

Thirdly, the public and employer are affected because the issuance of a certification order entitles the union, after having fulfilled the statutory requirements, to undertake a lawful strike (s. 180)....

In this case the unit proposed by the union is a single location unit—a unit of employees of the employer employed at a branch of the employer's operations. That unit is a unit because it is a 'group of two or more employees' (s. 107(1) 'unit'). Is it an appropriate bargaining unit?

It is the experience of this and other labour relations boards that employees consider the single location unit to be a natural unit, because this is where the employees work. In this case, the employees daily or regularly attend to work at the branch location. They work under the supervision of the branch manager and other personnel who, in turn, work in the branch. They have social interchange during the day, develop friendships and acquaintances among fellow employees in the branch, get to know the branch's customers, and perhaps engage in after-hours athletic or social activities.

It is also the common practice of labour relations boards to hold that the single location unit is an appropriate bargaining unit. Provincial boards make this determination when dealing with retail outlets, manufacturing operations, mines and other operations. This Board makes this determination when dealing with radio or television stations, atomic energy plants and others. It is the consensus among labour relations boards that the community of interest of employees at a single location is sufficient to hold that the single location unit is an appropriate unit.

The Commerce asks the Board to deviate from this natural inclination of employees and practice and consensus of labour relations boards. It asks the Board to find that the only appropriate unit is a unit of all employees of the bank. In this unit would be included most of the Commerce's 34,000 Canadian employees employed in 1,693 branch locations and several data centers, regional offices and head office. It would include tellers, clerks, loan officers and others employed in any one branch with keypunch operators, regional and head office clerical employees, administrators, instructors, security personnel and others.

Why is the bank asking for this unusually large, widespread and diverse unit? It requests this unit in the interest of administrative efficiency and convenience in bargaining, administrative convenience for lateral mobility of employees in a large unit, the desirability of common employment conditions, and a reduction of the potential incidents of industrial unrest....

The second reason it requests this unit is because in its view branch certification would create 'utter chaos' contrary to the public interest. In fact it maintains 'chaos was probably inadequate to describe' the branch unit proposition. The Commerce arrives at this unusual perception of single location unit designation because it perceives the banking industry as the fiscal fibre of the country. The argument is that branch unionization would affect the property rights of all Canadians, i.e., their right to deposit and withdraw money, and would disrupt the mechanism our society relies upon for the money necessary to sustain all elements of society....

Let us examine this position in the larger context of the duty the Board must discharge. The fundamental dilemma the Board confronts in each certification application and bargaining unit dispute is that the bargaining unit serves two basic purposes. It is the initial constituency which will decide whether an applicant union will acquire representational rights to commence collective bargaining. It is also the basis for the bargaining structure that may obtain in the future. This Board and other labour relations boards recognize that in difficult cases, such as this one, any judgment carries its cost. The freedom of choice of employees to group into self-determined units or the most rational, long-term bargaining structure is partially or totally sacrificed....

The express intention of Parliament is the 'encouragement of free collective bargaining' and to support labour and management who recognize and support collective bargaining 'as the bases of effective industrial relations for the determination of good working conditions and sound labour-management relations.' Parliament also 'deems the development of good industrial relations to be in the best interests of Canada in ensuring a just share of the fruits of progress to all.'

This legislative intent can best be achieved by facilitating collective bargaining for employees who choose this procedure for settling their terms and conditions of employment. That can be accomplished by this Board accepting or fashioning bargaining units that give employees a realistic possibility of exercising their rights under the Code. Too large units in unorganized industries will abort any possibility of collective bargaining ever commencing and defeat this express intention of Parliament. At the same time, this does not mean the Board will or should create artificial units based on [the] extent of organizing. This would ignore the purpose of the Board's role.

A real-life example of aborting the possibility of collective bargaining is the Board's decision 18 years ago in *Bank of Nova Scotia, Kitimat* ... In that case the Board found a single branch unit to be inappropriate....

The experience after the *Bank of Nova Scotia, Kitimat* decision demonstrates that bank employees and trade unions realistically perceived that any form of union organizing was virtually impossible on any basis other than the branch basis. There was some evidence that SORWUC supporters have the zeal to attempt organizing on a broader basis, but zeal is not the basis for interpreting legislative intention.

The practical reality of the employer's proposed bargaining unit is that only an organization or movement with the enormous financial resources to operate nationwide, in a concerted effort, for a long period of time, could make the rights of the Code meaningful for the Commerce employees. This in itself is a restriction of the freedom of employees 'to join the trade union of his choice' (s. 110(1)). Apart from this fact the history of union activity is that unions begin or are based in a particular locale. To organize on a national basis a union of bank employees would have to start to solicit members in one area and then move outward to other areas. By the time it had encompassed the expansive territorial boundaries of Canada the employees in the primary locales would have become disillusioned and perhaps lost interest in any expectation of achieving collective bargaining. Because of the turnover of employees at the Commerce and in the industry, a union seeking to act as a vehicle for bargaining would be on a constant treadmill of soliciting new employees and, at the same time, maintaining the support of members while expanding to new areas. And all of this would occur against the background of no tradition of collective bargaining in the industry.

Do the employer's arguments outweigh these considerations? Administrative convenience, lateral mobility of employees, and the desirability of common terms of employment are interests of the bank and employees. How much will these be compromised by a single branch unit?

The Commerce is an efficient, diversified organization responding to and leading in the complex world of commerce, finance and international business. It is a multi-resourced organization with specialists in banking as well as real estate, taxation, computer systems, government relations, personnel administration, etc. It operates across Canada and adapts to local business practices and labour markets. It structures its work environment, hours of business and wages to local conditions. Its employee benefit program is flexible to account for the differing wishes of its employees. It accepts and adopts changes in government regulation, markets and business practices.

Employees move from one branch to another, most often at their request or agreement. They are seldom required to move. Moves often accompany promotion or promotional opportunities which is a distinct interest of employees, perhaps even more than for the bank. Neither provincial boundaries, climatic conditions nor domestic situations prevent employee acceptance of movement.

These two factors of administrative convenience and lateral mobility of employees are significant to the bank, but we are not convinced that certification and collective bargaining at the branch level cannot result in agreements that accommodate these interests. Commonality of terms and conditions of employment does not entirely exist now. A multitude of employee classifications in a complex structure of delegated responsibility is reflected by varying pay ranges and merit steps in those ranges. Assorted benefit packages accommodate individual preferences. Differing local markets have necessitated different wage scales. We are satisfied that, under branch certification, centralized employer bargaining and the employees' interests in uniformity and equality can result in uniform terms and conditions of employment. This is the proven collective bargaining experience of multi-location employers.

The fourth factor, the reduction of the potential incidents for industrial unrest is linked with the employer's fears of chaos. This fear of hypothetical horribles is the foremost basis for the employer's position. The Commerce fears that an acceptance of SORWUC's position would create a 'monster' that could not be turned around. It points to the disruption resulting from a confusion of bargaining units that is recounted in *British Columbia Railway Company and CAIMAW et al.* . . . as an example, and says the approach of several other British Columbia public sector cases should be applied because the Commerce is akin to a public institution. The basic rationale of these decisions is capsulized in *British Columbia Ferry Corp. and B.C. Gov't Employees Union et al.* . . . .

The first distinguishing feature of these cases is that the unions applying for certification define their units in occupational terms. The future results of such a certification would have been that, when these employees withdrew their services, the employer's entire operation could be shut down because the occupations sought were employed in integrated operations employing several occupations. A cessation of work by one occupation could disrupt the entire system. This is not the case here where the unit sought is multi-occupational at a single location. A cessation of work at one location would not prevent the bank at its many other locations from continuing to operate. It would be essentially self-contained within the unit.

The second distinguishing feature of these cases is that they involve a truly public employer or an essential monopolistic enterprise (e.g., the British Columbia Railway Co. or the British Columbia Ferry Corp.). The impact of a work stoppage at these employers has a serious external impact on the public. The Commerce is not a public institution like a provincial monopolistic insurance corporation, a municipality, a workers' compensation board or a provincially run railway....

A collateral position the employer advances is that a branch unit will result in a multiplicity of unions representing a multiplicity of units. This is not the experience in other industries where craft unions have not been historically present. The experience is that unions grow and evolve with jurisdiction over employees in an industry. This is in the interest of employees and unions generally. New unionized sectors or industries often foster the creation of unions to care for their needs. Public sector and white-collar employee unions are recent examples. SORWUC and its Local No. 2 is an obvious example....

In conclusion, the Board has wrestled with the fundamental dilemma of the competing functions of the appropriate bargaining unit concept and its application in this case. We have decided that the single branch location of the Commerce encompasses employees with a community of interest and is an appropriate bargaining unit.

* * * * *

After the above decision, the union continued to organize bank branches for several months. In 1977 it made twenty-six more applications for branch certification in British Columbia and Saskatchewan, and was successful in sixteen. By the summer of 1978, however, it had withdrawn from bargaining for the vast majority of its units. By 1980, it had withdrawn entirely, and had lost all of its certifications.

What caused this turn of events? The banks had waged strong campaigns against unionization, to the extent of committing many unfair labour practices. Although the union tried to bargain with the banks on a multi-branch basis, the banks refused, pointing out that the union had been certified only on a branch-by-branch basis and was therefore entitled only to require branch-by-branch bargaining. This tactic stretched the union's resources to the breaking point. The banks also announced that their annual across-the-board pay increases would thereafter apply only to non-union branches. The Canada board initially dismissed the union's complaint that this was an unfair labour practice aimed at further undermining its already declining support (*Bank of Nova Scotia, Vancouver Heights Branch*, [1978] 2 CLRBR 181). The board reversed that decision a year later. However, the union had failed to conclude any collective agreements that would have improved terms and conditions, and it was unwilling to risk calling a strike. This led to its withdrawal from bargaining, and to requests for decertification. Other unions that subsequently attempted to organize in the banking sector were also unable to win better wages or benefits than those at non-unionized branches.

In the above excerpt, Elizabeth Lennon concluded that there were three reasons why the unions largely failed in their attempts to organize the banks. First, the small numbers of staff in each branch-based bargaining unit and the large number of such potential units meant that organizing and bargaining costs were huge. Second, the highly centralized nature of the banks and the enormous disparity between their bargaining power and that of a single-branch employee unit made it easy for them to resist giving unionized branches any wage increases and benefits not given to non-unionized employees. Finally, frequent transfer of personnel between branches, and high rates of staff turnover, often resulted in the swift disappearance of the initial majority that supported the union, and this led to pressure for decertification.

A more recent effort to unionize bank branches led to the following decision of the Canada Industrial Relations Board.

United Steelworkers of America v TD Canada Trust in the Greater City of Sudbury, 2005 CIRB 316

Michele A. Pineau, Vice-Chair; Laraine C. Singler and Alan D. Levy, Members.

I—The Application

[1] This is an application for certification filed by the United Steelworkers of America (the Steelworkers or the union) pursuant to section 24 of the *Canada Labour Code (Part I—Labour Relations)* (the Code) for a bargaining unit of all employees working in retail personal financial services at TD Canada Trust (TD or the employer) in Greater Sudbury, in the Province of Ontario. The bargaining unit scope being sought comprises eight branches and totals 111 employees....

[2] TD opposes the scope as applied for by the Steelworkers on the basis that the appropriate bargaining unit should be on a branch by branch basis. TD's submission is that the Board should determine that six bargaining units are appropriate for collective bargaining purposes....

II—The Parties' Submissions

[5] The parties' positions regarding the appropriateness of the bargaining unit are based on the following arguments:

a) Geographical Scope:
[6] In support of a single bargaining unit being appropriate, the Steelworkers submit that while the Greater Sudbury region comprises a wide area, the farthest branches to be included in this unit are no more than one hour's drive from each other. Moreover, the Board has in the past accepted the notion of a "cluster" bargaining units and certified single, multi-branch and municipality-wide bargaining units.

[7] TD argues that the Board has historically favoured single branch bargaining units. It states that Levack, Lively and Copper Cliff are separate communities outside

the City of Sudbury with separate individual and community interests. Apparently, the two sub-branches have specific local characteristics that would make them inappropriate for inclusion together in the same bargaining unit. TD points out that the branches of Greater Sudbury sought for inclusion are only one component of its "Northern Lights District" which comprises a total of 19 branches in various communities in the east-northern region of Ontario. Splitting this region as proposed by the union would neither make sense nor be appropriate.

b) The Business Unit and Operational Structure:

[8] The Steelworkers take the position that TD's arguments regarding different business units, branch levels, peer groups and operational structures do not factor, ultimately, into the determination of an appropriate bargaining unit.

[9] TD submits that the Board should consider the differences between the branches on a variety of fronts, including volume of business, mix of types of business, staff size, hours of operation, overall size, complexity and operational structure. TD emphasizes that the eight branches have different revenue targets with each location designed to serve separate and specific populations.

c) The Wishes of Employees:

[10] The Steelworkers submits that membership evidence supports the desire of the majority of this group of employees to be represented as a unit by the Steelworkers as their agent in collective bargaining.

[11] TD contends that not all the wishes or concerns of employees in every branch can be properly addressed in a single bargaining unit. For example the needs and wishes of employees in smaller branches could be significantly different from those in larger branches and potentially not realized if the bargaining unit scope is not tailored to the practical reality of the work environments.

d) Community of Interest:

[12] The Steelworkers submit that the classifications that are sought for inclusion in the bargaining unit have the same generic job descriptions in all the branches and that the employees perform the same duties, which speaks to the community of interest for them all.

[13] TD argues that the significant geographical distances between the branches, makes the interests of employees local to each branch. The independent and unique organizational, administrative and operational structure of each branch would support its position. . . .

[18] Since the principles that apply to decisions to certify bargaining units are now well established, it is not the Board's normal practice to issue reasons to explain its findings as such applications have largely become routine matters. However, the issues raised in this matter have not been addressed since the 1980's and it is appropriate here to refresh the principles that have applied to the banking industry.

V—Analysis and Decision

[19] The following provisions of the *Code* governing applications for certification are relevant to this application:

24. (1) A trade union seeking to be certified as the bargaining agent for a unit that the trade union considers constitutes a unit appropriate for collective bargaining may, subject to this section and any regulations made by the Board under paragraph 15(e), apply to the Board for certification as the bargaining agent for the unit.

28. Where the Board
(a) has received from a trade union an application for certification as the bargaining agent for a unit,
(b) has determined the unit that constitutes a unit appropriate for collective bargaining, and
(c) is satisfied that, as of the date of the filing of the application or of such other date as the Board considers appropriate, a majority of the employees in the unit wish to have the trade union represent them as their bargaining agent, the Board shall subject to this Part, certify the trade union making the application as the bargaining agent for the bargaining unit.

29. (1) The Board may, in any case, for the purpose of satisfying itself as to whether employees in a unit wish to have a particular trade union represent them as their bargaining agent, order that a representation vote be taken among the employees in the unit.

[20] As may be seen by the wording of section 24, the union has the freedom of defining the bargaining unit as it considers appropriate. The Board's role is to decide (i) whether the unit constitutes a unit appropriate for collective bargaining, and (ii) whether a majority of employees in the unit wish to have the trade union represent them as their bargaining agent.

[21] As the Board has stated on countless occasions, it is not required to define the most appropriate bargaining unit, but a unit appropriate for collective bargaining. The appropriateness of a bargaining unit is a matter of fact which rests on whether the bargaining agent is able to define a sufficient community of interest among the employees it seeks to represent to justify certifying such a bargaining unit. In essence, this determination involves a consideration of whether the employees share an appropriate structure of working conditions within the organization of the workplace.

Where employees are unorganized, the objective is to provide them with a meaningful opportunity to participate in collective bargaining.... The Board has also previously stated that in determining the appropriate bargaining unit, it may rely on past practice and conditions within the same or similar industries, but its hands are not tied by previous certifications. Each case is treated according to its particular facts....

[22] In *National Bank of Canada* (1985), 58 di 94, the Canada Labour Relations Board (CLRB), considered the issue of the appropriateness of certifying what it characterized as a "cluster" or geographical unit rather than a "city" unit. The Board noted that chartered banks have quite diverse structures, but rejected the notion that the "splinter" or individual branch rule applied by the National Labour Relations Board in the United States should prevail in Canada or that bargaining units should be configured according to a bank's administrative structures. Thus the Board found that a unit consisting of all branches in the Rimouski area constituted an appropriate unit. The Board also found that there was no need for the union to demonstrate majority support at each branch in

order to be certified for a cluster of branches. As well, in *Bank of Montreal, Sherbrooke, Quebec* (1986), 68 di 67 (CLRB no. 604), the CLRB found that a unit of all employees in the city of Sherbrooke to be an appropriate bargaining unit.

[23] In both these decisions, the Board recognized that following a history of certification of individual branches, unions began to break new ground by applying for larger units. In *Bank of Montreal, Sherbrooke, Quebec, supra* the Board restated its policy that "in determining that an individual branch was an appropriate unit, it never said that it was the only unit of bank employees appropriate for collective bargaining."

[24] In *National Bank of Canada, supra*, the Board stated the following principles as they apply to the banking industry:

> All labour boards in Canada have more or less abundantly written about the criteria to be applied in determining the appropriateness of a bargaining unit; certainly this Board has done so.
>
> This Board established the extreme limits of its discretion in this area in a fairly formal manner:
> 1. It is not required to determine the ideal unit.
> 2. There may be more than one appropriate unit, successively over time or at the same time.
> 3. It is not bound by any earlier finding, and it may change any such determination.
>
> It will not always be possible to determine the most appropriate unit, for a whole hose of reasons, the most important of which is undoubtedly that to do so would be to deprive a group of employees of their freedom to join the organization of their choice (section 110 of the *Code*).
>
> Generally speaking, ideal units, for reasons that have already been set out in a long line of cases, are those units that group the most employees possible. But this is not always possible, and is certainly not possible in the Canadian banking industry, with its own peculiar structure, as we have described in these reasons. It might never be possible to do this....
>
> One unit may be appropriate for the branches, and another unit for a data centre within the same bank, at the same time. One appropriate unit for one kind of branch could be joined by another different appropriate branch unit, and the two could coexist....
>
> This also makes it essential that we reject the concept of *stare decisis* in the exercise of this discretion by labour boards. A board must take into account developments and new needs in the field, and cannot be bound by an earlier determination if it is to respond rapidly and satisfactorily to the changes occurring in modern business.
>
> This Board has said before, and still believes, that it must take into account the employer's administrative structures, so long as by doing so it does not nullify the employees' right to freely choose an association.

[25] The Board finds that the facts submitted by TD in support of its position that individual branches with their sub-branches are appropriate units are not persuasive. It may be that the business at some branches is higher in deposits than others or that each branch has its own financial targets, performance incentive targets or sales revenue goals; however, this has no impact on the organization of the bargaining unit. How employee satisfaction or customer satisfaction is measured is not relevant to the community of interest of employees within the bargaining unit.

[26] Variances of hours of operation or shift schedules for the purposes of breaks and lunch or the availability of discretionary recreational or reward funds can certainly be addressed within the context of collective bargaining. The number of managers, the different reporting relationships or management duties within given branches is relevant to the administrative structure of the bank, but as stated earlier, is not decisive in how bargaining units are to be configured.

[27] Of greater relevance is the fact that the employees work in a general geographical area where the municipalities are proximate to each other. The 11 other branches that comprise the Northern Lights District are considerably further than the eight branches proposed for inclusion in the bargaining unit. The City of Greater Sudbury is the financial centre for northeastern Ontario and it is not disputed that the branches proposed for inclusion serve the same customer base. TD's products and services are available at all these branches. The fact that some branches may have a more rural base than others may affect the bank's clientele, but does not generally affect employees' working conditions. While there may be differences between branches, operating procedures and levels of service are standardized for all TD's customers.

[28] The volume of business does not fundamentally change the basic job descriptions and classifications since as these are similar, if not identical, regardless of the branch. The volume of business may determine whether a job classification exists at a particular branch and the number of employees filling such job classifications. Variations in job duties (generalists vs. specialists) because of branch size do not impact the general structure of employees' working conditions. The salary ranges that apply to job classifications are consistent between branches. Employee mobility between branches is not an issue since employees apparently enjoy access to the same job opportunities. The same human resource policies, bonus incentive plan, health, welfare and insurance and vacation benefits apply to all. While hiring and training practices may not be uniform between branches, such issues can be addressed within the collective bargaining context. Consequently, in spite of some minor differences, the working conditions of employees at the 8 branches sought for inclusion in the bargaining unit are sufficiently similar for the Board to decide that there should be a single bargaining unit.

[29] TD's submission that a single bargaining unit may be contrary to employee wishes is not supported by the evidence. Whether from smaller or larger branches, employees have elected, as it is their right to do so, to be represented by a single bargaining agent. To the extent that the Board determines that a unit is appropriate for collective bargaining, the employer has no say in respect of the employees' wishes. Bargaining units are not configured to accommodate the employer's administrative structure, but in view of giving employees access to collective bargaining rights.

[30] A number of employees filed letters of concern with the Board with respect to this application. In its submissions, the employer also raised the issue that there had been coercion and intimidation during the union's certification campaign, but did not provide the union with its allegations. The Board's Investigating Officer conducted interviews of a random sample of employees and filed a confidential report of these interviews for the Board's consideration. Upon review of the employee letters and the

confidential report, the Board has concluded there was no coercion or intimidation of employees associated with the union's membership campaign....

[31] There is one further point that should be addressed. In certification proceedings, the wishes of employees, including their motives for joining a union are not the employer's concern. Any disquiet about undue influence or coercion into signing membership concerns should be brought to the Board's attention by the employees themselves. Under section 96 of the *Code*, such allegations are within the Board's mandate to adjudicate and no useful purpose is served by the employer raising such an issue in an attempt to oppose an application for certification....

[36] This panel of the Board finds it appropriate to follow the policy established by the CLRB in *National Bank of Canada, supra*, whereby there is no need for the union to demonstrate majority support of each branch in order to be certified.

[37] In this case, the Board is satisfied that the Steelworkers have the support of the majority of employees within the bargaining unit and, accordingly, certifies them to represent a bargaining unit of employees to be described as follows:

> all employees of TD Canada Trust in the City of Greater Sudbury, save and except for managers and persons above the rank of manager and employees in the Business Banking and Insurance Group.

Even within single-jurisdiction, single-employer enterprises, highly particularistic units may be certified. In a university, for example, there may be separate units for full-time library staff, part-time library staff, electricians, carpenters, machinists, operating engineers, stagehands, security guards, plumbers, sheet metal workers, typesetters, day care workers, faculty, office staff, and teaching assistants. In hospitals, labour boards have segregated service employees, technicians, nurses, security guards, and operating engineers into separate units. In the mining industry, each mining property is generally recognized as a separate bargaining unit.

Whatever the deficiencies of single-branch or single-plant units in terms of employee bargaining power vis-à-vis a multi-location employer, unions often seek certification for such units because they may be easier to organize. In *Michelin Tires (Canada) Ltd*, excerpted below, the company had two plants in Nova Scotia—in Granton and Bridgewater—250 kilometres apart. The Nova Scotia Labour Relations Board followed the reasoning in the SORWUC case, above, in holding that a unit comprising only the employees at the Granton plant was appropriate. The board rejected Michelin's argument that the only appropriate unit would comprise both plants. The interest in allowing employees to unionize in the first place favoured the conclusion that Granton was an appropriate unit on its own.

United Rubber, Cork, Linoleum & Plastic Workers of America, Local 1028 v Michelin Tires (Canada) Ltd, [1979] 3 CLRBR 429 at 440–41

> It is undeniable that there is a sacrifice of stability and the likelihood of a strike is increased somewhat by creating a potential for two separate bargaining units. The Board accepts that a strike at one plant would inevitably bring a halt to work at the other. We do not belittle the importance of this consideration, but, simply, have concluded that the other factors favouring Granton as a separate bargaining unit are overriding. While the interdependence

of the Granton and Bridgewater plants is physically demonstrable to a somewhat unusual degree, it is not uncommon for separate operations of the same employer to be heavily dependent on one another in an economic sense. Thus a fish plant cannot operate without supplies of fish and a retail outlet cannot operate if there are no shipments from the warehouse. Nobody can fail to be aware of how dependent economic units in today's world are on each other, even where they are not owned by the same employer, but these facts of economic life have never been held to dictate single province-wide bargaining units.

No case was cited to us and we know of none in Nova Scotia where a unit of, essentially, all employees at a single plant has been held not to be appropriate.

* * * * *

Michelin, which never made a secret of its desire to remain union-free, found a more sympathetic ear in the provincial legislature, which passed section 24A (now section 26) of the *Trade Union Act*, commonly known as the Michelin Amendment, to overturn the board's decision. Under section 26, when an employer operating interdependent manufacturing locations so requests, the board must find that the appropriate unit is one that combines employees from all of the locations.

Brian Langille, "The Michelin Amendment in Context" (1981) 6 *Dalhousie Law Journal* 523 at 546–52

[D]epending upon one's view of the motives underlying [the Michelin Amendment], it either makes a serious and unnecessary error in reconciling the tension between the two functions of bargaining units, or recognizes that tension and exploits it in order to render organization extremely difficult. The Michelin Amendment, and the Labour Relations Board's order made pursuant to it declare that the appropriate unit consists of both the Granton and Bridgewater plants. If we assume that the purpose of the amendment and the link between it and jobs and development is that industry will be attracted to the province because of the stable (broad base) bargaining structures created by the labour relations board's bargaining unit orders, then it seems clear that the legislation has struck the balance between the conflicting tensions in bargaining unit theory totally in favour of long-term industrial relations stability at the expense of the other value at stake, the ability to organize at all....

This error may be an unnecessary one. Recent developments in bargaining unit determination in British Columbia demonstrate that it may be possible to reconcile the two functions of a bargaining unit in a most interesting way. It may be possible to both ensure that organization takes place and a broad based and stable bargaining structure results for collective bargaining purposes. It may be possible to have your cake and eat it too. How is this achieved?

In *Amon Investments Limited* (1978) B.C.L.R.B. No. 39/78, the employer had 13 locations within Victoria and Vancouver. The union applied for a unit at one location. The employer, of course, urged that the appropriate unit was one consisting of all thirteen locations, relying on the reasons set out in the *Insurance Corporation of British Columbia* [1974] 1 Can. L.R.B.R. 403, case favouring large units and stable unfragmented bargaining relationships. The union [argued] ... that a single location was appropriate in order to permit collective bargaining to take place. After reviewing the evidence and the countervailing pressures, the Board concluded that a single location was an appropriate unit but went on to add the following crucial qualification:

> Any union other than the [Applicant] seeking to represent employees of this Employer will be required to gain the support of those employees already represented by the [Applicant]. Further certification applications received from the [Applicant] (and there is one pending at this time) will, if the union has the required support, be disposed of by enlarging the existing unit rather than creating a new additional unit.
>
> Our decision to uphold the present certification, subject to the proviso that future organization of the employees must be accomplished by a variance of the presently certified unit, serves to allow the employees who now desire collective representation to exercise their rights and, at the same time, accommodate the employer's concerns.

What I refer to as the '*Amon* Principle' in my view successfully achieves a reconciliation of the conflicting purposes of the bargaining unit. It enables organization to take place while at the same time ensuring that an unfragmented and thus stable and broad base bargaining structure results in the long run....

If the legislature has determined that long-term stable and broad base bargaining structures are crucial in multi-location manufacturing plants, then it seems to me that the '*Amon* Principle' could profitably be invoked to ensure that that end is achieved without totally ignoring the other function of bargaining unit determination.

But there is one feature of the Michelin case which separates it and makes it a more difficult case than those which we have been discussing. The overwhelming majority of cases involving multi-location employers involve retail chains, fast food outlets, and banks. There is little jurisprudence concerning the manufacturing industry. But more especially there is little jurisprudence on functionally interdependent operations. The chain store, fast food outlet and bank cases are distinguishable because the locations there, although they may be dependent upon other parts of the employer's organization to continue to operate, are not functionally interdependent. The operations of Michelin Tire's two plants in Nova Scotia are unquestionably interdependent as was explained by the Nova Scotia Labour Relations Board....

The thrust of these discussions is that because of the Board's interest in long range industrial stability, functional interdependence is an important element in unit determination. Certifying separately a number of units which are functionally interdependent would lead to instability. Although not well articulated in the House of Assembly Debates, Michelin Tire itself took this argument one step further. It argued that because of functional interdependence a fundamental question of democracy arose in the attempted unionization of Michelin's plants. The focus was not upon the long term but upon the present. The argument was not based upon industrial stability in the future but rather upon a present question of fairness. Because a strike at Granton would put employees at Bridgewater out of work, it would be undemocratic to allow only those employees at Granton to vote upon a decision which would have such an impact on employees at both plants. In abstract form there is certainly merit in this contention. However, there are several problems with this contention as well. First, functional interdependence is pervasive in modern industrial society and crosses employer lines....

Secondly, there is a fundamental problem with this argument from democracy in that it too ignores the basic dilemma faced by labour relations boards in unit determinations. While in some sense it might seem abstractly more democratic to consult all employees at the outset, this ignores the real pragmatic difficulties confronting trade unions in organizing very large bargaining units, especially in the face of an organized employer campaign against unionization. The abstract appeal to the merits of democracy rings very hollow where there is no real equal opportunity to convey information and to consult all sides of the question. This has particular relevance in Michelin's case where the no solicitation rule is still in force. . . . It seems to me that the labour relations boards in striking the balance that they have achieved between the two functions of the bargaining unit are seeking to ensure a fairer degree of political equality.

It also seems to me that the '*Amon* Principle' also removes the potency of the argument from democracy. In the end all are consulted and in a meaningful manner without the sacrifice of long term stability.

[Reprinted by permission.]

6:240 Labour Relations Board Powers to Amend the Scope of the Bargaining Unit Post-certification

Given the tension, discussed above, between the effects of bargaining unit scope on the organizing process on the one hand, and the bargaining process on the other, one way to address this tension is to allow for amendment to the scope of a given bargaining unit over time. This may also assist union efforts to organize certain sectors characterized by employers that maintain large numbers of small workplaces. However, not all jurisdictions allow for this, as discussed in the excerpt below.

C Michael Mitchell & John C Murray, *Changing Workplaces Review: Special Advisors' Interim Report* (Ontario: Ministry of Labour, July 2016) 85–87

> The OLRB has historically taken the position that after it has issued a certificate and the parties have entered into a collective agreement, the certificate is "spent" and the OLRB has no general jurisdiction to reconsider or revise it, except where specifically authorized by the Act. Thus, with minor exceptions, as bargaining units are added over time, the only way to change the configuration of bargaining units now is for parties to voluntarily agree to changes. While the parties are free to expand or to reduce the scope of bargaining units, it is an unfair labour practice to take such issues to impasse (i.e., to make such a dispute the subject of a strike or lock-out). This is an effective bar to changing the bargaining unit structure where one party resists it.
>
> The issue, therefore, is whether there ought to be an explicit power to revise, amend and consolidate bargaining units for the rationalization or modernization of bargaining unit structures in circumstances where the original bargaining structure is no longer appropriate, where bargaining units are overly fragmented, or for other industrial relations reasons.
>
> The power to revise and revamp bargaining units involves not only the issue of the rationalization and modernization of bargaining unit structures, but also the possible

tension and interplay between organizing and bargaining in areas of the economy that have been traditionally difficult to organize, such as where employers have many smaller retail locations, in which cases it may only be possible to organize in smaller units. However, a small unit is likely to have little bargaining power; viable, effective and stable bargaining may be possible only where there is a larger unit. If units can be organized on a smaller basis and then consolidated afterwards, this could make collective bargaining in those industries viable....

Other Jurisdictions

It appears that labour boards have an express, general power to redefine bargaining units (which could include consolidating existing units) in British Columbia, Alberta, New Brunswick, Newfoundland and Labrador, Prince Edward Island, Nova Scotia, and the federal jurisdiction.

The test for applications to redefine bargaining units varies among jurisdictions. For example, the power of the federal labour relations board to consolidate bargaining units was previously quite broad until the Sims Task Force recommended, and Parliament accepted, that bargaining unit reviews should be restricted to situations where there are serious problems with bargaining unit structures, barring which, the employees' choice of bargaining agent should prevail. The *Canada Labour Code* was subsequently amended in 1999 to provide that, in order for a review to take place, the Board must now be satisfied that the existing bargaining unit structures are no longer appropriate for collective bargaining.

Even if the corresponding labour legislation does not expressly provide the power to amend a bargaining unit, some labour relations boards may modify the bargaining unit or certification order pursuant to their general powers. The OLRB, however, has maintained consistently that it does not have the jurisdiction to do so.

[© Queen's Printer for Ontario, 2016. Reproduced with permission.]

* * * * *

6:300   DETERMINING EMPLOYEE SUPPORT

The certification process is built around the concept that the choice of whether or not to have collective bargaining is given to the majority of employees in the bargaining unit. Nonetheless, there are divergences in how the presence or absence of majority support is assessed.

Across North America there are basically four models for determining whether most of the employees in a bargaining unit wish to be represented by a trade union. In the United States there is a representation vote in every case, preceded by a fairly long campaign in which the employer is allowed to be a full participant. In Canada, various approaches have been used in an effort to limit the opportunity for unfair labour practices by employers or undue influence on employees. The three Canadian models are:

1) a quick vote in every case;

2) primary reliance on membership evidence (generally in the form of signed membership application cards), with a brief period after the certification application is filed to allow for change-of-heart petitions; and
3) primary reliance on membership evidence as of the date of application.

Nova Scotia pioneered the quick-vote method. Under section 25 of that province's *Trade Union Act*, a vote is normally held within five days of the filing of an application for certification. The rationale for the quick vote is that it has the perceived reliability of a secret-ballot vote but reduces the time in which the employer may bring pressure on employees. In 1995, Ontario followed Nova Scotia's lead, providing for a vote in every case (other than in the construction industry, in which certification by membership "card-check" is still available) within five days of application unless the OLRB directs otherwise. British Columbia requires a vote to be held in every case, within ten days of the application, unless the vote is to be held by mail, in which case the board has the discretion to set the length of time. Section 32(1)(d) of the Alberta *Labour Relations Code* also requires a vote in every case, with no legislative stipulation on timing, although votes are typically held within two weeks of application. Since 2008, the Saskatchewan *Trade Union Act* (subsequently section 6(12) of *The Saskatchewan Employment Act*) has required a vote in every case, with no time limit specified. In 2017, the federal Bill C-4 restored the longstanding "card-check" mechanism that had been removed from the *Canada Labour Code* in 2015. In November 2016, section 40 of the Manitoba *Labour Relations Act* was revised to impose a mandatory vote in every case.

In other Canadian jurisdictions, votes are possible but are not required. The procedures under the *Canada Labour Code* are premised on the notion that "petitions" reflecting a change of heart on the part of employees are inherently suspect, even if they are not proven to have been inspired by the employer. In general, under the *Canada Labour Code*, such petitions are taken into account only if it is alleged that there was something improper in how the union obtained its membership evidence. Normally, a union is certified if its membership evidence shows that it had majority support at the date of application. The federal Board may also choose a date preceding the date of application if it concludes that employer interference caused the union to lose majority support shortly before the application was brought.

The following readings discuss the merits and effects of different ways of determining the level of employee support for unionization.

Paul Weiler, "Promises to Keep: Securing Workers' Rights to Self-Organization under the NLRA" (1983) 96 *Harvard Law Review* 1769 at 1775–78 and 1808–16

> American labor law has created an elaborate formal procedure for the representation contest. In order to make a sufficient showing of interest for a certification application to the NLRB a trade union must convince at least 30% of the employees in a unit to sign membership or authorization cards. The Board investigates the union's petition, defines the scope of the appropriate bargaining unit, decides whether the conditions for a valid election have been satisfied, and, if they have, conducts a secret ballot vote among the eligible employees. Before the election, both union and employer vigorously campaign in an effort to influence the vote; an extensive battery of legal regulations is aimed at preventing any improper interference with the employees' choice. Assuming that its

'laboratory conditions' for an informed and unrestrained verdict have been satisfied, the Board will either certify the victorious union as the exclusive bargaining representative for the employees (and impose on the employer a corresponding duty to bargain), or, if the union has lost, bar any further elections in the unit for at least twelve months.

In their halcyon days of the early 1940s, American unions fared very well under the formal certification procedure of the NLRA; elections involved more than one million eligible voters annually, and trade unions won approximately 80% of those elections. Union success rates were still high in 1950; but ... there has been a steady and stark decline ever since, both in the union victory rate in certification elections (from 74% in 1950 to 48% in 1980) and, even more dramatically, in the percentage of voters included in union victories (from 85% to 37%). The result of these trends is that the number of employees successfully organized each year has dropped from 750,000 to fewer than 200,000. In 1950, new certifications raised the level of union representation in the private sector work force by 1.92%; in 1980, the entire organizational effort of American unions under the NLRA increased union density by a near-infinitesimal 0.24%, a rate just one-eighth that of thirty years earlier (and one that was far outstripped by natural attrition from job loss in unionized firms). ...

To a dispassionate observer, the simplest explanation for the drop in the union victory rate would be that it represents a corresponding drop in interest in collective bargaining among American workers. My thesis, however, is that the decline in union success in representation campaigns is in large part attributable to deficiencies in the law: evidence suggests that the current certification procedure does not effectively insulate employees from the kinds of coercive anti-union employer tactics that the NLRA was supposed to eliminate.

It is the time lag between the filing of a representation petition and the vote, usually about two months, that gives the employer the opportunity to attempt to turn its workers against the union. Typically, the firm will mount a vigorous campaign to fend off the threat of collective bargaining. It will emphasize to its workers how risky and troubled life might be in the uncharted world of collective bargaining: the firm might have to tighten up its supervisory and personnel practices and reconsider existing, expensive special benefits; the union would likely demand hefty dues, fines, and assessments, and might take the employees out on a long and costly strike with no guarantee that there would be jobs at the end if replacements had been hired in the meantime; if labor costs and labor unrest became too great, the employer might have to relocate.

The employees might well dismiss this message as mere bluffing were it not that a determined anti-union employer has at its disposal a potent weapon with which to demonstrate its power over the lives of its employees: the dismissal of selected union activists, in violation of section 8(a)(3) of the NLRA. Dismissal has the immediate effect of rendering these union supporters unable to vote—a consequence that by itself might tip the balance in a close election—and also excludes the discharged employees from the plant, the setting in which they could have campaigned most effectively among their fellow employees. Even more importantly, the dismissal of key union adherents gives a chilling edge to the warning that union representation is likely to be more trouble for the employees than it is worth.

CHAPTER 6: THE ACQUISITION AND TERMINATION OF BARGAINING RIGHTS

Perhaps the most remarkable phenomenon in the representation process in the past quarter-century has been an astronomical increase in unfair labor practices by employers....

The purpose of a representation system, of course, is neither to chalk up a high union victory rate in certification drives nor to channel as many employees as possible into unions. Rather, it is to nurture and protect employee freedom of choice with respect to collective bargaining. Reflection on the differences between the legal techniques used by the United States and Canada to achieve this purpose reveals the crucial assumptions of the American model.

The assumption of the Canadian scheme is that the labor board simply licenses unions to bargain on behalf of employees. Thus, although the system includes a number of safeguards designed to ensure that the union card majority reflects actual employee wishes, its primary objective is a smooth-running administrative procedure that, without much fanfare, will get the parties to the negotiating table as quickly as possible.

By contrast, an ingrained premise of the American model is that certification confers on the trade union a quasi-governmental authority over the employees and therefore requires a procedure comparable to that by which a government is chosen.... This view is misleading insofar as it equates the limited role of the union with the role of a legislative body. A trade union does not govern the employees in the unit. Unlike an elected legislature, the union does not have the authority to prescribe conditions in the workplace. All it can do is negotiate with the employer to try to obtain some of the improvements that the union promised the employees in the representation campaign. Only if a contract is achieved will there be any tangible effects on the employees—changes in the distribution of the compensation package, union control over the prosecution of grievances, a union security clause, and so on. But achieving a first contract is a very different challenge for the union from that of simply obtaining certification.

The certification of a union in no way guarantees that the employees will be able to secure a collective bargaining agreement, even if the union has satisfied the most painstaking of representation procedures and won a secret ballot vote. Once the certification stage is passed, the guiding principle of the NLRA is freedom of contract. The employer is under no obligation to offer any tangible benefits to the union....

After administering a card-based system for five years [in British Columbia], I am satisfied that it not only rests on a more realistic appreciation of the tangible value of legal certification, but also permits a true reading of employees' sentiments about union representation. The system does, however, have one major drawback. Although both the union and the labor board may know that the union has the real support of the employees, the employer—who is prone to genuine self-deception on this score—often remains unconvinced on the basis of cards alone. A secret ballot vote has a symbolic value that a card check alone can never have. It clears the air of any doubts about the union's majority and also confers a measure of legitimacy on the union's bargaining authority, especially among minority pockets of employees who were never contacted in the initial organizational drive.

The Province of Nova Scotia has devised a procedure—the 'instant vote'—that achieves these values while still avoiding the trauma of the bitter representation battle. The Nova Scotia Labour Board must conduct an election no more than five days after it receives a certification petition. In this highly compressed interval, it is nearly impossible for the employer to mount a sustained offensive aimed at turning employee sentiments around through intimidation and discrimination....

[Copyright © 1983 by the Harvard Law Review Association.]

* * * * *

Taking Weiler's thesis as a starting point, various scholars have examined the relationship between union growth, union density, and the type of union certification procedure imposed by labour law. Some of the key findings suggested by this research are summarized below.

1) Fewer certification applications filed by unions
The imposition of a mandatory vote (in place of automatic certification) has been found to be associated with significant declines in the number of union organizing attempts that result in applications for certification being filed. See Felice Martinello, "Mr. Harris, Mr. Rae, and Union Activity in Ontario" (2000) 26 *Canadian Public Policy* 17 at 26; Timothy J Bartkiw, "Manufacturing Descent? Labour Law and Union Organizing in the Province of Ontario" (2008) 34:1 *Canadian Public Policy* 111.

2) Shifts in types of applications filed and certified
Introduction of the mandatory vote in Ontario was associated with lower levels of organizing activity and lower levels of success in organizing more vulnerable employee groups, including part-time workers, workers in hard-to-organize industries, private sector workers, and smaller units. See Sara Slinn, "An Analysis of the Effects on Parties' Unionization Decisions of the Choice of Union Representation Procedure: The Strategic Dynamic Certification Model" (2005) 43 *Osgoode Hall Law Journal* 407 at 436–38.

3) Lower certification success rate
Several studies have concluded that the introduction of mandatory representation elections has itself had a significant negative effect on certification success rates, with estimated declines in success rates ranging from 9 to 19 percentage points. See Chris Riddell, "Union Certification Success Under Voting Versus Card-Check Procedures: Evidence from British Columbia, 1978–1998" (2004) 57 *Industrial & Labor Relations Review* 493; Sara Slinn, "An Empirical Analysis of the Effects of the Change from Card-Check to Mandatory Vote Certification" (2004) 11 *Canadian Labour and Employment Law Journal* 259 at Table 6; Felice Martinello, "Mr. Harris, Mr. Rae, and Union Activity in Ontario" (2000) 26 *Canadian Public Policy* 17 at 24; Susan Johnson, "Card Check or Mandatory Vote? How the Type of Union Recognition Procedure Affects Union Certification Success" (2002) *The Economic Journal* 344; and Timothy J Bartkiw, "Manufacturing Descent? Labour Law and Union Organizing in the Province of Ontario" (2008) 34:1 *Canadian Public Policy* 111.

4) More effective employer unfair labour practices
The study by Riddell referred to under the previous heading found that in British Columbia, employer unfair labour practices were about twice as effective at defeating union organizing

attempts under a mandatory vote system than under a card-based system, and that one-quarter of the approximately 19 percent reduction in certification application success associated with the vote system was due to such employer practices. However, some studies have also found that where a mandatory vote system was imposed, there was also a major decline in the volume of unfair labour practice complaints filed. This may reflect unions' assessment of the value of pursuing a complaint, especially if other legal reforms in certain contexts may have simultaneously expanded the scope of permissible employer behaviour, and/or reduced the scope of labour board remedies available to redress unfair labour practices. See Ron Lebi & Elizabeth Mitchell, "The Decline in Trade Union Certification in Ontario: The Case for Restoring Remedial Certification" (2003) 10 *Canadian Labour & Employment Law Journal* 473; Chris Riddell, "Union Certification Success Under Voting Versus Card-Check Procedures: Evidence from British Columbia, 1978–1998" (2004) 57 *Industrial & Labor Relations Review* 493; and Timothy J Bartkiw, "Manufacturing Descent? Labour Law and Union Organizing in the Province of Ontario" (2008) 34:1 *Canadian Public Policy* 111.

5) *The role of delay*
A key criticism of mandatory vote systems is that it takes longer for the certification application to be processed, thereby giving employers more time to influence employees. The "quick vote" is posed as a solution to this concern. Statutory provisions or board policies generally specify the maximum number of days that may pass between a certification application and a vote.

Research in British Columbia and Ontario has found that delay has a strong negative effect on the likelihood of certification. In Ontario between 1995 and 1998, when there was poor compliance with election time limits (15.8 percent of votes were delayed), a delayed election meant a 32 percent reduction in the odds of success. In British Columbia in 1986–1987, 25.5 percent of votes were delayed, and there was a 10 percent reduction in the likelihood of certification for every five days of delay. See Chris Riddell, Michele Campolieti, & Sara Slinn, "Labor Law Reform and the Role of Delay in Union Organizing: Empirical Evidence from Canada" (2007) 61 *Industrial & Labor Relations Review* 30.

6:400 TIMELINESS OF CERTIFICATION AND DECERTIFICATION APPLICATIONS ("OPEN SEASONS")

The basic principle with respect to the timeliness of a certification application is that a union may apply at any time to be certified as bargaining agent for a unit of employees who are not already covered by collective bargaining. However, Canadian labour relations statutes set out a number of important and often complex exceptions, commonly known as bars to certification, which vary considerably from jurisdiction to jurisdiction. Those bars are designed to balance the need for stability in a collective bargaining relationship with the employees' right to get rid of a bargaining agent with which they are unhappy, and with the employer's interest in not having its work force targeted by overly frequent certification campaigns.

Generally speaking, a union which failed in an earlier attempt to establish majority support in a particular bargaining unit, or withdrew a certification application either before or after a vote was held, is barred for a certain period (either by statute or by board practice) from applying again for certification for the same unit. Similarly, because it is unlawful to strike in order to obtain recognition, a board will often dismiss a certification application made with respect to employees who are engaging in an unlawful work stoppage, or will simply adjourn the application until the strike ends.

If the unit of employees in question is already represented by another union, there are tighter bars to a certification application by a rival union. To give newly certified unions a chance to get established, most labour relations statutes allow a union a ten or twelve-month period after certification in which to reach a collective agreement with the employer. During that period, other unions or dissident employees may not apply to displace the new bargaining agent. This bar may be extended by the advent of the statutory conciliation process or by a legal strike or lockout. Unions that have been voluntarily recognized generally enjoy less protection than certified unions during the early part of the collective bargaining relationship, to limit the risk of entrenchment of employer-influenced bargaining agents.

If the union concludes a collective agreement, an application to terminate its bargaining rights can still be brought by another union or by employees within the bargaining unit, but only during certain periods (informally called the "open season") — for example, in Ontario, during the last three months of the agreement's term and in British Columbia during the seventh or eighth month of each year. Additional open season periods arise each year in the case of very long collective agreements, or agreements which provide for automatic renewal.

A bargaining agent will be decertified, and any collective agreement it may have negotiated will be void, if it is established at any time that the certification was obtained by fraud. This type of challenge is more likely to be brought in jurisdictions that allow the assessment of support through a card system than in those where elections by secret ballot are always required.

In some jurisdictions, such as Ontario (except in its construction sector), statutory amendments in recent years have made it slightly easier for employees in the bargaining unit to apply for decertification by extending the length of the open season. Decertification applications by employees are, however, subject to the same timeliness requirements as decertification applications by rival unions. If a board is given evidence in a timely application that a certain percentage of employees in the unit no longer support the union, the board will generally order a decertification vote.

Statutes also typically provide that a union can also have its bargaining rights extinguished if it has abandoned them, for example, by failing for a long time to make efforts to negotiate, renew, or administer a collective agreement.

6:500 DECERTIFICATION APPLICATIONS

Interesting procedural issues may arise on decertification applications — issues which go well beyond the question of timing. They include the question of who may apply for decertification, who may cast a ballot in a decertification vote, and how labour relations boards ought to exercise the statutory discretion that is given to them in such cases.

Employees of Kelly's Ambulance (1982) Ltd and Canadian Union of Public Employees v Kelly's Ambulance (1982) Ltd, 19 August 1993 (NSLRB)

B. Archibald (ViceChair), A. R. Harrington, L. Wark, P. Wedge, and S. Whitehead

This case squarely raises the issue of whether replacement workers may apply to decertify a trade union during the course of a lockout. The basic facts are relatively simple. The Respondent Union was certified on April 16, 1991....

On September 4, 1992 the Employer locked out its employees. On February 22, 1993 the Applicants filed their application for revocation of certification.

Since the outset, relations between the parties have been tense. The dispute has made local headlines, the parties have been before this Board concerning complaints which were settled without a hearing, and this present application for revocation of certification is coupled with a complaint by the Respondent that the Employer has failed to bargain in good faith....

The present application for decertification is pursuant to Section 29(b) of the *Trade Union Act*. The section reads as follows:

> Where certification of a trade union as bargaining agent has been in effect for not less than twelve months and no collective agreement is in force, or where an application can be made pursuant to subsection (4) or subsection (5) of Section 23, and the Board is satisfied that
> (a) a significant number of members of the trade union allege that the trade union is not adequately fulfilling its responsibilities to the employees in the bargaining unit for which it was certified; or
> (b) the union no longer represents a majority of the employees in the unit,
>
> the Board upon application for revocation of certification may order the taking of a vote to determine the wishes of the employees in the unit concerning revocation of the existing certification and may revoke or confirm the certification in accordance with the result of the vote. 1972 c. 19, s. 27.

There was virtually no evidence brought forward by the Applicants concerning Section 29(a). The contention of the Applicants was that they form a majority of "the employees in the unit" and they no longer want the Union. Hence the application falls to be determined by interpreting the meaning of "an employee of the [bargaining] unit" under Section 29(b) of the Act. However, these words can only be given intelligent meaning by a purposive analysis which takes into account the context and framework of the Trade union Act as a whole....

The replacement driver/attendants take the view that because they are doing the work, they are "employees in the unit" for the purposes of the Trade Union Act and are therefore entitled to apply for decertification of the Union under section 29. Not surprisingly the Intervener agrees. Members of the Gould family [who own the employer] make no bones about the fact that they would like to be rid of the Union. Of course section 58(2) of the *Trade Union Act* states that nothing in the Act "shall be deemed to deprive an employer of his freedom to express his views so long as he does not use coercion, intimidation, threats, or undue influence." Moreover, the Employer was granted Intervener status and availed itself of the opportunity to participate in the hearings, since the actions of management representatives were said to constitute employer interference with the decertification process. Suffice it to say that we find that any allegations of employer interference with the present application by the replacement employees have not been proved. While the Gould family members are clearly sympathetic to the application, we are convinced that the impetus for the application comes from the Applicants, and in particular from the somewhat idiosyncratic motivations of Mr. Soward (who has since withdrawn from the proceeding subsequent to his having been discharged by the Employer). We are thus not moved to exercise any statutory discretion which might be available to the Board under section 29 to refuse a decertification on grounds of employer interference. The matter therefore stands to be decided simply upon the issue of whether replacement workers may apply for revocation of certification under the *Trade Union Act* during the course of a lockout.

The Respondent, of course, argues that replacement workers ought not to be seen as employees in the bargaining unit, and argues that to allow an application for decertification by replacement workers undermines the policy of the Act.

The legal status of replacement workers is a matter of some controversy in labour relations throughout North America, and different jurisdictions have adopted different legal rules concerning the various issues surrounding replacement workers... Most Canadian jurisdictions allow employers to hire replacements for striking or locked out workers in order to carry on business, just as striking or locked out employees may seek other employment to tide them over the period of strike or lockout.... In this way both sides may attempt to lessen the impact of the economic loss inflicted by the other in seeking to force the other to agree, and gain greater advantage for its own position.

The issue to be decided here is whether workers replacing unionized employees locked out during a labour dispute are "employees in the bargaining unit" with status under the *Trade Union Act* to decertify the union. The Applicants, with the approval of the Intervener in argument, assert that they are "employees" within the meaning of the Act. Section 2(1)(b) states in part: "'employee' means a person employed to do skilled or unskilled manual, clerical or technical work."

The Board, by virtue of its certification order, among other things accepted that ambulance driver attendants or E.M.A.'s are skilled or technical workers who qualify as employees under the Act. However, the recognition that the Applicants are employees of Kelly's Ambulance (1982) Ltd., with legal rights under their contract of employment, does not necessarily mean that such employees are full-time or regular part-time employees pursuant to the certification order of this Board, or that they are thus employees within the bargaining unit with procedural rights to decertify the union under section 29.

In order to maintain the coherence of collective bargaining, this Board's general practice in certification has been to certify bargaining units of "full-time and regular part-time employees" as "appropriate for collective bargaining" in accordance with the definition of "unit" in section 2(1)(x). It is the Board's view that full-time and regular part-time employees usually have the kind of "community of interest among employees" which is referred to in section 25(14) of the Act. This approach has generally meant that temporary or casual employees are excluded from the bargaining unit for a variety of reasons, including the fact that such employees have no longterm commitment to or status in the employer's organization which would give them the kind of "stake" or ongoing community of interest common to full-time or regular part-time employees.

Critical to an understanding of the resolution of this case is that locked out employees, like those on strike, maintain their status as employees in the bargaining unit throughout the strike or lockout. Section 14 of the Act states:

> No person ceases to be an employee within the meaning of this Act by reason only of his ceasing to work for his employer as the result of a lockout or strike or by reason only of dismissal by his employer contrary to this Act or to a collective agreement. 1972, c. 19, s. 13.

Moreover, since the employee who is striking or locked out was in the bargaining unit at the time the strike or lockout began, and is being represented by the certified bargaining agent for the purpose of collective bargaining under the Act, he or she must continue as a member of the bargaining unit during the course of the strike or lockout. Indeed, this proposition is so obvious that it was assumed in argument by all participants.

The consequences which flow from this proposition, however, are quite far reaching. If striking or locked out employees are members of the bargaining unit with statutory rights connected to their status as an employee, the logic of the Act must be to view replacement workers as temporary employees whose jobs terminate, at least in principle, at the end of the strike or lockout if, and/or when, the full-time or regular part-time employees return to work. It will be recalled that section 53(3) of the Act prohibits an employer from refusing to employ or continuing to employ or otherwise discriminate against any person in regard to employment or any condition of employment because the person has participated in a strike that is not prohibited by the Act or exercised any right under the Act.

The Board thus concludes that the Applicant replacement employees in this case are not members of the bargaining unit by virtue of the fact that they must, of necessity, be temporary or casual employees for the duration of the strike or lockout. The Board is fortified in its conclusions by the knowledge that this approach is also adopted in other Canadian jurisdictions. Early on, the Manitoba Queen's Bench found that striking workers were part of the bargaining unit under Manitoba legislation in *Re Brandon Packers Limited* (1960), 33 W.W.R. 58....

This approach has also been adopted in other Canadian jurisdictions, notably by the Canada Labour Relations Board....

As counsel for the Intervener rightly pointed out, not all jurisdictions have taken this approach. In Ontario, under older legislation, replacement workers were, under certain circumstances, given status within the bargaining unit for certain purposes.... However, even in the United States where replacement workers have been accorded permanent status when they replace workers who have gone on strike, workers who replace locked out employees are considered temporary workers.... Surely this must be right. Otherwise an unscrupulous employer could subvert the purposes of the Act by declaring a lockout and then hiring antiunion workers whom it could be certain would apply for decertification. The lockout would no longer be the Employer's most powerful weapon in the process of collective bargaining, but rather the first step in the process of stripping unionized employees of their collective bargaining rights under the *Trade Union Act*.

How are these principles to be applied in relation to the facts of this case? Full-time and regular part-time employees who, in the words adopted by the Canada Labour Relations Board in *Arthur T. Ecclestone supra*, "were employed on the day of the commencement of the strike and who still have an interest in the issue" are members of the bargaining unit for the purposes of determining whether the "union represents a majority of employees in the unit" pursuant to section 29 of the Act. On the evidence, ... the Board must conclude that the union represents a majority (that is, two of the three) full-time or regular part-time employees in the bargaining unit. Therefore, the Board, not being satisfied that the union no longer represents a majority of the employees in the unit, hereby dismisses the Application.

After a similar issue arose in *Canadian Association of Smelter and Allied Workers v Royal Oak Mines et al and British Columbia Federation of Labour* (1993), 21 CLRBR (2d) 55, the following provision (s 29(1.1)) was added to the *Canada Labour Code* by SC 1998, c 26, s 13:

> Any person who was not an employee in the bargaining unit on the date on which notice to bargain collectively was given, and was hired or assigned after that date to perform all or part of the duties of an employee in the bargaining unit on strike or locked out, is not an employee in the unit.

International Association of Machinists and Aerospace Workers and Courtesy Chrysler, 5 September 2001 (NSLRB) [*Courtesy Chrysler #1*]

Vice-Chair Bruce Archibald (for the Board):

31. Applications for revocation of certification, or decertification applications as they are more frequently known, are covered by section 29 of the *Trade Union Act*....

49. The real issue among the parties on the section 29 decertification application is the question of the interference by the Employer in the process, and whether there is evidence of such sufficient to vitiate the voluntariness of the vote. The Employer denied any knowledge of or involvement in the decertification process, and the Union acknowledged that it did not have any "smoking gun" evidence in the sense of directly influential statements from management or observations of managers' positive acts in support of the decertification application. However, the Union argues that it is apparent from the evidence of Mr. Chapman's activities that the Employer was giving its obvious, tacit support for the decertification in a fashion that could not be lost upon its employees.

50. This Board, like other labour relations boards across the country, requires that Employers adopt an attitude of strict neutrality in respect of applications for revocation of certification. Employees under section 13(a) of the *Trade Union Act* have a right to join a trade union, and by section 29 may rid themselves of one. However, the matter is for employees alone. Boards have and must respond seriously to employer interference in the rights of employees in this regard....

Moreover, the British Columbia jurisprudence makes clear that the proper test in the circumstances is an objective one:

> The test is an objective one, not subjective. It is sufficient that the conduct could have that effect on a reasonable person...

In other words, the question is whether there is conduct, either an act or omission, on the part of the Employer from which reasonable employees would infer employer support for the decertification, and which would likely have an impact on whether the vote expresses the "true wishes of employees in the unit." If this is the case, the Board must exercise its discretion under section 29 to determine whether it shall "revoke or confirm the certification in accordance with the result of the vote." Under the old Board practice, ... the Board might decide in the face of employer interference not to hold a vote. Under the new pre-hearing vote practice, the Board may determine not to count a vote which it concludes has been the subject of improper employer influence, and therefore does not represent a true reflection of the democratic will of the employees in the unit....

51. On the facts of this case, the critical matters in relation to the above jurisprudence in decertification cases are the activities of Scott Chapman and the Employer's response, or more properly, lack of response to them. Mr. Chapman claims to have acted independently of Employer influence. He says he doesn't like unions, didn't like the impact the unionization drive was having on the Employer's workplace, and feared what he understood to be a threat from the Union to force employees to accept the 17% roll-back....

It does indeed seem curious that Mr. Chapman, who claims merely to have looked up law firms in the telephone book, should have chanced upon a predominately employer-side labour relations law firm. The Board takes judicial notice of the contents of local telephone books for the last two years. The firm's yellow page ads and listings (unlike some other firms) make no mention of a labour relations specialization. Moreover, it may stretch credibility to think that a retired gentleman working for the Employer as a valet at $7.00 per hour would bankroll the Applicants' efforts. However, the Union did not subpoena Mr. Behrsin to check out the story, and the only evidence on the issue is from Mr. Chapman. The Board is not prepared to draw negative inferences merely from the Applicants' fortunate choice of excellent legal counsel, in the absence of clear evidence of Employer influence in this regard....

53. Despite the undoubtedly fine legal advice Mr. Chapman may have received, the Board concludes that Mr. Chapman's conduct failed to avoid certain legal pitfalls and the Employer gave tacit encouragement in these matters. The evidence shows that early in the game, Mr. Chapman did some decertification organizing on company time and company premises.... The Board's conclusion is that the Employer was giving its tacit support to Mr. Chapman's revocation efforts, and that this was obvious to all concerned.... He worked extra hours on a regular basis, sometimes paid and sometimes unpaid. He went to lunch regularly with the Service Manager, and was apparently singled out for assignment to pleasant tasks, such as vehicle deliveries. While it is obviously no sin to be a helpful, co-operative and enthusiastic employee, Mr. Chapman's status in this regard seemed particular. We believe he exaggerates his reports that employees could, like him, get personal time off whenever they wanted it, virtually without explanation. This was not the testimony of other witnesses. When combined with his unhindered and zealous

activities in the organization of the decertification on company time (if not always on company property) both Saturday and Monday, the only reasonable conclusion for the reasonable employee, as for the Board, was that Mr. Chapman was acting, and was seen to be acting, with management approval. This is not an attitude of strict neutrality, and it contravenes section 35 of the *Trade Union Act*....

With respect to the application for revocation of certification under section 29:

(1) The Board declares that the pre-hearing vote on the revocation is a nullity by virtue of the Employer's tacit support and influence for the reasons expressed in this decision, and the Board hereby confirms the certification in L.R.B. No.4796 dated April 5, 2000; and

(2) The Board, pursuant to section 78, orders a time bar of six months from the date of this decision, on any subsequent application by employees for revocation of certification, unless the Union formally signifies its intention to abandon its bargaining rights under the certification. In the event of such notification from the Union, the Board will receive an application under section 29 at an earlier date.

6:600 ALTERNATIVES TO THE *WAGNER ACT* MODEL

In its heyday from the 1940s to the 1960s, collective bargaining was premised on a paradigmatic form of employment—embracing semiskilled factory work, mining, construction, and transportation—in which workers generally filled specific, stable jobs, in large organizations. This stability enabled employees to claim a range of very important "job rights"—pay scales, promotion opportunities, layoff protection—based on their seniority and skills. Unions were often able to negotiate elaborate collective agreement language regulating the acquisition and exercise of such rights within each bargaining unit. Workers were prepared to support unions because unions were able to protect job rights.

Today, changes in technology, especially in information technology, have radically altered the means of production, the nature of work and employment, and management strategies. Machines can be more easily retooled to produce new products, so manufacturers are more able to implement "flexible production." Volatile consumer demand, and the increased expectation that demand will drive production, have persuaded manufacturers not to maintain large inventories but to develop networks of suppliers and contractors to provide components as needed—"just in time" production. This in turn allows for rapid expansion or contraction of production without having to invest in a plant, or in employees who may be standing idle as production fluctuates. The risks resulting from volatility are shifted to the suppliers, whose employees are not in the original bargaining unit and thus cannot benefit from the job rights negotiated by the union.

Changes in technology also permit corporations to control technical specifications and quality when the actual production takes place thousands of kilometres away—in Asia or Latin America, for example. Thus, unionized employers can reduce the amount of work actually done within the bargaining unit in order to cut labour costs. The knowledge that this exit option is available to employers puts great pressure on workers and their unions to lower their demands, and often to surrender job rights and economic benefits.

Aside from their power to engage in workplace fissuring, thereby externalizing work to other firms, perhaps in other countries, firms may additionally argue that workers must become more adaptable or flexible in order for the firm to take full advantage of changes in technology. Flexibility, employers say, is impaired by the old job rights, which are based on the premise that jobs can remain essentially the same for many years. And finally, because new technologies require a greater degree of technical sophistication on the part of workers, employers argue that learning which is derived from and tied to the performance of a given set of operations unique to the bargaining unit is less relevant than general knowledge and skills, which enable employees to perform a wider range of tasks and effectively operate new machinery.

All of these developments have, over time, helped to undermine not only the old system of bargaining based on job rights within large firms, but more generally have increasingly undermined the potentiality of collective bargaining for private sector workers under North American *Wagner Act* models of labour law that impose highly decentralized bargaining structures, with bargaining units defined only at the level of a single employer, with yet further potential limits to bargaining unit scope. Arguably, reforms that enable broader-based bargaining structures are required in order to enable collective bargaining, in one form or another, to take place in the "new" economy described above.

North American collective bargaining, being highly atomized and decentralized, has a tradition of autonomous and uncoordinated action. This aspect of our collective bargaining system is a key factor in why a large body of scholarship comparing different societies characterized by different "Varieties of Capitalism" refer to both Canada and the United States as "liberal market economies" (LMEs), while certain societies with more centralized forms of collective bargaining are typically considered to be "coordinated market economies" (CMEs). If Canada is currently a LME overall, many of its other related labour market institutions, as well as firms, unions, and government actors, might be highly challenged to adapt to new broader-based models of collective bargaining. The notion that collective bargaining processes and rights should be constructed so as to reach across organizational (let alone jurisdictional) boundaries, remains a daunting challenge for policy makers to come to terms with. In contrast, in some northern European economies that are considered to be CMEs, labour law enables more broadly based forms of collective bargaining in many contexts.

In the following sections, various potential alternatives to the dominant *Wagner Act* model are discussed.

6:610 Minority and Occupational Unionism

The readings in this section question the principles of majority rule and exclusivity of bargaining rights that underpin the *Wagner Act* model. Clyde Summers advocates allowing unions to play a role in representing pro-union minorities in particular workplaces. Roy Adams recommends the adoption in Canada of a variant of the minority unionism concept, in which existing *Wagner*-type legislation could be revised such that in addition to allowing for union certification based on exclusive-majoritarianism, as they do currently, statutes could also provide for certification based on the concept of a "most representative" union. Dorothy Sue Cobble evokes the pre-*Wagner* phenomenon of occupationally organized unions as a possible way to facilitate the organization of service sector workers.

Clyde Summers, "Unions without Majority: A Black Hole?" (1990) 66 *Chicago-Kent Law Review* 531 at 532–34, 539–40, 542–43, 545, and 547–48

Unions, by their focus on organization campaigns for the purpose of winning elections, have helped foster the assumption that a union without a majority have [sic] no significant role to play. The dominant, if not exclusive, emphasis in organizing is not to increase membership, but to obtain majority status. Indeed, during an organizational campaign employees are commonly not asked to join the union, but only to sign cards authorizing the union to represent them. The objective is to obtain the status of exclusive representative through voluntary recognition by the employer or through a Board election. If the union fails in this objective it commonly assumes that it has no continuing role except, perhaps, to try again another year. Unions, thereby, tacitly accept the Board's characterization that if they are not the exclusive representative they have no representation function. In the absence of a majority, the union is not 'present' in the plant....

When the union loses the election, it commonly abandons the field, seldom attempting to maintain a functioning organization in the plant, except where there is hope that the union can mount a winning campaign the next year. The union ceases to exist as an organization representing the interests of those who supported it, and leaves the local leaders in the plant who declared their support of the union to the tender mercies of the employer.... All that is left is a black hole.

In the reports and legislative debates, preceding the Wagner Act, the arguments for majority rule were made in the context of competing unions and the necessity that the majority union have exclusive authority to negotiate for all employers. The purpose of an election was to determine which, if any, union was to be given exclusive representation rights, thereby empowering it to represent non-consenting employees. There was no suggestion that a majority, by preferring individual bargaining, could deprive a minority of their right to bargain collectively for themselves through representatives of their own choosing.

Bargaining collectively with a non-majority union for its own members is not impracticable. Indeed, it is practiced, if not legally required, in almost every country which has a system of free collective bargaining. The American notion that an employer has no duty to bargain with a union until it has obtained a majority is unknown and unthinkable in most other countries. In those countries the collective agreement is legally binding only for union members; the employer remains free to provide more, less, or different benefits to non-members and to settle their grievances without the intervention by the non-majority union.

To be sure economic strength of a non-majority may not be great, and the employer might resist agreeing to benefits for members which it was not prepared to extend to other employees. The non-majority union's position, however, would not be significantly different from that of a union which had a majority in a bargaining unit encompassing only a minority of the employer's work force. Negotiation with a non-majority union could serve the purpose of leading each side to understand better the needs and desires of the other side, and help find solutions which might be mutually accepted. More importantly, it could provide a grievance procedure to which individual employees could resort with assurance of an uncompromised advocate....

A more fruitful role for the non-majority union is to help employees know and enforce their individual employment rights. For example, many employees do not know the full scope of their rights under workmen's compensation....

Similarly, in-plant committees could help employees know and enjoy the full measure of their other entitlements such as medical benefits, sick leave, severance pay and pensions provided by employer established plans. The union could help employees claim and collect statutory entitlements such as unemployment compensation, disability pay, social security and various welfare benefits....

The most important potential function of a non-majority union is enforcement of the Occupational Safety and Health Act ('OSHA'). Statutory enforcement procedures provide a series of openings to a union which establishes an active in-plant safety committee....

There is neither time nor need to canvass the functions which non-majority unions could fulfill in making real other individual employment rights under the evolving common law or under statutes, such as plant closure laws, pregnancy leave acts, polygraph and privacy laws, and whistleblowing statutes. There is need, however, to point out that judicially created doctrines establishing employment rights and employment protection statutes are proliferating at a rapid rate, largely because of the recognition that the shrinking sphere of collective bargaining cannot provide protection. The failure of unions to achieve and maintain majorities is increasing the necessity for non-majority unions to play a significant role. When unions cannot represent employees for the purpose of collective bargaining, non-majority unions can represent employees for the protection of individual employment rights....

Obviously, a non-majority union is no substitute for an economically strong union with complete, recognized bargaining rights. Even at best, a non-majority union can provide less than half a loaf of economic justice and industrial democracy. But a union without a majority can provide workers a measure of protection, either by collective action or legal representation. It can maintain the bonds between those who believe in unions and want to belong, and it can offer a continuing visible presence in the workplace. [Copyright © 1990. Reprinted by permission of Chicago-Kent College of Law, Illinois Institute of Technology.]

Roy Adams, "Bringing Canada's Wagner Act Regime into Compliance with International Human Rights Law and the *Charter*" (2016) 19 *Canadian Labour and Employment Law Journal* 365 at 393–94

It is clear that both management and labour in Canada are uncomfortable with the prospect of the proliferation of unregulated labour organizations. Instead of abandoning the Wagner Model, as I urged in 1995, I suggest that we revise it in accordance with the second ILO-compliant option noted above. Specifically, every Canadian jurisdiction should revise its Wagner Model to provide for certification of "most representative" unions. The option of certifying an exclusive agent through a majoritarian procedure would continue to exist but it would no longer be the only form of certification available to workers. In an appropriate bargaining unit, the most representative union (or coalition of unions) with, perhaps, 30% support and a minimum membership to make it credible, could be certified by the labour law authority in each Canadian jurisdiction as the primary bargaining agent. It would have all of the rights and duties of exclusive agents but it would not have exclusive representation rights. In enterprises with certified "most representative" unions, minority unions would have the legal rights to speak for their own members, to present and pursue the grievances of their members, and to organize legal strikes, all of which are consistent with ILO norms. Collective agreements would have to allow minority unions to exercise those rights, but only within the terms of the agreement (and the law). Thus, for example, minority unions would have to respect the requirements of the grievance system laid out in the negotiated collective agreement and, should the minority association set out to organize a strike, the requirements in both the agreement and the law would have to be honoured. The law would also need to provide for replacement, at appropriate times, of the certified most representative union by another union that had acquired greater support, and for decertification.

This proposal would have the great advantage of requiring minimal change to existing procedures. The disruptions feared by Justice Winkler in *Fraser* would be kept at a minimum because of the requirement that minority unions operate within the bounds of the collective agreement and the law. Employers would not be continually accosted with demands that were inconsistent with one another. The competition from employer-sponsored "company unions," feared by organized labour as a consequence of legitimizing minority unionism, would also be minimized since such unions, unable to pass the independence test, would not be certifiable and any bargaining arrangements established with them could be nullified by the certification of a legitimate most representative union. The result would be that the processes and regulations now in effect under existing Wagner statutes will require only minor adjustment.

[Originally published in (2016) 19:2 CLEJ 365. Reproduced with the permission of Lancaster House.]

Dorothy Sue Cobble, "Making Postindustrial Unionism Possible" in Sheldon Friedman et al, eds, *Restoring the Promise of American Labor Law* (Ithaca: ILR Press, Cornell University, 1994) 285 at 292–94

Much of the current critique of the New Deal system falsely equates all unionism with the form of unionism that became dominant by the 1940s. Thus, the argument goes, if industrial unionism is obsolete, so is unionism per se. This historical amnesia hampers attempts to create new forms of collective representation. Postindustrial unionism does not need to be invented out of whole cloth: it can be reassembled, reshaped, and extended from elements of past and current institutional practice. The institutional practices of what I have termed 'occupational unions' and the nontraditional approaches to representation taken by female-dominated professional and semiprofessional groups such as teachers, nurses, and clericals offer the best guide to the formulation of a postindustrial unionism.

Occupational unionism, the primary model of unionism before the New Deal, was neither Taylorist nor worksite-based.... Although not every trade adopted 'occupational unionism' in toto, before the New Deal the majority of organized trades and virtually every single trade that successfully organized mobile workers relied on some elements of occupational unionism. Occupational unions recruited and gained recognition on an occupational or local market basis rather than by industry or individual job site. Their representational systems emphasized occupationally based rights, benefits, and identity rather than worksite-based protections. Longshoremen, janitors, agricultural laborers, food servers, and garment workers, as well as such classic craft unionists as printers, building tradesmen, and performing artists, strove for control over hiring through closed-shop language and through union-run employment exchanges, rosters, and hiring halls; stressed employment security rather than 'job rights' at individual worksites; offered portable benefits and privileges; and took responsibility for monitoring workplace performance.

Occupational unionism flourished because it met the needs of workers and employers outside of mass-production settings. In local labor markets populated with numerous small employers, the unionization of garment workers, restaurant employees, teamsters, and others brought stability and predictability, inhibiting cutthroat competition. Employers gained a steady supply of skilled, responsible labor and an outside agency (the union) that ensured the competence and job performance of its members. In many cases, the union took responsibility for expanding the customer base for unionized enterprises. A floor for minimum wage and working conditions was established. Workers did not gain long-term job tenure but the opportunity to invest in their own 'human capital' through training and experience at a variety of worksites. As long as the unionized sector remained competitive—a goal to which both labor and management were committed—unionized workers also gained real employment security, in that the union helped make them more employable individually and helped ensure there would be a supply of high-wage, 'good' jobs. This unionism, then, in contrast to industrial unionism, never developed rigid seniority rules at individual worksites; it was committed to maintaining employee productivity, high-quality service and production, and to ensuring the viability of unionized firms. In short, it was flexible, cooperative as well as adversarial, and dedicated to skill enhancement and to the creation of a high-performance workplace. . . .

Occupational unionism declined dramatically in the postwar era, in part because of shifts in union institutional practice. . . . Legislative and legal decisions also severely hampered the ability of occupational unions to exert control over their members, to pressure employers for recognition, and to provide services to members and employers. Closed-shop, top-down organizing, secondary boycotts, the removal of members from the job for noncompliance with union bylaws and work rules, and union membership for supervisors all became illegal. Unions lost their ability to organize new shops, to maintain multiemployer bargaining structures, to set entrance requirements for the trade, to oversee job performance, and to punish recalcitrant members. . . .

By the 1960s, occupational unionism was but a mere shadow of its former robust self. Only the building and construction trades (which obtained special legislative language exempting them from some of the new postwar legal restrictions on unions) and certain highly specialized professional groups (such as the performing arts occupations) retained some degree of power and influence. . . . Yet, by the 1960s other alternatives to mass-production unionism were emerging. The professional and semiprofessional employee organizations built primarily by women, for example, initially focused less on extracting economic concessions from individual enterprises and more on the well-being of their industry or sector and on responding to the 'professional' interests of their members. As state bargaining laws and other forces moved them toward more traditional 'bargaining' relations with employers, they shed some of their occupational and associational orientation. Yet, as Charles Taylor Kerchner and Douglas E. Mitchell ... have argued for teacher unions, many are now moving toward a third stage of labor relations, in which they are as concerned with the welfare of the overall educational system and with meeting the needs of their clients as with protecting their own interests as employees. It is these alternative models of unionism that hold promise for the future. [Copyright © 1994 by Cornell University. Used by permission of the publisher, Cornell University Press.]

6:620 Broader-Based Bargaining

In recent decades, there has been widespread advocacy (particularly among academics) of broader-based bargaining as a way of addressing the lack of fit between the modern economy characterized by widespread organizational fissuring and the *Wagner Act* model. Broader-based bargaining implies collective negotiations between a representative employers' association or bargaining agency on one side, and a union or association of unions on the other, covering employment relationships in a local, regional, or national labour market.

Proponents of such a system attribute many advantages to it. Uniform industry-wide working conditions might remove wages as a competitive factor and focus attention on other factors such as efficiency, design, and quality. Moving collective bargaining above the level of the individual workplace may produce a more statespersonlike approach on both sides, by facilitating the use of dispassionate professionals insulated from the emotional and political pressures of their immediate labour or management constituencies. Another argument is that the potential costs of industry-wide strikes are so great that public opinion will not tolerate them. Moreover, in many industries where small-scale firms predominate, organization on the employer side is needed to counterbalance union bargaining power. Finally, an employers' organization may help to bring order to an industry by enforcing compliance with industry-wide standards, thereby avoiding the necessity for legal or economic sanctions by the union.

Broader-based bargaining, especially if it is industry-wide, may also mitigate the problem of the contracting out of work by employers to non-union firms. As we have seen in Chapter 4, labour relations boards have generally refused to find that firms to which work is contracted out are successor employers bound by any bargaining rights that attached to the work before it was contracted out.

On the other hand, broader-based bargaining has its risks and disadvantages. Taking labour costs out of competition may decrease labour mobility. Industry-wide or regional standards may be unsuitable for particular firms with unique problems. Even more important, perhaps, employers' organizations formed for collective bargaining purposes may become vehicles for the suppression of commercial competition. Finally, the costs of industry-wide strikes, should they occur, are likely to be very great.

Of the multi-employer or industry-wide bargaining relationships that exist in North America, most are private arrangements not required by law. The authority of a bargaining agent to act on behalf of multiple employers or unions rests on ordinary agency principles, and such arrangements may prove to be unsatisfactory for a number of reasons. For one thing, voluntary coalitions are difficult to sustain; individuals have an incentive to refuse to participate in measures designed to further collective goals whenever such measures are detrimental to their particular interests. Those who break ranks may not only protect their own position but also enjoy any enhancement in the general climate produced by the collective action of others—the classic "free rider" problem well known to economists. Finally, the public interest may not be served when a private choice is made between individual and joint bargaining. Voluntarism does not always work.

Even if management or labour is able to maintain a strong coalition on its side, those on the other side may refuse to engage in joint bargaining. Economic action to enforce demands for multiparty bargaining may not be lawful in most Canadian jurisdictions, where certification orders are statutorily limited to one employer. In the few jurisdictions where multiparty certification is available, expanding the scope of the certified unit can help to meet the problem of unstable coalitions.

The following excerpt reviews some of the alternative models being considered in a significant labour law reform process that was ongoing at the time of writing in the province of Ontario.

C Michael Mitchell & John C Murray, *Changing Workplaces Review: Special Advisors' Interim Report* (Ontario: Ministry of Labour, July 2016) 115–19

There are various models for broader or sector-wide bargaining in Canada.

Construction Sector

In the construction industry, for example, reforms of the industrial relations system came at the request of employers to counter strong unions that were seen as engaging in bargaining tactics known as "whipsawing" and "leapfrogging" to advance pay and benefits. In this context, a multitude of employers with weak bargaining power as individual companies sought structural industrial relations relief to permit them to band together and force the union to bargain with one employer entity.

Multi-employer bargaining along trade lines has existed under Ontario's labour relations legislation for the construction industry since the 1970s and on a compulsory basis in the industrial, commercial and institutional (ICI) sector since 1977. The accreditation and province-wide bargaining provisions in the ICI sector were employer initiatives designed to equalize bargaining power with then-stronger unions. Unlike the general approach under the LRA, construction industry certificates include all of the operations of a single employer in either the province and/or geographic areas set by the OLRB in construction industry certification cases ("Board Area").

In the case of the ICI sector of the construction industry, the LRA imposes a system of single-trade, multi-employer, province-wide bargaining. The Minister of Labour designates employee bargaining agents and employer bargaining agents (representing all unionized employers in the province with respect to a single trade). There can be only one provincial agreement between these parties (bargaining outside the designated structures is prohibited). All provincial agreements have a common duration and a common expiry date. When a new bargaining unit is certified for a non-union employer, the parties automatically become bound to the provincial agreement.

The accreditation of a multi-employer bargaining agency is designed to offset the power of the unions and compel a union in a sector to bargain with the single employer bargaining agency rather than individual employers.

Arts Sector

The federal *Status of the Artist Act* (SAA) provides another example of sectoral or multi-employer approaches to collective employee representation and bargaining. The SAA permits a broad array of professional artists in the federally regulated cultural sector to form associations and bargain collectively with the producers who engage their services. It allows for the certification of artists' associations that meet certain criteria, in sectors within this industry that are considered suitable for bargaining. It is not necessary for an artists' association to provide proof that it represents more than 50% of artists working in a given sector (recognizing that it is often difficult or impossible to determine the exact size of the sector).

In addition, the SAA allows for the creation of producers' associations for bargaining with artists' associations. Certification gives an artists' association the exclusive authority to bargain a scale agreement on behalf of the artists in the sector.

Scale agreements are different from other collective agreements in that they establish only the minimum terms and conditions of engagement. Private negotiations between employees and employers for terms and conditions above and beyond scale agreements are permitted. This reflects the unique situation of the cultural industry, including the varying talent levels of individuals in the broadcasting industry. It appears that this practice has generally worked well in other sectors, such as in the areas of sports and entertainment.

The SAA model holds the potential to extend collective bargaining to types of workers who may not conventionally be thought of as "employees." It aims to create a safety net for the majority of working artists while not depriving artists of the ability to bargain better terms. A weakness of the legislation is that producers are not required to form associations for bargaining, potentially leaving artists' associations with no sector-wide group with which to bargain. Only producers bound to the agreement are subject to the terms and conditions established by scale agreements, and there is no process for binding a producer not voluntarily bound to the scale agreement.

Primarily as a result of the artists' and performers' need or desire to have independent contractor status for tax purposes, the performers are presumed not to be employees under the LRA and, therefore, the sector is not governed by the Act. As such, the agreements appear to fall outside the scope of the LRA. If there is no provision for binding individual producers to a scale agreement, and if the LRA does not apply, a producer who is not a party to an agreement cannot be compelled to negotiate with the association or sign the scale or other agreement.

Other Sector Arrangements

Another approach, common in Europe but generally absent in North America (except for the decree system in Quebec, which is much smaller in its application today than previously), is to institute a system by which certain terms (negotiated through a collective agreement or at a sectoral table) can be extended by decree to cover all workers, both union and non-union, within a specific sector. An example of this approach is Ontario's *Industrial Standards Act* (ISA), which was introduced in 1935 and repealed in 2000.

The ISA provided a mechanism for establishing a schedule of wages and working conditions that was binding on all employers and employees in a particular industry across a given geographical zone. Employers or employees in a particular industry could petition the Minister of Labour to call a conference of employers and employees in that industry, for the purposes of negotiating a schedule of minimum standards, including wages, hours of work, holiday pay, and overtime. The schedule would be submitted to the Minister, who could approve it if it had been agreed to by a "proper and sufficient representation of employers and employees." An approved schedule would be made as a regulation and would be binding across the entire industrial sector.

The ISA largely fell into disuse after the ESA was introduced in 1968. By 2000, when it was repealed, there were only two ISA schedules remaining, covering subsectors within the garment industry in Toronto.

Over the years, various proposals have come forward in relation to the concept of broader based bargaining. One that is frequently cited is a proposal put forward by a majority of special advisors appointed by the British Columbia government in 1992 to review the province's *Industrial Relations Act*. In its report, a majority of the sub-committee endorsed the introduction of a form of sectoral certification for "those small enterprises where employees have been historically underrepresented by trade unions."

The sectoral certification model proposed in British Columbia would be available only in sectors that were determined by the Labour Relations Board to be historically underrepresented by unions and where the average number of employees at work locations within the sector was fewer than 50. To determine whether a sector met these criteria, the Labour Relations Board would be required to hold public hearings and accept submissions not only from the parties but other employers and unions within the sector.

Sectors under this model would be defined by two characteristics—geographical area and similar enterprises—with employees performing similar tasks within that geographic area. For example, a sector could comprise "employees working in fast food outlets" in a city.

The recommendation stated that a union with the requisite support (e.g., 45% of employees) at more than one work location within a sector could apply for certification of the employees at those locations. To be certified, the union would have to establish majority support at each location and, in a representation vote, win majority support among all employees at the work locations where certification was being sought.

Once the union obtained a sectoral certificate under the British Columbia model, collective bargaining would take place between the union and the various employers subject to the certificate. A standard agreement would be worked out and, subsequently, if the union could demonstrate sufficient support at additional locations within the sector, it would be entitled to a variance of its bargaining certificate to encompass the new employees. Although the standard agreement would then apply to the new employees, the Labour Relations Board would have the option of tailoring this agreement to the exigencies of any particular location. Once a sector had been declared "historically underrepresented," any union would be able to apply for certification within the sector. The authors of the proposal point out that under their model, three or four different unions could end up representing employees within a sector or geographic area, each administering its own collective agreement. No union would have a "monopoly" on representation rights within a sector."

[The authors then proceed to outline various reform options under consideration, including the following additional model of their own design that departs somewhat from the BC proposal discussed above.]

5. Adopt a model that would allow for multi-employer certification and bargaining in an entire appropriate sector and geographic area, as defined by the OLRB (e.g., all hotels in Windsor or all fast-food restaurants in North Bay). The model would be a master collective agreement that applied to each employer's separate place of business, like the British Columbia proposal, but organizing, voting, and bargaining would take place on a sectoral, multi-employer basis. Like the British Columbia proposal, this might perhaps apply only in industries where unionization has been historically difficult, for whatever reason, or where there are a large number of locations or a large number of small employers, and, perhaps only with the consent of the OLRB. The following could be the technical details.
   a) A sectoral determination by the OLRB would precede any application for certification.
   b) To trigger a sectoral determination by the OLRB, itself a serious undertaking, a union (or council of unions), would have to demonstrate a serious intention and commitment to organize the sector, including a significant financial commitment.
   c) The OLRB would be required to define an appropriate sector, both by industry and geography, or could find that there was no appropriate sector. All interested parties could make representations on the appropriateness of the sector (e.g., all hotels in Windsor, or all fast-food outlets in North Bay).
   d) Employers in the sector would be required, at some stage of the sectoral proceedings, to produce employee lists to demonstrate the scope of the proposed sector and the union's apparent strength, or lack thereof.
   e) A secret ballot vote and a majority of ballots cast (the current rule) would be required for certification.
   f) Instead of the double majorities that could be required in the British Columbia model, this model would require only a single majority of employees because, as a result of certification, all employers in the sector would be covered by the master agreement, whereas in the British Columbia-based proposal, almost by definition, there would be a non-union portion of the sector.
   g) In the special case of an application for an entire sector in a large, multi-employer constituency, given the difficulties inherent in determining an accurate constituency as of any given date and, therefore, whether a numerical threshold to trigger a vote has been met, the union(s) in this model would not be required to meet a numerical threshold to be entitled to a vote. Rather, to be entitled, the union(s) would be required to persuade the OLRB that it had significant and sufficient broad support in the sector. The union would have the obligation to make full, confidential, disclosure to the OLRB, as is required now, with respect to its

membership evidence, including all of its information on the size of the unit, the number of employers, etc. Any effort to misrepresent the size of the unit could lead to the dismissal of the application.

h) Cards could be signed electronically, with the same safeguards now used by the OLRB for mailed membership evidence.

i) An OLRB-supervised secret ballot vote would take place electronically. Voters would "register," at the time they voted, listing their employer, work and home address, last hours worked, etc. The OLRB would have the authority and responsibility to quickly and administratively determine the eligibility of voters, including any status issues, and ensure that only eligible voters voted.

j) Such applications could only be brought at fixed intervals, and, if unsuccessful, could not be brought again, either by the same applicant or by any other applicant, for a period of one or two years.

k) If the union was certified, the OLRB would have the authority to accredit an employers' organization to represent the employers and to conduct the bargaining, directing that dues be paid from each employer on a pro-rata, per-employee basis.

[© Queen's Printer for Ontario, 2016. Reproduced with permission.]

* * * * *

6:621 Broader-Based Bargaining in Quebec

Patrice Jalette, "When Labour Relations Deregulation Is Not an Option: The Alternative Logic of Building Services Employers in Quebec" (2006) 23:2 *International Journal of Comparative Labour Law and Industrial Relations* 329 at 330–36 and 344–46

In contrast with the convergence thesis, the new institutionalism literature demonstrates that economic and technological pressures do not necessarily compel a national IR system to adopt one universal set of rules; it is instead the institutional arrangements characteristic of this IR system that will determine in which ways these pressures will be reflected in IR rules. In this stream of literature, the varieties-of-capitalism approach as formulated by Hall and Soskice, built on the distinction between two ideal types of economic systems, each at either end of a continuum, may help to account for the actual diversity observed in national IR systems. Thus, at one extremity are the liberal market economies, best characterised by the US and UK, and at the other, the coordinated market economies, best characterised by Germany. It is argued that liberal market economies (LMEs) rely on decentralised wage bargaining, limited vocational training, the limited role of unions and collective bargaining, no job security, competitive inter-firm relations and market-based standard setting. In contrast, coordinated market economies (CMEs) are characterised by centralised wage bargaining systems, the central role of unions, cooperative industrial relations, considerable job security, interfirm cooperation in education/training, and the important role of business associations.

What is central in this approach is that, in any type of economy, firms take advantage of the institutional support available. Different logics may help them to develop distinctive business strategies and competitive advantages. The varieties-of-capitalism approach highlights the important role of social policies in supporting the strategies of firms. While social policies are traditionally seen as a constraint on firms, in terms of both higher costs and labour market rigidities, supporters of the varieties-of-capitalism theory see them as potential ways to improve firm operation and performance. For example, unemployment benefits can improve the ability of the firm to attract and retain a pool of skilled workers in which it has invested, while early retirement can help the firm to avoid dismissals during economic downturns. Besides welfare regimes, are there other types of social policies such as labour relations policies that help employers to create a competitive advantage? Does labour relations regulation merely generate unnecessary costs and rigidities or can it provide employers with concrete advantages? In this paper, we seek to identify the institutional advantages that result from a labour relations policy and determine whether the benefits provided by this particular type of social policy outweigh its costs.

Quebec provides a particularly interesting case for those who wish to compare LME labour policies with CME labour policies, since this Canadian province is at the confluence of the USA and Europe in many respects. Even though located in a country classified as a liberal market economy and on a continent dominated by the USA, which represents the archetype of this type of economy, Quebec has a strong tradition of state intervention in the economy and some of the most progressive labour laws in North America. Both of these reinforce the idea of a distinctive form of capitalism in Quebec, one that is closer in many respects to a CME. Because the decree system is unique on the North American continent, many people in Quebec had concerns about the competitiveness of this regime. The globalisation argument has put a lot of pressure on the decree system, which led the government to abolish decrees in the manufacturing industry, but not in the building services where employers were more prone to support the system. In this article, we will examine this alternative logic of employer strategies in a liberal market economy, an issue that, according to Thelen, has not received sufficient attention in the literature. Above all, the most interesting finding of this case study is that, in spite of stringent working conditions regulation, the building services industry in Quebec is growing, dynamic and competitive. As will be demonstrated in this article, the explanation for this lies in the fact that employers have taken advantage of the labour relations regulation. The particular case of labour relations regulation presented here fits in precisely with the theoretical perspective that we propose.

3. The System of Working Conditions Extension in Quebec

In Canada, as in the United States, collective bargaining takes place at the level of the establishment. Thus, working conditions are negotiated between a local union and an employer and apply directly to the employees of this establishment, which is part of the union certification unit. Working conditions concern, among other things, wages, employee benefits, working hours, staff movements, and grievance resolution procedure, and are recorded in the local collective agreement. In Quebec, the current mechanism for extending the provisions of collective agreements is thus a remarkable exception to the prevailing employment relations system since, through an extension, the provisions of a collective agreement concluded between private parties are extended to third parties, making these working conditions obligatory for employers and workers who otherwise would not be subject to them. Quebec is the only place in North America with a strict extension mechanism. In contrast, a recent review of 20 European countries by Traxler and Behrens showed that 15 of them have some type of strict extension mechanism.

What are the characteristics of the extension mechanism in force in Quebec? The Act respecting Collective Agreement Decrees —or the Decrees Act—came into force in 1934 at a time when there was heavy unemployment and limited state regulation of working conditions. The Act was a product of social corporatism, a doctrine defended by the Catholic Church, under the terms of which Catholic employers and employees are not enemies and must develop harmonious relations.

Essentially, the Decrees Act allows the Quebec Minister of Labour to issue a decree extending the conditions of employment negotiated in a collective agreement to all employees in other firms within the same sector. In practice, this system allows for the extension of wages and certain conditions of employment to a given sector, not the extension of all provisions contained in the collective agreement. Any party to a collective agreement may request a juridical extension of the collective agreement. The conditions for extension are related to the scope of application and the provisions of the agreement. Section 6 of the Decrees Act thus specifies that the Minister may recommend that the government pass a decree for the extension of the agreement if he deems that:

1. the proper field of activity is defined in the application;
2. the provisions of the agreement:
   (a) have acquired a preponderant significance and importance for the establishment of conditions of employment;
   (b) may be extended without any serious inconvenience for enterprises competing with enterprises established outside Quebec;
   (c) do not significantly impair the preservation and development of employment in the defined field of activity;
   (d) do not result, where they provide for a classification of operations or for various classes of employees, in unduly burdening the management of the enterprise concerned.

The geographical territory to which the decree applies depends, among other things, on competition. Thus, if the competition is local or regional, that is, because the service can only be produced and consumed on the spot, for example, in the field of building services, the decree will have an equivalent scope. If, on the other hand, the competition takes place on a broader national or international scale, as was the case of the clothing industry, the decree will apply to Quebec as a whole.

By making the standards of working conditions obligatory in firms other than those that are signatories to the collective agreement, this labour relations system not only improves the working conditions of nonunionized workers, but also protects employers from unfair competition. It is easy to understand that, in a fiercely competitive market, an employer who wants to provide more advantageous working conditions to his employees will literally be knocked out of the market because he is not in a position to compete with other employers who provide less favourable working conditions. This is all the more true of an employer who must deal with a collective agreement and a union. The stated goal of the Act was to ensure that unionised and non-unionised firms would not compete solely on the basis of wages.

During the 1990s, strong pressures to abolish decrees in the manufacturing industry led the government to amend the law, leading to the abolition of many decrees. The number of decrees went from 34 in 1990 to 17 today: metalwork, building materials industries, garage (7 regions), cartage (Montreal and Quebec), installation of petroleum equipment, solid waste removal (Montreal), security guards (Montreal), hairdressing (Hull), and building services in Montreal and Quebec. The number of employees and employers covered also decreased by about half. According to the latest data issued by the Quebec Ministry of Labour, around 9,000 employers and 77,000 employees are currently covered by a decree. Over the decades, the number of workers covered by a decree has fluctuated between 5 per cent and 10 per cent of the Quebec labour force, but today it is about 3 per cent.

4. Application of the Decree System in the Building Services Sector

The Decree respecting building service employees in the Montreal region was first adopted in 1974. The Decree is the regulation adopted by the Quebec Government that applies certain sections of a collective agreement to all employees in the building services sector. The contracting parties who petitioned the Minister of Labour to render their labour agreement obligatory are, on the one hand, the Association des entrepreneurs de services d'édifices publics Inc. and, on the other hand, the Service Employees' Union, Local 800, affiliated to the Quebec Federation of Labour, the largest union in the province. The Association des entrepreneurs has 16 members, 11 of whom have a union certification. The contractors represented by the Association are among the sector's largest employers since they alone employ 51 per cent of employees covered by the Decree. The union, for its part, has 50 or so certification units and represents 5232 employees, or approximately 50 per cent of employees in the sector.

The Decree's field of application has two dimensions, one industrial and the other territorial. The Decree concerns employers in building services, that is, contractors who provide maintenance services to customers or, in other words, who perform maintenance services for others (section 2.02). Generally, all buildings are covered by the Decree, with the exception of private homes. It covers any work related to washing, cleaning and sweeping performed inside or outside a building. The building services sector is clearly a low-tech and low-skills industry. As regards the territorial dimension of the Decree jurisdiction, the Decree applies to employers whose operations are located in the Greater Montreal Region (section 2.01). In 2004, the Decree in this industry covered 891 employers and 10,342 employees who worked approximately 275,500 hours for a wage bill nearing CAD$193 million.

The Decree determines the minimal conditions of labour that all employers in the building services sector must grant their employees. These minimal conditions relate to: wage rates; working hours; meal and rest periods; call-back and call in; paid general holidays; paid vacations; special leave of absence; payment of wages; uniforms; sick leave; notice of termination of employment or layoff. Though they essentially cover the same working conditions, the Decree's standards are often higher than those provided for in the Act respecting Labour Standards which applies to non-unionised workplaces without a decree. It should be mentioned that the Decree establishes minimum working conditions and there is nothing to prevent an employer from providing more advantageous working conditions to its unionised or non-unionised employees.

One particularity of the decree system is that it makes the parties themselves responsible for administering and enforcing the Decree. The Parity Committee is an organisation put in place to ensure the application of the Decree. It is administered by both union and employer representatives. The fundamental principle that underlies the creation of the Parity Committee is that nobody but the contracting parties can more effectively monitor the application of the Decree. A board of directors made up of five persons representing the contractors and five persons representing the employees and the union governs the Parity Committee. The Board meets every month and discusses employers and employees' concerns in order to find concrete solutions to the problems of the building services industry. The Committee appoints a general manager, a secretary and inspectors....

CONCLUSION

This paper shows that employers do not automatically support labour relations deregulation, and adopt another logic of competition not solely based on low wages. As predicted by the varieties-of-capitalism approach, the stance of employers operating in the building services industry in Quebec was motivated by the fact that they benefit from the institutional characteristics of the labour relations system in place, the collective agreement decree system. At first sight, the system's resolutely distinctive character in North America, its underlying regulation and state intervention, the higher-than-labour-standards wages and working conditions it implies, and its constraint on the freedom to manage labour relations locally were not exactly appealing for employers. In general, employers come to terms with this labour relations system and adopt another competition logic based on factors other than wages and working conditions. This was possible because, over the years, they realised that costs associated with the decree system do not outweigh the benefits they derive from this labour relations regulation: industry-level wage coordination, a stable work force, a pool of valuable workers, enhanced productivity of factors, and constructive relations with employee representatives.

The presence of these comparative institutional advantages explains the adoption of this alternative logic of competition by employers and their satisfaction with this labour relations regulation, which leads to attractive results like labour market stability and low-inflation wage settlements. In addition, the economic performance of the industry also shows that it is dynamic and expanding. The direct evidence available also shows that Quebec's firms are actually more efficient than Toronto's firms. This seems to indicate that labour relations regulation and economic performance are not necessarily incompatible, contrary to what the deregulation thesis predicts. It is clear that employers in this case study do not believe that deregulation is the best route to get what they need.

The local nature of the market in the building services industry may also partly explain the results achieved under the decree system and its viability in this industry in Quebec. This thesis is supported somewhat by the comparison of this industry's experience with the very different situation observed in the manufacturing sector during the 1990s. During the process that led to the repeal of numerous decrees in the manufacturing sector, it was obvious that the government and employers considered the decrees to be impediments to the competitiveness of Quebec manufacturers since firms outside the province did not have to comply with the decree regulation. The increasingly global nature of the competition and the consequent need for Quebec firms to remain competitive in such a globalised market represented major arguments supporting the abolition of the decrees in manufacturing, especially in the clothing industry, probably one of the most internationalised industries. By contrast, in the building services sector, foreign competitors that want to compete with Quebec firms in the local market have to respect standards established by the Decree. In such a market, it seems easier to implement and enforce labour relations regulation seeking to reduce wage-based competition practised 'on the backs of employees.' Further research is nevertheless needed to explain more thoroughly the different fate of the decree system in each of these sectors, and the role played by the nature of their respective markets in the observed lack of convergence between their respective IR systems.

The last aspect to be addressed here relates to the main objective of the decree system, which is to give employees access to favourable wages and working conditions through participation in their determination in parts of the private sector where it is difficult for employees to unionise. Since the employers clearly benefit from the decree system in this industry, one can ask: what's in it for workers? Wage increases provided for in the Decree were not enough to compensate for the increase in prices and services, indicating that the sector's employees have suffered a purchasing power loss during the period studied. Also, wage levels are notably lower than those paid in large firms in Quebec. One can thus wonder if the failure of the system to generate better wages and working conditions for workers will undermine the viability of the decree industry. Maybe there are other advantages of being covered by a decree for employees that we were not able to measure in this study. The workers are probably in a better situation with a decree than without since they earn more than the minimum wage, which could be the standard without the decree, given their low level of skills. But one can certainly call into question a labour relations system that fails to significantly improve the working conditions of employees while contributing to a firm's competitiveness and economic performance. The threat of a repeal of the Decree in the building services industry in the future may come from its inability to serve the interest of employees and not only from pressures exerted by the deregulation lobbies which, for ideological reasons, want Quebec to make the transition to an LME.

6:630 Alternative Worker Voice Mechanisms: Workplace Councils?

Some scholars have argued that a major problem with the *Wagner Act* model is the fact that it does not provide workplace representation for all employees, but only for those within bargaining units that have voted on a majority basis in favour of unionization under existing certification procedures. Given the decline in union density over time, some scholars suggest alternative mechanisms to support workers' voices, such as the adoption of an *employee works council* in every workplace, with employees having the right to choose the members of that council but not the right to vote it out of existence. In the following excerpt, the authors propose the adoption of such a model, as an extension of an already existing statutory voice mechanism in Canada; namely, requirements for internal joint committees established by workplace safety legislation.

Rafael Gomez & Juan Gomez, *Workplace Democracy for the 21st Century: Towards a New Agenda for Employee Voice and Representation in Canada* (Ottawa: Broadbent Institute, 2016) at 56–58

> 3.3.5 Legislating for the Possibility of Employee-Management Workplace Councils
> Another approach towards workplace representation is advancing the idea of a "made-in-Canada" version of German-style workplace councils. In their basic form, these are bodies elected by all non-managerial employees and entitled to meet with management in establishments and firms operating above a certain size (these range from 20 to 50 employees in most cases). Typically, under this framework, work councils are apprised of and consulted with on all matters impacting employees and can participate to some degree in management. Work councils are a mainstay of workplace democracy in many European jurisdictions where they are integrated into larger labour relations systems covering collective bargaining and in countries such as Germany are part of the codetermination model (i.e., worker representation on company boards of directors). As such, they are seen as a complement to collective bargaining and not a replacement. In Canada, work councils could build on the experience of existing statutory health and safety committees and could be expanded along the lines suggested by Adams to "... codetermine specified critical aspects of work such as training, employment equity, technological change, job sharing and the terms of plant shutdowns and to co-operate with management in improving the efficiency and competitiveness of the enterprise". Though, in principle, any workplace council legislation would not mandate the particular duties of the committee, as a starting point for their introduction in Canada, employee-management workplace councils could be established in all non-union workplaces to promote compliance with existing employment standards and to deal with innovation and productivity issues, giving employees and managers a forum for developing and implementing solutions and strategies to improve employee welfare and firm performance. This would lower business sector opposition and showcase the forum as a win-win for employees and employers alike.

6:640 Alternative Worker Voice Mechanisms: Protecting "Concerted Activities" of Non-unionized Workers?

Recently, there has been increased discussion of the importance of providing, under section 7 of the *National Labor Relations Act*, a broadly defined protection for worker collective action to non-unionized workers in the United States. This provision states:

7. Employees shall have the right to self-organization, to form, join, or assist labor organizations, to bargain collectively through representatives of their own choosing, *and to engage in other concerted activities for the purpose of collective bargaining or other mutual aid or protection.* [Emphasis added.]

In the United States, this section has recently been used to provide a degree of protection from employer retaliation for workers engaged in forms of worker expression, voice or activism, in contexts where there was no union certified under the NLRA to represent such workers. In Canada, there appears to be no comparable express statutory protection for non-unionized workers engaged in forms of collective action, other than unfair labour practice provisions that protect workers engaged in union organizing and related activity (see Chapter 5). The *Changing Workplaces Review, Special Advisors' Interim Report* (Ontario: Ministry of Labour, 2016), sees the adoption of such a provision as an additional option to be considered.

Chapter 7: Negotiating a Collective Agreement

7:100 INTRODUCTION

Collective bargaining law is concerned with the substantive requirements and procedural standards of *bargaining between the employer and the employees seen as a unit*. Collective bargaining is one of the principal reasons why employees join a union and why unions secure the right to represent employees through certification or voluntary recognition. Once a union secures the status of exclusive bargaining agent, it supersedes individual bargaining between employer and employee and carries with it the constraint that an employer cannot bargain with another union.

But the fact that circumstances of bargaining are legally enumerated raises some difficult problems. We tend to think of bargaining as a voluntary exercise between willing participants who seek particular outcomes (a sale or purchase, for example) and who, if things do not go to their liking, are entitled to walk away from the table and seek a better deal elsewhere. Collective bargaining does not quite conform to this model. The employer is often an unwilling party to negotiations; outcomes are open-ended in the sense that collective agreements are almost infinitely variable; the parties cannot simply terminate their relationship and seek other buyers or sellers of labour; and the pressure each can apply to the other—by means of strikes and lockouts—has few counterparts in other bargaining contexts.

All of these peculiarities of collective bargaining law raise a fundamental issue: to what extent can and should the law seek to regulate bargaining behaviour? This issue presents itself in a variety of forms. For example, should the law attempt to prevent a truly recalcitrant employer from merely going through the motions of bargaining? Should it permit the parties to establish whatever terms of employment are mutually agreeable? To what extent should it regulate the use of pressure tactics in the name of the public interest? And assuming the law ought to proscribe some forms of bargaining behaviour, what kind of remedies will effectively keep the bargaining process within appropriate limits?

7:200 THE STATUTORY TIMETABLE

Collective bargaining legislation subjects negotiations to a fairly detailed statutory timetable. This timetable is set in motion, for the first collective agreement, by the certification of a trade union as exclusive bargaining agent; certification entitles the union to serve a notice to bargain on the employer, or the employer to serve a notice to bargain on the union. In relationships that have already seen the negotiation of at least one collective agreement, either party can serve a notice to bargain on the other party when an existing agreement has expired, or within a certain period before its expiry date. The precise period during which notice to bargain for the renewal of an agreement varies from jurisdiction to jurisdiction.

The service of a notice to bargain triggers the start of the statutory "duty to bargain." Under Canadian labour relations statutes, that duty generally has two interrelated branches: a duty to bargain "in good faith," and a duty to make "every reasonable effort" to reach a collective agreement. The Supreme Court of Canada in *Royal Oak Mines v Canada (Labour Relations Board)*, [1996] 1 SCR 369, excerpted in Section 7:421 described the "good faith" requirement as the subjective element of the duty to bargain, and the "reasonable efforts" requirement as the objective element. Statutes in the three Maritime provinces refer only to "reasonable efforts," and do not mention "good faith," but in those provinces the duty to bargain has been interpreted as having the same subjective and objective elements as in the rest of the country: see *Canadian Union of Public Employees v Labour Relations Board (Nova Scotia)*, [1983] 2 SCR 311 (the *Digby School Board* case).

Once a notice to bargain has been served, the parties remain under a duty to bargain until they reach a collective agreement. The duty does not require that they succeed in negotiating an agreement, but only that they try. Sometimes, no matter how hard they try, they may reach an impasse. Normally, before they may resort to a strike or lockout, labour relations legislation requires them to go through a conciliation or mediation process, usually under the auspices of the labour ministry. This requirement of conciliation or mediation, which is a long-standing feature of Canadian labour law, is predicated on the idea that the parties acting alone will often be unable to reach an agreement, not because there isn't any overlap in their respective positions, but because bargaining strategies and various obstacles to communication obscure potential points of agreement.

Although the state will intervene to try to help the parties reach an agreement, in general it will not impose one on them. The most important exception to this principle is what is called "first contract arbitration," which allows for state imposition of the terms of the first collective agreement after certification if the parties cannot settle those terms themselves. First contract arbitration is now provided for in most Canadian jurisdictions, and is discussed in Section 7:700. Other exceptions to the general principle that the state will not impose a bargain on the parties include ad hoc back-to-work legislation and specific statutes requiring compulsory interest arbitration in certain sectors. The use of these types of legislation varies widely across the country, and will be discussed briefly in Chapter 8 (Section 8:900).

Once a work stoppage (a strike or lockout) becomes legal, the duty to bargain continues, even while a stoppage is actually underway. However, the content of the duty changes significantly in those circumstances. If a party has complied with the duty to bargain but an impasse has nonetheless been reached at the bargaining table, that party is allowed to break off negotiations on the basis that there is no current prospect of progress. In a strike or a lockout, each side hopes that the economic pressure it puts on the other side will prompt concessions. Conversely, a party that thinks it is winning a strike or lockout can take advantage of that situation to toughen its stance. "It would be naive in the extreme," in the Ontario Labour Relations Board's words, "for parties to collective bargaining to expect that conditions which prevailed before a strike or lockout to still prevail afterwards": *Toronto Jewellery Manufacturers Association*, [1979] OLRB Rep July 719 at 723.

Normally, a collective agreement will eventually be reached, with or without the assistance of conciliation, and with or without resorting to a strike or lockout. Once a collective agreement has been signed, labour relations statutes explicitly provide that (with very few exceptions) conflict in the form of a work stoppage is no longer allowed, and the duty to bargain is suspended until it is time to negotiate a new agreement. It should be noted that American law is different in this respect; in the United States, the duty to bargain does continue during the lifetime of the collective agreement, on matters not dealt with in the agreement.

During the life of a collective agreement, the law across Canada entitles the parties to make changes to the agreement if they wish, but only by mutual agreement; neither party can require the other even to discuss any such changes. Every labour relations statute in the country now requires that a process of third-party arbitration, known as grievance arbitration or rights arbitration, must be provided for in every collective agreement in order to resolve differences over the meaning of the agreement; strikes and lockouts are not allowed while a collective agreement is in effect. Chapter 9 deals at length with the enforcement of the collective agreement. However, it should be noted here that under the "management rights" doctrine, to be discussed in Chapter 9, grievance arbitration has traditionally been understood as applying only to disputes over matters that are dealt with in the collective agreement, and management generally retains a right to act unilaterally on matters on which the agreement is silent. As we will see later in this chapter, for some commentators, the fact that the prohibition against strikes during the life of a collective agreement is broader than the reach of grievance arbitration means that a more rigorous duty to bargain should be imposed on management during the negotiation of the agreement.

The only significant exception to the prohibition against strikes or lockouts during the term of a collective agreement is the provision in a few statutes (for example, the *Canada Labour Code*, sections 51–55) that allows for the reopening of the duty to bargain if the employer introduces a technological innovation that is likely to affect the terms and conditions or security of employment of a significant part of the bargaining unit.

7:300 THE BARGAINING FREEZE

Complementary to the statutory duty to bargain are provisions that prohibit changes in terms and conditions of employment after notice to bargain has been given (what can be called the "bargaining freeze"). This is closely related to the "certification freeze," which prohibits changes in terms and conditions during a certification campaign. The basic principles underlying both the certification freeze and the bargaining freeze have been discussed in Chapter 5 (Section 5:300), and will not be dealt with again here.

Jurisdictions across Canada are consistent in tying the start of the bargaining freeze to the serving of notice to bargain, and are also consistent (either expressly or by implication) in bringing the freeze to an end when a new collective agreement is signed or when the union's bargaining rights are terminated. However, the statutes differ significantly as to exactly when the freeze ends if there has been neither a new agreement nor a termination of bargaining rights. A few statutes (Alberta *Labour Relations Code*, section 128; British Columbia *Labour Relations Code*, section 45(2)) state that the freeze remains in force until a lawful strike or lockout actually occurs; if the union is not ready to strike as soon as the law allows strike action to be taken, the employer must institute a lockout if it wants to bring the freeze to an end. In other jurisdictions, the freeze remains in force only until a strike or lockout would be lawful (for example, Ontario *Labour Relations Act, 1995*, section 86(1); Newfoundland *Labour Relations Act*, sections 74(b) and 75(b)). In the latter jurisdictions, if the union does not call a strike as soon as the law allows, the employer (though still subject to the duty to bargain with the union) can unilaterally change terms and conditions without actually instituting a lockout. The rationale for allowing such unilateral changes is that the employees are not forced to accept them, as they are free to strike. The differences between jurisdictions as to when the statutory freeze ends, and the courses of action that are open to the parties when it has ended, are canvassed in *United Steelworkers Local 2693 v Neenah Paper Company of Canada*, [2006] OLRD No 1132 (OLRB).

7:400 THE DUTY TO BARGAIN IN GOOD FAITH

7:410 Purposes of the Duty to Bargain

Archibald Cox, "The Duty to Bargain in Good Faith" (1958) 71 *Harvard Law Review* 1401 at 1407–9

Section 8(a)(5) of the *National Labor Relations Act* provides that it shall be an unfair labor practice for an employer "to refuse to bargain collectively with the representatives of his employees." ... By reading the testimony, the debate, and the history of the times with a large measure of hindsight one can discern four purposes which entered into the enactment of section 8(5).

1) The simplest and most direct purpose was to reduce the number of strikes for union recognition. Prior to 1935 [when the *National Labor Relations Act* was passed] the outright refusal of employers to deal with a labor union was a prolific cause of industrial strife.... The cause could be eliminated by placing an employer under a statutory duty to acknowledge as the legal representative of all his employees any union designated by the majority. In arguing that the act was constitutional the Government placed great stress upon this purpose....

2) The most important purpose of the *Wagner Act* was to create aggregations of economic power on the side of employees countervailing the existing power of corporations to establish labor standards. When the authors of the act spoke of "inequality of bargaining power" between employee and employer, they had in mind the famous dictum of Mr. Chief Justice Taft:

> [Labour unions] were organized out of the necessities of the situation. A single employee was helpless in dealing with an employer. He was dependent ordinarily on his daily wage for the maintenance of himself and family. If the employer refused to pay him the wages that he thought fair, he was nevertheless unable to leave the employ and to resist arbitrary and unfair treatment. Union was essential to give laborers opportunity to deal on equality with their employer.

The denial of recognition is an effective means of breaking up a struggling young union too weak for a successful strike. After the enthusiasm of organization and the high hopes of successful negotiations, it is a devastating psychological blow to have the employer shut the office door in the union's face. Imposing a legal duty to recognize the union would prevent such anti-union tactics and thereby contribute to the growth of strong labor organizations.

3) Section 8(5) was also intended to implement the basic philosophy of the act by imposing the duty to engage in collective — as distinguished from individual — bargaining. The courts exemplified the obligation by holding that after a representative has been designated, it is an unfair labor practice for an employer to negotiate wages or other terms of employment with individual employees. It is also possible that Congress meant that the duty to deal with the group — with the collectivity — included a more far-reaching idea usually expressed in metaphors. An employer must look upon labour as an equal partner, and "when we have such a partnership ... then one partner cannot do anything without consulting the other partner." Or to change the figure, the divine right of the king must yield to a constitutional monarchy, in which a large measure of industrial democracy will prevail. Wages, hours, and conditions of employment should be determined by mutual consent.

4) There were also those who looked upon collective bargaining as a rational process of persuasion. Collective bargaining, it was thought, enables employers and employees to dig behind their prejudices and exchange their views with the result that agreement is reached on many points while on others it is discovered that the area of disagreement is so narrow that compromise is cheaper than battle. As early as 1902 an industrial commission reported:

> The chief advantage which comes from the practice of periodically determining the conditions of labor by collective bargaining directly between employers and employees is, that thereby each side obtains a better understanding of the actual state of the industry, of the conditions which confront the other side, and of the motives which influence it. Most strikes and lockouts would not occur if each party understood exactly the position of the other.

Although there is little doubt that the sponsors of the *Wagner Act* hoped that the statute would accomplish all four purposes, only the first two can be said to have been written into law. There is no real evidence whether the sponsors intended to write the third and fourth directly into the statute or counted upon time and human nature to realize these objectives. Collective bargaining is curiously ambivalent even today. In one aspect collective bargaining is a brute contest of economic power somewhat masked by polite manners and voluminous statistics. As the relation matures, Lilliputian bonds control the opposing concentrations of economic power; they lack legal sanctions but are nonetheless effective to contain the use of power. Initially it may be only fear of the economic consequences of disagreement that turns the parties to facts, reason, a sense of responsibility, a responsiveness to government and public opinion, and moral principle; but in time these forces generate their own compulsions, and negotiating a contract approaches the ideal of informed persuasion.

The purpose of the original *Wagner Act* was to create a necessary balance of economic power. The act also aimed at ideal bargaining. It intruded at least so far as to protect unionization from interference by employers and to compel them to recognize the employees' representatives. Did the statute leave the further consequences to develop without government regulation or did it legislate some of the state of mind and habits of conduct which make up the ideal bargaining relation?

[Copyright © 1958 by the Harvard Law Review Association.]

7:420 Content of the Duty to Bargain

In 1935, Senator Walsh, one of the sponsors of the *Wagner Act* in the American Senate, in defending the inclusion in the statute of a requirement that the employer bargain collectively, described that requirement in minimalist terms:

> When employees have chosen their organization, when they have selected their representatives, all the bill proposes to do is to escort them to the door of the employer and say, "Here they are, the legal representatives of your employees." What happens behind those doors is not enquired into, and the bill does not inquire into it.

As you read the materials that follow, consider to what extent (if at all) that minimalist perception still prevails.

United Electrical, Radio and Machine Workers of America v DeVilbiss (Canada) Ltd (1976), 76 CLLC para 16,009 at 404–5 (OLRB)

> ADAMS, Vice-Chair: [A] very important function of section 14 [now section 17 of the Ontario *Labour Relations Act*] is that of reinforcing an employer's obligation to recognize a trade union lawfully selected by employees as their bargaining agent. Certainly the freedom to join a trade union of one's choice declared in section 3 of the legislation would be but an edict "writ on water" if an employer could enter into negotiations with no intention of ever signing a collective agreement. But we believe the duty to meet and make every reasonable effort to make a collective agreement has an even more important function in a modern society that for the most part accepts that trade unions have legitimate and important roles to play. That is to say that the duty assumes that when two parties are obligated to meet each other periodically and rationally discuss their mutual problems in a way that satisfies the phrase "make every reasonable effort," they are likely to arrive at a better understanding of each other's concerns thereby enhancing the potential for a resolution of their differences without recourse to economic sanctions—the impact of which is never confined to the immediate parties of an industrial dispute. At the very least rational discussion is likely to minimize the number of problems the parties are unable to resolve without the use of economic weapons thereby focusing the parties' attention in the eleventh hour on the "true" differences between them.... Hence it is our belief that the duty described in section 14 has at least two principal functions. The duty reinforces the obligation of an employer to recognize the bargaining agent and, beyond this somewhat primitive though important purpose, it can be

said that the duty is intended to foster rational, informed discussion thereby minimizing the potential for "unnecessary" industrial conflict.

Graphic Arts International Union Local 12-L v Graphic Centre (Ontario) Inc, [1976] OLRB Rep 221 at 229–31

[The employer served notice on the union to renegotiate the collective agreement. The parties met, and the union tabled a list of twelve proposals. The employer responded that it wanted to maintain the status quo. The union subsequently applied for conciliation, which did not resolve the dispute. The minister of labour decided not to appoint a board of conciliation, thereby setting in motion the statutory "countdown" which would lead to the point at which a strike or lockout could legally be called. The union rejected a compromise proposal made by the employer. A subsequent employer proposal was put to the union members, who voted to accept it, and the results of the vote were conveyed to the employer.

In the middle of the negotiations, the union brought a grievance (the MacDonald grievance) under the old collective agreement, alleging that the employer had breached that agreement by hiring a certain person. The union claimed that it had waited until this point to bring the grievance so as not to jeopardize the negotiations. The employer refused to sign a renewal agreement unless the grievance was dropped. Although the parties appeared to have settled all of the outstanding issues between them, the ill feeling generated by the filing of the grievance led the employer to put forward sixteen new demands for changes to the collective agreement. In these proceedings, the union alleged, among other things, that the employer had failed to make every reasonable effort to conclude a collective agreement.]

BURKETT, Vice-Chair: The requirement for rational discussion and full consideration of the issues between the parties is of particular importance in assessing the conduct of the respondent employer in the instant case. The evidence clearly establishes that the respondent took an initial position that it wished to renew the existing collective agreement without change....

The requirements for open and rational discussion of all the issues in dispute stems from the fact that collective bargaining is in essence an exercise in *decision making*. The parties make hard decisions as to the content and timing of their offers and counter offers as they attempt to conclude an agreement. Frequently the most difficult decision facing the parties and often a decision with far-reaching public ramifications, is the resort to economic sanctions. Decisions which determine terms and conditions of employment and which may precipitate strike or lock-out obviously require, as a matter of public policy, open and full discussions. Conduct by one of the parties to the process which inhibits or undermines the decision-making capability of the other is conduct which is contrary to the requirement to bargaining in good faith and make every effort to reach a collective agreement. The failure of the employer to supply the requested wage data in the *DeVilbiss* case *supra* undermined the decision-making capability of the union in that situation and the Board commented that:

> It is patently silly to have a trade union "in the dark" with respect to the fairness of the employer's offer because it has insufficient information to appreciate fully the offer's significance to those in the bargaining unit.

Lack of full discussion obviously impedes the decision-making capability to the detriment of the collective bargaining process and the relationship of the parties....

The decision-making capability of the parties depends upon not only a full and open discussion of the items which are in dispute but also upon an awareness that the scope of the dispute is limited to those items which have been put into dispute in the early stages of the bargaining process. Decision making does not take place in a vacuum. The parties set the parameters with their early exchange of proposals thereby establishing the framework within which they negotiate. A party which holds back on an item or number of items and then attempts to introduce these matters into the negotiations as the process nears completion, effectually destroys the decision-making framework. A party cannot rationally or properly consider its bargaining position in the absence of absolute certainty that the full extent of the dispute has been revealed. The tabling of additional demands after a dispute has been defined must, in the absence of compelling evidence which would justify such a course, be construed as a violation of the duty to bargain in good faith.

In the instant case the union was not altogether forthright in holding back the Mac-Donald grievance until it thought the bargaining had concluded. Nevertheless, the action of the employer which gave rise to that grievance occurred during the bargaining process thereby justifying a response by the union within the context of the bargaining process. The evidence establishes that the matter was verbally settled to the satisfaction of all parties and that subsequent to this verbal settlement the company tabled its revised list of demands. The tabling of the grievance did not justify the employer's response especially in light of the fact that the response occurred after a verbal settlement had been achieved. The employer's conduct is in violation of section 14 of the Act in so far as that section requires that the parties act in such a way as to foster rather than undermine the decision-making capability of the parties.

Canadian Association of Industrial, Mechanical and Allied Workers v Noranda Metal Industries Ltd, [1975] 1 CLRBR 145 at 162 (BC)

[The dispute between Noranda, the employer, and CAIMAW, the union, arose during the collective bargaining process wherein neither of the parties were ready to concede much ground to the other. After hard bargaining, the parties reached a deadlock, although they kept negotiation possibilities open. CAIMAW alleged to the Labour Relations Board of British Columbia that Noranda violated section 6 of the British Columbia *Labour Code* during the bargaining process. Section 6 reads: "No trade-union or employer shall fail or refuse to bargain collectively in good faith in the Province [of BC] and to make every reasonable effort to conclude a collective agreement." The action giving rise to the alleged unfair labour practice is a letter that Noranda wrote (on 5 September 1974) to its employees bypassing the union wherein it offered an inaccurate description of and insinuations about the bargaining process between Noranda and the union. Although the board did not find Noranda liable under section 6 for its letter offering an inaccurate description of the bargaining process, it found Noranda responsible for violation of section 6 for another communication to its employees wherein it "deliberately withheld factual data" on fringe benefits from the union. What is also important to note in this decision is the board's dismissal of Noranda's contention that once the board finds that the bargaining parties have made a sincere effort to reach a collective agreement, it cannot reasonably find a party liable under section 6 for specific objectionable incidents that were part of the bargaining process. Following are excerpts from the board's decision.]

Paul C. WEILER, Chair:

[...]

The crucial, undefined standard in [the] legal framework is the duty "to bargain collectively in good faith ... and to make every reasonable effort to conclude a collective agreement." This obligation originally evolved within American law and formed an important element in the original Wagner Act. The various Canadian statutes have followed this American lead in more or less the same language as [it] now exists in the Code....

Noranda has made a considerable and continuing effort to achieve [collective agreement with CAIMAW] (as, we should add, has CAIMAW).

The reason why agreement has not been reached, despite the efforts of both parties, is because each side wants to reach an agreement at or near its own terms and these opposing positions remain some distance removed. A failure to reach a collective agreement because of a determination not to make the concessions necessary to secure the consent of the other side is not, in and of itself, an unfair labour practice. It would be inconsistent with the fundamental policy of the Code—the fostering of free collective bargaining—for the Board to evaluate the substantive positions of each party, to decide which is the more reasonable, and then to find the other party to be committing an unfair labour practice for not moving in that direction. That interpretation of Section 6 would amount to compulsory arbitration in disguise ...

Thus far there was no dispute about the confines of Section 6. But within those parameters a serious issue is raised as to the scope of the duties imposed under that provision. Noranda's position was that once it is established that a party has made a sincere effort to reach agreement, the Board should not find a violation of Section 6 stemming from particular incidents, no matter how objectionable they might be....

We are not able to accept this "minimum" interpretation of Section 6.... First of all, it does not square with the language of the statute, which directs not only that a party "bargain collectively in good faith" but also that it "make every reasonable effort to conclude a collective agreement." Subjective motivation does seem to be the focus of the first clause, but the second places further limits on the objective means which each side is entitled to use in carrying out their intentions. The statute recognizes that a party, while waiting to secure a collective agreement, may adopt tactics[,] which unreasonably inhibit the process of achieving agreement.... While this Board must not appraise the reasonableness of the contract proposals by either side, it may assess the reasonableness of certain conduct adopted in an effort to achieve agreement....

[W]hile we interpret Section 6 as requiring adherence to certain fundamental principles of reasonable bargaining procedure, we also consider that this Board must exercise considerable restraint in intervening in negotiations between parties who are committed to reaching a collective agreement.

The facts of this case present two important issues to the Board about the collective bargaining procedure required under Section 6 of the Code. We shall deal first with the meeting of September 5th and the letter it spawned, an incident which puts in question the propriety of direct employer communication with its employees during a strike. CAIMAW did not suggest that it is illegal, as such, for an employer to write its employees, giving its own version of the negotiations, and hoping this will ultimately influence the trade-union to draw closer to the employer position for a settlement.... That letter may have been defamatory.... However, we cannot conclude that it was a failure "to bargain collectively in good faith ... and to make every reasonable effort to conclude a collective agreement." If this Board were asked to evaluate every distortion of fact or inflation of opinion contained in material written during heated collective bargaining disputes, we would be doing little else....

The union put its case regarding the September 5th letter in an alternative fashion. It argued that the contents of the letter could not be separated from Noranda's immovable bargaining position: "the Company appears to have retreated into 'neo-Boulwarism'—maintaining an intractable position, going through the motions of negotiations, and attempting to 'bargain' directly with the employees." In principle, we agree that an employer's stance which is destructive of the union's role as the exclusive bargaining agent for the employees—reducing the union's role to that of advisor rather than of full participant—does not fulfill the employer's obligation to bargain *collectively* under Section 6. However, the facts in this case are worlds removed from the practice of Boulwarism which [has been] found illegal.... Notwithstanding its firm position during the strike, Noranda had tried, both in the September 5th and October 1st meetings, to provide CAIMAW with a formula[,] which it might use as a basis for a somewhat different settlement. It is clear that the Company has bargained consistently and solely with the Union, although it has tried to sell its position to the employees as well. The one offending communication of September 5th was an isolated example and was no serious threat to the Union's status as bargaining agent. We find no violation of Section 6 in the events of September 5th.

The second important issue stems from the meeting of August 13th, and concerns the duty of party to produce and to discuss information relating to the claims[,] which are being made in negotiations. It is a long-established principle of American labour law that a party commits an unfair labour practice if it withholds information relevant to collective bargaining without reasonable grounds.... That principle does fit comfortably within the language of Section 6. One would hardly say that an employer who deliberately withheld factual data[,] which a union needed to intelligently appraise a proposal on the bargaining table was making "every reasonable effort to conclude a collective agreement." The policy behind the American rule has been summed up in this comment: "Negotiation nourished by full and informal discussion stands a better chance of bringing forth the fruit of collective bargaining agreement than negotiation based on ignorance and deception." Having said that, we want to make clear that we are not deciding in this case that this entire body of American doctrine is to be imported into British Columbia. The scope of the obligation[,] which we find in Section 6 of the [BC] Labour Code will be developed on a case-by-case basis. But here we do have a particularly arresting situation for the application of that principle. First of all, Noranda's letter of July 5th to the employees raised the issue of the cost of fringe benefits and made this issue a public obstacle to settlement. By that same letter, the Company indicated it did have the data available to make those calculations. Finally, in its letter of July 26th, the Company led the Union reasonably to believe there would be a fruitful discussion of the factual underpinnings of the fringe issues. In our judgment, Noranda could not suddenly reverse gears, as it did in the meeting of August 13th, without significantly prejudicing an opportunity to dissolve this important bar to a settlement. In this respect, we do find that Noranda Metal Industries was in violation of Section 6 of the Labour Code.

Simon Fraser University v CUPE, Local 3338, 2013 CanLII 2940 (BCLRB)

[Once collective bargaining commenced between CUPE (the union) and the university (the employer), and the parties exchanged their respective final proposals exhausting the possibility of introducing any further proposal at the bargaining table, the employer proposed changes to the pension plan. The university had previously discussed proposed amendments to the pension plan with the employees (wherein employer wanted salary increase to be tied to the pension plan), which the employees rejected. The parties agreed that an empowered group constitutive of employees represented by several unions would negotiate with the university insofar as modifications to the pension plan were concerned. Although none of the unions, including CUPE, could unilaterally agree to a pension plan during the negotiation, the university insisted that CUPE agree to amendments to the plan. As a result, CUPE applied to the British Columbia Labour Relations Board for a declaration that the employer (that is, the university) was bargaining in bad faith.]

[Excerpt from the decision]

Richard S Longpre, V-Chair:

[...]

29. [CUPE argued,] the parties are at an impasse. The University's three offers addressed changes to the Pension Plan. CUPE cannot respond to such changes. [The university] testified that [it] did not believe the parties are at an impasse. The University understands the agreement of APSA, the PolyParty and the EJPC [i.e., other representative bodies] are necessary for CUPE to be bound by any change to the Pension Plan. If CUPE refuses further discussion on the Pension Plan then such discussions are over. As noted in the University President's letter, he expects the parties will continue bargaining once this decision is rendered. . . .

IV. ANALYSIS AND DECISION

46. Section 11(1) of the Code reads:

> 11 (1) A trade union or employer must not fail or refuse to bargain collectively in good faith in British Columbia and to make every reasonable effort to conclude a collective agreement.

47. Most often, Section 11 applications address an overview of collective bargaining. In this case, bargaining prior to the summer of 2012 resolved virtually all non-monetary issues. The cessation in negotiations in the summer of 2012 was a result of a number of factors including the legitimate disagreement over CUPE's access to the Savings Plan,

the University's notice to CUPE that amendments to the Pension Plan would be a factor in monetary bargaining and the cancellation of scheduled bargaining days by both parties. The case management meeting on October 31, 2012 addressed these issues and the hearing went from there.

48. Idler [CUPE representative] testified that CUPE made its first proposal on November 4, 2012. Nonis [employer representative] testified that he did not receive CUPE's monetary proposal. A number of points support Idler. CUPE introduced a copy of that proposal as an exhibit. On each of CUPE's bargaining proposals, was a handwritten note showing the date and the time the proposal was given to Nonis and mediator Ready. This proposal was marked November 4, 2012 at 1:35 p.m. Nonis agreed they discussed the contents of CUPE's November 4, 2012 proposal, notably the proposed letter of agreement. If CUPE had not made the November 4, 2012 proposal then the Employer would have made two offers in a row—one on November 3, 2012 at 12:15 p.m. and the next one on November 4, 2012 at 1:35 p.m. Two offers in a row is unlikely to happen and Nonis did not suggest that it did happen. On November 4, 2012, Nonis was involved in two sets of negotiations at the same time. On balance, I am satisfied that Idler gave the November 4, 2012 proposal to Nonis who subsequently misplaced it.

49. Idler was upset at the statements made by Nonis at his meeting with the EJPC on November 8, 2012. Nonis met with the EJPC, absent Idler's presence, and told them that CUPE had been bargaining amendments to the Pension Plan. In their respective emails, Palmier of Local 1611 and Blackwell, the chair of the EJPC, described Nonis' comments in much the same way. In the three previous days of bargaining, discussions had been between mediator Ready, Idler and Nonis. All of the University's offers received by Idler were marked "confidential." Most importantly, CUPE's two proposals on November 4, 2012 (at 11:20 a.m. and 6:44 p.m.) did not suggest CUPE was agreeing to, or even proposing, a succession from the Pension Plan. I understand Idler's response, however, I do not see Nonis' comments at the EJPC meeting as being in breach of Section 11.

50. In the Protocol Agreement, the parties were agreeing that "following the initial exchange of proposals new items may only be raised by mutual agreement." Generally, parties are expected to comply with the terms of their protocol agreement. In this case, the Protocol Agreement was signed two years before the parties discussed monetary issues. Leaving aside the University's actual Pension Plan proposals, it is understandable that either party, two years from the time proposals were exchanged, might find it necessary to raise issues not considered when their original proposals were drafted and placed on the bargaining table. From the evidence, the University had good reason to raise the Pension Plan in November 2012. In 2011 and 2012, the University communicated the significant increase in Pension Plan costs and the urgency to address the Pension Plan's viability. CUPE expected the Pension Plan to be raised when monetary discussions began. And perhaps equally important, CUPE willingly discussed solutions to the Pension Plan that it could support.

51. Finally, the University relied upon British Columbia Hydro. In that case, the unions were seeking to bargain amendments to their pension plan. In its bargaining in bad faith complaint, the employer argued pension demands could not be raised at the bargaining table because any amendment to the pension required government approval.

The Board dismissed the employer's argument. The court of appeal upheld the Board's decision stating:

> I do not think complete freedom of action on the part of the employer is a prerequisite to bargaining. Agreements between an employer and a union will often be subject to others having authority to enforce rules concerning inflation, discrimination, health hazards, hours of work, and so forth. In such cases the employer may have limited power to contract but it is not relieved of the obligation to bargain. (para. 9) (QL)

The University argued the same applies in this case. The fact amendments to the Pension Plan would have to be approved by the EJPC did not restrict the University from raising amendments with CUPE in collective bargaining.

52. *Vancouver Symphony* assists in considering the University's argument. In *Vancouver Symphony*, the language in the collective agreement gave the union jurisdiction over the employers' home theatre. When the employers travelled to other locations, union employees were not required. In bargaining, the union sought to require the employers to use union members for all performances and rehearsals, regardless of location. *Vancouver Symphony* discussed the exceptions to the Board's hands off approach recognized in *Noranda*:

> Exceptions to the "hands off" approach established by *Noranda, supra,* have since been recognized: certain demands will in and of themselves be contrary to s. 6 of the Act. Those proposals which violate the duty to bargain in good faith fall into two categories. Some will be "illegal" from the outset, as they are expressly prohibited by the Act or some other applicable enactment (*e.g.*, human rights legislation). Even where agreed to by the parties and incorporated in their collective agreement, such proposals are not enforceable: see *MacDonalds Consolidated Ltd. and R.W.D.S.U., Local 580*, [1976] 2 CLRBR 292 (BCLRB No. 51/76). The second category is comprised of proposals which may be tabled, made the subject of negotiations and agreed to by the parties; however, they cannot be pressed to impasse: see, for example, *Northern-West Elevator Ltd. and Int'l Union of Elevator Constructors, Local 82*, B.C.I.R.C. (No. C127/91) [reported 12 CLRBR (2d) 308], and *Altech Architectural Products Ltd.*, B.C.I.R.C. (No. C20/89). These proposals become "improper" when taken to impasse, and a violation of s. 6, as their attainment through the use of economic sanctions would be inconsistent with the law and policy of the statute. (p. 172, added text in C.L.R.B.R.).

53. The principles in *Vancouver Symphony* were reiterated in *Northwood Pulp & Timber*. The *Northwood Pulp & Timber* panel summarized the distinction between the process of collective bargaining and the substantive proposals that arise in bargaining:

> In regulating the statutory duty to bargain in good faith now contained in s. 11 of the Code, the Board is primarily concerned with the process of collective bargaining. There may nonetheless be occasions where the substance of collective bargaining (*i.e.*, a proposal being advanced by one of the parties) overlaps with process or otherwise calls for scrutiny. The circumstances in which the Board will intervene are where specific demands are illegal, are inconsistent with the law and policy of the statute, or constitute evidence of bad faith bargaining. (pp. 319–320)

54. The question, in the present case, is whether the University's offers on November 3, 4, and 7, 2012, at this stage in bargaining, call for the scrutiny referred to in *Northwood Pulp & Timber*. I start with a review of the University's three offers.

55. The University's November 3, 2012 offer supports Nonis' evidence: all amendments sought by the University required the EJPC's agreement. The University's offer addressed two circumstances: if an agreement with the EJPC to change the Pension Plan could be reached, and an agreement with the EJPC to change the Pension Plan could not be reached. In either event, all discussions would occur "through the EJPC or whatever mutually agreeable forum is deemed necessary."

56. In the University's November 4, 2012 offer, Paragraphs (a), (b) and (c) are somewhat different but remain consistent with the previous offer. Paragraphs (d) and (e) are different from the previous offer. Paragraph (d) proposes that the members of the Pension Plan—including CUPE members—"will be responsible for all costs in excess of the University's 12% contribution." In Paragraph (e), the University proposes that "CUPE agrees to amend the Pension Plan to eliminate" specific terms of the Pension Plan. It is not apparent from the language of the offer that the EJPC's agreement on Paragraphs (d) and (e) was necessary.

57. On November 7, 2012, the University proposed that CUPE agree to implement a new pension plan. While the proposed plan was similar to the Pension Plan, funding for the new pension plan ensured the University's contribution was capped at 12%. In evidence, Nonis agreed that the new pension plan, while legally possible, could not be implemented without the EJPC's approval; however, the offer contains no such settlement.

58. I accept the Union's argument that the University's second offer dated November 4, 2012, and certainly its third offer, dated November 7, 2012, fit well within the concept of a receding horizon. The University was moving from CUPE assisting in discussions with the EJPC on amendments to the current Pension Plan—to CUPE agreeing to an entirely new pension plan covering CUPE members. Equally important, the second offer and certainly the third offer propose that CUPE agree to the current Pension Plan amendments without stating that such an agreement would have to be made with the EJPC.

59. The University argued that as its proposed amendments to the Pension Plan were not accepted—the amendments should be considered "off the table." There was no proposal that reflected that decision by the University; nor do I understand Nonis ever making that point to Idler in collective bargaining.

60. Consistent with *Vancouver Symphony* and *Northwood Pulp & Timber*, the University was entitled to raise solutions to the viability of the Pension Plan. It was entitled to propose amendments that, on their face, might have gone beyond CUPE's authority. There comes a point, however, where negotiations reach an impasse. CUPE took a strike vote and issued 72 hour strike notice on October 1, 2012. Rotating strike activity took place throughout October and November 2012. CUPE has put the University on notice that it will not continue to discuss the Pension Plan. The EJPC has put the University on notice that Pension Plan discussions must be with the EJPC. I am satisfied collective bargaining between the parties is at an impasse.

V. SUMMARY

61. I am satisfied that the University's attempt to keep the Pension Plan on the bargaining table at this time is a breach of Sections 11 and 47 of the Code.

* * * * *

7:421 Substantive and Procedural Obligations Imposed by the Duty to Bargain

At one extreme, it would be a clear breach of the duty to bargain for a party to propose a term that could not legally be included in a collective agreement—for example, a wage rate below the minimum wage required by employment standards legislation, or a union security clause weaker than the minimum required by the labour relations statute. Such substantive statutory requirements are matters of public policy, and a party who proposes that they be violated can hardly be said to be making reasonable efforts to reach a collective agreement.

There is another type of proposal which either the employer or the union can put forward without necessarily violating the duty to bargain, and which the other side can lawfully accept, but which neither side can press to an impasse—that is, to the point of threatening a strike or lockout over it. Generally speaking, these are proposals on matters, which affect the parameters of the collective bargaining relationship. Examples are proposals to reduce or expand the size of the bargaining unit as set by the labour board, and proposals to institute or maintain multi-employer bargaining in a situation where bargaining rights exist only on a single-employer basis. See Donald Carter, "The Duty to Bargain in Good Faith: Does it Affect the Content of Bargaining?" in KP Swan & KE Swinton, eds, *Studies in Labour Law* (Toronto: Butterworths, 1983) 36 at 42–51.

Apart from these relatively narrow exceptions, the parties to collective bargaining have considerable freedom to exercise their own judgment about what matters to raise at the bargaining table and about which of those matters are worth pressing to (or beyond) the point of impasse, as well as about the tactics they will use in the bargaining process. However, in applying the subjective and objective branches of the duty to bargain, labour boards have developed an extensive body of jurisprudence which places certain restrictions on that freedom. The rest of this section will review and assess those restrictions.

Labour boards have drawn an important distinction between what they characterize as "surface" bargaining and "hard" bargaining. Surface bargaining is a breach of the duty to bargain; hard bargaining is not. The meaning of this distinction is explored in the following case.

United Steelworkers of America v Radio Shack, [1980] 1 CLRBR 99 at 123–28 and 145 (OLRB)

[The respondent employer was a branch of Tandy Electronics Limited (Alberta), a subsidiary of Tandy Corporation of Fort Worth, Texas. The complainant union had been certified without a vote under section 7(a) (now section 11) of the Ontario *Labour Relations Act*, for full-time employees in November 1978 and for part-time employees in March 1979, pursuant to a finding by the Ontario Labour Relations Board that the employer had engaged in extensive unfair labour practices designed to keep the union out. Among those practices were the respondent's failure to comply with a board order to reinstate an employee dismissed for union activity; its involvement in the circulation of an anti-union petition; its warning that it would "move out west" if the union was certified, its statements to employees disparaging the board's procedures; and its distribution of free anti-union T-shirts to employees. There was also evidence from a former Radio Shack security officer, Donald Gallagher, that the respondent's director of personnel and security, Roy Murden, had hired people to infiltrate the union and obtain information on its activities, and had engaged private investigators to photograph everyone who attended union meetings. Murden had told Gallagher that he had been instructed "by Fort Worth to get rid of the union, no matter what the cost." Those activities had apparently all taken place before the union was certified.

On 30 November 1978, the complainant union's staff representative, Frank Berry, served notice to bargain on the respondent. In December Berry asked the respondent for the name, classification, and seniority date of each employee in the unit, and for the details of existing fringe benefits. On 9 January 1979, the respondent sent all employees a memorandum ridiculing the union's request for such information. Two days later, after receiving the union's proposals for a collective agreement, the respondent sent another memorandum to its employees, purporting to assure them that despite the union's demand for a union shop clause, no employee would ever have to pay union dues to work at Radio Shack. On 19 January, right after the first collective bargaining session, management sent employees another memorandum commenting on issues discussed at the bargaining table. On 16 February, after the second bargaining session, a further memorandum of that sort went out.

The respondent's counterproposals, put forward early in 1979, included several highly unusual items. A "relationship" clause would have prohibited the union from publicly mentioning the respondent or any of its employees, orally or in writing, without prior written authorization from the respondent's president, and would have allowed an employer grievance over any such mention to go immediately to arbitration, with the arbitrator being required to order the public withdrawal of the statement and damages of $5,000 to $10,000 a day against the union. A list of "rules and regulations" included eleven heads of prohibited employee conduct, some of them very vague. Any violation would subject the offending employee to immediate discharge.

On 15 December 1978, the parent company sent an American lawyer, Stewart Gordon, to participate in the negotiations. Gordon testified that he did not at first attend the bargaining sessions because of the objections of the respondent's Ontario labour lawyer, Donald McKillop, but that in May 1979 it was decided that he should attend the sessions. This led to McKillop's withdrawal as counsel and to his replacement by Bruce Binning, who became spokesman for the respondent along with Gordon.

Between 7 June 1979, when Binning and Gordon first arrived at the bargaining table, and the end of July, many outstanding issues were settled. Among the few remaining unsettled were the proposed rules and regulations and the union's request for a compulsory dues checkoff (a Rand Formula clause). Gordon and Binning testified that they had by then dropped their demand for the relationship clause, but Berry testified that the union was never told of this. The evidence was unclear on the respondent's willingness to modify its proposed rules and regulations.

Berry testified that Binning and Gordon told him in July 1979 that the respondent was unlikely to give any more ground on the outstanding issues unless the complainant threatened to strike. The parties therefore informally agreed to allow the mediator to time his report so that the employees would be in a legal strike position on 1 August. However, no settlement was reached. A strike began on 8 August and was still on when this matter was heard by the board.

Striking employees testified that during the strike, Jack MacDonald, a security consultant engaged by the respondent, photographed them on the picket line and told them—falsely—that a decertification application was being prepared. MacDonald testified that he said nothing about a decertification application. During the strike, Jerry Colella, vice-president and general manager of the respondent's Canadian operation since February 1979, published in the respondent's in-house publication (entitled *Watts Up*) a letter headed "A Debt of Gratitude." The letter gave profuse thanks to "those Radio Shack employees who have demonstrated their courage and fortitude by exercising their right to work in the face of a strike called by a minority of workers."

The complainant alleged that the respondent had breached sections 14, 56, 58, 59, and 61 (now sections 17, 70, 72, 73, and 76) of the Ontario *Labour Relations Act*, and asked for various remedies.]

ADAMS, Chair: [W]e have no hesitation in concluding that the respondent from November 1978 until June of 1979 utterly failed in its duty to bargain in good faith and make every reasonable effort to make a collective agreement. We are also of the view that its negotiating conduct during this period was a blatant continuation of its earlier anti-union animus and clearly aimed at further dividing its employees and undermining the trade union's statutory role in violation of sections 56, 58, and 61 of the *Labour Relations Act and their underpinning principles discussed above.*

This brings us to the months of June, July and August of 1979 and the Respondent's conduct at that time. There can be no doubt that the parties made "progress" after the insertion of Bruce Binning. A substantial portion of the language that would go into any collective agreement was agreed to between June and August and by the end of July the outstanding central issues had been narrowed to union security, merit wage increases, the transfer clause and the rules and regulations of the Respondent. Gordon testified that he had become dissatisfied with the "direction" of the negotiations by May and in retaining Bruce Binning wished to avoid the commission of any further unfair labour practices. Binning testified that the Respondent's position was not rigid on union security, that it was willing to submit disputed merit increases to arbitration; and that it was willing to review any rule the Complainant thought unreasonable. On the surface all of this evidence appears consistent with the Respondent's claim of a complete "change in heart."

So too, some of Berry's evidence is consistent with this theory. After narrowing the issues to four, Berry agreed to the issuance of a no-board report by the Minister apparently to facilitate the mutual need for a strike deadline. This could be said to be a peculiar approach to take with respect to an employer the Complainant thought was bargaining to destroy it. As the strike deadline approached Berry said that if there could be an agreement on union security and the rules, "everything else would fall into place." The union then waited until it was at least three weeks into its strike before commencing this complaint—a timing which might suggest the Complainant simply miscalculated its capacity to strike the employer, its strength having been dissipated by the Respondent's earlier lawless conduct.

We have, however, a number of serious misgivings which preclude adopting this view. For one thing, neither Gordon nor Binning had the final say in developing the Respondent's negotiating position. Apparently, Jerry Colella had the ultimate responsibility in this respect and Colella was not called to testify. The evidence indicates that Colella was in control of the Respondent from February of 1979 and, thus, would have been party to the earlier bad faith bargaining which we have found occurred up until at least June of 1979. We further note the recent publication of the letter of "thank you" bearing Colella's picture and signature to those employees who have continued to work during the strike and its resemblance to earlier improper tactics aimed at dividing the employees and undermining the Complainant. By itself the letter could be viewed as no more than an emotional response to a heated strike situation, but the overall conduct of the Respondent makes it difficult for the Board to be confident in characterizing the letter this way. Viewed in the totality of the Respondent's conduct, Colella's "thank you" is more suggestive of an unmitigated desire to destroy the Complainant by fostering employee opposition and belies any apparent change of heart. In the context of this case, the publication also constitutes a violation of section 56 as well as casting light on the proper construction to be given the Respondent's other actions.

Apart from Jerry Colella, there has been no significant change in the identity of those people managing the Respondent since the issuance of the certificate for the full-time unit, and yet, no one from the Respondent's management came forward to testify about the underlying basis to the instructions given to Gordon and Binning from June to August in contradistinction to the style of bargaining the Respondent had engaged in before that. Of additional concern is Gallagher's testimony that Murden told him "Fort Worth" wanted to get rid of the union at any cost and that the union would not get a contract within the year following notice to bargain. This testimony was inconsistent with Gordon's evidence that the American parent had been kept in the dark. Indeed, the insertion of Colella by the American parent in February of 1979 is inconsistent with Gordon's view of the Respondent as an independent Canadian subsidiary which was keeping its parent and its advisor in the dark. We are also concerned that neither Murden nor anyone associated with the parent came forward to rebut Gallagher's testimony or to explain to the Board firsthand that such deep-seated attitudes no longer permeated the Respondent's actions. Gordon explained his understanding of the change in attitude, but he is not an officer of either the American parent or the Respondent and his evidence about the change in attitude was, by and large, hearsay. Furthermore, he had no direct knowledge of any communication links between the Respondent and its parent and the role the parent was playing, if any, in the negotiations. Berry dealt exclusively with Gordon and Binning and even in the eleventh hour of the negotiations he doubted the sincerity of the Respondent. With the insertion of a new face in the negotiations, it is not surprising that the union delayed bringing this complaint and instead made a serious effort to test and judge the Respondent's apparent change in heart. That the Complainant called a strike before launching this complaint is not irrelevant to the issues before us but may only reflect its stated uncertainty over the Respondent's true intentions. After hard reflection on this issue, we have come to the conclusion that any ambivalence it may have had over the actual intentions of the Respondent was not unreasonable in the circumstances and ought not to deprive it from asking this Board to make its own judgment about the Respondent's sincerity in light of all the evidence.

In making our assessment, the absence of direct testimony from company officials is of great significance because of the rigid positions taken by the Respondent on the central issues in the negotiations. There can be little doubt that its positions on wages, transfer, union security and rules of conduct cut to the very heart of a collective agreement. That they would be strike issues with the Complainant in the context of this dispute is hardly surprising. That the Complainant would see an anti-union animus connecting the Respondent's position on each of these issues is also not unreasonable given the history to this relationship. Against the background of the Respondent's earlier misconduct, this Board is entitled to a detailed explanation justifying the Respondent's position on each item in order to be satisfied that the positions were not taken for the purpose of provoking the Complainant into an untenable strike.

To be fair to Bruce Binning and Stewart Gordon, they tried to give a rationale for some of the positions taken, but it was clear that they were merely giving their personal interpretations of what they thought the Respondent's intent was. The fact that they told Berry a strike deadline might affect the Respondent's resolve is demonstrative of their limited direct knowledge of the Respondent's motives.

The absence of direct testimony on motivation is of particular importance on the issue of union security because the Respondent's position on this issue fits hand in glove with the entire pattern of earlier unlawful conduct aimed at fostering employee opposition to the Complainant to undermine its status as exclusive bargaining agent for all of the employees in the bargaining unit. Binning testified that the Respondent's position was not rigid on this issue, but saying this does not make it so. The rigidity in a party's position must be gleaned as much from its conduct as from what it says to this Board. While we have no doubt that Bruce Binning thought his client might react differently in the face of a strike, the fact is that it did not. It is also a fact that Colella was the decision maker and he did not come forward to provide the Board with his understanding of the Respondent's current position on this issue and to explain how it differs from the Respondent's intemperate declaration on union security published in its January 11, 1979 newsletter. Nor was he called to explain how his "thank you" note to employees not honouring the picket lines related to the Respondent's earlier improper tactics aimed at discouraging support for the Complainant. From the Respondent's bargaining conduct one can detect no change on the union security issue from the period during which its actions were rife with anti-union animus to the more recent summer period where it claims to have engaged in hard bargaining. Furthermore, we have difficulty with Bruce Binning's explanation that the Respondent's position on union security is simply an unwillingness to agree to a Rand Formula where the union lacks a very large degree of employee support. Where the employer adopting this position has played no significant role in unlawfully contributing to the absence of such support, the position is unobjectionable. Such a difference in principle is not foreign to collective bargaining and cannot, by itself, be considered a product of bad faith bargaining.... But where an employer adopts this stance after having engaged in the kind of pervasive unlawful conduct that the Respondent has engaged in, the underlined caveat in the following excerpt from *The*

Daily Times leaps out from the rest of the paragraph which the Respondent asked the Board to take note of:

> The union claims that the company has coupled its wage offer with an offer of union security which it knows the union cannot accept and which, therefore, is designed to make it impossible to conclude an agreement. Section 36a [now 47] of the *Act* provides that on written request of the trade union there shall be included in the collective agreement a clause providing for voluntary revocable check-off. An offer of the form of union security provided for in Section 36a of the *Act* cannot be in violation of the *Act. This is not to say that an intransigent offer of this form of union security coupled with other relevant facts might not cause the Board to conclude in a given case that an employer had failed to bargain in good faith.* Even if the Board were to make such a finding, however, it could not impose a form of union security different than that set out in section 36a of the Act. If the Board was to make an order of the type sought by the trade union in this case, it would be ignoring the policy of voluntarism which is embodied in the Act and, having regard to the provisions of Section 36a, it would be thrusting itself into the role of legislator; a role which it cannot assume. [Emphasis added.]

It is not unusual for the ranks of a union to be swelled by bargaining unit employees after the issuance of a certificate. In fact, Bruce Binning made this point during his testimony. Employees who have been noncommittal may subsequently support the union once it has been certified by the Board. And this is true even for those employees who may have opposed the union prior to certification. But the Respondent did not refrain from the commission of unfair labour practices in November of 1978 after the issuance of the full-time bargaining unit certificate and did not commence to bargain in good faith. For the Respondent to then base its position on union security on an absence of employee support in August of 1979 tends to taint its motivation on this issue with its earlier unlawful conduct. Without persuasive evidence to the contrary, there is no reason for not concluding that the Respondent's rigid position on union security continues to be part and parcel of a longstanding scheme to undermine the statutory role of the Complainant as exclusive bargaining agent.

In coming to this conclusion we are particularly sensitive to the nature of section 36a, the benefit of which a trade union is entitled to as a matter of right and which is all the Respondent has ever been prepared to offer. Section 36a requires an employee to come forward and advise his employer that he wishes union dues to be deducted from his wages. Where an employer has acted as the Respondent has and over so long a period of time, it may require a particularly courageous employee to make such a request. Therefore, when this same employer rigidly ties his position to voluntary revocable checkoff, his conduct is open to the inference that he is motivated by a desire to deter his employees from supporting the union in this manner. The Respondent has, in the circumstances, failed to adduce sufficiently cogent evidence to rebut this inference. It is simply wrong to conclude that offering what the statute requires as a bare minimum in the area of union security cannot be held to constitute bargaining in bad faith. Standing alone this may be the case. But when considered in the light of other employer actions, it can be one of the most coercive elements of a scheme to discourage and undermine trade union support. Surely the Legislature did not intend to preclude the Board from so finding. We therefore find that the Respondent's position on union security violates sections 14, 56, 58 and 61 of the *Labour Relations Act*. As for counsel's argument that employees have to identify themselves when they go on strike in any event, this submission does not respond to the coercive significance of section 36a to non-member employees and, if the Respondent's own assessment of strike support is accurate, it may be telling that fewer employees than originally supported the Complainant's application for certification are now on strike. In fact, we find it quite remarkable that the Respondent could seriously rely on the "intelligence" about union support gathered by supervisors in developing its position on union security. With the history to this complaint, an employee would have to consider the wisdom of admitting support for the Complainant to the Respondent's supervisors and, as a Board, we are concerned that the Respondent is even monitoring employee sentiment in this respect in these circumstances.

To the extent that absolute rigidity is inconsistent with good faith bargaining and reasonable effort, it should be clear from our reasoning above that we are of the view that an employer can be no more rigid and unbending on union security than he can be on any other issue. Section 36a simply provides the union with a very limited form of union security as a matter of right. Any other form of union security is still clearly negotiable and, thus, an employer's bargaining obligation remains unchanged. Indeed, the very fact that the Legislature thought it necessary to enact section 36a conveys a statutory recognition of how important this issue is to trade unions and the problems associated with employer opposition. It would therefore be strange for this Board to interpret the presence of a provision benefiting trade unions to some limited degree in a manner which would encourage employer resistance and thereby exacerbate collective bargaining conflict in relation to this very sensitive issue. The issue is easily manipulated by an employer intent on undermining the exclusive role of a certified bargaining agent arising as it does in first agreement controversies. The Board must therefore judge bargaining with this fact clearly in mind.

After the long period of bargaining in bad faith that has been established in this case (together with the other unfair labour practices committed by the Respondent), there is an onus to prove the alleged change of heart in the latter stages of negotiations with the most cogent evidence available. This must be so because of the labour relations reality that apparent changes in heart may be little more than an awareness that "hard bargaining" is now sufficient to preclude the execution of any agreement or to cause so unsatisfactory a contract that continued employee support of the Complainant will be impossible. Neither of these approaches to "hard bargaining" is permissible and the Respondent is in the best position to explain its motivation in adopting the bargaining postures that it has.

After carefully analyzing all of the evidence, we have also come, on balance, to the more general conclusion that the Respondent was not bargaining in good faith and making every reasonable effort to enter into a collective agreement from June to August. This is not to deny that "progress" was made in negotiating the language of a possible agreement. But we think it more likely than not that the Respondent's rigid position on union security, as well as other items central to the negotiations, had the purpose of avoiding a collective agreement and was part and parcel of its earlier conduct aimed at undermining the trade union in the eyes of the employees in order to foster its early demise. This conclusion relies heavily on the totality of the evidence, arising as it does in a first agreement context, and draws its conceptual support from the following description of "surface bargaining" found in *The Daily Times*. . . .

> "Surface bargaining" is a term which describes a going through the motions, or a preserving of the surface indications of bargaining without the intent of concluding a collective agreement. It constitutes a subtle but effective refusal to recognize the trade union. It is important, in the context of free collective bargaining, however, to draw the distinction between "surface bargaining" and hard bargaining. The parties to collective bargaining are expected to act in their individual self interest and in so doing are entitled to take firm positions which may be unacceptable to the other side. The Act allows for the use of economic sanctions to resolve these bargaining impasses. Consequently, the mere tendering of a proposal which is unacceptable or even "predictably unacceptable" is not sufficient, standing alone, to allow the Board to draw an inference of "surface bargaining." This inference can only be drawn from the totality of the evidence including, but not restricted to, the adoption of an inflexible position on issues central to the negotiations. It is only when the conduct of the parties on the whole demonstrates that one side has no intention of concluding a collective agreement, notwithstanding its preservation of the outward manifestations of bargaining, that a finding of "surface bargaining" can be made.

We therefore find that the Respondent's more general bargaining posture during the months of June to August was in violation of sections 14, 56, 59, and 61 of the *Labour Relations Act*.

BOURNE, Board Member, dissenting: The history of events at the respondent's location in Barrie, up until May 1979, is unsavoury, to say the least. But it must surely be the events subsequent to that time which are the subject of bad faith bargaining in this instance. . . .

The shadow of negotiations before the entrance of Gordon and Binning has convinced the other members of the Board that the leopard hasn't changed its spots. Yet the evidence persuades me that both parties had entered into "hard bargaining" and had run across intractable positions on both sides by August 8—the company's stance with regard to the dues check-off being countered by the union's adamant position on rules and regulations as well as the check-off . . .

Events speak louder than words and [the respondent's] new team, which brought a whole grab-bag of unresolved issues down to three between June 7 and August 8, 1979, surely gives an indication of bargaining in good faith.

* * * * *

Canadian Union of United Brewery, Flour, Cereal, Soft Drink & Distillery Workers, Local No 304 v Canada Trustco Mortgage Company, [1984] OLRB Rep 1356 at 1363–65

[The union had been certified as bargaining agent at only two of the many branches of Canada Trust in Ontario—the St Catharines and Cambridge branches. The parties had negotiated a collective agreement for the St Catharines branch, generally embodying the terms that prevailed in the employer's non-unionized branches, with only marginal improvements. Then, in negotiations for the Cambridge branch, the employer was willing to offer only very minor improvements over the terms in the St Catharines agreement.

The union brought a complaint that the employer was bargaining in bad faith in the Cambridge negotiations. The employer's approach, the union argued, was the antithesis of real bargaining, which ought to have given the union the right to participate in or challenge employer decisions that adversely affected employees. After citing its *Radio Shack* decision (above), among others, the board concluded that the employer's behaviour was an example of hard but legitimate bargaining rather than surface bargaining.]

MACDOWELL, Vice-Chair: In recent years the Board has been scrupulous to protect the framework of collective bargaining: the independence of the union, the integrity of its role as the employees' exclusive bargaining agent and the right to information necessary for it to properly perform its statutory role. But the Board has been equally clear that it will not act as interest arbitrator, or prescribe the precise contents of the parties' collective agreement—even in the face of an "egregious" breach of the duty to bargain in good faith (see *Radio Shack* ...). The content of the agreement is for the parties to determine, in accordance with their own perceived needs and relative bargaining strengths. The legislation enables employees to combine together to bargain collectively and compels the employer to recognize their bargaining agent. It further provides a framework within which there can be an exploration of the parties' differences and a sincere effort to reach some accommodation. Despite the adversarial aspects of collective bargaining, there are substantial areas of mutual interest between employers and employees which informed discussion may reveal. But the statute does not *require* any particular concessions, nor does it stipulate the content of a collective agreement, or even that a collective agreement always must be the necessary outcome of the parties' bargaining.

One cannot quarrel with the proposition that the "duty to bargain in good faith" must encompass an obligation to engage in informed and rational discussion, and in exceptional circumstances an employer's position at the bargaining table may be so patently unreasonable or devoid of apparent business justification as to evidence a desire to avoid any collective agreement altogether. So may an unexplained retreat from a previous agreed position, or the untimely insertion of new issues into the bargaining process. However, the Board must be careful that in adjudicating disputes and giving a reasoned elaboration for its decisions, it does not impose its own model of decision-making as the normative standard for the collective bargaining process. Collective bargaining is not simply a matter of presenting proofs and reasoned arguments in an effort to achieve a favourable outcome, nor is that outcome necessarily arrived at, or explained, by a logical development from given and accepted premises. It is a process in which reason plays a part—but not the only part. There may be a range of potential outcomes or solutions and the ultimate result may have more to do with economic strength than abstract logic. In particular collective bargaining situations there simply may not be any commonly accepted principles or criteria and, in consequence, no objective basis for distinguishing a "claim of right" from a "naked demand." Reason and self-interest are inextricably intertwined. Ultimately the parties may reach agreement only because of a realistic appraisal of the value of their objectives in relation to their ability to obtain them, including the costs they are able to inflict on one another. It may have little to do with what some outsider might consider a "fair" settlement, or a just allocation of rewards to capital and labour.

Rational discussion is an important aspect of the bargaining process. So is power. Persuasion is an effective tactic to gain one's bargaining objectives. So is economic pressure. Whether that system actually results in a "just wage" or "distributive justice," we leave for others to debate. Collective bargaining permits that outcome, but it does not compel it. (For an interesting analysis of the impact of collective bargaining see: *What Unions Do*, by R.B. Freeman & J.L. Medoff....)

The facts of this case provide a graphic illustration of the absence of shared principle, and the predominance of bargaining power as a means of settling the parties' collective bargaining differences. The union seeks to limit the exercise of managerial authority and achieve for its supporters, terms and conditions of employment not only more generous than the employer is willing to pay, but also more generous than the employer is currently paying to hundreds of other employees in identical circumstances. The employer seeks to maintain its managerial prerogatives and provide levels of remuneration consistent with its own assessment of its needs, its own organizational imperatives, and its own perception of the dictates of the market place. There is no obvious way of reconciling these competing interests, nor is there any reservoir of principle to which one can resort to provide the "right answer." No amount of rational discussion or reasoned elaboration will necessarily produce an accommodation. Nor can there always be such accommodation in our system of free collective bargaining which ultimately rests, as it must, on the right of parties to resort to economic sanctions in pursuit of their own self-interest as they define it. Under our statute their only obligation is to endeavour to conclude a collective agreement and if that is the true intent, neither the content nor the consequences of that agreement are of any concern to the Board.

This is not to say that collective bargaining must always be a "zero sum game," or that there cannot be substantial areas of mutual accommodation and joint decision-making. But our statute mandates collective bargaining, not co-determination. Co-determination, or co-partnership may be the result of collective bargaining, but it is not an outcome required by law. Nor was the duty to bargain in good faith designed to redress an imbalance of bargaining power. A party whose bargaining strength allows it to virtually dictate the terms of the agreement does not thereby bargain in bad faith, and that proposition is applicable whether it is the union or the employer which "has the upper hand."

In the circumstances of this case, we are satisfied that the employer's conduct is properly characterized as hard bargaining in pursuit of its own self-interest and legitimate business objectives. It was, and remains, prepared to sign a collective agreement on terms similar to those agreed to in St. Catharines, and, in our view, it was entitled to take into account the relative insignificance of this bargaining unit in its overall organizational scheme. If its rigid insistence on the preservation of management rights has a certain ideological cast, it is one which in our system is recognized as legitimate. There has been no breach of section 15 of the Act. The complaint is therefore dismissed.

* * * * *

CHAPTER 7: NEGOTIATING A COLLECTIVE AGREEMENT

The authors of the following excerpt offer a critique of what they describe as the dominant approach to the duty to bargain—the approach taken by the Ontario board in *Canada Trustco* and in its subsequent decision in *Eaton's* [1985] OLRB Rep March 491.

Brian Langille & Patrick Macklem, "Beyond Belief: Labour Law's Duty to Bargain" (1988) 13 Queen's Law Journal 62 at 80–87 and 91–92

We wish to suggest that this whole structure and way of thinking about the duty to bargain is seriously mistaken. We do not say that this dominant understanding is incapable of processing any complaints in a rational manner. We believe it does so, and this explains, in part, the longevity of this point of view. However, at the heart of the conception lies a serious flaw, a flaw which renders the duty impotent where it is needed the most, in a category of truly hard cases which the current understanding does not even recognize. *Canada Trustco Mortgage* is such a case.

Returning to the opening words of the *Canada Trustco* decision, we find the Board articulating the views of the parties in terms which are perfectly understandable within the prevalent mode of thinking. The union alleges bad faith; the employer replies that it is simply acting in its self-interest. The point to make is that such a conception of the duty to bargain, which assumes or rests upon a supposed distinction between bad faith and self-interest, is bound to fail. It is bound to fail because, by and large, there is no such distinction. Any labour law rule which assumes, draws, or depends upon a distinction between bad faith and self-interest, or between anti-union animus and self-interest, in our view, will not work. In a contractualist bargaining world, self-interest is the only operable notion, the only gauge against which conduct can be measured. By definition, one's self-interest can include an anti-union animus. Acting under an anti-union animus is merely playing the contractualist game.

Now it is true that the current understanding of the duty to bargain in good faith will cover a number of particularly unattractive factual situations—represented, perhaps, by the *Radio Shacks* of this world. The current conception, as has been pointed out, does make one—but only one—change in the pre-existing rules governing contractual bargaining. The duty compels an employer to deal with a trade union. At common law there was no obligation to deal with anyone if one did not want to, regardless of one's reasons for not wanting. By contrast, under a collective bargaining regime, you must be willing to bargain and you must be willing to enter a collective agreement.

Thus it is clear that the duty is not without content. It can capture those employers who view it in their self-interest not to recognize the trade union. If your intent is not to sign a collective agreement because this is your view of how to maximize your self-interest then you are, if the evidentiary problem is overcome, caught by the duty. However, if you are willing to sign a collective agreement, then you can maximize your self-interest. The problem with this neat view of the world is that it captures only: (a) the rational but less powerful, and (b) the irrational but more powerful, employers of this world. It does not capture the rational and powerful employer. That is, a rational and powerful employer will always be willing to sign the collective agreement which maximizes its self-interest. It is simply wrong to think that one can only maximize one's self-interest by not signing a collective agreement. If the content of the agreement is totally "up for grabs" then there is no rational disincentive to signing. If self-interest backed by economic clout can produce any agreement, what disincentive is there to signing? Under our model, once you are willing to sign, all else becomes a matter of "self-interest." Once you cross that hurdle all is relegated to the tautology that whatever is in your self-interest is by definition legitimate; no further reason need be given—none whatsoever. Freedom of contract is absolute.

Our thesis is simply the following: the law has gradually come to grips with the irrational and powerful employers. Our existing conception captures this case. The hole in the heart of the theory is its inability to deal with the rational and powerful employer. And, as we all know, rational employers have appeared on the scene. The bottom line for our labour law must be that there is no distinction, from the point of view of regulating bargaining, between the rational and the irrational employer. Both achieve the same effect and both do so for the same motive. One is simply more rational in its pursuit of its objective than the other. It makes no sense to relegate the duty to the role of regulating the irrational powerful anti-union employers of this world, but not the rational ones.

Without substantive content, and with the principle of maximizing one's self-interest, a willingness to enter some collective agreement is merely the requirement of rationality upon the part of the employer. An employer who has superior bargaining power, such that it can dictate the terms of a collective agreement, need not act in an irrational way. There is no difference between refusing to sign any collective agreement and signing a collective agreement the terms of which can be completely dictated and which represent no change from the status quo. In the former situation, the employer refuses to recognize the union; in the latter, the employer refuses to permit the union to be recognized in the collective agreement. One simply achieves through the front door what one could not achieve through the back. Our current conception of the duty simply ignores this point. A powerful, rational, anti-union employer can thus plead self-interest and escape the strictures of the duty. This is what the opening words of *Canada Trustco* tell us, and this is what we all assume....

Thus our current conception of the duty to bargain ignores a whole category of employer behaviour. By relying on a distinction between good faith and self-interest which has the effect of upholding rational anti-union employer tactics, this conception threatens the integrity of legislative schemes designed to "encourag[e] the practice and procedure of collective bargaining" by subjecting their dictates in situations of this sort to an overriding defence of self-interest. In what can be characterized as a series of attempts to mediate the radical potential of this unruly affirmation of freedom of contract, jurisprudence under the duty to bargain contains certain exceptions to the automatic equation of good faith with self-interest—exceptions which, in our view, operate as avoidance techniques and which are only as coherent as the principle which engenders them.

An example of such exception and avoidance can be found in the recent Eaton's decision of the Ontario Board. In that case, the Board was faced with an employer who refused to give more at the bargaining table to unionized employees than what it was willing to give its non-unionized employees at other locations. In upholding such a position, the Board relied on the distinction between bad faith and self-interest outlined previously, accepting the argument that an employer is acting according to self-interest when it formulates bargaining proposals designed to minimize the likelihood of unionization at its non-unionized locations and rejecting the view that this constitutes bad faith. The Board stated the following:

> Nothing in the *Labour Relations Act* requires an employer to agree to wages and employee benefits for unionized employees that are superior to those being received by non-unionized employees. See *Canada Trustco*.... Neither is there any provision which prohibits an employer when formulating its bargaining position to take into account the likelihood that improvements in the terms of employment for one group of employees will likely impact on other groups. Indeed, logic suggests that this is a consideration frequently taken into account by employers, since an improvement in the employment conditions of one group of employees will logically lead to similar improvements for other employees of the same employer, whether they be unorganized or included in a different bargaining unit.

Stripped to its essentials, the above asserts that employers frequently consider the likely impact of improvements in terms of employment for one group of employees upon another (not yet organized) group of employees. Therefore, the cost of future unionization is part of the calculus of bargaining and affects the content of proposals. The paragraph is telling of the fact that jurisprudence under the duty simultaneously recognizes that minimizing the cost of unionization is self-interested action but represses the idea that such behaviour also amounts to an anti-union animus. The implication of such repression, of course, is that it potentially renders the notion of anti-union animus meaningless. The Board appears to recognize this implication and attempts to mediate it by introducing the following caveat:

> Further, the fact that an employer refuses to give more to unionized employees, does not, by itself, necessarily mean that the employer is seeking to interfere with the formation of trade unions. Such a conclusion might be justified if the terms being offered to organized employees were inferior to those being enjoyed by comparable non-union employees, for this would indicate an intent to punish employees because they had selected trade union representation. Such, however, is not the case here.

Thus the Board quickly distances itself from the idea that, even though an employer can factor in and attempt to minimize the cost of unionization during bargaining in an attempt to reduce the likelihood of future unionization, the employer does not breach the duty by attempting to enshrine terms in a collective agreement *inferior* to those being enjoyed by non-unionized employees. This, in the Board's view, would be acting in bad faith.

The question which presents itself is, of course, why? If one is entitled to take a hard line during bargaining to eliminate incentives on employees at other locations to organize, why is it that an employer cannot demand that unionized employees accept an offer inferior to what non-unionized employees receive? It is presumably in the employer's self-interest to do so, and there is nothing in the logic and rhetoric of our dominant conception of the duty to bargain, so long as the employer was willing to sign the agreement, which would prevent such an action. The notion that the latter move is punitive, while the former is self-interested, avoids the fact that both are punitive, both are self-interested, and both have the same motive and effect. . . .

In sum, the claim made here is that our dominant conception of the duty to bargain is fraught with inconsistency. This is not to say that it is totally useless. But there are serious problems. First, it relies on a distinction between self-interest and bad faith which does not hold up to scrutiny. Acting in one's economic self-interest and acting with an anti-union animus are ultimately indistinguishable: in theory, the former includes the latter and, in practice, it is widely thought that it is in one's economic self-interest to have a non-unionized workplace. The upshot is that our conception of the duty to bargain legitimates bargaining positions designed to eliminate the union from the workplace simply because the employer is amenable to the signing of a contract which ensures that result. Second, our conception of the duty engenders caveats to the equation of good faith and self-interest which, insofar as they rely on the validity of that equation but at the same time attempt to restrain its radical implications through exception and avoidance, are ultimately incoherent....

[T]he purpose of our collective bargaining law is not to promote contractualism, it is to seek justice. Contractualism is a means to the end, not the end itself. Indeed, pure common law contractualism is what we modified and rejected in the name of justice. We say, this method will not get us where we wish to go. Therefore, we create other modes of regulation, including that of the restructured market. Our misunderstanding has been to articulate the means of achieving justice in a way which denies the end in the name of which we utilize those means in the first place. At the same time, and as a result, we achieve the incoherence evident in *Canada Trustco* and *Eaton's*.

Earlier it was argued that there is no distinction between the irrational and rational powerful anti-union employer. Both seek to achieve the same effect and with the same motive. However, under our current conception of the duty, one is excused and the other is not. This cannot be correct. The point is that if the current conception of the duty demands only willingness to sign an agreement (that is, no intent not to sign any agreement) then a rational employer is indifferent to signing a collective agreement which merely embodies the status quo or not signing a collective agreement and thus guaranteeing the status quo. As long as you are willing to sign, any content can be justified in the name of self-interest backed by economic power. The collective agreement need not contain anything but what the statute demands. That is, until recently, almost nothing. There need be no recognition of the role of the union stewards, committees, or other institutions. Not even a bulletin board. Even if these institutions are created they need be given no role, no say, no process, no input, no control. Further, there need be no reduction of arbitrary employer power, no rule of law, no rights of citizenship, no recognition of seniority at all or in any form, no just cause provision, no inroads upon other arbitrary employer actions. What the employer gets is exactly what the employer gets without a collective agreement, and for the same reasons. The statute calls for an arbitration process but that process will not guarantee substantive rights. Assuming grievances even reach arbitration, the employer will win all the cases. When we witness the use of superior bargaining power to destroy the institutions and processes of collective representation of employees, then we witness the tragedy of the sacrifice of ends of the civilized and democratic workplace to the means of contractualism. We are in effect arguing for minimum substantive content of the duty to bargain— a minimum set of rights to ensure collective voice.
[Reprinted by permission.]

CHAPTER 7: NEGOTIATING A COLLECTIVE AGREEMENT

* * * * *

In *Royal Oak Mines Inc*, excerpted below, the Supreme Court of Canada considered the extent to which labour boards can scrutinize the contents of bargaining proposals. The majority of the Court found that where a party refuses to include in its proposals terms which have been widely accepted in other agreements throughout the particular industry, it may be appropriate for the board to find that party to be in breach of its duty to make every reasonable effort to reach a collective agreement. Consider how far this judgment goes to address the concerns raised by Langille and Macklem.

Royal Oak Mines v Canada (Labour Relations Board), [1996] 1 SCR 369 at 369–89

[The unionized workers of Royal Oak Mines, a company based in Yellowknife, NWT, voted overwhelmingly to reject a tentative agreement put forward by the employer. A bitter and violent eighteen-month strike followed, which affected the whole community of Yellowknife and resulted in nine deaths in a bomb explosion. Various attempts to bring about a settlement were made during the strike, through mediation and the appointment of an industrial commission under the *Canada Labour Code*. The Canada Labour Relations Board found that the employer had failed to bargain in good faith by refusing to bargain until a particular certification issue had been resolved and by attempting to impose a probationary period on all returning strikers. However, the board based its decision mainly on what it found to be the employer's most serious violation: the employer's refusal to negotiate until the issue of reinstatement and discipline of several employees accused of serious picket line violence had been resolved.

In light of the long history of intransigence and bitterness between the parties, the board ordered the employer to put back on the table the tentative agreement which it had put forward earlier (and which the union had rejected), with the exception of four items on which the employer had changed its position. The parties were given a thirty-day period to settle those items, after which compulsory arbitration was to be imposed.

An application by the employer for judicial review of the board's order was dismissed by the Federal Court of Appeal. The employer appealed to the Supreme Court of Canada.]

CORY J. (L'Heureux-Dubé and Gonthier JJ. concurring): Section 50(a) of the *Canada Labour Code* has two facets. Not only must the parties bargain in good faith, but they must also make every reasonable effort to enter into a collective agreement. Both components are equally important, and a party will be found in breach of the section if it does not comply with both of them. There may well be exceptions but as a general rule the duty to enter into bargaining in good faith must be measured on a subjective standard, while the making of a reasonable effort to bargain should be measured by an objective standard which can be ascertained by a board looking to comparable standards and practices within the particular industry. It is this latter part of the duty which prevents a party from hiding behind an assertion that it is sincerely trying to reach an agreement when, viewed objectively, it can be seen that its proposals are so far from the accepted norms of the industry that they must be unreasonable.

Section 50(a)(ii) requires the parties to "make every reasonable effort to enter into a collective agreement." It follows that, putting forward a proposal, or taking a rigid stance which it should be known the other party could never accept must necessarily constitute a breach of that requirement. Since the concept of "reasonable effort" must be assessed objectively, the Board must by reference to the industry determine whether other employers have refused to incorporate a standard grievance arbitration clause into a collective agreement. If it is common knowledge that the absence of such a clause would be unacceptable to any union, then a party such as the appellant, in our case, cannot be said to be bargaining in good faith. On this it is significant that the special mediators made the following observation in their second interim report:

> the employer must restrain itself from taking bargaining positions which it surely must know would be unacceptable to virtually any organization of workers. It is one thing to say that circumstances have changed such that the content of the tentative agreement is no longer good enough. It is another to construct unmanageable bargaining gaps.

In some cases a party's behaviour may be so egregious that it can be reasonably inferred that there is an unwillingness to make a real effort to reach an agreement. In those circumstances, while a party may express a desire to reach a collective agreement their actions may clearly indicate that they do not wish to intend to reach an agreement. A refusal to include such basic and standard terms in an agreement as a requirement of a just cause for dismissal clause, or a refusal to negotiate about pensions, or as in this case, a refusal to consider a grievance arbitration clause, leads to the inference that despite any "sincerely and deeply held" beliefs the party claims to have, by taking a rigid stance on such a widely accepted condition, it becomes apparent that the party (here the employer) has no real intention of reaching an agreement. In other words, the employer is breaching the duty to "make every reasonable effort to enter into a collective agreement."

If a party proposes a clause in a collective agreement, or conversely, refuses even to discuss a basic or standard term that is acceptable and included in other collective agreements in comparable industries throughout the country, it is appropriate for a labour board to find that the party is not making a "reasonable effort to enter into a collective agreement." If reasonable parties have agreed to the inclusion of a grievance arbitration clause in their collective agreement, then a refusal to negotiate such a clause cannot be reasonable. The grounds on which an employer may dismiss an employee is of fundamental importance for any association of employees. For an employer to refuse an employee a grievance procedure or some form of due process, by which the employee can challenge his or her dismissal on the ground that it was not for just cause, is to deny that employee a fundamental right. In those circumstances it would be reasonable for a board to infer that no reasonable union would accept a collective agreement which lacked a grievance arbitration clause and that the employer's failure to negotiate the clause indicated a lack of good faith bargaining....

The more appropriate approach would have been for the appellant to agree to the inclusion in the new collective agreement of some form of a grievance arbitration clause for the dismissed employees. It is certainly significant that after the Board decision, once a grievance arbitration process for the dismissed employees had concluded, the process resulted in 44 of the 49 employees being reinstated and/or awarded severance pay.

In summary, on the issue of the Board's finding that the appellant failed to bargain in good faith, I am of the view that this precise issue was by the provisions of the *Canada Labour Code* granted to the Board to decide, and that the courts should not set aside the Board's decision unless it was patently unreasonable. There is overwhelming support for the Board's finding that the appellant breached its duty to bargain in good faith by imposing an unreasonable condition to the collective bargaining process. Accordingly, the decision was clearly not patently unreasonable and the Federal Court of Appeal, recognizing this, properly deferred to the Board's finding.

* * * * *

National Automobile, Aerospace Transportation and General Workers Union of Canada (CAW-Canada) and its Local 2224 v Buhler Versatile Inc, [2001] MLBD No 9 at para 2ff

KORPESHO, Chair:

[…]

CAW-Canada alleged that B.V.I. had failed to bargain in good faith and failed to make every reasonable effort to conclude a collective agreement with the Applicant Union....

The original "Versatile" plant began as a family operation in Winnipeg, in 1952, as a manufacturer of tractors and drag-behind equipment. In or around 1987, the plant was purchased by Ford New Holland Canada, Ltd.... New Holland was subsequently sold to IHF—Internazionale Holding Fiat S.A....

The plant, throughout its history, experienced the cyclical nature of the agricultural industry, at one time employing up to 1,150 and as few as 70 employees. The current work force in the plant unit numbers approximately 250.

In 1999, New Holland purchased Case International..., another major farm tractor and implement manufacturer. The proposed purchase came under the scrutiny of the U.S. Department of Justice, in Washington, D.C., in regard to the potential loss of competitiveness in the industry as a result of this sale. The U.S. Department of Justice subsequently informed New Holland that the Versatile plant had to be sold as a condition of the New Holland-Case merger. At the time of the merger, the Versatile plant produced three tractors: a two-wheel drive model known as the G-70 Genesis; a four-wheel drive model; and a bidirectional model known as the TV140....

After some nine months of negotiations and meetings with the U.S. Department of Justice, as well as a representative of the Federal Government of Canada ... B.V.I. purchased the plant in July of 2000....

It is within this backdrop that we get to the allegations before us. There is no question that the CAW-Canada also had serious reservations as to the purchase of New Holland by B.V.I. The CAW-Canada had made it quite clear that B.V.I. was not its purchaser of choice as the Union felt Buhler did not have the corporate presence to enter into a purchase of this size. Having said that, B.V.I. became a party to the Collective Agreement covering the plant employees, which expired September 2000.

The parties' first bargaining session took place on September 29th, 2000, ... at which time proposals were exchanged....

It was at this meeting that Buhler stated, "My first offer is always my last offer." ...

There is no doubt in our minds that the CAW-Canada, from the initial meeting of September 29th, 2000, modified and withdrew certain bargaining proposals, and at the same time asked for written clarification so they could rationally consider certain proposals put forth by Buhler. The Employer, on the other hand, offered less each time they met and failed to provide, as requested, information in relation to its proposals....

The Alberta Labour Relations Board, in *Alberta Projectionists and Video Technicians Local 302 of the International Alliance of Theatrical Stage Employees and Moving Picture Machine Operators of the United States and Canada v. Famous Players Inc.* . . . , states:

> The duty to bargain in good faith is a cornerstone of the Labour Relations Code. It "gives life and substance to the rights of employers and employees" contained in sections 19.

That board went on to say, at page 12:

> The duty to bargain in good faith has many aspects; breach of one aspect does not imply a breach of all aspects. However, a breach of even one aspect may result in the Board finding a breach of s. 58. Decisions of this Board reveal the variety of obligations inherent in the duty to bargain in good faith. A summary of those obligations include the obligation on:
> - the employer to recognize the trade union as the bargaining agent;
> - the parties to meet;
> - the parties to bargain;
> - the parties to act with the intent of concluding, revising or renewing a collective agreement;
> - the parties to make every reasonable effort to enter into a collective agreement;
> - the parties to engage in full, rational, informed discussion about the issues;
> - the employer to disclose decisions that have been made affecting the bargaining unit;
> - a party, upon request, to provide the other party with information relevant to the issues involved in bargaining;
> - the parties to avoid deception in their representations to each other;
> - the parties to avoid surface bargaining.

[...]

The parties met and bargained on six occasions prior to the strike. We do not agree with counsel for the Employer that the limited number of meetings should be a significant issue in considering if bad faith bargaining had occurred. On the contrary, the Board is more interested in the quality of negotiations as opposed to the quantity of time expended....

Buhler, with the exception of the Buhler benefit package, put forth proposals without providing any justification or documentation to support his demands. It is also clear that Buhler was not prepared to discuss, in any rational way, any of the positions put forth by the CAW-Canada. One only has to review the notes of the last bargaining session, held on November 2nd, 2000, where most of Buhler's answers were either: "No; my answer is no; that's a definite no; and you've got to be kidding; no." to almost every query or proposal raised by the CAW-Canada.

It is also our view that Buhler knew, or ought to have known, that certain of his demands that would eliminate a number of longstanding provisions in the existing Collective Agreement, including the current health and welfare benefits and seniority, could not have been accepted by the Union and still have them maintain credibility with its members.

As Adams states [in] ... his text, *Canadian Labour Law* ... :

> The deliberate tabling of inflammatory proposals which would likely provoke a breakdown in negotiations may violate the duty. This must be contracted [sic] with the "hard-bargaining" situation where one party insists on onerous terms the other refuses to accept.

[...]

In assessing Buhler's demands, we are satisfied that his bargaining tactics went beyond that of "hard bargaining" and contravened the intent of section 63(1) of the Act [the duty to bargain requirement].

Although we are unaware of the negotiating tactics utilized by Buhler with other bargaining agents, we are troubled that his strategy with the CAW-Canada was based on his constant threats of plant closure. Buhler's proposals seemed, at times, to be irrational, to say the least, and at certain times took on a "bait and switch" type of strategy. A number of times through the bargaining sessions Buhler insisted that he would not lock out the employees, yet in those same discussions, threatened to padlock the doors.

The Board understands that parties, from time to time, engage in what has been described as "hard bargaining" to try to persuade the other side to accept a position on a particular issue. This, in our view, is not the case in the matter before us. Buhler consistently displayed an unwillingness to enter into any rational and informed discussions and provide supporting arguments throughout those negotiations. The evidence is clear that each time the CAW-Canada modified its position, Buhler proceeded to offer less. This, in itself, satisfies the Board that he breached the duty to bargain in good faith by purposely avoiding attempts to find some "common ground" to resolving the outstanding issues.

As previously mentioned, Buhler's tactics throughout can only be described as an attempt to bully the CAW-Canada into submission, by threats of selling the operation or padlocking the doors. Buhler and Engel were also quick to place the blame of the failed negotiations on the failure of both the Conciliation Officer and the Mediator for either not transmitting information or not holding face-to-face meetings with the parties. We find these comments unacceptable and consistent with Buhler's attitude that everyone else is responsible for the present situation except Buhler.

There is no doubt, in analyzing this situation, that B.V.I. placed the CAW-Canada in a situation where negotiations were going nowhere and, in fact, in a situation where each time they met, the Employer's offer worsened. Buhler's proposals could best be described as a "moving target."

Counsel for the Employer argued that the CAW-Canada didn't have to go on strike, as other options were available. She argued, for instance, that they could have continued working, and at the same time file an application with the Board alleging the very same bargaining in bad faith allegations. Although that may well have been an option for the CAW-Canada, that is not the question before the Board. The issue is simply, did the actions of the Employer cause the strike to take place. Having heard the evidence of both parties, the answer to that, in the Board's opinion, is an unequivocal yes.

We are satisfied, after considering the totality of the evidence, that the Employer's conduct during the bargaining sessions, up to and including November 2nd, 2000, were such that they contravened the duty to bargain in good faith and to make every reasonable effort to enter into a collective agreement....

The Board is satisfied that the action of this Employer went beyond hard bargaining. The constant threat of sale and closure; the lack of supporting material to justify Buhler's demands; the switching of positions in the middle of bargaining; the continued deterioration of Buhler's initial offer; Buhler's failure to disclose vital decisions; and his total lack of attempt to seek some common ground can only lead the Board to one conclusion — a breach of section 63(1) of the *Labour Relations Act*.

* * * * *

The Manitoba board noted above that the employer's chief executive officer (Buhler) had said at the very first bargaining meeting, "My first offer is always my last offer." This approach on the employer's part has echoes of a tactic known as Boulwarism, developed by General Electric in the United States in the 1940s. That tactic consisted of the employer's placing of a detailed offer on the table at the start of negotiations, and announcing that it would listen to what the union had to say but would not change the offer in any way unless economic conditions changed. *NLRB v General Electric Co*, 418 F2d 736 (2d Cir 1969), *certiorari* denied 397 US 965 (1970).

Should it be a breach of the duty to bargain for an employer to work out carefully in advance exactly how far it is willing to go in order to reach a collective agreement, then state that position at the start of negotiations and stick firmly to it? Conversely, should it be a breach of the duty for a union to insist that the employer accept the same terms that the union has negotiated with other employers in the particular industry?

* * * * *

United Food & Commercial Workers Canada, Local 175 v WHL Management Limited Partnership, 2014 CanLII 76990 (OLRB)

[In this dispute, the employer and the union were made to repeatedly engage in good faith collective bargaining by the Ontario Labour Relations Board. The production employees' trade union was certified as bargaining agent in August 2008. Eleven months after the certification, the parties entered into their first four-year collective agreement. By the fourth year of their collective agreement, the board observed, that bargaining relationship between the parties had deteriorated. Before the commencement of bargaining for the renewal of collective agreement between the parties, the unionized workers were already contemplating striking in the event the bargaining failed. On 29 April 2013, the union served the employer a notice to bargain, to which the employer responded by delivering documents on enterprise operations. During July and August 2013, mostly in the presence of a conciliation officer, the parties exchanged their proposals. On 13 August, the employer made a final offer, which was rejected by the union before it commenced its strike action. The strike continued until the date of the board's decision on 9 December 2014.

In spite of the strike, the parties continued bargaining from September 2013 through February 2014. When the matter came to the board on 5 March 2014, the board was advised that the parties were interested in continuing bargaining. It was then, with the consent of both parties, that the board encouraged mediation of outstanding issues between them. The board granted the parties until 25 April 2014, for mediated resolution of outstanding issues in the bargaining process. If the mediation failed, the board would hear the dispute on merits on 25 April. A mediated negotiation failed between the parties before the hearing on 25 April. The matter was then scheduled to be decided on merits in May. But, when the board convened on 6 May, the parties wanted to resolve their outstanding issues through a board-mediated process. After another failure in mediated bargaining, the board reconvened on 8 May, advising—with the consent of the parties—that the mediated bargaining should continue through 9 May. This latest mediated bargaining also reached an impasse. The board then went on to hear the issue on merits.

Objecting to the board's hearing on merits, the employer's counsel noted that it would be a violation of the natural justice principle if the board were to decide the dispute only on the basis of submitted documents without allowing oral evidence to examine the dispute. The employer's counsel also emphasized that in view of the turn of events (described above), the parties could not be said to have reached an impasse; the parties, instead, were still in the process of continuing their collective bargaining. It would, therefore, be improper for the board to intervene to resolve the disputed issues during the continuing bargaining process. The following paragraphs document the board's response to these issues. (Also note that the issues related to strike and employability of striking employees and replacement workers have constitutional implications.)]

The Decision on Process

Underlying Considerations
45. The Board declined to recuse itself for reasonable apprehension of bias or breach of its duty of fairness, as urged by counsel for the Employer in its post-hearing written submissions. It gives here its reasons for rejecting those submission and for proceeding as it has done. Our legal tradition countenances the addressing of a challenge to the integrity of its process by a quasi-judicial decision-maker, both in its own proceedings as well as before the courts [footnote omitted]. Nevertheless, in doing so the Board must be acutely aware that its relationship with the parties is not an adversarial one, nor should it appear to be so. . . . It must satisfy not only the parties appearing before it in the particular case, but parties generally who appear before it, that its process accords with the principles of natural justice—that before the Board they will receive a fair hearing. The Board addresses first the challenge alleging breaches of the duty of fairness; then that of reasonable apprehension of bias.

Duty of Fairness
46. The Board commences with the observation that the Act confers upon it the jurisdiction to determine its own practice and procedure so long as it gives to the parties' full opportunity to present their evidence and make their submissions [footnote omitted]. . . .

47. The procedure before the Board generally is informal and flexible, the object being to further one of the over-arching statutory purposes articulated at LRA [Labour

Relations Act] section 2.7—"to promote the expeditious resolution of workplace disputes." Settlement by the parties of the dispute between them is always preferable to resolution by Board decision and to that end the Board is committed, again in furtherance of an over-arching statutory purpose articulated at LRA section 2.6—"to encourage co-operative participation of employers and trade unions in resolving workplace issues." Within the context of its Rules of Procedure, the Board's process can be said to encompass elements of what has come to be termed 'active adjudication'—it endeavours to assist the parties before it to come to an expeditious resolution of their disputes. ...

49. The Board turns now to the allegations here of breach of its duty of fairness owed generally and to the employer in particular. First, it wishes to correct a misapprehension on the part of counsel as to the nature of the mediated bargaining[,] which took place over four days in early May under its auspices—May 6, 7, 8 and 9, 2014. Far from being a "forced mediation" as counsel reiterates thrice in his written submissions of May 14, 2014, the Board was insistent on obtaining the consent of the parties before it remitted the matters over to mediated bargaining with the assistance of two Labour Relations Officers.... [T]his it did twice—first on the afternoon of May 6 and then again at the end of the day on May 8—in each instance its decision to do so precipitated by the Employer having advised that it had further bargaining proposals to present to the Union. Consent to proceed in this fashion was given by both counsel *in camera*, and the parties advised in open hearing following, with the Board giving oral direction how such mediated bargaining was to proceed. Throughout this process the Board, ... keeping a 'watching brief,' was careful not to become engaged in the mediated bargaining directly, and was cautious always to address counsel and the parties together as the mediated bargaining proceeded, whether in camera or in open hearing, never separately with either one.

51. ... True, counsel for the Employer made the motion to strike at the commencement of hearing on May 6, but at the same time—having filed as an exhibit the Employer's latest proposal, having received the Union's proposal in response (also filed as an exhibit), having consented to return to mediated negotiations rather than continue with the formal hearing whether on the motion or the merits of the discharge cases—the Employer had become an active participant in that changing dynamic.... The Employer having consented to forego hearing of its motion to strike and a full hearing on the merits in order to engage in mediated bargaining cannot now assert that the Board has refused to hear it on the merits as originally pleaded in the radically changed circumstances following four days of such mediated bargaining in which it had participated fully.

53. It is inaccurate to assert that the Board heard submissions, and hence proceeded to determine this matter, in an evidentiary vacuum. True, apart from the testimony of Ms. Weinkove, it had no *oral* evidence going to the failure to bargain in good faith complaints. But it had before it a voluminous amount of *documentary* evidence on which it could and did rely in assessing the final positions of the parties on the issues outstanding at the point of impasse reached on May 9. ...

54. From experience the Board is aware that oral evidence in support of a complaint of failure to bargain in good faith may stretch out the hearing process excessively and needlessly hinder the expeditious resolution of the dispute to the detriment of labour relations between the parties.

55. The Board concludes by noting that, in its estimation, in order to address fully the complaints of failure to bargain in good faith, it saw no need of oral testimony to supplement the expansive documentary record[,] which had been filed into evidence as exhibits by the parties. There were no material facts in dispute on which oral testimony needed to be called. The documentary record itself spoke to the rationales underlying the proposals of the parties at the point of impasse.

The Decision on the Merits

Underlying considerations

63. This Board has repeatedly stated that its principal role on a failure to bargain in good faith inquiry is to monitor *the process* of bargaining, not its *content*[,] which is left to the interplay between the relative economic strength of the bargaining parties and the shaping of collective agreement terms and conditions which are reflective of their contrasting economic strength.... That said, the Board has recognized that in certain circumstances the *content* of bargaining proposals may impinge upon the integrity of the bargaining *process* such as to signal breach of the good faith bargaining duty. Such would include *illegal* proposals or proposals that are *contrary to public policy* informing the Act as well as *bargaining techniques* such as surface or receding horizon bargaining[,] which signal a refusal to bargain in good faith whatsoever ...

The Law Applied

66. [T]he Board has determined that, based upon the position it has taken on the outstanding issues as of the point of impasse reached on May 9, 2014, the Employer has failed to bargain in good faith and make every reasonable effort to make a renewal collective agreement contrary to sections 17 and 60 of the Act. ...

73. ... The Board discerns a disturbing pattern in the Employer's approach to bargaining. As serious impediments to reaching an agreement are overcome, minor language issues invariably proposed by the Employer are elevated into major points of contention.

74. More disturbing, the Board discerns a common theme running through several of the remaining outstanding issues—an attempt by the Employer to undermine the integrity and credibility of the Union as the certified bargaining agent of the employees in the bargaining unit vested with the exclusive right to represent them and their interests vis-à-vis the Employer. Such an approach bespeaks interference by the Employer with the representation of employees by the Union contrary to LRA section 70 and as such is violative of the bargaining in good faith component of the statutory directive [footnote omitted].

The Back-to-Work Protocol

92. The Union complaint over the Employer's back-to-work protocol proposal calls on the Board to revisit its earlier jurisprudence on the entitlement of striking employees to return to active production in the workplace over ... that of replacement workers to retain the positions they have taken up in their stead.

96. [T]he Board is aware that several of its decisions from the 1980s which pre-dated *Royal Oak Mines* had found acceptable in principle employer privileging of replacement

workers over returning strikers. However the bargaining climate has changed in the intervening thirty plus years. Today, employer refusal to reintegrate striking employees into production at the workplace with all due haste upon cessation of the strike and entry into a renewal collective agreement, because replacement workers are engaged in performing the available work, is one of those conditions of settlement which by common knowledge is unacceptable to any trade union. . . .

98. Solidarity of workers when engaged in economic conflict with their employer during a legal strike is critical to a successful outcome in their interest. Our law permits an employer to pierce that solidarity by engaging replacement workers to perform the production work[,] which the striking workers have lawfully ceased to perform. Replacement workers then are allied with the employer . . . against the striking workers in the underlying economic conflict—a conflict without which they would have had no opportunity at all to engage in production work for the employer. Nevertheless, the Act preserves the employment status of workers who engage in lawful strike activity and that status continues despite the engagement of replacement workers by the employer [footnote omitted]. By definition the replacement worker is junior in seniority—measured from initial engagement at the workplace by the employer—to the striking worker. The employment status of replacement workers commences upon hire on such terms as are agreed to between replacement worker and employer, following commencement of the strike. But significantly, these are subject always to such terms as the employer and the union representing striking workers negotiate in settling the strike and entering a renewal collective agreement.

* * * * *

7:422 Disclosure of Decisions or Plans Substantially Affecting the Bargaining Unit

In the early 1980s, the Ontario board considered the extent to which the duty to bargain in good faith required the employer to disclose to the union information concerning plans for closing or reorganizing plants. In *Westinghouse Canada Ltd*, [1980] 2 CLRBR 469 at 489 (OLRB), during negotiations for the renewal of a long-standing agreement, the company had been considering a plan to move one of the manufacturing operations covered by that agreement from its existing location in a highly-unionized area (Hamilton) to several less unionized areas of Ontario. The move, according to the testimony of a company officer, was an "unevaluated likelihood" during the period of the evaluations. At the bargaining table, the union did not ask whether the company had any relocation plans, nor did the company mention that it was considering the matter. Shortly after the renewal agreement was signed, the company announced the move and proceeded to implement it. The union then brought a complaint that the company had breached the duty to bargain in good faith by not informing the union of its plans before the agreement was signed. The union further argued that the decision to move was motivated by an anti-union animus, and therefore constituted an unfair labour practice. The board found that the company had committed an unfair labour practice by moving the plant, but dismissed the complaint of failure to bargain in good faith. The board said that the duty to bargain places an obligation on the employer to respond honestly to union inquiries at the bargaining table about the existence of company plans that may have a significant impact on the bargaining unit, but does not place the employer under a duty to reveal, on its own initiative, plans that have not yet ripened into at least *de facto* final decisions.

In *Sunnycrest Nursing Homes Limited*, [1982] 2 CLRBR 51 (OLRB), the Ontario board, on the principles enunciated in *Westinghouse*, found a violation of the duty to bargain in circumstances where it was clear that a decision to contract out a substantial portion of the bargaining unit's work had been taken before or during negotiations with the union. In *Plastics CMP Limited*, [1982] OLRB Rep May 726, a similar result was reached although most of the laid off employees were subsequently hired by the firm that the employer chose to do the work. Consider the following critique of this line of cases, and in particular of the *Westinghouse* decision.

Brian Langille, "Equal Partnership in Canadian Labour Law" (1983) 21 *Osgoode Hall Law Journal* **496 at 517 and 519–20**

Now the one simple point that needs to be made before turning to *Westinghouse* is this: it is much easier to get away with an agreement which says nothing about issues like plant shutdown or contracting out if the probability of such occurrences is perceived as low. Further, one aspect of perception of low probability is ignorance that future occurrences, contemplated or decided upon, are in the works. In short, the statutory timetable offers the employer not only the *Sunnycrest* incentive not to implement changes, but the further incentive (referred to as *Westinghouse* incentives) not to reveal possible or actual decisions upon changes. Rather, the incentive to the employer is to remain silent, lock the union into the agreement, and then reveal the plans or act upon them. It is a system geared to non-disclosure. It is this structuring of incentives, flowing from our statutory timetable and (partially) our arbitration jurisprudence, which generated the *Westinghouse* case. The *Westinghouse* decision and a rash of similar cases reveal that these thoughts about incentives are not idle speculations. Employers have attempted to exploit these incentives to non-disclosure. This, in itself, should lead us to question, for example, Canadian arbitration law on contracting out. Yet non-disclosure is in direct conflict with the duty to bargain in good faith. *Westinghouse* addresses this conflict. As a starting point, it may be noted that under the general law of contract bargaining, non-disclosure (of latent defects for example) is generally accepted unless there is a duty to disclose. This state of the general law is said to instance the general proposition that there is no duty of good faith in our law of contract. But, of course, under Canadian labour law the parties are under that precise duty of good faith. This can be viewed as the second purpose outlined in *DeVilbiss (Canada) Ltd. . . .* , "to foster rational, informed discussion thereby minimizing the potential for unnecessary industrial conflict." The question left by *Westinghouse* is how well has the Board explicated the content of the duty to bargain over planned changes in the face of the incentives to non-disclosure.

The second objection is much more substantial and it concerns the reasoning invoked by the Board to justify limiting disclosure on the employer's own initiative to cases where the decision has been finalized. This reasoning was determinative of the actual decision in *Westinghouse*. The Board's sole justification for its decision that the silence of the employer about relocation plans under corporate discussion did not violate the bargaining duty is contained in a single extraordinary paragraph.

The competitive nature of our economy and the ongoing requirement of competent management to be responsive to the forces at play in the marketplace result in ongoing management consideration of a spectrum of initiatives which may impact on the bargaining unit. More often than not, however, these considerations do not manifest themselves in hard decisions. For one reason or another, plans are often discarded in the conceptual state or are later abandoned because of changing environmental factors. The company's initiation of an open-ended discussion of such imprecise matters at the bargaining table could have serious industrial relations consequences. The employer would be required to decide in every bargaining situation at what point in his planning process he must make an announcement to the trade union in order to comply with section 14 [now section 17]. Because the announcement would be employer initiated and because plans are often not transformed into decisions, the possibility of the union viewing the employer's announcement as a threat (with attendant litigation) would be created. If not seen as a threat the possibility of employee overreaction to a company initiated announcement would exist. A company initiated announcement, as distinct from a company response to a union inquiry may carry with it an unjustified perception of certainty. The collective bargaining process thrusts the parties into a delicate and often difficult interface. Given the requirement upon the company to respond honestly at the bargaining table to union inquiries with respect to company plans which may have a significant impact on the bargaining unit, the effect of requiring the employer to initiate discussion on matters which are not yet decided within his organization would be of marginal benefit to the trade union and could serve to distort the bargaining process and create the potential for additional litigation between the parties. The section 14 duty, therefore, does not require an employer to reveal on his own initiative plans which have not become at least de facto decisions.

Does this sound familiar? Assumptions are made here in the guise of practical industrial relations thinking. The major one is that the Board can and should predict that any effort to bargain collectively (and thus possibly co-determine outcomes) would not have a desirable but rather an adverse effect because the union would act irrationally....

Nondisclosure of plans (not finalized) to shutdown, relocate, or contract out work is simply inconsistent with a duty to bargain in good faith. In *Westinghouse*, the Board avoided this conclusion by wrongly assuming that some issues were not within the scope of the duty. The Board did respond that the union position is adequately protected by the ruling that the employer must respond truthfully to union inquiries about any plans. But the whole point of a duty of disclosure is to put the onus on a party to reveal the information requested. It has always been a deceit to lie in response to a question, even before the Board's holding in *Westinghouse*. As the Board explained in a later decision, "[i]n *Westinghouse* the employer was silent on a substantial issue about which the employer had exclusive knowledge." Well, exactly. Under a system with a duty to bargain in good faith, this provides a complete rationale for disclosure.

From this perspective, the holding in *Westinghouse* that finalized plans must be disclosed looks very peculiar. If we hold that plant relocation is contemplated by our legislation as a fit subject for collective bargaining, then what rational ground can there be for inducing "bargaining" after one party has "finalized its plans?" This remains a mystery. Mac Neil recently and accurately summarized the defects of the *Westinghouse* decision as follows:

> The reason for not requiring the employer to give notice that this type of decision is being considered is said to be that notice would be of marginal benefit to the trade union and would only serve to distort the bargaining process. *The Board seems misguided in its approach.* Firstly, it is acting upon the assumption that the union has and should have no say in the decision-making process. Secondly, it fails to see that rather than distorting the bargaining process, such information rationalizes the process. Both parties should bargain from positions where they each can at least understand the goals and limitations of the other. The bargaining process is distorted if this information is known by only one party. Furthermore, even if the union cannot by reason of inexperience effectively provide useful input into the decision-making process, it will have a greater opportunity to protect the interests of its members by including provisions in the agreement to help through the transition process. By forcing the employer clearly to realize its duty toward the employees that will be affected by a decision to alter operations, the union can help internalize the social costs of the decision.

In summary, if the commitment to the rejection of the limited American approach, and the reasoning underpinning it, regarding the issue of the scope of the duty to bargain is taken seriously, that reasoning should not be let in the back door to limit the *functional content* of that duty.

[Reprinted by permission.]

* * * * *

Slightly later, in the *Consolidated Bathurst* case below, the Ontario board attempted to respond to some of the criticisms levelled against its *Westinghouse* decision.

International Woodworkers of America, Local 2-69 v Consolidated Bathurst Packaging Ltd, [1983] OLRB Rep 1411 at 1435–45

[From November 1982 until 13 January 1983, the union and the employer negotiated a renewal of the collective agreement covering an all-employee unit in the employer's Hamilton plant. During negotiations, the union sought to persuade the employer to tighten the provisions in the expired agreement dealing with plant closures and severance pay. In the end, the union dropped those demands, and the old provisions were simply renewed. At no point during the negotiations did the company indicate that its Hamilton plant might or would be closed during the term of the collective agreement. On 1 March 1983, a few weeks after the agreement was signed, the employer announced that it was shutting down its Hamilton operation on 26 April 1983.

The union complained that the employer breached its duty to bargain, and advanced three arguments in support of that complaint. First, the union argued that the employer's decision to close the plant had been finalized during bargaining, and therefore had to be communicated to the union under the *Westinghouse* principle. Alternatively, the union argued that the board ought to reconsider its decision in *Westinghouse* and require disclosure whenever an employer was "seriously considering an action which if carried out will have a serious impact on employees." Finally, the union urged the board to find a duty to bargain with a union over major and unexpected changes introduced or intended to be introduced during the lifetime of an agreement.

The board refused to extend the duty to bargain into the lifetime of the collective agreement, but after carefully scrutinizing internal and external employer communications on the matter, it held that the employer had in fact made the decision to close the plant before the collective agreement was signed, and that it had therefore violated the duty by failing to disclose that decision during bargaining.]

ADAMS, Chair: Clearly, collective bargaining is an appropriate tool for dealing with the impact of industrial change in a work environment although it is by no means a complete answer to the difficulties thrown up for both labour and management. It enables solutions to be tailored to the needs of the individual participants; trade-offs can be made; and, at the very least, there is the sense of participation in the eventual outcome. Of course, the difficulty with the legal background in Ontario is that the requirement of compulsory no strike clauses together with the absence of a continuing duty to bargain during the term of the agreement, minimizes the likelihood that parties will engage in collective bargaining about these issues. Indeed, it has been pointed out that against the backdrop of the arbitral and collective bargaining framework discussed to this point, there is a real incentive for employers not to make decisions with respect to major change until a union is locked into a collective agreement.... Other jurisdictions such as British Columbia, Manitoba, Saskatchewan and the Federal Government have enacted specific provisions to permit bargaining over various types of mid-contract change....

In considering the application of the bargaining duty in this context the Board needs to be sensitive to the limited time span of the duty and the potential for unilateral employer action once the duty ends and a collective agreement is signed. The incentive for non-disclosure or manipulation of decision-making should also be kept in mind when assessing evidence and an employer's stated justification. On the other hand, this Board must be sensitive to the limits of adjudicating policy responses to the general problem of industrial change. The history and complexity of the problem together with the competing values at stake has attracted legislated solutions in other jurisdictions after considerable debate and reflection. An isolated fact situation arising in the context of an unfair labour practice complaint is not a comparable format for fashioning a meaningful policy contribution. The Board must also be sensitive to the statutory purpose of the bargaining duty, the language describing that duty, and the industrial relations implications of one approach over another. A single-minded pursuit of disclosure is inconsistent with the scheme of the Act and sound collective bargaining practices. The same can be said of the opposite direction. The experience before the N.L.R.B. does little to dispel this caution....

We have seen that collective bargaining in Canada has significant temporal as opposed to substantive limitations. These temporal limitations become important in considering and assessing the disclosure requirements Canadian labour boards, such as this one, have begun to fashion through the bargaining duty....

A bargaining agent can claim entitlement to information necessary for it to reach informed decisions and thereby to perform effectively its statutory responsibilities.

Disclosure encourages the parties to focus on the real positions of both the employees and the employer. And hopefully with greater sharing of information will come greater understanding and less industrial conflict. Although Canadian experience is limited, the American cases reveal that the employer is under no duty, as a general matter, to provide information until the union makes a specific request for the relevant information.... A request identifies a union's interest in specific information and then permits a discussion by the parties on the relevance of the data. The requirement of a request also sharpens a disclosure obligation. Without a request, an employer will be unclear what is needed and why. Indeed, a request is a basic method for receiving information particularly in an adversarial context. A general duty of unsolicited disclosure would be costly, unclear and potentially counter-productive. However, a second and more limited way the bargaining duty requires disclosure arises out of its good faith purpose and does not require a specific request....

One does not have to expand this principle significantly to conclude further that it is "tantamount to a misrepresentation" for an employer not to reveal during bargaining a decision it has already made which will have a significant impact on terms and conditions of employment such as a plant closing and which the union could not have anticipated. Indeed, this is what the Board held in *Westinghouse Canada Limited in stating*:

> Similarly can there be any doubt that an employer is under a section 14 [now section 17] obligation to reveal to the union on his own initiative those decisions already made which may have a major impact on the bargaining unit. Without this information a trade union is effectively put in the dark. The union cannot realistically assess its priorities or formulate a meaningful bargaining response to matters of fundamental importance to the employees it represents. Failure to inform in these circumstances may properly be characterized as an attempt to secure the agreement of the trade union for a fixed term on the basis of a misrepresentation in respect of matters which could fundamentally alter the content of the bargain.

[After reviewing its decision in *Westinghouse*, the board asked itself whether the rulings in that case ought to define the extent of the duty to disclose in the absence of a specific request from the union.]

Against the backdrop of these cases some further reflection is merited. Corporate planning, it is argued, is necessarily complex and dynamic while collective bargaining is an adversarial and tactical process. Typically, unions bargain out provisions on the basis of a work force's experience. For example, as technological change becomes apparent, provisions are sought to cushion the effect. Day to day layoffs are expected and general seniority, recall and severance provisions are negotiated. It is also argued that the parties usually have enough real roadblocks to reaching an agreement without taking to impasse issues which "may" need a collective bargaining response. This may explain why in the *Westinghouse, Sunnycrest*..., and *Amoco*... cases questions about possible management changes in the future were not asked by *the unions* themselves. Indeed, no request for information was made in the facts at hand. Another disincentive to revealing other than firm decisions without solicitation, it is pointed out, is the uncertainty over when the disclosure obligation arises. At what stage in an employer's thinking about major change is he obligated to reveal "this thinking" to the trade union? Is a recommendation from a corporate planning division sufficient grounds? What if those with the ultimate say have not seen the proposal or have deferred its consideration? What if the planning document contains sensitive information which, on disclosure to the union, might be learned by competitors, customers or suppliers? Premature disclosure may force an adverse decision to be taken that might have been avoided if events had been left to take their course. Corporate thinking about possible closings or relocations may also not be in direct response to labour related costs but rather potential loss of customers, need for expansion or a more advantageous market location. Until a decision is made, is the matter sufficiently ripe for collective bargaining discussions? Another problem relates to the potential severity of labour board remedies. For example the N.L.R.B.'s usual backpay order from the date when disclosure should have been made until an actual impasse is arrived at under a Board bargaining order frequently puts employees in a better position than if the company had met its bargaining obligations, particularly if the plant would have closed anyway. In fact, with this type of order, a trade union might be encouraged not to ask questions about future planning and simply rely on the subsequent assistance of a labour board remedy. It could be reasonably suggested that these types of problems may have contributed to the United States Supreme Court eventually taking plant closure decisions off the bargaining table altogether. What policy justification then supports greater unsolicited disclosure and merits the Board's intervention in the face of these potential difficulties?

Those who argue for unsolicited disclosure beyond firm decisions marshal their arguments along the following lines. They point out that collective bargaining is valuable because of the "say" it gives employees in the decisions which affect them. When an employer fails to disclose changes which are being contemplated, employees are not put on notice of problems which may arise during the term of the agreement. The trade union will, in the usual case, enter into a collective agreement silent on the point which has the effect of providing for unilateral employer initiatives. Secondly, they point out unsolicited disclosure based only on firm decisions is a standard too subject to manipulation. Planning, proposals and decisions can be easily arranged around collective bargaining schedules particularly with the legal onus of proof in an unfair labour practice case involving section 15 residing with the complainant trade union. In response to claimed inherent uncertainty of proposals or plans, they submit that many decisions should not be made without first getting the trade union's response. They argue that in the face of cost-related problems, employees have frequently played a pivotal role in keeping a business functioning or a plant open. They further submit that if such plans are sufficiently concrete to be disclosed when an employer is asked about his intentions by a trade union, as the *Westinghouse* case suggested, then why is it a factor in the context of disclosure without being asked? In any event, it is submitted that an employee's commitment to a company usually involves years of training, the development of specialized skills and the ordering of his entire life around the employer's business. A decision to shut a plant destroys these human investments in as real a manner as shareholders are affected. It is submitted that some disruption at the bargaining table is a small price to pay for trying to provide workers with a meaningful opportunity to participate in such a fundamental decision. They further point to the fact that from 1966 until just recently the United States labour relations system operated under the *Ozark Trailers Inc.* . . . standard of disclosure which required disclosure once management had "reached the point of thinking seriously about taking such an extraordinary step as relocating or terminating a portion of the business. . . ." It is also pointed out that disclosure of only firm decisions is not likely to set the stage for productive "decision" bargaining. While bargaining does not demand that management ignore its own interests, bargaining is likely to be less productive if management already has its mind made up. It is further emphasized that the bargaining duty only imposes a duty on management to meet and discuss matters with a union. After that, it is free to do as it wishes. Finally, it is submitted that the very unusual and unexpected nature of major business decisions affecting employees explains why trade unions often fail to ask questions about such matters. It is asserted that the failure to ask should be treated, at most, as a technical oversight.

To be accurate, this Board has not said that unsolicited disclosure is only obligated after a board of directors has given its approval. In *Westinghouse*, the Board used the term *de facto* decision and, we might add, in the context of a decision that was not primarily cost related. In the same decision it also pointed out the supplementary obligation of a company to respond honestly to questions. In this respect we would observe that the bulk of solicited disclosure cases in the United States and the few in Canada that exist have related to factual information or data—wage rates, wage surveys, time studies, insurance costs and other employment related activity. (We point out that this Board has not yet had to set the ground rules to such requests. . . .) Accordingly, it is not at all clear what a company's obligation is, if any, with respect to requests over plans. In *Westinghouse* the Board's reference to requests for such material emphasized the employer's duty to respond "honestly" thereby pointing out that a request could well trigger a misrepresentation which may later be relied upon. Moreover, questions by a trade union on specific plans for significant changes permit the trade union to assess the employer's response and decide whether the issue should be pursued. An equivocal employer response may encourage a bargaining proposal which will not be removed until an acceptable assurance is forthcoming. In short, requests and answers provide a self-regulatory mechanism and permit collective bargaining to resolve these problems, minimizing the need for labour board intervention. A failure to request information of this kind may also, in certain circumstances, suggest the union is satisfied with the appropriateness of a collective agreement (as it will stand) or that it believes it can do little about such significant change—a "What will come, will come" type of attitude. There is also an inherent uncertainty in defining the extent of an unsolicited disclosure duty beyond firm decisions. There is the problem of confidentiality surrounding such plans. And there is the collective bargaining impact of dropping such "incomplete thinking" on a bargaining table. These problems cannot be denied or minimized.

On the other hand, plans and decisions to close a plant can effectively extinguish a bargaining unit and the relevance of the usual terms of a collective agreement. In this context, where a decision to close is announced "on the heels" of the signing of a collective agreement, the timing of such a significant event may raise a rebuttable presumption that the decision-making was sufficiently ripe during bargaining to have required disclosure or that it was intentionally delayed until the completion of bargaining. It can be persuasively argued that the more fundamental the decision on the workplace, the less likely this Board should be willing to accept fine distinctions in timing between "proposals" and "decisions" at face value and particularly when strong confirmatory evidence that the decision-making was not manipulated is lacking. This approach is sensitive to the positive incentive not to disclose now built into our system, and the potential for manipulation. Indeed, a strong argument can be made that the de facto decision doctrine should be expanded to include "highly probable decisions" or "effective recommendations" when so fundamental an issue as a plant closing is at stake. Having regard to the facts in each case, the failure to disclose such matters may also be tantamount to a misrepresentation. We might also point out that there are decisions taken because of costs which really ought not to be made until the underlying problem is discussed with the union to see if adjustments can be made and the decision avoided. However, for the reasons discussed above, we are not willing to adopt the *Ozark Trailers* test of "thinking seriously" for unsolicited disclosures as urged upon us by the complainant. The failure to reveal such "possibilities" as a general matter is not tantamount to a misrepresentation and therefore lacks the bad faith rationale developed in *Westinghouse* justifying unsolicited disclosure. The purpose of such information would be investigative and to facilitate the rational discussion purpose of the bargaining duty. Accordingly, the purpose of the information and the difficulties detailed above with unsolicited disclosure militate against any substantial expansion of the unsolicited disclosure obligation as elaborated to date. The interests of employees are real but the Board is not ignoring these interests by requiring a questioning approach to disclosure as a general matter. The position urged upon us by the complainant has too much potential for "greater heat than light" at the bargaining table. There is already enough uncertainty over precisely how significant and what nature a decision must be to trigger the unsolicited disclosure duty. Unsolicited disclosure must be understood to be exceptional and centered essentially on a bad faith rationale.

* * * * *

Applying this reasoning to the facts before it, the board concluded that a *de facto* decision to close the plant had been made by the employer during negotiations, and that the company's silence amounted to a misrepresentation within the meaning of the *Westinghouse* doctrine. By way of remedy the board declined, on grounds of practicality, to order the employer to reopen the plant. Instead, it ordered the employer to indemnify the union for the damages it suffered from the loss of opportunity to negotiate on the matter of the plant's closing.

For a recent application of the approach in *Consolidated Bathurst*, see *Canadian Union of Public Employees, Local 1251 v Her Majesty in Right of the Province of New Brunswick,* 2009 CanLII 74885 (NBLEB). The New Brunswick Labour and Employment Board held (at para 46) that the employer's duty of disclosure arises only at the point when "mere ideas" that emerge in the course of a planning exercise "move to the verge of implementation." In the board's view (at para. 48), "any inference that an employer, during bargaining, must bring to the table every matter of discussion or initiative in its contemplation could unreasonably raise non-issues to the level of issues, and interfere with the ability of parties to finalize a collective agreement."

In a world of intensified international competitive pressures, increasingly rapid technological change, and growing market uncertainties, restructuring of operations has become increasingly common. But restructuring may run up against some of the assumptions underlying fixed-term collective agreements, which generally have a lifetime of one to three years and have often evolved through several rounds of negotiations to embody a complex regime of employment rules and entitlements. Should Canadian labour relations legislation abandon the idea of closed collective agreements, thereby putting the onus on the parties to address the fallout of restructuring by resuming collective bargaining before the agreement's term runs out? Or are there social and economic advantages to accepting the current limits on the duty to bargain, and looking instead to other employment-related regimes to provide cushions for workers who lose their jobs through restructuring (regimes such as labour standards, insolvency law, employment insurance, and workforce retraining)? This question is discussed in some depth, though from the perspective of employment standards rather than that of collective bargaining, in Federal Labour Standards Review, *Fairness at Work: Federal Labour Standards for the 21st Century* (Gatineau: Human Resources and Skills Development Canada, 2006) c 11 ("Labour Standards in a Dynamic Economy").

7:500 REMEDIES FOR VIOLATING THE DUTY TO BARGAIN

In *Radio Shack*, Section 7:421, in addition to dealing with the content of the duty to bargain, the Ontario board outlined its position on remedies for breach of the duty. The board first stressed that a remedy should not be seen as a penalty. To that end, it held that it would award monetary relief only as compensation to an injured union for pay increases and other benefits it had failed to win as a result of the employer's actions, and not as punitive damages for the employer's breach of the duty to bargain. Second, it held that it could not simply impose a collective agreement on the parties by way of remedy, as this would exceed its statutory mandate and would deviate too far from the principle of free collective bargaining. Instead, the board said, it would resort to other measures such as cease-and-desist orders and orders to bargain in good faith, orders to publish retractions of false or prejudicial statements, and orders to pay the injured party's negotiating costs.

Critics argue that the sorts of relief fashioned by the board in the *Radio Shack* case are not sufficient to secure the objectives of the legislation, and that more far-reaching regulation of bargaining is required. According to those critics, the inability of many groups of employees to negotiate effective rules on matters central to their work relationships, and the poor distributive outcomes they experience under free collective bargaining, point to the need for substantive regulation of bargaining proposals on a standard of reasonableness.

Would it be a good idea for labour boards to move toward such an approach? Does the Supreme Court of Canada's decision in *Royal Oak Mines*, as reflected in the following excerpt, allow for such an approach?

Royal Oak Mines v Canada (Labour Relations Board), [1996] 1 SCR 369 at 402–23

> [A summary of the facts is given in Section 7:421. Justice Cory set out the test for determining whether a labour board has exceeded its jurisdiction in imposing a particular remedy.

The remedy in question was an order that the employer put an offer back on the table (with certain modifications) that it had made earlier in the negotiations—principally, the addition of a back-to-work protocol specifying that arbitration would be available for grievances brought by employees who were discharged by the employer during the bitter strike which had occurred during bargaining.]

CORY J. (L'Heureux-Dubé and Gonthier JJ. concurring): In examining the legislation itself it is apparent that Parliament has clearly given the Canada Labour Relations Board a wide remedial role. The wording of s. 99(2) does not place precise limits on the Board's jurisdiction. In fact, the Board may order anything that is "equitable" for a party to do or refrain from doing in order to fulfil the objectives of the Code. In my view, this was done to give the Board the flexibility necessary to address the ever changing circumstances that present themselves in the wide variety of disputes which come before it in the sensitive field of labour relations. The aims of the *Canada Labour Code* include the constructive resolution of labour disputes for the benefit of the parties and the public. The expert and experienced labour boards were set up to achieve these goals. The problem before the Board was one which Parliament intended it to resolve.

The requirement that the Board's order must remedy or counteract any consequence of a contravention or failure to comply with the Code imposes the condition that the Board's remedy must be rationally connected or related to the breach and its consequences. This requirement is also consistent with the test established in *National Bank of Canada v. Retail Clerks' International Union* . . . , which required that there be a relation between the breach, its consequences and the remedy. Section 99 also provides that the Board may remedy breaches which are adverse to the fulfilment of the objectives of the Code. This empowers the Board to fashion remedies which are consistent with the Code's policy considerations. Therefore, if the Board imposes a remedy which is not rationally connected to the breach and its consequences or is inconsistent with the policy objectives of the statute then it will be exceeding its jurisdiction. Its decision will in those circumstances be patently unreasonable. . . .

In my view the remedy directed by the Board was not patently unreasonable, rather it was eminently sensible and appropriate in the circumstances presented by this case. A judicial review of the order must take into consideration both the complex factual background, and the prior involvement of the Board in this dispute. In this case, the factual background presented to the Board was such that it cried aloud for the imposition of a remedial order.

The unparalleled severity of this labour dispute was well articulated by Dr. Nightingale, a professor at Queen's University who was commissioned by the appellant to study the dispute and advise it as to whether to accept the recommendations of the mediators. He described the course of the dispute in the following terms:

> The complexities of this dispute—including failed conciliation, failed mediation, the rejection of a tentative agreement, a representational dispute within the union, a decertification drive while the strike continues and the continued operation of the mine by the replacement workers—are unusual enough. Add to these, the murder of 9 workers, an ongoing RCMP investigation, intimidation and death threats directed toward miners and their families, violence, including beatings which have spilled over into the community

and the Mayor of Yellowknife discussing the possible need for martial law and we have a tragedy without precedent in Canadian labour history. The Black Tuesday clash in the Souris, Saskatchewan coal fields in 1931, the 1969 Inco strike, the 1990 Placer Dome strike and the more recent Brunswick Mining and Smelting strike pale in comparison.

In fashioning an order the Board was obliged to take into account the long violent and bitter history of the dispute. Moreover, the facts in this case are so extraordinary that, if it were necessary, the Board was justified in going to the limits of its powers in imposing a remedy. The appellant's suggestion, that the Board should have rectified the breach by simply ordering the appellant to cease taking such an intractable position on the issue of the dismissed employees and then requiring the parties to recommence bargaining is hopelessly inadequate. In light of the long and turbulent history of the parties' attempted negotiations the typical "cease and desist" order would have been, as the Board described it, "unrealistic and even a cruel waste of time".... It was clear that the parties would never come to an agreement on their own with respect to the issue of the dismissed employees. In fact, the Industrial Inquiry Commissioners concluded in their final report that everyone had to be realistic enough to acknowledge that on some of the matters in dispute, "the parties are not likely ever to come to an agreement on their own." Therefore, taking into account this prediction, the unfortunate bargaining history and the effect of the dispute on the community, the Board was correct in recognizing that a more effective remedy was required.

Section 99(2) of the *Canada Labour Code* gives the Board jurisdiction to require an employer "*to do or refrain from doing any thing that it is equitable* to require the employer ... to do or refrain from doing in order to remedy or counteract any consequence of the contravention or failure to comply that is adverse to the fulfilment of [the] objectives" of the Code....

The breadth of the remedial section gives a clear indication that it was the intention of Parliament that the Board should be given the necessary flexibility to fashion remedies which will best address the entire spectrum of problems and of factual situations which it must confront. It is noteworthy that the section was amended in 1978. Prior to that date, the Code allowed the Board to impose only those remedies which were specifically enumerated. Section 189 (now s. 99(2)) was added in 1978. This provision authorizes the Board to make orders based on the principles of equity. The section now gives the Board both the flexibility and the authority to create the innovative remedies which are needed to counteract breaches of the Code and to fulfil its purposes and objectives. The granting of such a broad discretion to the Board demonstrates that Parliament wished the courts to defer to the Board's experience and expertise in making remedial orders so long as they were not patently unreasonable....

The appellant's prime objection to the Board's remedial order is based on the premise that the Board imposed a collective agreement on the parties, and that in so doing, the Board exceeded its remedial jurisdiction. I cannot accept this contention. The Board did not impose a collective agreement. Instead, the Board made its best effort to identify what the appellant's last offer to the Union had been. The tentative agreement offered by the appellant and thus acceptable to the appellant in April 1992 was the last identifiable proposal put forward by the appellant. While the Union had initially rejected this agreement by an overwhelming majority, the membership had subsequently reconsidered the offer and was prepared to accept it. Therefore, the Board used this tentative agreement, drafted by the appellant, on terms which the appellant was obviously willing to accept as the foundation of its order. The Board ordered the appellant to offer this agreement to the Union, at which time the Union could decide whether or not to ratify it. The Board recognized that the appellant had changed its position regarding some aspects of the tentative agreement. On these, the Board directed the parties to bargain for 30 days and if they failed to reach agreement, they were to be subject to binding arbitration.

It cannot be said that the requirement of the Board that the employer tender the tentative agreement subject to the issues to be negotiated constituted the imposition of a collective agreement. A board is ordinarily acting within its remedial authority in ordering a party to present once again its last offer from which any improper or illegal demands have been deleted.... [That] was accomplished by the Board's reinvoking the tentative agreement. Similarly, a Board generally acts within its remedial jurisdiction when it imposes upon the parties certain terms and conditions of a collective agreement. These two legitimate remedies cannot be added together in order to contend that they constitute an illegal order. There is nothing to suggest that the two remedies are alternatives to each other. In the usual case, one of these remedies would suffice. However, since other efforts to resolve the dispute had been exhausted, the Board concluded that both facets of the order were needed in order to effect a constructive settlement of the dispute.

There are four situations in which a remedial order will be considered patently unreasonable: (1) Where the remedy is punitive in nature; (2) Where the remedy granted infringes the *Canadian Charter of Rights and Freedoms*; (3) where there is no rational connection between the breach, its consequences, and the remedy; and (4) where the remedy contradicts the objects and purposes of the Code. The appellant argued that the Board's order, in this case, failed on both the third and fourth of the above prohibited grounds. Namely, that the order failed both the "rational connection" test and the "policy consistency" test respectively.

(a) Rational Connection
The case of *National Bank* ... held that there must be a relation between the breach, its consequences and the remedy. However, the necessity for a rational connection is evident from the wording of s. 99(2) which requires that the remedy imposed by the Board be designed to counteract any consequence of the contravention or failure to comply found by the Board. In other words, the Board must be concerned about remedying a specific breach of the Code, and in so doing there must be a relationship between the unfair practice which has occurred, its consequences to the bargaining process, and the remedy imposed.

In the case at bar, there was a clear causal connection between the breach, its consequences and the remedy imposed by the Board. To begin with, the Board identified the breach as being the appellant's intractable position with respect to a form of due process for the dismissed employees. The consequence of this breach was that bargaining was blocked so completely that no collective agreement could ever be reached. As a result of the impasse the serious damage to the community of Yellowknife continued unabated. The nature, extent and effect of the failure to bargain in good faith may in certain circumstances justify, in itself, the imposition of a remedial order. To be valid, such an order must deal with the effect of the breach and comply with the aims and objects of the *Canada Labour Code*. Perhaps more often it will be the failure to bargain in good faith coupled with other factors which will justify a remedial order.

Yet a further consequence of the appellant's intractable position was the frustration of the efforts of the Industrial Inquiry Commission to achieve a settlement. The Commission had recommended that the parties reach an agreement similar to the appellant's April 1992 offer (the tentative agreement), and also suggested that in the four unresolved areas where the appellant had changed its position that the parties should continue to negotiate, with the possibility of binding arbitration if the negotiations failed. The Commission also recommended that the fate of the dismissed employees should be determined in the usual way by third party arbitration. While the Union agreed to the Commission's proposals, the appellant rejected them, primarily because it refused to consider any proposal which would result in the dismissed employees returning to work. Were it not for this the appellant would have, in principle, accepted the recommendations. Accordingly, the Board ordered the appellant to table an agreement based on its own tentative agreement and the final report of the Commission, including a grievance arbitration clause. This achieved the result that the parties were put back in the position they would have been in were it not for the appellant's violation; namely, with a collective agreement tabled for the Union's consideration. Therefore, there is a clear relation between the appellant's breach of its duty to bargain in good faith, the consequences of that breach and the remedy imposed by the Board.

(b) Policy Consistency
[...]

The appellant contends that the promotion of *free* collective bargaining supersedes all the other objectives of the statute and that the Board's remedial order did not respect the principle of free collective bargaining. This position is untenable. It fails to take into consideration all the other factors which made this dispute in the opinion of two very experienced mediators the worst they had known....

Clearly it can never be forgotten that free collective bargaining is a corner stone of the *Canada Labour Code* and of labour relations. As a general rule it should be permitted to function. Nonetheless, situations will arise when that principle can no longer be permitted to dominate a situation. Where the dispute has been bitter and lengthy; the parties intransigent and their positions intractable; when it has been found that one of the parties has not been bargaining in good faith and that this failure has frustrated the formation of a collective bargaining agreement; and where a community is suffering as a result of the strike then a Board will be justified in exercising its experience and special skill in order to fashion a remedy. This will be true even if the consequence of the remedy is to put an end to free collective bargaining. This follows in part because it is the lack of good faith bargaining by a party which is frustrating the bargaining process and in part because of the other principles and factors the Board is required to consider pursuant to the provision of the *Canada Labour Code*.

In the case at bar, the strike had been bitter and long. The intractable position of the appellant that it would not consider some form of due process for dismissed employees was found to constitute lack of good faith. This position of the appellant certainly put an end to any possibility of true bargaining between the parties. The community of Yellowknife was obviously suffering. In those circumstances it was appropriate for the Board to fashion a remedy. The remedy put forward did not impose a collective agreement on the appellant. Rather the Board used as a basis for the bulk of its remedy the tentative agreement drafted and put forward by the appellant. Obviously this agreement was acceptable to the appellant in April 1992. It is true that it had changed its mind with regard to four matters. On those matters the parties were directed to bargain for 30 days and if they failed to reach agreement they would be subject to binding mediation on those issues. In light of the past history of the intransigence of the parties, no other solution was feasible....

The appeal should be dismissed with costs.

* * * * *

In *Buhler Versatile Inc*, excerpted in Section 7:421, the Manitoba Labour Board found that a legal strike which lasted for more than four months had been precipitated by the employer's serious breaches of the duty to bargain. The major remedy granted by the board was the following: that the employer "immediately compensate each employee who is a member of the bargaining unit represented by the union and who was employed by the Employer/Respondent at the time the strike commenced for all lost wages and employment benefits they would have earned had the strike not occurred." As there were 250 employees in the bargaining unit, this amounted to an award of several million dollars in damages—by far the largest award for breach of the duty to bargain ever made in Canada.

If a union responds to an employer's illegal bargaining tactics not only by bringing a complaint before the labour board, but also by calling a strike, is it appropriate for the board to require the employer to indemnify employees for wages lost as a result of the strike?

As discussed in Section 7:600 below, a labour board can direct the parties to mandatory arbitration to settle their very first collective agreement as a remedy when parties are unable to conclude a contract for various reasons. However, labour boards may, in some circumstances, direct parties to arbitration as a remedy for bad faith bargaining even if it is not their first collective bargaining (that is, first contract). The decision in *Egg Films* is instructive in this respect.

International Alliance of Theatrical Stage Employees, Local 849 v Egg Films, Inc, 2015 NSLB 213

[The employer (Egg Films) bitterly but unsuccessfully contested certification of the newly formed trade union as a bargaining unit at their establishment. The judicial decision went in favour of certification of the union. The labour board determined the terms and conditions of the first collective agreement. At the expiration of the first collective agreement, when the parties negotiated for a second collective agreement, the union complained that the employer, Egg Films, breached its duty to bargain in good faith by employing various subversive strategies intended to avoid a collective agreement.

Finding that Egg Films breached its duty to bargain in good faith, the Nova Scotia Labour Board ordered the parties to return to collective bargaining and use the previous collective agreement (first contract) as a basis for their negotiation. It further delineated certain limits on the new negotiation (that is, non-negotiable terms) apart from asking Egg Films to compensate its employees for their loss of wages due to unemployment resulting from the lock out by the employer. Even though the board did not grant an award for arbitration, it noted that according to the *Trade Union Act*, RSNS 1989, c 475, under certain circumstances the board is empowered to direct the parties to settle their collective agreement through arbitration as a remedial order.]

[Excerpt from the decision]

Mary-Lou Stewart, Member:

137. The Board is accordingly satisfied that Egg Films' breached its duty under s.35 of the *Act* to make every reasonable effort to arrive at a collective agreement. In fact, it made no effort at all. The positions it took on November 27th and 28th were designed not to foster rational discussion but rather to wage by other means a war it had been waging against the Union since 2011. It was looking to unseat the Union rather than negotiate with it. It sought to achieve that goal by making proposals designed to exclude the Union from any meaningful role as a bargaining agent. It made proposals that were unlawful on their face even if, perhaps, not unlawful in intent. It refused to provide information that would support the positions it said were necessary for its survival. It retained a negotiator whose apparent recommendations it refused to accept. This was surface bargaining at its worst....

140. Did the parties "bargain collectively"? The Union says that Egg Films did not satisfy this condition because it failed to comply with its obligation under s.35(a) to "make every reasonable effort to conclude and sign a collective agreement." The Board agrees with this submission. The intent and purpose of the *Act* is to ensure that resort to industrial strife is authorized only when the parties have made a good faith effort to resolve their differences by peaceful negotiation. That purpose would be negated if parties paid only lip service to the requirements of s.35(a). In this case the Board is satisfied that Egg Films had no intention of reaching any agreement with the Union. It wanted the Union gone. It insisted on the upper threshold as means of neutering and sidelining the Union. It knew or should have known that the Union could not agree to such terms. To attempt to negotiate a collective agreement that one knows—or should know—that the other cannot accept is not to negotiate at all. It is to bargain with the intent that the result be an impasse rather than an agreement....

143. There are two questions here. First, can the Board make mandatory arbitration a part of any remedial order it makes. Second, if not, what order should the Board make with respect to the bargaining that is to take place.

1: Can the Board Make Mandatory Arbitration a Term of its Order to Return to the Bargaining Table?

[...]

146. The first question to address then is whether the Board has jurisdiction to order mandatory arbitration at all. Section 36(2) of the *Act* provides that where a party has breached its obligations under s.35 the Board "may make an order requiring any party to

the collective bargaining to do the things that, in the opinion of the Board, are necessary to secure compliance with section 35." Could the power to make an order requiring Egg Films and the Union "to do the things . . . necessary to secure compliance" with the duty to bargain in good faith include an order for mandatory arbitration?

147. At first glance such a conclusion would appear to negate the basic principle of labour relations legislation, which is that the parties should be free to bargain as they see fit. . . .

148. In the Board's opinion the law does recognize that labour boards do have a power to impose arbitration on parties in order to secure compliance with their obligation to bargain in good faith. While the relevant statutory provisions in various jurisdictions with respect to remedies for the failure to bargain in good faith vary somewhat, we believe the wording of s.36(2) is arguably broad enough either to include the jurisdiction to make such an order or, if not, and as suggested earlier by this Board in *Courtesy Chrysler v. IAM, Lodge 1763*, 2002 CarswellNS 763 (NS LRB) at para.52, to impose strict terms on what the parties can bargain about.

149. It is also clear, however, that precisely because such a power undercuts the principle of free collective bargaining it can be employed only in the most dire and exceptional of circumstances—only where, for example, there is no other way to secure the various social policies that underlie labour relations legislation. So, for example, where the failure to bargain in good faith, in part, led to labour strife marked by violence, bombings and death such an order can be made: *Royal Oak Mines Inc. v. Canada Labour Relations Board*, [1996] 1 SCR 369; see also *Telus Communications Inc. v. Telecommunications Union*, 2005 FCA 262 at paras.76-79. Another example may arise where the employer's bad faith and anti-union animus following certification and the negotiations over a first collective agreement has led to the decimation of the bargaining unit represented by the union, such that the latter's ability to negotiate was undermined by "the task of having to organize the workplace once again:" *Teamsters, Local 91 v. D.H.L. International Express Ltd.*, [2001] CIRB No. 129 at paras.135-36; and see *Teamsters, Local 91 v. D.H.L. International Express Ltd.*, [2002] CIRB No. 159 at paras.7, 23 and 27. Such an order may also be made *if* the party that engaged in bad faith bargaining had in fact made binding arbitration a part of its proposals during collective bargaining. In such a case the order would affirm rather than negate the principles of free collective bargaining since it is what the party itself was prepared to accept prior to its lapse into bad faith conduct: see *Teamsters, Local 91 v. Boldrick Bus Services Ltd.*, 2010 CanLII 51873 (ON LRB). As well, a labour relations board may retain jurisdiction to declare by way of binding arbitration (final offer selection) any term that the parties still cannot agree upon following a return to collective bargaining—but, we note, as a last rather than as a first resort: see, for e.g., *Intek Communications Inc. and CEP, Re*, 2013 CCRI 683; see also *Navistar Canada Inc. v. Unifor, Local 127*, 2015 CanLII 16341 (ON LRB).

150. This Board is not satisfied that the impact of Egg Films' bad faith bargaining has been as drastic as in *Royal Oak* or in *DHL International*. . . .

151. For these reasons the Board does not feel that mandatory arbitration should be part of its order in this case *at this point*. The parties are directed to return to the bargaining table. Egg Films deserves a chance to remedy its breach of its duties, and thereby, hopefully,

learn how to bargain in the appropriate way. The parties accordingly have the opportunity to return to the bargaining table to negotiate freely, subject to what we say below.

* * * * *

7:600 FIRST CONTRACT ARBITRATION

Apart from Alberta and New Brunswick, nine other jurisdictions in Canada have devised statutory provisions securing first contract arbitration (FCA), wherein an arbitrator finalizes the very first contract between a newly certified trade union and an employer when the parties fail to reach a negotiated agreement. The arbitrated first contract is normally mandated for either one or two years. The justification for imposing the first contract is two-pronged. First, FCA consolidates the legitimate role of trade unions as bargaining agents for employees in an establishment. Once employees have chosen a trade union to represent them and the union has received certification, the union is more likely to maintain long-term support (and retain its certification) when it can point to a collective agreement to demonstrate the advantages of collective action. If employers, on the other hand, are successful in thwarting trade union efforts in securing a first contract, they are more likely to be successful in eroding support for the union.

Secondly, FCA seeks to normalize collective labour relations, which is often difficult for employers to value. By mandating a first contract, employers are not only sensitized to the realities of industrial relations, but it is hoped that they also become more receptive of the role of trade unions in shaping employer-employee relations. Once they are so sensitized, this collective bargaining relationship becomes established as the predominant mode of such relations. The FCA, it must be noted, is not a remedy for an unfair labour practice by the employer. It is a remedy for the failure of the bargaining parties to arrive at an agreement. In *Yarrow Lodge Ltd v Hospital Employees' Union* (1993), BCLRB No B444/93 (BCLRB), the BC labour board noted (at para 122) that although collective bargaining is the preferred manner of concluding the first contract between employer and employees, when collective negotiations break down, the FCA helps to repair the relationship between the parties, unlike remedies for unfair labour practices.

FCA may pertain to two scenarios—fault and no-fault. When one or both of the parties are at fault (normally the employer)—for example, through resorting to unfair labour practices or delaying tactics in order to avoid having to conclude a negotiated agreement—a mediator or a labour board may order FCA as a remedy to overcome the disagreement and conclude a contract. However, it must be noted that FCA is not a penalty for fault; it is only a remedy for overcoming the negotiation deadlock. On the other hand, when negotiation deadlock is not a result of either party's fault, but the parties are nevertheless unable to agree on a final contract, FCA overcomes a no-fault collapse of bargaining. In this context, it is important to emphasize the difference between hard bargaining and surface bargaining. Hard bargaining is when bargaining parties, using their legitimate bargaining power, try to get the maximum out of a negotiation. Surface bargaining occurs when either (or rarely, both) of the parties bargain—not in order to agree on a contract, but only as a statutory obligation before moving on to other statutory remedies. In this latter situation, the real intention is to avoid bargaining and instead rely on other mechanisms to shape employer-employee relation. These FCA provisions, which normally do not apply to subsequent rounds of negotiations, differ across the country on such matters as these:

1) whether the labour ministry screens applications for first contract arbitration, to decide which cases will proceed;
2) whether the labour board ultimately has discretion as to whether to impose a collective agreement;
3) whether the terms of the agreement are decided upon by the labour board or by an arbitrator; and
4) whether a finding of breach of the duty to bargain is a prerequisite to the invocation of first contract arbitration.

Manitoba is the only jurisdiction that provides not only for first contract arbitration but also for the imposed arbitration of subsequent collective agreements in cases where there has been bad faith bargaining or where it is unlikely that a settlement will be reached: Manitoba *Labour Relations Act*, sections 87.1–87.3.

Yarrow Lodge Ltd v Hospital Employees' Union (1993), BCLRB No B444/93 (BCLRB)

STAN LANYON, Chair:

[T]he principles which we draw from the past experience of the British Columbia Labour Relations Board, our examination of other jurisdictions in Canada, and the policies which now underlie Section 55 [the first contract arbitration provision of the British Columbia *Labour Relations Code*], are as follows:

1. First collective agreement imposition is a remedy which is designed to address the breakdown in negotiations resulting from the conduct of one of the parties. It is not simply an extension of the unfair labour practice remedies for egregious employer conduct.
2. The process of collective bargaining itself, to whatever extent possible, is to be encouraged as the vehicle to achieve a first collective agreement.
3. Mediators should be assigned early into first collective agreement disputes in order to facilitate and encourage the process of collective bargaining and to educate the parties in the practices and procedures of collective bargaining.
4. The timing of the imposition of a first collective agreement (if it is deemed appropriate that one be imposed) should not be at the end of the negotiation process when the relationship has broken down and is irreparable, but rather should take place in a "timely fashion," after the mediator has identified "the stumbling blocks" in the dispute and what is needed in order to "avoid" an irreparable breakdown in the collective bargaining relationship.

In applying these principles, we now set out the following factors which the Board will employ in assessing the conduct of the parties in making its determination under Section 55(6)(b)—whether or not to impose a first collective agreement. The factors are as follows:

a) bad faith or surface bargaining;
b) conduct of the employer which demonstrates a refusal to recognize the union;
c) a party adopting an uncompromising bargaining position without reasonable justification;
d) a party failing to make reasonable or expeditious efforts to conclude a collective agreement;
e) unrealistic demands or expectations arising from either the intentional conduct of a party or from their inexperience;
f) a bitter and protracted dispute in which it is unlikely the parties will be able to reach settlement themselves.

This list is not exhaustive. The Board will monitor first contract applications to possibly refine or amend these factors in the future....

In reviewing the past policy of the Board and the policy of other jurisdictions in Canada, we set out the following criteria to be used by arbitrators in determining the terms and conditions of a first collective agreement. These criteria are in addition to the points made above concerning the term of an imposed collective agreement and the inclusion of certain fundamental collective agreements rights.

Our objective is to provide arbitrators with both guidance and flexibility in determining the actual terms and conditions of employment. These factors are as follows:

1. A first collective agreement should not contain breakthrough or innovative clauses; nor as a general rule shall such agreements be either status quo or an industry standard agreement.
2. Arbitrators should employ objective criteria, such as the comparable terms and conditions paid to similar employees performing similar work.
3. There must be internal consistency and equity amongst employees.
4. The financial state of the employer, if sufficient evidence is placed before the arbitrator, is a critical factor;
5. The economic and market conditions of the sector or industry in which the employer competes must be considered.

Communications, Energy and Paperworkers Union of Canada, Local, 87-M v Ming Pao Newspapers (Canada) Ltd, 2011 CanLII 77758 (OLRB)

[In *CEP Local, 87M*, after filing unfair labour practice complaints against the employer, the trade union applied to the Ontario Labour Relations Board for FCA. Noting that the two actions (unfair labour practice and FCA) could be pursued simultaneously as separate complaints, the board observed, what matters for an FCA application to be successful is whether, because of a wide array of reasons ranging from intentional non-cooperation to genuine disagreements, the parties to bargaining are unable to finalize an agreement. In order to ascertain whether there is a deadlock in the bargaining, the board needs to examine the "totality" of the parties' conduct during the bargaining process (para 14). The FCA remedy seeks to facilitate—in the long run—good faith bargaining in sustaining robust collective industrial relations.]

Lyle Kanee, V-Chair:

[...]

39. The above description of some of the events that have occurred since the Union announced its organizing drive in late August 2010 support the Board's conclusion that it appears collective bargaining has been unsuccessful because of the Employer's refusal to recognize the bargaining authority of the trade union. These events appear to reveal a prolonged recognition dispute. This is not a situation, like some, where an employer initially reacts negatively to the news of its employees' desire to unionize but with the passage of time accepts their decision and the role of the union in representing them. Here, on the undisputed facts, the Employer appears to have refused to accept the reality that its employees have chosen a union to represent them. Its conduct, intentionally or otherwise, could only serve to undermine the authority of the Union. The payment of significant wage increases when the union drive is announced followed by threats of job reductions, and the subsequent lay- off of employees, conveys the message to employees that they would be better off without a union. Challenging, for the first time, the employee status of individuals chosen by the employees to represent them in bargaining conveys the message that the Employer will not respect their choice of representative. Laying off employees, and in particular, the chair and vice-chair of the Union's bargaining committee, without any prior notification or discussion with the Union, conveys the message that the Union is irrelevant and has no ability to protect the job security of its supporters—its leaders are expendable. Repeated direct communications with employees about unionization, the financial circumstances of the company and the leaner workforce of its unionized competitor while the Employer is bargaining with the Union, also convey the message that the Union is irrelevant, that it does not speak on behalf of the employees and it will cause employees to lose jobs. In all of the circumstances, it appears to the Board that the Employer refuses to accept the bargaining authority of the Union and has persisted in efforts to undermine it. This appears to have caused collective bargaining to be unsuccessful.

* * * * *

In a recent quantitative research, Bradley R Weinberg notes that statutory FCA reduces the possibility of decertification of trade unions than in jurisdictions where FCA is absent.

Bradley R Weinberg, "A Quantitative Assessment of the Effect of First Contract Arbitration on Bargaining Relationships" (2015) 54:3 *Industrial Relations* **449 at 450, 452, 457, 466–67, and 473–74**

> Advocates of FCA claim it will allow newly certified employees the opportunity to participate in meaningful collective bargaining that will result in a contract, even in the face of a determinedly antiunion employer. Furthermore, proponents hope the presence of a collective agreement will stabilize new bargaining relationships, allowing them to develop and be maintained in the long term. Opponents of FCA, on the other hand, contend that it will hinder free collective bargaining and that imposing contracts on parties will not result in long-term bargaining relationships because the agreements were not produced voluntarily....

Even though the system of industrial relations in Canada is provincial (as opposed to national, as in the United States), Canadian labor law is largely based upon the NLRA, such that it adheres to the same model of a free system of collective bargaining with the duty to bargain in good faith. Numerous researchers have used Canada as a comparison to the United States due to the similarities in their systems of industrial relations, but also due to the likeness of their economies, labor markets, and institutions (Colvin 2006; Kuhn and Riddell 2010). These similarities mean that an analysis of Canadian data may be able to inform the policy of both countries (Johnson 2010)....

Those who designed the first FCA model in British Columbia assumed what the above survey showed: employers were resisting bargaining due to inexperience with unions. It was hoped that if a contract were imposed on a resistant employer then this "trial marriage" would familiarize the parties with collective bargaining and would provide the groundwork for a lasting bargaining relationship. Despite having this goal at the outset, one of the creators of FCA, Paul Weiler, became skeptical of it a few years after enactment because every case in which a contract was imposed resulted in decertification (Weiler 1980). McDonald's (1987) analysis of the same period led him to conclude that Weiler's "'trial marriage' concept of first contract arbitration generally ended in divorce" (McDonald 1987: 21). However, later studies questioned Weiler's skepticism for various reasons, including the small population from which Weiler drew his conclusions and the shortcomings of the fault form of FCA (McDonald 1987; Sexton 1987a). Indeed, these shortcomings may explain why many provinces subsequently switched to or enacted other forms of FCA....

[There is] some evidence, both through the qualitative results of the test (the directions of the coefficients) and the quantitative results (the statistical significance of the coefficients), that FCA is exogenous. Therefore, it would appear that the introduction of an FCA provision is related to the decrease in decertifications in those provinces that have such provisions and that this relationship is not spurious due to a pre-existing trend of decreasing decertifications....

Whereas the previous studies investigated the goals of ending work stoppages and securing a first agreement, respectively, this study is the first to examine FCA's effect on decertifications, which provides an evaluation of the goal of creating lasting bargaining relationships. This study presents evidence that more bargaining relationships exist under an FCA regime on aggregate due to its effect on decertifications than in provinces that lack such a provision. When the different types of FCA are modeled, the results show that the automatic and fault forms of FCA have the most robust effect on decertifications and this holds across all specifications. Furthermore, the mediation-arbitration form of FCA is shown to result in fewer decertifications, and therefore more bargaining relationships, in a number of the specifications....

[© 2018 Regents of the University of California. Published by Wiley Periodicals, Inc.]

Moreover, there is evidence that FCA acts as a deterrent, and thereby promotes collective bargaining. It also substantially reduces strikes and lockouts.

* * * * *

Susan Johnson, "First Contract Arbitration: Effects on Bargaining and Work Stoppages" (2010) 63:4 *ILR Review* 585 at 585, 586–87, and 602

Using a panel of Canadian jurisdictions that have introduced FCA legislation at different times over several decades, the author addresses three questions: (1) How does this legislation affect the incidence of first agreement work stoppages? (2) Does FCA encourage or discourage collective bargaining in the negotiation of first agreements? (3) Does FCA influence the duration of first agreement work stoppages? ...

When bargaining reaches an impasse a union has the option of calling a strike. Strikes that occur in this context fundamentally concern union recognition and can be very bitter and protracted disputes. Under these circumstances, in a legal environment that permits employers to hire permanent replacement workers, the risks associated with calling a strike are very high. ...

Recap: Lessons Learned from Canadian Experience
This empirical analysis of Canadian experience with first contract arbitration legislation yields the following lessons. First, cross-sectional time-series analysis shows that the introduction of first contract arbitration legislation reduces the incidence of work stoppages associated with the negotiation of first agreements by a substantial, statistically significant amount. Second, there is no evidence to suggest that the parties involved in the negotiation of a first agreement rely on arbitration to settle their differences—application rates and imposition rates are low across all jurisdictions. It appears the presence of first contract arbitration legislation creates an incentive for the parties to reach agreement without resorting to work stoppages or arbitration. Although application rates and imposition rates are low across all jurisdictions, there is some evidence to suggest that parties are more likely to apply for FCA in jurisdictions where there are less stringent requirements to access FCA—where automatic or mediation-supported FCA is in effect. Evidence also suggests that parties are less likely to apply for FCA in jurisdictions where it is more difficult to access FCA—where fault or no-fault FCA is in effect. There is no empirical evidence to support the notion that first contract arbitration legislation affects the duration of first agreement work stoppages.
[Copyright © 2010 by *ILR Review*. Reprinted by Permission of SAGE Publications, Inc.]

Chapter 8: Industrial Conflict

8:100 INDUSTRIAL PLURALISM AND INDUSTRIAL CONFLICT

As we have seen in the preceding chapter, labour boards have increasingly regulated the bargaining process in recent years. Nevertheless, under general labour relations legislation everywhere in Canada, the ultimate means of dispute resolution is the use of economic sanctions. Thus, the ability to maintain or withstand a work stoppage remains central to collective bargaining. If a union cannot win a strike or lockout, it will probably not get a favourable agreement, and it might not get an agreement at all. In the end, though, only a small minority of bargaining rounds actually lead to strikes or lockouts. For example, between 1990 and 1998, only 3 percent of public sector and 9.5 percent of private sector negotiations for major collective agreements resulted in a work stoppage.

Although the prospect of economic sanctions is generally considered to be a crucial part of the bargaining process, a primary factor driving the evolution of Canadian labour law has been a desire to limit what are seen as the detrimental effects of strikes. The earliest efforts at labour regulation in Canada involved a unitary approach which tended simply to repress strikes, leaving employees unable to withdraw their labour collectively. When this approach proved incapable of containing industrial unrest, Canadian governments (from the late 1800s on) began to move toward a pluralist approach, relying more on dialogue and accommodation as the principal road to industrial peace.

Over the years, this pluralist approach came to predominate in Canadian public policy. Negotiation and compromise are encouraged, while repression is used more sparingly, in the background. Employers are required to recognize and bargain with certified bargaining agents, and recourse to economic sanctions is hedged about with a set of legal restrictions. On occasion, non-binding third-party intervention by mediators, conciliators, fact finders, and others, pushes the parties toward agreement.

The Supreme Court of Canada confirmed in *Saskatchewan Federation of Labour v Saskatchewan*, [2015] 1 SCR 245 (which is considered fully in Chapter 12) that the right to strike is included in the *Charter* right to freedom of association. Prior to the constitutionalization of the right to strike, some analysts argued that legislatures should ban strikes altogether and substitute third-party interest arbitration of the terms of employment (see, for example, David Beatty's criticisms of collective bargaining in "Ideology, Politics and Unionism," excerpted in Chapter 1, Section 1:320). Even before the decision in *Saskatchewan Federation of Labour*, Canadian policymakers rejected this option, except in "essential services" and, in some provinces, in other public services. Canada has frequently been criticized by the International Labour Organization's (ILO) Committee on Freedom of Association and

Committee of Experts for banning or limiting public strikes and ordering interest arbitration instead. Essential services legislation and other restrictions on the right to strike are still possible, but if challenged, will now be subject to the Court's analysis in *Saskatchewan Federation of Labour*.

The Canadian government's rejection of a general system of interest arbitration, combined with a continuing desire to prevent industrial disruption, has led to persistent tension in Canadian labour regulation. On the one hand, governments try to push the parties to settle their disputes without strikes, by imposing a series of hurdles that must be overcome before economic sanctions can lawfully be invoked. On the other hand, governments generally (though decreasingly) disclaim any influence over the content of settlements.

This distinction between process and outcome is difficult to maintain. In Chapter 7, we saw that labour relations boards, despite misgivings, do to some extent scrutinize substantive bargaining positions in administering the duty to bargain, and in first-contract arbitration they do indeed impose collective agreement terms. Even when boards do not rule on the parties' bargaining positions, the regulation of the process cannot help but influence the outcome. In the following works on strike regulation, you will find echoes of the debate on the purpose and scope of the duty to bargain. In the pluralist literature, the discussion of strike law is frequently cast in terms of furthering equality of bargaining power. A particular regulatory structure is said to be justified because it promotes equality of bargaining power; another is rejected because it would tip the balance excessively.

The following excerpt sets out the classic pluralist conception of the role of strikes in collective bargaining.

Paul Weiler, *Reconcilable Differences: New Directions in Canadian Labour Law* (Toronto: Carswell, 1980) at 64–66

> It is understandable that there is growing exasperation among the press, the politicians and the general public, about Canada's dismal record of industrial unrest. Nor is it any consolation to explain that much of the recent trend is due to the fact that many of our public sector bargaining relationships were new and immature. Loss of public services due to strike action is not the answer to the problem; to many people that *is* the problem. We hear again the refrain that economic warfare is an outmoded and atavistic method of settling labour disputes. The law must provide a better way to replace such crude, primitive methods of self-help. We have already banned strike action as the means of settling recognition issues or contract grievances. Why should we not complete the circle and ban strikes about negotiating disputes as well, at least in a wide range of important industries? And of course, no one would want to single out just the trade unions for such restrictive action. It is assumed that lockouts by employers would be prohibited as well.
>
> I dare say that there would be near unanimous consensus among the professionals in labour-management relations that that kind of proposal is terribly unwise. They believe that there is, if not a logical necessity, at least a natural affinity between the right to strike and the system of free collective bargaining. Although the elements in that argument are rather commonplace, perhaps it is still worthwhile to spell them out, as a prelude to my discussion of the legal meaning of the right to strike.

The basic assumption of our industrial relations system is the notion of freedom of contract between the union and the employer. There are powerful arguments in favour of that policy of freedom of contract. We are dealing with the terms and conditions under which labour will be purchased by employers and will be provided by employees. The immediate parties know best what are the economic circumstances of their relationship, what are their non-economic priorities and concerns, what trade-offs are likely to be most satisfactory to their respective constituencies. General legal standards formulated by government bureaucrats are likely to fit like a procrustean bed across the variety and nuances of individual employment situations. Just as is true of other decisions in our economy—for example the price of capital investment or of consumer goods and services—so also unions and employers should be free to fix the price of labour at the level which they find mutually acceptable, free of intrusive legal controls.

The freedom to agree logically entails the right to disagree, to fail to reach an acceptable compromise. Most of the time good faith negotiation does produce a settlement at the bargaining table, often without a great deal of trouble. But often enough it does not; and of course it is the failures which generate the visible tumult and shouting. And at that point the collective bargaining system diverges sharply from other components in the market economy.

For instance, if a customer does not like the price for the sale of a car, or a businessman does not like the terms for a bank loan, the assumption is that each will go his own separate way and try to find a better deal elsewhere. The fact that they have reached a deadlock in their individual dealings is not a social problem. That competition among buyers and sellers, lenders and businesses, et al., is the necessary lubricant in the operation of a market economy. But that solution is totally at odds with the system of free collective bargaining. It is precisely because we do not want to allow the employer to quote his price for labour, and to invite his employees to accept those terms or go elsewhere (that is, 'to take it or leave it'), that as a matter of public policy we have fostered the development of collective organization of the employees, to provide a countervailing lever to the bargaining position of their employers (especially of large organizations and aggregations of capital). The whole point of a union is to act as a cartel in the supply of labour, to deny the employer an alternative source, and to force it to reach a mutually acceptable agreement about the terms and conditions of employment. The tacit premise underlying the system is that both employment status and collective bargaining relationship will persist indefinitely through one series of negotiations after another. And it is precisely for that reason that the means of resolving deadlocks in negotiations between union and management becomes a serious social issue.

At the same time we must appreciate the very different perspectives of the employer and the union on that subject. The employer typically has no direct and immediate interest in successfully getting the new contract settlement. That settlement almost invariably will provide for compensation increases, often in sizable amounts. All other things being equal, the employer would just as soon stick with the status quo. (Indeed in an inflating economy unchanged money wage rates mean real gains to the employer and real losses to its employees.) It is the union which ordinarily must take the initiative to move negotiations off dead centre. True, that is not always the case. Sometimes the status quo may be distasteful to the employer. It may have lost an arbitration award interpreting the previous agreement, an award now giving a monetary windfall to its employees. Or it may have had to use unnecessary and costly levels of manpower in its operations (for example manning the presses of a newspaper). Suppose the employer cannot get an agreement from the union to change these requirements in a new contract. In that event, management is entitled to act unilaterally. It can simply post an announcement to its employees that it is reducing the price it will pay for labour and the amount of labour that it is going to use. That is what it means for management to exercise the rights of property and of capital; to be able to propose the terms upon which it will purchase labour for its operations.

What rights and resources do the employees and their union have in response? In essence, they have only the collective right to refuse to work on those terms, to withdraw their labour rather than to accept their employer's offer. That is what a strike consists of. What is its function in the larger collective bargaining system? What contribution does the strike make to resolving the impasse? The employer's operations are shut down without any employees to run them. The employer loses the flow of revenues. In turn the employees are out of work, deprived of their earnings. Thus both sides are being hurt economically. They experience viscerally the pain of disagreement with their opposite numbers at the bargaining table. Soon they realize that it is much less painful to agree, even if they do have to move considerably closer to the terms proposed by the other side. In that way strike action plays an indispensable role in resolving deadlocks in a collective bargaining relationship.

... It is a common experience in industrial relations to achieve a midnight settlement on the eve of the strike deadline in difficult negotiations. The ability to compromise simply would not be there unless the parties were both striving mightily to avoid the harmful consequences of a failure to settle. In the larger system it is the credible threat of the strike to both sides, even more than its actual occurrence, which plays the major role in our system of collective bargaining.

Thus a simple legal ban on strike action is totally unacceptable if we are going to have free collective bargaining. I do not mean to suggest that the right to strike is a fundamental, inalienable, personal right, as many trade-unionists assert. The legal right to strike is justified not on account of its intrinsic value, but because of its instrumental role in our larger industrial relations system. We can, and we have, prohibited strikes at many points in the system; for example in the administration of the collective agreement, because we have concluded that there are better techniques for performing that task of dispute resolution: grievance arbitration. But so far we have not been able to agree on an acceptable alternative for contract negotiation disputes, and thus the strike continues to be the indispensable lesser evil in that setting.
[Reprinted by permission.]

* * * * *

Weiler began the above discussion by referring to Canada's "dismal record" of strikes and lockouts. He was writing at the end of the 1970s, which saw considerable labour upheaval, due in part to inflationary pressures and to the impact of federal anti-inflation legislation. The incidence of strikes has decreased markedly in more recent decades, particularly in the private sector. A comparison of the figures during and after the economic slowdowns of 1982 and 1991 shows us, among other things, that collective bargaining is not insulated from general market forces. The ability to win a strike depends in part on the employer's ability to replace strikers with new workers. This in turn depends on such factors as the rate of unemployment and the skill level of the workforce. The employer's ability to withstand a strike also depends on its position in the product market. At a time of low demand for its goods, the employer may lose little from a temporary shutdown. Striking employees may also find it harder to maintain a strike when other work is scarce. Increasingly, especially in the private sector, unions have had to take account of the fact that international competition may reduce the employer's ability to pay higher wages or to improve other terms and conditions. Because willingness to begin job action often depends on the likelihood of success, strike rates tend to reflect changes in general economic conditions.

What is the true impact of strikes in terms of lost production, profits, and wages? In the mid-1980s the average Canadian worker lost a little less than half a day's work per year because of industrial disputes. But because of the disproportionate effect of strike losses on certain sectors, this small figure represents a considerable social loss, though how much of a loss is difficult to calculate.

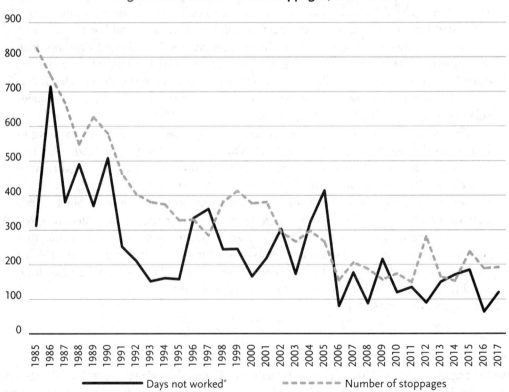

Figure 8.1. Canada—Work Stoppages, 1985–2017

* Days not worked are measured in units of 10,000
Source: Statistics Canada, CANSIM table 278-0015

8:200 THE CONSTITUTIONAL RIGHT TO STRIKE

The right to strike is not expressly guaranteed in the *Charter*, but since the Supreme Court of Canada's 2015 decision in *Saskatchewan Federation of Labour v Saskatchewan*, the right to strike has been recognized as an essential component of the right to a meaningful process of collective bargaining included in section 2(d) of the *Charter*. In the *Saskatchewan Federation* case the Supreme Court struck down essential services legislation which prohibited strikes by public service workers and gave the provincial government significant discretion to determine which workers would be captured by the prohibition. It remains to be seen how *Saskatchewan Federation* will shape other essential services regimes, mandatory arbitration requirements, or statutory provisions regulating the right to strike. This case, and questions posed by the constitutionalization of the right to strike, are fully canvassed in Chapter 12 in this book.

8:300 LEGAL FORUMS REGULATING INDUSTRIAL CONFLICT: AN OVERVIEW

A strike traditionally takes the form of a complete cessation of work. However, there are a wide variety of employee pressure tactics that fall short of a complete shutdown, and which have become relatively more important in recent years. These include rotating or selective strikes, go-slows, work-to-rule campaigns, "study sessions," overtime bans, coordinated sick days, consumer boycotts, picketing, hot declarations, and mass resignations. Many of these seek to restrict or disrupt the amount of work done. Others try to induce people not directly involved in the dispute to cease doing business with the target employer. In inflationary times, unions may strike to obtain better terms; in deflationary times, they may strike to prevent the imposition of worse terms.

On the employer's side, the lockout (where the employer closes the enterprise, or a part of it, to try to compel the union to come to terms) is usually cited as the counterpart to the strike. This is somewhat misleading. Employers do not often initiate conflict by shutting down. Usually, the employer simply resists the strike tactics, either by waiting them out or by trying to continue its operations through the use of supervisory personnel, replacement workers (where allowed by law), or bargaining unit members who do not heed the strike call. Even when the employer wants to modify an existing collective agreement, a lockout is not usually its first line of attack. It can impose new terms unilaterally, as long as it does so at the proper time and under certain conditions. This option is discussed below, in Section 8:422. However, in recent years there have been a number of high profile, bitter lockouts in Canada, including a lockout of 420 employees in 2012 at a Caterpillar Inc factory near London, Ontario, of over 1,000 employees in 2012 at a Rio Tinto Alcan smelter in Quebec, and of 900 employees of Stelco Steel in 2010 in Hamilton, Ontario, to provide a few examples.

The responsibility for deciding whether a strike or lockout has occurred, and if so, whether it is "timely," is usually assigned to the relevant labour relations board. Since the enactment of labour relations legislation after World War II, industrial action has been heavily regulated in labour relations statutes. Before that time, strikes were used by Canadian workers to resolve virtually all types of employment-related disputes — those over the recognition of unions for collective bargaining, the negotiation of new terms of employment, the reinstatement of discharged employees, the enforcement of collective agreements, and the drawing of jurisdictional boundaries between unions. This resort to the strike for many different purposes did not result from any affirmative legal recognition of a right to strike, but from the determination of employees and unions to use the one powerful industrial weapon available to them, often in defiance of legal restrictions. The law began to accommodate the exercise of employees' collective power, often in an unsystematic way, leading to a regime of qualified "collective *laissez-faire*" in pre-war Canadian labour relations. Collective bargaining and strikes occurred without express legal authorization, and legal intervention was sporadic.

During World War II, Canadian labour policy took a dramatically new turn. In response to demands for continuous war production, Canadian governments instituted a more intensely regulated system of collective bargaining. As explained in earlier chapters, this new system was a modified version of the US *Wagner Act* model — and in the area of the regulation of industrial conflict, it was stricter than the American prototype. The use of strikes was strictly limited to disputes over the negotiation of collective agreements. In all other circumstances, strikes were banned. Often, the use of economic force was replaced by a new set of mechanisms that were expected to play the role previously played by strikes. These included the certification process for initiating collective bargaining, the duty to bargain, the prohibition of unfair labour practices, and the grievance arbitration process for enforcing collective agreements. Employees were no longer allowed to strike in order to force the employer to recognize a union or to engage in bargaining, or perhaps most importantly, to enforce their interpretation of the terms of a collective agreement.

The only significant exception to the ban on strikes and lockouts during the lifetime of a collective agreement is found in Manitoba, Saskatchewan, New Brunswick, and federal labour relations statutes (and the British Columbia Public Service Labour Relations Act, but not its general Labour Code), which require the employer to give the union advance notice of any technological change during the lifetime of the collective agreement. A duty to bargain then arises over matters arising out of such change, and the bargaining can eventually result in a legal work stoppage.

Additional procedural prerequisites to industrial action were also introduced through statute, including the requirement, dating back to the early years of the twentieth century, that the parties talk to each other before resorting to a strike or lockout. Today, labour relations statutes in most jurisdictions provide that a dispute must be submitted to conciliation or mediation before a work stoppage may begin, permit the labour ministry to impose conciliation or mediation, or allow parties to elect mediation, which then becomes mandatory before a strike or lockout is allowed. Other more recent requirements in some Canadian jurisdictions include compulsory strike votes and the right of the employer or the labour ministry to demand an employee vote on whether to accept the employer's last offer.

The legality of a strike or lockout depends above all on whether the various statutory prerequisites in the relevant jurisdiction have been met. A strike or lockout is only "timely" if all statutory requirements have been met, and it must be "timely" in order to be legal. The remedial authority of labour boards generally includes the power to make cease and desist orders against strikes and lockouts which are not "timely" and to award compensation for losses resulting from such action.

While labour boards today play a principal role in the regulation of industrial conflict, courts and labour arbitrators also have a role. Before the advent of labour relations statutes and other modern employment legislation, the courts were often the only forum regulating strikes and other forms of industrial action. In those days, the study of labour law consisted mainly of the study of criminal law and common law tort doctrines restricting industrial action and picketing, and of such related matters as whether trade unions had the legal status to sue and be sued in the courts. In certain respects, as we will see below, those issues remain relevant, and courts continue to play an active and important role in regulating industrial conflict, though a much narrower one than in the nineteenth and early-twentieth centuries.

Finally, grievance arbitrators also play an important role in the governance of industrial conflict. Originally through convention but now because of the explicit requirements of statutory provisions such as section 48(1) of the Ontario *Labour Relations Act, 1995*, collective agreements contain no-strike clauses which are enforced through the agreement's grievance procedure and ultimately through arbitration. Arbitrators can award damages for violation of a no-strike clause, and may also have the authority to issue orders prohibiting the recurrence of industrial action. Some collective agreements include provisions permitting employees to respect lawful picket lines or otherwise to support striking workers: see Section 8:413.

Accordingly, a strike or lockout, or an episode of picketing or other activity in support of a strike or lockout, can give rise to proceedings in several forums—an action in the civil courts, a labour relations board proceeding, a prosecution in the criminal courts, and an arbitration proceeding involving an employer claim for damages or an employee grievance against discipline imposed by the employer against strikers or picketers. Because each of those forums applies a different subset of the broad array of legal rules that govern industrial conflict, whether a remedy will be given may well depend on where relief is sought. Finally, the constitutionality of the legal rules in question may be challenged under the *Canadian Charter of Rights and Freedoms*, and such a challenge may be brought in any of the proceedings just mentioned. In the following section, we will review the roles of labour relations boards, courts, and arbitrators in the governance of industrial conflict.

8:400 THE ROLE OF LABOUR RELATIONS BOARDS IN REGULATING INDUSTRIAL CONFLICT

8:410 Regulating Strike Activity

8:411 Defining "Strike" Activity

As noted above, labour boards are assigned the task of determining whether the many regulatory prerequisites to a lawful strike have been satisfied (whether the strike is "timely"). Those boards must also decide whether a "strike" has in fact occurred within the statutory meaning of that term. For example, section 3(1) of the *Canada Labour Code* sets out this definition:

> "[S]trike" includes a cessation of work or a refusal to work or to continue to work by employees, in combination, in concert or in accordance with a common understanding,

and a slowdown of work or other concerted activity on the part of employees in relation to their work that is designed to restrict or limit output.

The definitions of a strike in other Canadian jurisdictions are quite similar. All apply (expressly or, as discussed below, by interpretation) to a broad range of tactics that restrict production, including conduct short of a full-scale work stoppage. All require some measure of common action by employees. In three provinces—Alberta, Manitoba, and Nova Scotia—the definition of a strike includes the qualification that the job action must be for the purpose of compelling an employer to agree to terms or conditions of employment. As is indicated below in Sections 8:413 and 8:414, the statutes of some other jurisdictions (including British Columbia and the federal jurisdiction) included that qualification at one time but no longer do.

8:412 Actions Constituting a Strike: Common Action or Concerted Activity

What kinds of conduct fall within the definition of a strike? The following case gives an idea of the breadth of the answer to that question. It also addresses the question of the options open to an employer in responding to protected strike activity.

Communications, Electronic, Electrical, Technical and Salaried Workers of Canada v Graham Cable TV/FM (1986), 12 CLRBR (NS) 1 at 2–4 and 9–14

JAMIESON, Vice-Chair:

On July 18, 1985, the Communications, Electronic, Electrical, Technical and Salaried Workers of Canada (CWC) ... filed this complaint alleging that Graham Cable TV/FM ... had violated s. 184(3)(a)(vi) [now s. 94(3)(a)(vi)] of the *Canada Labour Code* by taking disciplinary action against some of its members because they were participating in lawful strike activities. The employer denied the allegations claiming that discipline had only been imposed on some employees who had reported for work but who had failed or refused to perform the functions of their job descriptions....

[At the time of the relevant events, the union was in a legal position to strike. Because of the nature of the employer's operations, the union believed that a traditional strike would fail, as management personnel could maintain service for a long time unless there was a major equipment failure. The union therefore decided to work to rule.]

Ms. Cynthia Down, a union steward and a member of the negotiating committee described the programme that was adopted and how it was to be put in place. The job action that was contemplated included slowdowns in some areas and a speed up in others. For example, in the marketing and sales department inside work was to slow down and outside sales were to speed up generating more work for the inside workers. No overtime was to be worked and employees would cease the practice of training others to perform their job functions. In the customer service area only four calls an hour were to be accepted with other incoming calls to be diverted to management persons. Dispatchers would screen orders going to technicians and servicemen were to request audit checks which would slow down the dispatchers. Installers would cease collecting money from customers. The employees also decided that they would no longer whisper amongst themselves about the union, they would speak up. To that end study sessions would be held on each floor to convince management that they were openly standing up for their rights.

The job action programme commenced on the morning of July 4, 1985. Ms. Down was the overall co-ordinator with eight to ten other co-ordinators reporting to her from other areas of the work place. Employees were given strict instructions to act only on the directions of the official co-ordinators. That way there would be some measure of control and there would be absolutely no doubt that the actions were being done in a concerted fashion.

[This kind of job action occurred, with some modifications, from 4 July until 26 July. Beginning on 15 July, the employer warned its employees that they must do the work required by their job descriptions or face discipline. Some employees who continued the job action were suspended. On 26 July the employer required all employees who wished to work to sign the document that follows.]

July 26, 1985
MEMO TO: Graham Cable
FROM:

I am reporting for work and desire to continue to work at Graham Cable TV/FM, commencing 26 July, 1985 as a _____, in accordance with my job description (see attached), Graham Cable standard procedures, Graham Cable practices and Graham Cable standards.

I agree as a condition to being permitted to enter the premises and report for work that I shall complete my work assignments, as set out above.

_____

Signature

[Those who did not sign were excluded from the premises.]

The issues before us really come down to what is a strike under the Code? If the work related activities by the employees fall within the definition of a strike they are then protected under s. 184(3)(a)(vi) of the Code and the imposition of discipline by the employer for having participated in those activities would amount to an unfair labour practice.

A strike is defined in s. 107(1) of the Code:

> 'strike' includes (a) a cessation of work or a refusal to work or to continue to work by employees, in combination or in concert or in accordance with a common understanding, and (b) a slowdown of work or other concerted activity on the part of employees in relation to their work that is designed to restrict or limit output;

The protection against discipline or other forms of penalty for having participated in a lawful strike is extremely broad and if one looks at the construction of s. 184(3)(a)(vi) it becomes readily apparent that Parliament intended it to be so:

> 184. (3) No employer and no person acting on behalf of an employer shall (a) refuse to employ or to continue to employ or suspend, transfer, lay off or otherwise discriminate against

any person in regard to employment, pay or any other term or condition of employment or intimidate, threaten or otherwise discipline any person, because the person ... (vi) has participated in a strike that is not prohibited by this Part or exercised any right under this Part;

There are strict limitations in the Code when a strike can legally occur. Section 180 sets out all of the conditions which have to be met before a strike becomes legal. The same restrictions apply equally to a lockout....

Frequently, when job action has been taken in response to mid-contract disputes or during negotiations where trade unions or employees have simply jumped the gun and have initiated job action before they are lawfully entitled to, employers have come to the Board under s. 182 of the Code seeking declarations of unlawful strikes and corresponding cease and desist orders. Through those procedures the definition of a strike in the federal jurisdiction has evolved to the extent that it encompasses a wide range of activities. It can even extend to a refusal to cross a legal picket line which is considered to be a right as a matter of routine in most jurisdictions.... In *Canadian Broadcasting Corp.* (No. 236) and *Air Canada*, the Board found that concerted refusals to work overtime were unlawful strikes notwithstanding that the overtime assignments in question were considered to be voluntary under the relevant collective agreements.... In the *Air Canada* case the Board also found a concerted refusal to accept acting supervisory assignments to be an unlawful strike regardless of the fact that the assignments being refused were again voluntary under the collective agreement.... Other job-related action that has been found to be an illegal strike includes, a concerted work to rule ... and booking off sick or being otherwise unavailable for assignments.... One of the best examples of how wide a net is cast when the Board is assessing the legality of job action is the decision in *Canada Post Corp.*.... There, the Board declared that an unlawful strike had been declared when the Canadian Union of Postal Workers announced that over the Christmas period its members would accept and process mail bearing ten cent stamps which was less than the postage rate required at that time. The key to the Board's apparent strict enforcement of s. 180 lies in the consistent presence of the few factual elements which go to make up a strike under the Code. All of the activities have taken place when the conditions set out in s. 180 have not been met, they were all found to have been done in combination or in concert or in accordance with a common understanding and, they were designed to restrict or limit output. That is all it takes for an unlawful strike to have occurred in the federal jurisdiction.

The broad interpretation of strike that has evolved under the Code really reflects the growing attitude of bargaining agents in today's work environment. As tough economic times continue and jobs are hard to come by, trade unions are looking for ways other than the traditional strike to apply pressures on employers. Particularly in industries where replacement workers are readily obtainable, rotating strikes, overtime bans, work to rule campaigns, slow-downs and many other more imaginative job-related activities are becoming the strike weapon of the day. Besides being less predictable, the strategy of limited or sporadic job action has one main advantage, the union members are not deprived of their income over long periods of time. Having repeatedly told trade unions and other members that those activities are unlawful when they are done at the wrong time, are we now going to tell them that the same activities are not lawful strike activities when they are in a legal strike position? Surely when we are faced with the reverse situation to an unlawful strike as we are now and are being asked to extend the protection of s. 184(3)(a)(vi) to concerted job related activities that have been taken when a strike can lawfully occur, the same standards must apply. It must then naturally follow if the same standards are applied to determine lawful strike activities as the Board has applied to unlawful strikes in the past that almost any concerted activity on the part of employees in relation to their work would fall within the protection contemplated by s. 184(3)(a)(vi) of the Code. We say almost any activity because it goes without saying that however broad the protection under the Code, it cannot be used to shield criminal or other unlawful acts.

Where does that leave employers? Are they left defenceless once a trade union is in a lawful strike position? We think the Ontario Labour Relations Board's comments, when they were faced with similar circumstances to what we have here, are most appropriate (*The Corporation of the City of Brampton* . . .):

> An employer, for its part, is free to take measures designed to limit the disruptive effect of this type of strike activity, such as the increased use of managerial personnel and non-striking employees. An employer is also free to take responsive action through its right to lock out employees. *An employer is not, however, free to discipline or punish employees for engaging in a lawful strike.* [Emphasis added.]

We concur with that assessment of the situation and adopt it as our own. Disruption of an employer's normal operations is what a strike is all about and provided the employees are participating in lawful strike activities their employer is prohibited from taking any of the actions against them that are spelled out in s. 184(3)(a)(vi). . . .

* * * * *

In 1992 the Canada Board was forced to return to the question of what measures an employer could take in response to rotating or partial strikes. In *CUPW v Canada Post Corporation* (1992), 16 CLRBR (2d) 290, the union over the course of one day had engaged in various concerted activities designed to decrease production; at the time, it was in a position to engage in a lawful strike. One such activity was a refusal by employees at a postal station to deliver anything but first class mail. The union handed out summaries of the *Graham Cable* decision, in an effort to persuade its members that the *Canada Labour Code* protected them from being punished for such activities. When the employer responded by refusing to allow employees who had participated in the partial strikes to work the following day, the union filed an unfair labour practice complaint alleging that the employer had discriminated against those employees because they had participated in a lawful strike.

The board held that *Graham Cable* meant that employers could defend their interests by imposing lockouts in response to concerted employee activity in the workplace. It went on to hold that it must try to distinguish employer conduct that was merely a (permissible) defensive lockout from conduct which (impermissibly) discriminated against or disciplined employees for the exercise of their rights under the *Code*. The Board found that the employer's conduct in this case was merely a rotating defensive lockout, despite the fact that in one instance only those employees who had engaged in strike activity were denied entry to the workplace the next day. The *Canada Post* decision indicates that a lockout might indeed be an effective weapon to counteract partial strike action.

* * * * *

What precisely does it mean that in order to be a strike, the industrial action must, in the words of the statutory formulation, be "in combination, in concert or in accordance with a common understanding"? In the two cases excerpted immediately above, there was no doubt that the action was coordinated by the union and that the strikers were acting with a common understanding. However, what about situations where there is no clear evidence that the action was coordinated?

British Columbia Terminal Elevator Operators' Association on Behalf of the Saskatchewan Wheat Pool v Grain Workers' Union, Local 333 (1994), 94 CLLC para 16,060 at 14,500 (CLRB)

[The employer sought an unlawful strike declaration and other remedies. The employer argued that there had been a concerted refusal by its employees to work voluntary overtime following the temporary layoff of ten employees in the bargaining unit. The collective agreement explicitly stated that employees could refuse overtime work.]

No direct evidence was presented that the union authorized or orchestrated the employees' refusal to work overtime. However, it is not necessary to prove that point through direct evidence; circumstantial evidence will suffice....

Here the parties were in the midst of collective bargaining. The employees in the bargaining unit had engaged in a concerted refusal to work overtime in circumstances where, in the normal course, a sufficient number would have accepted work. In addition, the employer had been told that the union was clearly opposed to the concept of resorting to overtime when lay-offs were in effect. In light of the above, and in the absence of any evidence to the contrary, the Board must conclude that the union was the architect of the employees' concerted refusal. We found therefore that a strike contrary to section 89 was in effect....

[I]t must be clear that the statutory definition of 'strike' cannot be changed by an agreement of the parties. Nor can the public purpose of 'industrial peace' behind the no-strike provision be avoided by 'contracting out' of the legal obligations of the Code.... Of course, the parties can negotiate an employee's individual right to refuse to work and these clauses will be applied in accordance with their given interpretation, subject to arbitration. However, the union or its members cannot use such a clause to circumvent the Code by giving employees the right to refuse collectively to work contrary to section 89. Each separate segment of the Code definition of 'strike' is significant and must be read in conjunction with the other segments. Actions which are acceptable, for individual employees, because of the collective agreement provisions, may constitute an unlawful strike when done 'in combination, in concert or in accordance with a common understanding,' that is aimed, in relation to their work, at restricting or limiting output.

8:413   The Strike Prohibition and Sympathetic Action

Because the timing of strikes is strictly regulated by statute, the strike ban poses significant obstacles to "sympathetic action" by one group of workers designed to help another group that is involved in a strike or lockout. Any sympathetic action of this sort is likely both to constitute a strike and to be untimely. An exception to this is found in British Columbia, where cessation of work due to lawful picketing is specifically excluded from the definition of "strike" in section 1 of that province's Labour Code. Similarly, Manitoba's *Labour Relations Act* (section 15) protects an employee from discipline who refuses to perform work that "would directly facilitate the operation or business" of an employer whose employees are on strike or locked out. In Alberta, the *Labour Relations Code* allows "anyone" to participate in peaceful picketing during a lawful strike at the location of the struck employment. Newfoundland and New Brunswick allow "expressions of sympathy or support otherwise than by picketing" by those who are not party to the dispute. The following case in the federal jurisdiction considers the refusal of employees to cross a picket line when they are not themselves in a position to strike legally.

Local 273, International Longshoremen's Association v Maritime Employers' Association, [1979] 1 SCR 120 at 123, 125–26, and 137–39

> ESTEY J.: The issuance of an injunction against three trade unions certified under the Canada Labour Code ... is challenged principally on the grounds that ... refusal by members of the appellant Locals to cross a lawful picket line is not a strike and therefore there is no proper basis for the issuance of an injunction, ...
>
> Prior to the incidents giving rise to these proceedings, a legal strike was commenced by the members of the National Harbours Board Police employed in the Port of Saint John, and the police, in the course of that strike, established picket lines in the entrance to the port's facilities. The employers of the police were not, of course, the employers of the members of the appellants; the conflict here arose because of the common *situs* of employment around which the police placed a picket line. The members of the three Locals refused to cross the police picket lines and on their failure to do so and to report to work, shipping operations in the Port of Saint John were closed down....
>
> The Locals submitted in this Court that by reason of the universally understood doctrine of 'union solidarity,' it could not have been the intention of Parliament in enacting the Code to have included, in the meaning of 'strike,' the refusal to cross a lawful picket line drawn up around the employees' place of work. Presumably the same argument is extended by the Locals to the terms of their Collective Agreements where the same definitions of 'strike' are employed. This approach to the problem at hand found support in proceedings before the B.C. Labour Relations Board in *MacMillan, Bloedel Packaging Ltd. v. Pulp, Paper & Woodworkers of Canada, Local 5 and Local 8, et al*, where the Board interpreted the statutory definition of strike as including a
>
>> subjective element: a concerted effort by employees undertaken for the specific purpose of compelling an employer to settle a dispute about terms of employment. It is just that motivation which is absent in the normal case of employees honouring a picket line.
>
> The response to this submission is found in the history of the federal labour statute itself. The *Industrial Disputes Investigation Act*, R.S.C. 1927, c. 112, provided in s. 1(k) a definition of strike as follows:
>
>> 'strike' or 'to go on strike,' without limiting the nature of its meaning, means the cessation of work by a body of employees acting in combination, or a concerted refusal or a refusal

under a common understanding of any number of employees to continue to work for an employer, in consequence of a dispute, done as a means of compelling their employer, or to aid other employees in compelling their employer, to accept terms of employment;

This statute was replaced in 1948 by the *Industrial Relations and Disputes Investigation Act*, 1948 (Can.), c. 54, which deleted the qualification that the withholding of services be done for the purpose of compelling the employer to accept the proposed terms of employment. The definition, [s. 2(p),] was as follows:

(p) 'strike' includes a cessation of work, or refusal to work or to continue to work, by employees, in combination or in concert or in accordance with a common understanding;

The Code, in its present form, repeats the 1948 definition. There is no room for doubt now that Parliament has adopted an objective definition of 'strike,' the elements of which are a cessation of work in combination or with a common understanding. Whether the motive be ulterior or expressed is of no import, the only requirement being the cessation pursuant to a common understanding. Here, the concurrent findings foreclose this aspect of this submission.

Refusal to cross a picket line lawfully established by another union cannot be a strike unless it falls within the definition of 'strike' which fortunately for the purposes of this appeal is in substance the same in both statute and contract. This definition requires a cessation of work (a) in 'combination' or (b) in 'concert' or (c) 'in accordance with a common understanding.' In this case the 'concert,' the 'combination' or the 'common understanding' may be considered to have a common root in the principle of labour organization which forbids the crossing of picket lines. Section X(b) of the agreement with Local 1039, Article 12:02 of Local 273, and the definition in the Code, when given the ordinary meaning of 'common understanding,' seem to be an attempt by the authors to provide for the very situation where the 'cessation of work' results from a concept jointly held by the employees, such as the principle against the crossing of picket lines. The contract might have been more precise and included in the 'strike' definition, the cessation of work resulting from a refusal to cross a picket line. However, the question is simply: do the words 'in accordance with a common understanding' embrace the more specific provision that a cessation of work resulting from the application of the commonly understood principle of the labour movement that members of unions should not cross picket lines?' The argument is made more complex here because one of the three Collective Agreements does not define 'strike' and none of the Agreements defines 'stoppage of work.' Given the ordinary meaning of these words, there is no room to import a qualification which would exclude a stoppage of work resulting from one circumstance only, namely the honouring of a picket line by the employees comprising the bargaining unit.

In the above case, the Supreme Court of Canada held that it could infer a "common understanding" where unionized employees respect another union's picket line. This inference is based in the idea that unionized workers respect picket lines as a show of solidarity. Does the same presumption apply when the employees that refuse to cross the picket line are not unionized?

Unilux Boiler Corp v United Steelworkers of America, Local 3950, [2005] OLRD No 2471 at para 14ff

[The company's non-unionized office employees refused or were unable to cross a picket line established by its striking unionized employees. The picketers were hostile, and even the police had been unable to escort the office employees through the picket line. The employer argued that the picketers and the union had caused them to strike unlawfully. The union's reply was that the office employees had not engaged in a strike, because their refusal to work was neither "concerted" nor done in pursuit of a "common understanding."]

MACLEAN, Vice-Chair: Since none of the employees at the picketed worksite are represented by a trade union (except those Steelworkers' members who crossed the picket line and are permitted to strike anyway), the Board's normal assumptions about the effect of picket lines do not apply. Non-union office workers and replacement workers cannot be expected to respect picket lines or act in concert. In fact, if anything, the opposite assumptions apply. That is, such workers are expected to cross the picket line and attend at work or make individual decisions not to do so.

In cases such as this, where no presumption as to the employee motivations can apply, it is critical to determine if there is a "refusal to work" in "combination," "in concert" or "in accordance with a common understanding." Here there is no allegation that the employees who refused (or were prevented) from crossing the picket line did so in concert in combination or in accordance with a common understanding as these terms have previously been understood. That is a necessary component of a strike.... The Board has found that employees who made an individual decision not to cross the picket line either because they are afraid or out of respect for the picket line, are not engaged in a strike ...

Even accepting there was a refusal to work in this case, such refusal is not alleged to have been done in concert or to limit the applicant's business.... For all of these reasons, I am satisfied that the employees of the applicant were not engaged in an illegal strike as alleged by the applicant.

What if a collective agreement expressly permits the employees covered by it to refuse to cross a lawful picket line? Are employees who do refuse to cross engaged in a strike?

Nelson Crushed Stone and United Cement, Lime & Gypsum Workers' International Union, Local Union 494 v Martin, [1978] 1 CLRBR 115 at 119–20, 125, and 128–29 (OLRB)

HALADNER, Vice-Chair: The facts of this case—a refusal by members of one union to cross a picket line maintained by members of another union who are legally on strike against a common employer, where the collective agreement between the employer and the 'non-striking' union contains a provision stating that it shall not be a violation of the agreement (or cause for discharge or discipline) if any employee refuses to cross a legal picket line—raise again the question of the precise scope of the strike definition contained in section 1(1)(m) of the Labour Relations Act....

The Board, when applying the statutory definition, has not drawn a distinction between a refusal by employees to cross a picket line and other types of employee activity which result in a disruption of an employer's operation. In all cases, the question is whether the refusal to work on the part of the employees is in combination, in concert, or in accordance with a common understanding within the meaning of section 1(1)(m). In this regard, the Board has held that the definition of 'strike' is not restricted or qualified by the purpose underlying the work stoppage. The Board, moreover, does not allow the parties to qualify the no-strike provision deemed to be contained in every collective agreement. The Board has held that provisions which purport to legalize strike activity during the contract term embody attempts by the parties to contract out of the Labour Relations Act and are, to that extent, invalid....

It is difficult to see any difference in principle between a clause which provides that it will not be a violation of the collective agreement for employees to refuse to cross a legal picket line and a clause which provides that employees will not be so required. Neither clause can make unlawful [sic] that which would otherwise be unlawful—that is, a concerted refusal on the part of employees to work when there is work scheduled....

To conclude that clauses such as Article 4.02 cannot authorize a work stoppage which, in the absence of such a clause, would amount to a 'strike' is not, however, to conclude that such clauses are of no legal effect ... such clauses, while invalid to the extent that they purport to contract out of the *Labour Relations Act*, may nevertheless limit the liability of employees and/or the union under the terms of a collective agreement. In addition, such clauses may ... be sufficiently exculpatory to persuade the Board to decline to grant consent to prosecute where the employees or the union, relying on such a clause, engage in a 'strike.' Whatever the precise extent of the 'collective agreement' protection which such clauses may afford, such clauses can probably be expected to provide a defense to individual employees who may be discharged or disciplined as a result of their refusal, on an individual basis, to cross a legal picket line.

* * * * *

A "hot cargo" or "hot declaration" clause in a collective agreement typically purports to allow employees to refuse to do any work coming from or destined for another employer who has been declared unfair by the union. Where the strike definition does not include a purpose component, respecting a "hot cargo" clause would amount to a strike unless the statute exempted this behaviour from the strike definition. Most provinces do not include such an exemption. However, in British Columbia, from 1973 to 1987 and again since 1992, the provincial labour relations statute has allowed the labour board to give effect to hot cargo clauses, with certain limitations: *Labour Relations Code*, sections 64 and 70: see *Victoria Times Colonist v CEP, Local 25-G*, 2008 BCSC 109. See also section 15 of the Manitoba *Labour Relations Act*, which permits unionized employees covered by a collective agreement to refuse to facilitate the operation or business of an employer who has locked out its employees or whose employees are on strike.

8:414   The Strike Prohibition and Political Protests

Whether a purposive restriction should be read into the definition of a strike has been controversial over the years. Should it matter *why* workers are striking? As we have just seen, with some exceptions (British Columbia and Manitoba), Canadian lawmakers have tended not to permit untimely *sympathy* strikes. Another reason why workers may engage in a strike not directly related to collective bargaining is as a form of *political expression or protest*. In a series of cases dealing with the 1976 National Day of Protest, which was a one-day work stoppage called by the Canadian Labour Congress to protest against federal anti-inflation legislation limiting wage increases, labour boards focused on whether the statutory definition of "strike" included a purpose clause.

In British Columbia at the time, the legislation did include a purpose clause; to meet the definition of a "strike" collective employee action had to be "for the purpose of compelling their employer to agree to terms or conditions of employment." Applying that language, the BC Labour Board found that the Day of Protest stoppage was not a strike. See *British Columbia Hydro and Power Authority and International Brotherhood of Electrical Workers, Local 258 and Local 213*, [1976] 2 CLRBR 410. But see *Re Robb Engineering and United Steelworkers of America, Local 4122* (1978), 86 DLR (3d) 307 (NSCA) where, on similar statutory language, that stoppage was held to be an unlawful strike. Justice MacKeigan of the Nova Scotia Court of Appeal in *Robb Engineering* concluded: "Four men deciding to go fishing together would not be striking, but if forty men all agreed to quit at the same time, purporting to go fishing, that might well be a strike." In jurisdictions where the definition of a strike had no purposive component, stoppages on the Day of Protest were invariably held to be strikes. See, for example, *Domglas Ltd* (1976), 76 CLLC para 16,050 (OLRB), aff'd (1978), 78 CLLC para 14,135 (Ont Div Ct).

More recently, unions have challenged the prohibition of political protest strikes during the term of a collective agreement as a violation of *Charter* rights, particularly the right to freedom of expression. These arguments have so far failed. See *British Columbia Teachers' Federation v British Columbia Public School Employers' Assn*, 2009 BCCA 39, leave to appeal to SCC refused, 2009 CanLII 44624. However, it is possible that the future *Charter* challenges of this type of strike activity may be informed by the Supreme Court of Canada's reasons in *Saskatchewan Federation*, discussed above and in Chapter 12.

8:420 Regulating Economic Sanctions Available to the Employer

8:421 Regulating Lockouts

As with strikes, labour relations statutes impose restrictions on when employers can declare lockouts. Generally speaking, the same timeliness restrictions that are imposed on the right to strike are also imposed on the right to lock out. In other words, a lockout is timely whenever the employees can legally strike. However, unlike the definition of a strike in most jurisdictions, the definition of a "lockout" invariably does include a purpose limitation. The definition in the *Canada Labour Code* is typical:

> "[L]ockout" includes the closing of a place of employment, a suspension of work by an employer or a refusal by an employer to continue to employ a number of their employees, *done to compel their employees, or to aid another employer to compel their employees, to agree to terms or conditions of employment* ... [Emphasis added.]

Thus, for an employer action to be a lockout, it must seek to influence employee and union views on collective bargaining issues. Therefore, an unconditional plant closure that leads to the permanent layoff of the workforce is not a lockout, unless the union can prove that the company intends to reopen and is using the closure as a bargaining ploy. See *Humpty Dumpty Foods Ltd*, [1977] 2 CLRBR 248 (OLRB).

8:422 Changes to the Employment Contract Without Union Consent

Canadian labour legislation is usually structured so that the end of the statutory collective bargaining freeze (discussed in Chapter 7, Section 7:300) coincides with the commencement of the lawful strike and lockout period. Therefore, in addition to the right to lock out employees, the employer has another weapon at its disposal once the right to strike or lockout arises: that is, the right to make changes to the terms and conditions of employment without the union's consent. This employer right was recognized in *Canadian Association of Industrial, Mechanical and Allied Workers, Local 14 v Paccar of Canada Ltd*, [1989] 2 SCR 983 at 1007–15, La Forest J, and was affirmed by the Ontario Labour Relations Board in *Neenah Paper Co of Canada*, [2006] OLRB Rep March/April 224, summarized below. In some jurisdictions, including British Columbia and Alberta, the right of employers to unilaterally impose contract terms only exists once a work stoppage has commenced.

United Steelworkers 1-2693 v Neenah Paper Company of Canada, 2006 CanLII 9888 (OLRB)

[The collective agreement between the union and employer, a lumber company, expired on 31 August 2005. The employer told the union that it was losing money and that it would require employees to accept a pay cut. The parties met with a government conciliation officer, but no deal was reached and as of 5 December 2005, the parties were in a legal strike/lockout position. Prior to that date, the employer sent the union a letter that advised the union that unless a deal was reached before 5 December, it intended on that date to implement new terms of employment, including a 6.4 percent wage cut and a substantial change to the pension plan, among other changes that had been proposed to the union in bargaining. On 5 December, the employer began to apply the new terms. The employees continued to work but advised the employer that they did not accept the change. The union filed an unfair labour practice complaint, arguing that the employer was unlawfully bargaining directly with employees, and that by unilaterally changing terms of employment without the union's consent and before it had locked out its employees, the employer was in violation of the "statutory bargaining freeze" (s 86) in the Ontario *Labour Relations Act*.]

McLean, Vice-Chair:

21. The employer ... relies on the Supreme Court of Canada decision in PACCAR OF CANADA LTD. [1989] 2 S.C.R. 983, (1989) 62 D.L.R. (4th) 437.... The issue on appeal was whether the decision of the respondent Labour Relations Board of British Columbia permitting an employer, after the termination of a collective agreement, to unilaterally alter terms and conditions of employment was patently unreasonable and subject to review by the Court....

27. After reviewing the history of the case, the Supreme Court ultimately decided the issue in the Board's favour. According to the Court, while the [B.C. *Labour Relations Code*] does not expressly provide the employer with the power to change the terms of which it makes employment available, it was not unreasonable for the Board to find that the power existed....

29. LaForest J., in finding that the Board's decision was reasonable stated at p. 451:

However, denying to the employer the power within the context of a collective bargaining relationship to, subject to its duty to bargain in good faith, change the terms on which it will make employment available denies almost all effect to the termination clause agreed to by the parties. Instead of terminating the agreement in any real sense, it simply would signal the commencement of a new bargaining session, coupled with the threat of strikes or lock-outs. The position taken by Judson J. in *C.P.R. Co. v. Zambri* 1962), 1962 CanLII 11 (SCC), 34 D.L.R. (2d) 654 at p. 666 [1962] S.C.R. 609, 62 C.L.L.C. 450, that "When a collective agreement has expired, it is difficult to see how there can be anything left to govern the employer-employee relationship" seems more satisfying. The relationship continues, of course, to be subject to the requirements contained in the appropriate statutory scheme. [Emphasis in original.]

While it is true that the Act does not expressly provide that the employer has the power contended for, it was not unreasonable for the board to find that the power existed. . . .

31. The union argues that the employer may not impose terms and conditions of employment until after it has locked out employees—which the employer has specifically decided not to do. Any implementation of terms and conditions of employment prior to a lock-out constitutes direct bargaining with employees in violation of s. 73(1) of the Act. The union argues that the words in s. 86 are to be read in conjunction with and subject to the prohibition against bargaining directly with bargaining unit employees. To impose terms and conditions of employment prior to a lock-out is to bargain directly with bargaining unit employees. In the union's submissions, once the employees are locked out and go to work after the lock-out takes place they are no longer employees in the bargaining unit and the employer's right to implement new terms and conditions with respect to these employees and other employees who may be hired commences. . . .

38. Given that the employer's case rests in large part on a plain reading of s. 86 of the Act, it is useful to start with an analysis of that section. On its face s. 86 prohibits an employer from altering terms and conditions of employment until after a party has given notice to bargain, the collective agreement has expired and the parties are in a strike/lock-out position. In my view it is clear that once the parties are in a strike/lock out position, s. 86 does not prevent an employer from altering terms and conditions of employment without the union's consent.

39. The union generally argues that the Board should, in effect, find a sort of rule, that being that terms and conditions cannot be changed until a lock-out. However, there is no support for that rule in s. 86. Had the Legislature intended such a rule it could have, as did the Alberta Legislature, easily drafted s. 86 in such a way to accomplish that result. In fact it appears that the Legislature took another approach. . . . In this case, the employer altered terms and conditions of employment only after the strike/lock-out period had commenced. I conclude, therefore, that the employer has not violated s. 86.

[The board then considered whether the employer's unilateral change to working conditions violated section 73 of the OLRA, which prohibited unionized employers from bargaining directly with employees.]

46. Under the union's theory, the employer cannot change the terms and conditions of "employees in the bargaining unit" until there is a strike or lock-out. To do otherwise would be to bargain directly with employees in the bargaining unit contrary to s. 73(1). The next aspect of the union's argument is novel. It asserts that once a strike/lock out occurs, employees who continue to work (whether they are employees who cross the picket line or new replacement workers) are not or are no longer "employees in the bargaining unit" so that the employer is free to deal with them as it sees fit.

47. The first problem with the union's interpretation becomes apparent when s. 73 is analysed in the context of s. 86. As discussed above, if that had been the Legislature's intention with respect to s. 73, it would have been easy to draft s. 86 in such a way to reflect that intention. Indeed the language of s. 86 suggests a different intention. The fact that s. 86 uses the phrase "alter rates of pay" suggests that, once the strike/lock out period has commenced, the employer's unilateral implementation of new terms and conditions of employment is not, under those circumstances, the same as "bargaining". The use of the word "alter" suggests a distinction between "bargaining" and the unilateral imposition of new terms and conditions of employment, the first of which is always prohibited, while altering terms of conditions is prohibited while the collective agreement is in operation and during the statutory "freeze", but is permitted once the parties are in a strike/lock-out position.

49. Moreover, while s. 86 does not use the term "employees in the bargaining unit" that is clearly whose terms and conditions are frozen. Were it otherwise, the requirement that the employer obtain the trade union's consent before altering terms and conditions would not make sense. If the union's interpretation is correct the term of the collective agreement, and the termination of the collective agreement would have no significance or even meaning. As LaForest, J. said [in *Paccar*], the end of the term would simply "signal the commencement of a new bargaining session, coupled with the threats of strikes or lockouts". It is difficult to believe, given the entire statutory context, that is what the Legislature intended....

50. If union employees who cross the picket line are not employees in the bargaining unit as the union argues, then they would not be entitled to vote whether to strike or to ratify a collective agreement. That is not the Board's understanding of the practice in Ontario. The union's suggestion that such employees momentarily return to the bargaining unit in order to cast their ratification ballot and then exit the bargaining unit if a collective agreement is not ratified and the employees return to work is wholly unsatisfying. Moreover, if union employees who cross the picket line are not employees in the bargaining unit, the employer would be permitted to "bargain" directly with such employees, an outcome which makes little labour relations sense. I am therefore satisfied that union employees who cross the picket line during a strike or lock-out remain employees in the bargaining unit and that the union's argument on this point must be rejected.

57. ... At Neenah Paper the union has the ability to respond. If it and the employees are unhappy with the new terms and conditions of employment they can simply go on a full-blown strike or engage in other activity to restrict production. In Ontario, the Act is premised on the fact that the parties may engage in economic warfare once the strike/lock out conditions have been met. Such economic warfare can, so long as it does not otherwise constitute a violation of the Act, take a variety of forms. Unions can legally engage in strikes. They also may engage in other activity which does not amount to a full blown work

stoppage, in order to put pressure on the employer. Included in these tactics are rotating strikes, overtime bans, "work to rule" activities etc. The employer has a similar broad range of economic weapons at its disposal (all of which must be exercised subject to the Act's unfair labour practice provisions). It can lock out. It can hire replacement workers to replace locked out or striking workers. I see no reason why, subject to the other provisions of the Act, a unilateral implementation of new terms and conditions (which have been offered to the union in collective bargaining) cannot form part of the employer arsenal. As has already been stated: if the union and the employees do not wish to operate under the new terms and conditions they do not have to. In short, on balance it appears that the statute contemplates exactly what occurred in this case. Had the interpretation advanced by the union been intended, the Legislature could have simply said so ...

[Finally, the board considered briefly whether the employer's actions constituted a failure to bargain in good faith, ruling that they did not.]

61. The union did not specifically allege a breach of s. 17 in its application. However, since the PACCAR decision, which was a case partially about the obligation to bargain in good faith, was heavily relied on by the union, it is appropriate to directly consider this aspect as well.

62. I start by noting that the union does not allege that the employer has bargained in bad faith in the traditional sense. That is, on the facts there can be no doubt that the employer met and sought to meet with the union for the purpose of collective bargaining. There is no allegation that it did not wish to conclude a collective agreement, albeit one that was satisfactory to it.

63. It is also notable that it is not alleged that the employer did any of the activities which form the basis of this complaint behind the union's back. It first gave the proposals it intended to implement to the union before giving them to the employees. It told the union what it intended to do if those proposals were not accepted by the union. Employees were advised to seek the union's assistance if they had any questions about the new terms and conditions.

64. The Board discussed the employer's "right" to implement new terms and conditions in the context of its obligation to bargain in good faith in *Devilbiss* [[1976] OLRB Rep March 49]. In that case the Board held that the employer's "right" to impose terms and conditions of employment arises after the time periods established by s. 86 have run their course and the parties are at an impasse, or when there is *a bona fide* business reason for such immediate action. I accept that proposition. It would be an unfair labour practice for an employer to implement new terms and conditions while the parties are in active bargaining without a good business reason for doing so and without notifying the union first. ... For all the reasons, the application is dismissed.

* * * * *

8:423 Employer Economic Weapons, the Duty to Bargain, and Unfair Labour Practices

The right of an employer to use either of these economic weapons — a lockout or a unilateral change to working conditions — is subject to the unfair labour practice provisions we have

CHAPTER 8: INDUSTRIAL CONFLICT

looked at in previous chapters, including the duty to bargain and the prohibition against punishing or otherwise discriminating against employees for exercising their lawful statutory rights. Thus, if a labour board found that an employer was using one of those weapons with anti-union *animus*, or that it had no intention of reaching a collective agreement, it would be in breach of the legislation.

It might be argued that any unilateral alteration of working conditions amounts to a breach of the duty to bargain, as it is tantamount to bargaining with the employees individually. However, this argument was rejected in *Paccar of Canada Ltd*, discussed above. The duty to bargain appears to require only that the employer must first give the union an opportunity to accept the proposed unilateral changes after the end of the statutory freeze before moving to implement them, and that the employer must otherwise show a willingness to conclude a collective agreement. See *Canadian National Railway Co and Council of Railway Unions* (1993), 23 CLRBR (2d) 122 and *Neenah Paper*, mentioned above.

The following case discusses the relationship between the right to lockout and hire replacement workers and the employer's duty to bargain and to avoid anti-union *animus*.

Westroc Industries Ltd v United Cement, Lime and Gypsum Workers International Union, [1981] 2 CLRBR 315 at 324–29 (OLRB)

[The company had manufacturing operations in several provinces. During negotiations for renewal of the collective agreement at its Mississauga, Ontario, plant, the company concluded that the union was deliberately prolonging discussions in order to conduct simultaneous strikes in other locations, where the collective agreements had later expiry dates. Attempts to bring the Mississauga negotiations to a more rapid conclusion failed, and after the exhaustion of conciliation proceedings, the company locked out the Mississauga employees. Over a period of several weeks, the company hired replacement workers and resumed certain operations. The OLRB found that during negotiations both before and after the lockout, the employer met the standard of good faith required by the legislation. The union complained that the lockout and the hiring of replacements were breaches of the *Ontario Labour Relations Act*.]

ADAMS, Chair: We have come to the conclusion that both complaints must be dismissed in their entirety. From a review of all of the evidence, we are satisfied that none of the impugned conduct of the respondent company violates sections 14, 56, 58 or 61 of the Act. ...

We begin by observing that an employer may properly decide to continue his operations in the face of a strike and, to that end, may hire fresh employees. Section 64 of the Act would appear to contemplate that possibility in that it explicitly provides for the job security of striking employees for a finite period. ...

Thus, as long as an employer's motive is free of anti-union animus, it seems clear that strike replacement employees can be hired and such action can be a powerful economic weapon in many cases. ... This being clear, it is of some interest to note that the almost parallel treatment of strike and lockout activity by the statute—a treatment that tends to suggest that, for the most part, they are but two sides of the same coin. For example, section 1(2) provides, *inter alia*, that no person shall cease to be an employee by reason only of his ceasing to work for his employer as the result of a lockout or strike.

Similar dual references can be found in, *inter alia*, sections 34b, 34d, 34e, 36, 53(3), 63, sections 65 and 66 when read together, 67, 68, sections 82 and 83 when read together, sections 119 and 134a. Indeed, section 64 is the only section of consequence where the dual reference is missing although our later analysis of the lockout replacement capacity of an employer will illustrate why we do not think this discloses a fundamental flaw in the statutory scheme. This parallel treatment, we think, goes some way to suggest that the Legislature saw each party in collective bargaining having a range of economic weapons in its arsenal and that it intended no ground rules with respect to the utilization of such weapons or the initiation of industrial conflict. The legislative scheme, on this latter point, clearly envisages the possibility of an employer locking out his employees before being struck. ... Moreover, while a lockout singles out those persons employed by an employer who are engaging in collective bargaining, the statute explicitly recognizes this result and makes a distinction between two classes of employer motivation in causing a lockout. Section 1(1)(i) of the Act defines a lockout as including:

> the closing of a place of employment, a suspension of work or a refusal by an employer to continue to employ a number of his employees or to aid another employer to compel or induce his employees, to refrain from exercising any rights or privileges under this Act or to agree to provisions respecting terms or conditions of employment or the rights, privileges or duties of the employer, an employees' organization, the trade union, or the employees;

A timely lockout aimed at inducing employee agreement over terms and conditions of employment is part of the very process of collective bargaining which the Act contemplates. See section 63(2) in the light of sections 14 and 45. On the other hand, a lockout aimed at dissuading employees from exercising rights under the Act is never lawful and the concept of timeliness simply had no application to such activity. ... A collective bargaining lockout, then, while in some real sense discriminating between those engaged in negotiations and those employees who are not, does not contravene sections 56, 58 or even section 61 because the employer's intent is directed at achieving a collective agreement and not at penalizing his employees for having exercised a right under the statute. Unlawful intent is the hallmark of these sections and a close analysis of the evidence before us in this case discloses no such motivation. As the United States Supreme Court observed in American *Shipbuilding Co. v. NLRB* ...

> [t]he lockout may well dissuade employees from adhering to the position which they initially adopted in the bargaining, but the 'right' to bargain collectively does not entail any 'right' to insist on one's position free from economic disadvantage.

Employers can lockout to apply economic pressure in order to achieve a collective agreement on the terms they want and, in the instant case, the employer continued to be driven by this purpose. There is also no evidence that the lockout was intended as a 'cheap layoff' or in any way unrelated to the bargaining differences between the parties. We also note that throughout the lockout the respondent has respected the exclusive authority of the complainant as bargaining agent.

Does this analysis change if the employer, after locking out his employees, goes on to replace them in order to operate? Clearly if the employer's motive is directed at avoiding a collective agreement or the punishment of his employees for having exercised rights under the Act, the hiring of replacements should be struck down. In fact, this Board has held that the permanent replacement of an employee does not constitute a lockout because there is nothing conditional in the employer's action.... The action is, instead, a dismissal or termination. The permanent replacement of locked out employees would likely amount to a unilateral destruction of the bargaining unit and the withdrawal of recognition of their duly certified bargaining agent.... This is the feature of a lockout that makes reference to it in section 64 unnecessary. A permanent lockout of bargaining unit employees would be very difficult to characterize as employer conduct aimed at achieving a collective agreement. But in the instant case, the company clearly hired temporary replacements and paid them at rates found in the expired collective agreement. Full benefit entitlement was not extended to these persons and formal recruitment procedures were not employed. The arrangement was therefore clearly temporary and locked out employees as a group can have their jobs back at any time their bargaining agent is prepared to agree with the respondent....

Counsel for the trade union submits that any form of replacement is unlawful because of the manifest distinction made between unionized employees and other workers, but this ignores the fact that the use of temporary replacements is only marginally more discriminatory than the lockout itself and clearly, in the facts at hand, has the same collective bargaining purpose. Indeed, the temporary replacement of locked out employees may allow an employer to maintain key customers (as was part of the employers' motivation in the case at bar) and, to some degree, ensure that locked out employees will have jobs to return to. But, more fundamentally, the trade union's position is totally at odds with the dynamics of collective bargaining and, if adopted, would permit trade unions to control the timing of economic conflict — the latter being an inestimable strategic advantage and one nowhere explicitly sanctioned in the statute....

For the same reasons that we have found the lockout itself to be lawful, therefore, we find the respondent's use of temporary lockout replacements; its deployments of non-unit personnel; and its subcontracting of bargaining unit work, do not violate any provision of the Labour Relations Act. The initial use of supervisors, clerical employees and subcontractors was aimed at protecting the patronage of key customers against its two major competitors who had substantial excess capacity. The use of temporary replacements was similarly motivated and implemented only after a lengthy lockout and a resulting perception by the employer of the trade union's unresponsiveness. A distinction made by an employer between employees engaged in protected activity and others who are not is, standing alone, sufficient to violate sections 56, 58, or 61. Rather, the basis to an impugned distinction has to be one of hostile purpose aimed at punishing employees or persons for having exercised their rights under the Act. As the definition of lockout reveals, this labour relations concept involves employer conduct that may be based on a proper or improper purpose. Which purpose is in fact the case must be determined on a careful review of all the evidence. In many earlier decisions we have said that first agreement situations are to be subjected to detailed scrutiny by this Board and a lockout with replacements will particularly merit such an approach in a first agreement context. However, in the instant case, the parties have had a longstanding relationship and there is simply no hint of anti-union animus on the evidence before us....

Lastly, regardless of the outcome of these negotiations, we are satisfied that individual employees locked out and replaced by temporary employees continue to have important job security rights under the general unfair labour practice provisions of the statue. After the imposition of a lockout for some considerable duration and without a collective agreement materializing, affected employees may wish to abandon the conflict and return to work despite the apparent continuing resistance of the bargaining agent. The employer's response to such a situation would be closely scrutinized under section 58, *inter alia*, of the Act. However, at present, such rights are not in issue between the parties.

For all of these reasons the matters consolidated herein are dismissed. . . .

8:430   Labour Board Remedies

For several decades, Canadian labour boards had little or no specific remedial authority over illegal strikes. In Ontario, for example, the OLRB could do no more than declare a strike to be illegal. Oddly, perhaps, this declaratory remedy proved reasonably effective. When the parties were in doubt about whether their actions were lawful, the declaration enlightened them, and they usually complied. When there was no such doubt, as in the case of a wildcat strike during the term of a collective agreement, the declaration alerted them to potential consequences such as a claim for damages, a criminal prosecution, or the discharge of illegally striking employees. This often altered the dynamics within the bargaining unit, encouraging some members to urge a return to work and giving those who were more militant a reason to back down.

Other advantages of declaratory relief over directive orders, especially in the context of politically motivated strikes of the sort that characterized the 1995 and 1996 Days of Protest in Ontario, were spelled out by Chair MacDowell of the OLRB in *General Motors of Canada Limited*, [1996] OLRB Rep May/June 409 at 452–54. Among them were the avoidance of the spectre of criminal contempt proceedings and the affirmation of the basic assumption of collective bargaining legislation that "self-regulation and private ordering are an appropriate (and perhaps the best) method of workplace governance."

The declaratory authority of some labour relations boards has in recent decades been supplemented by very broad and flexible remedial powers. For example, section 100 of the Ontario *Labour Relations Act, 1995*, reads as follows (the italicized passage was added in 1984):

> 100. Where, on the complaint of a trade union, council of trade unions, employer or employers' organization, the Board is satisfied that a trade union or council of trade unions called or authorized or threatened to call or authorize an unlawful strike or that an officer, official or agent of a trade union or council of trade unions counselled or procured or supported or encouraged an unlawful strike or threatened an unlawful strike or that employees engaged in or threatened to engage in an unlawful strike *or any person has done or is threatening to do an act that the person knows or ought to know that, as a probable and reasonable consequence of the act, another person or persons will engage in an unlawful strike*, the Board may so declare and it may direct what action, if any, a person, employee, employers' organization, trade union or council of trade unions and their officers, officials or agents shall do or refrain from doing with respect to the unlawful strike or threat of an unlawful strike.

CHAPTER 8: INDUSTRIAL CONFLICT

Labour boards have interpreted these statutory remedial powers as empowering them to seek sustainable industrial relations solutions in cases of illegal industrial action, as the following case indicates.

National Harbours Board v Syndicat national des employés du Port de Montréal, [1979] 3 CLRBR 502 at 503–18

[The union had called two one-day work stoppages while a conciliation commissioner was attempting to bring about a new collective agreement, and had also instituted an overtime ban. This affected the transshipment of grain through the Port of Montreal, disrupting export shipments. The employer complained that the union's actions were untimely and unlawful, and sought relief under the *Canada Labour Code*, section 182 (now section 91). The union argued that its members had become impatient with the slowness of the conciliation commissioner, that its use of limited sanctions was an attempt to "channel" employee discontent, and that it had to prove to the employer that it enjoyed support among the employees. The union acknowledged that the Canada board's officer had managed to speed up the actions of the conciliation commissioner, and that the union was now satisfied with his diligence. Finally, the union argued that the employer had violated the overtime provisions of the collective agreement, and also that the protest tactics had no serious consequences.]

LAPOINTE, Chair: It should be explained here that the Board's jurisdiction as created by the provisions of ... section 182 has existed only since Parliament's adoption of Bill C-8 and its implementation on June 1, 1978.

Being aware of the positive role that Parliament intended the Board to play in cases involving work stoppages, the latter therefore immediately developed a policy for applying this new jurisdiction. This policy bears the mark of the desire not only to remedy the symptoms of problems arising in labour relations but also to do so in particular by determining the source of the malady causing the problems.

The Board has now an experienced, dedicated support team composed of labour relations officers, and in the case of every application filed under section 182 or 183 (which, as the counterpart of section 182, deals with lockouts), it can rapidly establish a date for a public hearing. However, at the same time, it immediately sends one of its officers to the scene of the dispute. The latter will then do his utmost, by meeting with the parties and using the method of his choice, to discover where the shoe pinches in the case of an unlawful work stoppage (strike or lockout). He has complete authority with the full support of the Board to resolve the problem in order to avoid a public hearing.

If he fails, he merely reports this fact to the Board panel assigned to hear the case and then the Board sits and hears the parties.

The judiciousness of this approach seems clear in that to date, the Board has heard only three of over twenty applications of this nature. . . .

This practice and the policy underlying it are based on the Board's conviction that Parliament did not intend, by giving this new jurisdiction [to issue cease-and-desist orders] to the Board, to create a remedy that was identical and parallel to that still offered by the courts of the land.

It should be remembered, moreover, that Parliament's action in part reflected a reiterated request by central labour bodies in Canada ... that the legislator transfer to labour tribunals the jurisdiction of regular courts as regards injunctions. These labour bodies alleged that only specialized tribunals could really unravel problems in the case of bitter labour disputes characterized by work stoppages....

After giving the party in question the opportunity to be heard, the Board may decide not to issue an order even when faced with facts showing that an unlawful work stoppage exists. Everything depends on the higher interests to be satisfied in given circumstances: these higher interests may be summarized very simply. They involve creating or helping to create the factual situation most likely to promote healthy and orderly labour relations. In order to accomplish this, the Board believes that in cases of unlawful work stoppages which are the result of disturbances in the relations between the parties, it is important to identify the cause in order to determine the remedy. This is what it has instructed its officers to do in their meetings with the parties before the public hearing.... However, even in the event that the Board's officer fails, it may happen that the board will conclude after a public hearing that it may take the same action either by issuing an order containing specific directives conducive to remedying the cause of the disturbance or by refusing to issue an order.

It seems that this view of the Board corresponds to that of the regular Courts. In fact, in *McKinlay Transport Limited v. Goodman* ..., a case in which a party wanted the Federal Court to issue an injunction and for which the judgment is dated July 27, 1978, shortly after implementation of Bill C-8, Thurlow J. stated the following: ...

> [E]ven though the legislation does not specifically purport to withdraw from the Superior Courts' jurisdiction to issue injunctions in respect of conduct arising out of labour disputes, it seems to me that the Court can and ought to take into account in exercising its discretion that Parliament has shown its disposition that such matters be dealt with by the Board on the principles which it applies of the legislation rather than by the Courts. It is perhaps unnecessary to add that Court injunctions have not been notoriously successful as a device for achieving harmonious labour relations or for resolving labour disputes.
>
> A further aspect of the matter with respect to the exercise of discretion is that there is nothing before me to show that prompt and effective relief is not obtainable by the plaintiff in appropriate proceedings therefor before the Canada Labour Relations Board.

In effect, as the late shipping season delayed delivery of grain in the ports on the St. Lawrence, one of which was Montreal, there was a rapid increase in activities involving the unloading of vessels from the Great Lakes and the loading of ocean-going vessels. The employer has been very vulnerable for the last few weeks and will continue to be for a while yet. A large number of vessels are waiting to be loaded or unloaded.

The union's interests would be best served by collective bargaining in a situation of extreme pressure, namely the strike situation, if said bargaining and the strike occurred during this very peak of activities at the Port of Montreal. There is nothing inherently wrong with this union viewpoint.

Consequently, when the Board discovered between April 12 and 18, 1979, through the services of its labour relations officer, that what was bothering the union was the slowness of the conciliation commissioner's procedure, it anchored the re-establishment of the status quo by its interventions in obtaining a speed up of this procedure prior to the parties acquiring the right to stage a lawful work stoppage. The Board was successful in its attempts and even the union stated through its chief negotiator that it was satisfied in this regard on May 8, 1979, the date of the hearing regarding the employer's amended application. However, the employer complained that this status quo was again upset on May 4, 1979 and that it was in danger of remaining upset, depending on certain of the respondents' activities. On May 8, 1979, everyone was waiting from one moment to the next for the conciliation commissioner to file his report.

It is thus clear that in spite of the agreement concluded, which allowed the Board to help accelerate the process without intervening, the respondents or some of them again lost their patience on May 4, 1979 and a restive atmosphere prevailed subsequently from this date until May 8, 1979 inclusive....

In short, the respondent employees and their union began before the time stipulated in the Code to partially exercise the ultimate form of pressure in collective bargaining. This is prohibited by the legislator.

The respondent union sought through its main spokesman to transform these transgressions into virtues when it endeavoured to justify them by saying that it had attempted in this way to channel the discontent, prove to the employer that the 'troops' were following it and thus avoid the worst, presumably, a complete unlawful strike.

We can neither close our eyes to these violations nor excuse them in the current circumstances because over and above the plain fact of the violations per se, we must take into account the fact that by imposing time periods and interposing third parties, the legislator was seeking to achieve a well-defined goal, namely, to increase the opportunities for the parties to settle their differences without resorting to the ultimate sanction. But, he wanted still more. He also wanted the two parties to be on an equal footing at all times with respect to the means of exerting pressure that each of them had at its disposal....

Some people try to justify these transgressions by claiming that the insertion of the stages calling for the intervention of third parties constitutes poor labour legislation. It is not for us to form an opinion on this matter. However, it must be understood that if people are not happy with the legislation, the solution is to get it amended. In the meantime, parties must act honestly and legally.

*****

The board issued an order requiring that the workers "perform the duties of their employment and ... refrain from any concerted illegal activity," that the union refrain from authorizing or declaring such activity, and that the union distribute the order to its members. After that order was made, employees still refused to do overtime work. The employer sought the board's consent to prosecute the strikers and the union. The board authorized prosecution, but only against the union. The board also directed that any prosecution must be brought before the collective agreement was signed, to avoid allowing the prospect of a prosecution "to become a sword of Damocles during the term of the next collective agreement." (See Re National Harbours Board, [1979] 3 CLRBR 86.)

8:500 THE ROLE OF THE COURTS

8:510 Criminal Jurisdiction

Courts continue to play a role in some labour disputes through the general criminal law. Today that role consists almost exclusively of regulating the conduct of picketing that accompanies strikes and lockouts, rather than regulating the strikes and lockouts themselves. We will examine the courts' role in governing picketing more closely in Section 8:700. Basic *Criminal Code* prohibitions against assault, mischief, and other forms of trespass to persons and property, which we will not examine here, may be violated by conduct engaged in during a labour dispute. See Jonathan Eaton, "Is Picketing a Crime?" (1992) 47 *Relations Industrielles* 100.

There is also a less familiar criminal offence, called "watching and besetting," which is particularly relevant to industrial conflict. Section 423 of the *Criminal Code* states:

> (1) Every one who, wrongfully and without lawful authority, for the purpose of compelling another person to abstain from doing anything that he has a lawful right to do, or to do anything that he has a lawful right to abstain from doing, ... (f) besets or watches the dwelling-house or place where that person resides, works, carries on business or happens to be, ... is guilty of an offence punishable on summary conviction.
>
> (2) A person who attends at or near or approaches a dwelling-house or place, for the purpose only of obtaining or communicating information, does not watch or beset within the meaning of this section.

Most labour picketing at places of work is saved by section 423(2). However, this section has been applied to picketing that targets the homes of company officials and employees. See *Industrial Hardwood Products v IWAWC, Local 2963* (2000), 62 CLRBR (2d) 98 (ON SCJ)

Except in cases of violence, criminal provisions are no longer frequently used in labour picketing situations. Since an illegal strike or lockout constitutes a breach of statute, it is possible for the matter to be tried before the courts. However, every Canadian jurisdiction requires that consent to prosecute be obtained from the labour board or the labour ministry. As noted by Eaton at 102–10 of the paper cited above, such consent is rarely granted.

Penal prosecutions under labour relations legislation provide another potential avenue for court involvement in strikes. This avenue has remained significant in Quebec, where any interested party can bring a prosecution for contravention of the *Labour Code*, including the ban on strikes. These prosecutions are heard by the Labour Court (a division of the Court of Quebec), with an appeal to the Superior Court by way of trial de novo. Only penal sanctions, principally fines, are available as remedies. In British Columbia's Labour Relations Code, a declaration by the Labour Board that a strike or picketing action is unlawful gives rise to a right of action in court for damages suffered as a result of the strike or picketing activities (*British Columbia Labour Relations Code*, s 137(4)). In all other jurisdictions, access to penal prosecutions has been reduced or eliminated. Section 109 of the Ontario *Labour Relations Act 1995* is typical. Before a prosecution can be launched, consent must be obtained from the labour relations board (or in some jurisdictions, the Minister). This consent is seldom sought, and rarely granted save in egregious cases. Even when consent is obtained, prosecution is almost never proceeded with. Even a successful prosecution, coming to trial long after the events at issue and leading to fines payable to the Crown and not the victim, is very rarely thought to be worth the trouble.

8:520 Civil Jurisdiction

In practice, the courts' civil jurisdiction has been much more important in regulating industrial action than their criminal jurisdiction. Civil actions can bring immediate relief through injunctions forcing illegal strikers back to work, restricting picketing, or limiting the use of other economic sanctions, except in jurisdictions where (as will be discussed later) injunctions have been displaced to some degree by labour relations board remedies. Damages may also be available in certain circumstances. More will be said later in this chapter about injunctions and damages as remedies.

The interlocutory injunction is the remedy that was developed by the courts to make speedy relief available, not only in cases of industrial action but in many other contexts as well. This type of injunction was designed to preserve the status quo pending a full trial, in circumstances where the applicant was in danger of suffering irreparable harm that could not be adequately compensated for by money damages awarded after the event. In order to obtain an injunction, the plaintiff must first file a lawsuit in the court, then file a motion seeking an interlocutory injunction. In practice, the underlying lawsuit is rarely litigated in industrial action cases, because the substance of the employer-employee dispute is usually resolved long before a trial is scheduled. The main effect of an injunction is to reduce the adverse impact of industrial conflict on the employer and on third parties. The requirement that a lawsuit be brought means that a party seeking a labour injunction must identify and plead a legitimate cause of action and must also identify a proper defendant. Each of these requirements can pose difficulties in the context of an industrial conflict. We will now consider them both.

8:521 Pleading a Cause of Action: Tort Illegalities

Civil suits with respect to industrial action have sometimes been based on breach of contract, especially where no collective bargaining relationship exists, but in practice such suits are usually based on tort. Nominate torts such as assault, nuisance, trespass, and defamation, which protect basic interests in physical security of the person and property and in reputation, can ground such suits and sometimes do. More important in the area of industrial action, however, are a group of newer and more complex torts commonly known as the "economic torts." They were designed to provide redress against losses resulting from hostile use of the collective strength of economic adversaries, especially collective employee strength exerted through strikes and boycotts. The most well-established and most frequently used of these torts are conspiracy and inducing breach of contract.

The development of the economic torts by the English courts is a fascinating story, which we do not have the space to recount. An excellent account is given by KW Wedderburn, "Strike Law and the Labour Injunction: The British Experience, 1850–1966" in AWR Carrothers, ed, *Report of a Study on the Labour Injunction in Ontario*, vol 2 (Toronto: Ontario Department of Labour, 1966) at 603. Wedderburn describes how the English courts invented new economic torts, or relaxed the requirements of existing ones, in order to deal with outbursts of trade union militancy.

The doctrinal requirements of the economic torts will be summarized in the following paragraphs, in roughly the form in which they were developed by English courts up to about 1975, prior to major statutory changes in English labour law which are not relevant to Canada. As should become apparent by the end of this chapter, Canadian courts have not applied the requirements of the English court decisions rigorously or consistently, but have often bent or disregarded them in order to facilitate the granting of remedies against industrial action, especially in cases of secondary picketing.

The Tort of Conspiracy to Injure by Lawful Means
This requires:

1) a combination of two or more persons;
2) an intention to cause economic injury to the plaintiff and the causing of such injury; and
3) a predominant purpose or motive that the courts do not recognize as being a legitimate interest.

The courts have recognized the traditional collective bargaining activities of unions, including the demand for a closed shop, as legitimate interests. See *Crofter Hand Woven Harris Tweed Co v Veitch*, [1942] AC 435 (HL). In Ontario, section 3(1) of the *Rights of Labour Act*, RSO 1990, c R33, provides as follows:

> An act done by two or more members of a trade union, if done in contemplation or furtherance of a trade dispute, is not actionable unless the act would be actionable if done without agreement or combination.

This would appear to eliminate conspiracy to injure as a cause of action in labour cases, subject, however, to the fact that the courts have interpreted secondary picketing as going beyond the scope of a "trade dispute." This matter will be examined further in the discussion on secondary picketing in Section 8:420.

The Tort of Conspiracy to Injure by Unlawful Means
This requires:

1) a combination of two or more persons;
2) an intention to cause economic injury to the plaintiff; and
3) the use of unlawful means to cause the injury.

In *Rookes v Barnard*, [1964] AC 1129 (HL), the House of Lords held that any illegality (in that case, a breach of the defendants' contracts of employment) would suffice as unlawful means.

The Tort of Directly Inducing Breach of Contract
This requires:

1) an intention by the defendant to cause economic injury to the plaintiff;
2) knowledge by the defendant that there is a contract between the plaintiff and a third party;
3) the use of lawful means by the defendant to persuade the third party to breach the contract;
4) a breach of the contract; and

5) economic injury to the plaintiff as a reasonable consequence of the breach.

The requirements of knowledge and persuasion have been whittled away significantly in recent decades. The requisite knowledge will be found if the defendant ought reasonably to believe that a contractual relationship exists, even if she may not know of its terms, or if she acts "recklessly," without caring whether a contract exists. As for the element of persuasion, it is enough that the defendant conveys information to a third party whom the defendant would like to see act in a certain way (for example, to honour a picket line) and the third party does in fact act in that way. There is a defence of "justification" to this tort, but the pursuit of union objectives has traditionally not been considered to be justification. See Lord Pearce's judgment in *Stratford v Lindley*, [1965] AC269 (HL), and compare it with *Thomson v Deakin*, [1952] Ch 646 (CA).

The Tort of Indirectly Procuring Breach of Contract by Unlawful Means
This requires:

1) an intention by the defendant to cause economic injury to the plaintiff;
2) knowledge by the defendant that there is a contract between the plaintiff and a third party;
3) a threat by the defendant to use unlawful means against the third party unless the latter breaches his or her contract with the plaintiff, or the actual use of unlawful means for that purpose by the defendant;
4) a breach of the contract between the plaintiff and the third party; and
5) economic injury to the plaintiff as a necessary consequence of the breach.

The key to this tort is unlawful means. Under *Rookes v Barnard*, cited above, any technically illegal conduct can suffice for the purposes of the tort, whether that conduct be a crime, another tort, or a breach of contract. The defence of justification has traditionally not been available where unlawful means are present, but Lord Denning intimated otherwise in *Morgan v Fry*, [1968] 2 QB 710 (CA).

Direct Interference with Contractual Relations Falling Short of Breach
This tort was "discovered" by Lord Denning in *Torquay Hotel Co v Cousins*, [1969] 2 Ch 106 (CA). It requires the following:

1) an intention by the defendant to injure the plaintiff economically;
2) an action by the defendant that has the effect of hindering or preventing performance of a contract between the plaintiff and a third party; and
3) that the defendant's action was a direct cause of that result.

In *Acrow (Automation) Ltd v Rex Chainbelt*, [1971] 3 All ER 1175 (CA), Lord Denning added the qualification that the action causing the interference must be unlawful. Nonetheless, Canadian courts appear to be applying the tort according to Lord Denning's original, less rigorous formulation.

The Tort of Intimidation
This requires:

1) an intention by the defendant to injure the plaintiff economically;

2) a threat by the defendant to use unlawful means against a third party unless the latter takes action that will injure the plaintiff economically; and
3) action by the third party against the plaintiff which is lawful in itself but which causes the plaintiff economic injury.

The key element is again unlawful means. *Rookes v Barnard*, above, held that if the threatened act is illegal in any way, be it a crime, a tort, or a breach of contract, that is sufficient to constitute unlawful means.

The Tort of Intentional Injury by Use of Unlawful Means
This residual tort requires:

1) an intention by the defendant to injure the plaintiff economically; and
2) use by the defendant of unlawful means, in the *Rookes v Barnard* sense, to cause the injury.

No combination is needed.

* * * * *

The potency of these torts in the context of strikes and picketing becomes apparent if we imagine a fairly typical scenario of a union picketing a large construction site at which several other unionized trades are working. What sorts of tort illegalities might be present in this scenario?

Some provinces have enacted legislative provisions restricting or abolishing certain of the economic torts, particularly those that do not require illegal means. See, for example, the British Columbia *Labour Relations Code*, sections 66 and 69, and the Ontario *Rights of Labour Act*, section 3(1). Economic torts are also less important when industrial action constitutes a breach of a labour relations statute. This is because the courts have taken the position that the violation of a labour relations statute is enough to ground liability in tort, either because such a violation constitutes a tort in itself or because noncompliance with the statute constitutes the element of illegality necessary to make out the tort in question. A significant step in this direction was taken by the Supreme Court of Canada in *Gagnon v Foundation Maritime Ltd* (1961), 28 DLR (2d) 174 (SCC), where the violation of a statutory strike ban was held to constitute unlawful means for the purpose of the tort of conspiracy to injure by unlawful means. In *Maritime Employers' Association*, mentioned above in Section 8:413, the basis of liability again seems to have been violation of the labour relations statute and the applicable collective agreements, with no other cause of action being mentioned. See also *International Brotherhood of Electrical Workers v Winnipeg Builders Exchange*, [1967] SCR 628.

In other areas of law, it is not normally assumed that a violation of a statute which is silent on the question of civil suit automatically gives rise to a cause of action. Indeed, the contrary is true; if a statute prohibits certain conduct and provides its own form of recourse for those affected by such conduct, aggrieved parties are generally limited to pursuing the remedies provided by the statute, and cannot sue civilly. *Seneca College of Applied Arts and Technology v Bhadauria*, [1981] 2 SCR 181. In the context of industrial conflict, however, the courts have departed from that approach and have been willing to base civil actions on breach of the labour relations statute alone for the purposes of issuing a labour injunction.

CHAPTER 8: INDUSTRIAL CONFLICT

The economic torts remain especially important when the collective employee action in question does not constitute a breach of labour relations legislation or of any other statute (for example, where there is a legal strike supported by peaceful picketing). As we will see in Section 8:723, the Supreme Court of Canada decision in *Retail, Wholesale and Department Store Union, Local 558 v Pepsi-Cola Canada Beverages (West) Ltd*, 2002 SCC 8, affirmed a role for tort law (including the economic torts) in the regulation of industrial conflict and picketing, while at the same time making it more difficult to establish the requirements for at least some of those torts.

8:522 The Legal Capacity of Trade Unions to Sue and Be Sued

The foregoing brief outline of the civil jurisdiction of courts over industrial action raises the threshold issue of whether a trade union has the legal capacity to sue or be sued in a civil action. This question is significant in several areas of labour law other than industrial conflict, such as the enforcement of collective agreements and the law of internal union affairs — in short, wherever a court action is contemplated by or against a union. The legal status of unions to sue and be sued in the common law is dealt with in Chapter 11 in this book, but since this is the first point where the question arises in this book, we will briefly introduce the issues here.

At common law, a trade union was historically considered to be a voluntary unincorporated association, and therefore not a legal entity. It was deemed to be held together merely by a web of implied bipartite contracts between each member and every other member, and these contracts were deemed to incorporate the terms set out in the union's constitution. To avoid making unions and other unincorporated associations legally liable for the actions of members over whom they might have little or no control, the common law traditionally took the position that such associations could not be sued (or sue) in their own names unless a statute said they could. In *International Brotherhood of Teamsters v Therien*, [1960] SCR 265, the Supreme Court of Canada held that the traditional common law position had been implicitly overridden by the powers and responsibilities given to unions under modern Canadian labour relations legislation. Justice Locke wrote:

> In the absence of anything to show a contrary intention — and there is nothing here — the Legislature must be taken to have intended that the creature of the statute [i.e., the union] shall have the same duties and that its funds shall be subject to the same liabilities as the general law would impose on a private individual doing the same thing. . . . In my opinion, the appellant is a legal entity which may be made liable in name for damages either for breach of a provision of the *Labour Relations Act* or under the common law.

In *Therien*, Locke J held that the union had committed the tort of intentionally causing economic injury by unlawful means — that is, by breaching the labour legislation which required that disputes over the application of a collective agreement were to be settled by arbitration and not by industrial action or the threat of it.

More recently, in *Berry v Pulley*, 2002 SCC 40, which is discussed more fully in Chapter 11, Section 11:300, the Supreme Court ruled that union members have a contract with the union itself, in the form of the union's constitution, and that the contract can be enforced by legal action. The result of cases such as *Therien* and *Berry v Pulley* is that unions today do generally have legal status to sue and be sued in Canada at common law. However, as *Therien* indicated, this status flows from rights and obligations granted to or imposed upon unions by labour legislation, and it can be limited by legislation. Canadian legislatures have taken various approaches to the question of the legal capacity of unions for litigation purposes. At one end of the spectrum, some have made no mention of the matter in any statute, with the result that the holding in *Therien* governs. In the middle are those with provisions similar to section 23(1) of the Alberta *Labour Relations Code*, which provides that unions can sue or be sued "for the purposes of this Act." Proceedings arising from industrial action have been held to fall within those purposes.

Alone at the far end of the spectrum is Ontario, which since 1944 has had the following provisions in a unique statute called the *Rights of Labour Act*:

> Section 3(2) A trade union shall not be made a party to any action in any court unless it may be so made a party irrespective of this Act or of the *Labour Relations Act*.
>
> Section 3(3) A collective bargaining agreement shall not be the subject of any action in any court unless it may be the subject of such action irrespective of this Act or of the *Labour Relations Act*.

Section 3(2) has often been held to render the holding in *Therien* inapplicable in Ontario, and to preclude suits by or against unions in their own names. However, even these explicit provisions may no longer have the force they once had. In *Professional Institute of the Public Service of Canada v Canada (Attorney General)* (2002), 222 DLR (4th) 438 (Ont CA), Goudge J (for the court) held that the *Rights of Labour Act*, being a provincial statute, did not preclude a suit in the Ontario courts by a union operating in the federal jurisdiction. In an *obiter dictum*, Goudge J went further and expressed the view that it was time to do away totally with the restriction in section 3(2) on the capacity of unions to sue and be sued.

Where a statute prohibits a union from suing or being sued, it may nevertheless be possible to bring a "representative action" against named officers of the union, on the basis that they "represent" the interest of the entire membership in the particular matter. Courts have, however, often held "that it is not proper or convenient to allow a plaintiff to obtain what would in effect be a personal judgment against every member of an unincorporated body for the tortious act of one or some of its officers or members": *Body v Murdoch*, [1954] OWN 658 (HCJ). To avoid putting the personal assets of individual members in jeopardy, the courts have usually restricted representative actions to situations where the union has a trust fund, the terms of which would allow it to be used to satisfy a judgment—and very few unions have such funds.

8:523 Civil Remedies: Damages and Injunctions

As we have seen in Section 8:400, labour relations boards are clearly the principal forum for enforcing the limitations on strikes and lockouts set out in labour relations legislation. We have also seen, however, that courts have retained for themselves some role in assessing the statutory legality of strikes in civil actions for injunctions or damages, and the existence of an illegal strike or some other breach of statute may be held to provide the element of illegality required for a cause of action in tort. And as will be discussed later in Section 8:700, a rather confusing interplay between the roles of courts and boards still characterizes the regulation of picketing, especially peaceful picketing that occurs during a legal strike or lockout.

Only in British Columbia has an explicit legislative attempt been made to delineate the roles of the labour board and the courts in regulating industrial conflict, and to restrict the role of the courts. Other jurisdictions, including Ontario, have in recent decades amended their labour relations statutes to expand the board's remedial powers in cases involving industrial conflict, but they have not written any express limitations on the authority of the courts into those statutes (although some limitations on court injunctions are now found in civil justice statutes such as the Ontario *Courts of Justice Act*, which is referred to in several of the following sections of this chapter). As a result, courts continue to issue remedies in cases of illegal industrial action, although sometimes they will decline to act when a comparable remedy is available from a specialized tribunal. See, for example, *Attorney General for Ontario v OTF*, below, and *McKinlay Transport v Goodman* (1978), 78 CLLC para 14,161 (FC), referred to in the *National Harbours Board* judgment set out above in Section 8:430 and *Prince Rupert Grain v Grain Workers Union, Local 333* (2002), 8 BCLR (4th) 91 (BCCA).

a. Damages

Outside the labour context, the conventional remedy for a civil wrong is damages. Damages have on occasion been awarded in cases arising out of labour disputes. In *United Steelworkers of America v Gaspé Copper Mines Ltd*, [1970] SCR 362, a case decided under Quebec law where no equivalent of section 3(2) of Ontario's *Rights of Labour Act* exists, damages of $1.75 million (and thirteen years' interest) were assessed against a union for admittedly criminal and tortious conduct committed during an illegal strike. In 2003, the British Columbia Teachers' Federation was fined $500,000 for civil contempt when its members failed to comply with a court order to cease and desist from engaging in an illegal strike to protest legislative changes on the encouragement of union officials: *British Columbia Public School Employers Association v British Columbia Teachers' Federation*, 2005 BCSC 1490.

The deliberate commission of a tort—whether it is a nominate tort such as assault or trespass, or an economic tort such as conspiracy—gives rise not only to a claim for compensatory damages to make the injured plaintiff whole, but also possibly to punitive damages. Punitive damages are intended to discourage the defendant and others from repeating the tort, and may be assessed in whatever amount the court believes is necessary to accomplish that result. The potential of this kind of award in a labour dispute is easily imagined.

Nevertheless, employers have seldom pursued such claims right through to judgment, and have very seldom collected on them in full. More commonly, the existence of the suit, or the damage award if there is one, is used by the employer as a bargaining counter to obtain a settlement, either for lesser damages or for favourable collective agreement terms. Damages can be awarded by a civil court only after pleadings, discovery, and trial—a time-consuming process that can take years, during which time the union may continue to engage in the impugned conduct. Actions in damages became even rarer after the decision of the Supreme Court of Canada in *St Anne Nackawic*, set out later in this section, which ruled that grievance arbitrators have exclusive jurisdiction to award damages for a strike that violates a collective agreement.

b. Injunctions

In court proceedings arising from labour disputes, injunctions have always played a much more significant role than damages, because of the speed and relative ease with which an injunction can often be obtained and because it immediately prohibits the industrial action in question rather than merely granting a monetary remedy after the fact. Across Canada, injunctions used to be the principal means of enforcing legal limitations on industrial action. More recently, as noted above, labour legislation in several provinces has sought to replace injunctions with cease-and-desist orders issued by labour relations boards. But as we will see, in most of those jurisdictions injunctions nonetheless retain a crucial role in the regulation of picketing, especially but not solely where the picketing is conducted in an illegal manner.

The labour injunction was, and to some extent still is, a focal point for union hostility. It generated strong political controversy and academic criticism in Canada, as well as in the United States, where its use was largely suppressed by the *Norris-LaGuardia Act* of 1932. See AWR Carrothers, *The Labour Injunction in British Columbia* (Toronto: CCH Canadian, 1956), and AWR Carrothers, ed, *Report of a Study on the Labour Injunction in Ontario*, vol 1 (Toronto: Ontario Department of Labour, 1966). A number of serious concerns have been expressed over the years about the use of interlocutory injunctions in cases of industrial conflict. One concern focused on undue haste in the proceedings. In urgent cases, the courts had the power to grant an injunction *ex parte*, without notice to the defendants, and often did so on the mere allegation by the plaintiff that there was no time to give such notice. Even when normal notice rules were observed, the required period of notice (two days in Ontario) was often too short to allow the defendants to gather evidence in reply.

A related concern involved laxness with respect to proof. Normally, evidence has been given in interlocutory proceedings by means of affidavits, with the courts seldom exercising their power to hear oral evidence. Although the defendants (usually the union or the picketing employees) technically had the right to cross-examine whoever made the affidavits in question, in fact the time required to prepare for and do such cross-examination could only be purchased by an agreement on the defendants' part that the injunction should issue in the meantime. Given this virtual immunity both from cross-examination and from reply evidence, affidavits were often drafted in vague and inexact terms.

A third concern was that interlocutory orders are not normally appealable except with the consent of the court, which has rarely been given in labour relations matters. Accordingly, the great bulk of labour injunction decisions were by courts of first instance, and appeal courts had little opportunity to rationalize conflicting lines of trial decisions or even to correct errors. A fourth concern related to the broad scope of labour injunctions, which were typically directed against the named defendants, "their servants or agents, and anyone having knowledge of this order." This had the effect of binding persons who might have interests quite different from those of the named defendants, but who in any event had no opportunity to argue that they ought not to be bound by the order.

1. COMMON LAW TEST FOR AN INTERLOCUTORY INJUNCTION: *RJR-MACDONALD*

In response to these sorts of concerns, restrictions on the issuing of injunctions have been developed in recent decades by both courts and legislatures. The most important court-made restriction on the use of interlocutory injunctions is the three-stage test articulated by the Supreme Court of Canada in *RJR-MacDonald Inc v Canada (AG)*, [1994] 1 SCR 311—a test which applies not only in labour cases but governs the use of such injunctions in civil litigation in general. The *RJR-MacDonald* test was articulated in the following terms by Sopinka and Cory JJ, at 334:

> First, a preliminary assessment must be made of the merits of the case to ensure that there is a serious question to be tried. Secondly, it must be determined whether the applicant would suffer irreparable harm if the application were refused. Finally, an assessment must be made as to which of the parties would suffer greater harm from the granting or refusal of the remedy pending a decision on the merits.

If union members are engaged in an unlawful (untimely) strike or in activity that poses an immediate safety risk, courts will usually find that the requirements of *RJR-MacDonald* have been satisfied. See for example *Falconbridge Ltd v Sudbury Mine, Mill, & Smelter Workers Union, Local 598*, [2000] OJ No 4168 (SCJ). However, those requirements become more difficult to meet when the strike itself is lawful and the picketing in question is carried on in support of that strike. An injunction in a labour dispute almost always has the practical effect of determining the outcome of the dispute, since the matter rarely proceeds to a hearing on the merits. As a result, courts have taken the position that the party seeking a labour injunction must establish a *prima facie* case, or a "strong" *prima facie* case, rather than merely having to show that there is a "serious question to be tried." The application of *RJR-MacDonald* in the context of picketing activity is considered in Section 8:721 below.

2. STATUTORY REQUIREMENTS FOR OBTAINING A LABOUR INJUNCTION

Applicants for injunctive relief might also need to satisfy specific statutory requirements to obtain a labour injunction. For example, section 102 of the Ontario *Courts of Justice Act* provides that no injunction may be granted on an *ex parte* basis (that is, with no notice to the respondents). Where an injunction is given on an *inter partes* basis, that statutory provision sets out a number of safeguards: affidavit evidence is limited to facts "within the knowledge of the deponent," who may be required by the other side to appear for cross-examination; at least two days' notice of motion must be given to the union and any other persons affected by the injunction; and the maximum duration of the injunction is four days. An exception is made with respect to service of notice where the delay would result in "irreparable damage or injury, a breach of the peace or an interruption in an essential public service," and the judge believes that it is "otherwise ... proper" to dispense with notice. In that event, reasonable steps must be taken to put the other side on notice of the application, and material facts must be established by oral evidence. In addition, no injunction of any kind can be given unless the court is satisfied that "reasonable efforts to obtain police assistance, protection and action to prevent or remove any alleged danger of damage to property, injury to persons, obstruction of or interference with lawful entry or exit from the premises in question or breach of the peace have been unsuccessful." (See Section 8:721.)

However, the above protections apply only to actions "*in connection with a labour dispute*," which is defined as "a dispute or difference concerning terms ... of employment ... regardless of whether the disputants stand in the proximate relation of employer and employee" (s 102(1)). These provisions have given rise to considerable litigation over whether certain actions are taken "in connection with a labour dispute." This is a point of particular significance in cases of so-called secondary action (see Section 8:722).

British Columbia, alone among the Canadian provinces, decided as long ago as 1973 to adopt a more far-reaching solution than Ontario to the many problems posed by the labour injunction. The British Columbia *Labour Relations Code*, in sections 136 and 137, purports to abolish the courts' authority to grant injunctions in labour matters, providing instead for regulation by the labour board. The courts, however, may still grant an injunction when the conduct complained of "causes immediate danger of serious injury to an individual or causes actual obstruction or physical damage to property," and they have in fact claimed a jurisdiction broader than that expressly reserved to them by ruling that courts retain jurisdiction to issue injunctions to restrain breaches of the "general law," including torts and crimes. See *Better Value Furniture v Vancouver Distribution Centre Ltd* (1981), 122 DLR (3d) 12 (BCCA); *Insurance Corporation of British Columbia v Canadian Office and Professional Employees Union, Local 378*, 2012 BCSC 1244 (CanLII).

3. THE COURTS' JURISDICTION TO ISSUE LABOUR INJUNCTIONS

The *St Anne Nackawic* case, excerpted below, is the leading decision of the Supreme Court of Canada on two aspects of the law on the remedies available for illegal industrial action. One aspect deals with the very narrow scope that remains for civil actions for damages in respect of industrial action which contravenes a collective agreement. This matter will be looked at in Chapter 9 (Section 9:410), with respect to the enforcement of collective agreements. The other aspect, more central to the concerns of the present chapter, relates to the continued availability of court injunctions against unlawful industrial action, even when a collective agreement is in force and the arbitral forum is therefore available to the injured party. *St Anne Nackawic* thus bears witness to the entrenched status of the injunction in Canadian industrial dispute law, notwithstanding the thrust of modern labour relations legislation.

St Anne Nackawic Pulp & Paper Co Ltd v Canadian Paper Workers Union, Local 219, [1986] 1 SCR 704 at 708–14, 717–27, and 731

> [The respondent union represented two bargaining units—mill workers and office workers—at the appellant company's pulp and paper mill in New Brunswick. The office workers went out on a legal strike and picketed the mill. The mill workers, who could not legally strike because their collective agreement was in force, stayed out in sympathy with the office workers. The company began a court action three days after the strike began, and obtained an interlocutory injunction two days later. The mill workers did not return to work until after a finding of contempt of court was made against the union and three of its officers. Two weeks later the mill workers went out again. Despite another contempt order, they did not return to work until the office workers' strike was settled a few days later. The company then claimed damages against the union for the losses caused by the mill workers' strike.
>
> The New Brunswick court held that it had the authority to award damages against the union because of the illegal strike, and it fined the union for the two instances of contempt. On appeal, the union challenged the court's jurisdiction to award damages to enforce the collective agreement. The union did not challenge the court's jurisdiction to issue the interlocutory injunction, nor did it challenge the findings of contempt. However,

the Supreme Court of Canada considered whether the lower court could grant an injunction to enforce the no-strike clause of a collective agreement, as well as whether it could award damages for that purpose.]

ESTEY J.: This case raises for the first time in this Court the question whether a court of otherwise competent jurisdiction is authorized to receive a claim by an employer for damages against a trade union, the bargaining agent for its employees, by reason of a strike which was allegedly, and on the record before this Court, apparently, illegal under the applicable labour relations statute, and which was at the same time a breach of a collective agreement to which the employer and the trade union are parties....

There are numerous instances where the courts have issued injunctions in such circumstances, and the jurisdiction to do so was settled in *International Brotherhood of Electrical Engineers, Local Union 2085 v. Winnipeg Builders' Exchange*.... The courts have also awarded damages in similar circumstances ... but in those cases the issue of the jurisdiction of the court to do so was not challenged by the parties....

In its pleadings, the appellant based its claim on the following ground:

> The said unlawful strike referred to in paragraph 6, was in breach of the Collective Agreement between the Plaintiff and the Defendant and in violation of the *Industrial Relations Act*.

The collective agreement referred to was the one between the mill unit and the appellant. It ... provided that, 'There shall be no strike, lockout, stoppage, slow-down or restriction of output during the life of this Agreement.' The relevant sections of the *Industrial Relations Act*, R.S.N.B. 1973, c. 1-4, as amended, are as follows:

> 53(1) Every collective agreement shall provide that there shall be no strikes or lock-outs so long as the agreement continues to operate.
>
> 91(1) Where a collective agreement is in operation, no employee bound by the agreement shall strike....

The Act further provides, however, and this is what led to the trial judge's reservation of the question of the court's jurisdiction as a preliminary matter, that:

> 55(1) Every collective agreement shall provide for the final and binding settlement by arbitration or otherwise, without stoppage of work, of all differences between the parties to, or persons bound by, the agreement or on whose behalf it was entered into, concerning its interpretation, application, administration or an alleged violation of the agreement, including any question as to whether a matter is arbitrable.

Where a collective agreement does not so provide, a very comprehensive arbitration clause is, by s. 5(2), deemed to be a provision of the agreement. The collective agreement between the appellant and respondent in this case did provide for arbitration. Clause 8 provided a procedure to be followed in the 'Adjustment of Complaints' which culminated in the appointment of a three member arbitration board whose decision would be 'final and binding upon both parties to the Agreement.' ...

The preliminary question raised by the trial judge prior to trial, put simply, is whether, given the comprehensive provision for the submission to arbitration of all differences between the parties to a collective agreement, the court has any jurisdiction to hear a claim arising out of that agreement....

An early consideration of the relative jurisdictions of court and arbitration board to entertain claims for breach of a collective agreement is found in *McGavin Toastmaster Ltd. v. Ainscough* ..., where the employees claimed severance pay under their collective agreement after their employer had closed the plant during an illegal strike. Laskin C.J., writing for the majority, raised the issue of the Court's jurisdiction to hear a claim based on interpretation of a collective agreement which provided for grievance procedures and binding arbitration of such issues. He wrote ...:

> There was no contention in defence that the appropriate proceedings should have been by way of arbitration under the collective agreement, and it does not appear that any such position was taken either before the trial judge or in the British Columbia Court of Appeal. This Court refrained therefore in this case from taking any position on this question and is content to deal with the legal issue or issues as having been properly submitted to the Courts for adjudication.

The same approach was taken in the *Winnipeg Teachers' Association* case, ... per Martland J.... The majority of the Court in that case acknowledged as well founded an employer's claim for damages arising out of the employees' 'work to rule' under the collective agreement. Laskin C.J., however, writing in dissent, took the position that if the parties had raised the issue, he would have allowed the appeal solely on the basis that ...:

> the machinery for determining contract disputes as prescribed by the collective agreement is not only better suited than resort to the Court, but ought to have been resorted to here for resolving what emerged as a difference about the nature or scope of the contractual obligation of the appellant's members and of the appellant itself.

There are a significant number of decisions doubting the jurisdiction of the courts to hear claims based on the interpretation or application of collective agreements containing provision for binding arbitration. The earlier cases seemed to establish two exceptions to this principle. First, the courts have been held in a number of cases to have jurisdiction in a case where, although the claim depends entirely upon a right created by the terms of a collective agreement, the court is not required, in enforcing the right, to interpret the agreement. An example is *Hamilton Street Railway Co. v. Northcott*, ... in which a prior arbitration had established the right of a group of employees to unpaid wages, but had not settled the amounts owing to each member of the group. The latter issue was held to be within the Court's jurisdiction.

The second exception consists of cases where the claim can be characterized as arising solely under the common law, and not under the collective agreement. An example is *Woods v. Miramichi Hospital* ... a case involving a claim by an employee, a member of a bargaining unit, for damages for wrongful dismissal....

In cases where the claim concerned an entitlement originating in the collective agreement, and the proper interpretation of the agreement was disputed, the courts uniformly have denied that they have jurisdiction ....

If there were nothing more than the collective agreement between bargaining agent and employer, the courts might still have applied the common law to its enforcement at the suit of the bargaining agent or the employer. The collective agreement embodies a holding out, a reliance, a consent and undertaking to perform, mutual consideration passing between the parties, and other elements of contract which would expose the parties to enforcement in the traditional courts. There would be, of course, a basic difficulty as to the status of the absent third party, the employee, and perhaps the absence of an identifiable benefit in the bargaining agent. All this is overcome by the statute, and the question whether worthwhile enforcement could be realized at common law is, therefore, of theoretical interest only. The missing elements are the status of the members of the bargaining unit and the appropriate forum. The legislature created the status of the parties in a process founded upon a solution to labour relations in a wholly new and statutory framework at the centre of which stands a new forum, the contract arbitration tribunal. Furthermore, the structure embodies a new form of triangular contract with but two signatories, a statutory solution to the disability of the common law in the field of third party rights. These are but some of the components in the all-embracing legislative program for the establishment and furtherance of labour relations in the interest of the community at large as well as in the interests of the parties to those labour relations....

The collective agreement establishes the broad parameters of the relationship between the employer and his employees. This relationship is properly regulated through arbitration and it would, in general, subvert both the relationship and the statutory scheme under which it arises to hold that matters addressed and governed by the collective agreement may nevertheless be the subject of actions in the courts at common law. These considerations necessarily lead one to wonder whether the *Miramichi* case, *supra*, and cases like it, would survive an objection to the court's jurisdiction if decided today. The more modern approach is to consider that labour relations legislation provides a code governing all aspects of labour relations, and that it would offend the legislative scheme to permit the parties to a collective agreement, or the employees on whose behalf it was negotiated, to have recourse to the ordinary courts which are in the circumstances a duplicative forum to which the legislature has not assigned these tasks....

The courts have no jurisdiction to consider claims arising out of rights created by a collective agreement. Nor can the courts properly decide questions which might have arisen under the common law of master and servant in the absence of a collective bargaining regime if the collective agreement by which the parties to the action are bound makes provision for the matters in issue, whether or not it explicitly provides a procedure and forum for enforcement. There is, therefore, little practical scope left to the second general exception identified above. As to the first exception, that is, that the court may enforce the terms of a collective agreement where its meaning is not disputed, this Court decided in *Brunet* ... and *Shell Canada Ltd. v. United Oil Workers of Canada* [1980] ... that there is no difference in principle between a dispute over the 'application' of a collective agreement and one relating to its 'violation.' The jurisdiction of the courts ought not, therefore, to depend on whether the parties dispute the meaning or application of the terms of a collective agreement....

What is left is an attitude of judicial deference to the arbitration process.... It is based on the idea that if the courts are available to the parties as an alternative forum, violence is done to a comprehensive statutory scheme designed to govern all aspects of the relationship of the parties in a labour relations setting. Arbitration, when adopted by the parties as was done here in the collective agreement, is an integral part of that scheme, and is clearly the forum preferred by the legislature for resolution of disputes arising under collective agreements. From the foregoing authorities, it might be said, therefore, that the law has so evolved that it is appropriate to hold that the grievance and arbitration procedures provided for by the Act and embodied by legislative prescription in the terms of a collective agreement provide the exclusive recourse open to parties to the collective agreement for its enforcement.

This, however, appears to conflict with the long-settled jurisdiction of the courts to issue injunctions restraining illegal strike activity during the currency of a collective agreement: *International Brotherhood of Electrical Engineers, Local Union 2085 v. Winnipeg Builder's Exchange, supra, International Longshoremen's Association, Locals 273, 1039, 1764 v. Maritime Employers' Association*.... It can be surmised that many, if not all, of the cases in which injunctions have issued, started life as claims for an injunction together with other relief, including damages to compensate an employer for losses suffered during an illegal strike.... The history of labour law in our country since World War II reflects a rather straightforward pattern whereby the parties would take recourse to the superior courts by an action for injunction, declaration and damages in which an interlocutory or interim injunction was sought with a view to driving the other party back to the labour relations process prescribed by statute. Rarely would the action proceed beyond the interlocutory injunction stage.

An injunction is as much an action to enforce the no-strike clause in a collective agreement as is an action for damages. If the former is available, so in principle should be the latter. Thus, if it is confirmed that the courts have no business interpreting, applying or enforcing collective agreements in any way, the jurisdiction to enjoin strikes illegal by virtue of their occurrence during the term of a collective agreement, unquestioned since *Winnipeg Builder's Exchange, supra*, is called into doubt. This would have the unfortunate result of putting an employer whose assent to a collective agreement indicates his willingness to bargain in good faith with the union and to fulfill the expectations of the collective bargaining regime, in a more restricted position than an uncooperative employer who may never have signed an agreement, and who is not therefore subject to binding arbitration. This prejudice may be more apparent than real, however, as in fact it entails only a shift of forum and procedure, but not necessarily a real deprivation of ultimate remedy.

The statutory context may be viewed as ambiguous on this issue. Though setting out a scheme in which arbitration plays a central role, the legislation does not enact any privative clause explicitly ousting the jurisdiction of the courts to deal with breaches of collective agreements which clearly, under the legislation, regulate the legal rights of the parties and are binding and enforceable in the proper forum. This is in contrast to the practice in all provincial and federal labour relations statutes of expressly excluding the courts from any power of review by any procedure of the determinations by the statutory labour relations board. The absence of such legislative action in the case of the boards of arbitration established by contract, even in the provinces where such boards have been held to be statutory and not private, is perhaps revealing of the presence of a legislative intent to continue some role for the traditional courts in the labour relations pattern. What the statute does is to establish a preference for arbitration of a particular sort over other means of dispute settlement, by establishing a procedure to be followed where the parties do not expressly provide for any other method of resolving their differences. Where the parties so choose, however, the New Brunswick Act, in common with most of the other Canadian labour relations statutes, does not actually require the parties to resort to arbitration (the Ontario *Labour Relations Act*, R.S.O. 1980, c. 228 is an exception in this respect ...). It requires a provision in the collective agreement for 'final and binding settlement by arbitration *or otherwise*, without stoppage of work.' The emphasized words indicate that, if they so choose, the parties may validly provide for a variety of other sorts of settlement mechanisms, including recourse to the courts. ... Thus, even where the parties, as here, have chosen arbitration, it may be argued that s. 55(1) of the New Brunswick Act is insufficient to oust the inherent jurisdiction of the superior courts. ...

There is the further consideration that the Act appears to recognize concurrent jurisdiction to deal with aspects of illegal strikes in the statutory board, the courts, and arbitrators acting under the provisions of collective agreements. Section 102(3) provides:

> 102(3) A declaration made under this section does not affect any proceeding in any court or any proceeding under the provision of a collective agreement, where the question of a lawful or unlawful strike ... is in issue.

This may be seen to accord with the reason for enactment of the arbitration provisions. As suggested by Lord Russell in *Young v. Canadian Northern Ry. Co.* ...., the appropriate course of action for workers who had a grievance under a collective agreement at common law was to engage in concerted action, usually a strike, in order to force the employer's compliance. Labour legislation was enacted largely to regulate industrial relations with an eye to preserving industrial peace: per Cartwright J., as he then was, in Winnipeg Builders' Exchange, *supra*, at p. 640. A cornerstone in this legislative edifice was to make strike action or lock-out illegal during the currency of a collective agreement. In exchange for restricting the right to strike and lock-out, the legislation made collective agreements binding and enforceable. ...

This ... may be taken as indicated by the fact that grievances are directed to be settled by arbitration 'without stoppage of work.' It would, accordingly, be illogical to permit a union to plead in defence to court proceedings brought to restrain an illegal strike that the employer should have resorted to arbitration, when the conduct in issue is the very conduct which the provision for arbitration and the statutory prohibition were designed to prevent. ...

The avoidance of the disruptive effect of cessation of production of goods and services except in well defined circumstances is one of the basic design features of labour relations legislation. Another feature of labour legislation is the provision for rapid restoration of normal bargaining relations. Long or repeated abstentions of the parties from participation in the remedial processes of collective bargaining and grievance processing defeats the program. Slow and expensive processes of dispute resolution likewise render the statutory scheme less beneficial and perhaps unavailable to the community. The labour arbitration board came into being because of this reality.

In a limited role, the ready access by the parties to the court system provided by the community for the disposition of differences however arising in the community, can itself be another bulwark against the deterioration of employer-employee understanding. The interlocutory injunction by summary process but of limited life, for example as governed by the *Judicature Act* of Ontario, now the *Courts of Justice Act*, 1984 (Ont.), c. 11, s. 115, finds its origin in this reality. It is, of course, open to the legislature to close this access, as it has done in the case of the privative clauses relating to the labour relations boards themselves....

[I]t is apparent that the cases affirming the courts' injunctive power do not purport to create a power in the courts to enforce the terms of collective agreements. Rather, they enforce the general law as embodied in the statute, which includes both an express prohibition on strikes during the currency of a collective agreement and provision for binding and enforceable arbitration which, in many cases, would resolve the dispute underlying illegal strike activity. An injunction restraining a strike also upholds incidentally the rights of an employer under a collective agreement, and specifically enforces the individual obligations of the employees on whose behalf the collective agreement was negotiated pursuant to the *Industrial Relations Act* of New Brunswick, *supra*. Such incidental effects, as the *Winnipeg Builders' Exchange* case, *supra*, demonstrates, are not sufficient reason to deny an injunction to prevent immediate harm arising out of a clearly illegal act, where no adequate alternative remedy exists....

Therefore, I conclude that the courts below were correct in law in recognizing that the claim for damages must be advanced in the contractual forum of an arbitration board. This is so where legislation requires the parties to establish a mechanism for dispute resolution, and whether the arbitration board so established is 'statutory' or is private in nature. This appeal does not require comment upon the question of the range or remedies the board may apply in disposing of differences arising under the collective agreement, as we are here concerned only with a claim for damages. On the other hand, it should be said for clarity and completeness, because the issue of the availability of a court injunction and other judicial remedies was ever present in the arguments presented by the parties to this Court, that the initial process in injunction undertaken by the court in these proceedings was within the jurisdiction of the court, and that this jurisdiction has not been reduced by the labour relations statute or indeed by the presence of the collective agreement and its provision for arbitration.

The New Brunswick legislation on which *St Anne Nackawic* was based did not empower the labour board to issue cease-and-desist orders in the case of illegal strikes. The only remedy available from the New Brunswick board was a declaration that a strike was illegal. It was unclear whether Estey J's comments regarding injunctions would have been different had the cease-and-desist power existed. However, in subsequent decisions, courts decided that they retain residual jurisdiction to issue injunctions in cases of unlawful strikes unless the labour legislation expressly removes that jurisdiction. In *Weber v Ontario Hydro*, [1995] 2 SCR 929, the Supreme Court of Canada affirmed the "residual jurisdiction" of the courts to issue injunctions in labour matters. In *Attorney General for Ontario v OTF* (1997), 36 OR (3d) 367 (SCJ), the court refused the government's request for an interlocutory injunction to bring an end to a province-wide teachers' strike, in part because the government had made no attempt to use the Ontario Labour Relations Board procedures for that purpose before seeking a court injunction.

8:600 THE ROLE OF ARBITRATORS IN INDUSTRIAL CONFLICT

In this book, grievance arbitration is treated mainly in Chapter 9, which looks at the administration of collective agreements. However, grievance arbitrators play a central role in awarding damages for illegal strikes and in determining the justness of disciplinary measures imposed by employers for employee conduct in connection with both legal and illegal strikes. Therefore, these matters will be treated here.

8:610 Awards of Damages by Arbitrators

Most Canadian collective agreements contain a no-strike clause, which are generally required by legislative decree. Violation of a no-strike clause is a breach of the agreement and may be the subject of a grievance arbitration proceeding at the instance of the employer. As we saw in *St Anne Nackawic*, grievance arbitrators have the authority—indeed, the exclusive authority—to award damages against the union for such a breach. But they will do so only if the union itself, rather than employees acting on their own, is responsible for the breach.

Re Oil, Chemical & Atomic Workers & Polymer Corporation (1958), 10 LAC 31 at 33–35 and 37–39 (Ont Lab Arb)

> [A strike occurred during the lifetime of a collective agreement. The company brought a grievance under the agreement, alleging that the union had violated the no-strike clause (article 8.01) and claiming damages against the union for the losses that it suffered as a result of the strike.]
>
> LASKIN, Chair: Counsel for the company urged, with some vigour, that art. 8.01 involved an automatic liability of the union under each agreement upon mere proof of the occurrence of a strike ... this Board cannot accept the argument of automatic liability. On the other hand, it must equally reject the contention of the respondents herein that liability arises only if there is an official strike, that is one called or sanctioned under the prescriptions of the union constitution and by-laws....
>
> A union may contract (and for arbitration purposes a collective agreement is a contract) to accept liability for the conduct of a member but if it does so its ensuing responsibility does not arise under any principle of vicarious liability but by virtue of a contractual obligation. A union normally has officers and employees who, under varying circumstances, may implicate it in vicarious liability for tort and in so-called personal liability in contract. But members of a union are not, as members only, either employees or servants of a union, or its agents, and their actions are not the actions of the union for which the latter must respond either in tort or in contract. A union member cannot, as such, bind the union in

contract or make it liable vicariously for his tortious conduct merely by representing that he is acting for the union. Apart from principles of estoppel and kindred doctrines, upon which it is unnecessary to dilate here, his acts are no more the acts of his union than the acts of a mere shareholder in a corporation are the acts of the corporation. ...

[A]rt. 8.01 'must mean that the union undertakes that there will be no stoppages by persons in the bargaining unit whom it purports to control, that is the members. Or, that there will be no stoppages by any of the workers in the bargaining unit, whether members or not. Or that it will not through its proper officers sanction or direct or condone or encourage stoppages by any persons in the bargaining unit.' ...

This board agrees that the third alternative ... is the proper one to apply to the interpretation of art. 8.01. ... The board understands well enough how difficult it can be to pinpoint responsibility for the initiation of a work stoppage or, as here, a refusal to report for work, but the difficulty does not warrant accepting mere surmise as a substitute for evidence. In short, the real basis, and the only basis, for the company's grievances must be the alleged failure of the respondents to take prompt and necessary steps to bring the strike to an end. ...

Stewards or committeemen who are put forward by a union as its representatives for departmental or area grievance adjustment must be expected to know that their very status and function underlines the impropriety as well as the illegality of a strike while the collective agreement is in force. Thus it follows that a strike called or instigated by a steward or committeeman in his area is a strike for which the union must accept liability under art. 8.01. Steward action is union action in this respect. It does not follow, however, that given a situation where a strike arises by spontaneous employee action, or otherwise but without union complicity, that the stewards or committeemen implicate the union if they severally fail to take affirmative action to bring the strike to an end. Direction of 'back to work' efforts may be in the hands of officers on a higher level and the stewards would understandably be subordinate to them. If those officers did nothing towards the termination of the strike, union liability would be established by that fact and not by any inaction or passivity of the stewards as such. Two points are, however, important in connection with the position of stewards or committeemen in a situation, such as the one before this board, that calls for affirmative union action to bring a strike to an end. If the stewards or committeemen join the strikers in any demonstration, such as a picket line march, this would be evidence which might show, unless explained away, that the union was encouraging a continuation of the strike. Much would depend on the duration and other circumstances of the participation of the stewards or committeemen in the demonstration. Secondly, the presence of stewards or committeemen among the strikers at any mass demonstration would invite immediate action by union executive officers to procure their withdrawal as a tangible sign that the union is not supporting the unlawful strike.

* * * * *

In *Attorney General for Newfoundland v Newfoundland Association of Public Employees* (1977), 74 DLR (3d) 195 at 209 (SCTD), Goodridge J suggested a long list of measures which, in the circumstances before him, the union hierarchy might have taken to avoid liability when an illegal strike occurred:

1) Where a strike could have been foreseen, meetings of each unit involved should have been convened by the association executive who should have ordered the members not to strike;
2) After the strikes began the association should have convened unit meetings to order the members back to work;
3) Persuasive leaflets should have been placed in the hand of each employee outlining the legal and practical situation;
4) The special nature of their work—the care of those who could not care for themselves—should have been emphasized ...;
5) Association executive and staff members should have visited the picket lines to persuade the strikers to return to work;
6) Unit executive members should have been called on the carpet and told in no uncertain terms to return to work themselves, and to order the others to return;
7) Press, radio and TV coverage to the extent that it was available should have been used to persuade the employees to return;
8) The association should have forthwith suspended the shop stewards;
9) The association should have forthwith suspended the unit executives;
10) The association should have fined, suspended or otherwise disciplined any member who participated in the strikes; and
11) Finally, the association should have clearly indicated to all that in this dispute it was on the side of management and generally acted resolutely to determine the strike.

If damages are awarded against a union because of losses caused by an illegal strike, what is the proper measure of those damages? The normal contractual measure of compensation for breach? Some variant of compensatory damages permitting adjustment downward when the employer has provoked the strike by its own misconduct, or upward when the union's conduct was egregious? A non-compensatory measure calculated to discourage future misbehaviour and encourage good relations between the parties?

In *Limo Jet Gold Express* (2008), 171 LAC (4th) 28 (BC Coll Agree't Arb), a union was ordered to pay the employer more than $150,000 in damages after its officers encouraged and participated in an unlawful strike and attempted to bargain changes to the collective agreement rather than pressing workers to end the strike. That award included compensatory damages for lost revenues and expenses incurred by the employer, as well as $100,000 for aggravated damages. In *MacMillan Bloedel Ltd and Pulp, Paper & Woodworkers of Canada, Local 8* (1986), 2 CLAS 52, damages awarded against a union for participating in an illegal strike were reduced by the arbitrator because the employer's delay in applying for a cease and desist order meant that it had failed to mitigate its damages.

8:620 Employer Disciplinary Action against Strikers

Involvement by an employee in an illegal strike does not in itself rupture the employment relationship. However, it does expose the employee to discipline for cause, and leading an illegal strike will clearly be held by an arbitrator to justify heavier discipline than mere passive participation.

Involvement in a *legal* strike is quite different. The *Graham Cable* decision, excerpted in Section 8:411, makes clear that it is an unfair labour practice for an employer to discipline employees because of their participation in a legal strike. More difficult is the question of employer discipline imposed not for the act of striking but for the employee's conduct during a legal strike.

Rogers Cable TV (British Columbia) Ltd, Vancouver Division et al v International Brotherhood of Electrical Workers, Local 213 (1987), 16 CLRBR (NS) 71 at 77, 84–85, and 90–93

[The company had attempted to maintain operations during a very bitter legal strike. The union had picketed vigorously, blocking access to company premises and using flying picket squads to follow company vehicles and harass employees doing bargaining unit work. The company hired security guards, and the police were often called in to respond to picketing incidents. The company obtained three injunctions against picket line conduct, and a union business agent and twenty-two members were found guilty of contempt of court for disobeying the injunctions. The union then complained to the labour board that the company had committed an unfair labour practice by imposing disciplinary suspensions on eight employees for alleged misconduct on the picket line. Some of the eight were awaiting sentence for contempt, and three faced criminal charges for the acts for which the company disciplined them.]

JAMIESON, Vice-Chair: The specific allegations against the eight union members ranged from yelling, cursing and swearing, puncturing tires on company vehicles, pounding vehicles with pieces of wood, breaking mirrors on company vehicles, opening propane valves on vehicles, cutting cables to disrupt service to customers, to threatening persons with knives....

[Section 184(3)(a)(vi) of the *Canada Labour Code* provided that it was an unfair labour practice for an employer to take any reprisals against an employee for having "participated in a strike that is not prohibited by this Part or exercised any right under this Part...."]

The union ... took the position that an employer has no authority at law to discipline for any act committed during a lawful work stoppage. The logic for this argument is that an employer's right to discipline is a derivative of the employment contract whether it be collective or individual. Once a legal work stoppage is in progress by way of a strike or a lockout, there is no employment contract in effect. The employees no longer hold themselves out to be subject to employer discipline, thus the employer has no powers of discipline left to exert. The union says that picket line activities, legal or illegal, are a matter of public order and the employer's only recourse is to the courts through criminal or civil actions....

In the over-all scheme of the Code, strikes and lockouts are expected to be temporary suspensions in the employment relationship during which collective bargaining differences are ironed out. While these periods of economic sanctions last, employees have no obligation to report to work or to perform services on the employer's behalf. The employer on the other hand need not provide work to the employees, in fact, he has a legal right to call on others to perform the services necessary to keep the business operating....

Once a strike or lockout is over and when the full employer-employee relationship is restored, we can see nothing in the Code to prevent an employer from using its restored disciplinary powers to deal with acts of employees that occurred during the work stoppage, provided of course the discipline is not for reasons prohibited by s. 184(3)(a)(vi). Once employees do return to work they may find themselves accountable under employment law if they have participated in acts of violence or wilful damage against the property or persons of the employer.

This situation is not altogether dissimilar to where employees conduct themselves in a manner that is detrimental to their employment relationship while they are away from work on any other authorized leave of absence such as vacations, sick leave or just off duty for the week-end. In those instances, arbitration cases in general treat employers' powers of discipline as diminished in scope. The analysis seems to be directed at protecting the personal freedoms of employees and takes the form of imposing a higher standard of reasonableness on an employer's claim that discipline was justified. Arbitral jurisprudence on the scope of an employer's authority to discipline for off duty conduct appears to limit the exercise of disciplinary powers to circumstances where the conduct of the employee undermines the viability of the employment relationship....

In this complaint, the IBEW speaks about there being no duties or obligations remaining from the expired contract of employment, regardless if the contract is collective or individual. We would point out that in this case, like so many others where there is a lawful work stoppage, the new collective agreement was made retroactive to [a date] which was many months before the work stoppage occurred. The employer did not actually use its disciplinary powers until after the new collective agreement was entered into therefore we see no basis for the union's argument....

The facts before us show no indication of anti-union animus on the part of the employer. Certainly, the employer took a hard position at the bargaining table to achieve its collective bargaining goals, but there was never any suggestion that it was trying to rid itself of the union. This was further supported by the return-to-work arrangements entered into by the company and the union whereby all of the union members returned to work....

The evidence also clearly shows that the employer did not, or does not intend to discipline the eight union members because they participated in a lawful strike. The discipline has nothing to do with the withdrawal of their labour or their participation in normal picket line activities. Without in any way adjudicating upon the merits of the allegations against the union members affected by this complaint, we would like to make it clear that acts of violence or of wilful damage or any other such unlawful acts are not lawful activities of a trade union that are guaranteed as fundamental rights under s. 110 of the Code. Nor do they fall within the protection offered by s. 184(3)(a)(vi) of the Code.

Taking everything into consideration, we find that the employer has not contravened s. 184(3)(a)(vi) of the Code as alleged. The complaint is dismissed.

8:700 THE REGULATION OF PICKETING

In many strikes and lockouts, picket lines become the focus of the conflict. Strikers seek to disrupt the employer's operations by dissuading customers, suppliers, and other employees from doing business with their adversary. Employers, for their part, commonly attempt to maintain access to the premises, so supervisors and other non-striking employees can come to work and materials can be moved in and out. In hotly contested disputes, employers may bring in replacement workers.

A considerable body of common law and statute law has developed to regulate picketing. The diversity of sources, of means of enforcement, and of lawmakers' attitudes toward labour/management relations confounds any attempt to make definitive statements about what is permitted and what is not. Historically, the courts drew a distinction between two types of picketing: primary and secondary. Picketing was generally held to be primary if it was done at the struck employer's place of business, and secondary if it was done anywhere else (for instance, at the premises of a customer who continues to sell the struck employer's goods). This distinction between primary and secondary picketing was also reflected in the approach labour boards took to the regulation of picketing activity, and in the statutory schemes regulating picketing in some jurisdictions. Courts and labour boards tended to be much more permissive toward primary picketing than toward secondary picketing.

However, as we will see, in *Pepsi-Cola Canada* (excerpted in Section 8:723), the Supreme Court of Canada rejected the primary-secondary picketing distinction at common law. Instead, the Court crafted what it called a new "wrongful action" approach, which treats all picketing as being lawful unless it involves tortious or criminal behaviour. Although the distinction between primary and secondary picketing is therefore no longer significant at common law, it remains quite important in the approach taken in some Canadian jurisdictions to the statutory regulation of picketing. We will discuss these issues further in Section 8:724.

8:710 Regulatory Schemes Governing Picketing

8:711 The British Columbia Approach

Most Canadian labour relations statutes do not explicitly deal with picketing. This legislative silence has been interpreted as leaving the courts with the major role in the regulation of picketing, and labour boards with only a secondary role. British Columbia is the major exception. The British Columbia *Labour Relations Code* gives the board considerable power over picketing, to the substantial exclusion of the courts. Picketing is defined broadly in the *Code*:

> 1(1) "picket" or "picketing" means attending at or near a person's place of business, operations or employment for the purpose of persuading or attempting to persuade anyone not to
>
> (a) enter that place of business, operations or employment,
> (b) deal in or handle that person's products, or
> (c) do business with that person,
>
> and a similar act at such a place that has an equivalent purpose.

However, this definition of picketing has been held to be unconstitutional. In *United Food and Commercial Workers, Local 1518 v KMart Canada Ltd*, [1999] 2 SCR 1083, the Supreme Court of Canada found that this definition was broad enough to encompass expressive leafletting and therefore that it infringed section 2(b) [expression] of the *Charter*, and could not be saved by section 1. As of the date of printing of this text, no replacement definition had been enacted.

The Supreme Court did not strike down sections 65 and 67 of the same *Code*, which outline specifically when picketing is permitted, and make clear that picketing is unlawful if not specifically allowed by the *Code*. Picketing is allowed during lawful strikes and lockouts at the employer's place of business. On application, the *Code* allows the board to authorize picketing at secondary sites if they provide work, goods, or services that would normally occur at the struck employer's site, as well as at sites of the employer's "allies." The *Code* also grants the board the authority to determine the site of picketing within its exclusive jurisdiction to deal with picketing.

The following case reviews the policy background of British Columbia's statutory substitution of administrative for judicial regulation of picketing.

***Canex Placer Limited (Endako Mines Division) v Canadian Association of Industrial, Mechanical and Allied Workers, Local 10*, [1975] 1 CLRBR 269 at 272–75 (BCLRB)**

> [During a legal strike at the company's mine, large numbers of picketers completely blocked access to the mine by standing in the road and by uttering what the board described as "some isolated threats of violence." The company applied to the board for an order prohibiting such conduct.]

WEILER, Chair: The legal issue before us is whether the Board has the power to prohibit that behaviour.... Here the subject of the complaint ... was activity occurring on a picket line. [The board referred to the presence in the *Labour Code* of an earlier version of the provisions set out above.]

[T]he conduct [of the picketers] ... is illegal, at least at first blush, because it violates the requirements of quite different areas of the law of this province. These may include the *Criminal Code's* prohibition of assault or threats of violence, the *Highway Act* offence of obstruction of traffic, the common law torts of assault and battery, and so on. How may the Labour board, on a ... complaint under the Labour Code, exercise the power to enforce this entire body of the general law? ...

The ... *Code* ... creates a division of labour in the administration of the law that may affect picketing activity. Under the previous *Trade-unions Act*, the courts enforced both the labour law and the criminal or tort law facets of picketing. Now the Labour Relations Board is given exclusive jurisdiction over the industrial relations regulation of picketing while the courts remain charged with jurisdiction over its criminal or civil law features. The source of this change in the Code is found in the recommendations of the Woods Report, *Canadian Industrial Relations*, (1968):

> 621. The laws of industrial torts have particular relevance to conduct relating to the 'why,' 'where' and 'when' of picketing. The general law of torts and delicts (civil wrongs), of general application to society at large and generally designed to protect persons and property, relates to the 'how' of picketing. This distinction leads us into disparate recommendations for the 'why,' 'where' and 'when,' and for the 'how.' Briefly, because conduct relating to the first three facets of picketing is peculiar to the industrial relations system of collective bargaining, we recommend a form of codification of the law respecting 'why,' 'where' and when,' and a repeal of the common law of industrial torts in respect of cases where the code applies. We recommend also that adjudication under the Code be assigned to a reconstituted Canada

Labour Relations Board ... with a remedy, among other things, of restraining and mandatory orders to replace the equity injunction now available in the courts. ...

630. We would not change the substantive law relating to the form — that is, the 'how' — of picketing. Generally, we do not think there is a case for giving to persons who choose to engage in acts of picketing any relief from general laws for the protection of the person and property, such as assault, battery, defamation, trespass, nuisance, and so on. Nor do we think protection should be extended against civil liability for conduct that is a violation of the criminal law.

This is not to ignore what appeared to be the major support for the contrary conclusion, the policy argument that the Code should be interpreted as eliminating judicial injunctions entirely from labour disputes. The contention was that the distinctive process and atmosphere of a labour relations board should deal even with the problems of violence on the picket line.... Dean Arthurs put it this way:

> The practical difficulty is that in the course of deciding, for example, that messages disseminated by the pickets are defamatory, or that their behaviour constitutes an assault, the court is really determining the efficacy of the picketing. 'Defamation' may consist merely in a failure adequately to disclose that the primary focus of the dispute is at another of the employer's business premises. 'Assault' may consist merely in 'pointing, grimacing and staring.' And in determining that the tort of coercion has been committed, the court may well be defining the legitimate ambit of pressure available to a union seeking to enforce its collective agreement. By the astute selection of a cause of action ... the employer may bypass the whole integrated body of statutory rules administered by the labour relations board.

But ... there may be a serious constitutional issue in granting the Board jurisdiction over this kind of conduct. Apparently, the legislature can grant the Board power to enforce the strikes and picketing sections of the Code.... The reason is that the Board is simply directed to enforce an additional segment of the comprehensive Labour Code, rather than applying the traditional common law torts to the economic conflict.... Very different legal problems would be raised if a provincial administrative agency were empowered to enforce the general criminal or civil law, even if only in the labour relations context. Before the Code is interpreted as taking that constitutional risk, there should be a clear statement of the legislature that this is its intention.

In the preceding paragraph, Chair Weiler was referring to the effect of sections 96 to 100 of the *Constitution Act*, as interpreted by the Privy Council and the Supreme Court of Canada. The board ruled that it lacked jurisdiction to make an order in relation to the manner in which picketing is carried on, and could only regulate the place, timing, and object of picketing. In all jurisdictions, courts have retained the authority to deal with acts committed in the course of picketing which are illegal independent of the labour relations statute, including both criminal and tortious behaviour.

8:712 Other Regulatory Approaches: Ontario and Alberta

Although no other Canadian jurisdiction has opted as strongly for administrative regulation of picketing as British Columbia has, labour relations statutes in some other jurisdictions (including Alberta and Ontario) grant labour boards broad remedial authority with respect to illegal strikes and conduct which causes such strikes. This can include picketing. For example, the Ontario *Labour Relations Act, 1995*, includes the following section:

> 83. (1) No person shall do any act if the person knows or ought to know that, as a probable and reasonable consequence of the act, another person or persons will engage in an unlawful strike or an unlawful lock-out.
>
> (2) Subsection (1) does not apply to any act done in connection with a lawful strike or lawful lock-out.

Section 100 of the same Act grants the Ontario Labour Relations Board the power to issue cease and desist orders when, among other things, "any person has done or is threatening to do any act [and] the person knows or ought to know that, as a probable and reasonable consequence of the act, another person or persons will engage in an unlawful strike." The Alberta *Labour Relations Code*, sections 84 and 154, restricts picketing to the striking employees' place of employment, authorizes the board to regulate picketing at that location, and empowers the board to control a wide range of "dispute-related misconduct." Since the enactment of such provisions, labour boards and courts have been sharing the regulation of picketing, though somewhat uneasily.

On the eve of the 1996 "Days of Protest" called by the labour movement in Toronto against the policies of the Ontario government, senior officers of certain unions and labour federations publicly urged people to picket Toronto Transit Commission (TTC) sites so that the TTC would be unable to operate. In *Toronto Transit Commission*, [1996] OLRB Rep Sept/Oct 889, the Ontario Labour Relations Board declared that those officers had breached the statutory prohibition against doing anything that would likely lead to an illegal strike (section 83(1)). The Board also granted a limited cease and desist order against picketing at certain places that were critical to the movement of TTC employees and vehicles. Alternate Chair Herman wrote, at 892–93:

> [T]he Board does not have a general jurisdiction over picketing; rather, it deals, in circumstances such as those at hand, with questions of unlawful strikes or unlawful picketing, where the individuals on strike or likely to strike are not legally entitled to do so. If the strike itself is lawful, then the Board does not deal with particular picket line activity, and whether it might be unlawful. That jurisdiction is the courts'....
>
> It is important to understand what the Board is not dealing with in this application, and that is the question of whether the TTC can conduct its operations without interference from the protests.... The TTC asks only that no picketing occur prior to 6:30 a.m. on each day, because by that time its collectors will have been able to enter the stations. After 6:30 a.m., the TTC does not request that we issue any order. The remedy sought by the TTC in this respect reflects the jurisdiction and concern of this Board, that no unlawful strike occur. Except as is necessary or incidental to this issue, this Board does not deal with ensuring that the TTC can fully operate. Indeed, had the TTC sought a prohibition against picketing outside subway stations at any time during the day or night, the Board would not grant it, because there is nothing before us to indicate that such a remedy is necessary to ensure that employees do not have to cross picket lines.

The second point worth making is to re-emphasize that significant Charter rights are at issue in the circumstances. Even though the Board is satisfied that there must be some limits placed upon the rights of people to express themselves and to assemble, in order to ensure that no unlawful strike occurs, any limitation should be as narrow as possible, reflecting the significant and critical rights at issue. We are not dealing here with a typical employer-employee dispute, nor indeed, with a typical labour relations dispute. The provisions of section 83 have of course been breached, but any remedial response should restrict freedom of expression or freedom of assembly as little as possible in the circumstances. Just as the Board did in *Sarnia Construction Association*, ... where as a remedial response the Board established two gates around a construction site, one for striking employees and one for all other employees, similarly the Board should look here to establishing a remedial response that goes no further than is necessary to ensure that no unlawful strike occurs.

8:720 Primary and Secondary Picketing

As noted above, courts (and sometimes labour boards) traditionally distinguished between "primary" and "secondary" picketing. The Supreme Court's decision in *Pepsi-Cola Canada* (discussed in Section 8:723) has collapsed that distinction as it applies to the common law. However, as the distinction remains relevant in the regulatory models of several Canadian jurisdictions, we will now examine it and try to place it in its historical context.

8:721 Primary Picketing

Both labour boards and courts have tended to allow a wide scope for primary picketing in support of a legal strike, if the picketing is focused directly on the business of the struck employer and affects third parties only in their dealings with that employer. When these conditions are met, the only limitations tend to be those based in general tort law and criminal law, such as the prohibitions against physical obstruction, nuisance, assault, property damage, and trespass. Sometimes these issues are framed in terms of the watching and besetting provision of the *Criminal Code*, cited in Section 8:510. The question thus becomes whether the picketing is peaceful and informational or violent and obstructive. Because these restrictions on picket line conduct come from the general law, they are enforced by the ordinary courts.

It is clear in principle that assault, nuisance, trespass, obstruction, and the like are outside the limits of peaceful picketing and are not tolerated by the courts. However, the reality is somewhat more nuanced, as is reflected in these words of Sedgwick J of the Ontario Court (General Division) in *National Gallery of Canada v Public Service Alliance of Canada* (2001) Ontario Court (Gen Div) [unreported] at para 12:

> The courts recognize that implicit in picketing activities is some degree of interference with the civil and legal rights of others. Some give and take on the picket line, that goes beyond the bounds of normal polite conversation, is to be expected.

The next two cases explore the limits of this "give and take."

Harrison v Carswell, [1976] 2 SCR 200 at 202–5, 209, 212–13, and 216–20

DICKSON J.: The respondent, Sophie Carswell, was charged under *The Petty Trespasses Act*, of Manitoba, R.S.M. 1970, c. P-50, with four offences (one on each of four days) of unlawfully trespassing upon the premises of the Fairview Corporation Limited, trading under the firm name and style of Polo Park Shopping Centre, located in the City of Winnipeg, after having been requested by the owner not to enter on or come upon the premises. The appellant, Peter Harrison, manager of Polo Park Shopping Centre, swore the informations. The charges were dismissed by the Provincial Judge but on a trial de novo in the County Court Mrs. Carswell was convicted and fined $10 on each of the charges. The convictions were set aside by the Manitoba Court of Appeal....

With great respect, I am unable to agree with the majority reasons, delivered in the Court of Appeal by Chief Justice Freedman for I find it difficult, indeed impossible, to make any well-founded distinction between this case and *Peters v. The Queen* ..., decided by this Court four years ago in a unanimous decision of the full Bench....

It is urged on behalf of Mrs. Carswell that the right of a person to picket peacefully in support of a lawful strike is of greater social significance than the proprietary rights of an owner of a shopping centre and that the rights of the owner must yield to those of the picketer....

The submission that this Court should weigh and determine the respective values to society of the right to property and the right to picket raises important and difficult political and socio-economic issues, the resolution of which must, by their very nature, be arbitrary and embody personal economic and social beliefs. It raises also fundamental questions as to the role of this Court under the Canadian constitution. The duty of the Court, as I envisage it, is to proceed in the discharge of its adjudicative function in a reasoned way from principled decision and established concepts. I do not for a moment doubt the power of the Court to act creatively—it has done so on countless occasions; but manifestly one must ask—what are the limits of the judicial function? There are many and varied answers to this question. Holmes J. said in *Southern Pacific Co. v. Jensen* ...: 'I recognize without hesitation that judges do and must legislate, but they can do it only interstitially; they are confined from molar to molecular actions.' Cardozo, *The Nature of the Judicial Process* ..., recognized that the freedom of the Judge is not absolute in this expression of his review:

> This judge, even when he is free, is still not wholly free. He is not to innovate at pleasure. He is not a knight-errant, roaming at will in pursuit of his own ideal of beauty or of goodness. He is to draw his inspiration from consecrated principles.

Anglo-Canadian jurisprudence has traditionally recognized, as a fundamental freedom, the right of the individual to the enjoyment of property and the right not to be deprived thereof, or any interest therein, save by due process of law. The Legislature of Manitoba has declared in *The Petty Trespasses Act* that any person who trespasses upon land, the property of another, upon or through which he has been requested by the owner not to enter, is guilty of an offence. If there is to be any change in this statute law, if A is to be given the right to enter and remain on the land of B against the will of B, it would seem to me that such a change must be made by the enacting institution, the Legislature, which is representative of the people and designed to manifest the political will, and not by the Court.

I would allow the appeal, set aside the judgment of the Court of Appeal for Manitoba and restore the judgment of the County Court Judge.

LASKIN C.J.C. (dissenting): ... The locale is a shopping centre, in which a large number of tenants carry on a wide variety of businesses. The shopping centre has the usual public amenities, such as access roads, parking lots and sidewalks which are open for use by members of the public who may or may not be buyers at the time they come to the shopping centre. There can be no doubt that at least where a shopping centre is freely accessible to the public, as is the one involved in the present case, the private owner has invested members of the public with a right of entry during the business hours of his tenants and with a right to remain there subject to lawful behaviour. ...

An employee of a tenant in the shopping centre participated in a lawful strike and then proceeded to picket peacefully on the sidewalk in front of the tenant's premises. The struck employer took no action to prohibit the picketing and, on the record, an action by the employer would probably have been unsuccessful. The owner of the shopping centre introduced himself into the situation and told the picketer, the respondent in this appeal, that picketing was not permitted in any area of the shopping centre and if she did not leave she would be charged with trespass. He advised her to move to a public sidewalk which was some distance away. She continued to picket on the shopping centre sidewalk and charges against her under *The Petty Trespasses Act*, R.S.M. 1970, c. P-50, followed.

[*R. v. Peters*] also involved picketing in a shopping centre. However, the picketing there arose not out of a labour dispute with an employer tenant of premises in the shopping centre, but was by way of a boycott appeal against the selling of California grapes. ...

The first question put to this Court in the *Peters* case was framed as follows:

> Did the learned Judges in appeal err in law determining that the owner of the property had sufficient possession of the shopping plaza sidewalk to be capable of availing itself of the remedy for trespass under the *Petty Trespass Act* R.S.O. 1960 Chapter 294, Section 1(1) [now *Trespass to Property Act*, R.S.O. 1980, c. 511]?

This question, a strictly legal one without any context of fact, was answered unanimously in the negative by the full Court of which I was a member. The Court gave the briefest of oral reasons ..., and I regarded the answer as a response to a narrow question of whether a shopping centre owner can have sufficient possession of a sidewalk therein to support a charge of trespass under the provincial Act. The question, to me, was whether the owner had divested itself of possession so as to make the shopping centre sidewalk a public way upon which there could be no trespass as against such owner in any circumstances.

It is, of course, open to others to read this Court's disposition of the *Peters* case differently but I can say for myself that the brief reasons would not have sufficed had the question that was asked been put in a factual frame as is often done when questions are formulated for the consideration of this Court. For me, it follows that the Peters case is neither in law nor in fact a controlling authority for the present case which came to this

Court not upon specific questions of fact but at large so as to enable this Court to consider both law and fact as they bear on the position inter se of the shopping centre owner and of the lawful picketer in a legal strike. ...

This Court, above all others in this country, cannot be simply mechanistic about previous decisions, whatever be the respect it would pay to such decisions. What we would be doing here, if we were to say that the *Peters* case, because it was so recently decided, has concluded the present case for us, would be to take merely one side of a debatable issue and say that it concludes the debate without the need to hear the other side. ...

The respondent picketer in the present case is entitled to the privilege of entry and to remain in the public areas to carry on as she did (without obstruction of the sidewalk or incommoding of others) as being not only a member of the public but being as well, in relation to her peaceful picketing, an employee involved in a labour dispute with a tenant of the shopping centre, and hence having an interest, sanctioned by the law, in pursuing legitimate claims against her employer through the peaceful picketing in furtherance of a lawful strike.

* * * * *

The Manitoba Legislature amended the *Petty Trespasses Act* to overrule *Harrison v Carswell*: SM 1976, c 71, s 2 (RSM 1987, c P-50). Section 66 of the British Columbia *Labour Relations Code* provides that "No action or proceeding may be brought for (a) petty trespass to land to which a member of the public ordinarily has access ... arising out of strikes, lockouts or picketing permitted under this Code." The Ontario Labour Relations Board ruled in *T Eaton Co*, [1985] OLRB Rep June 491 that a mall owner violated the *Labour Relations Act*'s protection of the right to organize a union when it applied a blanket "no solicitation" rule to exclude union organizers from distributing literature to employees in the mall, since the union's activities did not interfere with a legitimate business interest of the mall owner.

As explained in the *Canex Placer* decision (above, in Section 8:711), courts still have the authority, everywhere in Canada, to restrain picketing activity that involves violence or other breaches of what the Woods Report called "general laws for the protection of the person or property." However, as explained earlier, even where such a breach is alleged, applicants seeking an injunction restraining picketing must still satisfy the common law test for an interlocutory injunction set out in *RJR-MacDonald*. They must also satisfy regulatory prerequisites such as that laid down in section 102(3) of the Ontario *Courts of Justice Act*, which states that the court "must be satisfied that reasonable efforts to obtain police assistance, protection and action to prevent or remove any alleged danger of damage to property, injury to persons, obstruction of or interference with lawful entry or exit from the premises in question or breach of the peace have been unsuccessful."

Cancoil Thermal Corp v Abbott, [2004] CLLC para 220-045 at para 1ff (Ont SCJ)

[The employees of Cancoil Thermal were engaged in a lawful strike that involved peaceful picketing at the entrance to the workplace. Thermal shared premises with a related company, Cancoil Corporation [Corporation], whose employees were not on strike. The picketers detained each person who attempted to cross the picket line for at least fifteen minutes. If a vehicle was occupied by several occupants, the fifteen minutes were multiplied by its number of occupants. This caused employees of Corporation to be late for work. Corporation responded by imposing a staggered entry schedule, which caused significant inconvenience to some of its employees. The police attended, but took the position that they would not interfere in a labour dispute unless there was a risk to public safety or the commission of a criminal offence, neither of which had occurred. The companies sought an interlocutory injunction to restrain the picketing.]

HACKLAND J: This is an application for an interlocutory injunction to restrain allegedly unlawful picketing activities on the premises of the applicant, Cancoil Thermal Corporation.... There has been a re-examination and clarification of the right to picket in recent appellate jurisprudence. The importance of picketing in the context of a labour dispute has been helpfully discussed by Goudge, J.A. of the Court of Appeal in *Industrial Hardwood Products (1996) Ltd. v. Industrial Wood and Allied Workers of Canada, Local 2693 et al*, reported at (2001) 52 O.R. (3rd) 694. The Court stated that in a case, such as the instant case, involving no property damage or personal injury, but obstruction of lawful entry or exit, the relevant considerations include the degree of obstruction, its duration on each occasion and the length of time the obstruction has occurred. Goudge, J.A. stated at page 699 of the report,

> First, there can be no doubt about the vital role that picketing plays in labour disputes. It provides striking workers with the collective opportunity to seek to persuade others of the rightness of their cause. It allows them to express through collective action their solidarity in pursuit of that cause. And it provides an important outlet for collective energy in what is often a charged atmosphere....

In order to establish an entitlement to injunctive relief, the employer must establish, as required by section 102 of the *Courts of Justice Act*, that reasonable efforts have been made to obtain police assistance and that these efforts, in the present context, to prevent obstruction of, or interference with lawful entry or exit from the premises in questions have been unsuccessful. In the present case the Kingston police have been summoned but have refused to become involved in dealing with the claimed interference with the entry to the business premises. Sergeant Charles Boyles of the Kingston Police has deposed that the force's policy is not to take sides or to intervene in relation to any issues that involve the blocking of access or exit from premises. They will deal with public safety issues or the commission of Criminal Code offences....

An interesting question arises as to the application of section 102(3) of the *Courts of Justice Act* when the police take the position, as in this case, that they will not, as a matter of policy, intervene in relation to issues that involve the blocking of access or exit from the company premises, in the absence of public safety concerns or criminal behaviour. The unwillingness of the police to become involved must not be allowed to preclude the Courts intervention in appropriate cases where, in the Court's view, tortious or criminal activity is occurring. As Justice Goudge noted in *Industrial Hardwood Product (1996) Ltd.*, that in cases involving obstruction of lawful entry or exit (not property damage or personal injury) the relevant considerations include the degree of obstruction, its duration on each occasion and how many days it has gone on. On the evidence in that case the Court of Appeal concluded that despite the company's reasonable efforts to obtain police assistance,

> the result was complete obstruction of lawful access for significant periods of time over a significant number of days.

In my view, the test in section 102 would be met having regard to the nonintervention policy of the Kingston police, but only if the employer can succeed in establishing a sufficiently serious ongoing obstruction in the manner contemplated by the Court of Appeal....

The evidence before the court establishes that this strike, in its 12th day, has been orderly and peaceful. There has been no violence or property damage. The principal moving party, Cancoil Thermal, has shut down its plant and is not currently attempting to carry on its business. The approximately 30 employees of Cancoil Corporation have adapted to the unions picket protocol so that vehicles are subject to 15 minute delays. I have no doubt that the sometimes very early or very late work schedules of the Cancoil Corporation employees operates as a hardship to them and their families. Similarly hardship is being experienced by the employees in the bargaining unit. There appear to have been several occasions (largely before Cancoil Corporation adapted its work schedule) when the picketers' activities delayed entry and egress from the company premises for an unwarranted amount of time. A civil nuisance may have occurred. I strongly doubt that the criminal offence of mischief has been made out in respect of the intermittent time limited obstructions which have occurred here. In short, at this early stage of this peaceful strike, I do not find that the level of obstructive conduct either in its nature, duration or effect, exists so as to establish the required *prima facie* case for the granting of injunctive relief, or to establish compliance with section 102 of the *Courts of Justice Act*.

In the context of picketing in a legal strike, which has been recognized as an important manifestation of the constitutionally protected right of freedom of expression, the court, on the record before it, does not consider that irreparable harm has occurred to the employer, either in the sense of criminal or tortious conduct or in the more traditional sense of losses not appropriately compensable in damages.

In assessing the balance of convenience, one weighs the union's right to picket for the purposes noted in the judgments, that I have referred to, against the company's right to the reasonable use of their premises, free from unlawful activities. The cases relied on by the applicants are all examples of far more egregious behaviour on the picket lines than anything to be seen in the present case. Many of the authorities arise in the context of violence and property damage, and those dealing strictly with obstruction of entry and egress usually involve a total obstruction lasting lengthy periods of time. In my view, the circumstances on this picket line, as they exist at this point in time, do not demonstrate a balance of convenience in favour of court intervention.

Even if the requirements of *R.J.R. MacDonald* had been fully met, which I have found not to be the case, I would, as a matter of discretion, have been disinclined to grant the prerogative relief requested. The company takes the position that there is an urgent, albeit limited, problem with the picket line protocol being utilized by the union, which requires the court's intervention. At the same time, the company continues to decline the union's ongoing, apparently good faith invitation to negotiate a mutually acceptable picket line protocol. As a matter of policy, the court's intervention in labour disputes must be characterized by restraint and reflect the objective, wherever possible, of encouraging or facilitating labour management negotiations. In particular, in the circumstances of this case I will not impose a picket line protocol in circumstances where the employer has declined to negotiate that issue with the union for no reason that was satisfactorily explained to the court.

For these reasons the application for an interlocutory injunction is dismissed.

* * * * *

In *Industrial Hardwood Products (1996) Ltd v International Wood and Allied Workers of Canada, Local 2693* (2001) 52 OR (3d) 694 (CA) [*Industrial Hardwood Products*], cited by Hackland J in *Cancoil*, the plaintiff employer had hired replacement workers and used vans to take them in and out of the plant. For about three months, picketers consistently obstructed the vans, except when police were present. The Ontario Court of Appeal rejected the union's argument that because the picketers obeyed police orders to move aside whenever the police did show up, the section 102(3) requirement of "unsuccessful efforts to obtain police assistance" had not been satisfied. Justice Goudge of the Court of Appeal wrote:

> [18] How then should the court determine whether the pre-condition set up by s. 102(3) has been met, particularly in a case like this where there is little or no evidence of property damage or personal injury, but where each day the picketers obstruct lawful entry until the police arrive?
>
> [19] The appellants argue that where, as in this case, the police respond on each occasion and on arrival are able to provide proper entry to or exit from the plant, the pre-condition is not met. They argue that police assistance has not failed to prevent obstruction of lawful entry or exit.
>
> [20] I do not agree. The section does not purport to assess the success of police assistance in preventing obstruction of lawful entry only once the police arrive. This would require the insertion into the subsection of the words "once the police arrive" after the word "prevent." Moreover, the Legislature surely did not contemplate that day after day a company could have access to its premises blocked until whenever the police arrive without being able at some point to resort to the court. The interpretation urged by the appellants would implicitly sanction an indefinite breach of the law. I do not think the Legislature intended this.

Justice Goudge of the Court of Appeal also upheld the prohibition in the order of the lower court against delaying vehicles for more than five minutes, but not the clause limiting to four the number of picketers at each entrance.

> [39] [O]nce the police arrived, the picketers, regardless of their numbers, complied with the requests of the police to provide access. The problem here was not the number of picketers but the delay in the arrival of the police. In these circumstances, limiting the number of picketers goes further than necessary to prevent a recurrence of the demonstrated obstruction of access. It unreasonably restricts an important aspect of the employees' right of expression.

CHAPTER 8: INDUSTRIAL CONFLICT

8:722 Secondary Picketing and the "Modified *Hersees*" Approach

Hersees of Woodstock Ltd v Goldstein (1963), 38 DLR (2d) 449 at 450–56 (Ont CA)

AYLESWORTH J.A.: The matter arises out of a labour dispute between Deacon Brothers Sportswear Ltd. of the City of Belleville, which may conveniently be referred to as the Deacon Company, and the Union.... The appellant [Hersees] is in no way interested in the dispute and has no difficulties with its own employees but in the ordinary course of its business as a retail merchant sells as part of its stock-in-trade from time to time, goods manufactured by the Deacon Company. Neither the respondents nor the Union of which they are members, have any business relationships whatsoever with the appellant and no quarrel with it unless it be appellant's refusal to accede to the request made of it by the respondents to which I shall later refer. On August 12, 1960, the Union was certified by the Ontario Labour Relations Board as the collective bargaining agent for the employees of the Deacon Company but following the report of a conciliation board that company refused and has continued to refuse to conclude a collective agreement with the Union.

The material before the Court consists of two affidavits—one by William Hersee of the appellant and the other by the respondent, Stanley Clair. Hersee deposes that on August 22, 1962, he was approached by Clair who represented himself to be the President of the Union Label Department of the Canadian Labour Congress; that upon Clair ascertaining that appellant did business with the Deacon Company, Clair requested appellant to cancel any orders it had with the Deacon Company; that Clair said if this were not done appellant's store would be picketed; that Clair's request was refused; that appellant then 'had no orders' with the Deacon Company; that on August 28th and following days, one or two pickets bearing placards stationed themselves in front of appellant's place of business. Hersee also deposes to his belief that the picketing thus carried on will have a detrimental effect on appellant's business....

While I am not prepared to disturb [the lower court's] findings negativing conspiracy and nuisance, I think with respect ... that there was a contract extant between appellant and the Deacon Company and that respondents, acting individually at least, tried to induce appellant to break it. I think further that the chief, if not only purpose of the subsequent picketing, was to force appellant's hand in this respect and thus indirectly to bring pressure to bear upon the Deacon Company.

In this day and age the power and influence of organized labour is very far indeed from negligible. 'Loyalty to the picket line' is a credo influencing a large portion of any community such as the City of Woodstock with its own District Labour Council and numerous member unions; nor does the matter rest there, for doubtless to many private citizens not directly interested in the labour movement the presence of pickets before business premises is a powerful deterrent to doing business at those premises....

To me, and I should think to anyone seeking to do business at the appellant's premises, the inference [to be drawn from the picketing] is unmistakable—Hersees is in a dispute of some kind with organized labour; don't become involved! I think any other conclusion is simply unrealistic and I would hold on the facts of the case that appellant's apprehension of damage to its business as a result of the picketing is completely justified.

Upon this branch of the case, therefore, I summarize my conclusions as follows: appellant had a contract with the Deacon Company; respondents knew of the contract and attempted to induce appellant to break it by picketing his premises; such picketing is a 'besetting' of appellant's place of business causing or likely to cause damage to appellant; not being 'for the purpose only of obtaining or communicating information' the picketing is unlawful— *Criminal Code*, 193-54 (Can.) c. 51, s. 366 [now s 423]—and it ought to be restrained.

But even assuming that the picketing carried on by the respondents was lawful in the sense that it was merely peaceful picketing for the purpose only of communicating information, I think it should be restrained. Appellant has a right lawfully to engage in its business of retailing merchandise to the public. In the City of Woodstock where that business is being carried on, the picketing for the reasons already stated, has caused or is likely to cause damage to the appellant. Therefore, the right, if there be such a right, of the respondents to engage in secondary picketing of appellant's premises must give way to appellant's right to trade; the former, assuming it to be a legal right, is exercised for the benefit of a particular class only while the latter is a right far more fundamental and of far greater importance, in my view, as one which in its exercise affects and is for the benefit of the community at large. If the law is to serve its purpose then in civil matters just as in matters within the realm of the criminal law, the interests of the community at large must be held to transcend those of the individual or a particular group of individuals. I have been unable to find clear and unequivocal precedent for this principle in any of the numerous decisions at all relevant to the question, to be found anywhere in Canada ... certain judicial observations would tend to support this conclusion but in each of such cases the secondary picketing which was the subject-matter under consideration, embraced one or more admittedly unlawful elements such as trespass, intimidation, nuisance or inducement of breach of contract.... Despite, however, the inclusion in these cases of secondary picketing of the unlawful elements I have mentioned, I deduce there from a trend toward if not a positive statement of the principle I have enunciated....

[C]ondemnations of the secondary picketing [by the Supreme Court of Canada in *AL Patchett & Sons Ltd v Pacific Great Eastern R Co*] as being illegal do not appear in a context which suggests that they are based upon the inclusion in the picketing of the extrinsic unlawful elements mentioned elsewhere in the judgments and I view them as declaring secondary picketing to be illegal per se. Upon this ground also I would restrain the respondents.

I would allow the appeal with costs, set aside the judgment and direct judgment against respondents with costs restraining respondents, their servants, agents and any persons acting under their instructions from watching, besetting or picketing or attempting to watch, beset or picket at or adjacent to appellant's place of business.

As a result of *Hersees*, secondary picketing came to be treated as "illegal *per se*" in Canadian common law. The stigma attached to secondary picketing was also reflected in the courts' approach to issues of statutory interpretation involving secondary picketing. For example, the prerequisites for obtaining an interlocutory injunction in Ontario's *Courts of Justice Act* were found not to apply to secondary picketing, which was held not to be an act "in connection with a labour dispute," as required by section 102 of that Act. See *Maple Leaf Sports & Entertainment* (1999), 49 CLRBR (2d) 285 (Ont Ct Gen Div). Similarly, the saving provision in section 83(2) of the Ontario *Labour Relations Act,* which protects acts that could cause an illegal strike (such as picketing) when done "in connection with a lawful strike or lawful lockout," was held by the OLRB not to apply to secondary picketing. See *Consolidated Bathurst Packaging Ltd,* [1982] 3 CLRBR 324 at 337–39.

The doctrine that secondary picketing was illegal *per se* was gradually relaxed by courts and labour boards to permit picketing against third parties who were aiding the struck employer in its dispute with strikers or locked out workers. Such third parties became known as "allies" of the struck employer, and the picketing of their operations was in essence treated as primary picketing, both under the *Courts of Justice Act* (see *683481 Ontario Ltd v Beattie et al* (1990), 73 DLR (4th) 346 (Ont HCJ)) and under section 83(2) of the Ontario *Labour Relations Act* (see *Consolidated Bathurst,* cited in the preceding paragraph).

In *Consolidated Bathurst,* the union had lawfully struck four of Ontario's five major manufacturers of cardboard cartons. Some of the customers of the four struck companies increased their orders from the fifth manufacturer (Consolidated Bathurst), whose employees were not on strike. The union then picketed Consolidated Bathurst's plants, and some of its employees refused to cross the picket line. In granting Consolidated Bathurst's application for a cease and desist order against the picketing, the OLRB found that it was not an "ally" of the struck employers for the reasons set out in the following excerpt, with the result that the picketing was held to be a violation of what is now section 83(1) of the Ontario *Labour Relations Act.*

> [A] customer or secondary employer may attempt to reduce the impact of the strike on his business as long as it does not reduce the impact of the strike on the primary employer by enabling him to continue his business. No alliance will usually exist where the impetus for substitutions comes solely from the customers of the struck primary employer and the services are not undertaken for the primary employer's account or his name.... But abstract pronouncements are not appropriate and the Board should be reluctant to develop per se rules in this area. Each case must be analyzed in light of the established facts, the industrial relations realities, and competing policy considerations.
>
> Against this analysis we cannot find that the facts established before us justify the finding that the applicant is an ally or has allied itself to the struck employers.... The applicant is a natural manufacturer for the customers to have recourse to in that the applicant was already performing work for such customers. There is no evidence that the customers are being directed to the applicant by the struck employers or that there is any kind of arrangement by which the struck employers will compensate the customer for any increased cost in having their work performed elsewhere. The applicant has also spurned completely new business. While there is some evidence to indicate that the customers may well return a portion of their patronage to the struck employers at the conclusion of the strike there is no clear understanding that this will be the case and we are satisfied that the applicant is interested in retaining this work if this is at all possible. The applicant also has *bona fide* concerns over customer reaction if it were to turn its large clients away in their time of need. We have been troubled by the joint meetings of the employers, including the applicant, in January and subsequently in August of this year. Employee suspicions of an arrangement are somewhat understandable in the context of these meetings. The applicant also has a real interest in the outcome of the negotiations involving the struck

employers in that this settlement has been a pattern settlement in previous rounds. But a thorough review of the 'minutes' produced does not disclose an understanding that the applicant perform struck work and that the meetings were anything more than informational in purpose. It must be remembered that the unions take an industry approach to their bargaining and it is natural for employers who are affected by their industry-wide efforts to exchange information, concerns and views. On the evidence before us we cannot find that the applicant has gone beyond this purpose or that it is acting in a manner other than as a true competitor to the struck employers in performing work that is clearly arising from the unavailability of the struck employers to perform work for their customers.... Accordingly, we find that the applicant is a neutral and that the picketing directed at it is not in connection with a lawful strike within the meaning of section 76(2).

* * * * *

Whether the "ally" doctrine was ever recognized at common law as a general exception to the "illegal *per se*" doctrine remains unclear. See *Air Canada v CALPA* (1997), 28 BCLR (3d) 159 (SC). However, in light of the Supreme Court's decision in *Pepsi-Cola Canada*, considered in Section 8:723, that issue is likely now moot. As noted earlier, British Columbia is the only Canadian jurisdiction with detailed legislative provisions on picketing. Section 67 of the BC *Labour Relations Code* says: "Except as provided in this Code, a person shall not picket in respect of a matter or dispute to which this Code applies." What sorts of picketing are permitted is set out in section 65. Section 65(3) of the BC *Code* allows primary picketing in support of a lawful strike at the site of the strike, and sections 65(2) and 65(4) permit (or authorize the board to permit) picketing at other sites of the struck employer or at the site of an ally as defined in section 65(1). Section 65(7) makes clear that the picketing of separate divisions of a struck corporation or firm is to be treated as secondary rather than primary. A leading discussion of the "ally" doctrine in the BC context is found in the reasons of Chair Paul Weiler in *Liquor Distribution Branch v Hiram Walker & Sons Limited*, [1978] 2 CLRBR 334 (BCLRB).

8:723 *Pepsi-Cola* and the "Wrongful Action Model"

Retail, Wholesale and Department Store Union, Local 558 v Pepsi-Cola Canada Beverages (West) Ltd, [2002] 1 SCR 156, 2002 SCC 8 at para 1ff

> [During a legal strike and legal lockout between the Saskatoon Pepsi-Cola distributor and its employees, strikers engaged in various types of picketing and other acts in support of their bargaining position. Some of those acts were clearly illegal because they involved violence or the picketing of private homes, which the Court ruled amounted to the torts of intimidation and private nuisance. However, the case dealt mainly with the peaceful picketing of a number of retail stores which sold Pepsi products but had no corporate connection to the Pepsi-Cola company, and only that part of the judgment is excerpted below.
>
> In the court of first instance, Pepsi-Cola applied for and was granted an interlocutory injunction prohibiting picketing "at any location other than [Pepsi's own] premises"—that is, prohibiting all secondary picketing. The Saskatchewan Court of Appeal struck down that prohibition. In a unanimous judgment written by McLachlin CJC and LeBel J, the Supreme Court of Canada upheld the Court of Appeal decision.]

McLachlin C.J.C. and LeBel J.:—This case raises the issue of when if ever secondary picketing—typically defined as picketing in support of a union which occurs at a location other than the premises of that union's employer—may be legally conducted....

For the reasons that follow, we conclude that secondary picketing is generally lawful unless it involves tortious or criminal conduct, and that the Saskatchewan Court of Appeal correctly disposed of the issues on this basis....

IV. ISSUES

The main issue in this appeal is the legality of secondary picketing at common law. A secondary issue is whether the employer, Pepsi-Cola, can apply for relief against secondary picketing, or whether only the third parties affected by secondary picketing may apply.

V. ANALYSIS

2. The Competing Values and Interests
[...]

(b) Picketing and Free Expression
[...]

Picketing represents a continuum of expressive activity. In the labour context it runs the gamut from workers walking peacefully back and forth on a sidewalk carrying placards and handing out leaflets to passersby, to rowdy crowds shaking fists, shouting slogans, and blocking the entrances of buildings. Beyond the traditional labour context, picketing extends to consumer boycotts and political demonstrations.... A picket line may signal labour strife. But it may equally serve as a physical demonstration of individual or group dissatisfaction on an issue.

For the purposes of this appeal, we find it unnecessary to define picketing in a detailed and exhaustive manner. We proceed rather on the basis that picketing may involve a broad range of activities, from the "traditional" picket line where people walk back and forth carrying placards, to the dissemination of information through other means.

Picketing, however defined, always involves expressive action. As such, it engages one of the highest constitutional values: freedom of expression, enshrined in s. 2(b) of the *Charter*. This Court's jurisprudence establishes that both primary and secondary picketing are forms of expression, even when associated with tortious acts: *Dolphin Delivery, supra*. The Court, moreover, has repeatedly reaffirmed the importance of freedom of expression. It is the foundation of a democratic society....

3. Potential Solutions—Surveying the Landscape

Picketing engages distinct and frequently clashing interests among the parties affected by a labour dispute. The present appeal casts the right of unions to freely express their views on the conditions of their employment and the facts of a labour dispute against the resulting potential for economic damage to third parties....

Three possible options emerge from the parties' submissions: (1) an absolute bar on secondary picketing (the "illegal *per se*" doctrine); (2) a bar on secondary picketing except for "allied" enterprises (the modified "*Hersees*" rule); and (3) permitting secondary picketing unless the picketing amounts to a tort or other wrongful conduct. We will consider each option in turn.

(a) The Illegal *Per Se* Doctrine

This view holds that secondary picketing is illegal *per se*, in the manner of an independent tort, even in the absence of any other wrongful or illegal act.

The doctrine turns on location. It rests on a distinction between picketing the premises of the employer against whom the union is striking (primary picketing) and picketing other premises (secondary picketing). Primary picketing is legal unless it involves tortious or criminal conduct, while secondary picketing is always illegal....

(b) Exceptions to *Hersees*—The Primary Employer and Ally Doctrines

Over time, necessary refinements to the bold "illegal *per se*" doctrine have riddled it with difficult exceptions. As a threshold matter, courts would refuse to enjoin picketing where the employees were found to be engaged in "primary" rather than "secondary" picketing. In some of these cases, the courts found that the location of the picketing, although not necessarily the primary workplace of the employees, was nonetheless owned by the same employer. The courts would also "lift the corporate veil" and refuse to enjoin picketing at the parent company, or at a company which shared corporate ownership with the primary employer.... The picketing would therefore not be characterized as "secondary"; hence the definition of secondary picketing referred to in these reasons.

However, forbidding picketing at any place other than the primary employer's workplace continued to create difficulty. For example, strict application of the *Hersees* doctrine would effectively deny a union the ability to picket its own employer if, by virtue of a shared driveway, for example, an otherwise unrelated employer would also be affected. Courts have nevertheless allowed picketing in these circumstances, provided it is primarily directed at the struck employer. However, the search for primary purpose may, at times, prove a rather subtle intellectual exercise, as some courts have found....

Another exception to the strict *Hersees* approach is the ally doctrine (although there is a significant degree of overlap between this doctrine and the other exceptions discussed in this section). Some courts, while suggesting secondary picketing may be illegal *per se*, have refused to enjoin picketing where the struck operation was effectively assisting the employer in carrying on business during a labour dispute....

Similarly, courts have refused injunctions where third parties allowed struck employers to conduct a business from their warehouse, on the basis that the secondary location was effectively a place of business for the employer.... Concerns such as these have required courts to make delicate distinctions regarding the amount of warehousing, for example, as evidence of the degree of co-operation between the primary and secondary employer....

These modifications to the *Hersees* doctrine have softened its harshest effects on unions and picketing, but have made the common law difficult to implement in a consistent, clear manner....

Despite these difficulties, the Ontario Court of Appeal and courts in some other provinces continue to apply the obiter of *Hersees* that secondary picketing is illegal *per se*....

On balance, few judgments reflect the *Hersees* doctrine in its strictest form, but some courts continue to apply a modified version.

(c) Permitting Secondary Picketing Unless it Involves a Tort or Crime
A third approach starts with the proposition that all picketing is permitted unless it can be shown to be wrongful or unjustified (the "wrongful action" model). It defines wrongful or unjustified picketing as picketing that involves a tort (a civil wrong) or a crime (a criminal wrong).

Even after *Hersees*, a number of Canadian courts have expressly declined to adopt its classification of secondary picketing as illegal *per se*; instead, they have refused injunctions to enjoin secondary picketing unless it involves tortious or criminal conduct.... This approach stems from the proposition, as articulated by Cameron J.A. for the majority in the court below, that "[g]enerally speaking, picketing constitutes an exercise of the fundamental freedom of expression which can only be circumscribed by laws, whether statutory, regulatory, or common, that accord with the constitutional norms of the *Canadian Charter of Rights and Freedoms*."

4. Resolving the Conflict: The Wrongful Action Model

[...]
We conclude that the third approach—the wrongful action model that makes illegal secondary picketing which amounts to tortious or criminal conduct—best achieves this goal. The following considerations, some of which involve overlapping themes, lead us to this conclusion.

(a) Conformity to *Charter* Methodology
While freedom of expression is not absolute, and while care must be taken in the labour context to guard against extending the more severe effects of picket lines beyond the employer, if we are to be true to the values expressed in the *Charter* our statement of the common law must start with the proposition that free expression is protected unless its curtailment is justified. This militates against a rule that absolutely precludes secondary picketing, whether harmful or benign, disruptive or peaceful. The preferred methodology is to begin with the proposition that secondary picketing is prima facie legal, and then impose such limitations as may be justified in the interests of protecting third parties....

(b) Protection of the Value of Free Expression
The wrongful action approach best protects the values of contemporary Canadian society as they find expression in the *Charter*.... The *Hersees* rule, even in its modified form, denies free expression any value outside primary picketing....

(c) Avoidance of Excessive Emphasis on Protection from Economic Harm
In *Hersees*, the Ontario Court of Appeal appears to have viewed the issue as a conflict between a public right to trade and the rights of a smaller group, the union, to advance its purely private interests. The public interest in free expression and societal debate on working conditions and labour conflict receives no mention. The *Hersees* doctrine

casts the economic protection of third parties from the effects of labour disputes as the pre-eminent concern of the law, regardless of the resulting incursion on free expression.

If the legal foundation of the hierarchy of rights proposed in *Hersees* was doubtful at the time, it is even more problematic in light of the enactment of the *Charter* and contemporary labour relations.

...

(f) Avoidance of the Primary-Secondary Picketing Distinction

It follows from this analysis that the difficult and potentially arbitrary distinction between primary and secondary picketing is effectively abandoned on a wrongful action approach to picketing. Secondary picketing has been, as we have seen, location defined. Indeed, many of the difficulties the courts have encountered over the years in defining secondary picketing flow from how to determine the relevant location. A conduct approach based on tortious and criminal acts does not depend on location. All picketing is allowed, whether "primary" or "secondary," unless it involves tortious or criminal conduct.

We should not lament the loss of the primary-secondary picketing distinction. It is a difficult and arbitrary distinction that deserves to be abandoned....

(g) Avoidance of Labour/Non-labour Distinctions

The wrongful action approach treats labour and non-labour expression in a consistent manner. The *Hersees* rule, by contrast, effectively creates an independent tort of secondary picketing that applies only in the labour context. This distinction is difficult to justify.... We can find no persuasive reason to deprive union members of an expressive right at common law that is available to all members of the public....

(h) Balance of Power

Pepsi-Cola argues that the potential harm to the employer from secondary picketing may be much greater than the harm that would result from primary picketing alone, and that allowing secondary picketing may tilt the balance of power too much in the unions' favour....

Judging the appropriate balance between employers and unions is a delicate and essentially political matter. Where the balance is struck may vary with the labour climates from region to region. This is the sort of question better dealt with by legislatures than courts. Labour relations is a complex and changing field, and courts should be reluctant to put forward simplistic dictums. Where specialized bodies have been created by legislation, be it labour boards or arbitrators, they are generally entrusted to reach appropriate decisions based on the relevant statute and the specific facts of a given situation. Mediation and arbitration are also assuming increasingly important roles in the resolution of labour disputes. If the Saskatchewan Legislature had enacted a comprehensive scheme to govern labour disputes, then it might be argued that allowing secondary picketing would disturb a carefully crafted balance of power. In the absence of a legislative scheme, however, we find it difficult to say that determining illegal picketing on the basis of tortious or criminal conduct—an approach that prevailed at common law prior to *Hersees*—will unduly undermine the power of employers *vis-à-vis* employees.

We emphasize that the validity of legislation is not at stake in this appeal. It is the absence of such legislation that requires us to look to the common law to resolve the issue of the legality of secondary picketing. Nothing in these reasons forestalls legislative action in this area of the law. Within the broad parameters of the *Charter*, legislatures remain free to craft their own statutory provisions for the governance of labour disputes, and the appropriate limits of secondary picketing.

[...]

(k) Does a Wrongful Action Rule Offer Adequate Protection?

[...]

At this point we may usefully review what is caught by the rule that all picketing is legal absent tortious or criminal conduct. The answer is, a great deal. Picketing which breaches the criminal law or one of the specific torts like trespass, nuisance, intimidation, defamation or misrepresentation, will be impermissible, regardless of where it occurs. Specific torts known to the law will catch most of the situations which are liable to take place in a labour dispute. In particular, the breadth of the torts of nuisance and defamation should permit control of most coercive picketing. Known torts will also protect property interests. They will not allow for intimidation, they will protect free access to private premises and thereby protect the right to use one's property. Finally, rights arising out of contracts or business relationships also receive basic protection through the tort of inducing breach of contract. . . .

[W]hile the wrongful action approach is grounded on conduct and hence less arbitrary than the per se illegal rule of *Hersees* . . . , the way torts or crimes are defined may introduce its own measure of arbitrariness. Some of the relevant torts require an unlawful act or the threat of an unlawful act. This makes the relevant inquiry circular: secondary picketing is unlawful if it is tortious but it is tortious only if it is unlawful. Other torts may end up drawing arbitrary lines. Inducing breach of contract, for example, requires (obviously) a contract. The result might be that a neutral employer who has a long-term contract with the primary employer may be protected from secondary picketing, whereas a neutral employer who sells the same products without a long-term supply contract would not be protected.

Despite some anomalies, it is safe to assert that a wrongful action-based approach will catch most problematic picketing—i.e. picketing whose value is clearly outweighed by the harm done to the neutral third party. Moreover, the law of tort may itself be expected to develop in accordance with *Charter* values, thus assuring a reasonable balance between free expression and protection of third parties.

[...]

5. Status to Seek an Injunction

In this case, Pepsi-Cola, the primary employer, sought an injunction to restrain picketing and demonstrations at the premises of independent third parties. Cameron J.A. for the majority of the Court of Appeal, held that picketing is not subject to injunctive relief unless accompanied by the commission of a tort actionable at the instance of the primary company (i.e. Pepsi-Cola). Wakeling J.A., in dissent, concluded that Pepsi-Cola had suffered adequate injury and loss by the secondary picketing and thus would have allowed it to maintain an action for injunctive relief.

We would favour Cameron J.A.'s approach for the following reasons.

First, this approach is consistent with the wrongful action approach to secondary picketing. Since the wrongful action approach recognizes that secondary picketing is lawful where there is no tortious or criminal conduct, it follows that Pepsi-Cola should only be allowed to initiate injunction proceedings where it has been subjected to a tort or a crime—not where it has merely been the target of peaceful secondary picketing.

The contrary view, espoused by Wakeling J.A., is based on accepting secondary picketing as an independent tort against the primary company. The approach we adopt is inconsistent with such a tort. It follows that allowing Pepsi-Cola to maintain an action for injunctive relief on the basis of secondary picketing alone should also be rejected.

This does not mean that Pepsi-Cola has no ability to maintain an action for injunctive relief in a secondary picketing situation. It simply means that Pepsi-Cola would have to base its claim on a specific tort. Not all torts limit the cause of action to the person primarily affected by the actions of another. Intimidation serves as a good example. The elements of intimidation include both intimidating the plaintiff and intimidating others, to the injury of the plaintiff. Thus, as Cameron J.A. points out, in the context of labour-management disputes, intimidation would be actionable at the instance of the employer whether the person intimidated be the employer or an employee. Hence, the tort-based approach only limits Pepsi-Cola's cause of action to the extent that it is limited by the tort itself.

The Court upheld the injunction banning picketing at the private homes of Pepsi-Cola employees, but quashed the prohibition of picketing at the other locations.

8:724 The Impact of *Pepsi-Cola Canada*

Several questions arise from the *Pepsi-Cola Canada* judgment. An important one relates to the statutory provisions found in some provinces which distinguish between primary and secondary picketing by providing greater protection for the former while treating the latter as illegal *per se* or illegal with exceptions (such as through the application of the "ally" doctrine). Are such provisions consistent with the Supreme Court of Canada's ruling in *Pepsi-Cola Canada* that there is nothing inherently unlawful about secondary picketing? The *Pepsi-Cola Canada* case dealt with the common law of picketing, and the Court was careful to note that "nothing in these reasons forestalls legislative action in this area." Nevertheless, the Court's ruling that common law doctrines which imposed a blanket prohibition on peaceful secondary picketing were inconsistent with *Charter* values may indeed create a tension with statutory schemes that treat secondary picketing less favourably than primary picketing merely because it is secondary.

Labour relations statutes in three provinces (Alberta, New Brunswick, and Newfoundland) prohibit all secondary picketing, even if the picketed party is an economic ally of the struck employer. For example, the Alberta *Labour Relations Code* states, in section 84(1), that picketing may take place at the "striking or locked out employees' place of work and not elsewhere." In *Alberta (Attorney General) v Retail Wholesale Canada, Local 285 (Brewers Distributors)*, [2001] 6 WWR 643 (Alta QB), decided before *Pepsi-Cola Canada*, the primary employer had in effect moved its business to the secondary employer's premises during a strike. The Alberta court upheld the opinion of the Alberta Labour Relations Board that the complete statutory ban on secondary picketing was in breach of the *Charter* protection of freedom of expression, because it went farther than was necessary to meet "the pressing and substantial objective of preventing economic damage to neutrals in a labour dispute." Since *Pepsi-Cola Canada*, the Alberta Labour Board appears to treat the ban on secondary picketing in section 84(1) in conjunction with the board's jurisdiction in section 84(2) and (3) to consider which locations constitute the "place of employment" as a presumptively valid scheme that departs from the common law (see *TransAlta Energy Corp v CEP, Local 707*, [2007] Alta LRBR LD-83).

The impact of *Pepsi-Cola* on less restrictive forms of legislative regulation of secondary picketing is not as clear. (See Bernard Adell, "Secondary Picketing after *Pepsi-Cola*: What's Clear and What Isn't?" (2003) 10 *Canadian Labour & Employment Law Journal* 135.) The distinctions between primary and secondary picketing found in court interpretations of the Ontario *Courts of Justice Act* and in the Ontario Labour Relations Board's interpretation of the "saving" provision in section 83(2) of the Ontario *Labour Relations Act* appear to be vulnerable to *Charter* attack after *Pepsi*. In *United Brotherhood of Carpenters and Joiners of America, Local 1030 v Labourers International Union of North America*, 2016 CanLII 30412 (ON LRB), the Ontario Labour Relations Board examined *Pepsi-Cola Canada*, and then expressed the opinion that, "it is difficult to see how a Board ban on expression and association through secondary picketing could survive Charter *analysis."*

The British Columbia legislation discussed above effectively bans secondary picketing except where struck work is performed by an "ally." In a case decided before *Pepsi-Cola Canada*, the Supreme Court of Canada ruled that insofar as that restriction prohibited *informational leafleting* at secondary locations, but not insofar as it prohibited picketing, it violated section 2(b) of the *Charter,* and the violation was not saved by section 1. (See *K Mart Canada Ltd v United Food and Commercial Workers, Local 1518*, [1999] 2 SCR 1083.) After *K Mart*, the BC Labour Board permitted secondary informational leafleting but continued to proscribe secondary (non-ally) "conventional" labour picketing (see, for example, paras 47, 50, and 55).

In *Overwaitea Food Group* (2003), 102 CLRBR (2d) 211 (BCLRB), although the union did not bring a direct *Charter* challenge to the BC legislative provisions on secondary picketing, it argued that as a consequence of *Pepsi-Cola Canada*, the board should cease to distinguish between informational picketing and "conventional" labour picketing, and should permit both at secondary locations. The board concluded:

> We find the continued regulation of conventional picketing at secondary sites to be the legislative intent of section 65 and 67 of the Code. In the absence of a *Charter* challenge to those provisions of the Code, we find we need not—and should not—consider whether the intention or legislative objective of regulating all forms of secondary picketing at secondary sites would survive a *Charter* challenge.

Pepsi-Cola Canada affirmed an important role for the economic torts in the common law regulation of picketing. (See Chris Rootham *et al*, "The Expanded Scope of Union Protection under the *Charter*" (2003) 10 *Canadian Labour & Employment Law Journal* 161 at 170–85.)

In *Telus Communications v TWU* (2005), 385 AR 43 (QB) (upheld on appeal in 2006 ABCA 397), an Alberta court, in dismissing an employer application to restrain picketing at the homes of non-striking employees, held that after *Pepsi-Cola Canada* the location of picketing can no longer determine its legality, and the mere fact that the picketing is secondary can no longer in itself supply the "unlawful means" required for most of the economic torts. The adoption of the "wrongful action" model in place of the "illegal per se" model means that applicants for injunctions to restrain picketing can no longer rely on the mere fact that the picketing is secondary to satisfy the "unlawful means" requirement for some of those torts. Furthermore, where an injunction has been issued based on the criteria in *Pepsi-Cola Canada*, the injunction may be enforced through contempt proceedings even when the tortious conduct has not resulted in a "completed tort."

Telus Communications Inc v Telecommunications Workers' Union, 2007 BCCA 413 at paras 23–24 and 27–28

[The union represented workers involved in a province-wide labour dispute. Union members engaged in picketing, and the employer obtained an injunction order prohibiting certain actions by the union's members. The injunction included picketing; watching and besetting; congregating at hotels and restaurants used by management and non-union employees; "molesting, assaulting, intimidating, obstructing, threatening, or interfering" with management and non-union employees; and following the cars of those employees within a distance of less than five car lengths in a "flying picket." The BC Supreme Court modified the order multiple times and eventually found two union members in contempt of court for breaching the terms of the injunction, finding that union members had followed non-union employees at very close physical distance; yelled and verbally harassed and threatened them; and approached within an unsafe distance while they were working, including while they were completing a job over a deep hole. The union appealed the contempt finding (but not the injunction itself), arguing that the "wrongful action" model endorsed in *Pepsi-Cola* effectively requires a "completed tort" to limit what is otherwise protected picketing. They argued that because the non-union employees were able to finish their work notwithstanding the actions of the union members, their actions did not amount to contempt of the order (because they did not "submit" to the intimidation, the tort was incomplete). In other words, the union argued that, following the decision in *Pepsi-Cola*, a "completed tort" should be an implied requirement in the interpretation of the injunction issued against the union. The BC Court of Appeal rejected this argument.]

Low, J.A.: The Pepsi-Cola case involved consideration of an injunction, not, as in the present case, an order finding picketers in contempt for breaching an injunction. In addition, it was found as a fact in that case that the secondary picketing under attack (other than at the homes of the management employees) was "peaceful informational picketing" (para. 116). On the findings of the chambers judge, the conduct of the appellants in the present case cannot be so described. Physical crowding of the Telus employees as they went about their lawful business coupled with the yelling of obscenities, the use of a disturbing racial slur in Mr. Nguyen's case, and informing Mr. Bigg that they knew where he lived was not peaceful picketing. It did not have an informational purpose.

This is the very conduct that can be enjoined under Pepsi-Cola and can be condemned under the law of contempt if enjoined. The language employed by the Court in that case does not support the contention of the appellants that all that can be enjoined and be contemptuous is an effective tort or a completed crime. The decision contemplates "curtailment" of freedom of expression "as may be justified in the interests of protecting third parties" (para. 67); it permits the court to "intervene and preserve the interests of third parties or the struck employer where picketing activity crosses the line and becomes tortious or criminal in nature" (para. 73); and it recognizes the importance of "the expressive activity involved in conveying information and trying to persuade" (para. 104) while also recognizing that the value of some picketing "is clearly outweighed by the harm done to the neutral third party" requiring "a reasonable balance between free expression and protection of third parties" (para. 106)....

In my opinion, this conclusion in Pepsi-Cola is fatal to this appeal. The conduct of the appellants described by the chambers judge and reproduced above is similar to the conduct that occurred in Pepsi-Cola at the homes of managerial employees: see the description of that conduct by Wakeling J.A. in his concurring reasons in the Saskatchewan Court of Appeal found at 1998 CanLII 12389 (SK CA), [1998] S.J. No. 727, para. 90.

As stated above, the argument of the appellants is that in order to attract a finding of contempt the conduct of the appellants had to amount to a completed tort. However, it is clear that what is required in a contempt application is proof of tortious (or criminal) conduct, not also proof of achievement of tortious intent or proof of actual damage to either the employer or to third parties, in this case the two non-union employees. The circumstances of the present case, where there had been escalating misconduct, including what the judge found to be prima facie breaches of earlier iterations of the injunction, required an order that would be responsive to the particular context of the dispute with a view to the prevention of harm and the preservation of the parties' respective rights. The terms of the injunction, including the conduct prohibited therein, must be understood with those purposes in mind.

8:800 JOB RIGHTS OF STRIKERS

8:810 Employee Status During a Strike

Canadian labour relations statutes do not explicitly grant a "right to strike," but (as we will see in Chapter 12) our courts have held that such a right is recognized by the *Canadian Charter of Rights and Freedoms*. However, a right to take lawful strike action in certain circumstances can be readily implied from the statutory right of employees to take part in the "lawful activities" of unions, from the statutory prohibition of strikes until such prerequisites as conciliation and strike votes have been met, and from the prohibition of employer retaliatory action designed to eradicate a union or to punish strikers.

The extent of the protection now afforded to striking workers depends on whether the strike is called in compliance with labour relations legislation. This section will examine employee status during a legal strike—that is, whether and to what extent employees retain a right to their jobs during such a strike. It will not discuss the effect of strikes on employment benefits such as pension entitlements, seniority rights, vacations, sick pay, and severance pay, although this question is often of great concern to striking employees. The following case (known as the *Royal York* case) provides the foundation for an analysis of employee status during a legal strike.

R v Canadian Pacific Railway Co (1962), 31 DLR (2d) 209 at 211, 216, and 218–20 (Ont HCJ)

[This was an appeal by way of stated case from a provincial criminal court's dismissal of an unfair labour practice charge against the Royal York Hotel. During the course of a legal strike, the hotel's management sent the following letter to strikers:

1. On June 26th I wrote you enclosing Form A—Resignation, and Form B—Return to Work, and asked you to sign either form and return it by July 15th. I again wrote you on July 10th in this same connection, and also outlined the new wage rates and working conditions now in effect.
2. As you did not indicate your availability for duty or otherwise, in accordance with paragraph 4 of letter dated 26th June, we are closing your employment record at the Royal York Hotel effective 16th July, 1961.

Chief Justice McRuer held that this letter amounted to an unfair labour practice. With respect to section 1(2) of the Ontario *Labour Relations Act*, which provided that no one "shall be deemed to have ceased to be an employee by reason only of his ceasing to work for his employer as the result of a lock-out or strike," he said:]

McRUER C.J.H.C.: This subsection preserves the relationship of employer and employee for the purposes of the statute notwithstanding a strike and even though the true relationship of employer and employee may have been terminated at common law on account of the strike....

I think the Act throughout recognizes that there may be employees who are reporting for work and employees who are on strike and it forbids the employer to dismiss or threaten to dismiss members of either class because they engage in lawful union activities....

One of the purposes of s. 1(2) is to preserve for employees their rights as such while they are on strike. The Act creates a statutory class of employees, *viz.*, employees on strike. In the United States of America it has been consistently held before and since the *Wagner Act*, which contains a provision somewhat similar to s. 1(2) of the Ontario Act, that the relationship of employer and employee continues notwithstanding a strike unless that relationship has been abandoned.... If I were to come to any other conclusion on the construction of section 1(2) the result would be that when a collective agreement comes to an end and conciliation proceedings have been exhausted an employer will be at liberty to lay down terms that employees could not be expected to accept with the consequence that if they went on strike they would lose all their pension rights, their insurance rights and seniority rights. To so interpret the law would destroy the security built up by old and experienced employees and leave it subject to the will of the employer. This would appear to be contrary to the whole course of the development of labour legislation for half a century....

CHAPTER 8: INDUSTRIAL CONFLICT

Counsel asks the question, 'If the law is as I have stated it to be, what is the legal position where a strike is never concluded by a settlement?' This is a question that it may not be necessary for me to answer. However, I think the answer is quite simple. In such a case the employees have either gone back to work, taken employment with other employers, died or become unemployable. Such employees could not any longer, adapting the language of s. 1(2), be deemed to have ceased to be employees by reason only of their ceasing to work for their employer as the result of a strike.

* * * * *

The decision of McRuer CJHC was affirmed by the Ontario Court of Appeal, and by the Supreme Court of Canada, *sub nom CPR Co v Zambri* (1962), 34 DLR (2d) 654 (Ont CA). Justice Cartwright wrote, at 664:

> It is said that the Act does not in terms declare the right to strike, but I find myself in agreement with [union counsel's] argument that the right is conferred by s. 3 which reads:
>
>> 3. Every person is free to join a trade union of his own choice and to participate in its lawful activities.
>
> It is clear on the findings of fact made by the learned Magistrate that the strike with which we are concerned was an activity of the union; I have already expressed my opinion that it was lawful; it follows that s. 3 confers upon the six employees, all of whom are members of the union, the right to participate in that lawful activity. I conclude therefore that the participation in the strike by the employees was the exercise of a right under the Act.

Justice Locke added this important *dictum*, at 657, with respect to the permanent replacement of lawful strikers:

> While unnecessary for the disposition of this appeal, I wish to express my dissent from the opinion that has been stated that if a strike is never concluded by settlement the relationship declared by ss. (2) of s. 1 continues until the employee has either gone back to work, taken employment with other employers, died or become unemployable. When employers have endeavoured to come to an agreement with their employees and followed the procedure specified by the *Labour Relations Act*, they are at complete liberty if a strike then takes place to engage others to fill the places of the strikers. At the termination of the strike, employers are not obliged to continue to employ their former employees if they have no work for them to do, due to their positions being filled. I can find no support anywhere for the view that the effect of the subsection is to continue the relationship of employer and employee indefinitely, unless it is terminated in one of the manners suggested.

In several Canadian jurisdictions, the use of "professional strikebreakers" has been expressly forbidden. See, for example, the Ontario *Labour Relations Act*, section 78. This prohibition is particularly significant for relatively small bargaining units of unskilled or semiskilled workers, where security firms and labour contractors could often undercut vulnerable unions by supplying temporary personnel to enable employers to maintain operations. In several well-publicized cases, these tactics were accompanied by other illicit devices such as the use of *agents provocateurs*.

Quebec and British Columbia have much broader provisions that forbid employers from hiring even temporary replacement workers or from using certain classes of ongoing employees to perform bargaining unit work. The BC provisions have survived several rounds of amendments to the *Labour Relations Code*. Ontario enacted anti-replacement worker legislation very similar to Quebec's in 1992, but it was repealed in 1995. See Section 8:820 for a discussion of legal restrictions on the use of replacement workers.

In other jurisdictions, where the hiring of replacements continues to be part of the employer's tactical arsenal, a controversial issue remained: can the employer maintain operations by using permanent replacements to fill the strikers' jobs without committing the unfair labour practice of refusing to employ someone because of his participation in the lawful activities of a trade union? Legislators in Ontario, Saskatchewan, Alberta, Manitoba, and the federal jurisdiction moved to protect employees by giving former strikers an explicit statutory right to return to their jobs even if replacement workers were in those jobs. The Manitoba provisions are the widest. They state that work being done by replacements at the end of a strike or lockout is work which "becomes available" for the purpose of allowing returning strikers to reclaim it, and that returning strikers must be recalled on the basis of their seniority, unless the parties agree otherwise. The Manitoba provisions also make it an unfair labour practice for the employer to hire or threaten to hire anyone to perform struck work "for any period of time longer than the duration of the lockout or legal strike" (Manitoba *Labour Relations Act*, sections 11–13). Section 87.6 of the *Canada Labour Code* provides as follows:

> At the end of a strike or lockout not prohibited by this Part, the employer must reinstate employees in the bargaining unit who were on strike or locked out, in preference to any person who was not an employee in the bargaining unit on the date on which notice to bargain collectively was given and was hired or assigned after that date to perform all or part of the duties of an employee in the unit on strike or locked out.

In Ontario, the protection is more limited in that the striker must make an "unconditional" application for reinstatement (*Labour Relations Act, 1995*, s 80). Following a bitter strike in which the entitlement of strikers to return to work was very much at issue, Alberta also enacted a general right to reclaim one's job (*Labour Relations Code*, s 90, enacted by SA 1988 c L-1.2, s 88). As the following extract reveals, even in the absence of an expressed statutory right of strikers to return to work at the conclusion of a strike, labour boards sometimes treated a refusal to reinstate strikers as an unfair labour practice.

Canadian Air Line Pilots' Association [CALPA] v Eastern Provincial Airways Ltd (1983), 5 CLRBR (NS) 368 at 407–10

> [During a lawful strike the company maintained operations by, among other things, hiring eighteen new pilots to fill the strikers' positions and promising those new employees that they would retain their jobs after the strike. Some nine weeks into the strike, the employer offered to conclude a return to work agreement with the striking union, clause 12 of which read as follows (at 409):

It is agreed that when the strike ends, all pilots presently involved in the strike will be considered on layoff due to a sudden cessation of work caused by a work stoppage of employees.... Pilots will be recalled to openings in accordance with their seniority. For these purposes, an opening is an available vacant position in a status according to operational requirements. However, it is understood that the problems of returning to normal operations and the requirements of retraining make it impractical to recall pilots in accordance with the provisions of the collective agreement for a temporary period. It is agreed, therefore, that pilots may be recalled out of seniority in accordance with operational requirements for a period of 60 days following the date of signing of this Return to Work Agreement. Following that, and unless the parties mutually agree to extend the period, the provisions of Article 7 of the Collective Agreement [regarding seniority] will apply for all further recalls.

It is agreed that no grievance shall be filed by CALPA or any pilot, as a result of the non-application of the Collective Agreement regarding recalls during the above mentioned period. Furthermore, it is agreed and understood that the reactivation of the provisions of the Collective Agreement regarding seniority shall not affect the status and base location of any pilot, who was already on active flying duty, or who had commenced, or been scheduled to commence training on the date of the signing of this Return to Work Agreement.

One of the union's claims was that this offer violated section 184(3)(a)(vi) [now s 94(3)(a)(vi)] of the *Canada Labour Code*, which made it an unfair labour practice for an employer to "refuse to employ or to continue to employ ... or otherwise discriminate against any person in regard to employment ... because the person ... has participated in a strike that is not prohibited by this Part ..." The board found in favour of the union.]

JAMIESON, Chair: EPA [Eastern Provincial Airways] takes the position that in the absence of statutory provisions providing for the reinstatement of employees at the end of a strike, and, where there is nothing to restrain an employer from operating during a strike or restricting the hiring of new employees, its insistence that the new pilots not be replaced by returning strikers, is not unlawful.

EPA relied on extensive North American industrial relations jurisprudence which would overawe any tribunal by the mere mention of the impressive list of prominent and respected authors and adjudicators in this field. Particular emphasis was placed on two Ontario Labour Relations Board decisions: *Mini-Skool Ltd.* ... and *The Becker Milk Company Limited*.... It is our view that there is nothing particularly relevant in those cases to the facts before us in this case. They deal primarily with the rights of employees under s. 73 of the Ontario legislation....

We shall not go through the other cases to distinguish them, they are all so clearly dependent upon the interpretation given the particular statutory provisions in the relevant jurisdictions.... If the Code only contained s. 107(2), which is a standard provision in most jurisdictions [preserving the 'employee status' of strikers], it would be open to argument that to retain 'employee status' does not necessarily mean a guarantee of a job. But, Parliament went much further than s. 107(2) to protect the continued employment of those who exercised their rights under the Code. The construction of s. 184(3)(a)(vi) could leave absolutely no room for doubt that employees cannot be deprived of any term or condition of employment whatsoever because of participation in a lawful strike. If an employee is so deprived, a reason, other than the exercise of the right to strike, must be present.

What reasons does EPA have for laying off some 18 pilots at the end of a lawful strike? The jobs are still there, the aircraft are the same and there has been no change in the equipment as far as we know. Other than the changes to the content of the collective agreement, the only difference there would be at the end of the strike from when it began ... is that there are 18 additional pilots. Pilots who have been lawfully hired in the same manner as any other pilot hired by EPA. They have the same working conditions, in fact, they are still on probation.... How does EPA propose to avoid laying off the new pilots rather than the strikers, keeping in mind that such lay-offs are normally governed by art. 7 of the collective agreement? ...

While we do not wish it said that we are interpreting the collective agreement, the effect of [the proposed] clause 12 is rather obvious. The seniority provisions which normally govern the employment relationship at EPA would be suspended long enough for EPA to accomplish what it could not lawfully do otherwise. That is, to keep the new pilots and those who crossed the picket lines to work during the strike on the active workforce out of seniority. Clause 12 also provides EPA with a 60 day opportunity to selectively recall whom it wishes, out of seniority or alternately, not to recall those that it does not wish to recall. And, to add insult to injury, CALPA and the pilots would be required to forego their right under the collective agreement to grieve their displacement by junior pilots. What could be more blatantly discriminatory? And, what is the reason for all of this? EPA cannot escape the answer!

Such conduct by EPA is contrary to s. 184(3)(a)(vi) of the Code, and we so find.

* * * * *

The *Canada Labour Code* provides, in section 87.6, that legal strikers or locked-out employees must be reinstated in preference to any replacement worker "who was not an employee in the bargaining unit on the date on which notice to bargain collectively was given." This would presumably apply even if the employer could establish that the replacement worker has superior skills.

The question of the applicability in Ontario of the reasoning in the *Eastern Provincial Airways* decision is complicated by section 80 of the Ontario *Labour Relations Act, 1995*, which allows strikers individually to return to their jobs during the first six months of a legal strike. If a strike is still on after six months, can the employer then decide to retain the replacement workers rather than take back the striking workers? In *Mini-Skool Ltd* (1983), 5 CLRBR (NS) 211, the Ontario Labour Relations Board held that it was not an unfair labour practice for an employer to retain junior employees who had returned to work before the six-month limit in preference to more senior employees who wished to return after that point. In *Shaw-Almex Industries Ltd* (1986), 15 CLRBR (NS) 23, on the other hand, the board held that the *Mini-Skool* decision depended on a finding that the employer had no improper motive for extending a preference to the junior employees. In *Shaw-Almex*, the employer's expression of feelings of loyalty to the replacement workers, and its failure to make out the claim that their skills had surpassed those of the returning strikers, led to a finding of improper motive in retaining the replacement workers in preference to the strikers, even though the strike had lasted longer than six months.

More recently, in *United Food & Commercial Workers Canada, Local 175 v WHL Management Limited Partnership*, 2014 CanLII 76990 (OLRB), the OLRB revisited the *Mini-Skool* and *Shaw-Almex* line of cases. The OLRB ruled in that case that an employer's insistence on a back-to-work protocol following a strike that permitted replacement workers to keep jobs over strikers seeking to return violated the duty to bargain in good faith as well as the prohibition against discrimination for exercising the lawful right to strike. The OLRB relied on the Supreme Court of Canada's 1996 decision in *Royal Oak Mines*, discussed in Chapter 7, in ruling that an employer who insists in bargaining on a clause that would protect less senior replacement workers over more senior employees who had exercised their legal right to strike is proposing a provision to which "no reasonable union" could be expected to agree. This amounted to a breach of the duty to bargain in good faith. In the *Fair Workplaces, Better Jobs Act, 2017*, SO 2017, c 22, the Ontario government eliminated the six-month limitation on the right of strikers to return to work and also added the following new provisions to section 80 of the Ontario *Labour Relations Act*:

> 80(3) Subject to subsections (5) to (7), at the conclusion of a lawful strike or lock-out, an employer of an employee who was engaged in a lawful strike or lawfully locked out shall reinstate the employee in the employee's former employment on such terms as the employer and the bargaining agent that represents the employee may agree upon.
>
> 80(5) Striking or locked out employees are entitled to displace any other persons who were performing the work of striking or locked out employees during the strike or lock-out if the length of service of the other person, as of the time the strike or lock-out began, is less than that of the striking or locked-out employee.

* * * * *

Do replacement workers have a right to participate in collective agreement ratification or "decertification" applications? In *Canadian Association of Smelter and Allied Workers, Local No 4 v Royal Oak Mines Inc* (1993), 93 CLLC para 16,063 at 14,510–14, a long and bitter strike was dragging on, and a rival employee association applied to decertify the striking union, as was allowed by the *Canada Labour Code*. The Canada Labour Relations Board held that replacement workers should not be considered to be in the bargaining unit or to be eligible to take part in the decertification vote, because they had only "a temporary, precarious status" and their interests were "not only divergent from but squarely opposed to those of the permanent workforce." In 1998, section 29(1.1) was added to the *Canada Labour Code* to make explicit the exclusion from the unit of anyone "hired or assigned after [notice to bargain was served] to perform all or part of the duties" of a striker or a locked out employee. The Ontario Labour Relations Board has also ruled that only employees whom the union represents are entitled to vote in ratification and decertification votes. This excludes people hired as replacement workers: see *Rescare Premier Canada*, [2003] OLRB Rep Nov/Dec 1077; *Sadyathasan v United Food and Commercial Workers International Union Canada Local 175*,

2015 CanLII 21273 (OLRB). On the status of employees during an *illegal* strike, see *McGavin Toastmaster Ltd v Ainscough*, [1976] 1 SCR 718, excerpted in Chapter 10, Section 10:220.

8:820 Replacement Worker Laws

Whether employers should be permitted to use replacement workers during a lawful strike or lockout has been a controversial question since the earliest days of collective bargaining legislation. Legislative responses have varied over time and across jurisdictions. For example, since 1977, Quebec's *Labour Code* has contained what are often called anti-strikebreaker provisions—provisions which have sharply restricted the use of replacement workers (ss 109.1–109.4). During a strike or lockout employers are forbidden to use most classes of employees to perform the work of the struck bargaining unit. All employees within the bargaining unit must cease work. The only employees who may fill their places are those who both fall within the managerial exclusion and were working in the struck operation before the beginning of the current negotiations. There is a limited exception for work designed to prevent the destruction or serious deterioration of property, and it may be permissible for an employer to have the work done by a subcontractor at another location. Thus, although these provisions do not explicitly require the employer to cease operations, they greatly curtail its ability to maintain production.

Perhaps because the anti-strikebreaker provisions met with very strong opposition from employers when they were introduced in 1977, only very limited redress was made available in the event of a breach of those provisions. The Quebec *Labour Code* expressly contemplates two kinds of redress: investigation leading to a non-binding report, and prosecution leading to a fine. An employer may well ignore the investigation and wait for the prosecution to come to trial, which only happens long after the dispute has ended. In the meantime, the employer's bargaining power will have been enhanced by the use of replacements. In practice, the only effective remedy has been injunctive relief from the ordinary courts, and this has not always served unions well. Despite the controversy which surrounded the anti-strikebreaker provisions in their early years, it is probably fair to say, many years later, that they have become well integrated into Quebec labour law. This is indicated by the fact that they were not called into question during the debate which led to amendments to the *Labour Code* in 2001.

Since 1992, the British Columbia *Labour Relations Code* (in section 68) has prohibited employers from using the services of paid or unpaid replacement workers. A replacement worker is defined as a worker:

(a) who is hired or engaged after the earlier of the date on which the notice to commence collective bargaining is given and the date on which bargaining begins,
(b) who ordinarily works at another of the employer's places of operations,
(c) who is transferred to a place of operations in respect of which the strike or lockout is taking place, if he or she was transferred after the earlier of the date on which the notice to commence bargaining is given and the date on which bargaining begins, or
(d) who is employed, engaged or supplied to the employer by another person, to perform
(e) the work of an employee in the bargaining unit that is on strike or locked out, or

(f) the work ordinarily done by a person who is performing the work of an employee in the bargaining unit that is on strike or locked out.

Unlike the Quebec provisions, the British Columbia provisions do not prohibit employees in the struck unit from returning to work while the strike continues. In Yukon, public service employers are prohibited from using replacement workers during a strike. In 2016, Alberta passed amendments to its *Labour Relations Act* in response to the *Saskatchewan Federation of Labour* case in which it will be required for all essential services agreements to contain a prohibition on the use of replacement workers. In Ontario, as was noted earlier in this chapter, anti-replacement worker provisions quite similar to those in Quebec were enacted in 1992 but repealed in 1995.

* * * * *

In 1995 the federal minister of labour appointed a task force to review Part I of the *Canada Labour Code*, which governs collective bargaining for private sector employers and unions in the federal jurisdiction. As part of its mandate, that task force considered proposals for the adoption of replacement worker legislation. Its report, known as the Sims Report, included the following.

Seeking a Balance: Canada Labour Code Part 1 Review (Ottawa: Supply and Services Canada, 1996) at 124–28 and 131

DIFFERENT PERSPECTIVES ON WORK AND WORK STOPPAGES

Part of the question involves the balance of power between labour and management. However, underlying the issue is a more fundamental difference between the parties about what bargaining rights entail. From an employer's perspective, the obligation to bargain is an obligation to bargain over the terms of work for their employees. They retain, in their view, the residual right to get the work done in other ways, restrained only by any commitments that they make through collective bargaining (for example, a prohibition on contracting out). Such commitments end, in any event, once a work stoppage takes place.

From the union's perspective, employees retain a permanent connection to their job until terminated. The Code maintains employees' status during a work stoppage, and protects them against retaliation for exercising their right to strike. Employees often perceive themselves as having almost a proprietary right not just to employment, but to the performance of the work. They therefore see it as an invasion of this proprietary right when someone else takes over their job.

There are also differences of view over what a strike is all about. Some see collective bargaining as an important market instrument. The strike or lockout tests competing views of the market value of work. The union maintains that the work is worth a specified price; the employer, in turn, believes it can get the work done for less. The availability of willing replacement workers and the efficiency with which they perform the work tests these assumptions. If replacement workers are unavailable or unsatisfactory, the employer is persuaded to raise its offer. If they work well, this pressures the employees, through their union, to reduce their demands to the market level.

Others see the strike as being fought on the more limited field of the financial ability of the employer to survive a shutdown versus the ability of the employees to survive without wages. Under this perception, the employer is seen as garnering an unfair advantage by maintaining a revenue stream during a shutdown. Employers argue that employees are not precluded from seeking alternative employment during a work stoppage and that to achieve balance, employers should not be prohibited from using alternate sources of labour.

THE POTENTIAL FOR VIOLENT CONFRONTATION

One argument advanced in favour of anti-replacement worker legislation is the need to avoid violent incidents that can arise when replacement workers attempt to cross picket lines set up by striking or locked out workers.

No one favours violence, however caused. But violence is not, and need not be, an inevitable consequence of the use of replacement workers. Unions advance this argument somewhat gingerly, and employers resent it being advanced at all. In the employer's view, to restrain its options because those on strike may become violent is seen as punishing the victim, not the perpetrator.

Neither side of this argument is fully justified. Experience shows that violence most often occurs when replacement workers and strikers come into contact with each other in a heated labour dispute. Sensible measures to reduce that potential should be considered seriously. Sometimes it is the strikers that instigate violence and sometimes, but by no means at all times, this is due to encouragement from their leadership. We recognize the important efforts taken by many union leaders to discourage violence in such situations. But it is not always the fault of the strikers or their union. Replacement workers and front line supervisors have also, on occasion, engaged in their fair share of provocative conduct.

In our experience, it is the threat of permanent job loss, and taunting about that between replacement workers and strikers, that raises picket line pressures towards the potential for violence. Creating a clear statutory right to return to work, eliminating the threat of permanent replacement, should moderate some of the deepest tensions.

In other areas of workplace regulation, employers and employees work hard to protect the personal integrity of the worker. We see this in our strict attitude towards safety hazards and the fact that we treat personal and particularly sexual harassment as intolerable actions. We recognize that it is simply unacceptable, no matter what the circumstance or alleged justification, to expose workers to physical harm or undue abuse. This same fundamental assumption must be accepted for the picket line. Labour and management must both take responsibility for the conduct of those they represent, or those who represent them, in such situations.

IMPACT ON INVESTMENT

Employers argue that any introduction of anti-replacement workers legislation will create an environment hostile to investment and scare away sources of capital, costing jobs and security.

A related, but more subtle argument, is that such legislation will gradually affect the way employers structure their business affairs, reducing their dependence upon their permanent workforce in favour of subcontracting and similar practices.

The investment argument arises partly because some provinces have anti-replacement workers legislation while others do not. Despite the vigour of the argument, we found disappointingly little research available on the impact that different provincial laws (particularly in Quebec) had on investment decisions.

Many investors are said to compare our laws to U.S. laws. U.S. laws currently permit the use not only of temporary but permanent replacement workers. However, these laws are also subject to an exception. U.S. law includes the concept of the unfair labour practice strike or lockout. If a dispute is engendered by illegal activities, such as ridding the workplace of the union, then an employer may not make permanent replacements and striking workers have a right to return to work.

IMPACT ON THE DURATION AND RESULTS OF STRIKES

How do anti-replacement workers laws affect the incidence, duration or results of labour disputes? We wish we could point to a conclusive answer but we cannot. Often labour and management supported their positions by referring to 'studies' which were neither named or filed with us for review. Closer analysis revealed that there are few definitive studies. Those that do exist arrive at somewhat different conclusions.

One 1993 study of Canadian manufacturing agreements, by John W. Budd of the University of Minnesota, entitled 'Canadian Strike Replacement Legislation and Collective Bargaining: Lessons for the United States,' concludes 'there is no evidence to support the contention that the presence of legislation affecting the use of strike replacements significantly alters relative bargaining power and the wage determination process or significantly impacts strike activity.'

A second study, however, by Peter Cramton, Morley Gunderson and Joseph Tracy, respectively of the University of Maryland, University of Toronto and Columbia University, entitled 'The Effect of Collective Bargaining Legislation on Strikes and Wages,' and published in 1994, finds that prohibiting the use of replacement workers during strikes is associated with significantly higher wages and more frequent and longer strikes. The Gunderson study compared private sector contract negotiations involving 500 or more workers from 1967 to March 1993. Particularly significant is their conclusion that 'As predicted by theory, the ban on replacement workers is associated with longer strike durations (a 37% increase).' The authors acknowledge however, that their conclusions are based only on a comparison with Quebec.

VARYING VULNERABILITY OF EMPLOYERS

Employers are unequally vulnerable to a prohibition on replacement workers. Some employers are vastly more susceptible to competition from non-union competitors. Other employers have a capital plant that requires regular maintenance even during a shutdown. Some can stockpile or reorganize during a shutdown, while others cannot. This alters the power balance and can thus skew wage settlements in different ways for different workplaces. The impact of a prohibition on employing replacement workers would therefore be quite uneven.

FREQUENCY OF USE

Some argue that the laws should prohibit replacement workers because so few employers use them anyway. For some employers, particularly with specialized work, there is no alternative workforce to call upon. In other industries, stockpiling (by suppliers or customers) gives sufficient protection against the full force of a strike. Many other employers choose not to risk the adverse labour management relationships that can result from using replacement workers. In the federal jurisdiction, external replacement workers were hired in about 25% of the 48 work stoppages under the *Canada Labour Code* which occurred during the period 1991 to 1994.

While it is true that most employers neither plan for nor use replacement workers, the law can nonetheless be an important consideration for collective bargaining strategies. Unions and employers may both modify their behaviour depending on their ability or lack of ability to operate with replacement workers. In this sense, it is not the actual use, but the threat of use and the perceived ability to use replacements that is important to the balance of bargaining power.

THREAT TO COLLECTIVE BARGAINING RIGHTS

Some argue that it is not the ability to use replacement workers itself that is objectionable so much as its frequent abuse. They point out the correlation between the use of replacement workers and efforts to undermine the trade union and destroy its bargaining agency.

This argument mirrors experience with the duty to bargain in good faith. Labour boards have moved to restrain bargaining proposals that indicate an intention to dislodge the union rather than to achieve a particular bargaining result. The distinction between this form of bad faith bargaining and hard bargaining is never easy to discern. However, such conduct is often accompanied by other conduct indicative of the same intention. While labour boards are reluctant to interfere with genuine bargaining positions, they are not, nor should they be, reluctant to intervene when bargaining positions become thinly disguised unfair labour practices aimed at undermining the union's right to represent employees....

Recommendations:
- There should be no general prohibition on the use of replacement workers.

- Where the use of replacement workers in a dispute is demonstrated to be for the purpose of undermining the union's representative capacity rather than the pursuit of legitimate bargaining objectives, this should be declared an unfair labour practice.
- In the event of a finding of such an unfair labour practice, the Board should be given the specific remedial power to prohibit the further use of replacement workers in the dispute.

[*Seeking a Balance* is a publication of Human Resources Development Canada. Reproduced with the permission of the Minister of Public Works and Government Services Canada, 1997.]

In 1998, the following provision was added to the *Canada Labour Code*, by SC 1998, c 26, s 42, pursuant to the above recommendations:

Section 94(2.1): No employer or person acting on behalf of an employer shall use, for the demonstrated purpose of undermining a trade union's representational capacity rather than the pursuit of legitimate bargaining objectives, the services of a person who was not an employee in the bargaining unit on the date on which notice to bargain collectively was given and was hired or assigned after that date to perform all or part of the duties of an employee in the bargaining unit on strike or locked out.

It remains unclear when the use of replacement workers is for the "demonstrated purpose of undermining" the union's representational capacity. The Canada Industrial Relations Board has noted the lack of direction in the statute in this regard, and has referred to the Sims Report's suggestion that "intention may be inferred from other conduct and unfair labour practices committed by the employer": *Telus Communications*, [2004] CIRBD No 12. For a discussion of section 94(2.1) of the *Canada Labour Code* see Luc Vaillancourt, "Amendments to the Canada Labour Code: Are Replacement Workers an Endangered Species?" (2000) 45 *McGill Law Journal* 757.

For an empirical study of the effect of anti-replacement worker legislation in Canada, see Peter Crampton, Morley Gunderson, & Joseph Tracy, "Impacts of Strike Replacement Bans" (1999) 50 *Labor Law Journal* 173.

8:900 ALTERNATIVES TO STRIKES?

We have already looked at many legal manifestations of the ambivalence of Canadian public policy toward strikes, such as extensive statutory restrictions on the timeliness of job action and court decisions denying *Charter* protection to the right to strike. Especially in the public and parapublic sectors, which we have not dealt with specifically in this book, Canadian legislatures have often gone much further and imposed a wide variety of standing and *ad hoc* statutory restrictions on strikes, sometimes with a view to balancing government budgets or limiting inflation and sometimes to maintain essential services. From the 1960s through the 1980s, such statutory intervention was quite frequently used, leading to what one study called "permanent exceptionalism": see Leo Panitch & David Swartz, *The Assault on Trade Union Freedoms: From Wage Controls to Social Contract* (Toronto: Garamond Press, 1993). It was used less often during the 1990s, when economic circumstances tended to discourage resort to strikes and to cast some doubt on the conventional view that the right to strike increases employee bargaining power.

The apparently declining efficacy of the strike led some governments, including that of Ontario, to bring an end to standing compulsory interest arbitration schemes for Crown employees and to give those employees the right to strike. Until 1993, provincial Crown employees in Ontario had no right to strike, and were covered by interest arbitration. Faced with a very large and growing budget deficit, and believing that arbitration meant higher wages and decreased managerial flexibility, a New Democratic Party government, against the wishes of the Ontario Public Service Employees' Union, passed the *Crown Employees Collective Bargaining Act, 1993*, SO 1993, c 38. That Act ended the system of interest arbitration for most of the public service, replacing it (in section 28) with a right to strike substantially more restricted than the equivalent right under the *Labour Relations Act*. Among the most important of the restrictions on the right to strike is a detailed procedure (sections 30 to 42) with respect to the designation and maintenance of essential services. That procedure includes a requirement that the parties attempt to negotiate agreements for the provision of essential services in the event of a strike. This requirement led to many months of arduous bargaining after the Act was passed, with frequent and often futile intervention by the labour board.

By the end of the 1990s, a revival of employee militancy in health care and in other parts of the public and parapublic sectors had led to the reemergence of *ad hoc* legislation to end or prohibit strikes. The common use of "back to work" legislation and mandatory interest arbitration to limit the right of public sector workers to strike has led to an ongoing tension between Canadian governments and the International Labour Organization, a point to which we will return in Section 8:930.

8:910 Essential Services Legislation

The rapid growth of collective bargaining in the public and parapublic sectors since the mid-1960s has led to more frequent conflict between the right to strike and lock out and the public right to the maintenance of essential services. This conflict has manifested itself in legislation restricting the opportunity to strike in services that are deemed essential. In the private sector too, the essential services issue has had to be confronted in jurisdictions that have banned the use of replacement workers during legal strikes—at present, only Quebec and British Columbia.

Widespread concern exists that the public will suffer undue hardship from stoppages by certain strategically placed groups of workers—most commonly, perhaps, health care workers, but also those who provide other services such as policing, public transit, electricity and water supply, garbage collection, snow clearing, and teaching. There is a countervailing view among other observers, including some who have been involved in such stoppages on both sides, that too wide a range of services are thought to be essential, and that even those which are truly essential can safely be reduced to a much lower level than usual for considerable periods. What about industries of substantial economic importance, where safety is not in issue? Back-to-work legislation has been used frequently on the railways, in the post office, and in such other sectors as the Saskatchewan dairy industry, the Quebec construction industry, and even at Air Canada, a private air carrier in a highly competitive industry. In 2011, the Ontario government passed legislation declaring employees of the Toronto Transit Commission essential and prohibiting their right to strike.

Employer representatives tend to favour removing the question of essential services from the bargaining table and addressing it elsewhere—that is, through direct legislative specification of the types and levels of services that must be maintained in the event of a work stoppage, or through a legislatively mandated adjudicative process. Unions, on the other hand, tend to be suspicious of any mechanism that limits the right of their most strategically placed members to withdraw services, because of the impact such limitations have on employee bargaining power.

There are three major models for dealing with the regulation of labour in essential services in Canada:

1) *The "unfettered strike" model.* In this model, strike action is available to workers in essential services in the same way as it would be available to any other unionized workers under the applicable labour statute; the statute does not single out essential services for a different strike regime. However, as Bernard Adell notes, when workers perceived as "essential" have the unfettered ability to strike, governments in Canada have frequently responded with separate back-to-work legislation, of which several examples are given below (see Bernard Adell, "Regulating Strikes in Essential (and Other) Services after the New Trilogy" (2013) 17 *Canadian Labour & Employment Law Journal* 413).

2) *The "no strike" model.* In this model, labour statutes include provisions that essential services are prohibited from going on strike. They are excluded from the strike ability to which other unionized workers are entitled under labour statutes. In this model, criteria for the definition of "essential services" are provided in the legislation, but governments retain the power to designate specific groups of workers as essential within the confines of those criteria. Labour disputes within essential services are resolved through binding arbitration. Broad versions of this model may breach the *Charter* right to freedom of association, as seen in the *Saskatchewan Federation of Labour* case, discussed in Chapter 12 of this book.

3) *The "designation" or "controlled strike" model.* In this model, certain groups of workers are designated as essential services, and their strike activity is limited by way of agreement between the parties or by a specialized tribunal or commission.

Within these models, there are a variety of legislative approaches in different jurisdictions across Canada, and sometimes even in different sectors in the same jurisdiction, with respect to the determination of essentiality and the manner of regulating strikes and lockouts once a particular service is deemed essential. Some jurisdictions, including Alberta, simply deny the right to strike to large parts of the public and parapublic sectors. Others give employees in those sectors a right to strike similar to that enjoyed by private sector workers, but do not refrain from using *ad hoc* legislation to prohibit or end work stoppages in what are considered to be essential services. Still others, including Quebec and the federal public service, give an adjudicative tribunal the responsibility for regulating such stoppages in accordance with legislatively specified criteria. The study by Adell, Grant, and Ponak, referred to above, outlines and evaluates the different approaches taken across the country (at 13–14 and 195–205). All legislative restrictions on the right to strike are now subject to the Supreme Court of Canada's reasons in *Saskatchewan Federation of Labour*, discussed more fully in Chapter 12.

Since the early 1980s, Quebec has relied on a specialized essential services tribunal called the Conseil des services essentiels, which has a detailed statutory mandate under the provincial *Labour Code* and has developed an extensive body of jurisprudence. The Conseil is generally thought to have been quite successful in ensuring the provision of essential services in what the *Code* (section 111.0.16) calls "public services"—municipal services, transit, electricity, garbage collection, and some others. British Columbia has for quite some time given the task of designating essential services and overseeing their maintenance to its Labour Relations Board, after having experimented with other adjudicative mechanisms. A hallmark of the current procedures in Quebec and British Columbia is that they put the employer and the union themselves at the forefront of the process, by requiring them to try to agree on what services are essential before the administrative tribunal steps in. As well, both provinces place much emphasis on mediation. For a discussion of the operation of the Conseil des services essentiels, see Adell, Grant, and Ponak, referred to above, at 36–40 and 67–106.

The structure and application of the British Columbia essential services provisions (sections 72 and 73 of the *Labour Relations Code*) are outlined in *School District No 54 v Bulkley Valley Teachers' Ass'n* (1993), 19 CLRBR 269 (BCLRB). In that case, the risk that students in their last year of high school would lose their year led the Labour Relations Board to hold that a strike by their teachers would pose "a threat to the health, safety or welfare of the residents of British Columbia" within the meaning of section 72 of the *Code*. After a change of government in 2001, section 72 was amended to allow the government to order the Labour Relations Board to designate as essential any services necessary "to prevent immediate and serious disruption of the provision of educational programs": see section 72(2.1), enacted by SBC 2001, c 33, s 11(b).

The designation of education as an essential service in BC led to a serious clash between the BC teachers' union and the government in 2003. In the fall of that year, the BC government passed Bill 12, which legislatively imposed a collective agreement on the teachers. In response, the teachers engaged in an illegal work stoppage, which led to a cease and desist order from the BC Supreme Court. When the teachers failed to comply with that order, they were fined $500,000 for contempt. See *British Columbia Public School Employers' Association v British Columbia Teachers' Federation*, 2005 BCSC 1490. While the contempt finding was not overturned with regard to the teachers' work stoppage, the government's action to legislatively rescind certain collective bargaining terms and prohibit their inclusion in future bargaining was eventually found to be contrary to the teachers' *Charter* rights and overturned by the Supreme Court of Canada (*British Columbia Teachers' Federation v British Columbia*, 2016 SCC 49, adopting the reasons of the dissent in *British Columbia Teachers' Federation v British Columbia*, 2015 BCCA 184).

8:920 Interest Arbitration

Interest arbitration, sometimes called compulsory arbitration, is designed to replace the strike as the mechanism for resolving bargaining disputes. If the parties cannot agree, work continues and an arbitrator sets the terms that will govern their future relations, in effect writing their collective agreement for them. In contrast, grievance arbitration, which will be examined in Chapter 9, involves the application of an existing agreement, where one party alleges that the other has violated that agreement.

Mediation is often used prior to arbitration, in order to clear away as many issues as possible. In a variant known as "med-arb," the arbitrator first tries to mediate the dispute, then adjudicates those issues that remain unresolved.

Allen Ponak & Loren Falkenberg, "Resolution of Interest Disputes" in Amarjit Sethi, ed, *Collective Bargaining in Canada* (Scarborough, ON: Nelson, 1989) 260 at 272–86 (references omitted)

> The rapid growth of public sector collective bargaining in the late 1960s and throughout the 1970s presented policy makers with a new dilemma. While the right to strike was well entrenched in the private sector, substantial reservations existed about permitting public employees to withdraw their services. The basis for these reservations was essentially twofold: (1) a belief that public sector work stoppages, involving irreplaceable and in some cases essential services, would place an intolerable burden on the public; and (2) a perception that the combination of political and economic pressure generated by public sector strikes would place too much power in the hands of public employee unions.
>
> The dilemma arose in finding substitutes for the right to strike. A number of American states had prohibited public sector work stoppages but had failed to provide mechanisms for the final resolution of impasses. This approach simply resulted in illegal strikes. Most Canadian jurisdictions, on the other hand, opted for some form of compulsory arbitration when the right to strike was removed by statute. By and large, arbitration accomplished the objective of eliminating work stoppages. Illegal strikes have occasionally taken place in the face of arbitration (a well-publicized example is the Montreal police strike in 1969), but such occurrences have constituted rare exceptions. Canadian public employees, albeit with great reluctance in some cases, have accepted the prohibition on strikes where arbitration is available as a substitute.
>
> Unfortunately, compulsory interest arbitration, while alleviating concern about public sector work stoppages, presents a number of problems of its own. Industrial relations systems in virtually all democratic countries place a high premium on permitting labour and management to negotiate their own collective agreements through the give-and-take of the bargaining process. Almost all available evidence suggests that compulsory arbitration systems reduce the likelihood that the parties will in fact be able to reach an agreement at the bargaining table....
>
> Three major reasons have been advanced to explain why compulsory arbitration reduces the likelihood of negotiated settlements. First, interest arbitration generally produces a lower cost of disagreement than does a strike. Put another way, the fear of going to arbitration is usually less than the fear of a work stoppage. Part of the reason parties settle in negotiations under right-to-strike systems relates to the substantial consequences of not settling. Strikes are usually expensive and painful propositions for the worker, the employer, or both. The same is less likely to be true in an arbitration system where the consequences of actually using an arbitrator may not be particularly onerous. In short, the threat of a strike is a powerful inducement to settle; arbitration systems lack such an inducement.

A second factor that is thought to inhibit negotiated settlements under arbitration systems is the fear that concessions made during bargaining may prove harmful if an arbitrated settlement is eventually required. Whether well-founded or not, a widespread perception exists that arbitrators 'split the difference' between the two parties' positions in arriving at their decisions. Accordingly, negotiators are reluctant to make bargaining concessions that might narrow the differences to their side's detriment; thus, there is a tendency to adopt extreme positions and maintain them. The inhibiting impact of arbitration on compromise activity is frequently referred to as the chilling effect.

The third major reason advanced for the reduced incidence of settlement under arbitration systems is that arbitration is habit forming. It is suggested that negotiators become accustomed to rely on arbitration as an easy way out of making difficult decisions and eventually lose the ability to settle in negotiations. This tendency has been referred to as the narcotic effect, with negotiators becoming 'addicted' to the arbitration process. As time passes, fewer and fewer settlements are achieved at the bargaining table as the temptation to rely on the 'quick fix' of an arbitrated agreement becomes irresistible.

USE OF ARBITRATION IN THE CANADIAN PUBLIC SECTOR

[A]rbitration is most likely to be obligatory for fire fighters, police, and civil servants. At the other end of the spectrum, it is not mandated in any jurisdiction for general municipal employees (i.e., inside and outside workers, local transit).

The most commonly used form of interest arbitration in Canada is the traditional or conventional form of arbitration. Under conventional arbitration procedures, the arbitration board is free, after receiving submissions from the union and the employer, to fashion its solution to the issues in dispute. The board is permitted to accept the union or the employer position, it can split the difference down the middle, or it can derive its own compromise position on the issues. Subject to very broad constraints of reasonableness, the arbitration board can issue the award it feels is most appropriate under the circumstances and that award becomes the new collective agreement.

Although rarely used in Canada, many jurisdictions in the United States use a form of arbitration called final offer selection (FOS). Final offer selection differs from conventional arbitration in that the arbitrator is required to choose the position submitted by management or by the union, without alteration. In other words, the arbitration board is not free to fashion its own solution by adopting a middle position; it is forced to choose one side's proposal or the other's. Depending on the jurisdiction, a total package format or more flexible issue-by-issue format is used. . . .

A third type of arbitration system, choice of procedures (COP) was pioneered in the 1967 Public Service Staff Relations Act, which granted collective bargaining rights to federal civil servants. It continues to be used in the federal sector as well as British Columbia, Saskatchewan, and some American states. Under a choice-of-procedures system, one of the parties (in Canada, the union) can specify at some point prior to or during negotiations whether an impasse will be resolved through a work stoppage or arbitration. . . . Experience has shown that arbitration is chosen much more frequently than the strike. . . .

SETTLEMENT RATE

There is little disagreement that arbitration systems reduce the incidence of negotiated settlements compared to strike-based systems. The most meaningful comparisons in this regard are among public sector jurisdictions....

The major variable of interest ... is settlement rate, defined as the proportion of negotiations that are settled by the parties without resort to the final mechanism of dispute resolution. Under arbitration systems, this would be the proportion of negotiations in which no arbitration award was issued; under right-to-strike systems, settlement rate means the percentage of negotiations where settlement was achieved without a work stoppage....

The broadest data set [for public sector systems with the right to strike] is for the province of Ontario and covers over 600 negotiations during a four-year period [1979–82] for teachers, hydro-electric utility workers, and municipal employees (including mass transit). The Ontario data show a settlement rate of 93 percent, a figure that appears to be a reasonable median rate for public sector strike-based systems....

Under conventional arbitration, the ability of labour and management to settle without the help of an arbitrator ranges between 65 and 82 percent. The average settlement rate would appear to be approximately 75 percent. The settlement rate goes up to the 85-percent range under final-offer selection, but still falls short of settlement rates achieved under strike-based systems.

The data, therefore, unequivocally supports the proposition that arbitration systems reduce the likelihood of negotiated settlements compared to strike-based dispute procedures. The gap between the two systems is approximately 18 percent under conventional arbitration and eight percent under final-offer selection procedures.

The data cannot answer the policy question, however, of whether the settlement rate difference between strike and arbitration systems is acceptable or not.... After all, even under the least productive arbitration systems, negotiators still manage to settle without arbitration two-thirds of the time. The fact that one out of three negotiations requires an arbitrator's intervention may well be a price that has to be paid for the overall public good. Such tradeoffs might be less palatable, however, in situations where settlement rates are much lower or where the groups involved are arguably less essential.

THE CHILLING AND NARCOTIC EFFECTS

The theoretical underpinnings of the perceived inadequacies of interest arbitration rest on two related concepts, the chilling and narcotic effects.... Chilling is assumed to occur when one or both parties are unwilling to compromise during negotiations in anticipation of an arbitrated settlement; the narcotic effect is an increasing dependence of the parties on arbitration, resulting in a loss of ability to negotiate.

[The authors then discuss several empirical studies on the chilling effect and narcotic effect, and observe that the findings of those studies were generally inconclusive.]

The most common method of assessing the narcotic effect is the proportion of units going to arbitration over time. It is assumed that if arbitration is addictive, more and more units will resort to it with each round of negotiations....

In summary, the empirical research suggests that: (1) a chilling effect may occur with conventional arbitration but is less likely with final offer selection; and (2) while some parties may become dependent on arbitration (narcotic effect), the majority does not repeatedly use the process. These conclusions notwithstanding, there remains considerable confusion among studies in terms of inferences drawn with much of the confusion relating to a lack of clarity over appropriate measures.

[From *Collective Bargaining in Canada*, 1st ed by AS Sethi. © 1989. Reprinted with permission of Thomson Learning: www.thomsonrights.com]

* * * * *

The authors of the following study examined collective bargaining in Ontario from 1984 to 1993, comparing bargaining outcomes where the right to strike and lockout existed with those where compulsory interest arbitration was the final dispute resolution method.

Robert Hebdon & Maurice Mazerolle, "Regulating Conflict in Public Sector Labour Relations: The Ontario Experience (1984–1993)" (2003) 58(4) *Relations Industrielles/Industrial Relations* **667**

This comprehensive data set has allowed researchers to look at the dispute resolution patterns of all bargaining units in the province of Ontario over a 10-year period. What have we learned from this? A central finding is that bargaining units covered by legislation requiring compulsory interest arbitration arrive at impasse 8.7 to 21.7 percent more often than do bargaining units in the right to strike sectors. Even after controlling for legislative jurisdiction, union, bargaining unit size, occupation, agreement length, time trend, and part-time status, strong evidence was found that compulsory arbitration has a chilling effect on the bargaining process. This failure to arrive at a negotiated settlement is particularly acute in the health care sector, especially among hospitals.

Our results call into question the use of interest arbitration in a central bargaining context. The centralized structure appeared to exacerbate the negative impact of the chilling effect. On the one hand, the 1984–93 period under study in this paper is atypical of public sector bargaining given the financial stresses and restructuring policy imperatives of governments of all political stripes. One could argue, therefore, that the results are not readily applicable to other North American jurisdictions. On the other hand, an important test of a system of dispute resolution is its ability to perform effectively under stress. The analysis of this paper suggests that conventional interest arbitration during this period in Ontario, when put to the test, failed to produce a satisfactory rate of freely agreed settlements. We found evidence that arbitration exerted a powerful influence over union bargaining behaviour by increasing rates of impasse. It was also significant that this effect was greater the more the union operates in the arbitration sector as a proportion of total bargaining activity. This finding is supportive of a dependency effect whereby a union's high usage of arbitration fosters an inability to freely negotiate settlements.

[Reproduced with permission.]

Chapter 9: The Collective Agreement and Grievance Arbitration

9:100   INTRODUCTION

If the collective bargaining process (discussed in Chapters 7 and 8) brings a settlement, the terms will be embodied in a collective agreement (sometimes informally called a "contract") between the union and the employer. This chapter deals with the enforcement of such agreements, first the common law history and then under modern labour relations legislation.

Disputes over the interpretation and application of collective agreements are commonplace. An employee may claim that the agreement was violated when he was disciplined, rejected for promotion, laid off, denied benefits, or subjected to some other unwelcome treatment. A union may challenge a management practice affecting the workforce at large, or affecting the union in its role as bargaining agent. Or, less commonly, an employer may claim that the union has not met its obligations under the collective agreement.

Modern Canadian labour relations legislation does not permit a contest of economic power over these disputes. Strikes and lockouts are banned during the term of a collective agreement, and every such agreement must provide a dispute settlement process to resolve disputes over whether the agreement has been complied with. Some statutes specify that this process must take the form of grievance arbitration. Until recently, even in jurisdictions where arbitration was not specifically mandated, it was used almost universally because no practical alternative had been found. This is changing now with the introduction of "or otherwise" language in final settlement provisions, such as section 42 of the Nova Scotia *Trade Union Act* and section 48 of the Ontario *Labour Relations Act*, and with developing practices under collective agreements leading to such alternatives as mediation, mediation-arbitration (med-arb), and restorative conferencing.

Collective agreements normally provide for an informal grievance procedure through which the parties attempt to resolve their disputes without resorting to an external, third party, expedited arbitration process. If a grievance is not resolved in that way, either party may invoke arbitration as a form of third-party adjudication. Arbitrators make legally binding rulings based upon evidence and argument presented by the parties in an adversarial hearing. The parties to a dispute normally choose the person who will act as arbitrator. Tripartite boards of arbitration (consisting of a union and employer nominee and an impartial chairperson) were widely used at one time, but single arbitrators are now much more common in most jurisdictions.

Mandatory grievance arbitration is often said to be the *quid pro quo* for the ban on mid-contract work stoppages, in the sense that a union is denied the right to strike as a means of enforcing the collective agreement but gains access to arbitration in exchange. However, as we will see, this idea of a *quid pro quo* overlooks the fact that if a matter in issue is not addressed by the collective agreement, neither arbitration nor a strike or lockout is legally available to resolve it. Although, in some instances, parties may resort to labour relations boards to resolve some mid-contract issues, such as disputes over configuration of bargaining units.

Lawyers often tend to see grievance arbitration as serving only an adjudicative function, but like the grievance procedure which precedes it, it performs other functions as well. Some of the purposes served by the grievance process (including arbitration) were described by Neil Chamberlain in *The Labor Sector* (New York: McGraw Hill, 1965) at 247:

> The grievance procedure is ... a many splendored thing. It is in part the judicial process of applying terms of the agreement to particular situations, as it is most frequently pictured. It is also the mechanism through which the first-line representatives of union and management engage in a continuing contest over the exercise of authority in the shop.... The grievance process is also a device which strategic groups within the union can use to engage in factional bargaining on their own behalf, sometimes challenging the authority of the union in the doing but more often able to clothe their purpose in "grievances" which have at least the air of legitimacy about them. And finally, the grievance process, in the hands of sophisticated practitioners, can be made an instrument for more effective administration within the shop.

The grievance arbitration process can also play an important role in the retention of employees. Allowing employees to air their complaints before an arbitrator might deter them from leaving. In *What Do Unions Do?* (New York: Basic Books, 1984) Richard Freeman and James Medoff found that turnover was lower in American workplaces with a union than in those without. They attributed the difference to the "collective voice" offered by unions—a voice that serves as a substitute for employee "exit."

Throughout this chapter, the reader should keep in mind the distinction between "grievance" or "rights" arbitration on the one hand, and "interest" arbitration on the other. This chapter addresses issues surrounding the former, while Chapter 8 addressed interest arbitration. This distinction is particularly important when reading the excerpts from Weiler and Beatty in Section 9:210 below.

9:110 The Common Law View of Collective Agreements

Before the advent of modern labour relations legislation in the 1940s, collective agreements were generally unenforceable at law. A system of binding arbitration had not yet developed, and Canadian courts were unwilling to entertain civil actions based on collective agreements.

Three major common law obstacles stood in the way of the enforcement of collective agreements by civil action—obstacles related to the fact the contractual parties to the collective agreement are the union and the employer, not the individual employees. First, as we saw in the preceding chapter, trade unions were not considered to have the legal capacity to make binding contracts or to sue or be sued in their own name. Because they sought to affect the operation of the labour market, they were thought to operate in illegal restraint of trade. Because they were unincorporated associations, they were treated as being without legal status. Second, the courts doubted that employers and unions intended their collective agreements to be legally binding, rather than mere informal understandings. Third, traditional rules of privity of contract were held to prevent individual employees from enforcing collective agreements to which they were not themselves parties.

Young v Canadian Northern Railway, [1931] 1 DLR 645 at 649–50 (PC)

[A collective agreement, called Wage Agreement 4, was in force between the Railway Association of Canada, representing employers, and Division 4 of the Railway Employees' Department of the American Federation of Labor, which negotiated on behalf of railway employees. The plaintiff was not a member of Division 4. The defendant railway hired him as a machinist, telling him that he would receive the going rate for machinists but not giving him a written employment contract. In addition to rules on hours and wages, Wage Agreement 4 provided that in the event of a workforce reduction, junior employees would be laid off first, in accordance with a seniority rule.

Young was laid off out of order of seniority. He sued for damages for wrongful dismissal, lost in the Manitoba courts, and appealed to the Judicial Committee of the Privy Council. At the time, no Canadian jurisdiction had labour relations legislation of the sort now in force across the country.]

LORD RUSSELL: . . . The fact that the railway company applied [Wage Agreement 4] to the appellant, is equally consistent with the view that it did so, not because it was bound contractually to apply it to him, but because as a matter of policy it deemed it expedient to apply it to all. If the conduct of the railway company in applying the provisions of the agreement to the appellant could only be explained by the existence of a contractual obligation to the appellant so to do, it would be not only permissible, but necessary to hold that the existence of the contractual obligation had been established. In the circumstances, however, of the present case, their Lordships find themselves unable so to decide. But the matter does not quite rest there. When Wage Agreement 4 is examined, it does not appear to their Lordships to be a document adapted for conversion into or incorporation with a service agreement, so as to entitle master and servant to enforce inter se the terms thereof. It consists of some 188 "rules," which the railway companies contract with Division 4 to observe. It appears to their Lordships to be intended merely to operate as an agreement between a body of employers and a labour organization by which the employers undertake that as regards their workmen, certain rules beneficial to the workmen shall be observed. By itself it constitutes no contract between any individual employee and the company which employs him. If an employer refused to observe the rules, the effective sequel would be, not an action by any employee, not even an action by Division 4 against the employer for specific performance or damages, but the calling of a strike until the grievance was remedied. If, in the present case, the appellant has suffered any injustice at the hands of the railway company, it was in the power of Division 4 to obtain justice for him had they chosen so to do. It is suggested that Division 4 chose not so to do, because the appellant was a member of a rival organization. Assuming the suggestion to be well founded, the moral thereby pointed would appear to be that in the case of an "open" shop, the protection which an agreement such as Wage Agreement 4 affords to a workman who is not a member of the contracting labour organization, is to be measured by the willingness of that body to enforce it on his behalf.... In the result their Lordships are of the opinion that this appeal should fail and be dismissed with costs, as they have already humbly advised His Majesty.

* * * * *

The courts' refusal to enforce collective agreements prompted legislative reform. In 1943, Ontario enacted the *Collective Bargaining Act*, SO 1943, c 4, creating a new branch of the Supreme Court of Ontario, called the Ontario Labour Court, with the power to render binding interpretations of collective agreements. However, resorting to the Ontario Labour Court was not compulsory.

In 1944, the federal government, using its wartime emergency powers to override provincial legislative jurisdiction in labour relations, promulgated the *Wartime Labour Relations Regulation*, PC 1003. Although PC 1003 basically adopted the *Wagner Act* model for the regulation of collective bargaining which had been adopted in the United States in 1935, its content differed in some important ways from that of the *Wagner Act*. One of those differences, which we have looked at in previous chapters, was the deferral of the right to strike during the negotiation of a collective agreement until the statutory conciliation process had been exhausted. Two other differences, more pertinent to the enforcement of collective agreements, were these: unlike the *Wagner Act*, PC 1003 imposed an outright statutory ban on the use of strikes or lockouts while a collective agreement was in force; and, again unlike the *Wagner Act*, it required that every collective agreement provide for the final and binding resolution, generally through a process of arbitration, of any disputes over the interpretation or application of the agreement.

These requirements have since become a standard feature of collective bargaining legislation across Canada. The fact that Canadian law takes a more restrictive approach than American law to strikes and lockouts, both during the negotiation of the collective agreement and during the agreement's lifetime, may be due in part to the fact that the Canadian version of Wagnerism was originally embodied in an emergency powers regulation designed to facilitate wartime production. However, the Supreme Court of Canada has recently made it clear that no single model of collective bargaining is guaranteed protection under section 2(d) of the *Canadian Charter of Rights and Freedoms*. In *Mounted Police Association of Ontario v Canada (Attorney General)*, 2015 SCC 1, the Court stated that a model of bargaining will receive constitutional protection so long as it respects the theoretical underpinnings of "choice" and "independence" and allows for the meaningful pursuit of collective bargaining (at paras 92–104). In short, section 2(d) guarantees individuals a right to "a process rather than an outcome or access to a particular model of labour relations" (at para 67). Were these views to encourage "minority unionism," there could be marked repercussions for the role of standard arbitration: see Roy J Adams, "Bringing Canada's *Wagner Act* Regime into Compliance with International Human Rights Law and the *Charter*" (2016) 19 *Canadian Labour & Employment Law Journal* 365–98.

9:120 Grievance Arbitration as a Distinctive Form of Adjudication

Proponents of grievance arbitration contend that it offers a very different form of adjudication than the courts do. Arbitrators are labour law or industrial relations specialists usually selected by the parties, whereas judges are appointed by the state and are usually legal generalists. The parties to a collective agreement are free not only to choose their arbitrator but also to design an arbitration process to meet their particular needs. This form of self-government is one of the hallmarks of Canadian collective bargaining law, as will be seen below in such cases as *Nor-Man Regional Health Authority Inc v Manitoba Association of Health Care Professionals*, 2011 SCC 59, where the Supreme Court vastly expanded arbitrators' remedial jurisdiction and ability to apply common law principles (Section 9:320).

As well as being labour law specialists, most arbitrators are lawyers trained in the common law. Arbitration awards are subject to review by judges who are steeped in the common law. As you work through this chapter, consider whether arbitral jurisprudence is shaped mainly by the labour relations environment or by the common law heritage of individual employment law. Can it be said that labour arbitration is the key element in what might be called the relative autonomy of labour law within the Canadian legal system? See Bruce P Archibald, "The Significance of the Systemic Relative Autonomy of Labour Law" (2017) 40 *Dalhousie Law Journal* 1.

9:200 THE ROLE OF GRIEVANCE ARBITRATION IN OUR COLLECTIVE BARGAINING REGIME—A STORY OF TRANSFORMATION

9:210 Different Visions of the Role of Arbitration

The following excerpts set out the contrasting views of two Canadian labour law academics on the role that arbitrators should play in helping the parties resolve mid-contract disputes. When reading them, keep in mind the important distinction between rights arbitration and interest arbitration.

Paul Weiler, "The Role of the Labour Arbitrator: Alternative Versions" (1969) 19 *University of Toronto Law Journal* **16**

> Two themes run through most discussions of the nature of the arbitrator's role. On the one hand, he is expected to act as a lawyer-judge, bringing 'legalist' tools to bear on the interpretation of the collective agreement, his only charter for action. On the other hand, he is alleged to have certain distinctive qualities, of expertise and experience, which legitimate actions that are based on peculiar 'nonlegal' criteria, in particular the maintenance of a peaceful, uninterrupted, and fair industrial enterprise.
>
> The first theory of the arbitrator as judge, contains within itself an essential ambiguity concerning the appropriate mode of judicial action. Some arbitrators feel that they must confine themselves to decisions which are based only on an explicit and specific provision in the collective agreement. In attributing a meaning to such a provision they restrict their assessment of the parties' will to the bare surface of the arrangement, the 'literal' or dictionary meaning of the words. Other arbitrators may feel that it is even more appropriate to delve beneath the surface of the text of a contract clause and assign a meaning which is most compatible with the purpose of the parties in selecting this text. When such a mutually agreed-to purpose is divined, these arbitrators may also feel it appropriate to develop and elaborate the principles it implies and then apply these principles to the instant case before them.

The second theory of the arbitrator's role, the arbitrator as 'labour relations physician,' holds that it is sometimes legitimate for an arbitrator to extend or limit what can fairly be said to be the meaning of an agreement (whether derived purposively or literally), in the light of certain overriding labour relations goals. This theory also contains within itself an essential ambiguity. Some advocate the arbitrator acting as a 'mediator,' attempting to get specific, individualized, consensual accords between the parties and thus enhancing the process of free, collective bargaining even during the administration of the agreement. Others argue that arbitrators must become aware of their necessary position as an 'industrial policy maker' and attempt intelligently to lay down authoritative, general policies, in the interests of the public as well as the immediate parties.

Each of these different theories, when worked out in detail in the literature, is sufficiently complex and sophisticated that it takes account of, and tends to shade into, each of the others. However, I am going to formulate abstract models in order to illustrate the institutional logic of each of the distinctive value judgments which lie at the roots of the different theories.... Each assumes that there is an intrinsic, reciprocal relationship between the job we ask arbitration to perform, the design of the institution within which arbitrators operate, and the manner in which we expect them to reach their decisions.

LABOUR ARBITRATION AND INDUSTRIAL CHANGE

Before going on to explicate each of these models in greater detail, I will briefly describe the substantive problem in connection with which I first worked them out. This problem concerns the legal consequences of management responses to changing economic, technological, and social conditions during the term of a collective agreement. Because of the substantial gains in security and stability in a collective bargaining relationship, there is a noticeable impetus in the direction of long term agreements. On the other hand, it is increasingly recognized that it is impossible to foresee in advance all the labour relations problems inherent in changing industrial conditions. Moreover it is believed undesirable to delay agreement in order to pin down, by specific language, the contractual consequences of changes foreseen from afar, and only in the abstract. For these reasons, the precise impact of the agreement in regard to industrial change must be ambiguous.

Management is required to take the initiative in ordering relations within the plant to best take account of the new demands posed by altered circumstances. This initiative can take various forms. Work may be subcontracted either within or without the plant or it may be transferred outside the bargaining unit or to a plant not covered by the agreement. Management may assign work previously performed by one employee to a new or different job classification or it may vary, or add to, the work assigned to the individual employee. It may close down unprofitable parts of the company's operation (or even the whole of its operations), or it may relocate the plant from an unprofitable site. Finally it may change work rules, or working conditions (e.g., by instituting a compulsory retirement age) which may not affect existing jobs as much as it does the overall amenities incident to the previous plant operation.

It is obvious that such unilateral initiative will affect adversely the interests of employees and unions who have built up certain expectations and attitudes concerning the status quo. In Ontario, by reason of the statutory policy requiring a no-strike clause in every agreement, the union is denied the remedy of self-help. As a consequence, grievances concerning these harmful effects of management-instituted changes are processed through to the arbitrator. The latter is faced with a problem which he must resolve without the aid of any concrete intention or specific language of the parties directed to its solution. This particular issue has formed the battleground over which the dispute about the appropriate role of the arbitrator has been largely conducted.

THE ARBITRATOR AS MEDIATOR

One of the models we can entitle 'the arbitrator as mediator.' This model conceives of arbitration as being at the end of a continuous spectrum, which extends backward through the mutual adjustment of grievances to the original negotiation of the terms of a collective agreement. The paradigm case for this model involved a complex industrial establishment, with many divergent, conflicting centres of interest, and requiring continual, intelligent adjustment of problems in the light of previously settled policies. Collective bargaining is the logical application of a free market economy to the problem of the terms and conditions of employment, when the latter is informed by a concern for industrial democracy. In other words, it allows the employees to wield sufficient power to participate in the determination of their conditions of employment, and makes the touchstone for the latter their mutual acceptability to the various interests inherent in the enterprise, and not their conformity to some governmental policy about the 'public interest.' Hence arbitration must first be perceived as an essential part of industrial (or economic) self-government.

The next important facet of the model is the recognition that collective bargaining is sharply distinguished from other forms of contract negotiation (and administration), because the parties at interest are inextricably wedded together in a permanent relationship.... [A]ny attempt to subject the ongoing enterprise to detailed prescriptions is not only impossible (because of the human incapacity to anticipate all problems for as far in the future as the normal collective agreement extends), but also undesirable (first, because of the unlikelihood of intelligent solutions to these problems in the abstract, and, second, because the necessity of arriving at final agreement requires statement in general and rather ambiguous principle, as opposed to specific detail)....

Into this situation is inserted the arbitrator, who is expected to settle those disputes, and solve those problems, left unresolved by mutual grievance adjustment ... the legalistic, adjudicative resolution of the dispute is unsuited for parties who must live together with each other following the decision, who will be affected in later negotiating situations by positions taken early in an adversary posture, and who will have to take the consequences of 'victories' which are not wisely addressed to the substantive problems.

Hence this model envisages the arbitrator as, ideally, performing the function of mediation. He can utilize private sources of information to get at the 'real' facts which define the labour relations substance of the grievance (rather than the 'artificial' case which filters through in the adversary context where the 'cards are not on the table'), and thus ensure that his decision does not impinge in a harmful way on the industrial relationship within which it becomes a precedent. The basic criterion for all decisions should be their 'mutual acceptability,' including especially the willing acquiescence by any 'losing party.' Of course the best evidence of such acceptability will be the actual agreement by the parties to the decision. The arbitrator should utilize all available resources to achieve this agreement, or at least to tailor the eventual decision in a way which preserves the essential interests of the losing party.

THE ARBITRATOR AS INDUSTRIAL POLICY-MAKER

[...]

For functional reasons an ever-growing gap has developed between ownership in the company or membership in the union and effective control of the decisions which are made on behalf of the institution. It is becoming more and more evident that it is fictional to speak of these decisions being 'private' only, with their effects confined only to those who participate immediately.

Since control by the market or by the affected constituencies is no longer possible, it becomes the function of legal and governmental policy to exert some control. One available representative of the public is the arbitrator. This is particularly true in jurisdictions where the parties have no untrammelled veto on the choice of an arbitrator (for instance, where they apply to a minister of labour who makes the appointment, rather than supplying panels of names). In Canada and in the United States the legal and social conditions no longer permit the arbitrator to believe he can fulfil his responsibilities by ensuring that his decisions are 'mutually acceptable' to each of the immediate parties. He has larger responsibilities to the 'public interest' of the society of which collective bargaining is an integral part. Out of this changing environment has emerged another model of the arbitration process, that of the 'arbitrator as industrial policymaker.'

This theory makes much the same assumptions about the necessarily ambiguous and 'open' quality of many of the provisions of the collective agreement, insofar as they apply to the types of problems raised in arbitration, if, as the arbitrator attempts to solve these problems, he cannot meaningfully base his decisions on principles that can be distilled from any actual, mutual agreement of the parties. Because of the legal and social developments described above, arbitrators have been delegated the power to make authoritative judgments, allocating values among the many different participants within the industrial community....

[T]he mode of decisionmaking which the arbitrator adopts must reflect the position he occupies. He is no longer justified in using 'conceptual' reasoning, deriving his conclusion from legal principles found within the agreement, the statutory or common law of the jurisdiction, or from a body of accepted, reported, arbitration precedents. The arbitrator should base his decisions on their functional relationship to what he believes to be the appropriate goals of the industrial society in whose government he is participating. Such goals include not only the maintenance of the productivity of the industrial enterprise, and the viability of collective bargaining as the technique for establishing working conditions, but also the commitments of the wider political community to the values of due process.

Although the need for general rules applicable to more than the instant case is also a concern for the arbitrator in some cases, it must often take second place to the latter's function as a flexible resolver of disputes.... The role of the arbitrator is peculiarly 'nonlegal,' and, as in early equity, his 'lay' judgment is sought 'to focus on a specific dispute and to reflect the contemporary conscience of the community in its resolution, with both utility and integrity.'

The distinctive value in this model is its perception of the fact that the arbitrator himself really decides those issues which are not reached by any meaning that can be honestly attributed to the agreement.... The 'policymaker' model lays bare the legal and social power attached to the office of the arbitrator, and the responsibilities to the wider public interest that this necessarily involves....

Yet I do not believe that those who have advocated this legal theory have fully appreciated the institutional significance of the fact that the imposition of implied restrictions on subcontracting, for instance, represents an authoritative value judgment by the arbitrator, and that his choice of the appropriate term in the agreement be adequately responsive not only to the private interests of the parties represented before him, but also the private interests of the subcontractor and his employees, and the public interest in a productive economy with fair conditions of employment....

THE ARBITRATOR AS ADJUDICATOR

Unlike the first two theories of the arbitrator's role, the adjudicative model rests its case largely on the design of the institution within which labour arbitration is carried on. It holds that the nature of the substantive policies which arbitrators should strive to achieve are and should be limited by the structural means within which they operate. Moreover, the maintenance of enduring institutions such as labour arbitration, and the continuance of wide acceptability for its decisions, is itself a sufficient reason for self-restraint, by participants in the institution in the pursuit of substantive goals such as job security. In other words, the fact that an institution such as arbitration is presented with an opportunity to relieve against more or less apparent industrial ills, even when there is no likelihood of short-run relief elsewhere, may not justify action that is inconsistent with established expectations about the proper limits of arbitral reasoning and decisionmaking. In the long run, the most important social value in industrial relations is the continued existence of procedures and institutions which shape and control the struggle carried on within them.

The distinctive role of adjudication is based on the assumption that arbitration is similar to the judicial process....

What are the reasons that purportedly justify the use of labour arbitration in its adjudicative form? Four are usually suggested: (1) inexpensiveness; (2) speed; (3) informality; and (4) arbitral expertise....

To summarize the model very briefly, it conceives of the arbitrator as an adjudicator of specific, concrete disputes, who disposes of the problem by elaborating and applying a legal regime, established by the collective agreement, to facts which he finds on the basis of evidence and argument presented to him in an adversary process. Hence, the arbitration process mirrors the division of functions conventionally adhered to in political life. There, a legislative body establishes the rules or principles which are to govern the private conduct of those subject to its enactments. Then, an adjudicative body settles disputes arising out of this private conduct, by evaluating the latter in the light of these established rules and principles. The key elements defining the adjudicative model are

(1) settlement of disputes, (2) adversary process, and (3) an established system of standards which are utilized in the process to dispose of the disputes....

This model, then, envisages the collective agreement as a more or less successful attempt to institute a governing legal system in the plant. The parties to the agreement are required to orient their own activity and relationships in the light of the standards established by the agreement. This does not mean that the parties are not entitled to change the rules as they go along, motivated by a sense of the need for accommodation of immediate goals in the light of long-range interests. However, the collective agreement furnishes the standards for evaluating their conduct as 'right' or 'wrong,' 'legal' or 'illegal.' ...

An adversary process of adjudication (by contrast with an umpire or inquisitorial system) entails a relatively passive role by the arbitrator who is expected to decide the case on the basis of evidence adduced, and reasoned arguments made, by the parties themselves. It is precisely because this is how the institutional structure is designed that it is illegitimate (within the confines of this model) to distinguish between the 'artificial' facts of the case, as prepared and presented by the parties, and the 'real' facts learned by the arbitrator through his resources outside the record (perhaps when his nominees 'put their cards on the table')....

Most important of all, it should be obvious why 'arbitration as adjudication' requires the existence of standards for decision, standards which are the objects of a consensus of all the participants in the process. This is due to the fact that the preparation and presentation of the case for decision is achieved by parties working separately from each other and from the person or group which is to decide the case. In order to single out and abstract from an undifferentiated concrete situation those facets which appear to be relevant to this resolution of the dispute, and argue for or against their use as reasons for a particular decision, there must be standards available which categorize certain types [of] situation as requiring certain legal results. For instance, suppose there is a promotion in a plant available, and two people want it, and the union supports one, and the company another. There must be some standards telling everybody which facets of the whole life history and present status of each are relevant for selection between them (i.e., training, or time with the company are usually relevant; union status or marital relationship to the supervisors are usually not relevant). Furthermore, the parties, at the time they prepare the case and while they present it, must have some awareness of the standards defining the arbiter's criteria for decision, in order that this enhance the quality of the results, and their sense of meaningfully participating in the process. The whole institution becomes a charade, absent such a consensus concerning standards for decision. Since the purpose of adjudication is to maintain the legal system set up by the agreement, by settling the disputes which occur in its administration, the standards to be used are those established by the agreement.

We can summarize the thesis of the ... [arbitrator as adjudicator] model as follows: the whole institutional structure of arbitration, its incidence, access to it, mode of participation in it, the bases for decision, the nature of the relief available in it, are all defined by and flow naturally from its function, which is to dispose of private disputes arising out of primary conduct by granting relief to parties on the basis of an evaluation of this conduct in the light of the 'legal' standards established by this agreement.

THE ARBITRATOR'S ROLE IN THE 'OPEN' OR 'UNWRITTEN' AREA OF THE AGREEMENT

[A]n arbitral decision is unacceptable as a mere 'fiat' of the arbitrator and finds its authoritative force or legitimacy in the reasoned opinion which justifies it. This tendency is based on real considerations of the function and makeup of arbitration which, as we have seen, presuppose 'objective' premises and standards as the starting point for arbitral argument. However, the premises relied on in the subcontracting and other analogous areas just do not have the mutually intended and established content necessary for those conclusions (limitation on unilateral change) to be derived from them. Nor is the arbitrator warranted in reasoning in accordance with what he believes to be most consistent with legislative policies and standards, to remake the parties' contract for them. The legislative presumption is that freedom of contract, not compulsory "interest dispute" arbitration, is the rule. Hence, the conclusion of the ... [arbitrator as adjudicator] model of the arbitral process, which I accept, is that these decisions are inconsistent with a proper conception of the arbitrator's role, and that any short-run substantive gains (which themselves are quite debatable) do not justify such misuse of grievance arbitration (with possible harmful consequences for the "acceptability" of the latter).

AN INSTITUTIONAL ANALYSIS OF ARBITRAL POLICY-MAKING

[I]n deciding whether a limited 'policymaking' role is suitable for arbitration, there are several dimensions along which the existing institution may be assessed: (1) accountability and legitimacy; (2) rationality and adequacy, and (3) effectiveness. At present, it seems safe to say that the institution is designed with the primary role of adjudication in mind. The issue is whether the existing structure is compatible, at certain key points, with the adoption of an overt policymaking role in this field of industrial change....

In the case of the ad hoc arbitration system, the arbitrator holds office completely at the pleasure of each of the parties....

Hence, subject to the limitation of the residual power of the minister of labour, the need for accountability in labour policymaking is substantially satisfied. What is not so apparent is the capacity of the arbitrator, acting within the framework of labour arbitration, to engage in intelligent development of a common law of the administration of the agreement. The vast majority of arbitration cases in Ontario are decided by men whose backgrounds are either in the judiciary, in law teaching, or on the labour relations board. All these men have either legal training or essentially legal experience. They are in a position to specialize in the labour relations field, and to become knowledgeable and surefooted in dealing with the typical problems posed in labour arbitration. However, as far as industrial relations as a whole is concerned, their interest is necessarily secondary, and their experience is essentially as an outsider. No one can seriously contend that, unaided, they are equipped to establish new, general policies adequately resolving the competing interests in job security and industrial change.

Is the institution of labour arbitration designed to furnish this aid? The typical hearing is conducted by lawyers on either side, or by labour relations consultants and/or international union representatives, or by personnel managers and/or union local business agents. Although the industrial background to a specific dispute may be thrashed out by cooperative discussion at the beginning of the meeting, the record for the decision is prepared through the examination of witnesses. Again I believe it a fair statement that the personnel who are presently available and involved in Ontario labour arbitration are unequipped to establish with any degree of probability the disputed policy facts which must underlie a new common law of labour arbitration.

Since, as we have already seen, the arbitrator does not have the expertise necessary to justify his taking 'official notice' of such controverted facts, he must rely on other resources. Yet he does not have the facilities or staff which are available to legislatures or administrative agencies, enabling him to make factual studies, evaluate proposals with the aid of experts, suggest legislative hypotheses in order to get the reaction of all interested parties, and then formulate a final compromise which takes adequate account of what has been learned. Because labour arbitration has been designed as adjudication, the arbitrator is essentially passive and dependent on the efforts of the parties to prepare a record and argument for him. Because they invited him in only when a dispute arises, his policymaking activity can only be sporadic and at random. Thus he does not have the opportunity to test and amend his policies and to avail himself of information feedback for this purpose....

Hence I conclude that, even on pragmatic grounds, there is no justification for the arbitrator stepping outside his appropriate adjudicative role and donning the cloak of industrial policymaker....

AN ALTERNATIVE VEHICLE: COLLECTIVE BARGAINING

I have argued that the type of limitations imposed by arbitrators on management initiatives are often a misconceived resolution of the conflicting interests involved.... Arbitration, because of its institutional and functional character, is suited for problems whose resolution can be achieved by the elaboration and application of established standards. Mutually accepted standards which could afford a sufficient basis for a reasoned solution to this problem simply do not exist in the conventional case of unilateral changes in working conditions. Here there is a framework of agreed-to principles and purposes from which we can reason to a more or less probable and plausible conclusion. However, in the job security situation, we leave this penumbral area of the agreement and embark on what are, essentially, the uncharted waters of the unwritten area of the relationship. Not only is there no consensus between union and management as a basis for a rational decision, but the arbitrator necessarily has a distorted perspective from whence it is difficult to perceive the claims of third parties and the general public.

I hope that my attempted justification of these conclusions has not been misinterpreted as a brief for the present legal regime. The existing institutional arrangements are radically deficient because they do not allow the interests of union and employees a fair access to the decisionmaking process. They constitute a disincentive to the use of the technique of free collective bargaining, which, after all, is the statutory policy for establishing working conditions. Moreover, because collective bargaining has given way almost completely to the unilateral prerogative of management, the substantive policies that have become established over a large portion of the economy are totally inadequate.

What is needed is a set of arrangements which allows the law in arbitration to be neutral as between the claims of union or management in this area. At present, the existence of the statutory, absolute, no-strike clause imposes a limitation on the employees' power to respond to employer initiatives and this furnishes a powerful attraction to arbitrators to imply a similar limitation on management's power to take these initiatives. We want a device which will allow arbitrators to declare, in a meaningful fashion, that, although employer conduct is not legally prohibited, neither is it legally permitted....

The logical solution to these problems is relatively simple, in principle, although there are many difficult questions of detail which must be settled. The duty to bargain must be held to continue during the terms of a collective agreement in a meaningful fashion. In this way, it will be made clear to both parties that the union has no right under the agreement to block employer initiatives but, at the same time, that the employer has no legal permission under the agreement to change working conditions. The terms under which changes are to be made are yet to be settled by negotiation. In order to facilitate collective bargaining the employer should be required to give notice of his intention to make changes affecting collective bargaining and then to make a good-faith attempt to reach an agreement about when and how the changes are to be made. Such a duty to bargain in good faith to an agreement or impasse can be enforced through the labour board with appropriate remedies. Of course, such a duty would be defeasible by agreement between the parties about such matters as subcontracting, etc.

However, because of the traditional inefficacy of such a legal duty to bargain, and because negotiations by themselves can be a charade on the employee's part, the union must be free to enforce their own claims through the traditional and legitimate weapon of the strike. Hence, the compulsory no-strike clause must be deleted from the collective agreement, at least to the extent that the strike is over a matter not 'covered' by the collective agreement. Such a legislative change would give the union a fair opportunity to make their interests felt in the process of decision-making leading up to technological or organizational changes. Moreover, it would give employers the incentive to deal with the problem of job security, and the minimization of the effects on employees of industrial change, in the original collective agreement. The union would be able to offer in exchange a more or less extensive promise not to strike. We could expect the same development that has occurred in the USA, where unions and employers have tailored the extent of the arbitration and no-strike clauses, and their provisions dealing with industrial change and job security, to their own individual needs.

The legal regime I have proposed is another alternative to the present options of unilateral management discretion or governmental imposition of the terms of the agreement (via a disguised form of compulsory, 'interest-dispute' arbitration). I believe it is the solution which is most compatible with the existing, legislatively-established policy of free, collective bargaining about employment conditions. This logical development of the statutory scheme will also serve to remove the arbitrator from the dilemma with which he is presently faced, a situation which often tempts him to go beyond his proper institutional role.

[Copyright © University of Toronto Press. Reprinted by permission of the University of Toronto Press Incorporated (www.utpjournals.com).]

Is there a significant risk that allowing unions to strike over matters not covered in the collective agreement would exacerbate the problem (discussed in earlier chapters) of bitter employer resistance to unionization? If so, how might the law best deal with that risk?

The following excerpt takes issue with Weiler's view that arbitrators should restrict themselves to the purely adjudicative role of interpreting and applying terms which were agreed to by the parties and incorporated into the collective agreement.

David Beatty, "The Role of the Arbitrator: A Liberal Version" (1984) 34 *University of Toronto Law Journal* 136

The issue of the nature and scope of management's rights in a collective bargaining relationship ... raising as it does questions about the legitimate and appropriate role of the arbitral process, is too important to leave unanswered. ...

Reduced to its essentials the legal or interpretative issue which is posed by a general recognition of authority in the internal bureaucratic procedures of management is whether decisions which are effected within them are absolute and beyond any form of impartial third-party review. The central question (to which the Court of Appeal in [*Metropolitan Toronto Board of Commissioners of Police* and *Council of Printing Industries of Canada*, excerpted in Section 9:220] has given two opposing answers) is whether management's 'right' to decide how to run its business is immune from any involvement by the persons most affected by such decisions, except in so far as the express language of the agreement provides otherwise or whether, alternatively, management's decision-making authority is impressed with implied obligations of fairness and reason. More pragmatically, the question is: when a collective agreement grants an employer a power of decision either in a broad delegation of managerial authority (as in *Re Metropolitan Toronto Board of Commissioners of Police*) or in a particular grant of discretion (as in *Re Council of Printing Industries of Canada*) and whether it does so explicitly or implicitly, is the employer thereby empowered to act in an arbitrary or even capricious way? For example, in the absence of any provision in the agreement explicitly prohibiting it from so doing, might an employer unilaterally introduce a surveillance system in its plant simply to satisfy a perverse curiosity to snoop on others unobserved, or might it require an employee to present herself in a costume it found pleasing to its eye? Alternatively, might management carry out a decision to reduce its labour costs by contracting out all or part of the work traditionally performed by its employees in the bargaining unit to a contractor who employed others at non-union rates or by integrating those duties in the functions performed by its own unorganized (supervisory) staff? Or, to take a final example, could employers choose to retire, layoff, or deny a leave of absence or an overtime opportunity to one employee rather than another simply in virtue of their preference for the colour of hair or political affiliation of the latter, unless it was explicitly constrained in the agreement not to do so?

At least in a system of industrial relations which grounds itself in the liberal-democratic tradition of law, it would seem inconsistent with and contrary to the most basic conceptions of justice and fairness if individuals could be treated in the ways just described. A commitment to liberal precepts of equality of liberty, to the basic entitlement of all individuals to be the authors of their own (occupational) plans in life seems to rule out decisions so central to one's existence being predicated on such idiosyncratic and subjective whims of others.... Liberal theory postulates an equality between individuals in their right to self-definition and self-government which renders intolerable rules and results in which, as with the examples I have used, some are given an authority to control others in an entirely arbitrary and discriminatory way....

ARBITRATION AS INTERPRETATION

[...]

The reserved rights thesis, with its particular assumptions as to the nature and scope of the collective agreement, has not, unsurprisingly, gone unchallenged. Indeed there has always been a competing thesis, sometimes characterized as the joint sovereignty theory of collective agreements, which rejected the historical, temporal analysis implicit in the reserved rights approach and which, envisaging the enactment of collective bargaining as making a complete break with the past, came to perceive the written terms of the collective agreement as representing a more limited grant of rule-making authority.... Advocates of this theory make the assumption that in addition to the express provisions of the collective agreement there will be ... 'a common law worked out empirically over [the] years ... to give meaning and consistency to the Collective Agreement on which it is based.' Rather than signalling a limit to the scope of their jurisdiction, silence on the face of agreements, alerts arbitrators to the task of discovering and 'working pure' this industrial, common law of the shop, from 'the customs and unwritten understandings, established practices and sound industrial relations standards' which are part of the ongoing enterprise. Parallelling precisely the role of the courts in the interpretation of commercial contracts or in constitutional adjudication, the role of the arbitrator in the interpretation, application, and administration of the collective agreement is not limited simply to the reading of documentary language. On this view, the context in which the collective agreement is negotiated is as essential to the task of discovering the most reasonable meaning of the agreement as are its written terms....

As a positivist description of the law which governs the role of the arbitrator, the reserved rights thesis and the cases which build on its assumptions can quite easily be shown to be wrong. Our courts' own pronouncements, however erratic they may have been, demonstrate a clear recognition that context (including a common law of the shop) must influence text; that no words stand by themselves admitting of a single unambiguous and absolute meaning.

The most obvious source of implied rights and obligations lying outside the written terms of an agreement which may constrain the exercise of management's, or indeed the union's, authority has always been the totality of established ('past') practices which have permeated the details of industrial life and which the express provisions of the agreement have, for the reasons touched on earlier, consciously avoided. It has always been understood that, simply because there are pragmatic reasons and external constraints which may cause the parties not to reduce all the rules and practices which regulate daily life in the workplace to writing, it does not follow as a matter of logical necessity (to say nothing of sound industrial relations standards) that in those areas and on those subjects the rule of law has been suspended. Indeed, quite the contrary. From the outset for many commentators, as a matter of interpretation and as a deduction from the theory of collective bargaining of which it was a part, a collective agreement was understood, "unless a contrary intention [was] manifest, to carry forward for its term the major terms and conditions of employment, not covered by the [written terms of] the agreement, which prevailed when the agreement was executed." ...

ARBITRATION AS AN EMPLOYMENT STANDARD

It would seem, then, that once it is established that the disputes which have traditionally arisen with respect to how management exercises a discretion delegated to it by the agreement are, both in theory and in practice, amenable to resolution by arbitration, the claim in favour of negotiation as the preferred process of social ordering collapses. Once the institutional integrity and practical viability of arbitration to resolve such matters is established, it makes no sense to argue for its displacement by negotiation. Quite the contrary. There is no reason to believe that the bargaining process which regulates labour relationships is so intrinsically superior to all other rulemaking or legislative procedures that it can dispense with an independent criterion to assess the justice of its outcomes. ...

Indeed, once the institutional legitimacy and capacity of the arbitral process has been established, the more coherent response is surely to recognize how, in acting more in the capacity of labour directors than that of managing directors, arbitrators can contribute towards, if not guarantee, the procedural fairness of the entire collective bargaining system of which they are a part. Whatever benefits the negotiation process might provide, the availability of arbitration would ensure that some minimum condition of procedural justice, like an employment standard of due process, was enjoyed by everyone contributing to the productive wealth of the society. As a minimum standard, an arbitral principle of fairness would enhance rather than derogate from the negotiation process. It would provide a limited but nonetheless effective means of individual involvement in decisions which affect a person's working life on which the negotiation process could build. Like a minimum wage, it would preclude those who are most vulnerable from trading what the rest of society regard as essential conditions of their autonomy. It would ensure that a basic feature of the rule of law, a minimum condition of justice, governed the working lives of everyone in society, and not just those who have the bargaining power to negotiate for it. ...

Realistically, however, the recent decisions of the courts in Ontario and the division of opinion in the arbitral community do not provide cause to be optimistic that these adjudicative processes have the will to work the law pure. The history of confusion and contradiction which distinguishes their collective treatment of the issue suggests that a legislative amendment will be necessary for the liberal theory of arbitration to be fully realized.
[Copyright © University of Toronto Press. Reprinted by permission of the University of Toronto Press Incorporated (www.utpjournals.com).]

Recent changes to legislation may be bearing out Beatty's interventionist vision. See, for example, sections 51–55 of the *Canada Labour Code*, which stipulate, *inter alia*, that collective agreements may be reopened for interest arbitration when technological changes affecting a significant number of employees are introduced.

CHAPTER 9: THE COLLECTIVE AGREEMENT AND GRIEVANCE ARBITRATION

* * * * *

9:220   Management Rights

As you read the materials below, particularly the materials on arbitral jurisdiction to apply the *Canadian Charter of Rights and Freedoms*, employment law statutes, and the common law, consider whether Weiler's vision of the most appropriate role for arbitrators has been supplanted by Beatty's more interventionist vision. To what extent are the views of those two authors reflected in the following cases on management rights?

Re United Steelworkers of America and Russelsteel Ltd (1966), 17 LAC 253 at 253–60 (Ont Lab Arb)

> ARTHURS, Chair: On October 25, 1965, three employees filed a grievance in the following terms:
>
> > The grievors contend that the company has violated our collective agreement by removing the regular truck drivers from their jobs and replacing them with persons who are not regularly employed in the bargaining unit.
> >
> > The Union requests that the truck drivers be immediately returned to their job as truck drivers and paid retroactively for all loss of earnings as a result of this violation and also all other bargaining unit employees suffering loss of earnings as a result of this action be returned to their jobs and paid retroactively for all loss of earnings.
>
> The facts underlying this controversy are hardly in dispute. Prior to the date of the grievance, the company leased trucks from another firm, but employed four truck drivers to drive them. Sometime during the week prior to the grievance, these leasing arrangements were terminated, and the company entered into a contract with another firm for the supply of both trucks and drivers. With this arrangement, the grievors' services as drivers became superfluous, and they were offered a choice of either going to work for the contractor, or remaining in the employ of the company as warehouse labourers. Each of these alternatives offered the grievors a lower wage rate than they were receiving in their capacity as truck drivers.
>
> We are thus confronted with a classic case of contracting out, complicated only by the fact that prior to the action here complained of, the company leased trucks rather than owned them. From the union's point of view, this latter fact is at best neutral and at worst presents additional support for the company's action as an extension of its earlier practice. Therefore, unless we hold the grievance otherwise valid, there will be no need for us to comment upon the effect of the prior leasing arrangement.
>
> There can hardly have been a more contentious issue in the field of labour arbitration in the past 10 years than that of contracting out. While in part, the controversy is prompted by the extremely serious repercussions of contracting out for both the employee and the union, it has, as well, assumed a symbolic significance which pervades the entire area of collective agreement administration. This significance stems from the fact that the divergent views of arbitrators as to the propriety of contracting out, represent polar positions in the approach to the construction of collective agreements. On the one side, there is

the 'reserved rights' school which permits contracting out in the absence of some express prohibition in the collective agreement. Arbitrators who have embraced this school take the position that the typical management rights clause reserves to the employer all of his precollective bargaining rights, save those which were expressly bargained away in collective negotiations. On the other hand, there is the school of which (formerly Professor) Laskin J. is perhaps the leading spokesman. As expressed in what has now become classic language in *Re United Electrical, Radio & Machine Workers of America, Local 527, and Peterboro Lock Mfg. Co. Ltd.* . . . , this view holds that . . . :

> The introduction of a Collective Bargaining regime involves the acceptance by the parties of assumptions which are entirely alien to an era of individual bargaining. Hence, any attempt to measure rights and duties in employer/employee relations by reference to the pre-collective bargaining standards is an attempt to reenter a world which has ceased to exist.

Inevitably, in a case of this kind, there are strong pressures upon a board of arbitration to declare its philosophical allegiances, to adopt a series of broad principles, and to derive a solution of the particular case on the basis of a general approach. However, we believe that so far as possible such pressures are to be resisted. Reliance on overbroad philosophical considerations may preclude the pragmatic and realistic solutions to particular problems which would be of most assistance to labour and management in a given bargaining relationship. By such an approach, there is a risk that the lessons of experience, the ever-changing industrial environment, the nuances of the particular situation, might disappear from view. This is not to say that a gradual and economical adumbration of principle ought not to occur. As principle emerges from particular situations, it assists the parties in resolving subsequent disputes without recourse to arbitration. As similar cases are decided over a period of years by a large number of arbitrators, the parties may be able to realistically evaluate the odds upon particular language being construed in a particular way. And as opposing statements of principle confront each other, there being no ultimate appellate tribunal, pressures are generated for compromise between the two positions.

Little purpose would be served by verbal analysis of the several dozen reported cases which constitute the Canadian jurisprudence on the subject. A statistical summary of these cases in a valuable paper presented in 1964 to the Labour Relations Section of the Canadian Bar Association showed that at that time 26 of the 32 reported cases favoured the company's position in the result, while only six favoured the union's. Extending this analysis down to the present day, an even more pronounced trend in favour of the company position is discernible, as 11 cases have since favoured the company's position while only two have favoured the union. The 'box score' since the issue first arose in the mid-1950s is 37 reported cases favouring the company's position, and only eight favouring the union's.

The fact that arbitrators have accepted management's right to contract out almost five times as frequently as they have denied it, does not in and of itself compel this board to a conclusion. As already noted, there is no appellate tribunal whose decisions can reconcile the conflicting awards of the many arbitrators who have considered this matter. Moreover, as is well known, no doctrine of stare decisis operates in labour arbitration. Thus, we are technically free to interpret the agreement as we think right. Looked at as an original question, there may have been much to recommend the 'Laskin' position;

indeed it is a position which is widely accepted in labour arbitration in the United States. But to whatever extent the collective bargaining climate may pervade contract interpretation in other areas, in the matter of contracting out, it can no longer be said to do so. Our reason for so holding is in fact rooted in the 'Laskin' approach, for Professor Laskin himself refers to the 'climate of employer/employee relations under a collective agreement.' In our view this 'climate' is of decided relevance, but it is not a climate solely generated by or confined to the relationships between the particular company and the particular group of employees. As well, the 'climate' reflects and in turn contributes to a broader climate prevailing throughout a particular industry, often extending generally to all collective bargaining relationships, and sometimes even borrowing general legal and social concepts from beyond the world of industrial relations. A few examples will suffice to demonstrate the relevance of this broader 'climate.' The traditional craft jurisdictions peculiar to the construction industry may, in a given case, be of extreme importance in interpreting the recognition and job assignment provisions of collective agreements in that industry. The need to vindicate a foreman's authority in order to ensure the orderly progress of work, is a concept well known and widely applied by arbitrators in all organized industries in determining the existence of 'just cause' for discipline or discharge under collective agreements. And broad notions of procedural fairness developed beyond the context of labour arbitration are frequently a guide to arbitrators called upon to decide similar questions in their special context.

In pursuing our task of industrial meteorology, then, we cannot ignore the fact that part of the 'climate' within which labour and management operate in Ontario is the controversy over contracting out. See in this regard Young, *The Contracting Out of Work*.... The wide notoriety given to labour's protests against this practice, the almost equally wide notoriety, especially amongst experienced labour and management representatives, of the overwhelming trend of decisions, must mean that there was known to these parties at the time they negotiated the collective agreement the strong probability that an arbitrator would not find any implicit limitation on management's right to contract out. It was one thing to imply such a limitation in the early years of this controversy when one could not speak with any clear certainty about the expectations of the parties; then, one might impose upon them the objective implications of the language of the agreement. It is quite another thing to attribute intentions and undertakings to them today, when they are aware, as a practical matter, of the need to specifically prohibit contracting out if they are to persuade an arbitrator of their intention to do so....

This brings us to the next, and crucial, question: did the parties by express language in the agreement restrict management's rights to contract out? The union drew the board's attention to art. 2 of the collective agreement:

> 2.01. The Company recognizes the Union as the sole collective bargaining agent for all its employees at its Plant in Vaughan Township, including employees formerly covered under separate agreements in Leaside and Rexdale, save and except foreman, persons above the rank of foreman, and office staff.
>
> 2.02. Persons whose regular jobs are not in the bargaining unit shall not work on any jobs which are included in the bargaining unit except for purposes of instruction, experimenting, or in emergencies when regular employees are not available.

The union contends that the employees of the independent contractor are 'persons whose regular jobs are not in the bargaining unit,' that in driving trucks for the company they are doing 'work on ... jobs which are included in the bargaining unit,' and that none of the exculpatory conditions which might relieve the company from complying with art. 2.02 are present. Accordingly, the union contends that art. 2.02 has been violated by the company's action in contracting out....

Over and against this interpretation, however, the company introduced evidence to demonstrate that in several contracts executed by locals of the United Steelworkers of America, and in contract proposals submitted to another company, Hugh Russel & Sons Ltd., Montreal, a clear distinction was drawn between a so-called 'working foreman' clause (such as art. 2.02) and a clause prohibiting contracting out. We must note, as persons familiar with collective agreements, that this distinction is frequently drawn. On the company's thesis, the union's knowledge of distinction between a contracting out clause and a 'working foreman' clause must lead this board to the conclusion that the union did not realistically expect the company to bargain away its right to contract out when it procured acceptance of the 'working foreman' clause....

On balance, we are persuaded by these arguments of the company and feel obliged to hold that art. 2.02 was not designed to bear the weighty load the union seeks to heap upon it. Rather, it was designed to preserve the integrity of the bargaining unit from any encroachment by foreman or non-bargaining unit employees. We must, therefore, hold that the agreement does not forbid the company to contract out work.

Finally, we think it important to note that our decision is based upon the interpretation of the agreement before us. We take no general position on the 'reserved rights' controversy. On the other hand, we do not foreclose the possibility that different problems may be presented by contracting out shown to flow from a desire to destroy the bargaining relationship, or from anti-union sentiments, or primarily prompted by a desire to subvert the wage structure of the agreement. Whether such situations give rise to arbitrable controversies, or whether relief must be sought under the *Labour Relations Act*, we do not consider. No evidence was presented to us as to any of these matters. Moreover, no argument was advanced to us that the violation might consist in failing to bargain with the union beforehand, rather than in the very act of contracting out.... The grievance is dismissed.

* * * * *

Russelsteel (Section 9:220, above) involved a consideration of the authority of the arbitrator where the collective agreement was *silent* on a particular matter. Subsequent Canadian arbitral jurisprudence has dealt with whether management rights *expressly recognized* in the collective agreement are qualified by an implied duty of fairness. The last edition of this book presented a series of three cases which sought to make sense of this question: *Re Metropolitan Toronto Board of Commissioners of Police v Metropolitan Toronto Police Association* (1981), 33 OR (2d) 476, 124 DLR (3d) 684 (CA) (in refusing an employee overtime when they had been assigned it in the past, there is no requirement of fair and non-discriminatory exercise of management rights where not express in the agreement); *Re Council of Printing Industries of Canada and Toronto Printing Pressmen and Assistants' Union No 10 et al* (1983), 42 OR (2d) 404 (CA), leave to appeal to the Supreme Court of Canada refused (1983), 52 NR 308n (in awarding temporary employees permanent status, there is no express requirement to follow seniority, but there was a "contractual intent" that the management exercise its discretion in "a reasonable manner, without discrimination, bad faith, or arbitrariness"; *Canadian Union of Public Employees, Metropolitan Toronto Civic Employees' Union, Local 43 v Metropolitan Toronto (Municipality of)* (1990), 74 OR (2d) 239 (CA) (the employer failed to exercise its discretion in a "reasonable fashion" when it implemented a policy with disciplinary consequences that required ambulance drivers to utilize certain warning lights and sirens for emergency calls, and this board finding was not patently unreasonable). This matter seems to have been resolved in the following case, without any reference by the Supreme Court to any of the above cases, or even the existence of the dispute itself.

Communications, Energy and Paperworkers Union of Canada, Local 30 v Irving Pulp & Paper, Ltd, 2013 SCC 34, [2013] 2 SCR 458

> [Irving, the employer, unilaterally implemented a policy for mandatory, random, alcohol and drug testing for 10 percent of employees in safety sensitive positions. A positive test for drugs or alcohol would lead to significant disciplinary action, up to and including dismissal. After weighing the employer's interest in the policy as a safety measure against the employees' privacy interest, the arbitration board allowed the union's grievance, stating that there was a lack of evidence of an existing problem to justify the policy. The award was set aside as unreasonable on review. The court of appeal dismissed the appeal. The Supreme Court of Canada understood the central issue of the case to be the interpretation of management rights within the specific context of a collective agreement with a clause stipulating management rights.]

Abella J (writing for LeBel, Fish, Cromwell, Karakatsanis and Wagner JJ):

[21] As the board recognized, the only possible source of the employer's asserted right to impose random alcohol testing unilaterally was the management rights clause in the collective agreement:

> 4.01. The Union recognizes and acknowledges that it is the right of the Company to operate and manage its business subject to the terms and provisions of this agreement.

The legal issue, as a result, is whether implementing a random alcohol testing policy was a valid exercise of the employer's management rights under the collective agreement.

[22] When employers in a unionized workplace unilaterally enact workplace rules and policies, they are not permitted to "promulgate unreasonable rules and then punish employees who infringe them" (*Re United Steelworkers, Local 4487 & John Inglis Co. Ltd.* (1957), 7 L.A.C. 240 (Laskin), at p. 247; see also *Re United Brewery Workers, Local 232, & Carling Breweries Ltd.* (1959), 10 L.A.C. 25 (Cross)).

[23] This constraint arises because an employer may only discharge or discipline an employee for "just cause" or "reasonable cause"—a central protection for employees. As a result, rules enacted by an employer as a vehicle for discipline must meet the requirement of reasonable cause (*Re Public Utilities Commission of the Borough of Scarborough and International Brotherhood of Electrical Workers, Local 636* (1974), 5 L.A.C. (2d) 285

(Rayner), at pp. 288-89; see also *United Electrical, Radio, and Machine Workers of America, Local 524, in re Canadian General Electric Co. Ltd. (Peterborough)* (1951), 2 L.A.C. 688 (Laskin), at p. 690; *Re Hamilton Street Railway Co. and Amalgamated Transit Union, Division 107* (1977), 16 L.A.C. (2d) 402 (Burkett), at paras. 9-10; Ronald M. Snyder, *Collective Agreement Arbitration in Canada* (4th ed. 2009), at paras. 10.1 and 10.96).

[24] The scope of management's unilateral rule-making authority under a collective agreement is persuasively set out in *Re Lumber & Sawmill Workers' Union, Local 2537, and KVP Co.* (1965), 16 L.A.C. 73 (Robinson). The heart of the "*KVP* test", which is generally applied by arbitrators, is that any rule or policy unilaterally imposed by an employer and not subsequently agreed to by the union, must be consistent with the collective agreement and be reasonable (Donald J. M. Brown and David M. Beatty, *Canadian Labour Arbitration* (4th ed. (loose-leaf)), vol. 1, at topic 4:1520).

[25] The *KVP* test has also been applied by the courts. Tarnopolsky J.A. launched the judicial endorsement of *KVP* in *Metropolitan Toronto (Municipality) v. C.U.P.E.* (1990), 74 O.R. (2d) 239 (C.A.), leave to appeal refused, [1990] 2 S.C.R. ix, concluding that the "weight of authority and common sense" supported the principle that "*all* company rules with disciplinary consequences must be reasonable" (pp. 257–58 (emphasis in original)). In other words:

> The Employer cannot, by exercising its management functions, issue unreasonable rules and then discipline employees for failure to follow them. Such discipline would simply be without reasonable cause. To permit such action would be to invite subversion of the reasonable cause clause. [p. 257]

[26] Subsequent appellate decisions have accepted that rules unilaterally made in the exercise of management discretion under a collective agreement must not only be consistent with the agreement, but must also be reasonable if the breach of the rule results in disciplinary action (*Charlottetown (City) v. Charlottetown Police Association* (1997), 151 Nfld. & P.E.I.R. 69 (P.E.I.S.C. (App. Div.)), at para. 17; see also *N.A.P.E. v. Western Avalon Roman Catholic School Board*, 2000 NFCA 39, 190 D.L.R. (4th) 146, at para. 34; *St. James-Assiniboia Teachers' Assn. No. 2 v. St. James-Assiniboia School Division No. 2*, 2002 MBCA 158, 222 D.L.R. (4th) 636, at paras. 19–28).

[27] In assessing *KVP* reasonableness in the case of unilaterally imposed employer rules or policies affecting employee privacy, arbitrators have used a "balancing of interests" approach. As the intervener the Alberta Federation of Labour noted:

> Determining reasonableness requires labour arbitrators to apply their labour relations expertise, consider all of the surrounding circumstances, and determine whether the employer's policy strikes a reasonable balance. Assessing the reasonableness of an employer's policy can include assessing such things as the nature of the employer's interests, any less intrusive means available to address the employer's concerns, and the policy's impact on employees. [I.F., at para. 4]

[The Court showed that the *KVP* test had been applied by courts and arbitrators in other contexts as a "balancing of interests" approach, beginning mainly in the context of disciplinary action and employee privacy, then branching into random drug and alcohol testing (at paras 28–31). This evolution culminated in a "blueprint" for applying the balancing of interests approach to dangerous workplaces in *Imperial Oil Ltd and CEP, Loc 900 (Re)* (2006), 157 LAC (4th) 225 (at para 32).

The Court found, however, that this approach still required extreme circumstances to justify the unilateral imposition of random testing by employers, and that there were no cases "in which an arbitrator has concluded that an employer could unilaterally implement random alcohol or drug testing, even in a highly dangerous workplace, absent a demonstrated workplace problem (at para 37). Reviewing the caselaw dealing with random alcohol testing (at paras 37–41), the Court found that the "arbitral consensus, which was carefully applied by the board, helps inform why its decision was reasonable on the facts of this case" (at para 42).

Applying this jurisprudential consensus to the board's decision, the Court framed the question as a balancing of interests: Was the benefit to the employer from the random alcohol testing policy in this dangerous workplace proportional to the harm to employee privacy?

With regard to the employer's interest in deterring alcohol abuse, the board found that previous reports of alcohol abuse from 1991 to 2006 were dated. It also inferred that, because two years of random testing had resulted in no positive results, there was no workplace alcohol abuse to deter in the first place. With regard to the employees' privacy interest, the board found that breathalyzer testing involved "coercion and restriction on movement. Upon pain of significant punishment, the employee must go promptly to the breathalyzer station and must co-operate in the provision of breath samples. ... Taking its results together, the scheme effects a loss of liberty and personal autonomy. These are at the heart of the right to privacy" (at para 49). The majority found that the board's balancing these two interests was not unreasonable. It allowed the appeal.]

The reasons of McLachlin CJ and Rothstein and Moldaver JJ were delivered by

[56] Rothstein and Moldaver JJ (dissenting)—Where labour and management fail to agree on the introduction of a new workplace policy, legislatures have delegated the task of adjudicating their dispute to labour arbitrators. In this case, a union challenged management's proactive adoption of a random alcohol testing policy at a paper mill, which the union accepts is inherently dangerous, carrying risks that go beyond the mill's four corners. An arbitral board struck down the policy.

[57] In striking down the policy, we conclude that the board departed from an arbitral consensus that has attempted to strike a balance between competing interests in privacy and safety in the workplace. The board put its thumb on the scales and upset the careful balance established in the arbitral jurisprudence. In so doing, it came to an unreasonable decision. Accordingly, we respectfully dissent from the majority opinion upholding the board's decision.

[Chief Justice McLachlin and Rothstein and Moldaver JJ agreed that the appropriate standard of review was reasonableness. They argued, however, that the arbitrator's award fell outside of the range of reasonable outcomes, in short because it "departed from the legal test emerging from the arbitral consensus by elevating the threshold of evidence Irving was required to introduce in order to justify a policy of random alcohol testing" without offering any explanation for that departure (at para 80). Distinguishing cases dealing with management policies that are neither "random" nor "testing for alcohol," the dissent found (at para 97) that there "is an arbitral consensus that an employer must demonstrate *evidence of an alcohol problem in the workplace* in order to justify a random alcohol testing policy." The board's decisions show that it was aware of this arbitral consensus requiring that an employer have "some" evidence of risk before implementing a policy of random alcohol testing. Despite this awareness, however, the board raised the standard to requiring a "significant" problem. As well, the board added an evidential requirement that the evidence of alcohol use be causally linked to an accident or injury. And finally, the board's adverse inference about a lack of risk was unreasonable because the employer tested only 10 percent of the employees in safety-sensitive positions. All of this together made the board's decision unreasonable. It is important to observe, however, that at no point did the dissenting judges challenge the notion, articulated so clearly by the majority, that management rights must be exercised reasonably, even where a management rights clause in a collective agreement fails to state this principle explicitly.]

9:300 SOURCES OF ARBITRAL LAW AND REASONING

9:310 The Collective Agreement—Contract Interpretation

Paul Weiler, *Reconcilable Differences: New Directions in Canadian Labour Law* (Toronto: Carswell, 1980) at 92–93 and 98

The collective agreement is, if not a unique, certainly an unusual kind of contract. It is vastly different from the individual sales transaction or employment engagement upon which the common law judiciary had cut its teeth in the contract arena. Modern collective agreements cover hundreds, even thousands of employees, not just in single locations or enterprises, but often across an entire industry. The parties deal searchingly with the entire relationship of employer and employee: not just with wages, but also with premium pay, holidays, vacations, leaves of absence, health and welfare plans, pension benefits, seniority rights and layoffs, promotions or transfers, protection from discharge, union security, occupational health and safety, technological change, and much more. And the parties must try to project into the future their views about what should be done about each one of these issues for contract periods which can last three years or even longer. To say the least, the task of interpreting that kind of agreement is a difficult and delicate one. Rarely is the answer to a hotly contested dispute found clearly expressed within the four corners of the written document. . . .

There are inevitable limits in the detail which the negotiators can draft and agree to. They are often under heavy pressure to reach a settlement at the eleventh hour to avoid a strike. The focus of their attention is on the amount of the wage increase, the economic impact of improvements and fringe benefits, the provision of greater job security for the workers, and so on. Each of the items could present any number of background issues about who is eligible, and for exactly what. For example, the memorandum of settlement may provide for an across-the-board percentage wage increase which is "retroactive to the expiry date of the last agreement." Does that increase apply to employees in the unit who may have worked a couple of months after the end of the previous contract, but whose employment was terminated shortly before this settlement was actually reached? The parties may have agreed to vacation pay of 6% of an employee's yearly "earnings." Does one include in earnings not just the regular hourly wages received, but also overtime and shift premiums, statutory holiday pay, sickness or accident indemnity, or the previous year's vacation pay itself? These are examples of the monetary provisions in the agreement which normally are phrased with some precision. The fundamental job security clauses are usually expressed as broad standards: "no employee shall be discharged or disciplined except for "just cause"; "preference in promotion (or layoff) will be given to the senior employee with the qualifications and ability to perform the job." Arbitration cases are replete with issues of principle which have arisen in the application of these standard discharge or seniority provisions. As to the literally tens of thousands of such penumbral issues which might arise in the operation of typical clauses in a sophisticated collective agreement, the negotiators for the parties have neither the foresight, nor the time, nor the inclination to canvass more than a handful of them and to try to reach mutual agreement about what they want done. [Reprinted by permission.]

* * * * *

When a dispute over one of these "penumbral issues" arises, how should it be resolved? Should the arbitrator seek to find a mutual understanding between the employer and union, perhaps by looking at what transpired between them when they negotiated the collective agreement ("negotiation history") or at how the now-contested issue was previously handled in the administration of the agreement ("past practice")? Use of such sources is often taken as evidence that collective agreements fall within the category of "relational contracts," as opposed to *ad hoc* commercial contracts, which seem to form the conceptual underpinnings for classical contract theory: see Douglas Brodie, "Relational Contracts" in Mark Freedland et al, eds, *The Contract of Employment* (Oxford: Oxford University Press, 2016) 145–66; Tamara Cohen, "The Relational Contract of Employment" in Rochelle de Roux & Alan Rycroft, eds, *Acta Juridica 2012: Reinventing Labour Law: Reflecting on the First 15 Years of the Labour Relations Act and Future Challenges* (Claremont: Juta and Co Ltd, 2012) 84; and Robert C Bird, "Employment as a Relational Contract" (2005) 8:1 *University of Pennsylvania Journal of Labour and Employment Law* 149.

9:311 Negotiation History

Re Noranda Metal Industries Ltd, Fergus Division v International Brotherhood of Electrical Workers (1983), 44 OR (2d) 529 at 530–38 (CA)

DUBIN JA: Pursuant to the terms of a collective agreement, dated September 1, 1981, effective to August 31, 1983, an arbitrator was appointed to resolve a grievance brought by the union. The arbitrator was called upon to interpret art. 3.02 of the agreement which provided as follows:

3.02. *During negotiations it was agreed* that the company has the right to subcontract, but in no case shall each subcontracting result in bargaining unit employees being laid off or losing their employment *or being likewise affected*. [Emphasis added.]

The union claimed that the company had violated that clause by subcontracting work to complete the replacement of an acid-waste line at its Fergus plant without offering those employees within the bargaining unit, qualified to do the work, an opportunity of performing that work on a voluntary basis and at overtime rates. Initially the work was performed by skilled tradesmen within the bargaining unit during normal working hours as part of the regularly scheduled non-overtime work of such tradesmen.

In determining whether the company had violated the clause, the arbitrator admitted and considered evidence as to what had transpired during negotiations and evidence of past practices as an aid in interpreting the meaning to be given to the article.

Briefly, the evidence relied upon was to the effect that the 'or being likewise affected' language of the article was expressly represented by the company to meet the concern expressed by the union, during negotiations, that union members could be denied overtime as a result of contracting out. As a result, the union withdrew a request to rephrase the article. The arbitrator relied upon the extrinsic evidence in holding that the company had violated the article. In arriving at his award, the learned arbitrator stated as follows:

> [...]
>
> *Upon due consideration of the evidence and argument of the parties, it is my conclusion that the 'or being likewise affected' language of art. 3.02 was intended to protect bargaining unit employees from losing overtime hours as a result of contracting out by the company....*
>
> The main evidence for the union regarding what was included within the scope of the 'or being likewise affected' language of art. 3.02, was given by Mr. A.W. Schaefer, the business manager of the local union. Mr. Schaefer testified that he was present at the negotiation of art. 3.02 into the collective agreement and that the article has remained the same since that time. In this regard, Mr. Schaefer testified that the first time that art. 3.02 appeared in the collective agreement was in the 1978 agreement. It was suggested by the company during 1977 negotiations leading to that agreement. He stated that it was submitted by the company to accommodate concerns expressed by the union regarding the possibility of maintenance people being denied opportunities to work as a result of contracting out by the company. The language of art. 3.02, he testified, was suggested by the company to cover this situation.
>
> *Mr. Schaefer further testified that the 'or being likewise affected' language of the article was expressly represented by the company to cover off an express concern of the union during those negotiations that union members could be denied overtime as a result of contracting out.* He was firm in his testimony that the company made that specific representation to him. This testimony was unshaken on cross-examination.
>
> Further, Mr. Schaefer testified that this interpretation of the 'or likewise affected' language was confirmed to him by the company during a union-management meeting sometime in 1978. According to his testimony, this meeting was called because the plant administration had changed, and there were indications to the union that line supervision on the floor did not understand the import of art. 3.02 in this regard. He recalled that in addition to himself at this meeting, there were Frank Wood, the then chairman of the union committee, and the chief steward of the union. He testified that he could not recall the names of management personnel at that meeting because 'the management changes

so often' that it is difficult for him to recall the precise persons to whom he spoke after the passage of so much time....

The sole witness for the company was Mr. Ken Faulconbridge, the personnel manager at the Fergus plant for the past 13 years. Mr. Faulconbridge testified that it was never apparent to him that in negotiations the company gave up the right to contract out as suggested by the union. He further testified that in the early stages of the current round of negotiations, the union proposed an amendment to art. 3.02 which specifically required the company to give work to bargaining unit employees on an overtime basis rather than to contract it out. He testified that the company rejected this more specific language because it would affect the efficiency with which the company could run its operation....

Both Mr. Schaefer and Mr. Faulconbridge agreed in their testimony that in response to these objections the union withdrew their proposed amendment at an early stage in negotiations. Mr. Schaefer testified that the union did so because the more specific language did not appear to be necessary in the light of assurances from management representation that they already had the coverage they desired. He further explained that the only reason that the union had proposed the more specific language in the first place was that, again, new line supervision on the plant floor did not appear to be conversant with the prior understanding of the parties regarding the overall effect of the article....

Upon due consideration of the foregoing arguments, I conclude that the 'or being likewise affected' language of art. 3.02 was intended, within reasonable bounds, to require the company to offer overtime to a member of the bargaining unit in the relevant skill group prior to engaging in contracting out. I accept the evidence of Mr. Schaefer regarding the existence of the understandings that, he testified, occurred during the negotiations and were confirmed on an informal basis in the meeting with management during the term of the 1978 collective agreement. Mr. Schaefer gave his testimony in a forthright and non-evasive manner. His evidence was unshaken on cross-examination. His inability to recall the identities of management personnel seemed to be understandable in light of the fact, which appeared to be acknowledged by all at the hearing, that there had been considerable turnover among management personnel at the Fergus plant. I do not attach considerable significance to Mr. Schaefer's inability to produce notes taken during the relevant negotiations, particularly in the light of the fact that the uncontradicted testimony of Mr. Johnson regarding the offering of overtime prior to contracting out confirmed in substantial respect Mr. Schaefer's testimony.... [Emphasis added.]

With respect, I think the majority of the Divisional Court erred in quashing the award of the arbitrator in this case. The arbitrator was called upon to interpret the article in issue in light of two competing submissions as to its meaning. The company contended that the clause related only to job security and, therefore, the phrase 'or being likewise affected' had to be construed in that light. The union contended that the article was to preserve income-producing opportunities for members of the bargaining unit and thus the term 'or being likewise affected' was designed to protect the employees from any loss of their income-producing opportunities by contracting out work. In determining the true intention of the parties as expressed by the language of the article, the arbitrator favoured the latter interpretation.

The majority of the Divisional Court concluded that the clause was unambiguous and thus extrinsic evidence could not be resorted to aid in its interpretation. Mr. Justice White was of the contrary view. It is apparent from the reasons of the arbitrator that he felt that both the contention of the company and of the union were plausible interpretations and thus the clause was ambiguous. It is difficult to conclude that he made a jurisdictional error in so concluding in light of the division of opinion of the Divisional Court on this very issue. I agree with Mr. Justice White that the clause was patently ambiguous and the arbitrator was entitled to resort to extrinsic evidence to assist him in ascertaining the true intentions of the parties, but, in any event, he was entitled to resort to extrinsic evidence to determine whether there was any latent ambiguity, or in applying it to the facts....

If the arbitrator in this case had refused to admit the extrinsic evidence and the article in question had been interpreted in the manner contended for by the company, there would have been a gross injustice. It is apparent that during negotiations the union was concerned that new management personnel were unfamiliar with the intent of the section and were dissuaded from seeking clarification on the express representation of the clause, as worded, met their concern and did protect their income-producing opportunities.

* * * * *

Did the arbitrator's use of negotiation history in this case lead to an outcome that was more acceptable to the parties?

9:312   Past Practice

In *Noranda Metal Industries*, excerpted immediately above, the arbitrator made passing mention of the employer's practice of contracting out work only if bargaining employees declined to put in the overtime needed to do the work. When should the parties' "past practice" be used to resolve an ambiguity in a collective agreement?

International Association of Machinists v John Bertram & Sons Co (1967), 18 LAC 362 at 367–68 (Ont Lab Arb)

> WEILER: If a provision in an agreement, as applied to a labour relations problem, is ambiguous in its requirements, the arbitrator may utilize the conduct of the parties as an aid to clarifying the ambiguity. The theory requires that there be conduct of either one of the parties, which explicitly involves the interpretation of the agreement according to one meaning, and that this conduct (and, inferentially, this interpretation) be acquiesced in by the other party. If these facts obtain, the arbitrator is justified in attributing this particular meaning to the ambiguous provision. The principal reason for this is that the best evidence of the meaning most consistent with the agreement is that mutually accepted by the parties. Such a doctrine, while useful, should be quite carefully employed. Indiscriminate recourse to past practice has been said to rigidify industrial relations at the plant level, or in the lower reaches of the grievance process. It does so by forcing higher management or union officials to prohibit (without their clearance) the settling of grievances in a sensible fashion, and a spirit of mutual accommodation, for

fear of setting precedents which may plague either side in unforeseen ways in future arbitration decisions. A party should not be forced unnecessarily to run the risk of losing by its conduct its opportunity to have a neutral interpretation of the terms of the agreement which it bargained for.

Hence it would seem preferable to place strict limitations on the use of past practice.... I would suggest that there should be (1) no clear preponderance in favour of one meaning, stemming from the words and structure of the agreement as seen in their labour relations context; (2) conduct by one party which unambiguously is based on one meaning attributed to the relevant provision; (3) acquiescence in the conduct which is either quite clearly expressed or which can be inferred from the continuance of the practice for a long period without objection; (4) evidence that members of the union or management hierarchy who have some real responsibility for the meaning of the agreement have acquiesced in the practice.

9:320 Promissory Estoppel

Nor-Man Regional Health Authority Inc v Manitoba Association of Health Care Professionals, 2011 SCC 59

[Ms Plaisier was employed by the Nor-Man Regional Health Authority for twenty years. Plaisier argued that she was entitled to a "bonus" week of vacation under articles 1004 and 1005 of the collective agreement. Nor-Man argued that Plaisier's years of casual work had not counted towards her seniority, and that she was therefore ineligible for the bonus. From 1998 to 2008, Nor-Man's practice had been to exclude casual work from seniority calculations.

The arbitrator found that Nor-Man's interpretation breached the collective agreement, but went on to bar the union's grievance because of its long-standing acquiescence to the employer's interpretation. On judicial review, the award was found reasonable. On appeal, the Court of Appeal found the standard of review to be correctness and set aside the arbitrator's estoppel award. The Supreme Court of Canada, applying *Dunsmuir* and making special note of the deference owed to labour arbitrators with respect to their expertise interpreting collective agreements, found that the appropriate standard of review in this case was reasonableness. The Court restored the award.]

FISH J (for the Court):

[43] In this case, as we have seen, the Court of Appeal found that the arbitrator's imposition of an estoppel was an aspect of the award that fell outside the protected zone of deference. With respect, I disagree.

[44] Common law and equitable doctrines emanate from the courts. But it hardly follows that arbitrators lack either the legal authority or the expertise required to adapt and apply them in a manner more appropriate to the arbitration of disputes and grievances in a labour relations context.

[45] On the contrary, labour arbitrators are authorized by their broad statutory and contractual mandates — and well equipped by their expertise — to adapt the legal and equitable doctrines they find relevant within the contained sphere of arbitral creativity.

To this end, they may properly develop doctrines and fashion remedies appropriate in their field, drawing inspiration from general legal principles, the objectives and purposes of the statutory scheme, the principles of labour relations, the nature of the collective bargaining process, and the factual matrix of the grievances of which they are seized.

[46] This flows from the broad grant of authority vested in labour arbitrators by collective agreements and by statutes such as the *LRA*, which governs here. Pursuant to s. 121 of the *LRA*, for example, arbitrators and arbitration boards must consider not only the collective agreement but also "the real substance of the matter in dispute between the parties". They are *"not bound by a strict legal interpretation of the matter in dispute"*. And their awards "provide a final and conclusive settlement of the matter submitted to arbitration".

[47] The broad mandate of arbitrators flows as well from their distinctive role in fostering peace in industrial relations (*Toronto (City) Board of Education v. O.S.S.T.F., District 15*, [1997] 1 S.C.R. 487, at para. 36; *Parry Sound (District) Social Services Administration Board v. O.P.S.E.U., Local 324*, 2003 SCC 42, [2003] 2 S.C.R. 157, at para. 17).

[48] Collective agreements govern the ongoing relationship between employers and their employees, as represented by their unions. When disputes arise—and they inevitably will—the collective agreement is expected to survive, at least until the next round of negotiations. The peaceful continuity of the relationship depends on a system of grievance arbitration that is sensitive to the immediate and long-term interests of both the employees and the employer.

[49] Labour arbitrators are uniquely placed to respond to the exigencies of the employer-employee relationship. But they require the flexibility to craft appropriate remedial doctrines when the need arises: Rigidity in the dispute resolution process risks not only the disintegration of the relationship, but also industrial discord.

[50] These are the governing principles of labour arbitration in Canada. Their purpose and underlying rationale have long been well understood by arbitrators and academics alike. More than 30 years ago, Paul C. Weiler, then Chairman of the British Columbia Labour Relations Board and now Professor Emeritus at Harvard University, underlined their importance in a dispute of particular relevance here. He explained in the following terms why the doctrine of estoppel must be applied differently in a grievance arbitration than in a court of law:

> a collective bargaining relationship is quite a different animal. The union and the employer deal with each other for years and years through successive agreements and renewals. They must deal with a wide variety of problems arising on a day-to-day basis across the entire spectrum of employment conditions in the workplace, and often under quite general and ambiguous contract language. By and large, it is the employer which takes the initiative in making operational decisions within the framework of the collective agreement. If the union leadership does not like certain management actions, then it will object to them and will carry a grievance forward about the matter. The other side of that coin is that if management does take action, and the union officials are fully aware of it, and no objection is forthcoming, then the only reasonable inference the employer can draw is that its position is acceptable. Suppose the employer commits itself on that assumption. But the union later on takes a second look and feels that it might have a good argument under the collective agreement, and the union now asks the arbitrator to enforce its strict legal rights

for events that have already occurred. It is apparent on its face that it would be inequitable and unfair to permit such a sudden reversal to the detriment of the other side. In the words of the Board in [*Corporation of the District of Burnaby and CUPE, Local 23*, [1978] 2 C.L.R.B.R. 99 at page 103]. It is hard to imagine a better recipe for eroding the atmosphere of trust and co-operation which is required for good labour management relations, ultimately breeding industrial unrest in the relationship—all contrary to the objectives of the Labour Code....

(*Re Corporation of the City of Penticton and Canadian Union of Public Employees, Local 608* (1978), 18 L.A.C. (2d) 307 (B.C.L.R.B.), at p. 320)

[51] Reviewing courts must remain alive to these distinctive features of the collective bargaining relationship, and reserve to arbitrators the right to craft labour specific remedial doctrines. Within this domain, arbitral awards command judicial deference.

[52] But the domain reserved to arbitral discretion is by no means boundless. An arbitral award that flexes a common law or equitable principle in a manner that does not reasonably respond to the distinctive nature of labour relations necessarily remains subject to judicial review for its reasonableness.

[53] Other contextual factors favour judicial deference to labour arbitrators as they adopt and apply common law and equitable principles within their distinctive sphere: Section 128(2) of the *LRA* contains a privative clause in respect of labour arbitrators and boards of arbitration. They benefit from *institutional expertise* in resolving disputes arising under a collective agreement (*O.S.S.T.F., District 15*, at para. 37), even if they lack *personal expertise* in matters of law. *Dunsmuir* makes clear that, "at an institutional level, adjudicators ... can be presumed to hold relative expertise in the interpretation of the legislation that gives them their mandate, as well as related legislation that they might often encounter in the course of their functions" (para. 68 (emphasis added)).

9:330 General Public Law: Employment-Related Statutes

The "employment bargain" is affected not only by the collective agreement but also by many statutory regimes, including those on human rights, employment standards, occupational health and safety, workers' compensation, and, in some jurisdictions, pay equity and employment equity. The extent of the authority of arbitrators to apply such regimes, particularly where there is no conflict between the collective agreement and the statute, has been a major issue in recent decades.

Parry Sound (District) Social Services Administration Board v Ontario Public Service Employees Union, Local 324, 2003 SCC 42

IACOBUCCI J. (McLachlin C.J., Gonthier, Bastarache, Binnie, Arbour, and Deschamps JJ. concurring):

[1] This appeal raises questions about the application of human rights and other employment-related statutes in the context of a collective agreement. More specifically, does a grievance arbitrator have the power to enforce the substantive rights and obligations of human rights and other employment-related statutes and, if so, under what

circumstances? As I discuss in these reasons, I conclude that a grievance arbitrator has the power and responsibility to enforce the substantive rights and obligations of human rights and other employment-related statutes as if they were part of the collective agreement. Consequently, I would dismiss the appeal.

I. BACKGROUND

[2] Joanne O'Brien was a probationary employee of the appellant District of Parry Sound Social Services Administration Board and a member of the respondent Ontario Public Service Employees Union (the "Union"). Her terms of employment were governed by a collective agreement negotiated between the parties. For the purposes of this appeal, the most important provision of the collective agreement is Article 5.01:

> ARTICLE 5—MANAGEMENT RIGHTS
>
> 5.01.
> The Union recognizes that the management of the operations and the direction of the employees are fixed exclusively in the Employer and shall remain solely with the Employer except as expressly limited by the clear and explicit language of some other provision of this Agreement and, without restricting the generality of the foregoing, the Union acknowledges that it is the exclusive function of the Employer to:
>
> ...
>
> (b) hire, assign, retire, promote, demote, classify, transfer, direct, lay off, recall and to suspend, discipline or discharge employees who have successfully completed their probationary period for just cause provided that a claim by an employee who has successfully completed his/her probationary period that she/he has been disciplined, suspended or discharged without just cause may be the subject of a grievance and dealt with as hereinafter provided;

[3] ... On its face, Article 5.01 is sufficiently broad to include the right of the employer to discharge an employee.... Article 8.06(a), under the heading "Grievance Procedures," states that "a probationary employee may be discharged at the sole discretion of and for any reason satisfactory to the Employer and such action by the Employer is not subject to the grievance and arbitration procedures and does not constitute a difference between the parties."

[4] Prior to the expiry of her probationary term, Ms. O'Brien went on maternity leave. Within a few days of returning to work, the appellant discharged her. On June 26, 1998, Ms. O'Brien filed a grievance with the Union. The grievance alleged as follows:

> I grieve that I have been discharged from my position without justification and that this decision was arbitrary, discriminatory, in bad faith and unfair.

At the arbitration hearing, the appellant objected on the basis that the Board of Arbitration (the "Board") did not have jurisdiction over the subject matter of the grievance. It was the appellant's submission that the collective agreement clearly expressed that it was the parties' intention that the discharge of a probationary employee was not arbitrable. The appellant submitted that the parties have the right to make such a bargain and that it would be a jurisdictional error for the Board to resolve the dispute.

II. RELEVANT LEGISLATIVE PROVISIONS

[5] *Employment Standards Act*, R.S.O. 1990, c. E.14

> 44. An employer shall not intimidate, discipline, suspend, lay off, dismiss or impose a penalty on an employee because the employee is or will become eligible to take, intends to take or takes pregnancy leave or parental leave.
>
> 64.5 (1) If an employer enters into a collective agreement, the Act is enforceable against the employer with respect to the following matters as if it were part of the collective agreement:
> 1. A contravention of or failure to comply with the Act that occurs when the collective agreement is in force.
>
> ...
>
> (2) An employee to whom a collective agreement applies (including an employee who is not a member of the trade union) is not entitled to file or maintain a complaint under the Act.
>
> (3) Despite subsection (2), the Director may permit an employee to file or maintain a complaint under the Act if the Director considers it appropriate in the circumstances.
>
> (4) An employee to whom a collective agreement applies (including an employee who is not a member of the trade union) is bound by a decision of the trade union with respect to the enforcement of the Act under the collective agreement, including a decision not to seek the enforcement of the Act.

Labour Relations Act, 1995, S.O. 1995, c. 1, Sch. A

> 48.(1) Every collective agreement shall provide for the final and binding settlement by arbitration, without stoppage of work, of all differences between the parties arising from the interpretation, application, administration or alleged violation of the agreement, including any question as to whether a matter is arbitrable.
>
> 48.(12) An arbitrator or ... an arbitration board, as the case may be, has power,
> (j) to interpret and apply human rights and other employment-related statutes, despite any conflict between those statutes and the terms of the collective agreement.

...

Human Rights Code, R.S.O. 1990, c. H.19

> 5.(1) Every person has a right to equal treatment with respect to employment without discrimination because of race, ancestry, place of origin, colour, ethnic origin, citizenship, creed, sex, sexual orientation, age, record of offences, marital status, same-sex partnership status, family status or handicap.

...

IV. ISSUES

[14] The principal question in this appeal concerns the Board's finding that Ms. O'Brien's grievance is arbitrable. In reviewing this finding, the primary substantive question to be answered is whether the substantive rights and obligations of the *Human Rights Code* are incorporated into a collective agreement over which the Board has jurisdiction. A

second question that arises is whether it was appropriate for the Court of Appeal to determine that the subject matter of the grievance is arbitrable on the basis that the substantive rights and obligations of the *ESA* are incorporated into the collective agreement.

[15] I also note that the Ontario Human Rights Commission has intervened in this appeal for the purpose of ensuring that its jurisdiction is not ousted because the aggrieved employee is a party to a collective agreement over which the Board has jurisdiction. The Commission submits that if the Court finds that the grievance is arbitrable, the Board and the Commission have concurrent jurisdiction. In my view, it is unnecessary to determine this matter at the present time. Consequently, in concluding that a grievance arbitrator has the power and responsibility to enforce the substantive rights and obligations of the *Human Rights Code* in this case, I make no holding on whether the jurisdiction of the Human Rights Commission is ousted by that of the Board.

V. ANALYSIS

A. What is the Appropriate Standard of Review?

[16] Where an arbitration board is called upon to determine whether a matter is arbitrable, it is well-established that a reviewing court can only intervene in the case of a patently unreasonable error. ...

[17] This high degree of curial deference to the decisions of arbitration boards is necessary to maintain the integrity of the grievance arbitration process. ... The protective clause found in s. 48(1) of the *LRA* is the legislative recognition that the basic nature of labour disputes requires their prompt and final resolution by expert tribunals. ...

B. Was the Arbitration Award Patently Unreasonable?

[19] ... the collective agreement is the "foundation" of a grievance arbitrator's jurisdiction. Absent a violation of the collective agreement, a grievance arbitrator has no jurisdiction over a dispute; if the alleged misconduct does not constitute a violation of the collective agreement, there is no basis on which to conclude that a dispute is arbitrable.

[20] In the present case, the parties are in agreement that the express provisions of the collective agreement in question impose no fetters on the employer's right to discharge a probationary employee. The Union, however, submits that s. 5(1) of the *Human Rights Code* is implicit in the collective agreement between the parties. If this is the case, there is no doubt but that the discriminatory discharge of a probationary employee is arbitrable. Under s. 5(1), every person has a right to equal treatment with respect to employment without discrimination. Ms. O'Brien's grievance—that she was discharged for discriminatory reasons—falls squarely within s. 5(1) of the *Human Rights Code*. ...

[21] Consequently, the critical issue to be determined at the arbitration hearing was whether or not the substantive rights and obligations of the *Human Rights Code* are incorporated into each collective agreement over which the Board has jurisdiction. ... If the critical question that the tribunal must answer is a question of law that is outside its area of expertise and that the legislature did not intend to leave to the tribunal, the tribunal must answer that question correctly.

[22] The question of whether the substantive rights and obligations of the *Human Rights Code* are incorporated into each collective agreement over which the Board has jurisdiction is not, in my view, a question that the legislature intended to leave to the Board. The Board's expertise does not lie in answering legal questions of general applicability, but, rather, in the interpretation of collective agreements and the resolution of factual disputes related to those agreements. ...

[23] For the reasons that follow, it is my conclusion that the Board was correct to conclude that the substantive rights and obligations of the *Human Rights Code* are incorporated into each collective agreement over which the Board has jurisdiction. Under a collective agreement, the broad rights of an employer to manage the enterprise and direct the work force are subject not only to the express provisions of the collective agreement, but also to statutory provisions of the *Human Rights Code* and other employment-related statutes.

(1) The Case Law

[24] The leading case regarding the effect of employment-related statutes on the content of collective agreements is *McLeod v. Egan*. ... Prior to *McLeod*, the prevailing view was that an arbitrator was not authorized to apply statutes in the course of grievance arbitration other than as an aid to interpreting a collective agreement. ... On this view, an arbitrator had no alternative but to construe and apply a collective agreement in accordance with its express terms and conditions. If the alleged misconduct did not constitute a violation of an express provision of the collective agreement, the subject matter of the dispute was not arbitrable. In *McLeod*, however, the Court established that it is necessary to look outside the collective agreement in order to ascertain the substantive rights and obligations of the parties to that agreement.

[25] In *McLeod*, the appellant employee alleged that he had been disciplined for refusing to work beyond 48 hours in a week. The collective agreement between the parties contained a broad management rights clause that expressly stated that the control of all operations and working forces, including the right to discipline employees and to schedule operations, is vested solely in the employer, subject only to the express provisions of the collective agreement. There were no provisions of the collective agreement that limited the right of an employer to require an employee to work overtime beyond 48 hours a week. In the absence of language limiting the broad power vested in the employer, the arbitrator concluded that insofar as the collective agreement was concerned the employer was entitled to discipline an employee who refused to work in excess of 48 hours a week.

[26] The Court, however, concluded that an arbitrator must look beyond the four corners of the collective agreement in order to determine the limits on an employer's right to manage operations. Under a collective agreement, this right is subject not only to the express provisions of the agreement, but also to statutory provisions such as s. 11(2) of the *Employment Standards Act, 1968*, S.O. 1968, c. 35 (the "*ESA, 1968*"). Martland J. held as follows, at p. 523:

> The basic provision of the Act is that which places a maximum limit upon the working hours of an employee of eight in the day and forty-eight in the week. Any provision of an agreement which purported to give to an employer an unqualified right to require working hours in

excess of those limits would be illegal, and the provisions of art. 2.01 of the collective agreement, which provided that certain management rights should remain vested in the Company, could not, in so far as they preserved the Company's right to require overtime work by its employees, enable the Company to require overtime work in excess of those limits.

Put another way, the absence of a provision that expressly prohibits an employer from requiring an employee to work in excess of 48 hours a week does not mean that the right to manage operations includes the right to violate s. 11(2) of the *ESA, 1968*. Management rights must be exercised not only in accordance with the express provisions of the collective agreement, but also in accordance with the employee's statutory rights. ...

[27] ... I believe it important to consider carefully what it was that made the collective agreement in *McLeod* objectionable. In *McLeod*, the collective agreement did not expressly state that the employer was authorized to require overtime beyond 48 hours a week. It did, however, contain a broad management rights clause that recognized the employer's right to control all operations and working forces, including the right to discipline employees and to schedule operations. The collective agreement was objectionable because the powers it extended to the employer were sufficiently broad to include the power to violate its employees' rights under s. 11(2) of the *ESA, 1968*.

[28] As a practical matter, this means that the substantive rights and obligations of employment-related statutes are implicit in each collective agreement over which an arbitrator has jurisdiction. A collective agreement might extend to an employer a broad right to manage the enterprise as it sees fit, but this right is circumscribed by the employee's statutory rights. The absence of an express provision that prohibits the violation of a particular statutory right is insufficient to conclude that a violation of that right does not constitute a violation of the collective agreement. Rather, human rights and other employment-related statutes establish a floor beneath which an employer and union cannot contract.

[29] As a result, the substantive rights and obligations of the parties to a collective agreement cannot be determined solely by reference to the mutual intentions of the contracting parties as expressed in that agreement. ...

[30] In some sense, *McLeod* is inconsistent with the traditional view that a collective agreement is a private contract between equal parties, and that the parties to the agreement are free to determine what does or does not constitute an arbitrable difference. But this willingness to consider factors other than the parties' expressed intention is consistent with the fact that collective bargaining and grievance arbitration has both a private and public function. ... This dual purpose is reflected in the fact that the content of a collective agreement is, in part, fixed by external statutes. Section 48(1) of the *LRA*, for example, dictates that every collective agreement must provide for final and binding settlement by arbitration of all differences arising under a collective agreement. Section 64.5(1) of the *ESA* provides that the Act is enforceable against an employer as if it was part of the collective agreement. In each collective agreement, certain procedural requirements and substantive rights and obligations are mandatory. In *McLeod*, the Court determined that these include the obligation of an employer to exercise its management rights in accordance with the statutory rights of its employees.

(2) Application of the Case Law

[31] As in *McLeod*, the collective agreement at issue in this appeal expressly recognizes the employer's broad right to manage the enterprise and direct the work force as it sees fit, subject only to express terms providing otherwise.... Under the traditional view, the management rights recognized therein are unlimited, except to the extent that the express provisions of the collective agreement provide otherwise. In the absence of a provision in the collective agreement that limits the right of the employer to discharge a probationary employee for discriminatory reasons, Ms. O'Brien's grievance is non-arbitrable.

[32] ... Just as the collective agreement in *McLeod* could not extend to the employer the right to require overtime in excess of 48 hours, the collective agreement in the current appeal cannot extend to the appellant the right to discharge an employee for discriminatory reasons....

[33] The one factor that distinguishes this case from *McLeod* is the fact that there is more evidence that the parties to the agreement specifically turned their minds to the subject matter of the grievance and agreed that it was not arbitrable.... Article 8.06(a) might be understood as an explicit expression of the parties' mutual intention that the discriminatory discharge of a probationary employee is not arbitrable.

[34] In response to this line of argument, I should state that I am not entirely comfortable attributing this intention to the parties. Although the language of Article 8.06(a) is broad, it cannot be established, as a matter of fact, that the parties reached a common understanding that the discriminatory discharge of a probationary employee is non-arbitrable. It is more likely, in my view, that the mutual intention was to affirm the right of the employer to discharge a probationary employee who did not perform his or her tasks to the employer's satisfaction.... I find it unlikely, however, that it was the parties' mutual intention to affirm the right of the employer to discharge a probationary employee on the basis of human rights grounds, namely, race, ancestry, place of origin, colour, ethnic origin, citizenship, creed, sex, sexual orientation, age, record of offences, marital status, same-sex partnership status, family status or handicap.

[35] But even if Article 8.06(a) does, in fact, reflect a common intention that the discriminatory discharge of a probationary employee is not an arbitrable dispute, I remain of the view that Ms. O'Brien's grievance is arbitrable. One reason I say this is that s. 48(1) of the *LRA* states that every collective agreement shall provide for the final and binding settlement by arbitration of all differences between the parties arising under the collective agreement. Section 48(1) prohibits the parties from enacting provisions stating that a violation of the collective agreement is non-arbitrable. By the operation of s. 5(1) of the *Human Rights Code*, the right of probationary employees to equal treatment without discrimination is implicit in the collective agreement, and thus the discriminatory discharge of a probationary employee constitutes a violation of that agreement. To the extent that Article 8.06(a) establishes that an allegation that the discriminatory discharge of a probationary employer is non-arbitrable, it is void as contrary to s. 48(1) of the *LRA*.

[36] More fundamentally, the interpretation of Article 8.06(a) that it reflects a common intention is inconsistent with the principle that under a collective agreement an employer's right to manage operations and direct the work force is subject not only to the express provisions of the collective agreement but also to the employees' statutory rights, irrespective of the parties' subjective intentions.... Even if the parties to the

agreement had enacted a substantive provision that clearly expressed that, insofar as the collective agreement is concerned, the employer possessed the right to discharge a probationary employee for discriminatory reasons, that provision would be void. Put simply, there are certain rights and obligation that arise irrespective of the parties' subjective intentions. These include the right of an employee to equal treatment without discrimination and the corresponding obligation of an employer not to discharge an employee for discriminatory reasons. To hold otherwise would lessen human rights protection in the unionized workplace by allowing employers and unions to treat such protections as optional, thereby leaving recourse only to the human rights procedure.

[37] The effect of my analysis is to modify Article 8.06(a). Under this analysis, it is only a probationary employee being discharged "at the sole lawful discretion of and for any lawful reason satisfactory to the Employer" that does not constitute a difference between the parties. Any exercise of this discretion otherwise than in accordance with a probationary employee's rights under the *Human Rights Code* and other employment-related statutes is an arbitrable difference under the collective agreement.

(3) Section 48(12)(j) of the LRA.

[38] Having determined that *McLeod* established that an employer's right to manage the operations and direct the work force is subject not only to the express provisions of the collective agreement but also to the right of each employee to equal treatment without discrimination, the question that arises is whether this principle applies under s. 48(12)(j) of the *LRA*. Put directly, did the enactment of s. 48(12)(j) displace or otherwise restrict the principles established in *McLeod*? ...

[40] ... I believe that the amendments to the legislation affirm that grievance arbitrators have not only the power but also the responsibility to implement and enforce the substantive rights and obligations of human rights and other employment-related statutes as if they were part of the collective agreement. If the right of an employer to manage operations and direct the work force is subject to both the express provisions of the collective agreement and the employee's statutory rights, then it follows that a grievance arbitrator must have the power to implement and enforce those rights.

[41] This conclusion is consistent with the modern approach to statutory interpretation. As this Court has repeatedly stated, the proper approach to statutory interpretation is that endorsed by the noted author E. A. Driedger, in *Construction of Statutes* (2nd ed. 1983), at p. 87: "the words of an Act are to be read in their entire context and in their grammatical and ordinary sense harmoniously with the scheme of the Act, the object of the Act, and the intention of Parliament." ...

(i) The Plain and Ordinary Meaning of Section 48(12)(j) of the LRA

[42] The primary factor that supports this conclusion is the very language of s. 48(12)(j), which provides that an arbitrator has the power "to interpret and apply human rights and other employment-related statutes, despite any conflict between those statutes and the terms of the collective agreement."

[43] The power to interpret and apply a particular statute would, in my view, ordinarily be understood to include the power to implement and enforce the substantive rights and obligations contained therein. . . .

[44] The appellant submits that the power to interpret and apply human rights and other employment-related statutes arises only when there is a direct conflict between the collective agreement and the statute....

[45] ... In any event, I am of the view that the inclusion of a management rights clause that is sufficiently broad to include the right of management to discharge a probationary employee for discriminatory reasons gives rise to a conflict between the statute and the collective agreement.

(ii) The Scheme of the Act

[46] The appellant's primary submission is that an arbitrator has the power to interpret and apply human rights and other employment-related statutes if, and only if, it already has been determined that the arbitrator has jurisdiction over the subject matter of the grievance. According to the appellant, an arbitrator's primary source of jurisdiction is s. 48(1), which states that each collective agreement shall provide for final and binding settlement by arbitration of a difference arising out of that agreement. Section 48(12)(j), on the other hand, sets out the powers that an arbitrator possesses once it already has been determined that a grievance is arbitrable. On this view, the power to interpret and apply other statutes is merely one among nine other incidental powers that an arbitrator may exercise for the purpose of resolving a difference over which she or he already has jurisdiction....

[49] Consequently, it cannot be inferred from the scheme of the *LRA* that it was the legislature's intention to displace or otherwise restrict the legal principles enunciated in *McLeod*. The appellant's submissions in respect of the structure of s. 48 are consistent with the conclusion that the substantive rights and obligations of the *Human Rights Code* are implicit in each collective agreement over which an arbitrator has jurisdiction. If an arbitrator is to enforce an employer's obligation to exercise its management rights in accordance with the statutory provisions that are implicit in each collective agreement, the arbitrator must have the power to interpret and apply human rights and other employment-related statutes. Section 48(12)(j) confirms that an arbitrator does, in fact, have this right.

(iii) Policy Considerations

[50] In respect of policy considerations, I first note that granting arbitrators the authority to enforce the substantive rights and obligations of human rights and other employment-related statutes advances the stated purposes of the *LRA*, which include promoting the expeditious resolution of workplace disputes. As this Court has repeatedly recognized, the prompt, final and binding resolution of workplace disputes is of fundamental importance, both to the parties and to society as a whole.... It is essential that there exist a means of providing speedy decisions by experts in the field who are sensitive to the workplace environment, and which can be considered by both sides to be final and binding.

[51] The grievance arbitration process is the means by which provincial governments have chosen to achieve this objective.... Recognizing the authority of arbitrators to enforce an employee's statutory rights substantially advances the dual objectives of: (i) ensuring peace in industrial relations; and (ii) protecting employees from the misuse of managerial power.

[52] Granting arbitrators the authority to enforce the substantive rights and obligations of human rights and other employment-related statutes has the additional advantage of bolstering human rights protection. Major J. [dissenting in this case] correctly observes that if the dispute is non-arbitrable, aggrieved employees have available the same mechanism for enforcing fundamental human rights as any other member of society: they may file a complaint before the Human Right Commission. But the fact that there already exists a forum for the resolution of human rights disputes does not mean that granting arbitrators the authority to enforce the substantive rights and obligations of the *Human Rights Code* does not further bolster human rights protection....

[54] ... in its submissions before this Court the intervener, Human Rights Commission, stated that it believes that the grievance arbitration process has an important role to play in the resolution of human rights issues. It did not intervene on the basis that arbitrators should not have the power to resolve human rights issues, but on the basis that arbitrators and the Board should have concurrent jurisdiction. This suggests that the Commission also is of the view that grievance arbitrators have sufficient expertise to hear alleged violations of the *Human Rights Code*.

(4) Conclusion

[55] For the foregoing reasons, the Board was correct to conclude that the substantive rights and obligations of the *Human Rights Code* are incorporated into each collective agreement over which an arbitrator has jurisdiction. Because of this interpretation, an alleged violation of the *Human Rights Code* constitutes an alleged violation of the collective agreement, and falls squarely within the Board's jurisdiction. Accordingly, there is no reason to interfere with the Board's finding that the subject matter of Ms. O'Brien's grievance is arbitrable. The Board's finding that the discriminatory discharge of a probationary employee is arbitrable is not patently unreasonable.

C. The Court of Appeal's Application of the *ESA*

[56] The foregoing analysis is sufficient to dispose of the appeal. The Board's finding that the subject matter of Ms. O'Brien's grievance is arbitrable was not patently unreasonable and should be upheld. However, even if there was no basis on which to conclude that the alleged violation of the *Human Rights Code* is arbitrable, I would still be of the opinion that the analysis furnished by the Court of Appeal would provide sufficient grounds to conclude that Ms. O'Brien's grievance is a proper subject of the arbitration process.

[57] In substantive terms, there is no doubt but that the application of ss. 44 and 64.5(1) of the *ESA* leads to the conclusion that the subject matter of Ms. O'Brien's grievance is arbitrable. Under s. 64.5(1), the terms and conditions of the *ESA* are enforceable against an employer as if they were part of the collective agreement. Under s. 44, an employer is prohibited from dismissing an employee because the employee intends to take or takes pregnancy leave. The joint effect of ss. 44 and 64.5(1) is that each collective agreement is deemed to contain a provision that prohibits the discharge of a probationary employee because she took or intends to take pregnancy leave. Thus, the subject matter of Ms. O'Brien's grievance clearly constitutes a dispute that arises under a collective agreement over which the Board has jurisdiction....

(2) Procedural Considerations

[63] The appellant's primary submission in respect of this argument is that the Union is statute-barred from relying on the *ESA*. Section 64.5(4) of the *ESA* states that:

> An employee to whom a collective agreement applies (including an employee who is not a member of the trade union) is bound by a decision of the trade union with respect to the enforcement of the Act under the collective agreement, including a decision not to seek the enforcement of the Act.

According to the appellant, s. 64.5(4) binds a union to a prior decision not to seek enforcement of the *ESA*. Under this view, the respondent Union is bound by its prior decision not to seek enforcement of s. 44 of the *ESA* at the initial hearing. However, this interpretation of s. 64.5(4) is inconsistent with both its words and its fundamental purpose.

[64] First, s. 64.5(4) clearly states that an employee is bound by a decision of the trade union with respect to the enforcement of the Act under the collective agreement. It does not, however, provide that the union is bound by a] decision not to seek enforcement of the *ESA*. If the purpose of s. 64.5(4) was to bind a trade union to its prior decision not to seek enforcement of the *ESA*, one would have expected the legislature to have used language indicating as much....

[65] This interpretation of s. 64.5(4) is consistent not only with its words but also with its basic purpose, namely, to ensure that the union has sole carriage over employment standards issues that arise during the currency of a collective agreement. This accords with established principles governing labour-management relations....

[66] Consequently, s. 64.5(4) has no effect in this appeal. This case does not involve an individual employee who seeks to file or to maintain a complaint under the *ESA* despite the fact that the Union has decided not to seek enforcement of her rights under the Act....

[73] MAJOR J (for himself and LeBel J, dissenting):

I respectfully disagree with the reasons of Iacobucci J.

[74] Are all employment and human rights statutes incorporated into every collective bargaining agreement? Collective agreements occupy an important role in Canadian management-union relations. As both parties are experienced in various components of labour law including grievance procedures, the courts should reluctantly interfere and only when necessary. In this case, there were alternatives available to the parties.... Because I believe that courts should assume that parties may set out the limits of their agreements absent express or implied legislative override, and because the parties should be bound by the form and substance of the grievance they chose, I would allow the appeal....

[93] ... Under *McLeod*, the parties attempted to explicitly "contract around" the protections conferred by statute, which is clearly impermissible. Here, the parties simply chose not to come to agreement on certain kinds of disagreements, explicitly choosing to remove the arbitrator's jurisdiction. The common law rule that parties may not contract in contravention of public policy does not require parties to agree to arbitrate violations of statutory rights.

[94] Under this more restrained reading of *McLeod*, ... explicit statutory directions override conflicting provisions of collective agreements, but they do not affect the

parties' ability to define the limits of their agreement. Parties remain free to exclude certain classes of employees, such as probationary, part-time, or temporary employees, from some of the provisions of the agreement, just as they remain free to exclude certain kinds of disputes from the jurisdiction of the arbitrator. They do this by limiting the scope of the grievance procedure on some matters or acknowledging that a party retains the right to make a unilateral final decision on certain questions.

[95] Although these labour agreements are entered into under the collective bargaining framework established by the *Labour Relations Act, 1995*, they are essentially private contracts of significant public importance. The decision to inject legislative protections into these private contracts is a serious one, though clearly one within the powers of a legislature. A court should not lightly infer such intent. When the Ontario legislature wishes to insert such protections directly into collective bargaining agreements, it knows how to do so explicitly and clearly. For example, s. 64.5(1) of the *Employment Standards Act* reads:

> If an employer enters into a collective agreement, the Act is enforceable against the employer with respect to the following matters as if it were part of the collective agreement:
> 1. A contravention of or failure to comply with the Act that occurs when the collective agreement is in force.

There is no equivalent provision in the *Human Rights Code*....

[100] Collective agreements reflect the outcome of a sometimes difficult process of negotiation. The content of the agreement may reflect the acknowledgment of the union that it should not be called upon to deal with matters it is not equipped to deal with or that might cause conflicts within its membership. Where remedies are available elsewhere, the silence of the agreement may reflect the wishes of the union that those remedies be used in preference to the remedies available under the agreement. Silence in the agreement does not indicate a denial of a right or its remedies. On the other hand, overloading the grievance and arbitration procedure with issues the parties neither intended nor contemplated channelling there, may make labour arbitration anything but expeditious and cost-effective. The present case speaks for itself in this respect.

[101] O'Brien's dismissal is not arbitrable because her Union and her employer agreed not to cover the dismissal of probationary employees in their collective agreement, and the legislature did not intend to require that they do so. She must seek the vindication of her rights before the Human Rights Commission, as would any employee not covered by a collective agreement.

9:340 General Public Law: The *Canadian Charter of Rights and Freedoms* and the Common Law

9:341 Arbitral Authority to Give *Charter* Remedies

At least where the arbitrator's powers are derived from statute, their exercise is subject to the *Charter*, since the arbitrator is a creature of statute who "does not have the power to make an order that would result in an infringement of the *Charter*." *Slaight Communications Inc v Davidson*, [1989] 1 SCR 1038, 59 DLR (4th) 416.

Whether the *Charter* applies to the arbitral dispute itself depends on whether there is a nexus with government. See *Douglas/Kwantlen Faculty Assn v Douglas College*, [1990] 3 SCR 570. The *Charter* applied to the dispute in *Douglas College* because community colleges were subject to government control to the extent that they could be considered part of the apparatus of government. Similarly, in *Lavigne v Ontario Public Service Employees' Union*, [1991] 2 SCR 211, the Supreme Court of Canada held that the application of the *Charter* to union security provisions in the collective agreement turned on a finding that the employer was a governmental actor and its acquiescence to a union request for a Rand Formula clause in the collective agreement was sufficient to constitute governmental conduct.

In the *Douglas College* case, the Supreme Court of Canada held that a grievance arbitrator had the jurisdiction to hear *Charter* challenges by virtue of section 52 of the *Constitution Act, 1982*, but left open the question of whether an arbitrator could be "a court of competent jurisdiction" within the meaning of section 24(1) of the *Charter*. That issue was addressed in the following case.

Weber v Ontario Hydro, [1995] 2 SCR 929 at paras 60–61 and 65–66

[Weber, an employee of Ontario Hydro, took an extended leave of absence because of back problems. Hydro paid him the sick benefits stipulated by the collective agreement. As a result of the information it obtained through private investigators who used false identities, Hydro suspended Weber for abusing his sick leave benefits. Grievances against Hydro were settled. Weber also commenced a court action based on the torts of trespass, nuisance, deceit, and invasion of privacy, as well as breach of sections 7 and 8 of the *Canadian Charter of Rights and Freedoms*, claiming damages for the surveillance. Section 45(1) (now section 48(1)) of the Ontario *Labour Relations Act*, stated that every collective agreement "shall provide for the final and binding settlement by arbitration ... of all differences between the parties arising from the interpretation, application, administration or alleged violation of the agreement."]

McLACHLIN J. (for the majority): ... *Douglas College* ... involved a grievance before a labour arbitrator. In that case, as in this, *Charter* issues were raised. It was argued, *inter alia*, that a labour arbitration was not the appropriate place to argue *Charter* issues. After a thorough review of the advantages and disadvantages of having such issues decided before labour tribunals, La Forest J. concluded that while the informal processes of such tribunals might not be entirely suited to dealing with constitutional issues, clear advantages to the practice exist. Citizens are permitted to assert their *Charter* rights in a prompt, inexpensive, informal way. The parties are not required to duplicate submissions on the case in two different fora, for determination of two different legal issues. A specialized tribunal can quickly sift the facts and compile a record for the reviewing court. And the specialized competence of the tribunal may provide assistance to the reviewing court. ...

Douglas/Kwantlen Faculty Assn. v. Douglas College also answers the concern of the Court of Appeal below that the *Charter* takes the issue out of the labour context and puts it in the state context. While the *Charter* issue may raise broad policy concerns, it is nonetheless a component of the labour dispute, and hence within the jurisdiction of the labour arbitrator. The existence of broad policy concerns with respect to a given issue cannot preclude the labour arbitrator from deciding all facets of the labour dispute.

This brings us to the question of whether a labour arbitrator in this case has the power to grant *Charter* remedies. The remedies claimed are damages and a declaration. The power and duty of arbitrators to apply the law extends to the *Charter*, an essential part of the law of Canada: *Douglas/Kwantlen Faculty Assn. v. Douglas College* ...; *Cuddy Chicks Ltd. v. Ontario (Labour Relations Board)* ...; *Re Ontario Council of Regents for Colleges of Applied Arts & Technology and Ontario Public Service Employees Union*.... In applying the law of the land to the disputes before them, be it the common law, statute law or the *Charter*, arbitrators may grant such remedies as the Legislature or Parliament has empowered them to grant in the circumstances. For example, a labour arbitrator can consider the *Charter*, find laws inoperative for conflict with it, and go on to grant remedies in the exercise of his powers under the *Labour Code*: *Douglas/Kwantlen Faculty Assn. v. Douglas College*.... If an arbitrator can find a law violative of the *Charter*, it would seem he or she can determine whether conduct in the administration of the collective agreement violates the *Charter* and likewise grant remedies....

It is thus Parliament or the Legislature that determines if a court is a court of competent jurisdiction; as McIntyre J. puts it, [in *Mills v The Queen*] the jurisdiction of the various courts of Canada is fixed by Parliament and the Legislatures, not by judges. Nor is there magic in labels; it is not the name of the tribunal that determines the matter, but its powers. (It may be noted that the French version of s. 24(1) uses '*tribunal*' rather than '*cour*.') The practical import of fitting *Charter* remedies into the existing system of tribunals, as McIntyre J. notes, is that litigants have 'direct' access to *Charter* remedies in the tribunal charged with deciding their case.

It follows from *Mills* that statutory tribunals created by Parliament or the Legislatures may be courts of competent jurisdiction to grant *Charter* remedies, provided they have jurisdiction over the parties and the subject matter of the dispute and are empowered to make the orders sought.

In *Nova Scotia (Workers' Compensation Board) v Martin*, 2003 SCC 54, the Supreme Court of Canada affirmed the authority of administrative tribunals to apply the *Charter* in cases involving governmental action. Justice Gonthier said, for the entire Court (at para 3):

> I am of the view that the rules concerning the jurisdiction of administrative tribunals to apply the *Charter* established by this Court in *Douglas/Kwantlen Faculty Assn. v. Douglas College* ..., *Cuddy Chicks Ltd. v. Ontario (Labour Relations Board)* ..., and *Tétreault-Gadoury v. Canada (Employment and Immigration Commission)* ..., ought to be reappraised and restated as a clear set of guidelines. Administrative tribunals which have jurisdiction—whether explicit or implied—to decide questions of law arising under a legislative provision are presumed to have concomitant jurisdiction to decide the constitutional validity of that provision. This presumption may only be rebutted by showing that the legislature clearly intended to exclude Charter issues from the tribunal's authority over questions of law.

"Canadians," Gonthier J said, "should be entitled to assert the rights and freedoms that the Constitution guarantees them in the most accessible forum available, without the need for parallel proceedings before the courts" (at para 29).

9:342 Arbitral Authority to Apply the Common Law

In *Weber v Ontario Hydro*, cited above in Section 9:341, the Supreme Court of Canada also held that arbitrators could apply common law doctrines to resolve claims based on those doctrines as long as the dispute, in its essential character, arose out of the collective agreement. See also *Nor-Man Regional Health Authority Inc v Manitoba Association of Health Care Professionals* cited above in Section 9:320.

9:400 REMEDIAL JURISDICTION OF ARBITRATORS

9:410 Damages

Re Polymer Corp and Oil, Chemical & Atomic Workers (1959), 10 LAC 51 at 54–65 (Ont Lab Arb)

> [The union had called a strike in breach of the collective agreement. The employer brought a grievance claiming damages for the losses caused by the illegal strike. The arbitration board held that it had the authority to award such damages to the employer. When the board reconvened to assess the quantum of damages, the union reopened the issue of whether the board had the power to award damages at all. The collective agreement said nothing about damages, and contained the following quite common limitation on arbitral authority:
>
>> Article 7.03. The Board of Arbitration shall not have power to alter or change any of the provisions of this Agreement or to substitute any new provisions for any existing provisions nor to give any decision inconsistent with the terms and provisions of this Agreement.
>
> Arbitrator Bora Laskin held as follows on the issue of the board's authority to award damages.]
>
> LASKIN: ... The burden of union counsel's argument against the board's authority to assess damages is that no such relief is stipulated in the governing collective agreement either generally or in particular relation to breach of a no-strike clause such as art. 8.01. Further, for the board to assess damages would be to add to the collective agreement in the teeth of art. 7.03 which forbids the board to alter, or change, or substitute new for any existing terms or to give a decision inconsistent with such terms. The collective agreement itself limits the issues which may be referred to a board, not only by art. 7.03 but also by art. 7.01. On the basis of this exposition, union counsel takes the stand that damages as a remedy for a collective agreement violation which results in loss to the innocent party cannot be awarded in the absence of clear agreement by the parties in that behalf, either generally in a collective agreement or specifically under a particular submission. Counsel emphasized that the collective agreement is a product of voluntary action, and the parties cannot be deemed to have committed themselves beyond that which they expressed in their contractual undertakings.
>
> For what it is worth this board must reject union counsel's contention that the award of this board is made final and binding only through the election of the parties and not through compulsion of legislation or regulation. Section 19 of the Industrial Relations and Disputes Investigation Act, R.S.C. 1952, c. 152, indicates a legislative policy of final

settlement by arbitration of what may be termed contract interpretation disputes; and while it is true that such a requirement depends on whether a party invokes s. 19 to have such a provision included in a collective agreement (where they have not mutually incorporated it), the fact is that its inclusion is not a matter of agreement only; it may be forced upon one party by the other.... It could not escape counsel's appreciation that if a union need not answer in damages for breach of a collective agreement obligation involving a company in pecuniary loss, neither need a company answer in damages for breach of a collective agreement obligation involving the union or an employee in pecuniary loss; unless, of course, in either or in both cases there is explicit provision for an award of compensation.

It seems to this board that fundamental to any approach to the issue is some understanding of the history and purpose of resort to 'final' or 'binding' arbitration, to use the terms which appear respectively in s. 19 of the Industrial Relations and Disputes Investigation Act and art. 7.04 of the governing collective agreement. As a matter of history, collective agreements in Canada had no legal force in their own right until the advent of compulsory collective bargaining legislation. Our Courts refused to assume original jurisdiction for their enforcement and placed them outside of the legal framework within which contractual obligations of individuals were administered. The legislation, which in the context of encouragement to collective bargaining sought stability in employer-employee relations, envisaged arbitration through a mutually accepted tribunal as a built-in device for ensuring the realization of the rights and enforcement of the obligations which were the products of successful negotiation. Original jurisdiction without right of appeal was vested in boards of arbitration under legislative and consensual prescriptions for finality and for binding determinations. In short, boards of arbitration were entrusted with a duty of effective adjudication differing in no way, save perhaps in the greater responsibility conferred upon them, from the adjudicative authority exercised by the ordinary Courts in civil cases of breach of contract. That the adjudication was intended to be remedial as well as declaratory could hardly be doubted. Expeditious settlement of grievances, without undue formality and without excessive cost, was no less a key to successful collective bargaining in day-to-day administration of collective agreements than the successful negotiation of the agreements in the first place. Favourable settlement where an employee was aggrieved meant not a formal abstract declaration of his rights but affirmable relief to give him his due according to the rights and obligations of the collective agreement. In some jurisdictions, as for example, Ontario, this view was emphasized by the fact of statutory withdrawal of the application of Arbitration Acts from labour arbitrations, thus excluding the kind of curial review which was open to the parties to commercial arbitration. To have proposed to union negotiators that collective agreements, so long ignored in law and left to 'lawless' enforcement by strikes and picketing, should continue to be merely empty vehicles for propounding declarations of right when the right to strike during their currency was taken away, would be to mock the policy of compulsory collective bargaining legislation which envisaged the collective agreement as the touchstone of the successful operation of that policy.

What was true in the case of aggrieved employees or aggrieved union could be no less true in the case of aggrieved employers. They too were sensitive to the need for stability which collective agreements could produce, and no less alive to the need for effective machinery to resolve disputes arising in the day-to-day administration of such agreements. In admitting their own responsibility for due observance of collective agreement obligations they could not be expected to agree to any lesser standard of performance by unions and employees. These considerations are aptly summed up in that part of art. 1 of the agreement between the parties herein which recites 'their desire to provide orderly procedure for collective bargaining, and for the prompt and equitable disposition of grievances.'

It is desirable at this point to point up a distinction between the imposition of penalties and the award of damages. It is a distinction taken, and in this Board's view, properly taken, in the award in *Re U.A.W. and C.C.M.*.... This board, sitting as a civil tribunal to resolve contract interpretation disputes, has no punitive function but is charged only with redressing private wrongs arising from breach of obligations assumed as a result of negotiation. The board's remedial authority, if it has any, must be addressed to the vindication of violated rights by putting the innocent party, so far as can reasonably be done, in the position in which he or it would be if the particular rights had not been violated. The redress, if any can be given, must be suited to or measured by the wrong done. A board of arbitration is not, however, a criminal court. True enough, it may play a role in passing upon or modifying a penalty imposed by an employer as a matter of discipline, but in so doing it is merely assessing the permissible limits of employer action taken under the collective agreement and not fashioning a penalty to reward an innocent party....

The pivotal issue is simply whether the exercise of arbitral authority encompasses the effectuation of the right and the enforcement of the obligation which are submitted for both original and final adjudication. One would ordinarily think, especially if seized of any knowledge of the history of collective bargaining and its legislative implementation, that if there is any area of adjudication where abstract pronouncements, devoid of direction for redress of violations, would be unwelcome it would be in labour arbitration. Such attenuation of arbitration authority must surely be found in explicit restriction rather than in implicit limitation.

It may be useful to pursue the point under discussion in relation to the 'intention of the parties' argument that is from time to time advanced in labour arbitration cases no less than in commercial contract adjudication. Thus, it is said that if the parties intended to make themselves answerable before a board of arbitration in damages they would have said so; and since many collective agreements contain specific reference to an arbitration board's remedial powers where discharge or lesser discipline is involved, the 'intention of the parties' argument is buttressed by reliance on the maxim *expressio unius exclusio alterius*. Whatever may be the intention of the parties as to the binding effect of their reciprocal rights and obligations, the statutory prescription of s. 18 of the Industrial Relations and Disputes Investigation Act makes the collective agreement terms binding on the union as well as on employer and employees covered thereby. Moreover, s. 19 carries the statutory policy further by reinforcing the binding character of a collective agreement with binding adjudication of disputes concerning its interpretation or violation. It seems to this board that whether one appraises the situation in terms of the statutory effects alone, or in terms of the intention of the parties (which must be viewed in the light of the statute), the result is the same; and there is nothing in the language of the agreement in this case to suggest that the parties have in any way tried to qualify this result. Indeed, they could not if they tried; and we are remitted again to consideration of the scope or meaning to be given to their (compelled) intention that the collective agreement shall be binding and that any alleged violation shall be submitted to binding arbitration.

As good an analogy as can be found on this issue lies in the field of international law and, particularly, in the effect given by international law to the voluntary submission of nations to adjudication of disputes arising under treaties to which they are parties. Thus, in the *Chorzow Factory* case of 1927 between Germany and Poland, the Permanent Court of International Justice said ...:

> It is a principle of international law that the breach of an engagement involves an obligation to make reparation in an adequate form. Reparation therefore is the indispensable complement of a failure to apply a convention and there is no necessity for this to be stated in the convention itself.

... One of the submissions of union counsel appears to be that there is a difference in an arbitration board's remedial authority where an employee claims redress under the collective agreement and where a company claims redress. The only differences, so far as this board can see any, are in the nature of the obligation which is allegedly violated and in the readier measure of loss, if loss is shown. The fact that a collective agreement stipulates the worth of an employee's labour in a wage schedule merely simplifies a tribunal's assessment of damages. It adds nothing to its powers. There is no need to emphasize that the difficulty of assessing damages has never been a reason for denying a claim thereto based on an established breach of contractual or other obligation owed to the claiming party....

It follows from what has been said that the union's challenge to this board's power to award damages for breach by the union of art. 8.01 is rejected and the board will proceed to assess the company's damages at a hearing to be convened by the board upon advice from the company that particulars as mentioned at the outset of this award have been furnished to the union and upon receipt of copies by members of the board.

*****

Arbitrator Laskin's views on arbitral authority to award damages for breach of the collective agreement were upheld on judicial review. See *Re Polymer Corporation & Oil, Chemical & Atomic Workers International Union, Local 16-14*, [1961] OR 176 (HCJ), aff'd [1961] OR 438 (CA), aff'd sub nom *Imbleau v Laskin*, [1962] SCR 338.

It is now well accepted that an arbitrator may award damages in accordance with general contract principles, even if there is no specific provision to that effect in the collective agreement. See *Nor-Man Regional Health Authority Inc v Manitoba Association of Health Care Professionals*, 2011 SCC 59, referred to in Section 9:320. See also *St Anne Nackawic Pulp & Paper Co Ltd v Canadian Paperworkers Union, Local 219*, [1986] 1 SCR 704, referred to on other matters in Chapter 8, Section 8:523 and in Sections 9:510 and 9:520.

9:420 Reinstatement

Almost all collective agreements provide that an employee is not to be disciplined or discharged except for just cause, even in jurisdictions where such a provision is not explicitly required by statute. In addition, labour relations legislation across Canada now includes provisions similar to section 48(17) of the Ontario *Labour Relations Act, 1995*, which gives arbitrators the discretion, where they find that an employee has been discharged or disciplined for cause, to substitute any other penalty that the arbitrator deems just and reasonable in the circumstances, as long as the collective agreement does not mandate a specific penalty for the misconduct in question.

As the following excerpt points out, the just cause requirement and the right to reinstatement represent radical departures from the common law approach to discipline and discharge. (The BC Labour Relations Board, unlike every other Canadian labour board, has the statutory authority to review arbitration awards.)

William Scott & Company Ltd v Canadian Food and Allied Workers Union, Local P-162, [1977] 1 Can LRBR 1 at 1–6 (BCLRB)

> WEILER, Chair: This is an application under s. 108 of the Labour Code. Section 108(1)(b) entitles the Board to set aside an award on the ground that it is 'inconsistent with the principles expressed or implied in the Code.' The Labour Code addresses itself directly to the issue of discharge of an employee. First, s. 93(1) requires that:
>
>> Every collective agreement shall contain a provision governing the dismissal or discipline of an employee bound by the agreement and that provision, or another provision, shall require that the employer have a just and reasonable cause for the dismissal or discipline of an employee;
>
> Then, in any grievances brought to challenge discharge under that clause of the agreement, the Code confers this statutory authority on the arbitrator:
>
>> 98. For the purposes set out in s. 92, an arbitration board has all the authority necessary to provide a final and conclusive settlement of a dispute arising under the provisions of a collective agreement, and, without limiting the generality of the foregoing, has authority . . .
>> (d) to determine that a dismissal or discipline is excessive in all the circumstances of the case and substitute such other measure as appears just and equitable.
>
> The wording of each of these provisions of the Code embodies the significant 1975 amendments contained in Bill 84. This explicit legislative attention to the problem of discharge and discipline testifies not only to the serious impact these measures may have on the individual employee, but also to the need to provide adequate, peaceful machinery for reviewing such cases as an antidote to possible industrial unrest in the bargaining unit.
>
> In this, the first s. 108 application in which the Board has analyzed this legislative language, we wish to emphasize the significance of the legal change from discharge as a pure matter of contract law, under the individual contract of employment, to discharge as the subject of legislative policy governing the collective agreement between employer

and trade union. Without reviewing the common law of master and servant in any detail, suffice it to say that the contract of employment allowed the employer to dismiss an employee without notice for cause (some relatively serious forms of misconduct which, in the eyes of the law, made the continuance of the employment relationship undesirable). But that particular doctrine of the common law can be appreciated only in light of two other features of the master-servant relationship. First of all, even in the absence of cause on the part of the employee, the employer could unilaterally dismiss an employee with reasonable notice, or with pay in lieu of notice. This meant that employees had no legal expectation of continuity of employment even if their performance was satisfactory and work was available. Secondly, if an employee was guilty of some misconduct at work, the employer had no other form of discipline available. The contract of employment did not entitle the employer to suspend the employee, for example. The presence of these two subsidiary doctrines naturally coloured the common law analysis of what constituted 'cause' for discharge, in two respects: first, the law concentrated on the immediate incident which triggered the discharge, rather than the situation of the individual employee; secondly, gradually the law took the view that certain serious forms of misconduct automatically justified discharge (e.g. insubordination, dishonesty, or disloyalty) on the grounds that these amounted to a fundamental breach of the contract of employment.

The nature of the legal right to discharge an employee has taken on a very different hue in the world of collective bargaining. A classic depiction of that new reality is contained in the award of the arbitrator in the crucial case of *Port Arthur Shipbuilding*:

> the collective agreement does create an entirely new dimension in the employment relationship: it is the immunity of an employee from discharge except for just cause, rather than the former common law rule of virtually unlimited exposure to termination. Whatever may have been the early views of labour arbitrators, it is common knowledge that over the years a distinctive body of arbitral jurisprudence has developed to give meaning to the concept of 'just cause for discharge' in the context of modern industrial employment. Although the common law may provide guidance, useful analogies, even general principles, the umbilical cord has been severed and the new doctrines of labour arbitrators have begun to lead a life of their own.

No doubt this legal shift is ultimately attributable to such socio-economic factors as the transformation of the personal relationship of 'master and servant' in a small firm into the impersonal administration of a large industrial establishment by a personnel department. But within the collective agreement itself, there were specific, contractual features which required from arbitrators a different conception of discharge.

First of all, under the standard seniority clause an employer no longer retains the unilateral right to terminate a person's employment simply with notice or pay in lieu of notice. Employment under a collective agreement is severed only if the employee quits voluntarily, is discharged for cause, or under certain other defined conditions (e.g. absence without leave for five days; lay-off without recall for one year, and so on). As a result, an employee who has served the probation period secures a form of tenure, a legal expectation of continued employment as long as he gives no specific reason for dismissal. On that foundation, the collective agreement erects a number of significant benefits: seniority claim to jobs in case of lay-off or promotion; service-based entitlement to extended vacation or sick leave; accumulated credits in a pension plan funded by the employer. The point is that the right to continued employment is normally a much firmer and more valuable legal claim under a collective agreement than under the common law individual contract of employment. As a result, discharge of an employee under collective bargaining law, especially of one who has worked under it for some time under the agreement, is a qualitatively more serious and more detrimental event than it would be under the common law. At the same time, the standard collective agreement also provides the employer with a broad management right to discipline its employees. If an individual employee has caused problems in the work place, the employer is not legally limited to the one, irreversible response of discharge. Instead, a broad spectrum of lesser sanctions are available: verbal or written warnings, brief or lengthy suspensions, even demotion on occasion ... Because the employer is now entitled to escalate progressively its response to employee misconduct, there is a natural inclination to require that these lesser measures be tried out before the employer takes the ultimate step of dismissing the employee, and thus cutting him off from all of the benefits associated with the job and stemming from the collective agreement.

Recognizing the cumulative impact of these contractual developments flowing from the modern industrial environment, Canadian labour arbitrators did gradually evolve quite a different analysis of discharge grievances. The essence of that approach was nicely conveyed by Mr. Justice Laskin, speaking for the Ontario Court of Appeal in upholding the arbitrator in Port Arthur Shipbuilding:

> The collective agreement leaves the extent of discipline (be it as light as a warning or as heavy as discharge) at large under the formula of "proper cause". By this I mean that there are no fixed consequences for specified types of misconduct. This is so even in respect of a violation of such a specific prohibition as is involved in article 11.03. The reason is simple; experience has shown that there must be a pragmatic and not a cut and dried, Medes and Persians approach to discipline. Employers and unions are, in my opinion, wise to leave room in collective agreement administration (which includes arbitration) for consideration of the worker as an individual, and not as simply part of an indistinguishable mass. The formulae of 'just cause' or 'proper cause' or 'reasonable cause' or 'just and proper cause' which are found in collective agreements join to the pragmatic case by case approach a sensible individualization in the assessment of punishment for misconduct. Whether the qualifying word be proper' or 'just', it expresses the duty to act according to the circumstances of the case in which an issue of discipline, reaching perhaps to discharge, arises. (1967) 67 CLLC 14,024 (at p.116)

[...]

Unfortunately, this indigenous arbitral solution was abruptly aborted by the Supreme Court of Canada, when it reversed the Ontario Court of Appeal and the arbitrator in *Port Arthur Shipbuilding Co. v. Arthurs et al*:

> The task of the board of arbitration in this case was to determine whether there was proper cause. The findings of fact actually made and the only findings of fact that the board could possibly make establish that there was proper cause. Then there was only one proper

legal conclusion, namely, that the employees had given the management proper cause for dismissal. The board, however, did not limit its task in this way. It assumed the function of management. In this case it determined, not whether there had been proper cause, but whether the company, having proper cause, should have exercised the power of dismissal. The board substituted its judgment for the judgment of management and found in favour of suspension.

The sole issue in this case was whether the three employees left their jobs to work for someone else and whether this fact was a proper cause for discipline. *Once the board had found that there were facts justifying discipline, the particular form chosen was not subject to review on arbitration.* [Emphasis added.]

On its face, that passage seemed to suggest that if an arbitrator found some employee misconduct, no matter how trivial, then management had a totally unreviewable discretion to select any form of discipline, no matter how heavy, up to and including the dismissal of a long service employee. Although some arbitrators attempted to mitigate the impact of such a draconian doctrine.... Canadian legislatures uniformly considered it necessary to overturn *Port Arthur Shipbuilding* by statutory reform. Section 98(d) of the Labour Code, the provision under analysis in this case, is the vehicle through which the B.C. Legislature has sought to place on a contemporary, industrial relations footing the law of discharge under a collective agreement.

We have reviewed this historical background to s. 98(d) to emphasize strongly its central thrust. The B.C. Legislature, in common with all other Canadian legislatures, wished to eradicate once and for all the residual traces of the common law of master and servant which had surfaced in *Port Arthur Shipbuilding* and which would prevent an arbitrator coming to grips with the 'real substance' and 'respective merits' of a discharge grievance (s. 92(3)) and thus impair the ability of arbitration to provide a satisfactory resolution of such disputes 'without resort to stoppages of work' (s. 92(2)). For that reason, it is not legally correct for an arbitrator in a discharge case to assume that the common law definition of 'cause' remains unchanged under the Code, subject only to the possibility that an arbitrator might exercise an ill-defined discretion to rescue an employee from the 'normal' legal consequences of discharge and substitute a lesser penalty on 'equitable' grounds. An arbitrator who approaches a discharge grievance with that reluctant state of mind simply is not proceeding in accordance with the principles of the Labour Code.

Instead, arbitrators should pose three distinct questions in the typical discharge grievance. First, has the employee given just and reasonable cause for some form of discipline by the employer? If so, was the employer's decision to dismiss the employee an excessive response in all of the circumstances of the case? Finally, if the arbitrator does consider discharge excessive, what alternative measure should be substituted as just and equitable?

Normally, the first question involves a factual dispute, requiring a judgment from the evidence about whether the employee actually engaged in the conduct which triggered the discharge. But even at this stage of the inquiry there are often serious issues raised about the scope of the employer's authority over an employee, and the kinds of employee conduct which may legitimately be considered grounds for discipline.... However, usually it is in connection with the second question—is the misconduct of the employee serious enough to justify the heavy penalty of discharge?—that the arbitrator's evaluation of management's decision must be especially searching:

i) How serious is the immediate offence of the employee which precipitated the discharge (for example, the contrast between theft and absenteeism)?
ii) Was the employee's conduct premeditated, or repetitive; or instead, was it a momentary and emotional aberration, perhaps provoked by someone else (for example, in a fight between two employees)?
iii) Does the employee have a record of long service with the employer in which he proved an able worker and enjoyed a relatively free disciplinary history?
iv) Has the employer attempted earlier and more moderate forms of corrective discipline of this employee which did not prove successful in solving the problem (for example, of persistent lateness or absenteeism)?
v) Is the discharge of this individual employee in accord with the consistent policies of the employer or does it appear to single out this person for arbitrary and harsh treatment (an issue which seems to arise particularly in cases of discipline for wildcat strikes)?

The point of that over-all inquiry is that arbitrators no longer assume that certain conduct taken in the abstract, even quite serious employee offences, are automatically legal cause for discharge. [The author then referred to recent awards holding discharge to be too severe a penalty, in the particular circumstances, for instances of theft, falsification of records and assault on a supervisor.] Instead, it is the statutory responsibility of the arbitrator, having found just cause for some employer action, to probe beneath the surface of the immediate events and reach a broad judgment about whether this employee, especially one with a significant investment of service with that employer, should actually lose his job for the offence in question. Within that framework, the point of the third question is quite different than it might otherwise appear. Suppose that an arbitrator finds that discharge and the penalty imposed by the employer is excessive and must be quashed. It would be both unfair to the employer and harmful to the morale of other employees in the operation to allow the grievor off 'scot-free' simply because the employer over-reacted in the first instance. It is for that reason that arbitrators may exercise the remedial authority to substitute a new penalty, properly tailored to the circumstances of the case, perhaps even utilizing some measures which would not be open to the employer at the first instance under the agreement (e.g. see *Phillips Cables*, ... in which the arbitration board decided to remove the accumulated seniority of the employee).

New Dominion Stores (cob Great Atlantic & Pacific Co of Canada) v Retail Wholesale Canada Canadian Service Sector, Division of USWA, Local 414 (McCaul Grievance) (1997), 60 LAC (4th) 308 (Beck)

[This was a grievance arbitration arising from the discharge of Carol McCaul by her employer, New Dominion Stores. McCaul was alleged to have stolen a half pint of berries by placing them in her calico bag. She claimed to have forgotten they were in there from when she had done some shopping for her dinner. Despite some evidence of McCaul's forgetful nature, the weight of the evidence suggested an intention to take the goods without paying for them. McCaul had twenty-three years of seniority.

The main issue was whether this behaviour led, in all circumstances, to automatic termination. The employer argued that it did because of the need for management to rely on the integrity and honesty of its staff, the vulnerability of food retailers to theft by employees, and the significant loss of profit theft can quickly represent given the slim mark-up of most supermarkets. The employer further argued that it had a clearly stated policy with regard to employee purchases. There were many cases that supported the employer's position. Arbitrator Beck noted, however, that with respect to theft in the retail industry there had been a marked shift from automatic dismissal to progressive discipline.]

26 ... This approach was elaborated upon in an earlier decision of Professor Harry Arthurs in Re Canadian Broadcasting Corporation and Canadian Union of Public Employees (1979) 23 L.A.C. (2d) 227, at p. 230:

> I have examined all authorities cited, and I believe that the following summary accurately reflects their significance. The older cases generally (but not inevitably) treated theft or dishonesty as an offence which warranted automatic discharge; more recent cases, especially those decided by arbitrators subscribing to the theory of "corrective discipline," do not treat dishonesty as per se grounds for discharge; and various mitigating factors have been identified as justifying the substitution of a lesser penalty for discharge in such cases.

27 Professor Arthurs listed the following factors which might be considered in mitigating a penalty:
(1) *bona fide* confusion or mistake by the grievor as to whether he was entitled to do the act complained of;
(2) the grievor's inability, due to drunkenness or emotional problems, to appreciate the wrongfulness of his act;
(3) the impulsive or non-premeditated nature of the act;
(4) the relatively trivial nature of the harm done;
(5) the frank acknowledgement of his misconduct by the grievor;
(6) the existence of a sympathetic, personal motive for dishonesty, such as family need, rather than hardened criminality;
(7) the past record of the grievor;
(8) the grievor's future prospects for likely good behaviour, and
(9) the economic impact of discharge in view of the grievor's age, personal circumstances, etc.

28 Most importantly, Professor Arthurs went on to note that the listed factors ought not be applied in some automatic way....

30 I do not wish to be understood to be saying that theft is simply another discipline matter and is to be treated as such. Clearly, theft may go to the root of the relationship of trust and confidence that is essential in many employment relationships. And a single instance of theft might lead to the conclusion that that relationship has been irretrievably broken. But that will very much depend on the facts of the particular case. To state the obvious, each case is unique on its facts and ought to be considered as such in imposing an appropriate penalty....

39 What are the relevant factors here which weigh for and against discharge? McCaul is 55 years old, has 23 years of service with the Company and has no prior record of

discipline. The value of the goods taken was nominal, $8.55. The grievor from start to finish stoutly maintained that she simply forgot that she had the items in her bag. Indeed, there was evidence that she is forgetful to the point where it is a matter of joking among her fellow employees. Nonetheless, I have found that there was clear and cogent evidence that the grievor knew what she was doing when she left the store with the unpaid for items in her bag on the afternoon of May 7, 1996.

40 Should the fact that McCaul did not admit her wrongdoing, but maintained her defence of forgetfulness throughout the entire piece, weigh against her to the extent that the penalty of discharge should be upheld? I am of the opinion that it should not, given her long record of service, her unblemished record and the nominal value of the goods taken. I agree with the holding of Arbitrator Bendel in Re Cannet Freight Cartage Ltd. and Teamsters Union (1993) 35 L.A.C. (4th) 314 (Bendel), at p. 326:

> Another matter that, according to some of the awards, bears on the appropriate disciplinary measure should be mentioned. In some of the cases to which I was referred, a grievor who was judged to have been untruthful in testifying has been regarded as deserving a more severe disciplinary penalty than one who has duly confessed to his misdeeds. I have doubts about the value of this factor in deciding the proper penalty. It must be remembered that the standard of proof in a case like this is upon the balance of probabilities. Although I have found that the grievor did throw a beverage at Mr. Plummer, I cannot state with absolute certainty that he did so. He has offered an explanation which I, upon a balance of probabilities, have rejected. Perhaps I am doing an injustice to the grievor since the possibility cannot be totally excluded that the grievor is relatively blameless in the whole altercation with Mr. Plummer.... In any event, the conduct for which the grievor has been disciplined is, in my view, much more relevant than his subsequent conduct, including his conduct at the hearing.

41 In making the above comment with respect to the grievor continuing to maintain his innocence, Arbitrator Bendel referred to the decision of the Ontario Court of Appeal in College of Physicians & Surgeons of Ontario v. Gillen (1993) 13 O.R. (3d) 385. The issue in that case was whether the doctor's licence to practice was properly revoked or whether some lesser form of discipline was appropriate. The Court found that the discipline committee had erred in attaching weight to the doctor's denial of professional misconduct:

> ... Any doctor is entitled to deny allegations made against him or her and to require the College to establish such allegations. If he or she chooses to admit the allegations, that may be taken into account in appropriate circumstances in setting a penalty, but in no circumstances should denial serve to increase what would otherwise be an appropriate penalty.

42 As I have noted, the standard of proof in a case like this is the balance of probabilities. While I have found the Company has satisfied that burden, the grievor was well within her rights to maintain her position of forgetfulness throughout. Although I have, on the balance of probabilities, rejected that explanation, she ought not to suffer in terms of the appropriate penalty for doing what she was entitled to do. Again, the impact of continuing denial will very much depend on the facts of the case, the weight of the evidence against a grievor, and the grievor's behaviour throughout the piece. That surely is the

sense of the direction of the Ontario Court of Appeal when it held that "... in no circumstances should denial serve to increase what would otherwise be an appropriate penalty."

43 In light of the above, I am of the opinion that the appropriate penalty here would be a suspension without pay, but without loss of seniority, for the some nine months that the grievor has been off work since her discharge on May 10, 1996. That is a very severe penalty for a person of the grievor's age and with 23 years of seniority. But it is not the only penalty. There is the shame and embarrassment of returning to the workforce, and her position as a Union Steward, having been found guilty of theft, and suspended for some nine months.

44 Accordingly, the grievance is allowed to the extent that the penalty of discharge is changed to a suspension without pay, but without loss of seniority, to the date of the receipt of this award.

* * * * *

Fourteen empirical studies of discharge cases, five of which used Canadian data, were summarized by Allen Ponak, "Discharge Arbitration and Reinstatement: An Industrial Relations Perspective" [1992] 2 *Labour Arbitration Yearbook* 31. Ponak noted that research findings on arbitral use of reinstatement have been remarkably consistent across time and space. He said (at 33):

> Discharge is upheld slightly less than one-half of the time, meaning that more than half of all grievors are reinstated. Approximately one out of five grievors receives a complete reinstatement [without any lesser penalty]. More often, however, if discharge is not upheld some grounds for discipline are found and approximately one of three grievors is reinstated with suspension substituted for termination.

As to the work experience of reinstated grievors, Ponak provided a capsule summary of the research results (at 38):

> [T]hose employees who return to work usually prove to be productive workers. As rated by their employers, well over half of reinstated grievors are deemed to perform satisfactorily or better. Only a very small proportion of returning employees are subsequently terminated for cause.

A more detailed discussion of the aftermath of reinstatement is found in an earlier study of Ontario discharge cases: George W. Adams, *Grievance Arbitration of Discharge Cases: A Study of the Concepts of Industrial Discipline and Their Results* (Kingston: Queen's Industrial Relations Centre, 1978). The core finding of this study is set out in the following passage (at 66):

> A summary of results pertaining to employee rehabilitation can be reported thusly. Of the 128 employees who returned to work with lesser discipline, 37.5 percent experienced some form of subsequent discipline including discharge, and 24.2 percent of the 128 employees were involved in a recurrence [of the same offence]. If a successful reinstatement is to be measured by the absence of any subsequent discipline, the collective success rate of the arbitration tribunals involved in this study is in the order of 63 percent. This 'rate of success' is comparable to earlier studies and, predictably, much at odds with the

poor results of rehabilitation in the criminal law field.... Therefore, while the correction and rehabilitation justifications for punishment in the criminal law field may be waning, this is not so in industrial relations. Indeed, as a general matter, these results appear to vindicate the corrective approach to discipline forged by arbitration tribunals....
[Reprinted by permission.]

* * * * *

In *Compagnie Minière Quebec Cartier v Quebec (Grievances Arbitrator)*, [1995] 2 SCR 1095, the Supreme Court of Canada considered whether arbitrators, in deciding whether to exercise their discretion to reinstate an employee and substitute a lesser penalty, should be allowed to rely on evidence of what happened after the employee was discharged. The arbitrator had held that the company was justified in discharging the grievor on the basis of the facts as they existed at the time of discharge, but that reinstatement should be ordered in light of the grievor's subsequent successful treatment for alcoholism. The Supreme Court found that the arbitrator had exceeded his jurisdiction by relying on "subsequent-event" evidence as grounds for reinstatement. Justice L'Heureux-Dubé, for the Court, wrote, at 1101–2:

> In my view, an arbitrator can rely on such evidence, but only where it is relevant to the issue before him. In other words, such evidence will only be admissible if it helps to shed light on the reasonableness and appropriateness of the dismissal under review at the time that it was implemented.

Applying this test in *Toronto (City) Board of Education v OSSTF, District 15*, [1997] 1 SCR 487, the Court quashed the decision of an arbitrator who excluded post-discharge evidence. At issue were three letters written by the grievor (a teacher) to his employer (a school board). The first letter contained what could have been perceived as veiled threats to the lives of the employer's director of education and others. It was written during the hearing of a complaint the grievor had filed with the Ontario Human Rights Commission alleging that the employer systemically discriminated against persons of the grievor's ethnic origin. The second letter was more explicitly threatening. The grievor was dismissed as a result of those two letters. Later, after the grievance was filed, he wrote the third letter, which was less abusive and threatening than the first two but which, in the Court's words (at 519 and 520), exhibited "the same extreme views, hyperbolic comparisons and total lack of judgment." The arbitration board, which was expressly empowered by the collective agreement to "modify the penalty" imposed by the employer, held that the grievor should be reinstated subject to stringent monitoring and to summary dismissal if the conduct recurred. The award took no account of the third letter written after the dismissal. In quashing the award, Cory J (for the Court), wrote (at 519):

> It is true that the third letter is, to some extent, "subsequent-event evidence" since it was written after the dismissal of [the grievor]. However it has been decided that such evidence can properly be considered "if it helps to shed light on the reasonableness and appropriateness of the dismissal": *Compagnie Minière Québec Cartier v. Québec (Grievances Arbitrator)*.... In this case, it would not only have been reasonable for the arbitrators to consider the third letter, it was a serious error for them not to do so.

A recent example of arbitral efforts to reconcile the Supreme Court's decisions in the *Québec Cartier* and *Toronto (City) Board of Education* cases is found in *London Civic Employees Local Union No 107 v London (City)*, [2010] OLAA No 270 at 31 (Snow):

> I read the *Board of Education* case as significantly limiting the application of the *Québec Cartier* decision. The Court's omission in its *Board of Education* decision of the phrase *"under review at the time that it was implemented,"* together with the conclusions actually reached in that case, indicate to me that the Court was not following its earlier *Québec Cartier* approach, but instead was adopting a different approach. The *Board of Education* decision appears to require consideration of the post-discharge evidence. [Emphasis in original.]

9:430   Rectification

As with damages, it was arbitrator Bora Laskin who led the way in asserting the authority of arbitrators to apply the general contract law principle of rectification (correcting a mutual error made by the parties when reducing the terms of the collective agreement to writing). See *W Harris & Company* (1953), 4 LAC 1531. However, arbitral authority in respect of rectification has had a more checkered history than in respect of damages. In *Re Metropolitan Toronto Board of Commissioners of Police and Metropolitan Toronto Police Ass'n* (1972), 26 DLR (3d) 672 (CA), aff'd on other grounds by the SCC, the Ontario Court of Appeal said:

> In 'applying the doctrine of rectification' the arbitrator made two separate and distinct errors:
> i) As a consensual arbitrator he had no power whatever to rectify the collective agreement. If the collective agreement did not represent the true bargain between the parties, the party asserting this to be so could bring an action [in court] for rectification, but as Judson J., said in *Port Arthur Shipbuilding Co. v. Arthurs et al.*, [1969] S.C.R. 85 ... the arbitrator '[had] no inherent powers to amend, modify or ignore the collective agreement.'
> ii) He ignored an express term of the agreement itself, cl. 17 of which reads:
>
>> 'An Arbitrator ... shall not have power to add to, subtract from, alter, modify or amend any part of this Agreement ...'

Many arbitrators declined to follow this ruling. They saw it as anomalous that arbitrators were allowed to invoke promissory estoppel and thus not to apply the strict letter of the agreement (see Section 9:320), but were not allowed to use rectification to correct simple mistakes in the wording of the agreement. It was also seen as inconsistent with the holding in *Polymer* (see Section 9:410) on arbitral authority to award damages.

More recently, in *PSAC v NAV Canada* (2002), 212 DLR (4th) 68 (Ont CA), the Ontario Court of Appeal held that an arbitrator had no authority to rectify a collective agreement where its written terms did not correspond to the parties' intentions. According to the Court of Appeal, contract clauses that prohibited an arbitrator from amending or modifying the collective agreement did not preclude the granting of a remedy by way of rectification, as that remedy did not operate to alter the agreement but simply to correct terms that were mistakenly drawn. The

CHAPTER 9: THE COLLECTIVE AGREEMENT AND GRIEVANCE ARBITRATION

court saw the arbitral authority to apply the equitable doctrine of rectification as flowing from the exclusive arbitral jurisdiction to resolve disputes arising under a collective agreement.

9:500 THE INSTITUTIONAL FRAMEWORK: COMPETING MODELS FOR ALLOCATING JURISDICTION AMONG MULTIPLE FORUMS

In Chapter 1, Section 1:200, the concept of three regimes of employment regulation was introduced. The existence of those three regimes means that a workplace-related incident or interaction between an employer and employee potentially gives rise to claims under a collective agreement, under other statutes, under the *Canadian Charter of Rights and Freedoms*, and under the common law. The employee may therefore want to bring a civil action or file a complaint under human rights legislation or another employment-related statute in addition to asking her union to take a grievance to arbitration. Whether arbitrators should have concurrent, overlapping or exclusive jurisdiction over such claims has resulted in much litigation.

9:510 Arbitration and Civil Actions Concerning *Charter* and Common Law Claims

St Anne Nackawic Pulp & Paper Co Ltd v Canadian Paperworkers Union, Local 219, [1986] 1 SCR 704, is set out in Chapter 8, Section 8:523, in connection with the availability of injunctions against strikes in breach of collective agreements. In *St. Anne Nackawic*, the employer had obtained an interim injunction against an illegal strike by the union, and then sued in tort for damages resulting from the strike. The decision of the Supreme Court of Canada in that case established that, with some exceptions, the grievance and arbitration procedure under the collective agreement has exclusive jurisdiction to deal with disputes arising between the parties to the agreement, and that the jurisdiction of the courts was therefore ousted. Justice Estey, for the entire Supreme Court, held that permitting concurrent actions would undermine the statutorily mandatory arbitration scheme, but that there remained a residual discretionary power in courts of inherent jurisdiction over matters such as injunctions.

The main issue in the later case of *Weber v Ontario Hydro*, the facts of which are summarized in Section 9:341, was the extent to which the arbitral regime had ousted the jurisdiction of the courts in civil and *Charter* matters. The following excerpts are from the majority judgment on this issue.

Weber v Ontario Hydro, [1995] 2 SCR 929 at para 37ff

> McLACHLIN J: . . . The crucial question we face is when employees and employers are precluded from suing each other in the courts by labour legislation providing for binding arbitration. It is common ground that s. 45(1) of the Ontario *Labour Relations Act* prevents the bringing of civil actions which are based solely on the collective agreement. . . . The cases reveal three different views on the effect of final and binding arbitration clauses in labour legislation. I shall deal with each in turn.
>
> [Justice McLachlin explained why, in her view, neither the concurrent model nor the model of overlapping jurisdiction was satisfactory. Under the concurrent model, the courts have

jurisdiction over common law or statutory claims even where they arise in the employment context. *St Anne Nackawic* stood for the principle that mandatory arbitration clauses in labour statutes deprive the courts of concurrent jurisdiction. However, in determining whether the arbitral regime has *exclusive* jurisdiction, "[t]he issue is not whether the action, defined legally, is independent of the collective agreement, but rather whether the *dispute* is one 'arising under [the] collective agreement.'" In this case, the Ontario *Labour Relations Act* made arbitration the only available recourse for differences arising out of the collective agreement. The word "differences" referred to the dispute between the parties, not to the legal actions one party might be entitled to bring against the other.

The object of the provision—and what is thus excluded from the courts—is all proceedings arising from the difference between the parties, however those proceedings may be framed. Where the dispute falls within the terms of the Act, there is no room for concurrent proceedings.

Furthermore, McLachlin J went on, permitting concurrent actions would undermine the goal of the collective bargaining regime, which was to resolve disputes quickly and economically with a minimum of disruption.]

On [the model of overlapping jurisdiction,] notwithstanding that the facts of the dispute arise out of the collective agreement, a court action may be brought if it raises issues which go beyond the traditional subject matter of labour law....

In so far as it is based on characterizing a cause of action which lies outside the arbitrator's power or expertise, [the overlapping spheres model] violates the injunction of the Act and *St. Anne Nackawic* that one must look not to the legal characterization of the wrong, but to the facts giving rise to the dispute. It would also leave it open to innovative pleaders to evade the legislative prohibition on parallel court actions by raising new and imaginative causes of action.... This would undermine the legislative purposes underlying such provisions and the intention of the parties to the agreement. This approach, like the concurrency model, fails to meet the test of the statute, the jurisprudence and policy....

The final alternative is to accept that if the difference between the parties arises from the collective agreement, the claimant must proceed by arbitration and the courts have no power to entertain an action in respect of that dispute. There is no overlapping jurisdiction.

On this approach, the task of the judge or arbitrator determining the appropriate forum for the proceedings centres on whether the dispute or difference between the parties arises out of the collective agreement. Two elements must be considered: the dispute and the ambit of the collective agreement.

In considering the dispute, the decision-maker must attempt to define its 'essential character,' to use the phrase of La Forest J.A. in *Energy & Chemical Workers Union, Local 691 v. Irving Oil Ltd.*.... In the majority of cases the nature of the dispute will be clear; either it had to do with the collective agreement or it did not. Some cases, however, may be less than obvious. The question in each case is whether the dispute, in its essential character, arises from the interpretation, application, administration or violation of the collective agreement.

Because the nature of the dispute and the ambit of the collective agreement will vary from case to case, it is impossible to categorize the classes of case that will fall within the exclusive jurisdiction of the arbitrator. However, a review of decisions over the past few years reveals the following claims among those over which the courts have been found to lack jurisdiction: wrongful dismissal; bad faith on the part of the union; conspiracy and constructive dismissal; and damage to reputation....

This approach does not preclude all actions in the courts between employer and employee. Only disputes which expressly or inferentially arise out of the collective agreement are foreclosed to the courts: *Elliott v. De Havilland Aircraft Co. of Canada Ltd.*...; *Butt v. United Steelworkers of America* ...; *Bourne v. Otis Elevator Co.*... Additionally, the courts possess residual jurisdiction based on their special powers, as discussed by Estey J. in *St. Anne Nackawic*....

Against this approach, the appellant Weber argues that jurisdiction over torts and *Charter* claims should not be conferred on arbitrators because they lack expertise on the legal questions such claims raise. The answer to this concern is that arbitrators are subject to judicial review. Within the parameters of that review, their errors may be corrected by the courts. The procedural inconvenience of an occasional application for judicial review is outweighed by the advantages of having a single tribunal deciding all issues arising from the dispute in the first instance. This does not mean that the arbitrator will consider separate 'cases' of tort, contract or *Charter*. Rather, in dealing with the dispute under the collective agreement and fashioning an appropriate remedy, the arbitrator will have regard to whether the breach of the collective agreement also constitutes a breach of a common law duty, or of the *Charter*.

The appellant Weber also argues that arbitrators may lack the legal power to consider the issues before them. This concern is answered by the power and duty of arbitrators to apply the law of the land to the disputes before them. To this end, arbitrators may refer to both the common law and statutes: *St. Anne Nackawic*; *McLeod v. Egan*.... As Denning L.J. put it, '[t]here is not one law for arbitrators and another for the court, but one law for all': *David Taylor & Son, Ltd. v. Barnett*.... This also applies to the *Charter*: *Douglas/Kwantlen Faculty Assn. v. Douglas College*....

It might occur that a remedy is required which the arbitrator is not empowered to grant. In such a case, the courts of inherent jurisdiction in each province may take jurisdiction. This Court in *St. Anne Nackawic* confirmed that the New Brunswick Act did not oust the residual inherent jurisdiction of the superior courts to grant injunctions in labour matters.... Similarly, the Court of Appeal of British Columbia in *Moore v. British Columbia* ... accepted that the court's residual jurisdiction to grant a declaration was not ousted by the British Columbia labour legislation, although it declined to exercise that jurisdiction on the ground that the powers of the arbitrator were sufficient to remedy the wrong and that deference was owed to the labour tribunal. What must be avoided, to use the language of Estey J. in *St. Anne Nackawic* ... is a 'real deprivation of ultimate remedy.' ...

APPLICATION OF THE LAW TO THE DISPUTE IN THIS CASE

On the interpretation outlined above, the question is whether the conduct giving rise to the dispute between the parties arises either expressly or inferentially out of the collective agreement between them.

The appellant contends that the dispute in this case falls outside the collective agreement. The act of hiring private investigators who used deception to enter his family home and report on him does not, he contends, relate to the interpretation, application or administration of the collective agreement. It is not in its essential character a labour matter; it is rather a matter of the common law and the constitutional rights of himself and his family. It follows, he submits, that the arbitrator does not have jurisdiction over the claims and that the courts may entertain them. . . .

Article 2.2 of the collective agreement extends the grievance procedure to '[a]ny allegation that an employee has been subjected to unfair treatment or any dispute arising out of the content of this Agreement. . . .' The dispute in this case arose out of the content of the Agreement. Item 13.0 of Part A of the Agreement provides that the 'benefits of the Ontario Hydro Sick Leave Plan . . . shall be considered as part of this Agreement.' It further provides that the provisions of the plan 'are not an automatic right of an employee and the administration of this plan and all decisions regarding the appropriateness or degree of its application shall be vested solely in Ontario Hydro.' This language brings the medical plan and Hydro's decisions concerning it expressly within the purview of the collective agreement. Under the plan, Hydro had the right to decide what benefits the employee would receive, subject to the employee's right to grieve the decision. In the course of making such a decision, Hydro is alleged to have acted improperly. That allegation would appear to fall within the phrase 'unfair treatment or any dispute arising out of the content of [the] Agreement' within Article 2.2.

I conclude that the wide language of Article 2.2 of the Agreement, combined with item 13.0, covers the conduct alleged against Hydro. Hydro's alleged actions were directly related to a process which is expressly subject to the grievance procedure. While aspects of the alleged conduct may arguably have extended beyond what the parties contemplated, this does not alter the essential character of the conduct. In short, the difference between the parties relates to the 'administration . . . of the agreement' within s. 45(1) of the *Labour Relations Act*.

* * * * *

Weber's union had settled the grievances brought on his behalf without settling his civil claims, but the Supreme Court of Canada held that he was now precluded from bringing a civil action. Thus, in a situation where a unionized employee might previously have had access to the courts, *Weber* leaves that employee more heavily dependent on the union's decision whether or not to take a grievance forward on his behalf. This problem will be discussed in Chapter 10, Section 10:230, in connection with the Supreme Court of Canada decision in *Allen v Alberta*, 2003 SCC 13.

The passages from the Supreme Court of Canada judgment in *Weber* set out in Section 9:341, and immediately above in this section, indicate that the Court saw the exclusive jurisdiction model as applying to *Charter* claims as well as common law claims. In *Weber*, the Ontario Court of Appeal had held that the exclusive jurisdiction model should be applied to common law claims, but could not apply to *Charter* claims because it would make a unionized employee's access to courts for enforcement of her most fundamental individual rights contingent upon support from the union as a collectivity. The majority judgment of the

Supreme Court of Canada in *Weber* did not address that very significant issue. For this and other reasons, *Weber* has been heavily criticized, as the following excerpt indicates.

Michel Picher, "Defining the Scope of Arbitration: The Impact of *Weber*: An Arbitrator's Perspective" (1999–2000) *Labour Arbitration Yearbook* 99, at 108–10, 114–17, and 144–47

> The decision of the Supreme Court of Canada in *Weber v. Ontario Hydro* in 1995, and its aftermath in a number of court decisions and arbitration awards, gives cause to wonder whether the success of arbitration may ultimately be its undoing. In Canada, in contrast to the United States, labour arbitration is a statutorily mandated procedure for the resolution of disputes concerning the application, interpretation or administration of the provisions of a collective agreement. Notwithstanding its statutory underpinnings, however, labour arbitration has evolved as an essentially private and consensual process whose procedures and scope have traditionally been controlled by the parties themselves. Before examining the reasoning and result in *Weber*, it is critical to appreciate the evolution of the limitations of arbitrability as fashioned by unions and employers, and long affirmed by arbitrators in Canada. The parties to collective agreements have always recognized that to make all workplace disputes arbitrable is unrealistic. While the enlightened participants in a collective bargaining relationship may wish to see justice and fairness in all things, they do not want to encourage all manner of grievances or surrender the day-to-day life of the workplace to micro-management by arbitrators. ...
>
> Central to [McLachlin J.'s] reasoning [in *Weber*] is the perception that the grievance and arbitration provisions of the collective agreement 'are broad, and expressly purport to regulate the conduct at the heart of this dispute.' Specifically, she notes that article 2.2 of the collective agreement allows a grievance to be filed in respect of '[a]ny allegation that an employee has been subjected to unfair treatment or any dispute arising out of the content of this Agreement.' ...
>
> Unfortunately, the Court failed to understand that broad allegations of unjust treatment were never intended to be arbitrated and that the grievance procedure, established under article 2 of the collective agreement, is distinct from the arbitration procedure, separately provided for under article 3. Of that there can be no doubt. Article 3.1 of the collective agreement then before the Court, titled 'Arbitration,' a provision not discussed by the majority or in dissent, expressly provides as follows:
>
> > This procedure shall not apply to Union allegations of unfair treatment. ...
>
> Although Ontario Hydro and the Power Workers' Union expressly agreed that allegations of 'unfair treatment' arising under the 'wide language of article 2.2 of the Agreement' were not arbitrable, the Court rested much of its decision requiring arbitration on this provision. In the result, the central reasoning of the Supreme Court of Canada in a decision of enormous importance to the labour relations community is reducible to a logical *non-sequitur*: because his collective agreement allows him to grieve unjust treatment, a board of arbitration has exclusive jurisdiction to arbitrate Weber's *Charter* and tort claims. However, claims of unjust treatment were, by the clear terms of the collective agreement, inarbitrable.
>
> The Court based its reasoning on the fact that the sick benefits, whose alleged abuse by Weber triggered the surveillance, were part of the collective agreement. McLachlin J.'s

comment that the dispute fell within the grievance procedure because 'the wide language of art. 2.2 of the agreement [unjust treatment], combined with item 13.0 [sick benefits], covers the conduct alleged against Hydro,' and her further observation that the employer's actions were 'directly related to a process which is expressly subject to the *grievance procedure*,' are beyond reproach (emphasis added). The Court's reasoning breaks down, however, when grievability is confused with arbitrability.

Further, as the subsequent court and arbitral jurisprudence ... demonstrates, the line of jurisdictional fence-plotting has been made extremely wobbly and unpredictable for judges and arbitrators attempting to apply *Weber* because of the ambiguity of the Court's two-fold test for vesting exclusive arbitral jurisdiction: the nature of the dispute and the ambit of the collective agreement. As is becoming painfully evident, courts and arbitrators are frequently at a loss to define those disputes which arise inferentially from the collective agreement. Bearing in mind that legislators in their wisdom have long required that collective agreements be in writing, and that arbitrators have generally been sensitive not to imply unduly rights and obligations not reduced to writing, absent some clear indication in the language or scheme of the collective agreement itself, the new concept of matters arising 'inferentially' from the collective agreement creates an unprecedented standard upon whose application honest adjudicators will inevitably differ, and in relation to which employers and unions may exercise less contractual control and predictability.

There is also a substantial argument to be made, which is in fact espoused in some quarters of the union movement, that far from being a victory for trade unions and collective bargaining, *Weber* will, in the end, prove to be an anti-union decision, at least in its consequences. As generally democratic institutions with relatively limited resources, unions have reason, after *Weber*, to fear the pressures that will now mount to pursue wide-ranging claims far beyond the scope of grievances traditionally brought to arbitration. They may be forced, under the threat of accusations of breach of their duty of fair representation, to bring or defend claims of defamation and negligence, as well as a multitude of statutory and *Charter* claims at arbitration. Labour arbitration itself, originally conceived as an informal and less costly alternative to the courts to resolve relatively simple contractual disputes, may increasingly become the forum for a much broader range of claims that are not contractual in their essence, involving more extensive and complex forms of evidence, resulting in awards and remedies of a kind which would have been unimaginable and would have been seen as undesirable by legislators and practitioners involved in the establishment and evolution of what, until now, has been the relatively efficient and expeditious labour arbitration process....

However, while it may be expected that the Supreme Court will have occasion to clarify, and indeed rectify, [*Weber's* obliteration of the fences erected by collective agreements to protect the privileged ground of arbitrability], it remains open for some to argue that the result in *Weber* demonstrates the Court's intention that grievable 'unfairness' complaints, including *Charter*, statutory and common law claims, are arbitrable, notwithstanding contrary language expressly negotiated within the terms of a collective agreement. It is to be hoped that, in the end, common sense will prevail, and that neither arbitrators nor courts will conclude that the parties to a collective agreement intended arbitration to be the exclusive forum for such open-ended claims, absent clear and unequivocal contractual language to support such a conclusion.

Few would question the value of single-forum efficiencies for the resolution of collective agreement-based claims having several facets, which might otherwise involve litigation before two or more tribunals or courts.... It is, however, an entirely different order of things for trade unions to take on the burden of enforcing statutory and *Charter* rights which have only a marginal employment connection, or for them to be compelled to vindicate common law rights traditionally protected by the courts, such as actions in defamation never before arbitrable. The wisdom of forcing employers to defend such claims in labour arbitrations is equally questionable....

In Canada, post-*Weber*, the concern is that arbitrators will assume jurisdiction beyond the intended scope of the collective agreement, based on an overly broad characterization of the 'nature of the dispute' and the 'ambit of the collective agreement,' to use the twofold terminology of McLachlin J. At first blush many, including this author, welcomed the single forum rationale of *Weber*. However, as demonstrated in the cases to date, the concept of disputes 'which expressly or *inferentially* arise out of the collective agreement' as a basis for exclusive arbitral jurisdiction has proven dangerously ambiguous, undermining the common law rights of individuals and threatening a long-established and rational understanding of the limits of arbitrability, so essential to sound labour relations and a viable labour arbitration process controlled by the parties themselves....

If *Weber* is broadly interpreted, the focus of arbitrators could shift from their traditional role of facilitating the smooth functioning of collective agreements to vindicating individual rights at the expense of long-term collective bargaining relationships. When the main subject-matter of labour arbitration expands from disputes about overtime provisions, call-in pay and statutory holidays to include bitter personal conflicts about negligence, defamation and other emotion-charged individual rights, arbitration itself may come to be perceived as an instrument that promotes conflict and human discord, in ways that do not ultimately serve the best long-term interests of employers, unions or employees....

Likewise, *Weber* can be a positive step forward if it is understood as a logical extension of *McLeod v. Egan*, facilitating the single-forum resolution of genuine collective agreement disputes which the parties themselves intended to be arbitrable, notwithstanding that those disputes have a related *Charter*, statutory or common law dimension. In Canada, it will be incumbent on the courts, arbitrators and practitioners of labour relations to appreciate the consequences for the arbitration process and the danger for collective bargaining itself in giving *Weber* too broad an interpretation. Subject to well-established precepts of public policy, the critical concept of arbitrability must never be allowed to go beyond the contractual control of the parties themselves.

In a healthy and responsive legal system, 'law' is not a moral imperative handed down from on high. Rather, it is the product of human interaction and mutual expectations developed at the grassroots, carefully nurtured over time. Recognizing that truth, labour arbitration will be better served if arbitrators, in the face of *Weber*, return to the first of first principles and ask, 'What did the parties intend?'

For their part, employers and unions would do well to be explicit in their collective agreements. They must appreciate the potential cost to their relationship, and to their respective resources, if the vindication of personal claims consumes the arbitration agenda. They should be clear if they do not intend tort claims such as defamation and negligence to be arbitrable. They should also specify that *Charter* and statutory issues are arbitrable only for the purposes of dealing with an alleged violation of their collective agreement, or as otherwise required by statute. With these adjustments, and a degree of understanding by the courts and arbitrators, labour arbitration will retain its proper focus of interpreting and applying collective agreements and facilitating the collective bargaining process. In the end employers, unions and employees will be better served. [Reprinted with permission of Lancaster House Publishing.]

For later discussions of the problems arising from the perceived vagueness of the standards laid down in *Weber* and how courts and arbitrators have been dealing with those problems, see Andrew Lokan & Maryth Yachnin, "From *Weber* to *Parry Sound*: The Expanded Scope of Arbitration" (2004) 11 *Canadian Labour and Employment Law Journal* 1; Brian Etherington, "*O.P.S.E.U. v. Seneca College*: Deference as a Two-Edged Sword—A Missed Opportunity to Address the '*Weber* Gap'" (2006-2007) 13 *Canadian Labour and Employment Law Journal* 301 (where the "*Weber* gap" is defined as "the gap between the existence of individual rights at common law and under the *Charter* on the one hand, and access to a forum for the effective pursuit of such rights on the other," at 303); and Elizabeth Shilton, "Enforcing Workplace Pension Rights for Unionized Employees: Is There a '*Weber* Gap'?" (2015) 19 *Canadian Labour & Employment Law Journal* 135 (where the author provides a short overview of the notion of the "*Weber* gap" and provides a comprehensive footnote citing the scholarship on the question).

Despite such concerns, a majority of the Supreme Court of Canada more recently indicated its intention to continue to apply *Weber* in a broad fashion to expand the scope of exclusive arbitral jurisdiction. In *Bisaillon v Concordia University*, 2006 SCC 19, the Court reaffirmed what the majority referred to (at para 33) as "a liberal position according to which grievance arbitrators have a broad exclusive jurisdiction over issues relating to conditions of employment, provided that those conditions can be shown to have an express or implicit connection to the collective agreement." An employee of the university who worked under a collective agreement had applied to bring a class action on behalf of members of the employee pension plan against the university for actions it had taken in the administration and use of the pension fund. Most of the members of the pension plan were employed in nine bargaining units subject to nine separate collective agreements with nine different unions. One of the nine unions agreed with what the university had done, but the other eight supported the application for a class action. The court of first instance declined to authorize the class action, holding that the subject matter of the dispute was within the exclusive jurisdiction of grievance arbitration under each of the nine collective agreements, because the pension plan was a benefit provided for under those agreements. The Court of Appeal reversed that decision, on the basis that the pension plan existed independently of any single collective agreement and a grievance arbitrator appointed under any one agreement would have no jurisdiction over the claims of employees covered by the other eight agreements.

The majority of the Supreme Court, in an opinion by LeBel J., reinstated the refusal to authorize a class action, on the basis that the disputes fell within the exclusive jurisdiction of grievance arbitrators because each of the collective agreements referred expressly to the pension plan. The parties had decided to incorporate into their collective agreements the conditions for applying the pension plan, and it would be incompatible with the exclusive representation rights of the nine unions for them to grant the status of class representative to the individual plaintiff in a class action — even though eight of the nine unions supported the application, and even though the majority of the Court acknowledged that each arbitrator would only have jurisdiction over the claims of employees who were subject to the collective agreement under which that particular arbitrator was appointed and that the process could lead to multiple proceedings and inconsistent results.

Justice Bastarache, dissenting, was of the view that in its essential character, the dispute did not arise out of the interpretation, application, or violation of the collective agreement. The pension plan, he said, transcended any single collective agreement, and superior courts were the only forum with jurisdiction to hear the claims. In his opinion, the presence of a single indivisible pension fund which predated the multiple collective agreements and employment contracts indicated that the claim arose essentially from the pension plan and not from the various agreements, and no one agreement could alter or affect the fund itself. Justice Bastarache also pointed to the inevitability of multiple proceedings and contradictory rulings, and to the fact that there would be no way of reconciling contradictory orders. This meant that, in his view, a class action in court was the only principled and practical way to resolve the matters in dispute.

For a critical discussion of the Supreme Court of Canada judgments in the *Bisaillon* case, in conjunction with the *Isidore Garon* case referred to in Section 9:520, see Jo-Anne Pickel, "*Isidore Garon* and *Bisaillon*: More Complications in Determining Arbitral Jurisdiction" (2006–2007) 13 *Canadian Labour & Employment Law Journal* 329.

9:520 Arbitration and Other Statutory Tribunals

The Supreme Court of Canada's ruling in *Weber* that arbitrators had exclusive jurisdiction over *Charter* claims as long as the dispute arose expressly or inferentially from the collective agreement led many (especially employers) to argue that the same test should be applied to jurisdictional overlaps between arbitration and other employment law forums, such as the human rights forum. The Court expressly declined to rule on that issue in the *Parry Sound* case, excerpted in Section 9:330, but did deal with it in the following decision.

***Quebec (Commission des droits de la personne et des droits de la jeunesse on behalf of Morin et al) v Quebec (Attorney General)*, 2004 SCC 39, [2004] 2 SCR 185**

> [Amendments negotiated during the lifetime of a collective agreement between a group of teachers' unions and the Quebec government adversely affected a subset of employees consisting primarily of younger and less-experienced teachers. The younger teachers complained to the Quebec Human Rights Commission that the amendments violated their equality rights under the Quebec human rights statute (the *Charter of Human Rights and Freedoms*) by treating them less favourably than older teachers. The commission brought the matter to the Human Rights Tribunal. The government asked the tribunal to decline jurisdiction on the ground that the matter was exclusively within arbitral jurisdiction. The

tribunal rejected the request, but was reversed by the Quebec Court of Appeal. The complainant teachers appealed to the Supreme Court of Canada.]

McLACHLIN CJ (Iacobucci, Major, Binnie and Fish JJ concurring):
[...]

B. ANALYSIS

6 The nature of Canadian labour-management relations changed dramatically following the Second World War. Federal and provincial legislation, seeking to create a better climate for the resolution of labour-management disputes, introduced grievance arbitration to provide for the quick and efficient resolution of disputes arising under collective agreements. Not surprisingly, this conferral of authority on grievance arbitrators sometimes leads to disputes about the proper scope of their jurisdiction.

7 There is no easy answer to the question of which of two possible tribunals should decide disputes that arise in the labour context where legislation appears to permit both to do so. As explained in *Weber v. Ontario Hydro*, [1995] 2 S.C.R. 929, three outcomes are possible.

8 The first possibility is to find jurisdiction over the dispute in both tribunals. This is called the "concurrent" jurisdiction model. On this model, any labour dispute could be brought before either the labour arbitrator or the courts or other tribunals.

9 The second possibility is the "overlapping" jurisdiction model. On this model, while labour tribunals consider traditional labour law issues, nothing ousts the jurisdiction of courts or other tribunals over matters that arise in the employment context, but fall outside traditional labour law issues.

10 The third possibility is the "exclusive" jurisdiction model. On this model, jurisdiction lies exclusively in either the labour arbitrator or in the alternate tribunal, but not in both.

11 *Weber* holds that the model that applies in a given situation depends on the governing legislation, as applied to the dispute viewed in its factual matrix. In *Weber*, the concurrent and overlapping jurisdiction approaches were ruled out because the provisions of the Ontario *Labour Relations Act*, R.S.O. 1990, c. L.2, when applied to the facts of the dispute, dictated that the labour arbitrator had exclusive jurisdiction over the dispute. However, *Weber* does not stand for the proposition that labour arbitrators always have exclusive jurisdiction in employer-union disputes. Depending on the legislation and the nature of the dispute, other tribunals may possess overlapping jurisdiction, concurrent jurisdiction, or themselves be endowed with exclusive jurisdiction ... As stated in *Weber, supra*, at para. 53, "[b]ecause the nature of the dispute and the ambit of the collective agreement will vary from case to case, it is impossible to categorize the classes of case that will fall within the exclusive jurisdiction of the arbitrator."

12 In the present case the complainants filed a complaint with the Quebec Human Rights Commission, which then decided to proceed with a claim before the Human Rights Tribunal. The Commission, on behalf of the complainants, asked for a declaration that the terms of the collective agreement violated the equality provisions of the Quebec *Charter*. That, on its face, is precisely the type of question, read in light of the legislation and in its factual matrix, that the Human Rights Tribunal is mandated to answer.

13 However, the unions, school boards and the Attorney General object to the Human Rights Tribunal resolving this issue. The basis of their objection is that s. 100 of the Quebec *Labour Code*, R.S.Q., c. C-27, gives arbitrators exclusive jurisdiction over grievances arising under collective agreements. The complaint, they suggest, is such a grievance, and therefore, the Human Rights Tribunal has no jurisdiction.

14 The case thus turns on whether the legislation confers exclusive jurisdiction on the arbitrator over this dispute. At this point, I diverge, with respect, from my colleague Bastarache J. who starts from the assumption that there is an "established principle" of arbitral exclusivity in Quebec. He formulates the principal question as whether "the principle of exclusive arbitral jurisdiction, a wellestablished principle in Quebec law, [should] be abandoned in favour of the jurisdiction of the Human Rights Tribunal in cases where a dispute between unionized workers and their employer raises a human rights issue" (para. 32). Thus framed, the question presupposes exclusivity. But, as we have seen, there is no legal presumption of exclusivity *in abstracto*. Rather, the question in each case is whether the relevant legislation applied to the dispute at issue, taken in its full factual context, establishes that the labour arbitrator has exclusive jurisdiction over the dispute.

15 This question suggests two related steps. The first step is to look at the relevant legislation and what it says about the arbitrator's jurisdiction. The second step is to look at the nature of the dispute, and see whether the legislation suggests it falls exclusively to the arbitrator. The second step is logically necessary since the question is whether the legislative mandate applies to the particular dispute at issue. It facilitates a better fit between the tribunal and the dispute and helps "to ensure that jurisdictional issues are decided in a manner that is consistent with the statutory schemes governing the parties," according to the underlying rationale of *Weber, supra*; see *Regina Police Assn. Inc. v. Regina (City) Board of Police Commissioners*, [2000] 1 S.C.R. 360, 2000 SCC 14, at para. 39.

16 Turning to the first step, s. 100 of the Quebec *Labour Code* requires that "[e]very grievance shall be submitted to arbitration in the manner provided in the collective agreement if it so provides and the certified association and the employer abide by it." This tells us that the arbitrator is competent to resolve all grievances under the collective agreement. The *Labour Code* s. 1(*f*), defines "grievance" as "any disagreement respecting the interpretation or application of a collective agreement." In other words, the arbitrator has jurisdiction over matters arising out of the collective agreement's operation. In *Weber*, this jurisdiction was found to be exclusive.

17 The Quebec *Charter* sets out a mechanism for the investigation and enforcement of human rights. It creates the Commission, which has the responsibility for investigating alleged violations of the *Charter* and which may, in turn, submit the allegations to the Human Rights Tribunal for remedy.

18 Section 111 of the Quebec *Charter* grants the Human Rights Tribunal a large jurisdiction over human rights matters in Quebec; see H. Brun and G. Tremblay, *Droit constitutionnel* (4th ed. 2002), at p. 991. The Tribunal is responsible for interpreting and applying the *Charter* in a wide range of circumstances. The importance of the Tribunal's mandate is underlined by the fact that the legislation provides that the president of the Human Rights Tribunal be chosen from judges on the Court of Québec having "notable

experience and expertise in, sensitivity to and interest for matters of human rights and freedoms"; see s. 101 of the *Charter*.

19 While the Tribunal enjoys generous jurisdiction over human rights violations, it is not exclusive. First, the Quebec *Charter* expressly exempts certain matters from the Commission's purview. Section 77 does so where a complainant or victim has personally pursued a remedy under s. 49 or s. 80 of the *Charter*. Similarly, s. 49.1 of the *Charter* removes the Human Rights Tribunal's jurisdiction over issues covered by the *Pay Equity Act*, R.S.Q., c. E-12.001. Second, the *Charter* permits, but does not oblige, the Commission to refuse to act or stop acting on behalf of a complainant in certain situations, including where "the victim or the complainant has, on the basis of the same facts, personally pursued a remedy other than those provided for in sections 49 and 80" (s. 77(4)). It follows that the Commission's and the Human Rights Tribunal's jurisdiction may be concurrent with that of other adjudicative bodies; see Brun and Tremblay, *supra*, at p. 992.

20 The second step is to look at the dispute in issue to determine whether it falls within the ambit of the arbitrator's exclusive jurisdiction. We must look at the dispute in its full factual context. Its legal characterization—whether it is a tort claim, a human rights claim, or a claim under the labour contract—is not determinative. The question is whether the dispute, viewed in its essential character and not formalistically, is one over which the legislature intended the arbitrator to have exclusive jurisdiction; see *Weber*, *supra*.

21 In *Weber*, this Court concluded that the dispute—a claim for tort arising from the employer's alleged trespass on the employee's land in the course of a dispute about sick-leave regulated by the collective agreement—fell under the collective agreement and hence within the scope of s. 45 of the Ontario *Labour Relations Act*, which provided:

> 45.(1) Every collective agreement shall provide for the final and binding settlement by arbitration, without stoppage of work, of all differences between the parties arising from the interpretation, application, administration or alleged violation of the agreement, including any question as to whether a matter is arbitrable.

This clause is arguably stronger than the clause conferring jurisdiction on the arbitrator in the case at bar. However, the critical difference between *Weber* and this case lies in the factual context that gave rise to the dispute.

22 In *Weber*, the dispute clearly arose out of the operation of the collective agreement. It was basically a dispute about sick-leave, which became encumbered with an incidental claim for trespass. In these circumstances, the majority of the Court concluded that it fell squarely within s. 45 and should be determined exclusively by the labour arbitrator.

23 Here, the same cannot be said. Taking the dispute in its factual context, as *Weber* instructs, the main fact that animates the dispute between the parties is that the collective agreement contains a term that treats the complainants and members of their group—those teachers who had not yet attained the highest level of the pay scale who were typically younger and less experienced—less favourably than more senior teachers. This, in turn, emerges from the fact that in the course of negotiating the collective agreement, disputes arose over how to meet the government's budgetary demands and how cutbacks in the budget should be allocated among union members. In its factual matrix,

this is essentially a dispute as to how the collective agreement should allocate decreased resources among union members. Ultimately, the decision was to impose the costs of the budget cutbacks primarily on one group of union members—those with less seniority. This gave rise to the issue in the dispute: was it discriminatory to negotiate and agree to a term that adversely affected only younger and less experienced teachers? The essence of the dispute is the process of the negotiation and the inclusion of this term in the collective agreement.

24 Viewed in its factual matrix, this is not a dispute over which the arbitrator has exclusive jurisdiction. It does not arise out of the operation of the collective agreement, so much as out of the pre-contractual negotiation of that agreement. This Court has recognized that disputes that arise out of prior contracts or the formation of the collective agreement itself may raise issues that do not fall within the scope of arbitration.... Everyone agrees on how the agreement, if valid, should be interpreted and applied. The only question is whether the process leading to the adoption of the alleged discriminatory clause and the inclusion of that clause in the agreement violates the Quebec *Charter*, rendering it unenforceable.

25 That is not to say that the arbitrator lacks the power to deal with all issues which involve a *Charter* claim. This Court has recognized that arbitrators may resolve legal issues incidental to their function of interpreting and applying the collective agreement: *Parry Sound (District) Social Services Administration Board v. O.P.S.E.U., Local 324*.... Moreover, s. 100.12 of the *Labour Code* specifically confers on the arbitrator the authority to interpret and apply any Act necessary to settle a grievance. But, at the same time, the dispute, viewed not formalistically but in its essential nature, engages matters which pertain more to alleged discrimination in the formation and validity of the agreement, than to its "interpretation or application," which is the source of the arbitrator's jurisdiction under the *Labour Code*, s. 1(f). The Human Rights Commission and the Human Rights Tribunal were created by the legislature to resolve precisely these sorts of issues.

26 Here the complaint was brought by the teachers to the Commission, which ultimately brought the matter before the Human Rights Tribunal. The Tribunal was entitled to exercise its jurisdiction over it. It was satisfied that the complainants had not "on the basis of the same facts, personally pursued one of the remedies provided for in sections 49 and 80" (s. 77 of the Quebec *Charter*), avoiding duplication. As noted, the Commission could have refused to proceed *as a matter of discretion* if the complainants had, on the basis of the same facts, "*personally* pursued a remedy *other than* those provided for in sections 49 and 80" (also s. 77 of the *Charter* (emphasis added)). But the complainants had not done so and thus the Commission was entitled to file the complaint before the Human Rights Tribunal. Moreover, for these same reasons, the Tribunal was entitled to exercise its jurisdiction over the claim under the governing legislation.

27 It is argued that the Tribunal should not have taken jurisdiction because the complainants could have asked their unions to "grieve" the alleged violation under the collective agreement. I cannot accept this argument. First, the nature of the question does not lend itself to characterization as a grievance *under* the collective agreement, since the claim is not that the agreement has been violated, but that it is itself discriminatory. Without suggesting that the arbitrator could not have considered these matters

incidentally to a different dispute under the collective agreement, the complainant cannot be faulted for taking this particular dispute to the Human Rights Commission, which then filed a claim before the Human Rights Tribunal.

28 Second, the unions were, on the face of it, opposed in interest to the complainants, being affiliated with one of the negotiating groups that made the allegedly discriminatory agreement. If the unions chose not to file a grievance before the arbitrator, the teachers would be left with no legal recourse (other than possibly filing a claim against their unions for breaching the duty of fair representation). This concern was summarized well by Abella J.A. in *Ford Motor Co. of Canada Ltd. v. Ontario (Human Rights Commission)* (2001), 209 D.L.R. (4th) 465 (Ont. C.A.) (leave to appeal refused, [2002] 3 S.C.R. x), at paras. 61–62 as follows:

> [T]here may be circumstances where an individual unionized employee finds the arbitral process foreclosed, since the decision whether to proceed with a grievance is the union's and not the employee's. Moreover, the alleged human rights violation may be against the union, as stipulated in the [*Human Rights*] *Code* in ss. 6 and 45(1)....
>
> In an arbitration under a collective agreement, only the employer and union have party status. The unionized employee's interests are advanced by and through the union, which necessarily decides how the allegations should be represented or defended. Applying *Weber* so as to assign exclusive jurisdiction to labour arbitrators could therefore render chimerical the rights of individual unionized employees.

29 Third, even if the unions had filed a grievance on behalf of the complainants, the arbitrator would not have jurisdiction over all of the parties to the dispute. Although the local unions and school boards were not involved in negotiating and agreeing to the clause impugned as discriminatory, the grievance and arbitration process set out in the collective agreement is directed at the resolution of disputes between the local unions and the school boards and not at those arising between the unions and the respondents that *did* actually agree to this provision. Although the Centrale des syndicats du Québec, the Fédération des syndicats de l'enseignement and the Minister are authorized to intervene in arbitration proceedings, there is no formal mechanism to bring these parties before the arbitrator.

30 Finally, because the complainants' general challenge to the validity of a provision in the collective agreement affected hundreds of teachers, the Human Rights Tribunal was a "better fit" for this dispute than the appointment of a single arbitrator to deal with a single grievance within the statutory framework of the *Labour Code*. In these circumstances the complainants cannot be faulted for taking their claim to the Human Rights Commission rather than to the union with the hope (but no guarantee) of having it filed as a grievance before a labour arbitrator.

C. Conclusion

31 I would allow the appeal and remit the matter to the Human Rights Tribunal.

[Justices Bastarache and Arbour dissented, arguing that proper application of the test from *Weber* should result in exclusive arbitral jurisdiction in this case because the dispute concerned the negotiation of clauses in the collective agreement and thus arose directly from that agreement.]

* * * * *

Competing viewpoints on the wisdom of maintaining concurrent jurisdiction between arbitration and human rights tribunals are set out by Faye Faraday, "The Expanding Scope of Labour Arbitration: Mainstreaming Human Rights Values and Remedies" (2005) 12 *Canadian Labour & Employment Journal* 419, and Peter Gall, Andrea Zwack, & Kate Bayne, "Determining Human Rights Issues in the Unionized Workplace: The Case for Exclusive Arbitral Jurisdiction" (2005) 12 *Canadian Labour & Employment Journal* 445.

In *Isidore Garon ltée v Tremblay; Fillion et Frères (1976) inc v Syndicat national des employés de garage du Québec inc*, 2006 SCC 2, the Supreme Court of Canada reviewed two Quebec awards in which grievance arbitrators took jurisdiction over termination notice claims under the *Civil Code of Quebec*. In neither case did the collective agreement say anything about plant closings. One of the agreements did make the employer responsible for pay in lieu of notice required under applicable legislation if employees were laid off for more than six months. The other agreement said nothing about termination payments. The Quebec Court of Appeal had upheld the arbitrators' findings of jurisdiction in both cases, largely on the strength of the Supreme Court's holding in *Parry Sound*, excerpted in Section 9:330, to the effect that the substantive rights and obligations set out in employment-related statutes are implicit in every collective agreement, whether or not the particular agreement makes reference to those statutes.

The decision of the Supreme Court in *Isidore Garon* imposes an important limitation on the extension of arbitral jurisdiction over statutory claims. Substantive rules from a statutory scheme that are incompatible with the collective labour relations regime cannot be incorporated into the collective agreement, and therefore do not come within the jurisdiction of a grievance arbitrator. If a statutory provision on the individual employment relationship is compatible with the collective bargaining regime and if it is a supplementary or mandatory norm, the arbitrator will have jurisdiction to apply it. However, only those parts of the statute that are compatible with the collective scheme are capable of being implicitly incorporated into the collective agreement.

In arriving at this conclusion, the majority of the Court noted the tension between two lines of authority on the relationship between the collective bargaining and statutory regimes designed to regulate the individual employment relationship. It pointed to a long line of cases, including *McGavin Toastmaster Ltd v Ainscough*, [1976] 1 SCR 718, excerpted in Chapter 10, Section 10:220, and *St Anne Nackawic Pulp & Paper Co Ltd v CPWU, Local 219*, [1986] 1 SCR 704, referred to in Section 9:510, which had recognized the autonomy of collective bargaining law and held that it had largely supplanted or displaced the general law on the individual employment relationship, particularly where the general law was inconsistent with the collective bargaining regime. The majority judgment then referred to the other line of authority, culminating in *Weber* and *Parry Sound*, where the Court had moved toward incorporating into collective agreements the norms set out in the *Canadian Charter of Rights and Freedoms*, in human rights legislation and in employment statutes. It noted that the two lines appeared to be in conflict, in that the first suggested that the general law had been excluded by the collective bargaining regime, while the second held that much of the general law was implicitly included in the collective agreement and was within arbitral jurisdiction. The majority sought to reconcile the two lines of authority by observing that the first dealt with the supplanting of individual rights which were incompatible with the collective bargaining regime, and the second dealt with the power of arbitrators to apply general law which was compatible with that regime and was incorporated into the collective agreement.

More recently, in Quebec, further questions have arisen concerning the Court's approach in *Isidore Garon*. In *Syndicat de la fonction publique du Québec v Quebec (Attorney General)*, 2010 SCC 28, the majority rejected the notion that statutes of public order are implicitly incorporated into collective agreements. The Court introduced the concept of a hierarchy of sources of Quebec labour law, which requires that the content of a collective agreement be modified by the effect of the public order provisions. This meant that a provision in the collective agreement that would have deprived probationary employees from their statutory right to grieve an unjust dismissal after two years of continuous service had to be considered unwritten. Some suggest that this latter approach better respects the intention of the parties by upholding their agreement insofar as it conforms to superior norms without implicitly injecting external norms into the agreements.

9:530 Criminal Courts Versus Arbitrators

The question of issue estoppel and abuse of process in the context of arbitrators and the criminal courts was addressed by the Supreme Court of Canada in *Toronto (City) v CUPE, Local 79*, 2003 SCC 63. The grievor was a union member who had been convicted of sexually assaulting a boy under his supervision as a recreation instructor in Toronto. He pleaded not guilty but was found not to be credible and was convicted. The City of Toronto fired the grievor a few days later. At the arbitration, the arbitrator found the conviction to be admissible evidence, but held that he was not bound to its conclusions on the question of whether the grievor had sexually assaulted the boy. The arbitrator found that the presumption raised by the criminal conviction had been rebutted, and therefore, the grievor had been dismissed by the City without just cause.

Justice Arbour, writing for the majority, relied upon the abuse of process doctrine; issue estoppel was inapplicable because the parties had changed (at para 32), and collateral attack did not apply because the union was not seeking to overturn the conviction itself in the different forum (at para 34). Justice Arbour found that under the abuse of process doctrine, the arbitrator was compelled to accept the conclusions of the criminal conviction. The "primary focus of the doctrine of abuse of process is the integrity of the adjudicative functions of courts," not so much the interests of the parties (at para 43). Here, "blatant abuse of process" occurred because the "grievor was convicted in a criminal court and he exhausted all his avenues of appeal" (at para 56). In effect, on a correctness standard, the arbitrator substituted his own finding for that of the court's, even though arbitrators are "considerably less equipped" than presiding criminal courts judges or juries to engage in a "fair search for the truth" (at para 58). In short, "[t]he arbitrator was required as a matter of law to give full effect to the conviction" (at para 58).

Toronto (City) v CUPE, Local 79, 2003 SCC 63 was relied upon by both majorities and minorities in *British Columbia (Workers' Compensation Board) v Figliola*, 2011 SCC 52 and *Penner v Niagara (Regional Police Services Board)*, 2013 SCC 19, discussed hereafter.

CHAPTER 9: THE COLLECTIVE AGREEMENT AND GRIEVANCE ARBITRATION

9:531 Arbitrators Versus Other Administrative Tribunals

In two recent cases, the Supreme Court of Canada has addressed the issues of *res judicata* in the context of concurrent jurisdiction of administrative tribunals: *British Columbia (Workers' Compensation Board) v Figliola*, 2011 SCC 52; and *Penner v Niagara (Regional Police Services Board)*, 2013 SCC 19.

Figliola was a judicial review of a decision of the British Columbia Human Rights Tribunal. Three claimants were injured while working and thereafter suffered from chronic pain. They applied to the British Columbia Workers' Compensation Board and received a fixed compensation award through the board's chronic pain policy. The claimants appealed the decision to the board's Review Division, claiming it was patently unreasonable, unconstitutional, and discriminatory on the grounds of disability under section 8 of the British Columbia *Human Rights Code*. The review officer held that he was statutorily barred from hearing the constitutional questions. He also found that the question of patent unreasonableness was reserved for consideration by the Workers' Compensation Appeal Tribunal (WCAT). Regarding the issue of exclusive jurisdiction, the review officer applied *Tranchemontagne v Ontario (Director, Disability Support Program)*, 2006 SCC 14, and found that the Human Rights Tribunal did not have exclusive jurisdiction over the *Human Rights Code* complaint. He then concluded that the chronic pain policy was not contrary to section 8 of the *Code*. Before the claimants could appeal this decision to the WCAT, the legislation amended the WCAT's authority to apply the *Code*. While the applicants could still apply for judicial review, they filed a fresh section 8 complaint with the Human Rights Tribunal instead.

At issue on appeal to the Supreme Court was section 27(1)(f) of the *Human Rights Code*, which allows the Human Rights Tribunal to dismiss a complaint where "the substance of the complaint or that part of the complaint has been appropriately dealt with in another proceeding."

The Court split 5:4. Justice Abella, writing for the majority, allowed the appeal, set aside the tribunal's decision, and dismissed the complaints. She found that section 27(1)(f) was the statutory reflection of the common law principles underlying the doctrines of issue estoppel, collateral attack, and abuse of process. The majority held that the primary concern is with "finality, the avoidance of multiplicity of proceedings, and protection for the integrity of the administration of justice, all in the name of fairness" (para 25). Section 27(1)(f) did not codify but did embrace these principles. The majority found that fairness of finality should guide the tribunal's decision (para 36). In determining whether a complaint has been appropriately dealt with under section 27(1)(f), the tribunal should ask itself three questions: "whether there was concurrent jurisdiction to decide human rights issues; whether the previously decided legal issue was essentially the same as what is being complained of to the Tribunal; and whether there was an opportunity for the complainants or their privies to know the case to be met and have the chance to meet it, regardless of how closely the previous process procedurally mirrored the one the Tribunal prefers or uses itself" (para 37). This analysis orients section 27(1)(f) "towards creating territorial respect among neighbouring tribunals, including respect for their right to have their own vertical lines of review protected from lateral adjudicative poaching" (para 38). The tribunal's strict adherence to a technical application of issue estoppel rather than applying its general principles through section 27(1)(f) was overly formalistic, which obstructed the goal of avoiding relitigation, and was, therefore, unreasonable (para 46).

Justice Cromwell wrote for the minority. He claimed that the majority characterized the finality doctrines too narrowly, ignoring the common law's focus on balancing the goals of finality and fairness (para 58). The minority agreed that the decision was unreasonable and allowed the appeal, but it would have remitted the Workers' Compensation Board's motion to dismiss under section 27(1)(f) to the tribunal for reconsideration under the principles Cromwell J articulated. The minority found that "in the administrative law context, common law finality doctrines must be applied flexibly to maintain the necessary balance of finality and fairness" (para 65). The amendments took away the complainants' rights to a review on the merits, as well as the review officer's authority to test the board's policies against the *Code* (para 73). These changes called for a more flexible application of the common law principles. The minority suggests that "[f]aced with a complaint, the substance of which has been addressed elsewhere, the Tribunal must decide whether there is something in the circumstances of the particular case to make it inappropriate to apply the general principle that the earlier resolution of the matter should be final" (para 93). When exercising this discretion, the decision maker should consider the mandate of the previous decision-maker, the purposes of the legislative schemes, the safeguards available to the parties in the earlier proceedings, the expertise of the previous administrative decision maker, and especially "whether giving the earlier proceeding final and binding effect will work an injustice" (para 95). Thus, per the minority, while the tribunal was entitled to look at the procedural limitations of the review officer's proceedings, it focused too narrowly on the strict application of issue estoppel. The tribunal had failed to consider the fundamental fairness of the earlier proceeding and whether the substance of the complaint had been addressed (para 97).

The Court revisited similar issues in *Penner*, splitting again by a narrow 4:3 margin. Justice Cromwell wrote this time with Karakatsanis J for the majority, while Abella and LeBel JJ wrote for the dissent. *Penner* dealt more specifically with issue estoppel in the context of administrative decisions. Penner had been forcibly removed from court and arrested for disruptive behaviour. He filed a complaint under the Ontario *Police Services Act* (PSA), alleging unlawful arrest and unnecessary use of force. Shortly after that, he began a civil action for damages arising from the same incident. Under the *PSA*, the chief of police appointed a hearing officer who heard evidence from Penner, who was present at the hearing. Ultimately, the hearing officer did not find the evidence credible, found the officers not guilty of misconduct, and dismissed the complaint. The Ontario Civilian Commission on Police Services reversed that decision on the basis that the arrest was unlawful. The Ontario Divisional Court restored the original decision. With this ruling, the officers successfully moved in the Superior Court of Justice to have Penner's civil action struck on the basis of issue estoppel. The Ontario Court of Appeal found that applying the doctrine, in this case, would not result in an injustice and dismissed Penner's appeal.

At the SCC, the majority upheld the appeal. It found that the requirements of issue estoppel were met: same issue, same parties, and the earlier decision had been a final judicial decision. However, the majority found that it would be fundamentally unfair in this case to disallow Penner's civil action. Echoing Cromwell J's arguments in *Figliola*, the majority held that unfairness could be worked in two ways: unfairness in the process of the original proceedings, or, even where the original proceedings were fair, unfairness in precluding the subsequent claim (para 39). In the opinion of the majority, the Court of Appeal erred because it had failed to "fully analyze the fairness of using the results of [the disciplinary hearing] to preclude the appellant's civil claims, having regard to the nature and scope of those earlier proceedings and the parties' reasonable expectations in relation to them" (para 49). The use of issue estoppel resulted in unfairness here because, among other things, the legislative scheme of the *PSA* does not foreclose civil action; the purposes and financial stakes of the proceedings are divergent; people in Penner's position could not reasonably contemplate that an acquittal would foreclose civil proceedings; and applying issue estoppel in these types of proceedings may risk turning the administrative process into a proxy for civil actions, delaying and defeating the expeditious operation of a disciplinary hearing.

The dissent drew heavily on *Figliola*. They argued that the appeal should be dismissed, stating the Court should endorse fairness of finality, as articulated in *Figliola*. The majority in *Figliola* "explicitly rejected an approach that suggests that fairness and finality are discrete objectives. Rather, the majority embraced the notion that preserving the finality of administrative adjudication and preventing relitigating better protected the fairness and integrity of the justice system and the interests of justice" (para 99).

These decisions seem to conflict on the question of *res judicata* for administrative tribunals of concurrent jurisdiction. On the one hand, *Figliola* suggests that when one tribunal decides an issue, fairness of finality requires barring subsequent tribunals from reconsidering the legal question. On the other hand, *Penner* suggests that, even if all the criteria of issue estoppel are met, the subsequent tribunal can reconsider the legal question because both finality *and* fairness are considerations. This ostensible confusion could be challenging in the future.

However, the cases may not be as divergent as they initially seem. In *Figliola*, the Court was addressing the interpretation of a statute and rested its conclusions on the idea that this provision and tribunal ought to incorporate underlying common law principles to further its purposes, a suggestion evocative of *Nor-Man*. In *Penner*, the question was narrower. There, the Court merely asked whether or not the common law doctrine of issue estoppel ought to apply. In answering in the affirmative, the majority in *Penner* elaborated that doctrine without reference to concepts such as deference to tribunals' interpretations of their enabling statutes.

9:600 JUDICIAL REVIEW OF ARBITRATION

As indicated in the previous sections, the scope of the arbitrator's role is delimited by the courts through judicial review of arbitration awards. Identifying the standards for judicial review of the decisions of administrative tribunals, including arbitration tribunals and labour relations boards, is a matter that is at the core of administrative law, and you will no doubt look closely at it when you study that field. Here we can give only a very brief overview.

By the 1960s, through judicial review, the courts had begun to intervene actively in the interpretation of collective agreements by arbitrators, as well as in the application of labour relations statutes by labour boards. The courts drew a distinction between so-called jurisdictional issues, which were subject to very strict review on a correctness standard, and issues involving the merits of the matter in dispute in the particular case, which were deemed to be within the adjudicative tribunal's jurisdiction and expertise and on which the courts purported to give the tribunal more leeway to carry out its legislative mandate. However, the distinction between jurisdictional and non-jurisdictional issues was never even tolerably clear, and the courts often held arbitrators and labour boards to a standard of correctness on matters that arguably were not jurisdictional at all but were well within the range of issues that the legislature had assigned to the tribunal. For a classic example, see *Metropolitan Life Insurance Co v International Union of Operating Engineers*, [1970] SCR 425.

In its watershed decision in *Canadian Union of Public Employees, Local 963 v New Brunswick Liquor Corporation*, [1979] 2 SCR 227, the Supreme Court of Canada directed the courts to take a very deferential approach to the decisions of labour relations boards, largely because of the high degree of specialized expertise of those boards—an approach which sought to dissuade the lower courts from reversing a board decision unless it was "patently unreasonable." Since that time, the Supreme Court has generally taken a similarly deferential approach to the decisions of grievance arbitrators, again mainly because of their specialized expertise. The correctness standard was to be reserved only for decisions on questions that were clearly jurisdictional in nature.

By the late 1990s, however, the Court had adopted a spectrum of three standards of review—correctness, simple unreasonableness, and patent unreasonableness—not only for arbitrators and labour boards, but for administrative tribunals in general. See *Canada (Director of Investigation and Research) v Southam Inc*, [1997] 1 SCR 748. With respect to arbitration awards, the courts generally applied the "patent unreasonableness" standard to arbitral interpretations of collective agreement language and of the provisions of labour relations legislation dealing with the arbitral process, but applied the "correctness" standard to arbitral interpretations of other statutes. See *Canada Safeway Ltd v Retail, Wholesale and Department Store Union, Local 454*, [1998] 1 SCR 1079.

This approach was abandoned in the following decision.

Dunsmuir v New Brunswick, 2008 SCC 9

The judgment of McLachlin CJ and Bastarache, LeBel, Fish and Abella JJ was delivered by

BASTARACHE AND LEBEL JJ—

I. INTRODUCTION

[...]

A. Facts

[Dunsmuir was a non-unionized officer in the New Brunswick public service, and his employment arrangements had both statutory and contractual elements. His wrongful discharge grievance, brought under a specialized statutory grievance resolution process, alleged (among other things) that the government had terminated his employment without following the procedures required for the discharge of a statutory appointee. The government argued that the applicable provincial statute recognized the predominantly contractual nature of his appointment, and that those procedures therefore did not have to be followed. When Dunsmuir's grievance reached adjudication under the specialized statutory procedure, the adjudicator rejected the government's argument and upheld the grievance.

On judicial review, the matter reached the Supreme Court of Canada, which held (among other things) that the adjudicator had acted unreasonably in holding that Dunsmuir had the procedural rights of a statutory rather than a contractual office holder. The majority of the Court (McLachlin CJ and Bastarache, LeBel, Fish, and Abella JJ) held that the wording of the statute (including the presence of a privative clause) indicated that the adjudication decision was entitled to more deference than the correctness standard would warrant, but that the decision could not stand because the adjudicator had acted unreasonably in finding that Dunsmuir was entitled to a higher standard of procedural fairness than was consistent with the contractual aspect of his appointment.

The details of the Supreme Court's finding that the adjudicator had acted unreasonably need not concern readers here. What should concern them, and what makes the *Dunsmuir* case so important, is the fact that the majority of the Court went on to abolish the division between "correctness," on the one hand, and the two standards of "patent unreasonableness" and "simple unreasonableness" on the other, replacing these former two reasonableness standards with a single standard of "*reasonableness*."]

II. ISSUES

[The Court reviewed the theoretical bases for judicial review, noting its constitutional dimension and its support for both the rule of law and respect for parliamentary supremacy. The Court decided the law around these principles had become "difficult to implement" (at para 32). In reviewing the jurisprudential origins of the three standards of review, the Court found that the distinction between patent unreasonableness and reasonableness *simpliciter* was difficult to apply in practice (at para 39). Furthermore, the Court argued that the distinction would allow irrational decisions to pass unaddressed because they were not irrational *enough* to meet the patently unreasonable standard (at para 42). The Court then elaborated its new two standard approach to standard of review.]

C. Two Standards of Review

[43] The Court has moved from a highly formalistic, artificial "jurisdiction" test that could easily be manipulated, to a highly contextual "functional" test that provides great flexibility but little real on-the-ground guidance, and offers too many standards of review. What is needed is a test that offers guidance, is not formalistic or artificial, and permits review where justice requires it, but not otherwise. A simpler test is needed.

(1) Defining the Concepts of Reasonabless and Correctness

[44] As explained above, the patent unreasonableness standard was developed many years prior to the introduction of the reasonableness *simpliciter* standard in *Southam*. The intermediate standard was developed to respond to what the Court viewed as problems in the operation of judicial review in Canada, particularly the perceived all-or-nothing approach to deference, and in order to create a more finely calibrated system of judicial review (see also L. Sossin and C. M. Flood, "The Contextual Turn: Iacobucci's Legacy and the Standard of Review in Administrative Law" (2007), 57 *U.T.L.J.* 581). However, the analytical problems that arise in trying to apply the different standards undercut

any conceptual usefulness created by the inherently greater flexibility of having multiple standards of review. Though we are of the view that the three standard model is too difficult to apply to justify its retention, now, several years after *Southam*, we believe that it would be a step backwards to simply remove the reasonableness *simpliciter* standard and revert to pre-*Southam* law. As we see it, the problems that *Southam* attempted to remedy with the introduction of the intermediate standard are best addressed not by three standards of review, but by two standards, defined appropriately.

[45] We therefore conclude that the two variants of reasonableness review should be collapsed into a single form of "reasonableness" review. The result is a system of judicial review comprising two standards — correctness and reasonableness. But the revised system cannot be expected to be simpler and more workable unless the concepts it employs are clearly defined....

[50] As important as it is that courts have a proper understanding of reasonableness review as a deferential standard, it is also without question that the standard of correctness must be maintained in respect of jurisdictional and some other questions of law. This promotes just decisions and avoids inconsistent and unauthorized application of law. When applying the correctness standard, a reviewing court will not show deference to the decision maker's reasoning process; it will rather undertake its own analysis of the question. The analysis will bring the court to decide whether it agrees with the determination of the decision maker; if not, the court will substitute its own view and provide the correct answer. From the outset, the court must ask whether the tribunal's decision was correct.

(2) Determining the Appropriate Standard of Review

[51] Having dealt with the nature of the standards of review, we now turn our attention to the method for selecting the appropriate standard in individual cases. As we will now demonstrate, questions of fact, discretion and policy as well as questions where the legal issues cannot be easily separated from the factual issues generally attract a standard of reasonableness while many legal issues attract a standard of correctness. Some legal issues, however, attract the more deferential standard of reasonableness.

[52] The existence of a privative or preclusive clause gives rise to a strong indication of review pursuant to the reasonableness standard. This conclusion is appropriate because a privative clause is evidence of Parliament or a legislature's intent that an administrative decision maker be given greater deference and that interference by reviewing courts be minimized. This does not mean, however, that the presence of a privative clause is determinative. The rule of law requires that the constitutional role of superior courts be preserved and, as indicated above, neither Parliament nor any legislature can completely remove the courts' power to review the actions and decisions of administrative bodies. This power is constitutionally protected. Judicial review is necessary to ensure that the privative clause is read in its appropriate statutory context and that administrative bodies do not exceed their jurisdiction.

[53] Where the question is one of fact, discretion or policy, deference will usually apply automatically (*Mossop*, at pp. 599-600; *Dr. Q*, at para. 29; *Suresh*, at paras. 29-30). We believe that the same standard must apply to the review of questions where the legal and factual issues are intertwined with and cannot be readily separated.

[54] Guidance with regard to the questions that will be reviewed on a reasonableness standard can be found in the existing case law. Deference will usually result where a tribunal is interpreting its own statute or statutes closely connected to its function, with which it will have particular familiarity: *Canadian Broadcasting Corp. v. Canada (Labour Relations Board)*, [1995] 1 S.C.R. 157, at para. 48; *Toronto (City) Board of Education v. O.S.S.T.F., District 15*, [1997] 1 S.C.R. 487, at para. 39. Deference may also be warranted where an administrative tribunal has developed particular expertise in the application of a general common law or civil law rule in relation to a specific statutory context: *Toronto (City) v. C.U.P.E.*, at para. 72. Adjudication in labour law remains a good example of the relevance of this approach. The case law has moved away considerably from the strict position evidenced in *McLeod v. Egan*, [1975] 1 S.C.R. 517, where it was held that an administrative decision maker will always risk having its interpretation of an external statute set aside upon judicial review.

[55] A consideration of the following factors will lead to the conclusion that the decision maker should be given deference and a reasonableness test applied:

- A privative clause: this is a statutory direction from Parliament or a legislature indicating the need for deference.
- A discrete and special administrative regime in which the decision maker has special expertise (labour relations for instance).
- The nature of the question of law. A question of law that is of "central importance to the legal system ... and outside the ... specialized area of expertise" of the administrative decision maker will always attract a correctness standard (*Toronto (City) v. C.U.P.E.*, at para. 62). On the other hand, a question of law that does not rise to this level may be compatible with a reasonableness standard where the two above factors so indicate.

[56] If these factors, considered together, point to a standard of reasonableness, the decision maker's decision must be approached with deference in the sense of respect discussed earlier in these reasons. There is nothing unprincipled in the fact that some questions of law will be decided on the basis of reasonableness. It simply means giving the adjudicator's decision appropriate deference in deciding whether a decision should be upheld, bearing in mind the factors indicated.

[57] An exhaustive review is not required in every case to determine the proper standard of review. Here again, existing jurisprudence may be helpful in identifying some of the questions that generally fall to be determined according to the correctness standard (*Cartaway Resources Corp. (Re)*, [2004] 1 S.C.R. 672, 2004 SCC 26). This simply means that the analysis required is already deemed to have been performed and need not be repeated.

[58] For example, correctness review has been found to apply to constitutional questions regarding the division of powers between Parliament and the provinces in the *Constitution Act, 1867*: *Westcoast Energy Inc. v. Canada (National Energy Board)*, [1998] 1 S.C.R. 322. Such questions, as well as other constitutional issues, are necessarily subject to correctness review because of the unique role of s. 96 courts as interpreters of the Constitution: *Nova Scotia (Workers' Compensation Board) v. Martin*, [2003] 2 S.C.R. 504, 2003 SCC 54; Mullan, *Administrative Law*, at p. 60.

[59] Administrative bodies must also be correct in their determinations of true questions of jurisdiction or *vires*. We mention true questions of *vires* to distance ourselves from the extended definitions adopted before *CUPE*. It is important here to take a robust view of jurisdiction. We neither wish nor intend to return to the jurisdiction/preliminary question doctrine that plagued the jurisprudence in this area for many years. "Jurisdiction" is intended in the narrow sense of whether or not the tribunal had the authority to make the inquiry. In other words, true jurisdiction questions arise where the tribunal must explicitly determine whether its statutory grant of power gives it the authority to decide a particular matter. The tribunal must interpret the grant of authority correctly or its action will be found to be *ultra vires* or to constitute a wrongful decline of jurisdiction: D. J. M. Brown and J. M. Evans, *Judicial Review of Administrative Action in Canada* (loose-leaf), at pp. 14-3 to 14-6. An example may be found in *United Taxi Drivers' Fellowship of Southern Alberta v. Calgary (City)*, [2004] 1 S.C.R. 485, 2004 SCC 19. In that case, the issue was whether the City of Calgary was authorized under the relevant municipal acts to enact bylaws limiting the number of taxi plate licences (para. 5, *per* Bastarache J.). That case involved the decision-making powers of a municipality and exemplifies a true question of jurisdiction or *vires*. These questions will be narrow. We reiterate the caution of Dickson J. in *CUPE* that reviewing judges must not brand as jurisdictional issues that are doubtfully so.

[60] As mentioned earlier, courts must also continue to substitute their own view of the correct answer where the question at issue is one of general law "that is both of central importance to the legal system as a whole and outside the adjudicator's specialized area of expertise" (*Toronto (City) v. C.U.P.E.*, at para. 62, *per* LeBel J.). Because of their impact on the administration of justice as a whole, such questions require uniform and consistent answers. Such was the case in *Toronto (City) v. C.U.P.E.*, which dealt with complex common law rules and conflicting jurisprudence on the doctrines of *res judicata* and abuse of process—issues that are at the heart of the administration of justice (see para. 15, *per* Arbour J.).

[61] Questions regarding the jurisdictional lines between two or more competing specialized tribunals have also been subject to review on a correctness basis: *Regina Police Assn. Inc. v. Regina (City) Board of Police Commissioners*, [2000] 1 S.C.R. 360, 2000 SCC 14; *Quebec (Commission des droits de la personne et des droits de la jeunesse) v. Quebec (Attorney General)*, [2004] 2 S.C.R. 185, 2004 SCC 39.

[62] In summary, the process of judicial review involves two steps. First, courts ascertain whether the jurisprudence has already determined in a satisfactory manner the degree of deference to be accorded with regard to a particular category of question. Second, where the first inquiry proves unfruitful, courts must proceed to an analysis of the factors making it possible to identify the proper standard of review.

[63] The existing approach to determining the appropriate standard of review has commonly been referred to as "pragmatic and functional". That name is unimportant. Reviewing courts must not get fixated on the label at the expense of a proper understanding of what the inquiry actually entails. Because the phrase "pragmatic and functional approach" may have misguided courts in the past, we prefer to refer simply to the "standard of review analysis" in the future.

[64] The analysis must be contextual. As mentioned above, it is dependent on the application of a number of relevant factors, including: (1) the presence or absence of a

privative clause; (2) the purpose of the tribunal as determined by interpretation of enabling legislation; (3) the nature of the question at issue, and; (4) the expertise of the tribunal. In many cases, it will not be necessary to consider all of the factors, as some of them may be determinative in the application of the reasonableness standard in a specific case.

[Two separate concurring opinions in *Dunsmuir* agreed with the majority view that the adjudicator's decision should be quashed, but disagreed on how the new "two standards of review" regime should be applied in the circumstances at hand and on the factors to be used in choosing the appropriate standard in a particular case. Justice Deschamps (supported by Charron and Rothstein JJ) took the position that the correctness standard should have been used, because the adjudicator's interpretation of the enabling statute called for significant application of the common law of employment, on which the courts had at least as much expertise as the adjudicator. Justice Binnie, writing only for himself, feared that the new reasonableness standard would continue to demand very subtle and difficult determinations on the appropriate level of deference in particular cases.]

It remains to be seen whether the attempt by the majority in *Dunsmuir* to simplify the law on the standard of review will succeed, or whether the distinction between correctness and reasonableness will remain as elusive as it has long been. The Supreme Court of Canada has now given the opportunity for intervenors to consider the nature and scope of judicial review. See *Bell Canada, et al v Attorney General of Canada*, 2018 CanLII 40808 (SCC).

For early empirical studies of the impact of the standard of review on the outcome of applications for judicial review of arbitration awards and labour board decisions, see Erika L Ringseis & Allen Ponak, "Judicial Review of Arbitration Awards in Alberta: Frequency, Outcomes and Standard of Review" (2007) 13 *Canadian Labour & Employment Law Journal* 301; Leonard Marvy & Voy Stelmaszynski, "Judicial Review of Ontario Labour Relations Board Decisions: From *CUPE* to *Dunsmuir* and Beyond" (2009–2010) 15 *Canadian Labour & Employment Law Journal* 555. More recently it has been suggested that there is increased intervention by reviewing courts in labour matters and some lack of consistency of approaches in implementing *Dunsmuir*: see Luba Yurchak, "Judicial Review of Labour Relations Board and Labour Arbitration Decisions in the Post-*Dunsmuir* Period in Ontario" (2017) 20 *Canadian Labour & Employment Law Journal* 447. However, this finding appears to be at odds with other research assessing the impact of *Dunsmuir* across the board in relation to a broad range of administrative tribunals: see William Lahey, Diana Ginn, David Constantine, & Nicholas Hooper, "How Has *Dunsmuir* Worked? A Legal-Empirical Analysis of Substantive Review of Administrative Decisions after *Dunsmuir v. New Brunswick*. Findings from the Courts of Nova Scotia, Quebec, Ontario and Alberta" (2017) 30 *Canadian Journal of Administrative Law and Practice* 317.

9:700 THE FUTURE OF THE GRIEVANCE RESOLUTION PROCESS

Labour arbitration, when introduced in the post–World War II era under Canadian *Wagner Act* models, was intended to be a quick, cost-effective, and expert means to resolve disputes in the workplace over the interpretation and application of collective agreements. The decisions of arbitrators, while formally binding only upon the parties, began to be seen as helpful examples for the resolution of analogous cases under the collective agreements of other parties. Parties and their counsel began to collect "arbitration awards" (as the decisions of arbitrators are known) and use them as precedents. Legal publishing houses saw a commercial opportunity and began to market labour arbitration reports series. For example, the Industrial Relations Institute first published its *Labour Arbitration Cases* in 1948. Legal academics, many of whom acted as labour arbitrators, organized and analyzed these arbitration cases in textbooks on labour arbitration: Donald J Brown & David M Beatty, *Canadian Labour Arbitration*, 4th ed (Aurora: Canada Law Book, 2006); Ronald M Snyder, *Collective Agreement Arbitration in Canada*, 5th ed (Markham: LexisNexis Canada, 2013); Morton Mitchnick & Brian Etherington, *Labour Arbitration in Canada*, 2d ed (Toronto: Lancaster House, 2006). In the French language, see Fernand Morin et al, *Droit de l'arbitrage de grief*, 6e éd (Montréal: Éditions Yvon Blais, 2012).

The growing body of jurisprudence began, in some quarters, to be called the "common law of the workplace" (Harry Arthurs, "The New Economy and the New Legality: Industrial Citizenship and the Future of Labour Arbitration" (1990) 7 *Canadian Labour & Employment Law Journal* 45). Arbitrators, in interpreting collective agreements, would not only refer to this non-binding but increasingly persuasive arbitral caselaw in their reasons for decisions, but began to assert that the parties in collective bargaining must be taken to be aware of well-settled principles of labour arbitration when negotiating their collective agreements.

Canadian administrative law treated labour arbitrators as expert decisional tribunals worthy of deference. The courts still defer to arbitrators on a standard of "reasonableness" in their interpretations of collective agreements and labour-related statutes, though the courts assert willingness to intervene to "correct" arbitrators who go astray on general propositions of law or non-labour statutes (see *Dunsmuir*, discussed above in Section 9:600). This, of course, occurs in a context where labour arbitrators have been given jurisdiction to adjudicate workplace disputes that may require the interpretation and application of the Constitution, human rights legislation, and even the common law, in order to achieve what the arbitrator considers to be a just result.

The upshot of all this has been a procedural "legalization and professionalization" of arbitration. Labour arbitration has become a very autonomous sphere of specialized dispute resolution, but it has also become increasingly dominated by lawyers presenting the cases for unions and employers, rather than lay union representatives or managers and human relations consultants. It is increasingly costly, time-consuming, and formalistic as a result. Arbitrators are now writing decisions with an eye as much to the possibility of judicial review as to the practical needs of the parties—in recognition that their autonomy is only relative and not complete. Respected observers complain that labour arbitration is no longer fulfilling its original role of giving quick, cost-effective justice in the unionized workplace; see Michel Picher, "The Canadian Railway Office of Arbitration: Keeping Grievance Hearings on the Rails" (1991) 1 *Labour Arbitration Yearbook* 37, and Warren Winkler, "Labour Arbitration and Conflict Resolution: Back to Our Roots" (Donald Wood Lecture, 2010).

Necessity being the mother of invention, the parties to arbitration and their counsel, and recently, governments, have gradually fashioned solutions to issues of the slow and expensive nature of formal arbitration. Various types of *expedited arbitration* have been tried. These have involved rules about hearings held within shortened delays of the date of the grievance, presentation of evidence through agreed-upon statements of fact, requirements for arbitrators to issue awards within certain times from the date of hearing, and agreements that such awards will not be used as precedents. Such efforts at expedited arbitration appear generally to have failed for a number of reasons, even when enshrined in statute; see Shannon Rae Webb, "Expedited Arbitration: Is it Expeditious? Evidence from Canada" (PhD Thesis, Saint Mary's University, 2015) [unpublished]. For more on the emergence and practice of expedited arbitration, see JB Rose, "The Emergence of Expedited Arbitration" (1999) *Labour Arbitration Yearbook* 13.

However, there seems to be agreement across Canada that *mediation-arbitration*, or "med-arb" as it is known, works to reduce time and expense in the resolution of grievances for a wide range of cases. The practice of med-arb can be seen as a somewhat formalized extension of the common and traditional efforts of arbitrators to assist the parties to achieve an informal settlement of their grievance dispute rather than to engage in a full hearing. In med-arb, the person appointed as an arbitrator will first make efforts to mediate a settlement through standard approaches, such as caucusing with the parties privately, trying to identify common interests, and doing shuttle diplomacy (and perhaps some arm-twisting) with respect to possible solutions. However, the parties will have agreed at the outset that, in the event they are unable to achieve a mediated settlement, the arbitrator will resume their role as adjudicator and decide the matter, giving reasons for their decision. For more detailed discussions of these processes, see David C Elliott, "Med/Arb: Fraught with Danger or Ripe with Opportunity?" (1995) 34 *Alberta Law Review* 163; and Bruce P Archibald, "Progress in Models of Justice: From Adjudication/Arbitration Through Mediation to Restorative Conferencing (and Back)" in Ronalda Murphy & Patrick Molinari, eds, *Doing Justice: Dispute Resolution in the Courts and Beyond* (Montreal: CIAJ, 2007).

To some extent, med-arb may be seen as a variant of what is becoming known in some administrative law circles as "active adjudication": see Michelle Flaherty, "Self-Represented Litigants, Active Adjudication and the Perception of Bias" (2015) 38 *Dalhousie Law Journal* 119; Michelle Flaherty, "Best Practices in Active Adjudication" (2015) 28:3 *Canadian Journal of Administrative Law and Practice* 291; and Lorne Sossin, "Administrative Justice & Adjudicative Ethics in Canada" (2012) 25:2 *Canadian Journal of Administrative Law and Practice* 131. There are risks that, in the mediation phase of a med-arb process, the arbitrator may have said or done things that give rise to a perception of bias. However, skilled practitioners of the art are usually able to maintain the confidence of the parties and avoid such pitfalls. Legislators in many Canadian jurisdictions have been persuaded of the value of med-arb and have given it statutory recognition. See, for example, the Nova Scotia *Trade Union Act*, s 43C; the British Columbia *Labour Relations Code*, ss 74–78; and the Ontario *Labour Relations Act*, s 50. Such legislative approval protects med-arbiters against specious allegations of bias merely for having agreed to and conducted such a proceeding, and clothes them with the authority to truncate the evidentiary phase by using information acquired in the process of mediation and by making orders for providing evidence on matters that require further clarification.

An additional benefit of med-arb is its respect for the autonomy of the parties in collective labour relations and the cost effectiveness, efficiency, and finality of the dispute resolution processes under collective agreements. To the extent that the system succeeds in keeping labour dispute resolution "in house" and away from the courts in judicial review proceedings, med-arb enhances the autonomy of Canadian labour law. As well, this innovative practice would appear to be rooted in restorative values that reflect the relational aspects of dispute resolution under collective agreements: see George Adams, *Mediating Justice: Legal Dispute Negotiations* (Toronto: CCH Publishing, 2003); and John Braithwaite, "Emancipation and Hope" in Valerie Braithwaite, ed, *Hope, Power and Governance* (2004) 592 *Annals of the American Academy of Political and Social Science* (Special Issue).

Another procedural labour relations innovation receiving recognition in some Canadian jurisdictions is *restorative workplace conferencing*: see Bruce P Archibald, "Progress in Models of Justice," above. This technique, rooted in restorative values and approaches to dispute resolution, goes beyond mediation to identify relational issues that may affect more than individual grievors or the union per se. It can be particularly valuable in resolving matters that extend beyond individual bargaining units, and which may involve workplace cultural dysfunctions, resulting in bullying, sexual harassment, abuse by authoritarian superiors, and the like. This approach is also being promoted by certain human rights commissions, and has had application by them in disputes arising out of workplaces. One example of this is the Nova Scotia Human Rights Commission's restorative dispute resolution process, which can be found online at humanrights.gov.ns.ca/content/restorative-approaches. This innovation, while in its infancy, may benefit from the relatively autonomous spaces created by the heterogeneous procedural patchwork that is Canadian labour law.

Chapter 10: The Individual Employee under Collective Bargaining

10:100 INTRODUCTION

Canadian labour relations law is wholly predicated on the twin concepts of majoritarianism and exclusivity. Once a trade union proves that it enjoys majority support in a bargaining unit, it becomes the exclusive bargaining agent for that unit, and no one else is allowed to bargain on behalf of any of the employees in the unit. As we will see below, the same principle of exclusivity governs the carrying of grievances to arbitration. We will also see how the law explicitly allows the negotiation and enforcement of union security provisions, including those that require union membership as a condition of employment. All of these features are based on the premise that trade unions need effective bargaining authority and a substantial degree of internal solidarity.

In principle, the individual employee's freedom of choice is given legal expression only through her vote for or against an applicant union. Once that vote and those of the other members of the bargaining unit have determined that there will be a bargaining agent, individual freedom is suspended for a substantial period. Majoritarianism, in other words, leads to exclusivity. In incurring the obligation to bargain collectively, the employer acquires the corresponding right to be confronted by only one adversary — one that can speak for every employee in the unit. Ever since they were first established under the American *National Labor Relations Act*, 29 USC §§ 151-169 (1935) [*Wagner Act*], the twin pillars of majoritarianism and exclusivity have been attacked by employers and by others who are opposed in principle to collective bargaining or who are concerned about what they perceive to be excessive union power. Many of these attacks have been framed as defences of individual workers' rights — the "right to work," for example. In reality, however, their main object has often been to weaken the representation rights of unions and to dilute their strength.

In more recent years, some supporters of collective bargaining and trade unions have increasingly been calling into question the principles of majoritarianism and exclusivity. (See, for example, Roy J Adams, "A Pernicious Euphoria: 50 Years of Wagnerism in Canada" (1995) 3 *Canadian Labour & Employment Law Journal* 321.) These principles, the argument runs, preclude the emergence (and the recognition by employers) of minority unions that seek to organize only certain categories of employees in a particular workplace, or those that (for one reason or another) are only able to obtain minority support — thereby making it impossible for a group of workers to have a collective voice if they do not want majority representation or cannot persuade most of their co-workers to opt for it. This situation is claimed to constitute a violation of employee freedom of association, contrary to section 2(d) of the *Canadian Charter of Rights and Freedoms* — a claim which has been given fresh vigour by the

Supreme Court of Canada's reference to international labour law in *Saskatchewan Federation of Labour v Saskatchewan*, 2015 SCC 4, excerpted at length in Chapter 12. On this matter, Roy Adams has argued the following in "Fraser v. Ontario and International Human Rights: A Comment" (2009) 14 *Canadian Labour & Employment Law Journal* 379 at 383–84:

> One of the most basic ILO principles on freedom of association is that all workers have a right to organize and to bargain collectively with their employers through agents of their own choice. Although majoritarian exclusivity denies a representative of their own choosing to those workers in a designated bargaining unit who are opposed to the certified agent, the ILO committees have nevertheless approved the system as a reasonable limit on the right to organize and bargain collectively. However, the ILO's position is that if workers decide to organize outside of the bounds of statutory majoritarian exclusivity, their organizations still ought to be recognized for bargaining purposes. In its 2006 Digest of Decisions, the [ILO] Committee on Freedom of Association had this to say: "Where, under a system for nominating an exclusive bargaining agent, there is no union representing the required percentage to be so designated, collective bargaining rights should be granted to all the unions in this unit, at least on behalf of their own members." On this reasoning, employees who want to be represented by minority unions have an international human right to bargain collectively, in Canada and elsewhere. In *B.C. Health Services* the Supreme Court said that Canadian workers should enjoy "at least the same level of protection" as that provided by "international conventions to which Canada is a party."
>
> [Reproduced with permission by Lancaster House.]

More recently, David Doorey has argued that the *Wagner Act* model in Canada needs to be supplemented by a graduated freedom of association that would offer a "thin" model of freedom of association to the minority of employees in a workplace who wish to have union representation where they work, but who cannot obtain the requisite majority employee support for the "thicker" Wagner model. Employees under this "thin" proposal would enable workers to have some access to union representation—for example, on issues such as individual grievances, collective representations to an employer on job conditions, and requests for wage and benefit improvements—without the right to engage in mandatory collective bargaining or collective agreement administration. Professor Doorey writes in "Graduated Freedom of Association: Worker Voice Beyond the Wagner Model" (2012) 38:2 *Queen's Law Journal* 511 at 544:

> The main purpose of the GFA [Graduated Freedom of Association] model is to give workers a more realistic chance to exercise at least the minimum freedoms that the Supreme Court has said are constitutionally guaranteed. As a concrete example, this model would have at least protected the employees who joined our fair workers' association from employer reprisals, and would have allowed us an audience with the employer. We cannot know whether that opening could have led to some measurable benefits with some creative advocacy. What is clear, however, is that protecting vulnerable workers in the future will require both creative advocacy and new forms of collective organization.

If majoritarianism and exclusivity are too firmly entrenched in our industrial relations system to be struck down by the courts or dismantled by legislatures, the issue then becomes the extent to which legitimate concern for individual and minority rights can be addressed within the existing structures. There may be no real evidence of widespread abuse of such rights, however, abuses clearly do occur at times. There is increasing acceptance of the view that more effective protection of minority and individual rights is implicit in the ideals of a democratic society, and also of the view that such protection is necessary to the effective functioning of the collective bargaining system and to its attractiveness to unorganized workers. It is very much open to debate whether protection of minority rights can best be achieved by reinvigorating grassroots democracy within unions, facilitating judicial intervention at the suit of aggrieved individuals, introducing closer administrative scrutiny of internal union affairs, or encouraging unions themselves to adopt new constitutional and institutional arrangements.

Before turning to that debate, we will consider some of the most common areas in which individual and collective interests collide under a regime of collective bargaining: the displacement of the regime of individual contracts when a union acquires bargaining rights, the union's authority in negotiating a collective agreement, and the union's authority in processing grievances under that agreement.

10:200 THE PRIMACY OF THE COLLECTIVE AGREEMENT

10:210 Bargaining with other Unions or with Individual Employees

Once a union has acquired majority support and has been certified or recognized as a bargaining agent, the employer is precluded from bargaining with any other union or any other person or organization on behalf of any employees in the bargaining unit, unless and until the union's bargaining rights are terminated pursuant to statute. This was confirmed many years ago in *International Brotherhood of Boilermakers v Sheafer-Townsend Ltd* (1953), 53 CLLC para 17,058 (OLRB).

Another long-established but perhaps less obvious rule is that an employer may not bargain directly with individual employees where there is a statutory bargaining agent. The North American *locus classicus* on this point is the United States Supreme Court decision in *JI Case Co v National Labor Relations Board*, 321 US 332 (1944). In that judgment, however, the court left open the possibility that an employer and an employee might make a binding contractual arrangement related to the employment relationship if the arrangement "is not inconsistent with a collective agreement or does not amount to or result from or is not part of an unfair labor practice." The leading Canadian case on this question is *Syndicat catholique des employés de magasins de Québec Inc v Compagnie Paquet Ltée*, [1959] SCR 206, where Judson J said:

> There is no room left for private negotiation between employer and employee. Certainly to the extent of the matters covered by the collective agreement, freedom of contract between master and individual servant is abrogated. The collective agreement tells the employer on what terms he must in future conduct his master and servant relations ... The terms of employment are defined for all employees, and whether or not they are members of the union, they are identical for all.

This blanket prohibition of bargaining between employers and individual employees on any matter dealt with in the collective agreement is virtually unknown outside of the United

States and Canada. But in recent years, interesting exceptions to the blanket prohibition have arisen, primarily in the sports arena in North America. In the four major North American sports leagues—baseball, hockey, football, and basketball—professional athletics have relied upon the *Wagner Act* model to create a hybrid approach, where strong player unions have bargained collective agreements with team owners to set a minimum floor for salaries and working conditions, but which also allow athletics to bargain individual contracts with their teams that improve upon the collective agreement minimums. For more information on this topic, see William Gould, *Bargaining with Baseball: Labour Relations in an Age of Prosperous Turmoil* (Jefferson, NC: McFarland & Co, 2011).

10:220 The Eclipsing of the Individual Contract of Employment

The collective agreement binds unions, the employees they represent, and employers. In the following case, the employer was trying to avoid the provisions of a collective agreement, but the decision has clear implications for similar attempts by individual employees.

McGavin Toastmaster Ltd v Ainscough, [1976] 1 SCR 718 at 721–33

> [The respondent employees worked at the appellant company's Vancouver plant. The collective agreement provided that any employees who lost their jobs because of a plant closure would be entitled to severance pay. The company decided that it would close the plant. In protest, and while the plant was still open, the employees went on strike. The strike was illegal because it occurred during the lifetime of the collective agreement. A few days later, while the strike was in progress, the company carried out its plan to close the plant. The closure was for legitimate economic reasons. The company refused to pay the respondent employees severance pay as required by the collective agreement, because it claimed that under the contract law doctrine of repudiation, the act of striking illegally had disentitled them to it. The employees sued the company for the severance pay and won in the British Columbia courts. The company appealed.]
>
> LASKIN C.J.C.:
>
> [2] This Court raised, *suo motu*, the question whether the matter in issue here ought properly to have been submitted to arbitration under the grievance and arbitration provisions of the collective agreement between the appellant and the plaintiffs' trade union. In correspondence exchanged between solicitors the question of arbitration was raised and then dropped, and Court proceedings were instituted on May 12, 1971. There was no contention in defence that the appropriate proceedings should have been by way of arbitration under the collective agreement, and it does not appear that any such position was taken either before the trial Judge or in the British Columbia Court of Appeal. This Court refrained therefore in this case from taking any position on this question and is content to deal with the legal issue or issues as having been properly submitted to the Courts for adjudication. . . .
>
> [6] [T]he issues taken both at trial and on appeal were: (1) whether there was a repudiation by each employee of his contract of employment, by reason of the unlawful strike,

entitling the company to terminate it and whether the company did so; (2) whether the concerted refusal to work terminated the employer-employee relationship; and (3) whether the unlawful strike constituted a breach of a fundamental term of the contracts of employment of the respective striking employees so as to disentitle them to call upon the company to perform its obligations, in this case the obligation to give severance pay ...

[...]

[8] ... I do not think that in the face of labour relations legislation such as existed at the material time in British Columbia, in the face of the certification of the union, of which the plaintiffs were members, as bargaining agent of a specified unit of employees of the company and in the face of the collective agreement in force between the union and the appellant company, it is possible to speak of individual contracts of employment and to treat the collective agreement as a mere appendage of individual relationships. The majority of this Court, speaking through Judson J. in *Syndicat Catholique des Employés de Magasins de Québec, Inc. v. Compagnie Paquet Ltée* ... said this in a situation where a union was certified for collective bargaining under Quebec labour relations legislation:

> There is no room left for private negotiation between employer and employee. Certainly to the extent of the matters covered by the collective agreement, freedom of contract between master and individual servant is abrogated. The collective agreement tells the employer on what terms he must in the future conduct his master and servant relations.

[9] The situation is the same in British Columbia where the legislation in force at the material time stated explicitly that a collective agreement entered into between a union and an employer is binding on the union, the employer and the employees covered thereby: see *Mediation Services Act*, s. 6.

[10] The reality is, and has been for many years now throughout Canada, that individual relationships as between employer and employee have meaning only at the hiring stage and even then there are qualifications which arise by reason of union security clauses in collective agreements. The common law as it applies to individual employment contracts is no longer relevant to employer-employee relations governed by a collective agreement which, as the one involved here, deals with discharge, termination of employment, severance pay and a host of other matters that have been negotiated between union and company as the principal parties thereto. To quote again from the reasons of Judson J. in the *Paquet* case, at p. 214:

> If the relation between employee and union were that of mandator and mandatary, the result would be that a collective agreement would be the equivalent of a bundle of individual contracts between employer and employee negotiated by the union as agent for the employees. This seems to me to be a complete misapprehension of the nature of the juridical relation involved in the collective agreement. The union contracts not as agent or mandatary but as an independent contracting party and the contract it makes with the employer binds the employer to regulate his master and servant relations according to the agreed terms.

[11] The collective agreement in the present case makes the foregoing abundantly clear. Wages and hours of work are, of course, dealt with, and persons who come into the employ do so on the terms of the collective agreement as to wages and hours. They also

come under the terms of the collective agreement as to promotion, layoffs, rehiring and preference of transfers to shifts, all of which are regulated in this case by art. XVI of the collective agreement, headed 'Seniority.' Article V deals with hiring procedure, and gives the union the prior right to supply staff subject to certain exceptions. Discharge is dealt with both in art. IV and in art. VII. Central to all the benefits and obligations that rest upon the union, the employees and the company under the collective agreement are the grievance and arbitration provisions, about which nothing more need be said here. Standing at the forefront of the substantive terms of the collective agreement is art. I under which the union is recognized by the company as "the sole collective bargaining agency for all employees coming under the jurisdiction of this agreement". There is in this collective agreement ample support for the observations of Judson J. in the *Paquet* case.

[12] In my view, therefore, questions such as repudiation and fundamental breach must be addressed to the collective agreement if they are to have any subject matter at all. When so addressed, I find them inapplicable in the face of the legislation which, in British Columbia and elsewhere in Canada, governs labour-management relations, provides for certification of unions, for compulsory collective bargaining, for the negotiation, duration and renewal of collective agreements. The *Mediation Services Act*, which was in force at the material time in this case, provided in s. 8 for a minimum one-year term for collective agreements unless the responsible Minister gave consent to earlier termination, and provided also for the making of collective agreements for longer terms, subject to certain termination options before the full term had run. Neither this Act nor the companion *Labour Relations Act*, R.S.B.C. 1960, c. 205, could operate according to their terms if common law concepts like repudiation and fundamental breach could be invoked in relation to collective agreements which have not expired and where the duty to bargain collectively subsists.

[13] In *Polymer Corp. v. Oil, Chemical and Atomic Workers International Union, Local 16-14* ... McRuer C.J.H.C. observed ... that a collective agreement "is not that sort of contract that can be terminated by repudiation by one party merely because the other party has broken one of its terms". In *C.P.R. v. Zambri*, ... this Court recognized that the common law relations of employer and employee had been altered by the labour relations legislation of Ontario that was involved in that case, legislation that was comparable to that in British Columbia to which I have referred. Judson J., speaking for four members of this Court said ... of the *Zambri* case that:

> When a collective agreement has expired, it is difficult to see how there can be anything left to govern the employer-employee relationship. Conversely, when there is a collective agreement in effect, it is difficult to see how there can be anything left outside except possibly the act of hiring.

[14] The references I have made to the collective agreement in this case, which was in force during the events that gave rise to this litigation, lends substance to the words of Judson J. What is, in truth, left for consideration on the appellant's submissions is whether, notwithstanding the existence and binding effect of the collective agreement, the plaintiffs had ceased to be employees by reason only of their unlawful strike and hence had by their own act excluded themselves from the benefits provided by art. XX of the collective agreement.

[15] The applicable legislation, the *Mediation Services Act*, s. 23, prohibits an employee who is bound by a collective agreement from striking during the term of the agreement. It was open to the company in this case to take disciplinary action against the plaintiffs for participating in an unlawful strike, and it is arguable (although this is not before this Court) that discharge would have been held to be for sufficient cause in the light of all the circumstances, if this issue had gone to arbitration. The company did not, however, take any action against the striking employees and, indeed, insisted in this statement of defence that the employees were not discharged but had, in effect, quit their jobs. No doubt they had quit work, but, far from quitting their jobs, the record shows that they had resorted to strike action as a means of emphasizing their concern for retention of jobs in the plant and as a means of persuading the company to reconsider its decision to curtail available jobs, a decision which was part of an overall plan to phase out the Vancouver operation. Even on the basis of common law concepts, the opinion was unanimous below that the unlawful strike did not per se terminate the employer-employee relationship, and I think this is plainly right, and a fortiori in the light of governing labour-management relations legislation. It was open to the company to act in relation to the unlawful strike by positive action against the strikers; and, whether or not it saw in the strike an opportunity to accelerate its longer term plan to close out its Vancouver operations, its failure to act against the employees save by closure of the plant brought it within the severance pay obligations at art. XX of the collective agreement.

[16] I would dismiss the appeal with costs.

10:230 The Pre-eminence of Grievance Arbitration

At the outset of the excerpt (immediately above) from his judgment in *McGavin Toastmaster*, Laskin CJC noted that the Supreme Court of Canada had itself raised the issue of whether the employees should have pursued their claim through the grievance and arbitration procedure rather than through a court action—but that because no objection was taken to court jurisdiction at any point in the litigation, the issue was not pursued in the particular case. Had the issue been dealt with, the Court might simply have concluded that the courts lacked the jurisdiction to consider the case brought by the employer—a conclusion that has been reached in a long line of cases where court jurisdiction was challenged.

Where disputes arise about the enforceability of rights arising from individual employment relationships, they raise both a question of forum (court versus grievance arbitration) and a consideration of whether the collective agreement can be bypassed. Can the collective agreement and its grievance and arbitration procedures be circumvented by characterizing the dispute as one outside its scope? The party seeking to do this may be the employer, the union, or an individual employee—either an employee who is acting in concert with the union or one who is trying to bypass the collective agreement as a means of challenging the union. No matter who is trying to avoid the grievance process or why, the courts have increasingly tended to foreclose that possibility, through reliance on provisions in labour relations statutes requiring final settlement of disputes between the employer and the union. Recall *Weber v Ontario Hydro*, [1995] 2 SCR 92, discussed in Section 9:341, in which a tort and *Charter* claim for invasion of privacy, beyond the settled grievance, was dismissed for want of jurisdiction. Court jurisdiction was similarly held to be lacking in the companion case of *New Brunswick v O'Leary*, [1995] 2 SCR 967, where the employer was told that grievance arbitration was the only channel through which it could pursue its claim against an employee for negligently damaging a vehicle by driving it with a flat tire.

In a more recent decision, the Supreme Court of Canada held that grievance arbitration was the appropriate legal forum for the resolution of employment disputes arising from a unionized workplace: see *Allen v Alberta*, 2003 SCC 1. In that case, the Court reaffirmed that labour arbitrators are granted broad jurisdiction over labour disputes, and found that the "essential character" of the dispute arose from a subject matter covered by the applicable collective agreement.

However, the principle enunciated in *Allen* has been held to not apply where the employee and employer had made an individual contractual arrangement before entering into the employment relationship (for example, an arrangement to the effect that the employee would continue to be paid at the level at which they were paid at a previous job, or that the job would last for a certain number of years). Several decisions have held that the employee may bring a civil action in the courts to enforce such a "pre-employment contract," whether or not its provisions are consistent with the collective agreement that applies to the employee once the employment relationship began. The Supreme Court of Canada affirmed that exception in *Goudie v Ottawa (City)*, 2003 SCC 14. In *Isidore Garon Ltée v Tremblay; Fillion et Frères (1976) inc v Syndicat national des employés de garage du Québec inc*, 2006 SCC 2, the Court cautioned against the inappropriate merging of collective bargaining schemes and legislated individual employment rights, holding that a grievance arbitrator had no jurisdiction to consider the applicability of individual employee notice rights set out in the *Civil Code of Quebec*, CQLR 1991, c CCQ-1991.

The Supreme Court of Canada restated the rule regarding the primacy of labour arbitration as the presumptive legal forum for the resolution of workplace disputes in the unionized employment relationship in the following case.

Bisaillon v Concordia University, 2006 SCC 19

[The majority of the employees at Concordia University were represented by unions, and were covered by nine different collective agreements. Mr Bisaillon, a unionized employee, initiated a motion before the Superior Court of Quebec seeking permission to launch a class action against the university to challenge its decisions regarding the administration and use of the employee pension plan. One of the nine unions opposed the class action and sought to have the motion dismissed, arguing that the Superior Court lacked jurisdiction to adjudicate the issue. The other eight unions supported Mr Bisaillon's motion.

The Superior Court of Quebec allowed the challenge to the class action and dismissed his motion. It ruled that the proper legal forum was a labour arbitration board, as the pension plan was a benefit provided for in the collective agreements. The Quebec Court of Appeal set aside that ruling, holding that the pension plan existed independently of the collective agreements, and the courts were therefore the appropriate forum. The Supreme Court of Canada allowed the appeal (4:3) and restored the ruling of the Superior Court.]

LeBel J. for the majority:

(2) Collective Representation System in Labour Law

[23] The *Labour Code*, R.S.Q., c. C27 ("*L.C.*"), recognizes that any association of employees having a representative character in relation to a separate group of employees within an employer's enterprise is entitled to be certified (s. 21 *L.C.*). This separate group—the bargaining unit—consists of one or more employees whose association is deemed appropriate for collective bargaining purposes .... The certification of an association of employees produces a variety of legal consequences, both for the association itself and for the employees and the employer.

[24] First, the *Labour Code* gives certified unions a set of rights, the most important of which is most certainly the monopoly on representation. When it is certified, a union acquires the exclusive power to negotiate conditions of employment with the employer for all members of the bargaining unit with a view to reaching a collective agreement. Once a collective agreement is in place, the union's monopoly on representation also extends to the implementation and application of the agreement. For example, a certified union holds a monopoly with respect to the choice of solutions for the implementation of the collective agreement. "The union's power to control the process includes the power to settle cases or bring cases to a conclusion in the course of the arbitration process, or to work out a solution with the employer, subject to compliance with the parameters of the legal duty of representation" (*Société d'énergie de la Baie James c. Noël*, [2001] 2 S.C.R. 207, 2001 SCC 39, at para. 45).

[25] Second, the monopoly on representation also has a significant impact on employees' rights. Our system of collective representation proscribes the individual negotiation of conditions of employment. A screen is erected between the employer and the employees in the bargaining unit (*Noël*, at para. 42). This screen prevents the employer from negotiating directly with its employees and in so doing precludes the employees from negotiating their individual conditions of employment directly with their employer (*Syndicat catholique des employées de magasins de Québec Inc. v. Cie Paquet Ltée*, [1959] S.C.R. 206 (S.C.C.); *Isidore Garon ltée v. Syndicat du bois ouvré de la région de Québec inc.*, [2006] 1 S.C.R. 27, 2006 SCC 2). Moreover, once a collective agreement is signed, it becomes the regulatory framework governing relations between the union and the employer, as well as the individual relationships between the employer and employees: *Hémond c. Coopérative fédérée du Québec*, [1989] 2 S.C.R. 962 (S.C.C.), at p. 975; *Noël*, at para. 43; *Isidore*, at para. 14.

[26] The system of collective representation thus takes certain individual rights away from employees. In particular, employees are denied the possibility of negotiating their conditions of employment directly with their employer and also lose control over the application of those conditions. In return, by negotiating with the employer with one voice through their union, employees improve their position in the balance of power with the employer (*Isidore*, at para. 38). Moreover, the individual interests of each member of the bargaining unit are protected in a system of collective representation. For example, in order to be certified to represent employees, a union must obtain the support of a majority of the employees in the bargaining unit (s. 28 *L.C.*). Furthermore, having regard to the provisions of s. 21 *L.C.*, it follows from the case law that employees must, *inter alia*, have a certain commonality of interests where labour relations are

concerned and that this helps to protect employees' individual interests. Lastly, while the monopoly on representation confers rights upon certified unions, it also imposes upon them a duty to act properly by, for example, taking into account the competing interests of all employees in the bargaining unit: s. 47.2 L.C.; *Noël*, at paras. 46–55.

[27] Finally, the collective representation system in labour law has a significant impact on the employer. It requires the employer to recognize the certified union and to enter into good-faith collective bargaining exclusively with it. However, the employer also derives various benefits from the collective representation system. In particular, employers acquire the right to industrial peace for the term of the collective agreement and can, in principle, expect that disagreements stemming from the implementation and application of the collective agreement will be negotiated with the union or settled through the grievance arbitration process. As I noted in *Noël*:

> The impact of this system on the employer is sometimes overlooked. Although the scheme imposes obligations on the employer relating to the employees and the union, it offers employers, in return, the prospect of temporary peace in their companies. An employer can expect that the problems negotiated and resolved with the union will remain resolved and will not be reopened in an untimely manner on the initiative of a group of employees, or even a single employee. This means that, for the life of a collective agreement approved by the bargaining unit, the employer gains the right to stability and compliance with the conditions of employment in the company and to have the work performed continuously and properly. However reluctant the members of a dissenting or minority group of employees may be, they will be bound by the collective agreement and will have to abide by it.
>
> In administering collective agreements, the same rule will apply to the processing and disposition of grievances. Administering the collective agreement is one of the union's essential roles, and in this it acts as the employer's mandatory interlocutor. If the representation function is performed properly in this respect, the employer is entitled to compliance with the solutions agreed on. [paras. 44–45]

[28] It is worth noting that the monopoly on collective representation is not limited to the context of the collective agreement but extends to all aspects of employee-employer relations (*Isidore*, at para. 41; *Noël*, at para. 57). The union's monopoly with respect to collective bargaining is based not only on the existence of a collective agreement, but also on the certification of the union (*Isidore*, at para. 38; *C.A.I.M.A.W., Local 14 v. Canadian Kenworth Co.*, [1989] 2 S.C.R. 983, at pp. 10078). For this reason, any negotiations regarding conditions of employment that are not mentioned in the current collective agreement must be conducted by the certified union.

(3) Jurisdiction of Grievance Arbitrators

[29] As Robert P. Gagnon explains, [TRANSLATION] "A grievance arbitrator's jurisdiction depends on two factors. The first has to do with the subject or the nature of the dispute; this is the subject-matter aspect of the arbitrator's jurisdiction. The second factor relates to the persons who are parties to the dispute; this therefore is the personal aspect of the arbitrator's jurisdiction" (p. 506). It should be noted however that subject-matter jurisdiction

includes the power to grant an appropriate remedy (*R. v. Mills*, [1986] 1 S.C.R. 863, at p. 890, and *Weber v. Ontario Hydro*, [1995] 2 S.C.R. 929, at paras. 63–66). Thus, in order to acquire jurisdiction in a given case, a grievance arbitrator must have jurisdiction over the essential subject matter of the dispute in order to ultimately grant an appropriate remedy.

(i) Subject-Matter Jurisdiction of Grievance Arbitrators

[30] I will begin by reviewing the subject-matter aspect of the jurisdiction of grievance arbitrators. The *Labour Code* gives the grievance arbitrator exclusive jurisdiction over "any disagreement respecting the interpretation or application of a collective agreement" (ss. 1(*f*) and 100.1 L.C.). To determine whether a dispute arises out of a collective agreement, it is necessary to follow the analytical approach adopted by this Court in *Weber*. As McLachlin J. explained, "The question in each case is whether the dispute, in its essential character, arises from the interpretation, application, administration or violation of the collective agreement" (*Weber*, at para. 52).

[31] The first stage of this approach consists in identifying the essential character of the dispute. On this point, the Court has stressed that what must be done is not limited to determining the legal nature of the dispute. On the contrary, the analysis must also take into account all the facts surrounding the dispute between the parties: *Regina Police Assn. Inc. v. Regina (City) Police Commissioners*, [2000] 1 S.C.R. 360, 2000 SCC 14, at paras. 25 and 29.

[32] At the second stage, it must be determined whether the factual context so identified falls within the ambit of the collective agreement. In other words, it must be determined whether the collective agreement implicitly or explicitly applies to the facts in dispute. In *Regina Police*, this Court explained this second stage of the analysis as follows:

> Simply, the decision-maker must determine whether, having examined the factual context of the dispute, its essential character concerns a subject matter that is covered by the collective agreement. Upon determining the essential character of the dispute, the decision-maker must examine the provisions of the collective agreement to determine whether it contemplates such factual situations. It is clear that the collective agreement need not provide for the subject matter of the dispute explicitly. If the essential character of the dispute arises either explicitly, or implicitly, from the interpretation, application, administration or violation of the collective agreement, the dispute is within the sole jurisdiction of an arbitrator to decide . . . [at para. 25].

[33] This Court has considered the subject-matter jurisdiction of grievance arbitrators on several occasions, and it has clearly adopted a liberal position according to which grievance arbitrators have a broad exclusive jurisdiction over issues relating to conditions of employment, provided that those conditions can be shown to have an express or implicit connection to the collective agreement: *New Brunswick v. O'Leary*, [1995] 2 S.C.R. 967; *Parry Sound (District) Welfare Administration Board v. O.P.S.E.U., Local 324*, [2003] 2 S.C.R. 157, 2003 SCC 42; *St. Anne Nackawic Pulp & Paper Co. v. C.P.U., Local 219*, [1986] 1 S.C.R. 704; *Allen v. Alberta*, [2003] 1 S.C.R. 128, 2003 SCC 13 (S.C.C.). . . .

(ii) Union's Monopoly on Representation

[56] To ascribe the status of representative to the respondent Bisaillon by granting his motion for authorization to institute a class action would be incompatible with

the legal mandates of representation accorded by the *Labour Code* to the nine certified unions representing Concordia employees. The Pension Plan, having been negotiated and incorporated into the collective agreement, became a condition of employment in respect of which the employees lost their right to act on individual basis, independently of the union representing them. As confirmed in *Noël*, the employees no longer have the power to apply to the ordinary courts to demand the application of provisions of the plan. Contrary to all these principles, a class action in the case at bar would jeopardize an explicit agreement—entered into within the framework set out in the *Labour Code*—between CUFA and Concordia with respect to the very subjects to which it applies.

[57] If the eight unions that disagreed with Concordia felt that their collective agreements had been violated, it was up to them to assert the rights of the employees they represent. As the disagreement arose, at least implicitly, out of the collective agreement, the unions should have pursued the collective bargaining process begun with the employer or filed a grievance with an arbitrator to defend the rights of their bargaining units. Their tactical decision to yield their power of representation to Mr. Bisaillon disregarded the legal mandates the *Labour Code* attributes to them as certified unions and the obligations it imposes on them in respect of the employees and the employer. ...

[64] ... To authorize a class action in the case at bar would be to deny the principles of the exclusivity of the grievance arbitrator's jurisdiction and of the union's monopoly on employee representation. The Superior Court was thus correct in granting the motion for declinatory exception and dismissing the respondent Bisaillon's motion for authorization to institute a class action.

V. DISPOSITION

[65] I would therefore allow the appeal, set aside the judgment of the Court of Appeal and restore the decision of the Superior Court, with costs throughout.

* * * * *

The requirement of recourse to grievance arbitration ties the fate of the individual employee to that of the union. Cases where such conflicts do arise are dealt with under the rubric of the union's duty of fair representation, discussed immediately below.

10:300 THE DUTY OF FAIR REPRESENTATION

A workforce is a matrix of differing interests and abilities. Skilled and unskilled, young and old, male and female, racial minorities and dominant groups, "social reformers," the exponents of "business unionism," anti-union activists—all perceive the terms and conditions of employment from quite different perspectives. Additionally, unions have a number of competing pressures, both internal and external, which shape their decision making and their actions. The American labour historian Melvyn Dubofsky has written in "Legal Theory and Workers Rights" (1981) 4:3 *Industrial Relations Law Journal* 496 at 500:

Unions have to be understood as peculiarly contradictory institutions. They are ... simultaneously town meetings and military formations. In one guise, unions are marked by rank and file participation where policy decisions are reached only after open democratic debate. In the other guise, they are fighting machines struggling for survival or victory through discipline, absolute loyalty to command and unbroken solidarity.

A certified union must reconcile these varying interests and pressures. It is assisted in this task by its statutory authority to bind all members of the bargaining unit, to exclude individual bargaining, and to administer the grievance arbitration machinery. The union's exclusive bargaining rights and its corresponding obligations put it in a position where it can (and indeed must) seek to compromise or otherwise adjust the important differences within its ranks. In the long run, a union's survival may depend as much on its ability to resolve these differences as on its ability to deal with the employer.

Beyond these inevitable tensions, minority and individual rights and interests are sometimes violated by oppressive or arbitrary union action—action that is qualitatively different from, for example, striking a compromise between employees who want more take-home pay and those who prefer higher pensions. In particular situations, moreover, the values underlying collective bargaining may point one way in support of a collective right or interest, while other fundamental social values may point to the vindication of the right or interest of a competing individual or minority. Finding legal standards to resolve such conflicts has been a slow and difficult process.

Within our statutory regime of labour relations, the primary mechanism for addressing these issues has been the union's duty of fair representation (DFR), which is the concomitant of the union's exclusive authority to bargain. Like the duty to bargain, the DFR applies not only with respect to the union's own members but also with respect to any non-members who may be in the bargaining unit.

The DFR was first formulated in the United States in the following case of blatant racial discrimination. It was created by the courts in the absence of any explicit statutory provision.

Steele v Louisville & Nashville Railroad Co, 323 US 192 at 199–208 (1944)

[The Brotherhood of Locomotive Firemen and Engineers was certified under the American *Railway Labor Act* as bargaining agent for all firefighters employed by the defendant railway. Under the union's constitution, black employees were explicitly denied the right to be members. In accordance with a demand by the union, new collective agreement provisions were negotiated limiting the percentage of black firefighters, and also limiting their seniority rights and employment opportunities. The purpose was to benefit the union's white members and ultimately to exclude all black employees, who were not given the opportunity to express their views on the matter.

The plaintiff, a black firefighter, sued for an injunction against the implementation of the collective agreement, and for damages. His action failed in the Alabama courts, and he appealed to the United States Supreme Court.]

STONE C.J.:

[W]e think that Congress, in enacting the *Railway Labor Act* and authorizing a labor union, chosen by a majority of a craft, to represent the craft, did not intend to confer plenary power upon the union to sacrifice, for the benefit of its members, rights of the minority of the craft, without imposing on it any duty to protect the minority....

Unless the labor union representing a craft owes some duty to represent non-union members of the craft, at least to the extent of not discriminating against them as such in the contracts which it makes as their representative, the minority would be left with no means of protecting their interests or, indeed, their right to earn a livelihood by pursuing the occupation in which they are employed. While the majority of the craft chooses the bargaining representative, when chosen it represents, as the Act by its terms makes plain, the craft or class, and not the majority. The fair interpretation of the statutory language is that the organization chosen to represent a craft is to represent all its members, the majority as well as the minority, and it is to act for and not against those whom it represents. It is a principle of general application that the exercise of a granted power to act in behalf of others involves the assumption toward them of a duty to exercise the power in their interest and behalf, and that such a grant of power will not be deemed to dispense with all duty toward those for whom it is exercised unless so expressed....

We hold that the language of the Act to which we have referred, read in the light of the purposes of the Act, expresses the aim of Congress to impose on the bargaining representative of a craft or class of employees the duty to exercise fairly the power conferred upon it in behalf of all those for whom it acts, without hostile discrimination against them.

This does not mean that the statutory representative of a craft is barred from making contracts which may have unfavourable effects on some of the members of the craft represented. Variations in the terms of the contract based on differences relevant to the authorized purposes of the contract in conditions to which they are to be applied, such as differences in seniority, the type of work performed, the competence and skill with which it is performed, are within the scope of the bargaining representation of a craft, all of whose members are not identical in their interest or merit.... Without attempting to mark the allowable limits of differences in the terms of contracts based on differences of conditions to which they apply, it is enough for present purposes to say that the statutory power to represent a craft and to make contracts as to wages, hours and working conditions does not include the authority to make among members of the craft discriminations not based on such relevant differences. Here the discriminations based on race alone are obviously irrelevant and invidious. Congress plainly did not undertake to authorize the bargaining representative to make such discriminations....

The representative which thus discriminates may be enjoined from so doing, and its members may be enjoined from taking the benefit of such discriminatory action. No more is the Railroad bound by or entitled to take the benefit of a contract which the bargaining representative is prohibited by the statute from making....

While the statute does not deny to such a bargaining labor organization the right to determine eligibility to its membership, it does require the union, in collective bargaining and in making contracts with the carrier, to represent non-union or minority union members of the craft without hostile discrimination, fairly, impartially, and in good faith. Wherever necessary to that end, the union is required to consider requests of non-union members of the craft and expressions of their views with respect to collective bargaining with the employer and to give to them notice of and opportunity for hearing upon its proposed action....

We conclude that the duty which the statute imposes on a union representative of a craft to represent the interests of all its members stands on no different footing and that the statute contemplates resort to the usual judicial remedies of injunction and award of damages when appropriate for breach of that duty.

The judgment is accordingly reversed and remanded for further proceedings not inconsistent with this opinion.

Building on the foundation laid in the above judgment of the US Supreme Court, American courts, and subsequently Canadian courts and legislatures, have defined the DFR as obliging a union with statutory bargaining rights not to act in a way that is arbitrary, discriminatory, or in bad faith when representing an employee vis-à-vis the employer. Most Canadian jurisdictions now expressly recognize the DFR, generally in almost exactly those terms, in their labour relations statutes. For example, section 74 of the Ontario *Labour Relations Act, 1995*, SO 1995 c 1, Schedule A, s 1(1), provides as follows:

> A trade union or council of trade unions, so long as it continues to be entitled to represent employees in a bargaining unit, shall not act in a manner that is arbitrary, discriminatory or in bad faith in the representation of any of the employees in the unit, whether or not members of the trade union or of any constituent union of the council of trade unions, as the case may be.

The labour board and court jurisprudence dealt with in the rest of this chapter all comes from jurisdictions with a statutory DFR.

Only New Brunswick and Prince Edward Island have no statutory DFR. In those provinces, however, an employee in a certified bargaining unit has access to what is known as the "common law duty of fair representation"—which is something of a misnomer because even where there is no statutory DFR, the duty has been held to arise not from the common law but (as in the US Supreme Court's decision in the *Steele* case itself) by implication from the powers over individual employee rights conferred on certified unions by labour relations legislation. Although the "common law DFR" is very similar in substance to the express statutory DFR, it is enforced by the courts rather than by the labour relations board, and (as with the common law contract of employment) the courts will award only monetary relief for a breach, rather than granting the broader range of remedies available to labour boards. This difference in forums and remedies appears to be important in practice, as DFR complaints are very numerous in jurisdictions with an explicit statutory DFR, but very few in jurisdictions where the complaint must be brought in the courts. The origin of the "common law duty" is found in *Canadian Merchant Service Guild v Gagnon et al*, [1984] 1 SCR 509.

10:310 The Duty of Fair Representation in the Negotiation of a Collective Agreement

In the American *Steele* case in which the DFR was born (excerpted in the preceding section), the complaint was about what the union had negotiated into the collective agreement, not about how it was administering the agreement. In Canada, most of the very large number of DFR complaints brought every year have been about collective agreement administration, which will be dealt with in Section 10:320. However, some of the most difficult and interesting DFR cases have involved decisions made by unions in the negotiation or renegotiation of collective agreement provisions—especially decisions that have affected the often divergent job security interests of different groups within the bargaining unit.

Bukvich v Canadian Union of United Brewery, Flour, Cereal, Soft Drink and Distillery Workers, Local 304 and Dufferin Aggregates (1982), 82 CLLC para 16,156 at 593–601 (OLRB)

M. PICHER, Vice-Chair:

[1] This is a complaint under section 68 [now section 70] of the [Ontario] *Labour Relations Act*. The five grievors were laid off from their jobs as dependent contractor owner-operators of tandem trucks working out of a quarry at Milton operated by Dufferin Aggregates. The unusual twist is that their layoffs were, in effect, initiated by the union. The grievors claim that the actions of the union which resulted in their layoffs were in violation of its duty of fair representation described in section 68 of the Act.

[2] The facts are not in dispute. In July of 1978 the respondent was certified by this Board as bargaining agent of all drivers working at or out of the Milton quarry ... The current agreement, the product of a strike in the summer of 1980, is in effect from June 15, 1980 until December 31, 1982.

[3] When the current collective agreement was executed, the unit numbered thirty-four drivers. Because of the nature of the services rendered, with drivers being paid by the load, the company is indifferent as to the number of drivers in the quarry as long as there are enough to handle the work available. The drivers on the other hand, who own their own trucks and have considerable financing costs and operating expenses to meet, are concerned with keeping a limit on the number of trucks in the quarry, to maximize their own revenues. To that end the following provisions were negotiated into the collective agreement:

Article IV

4.01 The company will establish a drivers' list based on seniority. The number of drivers on such list shall not exceed thirty-four (34) ...

4.02 There shall be no layoff during the life of this Agreement, it being understood that the drivers will share available work in accordance with present practice.

4.03 Drivers will receive available loads in accordance with the practice presently in effect.

4.04 The Company is entitled to call in truckers not on seniority list as it sees fit provided that, so far as practicable and the requirements of the Company's customers can be met satisfactorily, drivers on the seniority list shall have first call on loads at all times.

[4] The evidence establishes that conditions in the industry have caused a continuing attrition in the number of drivers in the bargaining unit. At one time there were fifty-six drivers at work. There were forty-five at the time of certification. Shortly before the layoff that is the basis of this complaint, there were thirty-three drivers, three of whom quit. After the layoff, at the time of the hearing, there were twenty-one owner-operators at work.

[5] The dependency of the drivers in the bargaining unit on the work available at Dufferin is a matter of record. They do not obtain any meaningful income from alternative sources ...

[6] The hardship experienced by the drivers is due in part to a general decline in the construction industry and to an increased use of independent trucking contractors who operate larger tractor trailer units ... There was then little reason to doubt that the company would respond to an initiative of the union to amend the collective agreement to allow it to lay off junior drivers and distribute the available work among a smaller pool of senior drivers.

[7] A group of senior drivers began to act on that prospect through the early months of 1981. A petition favouring the insertion of a layoff provision in the collective agreement was circulated among the senior drivers. As a result a meeting of the bargaining unit was held on June 3, 1981 to entertain a motion which would have authorized the union executive to re-open negotiations with the company to amend the no-layoff provision of the agreement. The motion passed by a margin of 14 to 10. The union executive, however, under the direction of Mr. Cameron Nelson, the full-time union officer who chaired the meeting, ruled that the vote was not sufficient to authorize re-opening the contract because it was passed by only a minority of the employees eligible to vote. It appears that under the union's rules a change of that magnitude requires a majority of all employees in the bargaining unit ...

[8] Undaunted, the senior drivers, led by shop steward, A. Levin, petitioned again. A further meeting was held on July 13, 1981 ...

[9] ... After some two hours of heated discussion a secret ballot vote was taken: the motion to re-open the contract carried 18 to 12, a majority of the employees in the bargaining unit.

[10] The inevitable followed. The union executive, bound to carry out the wishes of the majority, approached the company and negotiated an amendment of the collective agreement. The amendment, tentatively agreed to on August 14, 1981, provided:

[...]

4.02 Should the Company find it necessary to lay-off members of the bargaining unit due to lack of work, it shall do so in reverse order of seniority. During periods of lay-off, the Company shall maintain a lay-off list of drivers and shall recall them in order of seniority when work becomes available....

[11] On August 19, 1981, a final meeting of the bargaining unit was held to ratify the amendment. That meeting, again chaired by Mr. Nelson, is not irregular in respect of its procedures. The evidence establishes that adequate notice and a full opportunity to participate and vote was afforded all drivers in the bargaining unit. As expected, after a predictably stormy meeting, the amendment was ratified.

[12] Two weeks later, by letter dated September 3, 1981, the company notified the union that nine drivers were laid off effective 5:00 p.m., September 4, 1981. There can be little doubt that the layoff had a harsh impact on the drivers affected. One of the grievors, Mike D'Alonzo, was unable to find other haulage work and was forced to sell his truck because of an inability to meet his finance payments. Mr. Bukvich testified that because of

his financing obligations he may have to choose between losing his truck and losing his home. He is angry that the union could have permitted such a result through a process which he described as "the rich getting together ... voting member against member".

...

[22] In this case the complainants ask the Board to conclude that the decision to effectively eliminate the jobs of a minority is in itself a violation of the duty to fairly represent the members of the minority. Counsel for the complainants argues that the grievors had a contractual right and expectation to work out of the quarry over the life of the collective agreement, and that to re-open the contract to undo that right is a violation of their vested rights inconsistent with the duty of fair representation.

[23] As compelling as that argument may seem, in my view it does not assist the understanding of the issue to simply assert that the members of a minority have an absolute right to be protected against negative consequences to their job security. The collective agreement is a contract made between the employer and the union. They are the parties to it, and any benefits which it confers on individual employees are necessarily subject to the possibility of amendment between the parties. In this regard it should be recalled that a collective agreement is not "bundle of individual contracts between employer and employee negotiated by the union as agent for the employees" ...

[24] That is not to say that a trade union can with impunity disregard the interests of the employees it represents or take either a hostile or an indifferent attitude where employees' critical interests are at stake. In discharging its duty to fairly represent all of the employees in a bargaining unit a union must address its mind to the circumstances of those who may be adversely affected by its decision. It has a duty to weigh the competing interests of the employees it represents and make a considered judgment the procedure and result of which must be neither arbitrary, discriminatory nor in bad faith.

[25] Counsel for the complainants submits that in this case the union has not properly balanced the interests of the two groups of employees involved. He argues that if the union cannot show that the marginal advantage which the union's decision gives the majority outweighs the disadvantage to the minority, it has violated the duty of fair representation. In other words, he maintains that the union must justify its decision, and absent such justification the Board should conclude that the union's action is in violation of the duty of fair representation.

[26] That submission must be considered with great caution. To adopt that standard in an unqualified way risks placing the Board in the position of being the arbiter of the political correctness of a union decision. The weighing of competing interests and the ultimate choice as to which outcome is preferable is a highly subjective decision, inevitably influenced by the inherent values, viewpoints and preferences of the decision maker. In the collective bargaining context such choices are highly political, and to that extent unions are required to act as responsive political bodies.

[27] In bargaining changes that affect the competing interests of employees a union has a two stage involvement: firstly it must be the forum for resolving the conflict between sometimes irreconcilable employee interests; secondly it must act as the spokesman for the interests that carry the day. Once the internal choice is made the union must approach the employer with the force and conviction of a body with a single voice. To view the union

in this later stage as the antagonist of the minority is to misconceive the process. Professor Cox, in discussing the processing of grievances, usefully summarized this dimension of union activity as follows:

> When the interests of several groups conflict, or future needs run contrary to present desires, or when the individual's claim endangers group interests, the union's function is to resolve the competition by reaching an accommodation or striking a balance. The process is political. It involves a melange of power, numerical strength, mutual aid, reason, prejudice, and emotion. Limits must be placed on the authority of the group, but within the zone of fairness and rationality this method of self-government probably works better than the edicts of any outside arbiter. A large part of the daily grist of union business is resolving differences among employees poorly camouflaged as disputes with the employer.

[28] The weight of authority supports the view put forward by counsel for the complainants that special considerations attach to any decision by a union that alters or abrogates the job security of employees. That is especially true in relation to seniority rights. Seniority rights, built up over time, usually over a number of successive collective agreements, represent an employee's stake in critical interests such as promotion, pension rights and his rights of layoff and recall. The concept of seniority comes as close as any to approximating a form of industrial relations property right for the individual employee....

[30] This case involves the elimination of a work sharing guarantee in favour of a provision of layoffs by seniority. A work sharing provision is one of a number of means, like seniority, like provisions prohibiting the contracting out of bargaining unit work, or like classification schemes, whereby job security can be directly affected. It is obviously a fundamental provision in any collective agreement, expressing as it does the choice and expectation of the employees respecting the allocation of work in times of scarcity....

[31] Work sharing has deep and abiding importance for the employees who are under it. Because it impacts on job security it represents an employee interest just as critical as a seniority provision. Action by a union to change or eradicate a work sharing or no-layoff provision must, therefore, be viewed as seriously and be judged by the same standards as a change in seniority provisions. That is particularly so where, as here, employees have had the security and benefit of such a provision through successive collective agreements. The impact in this case is more dramatic still: as dependent contractors, the complainants do not contribute to the Unemployment Insurance scheme. For them the consequences of a layoff are particularly hard, and the analogy to a change in seniority ranking provisions is extremely close....

[37] ... The appropriate standard to be adopted by this Board is not unlike that expressed by the Court in the judicial review of the decisions of arbitrators: the Board should ask not whether the decision is right or wrong or whether it agrees with it—rather it should ask whether it is a decision that could reasonably be made in all the circumstances, even if the Board might itself be inclined to disagree with it. Used in this sense 'reasonable' must mean the rational application of relevant factors, after considering and balancing all legitimate interests and without regard to extraneous factors.

[38] In this case the evidence leaves little doubt that the union was faced with a deteriorating economic situation in early 1981. The number of trucks in the quarry had

been continuously reduced by attrition over the previous three years. Following the strike in the summer of 1980 conditions had continued to decline with some ten or eleven owner-operators leaving the quarry. In January of 1981 to remain competitive the drivers agreed to postpone the implementation of a negotiated rate increase from January 1, 1981 to April 1, 1981. In May the union agreed to drop the haulage rate by a further 25 cents in hopes of remaining competitive with independent truckers and retaining a larger volume of work. Because of the downturn in construction generally, and the increased use of larger independent trailer trucks, the drivers in the bargaining unit were only barely surviving.

[39] In this regard the evidence of Milovan Stanisic is particularly instructive. Called as a witness by the complainants, Mr. Stanisic has worked as a driver in the quarry for nine years. He believed he stood approximately 17th or 18th in seniority at the time the issue of re-opening the contract arose. Mr. Stanisic favoured the layoff provision. By his own unchallenged account, he did not know what number of employees would be laid off if the contract were re-opened and was given no assurance that he would not. He decided however, that he would be better off either out of the quarry entirely working elsewhere, or in the quarry sharing a viable volume of work among a smaller number of trucks. In his own words "I had to protect myself, sitting there doing little work with high costs — I had to protect myself from going out of business." For Stanisic marking time in the quarry was intolerable; he preferred the risk of layoff with the alternative chance of better work in the quarry, to the seemingly hopeless stagnation of the previous months.

[40] That is not to say that Stanisic's view was shared by everyone.... It would be unrealistic to think that most if not all drivers voted without giving some thought to their chances of survival. The fact, however, that some drivers in the position of Mr. Stanisic were willing to risk the unknown on the simple basis that the economic status quo was intolerable to them is in my view a compelling factor in understanding the decision which was made and assessing the objective justification for it.

[41] This was a crisis decision — like a decision about how to determine who will survive in an overcrowded lifeboat. If the union had decided to transfer work from the minority to the majority in a time of relative prosperity, where its obvious motive was to increase the already profitable position of some drivers at the expense of others, it would be difficult to avoid the conclusion that its decision was in violation of the duty to provide representation free of invidious favouritism. That is clearly not the situation....

[42] ... The only difference under work sharing as compared to under layoffs by seniority is that as the volume of work diminished attrition would be by order of poverty. Drivers with greater financial obligations would be less able to survive lean periods than those who owned their trucks outright. Under that system, given continual shrinkage, the poor would go first and the rich would go last.

[43] The drivers were in a 'no win' situation. Absent an upturn in the volume of business (in which case layoffs would not be a problem) someone was going to be hurt by the economic pressure. In these circumstances can the union be faulted for choosing an alternative by which those with the longest investment of service in the quarry should go last? The union was not content with a system which, in effect, gave the shrinking work in the quarry to those with the financial strength to bid for it. It chose instead to

let seniority prevail. In asking whether the ultimate decision is one that could be reasonably made I do not see how the union can be faulted for preferring what a particularly helpful study has called a political mode of allocation over a market mode of allocation in a time of scarcity. . . .

[44] This Board cannot conclude that in the difficult circumstances facing it, the union's decision to alter its system of work allocation was without objective justification. Without ignoring the hardship on the junior employees who were eventually affected by the union's decision, I must conclude that the decision to renegotiate the work sharing provision was one which the union was entitled to make in the circumstances, and that neither the motive nor the consequences of its decision violated its duty of fair representation. For reasons elaborated above, I am also satisfied that the procedure followed by the union was free of arbitrariness, discrimination or bad faith.

[45] For the foregoing reasons the complaint is dismissed.

Bukvich remains a leading case on the union's duty of fair representation during the negotiation of a collective agreement. For more recent examples where labour relations boards have upheld the decisions of a union during the negotiations of a collective agreement, see *Walters v CUPE, Local 5089*, [2014] OLRB Rep July/August 700 (loss of all seniority after transit employees took positions outside of the bargaining unit and then returned to the bargaining unit); *Pomietlarz v UFCW, Local 1000A*, [2013] OLRB Rep March/April 231 (union owes no duty to bargain future rights for employees who were not yet members of a bargaining unit); and *Vladyslav Logvynosky v Milk and Bread Drivers*, 2016 CanLII 20059 (OLRB) (duty is not breached where the union may not have fully understood the internal inconsistencies in the newly negotiated language at a membership ratification meeting).

The following decision was less deferential to the wishes of the majority.

Atkinson v CLAC, Local 66, [2003] BCLRBD No 422

[McRae, a company operating in waste pick-up, told its five employees that it was being sold to a competitor, Northwest. McRae's employees had been represented in a bargaining unit by the International Union of Operating Engineers (IUOE). About twenty-five employees of Northwest were in a bargaining unit represented by the Christian Labour Association of Canada (CLAC). As a result of the sale, the five McRae employees became Northwest employees, and it became necessary to determine where the five would be placed on the seniority list. CLAC called a union meeting, and a vote was held to determine whether the seniority of Northwest employees and McRae employees should be "dovetailed," or whether the McRae employees would all be put at the bottom of the seniority list ("endtailed"), which would give them less seniority than any of the Northwest employees. All five former McRae employees attended the meeting, where a secret ballot vote went twenty-four to five in favour of endtailing. CLAC representatives then met with Northwest and arranged for the creation of a seniority list endtailing the McRae employees. Soon afterward, Northwest announced that it was reorganizing all of its routes, and that the new routes would be posted and awarded on the basis of seniority. None of the McRae employees had enough seniority to obtain a regular route, so they worked only sporadically thereafter. They complained to the BCLRB that CLAC had violated its duty of fair representation.

[The board noted that a strict application of the successorship provisions of the *Labour Code* would lead to the conclusion that after the sale of McRae to Northwest, there were two bargaining units and two collective agreements—one for the original Northwest employees represented by CLAC and one for the former McRae employees represented by the IUOE. However, the IUOE had effectively abandoned its representation rights, and Northwest had effectively dealt with CLAC as the bargaining representative for both groups of employees. The board went on as follows.]

J.B. Hall, Vice-Chair:

[...]

35 To elaborate, the Complainants began working for Northwest on December 1, 1999 and there was no interruption in their duties. Atkinson (and, given the representative nature of his evidence, I assume all of the Complainants) became a member of CLAC as of that date. The IUOE was not on the scene at all, and Northwest dealt only with CLAC. The latter effectively assumed the role of bargaining representative for all employees working at Northwest after the successorship. The question of seniority was put to a vote by CLAC at the December 13 meeting and it later finalized the list with Northwest. The fact that the Complainants were allowed to participate in the vote implicitly confirms their status as members of the bargaining unit. In my view, the Reconsideration Decision accurately described CLAC during this period as "exercising its exclusive rights to represent the employees of Northwest, including the Complainants" (para. 46).

36 Having assumed the role of exclusive bargaining agent, and being recognized by the Northwest in that capacity, CLAC was statutorily obligated to act on behalf of all employees in accordance with the duty of fair representation. There was an obvious conflict between CLAC's pre-existing membership and the newly added ex-McRae employees over the latter's seniority. The Complainants may not have had seniority under the Northwest collective agreement at that point, but Kamphof [the CLAC representative] knew "dovetailing had been the practice." Instead of taking a reasoned view of the problem and making a thoughtful judgement about what to do, CLAC let the employees decide. The outcome was a foregone determination based on self-interest, as confirmed by the 24–5 vote against dovetailing.

37 The Complainants rely on *Bukvich v BFCSD, Local 304*, [1982] 1 Can. L.R.B.R. 422 (Ont L.R.B.), to argue it is not enough to say a decision was based on the will of the majority. The Complainants acknowledge the different factual setting of that decision, but say the reasoning applies equally here ...

[...]

39 In determining whether the evidence in *Bukvich* disclosed an objective justification, the Ontario Board said it would not ask whether the union's decision was right or wrong, or whether it agreed with the decision. Rather, it should ask whether the decision could be reasonably made in all of the circumstances, meaning "the rational application of relevant factors, after considering and balancing all legitimate interests and without regard to extraneous factors" (p. 431). That analysis is helpful in the present case, and I find the evidence does not disclose a rationale for endtailing the Complainants' seniority aside from the vote.

40 CLAC seeks to distinguish *Bukvich* and other decisions ... by arguing they all dealt with situations where seniority existed under a collective agreement and was being "gutted"; it says the decisions did not concern persons who had just come to the collective agreement. I find this distinction does not hold because of CLAC's conduct in accepting the Complainants as members and assuming authority to represent the entire unit ...

41 I acknowledge Kamphof telling Atkinson on December 1, 1999 that "if five guys were asking for dovetailing and 20 guys were against, he would have to take that into consideration." Even if this can be construed as a qualification on how the Complainants were brought into the bargaining unit, it wasn't respected—the vote became the sole and determinative factor. Further, the limited evidence indicates perfunctory conduct by CLAC: one Northwest employee indicated they had already made up their minds; Atkinson's offer to present the results of his research "fell on deaf ears"; and Kamphof attempted to suggest the Complainants had been terminated.

42 Does this mean CLAC was precluded from attempting to protect the seniority of the pre-existing Northwest employees? The short answer is "no." As demonstrated by those cases where incumbent unions have argued for endtailing, CLAC could have taken the same position and referred the issue to the Board. It could have also have declined to accept the ex-McRae employees into its bargaining unit (this might have caused Northwest to consider whether it had obligations to them under the IUOE collective agreement). The fundamental problem here was that CLAC assumed the role of exclusive bargaining agent for the Complainants but subordinated their interests to the will of the majority. Once the results of the vote were known, the usual practice of dovetailing was no longer a consideration. In all of the circumstances, I find CLAC's actions were arbitrary and discriminated against the Complainants.

* * * * *

Other decisions have given more weight to the existence of majority support within the bargaining unit, even where there is a sharp conflict of interest between majority and minority. An example is provided by *Ouellet v Syndicat des travailleurs et travailleuses de Deauville* (1983), 83 CLLC para 14,054 (Que Lab Ct). Before union certification in 1982 for the employees of a restaurant, the employer's practice was to take back an employee who had been on maternity leave as soon as an opening arose, even if the leave had been longer than the eighteen weeks envisaged in the labour standards statute. The complainant, who started to work at the restaurant in 1976, took an eleven-month maternity leave in 1979–80. When the first collective agreement was being negotiated in 1982, the union bargaining committee decided that any employee who had taken more than an eighteen-week maternity leave would be given a seniority date which coincided with her return from leave rather than her initial date of hire. The complainant asked the union to reconsider that rule in her case. Rather than putting the question to the entire bargaining unit, the union put it only to those employees who were junior enough to be directly affected by the outcome. Those employees voted to give the complainant a 1980 seniority date, which left her with much less job security than a 1976 date would have. In rejecting the complainant's DFR complaint, the Labour Court said (at 12,285):

[TRANSLATION] Having the matter voted on only by those members who were directly affected by it was a debatable course of action. On the other hand, when a union decides whether to make an exception in a particular case, it is perhaps normal to put the question only to those who are directly concerned. In any event, that was the choice which the union made, and intervention under the duty of fair representation is not appropriate.

Many, but not all, jurisdictions in Canada include the negotiation of a collective agreement within the scope of the duty of fair representation. Three jurisdictions—British Columbia, Ontario, and Quebec—expressly include this feature within their statutory definition. However, labour relations boards in a number of other jurisdictions have interpreted their DFR provisions broadly to include collective bargaining, including Canada, Alberta, and Saskatchewan.

10:320 The Duty of Fair Representation in the Administration of a Collective Agreement

In jurisdictions where the duty of fair representation clearly covers both negotiation and administration of the collective agreement, the bulk of the cases involve contract administration and grievance processing. Nonetheless, as the following often-cited decision on the nature of the duty in collective agreement administration indicates, an element of negotiation may be present in the form of a practice by the employer and the union of not enforcing the apparent meaning of the agreement in certain circumstances.

Rayonier Canada (BC) Ltd v International Woodworkers of America, Local 1-217, [1975] BCLRBD No 42

> [Employee Anderson complained that Rayonier had violated the collective agreement by denying him certain seniority rights due to him under that agreement, and that the union had breached its duty of fair representation by not carrying his resulting grievance to arbitration.]
>
> WEILER, Chair:
>
> [...]
>
> [4] ... Marpole Sawmill is a division of Rayonier. Its employees are represented by the IWA in a certification which also covers the employees of Rayflo Silvichemical plant, another division of Rayonier which is located on the same property as the sawmill. Both groups of employees are covered by the master collective agreement between the IWA and Forest Industrial Relations. However, they are treated as separate entities by the parties, each with its own elected Plant Chairman, Shop Committee, contract ratification votes, and separate seniority lists.
>
> [5] Last July 26, 1974, as a result of the serious economic condition of the lumber industry, there had to be a massive work reduction in the sawmill. This produced a layoff of more than 200 men, including almost all of the maintenance tradesmen. In particular, it affected the two main subjects of these proceedings, Ross Anderson and Angelo Nasato, both of whom were journeymen welders in the sawmills. Nasato's seniority date was listed as April 19, 1957, while Anderson, the next welder on the list, is dated November 17, 1964. In accordance with its previous practice, Rayonier had arranged to offer

some work at Rayflo to the employees at Marpole who were being laid off. On this occasion it had a job for Nasato, but not for Anderson.

[6] A few days later, Rayonier decided that it could conveniently proceed with a new scrubber-barker installation at Marpole during the Mill shutdown. This meant there would be work for some tradesmen, including two welders, and the work would be paid for at new construction rates. However, when Tribe, the foreman, phoned Nasato and offered him this work, Nasato was reluctant to return to Marpole for a short-term project and give up his steady job at Rayflo which would likely last throughout the layoff at the sawmill. Tribe did not insist that Nasato return; instead, he contacted Anderson and the next junior welder on the seniority list, and the latter two were recalled to Marpole for work during August.

[7] Eventually, the sawmill returned to production in mid-fall. However, Nasato remained at Rayflo until November 15, when he was laid off there. He returned to Marpole Sawmill on the date. A week later, on November 22nd, there was another layoff in the sawmill, again affecting the welders. This time, though, there was no work available at Rayflo because of the reduction in effect there. As a result, Nasato was retained at Marpole and Anderson was laid off until his recall on December 5th (losing a total of six working days in that period).

[8] It was this last occurrence and its aftermath which produced these complaints. Accordingly, it is important to be aware of its background. For years, Rayonier and the IWA have operated under an informal arrangement for layoffs and recalls at Marpole. The senior employee is entitled under the agreement to be recalled before the junior employee. However, it is not unusual, especially for tradesmen, for there to be intermittent recalls for short-term jobs during a protracted slowdown. A senior employee may have secured a steady alternate job, perhaps outside of the Lower Mainland, which will probably continue during the entire foreseeable layoff at Marpole. Naturally, he will be reluctant to give up this job to respond to a recall for work at Marpole which may last for just a few days. Recognizing this, Marpole has adopted the practice of allowing the senior employee to decline to return to work in these circumstances and going on to the next man on the seniority list. There may be an exceptional case where the senior man has special qualifications required by Rayonier for its work, in which case Rayonier will insist that he accept the recall, but this is a rare occurrence. We were given a list of 17 employees who had used this arrangement dating back to 1958. The Union knows of and approves the practice, and it had been reaffirmed in August 1974 in discussions between Murray, the Plant Chairman, and Fleming, the Personnel Supervisor, about the Nasato case itself.

[9] Anderson was aware of the long-standing practice and knew that this was the reason why Nasato had not reappeared at Marpole in August. However, for his own reasons, he decided to challenge the contractual basis of the practice on the occasion of the second layoff in November. In his view, when Nasato did not return to Marpole in August, he lost his place on the seniority list. When he did return on November 15th, he should be placed on that list far below Anderson. Hence, when the next work reduction occurred on November 22nd, it was Nasato who should have been laid off and Anderson who should have been retained.

[10] Naturally enough, Anderson did not find a very sympathetic ear in the Union to listen to this claim.

[Anderson filed a grievance, which the union, after normal internal discussions, decided to drop. He then brought this complaint to the board.]

[15] What is the content of the duty of fair representation imposed on a union? Section 7(1) requires that a trade union not "act in a manner that is arbitrary, discriminatory or in bad faith in the representation of any of the employees" in the unit ...

[...]

[17] ... The union must not be actuated by bad faith in the sense of personal hostility, political revenge, or dishonesty. There can be no discrimination, treatment of particular employees unequally whether on account of such factors as race and sex (which are illegal under the Human Rights Code) or simple, personal favouritism. Finally, a union cannot act arbitrarily, disregarding the interests of one of the employees in a perfunctory matter. Instead, it must take a reasonable view of the problem before it and arrive at a thoughtful judgment about what to do after considering the various relevant and conflicting considerations.

[18] These phrases express the duty imposed on the union in general and abstract terms. The case before us ... typifies the most intractable and the most litigated specific issue raised in the fair representation area. Does the union have the authority to settle, or to refuse to press, a grievance which the affected individual employee wants to have proceeded with? It is argued that a collective agreement is a contract establishing the law of the plant. As such, it entitles the individual employee to certain rights and engenders the expectation that these will be secured. If the employee feels that his rights have not been respected by the employer, then he should have access to some neutral forum to obtain a binding adjudication of his claim. The preferred mode of adjudication under a collective agreement is arbitration, and customarily the union controls access to that forum through its authority over the grievance procedure. But it has been vigorously argued that if an employee wants to have his claim to some contract benefit established in arbitration, the union acts arbitrarily, and thus in violation of its duty of fair representation, in denying him that right. The leading exponent of this view expressed its rationale in these terms.

> "... the collective parties can change the general rules governing the terms and conditions of employment, either by negotiating a new agreement or by formally amending the old. The individual has no right to have the contract remain unchanged; his right is only to have it followed until it is changed by proper procedures. Although contract making (or amending) and contract administration are not neatly severable, they are procedurally distinct processes. Most union constitutions prescribe the method of contract ratification, and it is distinct from grievance settlement; the power to make and amend contracts is not placed in the same hands as the power to adjust grievances. Indeed, many union constitutions expressly bar any officer from ratifying any action which constitutes a breach of any contract. Through the ability to change the agreement, the collective parties retain a measure of flexibility. They are not free, however, to set aside general rules for particular cases, nor are they free by informal processes to replace one general rule with a contrary one."

Summers, C. W. "Individual Rights in Collective Agreements and Arbitration", (1962) 37 NYU Law Rev. 362, at pp. 396–397.

[19] Most courts, labour boards, and commentators have rejected this individual rights position. The contrary view—that the union retains control over grievances subject to a duty of fair representation—derived originally from a law review article by Cox, 'Rights under a Labour Agreement' ... and his analysis was accepted by the [United States] Supreme Court majority in *Vaca v. Sipes*:

> "In providing for a grievance and arbitration procedure which gives the union discretion to supervise the grievance machinery and to invoke arbitration, the employer and the union contemplate that each will endeavour in good faith to settle grievances short of arbitration. Through this settlement process, frivolous grievances are ended prior to the most costly and time-consuming step in the grievance procedures. Moreover, both sides are assured that similar complaints will be treated consistently, and major problem areas in the interpretation of the collective bargaining contract can be isolated and perhaps resolved. And finally, the settlement process furthers the interest of the union as statutory agent and as co-author of the bargaining agreement in representing the employees in the enforcement of that agreement. See Cox, *Rights Under a Labor Agreement*, 69 Harv. L. Rev. 601 (1956) ..."

[20] In turn, that conclusion was followed by the Ontario Labour Relations Board in the *Gebbie* decision ... interpreting an Ontario provision with language almost identical to our own:

> "One of the most difficult areas in applying the duty is in the settlement of grievances. We think it clear that the union's obligation to administer the collective agreement gives it the right to settle grievances. An employee does not have an absolute right to have his grievances arbitrated ..."

[21] In our judgment, that same view should be taken of the authority permitted to the union under s. 7 of the Labour Code in handling individual grievances.

[22] ... the administration of a collective agreement is not simply the enforcement of individual contract claims: it is also an extension of the collective bargaining process. As such, it involves significant group interests which the union may represent even against the wishes of particular employees. ...

[23] ... [Grievance procedures and arbitration] can function successfully only if the union has the power to settle or drop those cases which it believes have little merit, even if the individual claimant disagrees. This permits the union to ration its own limited resources by arbitrating only those cases which have a reasonable prospect of success. But even if the employee were willing to finance the union's share of arbitration himself, this would not protect management from the cost of having to defend against frivolous grievances. Such a protection for the employer is a necessary *quid pro quo* from the union if the latter expects management to be reasonable in conceding those other claims which are well-founded, rather than attempt to wear down the union by making it take every case to arbitration to get relief. It is important as a matter of industrial relations policy that a union must be able to assume the responsibility of saying to an employee that his grievance has no merit and will be dropped.

[24] There is a second group interest in the settlement of grievances which applies even to cases which might succeed in arbitration. While a grievance may originally be

brought by one individual, it is not unusual for it to involve a conflict with other employees as well as with the employer.... Rather than relying on the arbitrator's interpretation of the vague language of the agreement drafted a long time ago, it is normally more sensible for the parties to settle that type of current problem by face-to-face discussions in the grievance procedure, with the participation of those individuals who are familiar with the objectives of the agreement and the needs of the operation and are thus best able to improvise a satisfactory solution. Again, if the employees are to have the benefit of this process and of the willing participation of the employer in it, the law must allow the parties to make the settlement binding, rather than allowing a dissenting employee to finesse it by pressing his grievance to arbitration....

[25] ... There is an ample body of experience, both in the American cases and also under the Ontario Labour Relations Act, defining the kinds of situations in which it is proper and those in which it is wrong for the union to deny a grievor access to the arbitration process. The judgment in particular cases depends on the cumulative effect of several relevant features: how critical is the subject matter of the grievance to the interest of the employee concerned? How much validity does his claim appear to have, either under the language of the agreement or the available evidence of what has occurred, and how carefully has the union investigated these? What has been the previous practice respecting this type of case and what expectations does the employee reasonably have from the treatment of earlier grievances? What contrary interests of other employees or of the bargaining unit as a whole have led the union to take a position against the grievor and how much weight should be attached to them? ...

[26] ... This is almost a textbook example of a situation in which it was perfectly proper for the union to drop an individual grievance.

[27] Recall first that Anderson was objecting to the workings of the practice adopted by the Union and the Employer for short-term intermittent recalls during a lengthy layoff ... It is a significant benefit to the bargaining unit, one which is wholly compatible with the principle of seniority, to allow the employee the option of returning to work for [a short] period or asking his supervisor to try someone else ...

[28] Nasato had an even more dramatic interest in conflict with Anderson's position. Anderson claimed that he should have been retained at work on November 22nd and until December 5th in preference to Nasato. This was not on the basis that Anderson was entitled to longer seniority himself. Rather, it was because Nasato had allegedly lost all his seniority on the theory that his employment should have been treated as terminated in August. Instead of seniority dating back to 1957, Nasato's current seniority standing would begin running on November 15, 1974. Accordingly, while by the time his grievance was underway, Anderson was back at work and seeking only compensation for lost wages, his case was based on an interpretation of the agreement which would permit—indeed, would require—Marpole to treat Nasato as a brand new employee, on probation, and the junior person on the tradesmen's seniority list. Again unquestionably, the impact of an unfavourable decision about the case would fall much more heavily on Nasato than on Anderson. Because of its implications for the position of both Nasato as an individual and the employees in the unit as a whole, we can understand why the IWA would be reluctant to have Anderson succeed on his grievance.

[29] But was the I.W.A. deliberately sacrificing Anderson's firmly-established rights under the collective agreement?

[The board examined the seniority provisions of the collective agreement and held that they were not wholly clear on whether an employee had to return to work immediately when recalled or could postpone his or her return if the employer so allowed.]

[34] We have sketched the opposing arguments in this case but we do not believe we should go further and adopt one of them as the correct reading of the agreement. Under Article XXX, there is a special procedure for interpretation of this agreement, one which should not be pre-empted by this Board unless this is necessary for the performance of our statutory obligations.... One must not lightly assume that there is a "right" interpretation to be divined in the collective agreement of this issue. Rather, the parties to this agreement have been faced with the industrial relations problem of minimizing the impact of a layoff on the employees and they dealt with it in a spirit of co-operation, using the clauses of the contract as guideposts. While the balance struck by the parties in this case over-rode the immediate claim of Anderson, it did so for the quite legitimate reason of advancing the more pressing needs of the other employees. Under the language of this agreement, read in the history of its application, one could not argue that Anderson had any contrary rights clearly conferred by the collective agreement nor that he had any firm expectation that he would be treated as more senior than Nasato. The 'method of self-government' of these parties operated in this case "within the zone of fairness and rationality' and should not be reversed by 'the edicts of any outside tribunal'".

* * * * *

In the following decision, the Saskatchewan Labour Relations Board provided a detailed review of the key legal terms in the duty of fair representation before finding that the union in the case had breached its duty under section 2(1) of *The Trade Union Act* (now *The Saskatchewan Employment Act*, SS 2013, c S-15.1, s 6-60).

Lucyshyn v Amalgamated Transit Union, Local 615 (2010), 178 CLRBR (2d) 96 (Sask LRB)

[A transit driver with the City of Saskatoon was reassigned job duties after suffering a work-related injury. He filed a number of grievances against his employer, alleging breaches of the collective agreement pertaining to job postings and call-in procedures. The driver's union acknowledged during the DFR hearing before the Saskatchewan Labour Relations Board that it had not advanced the grievances and that they were viewed as "hot potatoes" by the local union executive. Eventually, the union told the driver that it had withdrawn all his grievances with no explanation for its decision. The driver filed a DFR complaint with the Saskatchewan board against his union.]

Chair Kenneth G. Love QC:

Relevant statutory provisions:
[25] Section 25.1 provides as follows:

25.1 Every employee has the right to be fairly represented in grievance or rights arbitration proceedings under a collective bargaining agreement by the trade union certified to represent his bargaining unit in a manner that is not arbitrary, discriminatory or in bad faith.

Analysis & Decision:

[...]

[27] The duty of fair representation was outlined by the Board in *Mary Banga v. Saskatchewan Government Employees' Union*, [1993] 4th Quarter Sask. Labour Rep. 88, LRB File 173-93, at 97 and 98:

> ... As we have pointed out before, the duty of fair representation arose as the *quid pro quo* for the exclusive status as bargaining agent which was granted to trade unions under North American collective bargaining legislation. Once a certification order is granted on the basis of majority support, members of the bargaining unit have no choice as to who will represent them, whether or not they were among those who supported the union. This exclusive status gave trade unions security and influence; it was, however, viewed as imposing upon them an obligation to represent all of those they represented in a way which was not arbitrary, discriminatory or in bad faith.
>
> The concept of the duty of fair representation was originally formulated in the context of admission to union membership. In the jurisprudence of the courts and labour relations boards which have considered this issue, however, it has been applied as well to both the negotiation and the administration of collective agreements. Section 25.1 of *The Trade Union Act*, indeed, refers specifically to the context of arbitration proceedings. This Board has not interpreted the section in a way which limits the duty to that instance, but has taken the view that the duty at "common law" was more extensive, and that Section 25.1 does not have the effect of eliminating that duty of fair representation in the context of union membership, collective bargaining, or the grievance procedure.

[28] The duty of fair representation requires the Union to act in a manner that does not demonstrate bad faith, arbitrary treatment or discrimination. The general requirements were set out by the Supreme Court of Canada in *Canadian Merchant Services Guild v. Gagnon*, [1984] 84 CLLC 12,181. In particular, the Court held that "the representation by the Union must be fair, genuine and not merely apparent, undertaken with integrity and competence, without serious or major negligence, and without hostility towards the employees."

[29] The onus of showing a breach of the duty of fair representation falls upon the Applicant in these proceedings.

[30] In *Hargrave, et al. v. Canadian Union of Public Employees, Local 3833, and Prince Albert Health District*, [2003] Sask. L.R.B.R. 511, LRB File No. 223-02, the Board set out the principles applicable to an analysis of the duty of fair representation, with a particular focus on arbitrariness and the scope of the Union's duty. The Board stated at 518 to 526:

> [...]
>
> [28] In *Toronto Transit Commission*, [1997] OLRD No. 3148, at paragraph 9, the Ontario Labour Relations Board cited with approval the following succinct explanation of the concepts provided by that Board in a previous unreported decision:

... a complainant must demonstrate that the union's actions were:
(1) "Arbitrary"—that is, flagrant, capricious, totally unreasonable, or grossly negligent;
(2) "Discriminatory—that is, based on invidious distinctions without reasonable justification or labour relations rationale; or
(3) "in Bad Faith"—that is, motivated by ill-will, malice hostility or dishonesty.

The behaviour under review must fit into one of these three categories.... [M]istakes or misjudgments are not illegal; moreover, the fact that an employee fails to understand his rights under a collective agreement or disagrees with the union's interpretation of those rights does not, in itself, establish that the union was wrong—let alone "arbitrary", "discriminatory" or acting in "bad faith".

The concept of arbitrariness, which is usually more difficult to identify than discrimination or bad faith, is not equivalent to simple errors in judgment, negligence, laxity or dilatoriness. In *Walter Prinesdomu v. Canadian Union of Public Employees*, [1975] 2 CLRBR 310, the Ontario Labour Relations Board stated, at 315:

> It could be said that this description of the duty requires the exclusive bargaining agent to "put its mind" to the merits of a grievance and attempt to engage in a process of rational decision making that cannot be branded as implausible or capricious.
>
> This approach gives the word arbitrary some independent meaning beyond subjective ill will, but, at the same time, it lacks any precise parameters and thus is extremely difficult to apply. Moreover, attempts at a more precise adumbration have to reconcile the apparent consensus that it is necessary to distinguish arbitrariness (whatever it means) from mere errors in judgment, mistakes, negligence and unbecoming laxness.

[...]

[34] There have been many pronouncements in the case law with respect to negligent action or omission by a trade union as it relates to the concept of arbitrariness in cases of alleged violation of the duty of fair representation. While most of the cases involve a refusal to accept or to progress a grievance after it is filed, in general, the cases establish that to constitute arbitrariness, mistakes, errors in judgment and "mere negligence" will not suffice, but rather, "gross negligence" is the benchmark. Examples in the jurisprudence of the Board include *Chrispen, supra*, where the Board found that the union's efforts "were undertaken with integrity and competence and without serious or major negligence...." In *Radke v. Canadian Paperworkers Union, Local 1120*, [1993] 2nd Quarter Sask. Labour Rep. 57, LRB File No. 262-92, at 64 and 65, the Board stated:

> What is expected of trade union officials in their representation of employees is that they will act honestly, conscientiously and without prejudgment or favouritism. Within the scope of these criteria, they may be guilty of honest errors or even some laxity in the pursuit of the interests of those they represent. In making decisions about how or whether to pursue certain issues on behalf of employees, they should certainly be alert to the significance for those employees of the interests which may be at stake.

[35] Most recently, in *Vandervort v. University of Saskatchewan Faculty Association and University of Saskatchewan*, [2003] Sask. L.R.B.R. 147, LRB File Nos. 102-95 & 047-99, the Board stated, at ... at 194–95, as follows:

...

[219] In *Rousseau v. International Brotherhood of Locomotive Engineers et al.*, 95 CLLC 220-064 at 143, 558-9, the Canada Labour Relations Board described the duty not to act in an arbitrary manner as follows:

Through various decisions, labour boards, including this one, have defined the term "arbitrary." *Arbitrary conduct has been described as a failure to direct one's mind to the merits of the matter; or to inquire into or to act on available evidence; or to conduct any meaningful investigation to obtain the data to justify a decision. It has also been described as acting on the basis of irrelevant factors or principles; or displaying an indifferent and summary attitude. Superficial, cursory, implausible, flagrant, capricious, non-caring or perfunctory are all terms that have also been used to define arbitrary conduct.* It is important to note that intention is not a necessary ingredient for an arbitrary characterization.

Negligence is distinguishable from arbitrary, discriminatory or bad faith behaviour. The concept of negligence can range from simple negligence to gross negligence. The damage to the complainant in itself is not the test. Simple negligence may result in serious damage. Negligence in any of its variations is characterized by conduct or inaction due to inadvertence, thoughtlessness or inattention. Motivation is not a characteristic of negligence. Negligence does not require a particular subjective stage of mind as does a finding of bad faith. There comes a point, however, when mere/simple negligence becomes gross/serious negligence, and we must assess when this point, in all circumstances, is reached.

When does negligence become "serious" or "gross"? *Gross negligence may be viewed as so arbitrary that it reflects a complete disregard for the consequences.* Although negligence is not explicitly defined in section 37 of the Code, this Board has commented on the concept of negligence in its various decisions. Whereas simple/mere negligence is not a violation of the Code, the duty of fair representation under section 37 has been expanded to include gross/serious negligence ... The Supreme Court of Canada commented on and endorsed the Board's utilization of gross/serious negligence as a criteria in evaluating the union's duty under section 37 in *Gagnon et al.* [1984 CanLII 18 (SCC), [1984] 1 S.C.R. 509]. The Supreme Court of Canada reconfirmed the utilization of serious negligence as an element to be considered in *Centre Hospitalier Régina Ltée v. Labour Court*, 1990 CanLII 111 (SCC), [1990] 1 S.C.R. 1330.

[36] In *North York General Hospital*, [1982] OLRB Rep. Aug. 1190, the Ontario Labour Relations Board addressed the relation of negligence to arbitrariness as follows, at 1194:

> A union is not required to be correct in every step it takes on behalf of an employee. Moreover, mere negligence on the part of a union official does not ordinarily constitute a breach of section 68 ... There comes a point, however, when "mere negligence" becomes "gross negligence" and when gross negligence reflects a complete disregard for critical consequences to an employee then that action may be viewed as arbitrary for the purposes of section 68 of the Act. ...

[37] In a subsequent decision, *Canada Packers Inc.*, [1990] OLRB Rep Aug. 886, the Ontario Board confirmed this position as follows, at 891:

> A review of the Board's jurisprudence reveals that honest mistakes, innocent misunderstandings, simple negligence, or errors in judgment will not of themselves, constitute arbitrary conduct within the meaning of section 68. Words like "implausible", "so reckless as to be unworthy of protection", "unreasonable", "capricious", "grossly negligent", and "demonstrative of a non-caring attitude" have been used to describe conduct which is arbitrary within the meaning of section .... Such strong words may be applicable to the more obvious cases but may not accurately describe the entire spectrum of conduct which might be arbitrary. As the jurisprudence also illustrates, what will constitute arbitrary conduct will depend on the circumstances.

[...]

[35] ... The question that the Board must determine is whether or not, on an objective standard, the Union has taken steps to investigate a potential grievance and has taken a measured view of that grievance and made a reasoned decision in respect thereof.

[36] This case, along with the other cases determined by the Board under s. 25.1, suggests a minimum standard of conduct by a Union in the handling of a grievance. There should be a clearly defined process followed by the Union which could include the following steps:

1. Upon a grievance being filed, there should be an investigation conducted by the Union to determine the merits or not of the facts and allegations giving rise to the grievance;
2. The investigation conducted must be done in an objective and fair manner, and as a minimum would include an interview with the complainant and any other employees involved;
3. A report of the investigation should go forward to the appropriate body or person charged with the conduct of the grievance process within the Union. A copy of that report should be provided to the complainant;
4. The Union, Grievance Committee, or person charged with the conduct of grievances, should determine if the grievance merits being advanced. Legal advice may be sought at this time to determine the prospects for success based on prior arbitral jurisprudence;
5. At this stage, the Union may determine to proceed or not proceed with the grievance. However, in making that determination, the Union must be cognizant of the duty imposed upon it by s. 25.1 of the *Act*;

6. At each stage of the grievance procedure, the Union will be required to make a determination as to whether to proceed with the grievance or not. Again, its decision to proceed or not must be made in accordance with the provisions of s. 25.1 of the *Act*; and
7. It must also be recognized that the Union has carriage of the grievance, not the grievor. There may be instances where the common good outweighs the individual grievor's interest in a matter. Where such a decision is made (*i.e.:* not to proceed with a grievance) which is not arbitrary, discriminatory, or in bad faith, that decision will undoubtedly be supported by the Board.

[37] As noted in *Rousseau supra*, arbitrary conduct has been described as:

A failure to direct one's mind to the merits of the matter, or to inquire into or act on available evidence; or to conduct any meaningful investigation to obtain the data to justify a decision. It has also been described as acting on the basis of irrelevant factors or principles or displaying an indifferent and summary attitude. Superficial, cursory, implausible, flagrant, capricious, non-caring or perfunctory are all terms that have also been used to define arbitrary conduct.

[38] The Board finds the conduct of the Respondent Union in this case to be arbitrary. The evidence discloses that it did not conduct any meaningful investigation of the complaints alleged by the Applicant. Furthermore, it took a superficial or cursory view of the grievances filed. They maintained no record of the grievances (as demonstrated by their inability to even locate copies of the grievances). Furthermore, they failed to communicate with the Applicant concerning his grievances after the initial meetings with Mr. Heusdens, where the majority of the grievances were denied, following up on only one grievance, which was subsequently accepted and paid out. Arbitrariness was further demonstrated when the grievances were withdrawn by the Respondent Union without consultation or communication with the Applicant. Nor was the Applicant offered any opportunity to be heard in respect of the Respondent Union's decision to withdraw his grievances.

[39] Throughout the hearing of this matter, the Board was shocked by the apparent lack of any defined process or procedure to deal with grievances. They appeared to be handled in an offhand and disjointed manner. There was clearly a lack of any process as described in paragraph [36] above.

[After finding that the union had breached its duty of fair representation, the Saskatchewan Labour Relations Board ordered the union to conduct an investigation into the mishandling of the grievances; to provide the transit driver with a copy of the investigator's report; to refer the report to the union executive to decide whether to proceed with the grievances; and, if it decides not to proceed, to allow the transit driver the opportunity to initiate an internal appeal of the decision under the union's constitutional appeal procedures.]

* * * * *

Labour relations boards have been on guard against collusion between the complaining employee and the respondent union. In *Crewdson and Stebeleski v International Brotherhood* of *Electrical Workers, Local 1541* (1992), 18 CLRBR (2d) 107 at para 10, Vice-Chair Jamieson wrote:

> Let us say immediately that it is not the practice of this Board to accept 'guilty pleas' in duty of fair representation complaints. If this were so, it would be an easy matter for trade unions to counsel members to file complaints when access to arbitration has lapsed for one reason or another. The union could then plead guilty and have the Board order the matter to arbitration. For example, many complaints to the Board rest on allegations that the bargaining agent has missed a crucial time limit in a collective agreement. If the Board were to accept guilty pleas in these situations, it would be a convenient way for trade unions to circumvent these time limits in the collective agreement. In fact, there have been instances in the past where trade unions have literally pled guilty in these situations and the Board has found that there was no violation of the Code.

It is clear from the decision of the Supreme Court of Canada in *Parry Sound (District) Social Services Administration Board v Ontario Public Service Employees Union, Local 324*, 2003 SCC 42, set out above in Chapter 9 (Section 9:330), that grievance arbitrators have the jurisdiction to hear and decide employee grievances that allege violation of statutes dealing with the employment relationship, including human rights statutes. When a union processes a grievance that involves a fundamental statutory right, such as the protection against discrimination on the ground of disability, does the DFR impose a higher standard of conduct on the union than when it processes other types of grievance? The answer is yes.

In *Bingley v Teamsters, Local 91*, 2004 CIRB 291, the Canada Industrial Relations Board ruled that a union had not taken the "extra measure of care" to fairly represent a member with skin cancer who required an accommodation with respect to the length of her daily shift. In its ruling, the board set out the guiding principles for measuring a union's heightened representational obligations in accommodation and human rights cases:

- whether the union's intervention was reasonable where the employer failed to implement appropriate accommodation measures;
- whether the quality of the process that allowed the union to come to its conclusion was reasonable;
- whether the union went beyond its "usual" procedures and applied an extra measure of care in representing the employee; and
- whether the union applied an extra measure of assertiveness in dealing with the employer.

In *Bingley*, the Canada Industrial Relations Board held that the union's intervention was not reasonable. The union had taken the employer's word at face value that, because the complainant could not work more than eight hours per day, she was unfit for work. According to the board, the union should have made a stronger effort to seek appropriate accommodation. It ruled that the union did not go beyond its usual procedures in representing the grievor; it did not apply "an extra measure of assertiveness" when dealing with the employer.

Should individual employees have the right to carry their grievances to arbitration over the objections of their bargaining agent? Consider the following.

Bernard Adell, "Collective Agreements and Individual Rights: A Note on the Duty of Fair Representation" (1986) 11 *Queen's Law Journal* 251 at 254–58

[I]t will be impossible to make the duty of fair representation into a basket strong enough to hold all of the individual rights eggs. The low standards which the duty imposes upon unions are only one problem. Long, cumbersome proceedings are another. The Ontario Labour Relations Board has developed a two-stage procedure for fair representation complaints involving grievance processing. In the first stage, the board decides whether the union breached its duty of fair representation in the way it handled the grievance. At that stage, the merits of the grievance are supposed to be gone into only as far as is necessary to enable the board to assess the legality of the union's conduct—but that is often quite far. If the board finds that the union was in breach of its duty, the board remits the grievance to the second stage: adjudication on the merits by an arbitration tribunal. Although this procedure shows impeccable respect for the jurisdictional boundary between the board and the arbitral process, it can require a great deal of repetition and it does nothing to speed the employee's way to a remedy.

The less sophisticated the employee, and the less well-connected he is with such guardian angels as rival unions, the more intimidating the substantive and procedural barriers will be to him. Most important of all, duty of fair representation proceedings have the inherent flaw of pitting employee against union, in what is too often a bitter internecine fight, before even getting to the main event: the employee's claim against the employer. Is it necessary to make a prolonged, three-sided donnybrook out of a controversy which might well yield quickly to a one-step, bipartite hearing on the merits between employee and employer?

That leads straight into the third possible channel of recourse—a right in the individual employee to carry his own grievance to arbitration if the union refuses or neglects to do so. Alfred Blumrosen argued in 1959 that employees should have control over what he called "critical job interest" grievances, which he defined as those involving discharge or "major disciplinary action which will substantially destroy the employment relationship," those involving a claim for payment for work already done, and those involving job seniority. Paul Weiler has suggested a modified version of that approach, confined to discharge cases. He would not extend it to seniority cases, not even job seniority cases, because, as he puts it, seniority grievances often involve "a legitimate conflict of interest between two members of the bargaining unit." Such conflicts of interest, Professor Weiler clearly feels, are better suited to resolution by the union than by an arbitrator.

There are good reasons, which seem to me to get better as time passes, for going farther and giving any grievor covered by a collective agreement the right to carry any grievance to arbitration himself if the bargaining agent will not. The fairly brief history of the duty of fair representation has shown how awkward it is for an outside tribunal—even as sophisticated a tribunal as a labour relations board—to police a union's internal deliberations. Although I have seen no empirical evidence on this point, it seems probable that requiring unions to build up files of the sort which will protect them from unfair representation complaints imposes a drain on their resources out of all proportion to any gains which may accrue to individual employees.

Additionally, I would argue that whenever the law gives a substantive right to someone, as it does to an individual employee to enjoy the fruits of collective bargaining as contained in a collective agreement, it ought (in the absence of compelling reasons to the contrary) to provide a procedural means of enforcing that substantive right. That argument gains strength, in the context of grievance handling, from the central role which collective agreement rights play in the lives of individual employees. It is not only job *retention* grievances that may be of critical importance to particular employees, but also what can be called job *tolerability grievances*—those over such matters as shift work, overtime scheduling and major working conditions, especially where health or safety is involved. Grievances affecting job *level*—for example, job posting and employee selection grievances—can also be critical to ambitious employees. If a good case can be made for allowing individuals to carry their job retention grievances to arbitration, is the case really much weaker for these other kinds of grievances?

Giving employees the right to take their own grievances to arbitration would undoubtedly pose some dangers. Whether the arbitrating was done in the usual way or by a special panel of arbitrators or a special tribunal, there would be a risk that the entire arbitration system might be overburdened by a large influx of new cases. However, I do not think that is likely to happen. Aggrieved individuals who cannot persuade their unions to act for them may at times be persistent and cantankerous, but they are not very numerous, nor do they tend to be very rich or powerful. They usually lack substantial resources unless they are supported by a rival union, whose primary objective may well be to discredit the incumbent bargaining agent. To grievors who are out to get the bargaining agent, a straightforward arbitration proceeding against the employer is likely to be less appealing than the three-party, two-stage circus provided by a duty of fair representation proceeding, where the union is cast as the principal defendant right from the outset. As for the other type of individual grievor—the type who is truly acting on his own—it should not take long to become widely known that grievances rejected by one's own union had little chance of succeeding at arbitration.

A high likelihood of losing might not in itself deter many grievors with strongly felt but wholly ill-founded grievances. However, a requirement that a losing grievor had to pay his own costs, perhaps on a scale appropriate to his means, should be quite an effective deterrent against frivolous use of the arbitration procedure. It would probably not be necessary to take the further step of requiring an unsuccessful grievor to pay the employer's costs as well as his own, and that step might place such a heavy financial disincentive on grievors of modest means as to make illusory the new right which I am arguing for. However, it could be kept in reserve in case a further disincentive turned out to be needed.

As for the employer, it is true that he is now largely free, in the short run at least, from any need to go behind the union's assurance that it will not pursue a grievance. In contrast, under the reform I am proposing, he would have to treat any grievance settlement worked out with the union as tentative until the individual grievor had exhausted or abandoned his right to proceed on his own. That would be an inconvenience to the employer. However, because I believe individuals would make only limited use of such a right, I do not expect it would be a very severe inconvenience.

It might be argued that the availability of arbitration over the objections of the bargaining agent would undermine the latter's authority and would make employees unappreciative of union representation. This strikes me as an argument of sound and fury, without much substance. No union which does a reasonably conscientious and competent job of screening grievances should have much fear that its rejects would be warmly received by arbitrators.

Citing the important 1978 *Canada Labour Code* amendments allowing unorganized employees with twelve months' service to have discharge grievances arbitrated, Paul Weiler suggests that it would be incongruous to continue to allow unions to deny that right to organized employees. This is a valid point, and one which is likely to become relevant to more than discharge grievances as the statutory rights of unorganized employees are increased. It is yet another reason for giving organized employees a broad right to invoke grievance arbitration themselves when their unions fail or refuse to do it for them.

Finally, I would like to make some mention of experience outside our borders. Most Western European countries have a standing tribunal, often called a labour court, the jurisdiction of which varies from country to country but which generally includes the adjudication of individual employee complaints against employers about the violation of employment rights. Access to those tribunals is not limited to unions or to individuals whose cases are supported by unions. In Sweden, for example, as Clyde Summers wrote some years ago, "the individual has rights under the collective agreement which his organization can neither bar nor barter away." A Swedish employee may take his claim to the courts if the union refuses to do so, even if the union has purported to settle the matter against his wishes. According to Professor Summers, the fears of those who opposed giving such a right to the individual have not materialized. Only a very small percentage of the Labour Court's cases have been brought by individuals acting on their own. In addition, "the fears that the parties would be deprived of needed flexibility in administering the collective agreement have not been realized," because the Swedish Labour Court, in interpreting collective agreements, has been sensitive to the interests of the collective parties. It is hard to imagine that Canadian arbitrators, who depend on the collective parties for most of their business, would be any more inclined to neglect such interests.

It is true that the concept of exclusivity of bargaining rights in Canadian collective labour law, together with the strong focus of Canadian union activity at the workplace level and the virtually complete withdrawal from individual employees of the right to negotiate terms of employment superior to those in the collective agreement, may give exclusive union control over grievance processing an appearance of rationality in our country which it could not have in Europe. Furthermore, the legitimacy of unions is more widely accepted by employers in most Western European countries than in Canada, with the result that European unions may have less reason to fear that an individual right to press grievances will be misused as a stick with which to beat the union. Still, despite such important differences as these, I think Western European experience supports the view that we exaggerate the risks of giving individual employees the right to take their own grievance to arbitration.

[Reprinted by permission.]

* * * * *

In some industries, such as longshoring, construction, and film production, unions control access to employment through hiring halls. In these industries, employers are highly fragmented, and a job with a particular employer usually does not last long enough for an employee to acquire substantial seniority rights. Rather than hiring their own employees, the employers commonly look to a union to provide the workers needed on a job-by-job or even a day-by-day basis. The union thus becomes, to a degree, employer as well as bargaining agent—a dual role that can provide an important element of job security to workers who would otherwise lack any such security. But this concentration of powers—inherently conflicting powers, perhaps—in the hands of the union exposes workers to abuses as serious as those perpetrated by the most autocratic employers in other industries. Unions that run hiring halls obviously have a strong interest in limiting admission to union membership, in order to limit the supply of workers and thereby keep up the demand for the services of their existing members. In administering a hiring hall, a union may act in a high-handed way in deciding who to admit to membership or in who to choose for a particular job, and the individual would have no recourse under the DFR because the union's actions would not involve representation of the individual *vis-à-vis* the employer. Three jurisdictions—British Columbia, Ontario, and the federal jurisdiction—address this problem by imposing what is called a duty of fair referral on unions in the administration of a hiring hall. These provisions mirror the DFR provisions of the statutes, by prohibiting unions from making decisions that are arbitrary, discriminatory, or in bad faith in referring workers to jobs.

* * * * *

There are high numbers and yet a very low success rate for complaints based on the duty of fair representation, which has prompted concerns that unfounded complaints are draining the time and resources of labour boards, unions, and employers. In response to such concerns, some jurisdictions have adopted filter mechanisms to enable boards to dispose of such complaints without an oral hearing. See British Columbia *Labour Relations Code*, RSBC 1996, c 244, s 13; *Canada Labour Code*, RSC 1985, c L-2, s 98; and Ontario *Labour Relations Act*, s 99(3). The British Columbia mechanism is discussed in the following excerpt.

Judd v CEP, Local 2000 (2003), 91 CLRBR (2d) 33

> 8 When it receives a complaint alleging a breach of Section 12, the Board must make an initial determination under Section 13 of the Code as to whether the complaint discloses an apparent breach of Section 12. Section 13 provides:
>
>> 13. (1) If a written complaint is made to the board that a trade union, council of trade unions or employers' organization has contravened section 12, the following procedure must be followed:
>> (a) panel of the board must determine whether or not it considers that the complaint discloses a case that the contravention has apparently occurred;
>> (b) if the panel considers that the complaint discloses sufficient evidence that the contravention has apparently occurred, it *must*

(i) serve a notice of the complaint on the trade union, council of trade unions or employers' organization against which the complaint is made and invite a reply to the complaint from the trade union, council of trade unions or employers' organization, and

(ii) dismiss the complaint or refer it to the board for a hearing.

(2) If the board is satisfied that the trade union, council of trade unions or employers' organization contravened section 12, the board may make an order or direction referred to in section 14(4)(a), (b) or (d). (emphasis added)

9 Section 13 was added to the Code in 1993. This amendment to the Code was a direction from the Legislature to provide the Board with a "process by which the Board could effectively adjudicate fair representation complaints without requiring submissions, or holding hearings, in every case": *Recommendations for Labour Law Reform*, p. 22. The intent of the direction can be seen in the mandatory terms (i.e., "must") in Section 13, emphasized above. In short, the intent was to streamline the process and reduce the amount of work generated by Section 12 complaints. That intention of the Legislature is readily understandable given the Board's experience with Section 12 complaints....

12 As noted earlier, Section 13 of the Code allows the Board to proceed with a Section 12 complaint only if it discloses "a case that the contravention [of Section 12] has apparently occurred." Stated another way, the Board may only proceed with a Section 12 complaint if there is "sufficient evidence" that Section 12 has been breached. If there is sufficient evidence of a Section 12 breach, the Board must then proceed to adjudicate the matter on its merits.

13 It is often difficult to obtain from Section 12 complainants material details of what they allege the union did or did not do in respect to representing them, especially since the vast majority of them are lay litigants who are unfamiliar with the Board's processes or jurisprudence.

14 As a result, it has proven difficult for the Board to give Section 13 the full scope and effect which was intended in the 1993 legislative amendment....

25 Every year the Board receives a far greater number of Section 12 complaints than are justified on the facts. This has resulted in excessive demands being placed on the resources of unions and the labour relations system as a whole, including the resources of the Board. While in part this may be due to an increased level of sophistication amongst employees in the workforce in general, in our view it may also flow from a fundamental misconception regarding the nature of the rights and obligations arising under Section 12....

98 In our view, a widespread misunderstanding of the Section 13 complaint process by unrepresented Section 12 complainants, and the Board's sympathy for that predicament, may have operated to challenge the Board's ability to fulfil its statutory mandate under the Code in two respects. First, complaints may have passed through Section 13 that have not satisfied the threshold of "sufficient evidence" of an "apparent contravention." The Board, likely on the basis that many complainants do not understand their responsibilities in the process, may not have dismissed the complaint (as a literal reading of Section 13 would require), but instead invited a response from the union and employer in order to get a better understanding of the situation.

99 While trying to be accessible to individuals who are unrepresented is very important, simply passing these types of complaints through to the next step without fully

engaging the Section 13 requirements is, in our view, inconsistent with the legislative emphasis of that section. Despite the Board's existing statutory ability to dismiss any complaint or application at any time for failure to make out a prima facie case (Section 133(4)), the Legislature has set a special mandatory threshold for Section 12 complaints. It has established a minimum that must be done before respondents are put to the difficulty and expense of being engaged in litigation. The Legislature has in fact emphasized the requirement of sufficient evidence of an apparent contravention at two points in the Section 13 process for Section 12 complaints. That legislative policy should be given effect.

100 Experience has also tended to cast doubt on whether passing such complaints through the Section 13 threshold is, ultimately, beneficial to complainants. In our experience the vast majority of complaints are still dismissed, but after a full process of exchanging written submissions, potentially holding a hearing or engaging in other processes with the parties, and all the cost and delay associated with this.

101 This leads us to the second way in which the Board's ability to fulfil its statutory mandate has been challenged: delay. The typical Section 12 complaint begins with the filing of the complaint form and some of the relevant documents. Time then passes while the Board's staff prompt the complainant to provide additional documents or details. The file then goes to a Vice-Chair for the first Section 13 determination. If the Vice-Chair decides that Section 13 threshold is satisfied, submissions are invited from the respondents, followed by a reply from the complainant. A Settlement Conference may be held. If there is no Settlement Conference (or if it is unsuccessful), the file will be adjudicated.

102 In many cases there is no need for an oral hearing and the complaint is then adjudicated from the written material on file. What often occurs, however, is that the complainant's allegations, information and documents are not set out in an organized fashion. The Vice-Chair must review the information and organize it into a coherent narrative. The Vice-Chair then writes a decision which sets out the narrative and adjudicates it against the jurisprudence relating to Section 12. If the complaint is unsuccessful, the decision explains in a comprehensive fashion why each of the complainant's allegations do not fall within the scope of Section 12. This is so even where, as often can be the case, the allegations are not in reality close to establishing a violation of Section 12. The whole process takes, on average, six to eight months.

103 We appreciate that much of this process stems from a desire to make the Board's processes accessible. As well, the lengthy decisions dismissing unmeritorious Section 12 complaints are directed at enabling the complainants to understand why Section 12 does not provide a remedy for their assertions.

104 In our view, however, complainants would be better served by a quicker decision that allows them to get on with their lives with some certainty. While their complaint remains outstanding, the complainant may experience considerable uncertainty and anxiety. Depending on the issue that is at stake, this uncertainty may even affect a complainant's life beyond his or her employment.

105 The outstanding complaint may also cause uncertainty for the union and the employer (whose current arrangements may ultimately be undone if the complaint is successful), and sometimes for other employees who could similarly be affected by the complaint if it is successful and the complainant's grievance is taken to arbitration. It

also may have a negative effect on relations between the complainant and the union upon whom he or she may still have to rely for representation.

106 Delay is generally contrary to good labour relations and this applies to Section 12 complaints as well as other matters under the Code. The Board is required under the Code to promote conditions favourable to the orderly, constructive and expeditious settlement of disputes: Section 2(e). Looked at from this perspective, the Board's current Section 13 practices may leave room for improvement in that regard.

107 The Board will therefore take steps to streamline its Section 12/Section 13 processes. First, the mandatory requirements in Section 13 of the Code will be more strictly applied and focused upon.

108 Second, by providing a clear explanation of the scope of Section 12 in this decision, we hope to largely eliminate the need for lengthy decisions in response to each complaint. As a part of this, Section 12 decisions may no longer provide a summary of the factual background, particularly where the case has been decided under Section 13 on the basis of the Section 12 application itself or the written submissions of the parties.

109 Third, if a complaint discloses an apparent contravention of Section 12 and therefore passes the Section 13 thresholds, wherever possible it will stay with the same Vice-Chair for adjudication on the merits.

* * * * *

In the following passage in *McRae Jackson v CAW*, [2004] CIRB No 290, the Canada Industrial Relations Board also made it clear that it did not consider itself obliged to hold a hearing before dismissing a duty of fair representation complaint.

55 Since the [*Canada Labour*] *Code* was amended in 1999, the Board has the unfettered discretion to decide a section 37 complaint without a public hearing. The scheme of section 16.1 of the Code and section 10(g) of the *Canada Industrial Relations Board Regulations, 2001* (the *Regulations*) foresees that the Board may decide a complaint on the basis of the material filed, unless it considers that it has insufficient information before it to determine the matter and that the parties should be given the opportunity to advance their respective positions by way of an oral hearing. One or the other of the parties may request an oral hearing; however, the Board is not compelled to grant this request.

56 There is no requirement for the Board to give notice to the parties of its intention not to hold a hearing.... The *audi alteram partem* rule, that is the requirement to hear both sides of a matter, does not require that an oral hearing be held in every case. The reviewing courts have clearly stated that the Board is only required to grant to the parties an opportunity to present their case, whether by written submissions, documents produced and its own inquiries.

The Ontario Labour Relations Board also has the authority to dismiss a complaint where no arguable case has been made out in support of the complaint. An additional procedural innovation in Ontario allows cases to be dealt with by a consultation rather than a full hearing. The board's Information Bulletin No 11 contrasts the two, in these terms:

Ontario Labour Relations Board, "Duty of Fair Representation Applications," Information Bulletin (Toronto: OLRB, March 2018) at 3–4

A consultation is meant to be more informal and less costly to the parties than a hearing, and the Vice-Chair plays a much more active role in a consultation than in a hearing. The goal of a consultation is to allow the Vice-Chair to expeditiously focus in on the issues in dispute and determine whether an employee's statutory rights have been violated.

While the precise format of a consultation varies depending on the nature of the case and the approach of the individual adjudicators, there are some universal features. To draw out the facts and arguments necessary to decide whether the statutory duty of fair representation has been violated, the Vice-Chair may: 1) question the parties and their representatives, 2) express views, 3) define or re-define the issues, and 4) make determinations as to what matters are agreed to or are in dispute. The giving of evidence under oath and the cross-examination of witnesses are normally not part of a consultation, and when they are, it is only with respect to those matters that are defined by the Board.

Because the opportunity to call witnesses and present evidence is limited, the Board relies heavily on the information that is provided in the application and response. As such, the employee and union (and employer and any other affected party that participates) are required to provide in their application and response all of the material facts that they intend to rely on. Parties who fail to do so may not be allowed to present any evidence or make any representations about these facts at the consultation.

Chapter 11: The Trade Union and Its Members

11:100 TRADE UNION STRUCTURES

Stephanie Ross, Larry Savage, Errol Black, & Jim Silver, *Building a Better World: An Introduction to Trade Unionism in Canada*, 3d ed (Halifax: Fernwood Publishing, 2015) 112–17

CHAPTER 7: HOW DO UNIONS WORK?

The internal and external structures and dynamics of unions shape and influence how unions interact with employers, their members, the broader labour movement and the general public. These structures are complex. They include the union local led by elected members and a professional paid staff, where many collective agreements are negotiated and administered. But most locals are part of a larger structure, a parent union that provides locals with various kinds of support and organizes political action. Finally, many union locals are connected through municipal, provincial and national federations of unions, the labour centrals within which the decisions about the labour movement's overall political direction are made. Unions strive to make these decisions about priorities, strategies and actions in a democratic fashion. How and how well the labour movement makes its decisions has a huge impact on the lives of workers, and on society in general.

Local Unions

The labour movement is built on local unions, which represent workers in a particular workplace or location. Individual workers first become involved in union activity at the local level. Sometimes they are directly involved through an organizing drive that results in the certification of a local at their workplace. More often they find employment at workplaces that are already unionized, and automatically become members of the union. In 2013, 4,735,367 workers in Canada — 30.0 percent of non-agricultural paid workers — belonged to 14,147 locals in 771 unions (Labour Program 2014). Between 2006 and 2013, the number of union members increased by 7 percent, though the number of unions declined (from 827 to 771) as did the number of union locals (from 15,479 to 14,147). This change was reflected in increases in the average number of members per union (from 5,370 to 6,142) and per local union (from 287 to 335) and is part of a larger trend wherein parent unions become fewer, and local unions become larger.

Normally, local unions are established at a particular workplace to represent one bargaining unit and have their own elected executives and governing structures. But there are locals with much more complicated structures. Some include several bargaining

CHAPTER 11: THE TRADE UNION AND ITS MEMBERS

Figure 7.1: Union Membership in Local and Parent Unions, 1998–2013

Year	Union Members (Percent)	Locals (Percent Change)	Unions (Percent Change)	Average Members/Union	Average Members/Local
1998	3,937,790 (32.9 percent)	16,631	1,031	3,819	237
2006	4,441,000 (30.8 percent)	15,479 (–7 percent)	827 (–20 percent)	5,370 (+41 percent)	287 (+21 percent)
2013	4,735,367 (30.0 percent)	14,147 (–9 percent)	771 (–6 percent)	6,140 (+14 percent)	335 (+17 percent)

Source: Labour Program, Workplace Information and Research Division 2014

units at a given workplace (each with their own collective agreement), which nonetheless share a union executive and other decision-making structures, as is common in the university sector. Others have broader regional locals that bring together workers in many workplaces under a centralized executive, as part of what is referred to as a composite local. The United Food and Commercial Workers (UFCW) and the Services Employees International Union (SEIU) are examples of unions that have large locals covering workers in the same industry or occupation within a province. The UFCW's Local 401 represents grocery store and meatpacking workers in Alberta, with five regional offices and province-wide collective agreements with major grocery chains. The SEIU's Local 2 represents janitors and security guards (amongst other workers) across the whole of Canada. The Canadian Union of Public Employees (CUPE), on the other hand, is much more decentralized, with thousands of locals across the country, and sometimes with multiple locals in the same workplace. The most common workplace to have multiple locals of the same union is the university. Most Canadian universities have separate locals for teaching assistants and contract professors, administrative staff, and custodial and maintenance staff respectively, even when these employee groups are all members of CUPE.

Whatever the precise nature of the local, membership provides opportunities for workers to gain a voice in the workplace and in their union. Members have the right to attend meetings, voice their opinions and participate in votes on union matters, volunteer for union committees, take part in union education programs and attend union-organized social functions. They can participate both as candidates and voters in elections for union stewards (who administer and defend the collective agreement on behalf of union members and carry forward complaints and grievances from members) and for the union executive (which manages the day-to-day affairs of the local).

In most cases, a local's general membership meeting (GMM) is the highest authority in the union and has the exclusive right to make many important decisions. The GMM is responsible for the election of officers, committee members and delegates to external bodies, and the discussion and ratification of the local's policies and positions, including bargaining demands and tentative collective agreements. Since every local union member is eligible to participate in and vote at a GMM, the meeting is a form of mass direct or participatory democracy. Most unions use formal rules of order to make decisions and to make and pass motions—proposals that, if supported, direct the union to do something.

Union activities are funded through union dues, the regular contribution that bargaining unit members make to the union's coffers. Since the Rand Formula became part of provincial and federal labour law, all union dues are deducted from members' paycheques by their employer and sent directly to the union. While some locals continue to have a set dues fee that is the same for everyone regardless of their income, the majority of unions have moved to a percentage dues structure—while everyone pays the same percentage of their wage, those making higher wages pay more in absolute dollars to the union. One of the GMM's major democratic responsibilities is to set the level of union dues, approve the annual union budget and plan for spending, and exercise oversight of the local's financial affairs.

Even though members have the right to participate in the union's decision-making bodies, not all of them become active in their union locals. A common complaint from those active in local unions is that most of the membership do not participate and the turnout at meetings is low—as low as 5 or 10 percent (Craig and Solomon 1993: 102). The exceptions are meetings at which issues that affect everyone, such as the progress of collective bargaining, the potential for a strike vote, the possibility of an increase in union dues, or employer initiatives that will alter conditions in the workplace, are on the agenda. Member participation in union activities also increases in crisis situations involving layoffs and plant closures or widespread dissatisfaction with the conduct of either the local or the parent union.

Yet low attendance at union meetings and low participation in union-organized functions does not necessarily indicate apathy or a lack of support for the union. Members can keep abreast of union activities by checking with union activists to find out what happens at meetings. They can also relay their concerns to union stewards and others in the union who do attend meetings on a regular basis. As well, many local unions produce regular newsletters or have websites that keep members informed of key developments, and an increasing number rely on social media to engage with members.

The conduct of local union sis prescribed by a union constitution and bylaws that set out the rights and responsibilities of members, define the roles of elected officials in the locals, and set the rules for making decisions. All locals have an elected executive. The key positions on the executive are the table officers—usually a president, a treasurer and a recording secretary—but there can be other officers with specific roles, like equity, communications, and member education, or representing different segments of the membership. The local union president is responsible for administering the affairs of the local, including chairing local meetings, ensuring the local's decisions are carried out, keeping members informed of activities in the broader union and labour movement, and representing the local in the community. The treasurer is responsible for managing the local's funds and maintaining complete and accurate records of all financial transactions. The recording secretary compiles meeting minutes—a written record of the proceedings and formal decisions—and handles the local's correspondence. Together, the local executive's role is to execute decisions made at general membership meetings, make decisions between GMMs and report regularly to the membership on these actions, and make recommendations for action to the members. Depending on the local's size, complexity and financial resources, some local officers have full-time duties—they go on union leave and are paid a salary to replace the wages from their job. Others serve only part-time—carrying out their union leadership role while continuing to work at their regular job—and are usually paid either an honorarium or for the work time spent doing union business. In addition, some well-resourced locals may hire their own paid staff, sometimes referred to as business agents.

Most locals also have union stewards, who are elected by their co-workers and are responsible for representing workers in particularly occupations or departments. Stewards play a key role in local unions: they are responsible for ensuring that the employer complies with the collective agreement; they do the initial processing of member grievances (writing up the grievance and attempting to get it resolved); they raise members' concerns at union meetings and inform them of events and issues within both the local and the parent union; and they help to mobilize members in support of union initiatives at the bargaining table and in strike action. Union stewards (along with members of the local executive) may also assist members in the filing of employment insurance, workers' compensation, disability insurance and other claims. In recognition of the vital role played by union stewards—in most cases on a voluntary basis—steward training is an important component of union education activities.

In addition, many unions have created other voluntary positions within locals that deal with specific issues or problems. A number of union shave established union counsellor positions, for example. These people identify and provide advice and guidance to members who are having problems with alcohol or drugs or personal problems that are undermining their performance on the job. Many Unifor locals, for example, have women's advocates, workplace representatives who support members experiencing workplace sexual harassment and domestic violence and help them access union and community resources. As well, unions that actively engage in political activities encourage local members to run political action campaigns aimed at persuading members to support labour-friendly political candidates in national, provincial and municipal elections.

Parent Unions

Almost all local unions are affiliated with a parent union, a national or international union that brings together many locals, sometimes in the same industry or sector and therefore subject to the constitution and bylaws of these larger organizations. Some parent unions are very large. In 2013 in Canada, eight unions (three international and give national) had memberships of over 100,000, which taken together accounted for 42.7 percent of total union membership. Another seventeen unions (five international and twelve national) have memberships of between 50,000 and 99,999, accounting for another 22.9 percent of total membership. Of the eight unions with 100,000 or more members, four are public sector unions, with a combined membership of 1,286,669. The other four predominantly private sector unions have a combined membership of 903,018. Still, of the 771 national and international unions active in Canada, 421 (54 percent) had memberships of less than 10,000 (Labour Program 2014).

In most cases, local unions pay a significant portion of their local dues to the parent union, usually called a "per capita" or "per head" charge because these payments are often linked to how many members a local union has. In exchange for these dues, the

Figure 7.2: The Ten Largest Unions in Canada, 2013

Union	Membership
Canadian Union of Public Employees (CUPE)	630,050
National Union of Public and General Employees (NUPGE)	340,000
UNIFOR	308,000
United Food and Commercial Workers Canada (UFCW)	245,327
United Steel Workers (USW)	30,700
Public Service Alliance of Canada (PSAC)	187,587
Fédération de la Santé et des Service Sociaux (CSN)	129,032
Service Employees International Union (SEIU)	118,191
Teamsters Canada	93,351
Alberta Union of Provincial Employees	80,107

Source: Labour Program 2014

parent union provides locals with various kinds of support: the expertise necessary to negotiate collective agreements, legal assistance, and educational programs that develop the capacities of both local executives and members. In most unions, the parent union maintains a strike fund that members can draw on when they are on strike or locked out, a very important motivator for locals to join a parent union. The parent union's support of its locals is provided by union staff, paid union employees who are responsible for providing them with ongoing support and advice, especially during collective bargaining, and are often recruited from the union's membership. Most parent unions also have full-time organizers whose job it is to organize new locals in the non-unionized workplaces in the sectors in which the union operates. As well, large unions either employ or retain lawyers, economists and researchers, journalists, educators and others with specialized expertise that they provide to the membership on an as-needed basis.

The parent union also lobbies governments for legislation favourable to the interests of its membership, which meets in convention, typically every few years, to chart the union's course. Conventions are the main policy-making body for unions, bringing together democratically elected delegates or workplace-based representatives to discuss, debate and vote on the union's strategic priorities and policy positions.

11:200 UNION LIABILITY FOR ACTIONS OF MEMBERS

As discussed below in Section 11:300, unions are now recognized as legal persons for many purposes. Yet the union acts through its officers and its members whose actions may cause harm for which the victim seeks redress through a civil action. The following case explores the question of when a union might be liable for the actions of its members and officers, and when a national union might be liable for the actions of a union local.

Fullowka v Pinkerton's of Canada Ltd, 2010 SCC 5

[During a bitter strike at the Giant Mine in Yellowknife, Northwest Territories, in 1992, a striking miner, Roger Warren, placed a bomb in an underground transport car carrying miners who were crossing the union picket line to work during the strike. The bomb killed nine miners. Mr Warren was convicted of nine counts of second-degree murder. The surviving families of the dead miners, and a tenth miner who witnessed the immediate aftermath of the explosion, subsequently sued the union for damages.

At the time of the strike, the unionized miners were represented by the Canadian Association of Smelter and Allied Workers, Local 4, which was affiliated with the Canadian Association of Smelter and Allied Workers (CASAW National). In 1994, after the explosion, CASAW National merged with the Canadian Auto Workers, and CASAW, Local 4 became CAW, Local 2304. The families sued CAW National, some union officials, and members of CASAW, Local 4, for failing to control Mr Warren and for inciting him. The surviving miner who witnessed the aftermath of the explosion and acquired post-traumatic stress disorder, sued Local 4. (The families and the tenth miner also sued the mining company, security company, and the Government of the Northwest Territories for negligence; those claims were either settled or dismissed.)

The plaintiffs' claims against the union were largely successful at trial, but they were dismissed by the NWT Court of Appeal. The plaintiffs appealed to the Supreme Court of Canada. The pertinent legal issue for present purposes was whether the union could be successfully sued for negligence for failing to prevent the fatal bombing. The unanimous decision by the Supreme Court of Canada dismissing the appeal lays out the contemporary Canadian law on the separate legal status of union locals and their parent union.]

Cromwell J. for the Court

(2) Were CASAW Local 4 and CASAW National Separate Legal Entities? ...

[113] The question of whether CASAW Local 4 and CASAW National were separate legal entities is an important one for two reasons. If, contrary to the trial judge's view, they are separate legal entities, it follows that when CAW National stepped into the shoes of CASAW National on merger, CAW National did not thereby assume the obligations and liabilities of CASAW Local 4. Moreover, the trial judge's findings of liability considered the conduct of all union participants cumulatively. If he erred in doing so, his conclusions would be seriously undermined.

[114] The trial judge found that a national union and its local make a "two-tiered structure of one entity" (para. 862) and therefore CASAW Local 4 was not a separate legal entity from CASAW National ... Nearly every aspect of his analysis of the negligence claimed against the unions was affected by that conclusion. Throughout the standard of care analysis in relation to the claims against the union, the trial judge treated the conduct of both CASAW Local 4 and CAW National cumulatively ... and held it liable for the torts of the others. ...

[115] The Court of Appeal found that the local and the national unions were separate legal entities. Assuming CASAW Local 4 could be found liable, its liability did not extend to CASAW National or to its successor, CAW National. As the court put it, "CAW National (the only named defendant in the *Fullowka* action) is not liable for the debts and obligations of Local 4" ...

[116] The appellants challenge this conclusion.

[117] However, in my view, the union constitution and the merger agreement between

CASAW National and CAW National, as well as the jurisprudence, support the view of the Court of Appeal that CASAW National and CASAW Local 4 were separate legal entities and that on merger, CAW National did not succeed to CASAW Local 4's tort liabilities.

[118] There is no dispute that in the circumstances of this case CAW National is a legal entity capable of being sued in tort. As Iacobucci J. wrote for the Court in *Berry v. Pulley*, 2002 SCC 40 ... at para. 3, "unions have come to be recognized as entities which possess a legal personality with respect to their labour relations role". The question to be answered is the narrower one of whether CASAW Local 4 was a separate legal entity from CASAW National, so that on merger, CAW National did not assume CASAW Local 4's liabilities.

[119] There is no doubt that union locals may have an independent legal status and obligations separate from those of their parent national unions. Whether they do depends on the relevant statutory framework, the union's constitutional documents and the provisions of collective agreements. For example, it has been consistently held that where, as in this case, the local union is a certified bargaining agent, it and not the national union assumes the statutory and contractual duties of a bargaining agent. The reasoning of the Court in *International Brotherhood of Teamsters v. Therien*, [1960] S.C.R. 265, is based on the fact that the local union, certified as a bargaining agent, was a legal entity that could be sued because it had statutory powers and responsibilities in relation to collective bargaining: Locke J., at pp. 275–76. ...

[120] It is clear taking this approach that CASAW Local 4 is a legal entity capable of being sued in actions relating to its labour relations role. CASAW Local 4 was the certified bargaining agent for the mine workers at the time of the strike and explosion. This is reflected in the collective agreement between it—and I would add *only* it—and Giant Yellowknife Mines Ltd. In the agreement, Giant recognized CASAW Local 4 as *exclusive* bargaining agent for all employees covered by the agreement (art. 2.01). The certification of CASAW Local 4 was pursuant to the *Canada Labour Code*, R.S.C. 1985, c. L-2 ("Code"). The Code defines a " bargaining agent" (in part) as a "trade union that has been certified by the Board as the bargaining agent for the employees in a bargaining unit" (s. 3(1)). A "trade union" is defined to mean "any organization of employees, of any branch or local thereof, the purposes of which include the regulation of relations between employers and employees" (s. 3(1)). Thus, CASAW Local 4 was a "trade union" as defined in the Code . As the certified bargaining agent, CASAW Local 4 had "exclusive authority to bargain collectively on behalf of the employees in the bargaining unit" (s. 36(1)(a)). CASAW National was not a party to the collective agreement and had no status as a bargaining agent under the Code.

[121] As the Court of Appeal rightly pointed out, there is binding authority from this Court that local unions who are certified bargaining agents under the Code are legal entities. That was the decision of a unanimous Court in *International Longshoremen's Association, Local 273 v. Maritime Employers' Association*, [1979] 1 S.C.R. 120. The Court considered whether the local unions were legal entities capable of being sued for an injunction prohibiting participation in an allegedly illegal strike. Estey J., for the Court, noted the Code "establishes in modern form an elaborate and comprehensive pattern of labour relations in all its aspects within the federal jurisdiction. The exercise of the rights and the performance of the obligations arising under that statute can only be undertaken efficiently and conveniently *by those groups acting as legal entities*" (pp. 136–37 (emphasis added)). He concluded at p. 137:

The Locals are legal entities capable of being sued and of being brought before the Court to answer the claims being made herein for an injunction prohibiting the participation in the activities found to constitute an illegal strike.

[122] I conclude, therefore, that CASAW Local 4 was a legal entity capable of being sued in its own right. For the reasons which follow, I also conclude that it had a separate legal existence from CASAW National. This, in my view, is confirmed by the Code, by the constitutional arrangements between the local and the national union and by the terms of the merger agreement between CASAW and CAW.

[123] As noted, under the Code and the collective agreement, CASAW Local 4 had *exclusive* bargaining rights. It therefore had legal rights and obligations distinct from those of the national union. This reality is also reflected in the CASAW National constitution and in the merger agreement between CASAW National and CAW National.

[124] The constitution deals with the establishment of local unions, and its provisions underline their separate and autonomous status. The constitution consistently differentiates between the national union and the locals and provides for a high measure of local autonomy. For example, s. 4b) provides that the funds and assets of any local belong to the local provided the constitution is complied with and s. 4f) provides that the local can make by-laws which are subject to national approval only with respect to whether they are consistent with the constitution. Section 13 provides that local union autonomy will be fostered and encouraged....

[126] In my view, and contrary to the findings of the trial judge and the appellants' submissions, nothing in the constitution or in the merger agreement supports the view that the local and the national unions are simply branches of the same entity. Each has its own management structure, areas of responsibility and assets and liabilities which are treated as such consistently in both documents.

[127] The appellants submit that the Court's decision in *Berry* supports their position that the local and national union are one legal entity ...

[128] At issue in *Berry* was whether a union member may be personally liable to other members in a breach of contract action based on the terms of the union constitution. The Court decided that it was time to move away from the notion that union members were joined together by a web of individual contracts. Instead, the relationship should be viewed as one in which a union member has a contractual relationship with the union itself. Taking this proposition as their starting point, the appellants submit that if local unions were entities distinct from their national unions, then a joining member would enter into two distinct agreements, one with the local union and one with the national union whereas in fact there is only one constitution and the member joins only once. This, it is submitted, shows that the Court in *Berry* viewed the local and national unions as one entity.

[129] I cannot accept this reading of *Berry*. Nothing in the Court's decision suggests that a local and national union are one entity simply because an individual joins a parent union at the same time as she joins the local. Moreover, the appellants' contention that a single constitutional structure cannot create two separate legal entities is not correct. Taken to its logical conclusion, this would mean that because there is a single

constitution creating a federation, the provinces cannot be separate legal entities. This, of course, is not so as the *Constitution Act, 1867* demonstrates. . . .

(5) Summary of Conclusions

[156] The appellants have not shown that the Court of Appeal erred in setting aside the trial judge' findings against CAW National. . . .

IV. DISPOSITION

[166] I would dismiss both appeals with costs and affirm the order of the Court of Appeal with respect to costs.

11:300 THE LEGAL PROTECTION OF UNION MEMBERSHIP RIGHTS

The duty of fair representation, discussed in Chapter 10, Section 10:300, allows any employee in the bargaining unit (even one who is not a union member) to bring a complaint against the union if the employee feels that it has not fairly represented her interests *vis-à-vis* the employer.

A different set of legal issues arise when a union member has a complaint about an internal union matter—for example, about the conduct of a union election, about a fine levied for crossing a legal picket line, about expulsion from the union for a breach of the constitution, or about a decision to merge with another union. With some statutory exceptions (referred to in Section 11:400 below) which vary considerably across the country, Canadian legislatures have generally refrained from regulating internal union affairs. Such regulation therefore remains largely in the hands of the courts, through contract law. The governing legal instrument—the source of contractual terms—in such matters is generally the union constitution, and the initial forum for vindicating membership rights is the union's internal trial and appeal procedure. If the member is dissatisfied with the fairness of that procedure, he can launch a court challenge, subject perhaps to the prerequisite of exhausting the union's internal procedures or showing that those procedures are fundamentally biased.

At common law, contract doctrine has by no means been an easy fit with internal union affairs. Unless a statute indicates otherwise, unions are unincorporated associations without legal personality. Historically, the courts therefore had to develop legal fictions in order to take jurisdiction over union-member disputes. Until quite recently, the prevailing legal fiction, articulated most prominently in the Supreme Court of Canada decision in *Orchard v Tunney*, [1957] SCR 436, held that the union's constitution was not a contract between the member and the union, but that its provisions were incorporated into a network of individual contracts between the member and each and every other member. This is often called the "web of contracts" or the fiction/concession theory. It is criticized in the following excerpt.

Michael Mac Neil, Michael Lynk, & Peter Engelmann, *Trade Union Law in Canada* (Aurora, ON: Canada Law Book) (loose-leaf updated 2018) at 1.1–1.3, 9.6

> The legal status of trade unions raises political, theoretical and practical legal questions going to the very heart of our system of organizing workplace relations. Our society

attempts to solve many of its disputes by framing issues in terms of legal rights, and the ascription of legal status is a means of translating political, social and cultural values into a form by which we can measure the worth of social actors ... With our social and political order largely committed to liberal values, it is not surprising that the dominant legal person is the individual human being. With our economic order committed to capitalism and market arrangements, it is not surprising that corporations are treated as if they were human beings, and are considered to be legal persons. However, the liberal capitalist premises on which much of our legal system is based, has had a much more difficult time in developing a coherent vision of how trade unions should be treated ... [T]he collectivist principles which are central to trade union action have caused the judiciary and legislatures to struggle to fit trade unions into the conceptual framework which guides our understanding of legal personality....

The legal status of trade unions arises in two contexts. One is the relation between the union and external actors such as employers, the state, or persons who claim to be affected by the actions of the trade union. The second is the relation between the union and its members....

... The fiction/concession theory describes the personality of the group as artificial, the product of authority given to the group either by its members or by the state. The group is seen as having only those powers which are conceded to it by the state. In the absence of state concession, the group is nothing more than a collection of individuals, and cannot effectively claim rights or be subject to obligations other than the rights and obligations of individual members. Those rights and obligations, in the absence of statutory provisions, arise from the contractual nexus among the members, and any claims they may have to property of the group. This theory helps to explain the view that dominated the common law, holding that unincorporated associations were not legal persons, but that legislative rules could grant legal personality within statutorily defined bounds. It also explains how the courts nevertheless allowed actions against union members as a group, through the device of representative or class actions, purporting to hold individuals collectively liable for the actions of the group....

[T]he fiction/concession theory ... best explains judicial and legislative approaches to the legal status of trade unions in Canada ...

A consequence of treating the relationship as contractual is that it invites the courts to act as appellate bodies, interpreting the contracts and providing relief to a member for any violation, no matter how trivial, of the constitution and by-laws. The threat to union autonomy is obvious.

[Reproduced by permission of Thomson Reuters Canada Limited.]

In 2002, in *Berry v Pulley*, excerpted immediately below, the Supreme Court of Canada did away with the fiction of a web of individual contracts of membership. As a backdrop to this case, see *International Brotherhood of Teamsters v Therien*, [1960] SCR 265.

Berry v Pulley, 2002 SCC 40

[This case arose out of a dispute between the pilots of Air Ontario and those of Air Canada. The two groups belonged to the same union—the Canadian Air Line Pilots Association

(CALPA) —which, like most unions, was an unincorporated association. Their respective employers were engaged in merger talks. The union constitution provided that in the event of such a merger, the two groups of pilots were to negotiate an integrated seniority list. In the course of those internal union negotiations, the two groups took positions similar to those of the two competing groups of employees in *Atkinson v CLAC, Local 66*, excerpted in Chapter 10, Section 10:310. The Air Canada pilots insisted that the Air Ontario pilots should be "endtailed" on the new seniority list, meaning that even the most senior Air Ontario pilots would have less seniority than the most junior Air Canada pilots. In contrast, the Air Ontario pilots insisted that the two seniority lists be fully "dovetailed," so that the service they had accumulated with Air Ontario would be fully recognized after the merger.

Arbitrator Michel Picher was appointed by the union to settle the dispute. His award fell between the positions of the two unions. He directed that 15 percent of the Air Canada pilots should be dovetailed with the most senior Air Ontario pilots, but that the Air Canada pilots should generally be higher on the seniority list than their years of service would indicate. The CALPA president accepted the Picher award, but the Air Canada pilots voted to reject it, insisting on no dovetailing at all. They subsequently left CALPA to form their own union, the Air Canada Pilots Association (ACPA). Because the Air Canada pilots refused to present the revised seniority list to their employer, the Picher award was never put into effect.

The Air Ontario pilots brought a class action against the Air Canada pilots, suing them personally for damages in contract and tort because of their refusal to accept the Picher award. The Air Ontario pilots argued that each CALPA member was a party to a contract with every other member, that those contracts incorporated the terms of the CALPA constitution, and that the refusal of the Air Canada pilots to abide by the Picher award breached those contracts, resulting in damages to the Air Ontario pilots.

A motion by the Air Canada pilots to dismiss the action was granted by the motions judge, whose decision was upheld by the Ontario Court of Appeal. The Air Ontario pilots appealed to the Supreme Court of Canada.]

IACOBUCCI J. (for the Court):

A. A Brief Overview of the Historical Development of the Union Contract and Union Status

[34] The use of a contractual model to characterize union membership arose in the early part of the 20th century as a consequence of the rising prominence of trade unions in England. The general rule at common law was that unions, as unincorporated associations, had no legal status. As a result, members could not bring suit against the union itself and courts would normally only engage in union affairs in order to protect the property interests of the members, refusing to interfere to enforce the rules of the association ... As the role of trade unions became more significant, and unions were able to exercise significant control over employers and employees alike, common law courts sought to establish a basis for a legally enforceable obligation on unions to follow their internal rules, thereby protecting the rights of individual union members....

[37] In the seminal Canadian case of [*Orchard v Tunney*, [1957] SCR 436] a union member sued members of the union's executive board in tort for infringing his rights

under the union constitution. In addressing the character of the rights and obligations relating to union membership, Rand J. (for the majority) looked to the *Taff Vale* and *Bonsor* decisions [of the House of Lords] for the basis of his judgment; however he noted that those decisions were grounded in the fact that the English *Trade Union Acts* had granted significant rights to trade unions, and that there was no comparable legislation in Manitoba. Thus, with no basis upon which to follow these English decisions, Rand J. was unable to find that trade unions in Manitoba had legal status or personality....

[39] Since the *Orchard* decision, legislatures have granted statutory rights to trade unions similar to those acknowledged by the House of Lords in *Taff Vale*, supra. Recognizing these statutory developments, this Court has come to hold the view that a trade union is a legal entity that can be sued in its own name. In *International Brotherhood of Teamsters v. Therien*, [1960] S.C.R. 265, at pp. 277–78, the Court held through the judgment of Locke J. that:

> The granting of these [statutory] rights, powers and immunities to these unincorporated associations or bodies is quite inconsistent with the idea that it was not intended that they should be constituted legal entities exercising these powers and enjoying these immunities as such....
>
> In my opinion, *the appellant is a legal entity which may be made liable in name for damages either for breach of a provision of the* Labour Relations Act *or under the common law.* [Emphasis added.]

[40] Although *Therien* is arguably restricted in its application owing to the fact that the Court relied on specific provisions of the British Columbia *Labour Relations Act*, S.B.C. 1954, c. 17, and *Trade-unions Act*, R.S.B.C. 1948, c. 342, in *International Longshoremen's Association, Local 273 v. Maritime Employers' Association*, 1978 CanLII 158 (S.C.C.), [1979] 1 S.C.R. 120, at pp. 135–37, Estey J. speaking for the Court made a more general statement with respect to the legal status of trade unions:

> Federal and provincial labour relations statutes alike have been interpreted by the courts in the same general way as Farwell J. interpreted the United Kingdom legislation in the *Taff Vale* case, supra and *over the years the concept has crystallized in our law whereby trade unions and employer organizations are deemed to have been constituted by the Legislature as legal entities for the purpose of discharging their function and performing their role in the field of labour relations*....
>
> The [Canada Labour] Code introduced by Parliament in 1972... establishes in modern form an elaborate and comprehensive pattern of labour relations in all its aspects within the federal jurisdiction. The exercise of the rights and the performance of the obligations arising under that statute can only be undertaken efficiently and conveniently by those groups acting as legal entities. The reasoning in the *Taff Vale* decision, *supra*, and the subsequent cases in this country apply with equal force and effect in the case of the Code. It is not necessary to decide as has been done in some of the judgments cited above whether any action might be maintained in the courts by or against these entities in respect of conduct outside the discharge of their obligations or the exercise of their rights under the Code. *It would take the clearest possible language in my view on the part of Parliament when enacting the Code to show that Parliament did not wish to establish the bargaining agent and*

the employer as legal entities for the purpose of employer relations regardless of the status of each under pre-existing statute law or the common law generally. In the result, the Association is a legal entity fully capable of bringing these proceedings; and the three Locals are likewise each legal entities fully capable at law of being added as a party defendant.

[Emphasis added.]

[...]

B. The Union Contract and Union Status in the Modern Context

[46] [T]he world of labour relations in Canada has evolved considerably since the decision of this Court in *Orchard, supra*. We now have a sophisticated statutory regime under which trade unions are recognized as entities with significant rights and obligations. As part of this gradual evolution the view has emerged that, by conferring these rights and obligations on trade unions, legislatures have intended, absent express legislative provisions to the contrary, to bestow on these entities the legal status to sue and be sued in their own name. As such, unions are legal entities at least for the purpose of discharging their function and performing their role in the field of labour relations. It follows from this that, in such a proceeding, a union may be held liable to the extent of its own assets.

[47] Viewed in this modern context, the proposition that a trade union does not have the legal status to enter into contracts with its members is implausible. The impediments that prevented Rand J. in *Orchard, supra*, from holding that by joining a union, the member contracts directly with the union as a legal entity, have been overcome. In order for trade unions to fulfill their labour relations functions, it is essential for unions to control and regulate their internal affairs. Since the regulation of union membership is a fundamental part of the role of trade unions, it is only logical that it should fall within the sphere of activities for which unions have legal status. It follows that unions must have sufficient legal personality to enter into contracts of membership, and that this is an aspect of union affairs for which legislatures have impliedly conferred legal status on unions. In addition, I agree with Lord Morton's statement in *Bonsor, supra*, that there are no "vital differences" between an action in tort and an action in breach of contract brought by a member against the union, and to draw a line between the legal status to be sued in tort and the legal status to enter into contracts with its members is arbitrary and illogical.

[48] In light of the above, the time has come to recognize formally that when a member joins a union, a relationship in the nature of a contract arises between the member and the trade union *as a legal entity*. By the act of membership, both the union and the member agree to be bound by the terms of the union constitution, and an action may be brought by a member against the union for its breach; however, since the union itself is the contracting party, the liability of the union is limited to the assets of the union and cannot extend to its members personally. I say that this relationship is in the *nature* of a contract because it is unlike a typical commercial contract. Although the relationship includes at least some of the indicia of a common law contract (for example offer and acceptance), the terms of the contractual relationship between the union and the member will be greatly determined by the statutory regime affecting unions generally as well

as the labour law principles that courts have fashioned over the years. With this in mind, for ease of reference I will refer to the membership agreement between the individual member and the union as a contract.

[49] Having said that there exists an enforceable contract between union members and the union, I believe it is worth elaborating on several factors which make this contract unique. First, it is essentially an adhesion contract as, practically speaking, the applicant has no bargaining power with the union. Moreover, in many situations, union membership is a prerequisite to employment, leaving the individual with little choice but to accept the contract and its terms. Finally, it must be borne in mind that a statutory labour relations scheme is superimposed over the contract between the member and the union, and can create legal obligations. Consequently, the contract must be viewed in this overall statutory context. For example, the statutory right of members to be represented by the union of their choice implies that the contract only exists as long as the members maintain that union as their bargaining agent, and no penalty could be imposed by the contract against members for exercising this statutory right. As it is not necessary to interpret the terms of the membership contract or determine its scope on the facts of this case, I decline from elaborating further on these matters. I simply note that the unique character and context of this contract, as well as the nature of the questions in issue, will necessarily inform its construction in any given situation.

[50] In my view, the above characterization not only fulfills the practical purpose of providing a basis from which the terms of the union constitution may be enforced, but it also serves as an accurate and realistic description of the nature of union membership. The individual applies for membership *with the union*. It is *the union*, represented by its agents, that accepts the individual as a member, and this individual agrees to follow the rules *of the union*. Aside from the fact that the relationship between the union and its members fits naturally into the contractual model, in today's labour relations context, the public has come to view unions as associations with the responsibility to discharge their obligations to members; it would be inconsistent with this view to deny unions the right to enter into legally enforceable contracts with these members.

[51] I emphasize that the above recognition of the legal status of trade unions does not automatically extend to other unincorporated associations. The unique status of trade unions is a consequence of the complex labour relations regime governing their existence and operations. By statute, labour unions have been endowed with significant powers and corresponding duties. They are granted the monopoly power to act as the exclusive bargaining agent for a group of employees, and they have a corresponding duty to bargain fairly on their behalf. As well, union membership is often a prerequisite to employment, forcing members to join the union based on its prescribed terms. By acceding to union membership, the individual agrees to be bound by the union constitution, the terms of which will almost inevitably include internal disciplinary provisions in the event of a breach by the member. In light of the significant powers and duties of the union *vis-à-vis* its members, and in particular its ability to enforce the terms of the membership agreement internally, it is only logical to hold that the legislature has intended unions to have the status at common law to sue and be sued in matters relating to their labour relations functions and operations.

C. Existence of a Contract Inter Se Between Union Members

[52] Given the recognition of the special form of contractual relationship which exists between a trade union and each of its members, the question remains whether there is any basis for maintaining the proposition that there exists a web of contracts between each of the union members *inter se*, and, if so, whether this relationship can form the basis for a breach of contract claim against union members.

[53] As discussed above, the idea that union members were joined to each other through a web of contracts arose as a legal fiction designed by courts as a way to exert jurisdiction over the internal affairs of a trade union. It allowed courts to circumvent the lack of legal status of unions and hold unions liable through the medium of its membership. By characterizing the liability as that of the group, the execution of the judgment was limited to the assets of the union.

[54] With the acknowledgment of the legal status of unions relating to the fulfilment of their labour relations role, I agree with the view that the legal fiction of a web of contracts between members is no longer necessary. A member wishing to sue his or her union for breach of the constitution is not impeded by a lack of legal status. Since the underlying problem which led to the establishment of the fiction has been resolved, in the absence of some compelling reason to maintain it, the idea that union members are contractually connected to each other should likewise be abandoned.

[55] As an initial matter, I would find it difficult, if not impossible, to conclude that the traditional indicia of a contract exist between the members of a union. For example, it stretches the imagination to suppose that each and every member of a union makes an offer of membership to an individual who then accepts these various offers, or vice versa, or that there takes place some mutual exchange of consideration between and among perhaps thousands of members. This is in contrast with the ease with which the relationship between the member and the union fits into the contractual model. In my view, it is simply unrealistic to posit that such a web of contracts exists between union members. Moreover, I agree with the courts below that it is not within the reasonable expectations of union members that they could be held personally liable to other members for breaching the union constitution. As well, the union constitution does not generally set out obligations which exist between individuals. It is mainly concerned with the obligations of the individual to the union (e.g. to pay dues, to participate in job action, etc.) as well as laying out how the union will be governed and conduct its affairs.

[56] The respondents argue that the concept of a contractual relationship between the members should be maintained and enforced in this case in order to fill a gap that would otherwise exist in the labour relations scheme. In my view, there is no gap in this case that needs to be filled; if the appellants were in fact wronged, there are remedies that were and are available to them that appear to be fair and reasonable.

[57] First, although the Air Canada pilots subsequently left CALPA, at the time the alleged wrongs were committed, they were still members of CALPA and internal remedies were available to the Air Ontario pilots....

[58] In addition to these internal procedures, if the appellants were of the opinion that CALPA was not adequately addressing the alleged misdemeanours by the Air

Canada MEC [master executive council], the appellants may have been able to bring a complaint before the CIRB against CALPA for failing in its duty under s. 37 of the Canada Labour Code, to fairly represent the appellants in the bargaining of seniority rights. Although the appellants and respondents disagreed on whether the duty of fair representation was broad enough to encompass this situation, the essential point here is that the appellants failed to pursue any of these internal or CIRB procedures. In this connection, the appellants conceded at trial that there were internal remedies available to them which they elected not to pursue ... In addition, aside from the availability of internal procedures and CIRB proceedings, it is well established that tort claims may lie between union members, and in this case, the tort actions have been allowed to proceed.

[59] However, apart from the fact that there were and are remedies available to the appellants in these particular circumstances, on a more general level, it seems problematic for a court to fill legislative gaps in the labour relations scheme by contorting what is essentially a contractual metaphor into a basis for a breach of contract action. Absent an independent basis for recognizing a breach of contract action between members, the mere argument that there exists a legislative gap is insufficient justification for transforming this contractual metaphor, initially created to provide a foundation for finding group liability, into a concrete basis which allows for personal liability to exist between union members.

[60] On a policy level, if courts were to allow disagreements between union members to result in claims against their personal assets absent the existence of an identifiable wrongdoer in breach of some duty, like the required elements of a tort action, this would have a chilling effect on union democracy. The importance of the democratic rights of union members, including the right to dissent, was pointed out in *Tippett v. International Typographical Union, Local 226* (1975), 63 D.L.R. (3d) 522 (B.C.S.C.), at p. 546:

> All members of trade unions have the unqualified right to speak out against the manner in which union affairs are conducted. There is a right of dissent. There is a right to seek decertification, subject to the condition that no member of a union shall conspire with his employer to injure his union. I point out, moreover, that dual unionism is a fact of life in this Province. No person can be expelled or penalized by a trade union for insisting on his rights.

Exposing the personal assets of dissenting union members to liability would be antithetical to this "unqualified right" of union members to speak out against the agenda of their bargaining agent. The result would be to discourage member participation in union affairs and to erode union democracy.

[61] As well, I agree with [the motions judge] that trade unions would find it difficult to recruit members or obtain certificates to bargain collectively if the act of joining a trade union exposed individuals to personal liability in damages to other members for alleged breaches of provisions of the constitution. Further, if union members were permitted to bring suit against other members instead of resorting to internal dispute resolution mechanisms where breaches of the constitution were alleged, the ability of unions to resolve internal conflicts would be hindered. This loss of control over internal affairs would undermine the ability of unions to present a united front to employers and pursue the collective interests of their members.

[62] To summarize, on grounds of both law and policy, I conclude that there is no contract between union members based on the terms of the union constitution. In light of the finding that the union itself can be held liable in breach of contract, there is no need to maintain the "complex of contracts" model. In addition, to interpret this model so as to allow for personal liability between union members would be contrary to its purpose and intent and would have negative consequences on the operation of the labour relations scheme in this country.

[63] However, this is not to say that union members do not have some obligations *inter se*. By joining a union, the member agrees to follow the rules of the union, and, through the common bond of membership, union members have legal obligations to one another to comply with these rules. If there is a breach of a member's constitutional rights, this is a breach by the union, and the union may be liable to the individual. Similarly, the disciplinary measures in the constitution can be imposed by the union on a member who contravenes the union's rules. A failure by the union to follow these disciplinary procedures may cause it to breach its contractual obligations to the other members, giving rise to corresponding contractual remedies.

[64] In addition to potential internal procedures, a failure by the union to insist on compliance with the constitution or impose disciplinary measures for its breach may allow members to initiate proceedings either at the CIRB, or the courts, depending on the nature of the complaint. Aside from actions against the union, a member who is harmed by the breach of the union's rules by another member may, if the requisite elements are present, have an action in tort against that member.

VI. CONCLUSION

[65] For these reasons, I would dismiss the appeal with costs.

* * * * *

Although the courts maintain final supervisory authority over internal union affairs through the law of contract, and although labour relations boards have been given limited statutory jurisdiction to hear complaints by members against their unions, not many cases have been decided in this area by the judiciary or by labour boards. Canadian legislatures, unlike those in the United States and Britain, have refrained from enacting legislation that intrudes deeply into internal union affairs. One reason, according to many observers (including the authors of the following excerpt), is that Canadian unions are generally democratic and not corrupt, so close public regulation is not needed to ensure that their affairs are kept in order.

Michael Mac Neil, Michael Lynk, & Peter Engelmann, *Trade Union Law in Canada* (Aurora, ON: Canada Law Book) (loose-leaf updated 2018) at 6.3–6.8

> The Canadian approach of statutory abstinence from the regulation of internal union elections and union officers is the product of four factors. First, Canadian unions have historically encouraged a culture of democratic practices, and they have been able to give voice to both the employment and the social aspirations of their membership. Most

industrial relations observers in Canada would concur with the conclusions reached by the 1996 federally appointed Task Force which reviewed the *Canada Labour Code* that: "Canadian trade unions exhibit a high level of internal democracy and genuinely represent the interests and wishes of their membership." Other recent independent reviews of labour legislation—most notably in British Columbia in 1993, Ontario in 1992 and, earlier, federally in 1968—have echoed the same views. Union leadership in Canada has changed office on a regular basis both on the national and local level, it has in the past few decades avoided most hard-left and hard-right splits, and its membership and leadership has of late become more racially and gender diverse. As well, many unions in Canada have strived to achieve not only collective bargaining gains, but also to encourage forms of social unionism that would build durable relations with other community and national organizations on a range of political and social causes.

Secondly, unions in Canada have generally avoided both the stain of corruption that has tainted some parts of the American labour movement, as well as the spectra of unbridled militancy that had, fairly or unfairly, characterized a number of British unions. Certainly, there have been alarming, if sporadic, incidents of corruption in Canadian union leadership, and occasional episodes of intimidation in union elections. The most serious episode involved the Seafarers' International Union in the 1950s and early 1960s, which, after having been actively encouraged by the federal government of the day to oust the left-leaning union that represented seafarers on the Great Lakes, initiated a reign of thuggery and corruption until its leadership was removed following a federal commission of inquiry. However, the unions that encouraged or tolerated patterns of corruption or violence in Canada were generally outside the mainstream labour congresses, or were expelled once the mainstream leadership was satisfied that the patterns were endemic. As a result, the record of corrupted labour authority in Canada has been infrequent.

Thirdly, as a consequence of these first two reasons, there has never been a sustained political or popular demand in Canada for a significant legislative intrusion into internal union affairs. The cry for "union democracy" has never acquired the hot-button persona in Canada that it achieved in the United States and Britain. Nor has the use of the term "union bosses" ever strongly resonated in the contemporary media or in popular speech. Canadian employers have generally, if reluctantly, accepted the fundamental premises of collective bargaining, and they have not either built up a significant anti-union consulting industry nor have they sought as a common strategy to undermine the legitimacy of unions as representatives of employees.

Conservative federal and provincial governments have been elected with some regularity since the *Wagner Act* model was introduced, but they have generally respected the prevailing consensus among the industrial relations parties that the present level of statutory oversight of union affairs has been appropriate. Even when conservative provincial governments have significantly re-written labour legislation in order to restrict the organizing abilities and other powers of unions—such as in British Columbia in 2002, in Alberta in 1988, and in Ontario in 1995—they have rarely touched the existing degree of regulation of the internal affairs of unions....

Part of this forbearance from interfering in internal union affairs emanates from the active presence of social democratic parties in Parliament and in most provincial legislatures—the New Democratic Party in English Canada, and the Bloc Québécois and the Parti Québécois in Québec—that have articulated the labour movement's positions on industrial relations. In turn, the political presence of these social democratic parties has depended, in part, on the relative strength of the labour movement—the 2017 union coverage rate was 31 percent—among the Canadian work force, and its assertive attention to social and political concerns beyond the workplace.

And fourthly, the traditional British common law concept of unions as voluntary organizations—and therefore entitled to self-government—has long influenced Canadian legislators and courts. This approach, articulated through a long line of English judicial caselaw and subsequently adopted by the courts into Canadian law, likened trade unions to voluntary associations such as social clubs and political parties. The English and Canadian courts viewed the membership relationships of these organizations as purely personal and contractual, and they therefore would not review an internal decision of a union except on narrow procedural grounds. The law in England changed directions judicially in the 1950s, and legislatively in the 1980s, to become more interventionist. However, the theory that unions are skin to a social club prevailed in Canada until the Supreme Court's 2002 decision in *Berry v. Pulley* finally recognized unions are entities with legal status. Despite this significant step, the Court's reasons in *Berry* emphasized that the relationship between the member and the union remains essentially contractual. The contract is simply between the member and the union, rather than between members.

However, whether there is a role for the statutory regulation of internal union elections and the conduct of union officers has been actively debated in legal academic literature. In Canada, Geoff England and Bill Rees have advocated a measure of statutory intervention to plug what they see as current gaps in the common law. Specifically, they suggest legislative safeguards to protect a member's right to oppose an incumbent leadership, and to ensure fair election procedures that would be regulated by a specialist tribunal. Their remarks echo earlier arguments made by James Dorsey and by the 1968 Woods Task Force on Industrial Relations, who each recommended some statutory form of a union member's bill of rights. This argument for greater legislative intervention is premised not so much upon any historic or current pattern of abuse of democratic rights, as it is upon the increasing political and social role of unions in society. The rationale is that, with this growing political and social role, the public now has a particular interest in the internal operations of unions.

Opposed to this view are several of the leading British scholars on labour law. The late Otto Kahn-Freund argued that a union, as a fighting body of working people susceptible to outside hostile forces working from within, cannot have an overdose of elective democracy imposed upon it. Trade unions are primarily organizations designed to defend and advance their members' working conditions, and not to provide an exercise in civic government. Between democracy and autonomy, he wrote, "the law must come down on the side of autonomy." In the 1980s, Lord Wedderburn wrote that the issue of trade union democracy must be placed within the power system of labour-management relations. The statutorily imposed forms of elective union democracy in the United States and Britain, he argues, have resulted in weakening the role of the labour movement as an engine of collective bargaining and as a force for social change, a result likely intended by the conservative governments that enacted the legislation.

Any legislative judgment in the future as to whether statutory intervention of any degree is warranted to regulate the conduct of trade union elections and officers in Canada should be determined with at least the following three aspects in mind: the efficacy of judicial oversight, the ability of trade unions to provide democratic self-regulation, and the necessity for the internal democracy of trade unions to be statutorily regulated in comparison to other socially influential organizations, such as corporations, political parties and religious institutions. Those few industrial relations studies that have examined the character of political life in Canadian unions have found that unions are as democratic as other organizations in Canadian society, and far more democratic than the companies that they face across the bargaining table. The most serious obstacle to greater democracy within Canadian unions appears to lie not in the character of their leaders, nor in any particular strictures in their constitutions and rules, but in the generally low participation of the membership in the political life of unions, except in moments of conflict or crisis. Democratic life in British and American unions, with much more extensive legislative intervention, appears to be no greater than in Canadian unions. This may well be an area that is not amenable to legal reform.
[Reproduced by permission of Thomson Reuters Canada Limited.]

11:310 The Protection of Local Union Officers When Representing Members

An integral feature in Canadian labour law on trade union affairs is the right of unions to select their own leaders and representatives without interference from management. As part of this right, local union officers are entitled to freely represent their membership—vigorously, if necessary—when dealing with the employer on industrial relations matters. As union officers (whether in a full-time or a voluntary position), they acquire a position of equality vis-à-vis management, and this means that they can engage in conduct as a union leader that otherwise might attract discipline for insubordination were it not for their union office. As the Saskatchewan Labour Relations Board stated in *CEP, Local 911 and ISM Information Systems Management Corp*, [1998] Sask LRBR 352 at 360:

> A union representative must be dealt with on an equal footing with the employer when functioning as union representative as he or she is the exclusive representative of employees under [section 3 of the Saskatchewan *Trade Union Act*].... As a result, it is necessary for the employer to differentiate between when an employee is an "employee" simpliciter, and when an employee is acting in a representative capacity as union president, shop steward, grievance committee member, occupational health and safety committee member and the like."

This general immunity from employer discipline extends to activities within the reasonable performance of their union responsibilities. It would cover the right of union officers to criticize management, whether in meetings with employer representatives, in union literature, and in public comments. The authors of *Trade Union Law in Canada* have observed that union officers maintain legal protection for their comments as long as their conduct satisfies three criteria: (1) they were acting in good faith; (2) their comments were not malicious, reckless, or patently untrue; and (3) their comments were broadly linked to issues of concern to the union and its membership, and not to the personal concerns of the union official (see Michael Mac Neil, Michael Lynk, & Peter Engelmann, *Trade Union Law in Canada* (Aurora, ON: Canada Law Book, 2018 update) at para 6.970).

In *Canada Post Corp and CUPW (Condon), Re* (2013), 116 CLAS 137 (Can Lab Arb), the employer had imposed a one-day suspension on a local union steward for using vulgar and insulting language towards a member of management. During a meeting with management regarding the disposition of several union grievances, the union steward had become frustrated and angry with the employer's response, and swore at the managers as he was leaving the meeting room: "You guys have your heads so far up your a**, you don't know what you are doing." He did not subsequently apologize, although he expressed regret that this was not an effective way to represent his membership.

In dealing with this case, arbitrator Allen Ponak first noted that, had the steward's insults been delivered to management as an ordinary employee, there would have been legitimate grounds for disciplining him on the grounds of insubordination. However, this incident involved a union steward in a union-management meeting. Accordingly:

> [25] Set alongside the value of civility is a long tradition of protecting union officials when they are acting in their representative role even when they: "occasionally express strong disagreement with the company and its officers, and do so in vivid and unflattering terms ... If union stewards are to have the freedom to discharge their responsibilities in an adversarial collective bargaining system, they must not be muzzled into quiet complacency by the threat of discipline at the hands of the employer ... The statements of union stewards must be protected" (*Burns Meats*, page 386)....
>
> [26] I have already expressed my views of the Grievor's comments. I consider them vulgar, unprofessional, and insulting. They do not advance labour relations or contribute to workplace respect. He certainly could have chosen other words to convey his feelings. My distaste notwithstanding, the remarks were made while the Grievor was conducting legitimate union business. He made a single comment to express his strong displeasure with management's position and turned away. The comment was not made in front of members of the bargaining unit (other than another union representative). Given the very high value placed on the right of union officials to freely lobby and challenge management, even in strong and unwelcome language, I cannot conclude that the Grievor's comment crossed the line into conduct that clearly fell outside his role as a union representative.

Arbitrator Ponak ultimately allowed the union's grievance and struck down the one-day discipline imposed on the union steward.

In those public-sector workplaces where the *Charter of Rights and Freedoms*, Part I of the *Constitution Act, 1982*, c 11 applies, union officers have an additional layer of legal protection for their industrial relations activities: the freedom of expression guarantee in section 2(b). In *British Columbia Public School Employers' Assn v British Columbia Teachers' Federation (Head Grievance)* (2010), 193 LAC (4th) 65 (BCLRB), a teacher, who also served as the local union representative, had installed a sign outside of her classroom which read "staff representative." When her employer saw the sign, she was ordered to remove it. Her union grieved the decision. Arbitrator John Steeves upheld the union's grievance. He ruled that:

> 162 ... The Union is a significant part of bringing democratic decision-making process to the workplace, as recognized by previous decisions of the Supreme Court of Canada. The sign represented the pride the Grievor and other staff representatives felt in being elected to that position and in representing the Union and its members....
>
> 163 ... The effect [of the removal] is to make the sign a symbol for the existence of the Union itself. In light of the expressive content of the sign and this effect, there is a violation of section 2(b) of the *Charter*.

Also see *Taylor-Baptiste v OPSEU*, 2015 ONCA 495, where the Ontario Court of Appeal upheld a ruling by the Ontario Human Rights Tribunal that union officers enjoy a broad protection for comments made in an industrial relations context, particularly where the employer is a state actor and the associational and expressive protections of the *Charter* apply.

11:400 UNION SECURITY AND UNION DISCIPLINE

Only a few Canadian jurisdictions provide for any significant degree of legislative oversight of internal union affairs. Three provinces—Alberta, British Columbia, and Saskatchewan—explicitly require by statute that internal union disciplinary hearings comply with the requirements of natural justice. For example, the BC *Labour Relations Code*, RSBC 1996, c 244, s 10(1) provides as follows:

> 10(1) Every person has a right to the application of the principles of natural justice in respect of all disputes relating to
> (a) matters in the constitution of the trade union,
> (b) the person's membership in a trade union, or
> (c) discipline by a trade union.

In *Office and Technical Employees' Union, Local 378* (1995), 28 CLRBR (2d) 1 [*Coleman*], the British Columbia Labour Relations Board looked at a number of cases on the duty of trade unions to apply the requirements of natural justice, and said:

> [118] From these cases we can draw the following requirements which the courts have implied into the constitution of trade unions, but which must now form a part of the legislative policy of this province with the enactment of s. 10 of the Code:
> (1) Individual members have the right to know the accusations or charges against them and to have particulars of those charges.
> (2) Individual members must be given reasonable notice of the charges prior to any hearing.
> (3) The charges must be specified in the constitution and there must be constitutional authority for the ability to discipline.
> (4) The entire trial procedure must be conducted in accordance with the requirements of the constitution; this does not involve a strict reading of the constitution but

there must be substantial compliance with intent and purpose of the constitutional provisions.
(5) There is a right to a hearing, the ability to call evidence and introduce documents, the right to cross-examine and to make submissions.
(6) The trial procedures must be conducted in good faith and without actual bias; no person can be both witness and judge.
(7) The union is not bound by the strict rules of evidence; however, any verdict reached must be based on the actual evidence adduced and not influenced by any matters outside the scope of the evidence.
(8) In regard to serious matters, such as a suspension, expulsion or removal from office, there is a right to counsel.

In *Coleman*, several former members of a local union executive had been disciplined by their union for opposing the decision to raid the membership of another union. In finding that their internal disciplinary hearing had largely complied with the dictates of natural justice as required by section 10(1) of the *BC Labour Relations Code*, the Board acknowledged the tension between individual and collective rights that frequently arises in such conflicts:

> [113] Individual members of a trade union must be permitted to pursue their own trade or profession, earn a living, participate in the internal affairs of their union, and not be interfered with in any manner other than a lawful one. Conversely, trade unions find their greatest strength in their collective nature, and this may involve compromises between the interests of individual members and the collective interests. It is the enforcement of these trade-offs, and the requirement of a strong and united front that may involve a degree of control or discipline over those who may be seen to threaten that collective good.
>
> [114] It is clear that the democratic tradition, which trade unions uphold, is strengthened, not weakened, by the fair balance which they strike in the administration of these trade-offs. It is this view of the nature and role of trade unions in our society that will inform the framework for our interpretation and administration of s. 10 of the Code.

The right of a union member to natural justice at an internal union discipline hearing was adjudicated in *Gould (Re)* (2010), BCLRB No B3/2010, [2010] BCLRBD No 3. Mr Gould had been suspended for thirty days by his union local for violating its dispatch rules. He worked in the cinema production industry in Vancouver, and his union operated a dispatch room, where it managed the assignment of union members to various jobs in the industry in the Lower Mainland. A suspension by the union meant that Mr Gould was not able to work during the period of suspension. Mr Gould sought to appeal the union's decision within the process established by the union constitution, but the union did not respond to his request for an internal hearing. He then complained to the British Columbia Labour Relations Board under section 10 of the *BC Labour Relations Code*.

The board ruled in Mr Gould's favour:

> [27] I ... accept the Union's submission that the principles of natural justice are flexible, but this consideration does not assist the Union here. The penalty assessed to Gould for violating the Dispatch Rules was to be suspended from dispatch for 30 days. This is

a serious penalty with considerable financial consequences. Local 155 did not provide Gould the most basic elements of natural justice in these circumstances before deciding he had violated the Dispatch Rules and should be suspended. It did not provide him with written notice of the alleged violation and an opportunity to respond to the allegations before imposing serious discipline. To the contrary, Local 155's letter of August 25, 2008 which states the particulars of the conduct alleged also summarily finds Gould guilty of violating the Dispatch Rules and imposes a 30-day suspension. Absent from that process was any adequate opportunity for Gould to be heard on the matter before the Union made that decision.

[28] Local 155 has not argued that the informal meeting between Gould and the Executive Board operated to cure any breach of natural justice arising from the initial finding. In the particular circumstances of this case, I would not find that it did, nor that it rendered the process fair overall. Gould had been summarily found guilty by the same party that made the allegations against him, in the same letter, without any intervening opportunity to be heard. There was no suggestion by Local 155 that this represented a mistake on its part; to the contrary, it maintained it was an appropriate process. In his subsequent correspondence, Gould insisted he was entitled to particulars of the charges against him and a trial, while Local 155 insisted he was not. At the meeting with the Executive Board, Gould brought a member in good standing to speak on his behalf but that member was not permitted by Local 155 to speak. I note that [*Coleman*] states that in regard to serious matters, such as suspension, there is a right to counsel. The informal meeting was not a substitute for a hearing, and did not remedy the denial of natural justice.

[29] In conclusion, I find that Local 155's conduct falls short of the natural justice requirements of Section 10(c) of the Code because it failed to give Gould proper notice of the allegations and to hear from him prior to imposing serious discipline.

[As a remedy, the Labour Relations Board ordered the union to withdraw Mr Gould's thirty-day suspension and to fully compensate him for his provable loss of income.]

For an elaboration of the view that the English and Canadian courts (under the influence of Lord Denning) have been too intrusive in their application of procedural fairness rules to internal trade union proceedings, see Michael Lynk, "Denning's Revenge: Judicial Formalism and the Application of Procedural Fairness to Internal Union Hearings" (1997) 23:1 *Queen's Law Journal* 115.

A number of Canadian labour relations statutes stipulate that trade unions cannot impose disciplinary penalties against members in a discriminatory manner. For example, the *BC Labour Relations Code* states:

10. (2) A trade union must not expel, suspend or impose a penalty on a member or refuse membership in the trade union to a person, or impose any penalty or make any special levy on a person as a condition of admission to membership in the trade union or council of trade unions

(a) if in doing so the trade union acts in a discriminatory manner, or

(b) because that member or person has refused or failed to participate in activity prohibited by this Code.

Other jurisdictions have comparable provisions, but with added stipulations designed to protect the job status of individuals who have been deprived of union membership for certain reasons. For example, the *Canada Labour Code*, RSC 1985, c L-2 s 95, provides as follows:

> 95. No trade union or person acting on behalf of a trade union shall
> [...]
> (e) require an employer to terminate the employment of an employee because the employee has been expelled or suspended from membership in the trade union for a reason other than a failure to pay the periodic dues, assessments and initiation fees uniformly required to be paid by all members of the trade union as a condition of acquiring or retaining membership in the trade union

The distinction between the effect of statutory provisions that do and do not have job status protection can be shown by the example of an employee who works during a lawful strike. It is generally accepted that if an employee has engaged in strikebreaking activity, a union has the right to refuse membership to that employee, expel her from membership, or impose discipline on her. In such circumstances, union actions of that sort do not breach section 10(2) of the *BC Labour Relations Code* or similarly worded statutory provisions. However, the implication of section 95 of the *Canada Labour Code* and parallel provisions in other jurisdictions is that an employee expelled from union membership for strikebreaking cannot be dismissed from his job for that reason, even if the collective agreement requires union membership as a condition of employment.

To understand the position of an individual employee, it is thus necessary to examine the interaction among the union's constitution and membership rules, the union security provisions in the collective agreement, and the statutory provisions on internal union affairs in the particular jurisdiction.

11:410 Union Security Clauses

Under the principles of majoritarianism and exclusivity, representation of an employee by a union does not necessarily require that the employee be a member of the union. The precise relationship between representation and membership generally depends on what sort of union security provision is included in the collective agreement, and that is normally a matter for negotiation between union and employer. Although the possible varieties of union security provisions are almost endless, they fall into five broad types:

1) The closed shop

A closed shop provision requires that one must be a union member before being hired. All Canadian jurisdictions permit closed shop provisions in collective agreements but limit their effects in certain ways. Whether a collective agreement contains such a provision is a function of the union's bargaining strategy and bargaining strength. In some industries, such as construction, closed shop provisions are quite common.

In appearance, a closed shop provision gives the union a great deal of control over who is eligible to be an employee. In practice, union discretion is substantially fettered by statutory regulation, to be discussed in Section 11:500.

CHAPTER 11: THE TRADE UNION AND ITS MEMBERS

2) The union shop

A union shop provision requires that employees must become union members in order to keep their jobs. The union shop differs from the closed shop in not using union membership as a screening device for determining who is eligible to be hired. Union shop provisions may be included in collective agreements if the parties so decide. As in the closed shop situations, the ultimate result of a union shop provision is a convergence between union membership and bargaining unit membership.

3) Maintenance of membership

A "maintenance of membership" provision does not require an employee to join the union. However, it does specify that once the employee does join, she must remain a member or lose her job. *The Saskatchewan Employment Act*, SS 2013, c S-15.1 s 6-42(1) provides for a model union security provision which must be included in a collective agreement at the union's request. It embodies a maintenance of membership requirement for existing employees and a union shop requirement for new employees.

4) The agency shop, or Rand Formula

What is known as the Rand Formula was first proposed by Justice Ivan Rand of the Supreme Court of Canada in his successful mediation of a major automobile strike in 1946. (See *Ford Motor Co of Canada v UAW—CIO*, [1946] OLAA No 1, reprinted in 1 CLLR 1245 at 1356–63 (Ont Lab Arb)). A Rand Formula clause does not require employees to be members of the union, but does require that they pay to the union an amount equivalent to union dues. The idea is that because each employee in the bargaining unit gets the benefit of the collective agreement, each should have to pay a share of the union's costs, but should be allowed to register opposition to the union and its goals by declining to join. The Rand Formula may in fact give some dissenters an incentive to join, so that they will have a voice in union decisions in return for their money. Subject to religious objector provisions, discussed below, several jurisdictions have made the Rand Formula a statutory minimum for private sector collective agreements, either automatically (Manitoba and Quebec) or at the union's request (Canada, Newfoundland, and Ontario).

The logic of the Rand Formula has been challenged, especially in respect of union expenditures directed toward purposes other than collective bargaining. A *Charter* challenge based on both freedom of expression and freedom of association failed in the Supreme Court of Canada in *Lavigne v Ontario Public Service Employees' Union*, below, Section 11:500.

5) Voluntary checkoff

A voluntary checkoff provision is the weakest form of union security clause. It requires the employer to deduct union dues from an employee's wages, if the employee so authorizes, and remit those dues to the union. The voluntary checkoff is the statutory minimum in Alberta, British Columbia, New Brunswick, Nova Scotia, and Prince Edward Island.

The following case considers whether a union can seek to have an employee dismissed by an employer if the employee has been expelled from the union for failure to pay a fine.

Speckling v Communications, Energy and Paperworkers' Union of Canada, Local 76, BCLRB Decision No B333/2003

[The respondent union insisted that, instead of assigning overtime, the employer should recall laid off employees and give them the work. The employer refused. The union then promulgated a policy prohibiting its members from working overtime when laid off employees were available and capable of doing the work. The applicant, Speckling, an employee and union member, was charged by other union members with violating the union constitution by refusing to abide by the union's policy. A disciplinary hearing was held in accordance with the union constitution, and Speckling was fined an amount equal to his overtime earnings plus $50. The union's bylaws stipulated that members must pay all fines within a specified time in order to maintain their status in the union. Speckling was informed of the union's disciplinary decision and of his right to bring an internal appeal, but he did not do so until long after the time limit has passed, and the union appeal body rejected his appeal as untimely.

When Speckling continued to refuse to pay the fine, the union told the employer that he was no longer a member in good standing. The collective agreement contained a union security clause that required employees to maintain membership in the union as a condition of continued employment. The employer refused to dismiss Speckling from his job, so the union filed a grievance demanding that he be dismissed. The union and the employer reached a settlement whereby the union dropped its grievance and agreed to readmit Speckling to membership in good standing if he paid his fine. The employer agreed that it would not let him return to work until he was readmitted to the union. However, he continued to refuse to pay the fine, and eventually the employer dismissed him. Speckling filed a grievance against the dismissal, but the union refused to take it to arbitration. He then brought a duty of fair representation complaint against the union, before the British Columbia Labour Relations Board.]

S. KEARNEY (Vice-Chair):

59 The union security clause in the collective agreement requires employees to maintain membership in good standing in the union as a condition of continued employment. Such clauses are a common feature of collective agreements, and have been for decades.... From time to time there are cases where a union seeks an employee's dismissal pursuant to the union security clause, because the employee is no longer a member in good standing.

60 The union obtains its power to discipline its members (e.g., fine or expel them) through its constitution, which establishes the contractual relationship between the union and the member when the member joins: *Berry v. Pulley*, [2002] 2 S.C.R. 493. The issue of whether the power is validly exercised under the union's constitution, and thus whether the employee has in fact lost his or her membership in good standing, is ultimately a question of contract law for the courts: *Berry v. Pulley, supra; Orchard v. Tunney*, [1957] S.C.R. 436. The Labour Relations Code gives the Board no jurisdiction to determine such issues....

64 In British Columbia, the *Labour Relations Code* expressly permits union security clauses and their enforcement, but stipulates that they cannot be enforced where

the ground for expulsion from the union is membership in another trade union. This restriction—which was also one of the restrictions in the Ontario legislation considered in *Walker, supra*—was first introduced in 1975. Today it is found in Section 15 of the Code, which provides:

> 15 (1) Nothing in this Code shall be construed as precluding the parties to a collective agreement from inserting in it, or carrying out, a provision
> (a) requiring membership in a specified trade union as a condition of employment, or
> (b) granting preference in employment to members of a specified trade union.
>
> (2) Despite subsection (1), a trade union or person acting on its behalf must not require an employer to terminate the employment of an employee due to his or her expulsion or suspension from that trade union on the ground that he or she is or was a member of another trade union.

[...]
68 ... Section 10 of the Code gives the Board jurisdiction to review union discipline on grounds of natural justice, discrimination, and refusal to participate in activity prohibited by the Code. Section 15 allows the inclusion and enforcement of union security clauses, but prohibits their enforcement on the grounds of membership in another union.

69 The matters before me are complaints under Section 12 of the Code, which prohibits a union from acting in a manner that is arbitrary, discriminatory or in bad faith in representing any of the employees in a bargaining unit ...

[...]
74 As is apparent from a reading of the section, the general purpose of Section 12 is to address a union's representation of employees in dealing with the employer. However, its application to union security clause dismissals can be more readily appreciated when it is considered that the word "representation" does not refer only to advocacy of a particular individual's interests, but rather more generally to the union's exercise of its exclusive bargaining agency on the employees' behalf. It has long been recognized that this duty does not necessarily require a union to advocate or act in the interests of a given employee in any given case. Indeed, situations commonly arise—such as job competitions, or employer discipline arising from inter-employee conflict—where a union finds it must take a position in favour of one employee and against another. Further, a union is well within its rights under the Code to take a position against an individual employee based on its legitimate assessment of the interests of the bargaining unit as a whole (e.g., an employee who seeks to make a special arrangement with the employer regarding pay or hours of work). It is a union's ability to act as a collective and unified whole, rather than merely an amalgam of various and conflicting individual interests, that ultimately gives it its effectiveness in representing the employees. The Code recognizes this by prescribing unions' exclusive bargaining agency only by the requirement that it not be exercised in a manner that is arbitrary, discriminatory or in bad faith.

75 In this context, the application of Section 12 to union security clause dismissals can be more readily seen. Section 12 prohibits unions from exercising their exclusive bargaining agency in a manner that is arbitrary, discriminatory or in bad faith. The

Union in the case at hand used its exclusive bargaining agency to negotiate the union security clause, and to apply it, and it therefore must not seek to apply it in a manner that is arbitrary, discriminatory or in bad faith.

76 The above principles also explain why such a demand per se does not violate Section 12 ... The Board has recognized that unions must sometimes use their constitutional disciplinary power in order to act effectively on behalf of the bargaining unit in respect of certain core concerns ...

77 In my view however, union security clause dismissals may well present a greater risk of breaching Section 12 than more conventional situations. A union causing an employee's termination based upon its assessment of the interests of the bargaining unit as a whole will need a cogent rationale for that assessment. It is, of course, not the Board's role under Section 12 to judge whether the union's assessment is correct or whether its decision is the one the Board would have made. However, if a union's conduct demonstrates blatant or reckless disregard for an employee's interests, it is "arbitrary" within the meaning of Section 12 ... A union without a cogent rationale for causing a circumstance as severe as an employee's termination runs the risk of such a finding.

78 As well, the Board has held it will apply closer scrutiny to a union's conduct in cases involving an employee's termination from employment. Although this principle is generally applied in the context of a union's decision not to take an employee's dismissal to arbitration, its rationale is the importance of employment to the employee. As such, it is no less applicable to a situation where the employee is terminated at the instance of the union....

88 Nonetheless, it is not difficult to see why the Union also engaged in its campaign among the working members, who were working a substantial amount of voluntary overtime. By exercising control over the members, first by persuasion and then by sanctions under its constitution, the Union could reduce overtime, making work available for laid-off employees, without engaging in litigation or attempting to alter its bargain with the Employer. Considering the benefits the Union was trying to achieve, I do not find that it was unreasonable for it to adopt and enforce such a policy using its constitutional disciplinary power....

98 [This process] is not an inquiry into whether the constitution was violated or breaches of natural justice committed, but whether the Union acted in a manner that was arbitrary, discriminatory or in bad faith *in representing* Ben Speckling. Specifically, it is whether the Union acted in any of these ways in demanding Speckling's dismissal under the collective agreement. That is what falls under the scope of Section 12; the process leading to the employee's loss of membership in good standing does not.... As well, the Board's general approach to Section 12 is to assess the union's conduct as a whole.... This leads to the same result: an assessment of whether the Union's demand for Ben Speckling's dismissal, considered as a whole, was arbitrary, discriminatory or in bad faith. Finally, even if Section 12 were broad enough to allow the Board to engage in a general review on the merits of a union's internal disciplinary process (i.e., beyond its relevance to the demand for dismissal under the union security clause), in my view it would be inappropriate to use it for that purpose, given the existence of Section 10 which addresses such matters directly....

Summary and conclusion

177 The Union found that its members were working substantial amounts of voluntary overtime at the Employer's premises, while others were laid off for lack of work. It interpreted the collective agreement as contemplating overtime only in situations where it was necessary, and this did not include situations where there were laid off employees available who were qualified to do the work in question. The Union therefore began a campaign to reduce unnecessary overtime, so that there would be employment for some of the laid off employees. It first tried persuasion, then adopted a policy under its constitution whereby members found guilty of working unnecessary overtime would be fined the amount earned plus $50. This policy was unanimously endorsed by the Union's membership at the regular membership meeting.

178 Charges can be laid under the Union's constitution by any member. Four employees were charged with violating the Union's overtime policy, including Ben Speckling. Over the course of the lengthy evidentiary hearing into this complaint, there was no evidence that any employees worked unnecessary overtime without being charged. In each case where charges were laid, the Union constituted a Disciplinary Committee to hear the charges. Ben Speckling was found guilty of violating the Union's overtime policy by a Disciplinary Committee and fined according to the policy adopted by the membership. Although Speckling has argued before me that the overtime work he did was necessary and therefore did not violate the overtime policy, he did not give this evidence to the Disciplinary Committee, nor did he make the legal arguments that he does now concerning the policy's validity. He did not file a timely appeal of the Disciplinary Committee's decision. However, he refused to pay his fine.

179 The Union demanded Ben Speckling's dismissal pursuant to the collective agreement's union security clause, which requires that employees maintain membership in good standing as a condition of continued employment. On the day this dispute was scheduled to go to arbitration, the Employer and the Union settled it with an agreement that Speckling could return to work, and the Union would no longer seek his dismissal, if he paid his fine. The Union was aware that Speckling knew he could pay his fine without prejudice to his ability to challenge its validity. There was no issue concerning his ability to pay it. The Union expected he would pay the fine and return to employment. However, Ben Speckling continued to refuse to pay his fine, and after approximately a year and a half, he was dismissed.

180 The issue of whether the Union could validly levy the fine under its constitution is one for the Union appeal process and, ultimately, the courts. Section 10 of the Code also gives the Board jurisdiction to determine if union discipline (such as a fine) is discriminatory, contrary to the principles of natural justice, or was levied for refusal to participate in activity prohibited by the Code. However, Ben Speckling has elected not to make any complaint under Section 10, and those matters are not before me. The complaint before me is under Section 12, which requires that a union not act in a manner that is arbitrary, discriminatory or in bad faith in representing an employee in the bargaining unit. In this case, which concerns dismissal under a union security clause, that entitles me to review whether the Union's demand for Ben Speckling's dismissal was

arbitrary, discriminatory or in bad faith. I have found it was not. I have found the Union acted reasonably, for a legitimate and compelling purpose (to provide work for the laid off employees), and not in a discriminatory fashion or for any improper purpose. Ben Speckling has also advanced a number of legal arguments before me, but I have found those do not alter this conclusion.

181 Ben Speckling's Section 12 complaint is dismissed.

The board's decision was affirmed on judicial review (See *Walter LM Speckling v Labour Relations Board of British Columbia*, 2006 BCSC 285). Speckling also brought a court action challenging the union's jurisdiction to impose the fine pursuant to its constitution, and its power to take away his membership as a result of his refusal to pay the fine. The British Columbia Court of Appeal determined that his action should be dismissed as an abuse of process, given that substantially the same issues had already been canvassed in the duty of fair representation complaint before the Labour Relations Board: *Speckling v Local 76 of the Communications, Energy and Paperworkers' Union of Canada*, 2006 BCCA 203 (Bernardus J).

Do you think Speckling would have had any success if he had made a complaint pursuant to section 10 of the British Columbia *Labour Relations Code*? Section 10 reads:

> 10 (1) Every person has a right to the application of the principles of natural justice in respect of all disputes relating to
> (a) matters in the constitution of the trade union,
> (b) the person's membership in a trade union, or
> (c) discipline by a trade union.
>
> (2) A trade union must not expel, suspend or impose a penalty on a member or refuse membership in the trade union to a person, or impose any penalty or make any special levy on a person as a condition of admission to membership in the trade union or council of trade unions
> (a) if in doing so the trade union acts in a discriminatory manner, or
> (b) because that member or person has refused or failed to participate in activity prohibited by this Code.
>
> (3) If a trade union charges, levies or prescribes different initiation fees, dues or assessments in respect of a person according to whether the person applies or has applied for membership in the trade union before or after an application for certification by the trade union to represent the person as bargaining agent, the fees, dues or assessments are deemed to be discriminatory for the purpose of subsection (2)(a).

Birch v Union of Taxation Employees, Local 70030, 2008 ONCA 809

ARMSTRONG J.A.:

[1] This appeal addresses the question of whether a trade union may invoke the jurisdiction of the court to enforce fines that it has imposed against its members for crossing a picket line.

[2] The respondents, Jeffrey Birch and April Luberti, were fined by the appellant union for crossing the picket line to attend work during a legal strike. In an application

to the Superior Court of Justice, Justice Robert Smith held that a provision in the appellant's constitution authorizing the fines was an unenforceable penalty clause. The appellant appeals that finding.

[3] For the reasons that follow, I would dismiss the appeal.

FACTS

[4] The parties proceeded on an agreed statement of facts in the Superior Court of Justice. Mr. Birch and Ms. Luberti, employees of the Canada Revenue Agency, crossed a picket line to attend work on three days during a legal strike by the Public Service Alliance of Canada ("PSAC") in the fall of 2004. Mr. Birch and Ms. Luberti were members of the appellant, the Union of Taxation Employees ("UTE"), a component of PSAC (UTE and PSAC are referred to from time to time as "the union"). The UTE brought disciplinary proceedings against Mr. Birch and Ms. Luberti for violating the PSAC constitution by working during a legal strike. The union suspended the membership of Mr. Birch and Ms. Luberti for three years (one year for each day that they crossed the picket line). The union also fined each member $476.75. The fine was equivalent to the total of each employee's gross salary for the three days they crossed the picket line.

[5] The relevant provisions of the PSAC constitution under which Mr. Birch and Ms. Luberti were fined are the following:

> Section 25(5)(n)
>
> A PSAC Regional Council, Component, Local, Area Council officer or member, is guilty of an offense against this constitution who:
>
> (n) is a worker in a legal strike position, who either crosses the picket line or is paid by the employer not to participate in strike action, or performs work for the employer, unless required to do so by law, or who voluntarily performs struck work;
>
> Section 25(3)
>
> Any disciplinary action taken under the provisions of Sub-Sections (1) and (2) of this Section for a cause listed in Sub-Section (5)(n) of this Section shall include the imposition of a fine that equals the amount of daily remuneration earned by the member, multiplied by the number of days that the member crossed the picket line, performed work for the employer or voluntarily performed struck work.

[6] Mr. Birch, Ms. Luberti and a number of other employees, who had been fined for crossing the picket line, refused to pay their fines. UTE sought to enforce the payment of the fines in the Small Claims Division of the Superior Court of Justice. The parties agreed that this matter should proceed by way of application brought by Mr. Birch and Ms. Luberti in the Superior Court on an agreed statement of facts as a test case. Mr. Birch and Ms. Luberti sought the following relief in their application:

a. A Declaration that the Superior Court of Justice of the Province of Ontario does not have the jurisdiction to enforce provisions set out in the constitution of a trade union that provide for fines/financial penalties against the trade union's members;

b. In the alternative, a Declaration that the Superior Court of Justice of the Province of Ontario does not have the jurisdiction to enforce the fine/financial penalty provisions as set out in the Constitution of the Public Service Alliance of Canada ("PSAC") and/or the By-Laws of the Union of Taxation Employees ("UTE") (referred to collectively as the "Union");

c. An order dismissing claims brought by the Union against the Applicants in the Small Claims Branch of the Superior Court of Justice[.]

[7] The application judge, in different wording, granted the relief sought by Mr. Birch and Ms. Luberti ...

[8] UTE appeals the judgment of the application judge on the ground that he erred in failing to find that the penalty clause in the PSAC constitution was not unconscionable and therefore could be enforced. UTE also asserts that Mr. Birch and Ms. Luberti should have appealed the fines under the provisions of the PSAC constitution and, if necessary, filed a complaint with the Public Service Labour Relations Board. According to the union, the failure of Mr. Birch and Ms. Luberti to exercise their internal rights of appeal and statutory complaint to the Public Service Relations Board precludes them from asserting by way of defence in the Superior Court that the fines are unenforceable....

[41] I start with a consideration of the test for unconscionability. There are cases in this court, other provincial courts of appeal and the Supreme Court of Canada that articulate a test for unconscionability in respect of the law of contract. There does not appear to be a single articulation of a test applicable to all situations. This is not surprising, given that the doctrine of unconscionability has been applied in a wide variety of cases.

[42] Professor Waddams in *The Law of Contracts*, 5th ed. (Toronto: Canada Law Book, 2005) at para. 515, describes Bradley Crawford's definition of unconscionability from his "Comment" (1966) 44 Can. Bar. Rev. as "an immoderate gain or undue advantage taken of inequality of bargaining power." Professor Waddams cites *Dyck v. Mann Snowmobile Association*, [1985] 1 S.C.R. 589 ... as a leading Supreme Court authority which adopted Crawford's definition. In *Dyck* at page 593, the Supreme Court described unconscionability as occurring in a transaction where "the stronger party has taken unfair advantage of the other."

[43] The union relies on the judgment of the British Columbia Court of Appeal in *Harry v. Kreutziger* (1978), 95 D.L.R. (3d) 231 at page 237 where McIntyre J.A. said ...:

> Where a claim is made that a bargain is unconscionable, it must be shown for success that there was inequality in the position of the parties due to the ignorance, need or distress of the weaker, which would leave him in the power of the stronger, coupled with proof of substantial unfairness in the bargain.

[44] Most, if not all, of the cases that discuss the doctrine of unconscionability refer to the inequality of bargaining power of the parties. However, this court in *Fraser Jewellers (1982) Ltd. v. Dominion Electric Protection Co.* (1997), 34 O.R. (3d) 1 ... noted that the inequality of bargaining power alone does not render a contract unconscionable or unenforceable. Robins J.A. speaking for the court said at, pp 11–12 O.R.:

> The trial judge was of the opinion that there was an inequality of bargaining position between the plaintiff, a small retailer, and the defendant, a large security protection firm, and treated this as militating in favour of striking the clause. While I agree that such

inequality is a relevant criterion, the fact that the parties may have different bargaining power does not in itself render an agreement unconscionable or unenforceable. Mere inequality of bargaining power does not entitle a party to repudiate an agreement. The question is not whether there was an inequality of bargaining power. Rather, the question is whether there was an abuse of the bargaining power.

[45] However one articulates the test for unconscionability, I am satisfied that it involves more than a finding of inequality of bargaining power between the parties to a contract. Both the test adopted by the application judge in *Eckstein* and the test in *Harry* of the British Columbia Court of Appeal recognize that a determination of unconscionability involves a two-part analysis—a finding of inequality of bargaining power and a finding that the terms of an agreement have a high degree of unfairness. I see little, if any, difference between a description of terms of a contract as "very unfair" or "substantially unfair." I am also of the view that "abuse of the bargaining power" identified by Robins J.A. in *Fraser Jewellers* is another way of describing substantial unfairness.

[46] I can find no error in the application judge's articulation of the test for unconscionability....

[49] Counsel for the union submits that the application judge erred in finding that there was inequality of bargaining power and substantial unfairness in this case. Relying on the strict language of the British Columbia Court of Appeal in *Harry*, he argues that the inequality of bargaining power must be linked with some "ignorance, need or distress" of the weaker party. Counsel suggests that inequality of bargaining power can result from old age, emotional distress, dependence, lack of business experience, or poverty. Counsel further submits that there is no evidence that such factors exist in this case. I do not accept this submission. There is no fixed set of criteria that establishes inequality of bargaining power.

[50] The application judge relied upon Iacobucci J.'s reasoning in *Berry* that in a contract of adhesion, a union member has no bargaining power with the union. Iacobucci J. also concluded that it is when the contract is formed that determines whether ... there was inequality of bargaining power. When Mr. Birch and Ms. Luberti joined the union, they took the union constitution as they found it with no ability to negotiate or change its terms until they became members. The fact that they could recommend and lobby for change after becoming members does not alter the analysis.

[51] I am satisfied that the application judge committed no error in concluding that there was inequality of bargaining power between the respondents on the one hand and the union on the other hand.

[52] I turn to the question of whether the application judge erred in finding that the fines levied against the respondents as provided for in the union constitution were "very unfair." As I read the reasons for judgment, the application judge considered all of the facts relevant to this issue.

[53] The application judge determined that there was no evidence to support the union's position that the fines were proportional to the damage suffered by the union as a result of Mr. Birch and Ms. Luberti crossing the picket line. Before the application judge, the union sought to justify the fines as a genuine pre-estimate of the damages suffered by the union. Although there was no evidence to support this position, the

union submitted that the damages amounted to one cent per member which produced an amount of $258.95 for the total union membership of 25,895. If $50 per day strike pay (for a total of $150.00) is subtracted from that amount, the total amount of the damages would be reduced to $108.95. The actual amount of the fine was $476.75 or 454 per cent greater than the union's estimate of its damages less the $150.00 for strike pay. I agree with the application judge that a fine of that magnitude can properly be described as excessive and unconscionable. Even if I did not agree with him, I am satisfied that a high degree of deference is owed to the application judge on that issue.

[54] In this court, the union did not advance the one cent per member theory but argued that a fine of $476.75 is a trivial sum. In all of the circumstances, I disagree.

[55] The application judge rejected out of hand the submission that a fine representing the gross pay of an employee was justified because it represented the value of the work to the employer. I agree with the application judge's conclusion that basing the fine on the value of the work to the employer does not make an excessive fine justifiable. It is the circumstances of the employee that determines whether the fine meets the test of substantial unfairness. In this case, the application judge determined ... that a fine, which exceeded an employee's take-home ... pay, "at a time when members may already be suffering financially as a result of strike action supports the conclusion that the fine provisions are very unfair." I note that counsel for the union argues that there was no direct evidence of members suffering financially as a result of the strike action. While that may be so, the application judge's general statement that members may be suffering financially appears to me to be a logical inference to draw from the circumstances of a cessation of work due to a strike.

[56] The fact that Saskatchewan is the only jurisdiction in Canada that has seen fit to authorize a trade union to levy a fine on a member who crosses the picket line during a legal strike, limited to a member's net pay, adds support to the conclusion of the application judge that a fine greater than that amount is excessive. While I do not think it is necessary to conclude, as did the application judge, that no fine is enforceable in the absence of legislation authorizing the imposition of a fine, I find the legislation in Saskatchewan is informative on the issue to be decided here.

[57] The application judge also considered whether the fines provided under the constitution were justified in order to deter members from taking the benefits of union membership without accepting the burden of a work stoppage due to a legal strike. He decided that there were more appropriate means than fines of the magnitude here to accomplish this end. I also note that the respondents were suspended from union membership for three years. In my view, a suspension of such duration is a significant penalty in itself. The respondents not only lose the benefits of union membership but risk ostracism and ridicule from their fellow employees who are members of the union.

[58] I recognize that a fundamental principle of the union movement and the collective bargaining process is union solidarity. I accept that the penalty provision in this case was aimed at preserving union solidarity. As important as that principle is, the means adopted to achieve it in this case have been found to be "very unfair."

[59] In my view, the application judge applied the correct test for unconscionability to the agreed facts and to the inferences which he drew from those facts. I can see no

basis upon which this court could or should interfere with his conclusion that the penalty clause in the constitution is unconscionable and therefore unenforceable....

Juriansz J. (Dissenting):

[...]

[103] In summary, I would find that the disciplinary provision is not unconscionable for two reasons. First, while there is inequality of bargaining power, no unfair advantage has been taken of the weaker party by the stronger. Second, the amount of the fine is not unfair when considered in the light of the actual ... damage suffered by the union. Further, I would find that the disciplinary provision is not inherently unenforceable as a penalty.

Do you think a union should ever be allowed to use the courts to enforce a fine that it has imposed on members for crossing a picket line? If so, what would be a reasonable fine?

11:500 UNION SECURITY PROVISIONS AND THE ROLE OF UNIONS IN SOCIETY

Unions obviously play a key role in our statutory regime of labour relations, and the involvement of individual employees in unions allows them to participate in determining conditions at work. But unions have a broader significance as institutions in civil society. In his essay, "Bowling Alone: America's Declining Social Capital" (1995) 6:1 *Journal of Democracy* 65, Robert Putnam used union membership as one of several indicators of social engagement in the United States. He suggested that such engagement was declining in virtually all spheres—politics, unionism, churches, and bowling leagues, the largest single collective activity in which Americans were engaged. Putnam located American unions within the larger, rather sorry, picture of declining civic participation throughout society. Ironically, during the 1996 US presidential election campaign, shortly after Putnam's essay was published, unions became more active than they had been for years—yet for the first time, less than half of all eligible voters exercised their right to vote for a presidential candidate.

Canadian unions have traditionally been much more active in politics, and remain so. They tend to support what they deem to be worthy causes locally, nationally, and abroad. They lobby for the adoption of legislation that directly favours union interests, such as amendments to labour relations statutes, and for the adoption of social and economic policies that favour workers, minorities, and the non-working poor. Many unions, both federally and provincially, have chosen to align themselves with the New Democratic Party (NDP), either formally or informally, and unions in Quebec have generally supported the Parti Québécois.

However, the relationship of unions to the NDP has become more contingent and more contentious. That party has come under fire for its dependence on union support, all the more so because unions have been losing public sympathy in recent years. Nor has union support necessarily delivered many votes to the NDP; in recent years, more and more workers have been voting for other parties, and a few high-profile union leaders have explicitly supported other parties. Nor, finally, are unions always pleased with policies adopted by NDP governments. In the case of the 1990–95 Ontario NDP government, many unions became very displeased, and some stopped supporting the party altogether.

All of these developments form part of the backdrop to the next case, in which Mervin Lavigne, an anti-union dissident, tried to limit the capacity of unions to participate in politics by seeking a court order prohibiting the use for political purposes of dues collected under union security arrangements. A right-wing lobby group, the National Citizens' Coalition, provided support for Lavigne throughout the course of the litigation.

Lavigne v Ontario Public Service Employees' Union, [1991] 2 SCR 211

[Lavigne was a teacher in a community college that had a collective agreement with the Ontario Public Service Employees Union. The agreement had a Rand Formula provision, which required teachers to pay the equivalent of union dues as a condition of employment but did not require them to join the union. Lavigne did not challenge the requirement to pay union dues. However, he claimed that his constitutional rights of freedom of expression and freedom of association under sections 2(b) and 2(d) of the *Canadian Charter of Rights and Freedoms* were violated by the union's use of some of its funds, of which his dues were a part, for purposes other than collective bargaining—for example, support of the NDP; aid to various causes, including nuclear disarmament and abortion rights; opposition to the construction of the Toronto SkyDome; and support for Oxfam, striking British mine workers, and Nicaraguan health care workers.

Because Ontario community colleges were under substantial government control, the Supreme Court of Canada held that they were governmental actors within the meaning of section 32 of the *Charter*, and that the provisions of the applicable collective agreement therefore had to respect employees' *Charter* rights. However, the Court unanimously dismissed Lavigne's claim that the union's use of a portion of his dues for political purposes violated his *Charter* rights.]

WILSON J. (L'Heureux-Dubé J. concurring):

... The fact that the appellant is obliged to pay dues pursuant to the agency shop clause in the collective agreement does not inhibit him in any meaningful way from expressing a contrary view as to the merits of the causes supported by the Union. He is free to speak his mind as and when he wishes. Nor does his being governed by the Rand formula have such an effect. It is a built-in feature of the Rand formula that union activities represent only the expression of the union as the representative of the majority of employees. It is not the voice of one and all in the bargaining unit. I find therefore that the appellant's s. 2(b) right has not been infringed....

Although it is not necessary for me to consider s. 1 of the *Charter* in light of my conclusion that neither s. 2(d) nor s. 2(b) has been infringed, I am considering its application in case my conclusion is in error and for the sake of completeness....

Mr. Lavigne maintains that, while compelling non-members to pay the equivalent of union dues is rationally connected to the objective of promoting industrial peace, this is so only in so far as those dues are put to pure 'collective bargaining' purposes. It is the appellant's position that to confer a complete discretion upon the union to spend the dues as it sees fit, and in particular to spend dues on political parties and issues unrelated to the particular workplace in which dues payers are employed, does not further the goal of industrial harmony. In other words, Mr. Lavigne contends that the provision is overbroad....

Some commentators have suggested that, even if the interests of unions are considered to be primarily economic, there is none the less plenty of justification for permitting them to contribute to causes removed from the particular workplace. For example, Professor Etherington ... states ... :

> The attempt to distinguish the economic and political concerns rests on the misguided premise that unions can represent the economic interests of workers effectively without engaging in political activity. If this was ever more than a myth, it is certainly not the case in a post *laissez-faire* society in which government intervention and regulation in most spheres of economic and social life is a daily event. In such a society, it is *necessary* for unions to engage in political activity to ensure that governmental regulation takes a form that is favourable, or at least not adverse, to the economic interests of its constituents. If they do not, they may find that their bargaining position *vis-à-vis* employers has been substantially weakened or undermined by government legislation or policy. [Emphasis in original.]

Similarly, Benjamin Aaron, in his article 'Some Aspects of the Union's Duty of Fair Representation' stated ... :

> The welfare of organized labour is affected not only by so-called 'labour legislation,' but also by executive, legislative, and judicial decisions with respect to monetary and fiscal policy, defence, education, health, and many other issues. Finally, policies are made by men, and it is sheer sophistry to argue that although a union may legitimately support certain legislative objectives, it may not spend its funds to secure the election of candidates whom it hopes or has reason to believe will work to achieve labor's goals.

I agree with Professors Etherington and Aaron that union involvement outside the realm of strict contract negotiation and administration does advance the interests of the union at the bargaining table and in arbitration. However, I do not believe that the role of the union needs to be confined to these narrow economic functions. In the past, this court has not approached labour matters from an exclusively economic perspective. For example, in *Slaight Communications* ..., Dickson C.J.C. adopted the expression of Professor David Beatty that 'labour is not a commodity'.... The idea that is meant to be captured by this expression is, I think, that the interests of workers reach far beyond the adequacy of the financial deal they may be able to strike with their employers ... [T]he Chief Justice made it clear that the interests of labour do not end at some artificial boundary between the economic and the political. He expressed the view that "'[a] person's employment is an essential component of his or her sense of identity, self-worth and emotional well-being'" (quoting from the *Alberta Reference* ...) and that viewing labour as a commodity is incompatible with that perspective. Unions' decisions to involve themselves in politics by supporting particular causes, candidates or parties, stems from a recognition of the expansive character of the interests of labour and a perception of collective bargaining as a process which is meant to foster more than mere economic gain for workers. From involvement in union locals through to participation in the larger activities of the union movement the current collective bargaining regime enhances not only the economic interests of labour but also the interest of working people in preserving some dignity in their working lives....

[I]f Mr. Lavigne's *Charter* rights have indeed been infringed, that infringement has been occasioned through measures that significantly modify its impact. Some of the key features of the scheme are worth repeating: the union may only compel the payment of dues from each member of the bargaining unit after a majority of those employees have exercised their choice to be represented by the union; all employees are free to join the union or not, and the bargaining agent may not discriminate against any member of the bargaining unit on the basis of union membership; and if the members of the bargaining unit find that they are unhappy with their bargaining representative, they may take a vote to decertify the union.

Taking these factors into account it seems to me that the legislature has opted for a very reasonable and fair compromise. The union, once certified, has been permitted to exercise authority over the members of the bargaining unit in many respects. However, with that authority comes a great deal of responsibility. As well, the entire process of union representation carries the hallmark of democracy. This is not a case of the heavy hand of government coming down and enforcing its will with little or no regard for the rights and freedoms of those affected. The features of the scheme suggest to me that, while other means might have been available to the legislature to achieve its objective, none is clearly superior in terms of both accomplishing the goal of promoting collective bargaining and respecting as far as possible the rights of individual employees.

The *Charter* does not require the elimination of 'minuscule' constitutional burdens ...

LA FOREST J. (Sopinka and Gonthier JJ. concurring):

[...]

To take the first step in the *Oakes* test ..., what can be said to be the state objective in compelling someone like the appellant to pay dues to the Union knowing that those dues could be used to fund activities not immediately relevant, or at all relevant to the representation of his interest at the bargaining table? There appear to be two closely interrelated objectives.

The first is to ensure that unions have both the resources and the mandate necessary to enable them to play a role in shaping the political, economic and social context within which particular collective agreements and labour relations disputes will be negotiated or resolved. The balance of power between management and labour at any given time or in any particular industry or workplace is a product of many factors. It is, in part, clearly a product of factors specific to the industry or workplace in question, such as productivity, and the existence or non-existence of a history of bitter strikes and sharp practice. But it is also in part a product of more general factors, such as the prevailing public sentiment as to the importance of unions or the state of the economy. It is also a product of the state of government legislation and policy, most obviously in the area of labour relations itself, but also in regard to social and economic policy generally. Government policy on day-care, for example, will affect what a union can achieve for its members at the bargaining table. If universal day-care is paid for by taxpayers as a whole, union negotiators in a particular workplace will not have to pay for it by making wage concessions as a way of convincing the employer to provide it. Even if the government introduces certain taxes, the balance of power between workers and management may be affected. Concerned to cushion their membership against a tax's inflationary effect, unions may have to make concessions in areas they would otherwise have fought for, such as vacation time or worker safety. This, then, is one of the principal objectives that lies behind the government's willingness to force contribution to union coffers knowing that it will be spent on things not immediately related to collective bargaining on behalf of the workers making the contributions.

The second government objective I have alluded to explains why government puts no limits on the uses to which contributed funds can be put. This objective is that of contributing to democracy in the workplace. The integrity and status of unions as democracies would be jeopardized if the government's policy was, in effect, that unions can spend their funds as they choose according to majority vote provided the majority chooses to make expenditures the government thinks are in the interest of the union's membership. It is, therefore, for the union itself to decide, by majority vote, which causes or organizations it will support in the interests of favourably influencing the political, social and economic environment in which particular instances of collective bargaining and labour-management dispute resolution will take place. The old slogan that self-government entails the right to be wrong may be a good way of summing up the government's objective of fostering genuine and meaningful democracy in the workplace.

* * * * *

In the following case, the Supreme Court of Canada confronted the even more controversial question of whether the *Charter* right to freedom of association was violated by a statute that compelled workers to join a union in order to be employed in a particular industry.

R v Advance Cutting & Coring Ltd, 2001 SCC 70

[The Quebec *Act Respecting Labour Relations, Vocational Training and Workforce Management in the Construction Industry*, CQLR, c R-20 (the *Construction Act*) set up a scheme of province-wide bargaining in the construction industry similar in some respects to statutory schemes applicable to that industry in other provinces. In certain ways, however, the Quebec statute went further than those in other provinces. It named five union federations as recognized bargaining agents, and it required every construction worker to join one of the five (the worker could choose which one) in order to obtain the "certificate of competence" that was a prerequisite to employment in the industry. A limited number of certificates of competence were available in each region of the province.

Several construction firms were convicted and fined under the *Construction Act* for employing workers who did not have the requisite certificates. A number of contractors, real estate developers, and construction workers brought a claim under the *Charter* that the convictions should be set aside on the ground that the Act violated employees' freedom of association—and more precisely, that freedom of association under the *Charter* included the right not to associate. The Quebec government and the unions defended the statutory scheme as the only practical response to a long history of strife, violence, and dysfunctional labour relations in the construction industry. The matter eventually reached the Supreme Court of Canada.

A fragmented Supreme Court upheld the legislation by the narrowest of margins. Four separate judgments were written. Justice L'Heureux-Dubé, speaking only for herself, was the only judge who held that the freedom of association did not include the right of non-association. In her view, such a right would be antithetical to the purpose and scope of freedom of association, which was to protect the collective pursuit of common goals. Alternatively, she said, if there was a right of non-association, it was not violated by this statutory scheme, but even if there were a violation, it was justified under section 1 of the *Charter*.

The other eight judges were all of the view that the freedom of association did indeed include the right of non-association. However, they split three ways on whether that right had been violated, and on the issue of justification under section 1.

What turned out to be the dissenting judgment, written by Bastarache J and concurred in by McLachlin CJ and by Major and Binnie JJ, held that the right not to associate had been violated, and that the violation was not justified under section 1. In Bastarache J's opinion, the compulsory unionization scheme established by the *Construction Act* in and of itself represented a form of ideological coercion not justified under section 1. No specific evidence of the ideological views of the unions in question was required, the dissenters said; the mere fact that workers were required to participate in and indirectly support a system of state-sponsored and forced association was enough. Justice Bastarache was also of the view that the historical problems of labour relations in the provincial construction industry could not justify such an incursion on freedom of association. He was very unimpressed by the device of certificates of competence; in his view (with which the majority did not really take issue), the statute envisaged that those certificates were to be given out not on the basis of competence but on the basis of residence in the particular region and past employment in the industry.

What was in effect the majority judgment was written by LeBel J and concurred in by Gonthier and Arbour JJ. Like the four dissenters, LeBel J held that freedom of association included the right not to associate. However, like L'Heureux-Dubé J, he held that the right not to associate had not been violated in this case, and that even if it had been violated, the violation was justified in light of the problems which had led to the enactment of the *Construction Act*.

The swing vote was cast by Iacobucci J. Writing only for himself, he agreed with Bastarache J that the *Construction Act* violated the right of non-association, making a total of five judges who found such a violation. However, Iacobucci J agreed with LeBel J and L'Heureux-Dubé J that the violation was justified under section 1, making a total of five judges who reached that conclusion.]

LEBEL J.:

[...]

[218] The *Construction Act* imposes an obligation to join a union group. The obligation remains, nevertheless, a very limited one. It boils down to the obligation to designate a collective bargaining representative, to belong to it for a given period of time,

and to pay union dues. The Act does not require more. At the same time, the Act provides protection against past, present and potential abuses of union power. Unions are deprived of any direct control over employment in the industry. They may not set up or operate an office or union hall (ss. 104 and 119 of the Act). No discrimination is allowed against the members of different unions. Provided they hold the required competency certificates, all workers are entitled to work in the construction industry without regard to their particular union affiliation. Specific guarantees against discrimination are found in ss. 94 and 102. Section 96 grants members clear rights of information and participation in union life. The law allows any construction worker to change his or her union affiliation, at the appropriate time. As it stands, the law does not impose on construction workers much more than the bare obligation to belong to a union. It does not create any mechanism to enforce ideological conformity.

[Turning to the political role of unions and union members in contemporary Canadian society, LeBel J said:]

[226] The fact that unions intervene in political social debate is well known and well documented and might be the object of judicial notice. Indeed, our Court acknowledged the importance of this role in the *Lavigne* case. Several ideological currents have criss-crossed the history of the Quebec labour movement. It was never unanimous about its direction, even about the need to enter the political arena or involve itself in broader societal issues beyond the horizon of the bargaining unit. (See P. Verge and G. Murray, *Le droit et les syndicats* ...) These authors underscore the weakness of the formal links between the Quebec unions and political parties ... They add that it is impossible to determine whether union political positions had any real influence on their members ... More recent studies of voting attitudes seem to indicate that, in fact, Canadian unions exert very little influence on the voting behaviour of their members, as at least one Canadian political party, the New Democratic Party, has found repeatedly to its sorrow (see A. Blais *et al.* "Making Sense of the Vote in the 2000 Canadian Election", ...).

[227] Taking judicial notice of the fact that Quebec unions have a constant ideology, act in constant support of a particular cause or policy, and seek to impose that ideology on their members seems far more controversial ... In this case, it cannot be said that some form of politicization and ideological conformity which allegedly flows from the political and social orientation of the labour movement is self-evident. Instead, such views evidence stereotypes about the union movement as authoritarian and undemocratic, and conjures images of workers marching in lock step without any free choice or free will, under the watchful eye of union bosses and their goon squads.

[228] In fact, democracy undergirds the particular form of union security provided for by the *Construction Act*. Throughout the conflicts and difficulties that marred the history of the construction industry, a critical flaw of the regime appeared to be the lack of participation in the life of unions and the need to re-establish and maintain member control over their affairs. While it also facilitated the evaluation of the representativeness of the unions, the obligation to choose and join a union answered this critical need in a way that a different union security arrangement, like the Rand Formula, would not have addressed. The dues check-off scheme, like the Rand formula, disposes of the free

rider problem, but the employee remains outside the life of the union. In other security arrangements, a member may choose to remain aloof and refrain from attending meetings, voting for union officers and taking part in discussions. Affiliation means that he or she has, at least, gained the ability to influence the life of the association whether or not he or she decides to exercise this right....

[230] Union members seem to act very independently from their union when it comes to the expression of their political choices and, even more so, to their voting preferences, come election time. Existence of attempted ideological conformity, let alone its realization, seems highly doubtful ...

[231] In this context, there is simply no evidence to support judicial notice of Quebec unions ideologically coercing their members. Such an inference presumes that unions hold a single ideology and impose it on their rank and file, including the complainants in this case. Such an inference would amount to little more than an unsubstantiated stereotype....

BASTARACHE J. (dissenting):

[...]

[9] ... In this case, the fundamental values that must be protected in the workplace include freedom of conscience, mobility, liberty, freedom of expression and the right to work. The necessity of considering the totality of the rights and values that are interrelated when dealing with forced association in the workplace, in my opinion, points to the need to take a broad view of the *Charter* right not to associate.

[10] This approach is supported by consideration of this freedom in light of international conventions and the jurisprudence of this Court.

[11] The United Nations *Universal Declaration of Human Rights* ... states:

Article 20

[...]

2. No one may be compelled to belong to an association.

In addition, the United Nations *International Covenant on Economic, Social and Cultural Rights*, 993 U.N.T.S. 3, provides that:

Article 8. 1. The States Parties to the present Covenant undertake to ensure:
(a) the right of everyone to form trade unions and join the trade union *of his choice*, subject only to the rules of the organization concerned, for the promotion and protection of his economic and social interests. No restrictions may be placed on the exercise of this right other than those prescribed by law and which are necessary in a democratic society in the interests of national security or public order or for the protection of the rights and freedoms of others; [Emphasis added.]

[12] This Court has regularly made reference to and relied upon the aforementioned international documents in interpreting fundamental freedoms in the *Charter*....

[17] ... To suggest that the unions in the present case are not associated with any ideological cause is to ignore the history of the union movement itself...

[23] ... The legislation in question here is complex; it creates an entire labour relations scheme which governs, amongst other matters, union membership, employers

associations, collective bargaining and the creation of the Commission de la construction du Québec and committees on construction and vocational training.

[24] The *mis en cause* argues that the action against the appellants was directed solely at their failure to obtain competency certificates. According to the *mis en cause*, there is a distinction between this requirement and the requirement to become a member of one of the five recognized employee associations. I disagree with this assertion. The scheme of the Act provides that both requirements must be met as conditions precedent to working in the construction industry in Quebec; these conditions are certified together on one document, referred to as the competency certificate, and the only way to receive such a certificate pursuant to s. 39 of the Act is if both conditions have been met ...

[...]

[27] ... It is because of the collective force produced by membership that unions can be a potent force in public debate, that they can influence Parliament and the legislatures in their functions, that they can bargain effectively. This force must be constituted democratically to conform to s. 2(*d*)....

[28] ... Ideological constraint exists in particular where membership numbers are used to promote ideological agendas and, as noted in *Lavigne* ..., this is so even where there is no evidence that the union is coercing its members to believe in what it promotes ...

[...]

[32] The vast majority of Canadians must work for a living and, as such, working is a compelled fact of life; however, in the present situation, the appellants are not arguing that being forced to work with a particular group or to participate in employment-related activities violates s. 2(*d*). This is not a case where workers dispute the payment of mandated union dues; the restrictions in this case are much more severe than that in *Lavigne*. The Rand formula mandates payment of union dues for the betterment of all workers; in this case, the workers are being forced to join a union ...

[...]

[38] ... [P]ursuant to s. 30, construction workers can only be placed on the employer's list and join a union pursuant to s. 32 if they were a resident of Quebec in the previous year, worked 300 hours in that year and were under 50 years of age. The Commission de la construction du Québec forwards a card to the workers on this list (s. 36). No employer may use the services of a person in the construction industry unless that person holds one of these cards (s. 39). Therefore, if the s. 30 requirements are not met, a person may not join one of the five unions and, as a result, cannot work in Quebec. In addition, as acknowledged by the Commission de la construction du Québec ..., at the material time, there were regional quotas in place which also limited the number of workers in each predetermined region within the province. For persons living in and outside the province of Quebec, their ability to join one of the unions and thereby work in the construction industry is severely restricted by these arbitrary requirements ... The same may be said for a person who has never left the province but simply did not work in the industry in the previous year or a person who wishes to train and start working in the industry for the first time....

[42] In summary, there are severe restrictions on the right of a person to join one of the five chosen unions in order to work in the construction industry in Quebec. Even if

the conditions imposed by s. 30 of the Act were permissible limitations on freedom of association, the regional quotas would still need to be justified under s. 1. They unduly infringe the ability of workers to join a union, which is a prerequisite for working in the construction industry in Quebec. As such, they are an infringement of the s. 2(d) freedom of association....

[46] ... I accept that it is in the public interest to have structured collective bargaining and to provide for competency requirements; these are no doubt pressing and substantial objectives. But I have difficulty accepting that these are the true objectives of the impugned provisions. The legislation brings into play restrictions on the admission to the industry, cancellation of the ability to have a non-unionized business, restrictions on bargaining rights, imposition of regional quotas and impingement of regional mobility....

[47] Regarding the relationship between forced association and the objective stated, the *mis en cause* submits that it is essential to collective bargaining in this area to limit the number of actors in this industry. This is an argument based on the history of labour relations in Quebec. However, as stated above, the *mis en cause* has failed to show that permitting structured collective bargaining is the true purpose of these provisions as drafted. Further, any justification based on competency is untenable. The actual requirements of s. 30 and the regional quotas have little if anything to do with the professional competence of workers in the construction industry. This was noted by Judge Bonin who stated that "[t]he certificate's main purpose was to maintain hiring priority." Being a resident of Quebec in the previous year, having worked a set number of hours in that year, and being less than 50 years old, do not verify competence. The same may be said for the regional quotas and control over regional mobility within the province. As such, I find there is no rational connection between the objective and the measures taken....

[50] Further, when considering the public interest nature of collective bargaining, I fail to see how s. 30 and the regional quotas minimally impair the positive and negative components of the freedom of association. While recognizing the importance of collective bargaining in the public interest, if this was in fact the objective of these provisions, there is no evidence that it need result in government control over admission to the work force based on the factors discussed above or result in a denial of the democratic principle. As was shown by the factual situation in *Lavigne*, there are other choices that a government can make which support collective bargaining. The imposition of a Rand formula, for instance, would allow for collective bargaining to continue without the requirement that workers actually join a union. Furthermore, with respect to a means to protect the negative right, had there been no problem with the positive right in this case, the government could possibly have instituted a clause allowing those who did not wish to join a union to simply abstain while continuing to pay union dues to the representative union in the majority or to a collective "pot" to be divided equally among all five representative unions.

11:600 THE UNION'S RIGHT TO COMMUNICATE WITH ITS MEMBERS

Communication has evolved rapidly in recent decades. Where unions in the 1990s would have depended on leaflets, newspapers, physical bulletin boards, and mailed letters as its primary means of reaching its members, today, they have adapted to the changing world. They rely primarily upon social media, email messages, and internet communications to stay in touch. All unions maintain an active website presence, where members can find their collective agreements, open forums on current industrial relations and political topics, and ways to contact their local and national leadership.

Still, some of the old ways of communicating remain important. Unions continue to mail letters and news bulletins to their membership, and continue to contact their members by telephone. So what happens when a member of a bargaining unit that a union represents does not want her home contact information made available to the union? Do individual privacy rights trump the union's capacity to be able to communicate with its members? The Supreme Court of Canada addressed this issue in the following case.

Bernard v Canada (Attorney General), 2014 SCC 13

[Ms Bernard was a member of a federal public service bargaining unit, but chose not to belong to the Professional Institute of the Public Service (PIPS), the union that was the exclusive bargaining agent for the bargaining unit members. As a Rand Formula member, she was entitled to the benefits of the collective agreement and representation by the union, and she was required to pay union dues.

In 2005, the *Federal Public Sector Labour Relations Act*, SC 2003, c 22, was amended. Among other things, the amendments significantly expanded the representational obligations of the union. Consequently, PIPS requested the employer to provide it with the home contact information for the members of the bargaining unit. The employer refused. PIPS brought an unfair labour practice complaint against the employer to the Public Service Labour Relations Board. The board largely upheld the complaint because the employer's refusal interfered with the union's representation of the employees. As a result, the employer agreed to provide the union with the home mailing addresses and telephone numbers of the bargaining unit members, subject to some conditions related to the privacy and security of the information. In receiving the information from the employer, PIPS agreed not to disclose the information to anyone other than the appropriate union officials, and not to use it for any other purposes. The employer and the union agreed to jointly explain the terms of the information disclosure to the bargaining unit membership.

Ms Bernard objected that the disclosure to the union of her home contact information breached her rights under the federal *Privacy Act*, RSC 1985 c P-21. At a subsequent redetermination hearing, the Public Service Labour Relations Board ruled that the union requiring the employees' home contact information in order to fulfill its representational duties was reasonable, and this requirement complied with the *Privacy Act*. The Federal Court of Appeal upheld the board's ruling. Ms Bernard appealed to the Supreme Court of Canada.]

Abella and Cromwell JJ:

Analysis

[21] It is important to understand the labour relations context in which Ms. Bernard's privacy complaints arise. A key aspect of that context is the principle of majoritarian exclusivity,

a cornerstone of labour relations law in this country. A union has the *exclusive* right to bargain on behalf of *all* employees in a given bargaining unit, including Rand employees. The union is the exclusive agent for those employees with respect to their rights under the collective agreement. While an employee is undoubtedly free not to join the union and to decide to become a Rand employee, he or she may not opt out of the exclusive bargaining relationship, nor the representational duties that a union owes to employees.

[22] The nature of the union's representational duties is an important part of the context for the Board's decision. The union must represent all bargaining unit employees fairly and in good faith. The *Public Service Labour Relations Act* imposes a number of specific duties on a union with respect to employees in the bargaining unit. These include a duty to provide all employees in the bargaining unit with a reasonable opportunity to participate in strike votes and to be notified of the results of such votes (s. 184). According to the Board, similar obligations apply to the conduct of final-offer votes under s. 183 of the *Act*.

[23] This is the context in which to consider the reasonableness of the Board's findings that disclosure of home contact information is required under the *Public Service Labour Relations Act* and authorized by s. 8(2)(a) of the *Privacy Act* ...

[24] The Board found that the employer's refusal to disclose employee home contact information constituted an unfair labour practice because it interfered with the union's representation of employees. Two rationales fueled this conclusion. The first is that the union needs *effective* means of contacting employees in order to discharge its representational duties. This was explained in *Millcroft*, where the Ontario Labour Relations Board extensively reviewed a union's duties and concluded that the union "must be able to communicate effortlessly with the employees" and "should have [their contact information] without the need to pass through the obstacles suggested by the employer" in order to discharge those representational duties: para. 33.

[25] The Board explained why employee work contact information was insufficient to enable the union to carry out its duties to bargaining unit employees: it is not appropriate for a bargaining agent to use employer facilities for its business; workplace communications from bargaining agents must be vetted by the employer before posting; there is no expectation of privacy in electronic communications at the workplace; and the union must be able to communicate with employees quickly and effectively, particularly when they are dispersed.

[26] The second and more theoretical rationale for the employer's obligation to disclose home contact information is that the union must be on an equal footing with the employer with respect to information relevant to the collective bargaining relationship. Disclosure of personal information to the union is not like disclosure of personal information to the public because of the tripartite relationship between the employee, the employer and the union. To the extent that the employer has information which is of value to the union in representing employees, the union is entitled to it. This was explained as follows in *Millcroft*:

> A consequence of the union possessing exclusive bargaining status on behalf of the employees is that the union is placed in an equal bargaining position with the employer

in its collective bargaining relationship. To the extent that the employer has information which is of value to the union in its capacity to represent the employees (such as their names, addresses and telephone numbers), the union too should have that information. The employees' privacy rights are compromised (no doubt legitimately) by the employer having details of their names, addresses and telephone numbers. The union's acquisition of that information would be no greater compromise, nor any less legitimate. [para. 31]

[27] The Board's conclusions are clearly justified. The union's need to be able to communicate with employees in the bargaining unit cannot be satisfied by reliance on the employer's facilities. As the Board observed, the employer can control the means of workplace communication, can implement policies that restrict all workplace communications, including with the union, and can monitor communications. Moreover, the union may have representational duties to employees whom it cannot contact at work, such as employees who are on leave, or who are not at work because of a labour dispute.

[28] The second rationale—equality of information between the employer and the union—further supports the Board's conclusion. The tripartite nature of the employment relationship means that information disclosed to the employer that is necessary for the union to carry out its representational duties should be disclosed to the union in order to ensure that the union and employer are on an equal footing with respect to information relevant to the collective bargaining relationship.

[29] Moreover, an employee cannot waive his or her right to be fairly—and exclusively—represented by the union. Given that the union owes legal obligations to *all* employees—whether or not they are Rand employees—and may have to communicate with them quickly, the union should not be deprived of information in the hands of the employer that could assist in fulfilling these obligations.

[30] This brings us to the intersecting privacy concerns. The *Privacy Act* imposes a ban on disclosure of government-held personal information, which includes home addresses and telephone numbers, subject to a number of exceptions listed in s. 8(2), including the consistent use exception:

> 8. . . .
> (2) Subject to any other Act of Parliament, personal information under the control of a government institution may be disclosed
> (a) for the purpose for which the information was obtained or compiled by the institution or *for a use consistent with that purpose*;

[31] A use need not be identical to the purpose for which information was obtained in order to fall under s. 8(2) (a) of the *Privacy Act*; it must only be *consistent* with that purpose. As the Federal Court of Appeal held, there need only be a sufficiently direct connection between the purpose and the proposed use, such that an employee would reasonably expect that the information could be used in the manner proposed.

[32] The Board concluded that the union needed employee home contact information to represent the interests of employees, a use consistent with the purpose for which the government employer collected the information, namely, to contact employees about the terms and conditions of their employment. The information collected by the

employer was for the appropriate administration of the employment relationship. As the Board noted, "[e]mployees provide home contact information to their employers for the purpose of being contacted about their terms and conditions of employment. *This purpose is consistent with the [union]'s intended use of the contact information in this case*": para. 168 (emphasis added).

[33] In our view, the Board made a reasonable determination in identifying the union's proposed use as being consistent with the purpose of contacting employees about terms and conditions of employment and in concluding that the union needed this home contact information to carry out its representational obligations "quickly and effectively": para. 167. . . .

[37] Ms. Bernard's freedom of association argument has no legal foundation. Her argument was that since the Board's order required the employer to provide her personal information to the union, she was thereby being compelled to associate with the union, contrary to s. 2(*d*) of the *Charter*. In our view, the compelled disclosure of home contact information in order to allow a union to carry out its representational obligations to all bargaining unit members does not engage Ms. Bernard's freedom not to associate with the union. This Court's decision in *Lavigne v. Ontario Public Service Employees Union*, [1991] 2 S.C.R. 211, is determinative and its conclusion is supported by the more recent decision in *R. v. Advance Cutting & Coring Ltd.*, 2001 SCC 70, [2001] 3 S.C.R. 209.

[The Supreme Court of Canada dismissed the appeal.]

Chapter 12: The Constitutionalization of Collective Bargaining Law

12:100 INTRODUCTION

The *Canadian Charter of Rights and Freedoms*, Part 1 of the *Constitution Act*, 1982, being Schedule B to the *Canada Act 1982* (UK), 1982, c 11 states:

> 2. Everyone has the following fundamental freedoms:
> (a) freedom of conscience and religion;
> (b) freedom of thought, belief, opinion and expression, including freedom of the press and other media of communication;
> (c) freedom of peaceful assembly; and
> (d) freedom of association.

For labour lawyers, the central question is: What are we to make of the constitutional guarantee of "freedom of association?" This constitutional provision, in force since 1982, has added an important and rapidly growing new dimension to the study and practice of collective bargaining law in Canada. At various points in the previous several chapters of this book, we have touched on that new dimension, but we have postponed in-depth discussion of it to this point, with a view to treating it in a more focused way. Most of the *Charter* jurisprudence dealing with our labour law has come under the rubric of freedom of association, and that is what almost all of this chapter will be about.

It is true that in the leading cases a minor note has been struck by claims (none of them successful) that certain aspects of collective bargaining law have violated the guarantee of equality rights in section 15(1) of the *Charter*. Although equality rights at work will be treated in depth in Chapter 14, we will not here consider the potential use of section 15(1) in the context of collective labour law. That is not to say there is no such potential. See, for example, Brian Langille, "The Freedom of Association Mess: How We Got into It and How We Can Get Out of It" (2009) 54 *McGill Law Journal* 177. The focus of this chapter is freedom of association.

The Canadian law of freedom of association has had a turbulent history and is dominated by a series of cases from the Supreme Court of Canada. The Court has elaborated its evolving view of section 2(d) in three sets of three cases—a "trinity of trilogies." The first trilogy was issued on one day in 1987; the second trilogy began in 2001 and ended in 2011; and the cases constituting the third trilogy were all decided in 2015.

1987: THE FIRST TRILOGY
- *Reference re Public Service Employee Relations Act (Alta)*, [1987] 1 SCR 313 [*Alberta Reference*]
- *PSAC v Canada*, [1987] 1 SCR 42 [*PSAC*]
- *RWDSU v Saskatchewan*, [1987] 1 SCR 460 [*RWDSU*]

2001–2011: THE SECOND TRILOGY

- *Dunmore v Ontario (Attorney General)*, 2001 SCC 94 [*Dunmore*]
- *Health Services and Support—Facilities Subsector Bargaining Association v British Columbia*, 2007 SCC 27 [*Health Services*]
- *Ontario (Attorney General) v·Fraser*, 2011 SCC 20 [*Fraser*]

2015: THE THIRD TRILOGY

- *Mounted Police Association of Ontario v Canada (Attorney General)*, 2015 SCC 1 [*MPAO*]
- *Meredith v Canada (Attorney General)*, 2015 SCC 2 [*Meredith*]
- *Saskatchewan Federation of Labour v Saskatchewan (Attorney General)*, 2015 SCC 4 [*Sask Fed*]

The problem addressed in this chapter is, essentially: what are we to make of these nine cases? They are some of the most important labour law cases in a lifetime. Yet there remains an extremely difficult legal question. At one level we can see that the Court has reversed its original approach and critical holdings (against a constitutional "right" to strike, for example). That much is clear. But much else is not. This chapter takes the view that in order to understand (to the extent it is understandable) recent law, we need to start at the beginning. By starting there, we stand a chance of getting a view of our current state of play, our current difficulties, and what may lie ahead.

12:200 FREEDOM OF ASSOCIATION

12:210 The First Trilogy (1987): The *Alberta Reference*, *PSAC*, and *RWDSU*

We begin our story of freedom of association under section 2(d) of the *Charter* in the labour relations context with the *Alberta Reference*, one of three decisions released simultaneously in 1987. The central question in the *Alberta Reference* was whether Alberta legislation prohibiting strikes in the public service, and substituting a regime of compulsory interest arbitration, infringed section 2(d) of the *Charter*, and if so, whether the infringement was justified under section 1. The brief majority judgment was written by LeDain J. A more detailed, and very important analysis was offered in McIntyre J's concurring opinion. But it is Dickson CJ's dissent to which special attention must be paid. In this regard, closely read both Dickson's legal account of the freedom and its normative importance.

Reference Re Public Service Employee Relations Act (Alberta), [1987] 1 SCR 313

> LE DAIN J.:
>
> ... I agree with McIntyre J. that the constitutional guarantee of freedom of association in s. 2(d) of the *Canadian Charter of Rights and Freedoms* does not include, in the case of a trade union, a guarantee of the right to bargain collectively and the right to strike ...
>
> In considering the meaning that must be given to freedom of association in s. 2(d) of the *Charter* it is essential to keep in mind that this concept must be applied to a wide range of associations or organizations of a political, religious, social or economic nature, with a wide variety of objects, as well as activity by which the objects may be pursued. It is in this larger perspective, and not simply with regard to the perceived requirements of

a trade union, however important they may be, that one must consider the implications of extending a constitutional guarantee, under the concept of freedom of association, to the right to engage in particular activity on the ground that the activity is essential to give an association meaningful existence.

In considering whether it is reasonable to ascribe such a sweeping intention to the *Charter* I reject the premise that without such additional constitutional protection the guarantee of freedom of association would be a meaningless and empty one. Freedom of association is particularly important for the exercise of other fundamental freedoms, such as freedom of expression and freedom of conscience and religion. These afford a wide scope for protected activity in association. Moreover, the freedom to work for the establishment of an association, to belong to an association, to maintain it, and to participate in its lawful activity without penalty or reprisal is not to be taken for granted. That is indicated by its express recognition and protection in labour relations legislation. It is a freedom that has been suppressed in varying degrees from time to time by totalitarian regimes.

What is in issue here is not the importance of freedom of association in this sense, which is the one I ascribe to s. 2(*d*) of the *Charter*, but whether particular activity of an association in pursuit of its objects is to be constitutionally protected or left to be regulated by legislative policy. The rights for which constitutional protection is sought—the modern rights to bargain collectively and to strike, involving correlative duties or obligations resting on an employer—are not fundamental rights or freedoms. They are the creation of legislation, involving a balance of competing interests in a field which has been recognized by the courts as requiring a specialized expertise. It is surprising that in an area in which this Court has affirmed a principle of judicial restraint in the review of administrative action we should be considering the substitution of our judgment for that of the Legislature by constitutionalizing in general and abstract terms rights which the Legislature has found it necessary to define and qualify in various ways according to the particular field of labour relations involved. The resulting necessity of applying s. 1 of the *Charter* to a review of particular legislation in this field demonstrates in my respectful opinion the extent to which the Court becomes involved in a review of legislative policy for which it is really not fitted.

McINTYRE J.:

[...]

The question raised in this appeal, stated in its simplest terms, is whether the *Canadian Charter of Rights and Freedoms* gives constitutional protection to the right of a trade union to strike as an incident to collective bargaining ...

The appellants do not contend that the right to strike is specifically mentioned in the *Charter*. The sole basis of their submission is that this right is a necessary incident to the exercise by a trade union of the freedom of association guaranteed by s. 2(*d*) of the *Charter*. The resolution of this appeal turns then on the meaning of freedom of association in the *Charter*.

Freedom of Association and s. 2(*d*) of the *Charter*

Freedom of association is one of the most fundamental rights in a free society. The freedom to mingle, live and work with others gives meaning and value to the lives of individuals and makes organized society possible. The value of freedom of association as a unifying and liberating force can be seen in the fact that historically the conqueror, seeking to control foreign peoples, invariably strikes first at freedom of association in order to eliminate effective opposition. Meetings are forbidden, curfews are enforced, trade and commerce is suppressed, and rigid controls are imposed to isolate and thus debilitate the individual...

It is clear that the importance of freedom of association was recognized by Canadian law prior to the *Charter*. It is equally clear that prior to the *Charter* a provincial legislature or Parliament acting within its jurisdiction could regulate and control strikes and collective bargaining. The *Charter* has reaffirmed the historical importance of freedom of association and guaranteed it as an independent right. The courts must now define the range or scope of this right and its relation to other rights, both those grounded in the *Charter* and those existing at law without *Charter* protection....

The Value of Freedom of Association

... While freedom of association like most other fundamental rights has no single purpose or value, at its core rests a rather simple proposition: the attainment of individual goals, through the exercise of individual rights, is generally impossible without the aid and cooperation of others...

[...]

Our society supports a multiplicity of organized groups, clubs and associations which further many different objectives, religious, political, educational, scientific, recreational, and charitable. This exercise of freedom of association serves more than the individual interest, advances more than the individual cause; it promotes general social goals. Of particular importance is the indispensable role played by freedom of association in the functioning of democracy...

Associations serve to educate their members in the operation of democratic institutions... Associations also make possible the effective expression of political views and thus influence the formation of governmental and social policy... Freedom of association then serves the interest of the individual, strengthens the general social order, and supports the healthy functioning of democratic government.

In considering the constitutional position of freedom of association, it must be recognized that while it advances many group interests and, of course, cannot be exercised alone, it is nonetheless a freedom belonging to the individual and not to the group formed through its exercise. While some provisions in the Constitution involve groups, such as s. 93 of the *Constitution Act, 1867* protecting denominational schools, and s. 25 of the *Charter* referring to existing aboriginal rights, the remaining rights and freedoms are individual rights; they are not concerned with the group as distinct from its members. The group or organization is simply a device adopted by individuals to achieve a fuller realization of individual rights and aspirations. People, by merely combining together, cannot create an entity which has greater constitutional rights and freedoms than they, as individuals, possess. Freedom of association cannot therefore vest independent rights in the group....

Collective bargaining is a group concern, a group activity, but the group can exercise only the constitutional rights of its individual members on behalf of those members. If the right asserted is not found in the *Charter* for the individual, it cannot be implied for the group merely by the fact of association. It follows as well that the rights of the individual members of the group cannot be enlarged merely by the fact of association.

The Scope of Freedom of Association in s. 2(d)

Various theories have been advanced to define freedom of association guaranteed by the Constitution. They range from the very restrictive to the virtually unlimited. To begin with, it has been said that freedom of association is limited to a right to associate with others in common pursuits or for certain purposes. Neither the objects nor the actions of the group are protected by freedom of association. This was the approach adopted in *Collymore v. Attorney-General* ...

[...]

A second approach provides that freedom of association guarantees the collective exercise of constitutional rights or, in other words, the freedom to engage collectively in those activities which are constitutionally protected for each individual. This theory has been adopted in the United States to define the scope of freedom of association under the American Constitution. Professor L.H. Tribe in his treatise, *American Constitutional Law* (1978), describes the American position, as follows ... :

> [Freedom of association] *is a right to join with others to pursue goals independently protected by the first amendment* — such as political advocacy, litigation (regarded as a form of advocacy), or religious worship.

It will be seen that this approach guarantees not only the right to associate but as well the right to pursue those objects of association which by their nature have constitutional protection.

A third approach postulates that freedom of association stands for the principle that an individual is entitled to do in concert with others that which he may lawfully do alone, and conversely, that individuals and organizations have no right to do in concert what is unlawful when done individually ...

A fourth approach would constitutionally protect collective activities which may be said to be fundamental to our culture and traditions and which by common assent are deserving of protection. This approach was proposed by Kerans J.A. in *Black v. Law Society of Alberta* ... The court held in that case that legislative restrictions against partnerships for the practice of law between Alberta solicitors and non-resident solicitors violated freedom of association. Speaking for himself, Kerans J.A. stated ... :

> In my view, the freedom [of association] includes the freedom to associate with others in the exercise of *Charter*-protected rights *and also those other rights which — in Canada — are thought so fundamental as not to need formal expression: to marry, for example, or to establish a home and family, pursue an education or gain a livelihood.* [Emphasis added.]

A fifth approach rests on the proposition that freedom of association, under s. 2(d) of the *Charter*, extends constitutional protection to all activities which are essential to the lawful goals of an association. This approach was advanced in *Re Service Employees'*

International Union, Local 204 and Broadway Manor Nursing Home ... by the Ontario Divisional Court. The court held that freedom of association included the freedom to bargain collectively and to strike, since, in its view, these activities were essential to the objects of a trade union and without them the association would be emasculated ...

The sixth and final approach so far isolated in the cases, and by far the most sweeping, would extend the protection of s. 2(d) of the *Charter* to all acts done in association, subject only to limitation under s. 1 of the *Charter*. This is the position suggested by Bayda C.J.S. in the *Dairyworkers* case.... He said in his reasons for judgment ...:

> To summarize, a person asserting the freedom of association under para. 2(d) is free (apart from s. 1 of the *Charter*) to perform in association without governmental interference any act that he is free to perform alone. *Where an act by definition is incapable of individual performance, he is free to perform the act in association provided the mental component of the act is not to inflict harm* ... [Emphasis added.]

... I would conclude that both the fifth approach (which postulates that freedom of association constitutionally protects all activities which are essential to the lawful goals of an association) and the sixth (which postulates that freedom of association constitutionally protects all activities carried out in association, subject only to reasonable limitation under s. 1 of the *Charter*) are unacceptable definitions of freedom of association.

The fifth approach rejects the individual nature of freedom of association. To accept it would be to accord an independent constitutional status to the aims, purposes, and activities of the association, and thereby confer greater constitutional rights upon members of the association than upon non-members. It would extend *Charter* protection to all the activities of an association which are essential to its lawful objects or goals, but, it would not extend an equivalent right to individuals ...

The sixth approach, in my opinion, must be rejected as well, for the reasons expressed in respect of the fifth ...

I am also of the view that the fourth approach, which postulates that freedom of association embraces those collective activities which have attained a fundamental status in our society because they are deeply rooted in our culture, traditions, and history, is an unacceptable definition. By focusing on the activity or the conduct itself, this fourth approach ignores the fundamental purpose of the right. The purpose of freedom of association is to ensure that various goals may be pursued in common as well as individually. Freedom of association is not concerned with the particular activities or goals themselves; it is concerned with how activities or goals may be pursued ...

Of the remaining approaches, it must surely be accepted that the concept of freedom of association includes at least the right to join with others in lawful, common pursuits and to establish and maintain organizations and associations as set out in the first approach. This is essentially the freedom of association enjoyed prior to the adoption of the *Charter*. It is, I believe, equally clear that, in accordance with the second approach, freedom of association should guarantee the collective exercise of constitutional rights. Individual rights protected by the Constitution do not lose that protection when exercised in common with others. People must be free to engage collectively in those activities which are constitutionally protected for each individual. This second definition of freedom of association embraces the purposes and values of the freedoms which were identified earlier. For instance, the indispensable role played by freedom of association in the democratic process is fully protected by guaranteeing the collective exercise of freedom of expression ...

One enters upon more controversial ground when considering the third approach which provides that whatever action an individual can *lawfully* pursue as an individual, freedom of association ensures he can pursue with others. Conversely, individuals and organizations have no constitutional right to do in concert what is unlawful when done alone. This approach is broader than the second, since constitutional protection attaches to all group acts which can be lawfully performed by an individual, whether or not the individual has a constitutional right to perform them. It is true, of course, that in this approach the range of *Charter*-protected activity could be reduced by legislation, because the Legislature has the power to declare what is and what is not lawful activity for the individual. The Legislature, however, would not be able to attack directly the associational character of the activity, since it would be constitutionally bound to treat groups and individuals alike. A simple example illustrates this point: golf is a lawful but not constitutionally protected activity. Under the third approach, the Legislature could prohibit golf entirely. However, the Legislature could not constitutionally provide that golf could be played in pairs but in no greater number, for this would infringe the *Charter* guarantee of freedom of association. This contrasts with the second approach, which would provide no protection against such legislation, because golf is not a constitutionally protected activity for the individual. Thus, the range of group activity protected by the third approach is greater than that of the second, but the greater range is to some extent illusory because of the power of the Legislature to say what is and what is not lawful activity for the individual. This approach, in my view, is an acceptable interpretation of freedom of association under the *Charter*. It is clear that, unlike the fifth and sixth approaches, this definition of freedom of association does not provide greater constitutional rights for groups than for individuals; it simply ensures that they are treated alike ...

It follows from this discussion that I interpret freedom of association in s. 2(*d*) of the *Charter* to mean that *Charter* protection will attach to the exercise in association of such rights as have *Charter* protection when exercised by the individual. Furthermore, freedom of association means the freedom to associate for the purposes of activities which are lawful when performed alone. But, since the fact of association will not by itself confer additional rights on individuals, the association does not acquire a constitutionally guaranteed freedom to do what is unlawful for the individual.

When this definition of freedom of association is applied, it is clear that it does not guarantee the right to strike. Since the right to strike is not independently protected under the *Charter*, it can receive protection under freedom of association only if it is an activity which is permitted by law to an individual. Accepting this conclusion, the appellants argue that freedom of association must guarantee the right to strike because individuals may lawfully refuse to work. This position, however, is untenable for two reasons. First, it is not correct to say that it is lawful for an individual employee to cease work during the currency of his contract of employment. Belzil J.A., in the Alberta Court of Appeal, in the case at bar, dealt with this point in these words:

... While it is true that the courts will not compel a servant to fulfil his contract of service, the servant is nevertheless bound in law by his contract and may be ordered to pay damages for the unlawful breach of it. It cannot be said that his cessation of work is lawful.

The second reason is simply that there is no analogy whatever between the cessation of work by a single employee and a strike conducted in accordance with modern labour legislation. The individual has, by reason of the cessation of work, either breached or terminated his contract of employment. It is true that the law will not compel the specific performance of the contract by ordering him back to work as this would reduce 'the employee to a state tantamount to slavery' (I. Christie, *Employment Law in Canada* (1980), p. 268). But, this is markedly different from a lawful strike. An employee who ceases work does not contemplate a return to work, while employees on strike always contemplate a return to work. In recognition of this fact, the law does not regard a strike as either a breach of contract or a termination of employment. Every province and the federal Parliament has enacted legislation which preserves the employer-employee relationship during a strike.... Moreover, many statutes provide employees with reinstatement rights following a strike ... and in the province of Quebec the employer is expressly prohibited from replacing employees who are lawfully on strike ...

Modern labour relations legislation has so radically altered the legal relationship between employees and employers in unionized industries that no analogy may be drawn between the lawful actions of individual employees in ceasing to work and the lawful actions of union members in engaging in a strike. As Laskin C.J. stated in *McGavin Toastmaster Ltd. v. Ainscough* ... :

> The reality is, and has been for many years now throughout Canada, that individual relationships as between employer and employee have meaning only at the hiring stage and even then there are qualifications which arise by reason of union security clauses in collective agreements. The common law as it applies to individual employment contracts is no longer relevant to employer-employee relations governed by a collective agreement which, as the one involved here, deals with discharge, termination of employment, severance pay and a host of other matters that have been negotiated between union and company as the principal parties thereto.

It is apparent, in my view, that interpreting freedom of association to mean that every individual is free to do with others that which he is lawfully entitled to do alone would not entail guaranteeing the right to strike ... Restrictions on strikes are not aimed at and do not interfere with the collective or associational character of trade unions. It is therefore my conclusion that the concept of freedom of association does not extend to the constitutional guarantee of a right to strike ...

[...]

Furthermore, it must be recognized that the right to strike accorded by legislation throughout Canada is of relatively recent vintage. It is truly the product of this century and, in its modern form, is in reality the product of the latter half of this century. It cannot be said that it has become so much a part of our social and historical traditions that it has acquired the status of an immutable, fundamental right, firmly embedded in our traditions, our political and social philosophy. There is then no basis, as suggested in the fourth approach to freedom of association, for implying a constitutional right to strike ...

While I have reached a conclusion and expressed the view that the *Charter* upon its face cannot support an implication of a right to strike, there is as well, in my view, a sound reason grounded in social policy against any such implication. Labour law, as we have seen, is a fundamentally important as well as an extremely sensitive subject. It is based upon a political and economic compromise between organized labour—a very powerful socio-economic force—on the one hand, and the employers of labour—an equally powerful socio-economic force—on the other. The balance between the two forces is delicate and the public-at-large depends for its security and welfare upon the maintenance of that balance. One group concedes certain interests in exchange for concessions from the other. There is clearly no correct balance which may be struck giving permanent satisfaction to the two groups, as well as securing the public interest. The whole process is inherently dynamic and unstable. Care must be taken then in considering whether constitutional protection should be given to one aspect of this dynamic and evolving process while leaving the others subject to the social pressures of the day.... To intervene in that dynamic process at this early stage of *Charter* development by implying constitutional protection for a right to strike would, in my view, give to one of the contending forces an economic weapon removed from and made immune, subject to s. 1, to legislative control which could go far towards freezing the development of labour relations and curtailing that process of evolution necessary to meet the changing circumstances of a modern society in a modern world....

To constitutionalize a particular feature of labour relations by entrenching a right to strike would have other adverse effects. Our experience with labour relations has shown that the courts, as a general rule, are not the best arbiters of disputes which arise from time to time. Labour legislation has recognized this fact and has created other procedures and other tribunals for the more expeditious and efficient settlement of labour problems. Problems arising in labour matters frequently involve more than legal questions. Political, social, and economic questions frequently dominate in labour disputes. The legislative creation of conciliation officers, conciliation boards, labour relations boards, and labour dispute-resolving tribunals, has gone far in meeting needs not attainable in the court system. The nature of labour disputes and grievances and the other problems arising in labour matters dictates that special procedures outside the ordinary court system must be employed in their resolution. Judges do not have the expert knowledge always helpful and sometimes necessary in the resolution of labour problems. The courts will generally not be furnished in labour cases, if past experience is to guide us, with an evidentiary base upon which full resolution of the dispute may be made. In my view, it is scarcely contested that specialized labour tribunals are better suited than courts for resolving labour problems, except for the resolution of purely legal questions. If the right to strike is constitutionalized, then its application, its extent, and any questions of its legality, become matters of law. This would inevitably throw the courts back into the field of labour relations and much of the value of specialized labour tribunals would be lost ...

A further problem will arise from constitutionalizing the right to strike. In every case where a strike occurs and relief is sought in the courts, the question of the application of

s. 1 of the *Charter* may be raised to determine whether some attempt to control the right may be permitted. This has occurred in the case at bar. The section 1 inquiry involves the reconsideration by a court of the balance struck by the Legislature in the development of labour policy. The court is called upon to determine, as a matter of constitutional law, which government services are essential and whether the alternative of arbitration is adequate compensation for the loss of a right to strike. In the *PSAC* case, the Court must decide whether mere postponement of collective bargaining is a reasonable limit, given the Government's substantial interest in reducing inflation and the growth in government expenses. In the *Dairy Workers'* case, the Court is asked to decide whether the harm caused to dairy farmers through a closure of the dairies is of sufficient importance to justify prohibiting strike action and lockouts. None of these issues is amenable to principled resolution. There are no clearly correct answers to these questions. They are of a nature peculiarly apposite to the functions of the Legislature. However, if the right to strike is found in the *Charter*, it will be the courts which time and time again will have to resolve these questions, relying only on the evidence and arguments presented by the parties, despite the social implications of each decision. This is a legislative function into which the courts should not intrude. It has been said that the courts, because of the *Charter*, will have to enter the legislative sphere. Where rights are specifically guaranteed in the *Charter*, this may on occasion be true. But where no specific right is found in the *Charter* and the only support for its constitutional guarantee is an implication, the courts should refrain from intrusion into the field of legislation. That is the function of the freely-elected Legislatures and Parliament.

I would, therefore, dismiss the appeal...

[Chief Justice Dickson delivered the reasons why he and Wilson J were dissenting. That dissent included the following discussion of the link between freedom of association and the right to strike in international law, and the relevance of that link to interpretation of the *Charter*.]

DICKSON C.J.C. (dissenting): ...

Four important jurisprudential sources warrant review. First, an extensive jurisprudence has developed in Canada on the scope of constitutional protection of freedom of association. Second, the Judicial Committee of the Privy Council has addressed the issue. Third, there are a number of United States cases on freedom of association, some of which have been decided in respect to labour relations. And, fourth, freedom of association in the labour relations context has received considerable attention under international law. ...

In assessing the relevant authorities, it is important to keep three considerations in mind. First, are trade unions accorded any constitutional protection at all?

Second, what approach is taken to the nature of freedom of association? More specifically, has the relevant tribunal adopted what I shall refer to as a "constitutive" definition of freedom of association whereby freedom of association entails simply the freedom to combine together but does not extend to the freedom to engage in the activities for which the association was formed? Alternatively, has a wider definition been adopted to the effect that freedom of association embodies both the freedom to join together *and* the freedom to pursue collective activities? In this appeal, the respondent adopts the former view while the appellants adopt the latter.

Third, if the wider definition is adopted, what is the scope of activities protected? Not all activities in pursuit of a collective purpose are constitutionally shielded simply by virtue of the fact that they are done in association. The constitutional principle informing the appropriate scope of freedom of association, therefore, must be examined to uncover the limitations imposed in different jurisdictions on associational freedom.

[After surveying the decisions of the Privy Council and Canadian and US courts, Dickson J turned to a consideration of international law authorities.]

International law provides a fertile source of insight into the nature and scope of the freedom of association of workers. Since the close of the Second World War, the protection of the fundamental rights and freedoms of groups and individuals has become a matter of international concern. A body of treaties (or conventions) and customary norms now constitutes an international law of human rights under which the nations of the world have undertaken to adhere to the standards and principles necessary for ensuring freedom, dignity and social justice for their citizens. The *Charter* conforms to the spirit of this contemporary international human rights movement, and it incorporates many of the policies and prescriptions of the various international documents pertaining to human rights. The various sources of international human rights law—declarations, covenants, conventions, judicial and quasi-judicial decisions of international tribunals, customary norms—must, in my opinion, be relevant and persuasive sources for interpretation of the *Charter*'s provisions.

In particular, the similarity between the policies and provisions of the *Charter* and those of international human rights documents attaches considerable relevance to interpretations of those documents by adjudicative bodies, in much the same way that decisions of the United States courts under the *Bill of Rights*, or decisions of the courts of other jurisdictions are relevant and may be persuasive. The relevance of these documents in *Charter* interpretation extends beyond the standards developed by adjudicative bodies under the documents to the documents themselves. As the Canadian judiciary approaches the often general and open textured language of the *Charter*, "the more detailed textual provisions of the treaties may aid in supplying content to such imprecise concepts as the right to life, freedom of association, and even the right to counsel." J. Claydon, "International Human Rights Law and the Interpretation of the *Canadian Charter of Rights and Freedoms*" (1982), 4 Supreme Court L.R. 287, at p. 293.

Furthermore, Canada is a party to a number of international human rights Conventions which contain provisions similar or identical to those in the *Charter*.... The general principles of constitutional interpretation require that these international obligations be a relevant and persuasive factor in *Charter* interpretation.... I believe that the *Charter* should generally be presumed to provide protection at least as great as that afforded by similar provisions in international human rights documents which Canada has ratified.

In short, though I do not believe the judiciary is bound by the norms of international law in interpreting the *Charter*, these norms provide a relevant and persuasive source for interpretation of the provisions of the *Charter*, especially when they arise out of Canada's international obligations under human rights conventions.

(a) The United Nations Covenants on Human Rights

[Chief Justice of Canada Dickson discussed the relevant United Nations declarations, principally the *Declaration of Human Rights*, as well as the *International Covenant on Civil and Political Rights* and the *International Covenant on Economic, Social and Cultural Rights*. Article 8 of the latter covenant guarantees the right to join a trade union with no restrictions other than those necessary for public order or national security, and guarantees the right of unions to strike "provided that it is exercised in conformity with the laws of the particular country."]

... This qualification that the right must be exercised in conformity with domestic law does not, in my view, allow for legislative abrogation of the right though it would appear to allow for regulation of the right: see *Re Alberta Union of Provincial Employees et al. and the Crown in Right of Alberta* (1980), 120 D.L.R. (3d) 590 (Alta. Q.B.) at p. 597 ...

[Chief Justice of Canada Dickson then discussed article 22 of the *Covenant on Civil and Political Rights*, which guarantees the right to freedom of association, including the right to join a trade union, with the same limitations as in article 8 of the *Covenant on Economic, Social and Cultural Rights*.]

[...]

(b) International Labour Organization (I.L.O.) *Convention No. 87*

As a specialized agency of the United Nations, with representatives of labour, management, and government, the I.L.O. is concerned with safeguarding fair and humane conditions of employment. In the present appeal, it is important to consider the *Convention (No. 87) Concerning Freedom of Association and Protection of the Right to Organize*, 67 U.N.T.S. 18 (1948), which was ratified by Canada in 1972 ...

[Chief Justice Dickson listed the various rights protected by ILO *Convention 87*, including the right of workers to organize, draft their own rules, call their own elections, and affiliate with international organizations. The convention also states that unions cannot be dissolved by national administrative agencies. However, the Convention calls for unions to only exercise their rights pursuant to the "laws of the land" (provided those laws are fair).]

These provisions have been interpreted by various I.L.O. bodies ...

[...]

The general principle to emerge from interpretations of *Convention No. 87* by these decision-making bodies is that freedom to form and organize unions, even in the public sector, must include freedom to pursue the essential activities of unions, such as collective bargaining and strikes, subject to reasonable limits ... The [ILO] Committee of Experts has ... pointed out that prohibitions on the right to strike may, unless certain conditions are met, violate *Convention No. 87*:

> In the opinion of the Committee, the principle whereby the right to strike may be limited or prohibited in the public service or in essential services, whether public, semi-public or

private, would become meaningless if the legislation defined the public service or essential services too broadly. As the Committee has already mentioned in previous general surveys, the prohibition should be confined to public servants acting in their capacity as agents of the public authority or to services whose interruption would endanger the life, personal safety or health of the whole or part of the population. Moreover, if strikes are restricted or prohibited in the public service or in essential services, appropriate guarantees must be afforded to protect workers who are thus denied one of the essential means of defending their occupational interests. Restrictions should be offset by adequate impartial and speedy conciliation and arbitration procedures, in which the parties concerned can take part at every stage and in which the awards should in all cases be binding on both parties. Such awards, once rendered, should be rapidly and fully implemented.

(*Freedom of Association and Collective Bargaining: General Survey by the Committee of Experts on the Application of Conventions and Recommendations*, Report III (Part 4(B)), International Labour Conference, 69th Session, Geneva, International Labour Office, 1983, at p. 66.)

[...]
These principles were recently applied in relation to a number of complaints originating in Canada, in particular, in Alberta, Ontario and Newfoundland. A number of the provisions impugned as being in violation of *Convention No. 87* are the subject of this Reference. It is helpful, in the present context, to look at the Freedom of Association Committee's conclusions and recommendations on the provisions relating to prohibitions on strike activity. These conclusions and recommendations were approved unanimously by the I.L.O.'s Governing Body.

The complaint (Case No. 1247) was launched by the Canadian Labour Congress on behalf of the Alberta Union of Provincial Employees against the Government of Canada (Alberta). In discussing s. 93 of the *Public Service Act*, which bans strike activity of provincial government employees, the Committee summarized the principles applicable to complaints about infringements of *Convention No. 87* as follows:

> 131. The Committee recalls that it has been called to examine the strike ban in a previous case submitted against the Government of Canada/Alberta (Case No. 893, most recently examined in the 204th Report, paras. 121 to 134, approved by the Governing Body at its 214th Session (November 1980). In that case the Committee recalled that the right to strike, recognised as deriving from Article 3 of the Convention, is an essential means by which workers may defend their occupational interests. It also recalled that, if limitations on strike action are to be applied by legislation, a distinction should be made between publicly-owned undertakings which are genuinely essential, i.e. those which supply services whose interruption would endanger the life, personal safety or health of the whole or part of the population, and those which are not essential in the strict sense of the term. The Governing Body, on the Committee's recommendation, drew the attention of the Government to this principle and suggested to the Government that it consider the possibility of introducing an amendment to the Public Service Employee Relations Act in order to confine the prohibition of strikes to services which are essential in the strict sense of the term. In the present case, the Committee would again draw attention to its previous conclusions on section 93 of the Act.

(*I.L.O Official Bulletin*, vol. LXVIII, Series B, No. 3, 1985, pp. 34–35.)
[...]

(c) Summary of International Law

The most salient feature of the human rights documents discussed above in the context of this case is the close relationship in each of them between the concept of freedom of association and the organization and activities of labour unions. As a party to these human rights documents, Canada is cognizant of the importance of freedom of association to trade unionism, and has undertaken as a binding international obligation to protect to some extent the associational freedoms of workers within Canada. Both of the U.N. human rights Covenants contain explicit protection of the formation and activities of trade unions subject to reasonable limits. Moreover, there is a clear consensus amongst the I.L.O. adjudicative bodies that *Convention No. 87* goes beyond merely protecting the formation of labour unions and provides protection of their essential activities—that is of collective bargaining and the freedom to strike....

I am satisfied, in sum, that whether or not freedom of association generally extends to protecting associational activity for the pursuit of exclusively pecuniary ends—a question on which I express no opinion—collective bargaining protects important employee interests which cannot be characterized as merely pecuniary in nature. Under our existing system of industrial relations, effective constitutional protection of the associational interests of employees in the collective bargaining process requires concomitant protection of their freedom to withdraw collectively their services, subject to s. 1 of the *Charter*.
[...]

All three enactments prohibit strikes and, as earlier stated, define a strike as a cessation of work or refusal to work by two or more persons acting in combination or in concert or in accordance with a common understanding. What is precluded is a collective refusal to work at the conclusion of a collective agreement. There can be no doubt that the legislation is aimed at foreclosing a particular collective activity because of its associational nature. The very nature of a strike, and its *raison d'être*, is to influence an employer by joint action which would be ineffective if it were carried out by an individual.... It is precisely the individual's interest in joining and acting with others to maximize his or her potential that is protected by s. 2(*d*) of the *Charter*....

These provisions directly abridge the freedom of employees to strike and thereby infringe the guarantee of freedom of association in s. 2(*d*) of the *Charter*.
[...]

2. The Meaning of s. 2(*d*)

At the outset, it should be noted that, contrary to submissions by the respondent and some of the interveners in support, the purpose of s. 2 of the *Charter* must extend beyond merely protecting rights which already existed at the time of the *Charter*'s entrenchment. This point was made clear in *Big M Drug Mart Ltd*.... In that case the appellant submitted that "freedom of religion" in the *Charter* had the same meaning as that given it by this court under the Canadian Bill of Rights in *Robertson v. The Queen*, [1963] S.C.R. 651. The court rejected this argument (pp. 342–44):

CHAPTER 12: THE CONSTITUTIONALIZATION OF COLLECTIVE BARGAINING LAW

> The basis of the majority's interpretation in *Robertson and Rosetanni* ... is the fact that the language of the *Canadian Bill of Rights* is merely declaratory: by s. 1 of the *Canadian Bill of Rights*, certain existing freedoms are "recognized and declared", including freedom of religion....
>
> It is not necessary to reopen the issue of the meaning of freedom of religion under the *Canadian Bill of Rights*, because whatever the situation under that document, it is certain that the *Canadian Charter of Rights and Freedoms* does not simply "recognize and declare" existing rights as they were circumscribed by legislation current at the time of the *Charter's* entrenchment. The language of the *Charter* is imperative. It avoids any reference to existing or continuing rights.... I agree with the submission of the respondent that the *Charter* is intended to set a standard upon which present as well as future legislation is to be tested. Therefore the meaning of the concept of freedom of conscience and religion is not to be determined solely by the degree to which that right was enjoyed by Canadians prior to the proclamation of the *Charter*.

It is clear from *Big M Drug Mart Ltd.* that the meaning of a provision of the *Charter* is not to be determined solely on the basis of pre-existing rights or freedoms. In the present appeal, therefore, whether or not a right or freedom to strike existed prior to the *Charter*, by virtue of the common law or otherwise, is not determinative of the meaning of s. 2(d) of the *Charter*.

Similarly, the scope of the *Charter's* provisions is not to be confined by the fact of legislative regulation in a particular subject area. In argument, counsel for the respondent seemed to suggest that if freedom of association were interpreted to include strike activity, this would "constitutionalize" a statutory right. His argument appeared to be premised on the proposition that, because the "right to strike" was a subject of legislative regulation prior to the *Charter's* entrenchment, it followed that strike activity could not be a matter for constitutional protection after entrenchment of the *Charter*. While it may be true that the *Charter* was not framed for the purpose of guaranteeing rights conferred by legislative enactment, the view that certain rights and freedoms cannot be protected by the *Charter's* provisions because they are the subject of statutory regulation is premised on a fundamental misconception about the nature of judicial review under a written constitution.

The Constitution is supreme law. Its provisions are not to be circumscribed by what the legislature has done in the past but, rather, the activities of the legislature—past, present and future—must be consistent with the principles set down in the Constitution. As stated in *Ref. re Man. Language Rights*, [1985] 1 S.C.R. 721 at 745:

> The Constitution of a country is a statement of the will of the people to be governed in accordance with certain principles held as fundamental and certain prescriptions restrictive of the powers of the legislature and government. It is, as s. 52 of the *Constitution Act, 1982* declares, the "supreme law" of the nation, unalterable by the normal legislative process, and unsuffering of laws inconsistent with it.

This is not to say, however, that the legislative regulation of collective bargaining and strikes is entirely irrelevant to the manner in which a constitutional freedom to strike may be given effect in particular circumstances: see, on this point, my reasons in the *Dairy Workers* case, released concurrently. But the present case does not involve a challenge to the general labour law of Alberta which permits strike activity, subject to regulation. This appeal concerns the substitution of an entirely different mechanism for resolving labour disputes for particular employees, and one which does not merely regulate the freedom to strike but abrogates it entirely.

One further preliminary consideration deserves mention. Section 2 of the *Charter* protects fundamental "freedoms" as opposed to "rights". Although these two terms are sometimes used interchangeably, a conceptual distinction between the two is often drawn. "Rights" are said to impose a corresponding duty or obligation on another party to ensure the protection of the right in question whereas "freedoms" are said to involve simply an absence of interference or constraint. This conceptual approach to the nature of "freedoms" may be too narrow since it fails to acknowledge situations where the absence of government intervention may in effect substantially impede the enjoyment of fundamental freedoms (e.g., regulations limiting the monopolization of the press may be required to ensure freedom of expression and freedom of the press). Nonetheless, for the purposes of this appeal, we need not determine whether "freedom" may impose affirmative duties on the state, because we are faced with a situation where overt government action in the form of legislation is alleged to interfere with the exercise of freedom of association. We are not concerned in this case with any request for affirmative state action.

A wide variety of alternative interpretations of freedom of association has been advanced in the jurisprudence summarized above and in argument before this Court.

At one extreme is a purely constitutive definition whereby freedom of association entails only a freedom to belong to or form an association. On this view, the constitutional guarantee does not extend beyond protecting the individual's status as a member of an association. It would not protect his or her associational actions.

In the trade union context, then, a constitutive definition would find a *prima facie* violation of s. 2(*d*) of the *Charter* in legislation such as s. 2(1) of the *Police Officers Act*, which prohibits membership in any organization affiliated with a trade union. But it could find no violation of s. 2(*d*) in respect of legislation which prohibited a concerted refusal to work. Indeed, a wide variety of trade union activities, ranging from the organization of social activities for its members, to the establishment of union pension plans, to the discussion of collective bargaining strategy, could be prohibited by the state without infringing s. 2(*d*).

The essentially formal nature of a constitutive approach to freedom of association is equally apparent when one considers other types of associational activity in our society. While the constitutive approach might find a possible violation of s. 2(*d*) in a legislative enactment which prohibited marriage for certain classes of people, it would hold inoffensive an enactment which precluded the same people from engaging in the activities integral to a marriage, such as cohabiting and raising children together. If freedom of association only protects the joining together of persons for common purposes, but not the pursuit of the very activities for which the association was formed, then the freedom is indeed legalistic, ungenerous, indeed vapid.

In my view, while it is unquestionable that s. 2(*d*), at a minimum, guarantees the liberty of persons to *be* in association or belong to an organization, it must extend beyond a concern for associational status to give effective protection to the interests to which the constitutional guarantee is directed. In this respect, it is important to consider the purposive approach to constitutional interpretation mandated by this court in *R. v. Big M Drug Mart Ltd.* at p. 344:

> This Court has already, in some measure set out the basic approach to be taken in interpreting the *Charter*. In *Hunter v. Southam Inc.* ... this Court expressed the view that the proper approach to the definition of the rights and freedoms guaranteed by the *Charter* was a purposive one. The meaning of a right or freedom guaranteed by the *Charter* was to be ascertained by an analysis of the *purpose* of such a guarantee; *it was to be understood, in other words, in the light of the interests it was meant to protect.*
>
> In my view this analysis is to be undertaken, and the purpose of the right or freedom in question is to be sought by reference to the character and the larger objects of the *Charter* itself, to the language chosen to articulate the specific right or freedom, to the historical origins of the concepts enshrined, and where applicable, to the meaning and purpose of the other specific rights and freedoms with which it is associated within the text of the *Charter*. The interpretation should be, as the judgment in *Southam* emphasizes, a generous rather than a legalistic one, aimed at fulfilling the purpose of the guarantee and securing for individuals the full benefit of the *Charter's protection*. At the same time it is important not to overshoot the actual purpose of the right or freedom in question, but to recall that the *Charter* was not enacted in a vacuum, and must therefore, as this Court's decision in *Law Society of Upper Canada v. Skapinker* ... illustrates, be placed in its proper linguistic, philosophic and historical contexts. [Emphasis added.]

A second approach, the derivative approach, prevalent in the United States, embodies a somewhat more generous definition of freedom of association than the formal, constitutive approach. In the Canadian context, it is suggested by some that associational action which relates specifically to one of the other freedoms enumerated in s. 2 is constitutionally protected, but other associational activity is not.

I am unable, however, to accept that freedom of association should be interpreted so restrictively. Section 2(d) of the *Charter* provides an explicit and independent guarantee of freedom of association. In this respect it stands in marked contrast to the First Amendment to the American Constitution. The derivative approach would, in my view, largely make surplusage of s. 2(d). The associational or collective dimensions of s. 2(a) and (b) have already been recognized by this court in *R. v. Big M Drug Mart Ltd.* ... without resort to s. 2(d). The associational aspect of s. 2(c) clearly finds adequate protection in the very expression of a freedom of peaceful assembly. What is to be learnt from the United States jurisprudence is not that freedom of association must be restricted to associational activities involving independent constitutional rights but, rather, that the express conferral of a freedom of association is unnecessary if all that is intended is to give effect to the collective enjoyment of other individual freedoms.

I am also unimpressed with the argument that the inclusion of s. 2(d) with freedoms of a "political" nature requires a narrow or restrictive interpretation of freedom of association. I am unable to regard s. 2 as embodying purely political freedoms. Paragraph (a), which protects freedom of conscience and religion, is quite clearly not exclusively political in nature. It would, moreover, be unsatisfactory to overlook our Constitution's history of giving special recognition to collectivities or communities of interest other than the government and political parties. Sections 93 and 133 of the *Constitution Act, 1867*, and ss. 16–24, 25, 27 and 29 of the *Charter*, dealing variously with denominational schools, language rights, aboriginal rights and our multicultural heritage, implicitly embody an awareness of the importance of various collectivities in the pursuit of educational, linguistic, cultural and social as well as political ends. Just as the individual is incapable of resisting political domination without the support of persons with similar values, so too is he or she, in isolation, incapable of resisting domination, over the long term, in many other aspects of life.

Freedom of association is protected in s. 2(*d*) under the rubric of "fundamental" freedoms. In my view, the "fundamental" nature of freedom of association relates to the central importance to the individual of his or her interaction with fellow human beings. The purpose of the constitutional guarantee of freedom of association is, I believe, to recognize the profoundly social nature of human endeavours and to protect the individual from state-enforced isolation in the pursuit of his or her ends. In the famous words of Alexis de Tocqueville in *Democracy in America*, vol. 1, P. Bradley ed. (1945), at p. 196:

> The most natural privilege of man, next to the right of acting for himself, is that of combining his exertions with those of his fellow creatures and of acting in common with them. The right of association therefore appears ... almost as inalienable in its nature as the right of personal liberty. No legislator can attack it without impairing the foundations of society.

As social beings, our freedom to act with others is a primary condition of community life, human progress and civilized society. Through association, individuals have been able to participate in determining and controlling the immediate circumstances of their lives and the rules, mores and principles which govern the communities in which they live. As John Stuart Mill stated, "if public spirit, generous sentiments, or true justice and equality are desired, association, not isolation, of interests, is the school in which these excellences are nurtured" (*Principles of Political Economy*, Appleton (1893), vol. 2, at p. 352).

Freedom of association is most essential in those circumstances where the individual is liable to be prejudiced by the actions of some larger and more powerful entity, like the government or an employer. Association has always been the means through which political, cultural and racial minorities, religious groups and workers have sought to attain their purposes and fulfil their aspirations; it has enabled those who would otherwise be vulnerable and ineffective to meet on more equal terms the power and strength of those with whom their interests interact and, perhaps, conflict. Emerson, "Freedom of Association and Freedom of Expression" (1964), 74 *Yale L.J.* 1, at p. 1, states that:

> More and more the individual, in order to realize his own capacities or to stand up to the institutionalized forces that surround him, has found it imperative to join with others of like mind in pursuit of common objectives.

What freedom of association seeks to protect is not associational activities qua particular activities, but the freedom of individuals to interact with, support and be supported by their fellow humans in the varied activities in which they choose to engage. But this is not an unlimited constitutional licence for all group activity. The mere fact that an activity is capable of being carried out by several people together, as well as individually, does not mean that the activity acquires constitutional protection from legislative prohibition or regulation.

I believe that Bayda C.J.S. was right in holding that s. 2(d) normally embraces the liberty to do collectively that which one is permitted to do as an individual, a proposition which one American writer, Reena Raggi, perceives to be the cornerstone of freedom of association:

> The basic principle for which recognition will be sought in the formulation of an independent constitutional right of association is that whatever action a person can pursue as an individual, freedom of association must ensure he can pursue with others. Only such a principle assures man that, in his struggle to be independent of government control, he will not be crippled simply because on occasion he strives to achieve that independence with the help of others.
>
> ("An Independent Right to Freedom of Association" (1977), 12 *Harv. C.R.-C.L.L. Rev.* 1, at p. 15.)

However, it is not in my view correct to regard this proposition as the exclusive touchstone for determining the presence or absence of a violation of s. 2(d). Certainly, if a legislature permits an individual to enjoy an activity which it forecloses to a collectivity, it may properly be inferred that the legislature intended to prohibit the collective activity because of its collective or associational aspect. Conversely, one may infer from a legislative proscription which applies equally to individuals and groups that the purpose of the legislation was a bona fide prohibition of a particular activity because of detrimental qualities inhering in the activity (e.g., criminal conduct), and not merely because of the fact that the activity might sometimes be done in association. The proposition articulated by Chief Justice Bayda is therefore a useful test of legislative purpose in some circumstances. There will, however, be occasions when no analogy involving individuals can be found for associational activity, or when a comparison between groups and individuals fails to capture the essence of a possible violation of associational rights. This is precisely the situation in this case. There is no individual equivalent to a strike. The refusal to work by one individual does not parallel a collective refusal to work. The latter is *qualitatively* rather than quantitatively different. The overarching consideration remains whether a legislative enactment or administrative action interferes with the freedom of persons to join and act with others in common pursuits. The legislative purpose which will render legislation invalid is the attempt to preclude associational conduct because of its concerted or associational nature.

I wish to refer to one further concern. It has been suggested that associational activity for the pursuit of economic ends should not be accorded constitutional protection. If by this it is meant that something as fundamental as a person's livelihood or dignity in the workplace is beyond the scope of constitutional protection, I cannot agree. If, on the other hand, it is meant that concerns of an exclusively pecuniary nature are excluded from such protection, such an argument would merit careful consideration. In the present case, however, we are concerned with interests which go far beyond those of a merely pecuniary nature.

Work is one of the most fundamental aspects in a person's life, providing the individual with a means of financial support and, as importantly, a contributory role in society.

A person's employment is an essential component of his or her sense of identity, self-worth and emotional well-being. Accordingly, the conditions in which a person works are highly significant in shaping the whole compendium of psychological, emotional and physical elements of a person's dignity and self-respect. In exploring the personal meaning of employment, Professor D.M. Beatty, in his article "Labour is not a Commodity" in Reiter and Swan (eds.), *Studies in Contract Law* (1980), has described it as follows, at p. 324:

> As a vehicle which admits a person to the status of a contributing, productive, member of society, employment is seen as providing recognition of the individual's being engaged in something worthwhile. It gives the individual a sense of significance. By realizing our capabilities and contributing in ways society determines to be useful, employment comes to represent the means by which most members of our community can lay claim to an equal right of respect and of concern from others. It is this institution through which most of us secure much of our self-respect and self-esteem.

The role of association has always been vital as a means of protecting the essential needs and interests of working people. Throughout history, workers have associated to overcome their vulnerability as individuals to the strength of their employers. The capacity to bargain collectively has long been recognized as one of the integral and primary functions of associations of working people. While trade unions also fulfil other important social, political and charitable functions, collective bargaining remains vital to the capacity of individual employees to participate in ensuring fair wages, health and safety protections and equitable and humane working conditions. As Professor Paul Weiler explains in *Reconcilable Differences: New Directions in Canadian Labour Law* (1980), at p. 31:

> An apt way of putting it is to say that good collective bargaining tries to subject the employment relationship and the work environment to the "rule of law". Many theorists of industrial relations believe that this function of protecting the employee from the abuse of managerial power, thereby enhancing the dignity of the worker as a person, is the primary value of collective bargaining, one which entitles the institution to positive encouragement from the law.

Professor Weiler goes on to characterize collective bargaining as "intrinsically valuable as an experience in self-government" (p. 33), and writes at p. 32:

> ... collective bargaining is the most significant occasion upon which most of these workers ever participate in making social decisions about matters that are salient to their daily lives. That is the essence of collective bargaining.

A similar rationale for endorsing collective bargaining was advanced in the *Woods Task Force Report on Canadian Industrial Relations* (1968), at p. 96:

> One of the most cherished hopes of those who originally championed the concept of collective bargaining was that it would introduce into the work place some of the basic features of the political democracy that was becoming the hallmark of most of the western world. Traditionally referred to as industrial democracy, it can be described as the substitution of the rule of law for the rule of men in the work place.

Closely related to collective bargaining, at least in our existing industrial relations context, is the freedom to strike. Professor Carrothers, *Collective Bargaining Law in Canada*, 1st ed. (1965), describes the requisites of an effective system of collective bargaining as follows at pp. 3–4:

> What are the requirements of an effective system of collective bargaining? From the point of view of employees, such a system requires that they be free to engage in three kinds of activity: to form themselves into associations, to engage employers in bargaining with the associations, and to invoke meaningful economic sanctions in support of the bargaining.

The Woods Task Force Report at p. 129 identifies the work stoppage as the essential ingredient in collective bargaining:

> Strikes and lockouts are an indispensable part of the Canadian industrial relations system and are likely to remain so in our present socio-economic-political society.

At p. 138 the Report continues:

> Collective bargaining is the mechanism through which labour and management seek to accommodate their differences, frequently without strife, sometimes through it, and occasionally without success. As imperfect an instrument as it may be, there is no viable substitute in a free society.

At p. 175 the Report notes that the acceptance of collective bargaining carries with it a recognition of the right to invoke the economic sanction of the strike. And at p. 176 it is said, "the strike has become a part of the whole democratic system".

The importance to collective bargaining of the ultimate threat of a strike has also been recognized in the cases. Lord Wright noted in *Crofter Hand Woven Harris Tweed Co. v. Veitch*, [1942] A.C. 435, [1942] 1 All E.R. 142 at 158 -59 (H.L.), "The right of workmen to strike is an essential element in the principle of collective bargaining." As the editors of *Kahn-Freund's Labour and the Law*, 3rd ed. (1983), point out in respect of this comment: "If the workers could not, in the last resort, collectively refuse to work, they could not bargain collectively" (at p. 292). See also *Broadway Manor*; *Dairy Workers* case; *Blount*, per Wright J. The necessity and lawfulness of strikes has also been acknowledged by this court: *Perrault v. Gauthier* (1898), 28 S.C.R. 241 at 256 [Que.]; *C.P.R. v. Zambri*, [1962] S.C.R. 609 at 618 and 621.

I am satisfied, in sum, that whether or not freedom of association generally extends to protecting associational activity for the pursuit of exclusively pecuniary ends—a question on which I express no opinion—collective bargaining protects important employee interests which cannot be characterized as merely pecuniary in nature. Under our existing system of industrial relations, effective constitutional protection of the associational interests of employees in the collective bargaining process requires concomitant protection of their freedom to withdraw collectively their services, subject to s. 1 of the *Charter*.

3. Application to the Alberta Legislation

All three enactments prohibit strikes and, as earlier stated, define a strike as a cessation of work or refusal to work by two or more persons acting in combination or in concert or in accordance with a common understanding. What is precluded is a collective refusal to work at the conclusion of a collective agreement. There can be no doubt that the legislation is aimed at foreclosing a particular collective activity because of its associational nature. The very nature of a strike, and its *raison d'être*, is to influence an employer by joint action which would be ineffective if it were carried out by an individual. Professor Harry Arthurs refers, correctly in my respectful opinion, to the "notion of collective action" as "the critical factor" in the definition of "strike": "The Right to Strike in Ontario and the Common Law Provinces of Canada" (1967), Proceedings of the *Fourth International Symposium on Comparative Law*, University of Ottawa, at p. 187. It is precisely the individual's interest in joining and acting with others to maximize his or her potential that is protected by s. 2(d) of the *Charter*.

[Chief Justice Dickson then considered whether the legislation could be justified under section 1 of the *Charter*. He concluded that it could not, because the legislation covered workers who did not perform essential services, because it excluded some matters from arbitration without sufficient reason, and because the employees did not have recourse to arbitration as of right.]

12:220 The Second Trilogy (2001–2011): *Dunmore, Health Services*, and *Fraser*

It was clear after the 1987 Trilogy that there was no constitutional protection of the right to strike. The somewhat less clear idea that the guarantee of freedom of association did not include the right to bargain collectively was affirmed by the Supreme Court of Canada in *Dunmore*.

At the same time, the judgment of the majority of the Supreme Court of Canada in *Dunmore* began a movement away from the approach in the 1987 Trilogy. For example, the Court in *Dunmore* distanced itself from the idea that freedom of association as set out in the *Charter* only protects the collective exercise of activities that can legally be carried out by an individual, and toward the idea that freedom of association can protect some aspects of employee organizing activity that are "inherently collective." *Dunmore* also represents a clear move toward another view expressed in Dickson CJC's dissent in the *Alberta Reference* case to the effect that s 2(d) should be interpreted with an eye to the meaning that it had acquired in international jurisprudence. These ideas turn out to have a powerful influence in later cases. Are they good ideas?

We begin with a brief excerpt from the lower court judgment, which provides helpful background regarding the case:

Dunmore v Ontario (Attorney General), 37 OR (3d) 287, 1997 CanLII 16229 (SCJ)

Sharpe J.:

[...]

The first legislation in Ontario creating a framework for the establishment of trade unions and collective bargaining was enacted in 1943: An Act to Provide for Collective Bargaining, S.O. 1943, c. 4. That Act, modelled on the American National Labor Relations Act ("Wagner Act"), contained a list of excluded classes, including "domestic servants", "members of any police force", certain other public employees, and "the industry of farming": s. 24. Although the statutory framework has changed, the exclusion of those engaged in agricultural work has continued to this day, with the exception of one brief period from June 23, 1994 to November 10, 1995. During that time, the union activities and collective bargaining rights of agricultural workers were governed by the Agricultural Labour Relations Act, 1994, S.O. 1994, c. 6, ("ALRA"), an initiative of the New Democratic Party government.... Agricultural workers were given the right to organize and bargain collectively. The Act did, however, recognize certain special characteristics of the agricultural sector and prohibited strikes and lockouts, substituting in their place a dispute resolution process, the final stage of which was binding final offer selection by an arbitration board.

The ALRA was repealed by the newly elected Progressive Conservative Government in 1995: Labour Relations and Employment Statute Law Amendment Act, S.O. 1995, c. 1 ("LRESLAA"). LRESLAA not only repealed ALRA but also provided that any agreements certified under ALRA were terminated, as were any certification rights of trade unions. LRESLAA did, however, prohibit employers from reprisals against workers on account of union activity under ALRA. The net effect of LRESLAA was to subject agricultural workers to the exclusion clause in the Labour Relations Act, 1995, S.O. 1995, c. 1 ("LRA"), s. 3(b) of which provides as follows:

3. This Act does not apply,

...

(b) to a person employed in agriculture, hunting or trapping;

The legislative record is unclear as to why agricultural workers were excluded when collective bargaining was first introduced in Ontario in 1943. As already noted, early Ontario legislation followed the pattern established by the U.S. Wagner Act which contained a similar exclusion. Expert evidence relied on by the applicants suggests that at the time the Wagner Act became law, agricultural workers lacked political representation while the farm lobby was powerful. In the southern states, where the issue was of particular interest and importance, the majority of agricultural workers were black.

In recent times, two principal reasons have been offered, both of which are said to flow from fundamental aspects of the farm industry, and both of which are relied upon by the Attorney General in resisting the applicants' claim. First is the seasonal nature of farming, the perishable nature of the product and the need for uninterrupted husbandry of crops and livestock....

The second factor is that most farms are owned and operated by family units. There is a perception, widely accepted in the farming community, that a collective bargaining regime would be incompatible with the effective operation of the family farm. Indeed, at the time of ALRA's enactment, even organized labour took the position that its main target were the larger "factory farm" production units and that it was unlikely that any significant effort would be made to organize workers on family farms. That position was reiterated by the applicants before this court.

The current government, having a very different perspective from that of its predecessor on appropriate economic and labour policy, considers farm production to be incompatible with a regime which accords agricultural workers collective bargaining rights. It rejects the contention that strikes and lockouts could be replaced with binding, final offer selection arbitration and places particular emphasis on the perception that collective bargaining is incompatible with the family farm.

The affidavit evidence filed in support of the application is to the effect that agricultural workers have been widely considered to be among Canada's "most economically exploited and politically neutralized individuals". The denial of statutory collective bargaining rights for agricultural workers, particularly for workers employed in factory-style operations, has been the subject of commentary and criticism. The 1968 federal study Canadian Industrial Relations: Report of the Task Force on Labour Relations stated that the exclusion of agricultural workers from collective bargaining was unjustified. Several labour law scholars have reached a similar conclusion: see Neilson and Christie, "The Agricultural Labourer in Canada: A Legal Point of View" (1975-76), 2 Dal. L.J. 330; Adams, Canadian Labour Law, 2nd ed. (Aurora, Ont.: Canada Law Book, 1996) at p. 6–50; Labour Law: Cases, Materials and Commentary, 5th ed. (Industrial Relations Centre, Queens University) at p. 230; Beatty, Putting the *Charter to Work: Designing a Constitutional Labour Code* (McGill-Queen's, 1987) at pp. 91–92. Most Canadian provinces now include agricultural workers in their labour law regimes; only Alberta and Ontario exclude them.

Dunmore v Ontario (Attorney General), 2001 SCC 94

BASTARACHE J. (McLachlin C.J., Gonthier, Iacobucci, Binnie, Arbour, and LeBel JJ. concurring):

1 This appeal concerns the exclusion of agricultural workers from Ontario's statutory labour relations regime. The appellants, individual farm workers and union organizers, challenge the exclusion as a violation of their freedom of association and equality rights under the *Canadian Charter of Rights and Freedoms*. In particular, they argue that the *Labour Relations and Employment Statute Law Amendment Act, 1995*, S.O. 1995, c. 1 ("*LRESLAA*"), combined with s. 3(*b*) of the Ontario *Labour Relations Act, 1995*, S.O. 1995, c. 1, Sched. A ("*LRA*"), prevents them from establishing, joining and participating in the lawful activities of a trade union. In addition, they claim that the *LRESLAA* and the *LRA* violate their equality rights under s. 15(1) of the *Charter* by denying them a statutory protection enjoyed by most occupational groups in Ontario.

[...]

VI. ANALYSIS

A. Freedom of Association

(1) Nature of the Claim

12 ... [T]he appellants direct their attack not at legislation restricting collective bargaining *per se*, but at legislation restricting the "wider ambit of union purposes and activities."

13 In order to establish a violation of s. 2(*d*), the appellants must demonstrate, first, that such activities fall within the range of activities protected by s. 2(*d*) of the *Charter*,

and second, that the impugned legislation has, either in purpose or effect, interfered with these activities...

(2) Scope of Section 2(d)

(a) General Framework

14 The scope of s. 2(d) was first decided by this Court in a landmark trilogy of labour cases, all of which concerned the right to strike (see *Reference re Public Service Employee Relations Act (Alta.)* ... ("*Alberta Reference*"); *PSAC v. Canada* ...; *RWDSU v. Saskatchewan* ... In the *Alberta Reference*, McIntyre J. . . . stressed the double-edged nature of freedom of association, holding that "while [freedom of association] advances many group interests and, of course, cannot be exercised alone, it is nonetheless a freedom belonging to the individual and not to the group formed through its exercise" ... On the basis of this principle, McIntyre J. confined s. 2(d) to three elements ... These three elements of freedom of association are summarized, along with a crucial fourth principle, in the oft-quoted words of Sopinka J. in *Professional Institute of the Public Service of Canada v. Northwest Territories (Commissioner)* ... ("*PIPSC*"):

> Upon considering the various judgments in the *Alberta Reference*, I have come to the view that four separate propositions concerning the coverage of the s. 2(d) guarantee of freedom of association emerge from the case: first, that s. 2(d) *protects the freedom to establish, belong to and maintain an association*; second, that s. 2(d) *does not protect an activity solely on the ground that the activity is a foundational or essential purpose of an association*; third, that s. 2(d) *protects the exercise in association of the constitutional rights and freedoms of individuals*; and fourth, that s. 2(d) *protects the exercise in association of the lawful rights of individuals*.
> [Emphasis added.]

The third and fourth of these principles have received considerably less judicial support than the others, having only been explicitly affirmed by three of six judges in the *Alberta Reference* and two of seven judges in *PIPSC*.... Most recently, in *Delisle* ... this Court did not have to rule on the validity of the existing framework because all of the activities involved fell within it. In that case, this Court clarified that s. 2(d) does not guarantee access to a particular labour relations regime where the claimants are able to exercise their s. 2(d) rights independently....

[...]

16 [T]he purpose of s. 2(d) commands a single inquiry: has the state precluded activity *because* of its associational nature, thereby discouraging the collective pursuit of common goals? In my view, while the four-part test for freedom of association sheds light on this concept, it does not capture the full range of activities protected by s. 2(d). In particular, there will be occasions where a given activity does not fall within the third and fourth rules set forth by Sopinka J. in *PIPSC* ... but where the state has nevertheless prohibited that activity solely because of its associational nature. These occasions will involve activities which (1) are not protected under any other constitutional freedom, and (2) cannot, for one reason or another, be understood as the lawful activities of individuals. As discussed by Dickson C.J. in the *Alberta Reference* ... such activities may be *collective* in nature, in that they cannot be performed by individuals acting alone.... To limit s. 2(d) to activities

that are performable by individuals would, in my view, render futile these fundamental initiatives. At best, it would encourage s. 2(*d*) claimants to contrive individual analogs for inherently associational activities, a process which this Court clearly resisted in the labour trilogy, in *Egg Marketing*... and in its jurisprudence on union security clauses and the right not to associate.... The collective dimension of s. 2(*d*) is also consistent with developments in international human rights law, as indicated by the jurisprudence of the Committee of Experts on the Application of Conventions and Recommendations and the ILO Committee on Freedom of Association.... Not only does this jurisprudence illustrate the range of activities that may be exercised by a collectivity of employees, but the International Labour Organization has repeatedly interpreted the right to organize as a collective right....

17 As I see it, the very notion of "association" recognizes the qualitative differences between individuals and collectivities. It recognizes that the press differs qualitatively from the journalist, the language community from the language speaker, the union from the worker.... [T]he law must recognize that certain union activities—making collective representations to an employer, adopting a majority political platform, federating with other unions—may be central to freedom of association even though they are inconceivable on the individual level. This is not to say that all such activities are protected by s. 2(*d*), nor that all collectivities are worthy of constitutional protection; indeed, this Court has repeatedly excluded the right to strike and collectively bargain from the protected ambit of s. 2(*d*).... It is to say, simply, that certain collective activities must be recognized if the freedom to form and maintain an association is to have any meaning....

[...]

(b) State Responsibility Under Section 2(d)

20 [H]istory has shown, and Canada's legislatures have uniformly recognized, that a posture of government restraint in the area of labour relations will expose most workers not only to a range of unfair labour practices, but potentially to legal liability under common law inhibitions on combinations and restraints of trade. Knowing this would foreclose the effective exercise of the freedom to organize, Ontario has provided a statutory freedom to organize in its *LRA* (s. 5), as well as protections against denial of access to property (s. 13), employer interference with trade union activity (s. 70), discrimination against trade unionists (s. 72), intimidation and coercion (s. 76), alteration of working conditions during the certification process (s. 86), coercion of witnesses (s. 87), and removal of Board notices (s. 88). In this context, it must be asked whether, in order to make the freedom to organize meaningful, s. 2(*d*) of the *Charter* imposes a positive obligation on the state to extend protective legislation to unprotected groups. More broadly, it may be asked whether the distinction between positive and negative state obligations ought to be nuanced in the context of labour relations, in the sense that excluding agricultural workers from a protective regime substantially contributes to the violation of protected freedoms.

21 This precise question was raised in *Delisle* ... in which the appellant failed to establish that exclusion from a protective regime violated s. 2(*d*).... [T]he *Delisle* majority focused instead on the fact that an interference with associational activity had not been made out on the facts of the case. Indeed, in making this finding, I deferred

judgment on the appellant's argument that underinclusion could have "an important chill on freedom of association because it clearly indicates to its members that unlike all other employees, they cannot unionize, and what is more, that they must not get together to defend their interests with respect to labour relations".... In addition, I left open the possibility that s. 2 of the *Charter* may impose "a positive obligation of protection or inclusion on Parliament or the government ... in exceptional circumstances which are not at issue in the instant case" ...

22 [I]t seems to me that apart from any consideration of a claimant's dignity interest, exclusion from a protective regime may in some contexts amount to an affirmative interference with the effective exercise of a protected freedom. In such a case, it is not so much the differential treatment that is at issue, but the fact that the government is creating conditions which in effect substantially interfere with the exercise of a constitutional right; it has been held in the s. 2(*a*) context, for example, that "protection of one religion and the concomitant non-protection of others imports disparate impact destructive of the religious freedom of the collectivity" (see *Big M Drug Mart* ...). This does not mean that there is a constitutional right to protective legislation *per se*; it means legislation that is *underinclusive* may, in unique contexts, substantially impact the exercise of a constitutional freedom.

23 This brings me to the central question of this appeal: can excluding agricultural workers from a statutory labour relations regime, without expressly or intentionally prohibiting association, constitute a substantial interference with freedom of association? ...

24 [C]laims of underinclusion should be grounded in fundamental *Charter* freedoms rather than in access to a particular statutory regime.... In my view, the appellants in this case do not claim a constitutional right to general inclusion in the *LRA*, but simply a constitutional freedom to organize a trade association. This freedom to organize exists independently of any statutory enactment, even though the so-called "modern rights to bargain collectively and to strike" have been characterized otherwise in the *Alberta Reference* ... per Le Dain J. ... While it may be that the effective exercise of this freedom requires legislative protection in some cases, this ought not change the fundamentally non-statutory character of the freedom itself ...

25 Second, the underinclusion cases demonstrate that a proper evidentiary foundation must be provided before creating a positive obligation under the *Charter* ... [I]t was concluded in *Delisle* that "it is difficult to argue that the exclusion of RCMP members from the statutory regime of the *PSSRA* prevents the establishment of an independent employee association because RCMP members have in fact formed such an association in several provinces".... In my view, the evidentiary burden in these cases is to demonstrate that exclusion from a statutory regime permits a *substantial* interference with the exercise of protected s. 2(*d*) activity....

26 Assuming an evidentiary foundation can be provided, a third concern is whether the state can truly be held accountable for any inability to exercise a fundamental freedom.... [I]t should be noted that this Court's understanding of "state action" has matured since the *Dolphin Delivery* case and may mature further in light of evolving *Charter* values.... Moreover, this Court has repeatedly held in the s. 15(1) context that the *Charter* may oblige the state to extend underinclusive statutes to the extent underinclusion licenses private actors to violate basic rights and freedoms.... Finally, there has been some suggestion

that the *Charter* should apply to legislation which "permits" private actors to interfere with protected s. 2 activity, as in some contexts mere permission may function to encourage or support the act which is called into question ... If we apply these general principles to s. 2(*d*), it is not a quantum leap to suggest that a failure to include someone in a *protective* regime may affirmatively permit restraints on the activity the regime is designed to protect. The rationale behind this is that underinclusive state action falls into suspicion not simply to the extent it discriminates against an unprotected class, but to the extent it substantially orchestrates, encourages or sustains the violation of fundamental freedoms.

27 The notion that underinclusion can infringe freedom of association is not only implied by Canadian *Charter* jurisprudence, but is also consistent with international human rights law. Article 2 of *Convention (No. 87) concerning Freedom of Association and Protection of the Right to Organize*, 67 U.N.T.S. 17, provides that "[w]orkers and employers, *without distinction whatsoever*, shall have the right to establish and ... to join organisations of their own choosing," and that only members of the armed forces and the police may be excluded (Article 9). In addition, Article 10 of *Convention No. 87* defines an "organisation" as "any organisation of workers or of employers for furthering and defending the interests of workers or of employers." Canada ratified *Convention No. 87* in 1972. The Convention's broadly worded provisions confirm precisely what I have discussed above, which is that discriminatory treatment implicates not only an excluded group's dignity interest, but also its basic freedom of association. This is further confirmed by the fact that Article 2 operates not only on the basis of sex, race, nationality and other traditional grounds of discrimination, but on the basis of any distinction, including occupational status ... Nowhere is this clearer than in Article 1 of *Convention (No. 11) concerning the Rights of Association and Combination of Agricultural Workers*, 38 U.N.T.S. 153, which obliges ratifying member states to secure to "all those engaged in agriculture" the same rights of association as to industrial workers; the convention makes no distinction as to the type of agricultural work performed. Although provincial jurisdiction has prevented Canada from ratifying *Convention No. 11*, together these conventions provide a normative foundation for prohibiting *any* form of discrimination in the protection of trade union freedoms....

28 In sum, while it is generally desirable to confine claims of underinclusion to s. 15(1), it will not be appropriate to do so where the underinclusion results in the effective denial of a fundamental freedom such as the right of association itself.... [T]he burden imposed by s. 2(*d*) of the *Charter* differs from that imposed by s. 15(1): while the latter focuses on the effects of underinclusion on human dignity (*Law v. Canada (Minister of Employment and Immigration)*) ... the former focuses on the effects of underinclusion on the ability to exercise a fundamental freedom....

[...]

(c) Summary of Discussion on Section 2(d)

30 In my view, the activities for which the appellants seek protection fall squarely within the freedom to organize, that is, the freedom to collectively embody the interests of individual workers. Insofar as the appellants seek to establish and maintain an association of employees, there can be no question that their claim falls within the protected ambit of s. 2(*d*) of the *Charter*. Moreover, the effective exercise of these freedoms may require not

only the exercise in association of the constitutional rights and freedoms (such as freedom of assembly) and lawful rights of individuals, but the exercise of certain collective activities, such as making majority representations to one's employer. These activities are guaranteed by the purpose of s. 2(d), which is to promote the realization of individual potential through relations with others, and by international labour jurisprudence, which recognizes the inevitably collective nature of the freedom to organize. Finally, while inclusion in legislation designed to protect such freedoms will normally be the province of s. 15(1) of the *Charter*, claims for inclusion may, in rare cases, be cognizable under the fundamental freedoms....

(3) Application to the Ontario Legislation
[...]

(b) Effects of the Exclusion
[...]

(ii) Without the Protection of the LRA, Agricultural Workers Are Substantially Incapable of Exercising the Freedom to Associate
[...]
41 ... Not only have agricultural workers proved unable to form employee associations in provinces which deny them protection but, unlike the RCMP officers in *Delisle*, they argue that their relative status and lack of statutory protection all but guarantee this result. Distinguishing features of agricultural workers are their political impotence, their lack of resources to associate without state protection and their vulnerability to reprisal by their employers.... Moreover, unlike RCMP officers, agricultural workers are not employed by the government and therefore cannot access the *Charter* directly to suppress an unfair labour practice....

42 [I]t is only the right to associate that is at issue here, not the right to collective bargaining. Nevertheless, to suggest that s. 2(d) of the *Charter* is respected where an association is reduced to claiming a right to unionize would, in my view, make a mockery of freedom of association. The record shows that, but for the brief period covered by the *ALRA*, there has never been an agricultural workers' union in Ontario. Agricultural workers have suffered repeated attacks on their efforts to unionize. Conversely, in those provinces where labour relations rights have been extended to agricultural workers, union density is higher than in Ontario.... The respondents do not contest this evidence, nor do they deny that legislative protection is absolutely crucial if agricultural workers wish to unionize.... For these reasons, I readily conclude that the evidentiary burden has been met in this case: the appellants have brought this litigation because there is no possibility for association as such without minimum statutory protection.

(iii) The Exclusion of Agricultural Workers from the LRA Substantially Reinforces the Inherent Difficulty in Exercising the Freedom to Associate
43 Their freedom to organize having been substantially impeded by exclusion from protective legislation, it is still incumbent on the appellants to link this impediment to state, not just private action (see *Dolphin Delivery* ...).
[...]

45 The most palpable effect of the *LRESLAA* and the *LRA* is, in my view, to place a chilling effect on non-statutory union activity. By extending statutory protection to just about every class of worker in Ontario, the legislature has essentially discredited the organizing efforts of agricultural workers.... [T]he effect of s. 3(*b*) of the *LRA* is not simply to perpetuate an existing inability to organize, but to exert the precise chilling effect I declined to recognize in *Delisle*.

46 Conversely, the didactic effects of labour relations legislation on employers must not be underestimated. It is widely accepted that labour relations laws function not only to provide a forum for airing specific grievances, but for fostering dialogue in an otherwise adversarial workplace ... [T]he wholesale exclusion of agricultural workers from a labour relations regime can only be viewed as a stimulus to interfere with organizing activity. The exclusion suggests that workplace democracy has no place in the agricultural sector and, moreover, that agricultural workers' efforts to associate are illegitimate. As surely as *LRA* protection would foster the "rule of law" in a unionized workplace, exclusion from that protection privileges the will of management over that of the worker. Again, a contrast to *Delisle* ... is apposite: a government employer is less likely than a private employer to take exclusion from protective legislation as a green light to commit unfair labour practices, as its employees have direct recourse to the *Charter*....

[...]

48 In sum, I believe it is reasonable to conclude that the exclusion of agricultural workers from the *LRA* substantially interferes with their fundamental freedom to organize. The inherent difficulties of organizing farm workers, combined with the threats of economic reprisal from employers, form only part of the reason why association is all but impossible in the agricultural sector in Ontario. Equally important is the message sent by s. 3(*b*) of the *LRA*, which delegitimizes associational activity and thereby ensures its ultimate failure. Given these known and foreseeable effects of s. 3(*b*), I conclude that the provision infringes the freedom to organize and thus violates s. 2(*d*) of the *Charter*.

[Justice Bastarache went on to find that the exclusion of agricultural workers from the *Labour Relations Act* (*LRA*) could not be saved under section 1 of the *Charter*, and he found that the protection of the family farm was a pressing enough objective to warrant the infringement of section 2(d) of the *Charter*. However, he concluded that the complete exclusion of all agricultural employers was not minimally impairing because it denied the right of association in every sector of agriculture and denied every aspect of freedom of association, including those that were necessary for the effective formation and maintenance of employee associations. He found that if the legislature sought the protection of the family farm, it should at the very least protect agricultural workers from the legal and economic consequences of forming an association. He therefore declared both the *LRESLAA* and section 3(b) of the *LRA* contrary to the *Charter*. He suspended the declarations of invalidity for eighteen months to allow the legislature to pass amending legislation if it saw fit do to so.]

Dunmore is a fascinating constitutional law case about private actors, positive state obligations, and underinclusion. It stands in contrast to *Alberta Reference*, which was a much more typical case of straightforward state interference. This is also what the *Health Services* case, in the second trilogy, dealt with.

CHAPTER 12: THE CONSTITUTIONALIZATION OF COLLECTIVE BARGAINING LAW

12:221 The *Health Services* Decision

The second decision in the 2001–2011 Trilogy was decided in 2007. In what might be the most startling of the nine decisions constituting the three trilogies, the Supreme Court of Canada overruled the 1987 *Trilogy* and recognized a constitutional "right" of collective bargaining under section 2(d). The Court also expressly left open the issue of the "right" to strike. The Court visited that issue in *Sask Fed*, one of the 2015 Trilogy cases.

Health Services and Support—Facilities Subsector Bargaining Association v British Columbia, 2007 SCC 27

McLachlin C.J. and LeBel J. (Bastarache, Binnie, Fish, and Abella JJ. concurring):

I. INTRODUCTION

A. Overview

1. The appellants challenge the constitutional validity of Part 2 of the *Health and Social Services Delivery Improvement Act*, S.B.C. 2002, c. 2 ("Act"), as violative of the *Canadian Charter of Rights and Freedoms* guarantees of freedom of association (s. 2(*d*)) and equality (s. 15).

2. We conclude that the s. 2(*d*) guarantee of freedom of association protects the capacity of members of labour unions to engage in collective bargaining on workplace issues. While some of the impugned provisions of the Act comply with this guarantee, ss. 6(2), 6(4) and 9 breach it and have not been shown to be justified under s. 1 of the *Charter*. We further conclude that the Act does not violate the right to equal treatment under s. 15 of the *Charter*. In the result, the appeal is allowed in part.

B. The Background

3. This case requires the Court to balance the need for governments to deliver essential social services effectively with the need to recognize the *Charter* rights of employees affected by such legislation, who were working for health and social service employers. The respondent government characterizes the impugned legislation as a crucial element of its response to a pressing health care crisis, necessary and important to the well-being of British Columbians. The appellants, unions and individual workers representing some of the subsectors of the health care sector affected by the legislation, by contrast, see the Act as an affront to the fundamental rights of employees and union members under the *Charter*, which they understand as including a collective right to pursue fundamental workplace goals through collective bargaining in respect of terms of employment.

C. The Act

4. The Act was adopted as a response to challenges facing British Columbia's health care system. Demand for health care and the cost of providing needed health care services had been increasing significantly for years . . .

5. The goals of the Act were to reduce costs and to facilitate the efficient management of the workforce in the health care sector. Not wishing to decrease employees' wages, the

government attempted to achieve these goals in more sustainable ways. According to the government, the Act was designed in particular to focus on permitting health care employers to reorganize the administration of the labour force and on making operational changes to enhance management's ability to restructure service delivery ...

[...]

7. There was no meaningful consultation with unions before it became law ...

[...]

10. [Part 2 of the Act] introduced changes to transfers and multi-worksite assignment rights (ss. 4 and 5), contracting out (s. 6), the status of employees under contracting-out arrangements (s. 6), job security programs (ss. 7 and 8), and layoffs and bumping rights (s. 9).

11. Part 2 gave health care employers greater flexibility to organize their relations with their employees as they see fit, and in some cases, to do so in ways that would not have been permissible under existing collective agreements and without adhering to requirements of consultation and notice that would otherwise obtain. It invalidated important provisions of collective agreements then in force, and effectively precluded meaningful collective bargaining on a number of specific issues. Section 10 invalidated any part of a collective agreement, past or future, which was inconsistent with Part 2, and any collective agreement purporting to modify these restrictions ...

[...]

13. Neither the trial court nor the British Columbia Court of Appeal was willing to recognize a right to collective bargaining under s. 2(d) of the *Charter*, although the Court of Appeal acknowledged that the Supreme Court of Canada had opened the door to the recognition of such a right. In the result, the Act was held to be constitutional under ss. 2(d) and 15.

[...]

III. ANALYSIS

A. Section 2(d) of the *Charter*

19. At issue in the present appeal is whether the guarantee of freedom of association in s. 2(d) of the *Charter* protects collective bargaining rights. We conclude that s. 2(d) of the *Charter* protects the capacity of members of labour unions to engage, in association, in collective bargaining on fundamental workplace issues. This protection does not cover all aspects of "collective bargaining," as that term is understood in the statutory labour relations regimes that are in place across the country. Nor does it ensure a particular outcome in a labour dispute, or guarantee access to any particular statutory regime. What is protected is simply the right of employees to associate in a process of collective action to achieve workplace goals. If the government substantially interferes with that right, it violates s. 2(d) of the *Charter*: *Dunmore*. We note that the present case does not concern the right to strike, which was considered in earlier litigation on the scope of the guarantee of freedom of association.

20. Our conclusion that s. 2(d) of the *Charter* protects a process of collective bargaining rests on four propositions. First, a review of the s. 2(d) jurisprudence of this

Court reveals that the reasons evoked in the past for holding that the guarantee of freedom of association does not extend to collective bargaining can no longer stand. Second, an interpretation of s. 2(d) that precludes collective bargaining from its ambit is inconsistent with Canada's historic recognition of the importance of collective bargaining to freedom of association. Third, collective bargaining is an integral component of freedom of association in international law, which may inform the interpretation of *Charter* guarantees. Finally, interpreting s. 2(d) as including a right to collective bargaining is consistent with, and indeed, promotes, other *Charter* rights, freedoms and values.

[...]

(1) Reasons for Excluding Collective Bargaining from Section 2(d) in the Past Require Reconsideration

22. In earlier decisions, the majority view in the Supreme Court of Canada was that the guarantee of freedom of association did not extend to collective bargaining. *Dunmore*, opened the door to reconsideration of that view. We conclude that the grounds advanced in the earlier decisions for the exclusion of collective bargaining from the *Charter*'s protection of freedom of association do not withstand principled scrutiny and should be rejected.

23. The first cases dealing squarely with the issue of whether collective bargaining is protected under s. 2(d) of the *Charter* were a group of three concurrently released appeals known as the labour "trilogy": *Reference re Public Service Employee Relations Act (Alta.)*, [1987] 1 S.C.R. 313 ("*Alberta Reference*"), *PSAC v. Canada*, [1987] 1 S.C.R. 424, and *RWDSU v. Saskatchewan*, [1987] 1 S.C.R. 460. The main reasons were delivered in the *Alberta Reference*, a case involving compulsory arbitration to resolve impasses in collective bargaining and a prohibition on strikes. Of the six justices participating in the case, three held that collective bargaining was not protected by s. 2(d); four held that strike activity was not protected. The next case to deal with the issue was *Professional Institute of the Public Service of Canada v. Northwest Territories (Commissioner)*, [1990] 2 S.C.R. 367 ("*PIPSC*"), in which the government of the Northwest Territories refused to enact legislation required in order for the PIPSC union to bargain collectively on behalf of nurses. A majority of four held that collective bargaining was not protected by s. 2(d).

24. In these cases, different members of the majorities put forth five main reasons in support of the contention that collective bargaining does not fall within s. 2(d)'s protection.

25. The first suggested reason was that the rights to strike and to bargain collectively are "modern rights" created by legislation, not "fundamental freedoms".... The difficulty with this argument is that it fails to recognize the history of labour relations in Canada ... the fundamental importance of collective bargaining to labour relations was the very reason for its incorporation into statute. Legislatures throughout Canada have historically viewed collective bargaining rights as sufficiently important to immunize them from potential interference. The statutes they passed did not create the right to bargain collectively. Rather, they afforded it protection. There is nothing in the statutory entrenchment of collective bargaining that detracts from its fundamental nature.

26. The second suggested reason was that recognition of a right to collective bargaining would go against the principle of judicial restraint in interfering with government regulation of labour relations.... The regulation of labour relations, it is suggested,

involves policy decisions best left to government. This argument again fails to recognize the fact that worker organizations historically had the right to bargain collectively outside statutory regimes and takes an overbroad view of judicial deference. It may well be appropriate for judges to defer to legislatures on policy matters expressed in particular laws. But to declare a judicial "no go" zone for an entire right on the ground that it may involve the courts in policy matters is to push deference too far. Policy itself should reflect *Charter* rights and values.

27. The third suggested reason for excluding collective bargaining from s. 2(*d*) of the *Charter* rested on the view that freedom of association protects only those activities performable by an individual.... This view arises from a passage in which Sopinka J. [in *PIPSC*] set out the scope of s. 2(*d*) in four oft-quoted propositions (at pp. 402–3): (1) s. 2(*d*) protects the freedom to establish, belong to and maintain an association; (2) it does not protect an activity solely on the ground that the activity is foundational or essential to the association; (3) it protects the exercise in association of the constitutional rights and freedoms of individuals; and (4) it protects the exercise in association of the lawful rights of individuals. If this framework and the premise that s. 2(*d*) covers only activities performable by an individual is accepted, it follows that collective bargaining cannot attract the protection of s. 2(*d*) because collective bargaining cannot be performed by an individual.

28. This narrow focus on individual activities has been overtaken by *Dunmore*, where this Court rejected the notion that freedom of association applies only to activities capable of performance by individuals. Bastarache J. held that "[t]o limit s. 2(*d*) to activities that are performable by individuals would ... render futile these fundamental initiatives" (para. 16), since, as Dickson C.J. noted in his dissent in the *Alberta Reference*, some collective activities may, by their very nature, be incapable of being performed by an individual. Bastarache J. provided the example of expressing a majority viewpoint as being an inherently collective activity without an individual analogue (para. 16) ...

29. The fourth reason advanced for excluding collective bargaining rights from s. 2(*d*) was the suggestion of L'Heureux-Dubé J. that s. 2(*d*) was not intended to protect the "objects" or goals of an association.... This argument overlooks the fact that it will always be possible to characterize the pursuit of a particular activity in concert with others as the "object" of that association. Recasting collective bargaining as an "object" begs the question of whether or not the activity is worthy of constitutional protection. L'Heureux-Dubé J.'s underlying concern—that the *Charter* not be used to protect the substantive outcomes of any and all associations—is a valid one. However, "collective bargaining" as a procedure has always been distinguishable from its final outcomes (e.g., the results of the bargaining process, which may be reflected in a collective agreement). Professor Bora Laskin (as he then was) aptly described collective bargaining over 60 years ago as follows:

> Collective bargaining is the procedure through which the views of the workers are made known, expressed through representatives chosen by them, not through representatives selected or nominated or approved by employers. More than that, it is a procedure through which terms and conditions of employment may be settled by negotiations between an employer and his employees on the basis of a comparative equality of bargaining strength.

("Collective Bargaining in Canada: In Peace and in War" (1941), 2:3 *Food for Thought*, at p. 8.)

In our view, it is entirely possible to protect the "procedure" known as collective bargaining without mandating constitutional protection for the fruits of that bargaining process. Thus, the characterization of collective bargaining as an association's "object" does not provide a principled reason to deny it constitutional protection.

30. An overarching concern is that the majority judgments in the *Alberta Reference* and *PIPSC* adopted a decontextualized approach to defining the scope of freedom of association, in contrast to the purposive approach taken to other *Charter* guarantees. The result was to forestall inquiry into the purpose of that *Charter* guarantee. The generic approach of the earlier decisions to s. 2(*d*) ignored differences between organizations. Whatever the organization — be it trade union or book club — its freedoms were treated as identical. The unfortunate effect was to overlook the importance of collective bargaining — both historically and currently — to the exercise of freedom of association in labour relations.

31. We conclude that the reasons provided by the majorities in the *Alberta Reference* and *PIPSC* should not bar reconsideration of the question of whether s. 2(*d*) applies to collective bargaining. This is manifestly the case since this Court's decision in *Dunmore*, which struck down a statute that effectively prohibited farm workers from engaging in collective bargaining by denying them access to the Province's labour relations regime, as violating of s. 2(*d*) of the *Charter*. *Dunmore* clarified three developing aspects of the law: what constitutes interference with the "associational aspect" of an activity; the need for a contextual approach to freedom of association; and the recognition that s. 2(*d*) can impose positive obligations on government.

32. *Dunmore* accepted the conclusion of the majority in *Canadian Egg Marketing Agency v. Richardson*, [1998] 3 S.C.R. 157, that only the "associational aspect" of an activity and not the activity itself are protected under s. 2(*d*). It clarified, however, that equal legislative treatment of individuals and groups does not mean that the "associational aspect" of an activity has not been interfered with. A prohibition on an individual may not raise associational concerns, while the same prohibition on the collective may do so....

33. Second, *Dunmore* correctly advocated a more contextual analysis than had hitherto prevailed. Showing that a legislature has targeted associational conduct because of its "concerted or associational nature" requires a more contextual assessment than found in the early s. 2(*d*) cases ...

34. Finally, *Dunmore* recognized that, in certain circumstances, s. 2(*d*) may place positive obligations on governments to extend legislation to particular groups. Underinclusive legislation may, "in unique contexts, substantially impact the exercise of a constitutional freedom" (para. 22). This will occur where the claim of underinclusion is grounded in the fundamental *Charter* freedom and not merely in access to a statutory regime (para. 24); where a proper evidentiary foundation is provided to create a positive obligation under the *Charter* (para. 25); and where the state can truly be held accountable for any inability to exercise a fundamental freedom (para. 26). There must be evidence that the freedom would be next to impossible to exercise without positively recognizing a right to access a statutory regime.

35. Bastarache J. reconciled the holding in *Dunmore* of a positive obligation on government to permit farm workers to join together to bargain collectively in an effective

manner with the conclusion in *Delisle v. Canada (Deputy Attorney General)*, [1999] 2 S.C.R. 989, that the federal government was not under a positive obligation to provide RCMP officers with access to collective bargaining by distinguishing the effects of the legislation in the two cases. Unlike the RCMP members in *Delisle*, farm workers faced barriers that made them substantially incapable of exercising their right to form associations outside the statutory framework ... Government measures that substantially interfere with the ability of individuals to associate with a view to promoting work-related interests violate the guarantee of freedom of association under s. 2(*d*) of the *Charter*.

36. In summary, a review of the jurisprudence leads to the conclusion that the holdings in the *Alberta Reference* and *PIPSC* excluding collective bargaining from the scope of s. 2(*d*) can no longer stand. None of the reasons provided by the majorities in those cases survive scrutiny, and the rationale for excluding inherently collective activities from s. 2(*d*)'s protection has been overtaken by *Dunmore*.

37. Our rejection of the arguments previously used to exclude collective bargaining from s. 2(*d*) leads us to a reassessment of that issue, discussed below.

(2) Collective Bargaining Falls Within the Scope of Section 2(*d*) of the *Charter*

38. The question is whether the s. 2(*d*) guarantee of freedom of association extends to the right of employees to join together in a union to negotiate with employers on workplace issues or terms of employment—a process described broadly as collective bargaining.

39. The general purpose of the *Charter* guarantees and the language of s. 2(d) are consistent with at least a measure of protection for collective bargaining. The language of s. 2(d) is cast in broad terms and devoid of limitations. However, this is not conclusive. To answer the question before us, we must consider the history of collective bargaining in Canada, collective bargaining in relation to freedom of association in the larger international context, and whether *Charter* values favour an interpretation of s. 2(d) that protects a process of collective bargaining.... Evaluating the scope of s. 2(d) of the *Charter* through these tools leads to the conclusion that s. 2(d) does indeed protect workers' rights to a process of collective bargaining.

(a) Canadian Labour History Reveals the Fundamental Nature of Collective Bargaining

40. Association for purposes of collective bargaining has long been recognized as a fundamental Canadian right which predated the *Charter*. This suggests that the framers of the *Charter* intended to include it in the protection of freedom of association found in s. 2(*d*) of the *Charter*.

41. The respondent argues that the right to collective bargaining is of recent origin and is merely a creature of statute. This assertion may be true if collective bargaining is equated solely to the framework of rights of representation and collective bargaining now recognized under federal and provincial labour codes. However, the origin of a right to collective bargaining in the sense given to it in the present case (i.e., a procedural right to bargain collectively on conditions of employment), precedes the adoption of the present system of labour relations in the 1940s. The history of collective bargaining in Canada reveals that long before the present statutory labour regimes were put in place, collective bargaining was recognized as a fundamental aspect of Canadian society. This is the context against which the scope of the s. 2(*d*) must be considered.

42. Canadian labour history can be summarized by borrowing words from the 1968 *Report of the Task Force on Labour Relations*. As society entered into the industrialized era, "workers began to join unions and to engage in collective bargaining with their employers. Although employers resisted this development with all the resources at their command, it eventually became apparent that unions and collective bargaining were natural concomitants of a mixed enterprise economy. The state then assumed the task of establishing a framework of rights and responsibilities within which management and organized labour were to conduct their relations" (Task Force on Labour Relations, *Canadian Industrial Relations: The Report of Task Force on Labour Relations* (1968) ("Woods Report"), at p. 13).

43. Canadian labour law traces its roots to various legal systems, most importantly to British and American law. Prior to the 1940s, British law had a significant influence on the development of our labour law. American law became an influential force when the United States passed the *Wagner Act* in 1935 (also called *National Labor Relations Act*). And a substantial part of Quebec's law governing labour relations and collective bargaining prior to 1944 was influenced by French law (see R. P. Gagnon, L. LeBel and P. Verge, *Droit du travail* (2nd ed. 1991), at pp. 26–27).

44. The development of labour relations law in Canada may be divided into three major eras: repression, toleration and recognition. . . .

(i) Repression of Workers' Organizations

45. Workers' associations have a long history. . . .

46. In Canada, workers' organizations can be traced back to the end of the 18th century. "As early as 1794 employees of the North West Fur Trading Company went on strike for higher wages." However, it was not until the industrial revolution that workers' organizations took on more than a marginal role, and that a real labour movement was born. . . .

47. From the beginning, the law was used as a tool to limit workers' rights to unionize. In England, through the 18th and 19th centuries, labour organizations were considered illegal under the common law doctrine of criminal conspiracy. . . . Statutes soon added new limits. After the French Revolution, the British Parliament, convinced that labour organizations were the nesting ground of potential revolutions, adopted the *Combination Acts* of 1799 and 1800, making it unlawful for two or more workers to combine in an attempt to increase their wages, lessen their hours of work or persuade anyone to leave or refuse work. The Acts, which made it "a criminal offence to be a member of a trade union, to call a strike, or to contribute money for trade union purposes," had the effect of suppressing a large series of collective actions . . . Combinations of workers were already illegal at common law. The *Combination Acts* reinforced the common law by providing faster and more effective tools to enforce criminal penalties upon workers. . . .

48. In 1824, the English *Combination Acts* were repealed. The repeal was immediately followed by a series of strikes. The British Parliament responded with a new Combination Act less than a year later, which reintroduced strong criminal sanctions against workers. The new *Combination Act* of 1825 made it legal for workers to bargain collectively with their employers. However, it made strikes a criminal offence. . . .

49. In the 1860s, two important events led the British Parliament to change course. First, a Royal Commission on Trade Unions was appointed in 1867. It recommended better legal recognition for trade unions. Second, a reform of suffrage law gave a large

segment of the working class the right to vote, enabling them to exert more influence over Parliament... In response to these events, in 1871 the British Parliament adopted the *Trade Union Act* and the *Criminal Law Amendment Act*, which were intended to immunize trade unions and their members from the criminal laws of conspiracy and restraint of trade. Nevertheless, British courts continued to view collective actions suspiciously, repressing strikes through the doctrine of criminal conspiracy and repressing other union activity through the application of economic torts. The British Parliament in turn responded on occasion by strengthening the legislative protection for trade unions in that country....

50. The question of whether the repressive common law doctrines and the *Combination Acts* of 1799 and 1800 were introduced into Canada is subject to controversy. Some scholars are of the opinion that the common law doctrines of conspiracy and restraint of trade were introduced into Canadian law.... Others, however, argue that the Canadian common law and the civil law of Quebec were more ambiguous and less oppressive to trade unions than the British common law.... It is unnecessary to resolve this debate. It suffices to recognize that, at least until 1872, Canadian laws "cast shadows on the legitimacy of trade unions...."

(ii) Tolerance of Workers' Organizations and Collective Bargaining
51. A major shift in Canadian labour law took place in the aftermath of the Toronto Typographical Unions' strike that occurred in 1872. The strike by the Toronto typographers, inspired by the call for a nine-hour work day, led to numerous arrests and charges against the strikers for common law criminal conspiracy. At that time, Canada had not yet adopted legislation immunizing trade union members from criminal charges for conspiracy or restraint of trade. The criminal charges against the Toronto strikers raised public concern and revealed that Canada was behind the times—at least compared to Britain—on the issue of union protection and recognition.

52. In consequence, Canada adopted its own legislation copied in part from the British *Trade Union Act* of 1871. The Canadian *Trade Unions Act* of 1872 "made it clear that no worker could be criminally prosecuted for conspiracy solely on the basis of attempting to influence the rate of wages, hours of labour, or other aspects of the work relation".... Through this legislative action, the Canadian Parliament recognized the value for the individual of collective actions in the context of labour relations. As Sir John A. Macdonald mentioned in the House of Commons, the purpose of the *Trade Unions Act* of 1872 was to immunize unions from existing laws considered to be "opposed to the spirit of the liberty of the individual" (*Parliamentary Debates*, 5th sess., 1st Parl., 7 May 1872, at p. 392, as cited by M. Chartrand, "The First Canadian Trade Union Legislation: An Historical Perspective" (1984), 16 *Ottawa L. Rev.* 267).

53. By the beginning of the 1900s, the main criminal barriers to unionism in Canada had been brought down. Criminal law no longer prohibited employees from combining for the purposes of ameliorating their working conditions.... However, courts continued to apply common law doctrines to restrain union activities.... Moreover, nothing in the law required employers to recognize unions or to bargain collectively with them. Employers could simply ignore union demands and even refuse to hire union members. As J. Fudge and E. Tucker explain:

While workers were also privileged to combine with other workers to advance their common interests, employers were free to contract only with those workers who were not part of a combination. In short, they could refuse to hire union members and could fire those who became union members after taking up employment.

(*Labour Before the Law: The Regulation of Workers' Collective Action in Canada, 1900–1948* (2001), at p. 2)

54. While employers could refuse to recognize and bargain with unions, workers had recourse to an economic weapon: the powerful tool of calling a strike to force an employer to recognize a union and bargain collectively with it. The law gave both parties the ability to use economic weapons to attain their ends. Before the adoption of the modern statutory model of labour relations, the majority of strikes were motivated by the workers' desire to have an employer recognize a union and bargain collectively with it ...

(iii) Recognition of Collective Bargaining

55. The first few decades of the 20th century saw Parliament's promotion of voluntary collective bargaining. The federal Parliament enacted a series of statutes to promote collective bargaining by conferring on the labour minister the power to impose conciliation on the parties in an attempt to bring them to compromise ... This model failed, mainly because employers had no real incentive to participate in the process ... Moreover, union members did not receive any protection against unfair labour practices undertaken by employers ... In search of a better model, Canadian governments looked at what was happening in the United States.

56. In the United States, courts also relied heavily on the doctrine of conspiracy under criminal and civil law as well as antitrust law to limit union activities ... In 1914, the American Congress immunized unions from the application of antitrust law and adopted a non-interventionist attitude in order to let workers and employers use their respective economic powers to manage their own labour relations. However, the Depression and resulting industrial tension of the 1930s rendered the old laissez-faire model inappropriate. The result was the *Wagner Act*, which explicitly recognized the right of employees to belong to a trade union of their choice, free of employer coercion or interference, and imposed a duty upon employers to bargain in good faith with their employees' unions....

57. K. E. Klare has identified the following main objects of the *Wagner Act*:

1. *Industrial Peace*: By encouraging collective bargaining, the Act aimed to subdue "strikes and other forms of industrial strife or unrest," because industrial warfare interfered with interstate commerce; that is, it was unhealthy in a business economy. Moreover, although this thought was not embodied in the text, industrial warfare clearly promoted other undesirable conditions, such as political turmoil, violence, and general uncertainty.
2. *Collective Bargaining*: The Act sought to enhance collective bargaining for its own sake because of its presumed "mediating" or "therapeutic" impact on industrial conflict.
3. *Bargaining Power*: The Act aimed to promote "actual liberty of contract" by redressing the unequal balance of bargaining power between employers and employees.
4. *Free Choice*: The Act was intended to protect the free choice of workers to associate amongst themselves and to select representatives of their own choosing for collective bargaining.

5. *Underconsumption*: The Act was designed to promote economic recovery and to prevent future depressions by increasing the earnings and purchasing power of workers.
6. *Industrial Democracy*: This is the most elusive aspect of the legislative purpose, although most commentators indicate that a concept of industrial democracy is embedded in the statutory scheme, or at the least was one of the articulated goals of the sponsors of the Act. Senator Wagner frequently sounded the industrial democracy theme in ringing notes, and scholars have subsequently seen in collective bargaining "the means of establishing industrial democracy, ... the means of providing for the workers' lives in industry the sense of worth, of freedom, and of participation that democratic government promises them as citizens."

("Judicial Deradicalization of the *Wagner Act* and the Origins of Modern Legal Consciousness, 1937–1941" (1978), 62 *Minn. L. Rev.* 265, at pp. 281–84)

58. By the end of the 1930s, most Canadian provinces had passed legislation incorporating the main objectives of the *Wagner Act* ... However, it is Order in Council P.C. 1003, a regulation adopted by the federal government to rule labour relations in time of war, that firmly implemented the principles of the *Wagner Act* in Canada and triggered further development of provincial labour laws ...

59. Fudge and Glasbeek emphasize the effects of P.C. 1003 on Canadian labour relations:

> For the first time in Canada's history, the government compelled employers to recognize and to bargain with duly elected representatives and/or trade unions. From the workers' perspective, this constituted a movement from having a right to state their interest in being represented by a union to having enforceable legal right to have their chosen representative treated as a union by their employer. There was no longer any need to use collective economic muscle—always seriously limited by the common law—to obtain the right to bargain collectively with employers. [p. 359]

60. P.C. 1003 was a compromise adopted to promote peaceful labour relations. On the one hand, it granted major protections to workers to organize without fear of unfair interference from the employers and guaranteed workers the right to bargain collectively in good faith with their employers without having to rely on strikes and other economic weapons. On the other hand, it provided employers with a measure of stability in their relations with their organized workers, without the spectre of intensive state intervention in the economy.... These elements of P.C. 1003 continue to guide our system of labour relations to this day....

61. In all the provinces except Saskatchewan, legislation inspired by the *Wagner Act* initially applied only to the private sector. Its extension to the public sector came later. Between 1965 and 1973 statutes were passed across the country extending labour protections to public sectors.... However, the rights conferred to public sector employees were more restricted than in the private sector:

> Some employees are not allowed to bargain about certain subjects, some employees are given the alternative of striking or accepting a compulsory arbitrated award, some

employees are not given the right to strike at all. Further, governments have retained the right to determine that, even if a public sector bargaining unit is given the right to strike, some of its members should be designated as being essential workers, that is, workers who must continue to deliver a governmental service during a lawful strike by their bargaining unit colleagues. Moreover, a government's assumed right and need to continue to look after the public's welfare makes it easy to pass legislation suspending or abrogating a trade union's previously granted strike rights. In the same vein, a government can always argue that, whatever collective bargaining rights its workers have, these can justifiably be curtailed to allow the government, not just to continue to deliver services, but also to pursue a major policy, such as the reduction of inflation or the balancing of the budget.

(Fudge et Glasbeek, at p. 385).

62. Moreover, on many occasions (and with increasing frequency during the 1980s and 1990s), governments used legislation to impose unilaterally upon their own employees specific conditions of employment, in most cases related to wages....

63. In summary, workers in Canada began forming collectives to bargain over working conditions with their employers as early as the 18th century. However, the common law cast a shadow over the rights of workers to act collectively. When Parliament first began recognizing workers' rights, trade unions had no express statutory right to negotiate collectively with employers. Employers could simply ignore them. However, workers used the powerful economic weapon of strikes to gradually force employers to recognize unions and to bargain collectively with them. By adopting the *Wagner Act* model, governments across Canada recognized the fundamental need for workers to participate in the regulation of their work environment. This legislation confirmed what the labour movement had been fighting for over centuries and what it had access to in the laissez-faire era through the use of strikes—the right to collective bargaining with employers.

(iv) Collective Bargaining in the Charter era

64. At the time the *Charter* was enacted in 1982, collective bargaining had a long tradition in Canada and was recognized as part of freedom of association in the labour context. The 1968 Woods Report explained the importance of collective bargaining for our society and the special relationship between collective bargaining and freedom of association:

> Freedom to associate and to act collectively are basic to the nature of Canadian society and are root freedoms of the existing collective bargaining system. Together they constitute freedom of trade union activity: to organize employees, to join with the employer in negotiating a collective agreement, and to invoke economic sanctions, including taking a case to the public in the event of an impasse....
>
> In order to encourage and ensure recognition of the social purpose of collective bargaining legislation as an instrument for the advancement of fundamental freedoms in our industrial society, we recommend that the legislation contain a preamble that would replace the neutral tone of the present statute with a positive commitment to the collective bargaining system. [p. 138]

65. The preamble of the *Canada Labour Code*, R.S.C. 1970, c. L-1, was later modified, in 1972 (S.C. 1972, c. 18), to express the benefits that collective bargaining brings to society:

Whereas there is a long tradition in Canada of labour legislation and policy designed for the promotion of the common wellbeing through the encouragement of free collective bargaining and the constructive settlement of disputes;

And Whereas Canadian workers, trade unions and employers recognize and support freedom of association and free collective bargaining as the bases of effective industrial relations for the determination of good working conditions and sound labour management relations;

66. Collective bargaining, despite early discouragement from the common law, has long been recognized in Canada. Indeed, historically, it emerges as the most significant collective activity through which freedom of association is expressed in the labour context. In our opinion, the concept of freedom of association under s. 2(d) of the *Charter* includes this notion of a procedural right to collective bargaining.

67. This established Canadian right to collective bargaining was recognized in the Parliamentary hearings that took place before the adoption of the *Charter*. The acting Minister of Justice, Mr. Robert Kaplan, explained why he did not find necessary a proposed amendment to have the freedom to organize and bargain collectively expressly included under s. 2(d). These rights, he stated, were already implicitly recognized in the words "freedom of association":

> Our position on the suggestion that there be specific reference to freedom to organize and bargain collectively is that that is already covered in the freedom of association that is provided already in the Declaration or in the *Charter*; and that by singling out association for bargaining one might tend to d[i]minish all the other forms of association which are contemplated—church associations; associations of fraternal organizations or community organizations.
>
> (Special Joint Committee of the Senate and of the House of Commons on the Constitution of Canada, *Minutes of Proceedings and Evidence*, Issue No. 43, January 22, 1981, at pp. 69–70)

68. The protection enshrined in s. 2(d) of the *Charter* may properly be seen as the culmination of a historical movement towards the recognition of a procedural right to collective bargaining.

(b) International Law Protects Collective Bargaining as Part of Freedom of Association

69. Under Canada's federal system of government, the incorporation of international agreements into domestic law is properly the role of the federal Parliament or the provincial legislatures. However, Canada's international obligations can assist courts charged with interpreting the *Charter*'s guarantees.... Applying this interpretive tool here supports recognizing a process of collective bargaining as part of the *Charter*'s guarantee of freedom of association.

70. Canada's adherence to international documents recognizing a right to collective bargaining supports recognition of the right in s. 2(d) of the *Charter*. As Dickson C.J. observed in the *Alberta Reference*, at p. 349, the *Charter* should be presumed to provide at least as great a level of protection as is found in the international human rights documents that Canada has ratified.

71. The sources most important to the understanding of s. 2(d) of the *Charter* are the *International Covenant on Economic, Social and Cultural Rights*, 993 U.N.T.S. 3 ("*ICESCR*"),

the *International Covenant on Civil and Political Rights*, 999 U.N.T.S. 171 (*"ICCPR"*), and the International Labour Organization's (ILO's) *Convention (No. 87) Concerning Freedom of Association and Protection of the Right to Organize*, 68 U.N.T.S. 17 (*"Convention No. 87"*). Canada has endorsed all three of these documents, acceding to both the *ICESCR* and the *ICCPR*, and ratifying *Convention No. 87* in 1972. This means that these documents reflect not only international consensus, but also principles that Canada has committed itself to uphold.

72. The *ICESCR*, the *ICCPR* and *Convention No. 87* extend protection to the functioning of trade unions in a manner suggesting that a right to collective bargaining is part of freedom of association. The interpretation of these conventions, in Canada and internationally, not only supports the proposition that there is a right to collective bargaining in international law, but also suggests that such a right should be recognized in the Canadian context under s. 2(*d*).

73. Article 8, para. (1)(*c*) of the *ICESCR* guarantees the "right of trade unions to function freely subject to no limitations other than those prescribed by law and which are necessary in a democratic society in the interests of national security or public order or for the protection of the rights and freedoms of others." This Article allows the "free functioning" of trade unions to be regulated, but not legislatively abrogated (per Dickson C.J., *Alberta Reference*, at p. 351). Since collective bargaining is a primary function of a trade union, it follows that Article 8 protects a union's freedom to pursue this function freely.

74. Similarly, Article 22, para. 1 of the *ICCPR* states that "[e]veryone shall have the right to freedom of association with others, including the right to form and join trade unions for the protection of his interests." Paragraph 2 goes on to say that no restriction may be placed on the exercise of this right, other than those necessary in a free and democratic society for reasons of national security, public safety, public order, public health or the protection of the rights of others. This Article has been interpreted to suggest that it encompasses both the right to form a union and the right to collective bargaining....

75. *Convention No. 87* has also been understood to protect collective bargaining as part of freedom of association. Part I of the Convention, entitled "Freedom of Association," sets out the rights of workers to freely form organizations which operate under constitutions and rules set by the workers and which have the ability to affiliate internationally. Dickson C.J., dissenting in the *Alberta Reference*, at p. 355, relied on *Convention No. 87* for the principle that the ability "to form and organize unions, even in the public sector, must include freedom to pursue the essential activities of unions, such as collective bargaining and strikes, subject to reasonable limits."

76. *Convention No. 87* has been the subject of numerous interpretations by the ILO's Committee on Freedom of Association, Committee of Experts and Commissions of Inquiry. These interpretations have been described as the "cornerstone of the international law on trade union freedom and collective bargaining".... While not binding, they shed light on the scope of s. 2(*d*) of the *Charter* as it was intended to apply to collective bargaining: *Dunmore*, at paras. 16 and 27, *per* Bastarache J., applying the jurisprudence of the ILO's Committee of Experts and Committee on Freedom of Association.

77. A recent review by ILO staff summarized a number of principles concerning collective bargaining. Some of the most relevant principles in international law are

summarized in the following terms (see B. Gernigon, A. Odero and H. Guido, "ILO principles concerning collective bargaining" (2000), 139 *Intern'l Lab. Rev.* 33, at pp. 51–52):

    A. The right to collective bargaining is a fundamental right endorsed by the members of the ILO in joining the Organization, which they have an obligation to respect, to promote and to realize, in good faith (ILO Declaration on Fundamental Principles and Rights at Work and its Follow-up).

. . .

    D. The purpose of collective bargaining is the regulation of terms and conditions of employment, in a broad sense, and the relations between the parties.

. . .

    H. The principle of good faith in collective bargaining implies recognizing representative organizations, endeavouring to reach an agreement, engaging in genuine and constructive negotiations, avoiding unjustified delays in negotiation and mutually respecting the commitments entered into, taking into account the results of negotiations in good faith.

    I. In view of the fact that the voluntary nature of collective bargaining is a fundamental aspect of the principles of freedom of association, collective bargaining may not be imposed upon the parties and procedures to support bargaining must, in principle, take into account its voluntary nature; moreover, the level of bargaining must not be imposed unilaterally by law or by the authorities, and it must be possible for bargaining to take place at any level.

    J. It is acceptable for conciliation and mediation to be imposed by law in the framework of the process of collective bargaining, provided that reasonable time limits are established. However, the imposition of compulsory arbitration in cases where the parties do not reach agreement is generally contrary to the principle of voluntary collective bargaining and is only admissible: [cases of essential services, administration of the State, clear deadlock, and national crisis].

    K. Interventions by the legislative or administrative authorities which have the effect of annulling or modifying the content of freely concluded collective agreements, including wage clauses, are contrary to the principle of voluntary collective bargaining. These interventions include: the suspension or derogation of collective agreements by decree without the agreement of the parties; the interruption of agreements which have already been negotiated; the requirement that freely concluded collective agreements be renegotiated; the annulment of collective agreements; and the forced renegotiation of agreements which are currently in force. Other types of intervention, such as the compulsory extension of the validity of collective agreements by law are only admissible in cases of emergency and for short periods.

    L. Restrictions on the content of future collective agreements . . . are admissible only in so far as such restrictions are preceded by consultations with the organizations of workers and employers and fulfil the following conditions: [restrictions are exceptional measures; of limited duration; include protection for workers' standards of living].

[. . .]

78. The fact that a global consensus on the meaning of freedom of association did not crystallize in the *Declaration on Fundamental Principles and Rights at Work*, 6 IHRR 285 (1999), until 1998 does not detract from its usefulness in interpreting s. 2(d) of the *Charter*. For one thing, the Declaration was made on the basis of interpretations of international instruments, such as *Convention No. 87*, many of which were adopted by the ILO prior to the advent of the *Charter* and were within the contemplation of the framers of the *Charter*. For another, the *Charter*, as a living document, grows with society and speaks to the current situations and needs of Canadians. Thus Canada's current international law commitments and the current state of international thought on human rights provide a persuasive source for interpreting the scope of the *Charter*.

79. In summary, international conventions to which Canada is a party recognize the right of the members of unions to engage in collective bargaining, as part of the protection for freedom of association. It is reasonable to infer that s. 2(d) of the *Charter* should be interpreted as recognizing at least the same level of protection: *Alberta Reference*.

(c) Charter *Values Support Protecting a Process of Collective Bargaining Under Section 2(d)*

80. Protection for a process of collective bargaining within s. 2(d) is consistent with the *Charter*'s underlying values. The *Charter*, including s. 2(d) itself, should be interpreted in a way that maintains its underlying values and its internal coherence ...

81. Human dignity, equality, liberty, respect for the autonomy of the person and the enhancement of democracy are among the values that underly the *Charter* ... All of these values are complemented and indeed, promoted, by the protection of collective bargaining in s. 2(d) of the *Charter*.

82. The right to bargain collectively with an employer enhances the human dignity, liberty and autonomy of workers by giving them the opportunity to influence the establishment of workplace rules and thereby gain some control over a major aspect of their lives, namely their work (see *Alberta Reference*, at p. 368, and *Wallace v. United Grain Growers Ltd.*, [1997] 3 S.C.R. 701, at para. 93). As explained by P. C. Weiler in *Reconcilable Differences* (1980):

> Collective bargaining is not simply an instrument for pursuing external ends, whether these be mundane monetary gains or the erection of a private rule of law to protect dignity of the worker in the face of managerial authority. Rather, collective bargaining is intrinsically valuable as an experience in self-government. It is the mode in which employees participate in setting the terms and conditions of employment, rather than simply accepting what their employer chooses to give them.... [p. 33]

83. In *R.W.D.S.U., Local 558 v. PepsiCola Canada Beverages (West) Ltd.*, [2002] 1 S.C.R. 156, 2002 SCC 8, we underlined the importance of protecting workers' autonomy:

> Personal issues at stake in labour disputes often go beyond the obvious issues of work availability and wages. Working conditions, like the duration and location of work, parental leave, health benefits, severance and retirement schemes, may impact on the personal lives of workers even outside their working hours. Expression on these issues contributes to self-understanding, as well as to the ability to influence one's working and non-working life. [para. 34]

84. Collective bargaining also enhances the *Charter* value of equality. One of the fundamental achievements of collective bargaining is to palliate the historical inequality between employers and employees....

85. Finally, a constitutional right to collective bargaining is supported by the *Charter* value of enhancing democracy. Collective bargaining permits workers to achieve a form of workplace democracy and to ensure the rule of law in the workplace. Workers gain a voice to influence the establishment of rules that control a major aspect of their lives....

86. We conclude that the protection of collective bargaining under s. 2(d) of the *Charter* is consistent with and supportive of the values underlying the *Charter* and the purposes of the *Charter* as a whole. Recognizing that workers have the right to bargain collectively as part of their freedom to associate reaffirms the values of dignity, personal autonomy, equality and democracy that are inherent in the *Charter*.

(3) Section 2(d) of the *Charter* and the Right to Collective Bargaining

87. The preceding discussion leads to the conclusion that s. 2(d) should be understood as protecting the right of employees to associate for the purpose of advancing workplace goals through a process of collective bargaining. The next question is what this right entails for employees, for government employers subject to the *Charter* under s. 32, and for Parliament and provincial legislatures which adopt labour laws.

[...]

89. The scope of the right to bargain collectively ought to be defined bearing in mind the pronouncements of *Dunmore*, which stressed that s. 2(d) does not apply solely to individual action carried out in common, but also to associational activities themselves. The scope of the right properly reflects the history of collective bargaining and the international covenants entered into by Canada. Based on the principles developed in *Dunmore* and in this historical and international perspective, the constitutional right to collective bargaining concerns the protection of the ability of workers to engage in associational activities, and their capacity to act in common to reach shared goals related to workplace issues and terms of employment. In brief, the protected activity might be described as employees banding together to achieve particular work-related objectives. Section 2(d) does not guarantee the particular objectives sought through this associational activity. However, it guarantees the process through which those goals are pursued. It means that employees have the right to unite, to present demands to health sector employers collectively and to engage in discussions in an attempt to achieve workplace-related goals. Section 2(d) imposes corresponding duties on government employers to agree to meet and discuss with them. It also puts constraints on the exercise of legislative powers in respect of the right to collective bargaining, which we shall discuss below.

90. Section 2(d) of the *Charter* does not protect all aspects of the associational activity of collective bargaining. It protects only against "substantial interference" with associational activity, in accordance with a test crafted in *Dunmore* by Bastarache J., which asked whether "excluding agricultural workers from a statutory labour relations regime, without expressly or intentionally prohibiting association, [can] constitute a substantial interference with freedom of association" (para. 23). Or to put it another way, does the state action target or affect the associational activity, "thereby discouraging the collective

pursuit of common goals"? (*Dunmore*, at para. 16) Nevertheless, intent to interfere with the associational right of collective bargaining is not essential to establish breach of s. 2(*d*) of the *Charter*. It is enough if the *effect* of the state law or action is to *substantially interfere* with the activity of collective bargaining, thereby discouraging the collective pursuit of common goals. It follows that the state must not substantially interfere with the ability of a union to exert meaningful influence over working conditions through a process of collective bargaining conducted in accordance with the duty to bargain in good faith. Thus the employees' right to collective bargaining imposes corresponding duties on the employer. It requires both employer and employees to meet and to bargain in good faith, in the pursuit of a common goal of peaceful and productive accommodation.

91. The right to collective bargaining thus conceived is a limited right. First, as the right is to a process, it does not guarantee a certain substantive or economic outcome. Moreover, the right is to a general process of collective bargaining, not to a particular model of labour relations, nor to a specific bargaining method.... Finally, and most importantly, the interference, as *Dunmore* instructs, must be substantial—so substantial that it interferes not only with the attainment of the union members' objectives (which is not protected), but with the very process that enables them to pursue these objectives by engaging in meaningful negotiations with the employer.

92. To constitute *substantial interference* with freedom of association, the intent or effect must seriously undercut or undermine the activity of workers joining together to pursue the common goals of negotiating workplace conditions and terms of employment with their employer that we call collective bargaining. Laws or actions that can be characterized as "union breaking" clearly meet this requirement. But less dramatic interference with the collective process may also suffice. In *Dunmore*, denying the union access to the labour laws of Ontario designed to support and give a voice to unions was enough. Acts of bad faith, or unilateral nullification of negotiated terms, without any process of meaningful discussion and consultation may also significantly undermine the process of collective bargaining. The inquiry in every case is contextual and fact-specific. The question in every case is whether the process of voluntary, good faith collective bargaining between employees and the employer has been, or is likely to be, significantly and adversely impacted.

93. Generally speaking, determining whether a government measure affecting the protected process of collective bargaining amounts to substantial interference involves two inquiries. The first inquiry is into the importance of the matter affected to the process of collective bargaining, and more specifically, to the capacity of the union members to come together and pursue collective goals in concert. The second inquiry is into the manner in which the measure impacts on the collective right to good faith negotiation and consultation.

94. Both inquiries are necessary. If the matters affected do not substantially impact on the process of collective bargaining, the measure does not violate s. 2(*d*) and, indeed, the employer may be under no duty to discuss and consult. There will be no need to consider process issues. If, on the other hand, the changes substantially touch on collective bargaining, they will still not violate s. 2(*d*) if they preserve a process of consultation and good faith negotiation.

95. Turning to the first inquiry, the essential question is whether the subject matter of a particular instance of collective bargaining is such that interfering with bargaining over that issue will affect the ability of unions to pursue common goals collectively ... The more important the matter, the more likely that there is substantial interference with the s. 2(d) right. ...

96. ... Laws or state actions that prevent or deny meaningful discussion and consultation about working conditions between employees and their employer may substantially interfere with the activity of collective bargaining, as may laws that unilaterally nullify significant negotiated terms in existing collective agreements. By contrast, measures affecting less important matters such as the design of uniform, the lay out and organization of cafeterias, or the location or availability of parking lots, may be far less likely to constitute significant interference with the s. 2(d) right of freedom of association. ...

97. [Then], the need for the second inquiry arises: does the legislative measure or government conduct in issue respect the fundamental precept of collective bargaining—the duty to consult and negotiate in good faith? ...

[...]

100. A basic element of the duty to bargain in good faith is the obligation to actually meet and to commit time to the process. ...

101. The parties have a duty to engage in meaningful dialogue and they must be willing to exchange and explain their positions. They must make a reasonable effort to arrive at an acceptable contract. ...

102. Nevertheless, the efforts that must be invested to attain an agreement are not boundless. "[T]he parties may reach a point in the bargaining process where further discussions are no longer fruitful. Once such a point is reached, a breaking off of negotiations or the adoption of a 'take it or leave it' position is not likely to be regarded as a failure to bargain in good faith" ...

103. The duty to bargain in good faith does not impose on the parties an obligation to conclude a collective agreement, nor does it include a duty to accept any particular contractual provisions. ... Nor does the duty to bargain in good faith preclude hard bargaining. The parties are free to adopt a "tough position in the hope and expectation of being able to force the other side to agree to one's terms" ...

104. In principle, the duty to bargain in good faith does not inquire into the nature of the proposals made in the course of collective bargaining; the content is left to the bargaining forces of the parties. ... However, when the examination of the content of the bargaining shows hostility from one party toward the collective bargaining process, this will constitute a breach of the duty to bargain in good faith. In some circumstances, even though a party is participating in the bargaining, that party's proposals and positions may be "inflexible and intransigent to the point of endangering the very existence of collective bargaining" ... This inflexible approach is often referred to as "surface bargaining." This Court has explained the distinction between hard bargaining, which is legal, and surface bargaining, which is a breach of the duty to bargain in good faith. ...

105. Even though the employer participates in all steps of the bargaining process, if the nature of its proposals and positions is aimed at avoiding the conclusion of a

collective agreement or at destroying the collective bargaining relationship, the duty to bargain in good faith will be breached....

106. ... Under Canadian labour law, all conditions of employment attract an obligation to bargain in good faith unless the subject matter is otherwise contrary to the law and could not legally be included in a collective agreement.... However, the refusal to discuss an issue merely on the periphery of the negotiations does not necessarily breach the duty to bargain in good faith....

107. In considering whether the legislative provisions impinge on the collective right to good faith negotiations and consultation, regard must be had for the circumstances surrounding their adoption. Situations of exigency and urgency may affect the content and the modalities of the duty to bargain in good faith. Different situations may demand different processes and timelines. Moreover, failure to comply with the duty to consult and bargain in good faith should not be lightly found, and should be clearly supported on the record. Nevertheless, there subsists a requirement that the provisions of the Act preserve the process of good faith consultation fundamental to collective bargaining. That is the bottom line.

[...]

109. In summary, s. 2(d) may be breached by government legislation or conduct that substantially interferes with the collective bargaining process. Substantial interference must be determined contextually, on the facts of the case, having regard to the importance of the matter affected to the collective activity, and to the manner in which the government measure is accomplished. Important changes effected through a process of good faith negotiation may not violate s. 2(d). Conversely, less central matters may be changed more summarily, without violating s. 2(d). Only where the matter is both important to the process of collective bargaining, and has been imposed in violation of the duty of good faith negotiation, will s. 2(d) be breached.

(4) Application of the Law to the Facts at Bar

110. ... Ultimately, we conclude that ss. 6(2), 6(4) and 9 of the Act are unconstitutional because they infringe the right to collective bargaining protected under s. 2(d) and cannot be saved under s. 1. The remainder of Part 2 of the Act (consisting of ss. 3, 4, 5, 7, 8 and 10) does not violate the right to collective bargaining and withstands constitutional scrutiny under s. 2(d).

(a) Does the Act Infringe the Right to Bargain Collectively Under Section 2(d) of the Charter?
[...]

112. On the analysis proposed above, two questions suggest themselves. First, does the measure interfere with collective bargaining, in purpose or effect? Secondly, if the measure interferes with collective bargaining, is the impact, evaluated in terms of the matters affected and the process by which the measure was implemented, significant enough to substantially interfere with the associational right of collective bargaining, so as to breach the s. 2(d) right of freedom of association?

(i) Does the Act Interfere with Collective Bargaining?

113. Sections 4 to 10 of the Act have the potential to interfere with collective bargaining in two ways: first, by invalidating existing collective agreements and consequently undermining the past bargaining processes that formed the basis for these agreements;

and second, by prohibiting provisions dealing with specified matters in future collective agreements and thereby undermining future collective bargaining over those matters. Future restrictions on the content of collective agreements constitute an interference with collective bargaining because there can be no real dialogue over terms and conditions that can never be enacted as part of the collective agreement.

114. [T]he right to bargain collectively protects not just the act of making representations, but also the right of employees to have their views heard in the context of a meaningful process of consultation and discussion.... While the language of the Act does not technically prohibit collective representations to an employer, the right to collective bargaining cannot be reduced to a mere right to make representations. The necessary implication of the Act is that prohibited matters cannot be adopted into a valid collective agreement, with the result that the process of collective bargaining becomes meaningless with respect to them. This constitutes interference with collective bargaining.

115. A more detailed examination of Part 2 of the Act suggests that some of the provisions substantially interfere with the process of collective bargaining. They affect matters of substantial importance to employees, and they fail to safeguard the basic processes of collective bargaining. In proceeding through this analysis, it is critical to bear in mind the relationship between ss. 4 to 9 and s. 10 of the Act, which has the effect of voiding provisions of any collective agreement to the extent that these provisions are inconsistent with Part 2 of the Act.

1. Sections 4 and 5

[...]

117. Sections 4 and 5 altered the provisions for transfer and reassignment, as they existed in some collective agreements prior to the Act. Specific rights in existing collective agreements that employees lost when ss. 4 and 5 were enacted included: a requirement that the employer consider enumerated criteria in making hiring decisions, a guarantee that temporary assignments would not exceed four months, some protections for seniority, and the right to refuse a transfer if the employee has other employment options with the original employer under the collective agreement.

118. However ... protections similar in part to what the employees had under existing collective agreements were preserved. Notably, the regulation provided employees with a right to refuse being transferred outside of their geographic location without their consent, and a right to reasonable relocation expenses.... These were substantially similar to entitlements that some employees previously had under their collective agreements. Thus although ss. 4 and 5 of the Act (together with s. 10) nullified some of the employee's entitlements under existing collective agreements, they appear to have preserved the substance of the central aspects of the provisions of existing collective agreements that dealt with those questions. We therefore conclude that ss. 4 and 5 may have had some impact on prior collective agreements, although the impact was not great.

119. Nevertheless, the effect of ss. 4 and 5, in conjunction with s. 10, is to render future collective bargaining over transfers and reassignments largely meaningless, since collective bargaining cannot alter the employer's right to make transfers and reassignments. Section 10 of the Act would render void any terms inconsistent with ss. 4 and 5. Because it is meaningless to bargain over an issue which cannot ever be included in a

collective agreement, ss. 4 and 5, considered together with s. 10, interfere with future collective bargaining.

2. Section 6

120. Section 6(2) gives the employer increased power to contract out non-clinical services. Prior to the enactment of the Act, all collective agreements in the health care sector contained provisions restricting the right of management to contract out work. These provisions were inconsistent with s. 6(2) when that section was passed. The effect of s. 6(2), together with s. 10, is to invalidate these provisions in prior collective agreements. Further, s. 6(4), in conjunction with s. 10, invalidates any provision of a collective agreement that requires an employer to consult with a trade union prior to contracting outside the bargaining unit . . .

121. The combined effect of ss. 6(2), 6(4) and 10 is to forbid the incorporation into future collective agreements of provisions protecting employees from contracting out, or the inclusion of a provision requiring the employer to consult with the union. The prohibition on including certain provisions in a collective agreement related to contracting out is reflected in explicit language in s. 6(2), that "[a] collective agreement . . . must not contain a provision" dealing with certain aspects of contracting out. The prohibition both repudiates past collective bargaining relating to the issue of contracting out and makes future collective bargaining over this issue meaningless. It follows that ss. 6(2) and 6(4) have the effect of interfering with collective bargaining.

[Chief Justice McLachlin and LeBel J then held that sections 6(3), 6(5), 6(6), 7, and 8 did not interfere with collective bargaining and did not infringe the right to collective bargaining under section 2(d).]

[. . .]

4. Section 9—Layoff and Bumping

126. Section 9, which applies only to collective agreements up until December 31, 2005, deals with layoff and bumping. During the currency of this section, collective agreements could not contain provisions dealing with certain aspects of layoff and bumping. With respect to layoff, no collective agreement could restrict the right of health care employers to lay off employees (s. 9(*a*)), nor require them to meet conditions before giving layoff notice (s. 9(*b*)), nor provide notice beyond the 60 days guaranteed under the *Labour Relations Code* (s. 9(c)). With respect to bumping, no collective agreement could contain a provision providing an employee with bumping options other than those set out in regulations pursuant to the Act (s. 9(d)).

127. Section 9 made collective bargaining over specified aspects of layoff and bumping meaningless and also invalidated parts of collective agreements dealing with these issues, up to December 31, 2005. This constituted interference with both past and future collective bargaining, albeit an interference limited to the period between the enactment of the Act and December 31, 2005.

128. We conclude that ss. 4, 5, 6(2), 6(4) and 9, in conjunction with s. 10, interfere with the process of collective bargaining, either by disregarding past processes of collective bargaining, by pre-emptively undermining future processes of collective bargaining,

or both. This requires us to determine whether these changes substantially interfere with the associational right of the employees to engage in collective bargaining on workplace matters and terms of employment.

(ii) Was the Interference Substantial, so as to Constitute a Breach of Freedom of Association?
129. To amount to a breach of the s. 2(d) freedom of association, the interference with collective bargaining must compromise the essential integrity of the process of collective bargaining protected by s. 2(d). Two inquiries are relevant here. First, substantial interference is more likely to be found in measures impacting matters central to the freedom of association of workers, and to the capacity of their associations (the unions) to achieve common goals by working in concert. This suggests an inquiry into the nature of the affected right. Second, the manner in which the right is curtailed may affect its impact on the process of collective bargaining and ultimately freedom of association. To this end, we must inquire into the process by which the changes were made and how they impact on the voluntary good faith underpinning of collective bargaining. Even where a matter is of central importance to the associational right, if the change has been made through a process of good faith consultation it is unlikely to have adversely affected the employees' right to collective bargaining. Both inquiries, as discussed earlier, are essential.

1. The Importance of the Provisions
130. The provisions dealing with contracting out (ss. 6(2) and 6(4)), layoffs (ss. 9(a), 9(b) and 9(c)) and bumping (s. 9(d)) deal with matters central to the freedom of association. Restrictions in collective agreements limiting the employer's discretion to lay off employees affect the employees' capacity to retain secure employment, one of the most essential protections provided to workers by their union. Similarly, limits in collective agreements on the management rights of employers to contract out allow workers to gain employment security. Finally, bumping rights are an integral part of the seniority system usually established under collective agreements, which is a protection of significant importance to the union ... Viewing the Act's interference with these essential rights in the context of the case as a whole, we conclude that its interference with collective bargaining over matters pertaining to contracting out, layoff conditions and bumping constitutes substantial interference with the s. 2(d) right of freedom of association.

131. The same cannot be said of the transfers and reassignments covered under ss. 4 and 5 of the Act. These provisions, as discussed above, are concerned with relatively minor modifications to in-place schemes for transferring and reassigning employees. Significant protections remained in place. It is true that the Act took these issues off the collective bargaining table for the future. However, on balance ss. 4 and 5 cannot be said to amount to a substantial interference with the union's ability to engage in collective bargaining so as to attract the protection under s. 2(d) of the *Charter*.

2. The Process of Interference with Collective Bargaining Rights
132. Having concluded that the subject matter of ss. 6(2), 6(4) and 9 of the Act is of central importance to the unions and their ability to carry on collective bargaining, we must now consider whether those provisions preserve the processes of collective bargaining. Together, these two inquiries will permit us to assess whether the law at issue here

constitutes significant interference with the collective aspect of freedom of association, which *Dunmore* recognized.

133. This inquiry refocuses our attention squarely and exclusively on how the provisions affect the process of good faith bargaining and consultation. In this case, we are satisfied that ss. 6(2), 6(4) and 9 interfere significantly with the ability of those bound by them to engage in the associational activity of collective bargaining.

134. It is true that the government was facing a situation of exigency. It was determined to come to grips with the spiralling cost of health care in British Columbia. This determination was fuelled by the laudable desire to provide quality health services to the people of British Columbia. Concerns such as these must be taken into account in assessing whether the measures adopted disregard the fundamental s. 2(d) obligation to preserve the processes of good faith negotiation and consultation with unions.

135. The difficulty, however, is that the measures adopted by the government constitute a virtual denial of the s. 2(d) right to a process of good faith bargaining and consultation. The absolute prohibition on contracting out in s. 6(2), as discussed, eliminates any possibility of consultation. Section 6(4) puts the nail in the coffin of consultation by making void any provisions in a collective agreement imposing a requirement to consult before contracting out. Section 9, in like fashion, effectively precludes consultation with the union prior to laying off or bumping.

136. We conclude that ss. 6(2), 6(4) and 9 of the legislation constitute a significant interference with the right to bargain collectively and hence violate s. 2(d) of the *Charter*. . . .

(b) Are the Violations of Section 2(d) Justified Under Section 1?

[. . .]

140. In this case, the infringement of the appellants' right to bargain collectively is unquestionably prescribed by law, since the interference with collective bargaining is set out in legislation . . .

[The judgment then held that the Act pursued a pressing and substantial objective, and that although evidence to this effect was somewhat lacking, there was a reasonable connection between that objective and the means adopted by the Act.]

(iii) Does the Act Minimally Impair the Charter *Rights of the Appellants?*

[. . .]

151. . . . The government provides no evidence to support a conclusion that the impairment was minimal. It contents itself with an assertion of its legislative goal—"to enhance management flexibility and accountability in order to make the health care system sustainable over the long term,"—adding that "the Act is a measured, reasonable, and effective response to this challenge, and . . . satisfies the minimal impairment requirement". . . . In the absence of supportive evidence, we are unable to conclude that the requirement of minimal impairment is made out in this case.

152. The provisions at issue bear little evidence of a search for a minimally impairing solution to the problem the government sought to address.

153. Section 6(2) forbids any provision "that in any manner restricts, limits or regulates the right of a health sector employer to contract outside of the collective agreement."

It gives the employers absolute power to contract out of collective agreements. There is no need or incentive to consult with the union or the employees before sending the work they normally perform to an outside contractor. To forbid any contracting out clause completely and unconditionally strikes us as not minimally impairing. A more refined provision, for example, permitting contracting out after meaningful consultation with the union, might be envisaged.

154. Section 6(4) makes void a provision in a collective agreement to consult before contracting out. The bite of s. 6(4) is arguably small; given the employer's absolute power to contract out under s. 6(2), there would appear to be no reason for an employer to agree to such a clause in any event. However, insofar as it hammers home the policy of no consultation under any circumstances, it can scarcely be described as suggesting a search for a solution that preserves collective bargaining rights as much as possible, given the legislature's goal.

155. Section 9 evinces a similar disregard for the duty to consult the union, in this case before making changes to the collective agreement's layoff and bumping rules. It is true that s. 9 was temporally limited, being in force only to December 31, 2005. However, this is scant comfort to employees who may have been laid off or bumped before this date, without the benefit of a union to represent them on the issue.

156. An examination of the record as to alternatives considered by the government reinforces the conclusion that the impairment in this case did not fall within the range of reasonable alternatives available to the government in achieving its pressing and substantial objective of improving health care delivery. The record discloses no consideration by the government of whether it could reach its goal by less intrusive measures, and virtually no consultation with unions on the matter.

157. Legislators are not bound to consult with affected parties before passing legislation. On the other hand, it may be useful to consider, in the course of the s. 1 justification analysis, whether the government considered other options or engaged consultation with the affected parties, in choosing to adopt its preferred approach. The Court has looked at pre-legislative considerations in the past in the context of minimal impairment. This is simply evidence going to whether other options, in a range of possible options, were explored.

158. In this case, the only evidence presented by the government, including the sealed evidence, confirmed that a range of options were on the table. One was chosen. The government presented no evidence as to why this particular solution was chosen and why there was no consultation with the unions about the range of options open to it.

159. The evidence establishes that there was no meaningful consultation prior to passing the Act on the part of either the government or the HEABC (as employer). The HEABC neither attempted to renegotiate provisions of the collective agreements in force prior to the adoption of Bill 29, nor considered any other way to address the concerns noted by the government relating to labour costs and the lack of flexibility in administrating the health care sector. The government also failed to engage in meaningful bargaining or consultation prior to the adoption of Bill 29 or to provide the unions with any other means of exerting meaningful influence over the outcome of the process (for example, a satisfactory system of labour conciliation or arbitration). Union

representatives had repeatedly expressed a desire to consult with government regarding specific aspects of the Act, and had conveyed to the government that the matters to be dealt with under the Act were of particular significance to them. Indeed, the government had indicated willingness to consult on prior occasions. Yet, in this case, consultation never took place. The only evidence of consultation is a brief telephone conversation between a member of the government and a union representative within the half hour before the Act (then Bill 29) went to the legislature floor and limited to informing the union of the actions that the government intended to take.

160. This was an important and significant piece of labour legislation. It had the potential to affect the rights of employees dramatically and unusually. Yet it was adopted with full knowledge that the unions were strongly opposed to many of the provisions, and without consideration of alternative ways to achieve the government objective, and without explanation of the government's choices.

161. We conclude that the government has not shown that the Act minimally impaired the employees' s. 2(*d*) right of collective bargaining. It is unnecessary to consider the proportionality between the pressing and substantial government objectives and the means adopted by the law to achieve these objectives. We find that the offending provisions of the Act (ss. 6(2), 6(4) and 9) cannot be justified as reasonable limits under s. 1 of the *Charter* and are therefore unconstitutional.

B. Does the Act Violate Section 15 Equality Rights?

[...]

164. At issue is whether the Act violates s. 15 of the *Charter*, and more specifically, that the Act discriminates against health care workers based on a number of interrelated enumerated and analogous grounds including: sex, employment in the health care sector, and status as non-clinical workers.

165. The courts below found no discrimination contrary to s. 15 of the *Charter*. We would not disturb these findings. Like the courts below, we conclude that the distinctions made by the Act relate essentially to segregating different sectors of employment, in accordance with the long-standing practice in labour regulation of creating legislation specific to particular segments of the labour force, and do not amount to discrimination under s. 15 of the *Charter*. The differential and adverse effects of the legislation on some groups of workers relate essentially to the type of work they do, and not to the persons they are. Nor does the evidence disclose that the Act reflects the stereotypical application of group or personal characteristics. Without minimizing the importance of the distinctions made by the Act to the lives and work of affected health care employees, the differential treatment based on personal characteristics required to get a discrimination analysis off the ground is absent here.

166. Accordingly, we see no reason to depart from the view of the trial judge that these effects on health care workers, however painful, do not, on the evidence adduced in this case, constitute discrimination under s. 15 of the *Charter*.

167. In summary, we find that the impugned Act does not violate s. 15 of the *Charter*. Therefore, there is no need to consider potential reasonable justification under s. 1

IV. CONCLUSIONS AND DISPOSITION

168. ... We conclude that ss. 6(2), 6(4) and 9 of the Act are unconstitutional. However, we suspend this declaration for a period of 12 months to allow the government to address the repercussions of this decision. ...

[Justice Deschamps, dissenting in part, accepted the majority's view on the scope of freedom of association under section 2(d) of the *Charter*. However, she rejected the majority's analysis both on the infringement of section 2(d) and on the justification of that infringement under section 1. She found the legislation to be rationally connected to the pressing and substantial objectives pursued, and that with the exception of section 6(4), those measures all met the requirement of minimal impairment and proportionate effects.]

* * * * *

12:222 The Final Case of the Second Trilogy: *Fraser v Ontario (Attorney General)*

Both *Dunmore* and *Fraser* are cases about the fate of Ontario's agricultural workers. Unlike *Health Services* or the cases of the 1987 Trilogy, these two cases involve private actors, positive obligations, and underinclusion. While *Health Services* was widely hailed as a positive development, an academic debate ensued about the legal reasoning used to arrive at the legal result—in particular, the Court's use of legal history, international law, and its basic approach to section 2(d). Much of that debate stalks and often surfaces in *Fraser*. Justice Rothstein's well-known dissent is essentially a (four-year late) "dissent" from *Health Services*, urging its overruling (Rothstein J was not on the Court at the time of *Health Services*) and relying on criticisms of the reasoning in *Health Services*. We have not included the majority's specific responses to Rothstein J's dissent.

We begin *Fraser* with the decision of the Ontario Court of Appeal, because the decision of Winkler CJO (who was one of Canada's leading management-side labour lawyers before being appointed to the bench) gives us insight into the large implications of the Supreme Court's decision in *Health Services*. Such insight is one of several necessary preludes to any attempt at understanding the Supreme Court's decision in *Fraser*, which follows.

Fraser v Ontario (Attorney General), 2008 ONCA 760

WINKLER C.J.O. (for the court):

[...]

5. In response to *Dunmore*, the government [of Ontario] enacted the *Agricultural Employees Protection Act, 2002*, S.O. 2002, c. 16 (the "AEPA"). The legislation, which came into force on June 17, 2003, excludes agricultural workers from the [Ontario *Labour Relations Act ("LRA")*] but provides certain protections for organizing.

6. ... After failing to engage factory farm employers in collective bargaining on behalf of farm employees, the [United Food and Commercial Workers Union Canada ("UFCW")] and the individual appellants brought an application disputing the constitutionality of the *AEPA* ...

CHAPTER 12: THE CONSTITUTIONALIZATION OF COLLECTIVE BARGAINING LAW

7. The application judge dismissed the *Charter* challenge. However, the legal landscape has been altered since the application was originally heard and determined. When the application judge was seized of the case, the prevailing higher authority was *Dunmore* and the so-called labour trilogy....

9. Reversing the labour trilogy on the issue of collective bargaining, the Supreme Court concluded in *B.C. Health Services* that freedom of association, as guaranteed by s. 2(d), protects "the right of employees to associate for the purpose of advancing workplace goals through a process of collective bargaining"....

10. Therefore, the central issues on this appeal are whether the impugned legislation violates s. 2(d) of the *Charter* by failing to provide agricultural workers in Ontario with sufficient statutory protections to enable them to exercise (a) their freedom to organize and (b) their right to bargain collectively.

11. In light of the combined effect of *Dunmore* and *B.C. Health Services*, I conclude that the *AEPA* breaches s. 2(d). While the application judge correctly found that the *AEPA* provides the minimum requirements necessary to protect the appellants' freedom to organize, he did not have the benefit of the Supreme Court's judgment in *B.C. Health Services* to guide him in his analysis of the claims concerning collective bargaining. Taking into account the change in the legal landscape, I conclude that the *AEPA* substantially impairs the capacity of agricultural workers to meaningfully exercise their right to bargain collectively. This is not surprising in that the legislation itself was drafted with an apparent view to complying with the more limited interpretation of s. 2(d) set out in *Dunmore*.

12. Moreover, the violation of s. 2(d) is not saved under s. 1 of the *Charter*. The objectives of protecting the family farm and farm production/viability are substantial and pressing goals, but the impugned legislation does not satisfy the *Oakes* proportionality test ... It is open to the government, however, to seek to draft new legislation that balances the rights of agricultural workers with the concerns about the family farm and the viability of the agricultural sector in a manner that can withstand s. 1 *Charter* scrutiny.

13. I would therefore allow the appeal and declare the *AEPA* constitutionally invalid. However, I would also suspend this declaration of invalidity for 12 months from the date of these reasons in order that the government may determine the manner in which it wishes to statutorily protect the collective bargaining rights of agricultural workers ...

[Chief Justice of Ontario Winkler then outlined the history of labour relations in Ontario's agricultural sector and the key features of the *AEPA*.]

36. While I agree with the application judge that the *AEPA* does not violate the appellants' freedom to organize, in light of the Supreme Court of Canada's decisions in *Dunmore* and *B.C. Health Services*, I cannot accede to the respondent's arguments when it comes to the right to bargain collectively. The failure of the *AEPA* to provide protections for collective bargaining constitutes a breach of s. 2(d) and demands a remedy if not justified by s. 1. I begin my s. 2(d) analysis with a detailed discussion of *Dunmore* and *B.C. Health Services*, which underpin my analysis.

ISSUE 1: Does the impugned legislation violate the appellants' s. 2(d) rights?

A. The Scope of s. 2(d)

[Chief Justice of Ontario Winkler then reviewed the Supreme Court of Canada decisions in *Dunmore* and *B.C. Health*.]

52. In summary, the combined effect of *Dunmore* and *B.C. Health Services* is to recognize that s. 2(d) protects the right of workers to organize and to engage in meaningful collective bargaining. The decisions also recognize that, in certain circumstances, s. 2(d) may impose obligations on the government to enact legislation to protect the rights and freedoms of vulnerable groups.

[...]

59. Following *Dunmore* and *B.C. Health Services*, I conclude that the appellants' claims are grounded in the fundamental freedom of association rather than in the denial of access to the *LRA*. ...

60. Section 2(d) does not protect against all interferences with the freedom of association, rather only substantial interferences ... A substantial interference can occur either through the purpose or the effect of government action, but it must "seriously undercut or undermine" an activity protected by s. 2(d).... As held in *Dunmore*, underinclusive legislation may substantially interfere with a claimant's rights under s. 2(d).

61. The appellants submit that the *AEPA* regime is underinclusive because it fails to provide adequate statutory protections to enable agricultural workers to organize and to bargain collectively in a meaningful way. Thus, they contend that both the purpose and the effect of the *AEPA* interfere with the freedom of agricultural workers to organize and their right to bargain collectively. While I do not accept this argument in its entirety, in my view, there is no doubt that, with respect to the right to bargain collectively, the interference with their s. 2(d) rights is substantial for the following reasons....

65. ... The *AEPA* does not, on its face, prohibit agricultural workers from collective bargaining. The respondent submits that the legislation's objectives include the protection of the family farm, farm production and farm viability. Recognizing the difficulties of assessing legislative intent in these circumstances, it is more appropriate to focus on the effect of the *AEPA*....

66. ... In my view, the appellants have demonstrated that the impugned legislation substantially interferes with the ability of agricultural workers to bargain collectively. However, I am not persuaded that it impairs agricultural workers' ability to exercise their freedom to organize.

67. Both the appellants and the respondent led evidence of the vulnerability of agricultural workers....

[...]

69. Based on this evidence, I agree with the application judge who found that agricultural workers remain a vulnerable group ...

70. Given the vulnerability of agricultural workers, the evidence shows that it has been virtually impossible for agricultural workers to organize and to bargain collectively with their employers without statutory supports. Except under the *ALRA*, the parties

have not pointed to any instance where a union or employees' association has successfully organized and then been able to engage in the process of good faith collective bargaining on behalf of agricultural workers in Ontario....

72. The appellants' evidence, which details the UFCW's attempts to organize and to bargain collectively on behalf of agricultural workers at Rol-Land and Platinum Produce, shows that agricultural workers have been unable to bargain collectively under the AEPA....

78. In my view, this evidence demonstrates that the *AEPA*—which excludes agricultural workers from the *LRA* and which provides no protections for collective bargaining—substantially impairs the ability of agricultural workers to engage in collective bargaining. When Rol-Land and Platinum Produce refused to bargain with the UFCW, the union and employees were left without any remedy under the *AEPA*, as the employers were under no statutory duty to bargain in good faith with the employees' chosen representative.

79. ... [T]he evidence demonstrates that the failure to provide any protections for collective bargaining seriously impairs the capacity of agricultural workers to come together and meaningfully engage in the very process of collective bargaining.

80. If legislation is to provide for meaningful collective bargaining, it must go further than simply stating the principle and must include provisions that ensure that the right can be realized. At a minimum, the following statutory protections are required to enable agricultural workers to exercise their right to bargain collectively in a meaningful way: (1) a statutory duty to bargain in good faith; (2) statutory recognition of the principles of exclusivity and majoritarianism; and (3) a statutory mechanism for resolving bargaining impasses and disputes regarding the interpretation or administration of collective agreements.

81. Without a statutory duty to bargain in good faith, there can be no meaningful collective bargaining process. To quote the Supreme Court in *B.C. Health Services*, s. 2(d) protects "the ability of a union to exert meaningful influence over working conditions through a process of collective bargaining conducted in accordance with the duty to bargain in good faith": para. 90. Good faith collective bargaining "requires both employer and employees to meet and to bargain in good faith, in the pursuit of a common goal of peaceful and productive accommodation": para. 90.

82. In keeping with that goal, legislation dealing with collective bargaining must also provide a mechanism for resolving bargaining impasses. The bargaining process is jeopardized if the parties have nothing to which they can resort in the face of fruitless bargaining. There exists a broad range of collective bargaining dispute resolution mechanisms. I reiterate that the appellants have stated that they do not seek the right to strike as the dispute resolution mechanism.

83. Once bargaining has concluded, there must also be a statutory mechanism to resolve disputes relating to the interpretation and administration of the agreement. If an employer is able to unilaterally interpret the agreement that results from bargaining, that bargaining might as well have never occurred.

84. Another key aspect of the collective bargaining process is the recognition of a representative organization ...

[...]

86. The respondent submits that employee representatives need not be selected based on the principles of majoritarianism and exclusivity. The respondent says that exclusivity provisions are simply a feature of certain statutory regimes, such as the *LRA*, and are not typically found in the labour legislation of most European countries. I reject the respondent's submission on this point for three reasons.

87. First, I am instructed by *Dunmore* and *B.C. Health Services* to apply a contextual approach that takes into account the history and current reality of labour relations in the Canadian context. Labour relations policy in Canada has long recognized that allowing multiple worker representatives for workers performing similar functions is conducive to employer influence over employee associations, and thus undermines collective bargaining. This policy is reflected in collective bargaining legislation across the country. A common element found within labour relations statutes across Canada is a mechanism to allow workers to select, on a majority basis, a trade union free of employer interference with exclusive bargaining rights to represent them. ...

89. Second, exclusivity is consistent with the *Charter* values underlying collective bargaining, as they are described by the Supreme Court in *B.C. Health Services*. Exclusivity provides workers with a unified, and thus, a more effective voice from which to promote their collective workplace interests. It therefore promotes workplace democracy and, thus, what the Supreme Court describes as "the *Charter* value of enhancing democracy": *B.C. Health Services*, at para. 85.

90. Exclusivity is also key to mitigating the historical inequality between employers and employees, bringing about a more equitable balance of power in the workplace. It thus enhances equality, which the Supreme Court recognized was an important *Charter* value promoted through collective bargaining: para. 84. "One of the fundamental achievements of collective bargaining," noted McLachlin C.J. and LeBel J., "is to palliate the historical inequality between employers and employees": *B.C. Health Services*, at para. 84.

91. Majoritarian exclusivity is essential to ensure this balance of power. Not only does it empower a bargaining representative in its dealings with the employer, at the same time it confirms to the employer that the bargaining representative speaks with the support of the preponderance of the employees. As such, the notion of majoritarian exclusivity is a core value in any vibrant collective bargaining system in Canada.

92. Third, for the collective bargaining process to be meaningful, it must be workable and fair for employees and employers. It is impractical to expect employers to engage in good faith bargaining discussions when confronted with a process that does not eradicate the possibility of irreconcilable demands from multiple employee representatives, purporting to simultaneously represent employees in the same workplace with similar job functions. It is not overstating the point to say that to avoid chaos in the workplace to the detriment of the employer and employees alike, it is essential that a representative organization be selected on a majoritarian basis and imbued with exclusive bargaining rights.

93. The notion of majoritarianism is essential to trade unions because, in order for a trade union to be effective, it must have the support of the majority of workers. Conversely, it is unrealistic to expect an employer to bargain in good faith with a trade union that does not enjoy the support of the majority of the employees it represents.

94. Moreover, I would reject the respondent's claim that the protections sought by the appellants—duties upon the employer to bargain exclusively with a majority-selected representative and to do so in good faith, as well as dispute-resolution mechanisms—are in fact provisions aimed at ensuring that the union can achieve its objectives, and thus deal with the substantive outcomes of collective bargaining, rather than the process.

95. This argument is based on a narrow, literal interpretation of isolated portions of the reasons in *B.C. Health Services* that is inconsistent with the decision read as a whole. To give effect to this argument would be to disregard entirely the context of the Canadian notion of collective bargaining, which was at the foundation of the Supreme Court's reasoning.

96. While it is true that the right to bargain collectively does not guarantee any particular outcome, it is disingenuous to characterize protections ensuring the effectiveness of the collective bargaining process as similarly ensuring any particular substantive outcome. Indeed, in *B.C. Health Services*, the Supreme Court stated that the right to bargain collectively must entail more than just the right to make representations, it must also protect "the right of employees to have their views heard in the context of a meaningful process of consultation and discussion": para. 114.

97. Turning next to the appellants' argument that the *AEPA* does not provide adequate statutory support for the freedom to organize, I would make the following comments.

98. Based on the evidence in this case, I am not persuaded that the *AEPA* substantially interferes with the ability of agricultural workers to organize. The evidence ... shows that the UFCW has been successful in organizing agricultural workers since the advent of the *AEPA*. The primary difficulty has been that the union has been unsuccessful in engaging employers, who have no statutory duty to bargain in good faith, in the process of collective bargaining. To the extent there have been issues relating to employer interference, intimidation or coercion, an employee or employees' association may bring a complaint to the Tribunal, alleging a contravention of ss. 8 to 10 of the *AEPA*....

100. With regard to the appellants' submission that the Tribunal is ineffective and that the *AEPA* does not provide sufficiently broad protection against interference, intimidation and coercion, I agree with the application judge that it is premature to address these issues, since there is no evidence of any attempts to bring forward any complaints to the Tribunal. That said, I agree with the appellants that robust protection from employer interference is critical to a meaningful labour relations scheme ...

101. I conclude, therefore, that the appellants have demonstrated that the AEPA substantially interferes with s. 2(d) in that it fails to provide sufficient protections to enable agricultural workers to engage in a meaningful process of collective bargaining.

(5) Is the government responsible for the inability to exercise the fundamental freedom?
[...]

103. ... Applying *Dunmore*, I am satisfied that the government's legislative actions in the realm of labour relations are responsible for the appellants' inability to engage in a meaningful process of collective bargaining....

107. ... The exclusion of agricultural workers from a collective bargaining regime has a chilling effect on their efforts to exercise their right to bargain collectively. Accordingly, the inability of agricultural workers to bargain collectively is linked to state action.

[...]

ISSUE 2: Does the impugned legislation violate the right to equality under s. 15 of the *Charter* by denying agricultural workers equal protection and equal benefit of the law based on their occupational status as agricultural workers?

[...]
111. I accept the appellants' argument that the *AEPA* perpetuates and reinforces the pre-existing disadvantage of agricultural workers, but agree with the respondent that the distinction is not based on an enumerated or analogous ground. This view is supported by the Supreme Court's decisions in *B.C. Health Services* and *Baier*.

...

114. Likewise, in view of the record in this case, there is no basis for finding that "agricultural worker" is an analogous ground. The *AEPA* identifies an economic sector and limits the access of workers within that sector to aspects of a particular labour relations scheme. "Agricultural worker" includes workers with different qualifications, personal backgrounds and occupations within an economic sector. The category of "agricultural worker" does not denote a personal characteristic of the type necessary to support a s. 15 discrimination claim.

115. Accordingly, I would dismiss the appellants' s. 15 claim.

ISSUE 3: Is the violation of s. 2(d) saved under s. 1?

[...]

(a) Pressing and Substantial Objective
[...]
122. Focusing on the objective of the omission in this case (i.e., the failure to provide agricultural workers with the necessary statutory protections to exercise the right to bargain collectively) and taking into account the *AEPA* as a whole, I find that the main objectives of the *AEPA* are to protect the family farm and farm production/viability. I conclude that these objectives are sufficiently pressing and substantial objectives to meet the first step of the *Oakes* test. While protecting employees' freedom of association is stated as one of the *AEPA*'s objectives, it is not relevant for the purpose of the s. 1 analysis, since the focus in characterizing the objective is on the infringement.

[...]

(b) Proportionality
[...]

(i) Rational Connection
[...]
129. ... In my view, the wholesale exclusion of agricultural employees from a collective bargaining scheme is not adequately tailored to meet the objective of protecting the family farm. As Bastarache J. indicated, the idea that employees should sacrifice their freedom to associate to maintain a flexible employment relationship should be carefully circumscribed. Accepting that collective bargaining "can, in certain circumstances,

function to antagonize the family farm dynamic," that "concern ought only be as great as the extent of the family farm structure."

130. Bastarache J.'s reasoning with regard to concerns about economic viability and farm production is also apposite. It is arbitrary to exclude all agricultural workers from a collective bargaining scheme on economic grounds, where collective bargaining has been extended to almost every other class of worker in Ontario, even in other industries that also face thin profit margins and unpredictable production cycles. Thus, I conclude the *AEPA* is not rationally connected to either of these stated objectives.

(ii) Minimal Impairment
[...]
132. The *AEPA* excludes *all* employees in the agricultural sector from a regime that provides for collective bargaining. There is no attempt to minimize the impairment by carving out family farms that are allegedly incompatible with a more formal labour relations regime. Rather, all farms, including factory farms, are excluded from collective bargaining.

133. The *AEPA* fails to recognize the evolving nature of Ontario agriculture, which includes an "increasing trend ... towards corporate farming and complex agribusiness": *Dunmore*, at para. 62. In discussing minimal impairment in *Dunmore*, Bastarache J. stated "it is not only over-inclusive to perpetuate a pastoral image of the 'family farm', but it may be that certain if not all 'family farms' would not be affected negatively by the creation of agricultural associations": para. 62.

134. As noted by Bastarache J., while a line-drawing process may be difficult, it is not impossible: para. 64. ...

135. In this case, the legislature made no attempt to engage in a line-drawing exercise to exclude family farms or to tailor a collective bargaining system that recognizes the challenges facing the agricultural sector. Before *B.C. Health Services*, there was clearly no effort to tailor appropriate protections for a feasible collective bargaining regime. Rather, the intent was to create an alternative process.

(iii) Proportionality between Effects and Objectives
136. As I am of the view that the government has not satisfied the first two components of the *Oakes* proportionality test, it is not necessary to balance the effects of this exclusion against its stated purposes—the final component of the *Oakes* proportionality inquiry.

137. I conclude that the violation of s. 2(d) under the *AEPA* cannot be justified under s. 1.

ISSUE 4: Remedy

138. For the foregoing reasons, I would allow the appeal and declare that the *AEPA* is unconstitutional in that it substantially impairs the right of agricultural workers to bargain collectively because it provides no statutory protections for collective bargaining. The *AEPA* is declared invalid and the government is ordered to provide agricultural workers with sufficient protections to enable them to exercise their right to bargain collectively, in accordance with these reasons.

139. However, I would suspend this declaration of invalidity for 12 months from the date of these reasons to permit the government time to determine the method of statutorily protecting the rights of agricultural workers to engage in meaningful collective bargaining.

Ontario (Attorney General) v Fraser, 2011 SCC 20

The Chief Justice and LeBel J. —

[1] This appeal raises anew the issue of the constitutionality of the labour relations regime that applies to farm workers in Ontario. Most Canadian provinces have brought the farming sector under their general labour relations laws, with some exceptions and restrictions. Except for a very short period of time, Ontario has always excluded farms and farm workers from the application of its *Labour Relations Act* (currently *Labour Relations Act, 1995*, S.O. 1995, c. 1, Sch. A) ("*LRA*"). In the present appeal, our Court must determine whether Ontario's latest attempt to frame a separate labour relations regime for the farming sector respects the constitutional guarantee of freedom of association, or violates it by failing to safeguard the exercise of collective bargaining rights. *The Agricultural Employees Protection Act, 2002*, S.O. 2002, c. 16 ("*AEPA*" or "Act"), was a response to this Court's decision in *Dunmore v. Ontario (Attorney General)*, 2001 SCC 94, which found that the previous legislative scheme violated s. 2(*d*) of the *Canadian Charter of Rights and Freedoms*.

[2] We are of the view that the *AEPA* has not been shown to be unconstitutional. Section 2(*d*) of the *Charter* protects the right to associate to achieve collective goals. Laws or state actions that substantially interfere with the ability to achieve workplace goals through collective actions have the effect of negating the right of free association and therefore constitute a limit on the s. 2(*d*) right of free association, which renders the law or action unconstitutional unless it is justified under s. 1 of the *Charter*. This requires a process of engagement that permits employee associations to make representations to employers, which employers must consider and discuss in good faith.

[3] The law here at issue, the *AEPA*, properly interpreted, meets these requirements, and is not unconstitutional. We would therefore allow the appeal.

[...]

(1) Freedom of Association in the Labour Context: The Jurisprudential Background
[...]

[40] The majority of the Court in *Health Services* affirmed that bargaining activities protected by s. 2(*d*) in the labour relations context include good faith bargaining on important workplace issues (para. 94; see also paras. 93, 130 and 135). This is not limited to a mere right to make representations to one's employer, but requires the employer to engage in a process of consideration and discussion to have them considered by the employer. In this sense, collective bargaining is protected by s. 2(*d*). The majority stated:

> Thus the employees' right to collective bargaining imposes corresponding duties on the employer. It requires both employer and employees to meet and to bargain in good faith, in the pursuit of a common goal of peaceful and productive accommodation. [para. 90]

[41] By way of elaboration on what constitutes good faith negotiation, the majority of the Court stated:

- Section 2(*d*) requires the parties to meet and engage in meaningful dialogue. They must avoid unnecessary delays and make a reasonable effort to arrive at an acceptable contract (paras. 98, 100–101);
- Section 2(*d*) does not impose a particular process. Different situations may demand different processes and timelines (para. 107);
- Section 2(*d*) does not require the parties to conclude an agreement or accept any particular terms and does not guarantee a legislated dispute resolution mechanism in the case of an impasse (paras. 102–3);
- Section 2(*d*) protects only "the right ... to a general process of collective bargaining, not to a particular model of labour relations, nor to a specific bargaining method" (para. 91).

[42] The Court in *Health Services* emphasized that s. 2(*d*) does not require a particular model of bargaining, nor a particular outcome. What s. 2(*d*) guarantees in the labour relations context is a meaningful process. A process which permits an employer not even to consider employee representations is not a meaningful process. To use the language of *Dunmore*, it is among those "collective activities [that] must be recognized if the freedom to form and maintain an association is to have any meaning" (para. 17). Without such a process, the purpose of associating in pursuit of workplace goals would be defeated, resulting in a significant impairment of the exercise of the right to freedom of association. One way to interfere with free association in pursuit of workplace goals is to ban employee associations. Another way, just as effective, is to set up a system that makes it impossible to have meaningful negotiations on workplace matters. Both approaches in fact limit the exercise of the s. 2(*d*) associational right, and both must be justified under s. 1 of the *Charter* to avoid unconstitutionality.

[43] In summary, *Health Services* applied the principles developed in *Dunmore* and explained more fully what is required to avoid interfering with associational activity in pursuit of workplace goals and undermining the associational right protected by s. 2(*d*). Its suggestion that this requires a good faith process of consideration by the employer of employee representations and of discussion with their representatives is hardly radical. It is difficult to imagine a meaningful collective process in pursuit of workplace aims that does not involve the employer at least considering, in good faith, employee representations. The protection for collective bargaining in the sense affirmed in *Health Services* is quite simply a necessary condition of meaningful association in the workplace context.

[...]

(iii) Purpose of Section 2(d)*: Individual Versus Collective Rights*
[...]

[64] Consistent with this framework, the majority decision in *Health Services* framed s. 2(*d*) as an *individual right* ("the right of employees", para. 87 (emphasis added)) that *may require the protection of group activity* (see also paras. 19 and 89). The fundamental inquiry is whether the state action would *substantially impair* the ability of "union

members to pursue shared goals in concert" (para. 96 (emphasis added)). As in *Dunmore*, the majority concluded that the realization of the individual right required a capacity to act in common, which may give rise to a need to protect group activities and, as a consequence, to recognize group rights.

[65] In summary, *Health Services* was consistent with the previous cases on the issue of individual and collective rights. It recognized, as did previous jurisprudence, that s. 2(*d*) is an individual right. But it also recognized, as did previous cases, that to meaningfully uphold this individual right, s. 2(*d*) may properly require legislative protection of group or collective activities.

[...]

*(iii) The Argument That Section 2(*d*) Is a Freedom, Not a Right*
[...]

[68] The majority in both *Dunmore* and *Health Services* held that freedom to associate may require the state to take positive steps. Bastarache J. in *Dunmore* underlined that "it may be asked whether the distinction between positive and negative state obligations ought to be nuanced in the context of labour relations" (para. 20). He further noted that

> history has shown, and Canada's legislatures have uniformly recognized, that a posture of government restraint in the area of labour relations will expose most workers not only to a range of unfair labour practices, but potentially to legal liability under common law inhibitions on combinations and restraints of trade.... In this context, it must be asked whether, in order to make the freedom to organize meaningful, s. 2(*d*) of the *Charter* imposes a positive obligation on the state to extend protective legislation to unprotected groups. [para. 20]

[69] This Court has consistently rejected a rigid distinction between "positive" freedoms and "negative" rights in the *Charter*. For example, it recently held that s. 2(*b*) may require the government to disclose documents to the public in order to enable meaningful discourse: *CLA*, at para. 37. As stated by L'Heureux-Dubé J. in *Haig v. Canada*, [1993] 2 S.C.R. 995:

> The distinctions between "freedoms" and "rights", and between positive and negative entitlements, are not always clearly made, nor are they always helpful. One must not depart from the context of the purposive approach articulated by this Court in *R. v. Big M Drug Mart Ltd.*, [1985] 1 S.C.R. 295. Under this approach, a situation might arise in which, in order to make a fundamental freedom meaningful, a posture of restraint would not be enough, and positive governmental action might be required. This might, for example, take the form of legislative intervention aimed at preventing certain conditions which muzzle expression, or ensuring public access to certain kinds of information. [p. 1039]

[70] A purposive protection of freedom of association may require the state to act positively to protect the ability of individuals to engage in fundamentally important collective activities, just as a purposive interpretation of freedom of expression may require the state to disclose documents to permit meaningful discussion.

[The majority then discussed the impugned provisions of the AEPA, holding that they did not breach section 2(d) because they imposed, by implication, a duty on agricultural employers to *consider* employee representations in good faith.]

(2) Application: Have the Respondents Established a Breach of Section 2(d)?
[...]

[100] Under the *AEPA*, the right of employees' associations to make representations to their employers is set out in s. 5. The relevant sections are ss. 5(1), (5), (6) and (7):

> 5. (1) The employer shall give an employees' association a reasonable opportunity to make representations respecting the terms and conditions of employment of one or more of its members who are employed by that employer.
>
> ...
>
> (5) The employees' association may make the representations orally or in writing.
>
> (6) The employer shall listen to the representations if made orally, or read them if made in writing.
>
> (7) If the representations are made in writing, the employer shall give the association a written acknowledgment that the employer has read them.

[101] Sections 5(6) and (7) are critical. They provide that the employer shall listen to oral representations, and read written representations, and acknowledge having read them. They do not expressly refer to a requirement that the employer consider employee representations in good faith. Nor do they rule it out. By implication, they include such a requirement.

[102] Three considerations lead us to conclude that any ambiguity in ss. 5(6) and (7) should be resolved by interpreting them as imposing a duty on agricultural employers to consider employee representations in good faith....

[107] These considerations lead us to conclude that s. 5 of the *AEPA*, correctly interpreted, protects not only the right of employees to make submissions to employers on workplace matters, but also the right to have those submissions considered in good faith by the employer. It follows that s. 5 of the *AEPA* does not violate s. 2(d) of the *Charter*.

[The majority went on to dismiss the section 15 equality claim as being premature, since the legislation had not been tested and there was inadequate evidence that the regime utilized unfair stereotypes or perpetuated existing prejudice and disadvantage. Justices Charron and Rothstein wrote separate reasons, arguing that *Health Services* should be overturned.]

Rothstein J.—

[...]

[121] The reasons of the Chief Justice and LeBel J. are based upon the majority decision in *Health Services and Support—Facilities Subsector Bargaining Assn. v. British Columbia*, [2007] 2 S.C.R. 391 ("*Health Services*"). The majority in *Health Services* found that s. 2(d) of the *Charter* confers constitutional status on collective bargaining. It concluded that collective bargaining as protected by s. 2(d) "requires both employer and employees to meet and to bargain in good faith, in the pursuit of a common goal of peaceful and productive accommodation" (para. 90). It further found that the requirement to bargain in good faith imposes a duty on employers to meet with employees and make a "reasonable effort to arrive at an acceptable contract" (para. 101)....

[124] I respectfully disagree with the Chief Justice and LeBel J. that collective bargaining enjoys constitutional status under the s. 2(d) freedom of association. I do not

agree that s. 2(d) requires the state to impose a complex set of statutorily defined reciprocal rights and duties on employers and workers associations, including a duty to bargain in good faith.

[125] In my view, s. 2(d) protects the liberty of individuals to associate and engage in associational activities. Therefore, s. 2(d) protects the freedom of workers to form self-directed employee associations in an attempt to improve wages and working conditions. What s. 2(d) does not do, however, is impose duties on others, such as the duty to bargain in good faith on employers.

[126] A constitutionally imposed duty to bargain in good faith strengthens the position of organized labour *vis-à-vis* employers. I express no opinion on the desirability of such an outcome for agricultural employees in Ontario. My point is only that courts are ill-suited to determine what is a matter of labour relations policy. Such policy decisions require a balancing of differing interests rather than an application of legal principles. Courts do not have the necessary expertise, or institutional capacity, to undertake a process which should involve consulting with and receiving representations from the various interested stakeholders and coming to an informed decision after balancing the necessary policy considerations. The decision to impose a duty of collective bargaining should be made by the legislature, and not by the court.

[127] Since the majority reasons are an application of the findings in *Health Services* to the circumstances of this appeal, the initial question that is raised is whether *Health Services* was correctly decided. As I have already suggested, and as I will explain below, I would find that *Health Services* was not correctly decided, to the extent that it constitutionalizes collective bargaining.

[128] In my opinion, overruling *Health Services* would dispose of the constitutional challenge in this case. The respondents' (Fraser's) argument that the *Agricultural Employees Protection Act, 2002*, S.O. 2002, c. 16 ("*AEPA*"), violates the *Charter* because it does not protect a right to collective bargaining would have no basis. I therefore turn first to the question of whether it would be appropriate that *Health Services* be overruled.

[Justice Rothstein then went on to elaborate these arguments in his judgment. Justice Deschamps would have allowed the appeal on the basis of the section 15 claim. He disagreed with the majority's interpretation of *Health Services* and their conclusion that it imposed a duty on governmental employers to bargain in good faith:]

Deschamps J.—

[...]

[304] In *Health Services*, the claimants asked this Court to declare that the government had interfered with their right to unite to achieve common goals. While they recognized that under most Canadian labour law statutes, employers had an obligation to bargain in good faith, the claimants were not seeking a declaration characterizing this obligation as a constitutional one. Neither the British Columbia Supreme Court nor the Court of Appeal dealt with a duty on employers to bargain in good faith, because this subject was quite simply not raised. Indeed, it was in its legislative capacity—not as an employer—that the government had interfered with the employee's rights. Therefore, the majority in *Health Services* did not need to comment on or make findings in respect

of whether the government, as an employer, had a duty to negotiate in good faith. There was thus no need to *impose* a *Charter*-based *duty* to bargain on employers. *A fortiori*, there was no need to import, together with this duty, the *good faith* element that is one of the hallmarks of the Wagner model and that inevitably entails a number of statutory components. I cannot therefore agree with the majority in the case at bar that *Health Services* imposes constitutional duties "on governments as employers" (para. 73).

[Justice Deschamps went on to argue that the case should more appropriately be resolved by broadening the scope of section 15:]

[319] To redress economic inequality, it would be more faithful to the design of the *Charter* to open the door to the recognition of more analogous grounds under s. 15, as L'Heureux-Dubé J. proposed in *Dunmore*. Such an approach is preferable to relying on a distinction that does not rest on a solid foundation. This, of course, would entail a sea change in the interpretation of s. 15 of the *Charter*. The majority in the instant case resist such a change, referring to "Canadian values" and to the need to take a "generous and purposive" approach when interpreting *Charter* rights (at paras. 32, 90, 92 and 97), but to ensure consistency with the approach of the majority in *Health Services* (at paras. 81–96), they refer to equality in the s. 2(*d*) context without mentioning s. 15. My point here is not that each *Charter* protection should be interpreted in a formalistic manner. Rather, it is that if the law needs to move away from *Dunmore's* distinction between positive and negative rights, this should not be accomplished by conflating freedom of association with the right to equality or any other *Charter* right that may be asserted by a litigant. An analysis based on principles grounding the protection of rights and freedoms offers a better prospect of judicial consistency than one based on the more amorphous notion of "Canadian values".

[In her forceful dissent, Abella J argued that the majority had inappropriately applied *Health Services* to the *AEPA*:]

Abella J. (dissenting) —

[321] I fully endorse the Chief Justice and LeBel J.'s discussion of *Health Services and Support — Facilities Subsector Bargaining Assn. v. British Columbia*, [2007] 2 S.C.R. 391. I agree with them that by including protection for the process of collective bargaining, *Health Services* enhanced the scope of s. 2(*d*) of the *Canadian Charter of Rights and Freedoms* beyond the formalism assigned to it by this Court's 1987 labour Trilogy (*Reference re Public Service Employee Relations Act (Alta)*, [1987] 1 S.C.R. 313; *PSAC v. Canada*, [1987] 1 S.C.R. 424; and *RWDSU v. Saskatchewan*, [1987] 1 S.C.R. 460). I am also in agreement with their criticisms of Rothstein J.'s decision to reconsider the correctness of *Health Services* on his own motion, in the absence of a request from any of the parties that he do so, and without an opportunity for them to address the issue.

[322] With the greatest respect, however, I do not agree that the *Agricultural Employees Protection Act*, 2002, S.O. 2002, c. 16 ("*AEPA*"), meets the new *Health Services* standard. I have great difficulty with stretching the interpretive process in a way that converts clear statutory language and express legislative intention into a completely different scheme. The *AEPA* does not protect, and was never intended to protect, collective bargaining rights.

Background

[323] The *AEPA* was enacted in 2002 to respond to this Court's 2001 decision in *Dunmore v. Ontario (Attorney General)*, [2001] 3 S.C.R. 1016, which held that s. 2(d) protected the right to *organize*. *Dunmore* was decided in accordance with the labour Trilogy, the then operative s. 2(d) paradigm. The Trilogy was widely taken as standing for the proposition that s. 2(d) did not include protection for collective bargaining (*Professional Institute of the Public Service of Canada v. Northwest Territories (Commissioner)*, [1990] 2 S.C.R. 367). The Trilogy was not challenged in *Dunmore*, and Bastarache J., writing for the majority, was explicit that he was not addressing whether collective bargaining was protected under s. 2(d). What *was* protected, in his view, was the following:

> ... I conclude that at minimum *the statutory freedom to organize* in ... the [*Labour Relations Act*, 1995, S.O. 1995, c. 1, Sch. A] ought to be extended to agricultural workers, along with protections judged essential to its meaningful exercise, such as freedom to assemble, to participate in the lawful activities of the association *and to make representations*, and the right to be free from interference, coercion and discrimination in the exercise of these freedoms. [Emphasis added; para. 67.]

[324] It is not surprising, therefore, that the 2002 *AEPA* contains no reference to a protection which made no appearance on the constitutional stage until 2007. Or that the trial judge's decision in 2006 in the case before us, applied the *Dunmore* "right to organize" template and found the legislation compliant with s. 2(d) ((2006), 79 O.R. (3d) 219).

[325] But by the time the Court of Appeal heard this case in 2008, *Health Services* had been decided, creating a completely different jurisprudential universe. That was the new s. 2(d) universe Winkler C.J.O. applied to the *AEPA*, (2008 ONCA 760, 92 O.R. (3d) 481). He found the legislation wanting. I agree with him.

Analysis

[326] In granting constitutional protection to the process of collective bargaining under s. 2(d), *Health Services* found the duty to consult and negotiate in good faith to be a "fundamental precept" (para. 97). This does not guarantee that a collective agreement will be achieved, but good faith bargaining does require that the parties meet, engage in a meaningful dialogue, and make reasonable efforts to arrive at a collective agreement (paras. 90 and 101). *Health Services* confirmed that this involves not only the employees' collective right, as confirmed in *Dunmore*, to organize and make representations, but also a corollary duty on the part of employers to meaningfully discuss, consult, and consider these representations:

> ... the right to bargain collectively protects not just the act of making representations, but also the right of employees to have their views heard in the context of a meaningful process of consultation and discussion.... [T]he right to collective bargaining cannot be reduced to a mere right to make representations. [Emphasis added; para. 114.] ...

[...]

[329] The process created by [the impugned] provisions is the following: an employees' association is entitled to make representations, either orally or in writing, about

the terms and conditions of employment. If the representations are made orally, the employer is required to "listen" to them. If they are made in writing, the employer must "read" them and give the "employees' association" a written acknowledgment that the representations have been read. That is the full extent of the employer's duties—to listen, to read, and to acknowledge receipt. No response is required.

[330] If we compare these duties under the *AEPA* to the linguistic markers set out in *Health Services*, we find that the following language is missing in action: "negotiate", "meet", "good faith", "engage", "exchange", "dialogue", "consultation", "discussions", "consideration", "accommodation" and "union". Nor does the key word "bargaining" appear.

[331] Noting the absence in the *AEPA* of *Health Services*' collective bargaining vocabulary is not a criticism of the government's motives. The *AEPA* was the government's good faith—and, as the trial judge found, successful—implementation of how *Dunmore* had defined the scope of s. 2(*d*) in 2001. This does not, however, assist in determining whether it complies with the *revised* scope described in *Health Services*. The Ontario government obviously cannot be held responsible for the redefinition of s. 2(*d*) that intervened between the enactment and appellate review of the *AEPA*, but neither can courts disregard the applicable law because of its infelicitous timing. Since the applicable law for s. 2(*d*) is now found in *Health Services*, the *AEPA* must be scrutinized for compliance with its principles. And since, on its face, *no* bargaining or consultation is required by the *AEPA*, let alone the good faith bargaining *Health Services* set out as a minimal constitutional protection, the *AEPA* violates s. 2(*d*) of the *Charter*.

[332] Not only is there clarity of language, there is also clarity of purpose. The government's intentions to exclude collective bargaining were forthright. The then Minister of Agriculture and Food, the Honourable Helen Johns, was unequivocal when she introduced the legislation in confirming that the legislation included *no* right to collective bargaining:

> However, I need to make one thing very clear here. While an agricultural employee may join an association that is a union, the *proposed legislation does not extend collective bargaining to agricultural workers.*
>
> (Legislative Assembly of Ontario, *Official Report of Debates (Hansard)*, No. 46A, October 22, 2002, at p. 2339 (emphasis added))

This was based on the legislative goal of complying only with the rights required by *Dunmore*, rights which, as the Minister correctly noted, addressed only the "right to associate", not the "right to collectively bargain":

> I'd like to say that the Supreme Court was very clear. They said that agricultural workers across the province *had the right to associate. They did not say that they had the right to collectively bargain.*
>
> (Legislative Assembly of Ontario, *Official Report of Debates (Hansard)*, No. 43A, October 16, 2002, at p. 2128 (emphasis added))

[333] Judging from their conduct, the parties involved in this appeal seem to have accepted there were no protections for the process and enforcement of collective

bargaining in the *AEPA*. The United Food and Commercial Workers Union Canada represented workers at Rol-Land Farms Ltd. After a vote in which an overwhelming majority voted in favour of certification, the union wrote to Rol-Land requesting a meeting to begin negotiations. The owner of Rol-Land Farms did not respond to the letter and refused to recognize the union. The same union also represented employees at Platinum Produce, where the employer gave the union the opportunity to make brief oral representations, but said it had no obligation to bargain towards a collective agreement. The meeting lasted 15 minutes.

[334] In the years since the *AEPA* was enacted in 2002, there is no evidence of a single successfully negotiated collective agreement or even of any negotiations. I appreciate that statutory interpretation does not draw on the perceptions of the statute's intended consumers, but where, as here, there is perfect harmony between statutory language, legislative intention, and public perception, the usual interpretative tools are vindicated.

[335] In addition to finding a violation of s. 2(*d*) based on the explicit failure, by text and by design, to include even a hint of a process of collective bargaining, let alone a duty to engage in meaningful and good faith efforts to arrive at a collective agreement, I also agree with Winkler C.J.O. that for agricultural workers, the absence of a statutory enforcement mechanism and of majoritarian exclusivity is an infringement of s. 2(*d*).

[336] *Health Services* recognized that s. 2(*d*) of the *Charter* obliged the state, either as employer or as legislator, to protect the process of collective bargaining (para. 88). The content of that protection will of course mean different things in different contexts. The determinative question will inevitably be, as Bastarache J. said in *Dunmore*, what protections are "essential" to the "meaningful exercise" of the right.

[337] The right at issue in *Dunmore* was the right to organize. Bastarache J. concluded that this required ancillary protection for the freedom to assemble, to participate in the lawful activities of the "employees' association" and to make representations, along with the right to be free from interference, coercion and discrimination in the exercise of those freedoms (para. 67). All of these protections found their way into the *AEPA*, which is why the trial judge gave it his stamp of constitutional approval.

[338] Now, as a result of *Health Services*, we are dealing with a right to a process of good faith collective bargaining and consultation. What protections are essential for the meaningful exercise of this right for agriculture workers?

[339] For a start, there is no point to having a right only in theory. Unless it is realizable, it is meaningless. There must therefore be an enforcement mechanism not only to resolve bargaining disputes, but to ensure compliance if and when a bargain is made.

[340] At the moment, there is in fact a statutory mechanism in place for the enforcement of the *AEPA*—the Agriculture, Food and Rural Affairs Appeal Tribunal. But the fact that this Tribunal exists is, by itself, of no consequence if it cannot address the rights constitutionally guaranteed by *Health Services*.

[341] Section 11 of the *AEPA* gives the Tribunal authority to grant a remedy for a contravention of the *AEPA*. But it is not a contravention of the *AEPA* to refuse to engage in a good faith process to make reasonable efforts to arrive at a collective agreement. It is therefore not part of the Tribunal's mandate. No mandate, no jurisdiction; no jurisdiction, no remedy.

[342] It strikes me as fundamentally contrary to our jurisprudence to invite the Tribunal to interpret its home statute in a way that contradicts the clear statutory language and legislative intent. If, on the other hand, the *AEPA* had included the protections set out in *Health Services*, the Tribunal would certainly have the authority to address and remedy any bargaining disputes and would therefore comply with what is required by s. 2(*d*).

[343] This brings us finally to whether the process of good faith bargaining for agricultural workers requires that the employer bargain only with the union selected by a majority of the employees in the bargaining unit. This is known as the principle of majoritarian exclusivity, a routine protection in Canada's labour laws. In the context of this case, and given the unique vulnerability of agriculture workers, I agree with Winkler C.J.O. that statutory recognition of such exclusivity is essential for them to exercise their bargaining rights meaningfully.

[344] As long ago as 1944, when labour ministers from across Canada agreed to the principles which found their way into the model *The Industrial Relations and Disputes Investigation Act*, S.C. 1948, c. 54, majoritarian exclusivity was a central protection. Most provinces quickly aligned their legislation with these principles ...

[345] With the exception of specific public services and the construction industry in Quebec ... majoritarian exclusivity has remained a defining principle of the Canadian labour relations model. ...

[346] The reason for the protection is grounded in common sense and the pre-1944 experience. A lack of exclusivity allows an employer to promote rivalry and discord among multiple employee representatives in order to "divide and rule the work force", using tactics like engaging in direct negotiations with individual employees to undercut "the credibility of the union ... at the bargaining table" (Paul Weiler, *Reconcilable Differences: New Directions in Canadian Labour Law* (1980), at p. 126; see also Adams, vol. 1, at para. 3.1750).

[347] Rol-Land Farms, for example, unrestrained by the legal requirement to bargain only with one bargaining agent, sponsored its own "employee association" in direct competition with the union that had the workers' majority support. That is precisely the kind of conduct that Bora Laskin identified in 1944 as the flaw in Canada's then existing labour legislation, namely that "it neither compelled employers to bargain collectively with the duly chosen representatives of their employees nor did it prohibit them from fostering company-dominated unions" ("Recent Labour Legislation in Canada" (1944), 22 *Can. Bar Rev.* 776, at p. 781). It also led Canada's labour ministers that same year to include exclusivity among what were considered to be indispensable protections for collective bargaining rights.

[348] The inevitable splintering of unified representation resulting from the absence of statutory protection for exclusivity is particularly undermining for particularly vulnerable employees. Professor David M. Beatty vividly observed that agricultural workers are "among the most economically exploited and politically neutralized individuals in our society":

> Because they are heavily drawn from a migrant and immigrant population, these workers face even more serious obstacles to effective participation in the political process. ... Denying agricultural workers the benefits of [collective bargaining] means that the legal

processes which enable much of the rest of our workforce to be involved in decision-making at the workplace in a realistic way are unavailable to the farm workers. Thus a group of workers who are already among the least powerful are given even less opportunity than the rest of us to participate in the formulation and application of the rules governing their working conditions.

(*Putting the Charter to Work: Designing a Constitutional Labour Code* (1987), at p. 89)

[…]

[349] These conclusions were echoed by the trial judge in *Dunmore*, Sharpe J., whose observations were endorsed in this Court by Bastarache J.:

Distinguishing features of agricultural workers are their political impotence, their lack of resources to associate without state protection and their vulnerability to reprisal by their employers; as noted by Sharpe J., agricultural workers are "poorly paid, face difficult working conditions, have low levels of skill and education, low status and limited employment mobility".... [para. 41]

[350] The conditions of singular employment disadvantage for workers in the agricultural sector, as the trial judge in this case acknowledged, remain operative today. Permitting multiple representatives of disparate individuals or groups in such a workplace effectively nullifies the ability of its workers to have a unified and therefore more cogent voice in attempting to mitigate and ameliorate their relentlessly arduous working conditions.

[351] I acknowledge that different models of labour relations exist globally, some of which do not recognize the principle of majoritarian exclusivity.... These models, however, have been developed in entirely different historical contexts and systems of collective bargaining and have yet to be seriously road-tested in the Canadian context outside of the construction industry in Quebec. This is not to say that there is no room for innovation in the modalities of the Canadian labour relations model. But to "innovate" by eliminating a fundamental protection for the most vulnerable of workers is nullification, not innovation.

[352] Can the absence of these statutory protections be justified under s. 1 of the *Charter*? In my view they cannot.

[353] Chief Justice Winkler found that the relevant objectives of the rights limitation—the failure to provide agricultural workers with the necessary statutory protections to exercise the right to bargain collectively—were "to protect the family farm and farm production/viability" (para. 122).

[354] These were found by this Court to be pressing and substantial objectives in *Dunmore* and are conceded to reach the necessary threshold in our case.

[355] Even assuming that there is a rational connection between at least the second objective and the limitation, I see the minimal impairment branch of the *Oakes* test as being determinative. Under this step we ask whether there are "less harmful means of achieving the legislative goal" (*Alberta v. Hutterian Brethren of Wilson Colony*, 2009 SCC 37, at para. 53). The *AEPA* has an absolute exclusion of any protection for a process of collective bargaining: all agricultural workers, in all sectors of agriculture, no matter the

size and nature of the agricultural enterprise, are precluded from exercising their s. 2(*d*) rights. If the government has impeded those rights more than is reasonably necessary to achieve its stated objectives, then this absolute exclusion is not constitutionally justified.

[356] The first governmental objective of the absolute exclusion is the protection of family farms. Is a one-size-fits-all exclusion responsive to protecting family farms? It seems to me clear that less harmful means than outright exclusion are readily available to achieve the objective. Two provinces, for example, Quebec and New Brunswick, have specific exemptions for farms employing less than three (*Labour Code*, R.S.Q., c. C-27, s. 21) or five (*Industrial Relations Act*, R.S.N.B. 1973, c. I-4, s. 1(5)(*a*)) workers.

[357] It is also worth remembering that we are dealing with a highly diversified sector, only some of which consists of family farms. As Bastarache J. noted, there is an "increasing trend ... towards corporate farming and complex agribusiness" (*Dunmore*, at para. 62). Rol-Land Farms, for example, is a mushroom farm that employs between 270–300 workers. The nature of this kind of farm, as described in *Wellington Mushroom Farm*, [1980] O.L.R.B. Rep. 813, does "not differ in any material respect from a typical manufacturing plant" (para. 29). The description in the reasons of Vice-Chairman R. O. MacDowell is telling:

> There is no close involvement with the family farm. The production process is not seasonal, but rather, resembles a production cycle. The labour force is neither casual nor transitory. The operation is of considerable size, employing close to 200 employees in a single location with a "factory atmosphere"; and the company is much less economically vulnerable than many other employers to which *The Labour Relations Act* applies. [para. 25]

[358] Preventing *all* agricultural workers from access to a process of collective bargaining in order to protect family farms, no matter their size or character, is the antithesis of minimal impairment. Such a limitation harms the s. 2(*d*) right in its entirety, not minimally.

[359] The other government objective is more general—the protection of the viability of farms and agricultural production. It is instructive to consider the 1992 recommendations of the Ontario government's consultative Task Force on Agricultural Labour Relations, composed of representatives from the agricultural community, organized labour, farm workers and government (*Report to the Minister of Labour* (June 1992); *Second Report to the Minister of Labour* (November 1992)). The Task Force's recommendations in its two reports are germane not because they should be seen as binding, but because they demonstrate that there are "less harmful means" than an absolute exclusion to achieve the government's objective of protecting agricultural production and viability.

[360] The Task Force considered whether—and how—agricultural workers should be entitled to bargain collectively, given the unique characteristics of the agricultural sector. It concluded that "all persons employed in agriculture and horticulture" should be able to engage in collective bargaining, including those on family or smaller farms, but in accordance with a separate labour relations scheme that is "sufficiently modified" to reflect the "particular needs" of the agricultural sector (First Report, at pp. 7–8).

[361] The "single most critical issue" raised by farm owners before the Task Force was the "threat of work stoppage" (First Report, at p. 3). In response to this and many

other submissions, the Task Force recommended that all forms of work stoppage be prohibited and replaced by a dispute resolution process that:

- emphasizes the preference for negotiated settlements between the parties.
- provides a conciliation and mediation service to assist the parties in reaching a negotiated settlement.
- provides an arbitration process for the final and binding resolution of all outstanding matters between the parties following exhaustion of the negotiation process. [First Report, at p. 10]

It also recommended that there be an Agricultural Labour Relations Act, to be administered by a separate Board (Second Report, at p. 17).

[362] The government adopted these recommendations in the *Agricultural Labour Relations Act*, 1994, S.O. 1994, c. 6 ("*ALRA*"). The *ALRA* included protection for collective bargaining, including exclusivity, but prohibited work stoppages (ss. 3, 10 and 11). The inherent compromise in that legislation is reflected in its preamble:

> It is in the public interest to extend collective bargaining rights to employees and employers in the agriculture and horticulture industries.
>
> However, the agriculture and horticulture industries have certain unique characteristics that must be considered in extending those rights. Those unique characteristics include seasonal production, climate sensitivity, time sensitivity, and perishable nature of agriculture and horticulture products, and the need for maintenance of continuous processes to ensure the care and survival of animal and plant life.

[363] The *ALRA* was repealed in 1995 (c. 1, s. 80). Thereafter, agricultural workers were left only with their pre-existing exclusion from the Ontario *Labour Relations Act*, *1995*, S.O. 1995, c. 1, Sch. A, creating the spark that ignited *Dunmore*.

[364] And since s. 1 of the *Charter* directs us to compare how other democratic governments limit a particular right, it is also helpful to look at how other Canadian jurisdictions deal with agricultural workplaces. Except in Alberta, agricultural workers in every province have the same collective bargaining rights as other employees, including exclusivity ...

[365] Reviewing the consequences of the near-universality of extending bargaining rights to Canadian agricultural workers, the 1992 Task Force concluded that the availability of the right to bargain collectively in these provinces has not "had a significant negative impact on farm economics" (First Report, at p. 3). This state of national affairs clearly does not preclude the government from offering a s. 1 justification unique to Ontario, but it has not, and perhaps realistically cannot, explain why Ontario's farming interests are *so* different as to warrant a complete exclusion rather than less intrusive means of achieving its objectives.

[366] The agricultural sector undoubtedly faces significant economic challenges, but so do many others, in none of which are employees deprived of access to a process of collective bargaining.

[367] The government has therefore not justified why achieving protection for agricultural viability and production requires so uniquely draconian a restriction on s. 2(*d*) rights. The limitation is, in fact, like its relationship to protecting family farms, not even

remotely tailored to meet the government's objective in a less intrusive way. It is, in fact, not tailored at all. As Winkler C.J.O. concluded:

> ... the legislature made no attempt to engage in a line-drawing exercise ... to tailor a collective bargaining system that recognizes the challenges facing the agricultural sector. [para. 135]

[368] On the other hand, it bears repeating that the *AEPA* was designed before *Health Services* was decided. The government could hardly be expected to tailor its legislation in accordance with a bargaining regime it had neither a duty nor an intention to implement at the time. Nonetheless, the fact is that *Health Services* intervened and changed the microscope under which the *AEPA* was scrutinized. And under the new lens, the complete absence of any statutory protection for a process of collective bargaining in the *AEPA* cannot be said to be minimally impairing of the s. 2(*d*) right.

[369] I would therefore dismiss the appeal without costs.

* * * * *

Is *Fraser* consistent with *Health Services*? What actually happens to the "duty to bargain in good faith"? Does the legislation comply with the demands of *Health Services*? What happened to the distinction between state and private actor interference with the freedom? What can one make of the claim that "impossibility" is the degree of constraint on the freedom required for a state violation? How did that idea enter the Court's thinking? For answers to at least some of these puzzles, we now turn to our third trilogy.

12:230 The Third Trilogy (2015): *MPAO*, *Meredith*, and *Sask Fed*

In 2015, the Supreme Court of Canada issued yet another Trilogy of section 2(d) cases. The contrast between the 1987 Trilogy and the 2015 Trilogy is now, it seems, complete—both in approach and result. This does not mean that it is easy to understand the current state of Canada's constitutional labour law. Given that the path between the first and third trilogies passed over the territory of the Second Trilogy (*Dunmore*, *Health Services*, and *Fraser*), which we have just traversed, this should not be surprising.

The most famous of the three 2015 decisions may be *Sask Fed*, where the Supreme Court of Canada took up the invitation it had extended to itself in *Health Services* when it decided, as we have seen, that there is a constitutional "right to collective bargaining" but expressly left open, and did not decide, the issue of the "right to strike." In *Sask Fed*, that invitation was accepted and the Court decided that there *is* a constitutional right to strike. But the central case in 2015 on the Canadian approach to the meaning of "freedom of association" is *MPAO*. The common view—held, it seems, by the SCC itself—is that it is in this case that Dickson's dissent in the 1987 *Alberta Reference* becomes the view of the majority. We have the advantage of reading both decisions and can investigate the truth of that assertion. Much of the future of Canada's law of freedom of association lies in the results of that inquiry.

12:231 *Mounted Police Association of Ontario v Canada (Attorney General)*

This case, known as *MPAO*, was a *Charter* challenge brought by several associations of members of the Royal Canadian Mounted Police (RCMP), who argued that the organization's labour relations system (called the Staff Relations Representative Program (SRRP)) violated their section 2(d) right to collectively bargain. Under the SRRP, RCMP members could not engage in traditional collective bargaining with management; rather, the SRRP represented them and provided elected representatives to engage and consult with management on workplace issues.

MPAO was preceded by an earlier case, *Delisle v Canada (Deputy Attorney General)*, [1999] 2 SCR 989. In *Delisle*, the Court had to determine whether the complete statutory exclusion of members of the RCMP from the federal *Public Service Staff Relations Act* was inconsistent with the *Charter* guarantees of freedom of association (section 2(d)) and equal treatment under the law (section 15). The majority judgment held that section 2(d) did not impose upon Parliament a positive obligation of protection or inclusion. *Dunmore*, where, as we have seen, a positive state obligation to protect was imposed, distinguished between the RCMP and agricultural workers at paragraph 41:

> Distinguishing features of agricultural workers are their political impotence, their lack of resources to associate without state protection and their vulnerability to reprisal by their employers; as noted by Sharpe J., agricultural workers are "poorly paid, face difficult working conditions, have low levels of skill and education, low status and limited employment mobility" (p. 216). Moreover, unlike RCMP officers, agricultural workers are not employed by the government and therefore cannot access the *Charter* directly to suppress an unfair labour practice.

The 2015 *MPAO* case addresses two issues—not just the exclusion of members of the RCMP from any protective regime (the *Delisle/Dunmore* issue), but also the imposition of the SRRP. For labour lawyers, this latter complaint looks very familiar—it looks like a standard "employer dominated/sweetheart union" unfair labour practice. Both the exclusion and the imposition of the SRRP were held to violate section 2(d).

But *MPAO* is also the case where the "heavy lifting" is done to provide a new view of the meaning of the section 2(d) freedom. The Court claims to be, as we have noted, returning to the philosophical foundations of section 2(d) set out in Dickson CJC's dissent in 1987. But is this true? We have read what Dickson CJC said in 1987. Here is what the Court said in 2015:

Mounted Police Association of Ontario v Canada (Attorney General), 2015 SCC 1

The judgment of McLachlin C.J. and LeBel, Abella, Cromwell, Karakatsanis and Wagner JJ. was delivered by

THE CHIEF JUSTICE AND LEBEL J.—

I. INTRODUCTION

[1] In this appeal, we must decide whether excluding members of the Royal Canadian Mounted Police ("RCMP") from collective bargaining under the *Public Service Labour Relations Act*, enacted by the *Public Service Modernization Act*, S.C. 2003, c. 22, s. 2 ("*PSLRA*"), and imposing a non-unionized labour relations regime violates the guarantee of freedom of association in s. 2(d) of the *Canadian Charter of Rights and Freedoms*. This requires us to review the nature and interpretation of the right guaranteed by s. 2(d) of the *Charter*, and to clarify the scope of the constitutional protection of collective bargaining recognized in

Health Services and Support—Facilities Subsector Bargaining Assn. v. British Columbia, 2007 SCC 27 ... and *Ontario (Attorney General) v. Fraser*, 2011 SCC 20 ...

[2] RCMP members are not permitted to unionize or engage in collective bargaining. They have been excluded from the *PSLRA* and its predecessor statute since collective bargaining was first introduced in the federal public service in the late 1960s. Instead, there exists a non-unionized labour relations regime with three core components. First, members can advance their workplace concerns through the Staff Relations Representative Program ("SRRP"). Second, members' concerns regarding pay and benefits are communicated to management through the RCMP Pay Council process. Third, RCMP members have created the Mounted Police Members' Legal Fund ("Legal Fund"), a not-for-profit corporation funded through membership dues, which provides legal assistance to RCMP members for employment-related issues.

[3] A little over 15 years ago, this Court held that exclusion of RCMP members from collective bargaining under the PSLRA's predecessor legislation did not infringe s. 2(*d*): *Delisle v. Canada (Deputy Attorney General)*, [1999] 2 S.C.R. 989. On this appeal we are asked to reconsider that decision as it relates to the *PSLRA*. Unlike this appeal, however, Delisle did not involve a direct challenge to the sufficiency of the SRRP: *Delisle*, at para. 34.

[4] This case was heard together with a related appeal, brought by two Staff Relations Representatives ("SRRs") on behalf of all members of the RCMP, challenging the constitutionality of federal wage restraint legislation: *Meredith v. Canada (Attorney General)*, 2015 SCC 2 ... While the factual background of both appeals overlap, they raise different legal issues. Meredith addresses the question of whether a piece of legislation and its implementation unconstitutionally interfered with the existing RCMP labour relations scheme, but does not challenge that scheme as a whole as constitutionally deficient under s. 2(*d*). The present appeal is directed at the constitutionality of the scheme comprising both the *PSLRA* exclusion and the SRRP process.

[5] We conclude that the s. 2(*d*) guarantee of freedom of association protects a meaningful process of collective bargaining that provides employees with a degree of choice and independence sufficient to enable them to determine and pursue their collective interests. The current RCMP labour relations regime denies RCMP members that choice, and imposes on them a scheme that does not permit them to identify and advance their workplace concerns free from management's influence. Accordingly, we allow the appeal and find that s. 96 of the *Royal Canadian Mounted Police Regulations, 1988*, SOR/88-361 ("*RCMP Regulations*"), which was in effect at the time of the hearing of this appeal, is inconsistent with s. 2(*d*) of the *Charter*. We also find that the exclusion of RCMP members from collective bargaining under para. (*d*) of the definition of "employee" in s. 2(1) of the *PSLRA* infringes s. 2(*d*) of the *Charter*. Neither infringement is justified under s. 1 of the *Charter*.

[...]

A. Evolution of Section 2(*d*) Jurisprudence Toward a Purposive and Contextual Approach

[30] The jurisprudence on freedom of association under s. 2(*d*) of the *Charter*—which developed mainly with respect to labour relations ...—falls into two broad periods. The

first period is marked by a restrictive approach to freedom of association. The second period gradually adopts a generous and purposive approach to the guarantee.

[31] In what has come to be known as the Labour Trilogy, a majority of this Court held that s. 2(d) does not protect the right to bargain collectively or the right to strike: *Reference re Public Service Employee Relations Act (Alta.)*, [1987] 1 S.C.R. 313 (the "*Alberta Reference*"); *PSAC v. Canada*, [1987] 1 S.C.R. 424; and *RWDSU v. Saskatchewan*, [1987] 1 S.C.R. 460.

[32] The reasoning is set out most fully in the three opinions issued in the *Alberta Reference*. There Le Dain J., in brief reasons supported by Beetz and La Forest JJ., endorsed an interpretation of s. 2(d) that would protect "the freedom to work for the establishment of an association, to belong to an association, to maintain it, and to participate in its lawful activity without penalty or reprisal" (p. 391). However, he described collective bargaining and the right to strike as "modern rights" created by statute, and hence not protected by s. 2(d)....

[33] McIntyre J. reached the same conclusion, but for somewhat different reasons. In his view, freedom of association rested on the following proposition: "... the attainment of individual goals, through the exercise of individual rights, is generally impossible without the aid and cooperation of others" (p. 395). Accordingly, McIntyre J. held that freedom of association protected a right to engage collectively in those activities which are constitutionally protected for each individual:

> The only basis on which it is contended that the *Charter* enshrines a right to strike is that of freedom of association. Collective bargaining is a group concern, a group activity, but the group can exercise only the constitutional rights of its individual members on behalf of those members. If the right asserted is not found in the *Charter* for the individual, it cannot be implied for the group merely by the fact of association. It follows as well that the rights of the individual members of the group cannot be enlarged merely by the fact of association. [pp. 398–99]

[34] After reviewing six possible approaches to the scope of s. 2(d), McIntyre J. concluded that freedom of association encompassed the right to form and join associations, the right to exercise other constitutional freedoms collectively, and the right to do in concert with others what an individual may lawfully do alone (p. 409). On the particular question before the Court, he found that an individual could not lawfully refuse to work, and that there was no individual equivalent of a strike conducted in accordance with labour legislation (p. 410). Accordingly, he concluded that the right to strike was not protected (p. 412).

[35] Dickson C.J., dissenting (Wilson J. concurring), would have allowed the appeal. He identified three possible approaches to s. 2(d). The first, which he termed the "constitutive" approach, protects the freedom to belong to or form an association (p. 362). The second, the "derivative" approach, goes beyond the constitutive approach to protect associational activity that relates specifically to other constitutional freedoms enumerated in s. 2 (p. 364). Dickson C.J. rejected these alternatives as too restrictive and opted for a third approach. In his view, a purposive approach to freedom of association was needed. He identified the purpose and scope of s. 2(d) as follows, at pp. 365–66:

> The purpose of the constitutional guarantee of freedom of association is, I believe, to recognize the profoundly social nature of human endeavours and to protect the individual from state-enforced isolation in the pursuit of his or her ends....
>
> ...
>
> As social beings, our freedom to act with others is a primary condition of community life, human progress and civilized society. Through association, individuals have been able to participate in determining and controlling the immediate circumstances of their lives, and the rules, mores and principles which govern the communities in which they live....
>
> Freedom of association is most essential in those circumstances where the individual is liable to be prejudiced by the actions of some larger and more powerful entity, like the government or an employer. Association has always been the means through which political, cultural and racial minorities, religious groups and workers have sought to attain their purposes and fulfil their aspirations; it has enabled those who would otherwise be vulnerable and ineffective to meet on more equal terms the power and strength of those with whom their interests interact and, perhaps, conflict....
>
> ...
>
> What freedom of association seeks to protect is not association activities qua particular activities, but the freedom of individuals to interact with, support, and be supported by, their fellow humans in the varied activities in which they choose to engage.

[36] Dickson C.J. recognized as a starting point that s. 2(d) protected the right to do collectively what one may do as an individual. But he would also have held that the *Charter* protected some collective activities that have no true individual equivalents, including the right to strike.

[37] The approach to freedom of association endorsed by the majority in the Labour Trilogy was affirmed three years later in *Professional Institute of the Public Service of Canada v. Northwest Territories (Commissioner)*, [1990] 2 S.C.R. 367 ("*PIPSC*"). In that case, the *Public Service Act*, R.S.N.W.T. 1974, c. P-13, subjected the employees' choice of bargaining agent to approval by the legislature of the Northwest Territories. Like the present appeal, *PIPSC* involved a challenge to a labour relations scheme that imposed a framework for collective bargaining on a group of public service employees, limiting their ability to represent themselves through a freely chosen association. But the association itself remained entirely independent from management (p. 408).

[38] The seven judges who heard the case wrote five separate opinions. The majority agreed with Sopinka J. who concluded that s. 2(d) protected only the ability to form and join unions, but did not protect the right to collective bargaining. Famously, he outlined four principles concerning the scope of s. 2(d) drawn from the *Alberta Reference*, at p. 402:

> ... first, that s. 2(d) protects the freedom to establish, belong to and maintain an association; second, that s. 2(d) does not protect an activity solely on the ground that the activity is a foundational or essential purpose of an association; third, that s. 2(d) protects the exercise in association of the constitutional rights and freedoms of individuals; and fourth, that s. 2(d) protects the exercise in association of the lawful rights of individuals.

[39] Sopinka J.'s disposition of the case was supported by Dickson C.J., La Forest J. and L'Heureux-Dubé J., but only L'Heureux-Dubé J. endorsed the third and fourth propositions as limiting principles under s. 2(d). Dickson C.J. and La Forest J. each found that the appeal could be resolved by application of the Labour Trilogy's conclusion that s. 2(d) did not protect collective bargaining, without deciding the broader question of its scope.

[40] Cory J. (Wilson and Gonthier JJ. concurring), dissented on the scope of freedom of association. In his view, freedom of association permits individuals to work together for the purpose of achieving common goals. This freedom is fundamental to a free and democratic society and extends into the workplace. He succinctly stated one aspect of freedom of association in the workplace:

> Whenever people labour to earn their daily bread, the right to associate will be of tremendous significance. Wages and working conditions will always be of vital importance to an employee. *It follows that for an employee the right to choose the group or association that will negotiate on his or her behalf with regard to those wages and working conditions is of fundamental importance.* The association will play a very significant role in almost every aspect of the employee's life at work, acting as advisor, as spokesperson in negotiations, and as a shield against wrongful acts of the employer. If collective bargaining is to function properly, employees must have confidence in their representative. That confidence will be lost if the individual employee is unable to choose the association. [Emphasis added; p. 380.]

[41] To recap, and notwithstanding noteworthy dissents, the majority of this Court in this early period maintained a narrow view of freedom of association, which protected only the bare formation of the association and the collective exercise of individual freedoms. This view prevailed for some time. Outside the labour relations context, the same approach was applied in *Canadian Egg Marketing Agency v. Richardson*, [1998] 3 S.C.R. 157. And in the labour relations context, this approach resulted in the majority of this Court holding that the exclusion of RCMP members from the *PSSRA* did not violate s. 2(d) in the 1999 case of *Delisle*.

[42] Parallel to these cases, the Court considered the "negative" aspect of freedom of association—the freedom not to associate: *Lavigne v. Ontario Public Service Employees Union*, [1991] 2 S.C.R. 211; *R. v. Advance Cutting & Coring Ltd.*, 2001 SCC 70 ...; affirmed in *Bernard v. Canada (Attorney General)*, 2014 SCC 13 .... But, *Lavigne* and *Advance Cutting* are significant because they applied a purposive approach to s. 2(d). In *Lavigne*, at p. 318, La Forest J. suggested that, in keeping with democratic ideals, the guarantee of freedom of association should be interpreted as protecting "the individual's potential for self-fulfillment and realization as surely as voluntary association will develop it". (See also *Lavigne*, at p. 344, per McLachlin J.; and *Advance Cutting*, at paras. 15–17, per Bastarache J., and at paras. 170–71, per LeBel J.) Both judgments emphasized the importance of a purposive interpretation of s. 2(d).

[43] These cases marked the beginning of a more generous, purposive approach to s. 2(d)—an approach that was resoundingly affirmed in *Dunmore v. Ontario (Attorney General)*, 2001 SCC 94.... In that case, agricultural workers challenged their exclusion from the collective bargaining regime created by the Ontario *Labour Relations Act, 1995*,

S.O. 1995, c. 1, Sch. A. Bastarache J., for the majority, began his analysis with a review of the existing case law, concluding that Sopinka J.'s four principles could not capture all of the potential scope of s. 2(d). Justice Bastarache wrote, at para. 16:

> In my view, while the four-part test for freedom of association sheds light on this concept, it does not capture the full range of activities protected by s. 2(d). In particular, there will be occasions where a given activity does not fall within the third and fourth rules set forth by Sopinka J. in *PIPSC, supra*, but where the state has nevertheless prohibited that activity solely because of its associational nature. These occasions will involve activities which (1) are not protected under any other constitutional freedom, and (2) cannot, for one reason or another, be understood as the lawful activities of individuals.

[44] This renewed focus on the collective aspect of freedom of association and on its purposive interpretation led to the express recognition of a s. 2(d) right to collective bargaining in *Health Services*. All seven judges who heard that appeal agreed that a purposive interpretation of s. 2(d) required constitutional protection for the right of employees to engage in a process of collective bargaining:

> Based on the principles developed in *Dunmore* and in this historical and international perspective, the constitutional right to collective bargaining concerns the protection of the ability of workers to engage in associational activities, and their capacity to act in common to reach shared goals related to workplace issues and terms of employment.

(Para. 89, per McLachlin C.J. and LeBel J.; see also para. 174, per Deschamps J.)

[45] Finally, in *Fraser*, this Court reaffirmed that s. 2(d) confers the right to a process of collective bargaining, understood as meaningful association in pursuit of workplace goals. This process includes the employees' rights to join together, to make collective representations to the employer, and to have those representations considered in good faith:

> What s. 2(d) guarantees in the labour relations context is a meaningful process. A process which permits an employer not even to consider employee representations is not a meaningful process.... Without such a process, the purpose of associating in pursuit of workplace goals would be defeated, resulting in a significant impairment of the exercise of the right to freedom of association. One way to interfere with free association in pursuit of workplace goals is to ban employee associations. Another way, just as effective, is to set up a system that makes it impossible to have meaningful negotiations on workplace matters. [para. 42]

[46] In summary, after an initial period of reluctance to embrace the full import of the freedom of association guarantee in the field of labour relations, the jurisprudence has evolved to affirm a generous approach to that guarantee. This approach is centred on the purpose of encouraging the individual's self-fulfillment and the collective realization of human goals, consistent with democratic values, as informed by "the historical origins of the concepts enshrined" in s. 2(d): *R. v. Big M Drug Mart Ltd.*, [1985] 1 S.C.R. 295, at p. 344.

B. Defining the Scope of the Section 2(d) Guarantee

(1) A Purposive, Generous and Contextual Approach

[47] As is the case with other *Charter* rights, the jurisprudence establishes that s. 2(d) must be interpreted in a purposive and generous fashion, having regard to "the larger objects of the *Charter*..., to the language chosen to articulate the ... freedom, to the historical origins of the concepts enshrined, and where applicable, to the meaning and purpose of the other specific rights and freedoms with which it is associated within the text of the *Charter*": *Big M Drug Mart*, at p. 344. In a phrase, in order to determine whether a restriction on the right to associate violates s. 2(d) by offending its purpose, we must look at the associational activity in question in its full context and history. Neither the text of s. 2(d) nor general principles of *Charter* interpretation support a narrow reading of freedom of association.

[48] This interpretative approach to freedom of association is consistent with the approach to other basic rights connected with human activities and needs. The scope of freedom of religion, for example, is derived from its history and the range of activities to which it applies—holding, proclaiming and transmitting beliefs in the bosom of a secular state (R. Moon, "Freedom of Conscience and Religion", in Mendes and Beaulac, 339). Similarly, the scope of freedom of expression is defined by the different forms it takes and the different interests it protects—including, notably, "the quest for truth, self-fulfillment, and an embracing marketplace of ideas": *Saskatchewan (Human Rights Commission) v. Whatcott*, 2013 SCC 11, ... at para. 171, per Rothstein J. for the Court; see also *R. v. Keegstra*, [1990] 3 S.C.R. 697, at p. 766; P. B. Schabas, "The Ups and Downs of Freedom of Expression—Section 2(b)", in R. Gilliland, ed., *The Charter at Thirty* (2012), 1; H. Brun, G. Tremblay and E. Brouillet, *Droit constitutionnel* (5th ed. 2008), at p. 1060. An activity-based contextual approach is equally essential for freedom of association. Freedom of association, like the other s. 2 freedoms—freedom of expression, conscience and religion, and peaceful assembly—protects rights fundamental to Canada's liberal democratic society.

[49] Freedom of association is not derivative of these other rights. It stands as an independent right with independent content, essential to the development and maintenance of the vibrant civil society upon which our democracy rests.

[50] The purposes underlying *Charter* rights and freedoms may be framed at varying levels of abstraction. At the broadest level, a purposive interpretation must be consistent with the "larger objects of the *Charter*", including "basic beliefs about human worth and dignity" and the maintenance of "a free and democratic political system": *Big M Drug Mart*, at pp. 344 and 346; see also *Health Services*, at para. 81. At the same time, however, while *Charter* rights and freedoms should be given a broad and liberal interpretation, a purposive analysis also requires courts to consider the most concrete purpose or set of purposes that underlies the right or freedom in question, based on its history and full context. That is the task to which we now turn with respect to s. 2(d).

(2) The Content of Section 2(d) Protection

[51] In his dissenting reasons in the *Alberta Reference*, Dickson C.J. identified three possible approaches to the interpretation of s. 2(d)—constitutive, derivative and purposive. We conclude that s. 2(d) protects each of the aspects of freedom of association with which these approaches are concerned.

[52] The narrowest approach, the "constitutive", would protect only the bare right to belong to or form an association. The state would thus be prohibited from interfering with individuals meeting or forming associations, but would be permitted to interfere with the *activities* pursued by the associations people form. This protection, while narrow, is not trivial; history is replete with examples of states that have banned associations or prevented people from associating, either absolutely or in terms of restrictions on the number of people who can associate for a particular purpose.

[53] The "derivative" approach would protect not only the right to associate, but also the right to associational *activity* that specifically relates to other constitutional freedoms. This approach prevails in the United States, where freedom of association is recognized insofar as it supports other constitutional rights, like freedom of religion and the political rights. Beyond this, however, associational activities would not be constitutionally protected.

[54] The purposive approach, adopted by Dickson C.J. in the *Alberta Reference*, defines the content of s. 2(*d*) by reference to the purpose of the guarantee of freedom of association: "... to recognize the profoundly social nature of human endeavours and to protect the individual from state-enforced isolation in the pursuit of his or her ends" (*Alberta Reference*, at p. 365). The object of Dickson C.J.'s words is a concrete one, not an abstract expression of a desire for a better life. Elaborating on this interpretive approach, Dickson C.J. states that the purpose of the freedom of association encompasses the protection of (1) individuals joining with others to form associations (the constitutive approach); (2) collective activity in support of other constitutional rights (the derivative approach); and (3) collective activity that enables "those who would otherwise be vulnerable and ineffective to meet on more equal terms the power and strength of those with whom their interests interact and, perhaps, conflict": *Alberta Reference*, at p. 366.

[55] The purposive approach thus recognizes that freedom of association is empowering, and that we value the guarantee enshrined in s. 2(*d*) because it empowers groups whose members' individual voices may be all too easily drowned out. This conclusion is rooted in "the historical origins of the concepts enshrined" in s. 2(*d*) (*Big M Drug Mart*, at p. 344).

[56] The historical emergence of association as a fundamental freedom—one which permits the growth of a sphere of civil society largely free from state interference—has its roots in the protection of religious minority groups.... More recent history also illustrates how the freedom to associate has contributed to the women's suffrage and gay rights movements....

[57] Historically, those most easily ignored and disempowered as individuals have staked so much on freedom of association precisely because association was the means by which they could gain a voice in society. As Dickson C.J. put it in the *Alberta Reference*:

> Freedom of association is most essential in those circumstances where the individual is liable to be prejudiced by the actions of some larger and more powerful entity, like the government or an employer. *Association has always been the means through which political, cultural and racial minorities, religious groups and workers have sought to attain their purposes and fulfil their aspirations*; it has enabled those who would otherwise be vulnerable and

ineffective to meet on more equal terms the power and strength of those with whom their interests interact and, perhaps, conflict. [Emphasis added; pp. 365–66.]

[58] This then is a fundamental purpose of s. 2(d) — to protect the individual from "state-enforced isolation in the pursuit of his or her ends": *Alberta Reference*, at p. 365. The guarantee functions to protect individuals against more powerful entities. By banding together in the pursuit of common goals, individuals are able to prevent more powerful entities from thwarting their legitimate goals and desires. In this way, the guarantee of freedom of association empowers vulnerable groups and helps them work to right imbalances in society. It protects marginalized groups and makes possible a more equal society.

[59] The flip side of the purposive approach to freedom of association under s. 2(d) is that the guarantee will not necessarily protect all associational activity. Section 2(d) of the *Charter* is aimed at reducing social imbalances, not enhancing them. For this reason, some collective activity lies outside the *Charter's* protection. For example, associational activity that constitutes violence is not protected by s. 2(d): *Suresh v. Canada (Minister of Citizenship and Immigration)*, 2002 SCC 1 ... at para. 107.

[60] Whether there are other categories of activity in addition to violence that are by their very nature entirely excluded from s. 2(d) protection need not be canvassed here. It suffices to note that a purposive interpretation of s. 2(d) confers *prima facie* protection on a broad range of associational activity, subject to limits justified pursuant to s. 1 of the *Charter*.

[61] The nature of a given associational activity and its relation to the underlying purpose of s. 2(d) may also be relevant to the s. 1 analysis, in the same way that the nature of particular expression is relevant in s. 2(b) cases. For instance, as Rothstein J. explains in *Whatcott*, at paras. 112 and 114:

> Violent expression and expression that threatens violence does not fall within the protected sphere of s. 2(b) of the *Charter*: *R. v. Khawaja*, 2012 SCC 69 ... at para. 70. However, apart from that, not all expression will be treated equally in determining an appropriate balancing of competing values under a s. 1 analysis. That is because different types of expression will be relatively closer to or further from the core values behind the freedom, depending on the nature of the expression. This will, in turn, affect its value relative to other *Charter* rights, the exercise or protection of which may infringe freedom of expression.
>
> ...
>
> Hate speech is at some distance from the spirit of s. 2(b) *because it does little to promote, and can in fact impede, the values underlying freedom of expression.* As noted by Dickson C.J. in *Keegstra*, expression can be used to the detriment of the search for truth (p. 763). As earlier discussed, hate speech can also distort or limit the robust and free exchange of ideas by its tendency to silence the voice of its target group. It can achieve the self-fulfillment of the publisher, but often at the expense of that of the victim. These are important considerations in balancing hate speech with competing *Charter* rights.... [Emphasis added.]

[62] Section 2(d), we have seen, protects associational activity for the purpose of securing the individual against state-enforced isolation and empowering individuals to achieve collectively what they could not achieve individually. It follows that the

associational rights protected by s. 2(d) are not merely a bundle of individual rights, but collective rights that inhere in associations. L'Heureux-Dubé J. put it well in *Advance Cutting*:

> In society, there is an element of synergy when individuals interact. The mere addition of individual goals will not suffice. Society is more than the sum of its parts. Put another way, a row of taxis do not a bus make. An arithmetic approach to *Charter* rights fails to encompass the aspirations imbedded in it. [para. 66]

[63] It has been suggested that collective rights should not be recognized because they are inconsistent with the *Charter's* emphasis on individual rights, and because this would give groups greater rights than individuals. In our view, neither criticism is well founded.

[64] First, the *Charter* does not exclude collective rights. While it generally speaks of individuals as rights holders, its s. 2 guarantees extend to groups. The right of peaceful assembly is, by definition, a group activity incapable of individual performance. Freedom of expression protects both listeners and speakers: *R. v. National Post*, 2010 SCC 16 ... at para. 28. The right to vote is meaningless in the absence of a social context in which voting can advance self-government: *Sauvé v. Canada* (Chief Electoral Officer), 2002 SCC 68 ... at para. 31. The Court has also found that freedom of religion is not merely a right to hold religious opinions but also an individual right to establish communities of faith (see *Alberta v. Hutterian Brethren of Wilson Colony*, 2009 SCC 37.... And while this Court has not dealt with the issue, there is support for the view that "the autonomous existence of religious communities is indispensable for pluralism in a democratic society and is thus an issue at the very heart of the protection" of freedom of religion (*Hutterian Brethren*, at para. 131, per Abella J., dissenting, citing *Metropolitan Church of Bessarabia v. Moldova*, No. 45701/99, ECHR 2001-XII (First Section), at para. 118)....

[65] It has also been suggested that recognition of a collective aspect to s. 2(d) rights will somehow undermine individual rights and the individual aspect of s. 2(d). We see no basis for this contention. Recognizing group or collective rights complements rather than undercuts individual rights, as the examples just cited demonstrate. It is not a question of *either* individual rights *or* collective rights. Both are essential for full *Charter* protection.

[66] In summary, s. 2(d), viewed purposively, protects three classes of activities: (1) the right to join with others and form associations; (2) the right to join with others in the pursuit of other constitutional rights; and (3) the right to join with others to meet on more equal terms the power and strength of other groups or entities.

C. The Right to a Meaningful Collective Bargaining Process

[67] Applying the purposive approach just discussed to the domain of labour relations, we conclude that s. 2(d) guarantees the right of employees to meaningfully associate in the pursuit of collective workplace goals, affirming the central holdings of *Health Services* and *Fraser*. This guarantee includes a right to collective bargaining. However, that right is one that guarantees a process rather than an outcome or access to a particular model of labour relations.

[68] Just as a ban on employee association impairs freedom of association, so does a labour relations process that substantially interferes with the possibility of having meaningful collective negotiations on workplace matters. Without the right to pursue workplace goals collectively, workers may be left essentially powerless in dealing with their employer or influencing their employment conditions. This idea is not new. As the United States Supreme Court stated in *National Labor Relations Board v. Jones & Laughlin Steel Corp.*, 301 U.S. 1 (1937), at p. 33:

> Long ago we stated the reason for labor organizations. We said that they were organized out of the necessities of the situation; *that a single employee was helpless in dealing with an employer;* that he was dependent ordinarily on his daily wage for the maintenance of himself and family; that if the employer refused to pay him the wages that he thought fair, he was nevertheless unable to leave the employ and resist arbitrary and unfair treatment.... [Emphasis added.]

[69] Similarly, this Court recently affirmed the importance of freedom of expression in redressing the imbalance inherent in the employer-employee relationship in *Alberta (Information and Privacy Commissioner) v. United Food and Commercial Workers, Local 401*, 2013 SCC 62 ... at paras. 31-32:

> A person's employment and the conditions of their workplace can inform their identity, emotional health, and sense of self-worth....
>
> Free expression in the labour context can also play a significant role in redressing or alleviating the presumptive imbalance between the employer's economic power and the relative vulnerability of the individual worker.... It is through their expressive activities that unions are able to articulate and promote their common interests, and, in the event of a labour dispute, to attempt to persuade the employer. [Citations omitted.]

[70] The same reasoning applies to freedom of association. As we have seen, s. 2(d) functions to prevent individuals, who alone may be powerless, from being overwhelmed by more powerful entities, while also enhancing their strength through the exercise of collective power. Nowhere are these dual functions of s. 2(d) more pertinent than in labour relations. Individual employees typically lack the power to bargain and pursue workplace goals with their more powerful employers. Only by banding together in collective bargaining associations, thus strengthening their bargaining power with their employer, can they meaningfully pursue their workplace goals.

[71] The right to a meaningful process of collective bargaining is therefore a necessary element of the right to collectively pursue workplace goals in a meaningful way (*Health Services; Fraser*). Yet a process of collective bargaining will not be meaningful if it denies employees the power to pursue their goals. As this Court stated in *Health Services*: "One of the fundamental achievements of collective bargaining is to palliate the historical inequality between employers and employees ..." (para. 84). A process that substantially interferes with a meaningful process of collective bargaining by reducing employees' negotiating power is therefore inconsistent with the guarantee of freedom of association enshrined in s. 2(d).

[72] The balance necessary to ensure the meaningful pursuit of workplace goals can be disrupted in many ways. Laws and regulations may restrict the subjects that can be

discussed, or impose arbitrary outcomes. They may ban recourse to collective action by employees without adequate countervailing protections, thus undermining their bargaining power. They may make the employees' workplace goals impossible to achieve. Or they may set up a process that the employees cannot effectively control or influence. Whatever the nature of the restriction, the ultimate question to be determined is whether the measures disrupt the balance between employees and employer that s. 2(d) seeks to achieve, so as to substantially interfere with meaningful collective bargaining: *Health Services*, at para. 90.

[73] Against this conception, the Attorney General of Canada, relying on *Fraser*, argues that collective bargaining is at best a "derivative right" from the basic or "core" right to associate (the constitutive approach). It follows, according to the Attorney General, that collective bargaining is protected only if state action makes it *effectively impossible* to associate for workplace matters. Here that impossibility is lacking, the Attorney General asserts, because the SRRP process is a means by which RCMP members can associate for workplace purposes. The Court of Appeal accepted this position. We disagree. We will address the terms "effectively impossible" and "derivative right" in turn.

[74] The reference in *Fraser* to the effective impossibility of achieving workplace goals must be understood with reference to the legislative schemes at issue. For instance, in discussing *Dunmore*, the majority in *Fraser* explained that Bastarache J. had "concluded that the absence of legislative protection for farm workers to organize in order to achieve workplace goals made meaningful association to achieve workplace goals impossible *and therefore constituted a substantial interference* with the right to associate guaranteed by s. 2(d) of the *Charter*" (para. 31 (emphasis added)). Similarly, the majority in Fraser explained that the legislation impugned in *Health Services*—legislation that unilaterally nullified terms concerning seniority and lay-offs in existing collective agreements and precluded future bargaining over those matters—"rendered the meaningful pursuit of [workplace] goals impossible and effectively nullified the right to associate of its employees" (para. 38).

[75] These passages from *Fraser* and *Health Services* use terms like "impossible" and "effectively nullified" to describe the effect of legislative schemes (including legislative exclusions), not the legal test for infringement of s. 2(d). Explaining the reasoning in *Dunmore*, the majority in *Fraser* states that: "The *effect* of a process that renders impossible the meaningful pursuit of collective goals is to substantially interfere with the exercise of the right to free association ..." (para. 33 (emphasis in original)). In *Fraser*, the majority further explains that there cannot "be *any doubt* that legislation (or the absence of a legislative framework) that makes achievement" of collective workplace goals "substantially impossible, constitutes a limit on the exercise of freedom of association" (para. 32 (emphasis added)). It is clear that such passages do not adopt "substantial impossibility" as the threshold test for finding an infringement of freedom of association. Rather, the passages demonstrate that the majority in Fraser adopts substantial interference as the *legal test* for infringement of freedom of association.

[76] Dissenting in the case at bar, Rothstein J. highlights the fact that the majority reasons in *Fraser* "referred to the test of impossibility—either effective or substantial impossibility—no less than 12 times, tracing its origins in the decisions of *Dunmore* and *Health Services* ... see *Fraser*, at paras. 31-34, 38, 42, 46-48, 62 and 98" (para. 213

(emphasis in original)). In virtually every case (see paras. 31–33, 38, 42, 46–48, 62 and 98), the "impossibility" in question refers explicitly to the *effect* of legislation or the absence of a legislative framework. A test of substantial interference or substantial impairment is also explicitly stated as the standard for finding a s. 2(*d*) infringement at paras. 31, 33, 47–48 and 62. Finally, the majority in *Fraser* reaffirmed the holding in Health Services that "[t]he fundamental inquiry is whether the state action would *substantially impair* the ability of '*union members* to pursue shared goals in concert' (para. 96 (emphasis added))": para. 64 (emphasis in original); see *Health Services*, at paras. 92 and 96.

[77] This said, we agree that some of the passages in Fraser seem to unnecessarily complicate the analysis by referring to both effective impossibility (as the effect of certain state action) and substantial interference or impairment (as the test for infringement of s. 2(*d*)). For the reasons just discussed, however, such references should be understood consistently with the majority reasons in *Fraser*, read in their entirety, and with this Court's precedents in *Dunmore* and *Health Services*. More generally, they must be understood consistently with this Court's purposive and generous approach to s. 2(*d*), as explained above.

[78] We turn now to use of the term "derivative right" in *Fraser*. On the Court of Appeal's interpretation of *Fraser*, the right to a meaningful process of collective bargaining is "derivative" in the sense that it exists only where employees establish that it is effectively impossible for them to act collectively to achieve workplace goals (paras. 110–11 and 135). However, in *Fraser*, the majority explained that "collective bargaining is a derivative right" in the sense that it is "a 'necessary precondition' to the meaningful exercise of the constitutional guarantee of freedom of association": para. 66. The majority cited *Criminal Lawyers' Association* where the Court stated, at para. 30: "Access [to information in government hands] is a derivative right *which may arise where* it is a necessary precondition of meaningful expression on the functioning of government" (emphasis added). The Court of Appeal understood this to mean that the right to collective bargaining similarly *may arise* as a necessary precondition to meaningful association in the workplace only where some other condition is first met. The Court of Appeal took that condition to be the effective impossibility of acting collectively to achieve workplace goals.

[79] However, the majority in *Fraser* did not qualify the right to collective bargaining in this way. It held that collective bargaining is "a 'necessary precondition' to the meaningful exercise of the constitutional guarantee of freedom of association": para. 66. Similarly, at para. 99, "the right of an employees' association to make representations to the employer and have its views considered in good faith" is described as "a derivative right under s. 2(*d*) of the *Charter*, *necessary to* meaningful exercise of the right to free association" (emphasis added). To the extent the term "derivative right" suggests that the right to a meaningful process of collective bargaining only applies where the guarantee under s. 2(*d*) is otherwise frustrated, use of that term should be avoided. Furthermore, any suggestion that an aspect of a *Charter* right may somehow be secondary or subservient to other aspects of that right is out of keeping with the purposive approach to s. 2(*d*).

[80] To recap, s. 2(*d*) protects against substantial interference with the right to a meaningful process of collective bargaining. Historically, workers have associated in order "to meet on more equal terms the power and strength of those with whom their interests interact and, perhaps, conflict", namely, their employers: *Alberta Reference*, at

p. 366. The guarantee entrenched in s. 2(d) of the *Charter* cannot be indifferent to power imbalances in the labour relations context. To sanction such indifference would be to ignore "the historical origins of the concepts enshrined" in s. 2(d): *Big M Drug Mart*, at p. 344. It follows that the right to a meaningful process of collective bargaining will not be satisfied by a legislative scheme that strips employees of adequate protections in their interactions with management so as to substantially interfere with their ability to meaningfully engage in collective negotiations.

D. Essential Features of a Meaningful Process of Collective Bargaining Under Section 2(d)

[81] We have concluded that s. 2(d) protects the right of employees to associate for the purpose of meaningfully pursuing collective workplace goals. The government therefore cannot enact laws or impose a labour relations process that substantially interferes with that right. This raises the question—what are the features essential to a meaningful process of collective bargaining under s. 2(d)? In this section, we conclude that a meaningful process of collective bargaining is a process that provides employees with a degree of choice and independence sufficient to enable them to determine their collective interests and meaningfully pursue them.

[82] Collective bargaining constitutes a fundamental aspect of Canadian society which "enhances the human dignity, liberty and autonomy of workers by giving them the opportunity to influence the establishment of workplace rules and thereby gain some control over a major aspect of their lives, namely their work" (*Health Services*, at para. 82). Put simply, its purpose is to preserve collective employee autonomy against the superior power of management and to maintain equilibrium between the parties. This equilibrium is embodied in the degree of choice and independence afforded to the employees in the labour relations process.

[83] But choice and independence are not absolute: they are limited by the context of collective bargaining. In our view, the degree of choice required by the *Charter* for collective bargaining purposes is one that enables employees to have effective input into the selection of the collective goals to be advanced by their association. In the same vein, the degree of independence required by the *Charter* for collective bargaining purposes is one that ensures that the activities of the association are aligned with the interests of its members.

[84] In the following subsections, we lay out the theoretical underpinnings of choice and independence and we explain how they are inherent to the nature and purpose of collective bargaining. We then explain how the requirements of choice and independence can be respected by a variety of labour relations models, as long as such models allow collective bargaining to be pursued in a meaningful way.

(1) Choice and Independence Are Inherent to the Nature and Purpose of Collective Bargaining

(a) *Employee Choice*

[85] The function of collective bargaining is not served by a process which undermines employees' rights to choose what is in their interest and how they should pursue those

interests. The degree of choice required by the *Charter* is one that enables employees to have effective input into the selection of their collective goals. This right to participate in the collective is crucial to preserve employees' ability to advance their own interests, particularly in schemes which involve trade-offs of individual rights to gain collective strength ...

[86] Hallmarks of employee choice in this context include the ability to form and join new associations, to change representatives, to set and change collective workplace goals, and to dissolve existing associations. Employee choice may lead to a diversity of associational structures and to competition between associations, but it is a form of exercise of freedom of association that is essential to the existence of employee organizations and to the maintenance of the confidence of members in them ...

[87] Accountability to the members of the association plays an important role in assessing whether employee choice is present to a sufficient degree in any given labour relations scheme. Employees choose representatives on the assumption that *their* voice will be conveyed to the employer by the people they choose ... A scheme that holds representatives accountable to the employees who chose them ensures that the association works towards the purposes for which the employees joined together. Accountability allows employees to gain control over the selection of the issues that are put forward to the employer, and the agreements concluded on their behalf as a result of the process of collective bargaining.

(b) Independence From Management

[88] The function of collective bargaining is not served by a process which is dominated by or under the influence of management. This is why a meaningful process of collective bargaining protects the right of employees to form and join associations that are independent of management (*Delisle*, at paras. 32 and 37). Like choice, independence in the collective bargaining context is not absolute. The degree of independence required by the *Charter* for collective bargaining purposes is one that permits the activities of the association to be aligned with the interests of its members.

[89] Just as with choice, independence from management ensures that the activities of the association reflect the interests of the employees, thus respecting the nature and purpose of the collective bargaining process and allowing it to function properly. Conversely, a lack of independence means that employees may not be able to advance their own interests, but are limited to picking and choosing from among the interests management permits them to advance. Relevant considerations in assessing independence include the freedom to amend the association's constitution and rules, the freedom to elect the association's representatives, control over financial administration and control over the activities the association chooses to pursue.

[90] Independence and choice are complementary principles in assessing the constitutional compliance of a labour relations scheme. *Charter* compliance is evaluated based on the *degrees* of independence and choice guaranteed by the labour relations scheme, considered with careful attention to the entire context of the scheme. The degrees of choice and independence afforded should not be considered in isolation, but must be assessed globally always with the goal of determining whether the employees are able to associate for the purposes of meaningfully pursuing collective workplace goals.

[91] We now turn to the practical implications of choice and independence for labour relations models.

(2) Labour Relations Models Must Permit Collective Bargaining to Be Pursued in a Meaningful Way

[92] A variety of labour relations models may provide sufficient employee choice and independence from management to permit meaningful collective bargaining. As discussed, choice and independence are not absolute in the context of collective bargaining. By necessity, a collective framework not only serves employees' interests, but imposes limits on individual entitlements in order to permit the pursuit of collective goals. Collective bargaining is "an exercise in solidarity in which individual interests are not simply aggregated but transformed in the process of democratic deliberation" (J. Fudge, "Introduction: Farm Workers, Collective Bargaining Rights, and the Meaning of Constitutional Protection", in F. Faraday, J. Fudge and E. Tucker, eds., *Constitutional Labour Rights in Canada: Farm Workers and the Fraser Case* (2012), 1, at p. 17 . . .). As Professor Wellington states: "Accommodating the interests of the dissenter and those of the majority is always difficult. The hallmark of a truly democratic society is its unwillingness to give up easily either majority rule or individual freedom" (*Labor and the Legal Process* (1968), at p. 129).

[93] This Court has consistently held that freedom of association does not guarantee a particular model of labour relations (*Delisle*, at para. 33; *Health Services*, at para. 91; *Fraser*, at para. 42). What is required is not a particular model, but a regime that does not substantially interfere with meaningful collective bargaining and thus complies with s. 2(d) (*Health Services*, at para. 94; *Fraser*, at para. 40). What is required in turn to permit meaningful collective bargaining varies with the industry culture and workplace in question. As with all s. 2(d) inquiries, the required analysis is contextual.

[94] The Wagner Act model of labour relations in force in most private sector and many public sector workplaces offers one example of how the requirements of choice and independence ensure meaningful collective bargaining. That model permits a sufficiently large sector of employees to choose to associate themselves with a particular trade union and, if necessary, to decertify a union that fails to serve their needs. The principles of majoritarianism and exclusivity, the mechanism of "bargaining units" and the processes of certification and decertification—all under the supervision of an independent labour relations board—ensure that an employer deals with the association most representative of its employees . . .

[95] The Wagner Act model, however, is not the only model capable of accommodating choice and independence in a way that ensures meaningful collective bargaining. The designated bargaining model (see, e.g., *School Boards Collective Bargaining Act, 2014*, S.O. 2014, c. 5) offers another example of a model that may be acceptable. Although the employees' bargaining agent under such a model is designated rather than chosen by the employees, the employees appear to retain sufficient choice over workplace goals and sufficient independence from management to ensure meaningful collective bargaining. This is but one example; other collective bargaining regimes may be similarly capable of preserving an acceptable measure of employee choice and independence to ensure meaningful collective bargaining.

[96] Labour schemes are responsive to the interests of the parties involved and the particular workplace context. Different models have emerged to meet the specific needs of diverse industries and workplaces. The result has been ongoing debate on the desirability of various forms of workplace representation and cooperation and on their coexistence ...

[97] The search is not for an "ideal" model of collective bargaining, but rather for a model which provides sufficient employee choice and independence to permit the formulation and pursuit of employee interests in the particular workplace context at issue. Choice and independence do not *require* adversarial labour relations; nothing in the *Charter* prevents an employee association from engaging willingly with an employer in different, less adversarial and more cooperative ways. This said, genuine collective bargaining cannot be based on the suppression of employees' interests, where these diverge from those of their employer, in the name of a "non-adversarial" process. Whatever the model, the *Charter* does not permit choice and independence to be eroded such that there is substantial interference with a meaningful process of collective bargaining. Designation of collective bargaining agents and determination of collective bargaining frameworks would therefore not breach s. 2(*d*) where the structures that are put in place are free from employer interference, remain under the control of employees and provide employees with sufficient choice over the workplace goals they wish to advance.

[98] The respondent argues that this view of s. 2(*d*) would require an employer, even a government employer, to recognize and bargain with every association chosen by employees, whatever the size. In our view, this result does not follow. Freedom of association requires, among other things, that no government process can substantially interfere with the autonomy of employees in creating or joining associations of their own choosing, even if in so doing they displace an existing association. It also requires that the employer consider employees' representations in good faith, and engage in meaningful discussion with them. But s. 2(d) does not require a process whereby *every* association will ultimately *gain* the recognition it seeks ... As we said, s. 2(*d*) can also accommodate a model based on majoritarianism and exclusivity (such as the Wagner Act model) that imposes restrictions on individual rights to pursue collective goals.

[99] In summary, a meaningful process of collective bargaining is a process that gives employees meaningful input into the selection of their collective goals, and a degree of independence from management sufficient to allow members to control the activities of the association, having regard to the industry and workplace in question. A labour relations scheme that complies with these requirements and thus allows collective bargaining to be pursued in a meaningful way satisfies s. 2(*d*).

[...]

E. Whether the Imposition of the SRRP Infringes Section 2(*d*) of the *Charter*

[105] This is not a case of a complete denial of the constitutional right to associate and of its related constitutional guarantees. It is rather a case of substantial interference with the right to associate for the purpose of addressing workplace goals through a meaningful process of collective bargaining, free from employer control, as understood by Dickson C.J.

in the *Alberta Reference*. We conclude that the flaws in the SRRP process do not permit meaningful collective bargaining, and are inconsistent with s. 2(d). The SRRP process fails to respect RCMP members' freedom of association in both its purpose and its effects.

[106] Section 96 of the *RCMP Regulations* imposed the SRRP on RCMP members as the sole means of presenting their concerns to management. Section 56 of the current-day *RCMP Regulations, 2014* continues to impose the SRRP under nearly identical terms. RCMP members are represented by an organization they did not choose and do not control. They must work within a structure that lacks independence from management. Indeed, this structure and process are part of the management organization of the RCMP. The process fails to achieve the balance between employees and employer that is essential to meaningful collective bargaining, and leaves members in a disadvantaged, vulnerable position.

(1) The Purpose of the Imposition of the SRRP Infringes Section 2(d)

[107] We earlier described the history of RCMP labour relations. This history evidences a long-standing hostility on the part of RCMP management and successive Canadian governments to unionization in the Force. In the early 20th century, the federal government deployed one of the RCMP's predecessor bodies—the Royal Northwest Mounted Police—to confront labour unrest, most famously in breaking the Winnipeg General Strike of 1919. At a time when municipal police forces in Canada were beginning to unionize, the Canadian government issued Order in Council P.C. 1918-2213, which prohibited members of the Dominion Police and the Royal Northwest Mounted Police from becoming "a member of or in any wise associated with any Trades Union Organization ... or with any Union, Society or Association ... connected or affiliated therewith" on penalty of immediate dismissal.

[108] This stance was softened in the early 1970s, with the repeal of P.C. 1918-2213 (P.C. 1974-1339), but the federal government continued to resist the formation of independent RCMP members' associations. The DSRRP, precursor to the present SRRP, was openly presented as an alternative to unionization. The year it was created, RCMP Commissioner Nadon commissioned a report on the effects of police associations and the advantages and disadvantages of implementing such an association in the RCMP: J. P. Middleton, *A Study Report on Police Associations* (1974). The Middleton report was largely supportive of the formation of an RCMP members' association or union. In circulating the report, however, Commissioner Nadon included a brief foreword, in which he stated:

> At the outset I wish to make the Force's position very clear; the Force is opposed to the formation of an association or union of members and this position has been made known to our Minister. [p. i]

[109] Section 3(2) of the *Commissioner's Standing Orders (Division Staff Relations Representative Program)*, which formed the legal basis of the DSRRP from 1974 to 2003, prohibited DSRRs from promoting "*alternate* programs in conflict with the non-union status of the Division Staff Relations Representative Program".

[110] Even before this Court, the Attorney General of Canada does not contend that the current-day SRRP provides RCMP members with an independent association.

Indeed, the Attorney General appears to concede that the SRRP continues to be imposed on members of the RCMP for the purpose of preventing collective bargaining through an independent association. Its position is rather that s. 2(d) does not guarantee RCMP members a right to form and bargain through an association of their own choosing. We have rejected this view. Accordingly, it follows that the purpose of the imposition of the SRRP, to prevent the formation of independent RCMP members' associations for the purposes of collective bargaining, is unconstitutional.

(2) The Effects of the Imposition of the SRRP Infringe Section 2(d)

[111] While it would be sufficient to find a violation of s. 2(d) solely on the basis of the purposes of the imposition of the SRRP as a labour relations regime (*Big M Drug Mart*), we also find that imposing this regime infringes s. 2(d) in its effects. Our inquiry here is directed at whether RCMP members can genuinely advance their own interests through the SRRP, without interference by RCMP management. We are satisfied, on the record before us, that they cannot.

[112] The organizational structure of the SRRP has evolved significantly since its predecessor was first established in 1974. These changes are detailed above. While these changes have expanded the SRRs' freedom to direct the program, they nonetheless fall short of respecting RCMP members' right to join associations that are of their choosing and independent of management, to advance their interests.

[113] At the level of institutional structure, the SRRP is plainly not independent of RCMP management. Rather, it is squarely under its control. It is a part of the labour-management structure of the RCMP. In 1989, the Government of Canada formalized the SRRP (then known as the DSRRP) by adding s. 96 to the *RCMP Regulations*: SOR/89-581. The Regulatory Impact Analysis Statement that accompanied the amendment to the *RCMP Regulations* expressly stated that the DSRRP was "co-ordinated and monitored at R.C.M.P. Headquarters" and "subject to biannual reviews at R.C.M.P. Divisions with reports to the Commissioner from the Internal Communications Officer". Although not determinative nor exhaustive of a regulation's purpose or interpretation, regulatory impact analysis statements are a useful tool to understand how regulations are intended to work: see *MiningWatch Canada v. Canada (Fisheries and Oceans)*, 2010 SCC 2 ... at para. 33; *RJR—MacDonald Inc. v. Canada (Attorney General)*, [1994] 1 S.C.R. 311, at pp. 352-53.

[...]

[118] Simply put, in our view, the SRRP is not an association in any meaningful sense, nor a form of exercise of the right to freedom of association. It is simply an internal human relations scheme imposed on RCMP members by management. Accordingly, the element of employee choice is almost entirely missing under the present scheme.

[119] While the Attorney General of Canada observes that adoption of the SRRP was endorsed by members in all divisions outside Quebec in a referendum in 1974, we do not consider this fact determinative, for two reasons. First, the referendum in question evidently offered the SRRP a "take it or leave it" proposition. It does not reflect whether members would have preferred representation through an independent association. Second, the referendum took place 40 years ago. Today, there is no opportunity for RCMP members to indicate their support for an alternative form of association. Members have

no ability to opt out of participation in the SRRP, and there is no other means for them to communicate their workplace concerns to management. As we have seen, the structure has no independence from management; it is but a part of management itself.

[120] These constitutional defects in the SRRP are not cured by the election of SRRs. On this point we agree with the conclusion of the application judge, that "agreeing to populate a structure created by management for the purpose of labour relations cannot reasonably be construed as a choice not to conduct labour relations through an association of the members' own making" (para. 63).

[121] In conclusion, s. 96 of the *RCMP Regulations*, which imposed the SRRP as the sole recognized vehicle for engagement between RCMP membership and senior management, constituted a substantial interference with freedom of association in both its purpose and effects. Before considering whether that infringement could be justified under s. 1 of the *Charter*, we consider the related challenge to para. (*d*) of the definition of "employee" in s. 2(1) of the *PSLRA*.

F. Whether Paragraph (*d*) of the Definition of "Employee" in Section 2(1) of the *PSLRA* Infringes Section 2(*d*) of the *Charter*

[122] The appellants challenge the exclusion of RCMP members from the application of the *PSLRA* and ask that para. (*d*) of the definition of "employee" in s. 2(1) of that Act be struck down. Most employees in federally regulated workplaces are governed by the *Canada Labour Code*, R.S.C. 1985, c. L-2 ("*CLC*"), but the collective bargaining regime established by Part I of the *CLC* is inapplicable to employees of the Crown, with limited exceptions: s. 6.

[123] For employees in the federal public service, the *PSLRA* provides the general framework through which they can join and participate in employee associations; these associations can be certified as bargaining agents, and good faith collective bargaining can occur. The *PSLRA* provides for mediation, conciliation and arbitration when problems arise during collective bargaining and provides remedies for unfair labour practices. While being significantly different from private-sector labour relations models in many ways, the *PSLRA* and its predecessor, the *PSSRA*, are generally referred to as a Wagner Act model of labour relations (C. Rootham, *Labour and Employment Law in the Federal Public Service* (2007), at pp. 19-20).

[124] Paragraph (*d*) of the definition of "employee" in s. 2(1) of the *PSLRA* excludes RCMP members from the application of the PSLRA. This Court in *Delisle* held that the exclusion of the RCMP from the *PSSRA*, the *PSLRA*'s predecessor legislation, did not violate s. 2(*d*) of the *Charter*. This raises a threshold question: Should the Court's decision in Delisle be reconsidered? In our view, it should, for two reasons.

[125] First, *Delisle* was decided before this Court's decisions in *Health Services* and *Fraser*, which marked a shift to a purposive and generous approach to labour relations. At the time *Delisle* was decided, the right to a meaningful process of collective bargaining was not recognized as part of the s. 2(*d*) *Charter* guarantee. All three sets of reasons in *Delisle* make clear that the Court in that case was *not* addressing the issue of whether the purpose of the PSSRA exclusion was to prevent RCMP members from engaging in collective

bargaining: para. 5, per L'Heureux-Dubé J.; para. 20, per Bastarache J.; paras. 51, 88 and 107, per Cory and Iacobucci JJ. As formulated by Bastarache J., writing for the majority, the question in *Delisle* was whether the purpose of the exclusion "was to prevent RCMP members from forming any type of independent association": para. 20. The question of an interference with the right to a meaningful process of collective bargaining was neither asked nor answered in *Delisle*.

[126] Second, in *Delisle*, only part of the scheme governing the labour relations of RCMP members—their exclusion from the *PSSRA*—was before this Court. In the present appeal, the challenge targets the entire labour relations scheme—the exclusion from the application of the *PSLRA* and the imposition of the labour relations regime that we have found is intended to deny RCMP members the right to form an independent association capable of engaging in a meaningful process of collective bargaining. In other words, the majority in *Delisle* found that the legislative exclusion, viewed in isolation, did not prevent the creation of an independent association, but the Court now considers the complete scheme which is clearly intended to prevent associational activity protected under s. 2(d) of the *Charter*.

[127] Overturning precedents of this Court is not a step to be lightly taken ... However, as explained, *Delisle* was decided before this Court's shift to a purposive and generous approach to the exercise of freedom of association and *Delisle* considered a different question and narrower aspects of the labour relations regime than those at issue here. It follows that the result in Delisle must be revisited.

[128] We therefore propose to examine whether para. (d) of the definition of "employee" in s. 2(1) of the *PSLRA* infringes s. 2(d) in its purpose.

(1) The Purpose of the *PSLRA* Exclusion Infringes Section 2(d)
[129] The statutory exclusion of RCMP members must be read and its constitutionality assessed in relation to P.C. 1918-2213, the Order in Council that constituted the labour relations regime that applied to members of the RCMP at the time of enactment of the *PSSRA*. The blanket prohibition of associational activity in pursuit of workplace goals imposed by P.C. 1918-2213 unquestionably violates s. 2(d) of the *Charter*. The implementation of this labour relations regime was made possible by the exclusion of the RCMP members from the labour relations regime governing the federal public service under the *PSSRA*.

[130] Although they originated from different legal sources, the *PSSRA* exclusion and P.C. 1918-2213, working together, constituted a labour relations regime that was designed to interfere with the right to freedom of association of RCMP members. The *PSSRA* exclusion cannot be viewed in the abstract, independently from the Order in Council. These two prongs of the predecessor labour relations regime shared a common purpose. They were both intended to deny to RCMP members the constitutional exercise of their freedom of association. Like P.C. 1918-2213, para. (e) of the definition of "employee" in s. 2(1) of the *PSSRA*, now re-enacted as para. (d) of the definition of "employee" in s. 2(1) of the *PSLRA*, is tainted by an improper purpose and breaches s. 2(d) of the *Charter*.

[131] The purpose of para. (d) of the definition of "employee" in s. 2(1) of the *PSLRA*, viewed in its historical context, thus violates s. 2(d) of the *Charter*. The *PSSRA* and, later, the *PSLRA* established the general framework for labour relations and collective

bargaining in the federal public sector. A class of employees, the members of the RCMP, has, since the initial enactment of this regime, been excluded from its application in order to prevent them from exercising their associational rights under s. 2(d). Thus the issue to be addressed is whether the purpose of excluding a specific class of employees from the labour relations regime impermissibly breaches the constitutional rights of the affected employees. The issue is not whether Parliament must impose a new statutory labour relations regime in the presence of a legislative void.

[132] Paragraph (d) of the definition of "employee" in s. 2(1) of the *PSLRA* excludes every person "who is a member or special constable of the Royal Canadian Mounted Police or who is employed by that force under terms and conditions substantially the same as those of one of its members".

[133] Before 1967, the concept of collective bargaining was unknown to the federal public service generally and, of course, to the RCMP specifically. Parliament adopted the *PSSRA* to implement a process of collective bargaining in the federal public service ... The *PSSRA*'s successor, the *PSLRA*, reflected a similar commitment to collective bargaining (see the preamble of the *PSLRA* and Advisory Committee on Labour Management Relations in the Federal Public Service, *Working Together in the Public Interest* (2001), at p. 14).

[134] The exclusion of RCMP members from the *PSSRA* in 1967—the only vehicle available for meaningful collective bargaining in the federal public service—was intended to prevent them from engaging in collective bargaining. The then-Commissioner of the RCMP acknowledged this in correspondence to the Solicitor General of Canada in 1980, stating: "There is no enabling legislation which allows members to collectively bargain and we must infer that Parliament has not intended that members of the Force have that right"....

[135] The *PSSRA*'s successor, the *PSLRA*, reduced the categories of excluded public servants. RCMP members, however, continued to be excluded in identical terms as under the PSSRA, and no other statute permitted RCMP members to engage in a process of collective bargaining (*Delisle*, at para. 85, per Cory and Iacobucci JJ., dissenting; R. MacKay, "The Royal Canadian Mounted Police and Unionization", Parliamentary Research Branch, September 3, 2003, at p. 20). Nothing indicated that the purpose of the initial exclusion of RCMP members from collective bargaining had changed: *Interpretation Act*, R.S.C. 1985, c. I-21, at s. 44(f) ... Indeed, the *PSLRA* exclusion makes possible the current imposition of the SRRP, which we have found to substantially interfere in both purpose and effect with RCMP members' right to a meaningful process of collective bargaining. Working in tandem with P.C. 1918-2213, the *PSSRA* exclusion had similarly sought to deny the members of the RCMP the exercise of their right to freedom of association. The simple re-enactment of this exclusion in the *PSLRA* did not cure this constitutionally impermissible purpose. The *PSLRA* exclusion is but a part of a constitutionally defective regime of labour relations, designed to prevent the exercise of the s. 2(d) rights of RCMP members. We therefore conclude that the purpose of the *PSLRA* exclusion infringes s. 2(d) of the *Charter*.

(2) Summary

[136] We conclude that the purpose of the exclusion in s. 2(1) of the *PSLRA* substantially interferes with freedom of association. At this point, we need not consider the effects

of the *PSLRA* exclusion independently from those of the imposition of the SRRP as a labour relations regime.

[137] This conclusion does not mean that Parliament must include the RCMP in the *PSLRA* scheme. As discussed above, s. 2(*d*) of the *Charter* does not mandate a particular model of labour relations. Our conclusion with respect to the constitutionality of the *PSLRA* exclusion means only that Parliament must not substantially interfere with the right of RCMP members to a meaningful process of collective bargaining, unless this interference can be justified under s. 1 of the *Charter*. For example, it remains open to the federal government to explore other collective bargaining processes that could better address the specific context in which members of the RCMP discharge their duties.

[138] We now turn to whether the infringements of s. 2(*d*) rights caused by the legislative imposition of the SRRP and by the exclusion of RCMP members from the application of the *PSLRA* are justified under s. 1 of the *Charter*.

G. Are the Limits Imposed on the RCMP Members' Section 2(*d*) Rights Justified Under Section 1 of the *Charter*?

[The Court went on to find that the *PSLRA* exclusion was not justified under section 1 of the *Charter*, as the infringement of section 2(d) bore no rational connection to maintaining a neutral, stable, and reliable police force; even if there were a rational connection, the Court went on, the government would need to establish that the RCMP is materially different from the provincial police forces in order for total exclusion from "meaningful collective bargaining" to be minimally impairing. Since a material difference has not been shown, the legislation would fail the section 1 analysis on this ground as well.]

H. Remedy

[154] Within the impugned legislative scheme, the imposition of the SRRP and the exclusion in s. 2(1) of the *PSLRA* deny members of the RCMP the right to any meaningful process of collective bargaining. And, while s. 2(*d*) does not protect the right to any *particular* process of collective bargaining, it does protect the right to a *meaningful* process. Having found that s. 96 of the *RCMP Regulations* and para. (*d*) of the definition of "employee" in s. 2(1) of the *PSLRA* infringe the freedom guaranteed to RCMP members under s. 2(*d*) of the *Charter*, and that these provisions cannot be saved under s. 1, we conclude that the appropriate remedy is to strike down the offending provision of the *PSLRA* under s. 52 of the *Constitution Act, 1982*. We would similarly strike down s. 96 of the *RCMP Regulations* were it not repealed.

[155] The Attorney General of Canada argues that this conclusion would go against the proposition, which we accept, that s. 2(*d*) does not guarantee a right to a particular labour relations process. The Attorney General argues that striking down the offending provision of the *PSLRA* would constitutionalize the labour relations process set out in that Act.

[156] This argument misconstrues our conclusion. We do not conclude that the *PSLRA* process is constitutionalized, but rather that the existing labour relations scheme and the purpose motivating the *PSLRA* exclusion are inconsistent with the *Charter* and

fail under s. 52 of the *Constitution Act, 1982*. This conclusion does not mandate a particular labour relations regime or bar the federal government from pursuing an avenue other than the *PSLRA* to govern labour relations within the RCMP. Should it see fit to do so, Parliament remains free to enact any labour relations model it considers appropriate to the RCMP workforce, within the constitutional limits imposed by the guarantee enshrined in s. 2(*d*) and s. 1 of the *Charter*.

VII. CONCLUSION

[157] We would allow the appeal, with costs to the appellants throughout, and answer the constitutional questions as follows:

1. Does s. 96 of the *Royal Canadian Mounted Police Regulations, 1988*, SOR/88-361, infringe s. 2(*d*) of the *Canadian Charter of Rights and Freedoms*?
   Yes.

2. If so, is the infringement a reasonable limit prescribed by law as can be demonstrably justified in a free and democratic society under s. 1 of the *Canadian Charter of Rights and Freedoms*?
   No.

3. Does para. (*d*) of the definition of "employee" at s. 2(1) of *Public Service Labour Relations Act*, S.C. 2003, c. 22, infringe s. 2(*d*) of the *Canadian Charter of Rights and Freedoms*?
   Yes.

4. If so, is the infringement a reasonable limit prescribed by law as can be demonstrably justified in a free and democratic society under s. 1 of the *Canadian Charter of Rights and Freedoms*?
   No.

[158] Had s. 96 of the *RCMP Regulations* not been repealed, it would have been declared to be of no force or effect. Paragraph (*d*) of the definition of "employee" in s. 2(1) of the *PSLRA* is of no force or effect pursuant to s. 52 of the *Constitution Act, 1982*. We suspend the declaration of invalidity for a period of 12 months.

* * * * *

Does the Court adopt Dickson CJC's account of section 2(d) or not? What are the consequences?

12:232 *Saskatchewan Federation of Labour*: **The Right to Strike**
The last case in the 2015 Trilogy dealt with whether section 2(d) included a "right to strike." *Saskatchewan Federation of Labour v Saskatchewan*, 2015 SCC 4 [*Sask Fed*], was released two weeks after the first two cases, and dealt with Saskatchewan's *Public Service Essential Services Act*, SS 2008, c P-42.2 [*PSESA*]. The *PSESA* was introduced by a newly elected Saskatchewan provincial government in 2007 as a statutory scheme to limit the ability of certain employees from going on strike by enabling public sector employers in Saskatchewan to designate certain employees as "essential" and prohibiting them from going on strike.

Prior to the *PSESA*, public-sector strikes were regulated on an *ad hoc* basis, and it was often difficult for the provincial government to ensure that essential services continued during labour disputes. In April 1999, 8,400 members of the Saskatchewan Union of Nurses participated in a province-wide strike, which seriously affected the provision of critical care to patients in many health care facilities throughout the province. Similarly, in 2001, health care employees represented by the Canadian Union of Public Employees withdrew their services, seriously affecting the delivery of health care. And from December 2006 to February 2007, a large number of highway workers, snow plow operators, and corrections workers participated in the Saskatchewan Government and General Employees' Union strike, causing public concerns about safety.

It was in this context that the newly elected provincial government introduced the *PSESA* in 2007. The legislation provided that designated "essential services employees" were prohibited from participating in any work stoppage against their public employer. In the event of a strike, those employees are required to continue "the duties of [their] employment with the public employer in accordance with the terms and conditions of the last collective bargaining agreement" and are prohibited from refusing to continue those duties "without lawful excuse." Contravening any provision under the *PSESA* is a summary conviction offence that can result in an increasing fine for every day the offence continues.

Under the *PSESA*, "essential services" included:

s. 2(c) **"essential services"** means:
(i) with respect to services provided by a public employer other than the Government of Saskatchewan, services that are necessary to enable a public employer to prevent:
   (A) danger to life, health or safety;
   (B) the destruction or serious deterioration of machinery, equipment or premises;
   (C) serious environmental damage; or
   (D) disruption of any of the courts of Saskatchewan; and

(ii) with respect to services provided by the Government of Saskatchewan, services that:
   (A) meet the criteria set out in subclause (i); and
   (B) are prescribed ["prescribed" services referred to in s. 2(c)(ii) are listed in Table 1 of the Appendix of *The Public Service Essential Services Regulations*, R.R.S., c. P-42.2, Reg. 1, enacted in 2009]

A "public employee" is defined in the *PSESA* under section 2(b), which states "employee" means an employee of a public employer who is represented by a trade union. The *PSESA* defines public employer as follows:

s. 2(i) **"public employer"** means:
(i) the Government of Saskatchewan;
(ii) a Crown corporation as defined in *The Crown Corporations Act, 1993*;
(iii) a regional health authority as defined in *The Regional Health Services Act*;
(iv) an affiliate as defined in *The Regional Health Services Act*;
(v) the Saskatchewan Cancer Agency continued pursuant to *The Cancer Agency Act*;
(vi) the University of Regina;
(vii) the University of Saskatchewan;

(viii) the Saskatchewan Polytechnic;
(ix) a municipality;
(x) a board as defined in *The Police Act, 1990*;
(xi) any other person, agency or body, or class of persons, agencies or bodies, that:
(A) provides an essential service to the public; and
(B) is prescribed [again, "prescribed" services referred to in s. 2(c)(ii) are listed in Table 1 of the Appendix of *The Public Service Essential Services Regulations*, R.R.S., c. P-42.2, Reg. 1, enacted in 2009]

Public employers and unions were to negotiate an "essential services agreement" to govern how public services are to be maintained in the event of a work stoppage. However, in the event that the negotiations break down, the public employer would have the authority to unilaterally designate, with notice, which public services it considers to be essential, the classifications of employees required to continue to work during a work stoppage, and the names and number of employees in each of the classifications. Further notice may be given by the public employer at any time, either to increase or decrease the numbers of employees required to maintain essential services.

Additionally, the Saskatchewan Labour Relations Board had limited jurisdiction to review the numbers of employees required to work in a given classification during a strike, and no authority to review whether any particular service was essential, which classifications involve the delivery of genuinely essential services, or whether specific employees named by the employer to work during the strike have been reasonably selected.

A 5:2 majority of the Supreme Court of Canada ruled that the *PSESA* violated section 2(d). Moreover, the majority expressly stated, for the first time, that the guarantee of freedom of association in section 2(d) includes a right to strike.

Saskatchewan Federation of Labour v Saskatchewan, 2015 SCC 4

Abella J.—

[1] In the *Alberta Reference (Reference re Public Service Employee Relations Act (Alta.)*, [1987] 1 S.C.R. 313), this Court held that the freedom of association guaranteed under s. 2(d) of the *Canadian Charter of Rights and Freedoms* did not protect the right to collective bargaining or to strike. Twenty years later, in *Health Services and Support—Facilities Subsector Bargaining Assn. v. British Columbia*, [2007] 2 S.C.R. 391, this Court held that s. 2(d) protects the right of employees to engage in a meaningful process of collective bargaining. The rights were further enlarged in *Ontario (Attorney General) v. Fraser*, [2011] 2 S.C.R. 3, where the Court accepted that a meaningful process includes employees' rights to join together to pursue workplace goals, to make collective representations to the employer, and to have those representations considered in good faith, including having a means of recourse should the employer not bargain in good faith. And, most recently, in *Mounted Police Association of Ontario v. Canada (Attorney General)*, [2015] 1 S.C.R. 3, the Court recognized that a process of collective bargaining could not be meaningful if employees lacked the independence and choice to determine and pursue their collective interests. Clearly the arc bends increasingly towards workplace justice.

[2] The question in this appeal is whether a prohibition on designated employees participating in strike action for the purpose of negotiating the terms and conditions of their employment amounts to a substantial interference with their right to a meaningful process of collective bargaining and, as a result, violates s. 2(d) of the *Charter*. The question of whether other forms of collective work stoppage are protected by s. 2(d) of the *Charter* is not at issue here.

[3] The conclusion that the right to strike is an essential part of a meaningful collective bargaining process in our system of labour relations is supported by history, by jurisprudence, and by Canada's international obligations. As Otto Kahn-Freund and Bob Hepple recognized:

> The power to withdraw their labour is for the workers what for management is its power to shut down production, to switch it to different purposes, to transfer it to different places. A legal system which suppresses the freedom to strike puts the workers at the mercy of their employers. This—in all its simplicity—is the essence of the matter.
>
> (*Laws Against Strikes* (1972), at p. 8)

The right to strike is not merely derivative of collective bargaining, it is an indispensable component of that right. It seems to me to be the time to give this conclusion constitutional benediction.

[4] This applies too to public sector employees. Those public sector employees who provide essential services undoubtedly have unique functions which may argue for a less disruptive mechanism when collective bargaining reaches an impasse, but they do not argue for no mechanism at all. Because Saskatchewan's legislation abrogates the right to strike for a number of employees and provides no such alternative mechanism, it is unconstitutional....

[24] ... Along with their right to associate, speak through a bargaining representative of their choice, and bargain collectively with their employer through that representative, the right of employees to strike is vital to protecting the meaningful process of collective bargaining within s. 2(d). As the trial judge observed, without the right to strike, "a constitutionalized right to bargain collectively is meaningless".

[25] Where strike action is limited in a way that substantially interferes with a meaningful process of collective bargaining, it must be replaced by one of the meaningful dispute resolution mechanisms commonly used in labour relations. Where essential services legislation provides such an alternative mechanism, it would more likely be justified under s. 1 of the *Charter*. In my view, the failure of any such mechanism in the *PSESA* is what ultimately renders its limitations constitutionally impermissible....

[27] The trial judge in this case relied on changes in this Court's s. 2(d) jurisprudence to depart from the precedent set by the majority in the *Alberta Reference*.

[28] The recognition of the broader purpose underlying s. 2(d) led the Court to conclude in *Health Services* that "s. 2(d) should be understood as protecting the right of employees to associate for the purpose of advancing workplace goals through a process of collective bargaining" (para. 87). In reaching this conclusion, McLachlin C.J. and LeBel J. held that none of the majority's reasons in the *Alberta Reference* which had

excluded collective bargaining from the scope of s. 2(d) "survive[d] scrutiny, and the rationale for excluding inherently collective activities from s. 2(d)'s protection has been overtaken by *Dunmore*" (*Health Services*, at para. 36).

[29] This Court reaffirmed in *Fraser* that a meaningful process under s. 2(d) must include, at a minimum, employees' rights to join together to pursue workplace goals, to make collective representations to the employer, and to have those representations considered in good faith, including having a means of recourse should the employer not bargain in good faith.

[30] The evolution in the Court's approach to s. 2(d) was most recently summarized by McLachlin C.J. and LeBel J. in *Mounted Police*, where they said:

> The jurisprudence on freedom of association under s. 2(d) of the *Charter* ... falls into two broad periods. The first period is marked by a restrictive approach to freedom of association. The second period gradually adopts a generous and purposive approach to the guarantee.
>
> ...
>
> ... after an initial period of reluctance to embrace the full import of the freedom of association guarantee in the field of labour relations, the jurisprudence has evolved to affirm a generous approach to that guarantee. This approach is centred on the purpose of encouraging the individual's self-fulfillment and the collective realization of human goals, consistent with democratic values, as informed by "the historical origins of the concepts enshrined" in s. 2(d). ... [paras. 30 and 46]

[31] They confirmed that freedom of association under s. 2(d) seeks to preserve "employee autonomy against the superior power of management" in order to allow for a meaningful process of collective bargaining (para. 82).

[32] Given the fundamental shift in the scope of s. 2(d) since the *Alberta Reference* was decided, the trial judge was entitled to depart from precedent and consider the issue in accordance with this Court's revitalized interpretation of s. 2(d): *Canada (Attorney General) v. Bedford*, [2013] 3 S.C.R. 1101, at para. 42.

[33] Dickson C.J.'s dissenting reasons in the *Alberta Reference* were influential in the development of the more "generous approach" in the recent jurisprudence. Recognizing that association "has always been vital as a means of protecting the essential needs and interests of working people" (at p. 368), and that Canada's international human rights obligations required protection for both the formation and essential activities of labour unions, including collective bargaining and the freedom to strike, Dickson C.J. concluded that "effective constitutional protection of the associational interests of employees in the collective bargaining process requires concomitant protection of their freedom to withdraw ... their services [collectively], subject to s. 1 of the *Charter*" (at p. 371) ...

[34] His views are supported by the history of strike activity in Canada and globally.

[Justice Abella then reviewed some of the history of strike action in England and Canada.]

[49] As Gilles Trudeau wrote, [TRANSLATION] "[t]he strike was at the heart of the industrial relations system that prevailed throughout most of the 20th century ... in Canada" (p. 5). Its significance as an economic sanction to collective bargaining—or threat thereof—is what led Dickson C.J. to conclude in the *Alberta Reference*, as previously noted,

that "effective constitutional protection of the associational interests of employees in the collective bargaining process requires concomitant protection of their freedom to withdraw collectively their services, subject to s. 1 of the *Charter*" (p. 371).

[50] The inevitability of the need for the ability of employees to withdraw services collectively was also accepted by McLachlin C.J. and LeBel J. in *R.W.D.S.U.*, where they recognized that the purpose of strikes—placing economic pressure on employers—is a legitimate and integral means of achieving workplace objectives:

> Occasionally, ... negotiations stall and disputes threaten labour peace. When this happens, it has come to be accepted that, within limits, unions and employers may legitimately exert economic pressure on each other to the end of resolving their dispute. *Thus, employees are entitled to withdraw their services, inflicting economic harm directly on their employer and indirectly on third parties which do business with their employer.* [Emphasis added; para. 24.]

[51] The preceding historical account reveals that while strike action has variously been the subject of legal protections and prohibitions, the ability of employees to withdraw their labour in concert has long been essential to meaningful collective bargaining. Protection under s. 2(*d*), however, does not depend solely or primarily on the historical/legal pedigree of the right to strike. Rather, the right to strike is constitutionally protected because of its crucial role in a meaningful process of collective bargaining. ...

[53] In *Health Services*, this Court recognized that the *Charter* values of "[h]uman dignity, equality, liberty, respect for the autonomy of the person and the enhancement of democracy" supported protecting the right to a meaningful process of collective bargaining within the scope of s. 2(*d*) (para. 81). And, most recently, drawing on these same values, in *Mounted Police* it confirmed that protection for a meaningful process of collective bargaining requires that employees have the ability to pursue their goals and that, at its core, s. 2(*d*) aims

> to protect the individual from "state-enforced isolation in the pursuit of his or her ends".... The guarantee functions to protect individuals against more powerful entities. By banding together in the pursuit of common goals, individuals are able to prevent more powerful entities from thwarting their legitimate goals and desires. In this way, the guarantee of freedom of association empowers vulnerable groups and helps them work to right imbalances in society. It protects marginalized groups and makes possible a more equal society. [para. 58]

[54] The right to strike is essential to realizing these values and objectives through a collective bargaining process because it permits workers to withdraw their labour in concert when collective bargaining reaches an impasse. Through a strike, workers come together to participate directly in the process of determining their wages, working conditions and the rules that will govern their working lives ([Judy Fudge & Eric Tucker, "The Freedom to Strike in Canada: A Brief Legal History" (2009–2010), 15 *Canadian Labour & Employment Law Journal* 235] at p. 334). The ability to strike thereby allows workers, through collective action, to refuse to work under imposed terms and conditions. This collective action at the moment of impasse is an affirmation of the dignity and autonomy of employees in their working lives.

[55] Striking—the "powerhouse" of collective bargaining—also promotes equality in the bargaining process: England, at p. 188. This Court has long recognized the deep inequalities that structure the relationship between employers and employees, and the vulnerability of employees in this context. In the *Alberta Reference*, Dickson C.J. observed that

> [t]he role of association has always been vital as a means of protecting the essential needs and interests of working people. Throughout history, workers have associated to overcome their vulnerability as individuals to the strength of their employers. [p. 368]

And this Court affirmed in *Mounted Police* that

> ... s. 2(d) functions to prevent individuals, who alone may be powerless, from being overwhelmed by more powerful entities, while also enhancing their strength through the exercise of collective power. Nowhere are these dual functions of s. 2(d) more pertinent than in labour relations. Individual employees typically lack the power to bargain and pursue workplace goals with their more powerful employers. Only by banding together in collective bargaining associations, thus strengthening their bargaining power with their employer, can they meaningfully pursue their workplace goals.
>
> The right to a meaningful process of collective bargaining is therefore a necessary element of the right to collectively pursue workplace goals in a meaningful way ... [The] process of collective bargaining will not be meaningful if it denies employees the power to pursue their goals. [paras. 70–71]

Judy Fudge and Eric Tucker point out that it is "the possibility of the strike which enables workers to negotiate with their employers on terms of approximate equality" (p. 333). Without it, "bargaining risks being inconsequential—a dead letter" (Prof. Michael Lynk, "Expert Opinion on Essential Services", at par. 20; A.R., vol. III, at p. 145).

[56] In their dissent, my colleagues suggest that s. 2(d) should not protect strike activity as part of a right to a meaningful process of collective bargaining because "true workplace justice looks at the interests of all implicated parties" (para. 125), including employers. In essentially attributing equivalence between the power of employees and employers, this reasoning, with respect, turns labour relations on its head, and ignores the fundamental power imbalance which the entire history of modern labour legislation has been scrupulously devoted to rectifying. It drives us inevitably to Anatole France's aphoristic fallacy: "The law, in its majestic equality, forbids the rich as well as the poor to sleep under bridges, to beg in the streets, and to steal bread."

[57] Strike activity itself does not guarantee that a labour dispute will be resolved in any particular manner, or that it will be resolved at all. And, as the trial judge recognized, strike action has the potential to place pressure on *both* sides of a dispute to engage in good faith negotiations. But what it does permit is the employees' ability to engage in negotiations with an employer on a more equal footing (see *Williams v. Aristocratic Restaurants (1947) Ltd.*, [1951] S.C.R. 762, at p. 780; *Mounted Police*, at paras. 70–71).

[58] Moreover, while the right to strike is best analyzed through the lens of freedom of association, expressive activity in the labour context is directly related to the *Charter*-protected right of workers to associate to further common workplace goals under s. 2(d) of the *Charter*: *Fraser*, at para. 38; *Alberta (Information and Privacy Commissioner)*, at para. 30.

Strike action "bring[s the] debate on the labour conditions with an employer into the public realm": *Alberta (Information and Privacy Commissioner)*, at para. 28 Cory J. recognized this dynamic in *United Nurses of Alberta v. Alberta (Attorney General)*, [1992] 1 S.C.R. 901:

> Often it is only by means of a strike that union members can publicize and emphasize the merits of their position as they see them with regard to the issues in dispute. It is essential that both the labour and management side be able to put forward their position so the public fully understands the issues and can determine which side is worthy of public support. Historically, to put forward their position, management has had far greater access to the media than have the unions. At times unions had no alternative but to take strike action and by means of peaceful picketing put forward their position to the public. This is often the situation today. [p. 916]

[59] As Dickson C.J. observed, "[t]he very nature of a strike, and its *raison d'être*, is to influence an employer by joint action which would be ineffective if it were carried out by an individual" (*Alberta Reference*, at p. 371).

[60] Alternative dispute resolution mechanisms, on the other hand, are generally not associational in nature and may, in fact, reduce the effectiveness of collective bargaining processes over time: Bernard Adell, Michel Grant and Allen Ponak, *Strikes in Essential Services* (2001), at p. 8. Such mechanisms can help avoid the negative consequences of strike action in the event of a bargaining impasse, but as Dickson C.J. noted in *RWDSU v. Saskatchewan*, [1987] 1 S.C.R. 460, they do not, in the same way, help to realize what is protected by the values and objectives underlying freedom of association:

> ... as I indicated in the *Alberta Labour Reference*, the right to bargain collectively and therefore the right to strike involve more than purely economic interests of workers.... [A]s yet, it would appear that Canadian legislatures have not discovered an alternative mode of industrial dispute resolution which is as sensitive to the associational interests of employees as the traditional strike/lock-out mechanism.... [pp. 476–77]

That is why, in the *Alberta Reference*, Dickson C.J. dealt with alternative dispute resolution mechanisms not as part of the scope of s. 2(*d*), but as part of his s. 1 analysis: pp. 374–75.

[61] The ability to engage in the collective withdrawal of services in the process of the negotiation of a collective agreement is therefore, and has historically been, the "irreducible minimum" of the freedom to associate in Canadian labour relations (Paul Weiler, *Reconcilable Differences: New Directions in Canadian Labour Law* (1980), at p. 69).

[62] Canada's international human rights obligations also mandate protecting the right to strike as part of a meaningful process of collective bargaining. These obligations led Dickson C.J. to observe that

> there is a clear consensus amongst the [International Labour Organization] adjudicative bodies that [*Convention (No. 87) concerning freedom of association and protection of the right to organize*, 68 U.N.T.S. 17 (1948)] goes beyond merely protecting the formation of labour unions and provides protection of their essential activities—that is of collective bargaining and the freedom to strike. [*Alberta Reference*, at p. 359]

[63] At the time of the *Alberta Reference*, Dickson C.J.'s reliance on Canada's commitments under international law did not attract sufficient collegial support to lift his

views out of their dissenting status, but his approach has more recently proven to be a magnetic guide.

[Justice Abella then went on to cite international instruments as well as international jurisprudence in support of a right to strike.]

[75] This historical, international, and jurisprudential landscape suggests compellingly to me that s. 2(d) has arrived at the destination sought by Dickson C.J. in the *Alberta Reference*, namely, the conclusion that a meaningful process of collective bargaining requires the ability of employees to participate in the collective withdrawal of services for the purpose of pursuing the terms and conditions of their employment through a collective agreement. Where good faith negotiations break down, the ability to engage in the collective withdrawal of services is a necessary component of the process through which workers can continue to participate meaningfully in the pursuit of their collective workplace goals. In this case, the suppression of the right to strike amounts to a substantial interference with the right to a meaningful process of collective bargaining.

[76] In their dissenting reasons, however, my colleagues urge deference to the legislature in interpreting the scope of s. 2(d). This Court has repeatedly held that the rights enumerated in the *Charter* should be interpreted generously ... It is not clear to me why s. 2(d) should be interpreted differently: *Health Services*, at para. 26; *R. v. Advance Cutting & Coring Ltd.*, [2001] 3 S.C.R. 209, at para. 162; *Mounted Police*, at para. 47. In the context of constitutional adjudication, deference is a conclusion, not an analysis. It certainly plays a role in s. 1, where, if a law is justified as proportionate, the legislative choice is maintained. But the whole purpose of *Charter* review is to assess a law for constitutional compliance. If the touchstone of *Charter* compliance is deference, what is the point of judicial scrutiny?

[77] This brings us to the test for an infringement of s. 2(d). The right to strike is protected by virtue of its unique role in the collective bargaining process. In *Health Services*, this Court established that s. 2(d) prevents the state from substantially interfering with the ability of workers, acting collectively through their union, to exert meaningful influence over their working conditions through a process of collective bargaining (para. 90). And in *Mounted Police*, McLachlin C.J. and LeBel J. confirmed that

> [t]he balance necessary to ensure the meaningful pursuit of workplace goals can be disrupted in many ways. Laws and regulations may restrict the subjects that can be discussed, or impose arbitrary outcomes. They may ban recourse to collective action by employees without adequate countervailing protections, thus undermining their bargaining power. ... Whatever the nature of the restriction, *the ultimate question to be determined is whether the measures disrupt the balance between employees and employer that s. 2(d) seeks to achieve, so as to substantially interfere with meaningful collective bargaining*. ... [Emphasis added; para. 72.]

[78] The test, then, is whether the legislative interference with the right to strike in a particular case amounts to a substantial interference with collective bargaining. The *PSESA* demonstrably meets this threshold because it prevents designated employees from engaging in *any* work stoppage as part of the bargaining process. It must therefore be justified under s. 1 of the *Charter*.

[Justice Abella went on to conclude that the legislation could not be saved under section 1 because it did not minimally impair affected workers' right to freedom of association. There were three main reasons why it was not minimally impairing:

1) There was no "adequate review mechanism" through which employer determinations of which employees were essential could be challenged;
2) The legislation was overbroad in that it required designated employees to perform all duties, and not just essential duties, during a work stoppage; and
3) The legislation did not include a "meaningful dispute resolution mechanism" for bargaining disputes.]

[94] Not surprisingly, Dickson C.J. was alive to the profound bargaining imbalance the union inherits when the removal of the right to strike is not accompanied by a meaningful mechanism for resolving collective bargaining disputes:

> Clearly, if the freedom to strike were denied and no effective and fair means for resolving bargaining disputes were put in its place, employees would be denied any input at all in ensuring fair and decent working conditions, and labour relations law would be skewed entirely to the advantage of the employer. It is for this reason that legislative prohibition of freedom to strike must be accompanied by a mechanism for dispute resolution by a third party. I agree with the Alberta International Fire Fighters Association at p. 22 of its factum that "It is generally accepted that employers and employees should be on an equal footing in terms of their positions in strike situations or at compulsory arbitration where the right to strike is withdrawn". *The purpose of such a mechanism is to ensure that the loss in bargaining power through legislative prohibition of strikes is balanced by access to a system which is capable of resolving in a fair, effective and expeditious manner disputes which arise between employees and employers.* [Emphasis added.]
>
> (*Alberta Reference*, at p. 380)

[...]

[96] Given the breadth of essential services that the employer is entitled to designate unilaterally without an independent review process, and the absence of an adequate, impartial and effective alternative mechanism for resolving collective bargaining impasses, there can be little doubt that the trial judge was right to conclude that the scheme was not minimally impairing. Quite simply, it impairs the s. 2(*d*) rights of designated employees much more widely and deeply than is necessary to achieve its objective of ensuring the continued delivery of essential services.

[97] *The Public Service Essential Services Act* is therefore unconstitutional.

[Justice Abella suspended the declaration of invalidity for a period of one year.]

Rothstein and Wagner JJ. (Dissenting in part) —

[...]

[104] This case requires the Court to consider whether the right to strike is constitutionally protected under s. 2(*d*) of the *Canadian Charter of Rights and Freedoms*. The

appellant unions challenge Saskatchewan's *The Public Service Essential Services Act*, S.S. 2008, c. P-42.2 ("*PSESA*"), which restricts the ability of public sector workers who provide essential services to strike. The majority finds that these workers do have a constitutional right to strike. We disagree.

[105] McLachlin C.J. and LeBel J., writing for a unanimous Court in *R.W.D.S.U., Local 558 v. Pepsi-Cola Canada Beverages (West) Ltd.*, 2002 SCC 8, [2002] 1 S.C.R. 156, cautioned that

> [j]udging the appropriate balance between employers and unions is a delicate and essentially political matter. Where the balance is struck may vary with the labour climates from region to region. This is the sort of question better dealt with by legislatures than courts. Labour relations is a complex and changing field, and courts should be reluctant to put forward simplistic dictums. [para. 85]

Thirteen years later, the majority in this case ignores this sage warning in reaching its conclusion. Our colleagues have taken it upon themselves to determine "the appropriate balance between employers and unions", despite the fact that this balance is not any less delicate or political today than it was in 2002. In our respectful view, the majority is wrong to intrude into the policy development role of elected legislators by constitutionalizing the right to strike.

[106] In the Labour Trilogy, this Court firmly rejected the proposition that the right to strike in Canada is constitutionally entrenched.... [I]n *Health Services and Support—Facilities Subsector Bargaining Assn. v. British Columbia*, 2007 SCC 27 ... and *Ontario (Attorney General) v. Fraser*, 2011 SCC 20 ... despite the evolution in the s. 2(*d*) jurisprudence, this Court rejected the idea that there is a constitutional right to a dispute resolution process. The majority (at para. 1) now casts off these and other precedents and injects a one-sided view of "workplace justice" into s. 2(*d*) of the *Charter*. The majority has so inflated the right to freedom of association that its scope is now wholly removed from the words of s. 2(*d*).

[107] The statutory right to strike, along with other statutory protections for workers, reflects a complex balance struck by legislatures between the interests of employers, employees, and the public. Providing for a constitutional right to strike not only upsets this delicate balance, but also restricts legislatures by denying them the flexibility needed to ensure the balance of interests can be maintained. We are compelled to dissent.

II. ANALYSIS

A. There Is No Right to Strike Under Section 2(*d*) of the *Charter*

[108] The majority purports to recognize a violation of s. 2(*d*) of the *Charter* only where a "prohibition on designated employees participating in strike action for the purpose of negotiating the terms and conditions of their employment amounts to a substantial interference with [the] right to a meaningful process of collective bargaining" (para. 2). It attempts to minimize the impact of its decision by stating that the right to strike is only protected where it interferes with the right to meaningful collective bargaining, a right which has already been recognized in *Health Services*, *Fraser*, and *Mounted Police*

Association of Ontario v. Canada (Attorney General), 2015 SCC 1.... But our colleagues' reasons, in their entirety, reveal the true ambit of this decision: they have created a stand-alone constitutional right to strike.

[109] The majority's reasons include numerous references to the right to strike as being "essential" to, "crucial", and an "indispensable" component of meaningful collective bargaining. The majority describes the right to strike as "vital to protecting the meaningful process of collective bargaining within s. 2(d)" (para. 24). If the right to strike is a necessary element of meaningful collective bargaining, it will not only apply on a case-by-case basis; logically, any limitation on the right to strike will infringe s. 2(d) of the *Charter*. With respect, to accept this decision as simply an espousal of the right to meaningful collective bargaining disregards the substance of the majority's reasons.

(1) The Historical Right to Strike That the Majority Invokes Does Not Justify Constitutionalizing the Modern, Statutory Right to Strike

[110] The majority attempts to ground its new-found constitutional right to strike in the long history of strikes. There is no dispute that, at common law, employees are permitted to refuse to work (see G. W. Adams, *Canadian Labour Law* (2nd ed. (loose-leaf)), at ¶ 11.90; H. W. Arthurs, "Tort Liability for Strikes in Canada: Some Problems of Judicial Workmanship" (1960), 38 *Can. Bar Rev.* 346, at p. 349)....

[111] But the majority conflates this common law right to withdraw labour with the modern, statutory right to strike, which imposes obligations on employers: "Historically, there was no legal 'right' to strike at common law, entailing a correlative obligation on an employer to refrain from retaliatory measures, but rather a common law 'freedom' to do so" (B. Oliphant, "Exiting the Freedom of Association Labyrinth: Resurrecting the Parallel Liberty Standard Under 2(d) & Saving the Freedom to Strike" (2012), 70:2 *U.T. Fac. L. Rev.* 36, at p. 41). Thus, at common law, employers are not obligated to refrain from terminating striking workers or from hiring replacement employees to perform their functions (see B. Langille, "What Is a Strike?" (2009–2010), 15 *C.L.E.L.J.* 355, at pp. 368–69)....

[112] This historical common law right to strike is a fundamental component of our legal system insofar as it reflects the idea that employees have no obligation to continue to work under conditions they consider to be unsatisfactory: no legislature can force an individual or a group into servitude. The majority correctly remarks that "[t]he ability to strike thereby allows workers, through collective action, to refuse to work under imposed terms and conditions" (para. 54). The majority, however, is not constitutionalizing this fundamental historical right. Rather, it constitutionalizes a *duty* on employers not to terminate employees who have withdrawn their labour, nor to hire replacement workers.

[113] In the words of Justice Richards of the Saskatchewan Court of Appeal (as he then was) the majority invokes "the *contemporary* right to strike, a right significantly bound up with, integrated into, and defined by a specific statutory regime" (2013 SKCA 43, 414 Sask. R. 70, at para. 61 (emphasis in original)). This statutory regime is not found in s. 2(d) of the *Charter* or anywhere else in Canadian constitutional law.

[Justice Rothstein went on to state that the courts must show deference in the field of labour relations to legislatures, who are better placed to undertake the complex balancing between public, employer, and employee interests. He then stated the implications of constitutionalizing a right to strike:]

[123] Constitutionalizing a right to strike introduces great uncertainty into labour relations. In Canada, the ability of workers to strike and the limits placed on this ability are essential to the balance between employers, employees, and the public interest. The majority's reasons will make all statutory limits on the right to strike presumptively unconstitutional, a significant concern since all labour relations statutes contain extensive limits on the conditions under which workers may strike. Will governments be forced to defend all of these limits under s. 1 of the *Charter*, no matter how ingrained they may be in Canadian labour relations? What is the true scope of this new, constitutionalized right to strike? Despite our general understanding of *Charter* rights applying broadly to all Canadians, has the majority now created a fundamental freedom that can only be exercised by government employees and the 17 percent of the private sector workforce that is unionized? ... Are workers without collective agreements able to exercise this new right? The majority sidesteps these fundamental questions.

[124] These unanswered questions reveal why courts must be deferential. The unbridled right to strike that the majority endorses has far-reaching consequences that are difficult to predict and even more difficult to address once that right is constitutionalized. By constitutionalizing this broad conception of the right to strike, the majority binds the government's hands and limits its ability to respond to changing needs and circumstances in the dynamic field of labour relations.

(3) The Court Must Not Constitutionalize Particular Political Positions in Labour Relations
[125] Under the rubric of "workplace justice", our colleagues, relying on a 19th century conception of the relationship between employers and workers, enshrine a political understanding of this concept that favours the interests of employees over those of employers and even over those of the public. While employees are granted constitutional rights, constitutional obligations are imposed on employers. Employers and the public are equally as entitled to justice as employees—true workplace justice looks at the interests of all implicated parties. ...

(4) The Right to Strike Is Not an Indispensable Component of Collective Bargaining as Defined by This Court

[128] The majority finds that "the right to strike is an essential part of a meaningful collective bargaining process" and that "[t]he right to strike is not merely derivative of collective bargaining, it is an indispensable component of that right" (para. 3). Such statements expressly contradict the right to meaningful collective bargaining as it was so recently recognized and defined by this Court in *Health Services* and *Fraser*.

[129] In *Fraser*, the majority explains that s. 2(*d*) of the *Charter* protects a right to collective bargaining, that is, "a process that allows employees to make representations and have them considered in good faith by employers, who in turn must engage in a process of meaningful discussion" (para. 54). Nothing in the concept of collective bargaining, as this Court has defined the term, includes a constitutional right for employees to strike with a concomitant constitutional obligation on employers to not hire replacement workers or to take the employees back at the end of the strike.

[130] The majority in Fraser found a constitutionally protected dispute resolution process unnecessary. The Court interpreted the *Ontario Agricultural Employees Protection Act, 2002*, S.O. 2002, c. 16 ("*AEPA*"), as including a requirement that employers consider employee representations in good faith. The Court noted that "the Minister ... stated that the *AEPA* was not intended to 'extend collective bargaining to agricultural workers'", but said that this statement

> may be understood as an affirmation that the *AEPA* did not institute the dominant Wagner model of collective bargaining, or bring agricultural workers within the ambit of the [*Labour Relations Act, 1995*, S.O. 1995, c. 1, Sch. A], not that the Minister intended to deprive farm workers of the protections of collective bargaining that s. 2(*d*) grants. [para. 106]

Despite the fact that the *AEPA* contained no dispute resolution mechanism, only a bare requirement that employers consider employee representations in good faith, the Court concluded that the Act did not violate s. 2(*d*) of the *Charter* (para. 107).

[131] The majority's reasons overlook this Court's findings in *Fraser*. The trial judge in this case held, and the majority agrees, that without the right to strike "a constitutionalized right to bargain collectively is meaningless" (2012 SKQB 62 ... at para. 92; majority reasons, at para. 24). With respect, this is plainly incorrect—it is not the threat of work stoppage that motivates good faith bargaining. Before *Health Services*, there was a legal duty on employers to bargain in good faith under various labour relations statutes ... After *Health Services*, this duty was constitutionalized. It is the statutory duty, and is now this *constitutional duty*, not the possibility of job action, that compels employers to bargain in good faith. To say that this constitutional right is meaningless without a concomitant constitutionalized dispute resolution process would be to say that individuals can never vindicate their rights through the courts or other public institutions.

[132] The goal of strike action is not to guarantee a right that was statutory and is now constitutionally guaranteed. Instead, it is to apply economic or political pressure on employers to meet union demands. As the majority of the Court stated in *Fraser*:

> ... legislatures are [not] constitutionally required, in all cases and for all industries, to enact laws that set up a uniform model of labour relations imposing a statutory duty to bargain in good faith, statutory recognition of the principles of exclusive majority representation and a statutory mechanism for resolving bargaining impasses and disputes regarding the interpretation or administration of collective agreements.... What is protected is associational activity, not a particular process or result. [para. 47]

[133] When the right to strike was simply statutory, both employers and employees were able to exercise economic and political power through labour action. In certain circumstances, employees had the right to strike, while employers had the right to lock out. Even when meaningful collective bargaining was constitutionalized, good faith was required of both sides of the bargaining table. In *Health Services*, the majority of the Court noted that the employees' right to collective bargaining "requires both employer and employees to meet and to bargain in good faith, in the pursuit of a common goal of peaceful and productive accommodation" (para. 90; see also *Fraser*, at para. 40). Now, by constitutionalizing only the ability of employees to exert economic and political pressure,

the majority disturbs the delicate balance of labour relations in Canada and impedes the achievement of true workplace justice.

[134] The majority asserts that employees must have some "means of recourse should the employer not bargain in good faith" (para. 29). In the event that bargaining does not occur in good faith, workers *have* recourse: they can bring a claim under the relevant statutory provision or, in some cases, directly under s. 2(*d*) of the *Charter*, which is precisely what was done in *Health Services*.

[135] The majority's conclusion that the right to strike is "an indispensable component" of collective bargaining (at para. 3) does not accord with recent jurisprudence. There is nothing in the concept of collective bargaining as it has been defined by this Court in *Health Services*, *Fraser* and *Mounted Police* that would imply that employees have a constitutional right to strike and that employers have a constitutional obligation to preserve the jobs of those employees.

[136] Contrary to *Fraser*, the majority now says that "[t]he right to strike is not merely derivative of collective bargaining, it is an indispensable component of that right" (para. 3). However, the majority also says that the right to strike is protected simply because "the right to strike is an essential part of a meaningful collective bargaining process" (para. 3). This must mean that the right is indeed derivative—a right to strike is protected only because it derives from the right to collective bargaining, a right which was itself derived from the protection of freedom of association (see *Fraser*, at paras. 46, 54, 66 and 99). As earlier noted, the result is to inflate the right to freedom of association to such an extent that its scope is now completely divorced from the words of s. 2(*d*) of the *Charter* themselves.

[Justice Rothstein went on to state that the Court should not depart from its precedents in this case, and that international law did not favour constitutionalizing a right to strike. He therefore concluded that the *PSESA* did not violate section 2(*d*) and should be upheld as valid.]

12:233 Meredith v Canada (Attorney General)

Although this case, known as *Meredith*, was the second case released in the 2015 Trilogy, it is the last one that we will review in this section. As in *MPAO*, this case also involved the RCMP. In *Meredith*, members of the National Executive Committee of the SRRP brought a constitutional challenge on behalf of all members of the RCMP, arguing that the December 2008 decision of the Treasury Board and the relevant legislation (*Expenditure Restraint Act*, SC 2009, c 2), violated their constitutional right to collective bargaining protected by section 2(*d*) of the *Charter* by rolling back scheduled wage increases for RCMP members without prior consultation.

Their claim failed. A majority of the Supreme Court justified that conclusion, in large part, as follows:

Meredith v Canada (Attorney General), 2015 SCC 2

The Chief Justice and LeBel J. (Cromwell, Karakatsanis and Wagner JJ. Concurring)—

[…]

[24] For the reasons given in the companion case, *MPAO*, s. 2(*d*) of the *Charter* protects workers' freedom to associate and pursue their workplace goals through collective

bargaining. In s. 2(d) cases, the courts must ask whether state action has substantially impaired the employees' collective pursuit of workplace goals. The test applicable to this question is set out in *Health Services*.

[25] Section 2(d) guarantees a right to a meaningful labour relations process, but it does not guarantee a particular outcome. What is guaranteed is the right of employees to associate in a meaningful way in the pursuit of collective workplace goals ...

[...]

[26] For the affected RCMP members, the *ERA* resulted in a rollback of scheduled wage increases from the previous Pay Council recommendations accepted by the Treasury Board, from between 2% and 3.5% to 1.5% in each of 2008, 2009 and 2010. The original increase would also have doubled service pay and increased the Field Trainer Allowance. Both of these were also eliminated by the *ERA*, subject to subsequent negotiations pursuant to s. 62 of that Act.

[27] The Attorney General of Canada acknowledges that wages are an important issue, but notes that the limits imposed by the *ERA* were time-limited in nature, were shared by all public servants, and did not permanently remove the subject of wages from collective bargaining. Accordingly, he suggests that the importance of the wage restraints does not rise to the level of a s. 2(d) violation. For the reasons that follow, we conclude that s. 2(d) was not breached.

[28] The facts of *Health Services* should not be understood as a minimum threshold for finding a breach of s. 2(d). Nonetheless, the comparison between the impugned legislation in that case and the *ERA* is instructive. The *Health and Social Services Delivery Improvement Act*, S.B.C. 2002, c. 2, Part 2, introduced radical changes to significant terms covered by collective agreements previously concluded. By contrast, the level at which the *ERA* capped wage increases for members of the RCMP was consistent with the going rate reached in agreements concluded with other bargaining agents inside and outside of the core public administration and so reflected an outcome consistent with actual bargaining processes. The process followed to impose the wage restraints thus did not disregard the substance of the former procedure. And the *ERA* did not preclude consultation on other compensation-related issues, either in the past or the future.

[29] Furthermore, the *ERA* did not prevent the consultation process from moving forward. Most significantly in the case of RCMP members, s. 62 permitted the negotiation of additional allowances as part of "transformation[al] initiatives" within the RCMP. The record indicates that RCMP members were able to obtain significant benefits as a result of subsequent proposals brought forward through the existing Pay Council process. Service pay was increased from 1% to 1.5% for every five years of service—representing a 50% increase—and extended for the first time to certain civilian members. A new and more generous policy for stand-by pay was also approved. Actual outcomes are not determinative of a s. 2(d) analysis, but, in this case, the evidence of outcomes supports a conclusion that the enactment of the *ERA* had a minor impact on the appellants' associational activity.

[...]

Abella J. (dissenting)—

[...]

[62] The unilateral rollback of three years of agreed-upon wage increases without any prior consultation is self-evidently a substantial interference with the bargaining process. This conduct was precisely what led this Court in *Health Services* to find an unjustified infringement of s. 2(*d*). I have difficulty seeing the distinction between that case and this one. The fact that the rollbacks were limited to a three-year period does not attenuate the key fact that they were unilateral. Nor does the fact that consultation was possible on other more minor compensation issues minimize the severity of the breach.

[63] The failure to engage in *any* discussion meant that the RCMP was denied its right to a meaningful negotiation process about wages, a central component of employment relationships generally and particularly for RCMP members whose other benefits—pensions, disability benefits, paid time off, and service pay—were tied to their wage amounts.

* * * * *

The majority judgment begins with a recitation of ideas familiar from *Health Services*: "Section 2(d) guarantees a right to a meaningful labour relations process, but it does not guarantee a particular outcome." Is this still true?

12:240 Conclusion: What Is the Current and Future Legal Content of Section 2(d)?

So, we return to our primary question—what are we to make of our nine cases? We can now appreciate that this is indeed a very difficult question. Constitutional labour law has evolved remarkably and rapidly. We have presented the cases largely in order of appearance because, we believe, that is the best way to follow the difficult and remarkable story of section 2(d)—to read the cases that give it life in, essentially, the order in which they came into this world, and in the same order in which Canadian labour lawyers and judges have had to come to grips with them.

This has real advantages. One has to read *Dunmore* then *Health Services*, then the Ontario Court of Appeal decision in *Fraser*, in order to have any chance of seeing the difficulties on display in *Fraser* at the Supreme Court, and in the third trilogy (2015) as the Court attempted to come to grips with at least some of the state of play the second trilogy had bequeathed to us.

But reading chronologically also comes with a cost. For example, it obscures the truth that there is not one single line of cases here—rather, there are a number of lines, two of which are fundamental. First, there are cases such as *Alberta Reference* and *Health Services* where the constitutional complaint is the straightforward and common one that the state has interfered with the exercise of the freedom.

Second, there are cases such as *Dunmore* and *Fraser* where the complaint is that the state has not constrained private actors (employers) who are interfering with the exercise of the freedom. These are two very different types of cases and the costs of failing to see this can be seen in the cases, perhaps particularly *Fraser* and *MPAO*. There is also the danger of following the official storyline, as contained in the Supreme Court's self-reporting on its own prior decisions, too closely, and skating over the real depth and difficulty of the matters under discussion. As a result, we risk not taking charge of our thinking here and squarely addressing these matters. For example, is the idea of "inherently collective activities" doing any work in these cases? Isn't there a difference between rights and freedoms? How do rights against private actors "work"? Is the test for private actor interference and state interference with the freedom the same? Are our judges in fact imposing the *Wagner Act* model, or, as they say, not doing that at all? Do we now have a constitutional version of the mandatory/permissive distinction? If so, why? Is there a freedom to strike, or a right to strike in Canada—does the *Charter* ban dismissals for striking? Can any group of Canadian workers now go on strike? Does an employer have a duty to bargain with a group of workers who show up, as in *Estevan*? Is exclusivity a constitutionally valid idea? Why do Canadian workers only have a right to a "degree" of independence? How could "designated bargaining agents" ever pass a test of freedom of association (as suggested in *MPAO*)? What role should international labour law have in our *Charter* life—is Dickson and the current Supreme Court's view a good one? What role is international law actually playing now? Did *MPAO* revive Dickson's dissent from the *Alberta Reference* or undermine it? Are these cases all really equality cases, and would that insight have solved all of this difficulty? Why is that the path not taken? Does it matter? And so on. Stay tuned.

* * * * *

As of the time of writing, perhaps the most cogent summary of the current jurisprudence on section 2(d) on this most basic of points was articulated by Donald JA of the BC Court of Appeal, in the recent case of *BCTF v British Columbia*, 2015 BCCA 184. The case was the last stage in a fifteen-year legal dispute between the British Columbia provincial government and the British Columbia Teachers' Federation (BCTF) regarding the constitutionality of legislation that narrowed the scope of collective bargaining in the province's public education sector. In November 2016, the majority of the Supreme Court of Canada simply adopted Donald JA's reasoning (excerpted below) and allowed the appeal in an unusual ruling from the bench: *BCTF v British Columbia*, 2016 SCC 49.

The *BCTF* case is the result of legislation enacted by the BC provincial government in early 2002: the *Health and Social Services Delivery Improvement Act*, SBC 2002, c 2; the *Education Services Collective Agreement Act*, SBC 2002, c 1; and the *Public Education Flexibility and Choice Act*, SBC 2002, c 3. The government stated that these statutes would help contain costs and provide greater flexibility and stability for those charged with managing the health care and public education sectors. Several provincial health care unions and the BCTF immediately filed *Charter* challenges to parts of the legislation, particularly the legislation's restrictions on collective bargaining.

The health care unions actively pursued their *Charter* claim, ultimately succeeding in the Supreme Court of Canada in the *Health Services* decision, above. After the *Health Services* decision was released, the BCTF proceeded with its own claim. On 13 April 2011, BC Supreme Court Justice Griffin issued a decision, largely in BCTF's favour, but suspended her declaration respecting the invalidity of certain aspects of the impugned legislation for a period of twelve months so that the government would have time to address the repercussions of the decision. After one year, the BC government enacted the *Education Improvement Act*, SBC 2012, c 3 (*EIA*). The *EIA* both ended an ongoing teachers' strike and essentially re-enacted several of the legislative provisions that Griffin J had struck down. It was this legislation that became the subject of the most recent litigation.

The BCTF challenged the new legislation in 2013, and succeeded once again before Griffin J, who held that the BC government had not engaged in good faith consultations and negotiations with the BCTF subsequent to her earlier decision. She invalidated certain provisions of the *EIA* and, in addition, awarded the BCTF $2 million in damages under subsection 24(2) of the *Charter*. This time, Griffin J refused to suspend the declaration of invalidity, stating that the effect of her decision was to reinstate several collective bargaining agreement provisions that had been excised by way of the impugned legislation (addressing such things as class size, class composition, staff levels and ratios, and workloads) retroactive to 1 July 2002: *British Columbia Teachers' Federation v British Columbia*, 2014 BCSC 121.

The BC Court of Appeal heard the government's subsequent appeal on an expedited basis in mid-October 2014 and overturned Griffin J's decision six months later, on 30 April 2015. Chief Justice Bauman and Harris J jointly authored the majority's reasons, holding that teachers were afforded a meaningful process by which to advance their collective aspirations. The majority also held that the province did not engage in bad faith negotiations or consultations and that Griffin J "should not have assessed the substantive merit or objective reasonableness of the parties' negotiating positions" because "courts are poorly equipped to make such assessments" (para 7).

Justice Donald, in his dissent, disagreed with the majority's view of section 2(d) and the practical implications of the Supreme Court of Canada's 2015 Trilogy:

British Columbia Teachers' Federation v British Columbia, 2015 BCCA 184

Donald J.A. (dissenting):

[...]

[330] Before moving on to a discussion of the trial judge's finding pertaining to good faith negotiation, I will discuss why the test for determining such good faith negotiation was accurately laid out by the Supreme Court of Canada in *Health Services* and *Fraser*, and it would not be appropriate for this Court to add additional requirements selectively culled from labour tribunal decisions made in a Wagner-style context.

[331] The Supreme Court of Canada described the components of good faith negotiation in *Fraser* at para. 41, as follows: "Section 2(*d*) requires the parties to meet and engage in meaningful dialogue. They must avoid unnecessary delays and make a reasonable effort to arrive at an acceptable contract." In *Health Services* at para. 98 this was described as parties "endeavoring to reach an agreement, engaging in genuine and constructive negotiations, avoiding unjustified delays in negotiation and mutually respecting the commitments entered into, taking into account the results of negotiations in good faith." Parties must be willing to exchange and explain their positions: *Health Services* at para. 101.

[332] The Supreme Court of Canada found that good faith negotiation is *not* determined by the traditional components of Wagner-style collective bargaining: *Fraser* at paras. 44–45. Importantly, although a court does not generally inquire into the content of bargaining positions, in some circumstances, even though a party is participating, "that party's proposals and positions may be 'inflexible and intransigent to the point of

endangering the very existence of collective bargaining'": *Health Services* at para. 104, citing *Royal Oak Mines Inc. v. Canada (Labour Relations Board)*, [1996] 1 S.C.R. 369 at para. 46. Parties must "honestly strive to find a middle ground between their opposing interests": *Health Services* at para. 101, citing *Royal Oak Mines* at para. 41.

[333] In *Fraser*, the Court found that the *Agricultural Employees Protection Act, 2002*, S.O. 2002, c. 16, provided a statutory system requiring consideration of an association's representations, which included an obligation to listen to oral representations, read written representations, and acknowledge having read them. The Court then read in an implicit requirement for the employer to consider those representations in good faith: at paras. 101–103.

[334] To summarize, good faith negotiation, from a constitutional perspective, has been described by the Supreme Court of Canada as requiring parties to meet and engage in meaningful dialogue where positions are explained and each party reads, listens to, and considers representations made by the other. Parties' positions must not be inflexible and intransigent, and parties must honestly strive to find a middle ground.

[335] Any vagueness in this description and definition is necessary as the assessment is always context specific and fact-based. A single, specific test for finding good faith would be inflexible and unable to assist in the fact-based and context specific assessment that a trial judge must carry out.

[336] However, my colleagues have expanded upon this test and adopted an additional principle that "[i]t is inappropriate, for reasons of institutional competence, for a court or tribunal to investigate the factual basis and internal logic of an employer's substantive bargaining proposals" when conducting a good faith analysis (at para. 149). This principle was derived primarily from a review of five decisions of the British Columbia Labour Relations Board: *Re Catholic Independent Schools Diocese of Prince George*, [2001] B.C.L.R.B.D. No. 112; *Re Naramata Centre Society*, [2014] B.C.L.R.B.D. No. 157; *Re Noranda Metal Industries Ltd.*, [1974] B.C.L.R.B.D. No. 149; *Re IKEA Canada Limited Partnership*, [2014] B.C.L.R.B.D. No. 155; and *Re Insurance Corp. of British Columbia*, [2012] B.C.L.R.B.D. No. 143. With respect, I must disagree with my colleagues that this is an appropriate component of the good faith test from a constitutional perspective. There are at least three reasons why such a component should not be included in the good faith analysis under s. 2(*d*).

[337] First, the decisions of the Labour Relations Board were not made in a constitutional context, but were instead made in the context of the *Labour Relations Code*. This code was expressly acknowledged as being traced to the U.S. "*Wagner Act*" in *Catholic Independent Schools Diocese of Prince George (Re)* at para. 23, one of the cases cited by my colleagues. In my opinion, incorporating selective elements of traditional good faith analyses under a Wagner-style scheme makes the same error as the Ontario Court of Appeal in *Fraser* when it suggested that *Health Services* constitutionalized traditional Wagner-style collective bargaining. As was later made clear by the Supreme Court of Canada, *Health Services* did no such thing.

[338] Instead, a good faith analysis from a constitutional perspective must be approached from a different perspective. The Supreme Court of Canada was not ruling out Wagner-style collective bargaining in *Fraser* because such standards would be too

onerous. Rather, the Court did so because the traditional approach to collective bargaining in the private marketplace is not equivalent to what is constitutionally protected. Wagner-style schemes are largely predicated on an antagonistic relationship between private parties. A government, in contrast to private sector employers, is elected to serve all of society's stakeholders, including labour. As my colleagues acknowledge in their reasons: "Governments are not businesses" (at para. 125).

[339] There is less of a need to inquire into the rationality of internal logic of substantive positions in the context of private parties because Wagner-style collective bargaining imagines resolution of impasse through mediation, arbitration, or the economic pressure of strikes. However, in the constitutional context, the government always has the power to unilaterally resolve impasse through legislation, or force workers to end a strike through constitutionally compliant back-to-work legislation. This is a huge power imbalance that fundamentally alters the calculus of how negotiations unfold.

[340] My colleagues state, "[j]ust as employees do not have a presumptive veto over changes to their working conditions, government does not have a free hand to make any unilateral changes it likes to public sector employees' working conditions" (at para. 130). But if courts were barred from inquiring into the substantive reasonableness of the government's position, a "free hand" is exactly what the government would have. The government could declare all further compromise in any context to be untenable, pass whatever it wants, and spend all "consultation periods" repeatedly saying "sorry, this is as far as we can go". This would make a mockery of the concept of collective bargaining. An impasse created by the Province through the adoption of unwavering, unreasonable positions and a lack of good faith is not a legitimate impasse. Section 2(d) of the *Charter* does not incorporate a traditional Wagner-style scheme; it especially does not incorporate selective excerpts of a traditional Wagner-style scheme.

[341] Second, the inapplicability of the "hands off" principle taken from these labour decisions is made even clearer if the decisions themselves are explored. In *Re Naramata Centre Society*, another case relied on by my colleagues, the Board makes clear that such a "hands off" approach does not apply to negotiating positions that would be "improper" when taken to impasse, including matters that would be "inconsistent with the law and policy of the Code": at para. 58. These include "bargaining demands for changes to the scope of a bargaining unit or the waiver of statutory rights such as access to adjudication at arbitration or before the Board": at para. 58.

[342] It should be clear that such an exception is a problem when applied to bargaining between an association and the government. The positions of the government, if taken to impasse and passed unilaterally through legislation, *become* the law, and therefore could never be "inconsistent with the law". If directly applied to constitutional analyses, therefore, this exception would never occur, and courts would be completely barred from assessing the respective positions of the parties. Certainly the scope of judicial review when it comes to *Charter* rights is not smaller than the scope of a tribunal's competence under the *Labour Code*.

[343] More importantly, if the facts of the case at bar are considered, it is clear that if this *were* a dispute to be considered by a labour tribunal under the *Code*, it would be one such exception where the tribunal would consider the respective substantive positions

of the parties. The Province in this case was advocating for a restriction on traditional collective bargaining rights. Throughout the negotiations, the Province suggested that it would not return the right to collective bargaining to the union, and would instead replace it with some unnamed alternative. The Province eventually proposed the "Learning Improvement Fund" ("LIF") as a component of such replacement legislation.

[344] The LIF, as passed in ss. 18–19 of Bill 22, established a legislative mechanism for teachers to have input into how additional funds were to be used in order to ameliorate the removal of the Working Conditions. The LIF regulations required school boards to submit spending plans to the Minister before any decisions were made on how to allocate the additional funds. The legislation and regulations provide for opportunities for teachers individually to have input into each board's proposed spending plans. Although the LIF legislation also contemplates a role for the BCTF in this consultation process by including the local union president as one of the several parties to be consulted, the trial judge found that this was "clearly a process meant to dilute the influence and role of the BCTF": Bill 22 Decision at para. 497. I would note that, in *MPAO* at para. 288 the majority of the Court said: "A process that substantially interferes with a meaningful process of collective bargaining by reducing employees' negotiating power is therefore inconsistent with the guarantee of freedom of association enshrined in s. 2(*d*)." As the trial judge acknowledged in this case, the LIF proposal appeared to seek BCTF's agreement to give up its negotiating power: Bill 22 Decision at para. 288.

[345] The LIF was originally proposed by the Province at a time when it continued to suggest that collective bargaining on the Working Conditions would not be restored: Bill 22 Decision at paras. 287–288. Therefore, if this were reviewed under the *Code*, much of the Province's positions could be seen as forcing the BCTF to accept a waiver of collective bargaining rights—precisely the kind of position that apparently cannot be taken to impasse and one in which the tribunal would investigate substantive positions, including the "factual basis" and internal logic of such.

[346] Third, in my opinion, the suggestion by my colleagues that a court should not investigate the factual basis and internal logic of the position of the government is inconsistent with the history of judicial review for *Charter* compliance. As is well-known, the *Oakes* test includes an analysis of whether the purpose of potentially unconstitutional legislation is pressing and substantial and has a "rational connection" to the means used.... Such an analysis cannot occur without considering the substantive position of the government, since the substantive position of the government is equivalent to the purpose of and the means used in the legislation.

[347] If a court were barred from examining the substantive position of the government, this could create a constitutional loophole: legislation deleting important work terms that would otherwise fail the s. 1 analysis, because the deletion has no rational connection to the stated policy goals of the government, would sometimes not even reach the s. 1 stage because the court was barred from probing the substantive position of the government and therefore took the government at its word that no alternative was possible.

[348] In summary, the constitutional test for bad faith on the part of government should be expressed in the same language used by the Supreme Court of Canada in *Health Services* and *Fraser*. Parties are required to meet and engage in meaningful dialogue where

positions are explained and each party reads, listens to, and considers representations made by the other party. Parties' positions must not be inflexible and intransigent, and parties must honestly strive to find a middle ground. In order to determine whether the government is bargaining in good faith, it may sometimes be necessary to probe and consider the government's substantive negotiating position.

[Justice Donald went on to find that the province had not consulted in good faith, and that the impugned legislation was not saved by section 1 of the *Charter*. Besides an increased monetary remedy and striking down the legislation, Donald JA ordered that the working conditions be reinstated into the teachers' collective agreement by section 24(1) of the *Charter*. This is the dissent the Supreme Court adopted on appeal as its own.]

* * * * *

How well has Donald JA done in coming to grips with our current state of play? How well has he answered the questions we started with?

Chapter 13: Statutory Minimum Standards

13:100 INTRODUCTION

In this chapter, the focus shifts from collective bargaining to statutory regulation of the individual employment relationship. As we have seen in Chapter 3, the common law of employment treats the relationship as one based in contract. In light of the disparity in bargaining power between most employers and employees, it is commonly argued that the law of contract, which rests upon notions of individual autonomy and market freedom, is ill-equipped to effectively and fairly govern the employer-employee relationship. Statutory intervention, such as legislated minimum standards of employment, is aimed at levelling the playing field by ensuring a basic floor of rights for workers. Employment standards legislation, such as the *Employment Standards Act*, SO 2000, c 41 in Ontario and Part III of the *Canada Labour Code*, RSC 1985, c L-2, in the federal jurisdiction, governs a wide range of terms and conditions of employment (such as minimum wages; deductions from pay; internships; hours of work and overtime; public holidays; vacation; pregnancy, parental, and other leaves of absence; termination of employment). This chapter examines the purpose and evolution of statutory minimum standards, some of the difficulties related to enforcement, and their relationship to the common law of contract. A selection of caselaw offers a sample of some of the substantive statutory entitlements (such as minimum wage, vacation pay, overtime pay, and, in the federal jurisdiction, the protection against unjust dismissal) alongside a consideration of some of the potential gaps in the legislation's coverage as it applies to "employees."

In his 2008 report on federal labour standards for the minister of labour, commissioner Harry Arthurs articulated the "decency principle" against which, he argued, statutory minimum standards ought to be judged [Canada, Commission on the Review of Federal Labour Standards, *Fairness at Work: Federal Labour Standards for the 21st Century* (Ottawa: Human Resources and Social Development Canada, 2008) at x–xi]. He writes,

> The fundamental principle of decency at work underlies all labour standards legislation and is the benchmark against which all proposals must be measured:
>
>> Labour standards should ensure that no matter how limited his or her bargaining power, no worker in the federal jurisdiction is offered, accepts or works under conditions that Canadians would not regard as "decent." No worker should therefore receive a wage that is insufficient to live on; be deprived of the payment of wages or benefits to which they are entitled; be subject to coercion, discrimination, indignity or unwarranted danger in the workplace; or be required to work so many hours that he or she is effectively denied a personal or civic life.

This decency principle must be read alongside a number of other important principles. For example, Canada must maintain the dynamism of its market economy in order to sustain high labour standards; regulatory interventions in that economy must be carefully considered and implemented in such a way as to ensure that competing employers operate on a level playing field; labour standards can and should balance the legitimate interests and concerns of workers and employers through a strategy of "regulated flexibility;" and legislation should be drafted and administered so as to achieve the highest possible levels of compliance consistent with the efficient use of public resources and the achievement of multiple public policies.

Statutory regulation of employment is often met with criticism by proponents of a free labour market. The following passage provides an historical overview of this debate, and the subsequent one considers challenges posed to realizing the principle of decent work in the contemporary economic and social situation.

Barry J Reiter, "The Control of Contract Power" (1981) 1:3 *Oxford Journal of Legal Studies* **347 at 348–53 [footnotes omitted]**

It is important to appreciate at the outset the implausibility of a claim that society should be organized on the basis of private contracting behaviour. The claim advocates apparent anarchy and amoralism. Never before the birth of faith in markets had gain been advanced as an inherently worthy motive. Nor had economic structures ever been sharply differentiated from social structures and relations. But in an effort to throw off feudal and religious shackles, to release energy and to give vent to new theories of social justice, a broad coalition was forged over the sixteenth through the nineteenth century. The coalition, including economic liberals, utilitarians, and classes rising in power politically and intellectually, adduced powerful arguments in support of the market. The central benefits they attributed to organization in this form included the following. First, the market would provide powerful incentives motivating individuals to work and to produce wealth in society. The resultant gain would improve the lot of all (or of most, depending on the economist) individuals in society. The notion of incentives could be, and indeed was, pushed to the point of urging the necessity of a substantial level of poverty in society and of starvation as a sharp stick to keep the incentive structure keen. Second, market organization offered promises of efficiency. The consumer would determine what society produced: the cheapest mode of production of the right quantities of goods and an efficient distribution network were explicit outcomes of the model. Third, market organization would allow for innovation. This was a particularly critical attribute given the substantial barriers to innovation that had been erected by the guilds and other local protective arrangements. Fourth, the market meant freedom from imposition by governmental or religious authorities. This freedom offered a consent basis to society, a basis seen both as good in itself and as a legitimating force. Finally, the market promised justice. The entire notion of market rewards and failures could be and was linked to a personal merit principle.

The case was powerful, but it was never wholly accepted. Instead, strange and shifting alliances of intellectual and political power combined to prevent the excesses of the market through the assertion of political power. Society reacted in a 'spontaneous outburst' to assert its primacy over economics. The details of the social reaction and the proof of what I assert about its success are provided in Polanyi's classic study, *The Great Transformation* and in Atiyah's interesting and extensive recent work, *The Rise and Fall of Freedom of Contract*. It may suffice to describe the nature of the rejection of market principles in one critical sector only, that of 'the supply of labour.' The commodification of labour was a critical step necessary to establish a market-based economy. Older feudal notions of the relationship between workers and those responsible for them had to give way if mobile labour was to be available to be bought and sold as supply and demand dictated. The commodification of labour was not really achieved even in theory until the repeal of the Poor Laws in 1834. However, as the momentum to turn labour into a commodity grew, the social reaction was already taking shape. It appeared in the form of the reassertion and the continued assertion of values limiting market values in respect of human labour. The force of the social reaction demonstrates that the nineteenth century was anything but an era of *laissez-faire*. The best known reactions involve those associated with the various Factory Acts, dating from 1833. The Acts dealt with employment of children, hours of work, and safety matters. Similar legislation regulated other important industrial sectors. A bureaucracy was created, industrial inspection Commissions were established, Reports were issued and legislation followed frequently. Combination laws were enacted early in the nineteenth century and Truck Acts were passed frequently thereafter.

All of this social reaction occurred early in the 'era of market economy.' Today, the dimensions of the reaction are even more apparent. Industrial codes and related legislation govern virtually every aspect of employment: hiring, union rights and responsibilities, hours of work, health and safety standards, compensation for injury, redundancy arrangements (in some cases), minimum or prescribed wage rates (in many cases), terms of payment, pension and unemployment benefits. In modern society, it is a fact that all but the most subsidiary features of the 'labour contract' are determined by institutions other than contract. The labour relationship is governed by political rather than market power. Similarly, the permitted uses of lands and of capital were never and are not now determined by other than a most tightly controlled market. The same may be said of all other significant features of modern life. Contract may be a medium, but as a social directing and organizing principle, it is left well to the margins.

In the face of the powerful case adduced by the 'market coalition' how could this be so? The answer has been provided by students of the social sciences. First, it is important to realize the historical fallacy on which the market economists built their theory. When Adam Smith said that the division of labour in society was dependent on the existence of markets, on 'man's propensity to barter, truck and exchange one thing for another' he was quite clearly historically wrong. This fact is not adduced so much to cast doubt on Smith's historical facility as to point out the striking nature of the theory he advanced. Nowhere before had society been subservient to economics, and a sharp break with the past would have been necessary in order to implement the dramatic change in the relationship between social and economic principles that the classical economists and the utilitarians were, therefore, advocating. Second, it became apparent early on that the classical economic-utilitarian theory did not work even in its own terms: the problem of ignorance among members of the public was a pervasive one and the liberals' hopes for education as the cure proved futile; the problem of monopolies (natural and otherwise) appeared quickly, and posed a major challenge. Third, the problem of inequalities threatened the moral basis of the theory. To the extent that individuals began with different endowments of money, opportunities, or even human abilities, the merit basis of the market system faltered. Fourth, it became apparent that contract was not simply a two-party affair. The market produced externalities of significant proportion: society must be and was concerned about injured workers, ruined social fabric, and ecological chaos. Fifth, the preservation of the institution of the market itself required vigorous suppression of market principles: total freedom had to be limited in order that there could be any freedom. Thus legislation was clearly necessary to prevent the exercise of monopoly power and some action was essential to prevent the enforcement of restrictive covenants that would serve to limit the participation the contract model was designed to foster. Intervention in the market was also necessary to slow the pace of change that might occur too rapidly thereby threatening to bring down the entire structure.

Finally, and most importantly, market theory simply did not take enough account of social values other than those concerned with efficiency and (measurable) net gains. On one hand, *a priori* values could be asserted against the anarchy of contract. Thus it could be argued that individuals and land were not commodities, or that they were not mere means but were, rather, ends. Or different visions of equality could be asserted. While contract may be said to foster certain forms of equality, it is apparent that other more levelling forms can be advocated in its place. On the other hand, less fundamental but nevertheless conflicting values could be asserted against 'market values.' Paternalistic notions could be advanced in support of the view that the consumer *cannot* choose best, and that choice by others might be preferable. Health, safety and moral values might claim priority on an other-than-market calculus. From the time of John Stuart Mill onward, it was apparent that classical economics had little to contribute on important issues of distribution though it could say much about efficiency.

Many of these difficulties were appreciated very early in the nineteenth century, and it was clear by the last quarter of that century (if not well before) that arguments founded on 'freedom of contract' would not carry much independent weight. In the end, and in respect of contract as a social organizing principle, we have witnessed a 'death of contract' quite different from that which has been the subject of intense debate of late. We have observed the replacement of the idea that contract alone might be the balance wheel of society by one suggesting that political institutions ought to perform this role instead. 'Contract' has become recognized as in need of extensive political manipulation. Ultimately, 'the market' turns out to have been a short term bridge philosophy carrying society from a period of organization in religious and feudal terms to the modern era of democratic political direction. A contemporary theory of contract must recognize these facts by rejecting 'the market' in favour of an institutionally mixed and discretionary measure of social progress.

[By permission of Oxford University Press.]

Judy Fudge, "The New Workplace: Surveying the Landscape" (2009) 33:1 *Manitoba Law Journal* 131 at 135–49

The changing nature of industry has meant the old "Fordist" paradigm of the mass of workers performing a standard set of skills in large-scale production enterprises is rapidly becoming a thing of the past. In industrialized countries, employment patterns and practices are now primarily determined not in manufacturing, but in the service sector, which since 2000 has accounted for over 60 per cent of total OECD employment and close to three-quarters of all employment in a number of major OECD countries....

... Union density in manufacturing has fallen from about one-half to one-third of all workers since the mid-1980s. Other industries that historically have sustained the standard employment relationship—primary industries, transportation, and, to a lesser extent, communications and utilities—have also experienced declining union density.

Unionization continues to be very low in private consumer services and in financial and business services....

Young workers' unionization rate showed the steepest decline. Union members are most likely to be prime age, between 45 and 54 years old, and are more likely than not to have postsecondary education. Moreover, the temporal dimension of the employment relationship—both in terms of hours worked on a weekly basis and the duration of the relationship—influences the likelihood of unionization. Full-time and permanent workers have a higher chance, one in three, of being union members than do part-time and temporary workers, who have only a one in four chance.

A shift in the occupational structure of the Canadian labour market has accompanied economic restructuring. The number of jobs requiring higher levels of formal education and skills has increased. Between 1989 and 2003, the share of all jobs in professional occupations rose from 18 per cent to 22 per cent. Yet, as Andrew Jackson notes, more than 40 per cent of men still work in traditional blue-collar jobs and one-third of women still work in pink-collar clerical, secretarial, and administrative jobs in offices. Moreover, one in five men and almost one in three women work in sales and service occupations—mainly lower paid and often part-time jobs in stores, hotels and restaurants—and as security guards and building cleaners.

The firms that employ labour have also reorganized. Today fewer employees work for large vertically integrated firms of the type that once formed a stable anchor for the standard employment relationship. Outsourcing and franchising fuel the disintegration of the vertically integrated firm, and networks are an alternative form of organization to bureaucracy. Thus, it is not surprising that the proportion of employees working in firms with less than 100 employees increased from 36 to 41 per cent between 1983 and 2001. This change in the structure of firms has affected employment. Jobs in smaller firms are less well paid than jobs in big firms. They are also less likely to provide benefits, security, and union representation than jobs provided by large firms.

One of the most significant impacts of the new economy on employment is the rise in non-standard, contingent, or precarious forms of work. This work departs from the normative model of the standard employment relationship, which is a full-time and year-round employment relationship for an indefinite duration with a single employer.

It includes self-employment, part-time work, temporary employment, contract work, and multiple-job holding. In 1989 these forms of nonstandard employment made up 33 per cent of jobs, whereas in 2002 these forms of employment made up 37 per cent of total employment. The further the form of employment departs from the normative model the more precarious it is. Temporary, part-time, and self-employment tend to be precarious both in terms of income and security. For example, temporary workers earned 16 per cent less per hour than permanent workers. In 2000, 30 per cent of workers who were paid under ten dollars an hour were employed in temporary jobs, compared to 16 per cent of workers paid between 10 and 20 dollars an hour and 9 per cent of workers who were paid more than 20 dollars an hour.

Social location—sex, race, immigration status, ethnicity, disability, and type of household—interacts with occupation and industry to channel vulnerable workers into precarious employment. Women and new immigrants, who tend also to be members of visible minorities, disproportionately perform precarious work.... Young men are also overrepresented in precarious employment.

Most employees who are in precarious employment remain in such jobs for extended periods of time because there are virtually no ladders into better jobs. Moreover, relative to other similar countries Canada has a high proportion of low-paid jobs. One out of ten persons aged 18 to 59 in 1996 and not a full-time student was a low-income worker for at least one year between 1996 and 2001. One in six Canadians working full-time earned less than $10 an hour (in dollars adjusted to 2001)....

Moreover, only a small proportion of new jobs are being unionized. Union coverage of newly hired men fell by almost 20 percentage points, from 38 per cent in 1981 to 19 per cent in 2004. This is twice the drop in union density observed among other male employees....

The cumulative impact of these changes—declining unionization, the increase in precarious employment, and the deterioration in the terms and conditions of new jobs—has been a polarization of earnings. The increase in earnings inequality during the second half of the 1990s is surprising given that it was a period of prosperity and economic expansion. The conventional theory that "a rising tide lifts all boats" predicts that wage differentials narrow and that lower-skilled workers disproportionately benefit from tighter labour markets. However, the result of the 1990s—increasing earnings inequality—suggests that a new paradigm based on the new economy is at play. Globalization, outsourcing, international trade, information technologies, work reorganization and new forms of employment relationships, especially in the high-growth and more manufacturing-orientated provinces, explain some of the earnings inequality....

The most profound change in the labour force over the past fifty years has been the flood of women into paid employment. The participation rate of women in the labour force has increased steadily since the 1960s, and Canada's female labour force participation rate is amongst the highest of the thirty member states of the OECD. In 2003 the labour force participation rate of women was 73 per cent, still below that of men, which stood at 83.2 per cent....

The increase in women's employment—both participation rate and working hours—has not been matched by a concomitant shift in unpaid domestic work to men, although men have increased their contribution to domestic labour....

The lack of fit between the organization of employment and the demands of domestic labour, especially caring for others, has resulted in a struggle to find a suitable work-life balance. Linda Duxbury and Chris Higgins analyzed two large-scale surveys of employees in large firms held ten years apart. They found rising levels of stress caused by too many demands on mothers' time, while fathers are increasingly reporting stress from work-life conflict. They have also quantified the costs to employees, their families, employers and society at large of this conflict between the demands of work and personal, family and community life.

The deterioration in employment and wages places households under pressure, which influences social cohesion and labour supply. Under the contemporary employability model of welfare, women with children and young families are especially vulnerable in the new economy. Women with young children are expected to work. However, the kind of employment that is compatible with caring for young children does not, generally, provide sufficient income or security for women to support dependents on their own earnings. Yet, household structures are changing, and families are less stable. Married couples with children are the only census family structure to experience a sharp decline in numbers compared to 2001. The percentage of divorces per 100,000 married couples rose from 180 in 1951, where it remained for the next decade, when it shot up in the 1970s and 1980s, reaching 1222 per 100,000 in 2001. One of the most visible social transformations since the 1950s is the rise in the number of lone-parent families created by divorce or childbearing outside marriage. Lone-parent families are at much higher risk of low income than other types of families.

Young people today have to work harder and longer to reach earnings achieved by previous generations. The earnings of younger adults under 35 have declined since the 1970s, which had a corresponding negative impact on young families. The result is that the fertility rate is below the rate necessary to replace the population, declining to 1.5 in 2001. However, the fertility rate does not reflect what people say they would prefer; when polled people say they want to have more children than they actually have....

Employment standards—such as longer maternity and parental leave and benefits as well as family responsibility leave—have been enacted to accommodate the increasing labour force participation of women and alleviate growing work-life conflict....

At the same time as the capacity of unions to represent the rights of workers has diminished, governments have also dismantled the public services needed to enforce labour standards and human rights. While courts have expanded their capacity to address violations of individual labour rights, either by allowing civil enforcement of a statutory right or by expanding the common law, litigation, even if class actions prove to be successful, is not an effective means of combating increasing inequality in the labour market.

The new economy has produced distinctive patterns of winners and losers when it comes to labour market outcomes such as types of jobs, wages, benefits and working hours. The consequences of a deregulated labour market accumulate along the ascriptive features of traditionally disadvantaged groups such as women and immigrants, especially those who are visibly different. Moreover, the evidence suggests that one of the consequences of deregulation has been to downgrade the norm for new jobs for all labour market participants.

In the new economy, the rising tide of economic prosperity has not lifted all boats; too many have been tethered to the bottom. Despite an annual rate of economic growth of 3 per cent, a thirty-year record low rate of unemployment (hovering about 6 per cent), and an all time high employment rate (over 63 per cent of the population is employed), a greater proportion of jobs are insecure and precarious and the standard employment relationship is deteriorating. Inequality in labour market outcomes, especially earnings, has grown. Precarious work and inequality undermine the sustainability of households and create fissures and tensions in social cohesion.

Over the last half century there has been a transformation both in employment and household structures. Thus, we need to reconsider for whom employment and labour law should be designed. The scope of employment and labour law is dwindling as the standard employment relationship shrinks. It is time to institutionalize a new standard employment relationship, one that achieves the traditional goals of protecting employees against economic and social risks, reducing social inequality, and increasing economic efficiency. But it should also be one that provides equal access for women and men to the employment system, supports lifelong learning and the new patterns of the life-course, and accommodates diversity without penalty. The construction of a new employment norm is necessary in order to revitalize labour law's distinctive contribution, which is to strengthen the bonds of social solidarity against the fragmentation of the market. The current economic crisis simply underscores the urgency of the need to institutionalize new, inclusive employment norms that protect workers from the risks inherent in the market.
[Reprinted with permission.]

What are the implications of these readings for the role of employment standards within Canada's system of labour and employment laws?

13:200 AN OVERVIEW OF MODERN EMPLOYMENT STANDARDS LEGISLATION

Employment standards legislation regulates a wide and growing range of terms and conditions of employment. This legislation has developed significantly in recent decades, responding to some extent to the social and economic pressures and needs discussed in Section 13:100, above. The following excerpt chronicles the development of employment standards legislation in Ontario. Similar developments can be traced in other Canadian jurisdictions.

Leah F Vosko, Eric Tucker, Mark P Thomas, & Mary Gellatly, "New Approaches to Enforcement and Compliance with Labour Regulatory Standards: The Case of Ontario, Canada." Commissioned Paper for Vulnerable Workers and Precarious Work (Law Commission of Ontario, 2012)

> [Employment Standards (ES)] are legislated standards that set minimum terms and conditions of employment in areas such as wages, working time, vacations and leaves, termination and severance. ES generally apply to most workers in a labour market but are often the only source of workplace protection for workers in non-unionized jobs. The majority of Ontario's over 6 million workers in over 370,000 workplaces rely on ES . . .

Ontario's [*Employment Standards Act* (ESA)] was enacted in 1969. The ESA provided a minimum wage for both men and women and established maximum hours of work at 8 per day and 48 per week. An overtime rate of time and a half was set for anything over 48 hours a week and the Act established the right to refuse overtime work. It also provided for time and a half on 7 statutory holidays and guaranteed 2 weeks of paid vacation per year ... the legislation was designed to set minimum standards for Ontario's labour market and provide legislative protection for those most vulnerable to employer exploitation.

The core standards of the ESA were altered through minor reforms in the 1970s, 1980s, and early 1990s, most of which added to the scope of legislative protections for workers in the province. Termination notice requirements were added in 1971. In 1972, a pregnancy leave provision was added that gave employees with at least 1 year of seniority in workplaces of 25 or more up to 12 weeks (6 and 6) of pre- and post-natal leave, and entitlement to their former or a comparable position. In 1975, the overtime pay (time-and-one-half) threshold was reduced from 48 hours to 44, and pregnancy leave provisions were expanded to cover up to 17 weeks of leave. In 1976, the province introduced a differential (lower) minimum wage rate for servers in the hospitality industry.

Severance pay provisions were introduced in 1981. These provisions provided employees with a minimum of 5 years of service with 1 week's pay for each year worked up to a maximum of 26 weeks in cases of mass termination. Under amendments made in 1987, employers were required to provide termination notices 1 week in advance for any employee employed longer than 3 months, with an additional week's notice for each year of employment, up to a maximum of 8 weeks. Workers with 5 years of employment at a business with an annual payroll of at least $2.5 million became eligible for severance pay. In addition, the new severance provisions were extended to workers whose temporary lay-off extended beyond 35 weeks in a 52-week period. Further, in the case of mass layoffs, the legislation required that employers provide the Ministry of Labour (MOL) with an explanation of the economic circumstances surrounding the termination, a summary of consultations with employees and the affected community, any proposed measures to help those laid off, and a statistical profile of affected workers.

Bankruptcy protection legislation was introduced in the Spring of 1991. The Employee Wage Protection Program was designed to provide employees with compensation for unpaid wages, commissions, overtime wages, vacation pay, holiday pay, and termination and severance pay, up to a maximum of $5000 per employee. The program was administered through the Employment Standards Branch of the MOL and Employment Standards Officers (ESOs) were given the ability to order payments under the program. The program was funded out of general provincial revenues. Upon payment of a claim, the government would attempt to recover funds from employers and businesses....

Beginning in 1995, Ontario's ES underwent a three-stage reform process. The reforms ... were designed primarily to promote 'flexibility' for employers, in particular through changes to working time standards introduced in 2001.

First, in 1995 the Employee Wage Protection Program was terminated and the minimum wage was frozen at $6.85, a wage freeze that would last for 9 years. Second, in 1996, the *Employment Standards Improvement Act* reduced the time limit for workers to register formal complaints from 2 years to 6 months, and placed a $10,000 limit on monetary awards for ESA violations, regardless of the value of lost wages. The Act also introduced a provision preventing unionized employees from filing ES complaints with the MOL, requiring employees with union representation to resolve ES complaints through the grievance arbitration process, placing the cost of administering ESA complaints in the hands of unions, rather than the Ministry.

[M]ajor legislative changes were implemented in the ESA, 2000. These amendments increased weekly maximum hours of work from 48 to 60 and allowed for the calculation of overtime pay to be based on an averaging of overtime hours across a 4-week period: employers could schedule overtime hours without compensation at time and a half provided the total for the 4-week period was less than 176 hours. They also revoked the system of government permits required for excess hours (more than 48 per week), introducing instead a requirement for employee "consent" to the new excess hours and overtime averaging provisions. The ESA 2000 also introduced anti-reprisal protections and family crisis leave. In addition, the government expanded the parental leave provisions of the Act, to bring them in line with federal amendments to the Employment Insurance program, allowing for up to 52 weeks of unpaid, job protected leave for birth mothers and up to 37 weeks for new parents (generally fathers or adoptive parents)....

Between 2004 and 2010, ES reforms displayed a partial return to decent work principles, with the introduction of ES legislation targeted at particular groups of 'vulnerable workers': specifically, workers employed through temporary help agencies and live-in caregivers. In developing this legislation, the government assumed that most employers will comply with minimum standards legislation and aimed to target legislative reforms at employers in sectors where violations are high.

The *Employment Standards Amendment Act (Temporary Help Agencies) 2009* developed new standards for workers in temporary help agencies. It introduced requirements that temporary agencies must provide information about the agency (name and contact information) and working conditions (incl. pay, hours, nature of work) to workers. It extended ESA coverage for public holiday pay and termination and severance to these workers. Finally, it introduced some prohibitions on charging fees to clients for entering into employment agreements with assignment employees. Specifically, agencies are permitted to charge clients a fee if an employee is offered a permanent position in first six months of an assignment with that client.

In 2010, the *Employment Protection for Foreign Nationals Act (Live-in Caregivers and Others)*, introduced a series of legislative protections for those employed as live-in caregivers. Specifically, it banned fees charged by recruiters and employers, allowed live-in-caregivers up to 3½ years to make a complaint to recover prohibited fees, prohibited reprisals against live-in caregivers for exercising their rights under the legislation, and prohibited an employer or recruiter from taking possession of a live-in caregiver's property (incl. documents such as passports). The Act also authorized ESOs to proactively enforce the legislation....

[T]he most recent reforms to the ESA were introduced through the *Open for Business Act, 2010* (OBA). This Act focused on enforcement, modifying enforcement practices with the stated aim of making these practices more 'efficient'. Specifically, the OBA alters ES enforcement procedures fundamentally by, among other things, requiring workers facing ES violations to first approach their employers for a resolution, mandating that workers and employers provide information on their claims before they will be accepted by the MOL, and giving new powers to ESOs to facilitate settlements between workers and employers, including unprecedented discretion over monetary compensation for workers. Like the ESA reforms of 2001, the OBA was a clear departure from the norms of *decent work* outlined above, prioritizing the efficient resolution of claims over the aim of protecting vulnerable workers.

First, employees are required to notify their employer before the MOL will initiate an ES claim. The assumption behind this requirement is that "[m]ost employers want to do the right thing and they will often remedy the situation promptly and voluntarily, if they agree there is a valid claim." Second, the amendments place responsibility on individual workers to collect the information for their complaints, reducing the requirements on the investigative procedure itself. If an ESO determines that there is insufficient evidence provided by an employee, then the officer may determine there is no violation. Finally, the amendments promote a voluntary approach to ES regulation, specifically through amendments that give ESOs a role in bringing employers and employees to a mediated settlement, with the Act stating that neither party would have to participate in such a settlement unless they agree to it.

[Reprinted with permission.]

Following *The Changing Workplaces Review* (Ontario, Ministry of Labour, *The Changing Workplaces Review: Special Advisors' Interim Report*, by C Michael Mitchell & John C Murray, (Ontario, July 2016)) —a comprehensive review of Ontario's labour and employment legislation in light of the changing nature of the workforce, the workplace, and the economy—the Ontario government passed the *Fair Workplaces, Better Jobs Act*, SO 2017, c 22. The new legislation includes a number of significant amendments to Ontario's *Employment Standards Act*, including an increased minimum wage; guarantees of equal pay for equal work for casual, part-time, temporary, and seasonal workers; one week's notice or pay in lieu of notice for employees of temporary help agencies; new scheduling rules; a minimum of three weeks' vacation after five years with the same employer; up to ten individual days of leave and/or up to fifteen weeks of leave, without the fear of losing their job when a worker or their child has experienced or is threatened with domestic or sexual violence; expanded personal emergency leave in all workplaces; and unpaid leave to take care of a critically ill family member.

13:300 COVERAGE: THE MEANING OF "EMPLOYEE" UNDER EMPLOYMENT STANDARDS LEGISLATION

Employment Standards statutes typically apply only to "employees," but the term "employee" is defined under the legislation in very general terms. Courts and tribunals have interpreted the meaning of that term purposively, in a way that brings within the legislation those workers who are in a position of economic subordination to their employer and are part and parcel of their employer's business, and which excludes those who are independent entrepreneurs running their own businesses. Legislatures have also created a patchwork of exclusions and exemptions of employees and employers from employment standards legislation. The relatively recent proliferation of self-employment and other forms of so-called atypical work such as home-based work, telecommuting, casual work, and part-time work, along with unpaid internships, means that many workers may appear to fall outside the scope of Employment Standards protections. However, rarely are these workers true entrepreneurs; indeed, they can be as economically vulnerable and dependent on their employers as regular "employees." The following cases illustrate the approach Boards and Tribunals have adopted to the determination of a worker's status under Employment Standards legislation and the associated Regulations is in dispute: in *Renaud*, a claim for overtime pay by a personal care attendant; in *Girex Bancorp*, a claim for wages and vacation pay by an intern; and in *New Jenny Nail and Spa*, a claim for minimum wage, public holiday pay and vacation pay sought by a spa worker classified by the employer as an independent contractor. On this last category of case, note that in an attempt to level the playing field, the recent legislative amendments in Ontario provide for penalties, including prosecution, public disclosure of a conviction and monetary penalties against employers who misclassify their employees. The legislation now also clearly places the burden on the employer to establish that any disputed worker is truly an independent contractor rather than an employee: *Labour Standards Act, 2000*, SO 2000, c 41, s 5.

Renaud (Re), [1999] BCESTD No 462

OVERVIEW

This decision deals with an appeal brought against a Determination issued on June 3, 1999, wherein the Director found that Mike Renaud owed $27,566.07 being overtime wages, statutory holiday pay and compensation for length of service to Ms. Candice Spivey whom he had hired as a personal care attendant. The grounds for the appeal ... is basically that the Director erred in finding that Ms. Spivey was not a "live-in home support worker" or a "sitter" as defined in the *Employment Standards Act Regulation (the Regulation)* and thereby excluded from *Employment Standards Act (the Act)*, or at least from the entitlement to overtime pay.

[...]

FACTS

Mike Renaud is a ventilator-dependent complete quadriplegic who requires personal care attendance on a 24 hour basis. His condition came about as a result of a motor vehicle accident.

Ms. Spivey was hired and paid directly by Mr. Renaud as a personal care attendant and she worked from September 30, 1998 to February 28, 1999. Ms. Spivey held no qualifications for this type of work and was trained on the job during the first two or three weeks she was there by Mrs. Nancy Renaud, Mike Renaud's mother.

Ms. Spivey worked at Mr. Renaud's residence three days per week, Sunday, Wednesday and Friday. The daily hours were 24 hours from 8.00 a.m. on the reporting day until 8:00 a.m. the following morning. Ms. Spivey was paid on the basis of a 13 hour day at the hourly rate of $16.00 per hour. The other 11 hours were considered to be her rest period. However, she was on call during the night to attend Mr. Renaud's needs. To facilitate this, Ms. Spivey slept on a couch in the living room at night and, in the event this becomes a consideration later, she was not charged for board and room.

The duties performed by Ms. Spivey included typical care giver functions such as bathing, dressing, feeding, lifting from bed to chair, chair to bed, tidying up and generally being there to help if an emergency arose. Other daily duties involved trachea care, suctioning, bowel care and changing the condom catheter. Ms. Spivey also accompanied Mr. Renaud on outings, doing the driving in his specially equipped vehicle to places like movies, shopping and to restaurants and bars.

In the Determination under review, the Director's Delegate concluded that on the basis of the foregoing facts, Ms. Spivey was not a "live-in home support worker" a "night attendant" or, a "residential care worker," which are all excluded by *the Regulation* from the hours of work and overtime provisions of *the Act*.

The Delegate then went to address the definition of work:

> One other definition under the Act needs to be examined in making a determination in this matter and that is the definition of "work." The complainant has alleged that she was required to be at the employer's place of residence for a 24 hour basis for which she received only 13 hours of pay. The employer states that although she was required to be there for 24 hours per day she wasn't required to perform work during the entire 24 hour period, in other words there was lots of down time that the complainant was not providing services for the employer. The Act defines "work" as follows:
>
> > "**work**" means the labour or services an employee performs for an employer whether in the employee's residence or elsewhere.
> > (2) An employee is deemed to be at work while on call at a location designated by the employer unless the designated location is the employee's residence.
>
> The complainant is required to remain at a specific location, that is, the employer's residence. She is required to be at the employer's residence to attend to his needs should they be required. As the complainant is still under the employer's direction and control and not free to pursue her own interests and is at a place designated by the employer she is entitled to be paid for the full 24 hours that she is at the employer's residence.
>
> I find that the complainant is entitled to be paid wages for 24 hours per day while on shift and that she is entitled to overtime wages pursuant to section 40 for all hours in excess of 8 in a day. As the complainant has been paid straight time for 13 hours each day the adjustment will be a half time adjustment for the hours of work between 8 and 11 hours per day and straight time for the hours between 11 and 13 hours. All hours in excess of 13 hours are owing at double time.

THE APPEAL

[...]

... Mr. Renaud submits that Ms. Spivey was a sitter as defined in *the Regulation*, and thus excluded from *the Act*:

"sitter" means a person employed in a private residence solely to provide the service of attending to a child, or to a disabled, infirm or other person, but does not include a nurse, domestic, therapist, live-in home support worker or an employee of
   a) a business that is engaged in providing that service, or
   b) a day care facility;"

In support of this position Mr. Renaud points out that Ms. Spivey does not fit into any of the exclusions in the definition, not being a nurse, therapist etc., and that she was employed in a private residence solely for the purpose of attending to the needs of a disabled or infirm person.

In response dated July 9, 1999, Candice Spivey, through Counsel ... denies she was a sitter within the meaning of *the Regulation*. In this respect, Ms. Spivey emphasizes that she was a full-time employee who was required to stay at the Renaud home 24 hours per day during which she provided much more than sitting services....

A major theme of the argument on Mr. Renaud's behalf goes to the amount Candice Spivey would earn if the Determination is upheld. This works out to about $600.00 per day, which is absurd according to Mr. Renaud, considering that the minimum daily wage for live-in home support workers under the Act is $70.00 per day. He submits that the money he has been allowed for this type of care would last only a few years instead of a lifetime if he is forced to pay these kinds of wages. This would result in him having to rely on government assistance programs which in his opinion could mean a loss of dignity and independence.

In response to this, Counsel for Ms. Spivey suggests that it is an option for Mr. Renaud to employ three care attendants for eight hour shifts and thus avoid paying overtime rates....

ANALYSIS

[T]he fact that Ms. Spivey was required to be there for a full twenty-four hour shift, three times per week, for which she was paid thirteen hours at a straight-time rate of $16.00 per hour is undisputed.

While the central issues here are clearly whether Candice Spivey was a ... sitter, I believe that it would be helpful in this case to take a brief look at where all of these differently defined classes of employees in the care attendant field fit into the overall statutory scheme of *the Act* and *the Regulation*.

"night attendant" means a person who,
   (a) is provided with sleeping accommodation in a private residence owned or leased or otherwise occupied by a disabled person or by a member of the disabled person's family, and
   (b) is employed in the private residence, for periods of 12 hours or less in any 24 hour period, primarily to provide the disabled person with care and attention during the night,

but does not include a person employed in a hospital or nursing home or in a facility designated as a community care facility under the *Community Care Facility Act* or as a Provincial mental health facility under the *Mental Health Act* or in a facility operated under the *Continuing Care Act*;

"residential care worker" means a person who,

(a) is employed to supervise or care for anyone in a group home or family type residential dwelling, and

(b) is required by the employer to reside on the premises during periods of employment,

but does not include a foster parent, live-in home support worker, domestic or night attendant; ...

Under Section 34 of *the Regulation,* live-in home support workers, night attendants and residential care workers are excluded from the hours of work and overtime requirements of Part 4 of *the Act.*

The basis for these exclusions would appear to be the common requirement for some degree of residency at the place of employment in these jobs, coupled with the long hours that employees in this field are considered to be on duty, while they may only be required to perform specific duties periodically. This makes it extremely difficult to distinguish actual working hours from down time.

Accordingly, Section 16(1) of *the Regulation* sets a daily minimum wage of $70.00 for live-in home support workers and Section 22 of *the Regulation* requires that residential care workers be allowed eight (8) consecutive hours as a rest period. For each interruption of this rest period, residential care workers must receive the greater of two (2) hours at the regular rate of pay or pay for the actual hours of work caused by the interruption.

Sitters are of course, excluded from *the Act* itself, by virtue of Section 32(1)(c) of *the Regulation.* ...

Looking at the Determination under review against that background, I must agree with the Delegate's conclusion that Ms. Spivey does not fall within the definitions of a live-in home support worker [defined as a person who is paid through a government program], a night attendant or, a residential care worker. ...

Dealing now with whether Ms. Spivey was a sitter and thereby excluded from *the Act,* I note that nowhere in the Determination does the Delegate entertain the possibility that the arrangements between Mr. Renaud and Ms. Spivey could fall within the definition of a "sitter." I will not speculate as to why not.

In any event, in light of the argument here about Ms. Spivey providing services beyond those contemplated by the definition of a sitter, and what was said in [*Mills (Re)*, [1997] BCESTD No 220] ..., regarding the meaning of "attend," this aspect of the definition has to be revisited to determine if there really is a meaningful distinction between providing "care and attention" and "attending."

Using Webster's Revised Unabridged Dictionary, (1998, Micra Inc.) and Webster's New World Thesaurus, it is readily apparent that the full meaning of attend goes well beyond waiting on, escorting or accompanying, especially when used in the context of health care attendants.

Attending, which is the actual term used in the definition of sitter, includes, "the work of caring for or attending to someone or something." Conversely, care also includes "the work of caring for or attending to someone or something." Clearly, for the purposes of giving the words in the definition their plain and ordinary meaning, these terms must be taken to be synonymous.

Consequently, Ms. Spivey cannot be eliminated from being a sitter on the basis of the argument that she did more than simply attend to Mr. Renaud's needs as interpreted in the Mills case. In fact, taking the evidence as a whole, sketched against the plain language of the text in the definition of a sitter in the Regulation, it is difficult to avoid the reality that Ms. Spivey falls squarely within this definition, i.e., she was hired to work in a *private residence, solely* to provide the service of *attending* to Mr. Renaud, who is a *disabled or infirm person.*

Granted, Ms. Spivey worked on more than a casual basis, which the Director says should be a persuasive factor against her being found to be a sitter. However, if we look back to [the Thompson Report (*Rights and Responsibilities in a Changing Workplace: A Review of Employment Standards in British Columbia* (Victoria, BC: Ministry of Skills, Training and Labour, 1994)], at pages 73 & 74, where sitters are discussed, it can be seen that this concern was specifically addressed:

> A sitter is defined as a person employed in a private residence solely to provide the service of attending to a child, or to a disabled, infirm or other person, but does not include a nurse, therapist, domestic, homemaker or an employee of a business providing that service or a day care facility. The Commission heard that the intent of this section was to exclude the occupation traditionally known as "babysitter" provided by school age children and adults.
>
> The Commission also learned that some live out domestics think that they are not covered by the Act because they or their employers believe that they are sitters as defined in the Act. Recommendations in this Report concerning domestics raised the matter of the relationship of their work with sitters. The intent of these recommendations is to ensure that they cannot be converted to the status of "sitters" at the end of the regular working day. The Report does not intend to extend coverage to persons providing services for children, parents or immediate family members on a casual basis. *Minimum standards of employment should be available for employees who provide personal care services on more than casual basis. The same distinction used for newspaper carriers and part-time employees, i.e., 15 hours per week, is appropriate to separate casual and regular work.* (Emphasis added)

The Commission then went on to recommend that a person who provides personal care services for 15 hours or less per week should be excluded from *the Act*.

Obviously, had this recommendation been adopted, the distinction that the Director asks me to imply between casual care givers and people who work more than on a casual basis, would appear in *the Regulation*. However, for whatever reasons, the recommendation was not adopted and I cannot read into *the Regulation* what is not there.

Consequently, I find myself in the same position as the Adjudicator in Dolfi. Being every bit as bound by the plain language of the definition of sitter, I must find albeit reluctantly, in the given circumstances that Ms. Spivey was indeed a sitter as defined in *the Regulation* and thus excluded from the minimum standards of employment prescribed by *the Act*.

Accordingly, the appeal must succeed....

[T]he Determination in question is hereby cancelled in its entirety.

***Girex Bancorp Inc v Lynette Hsieh*, 2004 CanLII 24679 (ON LRB)**

Tanja Wacyk, Vice-Chair

1. This is a director's application under section 116 of the *Employment Standards Act, 2000*, S.O. 2000, c.41, as amended, (the "Act") for the review of Employment Standards Officer Janis Zakoor's order to pay $10,000 to Ms. Lynette Hsieh and $7,681.60 to Mr. David-Paul Sip, in wages and vacation pay.

2. Mr. Schmidt maintains that Mr. Sip and Ms. Hsieh were not employees but rather were voluntary trainees.

Background

3. Mr. Schmidt is the owner and sole director of Girex Bancorp Inc. Girex Bancorp Inc. ("the Company") was incorporated in 1999 for the purpose of operating an e-commerce business. Mr. Schmidt initially hired three or four individuals who were paid to develop the required software program. However, due to the Company's lack of funds, those employees eventually left.

4. Mr. Schmidt then acquired the services of a number of recent immigrants through a program called "Jobstart." This program is sponsored by Human Resources Development Canada and pays the salaries of new immigrants to assist them in gaining Canadian work experience.

5. The individuals from Jobstart also worked on developing the software program for the Company but Mr. Schmidt indicated that it became apparent that the software program was more complex than he had initially appreciated, and that these individuals were unable to execute the task.

6. Consequently, in October, 2000, the Company began selling shares in order to raise capital to fund its development costs, including the salaries of individuals with the necessary skill set to develop the software program for the Company. Mr. Schmidt's financial advisors indicated the necessary funds would be available in three months' time following the public share offering.

7. Although the Company lacked the financial resources to hire employees prior to the financing becoming available, Mr. Schmidt made "training" opportunities available to students from the Institute of Computer Studies. Mr. Schmidt indicated that the Claimants were both students in the final phase of their theoretical and academic studies. They began their "training" with the Company on December 10, 2001.

8. It was Mr. Schmidt's intention to provide "training" for the Claimants during this three month period of time, and then offer them employment once the financing was available.

9. However, the anticipated financing did not materialise, and Mr. Schmidt offered the Claimants a contract to continue on as independent contractors. The Claimants subsequently claimed wages for the time they had worked with the Company.

10. The Company is no longer in operation and has been locked out of its rented premises for failure to pay the rent.

11. The investigating officer found that the Claimants came within the definition of "employee," contained in the Act, set out below:

CHAPTER 13: STATUTORY MINIMUM STANDARDS

Definitions

(1) In this Act

[...]

"employee" includes,

[...]

(c) a person who receives training from a person who is an employer, as set out in subsection (2),

(2) For the purposes of clause (c) of the definition of "employee" in subsection (1), an individual receiving training from a person who is an employer is an employee of that person if the skill in which the individual is being trained is a skill used by the person's employees, unless all of the following conditions are met:

1. The training is similar to that which is given in a vocational school.
2. The training is for the benefit of the individual.
3. The person providing the training derives little, if any, benefit from the activity of the individual while he or she is being trained.
4. The individual does not displace employees of the person providing the training.
5. The individual is not accorded a right to become an employee of the person providing the training.
6. The individual is advised that he or she will receive no remuneration for the time that he or she spends in training.

The Evidence

12. Mr. Schmidt focussed his evidence on the six elements set out above.

Similarity of training to that given in a vocational school

13. Mr. Schmidt advised that he is an engineer with 15 years of programming experience, and in the past was a "gild master" for many employees. He testified that he personally provided supervision to all the individuals being trained at the Company, and that everyday he "explained what the system was all about."

14. Mr. Schmidt testified that he explained the concept of what he wanted done, but did not tell the trainees how they were to do it. He maintained this was to teach them "the real office environment" in that one does not tell a programmer how to do his or her job—that is what the programmer brings to the job.

15. In cross-examination, Mr. Schmidt agreed that he was training the Claimants in "work experience"—not anything new in terms of technical skills.

The training is for the benefit of the individual

16. Mr. Schmidt maintained that the formal education students receive provides only theoretical training. However, he was providing the Claimants with an opportunity to apply that knowledge—which would enhance their employability.

The person providing the training derives little, if any, benefit from the activity of the individual while he or she is being trained

17. Mr. Schmidt denied that his company received any benefit from the training opportunity provided to the Claimants. Mr. Schmidt agreed, in cross-examination, that the

"training" which the Claimants received was "hands on experience" continuing the work on the software program. However, he maintained that because of their lack of experience the software they created was not useable. Mr. Schmidt also conceded that following the three months of "training," the nature of the work did not change and the Claimants would have simply continued to work on the software program.

The individual does not displace employees of the person providing the training
18. Mr. Schmidt maintained that the Claimants did not displace any employees. However, he agreed, in cross-examination, that the original employees who worked on the software program were paid.

The individual is not accorded a right to become an employee of the person providing the training
19. Mr. Schmidt testified that while he did not promise the Claimants they would become employees after the three months of training, he did indicate that this was a possibility, and that he subsequently offered them a job (presumably as independent contractors).

The individual is advised that he or she will receive no remuneration for the time that he or she spends in training
20. Mr. Schmidt testified that the Claimants received no remuneration and their "internship" was voluntary and free of charge. In exchange, they were to receive a letter of reference.
    21. The Ministry and the Claimants chose not to call any evidence.

Argument
22. Mr. Schmidt also relied on a document which was titled "Girex Internship Program" which purported to set out the terms of the voluntary training arrangement. However, while Mr. Schmidt testified that he had been advised that the Claimants had signed a copy of the document agreeing to the terms, he was unable to produce a copy. In any event, parties cannot, in law, contract out of the minimum standards of the *Employment Standards Act*.
    23. Mr. Schmidt argued that he had been well intentioned in offering the Claimants an opportunity to receive some practical work experience, and the Claimants should not be able to use the *Employment Standards Act* to escape an arrangement they freely entered into.
    24. The Ministry maintained that based on Mr. Schmidt's own evidence, all the preconditions set out in subsection 1(2) of the Act have not been met. The Ministry's submissions in this respect are reflected in the Analysis section, set out below.
    25. The Claimants made no additional submissions.

Analysis
26. Mr. Schmidt is the applicant in this matter and bears the onus of demonstrating that the Employment Standards Officer erred in issuing the Order to Pay. In order to bring the Claimants within the exclusion contained in subsection 1(2) of the Act, Mr. Schmidt must show that all of the six preconditions have been met. However, as set out below, Mr. Schmidt was able to show that only two of the six preconditions have been met.

Similarity of training to that given in a vocational school
27. It is apparent from Mr. Schmidt's evidence that the Claimants were brought into the Company to continue the work on the software program the Company needed in order

to be viable. While Mr. Schmidt testified that everyday he "explained what the system was all about" there was no evidence of any formal instruction, supervision, or evaluation. Consequently, the Board finds that the work experience the Claimants received cannot be characterized as "training similar to that which is given in a vocational school."

The training is for the benefit of the individual and the person providing the training derives little, if any, benefit from the activity of the individual while he or she is being trained
28. Nor can the training be said to be to the Claimants' benefit as it is not apparent that they received any benefit from their labours, aside from a letter of reference of dubious value. In any event, it was clear that the primary benefit was to be reaped by the Company, which needed the software program to be viable.

The Individual does not displace employees of the person providing the training
29. Furthermore, while it may be true that the Claimants did not displace any employees, as the employees had left some time earlier, it is clear that the work the Claimants had been brought in to perform had initially been done by employees who were paid for their labours. However, when the money ran out, Mr. Schmidt and the Company turned to the Claimants to achieve that end.

The individual is not accorded a right to become an employee of the person providing the training, and the individual is advised that he or she will receive no remuneration for the time that he or she spends in training
30. The Board finds that the last two prerequisites have been met, in that the Claimants did not have a "right" to become employees, and there was no issue they had been advised they would not be paid for their labour during the three months.

31. However, the Board also finds that Mr. Schmidt has failed to demonstrate that the other preconditions have been met.

32. As only two of the six preconditions have been met, the Board finds that in accordance with subsections 1. (1)(c) and 1.(2), the Claimants were employees under the Employment Standards Act and entitled to the minimum standards contained within.

DISPOSITION

33. The application is dismissed and the Officer's order affirmed.

New Jenny Nail & Spa v Qiurong Cao Jane and Director of Employment Standards, 2016 CanLII 28478 (OLRB)

1. This is an application under section 116 of the *Employment Standards Act*, 2000, S.O. 2000, c. 41 as amended (the "Act"). 8959757 Canada Inc. operating as New Jenny Nail & Spa ("New Jenny") seeks to review an Order to Pay in the amount of $1,109.84 to Qiurong Coa ("Coa") on account of the failure to pay the general minimum wage rate for all hours she worked, public holiday pay and vacation pay. Jenny Nail submits that Coa was at all relevant times an independent contractor and is therefore not entitled to the amounts claimed. Further, New Jenny disputes the amount of the Order since payment was ordered for days Coa did not work.

Facts

2. Xiaoxia Shoa ("Shoa"), the sole director and owner of New Jenny, and Coa each gave evidence. Many of the material facts are not in dispute.

3. Coa worked at New Jenny from April 11, 2015 to May 19, 2015 performing manicure and pedicure services. She was paid 50% of her gross sales. New Jenny set the prices that Coa charged the customers. New Jenny was open for business from 10:00 a.m. to 7:00 p.m. each day. Clients would book appointments in advance with New Jenny, or in some instances, simply walk in. Coa did not have any clients of her own.

4. Coa performed her work on the premises of New Jenny using a table and chair supplied by New Jenny. New Jenny also supplied some chemicals and nail polish. Coa supplied certain tools including nail clippers and a nail pusher. New Jenny provided a uniform although Coa did not always wear it. Coa had a key to the premises.

5. The significant area of dispute is the hours that Coa worked. New Jenny introduced a schedule showing the days on which Coa worked and the amount of her gross sales on each day. Shoa testified that Coa often did not start until 10:30 a.m. and frequently left before 7:00 p.m.. However, New Jenny did not keep any record of the hours which Coa worked.

6. Coa testified that she worked 5 days a week with Thursday and Sunday off. She worked every day from 10:00 a.m. until 7:00 p.m.. She denied that she started late or left early. She acknowledged that she did not start until 1:00 p.m. on April 16, 2015 because she picked her husband up at the airport. There were no formal breaks but she did take breaks when things were slow.

Principles

7. Section 1(1) of the Act defines an employee and employer as:

    "employee" includes,
    (a) a person, including an officer of a corporation, who performs work for an employer for wages,
    (b) a person who supplies services to an employer for wages,
    (c) a person who receives training from a person who is an employer, as set out in subsection (2), or
    (d) a person who is a homeworker,

    and includes a person who was an employee;

    "employer" includes,
    (a) an owner, proprietor, manager, superintendent, overseer, receiver or trustee of an activity, business, work, trade, occupation, profession, project or undertaking who has control or direction of, or is directly or indirectly responsible for, the employment of a person in it, and
    (b) any persons treated as one employer under section 4, and includes a person who was an employer.

8. In *2006515 Ontario Inc. (c.o.b. Greco Health Shack)*, [2005] O.E.S.A.D. No. 34 (January 12, 2005), the Board made the following observations concerning the question of employee status:

> 37. The test to be applied in determining whether an individual is an employee or an independent contractor at common law was recently reviewed by the Supreme Court of Canada in *671122 Ontario Ltd. v. Sagaz Industries Canada Inc.*, 2001 SCC 59 ... The Court reviewed the various tests which have been articulated at common law over time: the "control test"; the "fourfold test"; and the "organization test" or "integration test". The Court noted the difficulties that have emerged from the application of each of these tests. Of note, with respect to the "organization test", the Court referred favourably to the following statement by MacGuigan J.A. in *Wiebe Door Services Ltd. v. M.N.R.*, [1986] 3 F.C. 553:
>
> > Of course, the organization test of Lord Denning and others produces entirely acceptable results when properly applied, that is, when the question of organization or integration is approached from the persona of the "employee" and not from that of the "employer", because it is always too easy from the superior perspective of the larger enterprise to assume that every contributing cause is so arranged purely for the convenience of the larger entity. We must keep in mind that it was with respect to the business of the employee that Lord Wright [in *Montreal v. Montreal Locomotive Works Ltd.*, 1946 CanLII 353 (UK JCPC), [1947] 1 D.L.R. 161] addressed the question "Whose business is it?" ...
>
> 38. The Court concluded (at paragraph 46) that: "there is no conclusive test which can be universally applied to determine whether a person is an employee or an independent contractor". The Court continued, however, as follows:
>
> > Para. 47 Although there is no universal test to determine whether a person is an employee or an independent contractor, I agree with MacGuigan J.A. that a persuasive approach to the issue is that taken by Cooke J. in *Market Investigations*, supra [*Market Investigations Ltd. v. Minister of Social Security* [1968] 3 All E.R. 732]. The central question is whether the person who has been engaged to perform the services is performing them as a person in business on his own account. In making this determination, the level of control the employer has over the worker's activities will always be a factor. However, other factors to consider include whether the worker provides his or her own equipment, whether the worker hires his or her own helpers, the degree of financial risk taken by the worker, the degree of responsibility for investment and management held by the worker, and the worker's opportunity for profit in the performance of his or her tasks.
>
> > Para. 48 It bears repeating that the above factors constitute a non-exhaustive list, and there is no set formula as to their application. The relative weight of each will depend on the particular facts and circumstances of the case.
>
> 39. Finally, it is important to note that whether or not an individual is an employee or independent contractor is a question of law to be determined after consideration of all the relevant factors. The intention of the parties is relevant only to the extent that it is reflected in the actual arrangements they have made with each other in structuring their

relationship. Put another way, the parties cannot by their "agreement" render the relationship of an employee an independent contractor or vice versa : see for example *Greypoint Properties Inc.* [2000] OLRB Rep. May/June 479 at paragraph 15.

9. The Supreme Court of Canada in *McCormick v. Fasken Martineau DuMoulin LLP*, 2014 SCC 39 . . . recently commented on the indicia of an employment relationship:

> [23] Deciding who is in an employment relationship for purposes of the Code means, in essence, examining how two synergetic aspects function in an employment relationship: control exercised by an employer over working conditions and remuneration, and corresponding dependency on the part of a worker. In other words, the test is who is responsible for determining working conditions and financial benefits and to what extent does a worker have an influential say in those determinations? The more the work life of individuals is controlled, the greater their dependency and, consequently, their economic, social and psychological vulnerability in the workplace: . . .
>
> [27] Control and dependency, in other words, are a function not only of whether the worker receives immediate direction from, or is affected by the decisions of others, but also whether he or she has the ability to influence decisions that critically affect his or her working life. The answers to these questions represent the compass for determining the true nature of the relationship.

Decision

10. The Board finds that Coa was an employee of New Jenny, not an independent contractor. New Jenny was responsible for determining the working conditions and financial benefits under which Coa performed her work. New Jenny supplied the premises and much of the equipment used by Coa. It supplied the work through the booking of appointments. Coa had no independent source of work. New Jenny determined what Coa would be paid and the hours that she worked. There is no question that Coa was in a position of dependence on New Jenny.

Quantum of the Order to Pay

11. A schedule was introduced by New Jenny showing the days which Coa worked from April 11 to May 19, 2015, inclusive. The Employment Standards Officer in issuing the Order to Pay did not have the benefit of this schedule. Coa did not challenge this evidence.

12. May 18 was Victoria Day and the schedule establishes that Coa did not work on that day. The schedule establishes that Coa worked a total of 25 days during the period of her employment and the Board accepts this schedule as the best evidence of the days Coa worked. . . .

16. The Board accepts the evidence of Coa that she worked from 10:00 a.m. to 7:00 p.m. with time for breaks on each day that she worked, except April 16, 2015. She therefore worked 8.5 hours each day on 25 days (less 3 hours on April 16) during the period of her employment, a total of 209.5 hours.

17. There is no dispute that she was paid two payments of $961.50 and $700.00, a total of $1,661.50. She was not paid for the public holiday, May 18, nor did she receive

any vacation pay. If she had been paid the minimum wage, $11.00/hr., during this period, Coa would have earned $2,304.50. The Board therefore finds New Jenny in violation of the Act in failing to pay an employee the minimum wage, public holiday pay and vacation pay.

13:400 THE ENFORCEMENT OF EMPLOYMENT STANDARDS

Employment standards acts are primarily enforced through the investigation of worker complaints by labour ministry inspectors. The process under Ontario's *Employment Standards Act* (ESA) is similar to that found in other jurisdictions and was briefly outlined in John Grundy et al, "Enforcement of Ontario's *Employment Standards Act*: The Impact of Reforms" (2017) 43 *Canadian Public Policy* 190 at 193:

> For a worker to access the complaints system under the *ESA*, he or she must file a claim with the [Ministry of Labour, or] MOL. This process entails filling out a form that details the alleged violation, collecting supporting documents when possible, and submitting the material online or by mail. Once submitted, a claims processor verifies that the necessary information is provided and refers it to a manager for a decision if it appears that it does not fall under the jurisdiction of the *ESA*. Claims that fall under ESA jurisdiction are then forwarded to an [Employment Standards Officer, or] ESO who determines whether there are grounds for an investigation. An ESO can investigate a claim on the basis of written materials, by phone, by visiting the employer's premises, or by calling a meeting between the parties. On the basis of this investigation, the ESO assesses whether the complaint is substantiated in whole or in part and, if applicable, the amount of money owed to the complainant. An ESO can also assess entitlements that go beyond what was claimed in the original complaint.

Labour ministries also use proactive compliance and enforcement strategies, such as information dissemination and targeted inspection campaigns, usually aimed at sectors suspected to have high rates of non-compliance. In recent years there has been a growing recognition by researchers that reliance on complaint-driven enforcement is likely to be ineffective in ensuring high rates of compliance with employment standards in sectors employing the employees who are most likely to need the protection of such legislation. The following readings outline the reasons why this is so, and then propose alternative approaches to compliance and enforcement.

Kevin Banks, *Employment Standards Complaint Resolution, Compliance and Enforcement: A Review of the Literature on Access and Effectiveness* (Toronto: Ontario Ministry of Labour, 2015) at 6, 13–14, 41–42, 46–53, online: https://cirhr.library.utoronto.ca/sites/cirhr.library.utoronto.ca/files/research-projects/Banks-6B-ESA%20Enforcement.pdf

> [M]any workers, especially those who are most vulnerable to low pay and precarious working conditions, are likely to face barriers to accessing the complaints system. These include well-founded fears of employer reprisal, direct and opportunity costs of the

claims process, difficulties presenting and documenting their claims, and lack of access to professional advice or representation ...

[F]ear of reprisal and the challenges and opportunity costs associated with pursuing a claim can each be a significant barrier to pursuing claims, and that this is particularly so for workers who are low paid and lack job security. Such workers are disproportionately women and/or members of ethnic or racial minority groups who are more likely to face linguistic and cultural barriers or stereotyping ... They are more likely to be persons with disabilities, who often face stereotyping in the labour market and often do not have access to accommodations that they need in order to work with equal opportunity ... Low-wage workers are less likely to be unionized, or to have access to health and disability benefits that improve income security ... Workers in a temporary or otherwise insecure residency status, recent immigrants, racialized workers, and people with disabilities are all over-represented in precarious forms of employment....

The literature refers to such workers as vulnerable, a term that is now also commonly used in policy discourse. The concept of vulnerability refers to the effect of various disadvantages both on labour market participation and success — labour market vulnerability — and in impeding access to full benefit and protection of the law. The available evidence ... suggests that workers who are vulnerable in the former sense are also more likely both to experience employment standards violations and to face barriers to enforcing their rights, and that the two types of vulnerability are causally related ... US-based research finds that significant factors decreasing the likelihood that a worker will complain about an employment standards violation include immigration status, lack of union representation, lack of education or knowledge of basic rights, and costs of job loss, notably the local rate of unemployment ...

[...]

2. Effective Compliance and Enforcement Strategy

2.1 What we know about the extent and location of non-compliance

There are few reliable direct measurements of compliance with employment standards in Ontario or elsewhere. Labour ministries often track complaint statistics, but it is widely accepted in the literature that complaint statistics are not a reliable measurement of compliance.... For reasons discussed above, there are often significant barriers to filing complaints and therefore complaint activity is very unlikely to capture the full extent of non-compliance. It is possible that complaints activity may be very low in sectors with serious compliance problems.... Some have argued that for many workers the daily reality of labour-law violations have made them seem ordinary and expected, particularly in labour sectors where new immigrants, racialized, women and low-wage workers are predominant.... As a result, the threshold point at which workers register ES violations as a problem may be quite high, especially at the lower end of the labour market, where habituation to experiences such as work intensification, insecurity, low pay and coercion lower expectations of working life.... In the presence of persistent violations, keeping one's head down, "staying out of other people's business," and turning a blind eye to unfair treatment of others is a survival strategy.... Weil makes the analogy between such workplaces and neighbourhoods with "broken windows", i.e. in which property and other crimes are widespread. This perspective suggests that workers often do not complain when faced with the equivalent of "neighborhood disorder" at the workplace. In the face of deteriorating conditions and greater barriers to speaking out (e.g. from increased economic vulnerability), people retreat from the "unsafe street" and the likelihood of complaining decreases even further....

A recent report by the Law Commission of Ontario (LCO) stated that "the LCO's research and consultations revealed that most employers are compliant with the legislation".... The LCO did not undertake any new systematic empirical research on the extent of non-compliance, but its conclusion is plausible in light of the limited available evidence.... That evidence also suggests however that at least a significant minority of employers are not in compliance with some employment standards, and that vulnerable workers are most likely to be affected by non-compliance.

[...]

2.2 Causes of compliance and non-compliance

Non-compliance with employment standards, as with any other legal requirement, maybe due to inadvertence—mistakes in interpreting or applying the law or lack of awareness of the law—or due to deliberate decision making. There is very little research directly observing employer reasons for complying or not with employment standards. But the question of whether and why businesses will or will not comply with employment standards raises the same two fundamental issues that arise in many other fields of regulation: (1) to what extent do businesses understand and have the ability to implement what is legally required; and (2) why do businesses comply with regulations that impose costs on them.

2.2.1 Understanding and ability to implement what is legally required

Ministry compliance systems, like those in other jurisdictions, place significant emphasis on education and information dissemination, on the supposition that many employers can and will improve their compliance if they access such services.... There is ... research suggesting that in many fields of employment law smaller firms often lack information and capacity to comply.... Studies in the field of occupational safety and health indicate that smaller firms, which tend to have less in-house expertise in such matters, are more prone to non-compliance and that this is often for reasons of competence, that is, of lack of knowledge and developed capacities to implement legal requirements.... Moreover, 75 percent of businesses in Ontario have fewer than 10 employees. Many of these employ part-time, casual and seasonal workers, pay at or near minimum wage and have limited financial resources and narrow profit margins.... Even in larger enterprises, awareness at the level of human resource staff did not necessarily translate into awareness at the level of shop floor management....

It appears to be a reasonable supposition that a portion of total non-compliance is simply attributable to information and implementation problems. It is very difficult to estimate the extent of such problems with any precision.

2.2.2 Employer motivations

Literature reviews in the fields of occupational safety and health ... and environmental regulation ... indicate that both cost considerations (direct and reputational) and acceptance of normative duty influence employer decisions with respect to compliance. The nature of and interactions between these considerations are likely to vary widely across the employer population.

Fairly standard economic analysis suggests that employers will comply with costly regulations only if the probability of getting caught times the cost associated with getting caught is greater than the cost savings of non-compliance times the probability of not getting caught.... The relevant costs may extend well beyond the direct economic costs entailed by compensation required or sanctions imposed by regulators. Costs can also flow from damage to reputation ... Firms with an investment in and expected return on their brand image may fear loss of market share as consumers turn away from their products.... Firms aiming to recruit the best talent may fear the effects of reputation for non-compliance. Firms may also fear a loss of "social license". For example, studies suggest that manufacturing or resource extraction firms often fear that a reputation for non-compliance with environmental laws will undermine their ability to secure approvals to establish new facilities or expand existing ones....

There is considerable evidence that directly changing cost structures for regulated entities through sanctions and compensation orders can be effective. Researchers have found reductions in mining fatalities in the US following significant increases in enforcement budgets of federal mine inspection agencies.... Violations of occupational safety and water pollution regulations decline among firms that have recently been visited by inspectors and fined for violations....

On the other hand, many researchers argue that a direct cost-based incentive model cannot account for observed levels of compliance with many forms of regulation. For example, studies of environmental regulation have tended to find that in advanced industrial democracies most business firms, particularly large ones, tend to substantially comply with most environmental regulations most of the time. This is despite the fact that the likelihood of an inspection at any given firm is often very low, that compliance is often complex and costly, and the deterrent messages sent by penalties imposed on other firms often do not make it through the cacophony of information and urgent demands facing business managers.... One study of general deterrence of non-compliance with US environmental laws found that the magnitude, effort or expenditure of firms on compliance did not correlate with managers' estimates of the probability that a serious violation would be detected and punished....

Studies of environmental regulatory compliance suggest that for many firms reputational or social license concerns play a major role, and that managers believed that neighbours, employees, community groups, news media and environmental advocacy groups could generate adverse publicity damaging the firms' reputation leading to consumer defection, recruiting difficulties, promulgation of more stringent regulation, or declines in stock prices....

Socio-legal research also suggests that compliance often cannot be fully explained by direct cost or reputational cost considerations alone. Interview-based research has found that managers and business owners often report a strong sense of duty to comply with laws and rate its influence as more significant than fear of punishment.... Further, the sense of duty within one's social circle can exert influence. For example, a study of compliance with tax laws suggest people often fear disgrace in the eyes of family members or social peers in the event that they were caught violating the law.... The socio-legal literature thus suggests that such normative commitments can often exert an independent influence in favour of compliance.

A sense of duty may strengthen and in turn be reinforced by concerns for maintaining a good reputation. The extent of the sense of duty to observe legal norms appears to be tied to the perceived legitimacy of the norm in question. This in turn tends to depend not simply on the normative orientation of the individual manager or firm but also upon perceptions that the law will be consistently applied to others so as to provide a level playing field amongst competitors, and that cheaters will be punished. Some researchers, echoing what they have been told by regulatory officials in contemporary regulatory agencies, suggest that a population of regulated enterprises can often be conceptualized in the form of a bell curve, in which one tail is comprised of "duty-driven good apples", the other of "bad apples" with little sense of duty towards compliance or fear of consequences of non-compliance, and the bulk as "contingent good apples generally willing to comply but not when they think a regulatory requirement is unreasonable or excessively burdensome, or when they think that most of their competitors are cheating....

On the other hand, researchers have observed important limits on the influence of concern for reputation and normative duty.... Reputational pressures are naturally lesser where risks to brand value, social license, or human resource strategy are low ... There are also important limits to the potential influence of normative duty. In for-profit enterprises normative duty will also tend to yield at some point to the requirements of the "economic license" to operate: they are unlikely to trump the viability or profitability of the enterprise....

These general observations in the regulatory studies literature are consistent with observed patterns of compliance and non-compliance with employment standards, and with workplace law more generally.

Compliance with employment standards can be consistent with a firm's business and human resource management strategies. If a firm seeks to recruit and retain employees on the basis of working conditions better than those required by basic minima, labour market pressures may be sufficient to ensure its compliance with them. In a 1997 survey of federal jurisdiction employers, most agreed that compliance with federal labour standards imposed no significant costs on them, and a 2006 survey in the same jurisdiction found that most employers exceeded most code standards....

This is clearly not the case for all employers however, as the literature on minimum wages and the costs of other standards such as overtime rules suggests.... Even if such standards may lead to changes in human resource management practices that increase productivity, they may reduce profitability or require changes to methods of production that some employers may be reluctant to undertake. Moreover, for many such employers the potential reputational costs of proven non-compliance are likely to be low. This will be the case for many producers not having brands recognizable to consumers or customer bases sensitive to moral concerns about working conditions, not depending upon social or regulatory licenses to operate, and able to operate without recruiting employees with the skills or mobility options to resign and obtain better employment in the face of labour standards violations. As a result, cost considerations will create incentives for non-compliance.

In these circumstances employers may still comply out of a sense of normative duty. But they risk being undercut by less scrupulous competitors. If profit margins are thin, they may also face steady pressures to reduce costs. Enforcement action will likely be necessary both to maintain the legitimacy of employment standards norms that underpins the sense of duty to comply, and to deter those lacking this sense of duty from undercutting their competitors.

It is difficult to know the precise extent of such conditions in the Ontario economy. But there are good reasons to think that they are becoming more pervasive. In a growing number of industries with large concentrations of low wage workers lead firms that determine product market conditions have become separated from employment of the workers who provide the goods or services. Those workers are instead employed by firms operating in far more competitive markets that create conditions for non-compliance, a process that Weil's ... influential work labels "fissuring". Fissuring results from a wide variety of organizational methods: subcontracting, franchising, third party management, changing workers from employees to self-employment, and triangular employment relationships that change the employer of record. It has been driven by multiple motivations including:

- shifting costs and liabilities
- focusing on core competencies
- creating conditions of competition between those providing non-core services that lowers the cost at which they are supplied.

Fissured organizational structures reflect intents to lower costs while preserving sufficient control of conditions of production to ensure that brand standards are met and brand value is protected.... In some sectors, such as agriculture or garment production, these changes are also fueled by the competitive pressures of globalization. But they are more widespread, and indeed quite commonly found in non-traded sectors. While these shifts in the organization of production have been observed in North America for quite some time ... they appear to have grown in recent years....

These considerations provide a plausible and likely account of the patterns of compliance and non-compliance observed in the data discussed above. Many, perhaps even most employers probably have little reason not to comply with employment standards, may in fact have positive incentives to comply, or to varying degrees accept a normative duty to comply. This accounts for observations suggesting that most employers are in compliance with most standards most of the time. On the other hand, conditions for many employers, perhaps a substantial minority of the employer population, are such that competitive pressures create incentives not to comply, and labour and product market conditions create no countervailing reputational concerns. Bernhardt et al's 2009 US-based study finds that rates of non-compliance are much higher than average in many industries with a fissured structure: home health care; grocery stores; restaurants and hotels, residential construction, building and grounds security, and retail and drug stores .... Labour market forces combined with patterns of social exclusion are likely to leave the most economically vulnerable workers in these sectors of the economy. It is not surprising therefore that surveys of low wage workers report high rates of labour standards violations....

[...]

2.3 Maintaining compliance and responding effectively to non-compliance

The foregoing analysis of the likely extent and causes of compliance and non-compliance with labour standards has a number of broad implications for compliance and enforcement strategy. Specifically, it suggests that separate strategies are needed for each of three broadly defined groups of employers.

First, for many employers an effective compliance strategy simply entails dissemination of clear information on what compliance requires. These employers will probably tend to be those that provide terms and conditions well above minimum standards in order to pursue a competitive strategy based on retaining and rewarding employees with marketable skills and abilities. These employers have few if any incentives not to comply.

For others, compliance may impose moderate cost and administrative burdens. For such employers a sense of normative duty and/or reputational incentives may nonetheless be sufficient to maintain compliance. Compliance and enforcement strategy might therefore:

- enlist the support of respected industry and professional human resource associations;
- use an approach to enforcement that avoids the appearance of unreasonableness that can arise through sanctioning technical violations or stigmatizing unintentional violations;
- conversely, use an approach to enforcement that visibly and firmly deals with deliberate non-compliance so as to provide reminders and reassurance to the community of regulated employers that the government itself takes the rules seriously and is trying to provide a level playing field;
- use an approach to enforcement making use of publicity in cases of deliberate non-compliance in order to provide reassurance and reminders to the compliant members of the community and to provide incentives to those facing moderate incentives not to comply.

Finally, there is a significant and probably growing group of employers that operate under competitive conditions that place compliance with labour standards under continuous pressure. These pressures will often combine with weakness in reputational incentives to comply. With respect to this group, an effective enforcement strategy will likely require:

- reliable detection of violations;
- predictable imposition of monetary remedies and sanctions with significant deterrent value;
- problem-solving approaches that seek to relieve where possible some of the competitive pressures that lie at the roots of systematic non-compliance.

An effective compliance and enforcement strategy will therefore seek to inform about, strengthen normative commitment to, and detect, deter and where possible address

systemic root causes leading to violations of employment standards. Doing this requires a tool kit that combines information dissemination, outreach, persuasion to voluntarily comply, proactive detection of non-compliance, and enforcement of deterrent remedies and sanctions. Deploying these tools effectively to increase compliance requires intelligence gathering and the capacity to evaluate alternative strategies.
[© Queen's Printer for Ontario, 2015. Reproduced with permission.]

C Michael Mitchell & John C Murray, *The Changing Workplaces Review — Final Report* **(Ontario: Ministry of Labour, May 2017) at 57–72 [footnotes omitted]**

The Extent of and Reasons for Non-compliance

A report by the Law Commission of Ontario (LCO) confirms the conclusion that "most employers are compliant with the legislation". However, at least a significant minority of employers are not in compliance with some employment standards, and vulnerable workers are most likely to be affected by non-compliance.

In their research paper prepared for the CWR, Vosko, Noack and Tucker advise that the existence of complaints does not always accurately reflect the number or source of violations. However, in our view, complaint patterns and outcomes can nonetheless be helpful in considering compliance issues:

> Complaints related to the accommodation and food services industry are most likely to have violations, with 78% of assessed complaints resulting in violations.... Violations are also more likely to be found for complaints filed against small firms. The difference between large and small firms is most noticeable when comparing complaints relating to firms with 1–5 employees, that have a violation rate of 80%, and complaints relating to firms with more than 200 employees, which have a violation rate of only 49% ... The vast majority of these violations relate to monetary complaints. Among assessed complaints, 69% included monetary violations, and only 1.6% included non-monetary violations. The percentage of assessed complaints that result in a violation declined slightly in the 2014/15 year, though it is too soon to say whether this is part of a trend.

Simply put, there are too many people in too many workplaces who do not receive their basic rights.

A variety of factors contribute to non-compliance. Ignorance by both employees and employers of their rights and obligations contributes to non-compliance.

Many small employers and employees have no idea what the ESA requires. Educating employers about their responsibilities is as important as educating employees about their rights. The complexity of the law may contribute to a lack of understanding of the rights and obligations in the ESA, thereby exacerbating non-compliance. Some employers have an uncaring attitude towards their obligations and responsibilities and do not regard them as important enough to ensure compliance. Some employers violate the law as part of a deliberate business strategy — including situations where they think that their competitors are not complying. Some employers are confident that because their employees will not complain and the likelihood of government inspection is very low, non-compliance is a risk worth taking, calculating that if they are caught, they can extract themselves from the legal consequences of non-compliance without much difficulty and with trivial costs. The literature is also clear that fear of reprisals reduces the number of complaints that are made by employees. Unfortunately, there is a widespread fear of reprisal among employees if they complain about violation of their ESA rights, and this inhibition contributes to non-compliance. For this reason, the absence of complaints from some sectors of the economy or from some workplaces may be as consistent with non- compliance as it is an indication of substantial compliance.

Strategic Enforcement—A Combination of Existing and New Approaches

Strategic enforcement involves a set of policies and practices that have the goal of changing employer conduct so that breaches of the Act do not occur. It is designed to address non-compliance at a systemic level and not only on the basis of complaints. This is a change in emphasis that is required as a result of the changed workplace. As David Weil stated:

> The changing workplace environment . . . requires new, more strategic approaches to enforcement. Strategic enforcement policies aim to change employer behavior so that practices that result in underpayment of wages do not occur in the first place. This requires addressing the underlying factors that lead to lost wages and other violations of labor standards. Strategic enforcement also entails changing behavior of employers at the market level, rather than on a case-by-case basis.

In his research paper for this Review, Professor Kevin Banks described an integrated enforcement strategy with a variety of important elements in the toolkit of the Ministry of Labour including education, proactive auditing, and the effective use of deterrents and remedies:

> An effective compliance and enforcement strategy will . . . seek to inform about, strengthen normative commitment to, and detect, deter and where possible address systemic root causes leading to violations of employment standards. Doing this requires a tool kit that combines information dissemination, outreach, persuasion to voluntarily comply, proactive detection of non-compliance, and enforcement of deterrent remedies and sanctions. Deploying these tools effectively to increase compliance requires intelligence gathering and the capacity to evaluate alternative strategies.

David Weil and others argue that changes in the structure of the economy and in the complexity of employment relationships, together with the decline in unionization have meant that the traditional complaint driven approach to enforcement is less and less effective. Weil put it this way:

> The employment relationship in many sectors with high concentrations of vulnerable workers has become complicated as major companies have shifted the direct employment of workers to other business entities that often operate under extremely competitive conditions. This "fissuring" or splintering of employment increases the incentives for employers at lower levels of industry structures to violate workplace policies, including the FLSA. Fissuring means that enforcement policies must act on higher levels of industry structures in order to change behavior at lower levels, where violations are most likely to occur.

Strategic enforcement is increasingly important when the workplace environment is becoming more complex and governments with limited resources are faced with high public expectations. The Ministry must adopt proactive strategic enforcement tools to detect and target systemic violations of the act across the economy and in particular sectors. Responding to individual complaints alone cannot form a primary basis for enforcement and will leave most breaches of the Act undetected.

[...]

Proactive Inspections

A good starting point in the discussion of inspections is Professor Banks:

> For good reasons, the literature is essentially unanimous in concluding that labour standards compliance and enforcement agencies need to proactively and strategically detect and target non-compliance.
>
> As discussed above, the need for proactive detection arises because many workers are unlikely to complain about violations of their employment standards rights during the life of the employment relationship, or at all. Moreover, as Weil points out: "Although most complaints relate to real problems, there is nothing to say that they represent problems of the highest order if compared to the "dog that doesn't bark"—that is, those workplace problems which may exist but which, for one reason or another, are not reported via complaint processes.... Complaints are often driven by specific problems facing particular workers. They may or may not be related to more systemic issues. And even if they are, investigations arising from a complaint process may not be perceived as part of a wider systemic problem. This compounds their reactive nature." ...
>
> ... relying on complaints or legal actions to detect violations leaves much if not most non-compliance undetected. Without risk of detection, there can be little deterrence. To the extent that education and information initiatives are not enough to correct non-compliance, as is likely often the case, it will persist without remedy.
>
> [...]
>
> The consensus in favour of increased proactive inspection is essentially based on evidence of significant non-compliance ... and the proposition that proactive inspection is the most effective available means of addressing non-compliance not detected through complaints.... Proactive inspection campaigns can, if properly targeted, achieve "wholesale-level" economies of scale that cannot be matched by "retail" interventions in response to particular complaints. Further, the use of targeted campaigns stands to have a deterrent effect as it increases the risk of non-compliance detection.
>
> [...]
>
> Proactive inspections provide an effective means of detecting and remedying non-compliance. The [Law Commission of Ontario] notes that in 2011–12, Ministry figures show that 83% of such inspections detected violations. Vosko, Noack and Tucker find that the proportion of inspections that detected violations ranged from 75% to 77% in the years between 2011/12 and 2013/14, but dropped to 65% in 2014/15. They also point out that 92 to 99 per cent of confirmed unpaid wages were recovered through proactive processes, much higher than the 60% more typical in complaints investigations, though, as Ministry officials suggest, this difference is likely due in part to a higher proportion of insolvent employers among the population of employers that is the subject of complaints. Regular enforcement sweeps also provide low risk opportunities for workers to voice their complaints of alleged non-compliance ...

[...]

Targeted inspections can influence the behaviour of others in the same line of business and beyond....

[...]

Targeted inspections need to be maintained over time. They will likely not have sustained effects if they are seen as one-time events rather than part of an ongoing initiative. This means that re-investigations and\or inspections are an important component of an effective enforcement strategy. Not only do they serve as an unofficial quality check on prior past investigations\inspections but also as a check on problem employers — particularly where there is high turnover of employees — and as an assessment of whether there is repetitive non-compliance and whether there is a basis to decide whether further sanctions are warranted.

Other Strategic Initiatives

...

Weil recommends designing sectoral enforcement strategies, a central purpose of which — as with all enforcement strategies — is to deter violations before they occur. Implementation of a sectoral enforcement strategy requires analysis and understanding the structure of industries to provide insights into why there are higher levels of non-compliance in some industries than in others, and to help inform sector-based enforcement strategies designed to improve compliance. It is his view that an understanding of supply-chain relationships, franchising and other industry structures is an essential first step to the development and implementation of effective enforcement strategies.

Given the similarities between the structural changes in the US economy and those in the Ontario economy, serious consideration of the strategic approach recommended by Dr. Weil and others is a necessity.

The "fissured' workplace requires re-thinking compliance strategies that may engage entities other than the immediate employer. Weil and others have recognized the potential influence of leading firms (such as franchisors, leading brand, or major retailers) within fissured networks of employers on the compliance behavior of subordinate firms, and of engaging those firms in order to change systemic conditions that create incentives for non-compliance...

[...]

Good practices may also include "obtaining information from individual workers, anonymous sources, unions, community organizations and employer associations" in order to learn about "particular employers that are likely to be non-compliant, how fissured industries are organized, and the extent to which lead firms and employer associations might be engaged to alter systemic conditions fostering non-compliance."

[...]

Focusing at the Top

In addition to an expanded use of inspections, Weil and others advise focusing enforcement strategy so that it includes "lead firms" (i.e., firms at the top of the industry structure such as franchisors), as well as the employers directly responsible for labor standards violations. Weil argues that such a strategy requires changes to a variety of investigation protocols. As noted above, it requires sophisticated data collection and a commitment to investigations of multiple sites of a given employer or operating under a lead firm where wide scale violations are believed to be present.

Related to strategies designed to involve the top or lead firm, brand recognition and the need to protect the brand can be important factors in engaging a lead firm ...

[A] targeted group of firms would be pre-selected and screened and inspections of the targeted employers would start at the same time. These initiatives could be implemented in the hotel, restaurant and other sectors where there are a large number of vulnerable and precarious workers. For example, the outlets of a major franchisor could be inspected during a stipulated period in multiple locations. Such a coordinated effort would both create an impetus for establishing agreement with the franchisor to encourage ESA compliance with franchisees, as well as have potential ripple effects on other industry players ... Such a strategy is designed to engage the custodian of the "brand" in voluntary strategic partnerships to create "top-down" pressure to comply.

These "top down" compliance strategies are not based on concepts of joint liability, but rather on the fact that top of industry firms have a stake in protecting the name of the brand and its potential vulnerability if there is well-publicized non-compliance by those down the chain—franchisees for example.

There are similar approaches that have been used in other jurisdictions to engage the "top of industry" in strategic enforcement initiatives. As mentioned above, the Fair Work Ombudsman (FWO) in Australia has established a National Franchise Program that works with franchisors aiming to improve the employment standards compliance performance of their franchisees. The franchisor program is premised on the notion that non-compliance by an employer franchisee can result in serious legal consequences for the franchisee and that these consequences may impact the entire brand. As a result, the franchisor program encourages franchisors to take steps to minimize the risk to their brand by taking practical steps to help franchisees understand and meet their obligations. For example, the FWO encourages franchisors to:

- include in their franchise agreements a specific obligation requiring franchisees to comply with workplace laws;
- make sure that every franchise's business model takes into account the costs of lawfully employing adequate numbers of staff;
- incorporate the Fair Work Handbook into the business' operations manual or as a stand alone document for franchisees;
- develop internal processes to support compliance including making compliance easier for franchisees by providing human resource/industrial relations systems or software to help franchisees achieve consistent and compliant workplace practices;
- recruit and train franchisees who are committed to compliance on the applicable workplace laws including engaging appropriately qualified human resources/industrial relations staff to train, update and assist franchisees; or arrange corporate memberships with an employer association, or special rates with a professional adviser to help franchisees access reliable and cost effective advice;
- regularly check that franchisees are complying with workplace laws including audits to ensure franchisees are meeting their record-keeping obligations or require franchisees to conduct 'self-audits' and report the results.

The FWO also has entered into various "compliance partnerships" between the FWO and "top of industry" enterprises that may involve reviewing and monitoring supply chain and franchise relationships. These agreements are designed to establish a collaborative relationship between the regulator and businesses that want to publicly demonstrate their commitment to creating compliant and productive workplaces. To quote the office of the FWO: "Through a Compliance Partnership with us, businesses can ensure their systems and processes are working effectively to build a culture of compliance."

[...]

A Law Enforcement Agency

As effective as inspections and other strategic initiatives may be, they are just one element of a cohesive and a comprehensive strategic enforcement approach.

As part of strategic management, the Ministry must move closer to becoming a more traditional law enforcement agency and less an agency involved in customer service that also performs some enforcement activities. We do not mean to suggest that the MOL is not currently interested in and dedicated to Enforcement. It is. We do suggest that it needs to consider the implementation of new strategies and also that the Ministry needs more tools and more opportunity to pursue enforcement initiatives. A change in emphasis—to become more of a law enforcement agency—accompanied by legislative change should help create a culture of compliance in Ontario workplaces and help the MOL to carry out its mission more effectively.

[© Queen's Printer for Ontario, 2017. Reproduced with permission.]

Leah F Vosko, "'Rights Without Remedies': Enforcing Employment Standards in Ontario by Maximizing Voice Among Workers in Precarious Jobs" (2013) 50:4 *Osgoode Hall Law Journal* **845 at 869–73**

> Considering the existing array of initiatives emergent in other common law jurisdictions, what options are available for altering Ontario's [Employment Standards (ES)] regime to begin to counter the tendency to place enforcement in individual workers' hands? How might workers reliant on the [Employment Standards Act (*ESA*)] and their advocates have a stronger voice in its enforcement? Since almost all regulatory regimes rely on a mix of approaches and methods, Ontario's system could be improved by drawing insights from both the individual and collective voice mechanisms....
>
> [...]
>
> At a policy level, it is critical to recognize that an onerous and risky complaints process requiring the precariously employed to play the protagonist works against the exercise of voice. Maximizing the accessibility of the complaints process, and supports once it is accessed, is therefore necessary.
>
> The foremost failings of Ontario's ES enforcement system relate to the onus placed on individual workers to initiate and proceed through arduous claims processes, made more complex by the additional requirements (since 2010) that the claimant confront his or her employer about perceived violations and provide certain information in writing before he or she is permitted to make a formal claim. To maximize effective routes to individual claims-making and reduce its associated risks to workers, the involvement

of outside parties and external supports is critical in this context. Rather than making the complaints process more onerous, the ES enforcement regime could provide for anonymous and third-party complaints to initiate investigations and limit the potential for reprisals against workers whose rights are in question, changes which could be achieved largely through the straightforward adaptation of administrative measures. Here, the anonymous complaints process operating in Saskatchewan and the third-party complaints permissible in Australia offer preferable models. On the assumption that complaints may be shared among workers, in such situations Ontario could also follow Saskatchewan's lead and pursue expanded investigations.

Permitting anonymous and third-party complaints does not, however, resolve deficiencies in the support available to workers in the complaints process. Workers making claims under the Health and Safety, Workplace Safety and Insurance, and Human Rights regimes are eligible for significant supports from Occupational Health and Safety Clinics for Ontario Workers, the Office of the Workers' Advisor, and the Human Rights Legal Support Centre, respectively. Enhanced supports, ideally through devoting greater financial resources to legal aid, are necessary for the ES enforcement regime to function effectively, and for ES dependent workers not only to be deemed to be full members of the labour market in laws on the books but to be able to exercise their voice and participate in practice. Timely person-to-person support in the claims process is especially key given the six month time limit on claims-making and since studies of other jurisdictions (*e.g.*, British Columbia) show that the self-help model undercuts worker claims making altogether. To buoy such measures, relecting [sic] New York state's wage-theft legislation, the creation of an effective presumption of employer retaliation is also important. This would involve boosting the current onus of proof under Ontario's ESA through measures of interim reinstatement during claims investigation for workers fired for seeking their ES entitlements, establishing meaningful fines in cases of documented reprisal, and expanding the circumstances under which worker protections against retaliation apply as well as the actors that may be deemed to be engaging in retaliatory behavior.

In the complaints process, third-party representation of the sort possible in Australia offers another direction that Ontario could take. This sort of representation is crucial to the expression of individual voice and could contribute to augmenting workers' collective voice by, among other things, spawning new or supporting existing institutions (*e.g.*, unions) devoted to workers' realization of their rights. Furthermore, there is no principled reason that third-party representation should be a feature of some pieces of labour legislation and not others. Assistance through the complaints process, as well as outreach of the sort that labour inspectorates in other jurisdictions pursue in partnership with community organizations, would also make such representation more meaningful. So, too, would greater interagency coordination, that is, the facilitation of links between different government agencies, in a range of related areas where a worker may be in a position to complain (*e.g.*, Occupational Health and Safety, Human Rights, Employment Standards, et cetera). Such coordination has the potential to deliver fair compensation to workers if collections are simultaneously altered such that costs of enforcement shift to those that violate the law. Limited fines for employers and the financial burden of mounting a claim mute workers' voices in the complaint process, particularly the precariously employed, especially those facing other structural disadvantages such as migrant workers, for whom claims-making is also constrained by obligations to households and communities abroad. One potential remedy here is to require employers found in violation to cover administrative costs (*e.g.*, costs of investigation). This could act as a deterrent against avoiding compensating workers for what they are genuinely owed.

[…]

Repairing the complaint-driven system alone is insufficient in increasing voice amongst ES-dependent workers. Greater avenues for collective action are required, involving a diversity of actors and institutions in enforcement. From this perspective, practices emergent in other common law jurisdictions confronting similar problems highlight two channels to pursue in particular.

The first channel involves inventing new collaborations where workers' designates (*e.g.*, business agents from unions or representatives from entities supporting non-unionized workers such as workers' centres) are either deputized to assist in enforcement or involved in other formal arrangements directed towards similar ends. Such initiatives offer particular promise in segments of the labour market characterized by high levels of violation or evasive behaviour on account of the presence of immigrants and young or women workers, whose social location may impede their ability to voice complaints as individuals. Although deputization [sic] is ideal under many circumstances, given the limits that it can place on the actions of workers' advocates, collaboration between state inspectors and workers' advocates to enforce ES rights may be desirable. Initiatives organized by geography, of the sort evolving under the former New York Wage and Hour Watch, offer strong examples. They go a considerable distance in bringing the culture of enforcement to the streets, in giving voice to collectives of workers in a given region or neighbourhood.

Although little known, the MOL's *Administration Manual for Employment Standards (2010)* provides a vehicle through which Ontario could pursue community-based enforcement initiatives of these sorts. It mandates the existence of an Employment Standards Program Advisory Committee, whose roles include monitoring "changing circumstances and emerging issues" and assisting "in the development of strategies and best practices *to implement special projects.*" To fulfill its mandate, the Employment Standards Program Advisory Committee is also to review "stakeholder concerns;" this committee thereby offers a potential mechanism for communicating with workers' organizations and advocates in improving enforcement. Collectively, such provisions permit the committee to develop and advance initiatives augmenting the collective voice of workers in conjunction with diverse actors and institutions.

Another channel for increasing collective voice entails conducting regular enforcement sweeps of high-risk sectors of the sort undertaken by the US Department of Labor and expanded investigations carried out routinely in Saskatchewan. Both types of undertakings offer attractive models since they cover greater ground than the investigation of individual complaints and give workers voice by providing low risk opportunities for the expression of grievances.

[…]

The lack of effective individual and collective voice mechanisms amongst workers dependent on ES as their primary source of labour protection hinders their access to formal rights and entitlements. By requiring workers, a sizeable subset of whom are precariously employed, not only to come forward with their own grievances but to prepare and present their own cases, often with limited foreseeable pecuniary benefits beyond obtaining entitlements that they are already owed, Ontario's predominantly complaint-based system has a chilling effect. There are, however, other paths to follow. In other common law contexts, where conditions of work and employment have similarly deteriorated, there are a growing number of initiatives where the burden of enforcement does not rest predominantly on individual workers but is rather shared between different government agencies and external institutions. In such contexts, unions and community groups are increasingly playing supportive roles in knowledge-sharing about workers' rights and taking on substantive responsibilities linked to representation, investigations, and settlements. In making necessary adaptations to Ontario's ES enforcement regime, drawing from these examples of incremental change and especially their underlying principles could contribute to creating a context in which rights bearers have better access to meaningful remedies where collective improvements are also within closer reach. [Reprinted with permission.]

13:500 STATUTORY MINIMUMS, THE CONTRACT OF EMPLOYMENT, AND THE COMMON LAW

As we saw in Chapter 3, an employment contract of indefinite duration is presumed to be terminable by either party either with just cause or with reasonable notice. In the following case, Iacobucci J, writing for the Supreme Court of Canada in what has become one of the most widely cited employment decisions, considered the interaction between the common law right to reasonable notice of dismissal and the statutory minimum entitlements to notice of termination.

Machtinger v HOJ Industries Ltd, [1992] 1 SCR 986

IACOBUCCI J. (La Forest, L'Heureux-Dubé, Sopinka, Gonthier, and Cory JJ. concurring):

This appeal concerns the contractual rights of employees who are dismissed without cause by their employers. Specifically where a contract of employment provides for notice periods less than the minimum prescribed by the applicable employment standards legislation, which in this case is the *Employment Standards Act*, R.S.O. 1980, c. 137 (the "Act"), and absent any claims of unconscionability or oppression, is an employee entitled to reasonable notice of dismissal, or to the minimum statutory notice period? The answer to this question is of considerable importance to employees.

Indeed, it has been pointed out that the law governing the termination of employment significantly affects the economic and psychological welfare of employees ...

[The two appellants, Machtinger and Lefebvre, were dismissed after having been employed for seven years by the respondent car dealer, who acknowledged that the dismissals were without cause. Both appellants had written contracts of employment. One provided for a notice period of two weeks on termination; the other specified that no notice was required. The employer gave each appellant four weeks' pay in lieu of notice, which was the amount required by the Ontario *Employment Standards Act*. At common law the appellants would have been entitled to a significantly longer period of notice or pay in lieu of notice. They sued for the difference between the common law and statutory entitlements.]

The appellants acknowledged at trial that, save for the effect of the provisions of the Act, the termination provisions were valid. The appellants make no allegations of unconscionability or oppressive acts on behalf of the respondent...

[...]

STATUTORY PROVISIONS

Employment Standards Act, R.S.O. 1980, c. 137

1. In this Act,
    (e) "employment standard" means a requirement imposed upon an employer in favour of an employee by this Act or the regulations;

2. ...
    (2) This Act applies to every contract of employment, oral or written, express or implied,
    (a) where the employment is for work or services to be performed in Ontario; or
    (b) where the employment is for work or services to be performed both in and out of Ontario and the work or services out of Ontario are a continuation of the work or services in Ontario.

3. Subject to section 4, no employer, employee, employers' organization or employees' organization shall contract out of or waive an employment standard, and any such contracting out or waiver is null and void.

4. (1) An employment standard shall be deemed a minimum requirement only.

    (2) A right, benefit, term or condition of employment under a contract, oral or written, express or implied, or under any other Act or any schedule, order or regulation made thereunder that provides in favour of an employee a higher remuneration in money, a greater right or benefit or lesser hours of work than the requirement imposed by an employment standard shall prevail over an employment standard.

6. No civil remedy of an employee against his employer is suspended or affected by this Act.

40. (1) No employer shall terminate the employment of an employee who has been employed for three months or more unless he gives,

    ...

    (c) four weeks notice in writing to the employee if his period of employment is five years or more but less than ten years

    ...

    and such notice has expired.

    (7) Where the employment of an employee is terminated contrary to this section,

(a) the employer shall pay termination pay in an amount equal to the wages that the employee would have been entitled to receive at his regular rate for a regular non-overtime work week for the period of notice prescribed by subsection (1) ... and any wages to which he is entitled;

ISSUE ON APPEAL

This appeal raises one issue, namely:

if an employment contract stipulates a period of notice less than that required by the *Employment Standards Act*, R.S.O. 1980, c. 137 is an employee who is dismissed without cause entitled to reasonable notice of termination, or to the minimum period of notice required by the Act?

ANALYSIS

A. Introduction

At least on their face, the two contracts at issue in this case represent attempts to contract out of the minimum notice periods required by the Act. Under these circumstances, the question posed by this appeal is deceptively simple: of what significance is an attempt to contract out of the minimum notice requirements of the Act?

Howland C.J.O. held that, although the contractual terms were in breach of the Act, they were nonetheless relevant to determining the intention of the parties as to what the notice period should be. Specifically, Howland C.J.O. held that the terms of the contracts entered into by the parties were such as to make it unnecessary and improper for the court to imply a term of reasonable notice. Instead, Howland C.J.O. gave effect to the intention of the parties, as evidenced by the terms of the contracts they entered into, and held that the appellants were entitled only to the minimum notice period set out in the Act.

With respect, I cannot agree with the reasoning of the Chief Justice of Ontario, and I have come to the conclusion that the appeal must be allowed. I divide my analysis into three parts. In the first part, I discuss the common law presumption that reasonable notice is required to terminate contracts of employment for an indefinite term. In the second part, I review the impact of the provisions of the Act on the two contracts at issue in this appeal. Finally, I turn to a consideration of the policy dimensions of the issue before us.

B. Reasonable Notice at Common Law

... In Canada, it has been established since at least 1936 that employment contracts for an indefinite period require the employer, absent express contractual language to the contrary, to give reasonable notice of an intention to terminate the contract if the dismissal is without cause: *Carter v. Bell & Sons (Canada) Ltd* ...

... For the purposes of this appeal, I would characterize the common law principle of termination only on reasonable notice as a presumption, rebuttable if the contract of employment clearly specifies some other period of notice, whether expressly or impliedly....

What constitutes reasonable notice will vary with the circumstances of any particular case. The most frequently cited enumeration of factors relevant to the assessment of reasonable notice is from the judgment of McRuer C.J.H.C. in *Bardal* ... :

> There can be no catalogue laid down as to what is reasonable notice in particular classes of cases. The reasonableness of the notice must be decided with reference to each particular case, having regard to the character of the employment, the length of service of the servant, the age of the servant and the availability of similar employment, having regard to the experience, training and qualifications of the servant.

Hollingworth J. referred to the factors set out in *Bardal* in determining what would constitute reasonable notice for the two appellants. His determination in this respect was not challenged in this appeal.

C. The *Employment Standards Act*

It was acknowledged by the appellants and the respondent that, but for the possible effects of the Act, no issue as to the validity of the employment contracts would have arisen. The presumption at common law that a contract of employment for an indefinite term is terminable only on reasonable notice would have been rebutted by the clear language of the contract specifying shorter notice periods. But what is the effect of the Act?

The Act provides for mandatory minimum notice periods. The provision relevant to the appellants is set out in s. 40(1)(c) of the Act, which provides that an employer must give any employee who has been employed for five years or more but less than ten years four weeks' notice of termination. Section 40(7)(a) provides that, if the required notice is not given, the employer shall pay the employee an amount equivalent to his or her regular wages for the period of notice.

It is also clear from ss. 4 and 6 of the Act that the minimum notice periods set out in the Act do not operate to displace the presumption at common law of reasonable notice. Section 6 of the Act states that the Act does not affect the right of an employee to seek a civil remedy from his or her employer. Section 4(2) states that a "right, benefit, term or condition of employment under a contract" that provides a greater benefit to an employee than the standards set out in the Act shall prevail over the standards in the Act. I have no difficulty in concluding that the common law presumption of reasonable notice is a "benefit," which, if the period of notice required by the common law is greater than that required by the Act, will, if otherwise applicable, prevail over the notice period set out in the Act. Any possible doubt on this question is dispelled by s. 4(1) of the Act, which expressly deems the employment standards set out in the Act to be minimum requirements only.

What is at issue in this appeal is the effect, if any, to be given to a term of an employment contract which does not comply with the minimum notice requirements of the Act. Is such a term capable of displacing the common law presumption of reasonable notice? The effect of ss. 3 and 4 of the Act is to make any attempt to contract out of the minimum employment standards of the Act by providing for lesser benefits than those minimum employment standards, "null and void." The two contracts at issue on this appeal do attempt to contract out of the minimum notice period set out in s. 40(1)(c) of the Act by specifying notice periods shorter than the statutory minimum. Accordingly, the two contracts are not in compliance with the mandatory language of s. 3 of the Act, and those portions of the two contracts specifying the notice periods are "null and void."

In argument, the respondent accepted that the attempt to contract out of the provisions of the Act was "null and void," but argued that the documents should be considered as evidence "that contracts were entered into which expressed clearly the intention of the parties with respect to notice of termination." I cannot accept this argument. In *Rover International Ltd. v. Cannon Film Sales Ltd.* . . . , the Court of Appeal was faced with a contract which was entirely void. Kerr L.J. refused to look to the terms of the contract to limit the recovery of the appellant in *quantum meruit* . . . :

> . . . if the imposition of a "ceiling" in the present case were accepted, then the consequences could be far-reaching and undesirable in other situations which it would be impossible to distinguish in principle. It would then follow that an evaluation of the position of the parties to a void contract, or to one which becomes ineffective subsequently, could always be called for. We know that this is not the position in the case of frustrated contracts, which are governed by the Law Reform (Frustrated Contracts) Act 1943. It would cause many difficulties if the position were different in relation to contracts which are void ab initio. By analogy to [the respondent's] submission in the present case, in deciding on the equities of restitution the court could then always be called upon to analyse or attempt to forecast the relative position of the parties under a contract which is ex hypothesi non-existent. This is not an attractive proposition, and I can see no justification for it in principle or upon any authority.

In this case we are not faced with an entirely void contract, but a contract of which one clause is null and void by operation of statute. I would nonetheless apply the reasoning of Kerr L.J.: if a term is null and void, then it is null and void for all purposes, and cannot be used as evidence of the parties' intention. If the intention of the parties is to make an unlawful contract, no lawful contractual term can be derived from their intention. . . .

Moreover, because the Act declares the notice provisions of the contracts in dispute to be null and void, it seems to me that the proper question to ask in determining the parties' intention is: what did the parties intend should the notice provisions be found to be null and void? There is simply no evidence with which to answer this question . . .

POLICY CONSIDERATIONS

I turn finally to the policy considerations which impact on the issue in this appeal. Although the issue may appear to be a narrow one, it is nonetheless important because employment is of central importance to our society. As Dickson C.J. noted in *Reference Re Public Service Employee Relations Act (Alta.)* . . . :

> Work is one of the most fundamental aspects in a person's life, providing the individual with a means of financial support and, as importantly, a contributory role in society. A person's employment is an essential component of his or her sense of identity, self-worth and emotional well-being.

I would add that not only is work fundamental to an individual's identity, but also that the manner in which employment can be terminated is equally important.

Section 10 of the *Interpretation Act* ... provides that every Act "shall be deemed to be remedial" and directs that every Act shall "receive such fair, large and liberal construction and interpretation as will best ensure the attainment of the object of the Act according to its true intent, meaning and spirit." The objective of the Act is to protect the interests of employees by requiring employers to comply with certain minimum standards, including minimum periods of notice of termination. To quote Conant Co. Ct. J. in *Pickup [v Litton Business Equipment Ltd]* "the general intention of this legislation [i.e. the Act] is the protection of employees, and to that end it institutes reasonable, fair and uniform minimum standards." The harm which the Act seeks to remedy is that individual employees, and in particular non-unionized employees, are often in an unequal bargaining position in relation to their employers. As stated by Swinton ... :

> ... the terms of the employment contract rarely result from an exercise of free bargaining power in the way that the paradigm commercial exchange between two traders does. Individual employees on the whole lack both the bargaining power and the information necessary to achieve more favourable contract provisions than those offered by the employer, particularly with regard to tenure.

Accordingly, an interpretation of the Act which encourages employers to comply with the minimum requirements of the Act, and so extends its protections to as many employees as possible, is to be favoured over one that does not. In this regard, the fact that many individual employees may be unaware of their statutory and common law rights in the employment context is of fundamental importance. As B. Etherington suggests in "The Enforcement of Harsh Termination Provisions in Personal Employment Contracts: The Rebirth of Freedom of Contract in Ontario" ..., "the majority of unorganized employees would not even expect reasonable notice prior to dismissal and many would be surprised to learn they are not employed at the employer's discretion."

If the only sanction which employers potentially face for failure to comply with the minimum notice periods prescribed by the Act is an order that they minimally comply with the Act, employers will have little incentive to make contracts with their employees that comply with the Act. As Swinton and Etherington suggest, most individual employees are unaware of their legal rights, or unwilling or unable to go to the trouble and expense of having them vindicated. Employers can rely on the fact that many employees will not challenge contractual notice provisions which are in fact contrary to employment standards legislation. Employers such as the present respondent can contract with their employees for notice periods below the statutory minimum, knowing that only those individual employees who take legal action after they are dismissed will in fact receive the protection of the minimum statutory notice provisions.

In my view, an approach more consistent with the objects of the Act is that, if an employment contract fails to comply with the minimum statutory notice provisions of the Act, then the presumption of reasonable notice will not have been rebutted. Employers will have an incentive to comply with the Act to avoid the potentially longer notice periods required by the common law, and in consequence more employees are likely to receive the benefit of the minimum notice requirements. Such an approach is also more consistent with the legislative intention expressed by s. 6 of the Act, which expressly preserves the civil remedies otherwise available to an employee against his or her employer.

Moreover, this approach provides protection for employees in a manner that does not disproportionately burden employers. Absent considerations of unconscionability, an employer can readily make contracts with his or her employees which referentially incorporate the minimum notice periods set out in the Act or otherwise take into account later changes to the Act or to the employees' notice entitlement under the Act. Such contractual notice provisions would be sufficient to displace the presumption that the contract is terminable without cause only on reasonable notice ...

Finally, I would note that the Act sets out what the provincial legislature deems to be fair minimum notice periods. One of the purposes of the Act is to ensure that employees who are discharged are discharged fairly. In the present case, the employer attempted to contract with its employees for notice periods which were less than what the legislature had deemed to be fair minimum notice periods. Given that the employer has attempted, whether deliberately or not, to frustrate the intention of the legislature, it would indeed be perverse to allow the employer to avail itself of legislative provisions intended to protect employees, so as to deny the employees their common law right to reasonable notice.

CONCLUSION AND DISPOSITION

I would conclude that both the plain meaning of ss. 3, 4 and 6 and a consideration of the objects of the Act lead to the same result: where an employment contract fails to comply with the minimum notice periods set out in the Act, the employee can only be dismissed without cause if he or she is given reasonable notice of termination.

Accordingly, the appeal should be allowed.

13:600 STATUTORY PROTECTION OF NON-UNIONIZED EMPLOYEES AGAINST DISMISSAL FOR CAUSE

Labour and employment law is marked by a constant tension between protecting the employee's personal dignity and autonomy and establishing a legal framework that will allow employers to operate profitably. Nowhere is this tension more apparent than in the determination of what constitutes just cause for dismissal. It is widely accepted that the costs and delay of civil litigation often mean that non-unionized employees may in reality have little protection against unjust dismissal under the contract of employment. Unionized employees, on the other hand, usually enjoy relatively comprehensive, cheap, and fast safeguards against unjust dismissal under collective agreements, and have access to the remedy of reinstatement. The International Labour Organization's *Termination of Employment Convention, 1982* (entered into force 23 November 1985), which Canada has not ratified, provides as follows with respect to termination for cause:

> Article 4. The employment of a worker shall not be terminated unless there is a valid reason for such termination connected with the capacity or conduct of the worker or based on the operational requirements of the undertaking, establishment or service.

Article 8(1). A worker who considers that his employment has been unjustifiably terminated shall be entitled to appeal against that termination to an impartial body, such as a court, labour tribunal, arbitration committee or arbitrator.

Article 10. If the bodies referred to in Article 8 of this Convention find that termination is unjustified and if they are not empowered or do not find it practicable, in accordance with national law and practice, to declare the termination invalid and/or order or propose reinstatement of the worker, they shall be empowered to order payment of adequate compensation or such other relief as may be deemed appropriate.

In Canada, such rights have not been accorded to non-unionized employees except in the federal jurisdiction, Quebec, and Nova Scotia. The lack of trade union political pressure for such initiatives may be one explanation; a major reason why employees join unions is to secure protection against unjust dismissal. Others argue that from the employers' perspective, such legislation makes it too cumbersome and too expensive to fire unsatisfactory workers. The Thompson Report on employment standards legislation in British Columbia, excerpted on other matters in Sections 13:700 and 13:800 below, recommended (at 145) against incorporating protection against unjust dismissal.

Employer perceptions in this regard have been challenged by some studies in England, where such protection has been on the books since the mid-1970s. See Bob Hepple, "The Fall and Rise of Unfair Dismissal" in WEJ McCarthy, *Legal Intervention in Industrial Relations: Gains and Losses* (Oxford: Blackwell, 1992) ch 2.

Perhaps the most comprehensive statutory protection to be found in Canada against unjust dismissal of unorganized workers is set out in sections 240 to 246 of the *Canada Labour Code*, which provide for third party adjudication of claims of unjust dismissal. Parallel provisions in Quebec (*Act Respecting Labour Standards*, CQLR c N-1.1, s 124) and Nova Scotia (*Labour Standards Code*, RSNS 1989, c 246, s 71) are somewhat more limited than the federal scheme, in that they require, respectively, qualifying periods of two years and ten years of continuous service with the employer. The qualifying period in the federal jurisdiction is twelve months.

The just cause standards developed by adjudicators under the statutory provisions just mentioned are very similar to those applied by collective agreement arbitrators and discussed above in Chapter 9. Unlike arbitrators, however, adjudicators under the *Canada Labour Code* order reinstatement relatively infrequently, partly because of the practical difficulties of supervising such orders without the presence of a union in the workplace. In 1997–98, reinstatement was ordered in only sixteen of the fifty-three adjudications where dismissal was held to be unjust.

In "Section 240 of the *Canada Labour Code*: Some Current Pitfalls" (2000) 27 *Manitoba Law Journal* 17 at 29–30, Geoffrey England made the following observations on the weakness of the reinstatement remedy in a non-unionized workplace:

> [T]he practical difficulties of making reinstatement succeed in the face of employer opposition are almost insurmountable. Although flagrantly disobeying a reinstatement order may ultimately result in the employer being found in contempt of court, the employer may take the worker back, but make life so miserable that the employee is

eventually driven to resign. Indeed, a worker who resigns shortly after being reinstated may be worse off financially than if he or she had been initially awarded compensation on a "make whole" basis. The employer, therefore, may ultimately succeed in being rid of the employee. An important empirical study of the post-reinstatement experience of non-unionized federal workers in Quebec conducted by Professor Trudeau reported that approximately two-thirds of reinstated workers perceived that they had been "unjustly" treated by their employer. Approximately 38 percent of those employees had resigned by the time the study was carried out. In comparison, reinstatement is very successful in the unionized sector due to the presence of the union to police the order.

In the following case, the majority of the Supreme Court of Canada held that the *Canada Labour Code* does not permit dismissals on a without cause basis, even where adequate severance pay is provided.

Wilson v Atomic Energy of Canada Ltd, [2016] 1 SCR 770

[1] Abella J.—At common law, a non-unionized employee could be dismissed without reasons if he or she was given reasonable notice or pay in lieu. The issue in this appeal is whether Parliament's intention behind amendments to the *Canada Labour Code* in 1978 was to offer an alternative statutory scheme consisting of expansive protections much like those available to employees covered by a collective agreement. In my respectful view, like almost all of the hundreds of adjudicators who have interpreted the scheme, I believe that is exactly what Parliament's intention was.

Background

[2] In 1971, Parliament passed amendments to the *Canada Labour Code* [*Code*] setting out the notice requirements for firing non-unionized employees who had worked for three or more consecutive months. The amendments also stipulated a minimal rate of severance pay for those who had worked for 12 months. Employees dismissed for just cause are not entitled to either notice or severance pay.

[3] More fundamental reforms were enacted in 1978, when the *Code* was again amended by adding a series of provisions to Part III under the heading "Unjust Dismissal". They are found at ss. 240 to 246. This Unjust Dismissal scheme applies to non-unionized employees who have completed 12 consecutive months of continuous employment. Any such employee who has been dismissed has 90 days to make a complaint in writing to an inspector if the employee considers the dismissal to be unjust (s. 240).

[4] A dismissed employee or an inspector can ask the employer for a written statement setting out the reasons for the dismissal. The employer must then provide the statement within 15 days (s. 241(1)).

[5] An inspector is required to try to immediately settle the complaint (s. 241(2)). If the complaint cannot be settled within a reasonable time, the inspector can, at the request of the dismissed employee, refer the matter to the Minister (s. 241(3)), who may appoint an adjudicator to hear the complaint (s. 242(1)). The report of an inspector acts as a screening mechanism to prevent complaints which are frivolous, vexatious or

clearly unmeritorious from proceeding to adjudication: Harry W. Arthurs, *Fairness at Work: Federal Labour Standards for the 21st Century* (2006), at pp. 179-80 (Arthurs Report).

[6] The mandate of the adjudicator is to determine whether the dismissal was unjust (s. 242(3)). If it was, the adjudicator has broad authority to grant an appropriate remedy (s. 242(4)), including requiring the employer to

(a) pay the person compensation not exceeding the amount of money that is equivalent to the remuneration that would, but for the dismissal, have been paid by the employer to the person;
(b) reinstate the person in his employ; and
(c) do any other like thing that it is equitable to require the employer to do in order to remedy or counteract any consequence of the dismissal.

[7] No complaint can be considered by an adjudicator if the employee was laid off because of lack of work or the discontinuance of a function (s. 242(3.1)(a)).

Prior Proceedings

[8] Wilson was hired by Atomic Energy Canada Limited (AECL) as a Senior Buyer/Order Administrator in 2005 and was later promoted to Procurement Supervisor. He worked for four and a half years until his dismissal in November 2009. He had a clean disciplinary record.

[9] Mr. Wilson filed an "Unjust Dismissal" complaint in December 2009, claiming that he was unjustly dismissed contrary to s. 240(1) of the Code. In response to a request from an inspector for the reasons for Mr. Wilson's dismissal, AECL sent a letter in March 2010 saying that he was "terminated on a non-cause basis and was provided a generous severance package that well exceeded the statutory requirements. We trust you will find the above satisfactory."

[10] Mr. Wilson claimed that his dismissal was in reprisal for having filed a complaint of improper AECL procurement practices.

[11] A labour Adjudicator, Prof. Stanley Schiff, was appointed to hear the complaint. AECL sought a preliminary ruling on whether a dismissal without cause together with a sizeable severance package meant that the dismissal was a just one.

[12] The parties agreed that regardless of the Adjudicator's ruling on this preliminary issue, he retained jurisdiction to hear Mr. Wilson's allegations of reprisal.

[13] The Adjudicator concluded that he was bound by *Redlon Agencies Ltd. v. Norgren* 2005 FC 804 (CanLII), which had held that an employer could not resort to severance payments, however generous, to avoid a determination under the Code about whether the dismissal was unjust. Because AECL did not rely on any cause to fire him, Mr. Wilson's complaint was allowed.

[14] The Application Judge found this decision was unreasonable because, in his view, nothing in Part III of the Code precluded employers from dismissing non-unionized employees on a without-cause basis. The Federal Court of Appeal agreed, but reviewed the issue on a standard of correctness.

Analysis

[...]

[39] ... The issue here is whether the Adjudicator's interpretation of ss. 240 to 246 of the Code was reasonable. The text, the context, the statements of the Minister when the legislation was introduced, and the views of the overwhelming majority of arbitrators and labour law scholars, confirm that the entire purpose of the statutory scheme was to ensure that non-unionized federal employees would be entitled to protection from being dismissed without cause under Part III of the *Code*. The alternative approach of severance pay in lieu falls outside the range of "possible, acceptable outcomes which are defensible in respect of the facts and law" because it completely undermines this purpose by permitting employers, at their option, to deprive employees of the full remedial package Parliament created for them. The rights of employees should be based on what Parliament intended, not on the idiosyncratic view of the individual employer or adjudicator.

[40] Adjudicator Schiff's decision was, therefore, reasonable.

[41] As previously noted, Parliament passed amendments to the Code in 1971 which included provisions setting out the minimum remuneration owed to an employee whose employment had been terminated if that employee worked for a threshold number of consecutive months and was not dismissed for just cause. These provisions are now found in ss. 230(1) and 235(1) of the *Code*, both in Part III. The enactment of these provisions neither codified nor extinguished the common law; instead, it offered an alternative to going to court by setting out minimum entitlements for dismissed employees who wanted to avoid the expense and uncertainty of civil litigation: Arthurs Report, at pp. 172–74.

[42] In 1978, Parliament further amended the *Code* and established the Unjust Dismissal scheme, currently found in ss. 240 to 246 in Part III of the *Code*. The central question in this case is what effect the 1978 amendments had on the rights of non-unionized employees whose employment had been terminated. When the provisions were introduced, the then Minister of Labour, the Hon. John Munro, said:

> It is our hope that [the amendments] will give at least to the unorganized *workers some of the minimum standards* which have been won by the organized workers and which are now embodied in their collective agreements. We are not alleging for one moment that they match the standards set out in collective agreements, but we provide here a minimum standard. [Emphasis added.]

(*House of Commons Debates*, vol. II, 3rd Sess., 30th Parl., December 13, 1977, at p. 1831)

[43] He explained the purpose of the new "Unjust Dismissal" provisions to the Standing Committee on Labour, Manpower and Immigration in March 1978 as follows:

> The intent of this provision is to provide employees not represented by a union, including managers and professionals, with the right to appeal against arbitrary dismissal — protection the government believes to be a fundamental right of workers and already a part of all collective agreements.

(*House of Commons, Minutes of Proceedings and Evidence of the Standing Committee on Labour, Manpower and Immigration, Respecting Bill C-8, An Act to amend the Canada Labour Code*, No. 11, 3rd Sess., 30th Parl., March 16, 1978, at p. 46)

[44] The references in this statement to the right of employees to "fundamental" protection from arbitrary dismissal and to the fact that such protection was "already a part of all collective agreements", make it difficult, with respect, to draw any inference other than that Parliament intended to expand the dismissal rights of non-unionized federal employees in a way that, if not identically, then certainly analogously matched those held by unionized employees.

[45] Parliament's intentions were also on display when, the previous August, the Minister acknowledged that while the terminology of "just" and "unjust" was, on its face, ambiguous, the extensive arbitral jurisprudence from organized labour would illuminate the way forward for non-unionized federal employees who were dismissed:

> I realize that the terms "just" or "unjust" are sometimes difficult to define. However, we have a vast body of arbitral jurisprudence on dismissals in the organized sector. They contain precedents that will enable arbitrators to determine whether a firing is warranted or not. Each case has to be decided according to its circumstances, but the application of the principles of fairness and common sense have established pretty clearly what constitutes just or unjust dismissal.
>
> (The Hon. John Munro, "A better deal for Canada's unorganized workers" (1977), 77 *The Labour Gazette* 347, at p. 349)

[46] And this, in fact, is how the new provisions have been interpreted by labour law scholars and almost all the adjudicators appointed to apply them, namely, that the purpose of the 1978 provisions in ss. 240 to 246 was to offer a statutory alternative to the common law of dismissals and to conceptually align the protections from unjust dismissals for non-unionized federal employees with those available to unionized employees: Geoffrey England, "Unjust Dismissal in the Federal Jurisdiction: The First Three Years" (1982), 12 Man. L.J. 9, at p. 10; Innis Christie, *Employment Law in Canada* (2nd ed. 1993), at p. 669; Arthurs Report, at p. 172.

[47] The effect of the 1978 amendments was to limit the applicability of the notice requirements in s. 230(1) and the minimum severance provisions in s. 235(1) to circumstances that fell outside the Unjust Dismissal provisions. The notice and severance pay requirements under ss. 230(1) and 235(1), for example, apply to managers, those who are laid off due to lack of work or discontinuance of a function, and, in the case of s. 230(1), employees who have worked for the employer for more than 3 consecutive months but less than 12 months. In other words, ss. 230(1) and 235(1) are not an alternative to the Unjust Dismissal provisions in ss. 240 to 246, they apply only to those who do not or cannot avail themselves of those provisions: *Redlon Agencies*, at paras. 38-39; *Wolf Lake First Nation v. Young* (1997), 1997 CanLII 5057 (FC), 130 F.T.R. 115, at para. 50.

[48] The soundness of the consensus among adjudicators interpreting the Unjust Dismissal provisions was confirmed in Prof. Arthurs' 2006 report on Part III of the *Code*, commissioned by the then Minister of Labour. In preparing his report, Prof. Arthurs established a 16-person Commission Secretariat, consulted two advisory panels (one consisting of impartial experts and the other of labour and management representatives), held two academic round tables engaging 38 participants from almost 20 universities as

well as industry groups, and consulted 23 independent research studies conducted by leading Canadian and foreign experts. Nine additional studies were provided by Commission staff on topics such as comparisons between Part III and labour standards legislation across Canada and in other countries. The Commission heard from 171 groups and individuals at public hearings and received over 154 briefs and other submissions. The Commission also met with labour, management and community-based organizations, and labour standards administrators and practitioners.

[49] After this extensive review of Part III of the Code and its application, Prof. Arthurs confirmed that the goal of the new "Unjust Dismissal" provisions was meant to give "unorganized workers protection against unjust dismissal *somewhat comparable to that enjoyed by unionized workers under collective agreements*" (p. 172 (emphasis added)):

> ... over the years the adjudication system has not only remedied many of the procedural shortcomings of civil litigation, it has significantly modified the old civil and common law doctrines governing wrongful dismissal.... Adjudicators, borrowing extensively from the jurisprudence developed over the years by arbitrators in unionized workplaces, have built up their own distinctive doctrines that confer on unorganized federal workers quite extensive substantive and procedural protections.... [T]his has coincided with, and arguably hastened, the adoption of progressive attitudes and practices in the field of workplace discipline, many of which were also advocated by human resource and industrial relations professionals as a matter of best practice. [p. 178]

(See also Gilles Trudeau, "Is Reinstatement a Remedy Suitable to At-Will Employees?" (1991), 30 *Indus. Rel.* 302, at pp. 312–13.)

[50] The new *Code* regime was also a cost-effective alternative to the civil court system for dismissed employees to obtain meaningful remedies which are far more expansive than those available at common law. As Prof. Arthurs observed:

> At common ... law, employers who wish to reconfigure or reduce their workforce for business reasons are obliged to give "reasonable" notice to employees they intend to dismiss, unless the contract of employment provides otherwise. Of course, as with other protections supposedly enjoyed by workers under the general law, this one has always been difficult to enforce. Nonetheless, it remains the law today, and Part III does nothing to change it. What Part III does do is establish a different, more accessible procedure under which workers confronting discharge for business or economic reasons can claim notice and compensation without having to sue.
>
> ...
>
> In effect, then, one great merit ... is that it overcomes the main deficiencies of civil litigation. It provides effective remedies and it removes cost barriers to access to justice. It thereby translates a universally accepted principle—that no one should be dismissed without just cause—into a practical reality. Part III can therefore be understood as an exercise in the reform of civil justice. [pp. 172–73 and 177]

[51] The most significant arbitral tutor for the new provisions came from the way the jurisprudence defined "Unjust Dismissal". It is true, as the Federal Court of Appeal

noted, that the word "unjust" is a familiar one in the legal profession's tool kit and has a generic, even iconic role. In the collective bargaining context, however, it has a specific and well understood—and no less iconic—meaning: that employees covered by collective agreements are protected from Unjust Dismissals and can only be dismissed for "just cause". This includes an onus on employers to give reasons showing why the dismissal is justified, and carries with it a wide remedial package including reinstatement and progressive discipline. As in the 1978 provisions, there is no Unjust Dismissal protection in the case of layoffs or discontinuance of a job.

[52] Notably, adjudicators did not interpret their mandate as requiring the automatic application of the arbitral jurisprudence or any remedies. Instead, while they "have drawn heavily" from it, they also "modified it in order to reflect the differences at play in the non-unionized environment" ...

[53] The decision which continues to be the accepted theoretical template, was the 1979 decision of Prof. George W. Adams in *Roberts v. Bank of Nova Scotia* (1979), 1 L.A.C. (3d) 259 (Can.). It helps illuminate what is generally understood by the terms "just cause" and "Unjust Dismissal":

> I am of the view that when Parliament used the notion of "unjustness" in framing [ss. 240 to 246], it had in mind the right that most organized employees have under collective agreements—the right to be dismissed only for "just cause". I am of this view because the common law standard is simply "cause" for dismissal whereas "unjust" denotes a much more qualitative approach to dismissal cases. Indeed, in the context of modern labour relations, the term has a well understood content—a common law of the shop if you will: see Cox, "Reflections Upon Labour Arbitration", 72 Harv. L. Rev. 1482 (1958) at p. 1492. But having said that, I do not deny that the statute is silent on a whole host of important considerations that will, in any particular case, affect the precise meaning to be given to "justness". [pp. 264–65]

[54] He concluded that Parliament must also have had the concept of progressive discipline in mind (Roberts, at pp. 265–66). This concept generally requires employers seeking to justify the dismissal to demonstrate that they have made the employee aware of performance problems, worked with the employee to rectify them, and imposed "a graduated repertoire of sanctions before resorting to the ultimate sanction of dismissal": Arthurs Report, at p. 96; Christie at pp. 690–91.

[55] Prof. Adams explained why he thought progressive discipline was incorporated into the scheme:

> Under a collective agreement, arbitrators have adopted the concept of progressive discipline, subject to specific provisions under the collective agreement to the contrary...
>
> ... Parliament must have had this basic concept in mind when it enacted the instant provision because it is the very essence of "justness" in any labour relations sense.... [M]ore fundamentally, it would be my view that on the enactment of [ss. 240 to 246] all employers subject to this new provision were accorded the powers to meet the requirements of progressive discipline. With the greatest of respect, [a] more technical and contrary interpretation ... would simply frustrate and squander the purpose of this legislation. [Citations omitted.]

(*Roberts*, at pp. 265–66)

[56] But he also noted that adjudicators should be mindful of the varying employment contexts under the *Code*, so that the arbitral jurisprudence is not rigidly applied:

> However, this does not mean that Adjudicators should import the law of the collective agreement in discipline cases unthinkingly and without modification. They should be extremely sensitive to the varying employment contexts subject to this new provision of the *Code*, many of which may not fit comfortably within the "industrial" discipline model. In such cases appropriate modifications can be made as required. Thus, I must ask whether the use of suspensions in the banking industry ought not to be required.

(*Roberts*, at p. 266)

[57] Ultimately Prof. Adams concluded that while the dismissal in the case before him was unjust, he did not consider reinstatement to be an appropriate remedy in the circumstances. Instead, he awarded Ms. Roberts the equivalent of five months' wages.

[58] What turned out to be the consensus interpretation of the new provisions as reflected in the Roberts decision, was also the interpretation accepted by Prof. Gordon Simmons in a report commissioned by Labour Canada to explain the provisions:

> For some guidance as to what constitutes just or unjust dismissal we can turn to nearly three decades of dismissal decisions pursuant to collective agreements. There are no hard and fast rules as each situation must be determined according to the particular circumstances of each case. However, the arbitral jurisprudence which has been developed can act as a guide to what have traditionally been regarded as sufficient or insufficient grounds for just dismissal.

(C. Gordon Simmons, Meaning of Dismissal: The Meaning of Dismissals Under Division V.7 of Part III of the Canada Labour Code (1979), at p. 1)

[59] Until 1994, when Adjudicator T.W. Wakeling broke away in *Knopp v. Westcan Bulk Transport Ltd.*, [1994] C.L.A.D. No. 172 (QL), the adjudicative path was clear that an employee could only be dismissed for just cause as that term was understood in the collective bargaining context. Adjudicator Wakeling's revisionism led him to conclude that the common law approach applied, and that if the employer has satisfied the requirements in ss. 230(1) and 235(1) of the *Code* or according to the common law, whichever amount is higher, the dismissal would not be unjust. His is the interpretation accepted by the Federal Court of Appeal in this case.

[60] Out of the over 1,740 adjudications and decisions since the Unjust Dismissal scheme was enacted, my colleagues have identified only 28 decisions that are said to have followed the Wakeling approach.... Of these 28 decisions, 10 were rendered after this case was decided at the Federal Court and are therefore not relevant to determining the degree of "discord" amongst adjudicators before this case was heard....

[61] That leaves 18 cases that have applied the Wakeling approach. Three of them were decided by Adjudicator Wakeling himself. In other words, the "disagreement [that] has persisted for at least two decades" referred to by my colleagues consists of, at most, 18 cases out of over 1,700 (para. 74). What we have here is a drop in the bucket which is being elevated to a jurisprudential parting of the waters.

[62] Even AECL concedes in its factum that "[t]he majority of adjudicators have held that employees may only be dismissed for just cause." This consensus is hardly surprising given the unchallenged goals of the Unjust Dismissal scheme and their incompatibility with what is available under the common law.

[63] In fact, the foundational premise of the common law scheme—that there is a right to dismiss on reasonable notice without cause or reasons—has been completely replaced under the *Code* by a regime requiring reasons for dismissal. In addition, the galaxy of discretionary remedies, including, most notably, reinstatement, as well as the open-ended equitable relief available under s. 242(4)(c), are also utterly inconsistent with the right to dismiss without cause. If an employer can continue to dismiss without cause under the *Code* simply by providing adequate severance pay, there is virtually no role for the plurality of remedies available to the adjudicator under ss. 240 to 245.

[64] It is true that under s. 246, dismissed employees may choose to pursue their common law remedy of reasonable notice or pay in lieu in the civil courts instead of availing themselves of the dismissal provisions and remedies in the *Code*. But if they choose to pursue their rights under the Unjust Dismissal provisions of the *Code*, only those provisions apply. As Prof. Arthurs observed in his Report:

> ... the two types of proceedings differ most importantly in other respects.
>
> The first relates to remedies. If successful in a civil action, an employee is entitled to damages equivalent to whatever compensation he or she would have received if the employment contract had been allowed to run its natural course—that is, for whatever period of notice would have been "reasonable." If an employer has been unfair or highhanded in carrying out the discharge, the employee may be awarded additional damages. *By contrast, if successful before an Adjudicator under Part III, an employee is entitled both to reinstatement and to compensation, not only for the duration of the notice period, but for all losses attributable to the discharge. These are potentially more extensive and expensive remedies than those a court might award.* [Emphasis added; p. 177.]

[65] It is worth noting that the *Code*'s scheme, which was enacted in 1978, was preceded by similar Unjust Dismissal protection in Nova Scotia in 1975, and followed by a similar scheme in Quebec in 1979 ... Unlike other provinces, the Nova Scotia and Quebec schemes display significant structural similarities to the federal statute. They apply only after an employee has completed a certain period of service and do not apply in cases of termination for economic reasons or layoffs. Like the federal scheme, the two provincial ones have been consistently applied as prohibiting dismissals without cause, and grant a wide range of remedies such as reinstatement and compensation.

[66] It seems to me to be significant that in *Syndicat de la fonction publique du Québec v. Quebec (Attorney General)*, 2010 SCC 28 ... interpreting the Unjust Dismissal provision in the Quebec Act, this Court concluded that "[a]lthough procedural in form", the provision creates "a substantive labour standard" (para. 10). It would be untenable not to apply the same approach to the Unjust Dismissal provision in the federal *Code*, and instead to characterize the provision as a mere procedural mechanism.

[67] The remedies newly available in 1978 to non-unionized employees reflect those generally available in the collective bargaining context. And this, as Minister Munro

stated, is what Parliament intended. To infer instead that Parliament intended to maintain the common law under the *Code* regime, creates an anomalous legal environment in which the protections given to employees by statute—reasons, reinstatement, equitable relief—can be superseded by the common law right of employers to dismiss whomever they want for whatever reason they want so long as they give reasonable notice or pay in lieu. This somersaults our understanding of the relationship between the common law and statutes, especially in dealing with employment protections, by assuming the continuity of a more restrictive common law regime notwithstanding the legislative enactment of benefit-granting provisions to the contrary: *Machtinger v. HOJ Industries Ltd.*, [1992] 1 S.C.R. 986, at p. 1003; *Rizzo & Rizzo Shoes Ltd. (Re)*, [1998] 1 S.C.R. 27, at para. 36.

[68] AECL's argument that employment can be terminated without cause so long as minimum notice or compensation is given, on the other hand, would have the effect of rendering many of the Unjust Dismissal remedies meaningless or redundant. The requirement to provide reasons for dismissal under s. 241(1), for example, would be redundant. And, if an employee were ordered to be reinstated under s. 242(4)(b), it could well turn out to be a meaningless remedy if the employer could simply dismiss that employee again by giving notice and severance pay. These consequences result in statutory incoherence. Only by interpreting ss. 240 to 246 as representing a displacement of the employer's ability at common law to fire an employee without reasons if reasonable notice is given, does the scheme and its remedial package make sense.

[69] That is how the 1978 provisions have been almost universally applied, including—reasonably—by the Adjudicator hearing Mr. Wilson's complaint. It is an outcome that is anchored in parliamentary intention, statutory language, arbitral jurisprudence, and labour relations practice. To decide otherwise would fundamentally undermine Parliament's remedial purpose. I would allow the appeal with costs throughout and restore the decision of the Adjudicator.

13:700 HOURS OF WORK, OVERTIME, FAMILY CARE, AND FLEXIBILITY

Employment standards statutes across Canada take two somewhat different approaches to limiting working hours and overtime. The first is the "market" approach, which establishes a definition of "standard working hours" per day, week, or month and requires the employer to pay an overtime premium (usually 50 percent) for excess hours worked. This approach leaves it to the employer to decide whether overtime assignments are cost-effective. The second approach also specifies a threshold above which an overtime premium is payable, but goes further by setting a maximum number of hours that can be worked in a defined period—a limit that the parties cannot exceed even if they both want to. Some provinces combine features of both approaches in their legislation.

Before the Ontario *Employment Standards Act* was amended in 2000, it set the maximum number of hours an employee could work at forty-eight per week. The current Act raises this to sixty, but only if the employee agrees. For hours above forty-four per week, the Act requires overtime pay or, if the employee agrees, compensation in the form of one-and-a-half hours of paid time off for each hour of overtime worked. It is worth noting that the Act now subjects its protections concerning hours of work and overtime to modification by written or oral agreement between the individual employee and the employer. Some have questioned whether that approach is consistent with the commonly accepted statutory objective of protecting vulnerable workers from some of the consequences of unequal bargaining power.

The overtime provisions of employment standards legislation apply to salaried as well as hourly workers. When a salaried employee works hours for which an overtime premium should be payable, the employer must calculate the additional amount to which the employee is entitled. In recent years, groups of salaried employees have commenced civil class actions for recovery of unpaid overtime, claiming that they were routinely required to work extra hours for which they were not paid. For two Ontario decisions taking somewhat different approaches to the certification of such class actions, see *Fresco v Canadian Imperial Bank of Commerce*, 2012 ONCA 444, and *Fulawka v Bank of Nova Scotia*, 2012 ONCA 443.

In *Macaraeg v E Care Contact Centers Ltd*, 2008 BCCA 182, the British Columbia Court of Appeal refused to allow a civil action for overtime pay, holding as follows (at para 103): "In this case, the ESA provides a complete and effective administrative structure for granting and enforcing rights to employees. There is no intention that such rights could be enforced in a civil action." We will return below, in Section 13:1000 to the recurring question of the relationship between recourse under employment standards legislation and recourse under the common law.

Some employers face irregular production cycles (as in the trucking industry) or unusual labour and product marketing conditions that regularly call for working hours above the statutory ceiling or overtime threshold. To protect such employers from incurring undue labour costs, most provinces have a system averaging hours of work across a specified number of days for granting permits (which are widely used) to exempt them from the usual statutory restrictions. However, the legislation requires that account also be taken of the employee's need for adequate time off work.

Generally, a permit is granted at the discretion of the provincial ministry of labour. Some provinces require that a substantial majority of employees approve any variation from the statutory maxima. This may help to meet the concern that permits should not be granted for political reasons rather than for economic necessity.

Canadian employment standards statutes provide for three major types of leave: annual paid vacations; designated paid holidays; and maternity, parental, and adoption leave. Employers do not have to pay wages to employees who are on maternity, parental, or adoption leave. Instead, for employees who qualify, the federal employment insurance fund makes up for a percentage of insurable earnings during the leave, and it is for the employer to decide whether to top up the difference. (See the *Employment Insurance Act*, SC 1996, c 23, ss 22-23.) Leaves of absence for other reasons, such as a death in the family or voting in an election, are also provided for by some statutes.

There is a widely held view that the traditional approach to leaves of absence has not met the need of many Canadian workers for more flexible working hours. In that regard, the federal government has increased the combined period of maternity and parental benefits to fifty weeks, and most provinces have legislated corresponding increases. A number of jurisdictions also provide compassionate care leave. For example, section 50 of the Ontario

Employment Standards Act, now allows for two days of paid, and eight days of unpaid, annual emergency leave for employees who need to take care of a spouse, child, same-sex partner, or other family member.

The regulation of hours of work under employment standards legislation raises pressing issues for employees, employers, and policy makers. First, full-time employees in some occupations are working extremely long hours, while many other people are unemployed or working fewer hours than they would like. Second, many employees are now demanding more flexible hours of work than the traditional forty-four-hour week allows, and more flexible leaves of absence for educational, family, and other purposes. Third, employees who work part-time (usually defined as twenty-four hours or less per week) are generally treated less favourably under their employment contracts than full-time employees. They usually receive lower pay, they often are not entitled to fringe benefits such as medical and dental insurance and pensions, and they may find it harder to enforce their statutory rights. In British Columbia, the following recommendation was made by the Thompson Report (Ministry of Skills, Training and Labour, *Rights and Responsibilities in a Changing Workplace: A Review of Employment Standards in British Columbia* (Victoria, BC: Ministry of Skills, Training and Labour 1994) at 102):

> The Commission recommends that employees who work 15 hours or more for an employer continuously for 6 months or more should be eligible for proportional coverage by all nonstatutory fringe benefits available to full-time employees, except for pensions. Eligibility for pensions will be regulated by the *Pension Benefits Standards Act*. Part-time employees will be responsible for paying the costs of fringe benefit coverage not borne by employers. Employers should have no liability to pay wages in lieu of fringe benefit coverage for employees who are not eligible or who choose not to accept coverage. The Ministry should have the authority to grant variances to this requirement under appropriate circumstances.

Provinces are beginning to address the differences in treatment of part-time workers. For example, Ontario has recently amended section 42 of the *Employment Standards Act* to benefit part-time, casual, temporary, and seasonal workers who perform substantially the same work as full-time or permanent employees by requiring the same rate of pay: Bill 148, *Fair Workplaces, Better Jobs Act, 2017*, 2nd Sess, 41st Leg, Ontario, 2017, c 22 (assented to 27 November 2017). The Saskatchewan government has even legislated mandatory prorated benefits for part-time workers under the complex provisions in the *Labour Standards Regulations 1995*, RRS c L-1, Reg 5, Sask Gaz, ss 23–26, enacted pursuant to section 45.1 of the *Labour Standards Act 1995*, RSS c L-1, Reg 5.

On the employer side, escalating pressures from competitors, consumers and other sources often lead to a demand that employees be available for more flexible hours of work, though not always in a way that accords with the types of flexibility sought by employees.

The following excerpt from a comprehensive review of labour standards in the federal jurisdiction discusses some of these issues. Employment standards protections in the federal jurisdiction are found in Part III of the *Canada Labour Code*.

CHAPTER 13: STATUTORY MINIMUM STANDARDS

Harry W Arthurs, *Fairness at Work: Federal Labour Standards for the 21st Century* (Gatineau, QC: Government of Canada, 2006) at 108–14

CHAPTER 7, "CONTROL OVER TIME"

1. INTRODUCTION

The regulation of working time affects all employees every day, both in their relations with their employer and in the rest of their lives. It affects the way in which employers conduct business; produce goods and services; relate to their suppliers, clients or customers; in some circumstances, it may also affect the profitability of the enterprise. And, as I explain below, it affects the public in many ways as well. The importance of the issue can be gauged by the fact that limitations on working time were among the first labour standards established early in the 19th century in the United Kingdom, in several Canadian provinces in the late 19th century, and in federal legislation during the first third of the 20th century. The subject has grown in importance over the years to the point where provisions dealing with time—working hours, overtime, breaks, rest periods, leaves, holidays and vacations—now comprise about half of Part III, and is the subject as well of other statutes relating to social policy and economic activities. The regulation of working time was addressed in almost two-thirds of the submissions received by the Commission....

2. MODERN TIMES: WHY THE WORK–LIFE BALANCE IS IMPORTANT FOR CANADIAN WORKERS, EMPLOYERS AND THE REST OF US

Charlie Chaplin's famous film, *Modern Times,* portrays a man so overwhelmed by the demands of his job that he is, in effect, turned into a machine. Even when he stops working, his hands continue to perform the functions they performed while he was tightening bolts on an auto assembly line. Technology has changed since Chaplin made his film in the 1930s—indeed, since the *Canada Labour Code* was enacted in 1965. But if anything, the message of *Modern Times* has become even more relevant today: the requirements and rhythms of the workplace threaten to organize the rest of our lives. Pressures faced by workers Several key transformations have had a direct impact on the availability of workers' time to meet the demands of their paid work and those of competing family and personal responsibilities.

- The increased participation rate of women in the labour force and the growing proportion of dual earner couples have resulted in a rise in the average number of hours spent by household members in paid work.
- The increased instability of family units means that many single earner households are actually lone-parent families where an individual (usually a mother) must meet work and care giving responsibilities with limited support from the other parent.
- Population aging resulting from a declining birth rate and the growth in average life expectancy has led to a rising demand for elder care, a demand that must often be met by prime age workers, particularly those in the "sandwich generation."
- Older workers are a more significant presence in the workplace but are more likely than their younger counterparts to face health problems, to require special

- accommodations such as time off for medical reasons, and to gradually reduce their paid working time to facilitate their transition to retirement.
- Immigration from abroad and the internal mobility of workers have contributed to the wide dispersal of family members, thus weakening family support networks, which traditionally helped share the burden of child- and elder-care.
- While the average work week of Canadians has increased only marginally, significant differences are developing between the extremes. Many underemployed workers would like to increase their hours of paid work, but an increasing proportion of those who work long or very long hours are seeking more time off, or at least more control over the scheduling of their hours of work.
- A decreasing percentage of workers is now working regular nine-to-five schedules, Monday to Friday. Many more workers now work shifts, irregular hours, weekends or on a part-time or casual basis than 40 years ago. More also work under temporary employment contracts, normally for a short period of time or to complete a specific project or task, but sometimes over several years through a series of contract renewals.
- Developments in information and communication technology increasingly allow work to be performed outside the confines of the workplace and at any hour of the day or night. Although this may provide workers more personal freedom over the scheduling of their work, it may also make it possible for work demands to intrude on personal time. Many studies report that in recent years the work–life balance of Canadian workers, including those covered by Part III, has deteriorated significantly. While a solid majority of workers rate a good work–life balance as important to them, survey evidence suggests that only a fraction have been able to achieve it. This is a worrisome trend, since there is growing evidence that individuals who work overly long or unsociable hours, and those who have high levels of work–life conflict, are more likely to experience stress, strained relationships at home and at work, and various adverse health consequences. This has consequences not only for workers and their families, but also for employers who suffer the effects of absenteeism, staff turnover, loss of productivity, and increased benefit plan costs. Studies also suggest that employees who work excessive hours, whether voluntarily or not, help perpetuate a "culture of long hours," thereby exerting pressure on other employees to do the same, lest they be suspected of lacking commitment to their job.

Beyond actual health and economic impacts, excessive hours of work adversely affect workers' quality of life. They cannot find the time to engage in unpaid but socially desirable work related to family and other responsibilities, to study, to participate in community or civic life or simply to enjoy leisure pursuits. The result, according to surveys, is that many workers would be willing to accept lower levels of remuneration if they could reduce their current hours of work.

But not all workers feel that way. Some want and need more hours of paid work, not fewer. The availability of work is a major determinant of their economic security, their entitlement to statutory and contractual benefits, and more generally, their well-being and that of their families. Unduly rigid restrictions on hours of work can thus adversely affect the standard of living of vulnerable workers, such as those earning close to the minimum wage, seasonal workers and employees on short-term contracts. But of course, they are the very workers most likely to be unable to resist the opportunity or the requirement that they work longer than is lawful or desirable.

Finally, for many workers in search of a better work–life balance, the actual length of the workday or work week may be less problematic than the intensity of work, the unpredictability of work schedules, the difficulty of securing leave to deal with specific responsibilities or unexpected emergencies, and the absence of guaranteed sociable time off during the week.

Many employers are sensitive to their employees' needs and have put in place a wide array of arrangements, including generous leave and vacation provisions, family-friendly schedules, employee wellness programs, workplace childcare centres and elder-care referral services. However, even when employers have adopted well-defined and enlightened working time policies, employees may not take advantage of them because they do not know about them, are ineligible because of exclusions or stringent qualifying requirements, hesitate to irritate their supervisors or fellow workers, or fear becoming known as a person who cannot be depended upon to be available for work assignments. As well, many employees benefit from informal under-the-radar arrangements with their supervisors that accommodate their needs and preferences. However, such informal arrangements have obvious limitations. They may be impossible if either party stands on its rights, unfair if the stronger party (usually the employer) takes advantage, and on occasion difficult to reconcile with the requirements of Part III or other laws.

Many employers, then, have dealt with working-time issues by means of non-statutory policies and practices that range from the highly responsive to the barely acceptable. However, many have not adopted any such policies or practices at all because they are concerned about long-term costs, dubious about potential benefits, fearful that their employees will abuse them or simply ignorant of the need to do so. In the end, many workers depend wholly on the standards established by Part III to protect their work–life balance. How robust should such standards be? Before answering that question, it is necessary to examine claims by employers that they need a significant degree of "flexibility" in setting working time standards, both to meet their own operational requirements and to enable them to agree upon sensible arrangements with their employees.

Pressures faced by employers

Like workers, employers confront problems that were not foreseen when Part III was adopted over 40 years ago. Many employers face growing competitive pressures as a result of globalization, changing trade and capital flows, new technologies, deregulation of some key economic sectors, anticipated labour shortages and evolving consumer demands. Even companies that previously dominated some sectors are no longer immune from competition. In order to regain, maintain or improve their competitiveness, employers contend, they need greater flexibility concerning the scheduling of work and less burdensome requirements to provide leaves, vacations and other time-related benefits to employees. However, "flexibility" is a broad term that involves many aspects, not all of which are equally important to every employer.

Due to consumer demands, the need to amortize the cost of expensive capital equipment, the structure of their business operations, or the nature of the services they offer, more employers nowadays claim to need "timing flexibility"—the ability to schedule work so as to operate 24/7—or at least beyond the once-standard nine-to-five, five-day work week. To avoid having to hire extra staff to cope with extended hours of operation or unexpected situations, employers may require existing employees to work shifts, to accept longer workdays or variable schedules, to remain on call after their regular working hours or to work overtime.

"Numerical flexibility" is what other employers need: the ability to increase or decrease their labour force in order to respond to cyclical or seasonal fluctuations in the demand for their goods and services. It may be possible to cope with these fluctuations by laying off some workers as labour force requirements decline, or by bringing in extra workers on a short-term basis as requirements increase. But both of these strategies may be problematic in terms of employee morale, productivity and cost. A better strategy may be to schedule the existing workforce so that its hours of work grow or shrink in response to predictable peaks and valleys in labour force requirements.

However, this strategy may be difficult to implement if labour standards legislation imposes strict limits on maximum weekly hours and requires premium pay for overtime work. Many employers seek more "labour cost flexibility" to enable them to remain profitable in the face of enhanced domestic or international competition. While this concern involves many aspects of regulation and other matters, such as payroll taxes, in the present context they argue that their unit labour costs are increased by having to pay statutorily mandated benefits, and by having to abide by legal rules that hinder the optimal deployment of their workforce.

Another common complaint, particularly from small business owners is that, apart from its substantive content, the very complexity of working time regulation puts them at constant risk of unintentional non-compliance, forces them to incur the expense of hiring lawyers or HR advisors, wastes time, creates uncertainty and causes friction and frustration in the workplace. The flexibility they seek is fewer rules and greater freedom to depart from them in clearly defined circumstances. Finally, not all requests for less rigid statutory regulation of working time are driven by demands from employers for reduced costs or greater control over their workforce. Some employers argue that greater flexibility would allow them to accommodate the different lifestyle preferences and family needs of present or prospective employees. It is difficult, they contend, to work out flexible working time arrangements with their employees within the constraints imposed by legislation. Interestingly, a review of collective agreements on file with the Labour Program reveals considerable variation in working time provisions, at least one of which—time off in lieu of overtime pay—is not, strictly speaking, lawful. This suggests that workers and their representatives acknowledge that greater flexibility might sometimes be to their benefit as well as that of employers.

Broader societal concerns

These competing concerns of workers and employers are real and compelling, and somehow a way must be found to strike a fair balance among them. However, because working time policies and practices can have large, cumulative effects well beyond the boundaries of the workplace, they must also be assessed from a broader societal perspective. For example, there is evidence that stress and other problems related to work–life imbalance, entails direct costs to Canada's health care system. Excessive hours of work or shifts that disrupt workers' sleeping patterns have a public safety dimension; fatigued workers who operate dangerous equipment—trucks and airplanes, for example—may constitute a danger not only to themselves but also to others in their vicinity. Restrictions on employees' working time, such as maximum hours, minimum rest periods, and overtime premiums, may force employers to hire additional full-time staff, with implications for overall levels of unemployment and underemployment. In certain labour markets, additional hiring may not be possible, or it may have the effect of driving up the cost of labour. Conversely, at a time of rising dependency ratios (the ratio of children and seniors to working- age individuals) and anticipated shortages of skilled labour, flexible working time arrangements may help to attract groups of people, such as those with care giving responsibilities and older workers, back into the labour force. Studies submitted to the Commission also indicate that there may be a link between the regulation of working time and such issues as fertility rates and early childhood development. It is also often argued that appropriate working time policies and practices can help foster greater gender equality by allowing a more equitable sharing of domestic and family care responsibilities, with attendant improvements to women's employment prospects and earnings. Lastly, if employment-related obligations prevent working men and women from participating in parent-teacher groups, political parties, sports leagues or arts organizations, the social, cultural and political life of communities will be inhibited, even impoverished.

* * * * *

13:800 LOW PAY AND THE STATUTORY MINIMUM WAGE

The minimum wage is an important component of the statutory floor for many workers. The traditional view among economists is that increasing the minimum wage will not in itself be an effective remedy for low pay. They argue that if labour costs increase too much, employers will hire fewer workers or cut back on training and educational programs for existing employees, thereby harming the very people whom the minimum wage laws are designed to benefit. These negative effects, the argument runs, could be aggravated in industries where employers must compete against enterprises in other jurisdictions with much lower wages. Other economists, however, argue that increasing the minimum wage has little or no disemployment effect.

Mark Thompson, *Rights and Responsibilities in a Changing Workplace: A Review of Employment Standards in British Columbia* (Victoria: Ministry of Skills, Training and Labour, 1994) at 81–84

> Given the interest in the minimum wage, it is surprising how little information exists on who receives these wages, the impact of the minimum wage on compensation and the effects of raising the minimum wage on employment. The last topic is a complex one requiring sophisticated research techniques, but the first two call for rather simple data collection.
>
> One controversial aspect of the minimum wage is who actually receives it. Statistics Canada conducted a Labour Market Activity Survey from 1986 to 1990. Data from the

1989 survey, when the minimum wage in B.C. was $4.50 for adults and $4.00 for persons under 18 years, revealed that 3.2 percent of employed workers, about 45,000 persons were earning the minimum wage. Half of those workers were between 15 and 19 years old, two thirds of whom were females. The survey found that about 30 percent of low wage earners reported just one family member was working. By contrast 46 percent reported two family earners and 22 percent, three or more family members holding a job. There was no information on the level of compensation of the other family members who were employed. About 60 percent of low wage workers were employed in the service sector in the 1986 survey. Agriculture also employed a relatively large proportion.

The Commission heard many employers argue against raising the minimum wage and that differentials be retained or established. Yet when asked, very few of these employers actually paid the minimum wage. A few started workers there and then gave a raise a few weeks later. Most who discussed this point paid between $6.00 and $7.00 per hour. Their concern about the higher minimum wage was the impact an increase would have on those rates slightly above the minimum, as workers would expect to receive an increase approximately the same as any rise in the legal minimum. One exception to this generalization is the restaurant industry, where some of the more expensive restaurants pay their servers the minimum wage with the expectation that they will earn much more in gratuities. The major gap in knowledge is the link between the minimum wage and other rates of pay. National data from 1991, when the minimum wage was $5.00 in British Columbia, indicated that 5.6 per cent of full-time male workers, and 8.2 percent of full-time female workers earned less than $10,000 per year, and 5.7 percent of males and 11.5 percent of females earned between $10,000 and $15,000 for working between 49 and 52 weeks.

Thus, after looking at hourly wage rates and family income data, it is safe to assume that between 5 and 10 percent of full-time British Columbia workers earn more than the minimum wage, but less than $8.00 per hour, and that about 60 percent of these are female. A *relatively small* number of persons earn the minimum wage, and most of them are under 19 years of age. If only full-time workers are considered, there should be few persons under 19 years of age included in this group. However, some part-time workers receiving hourly wages in this range would prefer full-time employment. There is evidence that low wage earners frequently rely on welfare during the course of a year....

[T]he purchasing power of the adult minimum wage has varied considerably in the last 24 years. The high period was in 1972–1977, when the value of the minimum wage was approximately $8.00 in 1992 dollars. After that, the value of the minimum wage sank steadily through 1986, as the minimum did not rise between 1981 and 1986. By 1992, the minimum wage in constant dollars was lower than it was in 1981. Comparing the minimum wage with other compensation levels in the economy yields much the same result. Between 1970 and 1979, the 40 hours' work at the minimum wage was equal to about half of average weekly earnings. By 1990–1992, the same number of hours was about 40 percent of average weekly earnings ... much the same trend occurred in other provinces during the 1980s. Minimum wages rose slowly or not at all during and after the 1982–1983 recession, so that by the beginning of the 1990s, the minimum wage was equal to approximately 40 percent of average weekly earnings in all regions of the country.

There is evidence that increasing the minimum wage reduces employment, although the magnitude of the relationship is uncertain. In a review of the evidence on the relationship between minimum wages and employment prepared for the Canadian Association of Administrators of Labour Legislation, a policy specialist in the British Columbia government found that Canadian and American studies indicated that a 10 percent increase in the minimum wage causes a short-term decline in employment of 1 and 2 percent. Recent research in Ontario concluded that raising the minimum wage to 60 percent of the average weekly earnings (an increase of 13 percentage points) would raise the unemployment rate for women and young workers between 1.8 and 2 percent. The latest research done in the United States found that increases in the minimum wage of 10 percent may cause no declines in employment....

Academic research currently available typically addresses the impact on employment of increases in the minimum wage in the order of 10 percent. There are no estimates of the effects on employment levels of increases in the minimum wage of 25 or 30 percent, but the Commission has concluded that such changes would cause significant reductions in employment, especially in small businesses and the hospitality sector. The Commission heard from restaurant owners who explained how they had reduced employment by eliminating hostesses or bus persons after the minimum wage rose in this province. An Ontario study concluded that labour accounts for about 30 percent of the restaurant industry costs. The emphasis on declines in employment must be balanced by the increases in the incomes of low wage workers when the minimum wage rises. Over a longer term, the immediate employment effects of raising minimum wages are dissipated, since some persons' income rises and others' falls.

It is also necessary to point out that the purchasing power of the current minimum wage is now substantially below the levels of the 1970s and approximately 10 percent less than 1980. Low-paid workers in British Columbia felt the effects of the 1980s recession long after other workers had benefitted from the recovery.

[Copyright © 2004 Province of British Columbia. All rights reserved. Reprinted with permission of the Province of British Columbia. www.ipp.gov.bc.ca]

Jennifer Wells, "McJobs: Is Minimum Wage a Good Idea?" *Toronto Star* **(27 March 2010) 3**

"I've asked people, 'Where the hell did this $10 come from?'"

Morley Gunderson, professor of economics at the University of Toronto, is pondering the minimum wage, set to increase on Wednesday to $10.25 from $9.50. It's a breakthrough moment, one of those psychological barriers being crossed. (Or not crossed. If you're under 18 and work no more than 28 hours a week, your pay pops to a minimum $9.60 from $8.90; liquor servers see an increase to $8.90 from $8.25.)

Gunderson, a professor of economics at the University of Toronto, isn't much impressed. He knows that in large measure the answer to the question he poses can be found here at this very newspaper. "I call them the Star-induced minimum wage increases," he says, sounding somewhat bemused. "I think the Star was very effective," he adds, referring to a series of stories three years ago that pushed hard for the Ontario government to pledge a move to 10 bucks.

In the March 2007, budget, the Dalton McGuinty government announced a three-step, year-over-year increase from what was an $8-an-hour minimum wage. Gunderson's reaction: "I was surprised." His analysis: "I don't think it was the right thing."

Gunderson's deeper analysis had been submitted a month earlier to the Ministry of Finance, in the form of a 23-page commissioned report that cautioned the government as to the potential negative effects of a minimum wage bump. Specifically, Gunderson forewarned of a reduction in teen employment, not in the form of layoffs or termination but in the likelier slowing of low-wage employment growth.

Gunderson advocated instead for an "arsenal of weapons" - wage subsidies, tax credits. "Minimum wages are, at best, an exceedingly blunt instrument for curbing poverty," he wrote, "and the evidence suggests they essentially have no effect on reducing overall poverty and only a very small effect on reducing poverty amongst the working poor."

That sound bite garnered a good deal of media attention.

On the eve of the historic increase, Gunderson is sticking to his guns. "I think the bottom line is, minimum wages tend to be advocated as an anti-poverty device," he says. "I never jump up and down and say, 'Look, this is the stupidest thing you can do, stop this' ... I just say, 'Look it, I don't think it works in the way it's supposed to work.'"

The operative words there are "supposed to work."

Down in Atlanta, Bruce Kaufman is warming up for his appearance next Wednesday before the Federal Reserve Bank of Atlanta. The hot topic: legislated minimum wages. "Do you get Fox News up in Canada?" wonders Kaufman, an economics professor at Georgia State and a noted international expert in the field of industrial relations. "I feel that all the crowd that criticizes the minimum wage is sort of the Fox News of economics ... It's not like I'm a flaming Liberal, but I'm just trying to present the other side of the story."

In Georgia, understand, that makes him a heretic.

Professors Kaufman and Gunderson know one another and respect one another's work in that puckish way that economists do. ("No, we don't agree," says Gunderson. "We agree to disagree. I agree to point out where he's missing the boat.")

In Kaufman's assessment, the minimum wage critics are looking at the wrong end of the horse, as it were. Minimum wages were never designed as a means to eliminate poverty, he argues. Rather, the Fair Labor Standards Act, enacted in the U.S. in 1938, imagined that poverty reduction would be an indirect benefit. The direct goals of the FLSA, as synthesized in a paper that Kaufman is currently polishing for spring publication in the Industrial and Labor Relations Review:

1. Eliminate labour standards that are so low they harm the ongoing efficiency, health and well-being of workers.
2. Prevent unrestrained competition in labour markets from further lowering labour standards in affected industries, or spreading low standards to other industries.
3. Prevent low labour standards from interfering with attainment of full employment and sustainable economic growth.
4. Eliminate low labour standards because they lead to labour disputes and divide employers and employees, thus further harming economic activity.

"We need a minimum wage as part of an overall social safety net and human resource development policy," says Kaufman. "A minimum wage helps level the playing field for unskilled and immigrant workers that otherwise don't have bargaining power in the labour market due to education or skills ... When people were thinking way back when a century ago about protecting and promoting our nation's human resources, a minimum wage was the most obvious thing they came to."

To the argument that social policy of 100 years ago bears little relevance today, Kaufman points out that the United Kingdom only introduced a national minimum wage in the spring of 1999, citing the need to put a floor to wages to order to eradicate worker exploitation. "I suppose you can say a steering wheel in a car is a relic, but you know what? We still need it," he says.

Kaufman isn't sounding very economist-like. "Economists don't give a lot of credence to fairness," he acknowledges. "That's for somebody else to worry about." What economists are supposed to be worried about is efficiency, like those free market Chicago School Milton Friedman acolytes. But markets, says Kaufman, are imperfect. "So the more imperfect a market becomes, the more there's the case for legislation to bring up the bottom end and protect the people on the bottom from exploitation."

On this the two economists agree: there will be a slowing effect in job growth at the low end. But to what degree? "The critics will always point to the fact that when you raise the minimum wage, some people will lose their jobs, and that's a reality," says Kaufman.

"There's a big debate about how severe that is. I think the evidence is, it's relatively modest. The other side of the argument is that labour has to get enough to live on and reproduce itself and if you have to raise the minimum wage to provide that, that's simply a cost that has to be borne ... It's not only fair, it's economically efficient. Otherwise labour is subsidizing the consumer."

Kaufman adds that there's a fine economist at the University of Toronto who will offer the other side of the story. His name is Morley Gunderson.

"He's going to be focusing on the loss of jobs. You might say, 'Morley, if jobs are so important, why don't we just get rid of child labour laws?'"

Gunderson, gamely, laughs. He has a new study underway on the negative impacts of minimum wages. He's a year from sharing the results. Says Gunderson: "The mills of the gods grind slowly."

Don Pittis, "Ontario's Experiment With Minimum Wage Could Transform Canada's Economy" *CBC News* **(8 January 2018), online: www.cbc.ca/news/business/minimum-wage-experiment-1.4473095**

Reading any statement from an economist on the subject of minimum wage, you might think the eventual results are unequivocal and well understood.

The strongest critics of Ontario's sharp hike on Jan. 1 in the hourly rate from $11.60 to $14 use traditional economics to predict certain doom for an economy devastated by plunging employment.

Of course, supporters of the increase take the opposite view, saying it will stimulate the economy by putting money into the hands of the poorest, who will actually spend it.

In spite of research purporting to support these opposing sides, the issues are so complex, so entangled with other economic impacts, with politics, with emotion, that exactly how the rise in wages will play out is far from certain.

Economists around the world are enthralled by what is effectively a huge and radical real-life experiment. The laboratory is the Canadian economy. The lab rats are us.

And partly because Ontario's 21 per cent increase is so steep, no one is really sure how it will turn out, says labour economist David Green.

"Most economists, even economists on the left, are worried about how fast that is going up," says Green, a professor at the University of British Columbia who has made a career of studying how the price of labour affects other parts of the economy.

While this increase is happening in a single province, that province is Canada's most populous and most industrialized. It includes rich cities and rural backwaters. And if it damages the economy, it is reasonable to assume that damage will have an impact across the country.

Whether it succeeds or fails, and how, will stand as a lesson for other jurisdictions.

Unique opportunity for economists

For economists, used to having to extract meaning amid the noise of other economic forces, this sudden change in the price of labour is a unique opportunity.

"When you see a wage go up, you're like, is that because demand has increased? Is it because supply has increased? How are those things interacting?" Green explains. "Here somebody actually comes along and just moves a price for you. And so you get to see things that help us understand how the labour market works."

As Yale economist Robert Shiller observed last year, the things that move our economy are seldom clinical and mechanical. Often far more important is the story we tell ourselves about what is happening — what he calls "narrative economics."

Part of the current popular narrative is the growing gap between rich and poor, which, as polls have repeatedly shown, Canadians don't like.

Observe the astonishing reaction to the CBC News story broken last week by Aaron Saltzman, with the narrative of super-wealthy Tim Hortons bosses wintering at their southern estate while cutting the benefits of the minimum-wage workers who help generate their wealth.

Previous attempts to redistribute wealth through tax reform have faced a traditional-media backlash.

But this time, the social media narrative indicates a widespread acceptance of the wage increase as a means of improving the balance between rich and poor even if it results in an increase in consumer prices.

Previous studies have shown price increases will come, but economists say they should be small. For example, if minimum-wage labour contributes 10 per cent of a product's value, final prices would rise by about two per cent.

Sometimes outside forces such as competition or a consumer backlash mean business owners must swallow some of the cost increase out of their profits or look for savings elsewhere.

Will poor people be worse off?

A minimum-wage hike is not necessarily bad for business, because all businesses have to pay it. Some say businesses will move operations to lower-wage parts of the world, but even that is disputed. Others say the poor will be worst affected as consumer prices rise.

Other strange features have been observed following minimum-wage increases. One is that after a hike, layoffs actually go down. Companies known to profit by paying their workers well, such as B.C.'s White Spot restaurants and Costco, do better at the expense of those using a low-wage strategy, such as Tim Hortons or Walmart.

But at the heart of the increase is the political issue of social fairness, says Carleton University professor emeritus Allan Moscovitch, who says the minimum wage was initially intended to provide enough income to support a family.

That has slipped over the years so that working families who try to survive on a single minimum wage live in poverty.

Guided by the tradition of British poor laws, he says, social service payments are always held below minimum wage. That means sharply higher minimum wages may eventually result in welfare payments closer to the poverty line.

As Ontario Premier Kathleen Wynne said last week, businesses never think it is a good time to raise the minimum wage.

"Ontario is doing very, very well right now. Corporate profits are high," Wynne told the CBC News. "And so it just makes no sense that this is not the time."

"It is the time," she said.

* * * * *

Consider these questions about minimum wage laws:

1) British Columbia's minimum wage is about $2.00 an hour lower for the first 500 hours or six months that an employee works. Why? Is this a good policy?
2) As is mentioned in the preceding excerpt, some provinces set a lower minimum wage for all workers under the age of eighteen. Why? Is this a breach of section 15(1) of the *Canadian Charter of Rights and Freedoms*?
3) Some American cities have passed "living wage" laws that tie the minimum wage to the actual cost of living in the area. Many of those laws are the result of grassroots community campaigns on behalf of what is often called the "working poor." What arguments do you see for and against such laws? What would you need to know in order to evaluate these arguments? See Robert Pollin et al, *A Measure of Fairness: The Economics of Minimum Wages and Living Wages in the United States* (Ithaca: Cornell UP, 2008) and Lawrence Glickman, *A Living Wage* (Ithaca: Cornell UP, 1999).

13:900 TERMINATION PAY UNDER EMPLOYMENT STANDARDS LEGISLATION

13:910 Entitlement to Individual and Mass Termination Pay

During the various economic slumps in recent decades, there has been a marked increase in terminations for economic reasons (these are usually referred to as layoffs). In theory, as we have seen in Chapter 3, a non-unionized employee in such a situation has some protection under the employment contract: because redundancy does not provide just cause for summary dismissal at common law, the employer must provide "reasonable notice," or wages in lieu of notice, when laying an employee off. But as also noted in Chapter 3, that right may be of little practical value to most employees because it is enforceable only through a civil action, which may well be unrealistically slow and costly.

The basic level of protection in the event of termination is found in the provisions of employment standards legislation regarding notice of termination or wages in lieu. Generally, the length of required notice increases with the employee's service with the particular employer, up to a specified limit. This emphasis on length of service may reflect a limited form of property interest in the job, and may also support the view that the statutory notice period represents earnings that were deferred as a form of insurance against termination.

Another level of protection consists of the mass termination provisions found in all Canadian employment standards statutes. These provisions typically require the employer to give longer notice where large numbers are laid off within a defined period. The rationale is that it will be more difficult for employees to find other work if many of them are thrown onto the labour market simultaneously. Empirical evidence shows that receiving early notice of layoff makes it easier for employees to find alternative work and helps relieve some of the psychological stress of losing a job. See Christopher J Ruhm, "Advance Notice and Post-displacement Joblessness" (1992) 10:1 *Journal of Labor Economics* 1. The mass termination provisions commonly contain exemptions that roughly parallel the statutory exemptions in single-employee termination provisions.

Additionally, employers are usually required to notify the labour ministry of plans for a mass termination, so that the ministry can help the parties alleviate the impact of the layoffs. In many jurisdictions, including Ontario, Manitoba, New Brunswick, Quebec, British Columbia, and the federal jurisdiction, the ministry may appoint a joint committee, consisting of government, employer, and employee (or union) representatives, to formulate plans for coping with the mass termination. In all but one of these jurisdictions, it is the employer who finally decides what the plan will be when the committee has concluded its deliberations. The exception is the federal jurisdiction, where the ministry can appoint an adjudicator to impose an adjustment plan if the committee cannot agree on one. Nevertheless, the adjudicator has no authority to veto or delay an employer's decision to implement layoffs, but only to set the conditions under which the layoffs will proceed.

The federal scheme is unique in Canadian employment law because it gives even non-unionized workers a right to participate in collective decision-making with the employer. The fact that compulsory adjudication is available to impose an adjustment plan if the employer and the employees cannot agree gives teeth to what would otherwise be merely a form of non-binding joint consultation.

In Ontario and the federal jurisdiction, permanently displaced employees in defined mass-termination situations are entitled to a severance payment based on their length of service with the employer, in addition to their other statutory entitlements. In *Stevens v The Globe and Mail* (1996), 28 OR (3d) 481 (CA), the Ontario Court of Appeal held that severance pay had to be deducted from damages for wrongful dismissal. On the other hand, some courts have held that severance pay vests in the worker as a form of deferred wages and is therefore not deductible from damages for wrongful dismissal. Can you see any weaknesses in the deferred wages rationale?

As of yet, no province has given laid-off employees a statutory right to be recalled if work becomes available. Such a right is endorsed in the International Labour Organization's *Termination of Employment Recommendation, 1982* (Recommendation 166), art 24:

> 24 (1) Workers whose employment has been terminated for reasons of an economic, technological, structural or similar nature, should be given a certain priority of rehiring if the employer again hires workers with comparable qualifications, subject to their having, within a given period from the time of their leaving, expressed a desire to be rehired.
>
> (2) Such priority of rehiring may be limited to a specified period of time.

What difficulties might arise in implementing this right? Consider how collective agreements handle recall rights, as discussed in Donald JM Brown & David M Beatty, *Canadian Labour Arbitration*, 3d ed (Aurora: Canada Law Book) at 6:2354.

13:1000 THE INTERFACE BETWEEN THE EMPLOYMENT STANDARDS FORUM, COLLECTIVE BARGAINING, AND COMMON LAW LITIGATION

As we have seen at several points in this book, many different substantive areas of law touch on the employment relationship, and different substantive areas often give access to different enforcement forums. For example, in Chapter 9, we looked quite closely at the interfaces between grievance arbitration and the statutory human rights forum, and between grievance arbitration and common law litigation. Similarly, employment standards law and the employment standards forum have many interfaces with other areas of law and their forums, and to the extent that employment standards statutes across Canada deal at all with these interfaces, they do so in different ways. In Ontario, for example, the *Employment Standards Act*, 2000, says, in section 99(1), that in a workplace covered by a collective agreement, "this Act is enforceable against the employer as if it were part of the collective agreement with respect to an alleged contravention of this Act." Section 99(2) precludes an employee covered by a collective agreement from bringing a complaint under the Act, and sections 99(3) and 99(4) state that the employee "is bound by any decision of the trade union with respect to the enforcement of this Act under the collective agreement, including a decision not to seek that enforcement," whether or not the employee is a member of the union. However, section 99(6) gives the director of employment standards the authority to allow an employee to pursue a complaint in the statutory forum, "if the Director considers it appropriate in the circumstances." Section 100(1) allows the grievance arbitrator to grant any remedy that could have been granted in the employment standards forum.

A particularly vexing question has arisen from the fact that while the statutory employment standards forum provides employees with a relatively fast and inexpensive way to recover termination pay and other amounts owing under statute, resorting to that forum may deprive an employee of the chance to recover much larger amounts through a common law wrongful dismissal action. To use the Ontario example again, the *Employment Standards Act*, 2000, confronts this question by providing, in sections 97(2) and 97(3), that "[a]n employee who files a complaint under this Act alleging an entitlement to termination pay or severance pay may not commence a civil proceeding for wrongful dismissal if the complaint and the proceeding would relate to the same termination or severance of employment" — not even if "the amount alleged to be owing to the employee is greater than the amount for which an order can be issued under this Act." However, section 97(4) provides, by way of exception, that an employee who has filed such a complaint may bring a civil action "if he or she withdraws the complaint within two weeks after it is filed." Conversely, section 98(2) states that "[a]n employee who commences a civil proceeding for wrongful dismissal may not file a complaint alleging an entitlement to termination pay or severance pay or have such a complaint investigated if the proceeding and the complaint relate to the same termination or severance of employment."

The courts, while endorsing the general principle against relitigating a legal dispute, have regularly sought to refine the rules on issue estoppel and *res judicata* to allow for exceptions. For examples that predate the above provisions in the Ontario statute, see *Rasanen v Rosemount Instruments Ltd* (1994), 17 OR (3d) 267 (CA), and *Danyluk v Ainsworth Technologies Inc*, 2001 SCC 44. For further reading, see Sean Doyle, "The Discretionary Aspect of Issue Estoppel: What Does Danyluk Add?" (2002) 9 *Canadian Labour & Employment Law Journal* 291 and Craig Flood, "Efficiency v. Fairness: Multiple Litigation and Adjudication in Labour and Employment Law" (2001) 8 *Canadian Labour & Employment Law Journal* 383. In *Macaraeg v E Care Contact Centers Ltd,* 2008 BCCA 182, leave to appeal to SCC refused, [2008] SCCA No 293, referred to in Section 13:700 above, a non-unionized employee sought to enforce the overtime pay provisions of the British Columbia *Employment Standards Act* through a civil action in contract, arguing that the mandatory overtime provisions of that Act had been implicitly incorporated into her contract of employment. In refusing to allow the civil action to be brought, the BC Court of Appeal affirmed the following principle (at para 78): "The implication of terms is an adjunct to the conclusion, based on a consideration of the legislation as a whole, that the Legislature intended the rights could be enforced by civil action, a conclusion that may be derived from the absence of an effective statutory enforcement regime."

Chapter 14: Equality and Human Rights in Employment

14:100 INTRODUCTION

Labour law has long been grounded in equality considerations. Historically, the main issue has been diminishing the inequality of bargaining power between employers and employees through trade unions. Today, when we speak of equality rights in the workplace, we are more likely referring to protections against discrimination—to diminishing sexism, racism, and homophobia, and to enhancing the ease with which persons with disabilities can participate fully in the workforce. In this regard, labour relations are subject to the constraints of equality law. The equality provisions of the *Canadian Charter of Rights and Freedoms* apply to labour and employment legislation and to its application by administrative tribunals, as well as to any employment relationship that has a nexus with government. Human rights legislation applies to employers, unions, and employees in the public and private sectors, and it may take primacy over other legislation. As discussed in Chapter 9, grievance arbitrators have jurisdiction, to an increasing degree, to apply human rights legislation and the equality provisions of the *Charter*. Other statutes also explicitly promote particular aspects of equality. Pay equity legislation, for example, reflects important policy decisions about equality relationships in the workplace and about the social status of employees. Other important human rights issues, which have received a growing recognition, include workplace harassment and privacy in the workplace.

In this chapter, we address some of the most pressing equality issues involved in labour relations, a few of which were mentioned in earlier chapters. We begin with an overview of the meanings given to equality and the identification of equality-seeking groups. We then discuss specific areas of equality and human rights law, such as harassment law, pay equity law, the duty to accommodate, and privacy issues, as they apply in the labour and employment context. Some traditional labour relations principles, such as respect for seniority, must be reconciled with equality requirements.

14:200 THE CONCEPT OF EQUALITY

14:210 Theoretical Development of the Concept

Equality is a complex concept. It has evolved in many different arenas and it is highly contextual. "Equality and inequality," one writer has said, "are political constructions; both their conditions and their definitions vary across space, time, and philosophical families": Jane

Jenson, "Rethinking Equality and Equity: Canadian Children and the Social Union" in Edward Broadbent, ed, *Democratic Equality: What Went Wrong?* (Toronto: University of Toronto Press, 2001) 111.

Our contemporary understanding of social equality has its roots in a commitment to political and legal equality, which is embodied in principles such as "one person, one vote" and the right to equal treatment before the law. These are examples of formal equality; the capacity to enjoy them and use them effectively is often dependent on social or economic status.

Proponents of formal equality may go no further than to accept that arbitrary barriers should not be placed in the way of anyone's *opportunity* to improve his or her condition. Underlying the notion of formal equality is the objective of treating people more or less the same. However, if one begins with the assumption that, for example, only men are capable of being lawyers, high school principals, or skilled tradespeople, excluding women (explicitly or in practice) from those lines of work will not be seen as a denial of equality rights. Under this status-based approach to equality rights, anyone who is treated in a manner appropriate to his or her status is seen to be treated equally.

Taking the commitment to equality one step further leads to the idea that people should be judged on their individual merit and not be excluded from pursuing opportunities or receiving benefits because of particular characteristics, such as class, race, sex, religion, or disability. This idea of equality of opportunity represented a step forward from the earlier status-based concept to a liberal concept of equality based on the right of each individual to achieve whatever can be achieved through that person's own efforts. Yet when we look below the surface of this liberal ideal, it becomes obvious that because of their economic status, some people are better placed than others to develop their aptitudes.

As noted above, anti-discrimination law initially stressed "sameness," emphasizing the fact that all human beings share common characteristics simply because they are human beings. Whatever its strengths, that approach overlooked the ways in which people can be treated unequally under a veil of equal treatment. The gradual realization of this shortcoming in recent decades led to the development of the concept of substantive equality or equality of outcome. Key to this concept is the distinction between direct and indirect (or adverse effect) discrimination and the development of the legal duty to accommodate.

The distinction between direct and indirect discrimination was based on the recognition that there can be discrimination without an intention to discriminate. Ostensibly neutral job requirements are often developed without consideration of their impact on members of particular groups. A job requirement that an employee be able to lift heavy weights might have an adverse effect on women or on people with particular disabilities, even if the employer does not actually intend to exclude them from the job. Similarly, a requirement that employees work on Saturdays may not be intended to discriminate against those whose religion makes Saturday a day of rest. Human rights legislation imposes a duty to accommodate if it can be done without undue hardship to the employer or other employees. Facially neutral rules such as the examples just given will not be upheld as *"bona fide* occupational requirements" if the employee can be accommodated without undue hardship pursuant to human rights law.

This evolution in the concept of equality has been accompanied by an evolution in the identification of the groups protected by anti-discrimination law. Initially, a few categories were identified on the basis of seemingly immutable attributes such as race and sex. Human rights legislation now recognizes a much wider variety of grounds, which may include family status, marital status, sexual orientation and criminal record. This is in accord with the broadening view of the concept of equality and the acceptance of the idea that individual cases of discrimination and unequal treatment in employment do not exist in isolation from broader social conditions. Areas of contention at the borders of today's expanded grounds include immigration status and the status of being a temporary or part-time worker.

14:220 Application of the Concept of Equality by the Courts

Although understanding different approaches to the concept of equality requires some familiarity with the approaches taken by various disciplines—philosophical and political approaches, among others—we also need to understand how the law sees that concept. The main sources of equality law in the labour relations context are found in section 15 of the *Canadian Charter of Rights and Freedoms* and in human rights statutes, and in the interpretation of those instruments by appellate courts.

Until the enactment of human rights legislation, there was no way to challenge inequality directly where issues such as race or sex were involved. Provincial legislation prohibiting Chinese from working in mines was successfully challenged more than a century ago on division of powers grounds; it was held to trespass on federal authority over "naturalization and aliens" under section 91(25) of the *Constitution Act, 1867*. Not much later, however, a provincial statute prohibiting Chinese employers from hiring white women was held to be within provincial authority because its primary purpose was found to be protective. See *Union Colliery Co v Bryden*, [1899] AC 580 (PC) and *Quong-Wing v R* (1914), 49 SCR 440. The first detailed statute codifying equality in employment as a basic human right was the Saskatchewan *Bill of Rights Act*, SS 1947, c 35. It was quasi-criminal legislation that required proof of an invidious intent: its sanctions were penal, focusing on fines and imprisonment. Attacking discrimination by punishing the perpetrators of discrimination proved ineffective, however, and other provincial legislatures passed statutes designed to give victims compensation and relief. In 1951 Ontario passed the first human rights statute—the *Fair Employment Practices Act*, SO 1951, c 24.

Slowly, during the next two decades, the other provinces and the federal government enacted similar legislation. Over the years, the prohibited grounds of discrimination under those statutes were expanded, as were the areas of activity to which they applied, the administrative machinery for their enforcement, and the range of remedies available. In *Seneca College of Applied Arts and Technology v Bhadauria*, [1981] 2 SCR 181, Laskin CJ held that a civil action could not be brought to vindicate equality rights set out in human rights statutes, because those statutes themselves provided a comprehensive administrative and adjudicative regime for the protection of such rights.

Human rights legislation was the major source of equality law until section 15 of the *Canadian Charter of Rights and Freedoms* came into force in 1985. When the Supreme Court of Canada decided its first case under section 15—*Andrews v Law Society of British Columbia*, [1989] 1 SCR 143—it sought guidance from contemporary jurisprudence under human rights legislation. The idea that intention is not required for a finding of discrimination, the idea that discrimination need not be overt or direct but may result from an adverse effect on a particular group, and the idea that attaining equality may require treating people differently—these were all imported into the interpretation of section 15 of the *Charter* from the Supreme Court of Canada's human rights jurisprudence.

In the 1989 *Andrews* case referred to above, the Supreme Court of Canada rejected the formal equality approach that it had developed under the *Canadian Bill of Rights*, SC 1960, c 44, which was the non-constitutional predecessor to the *Charter*. In particular, the Court rejected the "similarly situated" test, under which "things that are alike should be treated alike, while things that are unalike should be treated unalike in proportion to their unalikeness [sic]." Equality, McIntyre J noted,

> is a comparative concept, the condition of which may only be attained or discerned by comparison with the condition of others in the social and political setting in which the question arises. It must be recognized at once, however, that every difference in treatment between individuals under the law will not necessarily result in inequality and, as well, that identical treatment may frequently produce serious inequality.

In holding that section 15 of the *Charter* guaranteed substantive and not merely formal equality, the Court said: "Consideration must be given to the content of the law, to its purpose, and its impact upon those to whom it applies, and also upon those whom it excludes from its application."

Andrews established a three-stage test for determining whether there had been a breach of subsection 15(1). To prove a breach, a plaintiff had to show that the impugned legislation or other governmental action did all of the following: that it (1) made a distinction, (2) which resulted in a disadvantage, (3) on the basis of an enumerated ground set out in section 15(1) or an "analogous" ground—that is, a personal attribute which is immutable (in that it is impossible or very difficult to change) and which is characteristic of a disadvantaged group. In *Andrews*, citizenship, which was a qualification for being called to the Bar of British Columbia, was held to be an analogous ground.

The test for determining whether there has been a breach of section 15 of the *Charter* has evolved over time and is still under great debate. We will not discuss it here as our focus is human rights laws. But before we delve into human rights laws jurisprudence, consider the following case, which provides another example of how the *Charter* may affect human rights laws.

Vriend v Alberta, [1998] 1 SCR 493.

[Throughout Delwin Vriend's employment as a laboratory coordinator by King's College in Alberta, his work had been evaluated positively. In 1990, in response to an inquiry by the president of the college, Mr. Vriend disclosed that he was gay. In 1991, after adopting a policy disapproving of homosexuality, the college dismissed him for non-compliance with the policy. Mr. Vriend tried to file a complaint with the Alberta Human Rights Commission under the *Individual's Rights Protection Act*, RSA 1980, c 1-2 [*IRPA*] but was unable to do so because the *IRPA* did not include sexual orientation as a protected ground. Mr. Vriend sued for a declaration that the omission of sexual orientation from the *IRPA* contravened section 15 of the *Canadian Charter of Rights and Freedoms*. He won at trial, lost in the Alberta Court of Appeal, and appealed to the Supreme Court of Canada. Justices Cory and Iacobucci wrote a joint judgment for the majority of the Court.]

B. Application of the *Charter*

[...]

54 ... McClung J.A. in the Alberta Court of Appeal criticized the application of the *Charter* to a legislative omission as an encroachment by the courts on legislative autonomy. He objected to what he saw as judges dictating provincial legislation under the pretext of constitutional scrutiny ...

55 There are several answers to this position. The first is that in this case, the constitutional challenge concerns the *IRPA*, legislation that has been proclaimed. The fact that it is the underinclusiveness of the Act which is at issue does not alter the fact that it is the legislative act which is the subject of *Charter* scrutiny in this case. Furthermore, the language of s. 32 does not limit the application of the *Charter* merely to positive actions encroaching on rights or the excessive exercise of authority, as McClung J.A. seems to suggest ...

59 The respondents contend that a deliberate choice not to legislate should not be considered government action and thus does not attract *Charter* scrutiny. This submission should not be accepted. They assert that there must be some "exercise" of "s. 32 authority" to bring the decision of the legislature within the purview of the *Charter*. Yet there is nothing either in the text of s. 32 or in the jurisprudence concerned with the application of the *Charter* which requires such a narrow view of the *Charter*'s application.

60 The relevant subsection, s. 32(1)(*b*), states that the *Charter* applies to "the legislature and government of each province in respect of all *matters within the authority of the legislature* of each province." There is nothing in that wording to suggest that a positive act encroaching on rights is required; rather the subsection speaks only of matters within the authority of the legislature ...

61 The *IRPA* is being challenged as unconstitutional because of its failure to protect *Charter* rights, that is to say its underinclusiveness. The mere fact that the challenged aspect of the Act is its underinclusiveness should not necessarily render the *Charter* inapplicable. If an omission were not subject to the *Charter*, underinclusive legislation which was worded in such a way as to simply omit one class rather than to explicitly exclude it would be immune from *Charter* challenge. If this position was accepted, the form, rather than the substance, of the legislation would determine whether it was open to challenge. This result would be illogical and more importantly unfair. Therefore, where, as here, the challenge concerns an Act of the legislature that is underinclusive as a result of an omission, s. 32 should not be interpreted as precluding the application of the *Charter*.

62 It might also be possible to say in this case that the deliberate decision to omit sexual orientation from the provisions of the *IRPA* is an "act" of the Legislature to which the *Charter* should apply. This argument is strengthened and given a sense of urgency by the considered and specific positive actions taken by the government to ensure that those discriminated against on the grounds of sexual orientation were excluded from the protective procedures of the Human Rights Commission. However, it is not necessary to rely on this position in order to find that the *Charter* is applicable....

75 The respondents have argued that because the *IRPA* merely omits any reference to sexual orientation, this "neutral silence" cannot be understood as creating a distinction. They contend that the *IRPA* extends full protection on the grounds contained within it to heterosexuals and homosexuals alike, and therefore there is no distinction and hence no discrimination. It is the respondents' position that if any distinction is made on the basis of sexual orientation that distinction exists because it is present in society and not because of the *IRPA*.

76 These arguments cannot be accepted. They are based on that "thin and impoverished" notion of equality referred to in *Eldridge* (at para. 73). It has been repeatedly held that identical treatment will not always constitute equal treatment (see for example *Andrews*... at p. 164). It is also clear that the way in which an exclusion is worded should not disguise the nature of the exclusion so as to allow differently drafted exclusions to be treated differently....

77 The respondents concede that if homosexuals were excluded altogether from the protection of the *IRPA* in the sense that they were not protected from discrimination on any grounds, this would be discriminatory. Clearly that would be discrimination of the most egregious kind. It is true that gay and lesbian individuals are not entirely excluded from the protection of the *IRPA*. They can claim protection on some grounds. Yet that certainly does not mean that there is no discrimination present. For example, the fact that a lesbian and a heterosexual woman are both entitled to bring a complaint of discrimination on the basis of gender does not mean that they have equal protection under the Act. Lesbian and gay individuals are still denied protection under the ground that may be the most significant for them, discrimination on the basis of sexual orientation....

80 If the mere silence of the legislation was enough to remove it from s. 15(1) scrutiny then any legislature could easily avoid the objects of s. 15(1) simply by drafting laws which omitted reference to excluded groups. Such an approach would ignore the recognition that this Court has given to the principle that discrimination can arise from underinclusive legislation. This principle was expressed with great clarity by Dickson C.J. in *Brooks v. Canada Safeway Ltd.*, [1989] 1 S.C.R. 1219, at p. 1240. There he stated: "Underinclusion may be simply a backhanded way of permitting discrimination." ...

84 Finally, the respondents' contention that the distinction is not created by law, but rather exists independently of the *IRPA* in society, cannot be accepted. It is, of course, true that discrimination against gays and lesbians exists in society ... The reality of society's discrimination against lesbians and gay men demonstrates that there is a distinction drawn in the *IRPA* which denies these groups equal protection of the law by excluding lesbians and gay men from its protection, the very protection they so urgently need because of the existence of discrimination against them in society. It is not necessary to find that the legislation creates the discrimination existing in society in order to determine that it creates a potentially discriminatory distinction....

96 The comprehensive nature of the Act must be taken into account in considering the effect of excluding one ground from its protection. It is not as if the Legislature had merely chosen to deal with one type of discrimination. In such a case it might be permissible to target only that specific type of discrimination and not another.... The case at bar presents a very different situation. It is concerned with legislation that purports

to provide comprehensive protection from discrimination for all individuals in Alberta. The selective exclusion of one group from that comprehensive protection therefore has a very different effect.

97 The first and most obvious effect of the exclusion of sexual orientation is that lesbians or gay men who experience discrimination on the basis of their sexual orientation are denied recourse to the mechanisms set up by the *IRPA* to make a formal complaint of discrimination and seek a legal remedy. Thus, the Alberta Human Rights Commission could not hear Vriend's complaint and cannot consider a complaint or take any action on behalf of any person who has suffered discrimination on the ground of sexual orientation. The denial of access to remedial procedures for discrimination on the ground of sexual orientation must have dire and demeaning consequences for those affected. This result is exacerbated both because the option of a civil remedy for discrimination is precluded and by the lack of success that lesbian women and gay men have had in attempting to obtain a remedy for discrimination on the ground of sexual orientation by complaining on other grounds such as sex or marital status. Persons who are discriminated against on the ground of sexual orientation, unlike others protected by the Act, are left without effective legal recourse for the discrimination they have suffered.

98 It may at first be difficult to recognize the significance of being excluded from the protection of human rights legislation. However it imposes a heavy and disabling burden on those excluded ...

99 Apart from the immediate effect of the denial of recourse in cases of discrimination, there are other effects which, while perhaps less obvious, are at least as harmful. In *Haig*, the Ontario Court of Appeal based its finding of discrimination on both the "failure to provide an avenue for redress for prejudicial treatment of homosexual members of society" and "the possible inference from the omission that such treatment is acceptable" (p. 503). It can be reasonably inferred that the absence of any legal recourse for discrimination on the ground of sexual orientation perpetuates and even encourages that kind of discrimination. The respondents contend that it cannot be assumed that the "silence" of the *IRPA* reinforces or perpetuates discrimination, since governments "cannot legislate attitudes." However, this argument seems disingenuous in light of the stated purpose of the *IRPA*, to prevent discrimination. It cannot be claimed that human rights legislation will help to protect individuals from discrimination, and at the same time contend that an exclusion from the legislation will have no effect.

100 However, let us assume, contrary to all reasonable inferences, that exclusion from the *IRPA*'s protection does not actually contribute to a greater incidence of discrimination on the excluded ground. Nonetheless that exclusion, deliberately chosen in the face of clear findings that discrimination on the ground of sexual orientation does exist in society, sends a strong and sinister message. The very fact that sexual orientation is excluded from the *IRPA*, which is the Government's primary statement of policy against discrimination, certainly suggests that discrimination on the ground of sexual orientation is not as serious or as deserving of condemnation as other forms of discrimination. It could well be said that it is tantamount to condoning or even encouraging discrimination against lesbians and gay men. Thus this exclusion clearly gives rise to an effect which constitutes discrimination.

101 The exclusion sends a message to all Albertans that it is permissible, and perhaps even acceptable, to discriminate against individuals on the basis of their sexual orientation. The effect of that message on gays and lesbians is one whose significance cannot be underestimated. As a practical matter, it tells them that they have no protection from discrimination on the basis of their sexual orientation. Deprived of any legal redress they must accept and live in constant fear of discrimination. These are burdens which are not imposed on heterosexuals.

102 Perhaps most important is the psychological harm which may ensue from this state of affairs. Fear of discrimination will logically lead to concealment of true identity and this must be harmful to personal confidence and self-esteem. Compounding that effect is the implicit message conveyed by the exclusion, that gays and lesbians, unlike other individuals, are not worthy of protection. This is clearly an example of a distinction which demeans the individual and strengthens and perpetuates the view that gays and lesbians are less worthy of protection as individuals in Canada's society. The potential harm to the dignity and perceived worth of gay and lesbian individuals constitutes a particularly cruel form of discrimination.

103 Even if the discrimination is experienced at the hands of private individuals, it is the state that denies protection from that discrimination. Thus the adverse effects are particularly invidious ...

104 In excluding sexual orientation from the *IRPA*'s protection, the Government has, in effect, stated that "all persons are equal in dignity and rights," except gay men and lesbians. Such a message, even if it is only implicit, must offend s. 15(1), the "section of the *Charter*, more than any other, which recognizes and cherishes the innate human dignity of every individual" (*Egan*, at para. 128). This effect, together with the denial to individuals of any effective legal recourse in the event they are discriminated against on the ground of sexual orientation, amount to a sufficient basis on which to conclude that the distinction created by the exclusion from the *IRPA* constitutes discrimination ...

Justices Cory and Iacobucci also held that the Alberta government had not shown that the omission of sexual orientation as a protected ground under the *IRPA* satisfied the "pressing and substantial objective," so it failed the *Oakes* test and was not saved under section 1. Nor did the judgment accept the government's argument that it could use incremental means to advance the purposes of the legislation. "[G]roups that have historically been the target of discrimination," Cory and Iacobucci JJ stated, "cannot be expected to wait patiently for the protection of their human dignity and equal rights while governments move toward reform one step at a time." The judgment concluded that this was an appropriate occasion for the Court to read the words "sexual orientation" into the relevant sections of the *IRPA*.

14:230 Establishing Discrimination U1072nder Human Rights Laws

A number of the leading early human rights cases involved the workplace. For example, in *Ontario (Human Rights Commission) v Simpsons Sears Ltd*, [1985] 2 SCR 536 (*O'Malley*), a department store employee objected to working on Friday nights and Saturdays on religious grounds. Although the employer had legitimate reasons for requiring employees to work at those times and did not intend to discriminate against O'Malley, the Supreme Court of Canada held the requirement to be discriminatory because it had an adverse effect on anyone of her religion. The Court ordered the employer to accommodate O'Malley by scheduling her time differently, as long as the rescheduling did not impose an undue hardship on the employer. Thus, *O'Malley* established that intention was not required for a finding of discrimination, and it also introduced the idea of the duty to accommodate. Justice McIntyre noted that:

> [14] ... To take the narrower view and hold that intent is a required element of discrimination under the Code would seem to me to place a virtually insuperable barrier in the way of a complainant seeking a remedy. It would be extremely difficult in most circumstances to prove motive, and motive would be easy to cloak in the formation of rules which, though imposing equal standards, could create ... injustice and discrimination by the equal treatment of those who are unequal ... Furthermore, as I have endeavoured to show, we are dealing here with consequences of conduct rather than with punishment for misbehaviour. In other words, we are considering what are essentially civil remedies. The proof of intent, a necessary requirement in our approach to criminal and punitive legislation, should not be a governing factor in construing human rights legislation aimed at the elimination of discrimination. It is my view that the courts below were in error in finding an intent to discriminate to be a necessary element of proof.

This case also provided an explanation of the distinction between direct discrimination and adverse effect discrimination and the burden of proof required in both cases:

> [18] ... Direct discrimination occurs in this connection where an employer adopts a practice or rule which on its face discriminates on a prohibited ground. For example, "No Catholics or no women or no blacks employed here." There is, of course, no disagreement in the case at bar that direct discrimination of that nature would contravene the Act. On the other hand, there is the concept of adverse effect discrimination. It arises where an employer for genuine business reasons adopts a rule or standard which is on its face neutral, and which will apply equally to all employees, but which has a discriminatory effect upon a prohibited ground on one employee or group of employees in that it imposes, because of some special characteristic of the employee or group, obligations, penalties, or restrictive conditions not imposed on other members of the work force. For essentially the same reasons that led to the conclusion that an intent to discriminate was not required as an element of discrimination contravening the Code I am of the opinion that this Court may consider adverse effect discrimination as described in these reasons a contradiction of the terms of the Code. An employment rule honestly made for sound economic or business reasons, equally applicable to all to whom it is intended to apply, may yet be discriminatory if it affects a person or group of persons differently from others to whom it may apply. From the foregoing I therefore conclude that the appellant showed a *prima facie* case of discrimination based on creed before the Board of Inquiry.
>
> [28] ... The complainant in proceedings before human rights tribunals must show a *prima facie* case of discrimination. A *prima facie* case in this context is one which covers the allegations made and which, if they are believed, is complete and sufficient to justify a

verdict in the complainant's favour in the absence of an answer from the respondent-employer. Where adverse effect discrimination on the basis of creed is shown and the offending rule is rationally connected to the performance of the job, as in the case at bar, the employer is not required to justify it but rather to show that he has taken such reasonable steps toward accommodation of the employee's position as are open to him without undue hardship. It seems evident to me that in this kind of case the onus should again rest on the employer, for it is the employer who will be in possession of the necessary information to show undue hardship, and the employee will rarely, if ever, be in a position to show its absence. The onus will not be a heavy one in all cases. In some cases it may be established without evidence; for example, a requirement that all employees work on Saturday in a business which is open only on Saturdays, but once the *prima facie* proof of a discriminatory effect is made it will remain for the employer to show undue hardship if required to take more steps for its accommodation than he has done.

* * * * *

The jurisprudence of human rights laws and of section 15 of the *Charter* have influenced each other over the years. Some adjudicators suggested that to establish a *prima facie* case of discrimination under human rights laws, the complainant must prove some elements of disadvantage that perpetuate stereotyping or prejudice similarly to the requirements under section 15 of the *Charter* (see, for example, *Ontario (Director, Disability Support Program) v Tranchemontagne*, 2010 ONCA 593); however, others strongly object to this proposition (see, for example, Denise Réaume, "Defending the Human Rights Codes from the *Charter*" (2012) 9 *Journal of Law & Equality* 67 at 68–72). As Réaume explains:

> The conventional human rights code analysis treats as discriminatory any differential treatment connected to a prohibited ground unless it passes both an efficacy and necessity test. The *Charter* test requires claimants to show substantive discrimination, in some sense, and this burden exempts some cases from a necessity assessment that the code test has conventionally imposed on respondents.
>
> The difference matters because the former conception of discrimination is potentially wider in scope; it is also the approach that makes the best sense of the human rights codes, both of their language and their purpose. It should therefore be protected from *Charter* encroachment . . .
>
> [. . .]
>
> The conventional account of the structure of a human rights code complaint holds that the applicant must establish a *prima facie* case of discrimination, after which the burden shifts to the respondent to demonstrate that the exclusionary requirement is a bona fide requirement, provided that such an exemption from the prohibition on discrimination is provided by the code on the facts . . . Traditionally, the burden to make out a *prima facie* case has been relatively light, one that is largely factual rather than normative. That is, the applicant need only establish certain facts to make out the *prima facie* case — need only show that there has been discrimination in effect or in a factual sense. This is not enough to establish *liability*, but it is enough for us to ask for an explanation from the respondent so that we can intelligently decide whether it is appropriate to

impose liability. The final determination of liability ultimately brings normative issues into the analysis, but the *prima facie* case is essentially a factual one.

[...]

This account gives us a simple, factual basis for establishing a *prima facie* complaint: if members of a group identified by reference to a ground in the code have been treated differently than others,' so as to deny full enjoyment of the activities covered by the spheres, this is sufficient to ground liability, absent an answer from the respondent that somehow negates/rebuts or justifies this result. It is important to note that on this approach, any case in which the respondent has explicitly used one of the grounds listed in the code as an exclusionary criterion for access to a protected sphere is one in which the applicant makes out a *prima facie* case of discrimination simply by pointing to that explicit criterion. The explicit use of the ground means that the applicant has suffered differential treatment in a way that is connected to a ground, and this factual case satisfies the conventional *prima facie* test, provided it falls within one of the spheres covered by the code.

The applicant's task can be more onerous in situations in which there is no explicit use of a prohibited ground, but rather a neutral rule is adopted that has a tendency to affect members of a group identified by one of the grounds more harshly than others. In these cases—adverse effects cases—the applicant must establish, either as a matter of logic, or common sense, or through factual evidence such as statistical patterns, the rule's tendency to have a worse effect on people in one group than it does on others. In a case in which an employment rule is completely inconsistent with the religious obligations of a particular group, the discriminatory tendency will require no more by way of evidence than testimony about the religious requirements of the group. By contrast, when the rule excludes on the basis of a characteristic or behavioural tendency that is generally true of members of a group identified by a ground but not necessarily true of all, statistical evidence may be needed. If the applicant cannot make out this differential effect, she has not established the *prima facie* case and the respondent has nothing to defend.

Recently, the Supreme Court applied a *prima facie* test which was consistent with the test formulated in *O'Malley*. In *Moore v British Columbia (Education)*, 2012 SCC 61 at para 33, the Court held that:

> to demonstrate *prima facie* discrimination, complainants are required to show that they have a characteristic protected from discrimination under the *Code*; that they experienced an adverse impact with respect to the service; and that the protected characteristic was a factor in the adverse impact. Once a *prima facie* case has been established, the burden shifts to the respondent to justify the conduct or practice, within the framework of the exemptions available under human rights statutes. If it cannot be justified, discrimination will be found to occur.

Note that the complainant must establish a connection between the differential treatment or effect and one of the enumerated grounds. The Supreme Court of Canada clarified that this connection does not have to be close or causally determinative in *Quebec (Commission des droits de la personne et des droits de la jeunesse) v Bombardier Inc (Bombardier*

Aerospace Training Centre), 2015 SCC 39 at para 52: "[T]he plaintiff has the burden of showing that there is a connection between a prohibited ground of discrimination and the distinction, exclusion or preference of which he or she complains or, in other words, that the ground in question was a factor in the distinction, exclusion or preference."

14:240 The "Unified Approach" to Discrimination

Once a *prima facie* case of discrimination under human rights laws is established, the burden shifts to the respondent to explain its action. One of the most important statutory defences is the bona fide occupational requirement. In the past, it was not clear whether the BFOR defence applied to both direct and indirect discrimination, and if so, how the tests might be different. In the 1999 *Meiorin* case, excerpted below, the Supreme Court of Canada tried to simplify the relationship between direct and indirect discrimination, bona fide occupational requirements (BFORs), and the duty to accommodate. In doing so, it articulated a new three-stage test for deciding whether a standard which appears to be discriminatory is in fact a BFOR.

British Columbia (Public Service Employee Relations Commission) v BCGSEU, [1999] 3 SCR 3 [*Meiorin*].

McLACHLIN J., for the Court:

[...]

II. FACTS

[4] Ms. Meiorin was employed for three years by the British Columbia Ministry of Forests as a member of a three-person Initial Attack Forest Firefighting Crew in the Golden Forest District. The crew's job was to attack and suppress forest fires while they were small and could be contained. Ms. Meiorin's supervisors found her work to be satisfactory.

[5] Ms. Meiorin was not asked to take a physical fitness test until 1994, when she was required to pass the Government's "*Bona Fide* Occupational Fitness Tests and Standards for B.C. Forest Service Wildland Firefighters" (the "Tests"). The Tests required that the forest firefighters weigh less than 200 lbs. (with their equipment) and complete a shuttle run, an upright rowing exercise, and a pump carrying/hose dragging exercise within stipulated times. The running test was designed to test the forest firefighters' aerobic fitness and was based on the view that forest firefighters must have a minimum "VO$_2$ max" of 50 ml·kg^{-1}·min^{-1} (the "aerobic standard"). "VO$_2$ max" measures "maximal oxygen uptake," or the rate at which the body can take in oxygen, transport it to the muscles, and use it to produce energy.

[6] The Tests were developed in response to a 1991 Coroner's Inquest Report that recommended that only physically fit employees be assigned as front-line forest firefighters for safety reasons. The Government commissioned a team of researchers from the University of Victoria to undertake a review of its existing fitness standards with a view to protecting the safety of firefighters while meeting human rights norms. The researchers developed the Tests by identifying the essential components of forest firefighting, measuring the physiological demands of those components, selecting fitness tests to measure those demands and, finally, assessing the validity of those tests.

[7] The researchers studied various sample groups. The specific tasks performed by forest firefighters were identified by reviewing amalgamated data collected by the British Columbia Forest Service. The physiological demands of those tasks were then measured by observing test subjects as they performed them in the field. One simulation involved 18 firefighters, another involved 10 firefighters, but it is unclear from the researchers' report whether the subjects at this stage were male or female. The researchers asked a pilot group of 10 university student volunteers (6 females and 4 males) to perform a series of proposed fitness tests and field exercises. After refining the preferred tests, the researchers observed them being performed by a larger sample group composed of 31 forest firefighter trainees and 15 university student volunteers (31 males and 15 females), and correlated their results with the group's performance in the field. Having concluded that the preferred tests were accurate predictors of actual forest firefighting performance—including the running test designed to gauge whether the subject met the aerobic standard—the researchers presented their report to the Government in 1992.

[8] A follow-up study in 1994 of 77 male forest firefighters and 2 female forest firefighters used the same methodology. However, the researchers this time recommended that the Government initiate another study to examine the impact of the Tests on women. There is no evidence before us that the Government has yet responded to this recommendation.

[9] Two aspects of the researchers' methodology are critical to this case. First, it was primarily descriptive, based on measuring the average performance levels of the test subjects and converting this data into minimum performance standards. Second, it did not seem to distinguish between the male and female test subjects.

[10] After four attempts, Ms. Meiorin failed to meet the aerobic standard, running the distance in 11 minutes and 49.4 seconds instead of the required 11 minutes. As a result, she was laid off. Her union subsequently brought a grievance on her behalf. The arbitrator designated to hear the grievance was required to determine whether she had been improperly dismissed.

[11] Evidence accepted by the arbitrator demonstrated that, owing to physiological differences, most women have lower aerobic capacity than most men. Even with training, most women cannot increase their aerobic capacity to the level required by the aerobic standard, although training can allow most men to meet it. The arbitrator also heard evidence that 65 percent to 70 percent of male applicants pass the Tests on their initial attempts, while only 35 percent of female applicants have similar success. Of the 800 to 900 Initial Attack Crew members employed by the Government in 1995, only 100 to 150 were female.

[12] There was no credible evidence showing that the prescribed aerobic capacity was necessary for either men or women to perform the work of a forest firefighter satisfactorily. On the contrary, Ms. Meiorin had in the past performed her work well, without apparent risk to herself, her colleagues or the public.

III. THE RULINGS

[13] The arbitrator found that Ms. Meiorin had established a *prima facie* case of adverse effect discrimination by showing that the aerobic standard has a disproportionately

negative effect on women as a group. He further found that the Government had presented no credible evidence that Ms. Meiorin's inability to meet the aerobic standard meant that she constituted a safety risk to herself, her colleagues, or the public, and hence had not discharged its burden of showing that it had accommodated Ms. Meiorin to the point of undue hardship. He ordered that she be reinstated to her former position and compensated for her lost wages and benefits.

[14] The Court of Appeal ... did not distinguish between direct and adverse effect discrimination. It held that so long as the standard is *necessary* to the safe and efficient performance of the work and is applied through individualized testing, there is no discrimination. The Court of Appeal (mistakenly) read the arbitrator's reasons as finding that the aerobic standard was necessary to the safe and efficient performance of the work. Since Ms. Meiorin had been individually tested against this standard, it allowed the appeal and dismissed her claim. The Court of Appeal commented that to permit Ms. Meiorin to succeed would create "reverse discrimination," i.e., to set a lower standard for women than for men would discriminate against those men who failed to meet the men's standard but were nevertheless capable of meeting the women's standard.

IV. STATUTORY PROVISIONS

[15] The following provisions of the British Columbia *Human Rights Code*, R.S.B.C. 1996, c. 210, are at issue on this appeal:

> *Discrimination in employment*
> 13 (1) A person must not,
> (a) refuse to employ or refuse to continue to employ a person, or
> (b) discriminate against a person regarding employment or any term or condition of employment because of the race, colour, ancestry, place of origin, political belief, religion, marital status, family status, physical or mental disability, sex, sexual orientation or age of that person or because that person has been convicted of a criminal or summary conviction offence that is unrelated to the employment or to the intended employment of that person.
>
> ...
>
> (4) Subsections (1) and (2) do not apply with respect to a refusal, limitation, specification or preference based on a bona fide occupational requirement.

V. THE ISSUES

[16] The first issue on this appeal is the test applicable to s. 13(1) and (4) of the British Columbia *Human Rights Code*. The second issue is whether, on this test, Ms. Meiorin has established that the Government violated the Code.

VI. ANALYSIS

[17] As a preliminary matter, I must sort out a characterization issue. The Court of Appeal seems to have understood the arbitrator as having held that the ability to meet

the aerobic standard is necessary to the safe and efficient performance of the work of an Initial Attack Crew member. With respect, I cannot agree with this reading of the arbitrator's reasons.

[18] The arbitrator held that the standard was one of the appropriate measurements available to the Government and that there is generally a reasonable relationship between aerobic fitness and the ability to perform the job of an Initial Attack Crew member. This falls short, however, of an affirmative finding that the ability to meet the aerobic standard chosen by the Government is necessary to the safe and efficient performance of the job. To the contrary, that inference is belied by the arbitrator's conclusion that, despite her failure to meet the aerobic standard, Ms. Meiorin did not pose a serious safety risk to herself, her colleagues, or the general public. I therefore proceed on the view that the arbitrator did not find that an applicant's ability to meet the aerobic standard is necessary to his or her ability to perform the tasks of an Initial Attack Crew member safely and efficiently. This leaves us to face squarely the issue of whether the aerobic standard is unjustifiably discriminatory within the meaning of the Code.

A. The Test

1. The Conventional Approach

[19] The conventional approach to applying human rights legislation in the workplace requires the tribunal to decide at the outset into which of two categories the case falls: (1) "direct discrimination," where the standard is discriminatory on its face, or (2) "adverse effect discrimination," where the facially neutral standard discriminates in effect: *O'Malley v. Simpsons-Sears Ltd.*, [1985] 2 S.C.R. 536 (S.C.C.) (hereinafter "*O'Malley*") at p. 551, per McIntyre J. If a *prima facie* case of either form of discrimination is established, the burden shifts to the employer to justify it.

[20] In the case of direct discrimination, the employer may establish that the standard is a BFOR by showing: (1) that the standard was imposed honestly and in good faith and was not designed to undermine the objectives of the human rights legislation (the subjective element); and (2) that the standard is reasonably necessary to the safe and efficient performance of the work and does not place an unreasonable burden on those to whom it applies (the objective element) ... It is difficult for an employer to justify a standard as a BFOR where individual testing of the capabilities of the employee or applicant is a reasonable alternative ...

[21] If these criteria are established, the standard is justified as a BFOR. If they are not, the standard itself is struck down ...

[22] A different analysis applies to adverse effect discrimination. The BFOR defence does not apply. *Prima facie* discrimination established, the employer need only show: (1) that there is a rational connection between the job and the particular standard, and (2) that it cannot further accommodate the claimant without incurring undue hardship ... If the employer cannot discharge this burden, then it has failed to establish a defence to the charge of discrimination. In such a case, the claimant succeeds, but the standard itself always remains intact.

[23] ... On the conventional analysis, I agree with the arbitrator that a case of *prima facie* adverse effect discrimination was made out and that, on the record before him and

before this Court, the Government failed to discharge its burden of showing that it had accommodated Ms. Meiorin to the point of undue hardship.

[24] However, the divergent approaches taken by the arbitrator and the Court of Appeal suggest a more profound difficulty with the conventional test itself. The parties to this appeal have accordingly invited this Court to adopt a new model of analysis that avoids the threshold distinction between direct discrimination and adverse effect discrimination and integrates the concept of accommodation within the BFOR defence.

2. Why is a New Approach Required?

[25] The conventional analysis was helpful in the interpretation of the early human rights statutes, and indeed represented a significant step forward in that it recognized for the first time the harm of adverse effect discrimination. The distinction it drew between the available remedies may also have reflected the apparent differences between direct and adverse effect discrimination. However well this approach may have served us in the past, many commentators have suggested that it ill-serves the purpose of contemporary human rights legislation. I agree. In my view, the complexity and unnecessary artificiality of aspects of the conventional analysis attest to the desirability of now simplifying the guidelines that structure the interpretation of human rights legislation in Canada.

[Justice McLachlin then discussed several difficulties with the conventional analysis, including the following:]

[40] Under the conventional analysis, if a standard is classified as being "neutral" at the threshold stage of the inquiry, its legitimacy is never questioned. The focus shifts to whether the individual claimant can be accommodated, and the formal standard itself always remains intact. The conventional analysis thus shifts attention away from the substantive norms underlying the standard, to how "different" individuals can fit into the "mainstream," represented by the standard.

[41] Although the practical result of the conventional analysis may be that individual claimants are accommodated and the particular discriminatory effect they experience may be alleviated, the larger import of the analysis cannot be ignored. It bars courts and tribunals from assessing the legitimacy of the standard itself. . . .

[. . .]

3. Toward a Unified Approach

[50] Whatever may have once been the benefit of the conventional analysis of discrimination claims brought under human rights legislation, the difficulties discussed show that there is much to be said for now adopting a unified approach that (1) avoids the problematic distinction between direct and adverse effect discrimination, (2) requires employers to accommodate as much as reasonably possible the characteristics of individual employees when setting the workplace standard, and (3) takes a strict approach to exemptions from the duty not to discriminate, while permitting exemptions where they are reasonably necessary to the achievement of legitimate work-related objectives. . . .

[52] Furthermore, some provinces have revised their human rights statutes so that courts are now required to adopt a unified approach: see s. 24(2) of the Ontario *Human Rights Code* . . .

[...]

4. Elements of a Unified Approach

[54] Having considered the various alternatives, I propose the following three-step test for determining whether a *prima facie* discriminatory standard is a BFOR. An employer may justify the impugned standard by establishing on the balance of probabilities:

(1) that the employer adopted the standard for a purpose rationally connected to the performance of the job;
(2) that the employer adopted the particular standard in an honest and good faith belief that it was necessary to the fulfilment of that legitimate work-related purpose; and
(3) that the standard is reasonably necessary to the accomplishment of that legitimate work-related purpose. To show that the standard is reasonably necessary, it must be demonstrated that it is impossible to accommodate individual employees sharing the characteristics of the claimant without imposing undue hardship upon the employer.

[55] This approach is premised on the need to develop standards that accommodate the potential contributions of all employees in so far as this can be done without undue hardship to the employer. Standards may adversely affect members of a particular group, to be sure. But as Wilson J. noted in [*Central Alberta Dairy Pool v. Alberta (Human Rights Commission)*], "[i]f a reasonable alternative exists to burdening members of a group with a given rule, that rule will not be [a BFOR]." It follows that a rule or standard must accommodate individual differences to the point of undue hardship if it is to be found reasonably necessary. Unless no further accommodation is possible without imposing undue hardship, the standard is not a BFOR in its existing form and the *prima facie* case of discrimination stands.

[56] Having set out the test, I offer certain elaborations on its application.

Step One
[57] The first step in assessing whether the employer has successfully established a BFOR defence is to identify the general purpose of the impugned standard and determine whether it is rationally connected to the performance of the job. The initial task is to determine what the impugned standard is generally designed to achieve. The ability to work safely and efficiently is the purpose most often mentioned in the cases but there may well be other reasons for imposing particular standards in the workplace. In [*Brossard (Town) v Quebec (Commission des droits de la personne)*] for example, the general purpose of the town's anti-nepotism policy was to curb actual and apparent conflicts of interest among public employees. In [*Caldwell v Stuart*], the Roman Catholic high school sought to maintain the religious integrity of its teaching environment and curriculum. In other circumstances, the employer may seek to ensure that qualified employees are present at certain times. There are innumerable possible reasons that an employer might seek to impose a standard on its employees.

[58] The employer must demonstrate that there is a rational connection between the general purpose for which the impugned standard was introduced and the objective requirements of the job. For example, turning again to *Brossard, supra*, Beetz J. held

... that because of the special character of public employment, "[i]t is appropriate and indeed necessary to adopt rules of conduct for public servants to inhibit conflicts of interest." Where the general purpose of the standard is to ensure the safe and efficient performance of the job—essential elements of all occupations—it will likely not be necessary to spend much time at this stage. Where the purpose is narrower, it may well be an important part of the analysis.

[59] The focus at the first step is not on the validity of the particular standard that is at issue, but rather on the validity of its more general purpose. This inquiry is necessarily more general than determining whether there is a rational connection between the performance of the job and the *particular standard* that has been selected, as may have been the case on the conventional approach. The distinction is important. If there is no rational relationship between the general purpose of the standard and the tasks properly required of the employee, then there is of course no need to continue to assess the legitimacy of the particular standard itself. Without a legitimate general purpose underlying it, the standard cannot be a BFOR. In my view, it is helpful to keep the two levels of inquiry distinct.

Step Two
[60] Once the legitimacy of the employer's more general purpose is established, the employer must take the second step of demonstrating that it adopted the particular standard with an honest and good faith belief that it was necessary to the accomplishment of its purpose, with no intention of discriminating against the claimant. This addresses the subjective element of the test which, although not essential to a finding that the standard is not a BFOR, is one basis on which the standard may be struck down.... If the imposition of the standard was not thought to be reasonably necessary or was motivated by discriminatory *animus*, then it cannot be a BFOR.

[61] It is important to note that the analysis shifts at this stage from the general purpose of the standard to the particular standard itself. It is not necessarily so that a particular standard will constitute a BFOR merely because its general purpose is rationally connected to the performance of the job ...

Step Three
[62] The employer's third and final hurdle is to demonstrate that the impugned standard is reasonably necessary for the employer to accomplish its purpose, which by this point has been demonstrated to be rationally connected to the performance of the job. The employer must establish that it cannot accommodate the claimant and others adversely affected by the standard without experiencing undue hardship. When referring to the concept of "undue hardship," it is important to recall the words of Sopinka J. who observed in *Renaud v. Central Okanagan School District No. 23* ..., that "[t]he use of the term 'undue' infers that some hardship is acceptable; it is only 'undue' hardship that satisfies this test." It may be ideal from the employer's perspective to choose a standard that is uncompromisingly stringent. Yet the standard, if it is to be justified under the human rights legislation, must accommodate factors relating to the unique capabilities and inherent worth and dignity of every individual, up to the point of undue hardship....

[64] Courts and tribunals should be sensitive to the various ways in which individual capabilities may be accommodated. Apart from individual testing to determine whether

the person has the aptitude or qualification that is necessary to perform the work, the possibility that there may be different ways to perform the job while still accomplishing the employer's legitimate work-related purpose should be considered in appropriate cases. The skills, capabilities and potential contributions of the individual claimant and others like him or her must be respected as much as possible. Employers, courts and tribunals should be innovative yet practical when considering how this may best be done in particular circumstances.

[65] Some of the important questions that may be asked in the course of the analysis include:

(a) Has the employer investigated alternative approaches that do not have a discriminatory effect, such as individual testing against a more individually sensitive standard?
(b) If alternative standards were investigated and found to be capable of fulfilling the employer's purpose, why were they not implemented?
(c) Is it necessary to have all employees meet the single standard for the employer to accomplish its legitimate purpose or could standards reflective of group or individual differences and capabilities be established?
(d) Is there a way to do the job that is less discriminatory while still accomplishing the employer's legitimate purpose?
(e) Is the standard properly designed to ensure that the desired qualification is met without placing an undue burden on those to whom the standard applies?
(f) Have other parties who are obliged to assist in the search for possible accommodation fulfilled their roles? As Sopinka J. noted in *Renaud, supra*, at pp. 992–96, the task of determining how to accommodate individual differences may also place burdens on the employee and, if there is a collective agreement, a union.

[66] Notwithstanding the overlap between the two inquiries, it may often be useful as a practical matter to consider separately, first, the *procedure*, if any, which was adopted to assess the issue of accommodation and, second, the *substantive content* of either a more accommodating standard which was offered or alternatively the employer's reasons for not offering any such standard ...

[67] If the *prima facie* discriminatory standard is not reasonably necessary for the employer to accomplish its legitimate purpose or, to put it another way, if individual differences may be accommodated without imposing undue hardship on the employer, then the standard is not a BFOR.... Conversely, if the general purpose of the standard is rationally connected to the performance of the particular job, the particular standard was imposed with an honest, good faith belief in its necessity, and its application in its existing form is reasonably necessary for the employer to accomplish its legitimate purpose without experiencing undue hardship, the standard is a BFOR. If all of these criteria are established, the employer has brought itself within an exception to the general prohibition of discrimination.

[68] Employers designing workplace standards owe an obligation to be aware of both the differences between individuals, and differences that characterize groups of individuals. They must build conceptions of equality into workplace standards ... To the extent that a standard unnecessarily fails to reflect the differences among individuals, it

runs afoul of the prohibitions contained in the various human rights statutes and must be replaced. The standard itself is required to provide for individual accommodation, if reasonably possible...

B. Application of the Reformed Approach to the Case on Appeal

1. Introduction

[69] Ms. Meiorin has discharged the burden of establishing that, *prima facie*, the aerobic standard discriminates against her as a woman. The arbitrator held that, because of their generally lower aerobic capacity, most women are adversely affected by the high aerobic standard. While the Government's expert witness testified that most women can achieve the aerobic standard with training, the arbitrator rejected this evidence as "anecdotal" and "not supported by scientific data." This Court has not been presented with any reason to revisit this characterization...

[70] Ms. Meiorin having established a *prima facie* case of discrimination, the burden shifts to the Government to demonstrate that the aerobic standard is a BFOR. For the reasons below, I conclude that the Government has failed to discharge this burden and therefore cannot rely on the defence provided by s. 13(4) of the Code.

2. Steps One and Two

[71] The first two elements of the proposed BFOR analysis, that is (1) that the employer adopted the standard for a purpose rationally connected to the performance of the job; and (2) that the employer adopted the particular standard in an honest and good faith belief that it was necessary to the fulfilment of that legitimate work-related purpose, have been fulfilled. The Government's general purpose in imposing the aerobic standard is not disputed. It is to enable the Government to identify those employees or applicants who are able to perform the job of a forest firefighter safely and efficiently. It is also clear that there is a rational connection between this general characteristic and the performance of the particularly strenuous tasks expected of a forest firefighter. All indications are that the Government acted honestly and in a good faith belief that adopting the particular standard was necessary to the identification of those persons able to perform the job safely and efficiently. It did not intend to discriminate against Ms. Meiorin. To the contrary, one of the reasons the Government retained the researchers from the University of Victoria was that it sought to identify non-discriminatory standards.

3. Step Three

[72] Under the third element of the unified approach, the employer must establish that the standard is reasonably necessary to the accomplishment of that legitimate work-related purpose. To show that the standard is reasonably necessary, it must be demonstrated that it is impossible to accommodate individual employees sharing the characteristics of the claimant without imposing undue hardship upon the employer. In the case on appeal, the contentious issue is whether the Government has demonstrated that this particular aerobic standard is reasonably necessary in order to identify those persons who are able to perform the tasks of a forest firefighter safely and efficiently. As noted, the burden is on the government to demonstrate that, in the course of accomplishing this

purpose, it cannot accommodate individual or group differences without experiencing undue hardship.

[73] The Government adopted the laudable course of retaining experts to devise a non-discriminatory test. However, because of significant problems with the way the researchers proceeded, passing the resulting aerobic standard has not been shown to be reasonably necessary to the safe and efficient performance of the work of a forest firefighter. The Government has not established that it would experience undue hardship if a different standard were used.

[74] The procedures adopted by the researchers are problematic on two levels. First, their approach seems to have been primarily a descriptive one: test subjects were observed completing the tasks, the aerobic capacity of the test subjects was ascertained, and that capacity was established as the minimum standard required of every forest firefighter. However, merely describing the characteristics of a test subject does not necessarily allow one to identify the standard *minimally* necessary for the safe and efficient performance of the task. Second, these primarily descriptive studies failed to distinguish the female test subjects from the male test subjects, who constituted the vast majority of the sample groups. The record before this Court therefore does not permit us to say whether men and women require the same minimum level of aerobic capacity to perform safely and efficiently the tasks expected of a forest firefighter.

[75] While the researchers' goal was admirable, their aerobic standard was developed through a process that failed to address the possibility that it may discriminate unnecessarily on one or more prohibited grounds, particularly sex. This phenomenon is not unique to the procedures taken towards identifying occupational qualifications in this case ....

[76] The expert who testified before the arbitrator on behalf of the Government defended the original researchers' decision not to analyse separately the aerobic performance of the male and female, experienced and inexperienced, test subjects as an attempt to reflect the actual conditions of firefighting. This misses the point. The polymorphous group's average aerobic performance is irrelevant to the question of whether the aerobic standard constitutes a minimum threshold that cannot be altered without causing undue hardship to the employer. Rather, the goal should have been to measure whether members of all groups require the same minimum aerobic capacity to perform the job safely and efficiently and, if not, to reflect that disparity in the employment qualifications. There is no evidence before us that any action was taken to further this goal before the aerobic standard was adopted.

[77] Neither is there any evidence that the Government embarked upon a study of the discriminatory effects of the aerobic standard when the issue was raised by Ms. Meiorin. In fact, the expert reports filed by the Government in these proceedings content themselves with asserting that the aerobic standard set in 1992 and 1994 is a minimum standard that women can meet with appropriate training. No studies were conducted to substantiate the latter assertion and the arbitrator rejected it as unsupported by the evidence.

[78] Assuming that the Government had properly addressed the question in a procedural sense, its response—that it would experience undue hardship if it had to accommodate Ms. Meiorin—is deficient from a substantive perspective. The Government has presented no evidence as to the cost of accommodation. Its primary argument is that,

because the aerobic standard is necessary for the safety of the individual firefighter, the other members of the crew, and the public at large, it would experience undue hardship if compelled to deviate from that standard in any way.

[79] Referring to the Government's arguments on this point, the arbitrator noted that, "other than anecdotal or 'impressionistic' evidence concerning the magnitude of risk involved in accommodating the adverse-effect discrimination suffered by the grievor, the employer has presented no cogent evidence ... to support its position that it cannot accommodate Ms. Meiorin because of safety risks." The arbitrator held that the evidence fell short of establishing that Ms. Meiorin posed a serious safety risk to herself, her colleagues, or the general public. Accordingly, he held that the Government had failed to accommodate her to the point of undue hardship. This Court has not been presented with any reason to interfere with his conclusion on this point, and I decline to do so. The Government did not discharge its burden of showing that the purpose for which it introduced the aerobic standard would be compromised to the point of undue hardship if a different standard were used.

[80] This leaves the evidence of the Assistant Director of Protection Programs for the British Columbia Ministry of Forests, who testified that accommodating Ms. Meiorin would undermine the morale of the Initial Attack Crews. Again, this proposition is not supported by evidence. But even if it were, the attitudes of those who seek to maintain a discriminatory practice cannot be reconciled with the Code. These attitudes cannot therefore be determinative of whether the employer has accommodated the claimant to the point of undue hardship....

[81] The Court of Appeal suggested that accommodating women by permitting them to meet a lower aerobic standard than men would constitute "reverse discrimination." I respectfully disagree. As this Court has repeatedly held, the essence of equality is to be treated according to one's own merit, capabilities and circumstances. True equality requires that differences be accommodated.... A different aerobic standard capable of identifying women who could perform the job safely and efficiently therefore does not necessarily imply discrimination against men. "Reverse" discrimination would only result if, for example, an aerobic standard representing a minimum threshold for *all* forest firefighters was held to be inapplicable to men simply because they were men.

[82] The Court of Appeal also suggested that the fact that Ms. Meiorin was tested individually immunized the Government from a finding of discrimination. However, individual testing, without more, does not negate discrimination. The individual must be tested against a realistic standard that reflects his or her capacities and potential contributions. Having failed to establish that the aerobic standard constitutes the minimum qualification required to perform the job safely and efficiently, the Government cannot rely on the mere fact of individual testing to rebut Ms. Meiorin's *prima facie* case of discrimination.

...

[Justice McLachlin concluded that the government had not shown that the *prima facie* discriminatory aerobic standard was reasonably necessary to identify forest firefighters who could work safely and efficiently, so the government could not rely on the BFOR defence.

She therefore restored the order of the arbitrator reinstating Ms Meiorin to her former position and compensating her for lost wages and benefits.]

* * * * *

It has been argued that the standard in *Meiorin* focuses the analysis more on the system than on the individual, and that it recognizes the need to restructure organizations: see Tamar Witelson, "From Here to Equality: *Meiorin, TD Bank,* and the Problems with Human Rights Law" (1999) 25 *Queen's Law Journal* 347.

14:300 SOME MAJOR EMPLOYMENT-RELATED EQUALITY ISSUES

14:310 Sex Discrimination

The law's treatment of claims of sex discrimination in the workplace illustrates how equality claims in the employment context have evolved, and how workplace discrimination issues reflect broader societal concerns.

Understanding the meaning of sex discrimination requires consideration of the societal impact of women's capacity to reproduce and the need to combine family care and work outside the home. In *Bliss v Attorney General of Canada*, [1979] 1 SCR 183, the Supreme Court of Canada held that discrimination on the basis of pregnancy was not discrimination on the basis of sex. In *Brooks v Canada Safeway*, [1989] 1 SCR 1219, the Court revisited that question. Canada Safeway's accident and sickness plan excluded pregnant women from benefits during the period prior to the birth and for seventeen weeks afterwards. Applying the test articulated under section 15 of the *Charter* in the *Andrews* case, mentioned above in Section 14:220, Dickson C.J. noted that the plan treated pregnant women less favourably than non-pregnant employees, and was thus discriminatory on the basis of pregnancy. Pregnancy itself was not a prohibited ground of discrimination under the applicable human rights statute (the Manitoba *Human Rights Act*, SM 1974, c 64), but sex was. Chief Justice Dickson held that "[d]iscrimination on the basis of pregnancy is a form of sex discrimination because of the basic biological fact that only women have the capacity to become pregnant." He said:

> Over ten years have elapsed since the decision in *Bliss*. During that time there have been profound changes in women's labour force participation. With the benefit of a decade of hindsight and ten years of experience with claims of human rights discrimination and jurisprudence arising therefrom, I am prepared to say that *Bliss* was wrongly decided or, in any event, that *Bliss* would not be decided now as it was decided then. Combining paid work with motherhood and accommodating the childbearing needs of working women are ever-increasing imperatives. That those who bear children and benefit society as a whole thereby should not be economically or socially disadvantaged seems to bespeak the obvious. It is only women who bear children; no man can become pregnant ... [I]t is unfair to impose all of the costs of pregnancy upon one-half of the population.... The Safeway plan was no doubt developed ... 'in an earlier era when women openly were presumed to play a minor and temporary role in the labor force'....

[...]

I am not persuaded by the argument that discrimination on the basis of pregnancy cannot amount to sex discrimination because not all women are pregnant at any one time. While pregnancy-based discrimination only affects parts of an identifiable group, it does not affect anyone who is not a member of the group. Many, if not most, claims of partial discrimination fit this pattern. As numerous decisions and authors have made clear, this fact does not make the impugned distinction any less discriminating.

[...]

Finally, on this point, the respondent referred to *Canada Safeway Ltd. v. Manitoba Food and Commercial Workers Union, Local 832*... in which this Court restored an arbitration award which found Safeway's "no beards" rule to be a "reasonable" rule. Safeway argues that, by analogy, this Court has already found that discrimination because of pregnancy is not discrimination because of sex. Reference was also made to *Manitoba Human Rights Commission v. Canada Safeway Ltd.*.... in which a panel of this Court dismissed the Human Rights Commission's application for leave to appeal the decision that Safeway's "no beards" rule was not discrimination because of sex. The Manitoba Court of Appeal in a unanimous decision stated that the "no beards" rule was 'definitely not a matter of sexual discrimination'.... It is contended that there is an analogy between that case and the present situation; beards are peculiar to men as pregnancy is peculiar to women; however, not all men grow beards and not all women become pregnant. I do not find these cases helpful; I cannot find any useful analogy between a company rule denying men the right to wear beards and an accident and sickness insurance plan which discriminates against female employees who become pregnant. The attempt to draw an analogy at best trivializes the procreative and socially vital function of women and seeks to elevate the growing of facial hair to a constitutional right.

* * * * *

Since the *Brooks* case was decided, human rights statutes have been amended to specify that discrimination on the basis of pregnancy is a form of sex discrimination.

From claims based on pregnancy itself have evolved claims based on experiences related to pregnancy. For example, *Carewest v Health Sciences Association of Alberta* (2001), 93 LAC (4th) 129, an employer's refusal to extend the maternity leave of a woman who wanted to breast-feed her baby at home was held by an arbitrator to be sex discrimination. Similarly, sex discrimination claims (including those related to pregnancy) may have to be reconciled with claims based on other grounds. For example, in *Quintette Operating Corp v United Steelworkers of America, Local 9113*, [1997] BCCAAA No 619 (BCDLA), the union and employer had agreed that temporarily disabled employees would be given preference for light work that was available within their own department. A pregnant employee grieved unsuccessfully that it was discriminatory not to include her in the scheme. The arbitrator held that the scheme was not discriminatory—that the grievor was being treated not as a pregnant woman but as an employee who could do only office work when no such work was available in her department.

14:320 Sexual Harassment

14:321 Sexual Harassment as Sex Discrimination

Workplace harassment on the ground of sex, race, disability, or any other ground specified in human rights legislation is recognized in law as a form of discrimination in employment. Legal recognition that harassment is a form of discrimination was not immediate, particularly in the case of sexual harassment. Some courts and tribunals considered sexual harassment not to be a form of sex discrimination, because not every woman in a given workplace was subjected to it or because it was considered to be an expression of personal attraction which with the law should not interfere. The Supreme Court of Canada considered the matter in the following case.

Janzen v Platy Enterprises Ltd, [1989] 1 SCR 1252

[The two complainants were waitresses at a restaurant. A male co-worker repeatedly kissed and touched them and made sexual advances toward them, despite their objections. When they complained to the manager, the sexual conduct ceased, but they were then subjected to verbal criticism and abuse from the co-worker and the manager. They quit their jobs and filed complaints of sex discrimination with the Manitoba Human Rights Commission. At the time, the Manitoba *Human Rights Act* prohibited sex discrimination but made no mention of sexual harassment.

The human rights adjudicator and the trial court upheld the complaint. The Manitoba Court of Appeal reversed, finding that the sexual harassment experienced by the complainants was not sex discrimination. They appealed to the Supreme Court of Canada.]

DICKSON C.J. (for the Court):

[...]

Without seeking to provide an exhaustive definition of the term, I am of the view that sexual harassment in the workplace may be broadly defined as unwelcome conduct of a sexual nature that detrimentally affects the work environment or leads to adverse job-related consequences for the victims of the harassment.... When sexual harassment occurs in the workplace, it is an abuse of both economic and sexual power. Sexual harassment is a demeaning practice, one that constitutes a profound affront to the dignity of the employees forced to endure it. By requiring an employee to contend with unwelcome sexual actions or explicit sexual demands, sexual harassment in the workplace attacks the dignity and self-respect of the victim both as an employee and as a human being.

[...]

There appear to be two principal reasons, closely related, for the decision of the Court of Appeal of Manitoba that the sexual harassment to which the appellants were subjected was not sex discrimination. First, the Court of Appeal drew a link between sexual harassment and sexual attraction. Sexual harassment, in the view of the Court, stemmed from personal characteristics of the victim, rather than from the victim's gender. Second, the appellate court was of the view that the prohibition of sex discrimination in s. 6(1) of the *Human Rights Act* was designed to eradicate only generic or categorical discrimination. On this reasoning, a claim of sex discrimination could not be made out unless all women were subjected to a form of treatment to which all men were not. If only some female employees were sexually harassed in the workplace, the harasser could not be said to be discriminating on the basis of sex. At most the harasser could only be said to be distinguishing on the basis of some other characteristic.

[...]

The fallacy in the position advanced by the Court of Appeal is the belief that sex discrimination only exists where gender is the sole ingredient in the discriminatory action and where, therefore, all members of the affected gender are mistreated identically. While the concept of discrimination is rooted in the notion of treating an individual as part of a group rather than on the basis of the individual's personal characteristics, discrimination does not require uniform treatment of all members of a particular group. It is sufficient that ascribing to an individual a group characteristic is one factor in the treatment of that individual. If a finding of discrimination required that every individual in the affected group be treated identically, legislative protection against discrimination would be of little or no value....

The argument that discrimination requires identical treatment of all members of the affected group is firmly dismissed by this Court in *Brooks v. Canada Safeway Ltd*.... In *Brooks* I stated that pregnancy-related discrimination is sex discrimination. The argument that pregnancy-related discrimination could not be sex discrimination because not all women become pregnant was dismissed for the reason that pregnancy cannot be separated from gender. All pregnant persons are women. Although, in *Brooks*, the impugned benefits plan of the employer, Safeway, did not mention women, it was held to discriminate on the basis of sex because the plan's discriminatory effects fell entirely upon women.

The reasoning in *Brooks* is applicable to the present appeal. Only a woman can become pregnant; only a woman could be subject to sexual harassment by a heterosexual male. ... That some women do not become pregnant was no defence in *Brooks*, just as it is no defence in this appeal that not all female employees at the restaurant were subject to sexual harassment. The crucial fact is that it was only female employees who ran the risk of sexual harassment. No man would have been subjected to this treatment...

... As the LEAF factum puts it, "... sexual harassment is a form of sex discrimination because it denies women equality of opportunity in employment because of their sex." It is one of the purposes of anti-discrimination legislation to remove such denials of equality of opportunity.

14:322 Defining Sexual Harassment

Around the time of *Janzen*, some legislatures amended their human rights or labour legislation to make specific reference to sexual harassment. Currently, four provinces (Manitoba, Newfoundland and Labrador, Ontario, and Quebec) and the federal jurisdiction have an explicit legislative prohibition against sexual harassment. The other provinces continue to rely on the general prohibition against discrimination in employment. Only the federal jurisdiction refers to sexual harassment in both human rights and labour legislation. The following decision makes it clear that sexual harassment is not limited to unwanted sexual advances.

Shaw v Levac Supply Ltd (1991), 91 CLLC 17,007 (Ontario Board of Inquiry)

[Shaw worked for Levac Supply for fourteen years as a bookkeeper. She was frequently teased by a male co-worker, Robertson, and her complaints to management went unanswered. The conduct included mimicking her speech, suggesting that she was incompetent, and making derogatory comments about her weight—for example, saying "waddle, waddle" when she walked around the office.]

H.A. HUBBARD, Chair:

[139] It seems to me incontestable that to express or imply sexual unattractiveness is to make a comment of a sexual nature. Whether the harasser says, "you are attractive and I want to have sex with you," or says, "you are unattractive and no one is likely to want to have sex with you," the reference is sexual. It is verbal conduct of a sexual nature, and it is sexual harassment in the workplace if it is repetitive and has the effect of creating an offensive working environment; it is sexual harassment in the form of an inappropriate comment of a sexual nature ...

[140] When a man chants "waddle, waddle" within her hearing every time an overweight woman walks about the office, or mimics the swishing sound made by her nylons rubbing together because of her weight, what purpose can he possibly have except to indicate that she is physically unattractive? Why draw attention to her bodily inelegance in such circumstances other than to indicate that she is sexually undesirable? What other way is the victim to take such comments? The respondent was not a disinterested observer simply making an objective comment upon someone's unfortunate condition. In my opinion, he knew, or ought to have known, that these gibes were ... a "sexual put-down" ...

[142] I turn now to the alternative submission of the Commission that, even if it were found that Mr. Robertson's conduct did not amount to sexual harassment so as to bring it within the scope of [s 6(2) of the Ontario *Human Rights Code* which prohibited sex discrimination and sexual harassment], it was aimed at the complainant because she is a woman, and gender harassment in the workplace is an infringement of that provision ...

[143] To begin with, the primary meaning of the word "sex" is the fact or character of being either male or female, "coitus" being a secondary meaning. Unless the context indicates otherwise, the word is to be given its primary meaning ... [E]arly decisions in the field of human rights found that sexual harassment was discrimination because of sex (i.e. "gender") in order to subject that conduct to provisions that prohibited discrimination but did not deal directly with sexual harassment. It would be odd to find that, now that harassment because of sex is dealt with in a separate provision, the word "sex" does not mean gender and that to harass a person non-sexually solely because of his or her gender does not come within the provision.

Similarly, for example, repeated sabotage by male employees of a female co-worker's safety equipment, due to resentment of the presence of a woman in the workplace, has been recognized as a form of sexual harassment. In such cases, the complainant must prove a link between the harassing conduct and her sex.

The difficult issues raised by same-sex harassment are discussed by Janine Benedet, "Same-Sex Sexual Harassment" (2000) 26 *Queen's Law Journal* 101.

14:330 Racial Discrimination

McKinnon v Ontario (Ministry of Correctional Services) (No 3), [1998] OHRBID No 10

[McKinnon was a First Nations man who had worked for the Ministry of Correctional Services as a Corrections Officer at the Metro Toronto East Detention Centre for several years. He claimed to have been subjected to racial harassment, slurs, and taunts, including the imitating of Native war cries when he entered a room, and claimed that he and his wife had been denied promotions. Eventually he filed complaints alleging that the employer had failed to prevent discrimination in the workplace, as required by Ontario human rights legislation. The Board of Inquiry found that there had been harassment, which had been condoned and indeed participated in by managers at the ministry. McKinnon and his wife had also been subjected to reprisals, including the assignment of undesirable work to him and the improper calculation of job competition test scores for her. The board also held that other employees had been targeted in racial incidents. The following passages set out some of the board's conclusions.]

H.A. Hubbard (Board of Inquiry) —

[...]

[282] The nature of the employer's duty when faced with problems of racist behaviour in its workplace and what it ought to do in order to fulfil that duty are considered in a number of cases ... In *Hinds v. Canada* ... what is involved was explained as follows ... :

> ... there is a duty upon an employer to take prompt and effectual action when it knows or should know of co-employees' conduct in the workplace amounting to racial harassment. [Citations omitted.] To satisfy the burden upon it, the employer's response should bear some relationship to the seriousness of the incident itself. To avoid liability, the employer is obliged to take reasonable steps to alleviate, as best it can, the distress arising within the work environment and to reassure those concerned that it is committed to the maintenance of a workplace free of racial harassment. A response that is both timely and corrective is called for and its degree must turn upon the circumstances of the harassment in each case.

[283] It is obvious from a review of the evidence that the workplace environment of the Centre was poisoned by racial harassment and discrimination, and that such sporadic efforts as were undertaken to address it were inadequate and often begrudged. The complainant's requests for action were viewed with suspicion and either ignored, mishandled or met with undue delay, as were the complaints of several others. The "race relations committee" (of which little has been said, as befits the matter) was ineffectual and scorned by its ostensible beneficiaries ... and nothing was achieved by the commissioning of one Natalie Bronstein to prepare a report reviewing the entire "labour relations situation" at the Centre which had apparently become something of a shambles ...

[284] For all the above reasons, it is my view that the Ministry has infringed the complainant's right to equal treatment without discrimination because of race, ancestry or ethnic origin through permitting a poisoned workplace environment as a condition of his employment....

[307] Under s. 41(1)(a) of the Code, an order awarding damages for mental anguish cannot be made unless the party whose conduct is in question acted wilfully or recklessly. It has been repeatedly held that the meaning of "wilfully" in this provision is "intentionally," "knowingly" or "deliberately".... Since I find that each of the Respondents acted in full knowledge of the unwelcome character of their conduct, it follows that such conduct was "engaged in wilfully" and that it attracts such an award.

[308] As to the quantum of general damages that ought to be awarded, counsel for the Commission said that "no specific amount is asked for [by the Commission], but it is submitted that it should be at the higher range." The position of counsel for the complainant, however, was more definite in this regard, in support of which submissions he reviewed the impact upon the complainant's health, family life and working relationships of his prolonged exposure to such abusive conduct.

[309] There was medical evidence in the form of letters from the complainant's physician in whose care he has been since 1990 ... indicating that the Complainant has been suffering from work-related stress and anxiety for which he is required to take medication. Both the Complainant and his wife spoke of the [e]ffect that these symptoms had on his appetite, his ability to sleep and his relationships with his family, and the complainant testified as to the reluctance of co-workers to be seen to associate with him and as to the damage to his relationships with supervisory staff. It was pointed out that he has had to suffer through nine years of waiting for his complaints to be resolved "throughout which time he has continued to work at the Centre and to face daily the poisoned environment"....

[310] [C]ounsel relied on the following passages from my decision in [*Ghosh v Domglas Inc*] as authority for the making of such orders:

> [116] ... It remains necessary for [boards of inquiry] to assess general damages as objectively as possible having regard to the unique circumstances of the case at hand, and in such a way as to reflect not only the mental anguish that willful or reckless conduct may cause, but elements of pain and suffering and injury to the complainant's dignity and self-worth as well. In this respect several cases have had regard to the following factors: 1. The nature of the harassment, that is, was it simply verbal or was it physical as well; 2. The degree of aggressiveness and physical contact in the harassment; 3. The ongoing nature, that is, the time period of the harassment; 4. The frequency of the harassment; 5. The age of the victim; 6. The vulnerability of the victim; 7. The psychological impact of the harassment upon the victim...
>
> [118] While the Code limits the *amount* of *an* award of monetary compensation in respect of mental anguish, it does not restrict the *number* of such awards a board may order after a hearing where it finds distinct rights to have been infringed in separate incidents, or series of incidents, and whether by the same or by different Respondents ...

The Board of Inquiry went on to award general damages against various individuals for the discriminatory conduct and reprisals. In addition, it ordered the ministry to do the following:

to compensate McKinnon for the difference between his salary and the pay he received while on "sick leave" for work-related stress; to promote both the complainant and his wife; to pay them the difference between their current salaries and what they would have received had they been promoted earlier; to move one of the respondents who had harassed McKinnon and ensure that neither he nor another respondent would work in the same facility as the complainant in the future; to amend its records to ensure that the complainant's stress-related absences would not be used against him in the future; and to give the Ontario Human Rights Commission access to the complainant's and his wife's personnel files so that it could verify that certain items had been removed and destroyed; to ensure that the orders were read on parade, attached to pay slips at Metro East Toronto Detention Centre and published in the institutional newsletter; and to establish at its own expense within six months a human rights training program approved by the commission. Extensive further proceedings ensued, with respect to implementation and allegations of contempt on the part of the ministry. See *McKinnon v Ontario (Ministry of Correctional Services)*, 2010 HRTO 1521.

14:340 Discrimination on the Basis of Disability

Concern about discrimination on the ground of disability has become much more pronounced in the past two decades. This reflects more understanding of different kinds of disabilities, and rising expectations on the part of people with disabilities. On the history of legal protection in this area, see Bernard Adell, "The Rights of Disabled Workers at Arbitration and under Human Rights Legislation" (1991) 1 *Labour Arbitration Yearbook* 167. As Adell pointed out, collective bargaining can only offer a limited response to the problem of disability discrimination because it focuses on people who are employed, and usually on full-time employees. People with disabilities, particularly severe disabilities, have a high rate of unemployment. Those who do have jobs tend to have held them for a relatively short time and to have a less stable connection with the workforce.

Disability (both mental and physical) is now listed among the prohibited grounds of discrimination in human rights legislation across the country, but it has unique features that distinguish it from other prohibited grounds.

Michael Lynk, "Disability and the Duty to Accommodate" (2001–2002) 1 *Labour Arbitration Yearbook* 51 at 53–54

> First, persons with a disability are characterized by greater heterogeneity than virtually any other group covered by the legislation. Even within the same injury, disease or condition, the varieties of disabling experience are extremely wide. Moreover, the social environment has a substantial capacity either to compound or to alleviate a disability. As the late Justice John Sopinka stated in one of his last decisions [*Eaton v. Brant County Board of Education*]:
>
>> It follows that disability, as a prohibited ground, differs from other enumerated grounds such as race or sex because there is no individual variation with respect to these grounds. However, with respect to disability, this ground means vastly different things depending upon the individual and the context.

Second, unlike the predominately fixed character of most other protected grounds, such as race or gender, the condition of disability is potentially quite mutable. A person with a disability may recover entirely, the particular condition may stabilize for an extended period of time, or the intervention of modern medicine and technology may permit the employee to work productively with few or no limitations. Conversely, a disability might deteriorate or fluctuate dramatically, both in the short and in the long term, thus rendering an employee's attempt to return to work unsuccessful. Furthermore, anyone—regardless of her or his present state of health—can potentially acquire a permanent, total or long-lasting disability, and the chances of becoming disabled increase with age.

And third, the modes of accommodation, short of undue hardship, required to extend equality to persons with disabilities, because of the greater heterogeneity of disabling conditions, are invariably broader and more complex than those required by other protected grounds. In the case of most protected grounds, accommodations can be accomplished through a change in policies or programs, together with a campaign to reform social attitudes. The responses necessary to ameliorate the social disadvantages of disablement, however, will frequently be more diverse, more individually tailored, more reliant upon technology, and probably more costly. This will often require more creativity and co-operation, and will likely necessitate a greater number of long-lasting alterations and commitments.

[Reprinted by permission of Lancaster House Publishing.]

Accommodating a disability in the workplace can be a very complex and painstaking process. In *Meiorin* (Section 14:240), the Supreme Court of Canada set out a demanding three-part test to evaluate whether workplace standards conform to human rights legislation. Under that test, an employer must meet a very high standard in order to satisfy its duty to accommodate a worker with a disability to the point of undue hardship. Potential accommodations may be as simple as making a washroom wheelchair-accessible and adjusting a shift schedule, or as complex as trying to transform attitudes to psychiatric disabilities and providing appropriate training for colleagues and managers. While the standard is high, note how the terminology around "impossibility" has evolved in the case law below.

Shuswap Lake General Hospital v British Columbia Nurses' Union (Lockie Grievance), [2002] BCCAAA No 21

INTRODUCTION

1 Ms. Sharon Lockie, the grievor, has been employed as a registered nurse ("RN") at the Shuswap Lake General Hospital (the "hospital") since May 1994. In April 1997 she was diagnosed with bi-polar mood disorder ("bmd"). She has experienced several episodes of "mania," a manifestation of her disorder, since then. One such episode occurred in early April 2000. On that occasion, one of her co-workers noted behavior consistent with mania, and, following an intervention at the workplace, the grievor went off work. There is no dispute the grievor is not fit to practice as a nurse when she is unwell.

[Although the grievor had been treated by her psychiatrist for several weeks, and in his opinion, was fit to return to work, the employer would not allow her to return to her position. The employer sought an assurance that she would not have relapse (or at least that any relapse could be accurately predicted), but the evidence indicated that bmd could not be accurately predicted. She filed a grievance and a human rights complaint, the latter being held in abeyance pending arbitration of the grievance.]

5 The Union's position is that by suspending the grievor from her nursing position due to the possibility of a relapse, the Employer is discriminating against her by reason of her mental disability contrary to Article 31 of the collective agreement, and has not discharged its duty to accommodate the grievor to the point of undue hardship. In Article 31, the parties agree to subscribe to the principles of the British Columbia *Human Rights Code*, R.S.B.C., c. 210 (the "Code").

6 The Employer advances a three-fold response to the grievance. It says it: 1) could not continue to accommodate the grievor in her position without incurring undue hardship; 2) canvassed and could not find any nursing position that would not similarly result in undue hardship; and, 3) offered to canvass the possibility of positions in the other two bargaining units in its facility, but the Union and the grievor were "not interested" in doing so pending the outcome of this proceeding....

18 Bmd is an incurable relapsing condition. Individuals with this disorder experience changes in mood state from either normality to mania, or normality to "depression." These changes in mood state are commonly referred to as "decompensations"....

20 Dr. Gibson testified that approximately two-thirds of patients with bmd experience "very significant improvement" in their disorders through treatment, and approximately 50 percent of such patients are employed. He said the duration of episodes of mania can be greatly reduced with medication. Dr. Collins and Dr. Gibson agree that work is therapeutic for individuals with bmd as it provides structure to the day/week/month. In Dr. Gibson's experience, treated bmd patients in the following occupations have all continued to be employed: specialist physicians (including the Head of Psychiatry at a Calgary-based facility), engineers, lawyers, social workers, nurses, mill workers, taxi drivers, and restaurant workers. In the health care facility where Dr. Gibson works in Alberta, he is aware of two staff members with treated bmd who have direct patient care responsibilities. He said these individuals "function well" in their positions.

The History of the Grievor's Disability and the Events Giving Rise to this Dispute

[Between October 1999 and October 2000, six of the grievor's family members died. On one occasion, she made medication errors in administering antibiotics, which she attributed to fatigue and for which she received a written warning. On the second occasion, she sought support when approached by a concerned co-worker, and was relieved by a replacement nurse. She went on sick leave in December 1999. Dr Gibson diagnosed her "decompensations," and adjusted her medications to help her cope with certain events in her life. She returned to work in February 2000 pursuant to an agreement between the employer and union, and worked without incident in her regular rotation until April, when she became overly stressed and upset at a patient who was in pain. The employer sought assurances from Dr Gibson that she would consistently meet the required standards of practice, but he balked at this because of the nature of bmd and the stresses she had been under. The employer concluded that it could not accommodate the grievor in her position, given the impossibility of predicting further relapses, and said that it could not accommodate her in any other nursing positions because they all involved direct patient care. The employer acknowledged that it did not consider potential accommodative measures involving closer medical scrutiny of the grievor.]

ANALYSIS AND DECISION

136 At issue in this dispute is whether the continued employment of the grievor as a nurse at the hospital would impose undue hardship on the Employer.

137 I accept the Employer's submission that this case does not involve general policy in health care; rather, it involves this grievor and this facility. I also accept the Employer's contention that it has accommodated the grievor's mental disability in the workplace in several ways since April 1997. The Employer has permitted various absences from work on sick leave ranging in duration from one week to approximately two months, and has replaced the grievor with casual RNs when she has had to go off work during a shift due to decompensation. The Employer designed and implemented a return-to-work plan including two weeks of supernumerary day shifts and certain reporting/monitoring mechanisms, some of which involved the grievor's co-workers. Following the April 2000 episode at work, the Employer sought further medical information to see if it could accommodate the grievor and canvassed all the nursing positions in its facility to see if the grievor could be accommodated in positions that did not entail direct patient care duties. Accordingly, this dispute involves an assessment of whether the Employer has reached the point of undue hardship in its efforts to accommodate the grievor as a nurse at its facility.

138 Applying the [*Meiorin*] principles to the evidence before me, I have no difficulty finding that a *prima facie* case of discrimination has been made out. The reason the Employer has refused to continue to employ the grievor as a nurse is her inability to assure management she will be able to accurately predict future relapses. As the inability to accurately predict relapse is a feature of bmd, I find the Employer's refusal to continue to employ the grievor is inextricably linked to her mental disability and is *prima facie* discriminatory.

139 The onus therefore shifts to the Employer to establish, on a balance of probabilities, that its standard constitutes a BFOR. The Employer's standard for the purposes of the BFOR analysis was succinctly summarized in Ms. Thompson's evidence. She said she would only permit a nurse with bmd to return to work in a position involving patient care duties if the nurse was "well controlled and no risk to patient safety and does not require other nurses to monitor [him or her] closely." In Ms. Thompson's and Mr. Jackson's opinion, the grievor did not meet this standard because she could not guarantee she would not relapse and could not assure them that relapse could be accurately predicted.

140 The Union only challenges the Employer's standard under the third part of the BFOR test. Thus, the question is whether the Employer has established that its standard is reasonably necessary by demonstrating it is impossible to accommodate the grievor in her nursing position without incurring undue hardship. . . .

141 In terms of a risk to patient safety, I find the Employer's standard is effectively one of absolute safety or perfection, not one of reasonable safety. To use the words of the Supreme Court of Canada in *PSERC*, the Employer's test of "no" risk to patient safety set an "uncompromisingly stringent standard." The Employer's relapse prediction standard effectively negates a fundamental characteristic of the grievor's mental disability. I accept the Union's contention that the Employer focused too narrowly on whether relapse could be accurately predicted. Given the medical information relating to the nature of bmd, the Employer ought to have acknowledged the fact that relapse cannot be accurately predicted, and ought to have engaged in a search for reasonable accommodative measures that would reduce any risk to patient safety to an acceptable level and still allow the grievor to work as a nurse. . . .

143 On the evidence before me, I cannot find the Employer has established either a "serious" or "unacceptable" risk to patient safety, or the "impossibility" of reducing that risk to an acceptable level through reasonable accommodative measures. The identity of those who bear the risk to safety is the patients on the unit. This undoubtedly poses a legitimate concern for the Employer. Patients reasonably expect the Employer to protect their health and safety while they are in hospital. But the evidence fails to establish that the magnitude of the risk to patient safety is serious or unacceptable. . . .

145 [T]here is no direct evidence of any specific loss or injury to any patient due to the grievor's medication errors, and no direct evidence relating to the seriousness of the loss or injury that may result . . . For these reasons, I find the Employer has failed to establish a serious or unacceptable risk to patient safety or, for that matter, to patient discomfort amounting to a safety risk due to medication errors.

146 In terms of the Employer's concern relating to patient disruption and/or nursing shortages leading to a direct risk to patient safety, I must again find the evidence falls short of establishing the Employer's factual contentions. . . .

[. . .]

151 Moreover, the evidence fails to demonstrate that it is impossible to reduce the identified risks to an acceptable level through reasonable accommodative measures. I find several material facts relating to the nature of the grievor's workplace, her disability and the way it manifests itself in the workplace must be considered.

152 First, the nature of the workplace provides certain implicit safeguards against any risk to patient health or safety escalating to a serious or unacceptable level. The grievor's duties are performed in a professional and team-based context. Unlike the solitary work of the fishing guide in [*Oak Bay Marina Ltd v British Columbia Human Rights Commission*] . . . , the grievor can be easily observed by her co-workers for approximately 30 minutes at the outset of each shift during report. The grievor is also in ongoing contact with her professional colleagues throughout a shift at the nursing station, medication carts and in the hallways. . . . On the evidence before me, I accept that it would not be a reasonable accommodative measure to impose on the grievor's co-workers an obligation to closely scrutinize her behavior in a formal monitoring system. RNs and LPNs nonetheless have a professional responsibility to observe and report co-workers' impairments to their supervisors, and I am satisfied the concerns expressed

by the grievor's co-workers in this regard can be satisfactorily addressed through the provision of an educational workshop on bmd and clear instructions from management.

153 Second, the grievor's particular indicators of relapse have, in the past, been readily observed by her co-workers and reported to supervisory or management staff...

154 Third, supervisory and/or management staff are available for reporting purposes. On day shift, a team leader is on the unit and both Ms. Thompson and Ms. Wherry are scheduled to work. For evening and night shifts, managers are available on an on-call basis.

155 Fourth, although bmd is characterized by a loss of insight as an episode evolves, the evidence is that when fellow RNs have confronted the grievor with a possibility that she may be unwell, she has accepted their observations and has agreed she needs to be replaced....

[...]

157 ... Over time, and more specifically since the April 2000 episode, the grievor and Dr. Gibson have become more familiar with the specific features of her disorder. Together, they have developed some very effective approaches to her illness in terms of treatment, monitoring and prevention of episodes of mania...

158 The grievor stabilizes quickly following an episode of mania, responds very well to treatment, and is entirely compliant to her medications. The medical evidence also establishes that the seasonal character of the grievor's illness is amendable to monitoring and medication. Moreover..., she has made significant strides since April 2000 in terms of self-education and self-identification of indicators for relapse. It is true, as the Employer submits, that the grievor's optimism in this regard has not yet been tested at its facility, but a significant fact remains. The grievor has experienced 14 months of relapse-free living during much of which she has been employed as an RN performing direct patient care duties for two different health care employers....

161 I find the Employer's willingness to engage in a meaningful search for reasonable accommodative measures enabling the grievor to return to her position as a nurse ceased when Dr. Gibson confirmed the impossibility of accurately predicting relapses. The Employer continued to focus on relapse prediction even after Dr. Gibson outlined various mechanisms that would assist in anticipating the grievor's decompensations. As I have said, the Employer's focus on relapse prediction was too narrow and its standard of "no" risk was too stringent. The evidence of both Dr. Collins and Dr. Gibson is that other nurses and doctors with bmd have returned to work and have performed their patient care duties safely with some workplace accommodations....

167 For all of the foregoing reasons, I find the Employer has failed to satisfy the third test outlined in [*Meiorin*]....

173 In all of the circumstances of this case, I find the grievor should be returned to work as a nurse on the following conditions. The grievor must:

1. continue to regularly attend her psychiatrist and physician and immediately report indicators for relapse to them;
2. continue to comply with her medical caregivers' testing, monitoring, treatment and medication recommendations;
3. continue to regularly use her familial support team to monitor her indicators for relapse;

4. authorize her psychiatrist, physician, and/or husband to contact her manager if any of them identifies indicators for decompensation or has a concern about the grievor's condition;
5. prepare a self-report of indicators of relapse and the need to increase medication and provide a copy of it to her manager, or designate, if and when requested to do so;
6. meet with supervisors or other administrative personnel to monitor her condition, if and when requested to do so;
7. not report for work if she has a suspicion she is not well;
8. agree to work predictable, routine shifts, and no night shifts;
9. agree not to work excessive overtime;
10. advise her co-workers and team leader about her disorder and the indicators for relapse;
11. comply with any reasonable accommodative measures the grievor, her Union representative and her manager negotiate for detecting early warning signs of decompensation in the workplace.

174 In terms of reasonable accommodative measures, the following will apply:
1. the grievor is to be scheduled for predictable, routine shifts with as few alterations as possible, and no night shifts;
2. the Employer is to provide the grievor's co-workers, supervisors, managers and other personnel such as the Occupational Health and Safety Officer, with an educational workshop on bmd and the detection of indicators for decompensation;
3. the Employer is to provide a facilitated discussion of co-worker concerns relating to the grievor's return to work;
4. in consultation with the grievor, her Union representative and Dr. Gibson, the Employer is to develop a procedure for staff to utilize if they detect signs of relapse at the workplace, and bring that procedure to the attention of the grievor's co-workers and supervisors;
5. the Employer is to permit the grievor to be absent from work if she identifies indicators of relapse;
6. the Employer may implement reasonable reporting mechanisms involving supervisors, other administrative personnel, or the local mental health unit to monitor the grievor's condition.

Hydro-Québec v Syndicat des employées de techniques professionnelles et de bureau d'Hydro-Québec, section locale 2000 (SCFP-FTQ), 2008 SCC 43

DESCHAMPS J.

[1] This appeal requires the Court to take another look at the rules protecting employees in the event of non-culpable absenteeism and the rules governing contracts of employment. In particular, the Court must consider the interaction between the employer's duty to accommodate a sick employee and the employee's duty to do his or her work. For the reasons that follow, I would allow the appeal and affirm the Superior Court's judgment dismissing the application for judicial review of the arbitration award in issue.

1. Facts and Procedural History

[2] The complainant's employment with the appellant, Hydro-Québec, was marked by numerous physical and mental problems: she suffered from tendinitis, epicondylitis and bursitis, had undergone a number of surgical procedures for various problems, took medication for various other physical problems (hypothyroidism, hypertension, etc.), and had episodes of reactive depression and a mixed personality disorder with borderline and dependent character traits.

[3] The complainant's record of absences indicates that she missed 960 days of work between January 3, 1994 and July 19, 2001, that is, during the last seven and a half years she was employed by Hydro-Québec. These absences were due to her many problems. One of the main problems was that her personality disorder resulted in deficient coping mechanisms and that, as a result, her relationships with supervisors and coworkers were difficult. Over the years, the employer adjusted her working conditions in light of her limitations: light duties, gradual return to work following a depressive episode, etc. As well, following an administrative reorganization in which the complainant's position was abolished and she became surplus, the employer assigned her to a position she was not owed, although the union had not consented to this.

[4] At the time of her dismissal on July 19, 2001, the complainant had been absent from work since February 8 of that year and had been seen by her attending physician, who recommended that she stop working for an indefinite period, [TRANSLATION] "until the work-related dispute is resolved". The employer had also obtained a psychiatric assessment, which included a conclusion that the complainant would no longer be able to [TRANSLATION] "work on a regular and continuous basis without continuing to have an absenteeism problem as in the past". The employer's letter informing the complainant of her administrative dismissal referred to her absenteeism, her inability to work on a [TRANSLATION] "regular and reasonable" basis and the fact that no improvement in her attendance at work was expected. The complainant filed a grievance, alleging that her dismissal was not justified.

[5] The arbitrator who heard the case dismissed the grievance. He was of the opinion [TRANSLATION] "that, in principle, the [e]mployer could terminate its contract of employment with the complainant if it could prove that, at the time it made that administrative decision, the complainant was unable, for the reasonably foreseeable future, to work steadily and regularly as provided for in the contract". The arbitrator stated that, according to the employer's experts, no medication can effectively treat a condition such as a personality disorder, and that psychotherapy can at most alleviate the symptoms very slightly. Those experts estimated the risk of depressive relapse at more than 90 percent. In their words, [TRANSLATION] "the future will mirror the past". On the other hand, the arbitrator noted that the expert for the Syndicat des employées de techniques professionnelles et de bureau d'Hydro-Québec, section locale 2000 (SCFPFTQ) ("Union"), which represents the complainant and is the respondent in this Court, was of the opinion that the complainant could

> [TRANSLATION] work in a satisfactory manner provided that it is possible to eliminate the stressors — both those related to her work and those arising out of her relationship with

her immediate family—that affect her and make her unable to work. He suggests a complete change in the complainant's work environment.

[6] The arbitrator concluded that, given the specific characteristics of the complainant's illness, if the suggestion of the Union's expert were accepted, [TRANSLATION] "the [e]mployer would have to periodically, on a recurring basis, provide the complainant with a new work environment, a new immediate supervisor and new coworkers to keep pace with the evolution of the 'love-hate' cycle of her relationships with supervisors and coworkers". The arbitrator added that some of the factors that contributed to the complainant's condition were beyond the employer's control and that the employer would not be able to eliminate stressors related to the complainant's family environment, as the suggestion of the Union's expert would require. The arbitrator found that the conditions suggested by the Union's expert would constitute undue hardship. In his view, the employer had acted properly—with patience and even tolerance—toward the complainant. He dismissed the grievance. The Union then applied for judicial review of the arbitrator's decision.

[7] Matteau J. of the Superior Court noted at the outset that the complainant's illness was a handicap within the meaning of the *Charter of human rights and freedoms* ... and that the decision to terminate her employment had been based on her inability to work regularly and steadily because of her health ([2004] Q.J. No. 11048 (QL), at paras. 2930). The judge considered the arbitrator's assessment of the duty to accommodate. She rejected the Union's argument that the employer had to show that the complainant's absences would have [TRANSLATION] "insurmountable consequences". In the judge's view,

> [TRANSLATION] [t]he arbitrator's findings on the duty to accommodate are therefore correct and are based on the opinions of the various psychiatrists who examined the employee. Although the arbitrator did not, in his reasons, refer clearly to the various steps established by the Supreme Court, he did reach the conclusion that the employer's decision was not discriminatory. This conclusion is consistent with the provisions of the *Charter* [of human rights and freedoms] and with what the Supreme Court has said on this question. [para. 51]

The Union responded by appealing the Superior Court's judgment.

[8] The Court of Appeal expressed the opinion that the complainant was not totally unable to work and that the arbitrator had misapplied the approach adopted in *British Columbia (Public Service Employee Relations Commission) v. BCGSEU*, [1999] 3 S.C.R. 3 ("*Meiorin*"). According to the Court of Appeal, the employer had to prove that it was impossible to accommodate the complainant's characteristics. Furthermore, in the court's view, the arbitrator should not have taken only the absences into account, since the duty to accommodate must be assessed as of the time the decision to terminate the employment was made ([2006] R.J.Q. 426 ...).

2. Issue

[9] The application of the *Meiorin* approach is central to this appeal. In the Superior Court and the Court of Appeal, only the scope of the duty to accommodate was really in issue, as both courts briefly noted that the employer in fact has such a duty (Sup. Ct.,

at paras. 2931; C.A., at paras. 6364). In this Court, the appellant also argued that there was no *prima facie* discrimination and that the rules on accommodation therefore did not apply. According to the respondent, however, the employer had not shown that its attendance standard was necessary for the business to be able to meet its objectives. The preconditions for the duty to accommodate are not really in issue. The real issue is instead the interpretation and application of the undue hardship standard.

3. Analysis

[10] Two problems are apparent upon reading the decision of the Court of Appeal. The first is that the standard that court applied to determine whether the employer had fulfilled its duty to accommodate was whether [TRANSLATION] "it was impossible to [accommodate the complainant's] characteristics", and the second is that, according to the court, the duty of accommodation must be assessed as of the time of the decision to dismiss.

A. Standard for Proving Undue Hardship

[11] Despite the large number of decisions concerning the rules developed in *Meiorin*, the concept of undue hardship seems to present difficulties. Certain aspects that have caused interpretation problems in the case at bar therefore need to be reviewed. First of all, it will be helpful to reproduce the explanation of the approach given in *Meiorin* (at para. 54):

> An employer may justify the impugned standard by establishing on the balance of probabilities:
>
> (1) that the employer adopted the standard for a purpose rationally connected to the performance of the job;
>
> (2) that the employer adopted the particular standard in an honest and good faith belief that it was necessary to the fulfilment of that legitimate work-related purpose; and
>
> (3) that the standard is reasonably necessary to the accomplishment of that legitimate work-related purpose. To show that the standard is reasonably necessary, it must be demonstrated that it is impossible to accommodate individual employees sharing the characteristics of the claimant without imposing undue hardship upon the employer.

[12] The relevance of the approach is not in issue. However, there is a problem of interpretation in the instant case that seems to arise from the use of the word "impossible". But it is clear from the way the approach was explained by McLachlin J. that this word relates to undue hardship (at para. 55):

> This approach is premised on the need to develop standards that accommodate the potential contributions of all employees in so far as this can be done *without undue hardship to the employer*. Standards may adversely affect members of a particular group, to be sure. But as Wilson J. noted in *Central Alberta Dairy Pool*, [[1990] 2 S.C.R. 489], at p. 518, "[i]f a reasonable alternative exists to burdening members of a group with a given rule, that rule will not be [a BFOR]". It follows that a rule or standard must accommodate individual differences *to the point of undue hardship* if it is to be found reasonably necessary. Unless no further accommodation *is possible without imposing undue hardship*, the standard is not a BFOR in its existing form and the *prima facie* case of discrimination stands. [Emphasis added.]

What is really required is not proof that it is impossible to integrate an employee who does not meet a standard, but proof of undue hardship, which can take as many forms as there are circumstances. This is clear from the additional comments on undue hardship in *Meiorin* (at para. 63):

> For example, dealing with adverse effect discrimination in *Central Alberta Dairy Pool*, supra, at pp. 52021 Wilson J. addressed the factors that may be considered when assessing an employer's duty to accommodate an employee to the point of undue hardship. Among the relevant factors are the financial cost of the possible method of accommodation, the relative interchangeability of the workforce and facilities, and the prospect of substantial interference with the rights of other employees. See also *Renaud*, [[1992] 2 S.C.R. 970], at p. 984, per Sopinka J. The various factors are not entrenched, except to the extent that they are expressly included or excluded by statute. In all cases, as Cory J. noted in *Chambly*, [[1994] 2 S.C.R. 525], at p. 546, such considerations "should be applied with common sense and flexibility in the context of the factual situation presented in each case".

[13] As these passages indicate, in the employment context, the duty to accommodate implies that the employer must be flexible in applying its standard if such flexibility enables the employee in question to work and does not cause the employer undue hardship. L'Heureux-Dubé J. accurately described the objective of protecting handicapped persons in this context in *Quebec (Commission des droits de la personne et des droits de la jeunesse) v. Montréal (City)*, [2000] 1 S.C.R. 665 ... at para. 36:

> The purpose of Canadian human rights legislation is to protect against discrimination and to guarantee rights and freedoms. With respect to employment, its more specific objective is to eliminate exclusion that is arbitrary and based on preconceived ideas concerning personal characteristics which, when the duty to accommodate is taken into account, do not affect a person's ability to do a job.

[14] As L'Heureux-Dubé J. stated, the goal of accommodation is to ensure that an employee who is able to work can do so. In practice, this means that the employer must accommodate the employee in a way that, while not causing the employer undue hardship, will ensure that the employee can work. The purpose of the duty to accommodate is to ensure that persons who are otherwise fit to work are not unfairly excluded where working conditions can be adjusted without undue hardship.

[15] However, the purpose of the duty to accommodate is not to completely alter the essence of the contract of employment, that is, the employee's duty to perform work in exchange for remuneration. The burden imposed by the Court of Appeal in this case was misstated. The Court of Appeal stated the following:

> [TRANSLATION] Hydro-Québec did not establish that [the complainant's] assessment revealed that *it was impossible to [accommodate] her characteristics*; in actual fact, certain measures were possible and even recommended by the experts. [Emphasis added; para. 100.]

[16] The test is not whether it was impossible for the employer to accommodate the employee's characteristics. The employer does not have a duty to change working conditions in a fundamental way, but does have a duty, if it can do so without undue

hardship, to arrange the employee's workplace or duties to enable the employee to do his or her work.

[17] Because of the individualized nature of the duty to accommodate and the variety of circumstances that may arise, rigid rules must be avoided. If a business can, without undue hardship, offer the employee a variable work schedule or lighten his or her duties—or even authorize staff transfers—to ensure that the employee can do his or her work, it must do so to accommodate the employee. Thus, in *McGill University Health Centre (Montreal General Hospital) v. Syndicat des employés de l'Hôpital général de Montréal*, [2007] 1 S.C.R. 161 ... the employer had authorized absences that were not provided for in the collective agreement. Likewise, in the case at bar, Hydro-Québec tried for a number of years to adjust the complainant's working conditions: modification of her workstation, part-time work, assignment to a new position, etc. However, in a case involving chronic absenteeism, if the employer shows that, despite measures taken to accommodate the employee, ... the employee will be unable to resume his or her work in the reasonably foreseeable future, the employer will have discharged its burden of proof and established undue hardship.

[18] Thus, the test for undue hardship is not total unfitness for work in the foreseeable future. If the characteristics of an illness are such that the proper operation of the business is hampered excessively or if an employee with such an illness remains unable to work for the reasonably foreseeable future even though the employer has tried to accommodate him or her, the employer will have satisfied the test. In these circumstances, the impact of the standard will be legitimate and the dismissal will be deemed to be nondiscriminatory. I adopt the words of Thibault J.A. in the judgment quoted by the Court of Appeal, *Québec (Procureur général) v. Syndicat de professionnelles et professionnels du gouvernement du Québec (SPGQ)*, [2005] R.J.Q. 944 ... : [TRANSLATION] "[In such cases,] it is less the employee's handicap that forms the basis of the dismissal than his or her inability to fulfill the fundamental obligations arising from the employment relationship" (para. 76).

[19] The duty to accommodate is therefore perfectly compatible with general labour law rules, including both the rule that employers must respect employees' fundamental rights and the rule that employees must do their work. The employer's duty to accommodate ends where the employee is no longer able to fulfill the basic obligations associated with the employment relationship for the foreseeable future.

B. Time of Accommodation

[20] The Court of Appeal held that the duty to accommodate had to be assessed as of the time the decision to dismiss the complainant was made. It stated the following:

> [TRANSLATION] Nevertheless, can it be affirmed that Hydro-Québec, having in its possession relatively unfavourable expert reports on [the complainant], has established that it had considered *all* [reasonably possible accommodation measures] <u>when it dismissed</u> [the complainant]? [Underlining added; italics in original; para. 78.]

It should be noted that the Court of Appeal's judgment was delivered prior to this Court's decision in *McGill University Health Centre*. In that case, this Court reversed a decision in which the Court of Appeal had adopted the date of dismissal as the relevant date. This Court opted to assess the duty to accommodate globally in a way that took into account the entire time the employee was absent (at para. 33):

> The Court of Appeal appears to have held that the duty to accommodate must be assessed as of the time the employee was effectively denied an additional measure (para. 31). In my view, this approach is based on a compartmentalization of the employee's various health problems. Undue hardship resulting from the employee's absence must be assessed globally starting from the beginning of the absence, not from the expiry of the three-year period.

[21] In the instant case, the Court of Appeal applied a compartmentalized approach that was equally inappropriate. A decision to dismiss an employee because the employee will be unable to work in the reasonably foreseeable future must necessarily be based on an assessment of the entire situation. Where, as here, the employee has been absent in the past due to illness, the employer has accommodated the employee for several years and the doctors are not optimistic regarding the possibility of improved attendance, neither the employer nor the employee may disregard the past in assessing undue hardship.

[22] The Court of Appeal's approach led it to criticize the employer for not trying to accommodate the complainant after February 8, 2001, the last day she reported for work. Even if the employer had not known the reasons for the complainant's absenteeism at the time it agreed to accommodate her, her personal file, including the record of her past absences, was nonetheless entirely relevant for the purpose of putting the experts' prognosis for the period after February 8 into context. The Court of Appeal found that the employer did not know the nature of the complainant's mental disorders and therefore could not have taken action in this regard. Believing that it had detected an error in the arbitrator's approach, the Court of Appeal reinterpreted the evidence and concluded that a gradual return to work was a possible accommodation. My view is that it is in fact the Court of Appeal that erred and that that court should not have interfered with the arbitrator's assessment of the evidence.

4. Conclusion

[23] I therefore conclude that the Court of Appeal's decision contains two errors of law, one relating to the standard for assessing undue hardship and the other relating to the time that is relevant to the determination of whether the employer has fulfilled its duty to accommodate. The arbitrator, on the other hand, did not err in law, and there was no justification for interfering with his assessment of the facts.

[24] For the above reasons, I would allow the appeal, set aside the judgment of the Court of Appeal and affirm the Superior Court's judgment dismissing the motion for judicial review, with costs throughout.

14:350 Who Is Under a Duty to Accommodate?

The employer and the union share the duty to accommodate. According to the Supreme Court of Canada in *Central Okanagan School District No 23 v Renaud* (excerpted below), the union may be liable for failure to accommodate not only if it has been involved in developing the impugned rule or practice, but also if it impedes the employer's efforts to accommodate. This view has been criticized because it treats the employer and the union as equal partners in collective bargaining. See Beth Bilson, "Seniority and the Duty to Accommodate: A Clash of Values—A Neutral's Perspective" (1999–2000) 1 *Labour Arbitration Yearbook* 73 at 77–79.

Central Okanagan School District No 23 v Renaud, [1992] 2 SCR 970

SOPINKA J.:—The issue raised in this appeal is the scope and content of the duty of an employer to accommodate the religious beliefs of employees and whether and to what extent that duty is shared by a trade union.... Is a trade union liable for discrimination if it refuses to relax the provisions of a collective agreement and thereby blocks the employer's attempt to accommodate? Must the employer act unilaterally in these circumstances? These are issues that have serious implications for the unionized workplace.

THE FACTS

[2] The appellant was employed by the Board of School Trustees, School District No. 23 (Central Okanagan) (the 'school board') and was a member of the Canadian Union of Public Employees, Local 523 (the 'union'). He had been employed by the school board since 1981 and in 1984 used his seniority to secure a Monday to Friday job at Spring Valley Elementary School ('SVE'). The gymnasium at SVE was rented out to a community group on Friday evenings and a custodian was required to be present for security and emergency purposes during this time. Pursuant to the employer's work schedule, which was included in the collective agreement, the job at SVE involved an afternoon shift from 3:00 p.m. until 11:00 p.m. during which only one custodian was on duty. As a Seventh-day Adventist, the appellant's religion forbade him from working on the church's Sabbath, which is from sundown Friday until sundown Saturday. The appellant met with a representative of the school board to try to accommodate his inability to work the full Friday shift. The school board representative was agreeable to the request but indicated that the school board required the consent of the union if any accommodation involved an exception to the collective agreement. Many of the alternatives discussed by the representative and the appellant involved transfer to 'prime' positions which the appellant did not have enough seniority to secure. The appellant was reluctant to accept a further alternative, that he work a four-day week, as this would result in a substantial loss in pay. In spite of these possibilities and other alternatives that could perhaps have been implemented without the union's consent, the employer concluded that the only practical alternative was to create a Sunday to Thursday shift for the appellant which did require the consent of the union.

[3] The union had a meeting to discuss making an exception for the appellant but instead passed the following motion:

> ... that the Kelowna sub-local of Local 523 demand that management of SD #23 rescind the proposal of placing any employee on a Sunday-Thursday shift. If, failing this agreement, a

Policy Grievance be filed immediately to prevent the implementation of this proposal due to the severe violations of the Collective Agreement.

The appellant was informed of the rejection of the proposed accommodation and the ongoing requirement to work on Friday nights. He was also informed of the intention of the school board to continue to seek a viable accommodation. After further unsuccessful attempts to accommodate, the school board eventually terminated the appellant's employment as a result of his refusal to complete his regular Friday night shift.

[4] The appellant filed a complaint pursuant to s. 8 of the British Columbia *Human Rights Act*, S.B.C. 1984, c. 22 (the Act), against the school board and pursuant to s. 9 against the Union. The proceedings were subsequently amended by the member designate (appointed by the British Columbia Council of Human Rights to investigate the complaints) to include a claim against the union under s. 8 as well.

[The member designate of the British Columbia Council of Human Rights upheld the complaints against both the respondent employer and the respondent union. The BC courts reversed that decision, and the complainant appealed to the Supreme Court of Canada.]

LEGISLATION

For convenience, the relevant legislation [the British Columbia *Human Rights Act*] is reproduced below:

8. (1) No person or anyone acting on his behalf shall
   (a) refuse to employ or refuse to continue to employ a person, or
   (b) discriminate against a person with respect to employment or any term or condition of employment, because of the ... religion ... of that person ...

   (4) Subsections (1) and (2) do not apply with respect to a refusal, limitation, specification or preference based on a *bona fide* occupational requirement.

9. No trade union, employers' organization or occupational association shall
   (a) exclude any person from membership,
   (b) expel or suspend any member, or
   (c) discriminate against any person or member, because of the ... religion ... of that person or member ...

[...]

THE ISSUES

[The issue before the Supreme Court of Canada was expressed as follows by Sopinka J:

Whether an employer or a labour union representing him is under any duty to effect a reasonable accommodation where, for reasons of religious belief, the employee is unable to work a particular shift

Justice Sopinka then considered the nature and extent of the employer's duty to accommodate "short of undue hardship" as outlined in the *O'Malley* case referred to in

Section 14:220. He rejected the employer's argument that the Court should hold, as the American Supreme Court had, that no accommodation requiring more than a *de minimis* cost could be required of an employer. "The use of the term 'undue,'" he said, "infers that some hardship is acceptable...." Justice Sopinka also rejected the employer's argument that no accommodation should be required which interfered at all with the rights of other employees. Impact of a proposed accommodation measure on other employees "is," he said, "a factor to be considered in determining whether the interference with the employer's business would be undue." However, he concluded:

> more than minor inconvenience must be shown before the complainant's right to accommodation can be defeated. The employer must establish that actual interference with the rights of other employees, which is not trivial but substantial, will result from the adoption of the accommodating measures. Minor interference or inconvenience is the price to be paid for religious freedom in a multicultural society.

Justice Sopinka then went on to consider the extent to which the union was also under a duty to accommodate in the circumstances at hand.]

Union's Duty to Accommodate

[39] The duty to accommodate developed as a means of limiting the liability of an employer who was found to have discriminated by the *bona fide* adoption of a work rule without any intention to discriminate. It enabled the employer to justify adverse effect discrimination and thus avoid absolute liability for consequences that were not intended. Section 8 of the Act, like many other human rights codes, prohibits discrimination against a person with respect to employment or any term or condition of employment without differentiating between direct and adverse effect discrimination. Both are prohibited. Moreover, any person who discriminates is subject to the sanctions which the Act provides. By definition (s. 1) a union is a person. Accordingly, a union which causes or contributes to the discriminatory effect incurs liability. In order to avoid imposing absolute liability, a union must have the same right as an employer to justify the discrimination. In order to do so it must discharge its duty to accommodate.

[40] The respondent union does not contest that it had a duty to accommodate but asserts that the limitations on that duty were not properly applied by the member designate. It submits that the focus must be on interference with the rights of employees rather than on interference with the union's business. It further submits, and is supported in this regard by the Canadian Labour Congress ("C.L.C."), that a union cannot be required to adopt measures which conflict with the collective agreement until the employer has exhausted reasonable accommodations that do not affect the collective rights of employees.

[41] These submissions raise for determination the extent of a union's obligation to accommodate and how the discharge of that duty is to be reconciled and harmonized with the employer's duty. These are matters that have not been previously considered in this court.

[42] As I have previously observed, the duty to accommodate only arises if a union is party to discrimination. It may become a party in two ways.

[43] First, it may cause or contribute to the discrimination in the first instance by participating in the formulation of the work rule that has the discriminatory effect on the complainant. This will generally be the case if the rule is a provision in the collective agreement. It has to be assumed that all provisions are formulated jointly by the parties and that they bear responsibility equally for their effect on employees. I do not find persuasive the submission that the negotiations be re-examined to determine which party pressed for a provision which turns out to be the cause of a discriminatory result. This is especially so when a party has insisted that the provision be enforced ...

[44] Second, a union may be liable for failure to accommodate the religious beliefs of an employee notwithstanding that it did not participate in the formulation or application of a discriminatory rule or practice. This may occur if the union impedes the reasonable efforts of an employer to accommodate. In this situation it will be known that some condition of employment is operating in a manner that discriminates on religious grounds against an employee and the employer is seeking to remove or alleviate the discriminatory effect. If reasonable accommodation is only possible with the union's co-operation and the union blocks the employer's efforts to remove or alleviate the discriminatory effect, it becomes a party to the discrimination. In these circumstances, the union, while not initially a party to the discriminatory conduct and having no initial duty to accommodate, incurs a duty not to contribute to the continuation of discrimination. It cannot behave as if it were a bystander asserting that the employee's plight is strictly a matter for the employer to solve ...

[45] The timing and manner in which the union's duty is to be discharged depends on whether its duty arises on the first or second basis as outlined above. I agree with the submissions of the respondent union and CLC that the focus of the duty differs from that of the employer in that the representative nature of a union must be considered. The primary concern with respect to the impact of accommodating measures is not, as in the case of the employer, the expense to or disruption of the business of the union but rather the effect on other employees. The duty to accommodate should not substitute discrimination against other employees for the discrimination suffered by the complainant. Any significant interference with the rights of others will ordinarily justify the union in refusing to consent to a measure which would have this effect. Although the test of undue hardship applies to a union, it will often be met by a showing of prejudice to other employees if proposed accommodating measures are adopted. As I stated previously, this test is grounded on the reasonableness of the measures to remove discrimination which are taken or proposed. Given the importance of promoting religious freedom in the workplace, a lower standard cannot be defended.

[46] While the general definition of the duty to accommodate is the same irrespective of which of the two ways it arises, the application of the duty will vary. A union which is liable as a co-discriminator with the employer shares a joint responsibility with the employer to seek to accommodate the employee. If nothing is done both are equally liable. Nevertheless, account must be taken of the fact that ordinarily the employer, who has charge of the workplace, will be in the better position to formulate accommodations. The employer, therefore, can be expected to initiate the process. The employer must take steps that are reasonable. If the proposed measure is one that is least expensive or

disruptive to the employer but disruptive of the collective agreement or otherwise affects the rights of other employees, then this will usually result in a finding that the employer failed to take reasonable measures to accommodate and the union did not act unreasonably in refusing to consent. This assumes, of course, that other reasonable accommodating measures were available which either did not involve the collective agreement or were less disruptive of it. In such circumstances, the union may not be absolved of its duty if it failed to put forward alternative measures that were available which are less onerous from its point of view. I would not be prepared to say that in every instance the employer must exhaust all the avenues which do not involve the collective agreement before involving the union. A proposed measure may be the most sensible one notwithstanding that it requires a change to the agreement and others do not. This does not mean that the union's duty to accommodate does not arise until it is called on by the employer. When it is a co-discriminator with the employer, it shares the obligation to take reasonable steps to remove or alleviate the source of the discriminatory effect.

[47] In the second type of situation in which the union is not initially a contributing cause of the discrimination but by failing to co-operate impedes a reasonable accommodation, the employer must canvass other methods of accommodation before the union can be expected to assist in finding or implementing a solution. The union's duty arises only when its involvement is required to make accommodation possible and no other reasonable alternative resolution of the matter has been found or could reasonably have been found.

[48] The member designate did not, therefore, err in applying the *O'Malley* definition of the duty to accommodate to the respondent union. Moreover, she found that the union was involved in the conduct which resulted in adverse effect discrimination and that its duty to accommodate arose by reason of this fact. The respondent union, therefore, owed a duty to accommodate jointly with the employer. The proposal for accommodation presented to the union was found to be reasonable. While it was submitted that the member designate failed to consider the trespass on the rights of other employees, I am satisfied that the only possible effect was the adjustment to the schedule of one employee to work the Friday afternoon shift in place of the appellant. The respondent union conceded in argument that there is no evidence that employees were canvassed to ascertain whether someone would volunteer to switch with the appellant. If this occurred, no employees' rights would have been adversely affected. The onus of proof with respect to this issue was on the respondent union. I agree with the member designate that it was not discharged.

[49] Finally, in view of the fact that the duty to accommodate of the union was shared jointly with the employer, it was not incumbent on the member designate to determine whether all other reasonable accommodations had been explored by the employer before calling upon the union. Nevertheless, it appears to me that the member designate was of the view that the special shift proposal was not only reasonable but the most reasonable. This view is fully supported by the evidence. Accordingly, the decision of the member designate must be upheld unless the respondents are correct that there was an error in law on her part with respect to the complainant's duty to facilitate accommodation of his religious beliefs.

Duty of Complainant

[50] The search for accommodation is a multi-party inquiry. Along with the employer and the union, there is also a duty on the complainant to assist in securing an appropriate accommodation.... To facilitate the search for an accommodation, the complainant must do his or her part as well. Concomitant with a search for reasonable accommodation is a duty to facilitate the search for such an accommodation. Thus, in determining whether the duty of accommodation has been fulfilled, the conduct of the complainant must be considered.

[51] This does not mean that, in addition to bringing to the attention of the employer the facts relating to discrimination, the complainant has a duty to originate a solution. While the complainant may be in a position to make suggestions, the employer is in the best position to determine how the complainant can be accommodated without undue interference in the operation of the employer's business. When an employer has initiated a proposal that is reasonable and would, if implemented, fulfil the duty to accommodate, the complainant has a duty to facilitate the implementation of the proposal. If failure to take reasonable steps on the part of the complainant causes the proposal to founder, the complaint will be dismissed. The other aspect of this duty is the obligation to accept reasonable accommodation. This is the aspect referred to by McIntyre J. in *O'Malley*. The complainant cannot expect a perfect solution. If a proposal that would be reasonable in all the circumstances is turned down, the employer's duty is discharged.

[52] In my opinion the member designate did not err in this respect. The complainant did everything that was expected of him with respect to the proposal put forward by the employer. It failed because the Union refused consent and the employer refused to proceed unilaterally. The appellant had no obligation to suggest other measures. Moreover, it is not suggested that the appellant turned down any reasonable proposal which was offered to him.

* * * * *

Where the provisions of a collective agreement are found to discriminate against some members of the bargaining unit on a prohibited ground, the union may be held to be in breach of its duty to accommodate even though it had tried (and failed) to persuade the employer to accept non-discriminatory terms: see *United Food and Commercial Workers, Local 401 v Alberta Human Rights and Citizenship Commission*, 2003 ABCA 246.

On the interface between the arbitral forum and the human rights forum in the enforcement of equality rights in unionized workplaces, see Chapter 9 (Section 9:420).

14:360 Systemic Discrimination

Systemic discrimination is the term used to refer to the operation of a web of factors which lead to the under-representation of particular groups in the workforce, or their over-representation in low-level jobs. As the following excerpts indicate, dramatic shifts in Canada's demographic profile have highlighted the degree of stratification in the workforce.

Statistics Canada, *"Earnings and Incomes of Canadians over the Past Quarter Century, 2006 Census,"* Catalogue number 97-563-X (Ottawa: Statistics Canada, 2008) at 21–24

Immigrants
As they integrate into the Canadian labour market, many recent immigrants initially face difficulties finding full-time full-year employment as well as locating jobs that pay relatively high wages....

[...]

Gap in earnings widens between recent immigrants and Canadian-born workers
During the past quarter century, the earnings gap between recent immigrants and Canadian-born workers widened significantly.

In 1980, recent immigrant men who had some employment income earned 85 cents for each dollar received by Canadian-born men. By 2005, the ratio had dropped to 63 cents. The corresponding numbers for recent immigrant women were 85 cents and 56 cents, respectively.

The gap widened even though the educational attainment of recent immigrant earners rose much faster than that of their Canadian-born counterparts, during this 25-year period.

Earnings disparities between recent immigrants and Canadian-born workers increased not only during the two previous decades, but also in recent years.

While recent immigrant men earned only about 63 cents for every dollar earned by their Canadian-born counterparts in 2005, the corresponding number was 67 cents in 2000.

Recent immigrant women also lost ground relative to their Canadian-born counterparts in recent years. In 2000, they earned 65 cents for each dollar received by Canadian-born women, compared to 56 cents in 2005.

The gap in median earnings between recent immigrant men and women and their Canadian-born counterparts widened both for individuals with a university degree and for those with no university degree.

[...]

Earnings gap between recent immigrants and Canadian-born larger among university graduates
The earnings gap between recent immigrants and Canadian-born workers was larger among individuals with a university degree than among their less educated counterparts.

In 2005, recent immigrant men with a university degree earned only 48 cents for each dollar received by Canadian-born male university graduates. In contrast, recent immigrant men with no university degree earned 61 cents for each dollar received by their Canadian-born counterparts.

Similar patterns were observed among recent immigrant women.

The larger earnings disparities among university graduates were observed as many recent immigrants with a university degree were employed in low-skilled occupations.

For instance, 29.8% of recent immigrant male university graduates worked in occupations normally requiring no more than high-school education in 2005. This was more than twice the rate of 11.5% among their Canadian-born counterparts.

Similarly, recent immigrant women with a university degree were more likely to work in low-skilled occupations than their Canadian-born counterparts.

This high propensity of recent immigrant university graduates to be employed in low-skilled occupations partly explains why the relative return to a university degree was smaller among recent immigrants than among Canadian-born workers.

In 2005, median earnings of recent immigrant male university graduates aged 25 to 54 were 24.0% higher than those of their counterparts with no university degree. The corresponding proportion among Canadian-born individuals was 55.5%, more than twice as high.

As a result, recent immigrant university graduates had lower median earnings than Canadian-born individuals of comparable age with no university degree. For instance, recent immigrant men with degrees had median earnings of $30,332, about 24.6% below the level of Canadian-born men without university degrees.

Derek Hum & Wayne Simpson, "Revisiting Equity and Labour: Immigration, Gender, Minority Status, and Income Differentials in Canada" in Sean P Hier & B Singh Bolaria, eds, *Race and Racism in 21st-Century Canada: Continuity, Complexity, and Change* **(Peterborough, ON: Broadview Press, 2007) 89 at 105–6**

Summary and Policy Implications

The extent to which visible minorities participate in the Canadian economy is an important public policy issue. Together with women, Aboriginal peoples, and persons with disabilities, visible minorities are a designated disadvantaged group under federal employment equity legislation. While these four social groups are very different, the matter of racial discrimination is central to visible minorities and strikes at the heart of Canada's image as a tolerant and liberal democracy. At the same time, immigrants to Canada increasingly come from "non-white" countries of origin; hence Canada's image as an accommodating, immigrant-welcoming nation is also at stake.

Our research reveals the danger of merely collating information on visible minorities to draw inferences concerning discrimination by colour. This type of exercise, typified by Table 5.1 ["Selected characteristics of Canadians by visible minority group"], is incomplete and, worse, misleading, because it combines all visible minority individuals without distinguishing their colour, ethnic origin, education, work experience, or degree of assimilation into the Canadian labour stream. A more accurate picture is presented in Table 5.3 ["Estimated wage gap between non-visible minority members and members of visible minority group: 2002 vs. 1993"], where it is apparent that, with the exception of black and Latin American men, there is no significant wage gap between visible minority and non-visible minority group membership for native-born workers. For all others, it is predominantly among immigrants that the question of wage differentials for visible minority status arises. But because two of every three new immigrants to Canada claim membership in a visible minority group, it is too easy to conflate disadvantage due to colour with disadvantage arising from immigration circumstances. At a conceptual level, appropriate ameliorative effort would require different policy responses according to whether the disadvantage is associated with colour or immigration adjustment.

What implications do these findings have for public policy? In this chapter, we have attempted to disentangle some of the determinants of wages for visible minority Canadians. It is primarily an economic—not a sociological or anthropological—examination of visible minority group membership. Yet, our findings should sound a warning bell with regards to treating visible minorities as a homogenous group for public policy formation, particularly employment equity. With more and more of Canada's immigrants belonging to a visible minority group, and with our evidence that the issue of skin colour is largely bound up with immigrant status, it may now be time to rethink Canada's emphasis on achieving equal opportunity in the labour market. Our findings suggest that efforts to achieve a colour-blind labour market, offering opportunities for all Canadian workers, may have to focus more on helping immigrants adjust and integrate rather than on the traditional prods embodying employment equity legislation. The caveat is the urgent need to examine the economic circumstances pertaining to native-born black men. Complacency that black-white differentials are more an issue for Americans than they are for Canadians should be forthrightly abandoned. American research has understandably framed the issue in terms of black-white comparisons for social and cultural reasons specific to that country's historical past. In Canada, we tend to approach the issue of race within a multi-ethnic and multicultural discourse, silently acknowledging the percolating issue of colour but remaining reluctant to privilege one non-white group over another. Yet, history shows that progression from economic and social marginalization towards full economic participation and social integration has been markedly different for Chinese and Japanese Canadians, for East Asians, and for blacks.

The persistent disadvantage facing black men in Canada (and, now, Latin American men) should neither be submerged in a multicultural discourse nor confined exclusively within a 'visible minority' context. The situation of native born black Canadians can no longer be regarded as simply one extreme end of the variation that exists across all visible minority groups in this country. The size of differential for native-born black men in Canada is too large, and too long lasting, to be viewed as a statistical outlier. Rather, the evidence is clear that economic disadvantage for blacks in Canada stems from unique structural features of Canadian society and economy, and it is hard to resist the suggestion that racial discrimination is an important factor. The statistically significant (and large) penalty for native-born Latin American men is also disturbing in this context. Will Latin American men, over time imitate the trajectory of Chinese male immigrants or that of native-born black men? These questions must be at the top of research agendas and policy priorities. Nonetheless, the necessary leitmotif of all enquiry concerning both race and immigrants in Canada bears repeating: visible minorities are an extremely heterogeneous category and should not be conflated in either statistical analysis or public policy. [Reprinted with permission.]

The Supreme Court of Canada's approach to equality under section 15 of the *Canadian Charter of Rights and Freedoms*, discussed above in Sections 14:220 and 14:230, does not see the prohibited grounds of discrimination as including economic grounds. In this regard, the Ontario Court of Appeal has held that section 15 does not require the provincial government to institute employment equity legislation: see *Ferrell v Ontario (Attorney General)* (1998), 42

OR (3d) 97 (CA), leave to appeal to SCC refused, [1999] SCCA No 79. Even if the *Charter* did require the government to take proactive measures to combat systemic discrimination in employment, that duty, in the Ontario Court of Appeal's view, had been met by the Ontario *Human Rights Code*, notwithstanding that statute's emphasis on individual rather than systemic complaints. The court added, in a dictum, that the *Charter* did not appear to impose a positive obligation on legislatures to enact measures to combat systemic discrimination.

However, section 15(2) of the *Charter* expressly allows laws and practices (in effect, affirmative action) that singles out particular groups in order to help them overcome historic inequities. In the following decision, the Supreme Court of Canada gave an affirmative action remedy for systemic discrimination in employment.

Canadian National Railway Co v Canada (Human Rights Commission), [1987] 1 SCR 1114 [*Action Travail des Femmes*]

[A human rights tribunal under the *Canadian Human Rights Act*, RSC 1985, c H-6, found Canadian National Railway (CN) guilty of discrimination on the basis of sex in its hiring practices for certain unskilled blue-collar jobs. Relying on the predecessor to section 53 of the Act (section 41(2)(a)), the tribunal ordered the company to cease certain discriminatory hiring and employment practices and to alter others, and also ordered it to set a goal of 13 percent female participation in targeted jobs in its St Lawrence region. The order established a requirement to hire at least one woman for every four job openings until the goal was reached. Finally, the company was required to file periodic reports with the commission. A majority of the Federal Court of Appeal set aside the measures dealing with hiring. The matter was appealed to the Supreme Court of Canada, which allowed the appeal.]

DICKSON C.J.C.:

By the end of 1981, there were only 57 women in 'blue-collar' posts in the St. Lawrence region of CN, being a mere 0.7 percent of the blue-collar labour force in the region. There were 276 women occupying unskilled jobs in all the regions where CN operated, again amounting to only 0.7 percent of the unskilled workforce. By contrast, women represented, in 1981, 40.7 percent of the total Canadian labour force. At the time, women constituted only 6.11 percent of the total workforce of CN. Among blue-collar workers in Canada, 13 percent were women during the period January to May 1982, yet female applicants for blue-collar jobs at CN constituted only 5 percent of the total applicant pool.

The markedly low rate of female participation in so-called 'non-traditional' occupations at Canadian National, namely occupations in which women typically have been significantly under-represented considering their proportion in the workforce as a whole, was not fortuitous. The evidence before the Tribunal established clearly that the recruitment, hiring and promotion policies at Canadian National prevented and discouraged women from working on blue-collar jobs. The Tribunal held, a finding not challenged in this Court, that CN had not made any real effort to inform women in general of the possibility of filling non-traditional positions in the company. For example, the evidence indicated that Canadian National's recruitment program with respect to skilled crafts and trades workers was limited largely to sending representatives to technical schools where there were almost no women. When women presented themselves at the personnel office, the interviews had a decidedly 'chilling effect' on female involvement in non-traditional employment; women were expressly encouraged to apply only for secretarial jobs. According to some of the testimony, women applying for employment were never told clearly the qualifications which they needed to fill the blue-collar job openings. Another hurdle placed in the way of some applicants, including those seeking employment as coach cleaners, was to require experience in soldering. Moreover, the personnel office did not itself do any hiring for blue-collar jobs. Instead, it forwarded names to the area foreman, and Canadian National had no means of controlling the decision of the foreman to not to hire a woman. The evidence indicated that the foremen were typically unreceptive to female candidates.

[...]

SYSTEMIC DISCRIMINATION AND THE SPECIAL TEMPORARY MEASURES ORDER

A thorough study of 'systemic discrimination' in Canada is to be found in the Abella Report on equality in employment. The terms of reference of the Royal Commission instructed it 'to inquire into the most efficient, effective and equitable means of promoting employment opportunities, eliminating systemic discrimination and assisting individuals to compete for employment opportunities on an equal basis.' ... Although Judge Abella chose not to offer a precise definition of systemic discrimination, the essentials may be gleaned from the following comments ... [from] the Abella Report:

> Discrimination ... means practices or attitudes that have, whether by design or impact, the effect of limiting an individual's or a group's right to the opportunities generally available because of attributed rather than actual characteristics ... It is not a question of whether this discrimination is motivated by an intentional desire to obstruct someone's potential, or whether it is the accidental by-product of innocently motivated practices or systems. If the barrier is affecting certain groups in a disproportionately negative way, it is a signal that the practices that lead to this adverse impact may be discriminatory. This is why it is important to look at the results of a system ...

In other words, systemic discrimination in an employment context is discrimination that results from the simple operation of established procedures of recruitment, hiring and promotion, none of which is necessarily designed to promote discrimination. The discrimination is then reinforced by the very exclusion of the disadvantaged group because the exclusion fosters the belief, both within and outside the group, that the exclusion is the result of 'natural' forces, for example, that women 'just can't do the job' (see the Abella Report ...). To combat systemic discrimination, it is essential to create a climate in which both negative practices and negative attitudes can be challenged and discouraged. The Tribunal sought to accomplish this objective through its 'Special Temporary Measures' Order. Did it have the authority to do so?

Section 41(2) of the *Canadian Human Rights Act* lists the orders that a Tribunal may make if it determines that a person has engaged in a discriminatory practice. Among the potential orders is an order for 'measures' to be taken under s. 41(2)(a) 'including adoption of a special program, plan or arrangement referred to in subsection 15(1), to prevent the same or a similar practice occurring in the future.' The 'program, plan or arrangement' referred to in s. 15(1) is any mechanism 'designed to prevent disadvantages that are likely to be suffered by, or to eliminate or reduce disadvantages that are suffered by, any group of individuals when those disadvantages would be or are based on or related to,' *inter alia*, sex.

Because of his stated emphasis upon the 'ordinary grammatical construction' of s. 41(2)(a), Hugessen J., for the majority in the Federal Court of Appeal, offered this reading of the paragraph ... :

> Reduced to its essentials, this text permits the Tribunal to order the taking of measures aimed at preventing the future occurrence of a discriminatory practice on the part of a person found to have engaged in such a practice in the past.

He stressed that '[t]he sole permissible purpose for the order is prevention' and that the text 'does not allow restitution for past wrongs.' Therefore, the 'program, plan or arrangement' authorized by reference to s. 15(1) would necessarily be limited by the language of s. 41(2)(a) to a mechanism designed 'to prevent the same or a similar practice occurring in the future.' Hugessen J. recognized the special difficulties involved in dealing with systemic discrimination ... :

> ... I recognize that by its very nature systemic discrimination may require creative imaginative preventive measures. Such discrimination has its roots, not in any deliberate desire to exclude from favour, but in attitudes, prejudices, mindsets and habits which may have been acquired over generations. It may well be that hiring quotas are the proper way to achieve the desired result.

Hugessen J. simply did not believe, without some precise factual showing, that specific hiring goals could be related to prevention, and thereby fall within s. 41(2)(a). The 'Special Temporary Measures' ordered by the Tribunal were struck down because the employment objectives imposed in the order were expressed in terms which, in Justice Hugessen's view, indicated that the objective was remedial and not preventive.

To evaluate this argument it is important to remember exactly what was ordered by the Human Rights Tribunal. The impugned section of the Order was headed 'Special Temporary Measures' and the heart of the employment equity programme was contained in paragraph 2:

> ... Canadian National is ordered to hire at least one woman for every four non-traditional positions in the future ... When it is in effect, daily adherence to the one-in-four ratio will not be required in order to give the employer a better choice in the selection of candidates. However, it must be complied with over each quarterly period until the desired objective of having 13% of non-traditional positions filled by women is achieved.

It should be underscored once again that the objective of 13 percent female participation was not arbitrary, for it corresponded to the national average of women involved in the non-traditional occupations.

In his dissenting opinion in the Federal Court of Appeal, MacGuigan J. accepted, as I do, that s. 41(2)(a) was designed to allow human rights tribunals to prevent future discrimination against identifiable protected groups, but he held that 'prevention' is a broad term and that it is often necessary to refer to historical patterns of discrimination in order to design appropriate strategies for the future. He noted the deep roots of discrimination against women at CN. It is an uncontradicted fact that the hiring and promotion policies of CN and the enormous problems faced by the tiny minority of women in the blue-collar workforce amounted to a systematic denial of women's equal employment opportunities.

Justice MacGuigan's point is made abundantly clear when one considers the context in which the challenged order was issued. It bears repeating that the tribunal had found that at the end of 1981 only 0.7 percent of blue-collar jobs in the St. Lawrence Region of Canadian National were held by women. The Tribunal found, furthermore that the small number of women in non-traditional jobs tended to perpetuate exclusion and, in effect, to cause additional discrimination. Moreover, Canadian National knew that its policies and practices, although perhaps not discriminatory in intent, were discriminatory in effect, yet had done nothing substantial to rectify the situation. When confronted with such a case of 'systemic discrimination,' it may be that the type of order issued by the Tribunal is the only means by which the purpose of the *Canadian Human Rights Act* can be met. In any program of employment equity, there simply cannot be a radical dissociation of 'remedy' and 'prevention.' Indeed there is no prevention without some form of remedy. The point was explained clearly by Professors Greschner and Norman in their Case Comment on the majority judgment of the Federal Court of Appeal in this case.... They emphasize that an employment equity program:

> ... tries to break the causal links between past inequalities suffered by a group and future perpetuation of the inequalities. It simultaneously looks to the past and to the future, with no gap between cure and prevention. Any such program will remedy past acts of discrimination against the group and prevent future acts at one and the same time. That is the very point of affirmative action.
>
> This point demands repetition.... When a program is said to be aimed at remedying past acts of discrimination, such as by bringing women into blue-collar occupations, it necessarily is preventing future acts of discrimination because the presence of women will help break down generally the notion that such work is man's work and more specifically, will help change the practices within that workplace which resulted in the past discrimination against women. From the other perspective, when a program is said to be aimed at preventing future acts of discrimination (again by bringing women into blue-collar occupations), it necessarily is also remedying past acts of discrimination because women as a group suffered from the discrimination and are now benefiting from the program.

Unlike the remedies in s. 41(2)(b)–(d), the 'remedy' under s. 41(2)(a) is directed towards a group and is therefore not merely compensatory but is itself prospective. The benefit is always designed to improve the situation for the group in the future, so that a successful employment equity programme will render itself otiose.

To see more clearly why the Special Temporary Measures Order is prospective, it would be helpful to review briefly the theoretical underpinnings of employment equity programs. I have already stressed that systemic discrimination is often unintentional.

It results from the application of established practices and policies that, in effect, have a negative impact upon the hiring and advancement prospects of a particular group. It is compounded by the attitudes of managers and co-workers who accept stereotyped visions of the skills and 'proper role' of the affected group, visions which lead to the firmly held conviction that members of that group are incapable of doing a particular job, even when that conclusion is objectively false. An employment equity program, such as the one ordered by the Tribunal in the present case, is designed to break a continuing cycle of systemic discrimination. The goal is not to compensate past victims or even to provide new opportunities for specific individuals who have been unfairly refused jobs or promotion in the past, although some such individuals may be beneficiaries of an employment equity scheme. Rather, an employment equity program is an attempt to ensure that future applicants and workers from the affected group will not face the same insidious barriers that blocked their forebears.

An employment equity program thus is designed to work in three ways. First, by countering the cumulative effects of systemic discrimination, such a program renders further discrimination pointless. To the extent that some intentional discrimination may be present, for example, in the case of a foreman who controls hiring and who simply does not want women in the unit, a mandatory employment equity scheme places women in the unit despite the discriminatory intent of the foreman. His battle is lost.

Secondly, by placing members of that group that had previously been excluded into the heart of the workplace and by allowing them to prove ability on the job, the employment equity scheme addresses the attitudinal problem of stereotyping. For example, if women are seen to be doing the job of 'brakeman' or heavy cleaner or signaler at Canadian National, it is no longer possible to see women as capable of fulfilling only certain traditional occupational roles. It will become more and more difficult to ascribe characteristics to an individual by reference to the stereotypical characteristics ascribed to all women.

Thirdly, an employment equity programme helps to create what has been termed a 'critical mass' of the previously excluded group in the work place. This 'critical mass' has important effects. The presence of a significant number of individuals from the targeted group eliminates the problems of 'tokenism'; it is no longer the case that one or two women, for example, will be seen to 'represent' all women ... Moreover, women will not be so easily placed on the periphery of management concern. The 'critical mass' also effectively remedies systemic inequities in the process of hiring:

> There is evidence that when sufficient minorities/women are employed in a given establishment, the informal processes of economic life, for example, the tendency to refer friends and relatives for employment, will help to produce a significant minority [or female] applicant flow.
>
> (Alfred W. Blumrosen, 'Quotas, Common Sense and Law in Labour Relations: Three Dimensions of Equal Opportunity' in Walter S. Tarnopolsky, ed., *Some Civil Liberties Issues of the Seventies* ...)

If increasing numbers of women apply for non-traditional jobs, the desire to work in blue collar occupations will be less stigmatized. Personnel offices will be forced to treat women's applications for non-traditional jobs more seriously. In other words, once a 'critical mass' of the previously excluded group has been created in the workforce, there is a significant chance for the continuing self-correction of the system.

When the theoretical roots of employment equity programs are exposed, it is readily apparent that, in attempting to combat systemic discrimination, it is essential to look to the past patterns of discrimination and to destroy those patterns in order to prevent the same type of discrimination in the future. It is for this reason that the language of the Tribunal's Order for Special Temporary Measures may appear 'remedial.' In any case, as was stressed by MacGuigan J. in his dissent, the important question is not whether the Tribunal's order tracked the precise wording of s. 41(2)(a), but whether the actual measures ordered could be construed fairly to fall within the scope of the section. One should look to the substance of the order and not merely to its wording.

For the sake of convenience, I will summarize my conclusions as to the validity of the employment equity program ordered by the Tribunal. To render future discrimination pointless, to destroy discriminatory stereotyping and to create the required 'critical mass' of target group participation in the workforce, it is essential to combat the effects of past systemic discrimination. In so doing, possibilities are created for the continuing amelioration of employment opportunities for the previously excluded group. The dominant purpose of employment equity programs is always to improve the situation of the target group in the future. MacGuigan J. stressed in his dissent that 'the prevention of systemic discrimination will reasonably be thought to require systemic remedies.' Systemic remedies must be built upon the experience of the past so as to prevent discrimination in the future. Specific hiring goals, as Hugessen J. recognized, are a rational attempt to impose a systemic remedy on a systemic problem. The Special Temporary Measures Order of the Tribunal thus meets the requirements of s. 41(2)(a) of the *Canadian Human Rights Act*. It is a 'special program, plan or arrangement' within the meaning of s. 15(1) and therefore can be ordered under s. 41(2)(a). The employment equity order is rationally designed to combat systemic discrimination in the Canadian National St. Lawrence Region by preventing 'the same or a similar practice occurring in the future.'

A secondary problem must now be addressed, the fact that the Order of the Tribunal was expressed in terms of an employment goal, rather than a hiring goal. This methodology might increase the belief that the Order was remedial and not, properly speaking, preventive. The Tribunal held, however, that the systemic discrimination at CN occurred not only in hiring but once women were on the job as well. The evidence revealed that there was a high level of publicly expressed male antipathy towards women which contributed to a high turnover rate amongst women in blue-collar jobs. As well, many male workers and supervisors saw any female worker in a non-traditional job as an upsetting phenomenon and as a 'job thief.' To the extent that promotion was dependent upon the evaluations of male supervisors, women were at a significant disadvantage. Moreover, because women generally had a low level of seniority, they were more likely to be laid off. For the employment equity program to be effective in creating the 'critical mass' and in destroying stereotypes, the goals had to be expressed in terms of actual employment. Otherwise the reasonable objectives of the scheme would have been defeated. The dominant purpose remained to improve the employment situation for women at CN in the future.

The call in *Action Travail des Femmes* for effective systemic remedies for systemic discrimination has since had a reality check. In *Moore v British Columbia (Education)*, 2012 SCC 61 (which was not an employment case), the Supreme Court interpreted the remedial authority of the human rights tribunal in a restrictive manner, holding that the remedy "must flow from the claim," and since the claim was made by one individual complainant (although it entailed some evidence of systemic discrimination), the remedy should be tied specifically to that individual. On the administrative and judicial barriers to effective crafting and enforcement of systemic remedies through adjudication, see Dianne Pothier, "Adjudicating Systemic Equality Issues: The Unfulfilled Promise of *Action Travail des Femmes*" (2014) 18 *Canadian Labour & Employment Law Journal* 177. Pothier concludes on pages 206–8:

> In *Action Travail des Femmes*, the Supreme Court of Canada seemed to have assumed that systemic remedies would be an effective response to systemic discrimination in the face of a recalcitrant respondent. The Canadian Human Rights Tribunal in that case had taken care to craft detailed orders which appeared to set out enough particulars to be readily enforceable, but barriers to the enforcement of the hiring quota proved to be insurmountable. CN's resistance was not effectively countered by the Canadian Human Rights Commission, and federal legislative intervention clamped down on future hiring quota orders. Developments since *Action Travail des Femmes* have not made the enforcement of systemic remedies in human rights cases any easier.
>
> Systemic remedies frequently give rise to complex issues regarding compliance with human rights legislation. As *McKinnon* and *Moore* have shown, it is no simple task to remedy a poisoned work environment, or a public school system that is not responsive to the needs of disabled students. That task poses major challenges to the crafting of remedies by human rights tribunals. Although we may expect tribunals to be expert in the matter of discrimination, they will unlikely be expert in the operational particularities of the specific context in which a case arises. If the respondent cooperates, setting out general principles may suffice to secure compliance with human rights obligations. But if the respondent resists, orders based on general principles may not give enough direction.
>
> Faced with that dilemma, how far can a tribunal go in specifying what must be done to comply with human rights legislation? When the tribunal reaches the limits of its expertise, third-party experts might be engaged, but their legitimacy may be challenged. The responsibility of respondents to manage their own affairs is subject to their human rights obligations, but reconciling the two remains very difficult when the respondent refuses to do what it is told. The more complex the issues of compliance with human rights legislation are in the particular case, the harder it is to draft orders that are detailed enough to be enforceable. Where an order is vague, determining whether it has been complied with is a laborious task. Where litigation is protracted, as in *McKinnon*, human rights enforcement gets lost in the shuffle; settlement after 23 years does not reflect well on its efficacy.
>
> The enforcement of human rights legislation in relation to fundamental public policy and budgetary allocations raises difficult questions about institutional roles. In *Moore*, the British Columbia Human Rights Tribunal had concluded that systemic remedies were necessary to hold both the province and the school district accountable for making public education accessible to students with learning disabilities. Those remedies

were never enforced, having been stayed pending judicial review and ultimately declared invalid at all court levels. The Supreme Court of Canada took a strong stand on the meaning of adverse-effects discrimination by finding that the school district had discriminated against Jeffrey Moore, but the Court gave short shrift to the Tribunal's systemic remedies by setting them aside in a superficial analysis. Insisting that remedies be tied directly to the individual complainant, the Court pulled back from its earlier jurisprudence which had emphasized the broadly-based transformative effect of human rights obligations. Nor did the Court seriously address how respondents, especially governments, can be held meaningfully accountable for compliance with their human rights obligations.

The Supreme Court of Canada's 1987 decision in *Action Travail des Femmes* represented a high-water mark in the invocation of systemic remedies in human rights cases. It held out the promise that systemic remedies could be realistically counted upon to redress discrimination. Unfortunately, that promise has not been fulfilled. Complex remedies have proven notoriously difficult to enforce where the respondent considers that its responsibility to manage is being undermined, and limitations on the availability of systemic remedies in general render issues of enforcement practically moot.

In light of *Moore*, the viability of systemic remedies is now an open question. Even when the merits of such remedies are acknowledged, crafting enforceable orders against recalcitrant respondents is made more difficult by considerations of institutional capacity and by the complexity of the particular context. The human rights adjudication process has not developed a broadly effective strategy to deal with those who are determined to resist strong remedies. Have we run up against the limits of what law can accomplish? [Originally published in (2015) 18:1 CLEJ 177. Reproduced with the permission of Lancaster House.]

For an alternative approach that the Court might have taken in the context of the *United Nations Convention on the Rights of Persons with Disabilities*, 30 March 2007, A/RES/62/170, see Ravi Malhotra & Robin F Hansen, "The United Nations Convention on the Rights of Persons with Disabilities and its Implications for the Equality Rights of Canadians with Disabilities: The Case of Education" (2011) 29 *Windsor Yearbook of Access to Justice* 73.

14:370 Pay Equity

The existence of a gap between the wages of men and women is well established. After closing for two decades, largely because of a decline in the median earnings of young men, the wage gap among new market entrants has remained constant since 2000: young women working full-time earn about 85 cents for each dollar earned by their male counterparts, despite a marked rise in the educational achievements of women. Overall, women working full time earn only 70 percent of what men do, down from 72 percent since the mid-1990s. See Statistics Canada, "*Earnings and Income of Canadians Over the Past Quarter Century*, 2006 Census," Catalogue number 97-563-X (Ottawa: Statistics Canada, 2006). The extent of the gap is due to many factors, including education, age, race, training, labour market experience, length of service, disability, marital status, and geographical region. It is also influenced by sex discrimination in the labour market and in society at large.

Prior to the earliest pay equity legislation, it was not uncommon for employers to maintain two wage rates for the same position on the basis of sex, partly on the reasoning that men needed more money because they were the family breadwinners. In the early 1950s, statutes began to address the relatively straightforward problem of unequal pay for equal work, by forbidding employers from paying women less when they did the same work as men.

The legislation did not address a far more significant contributor to the wage gap: the fact that women were overrepresented in lower-paying jobs. This problem of occupational segregation led to a campaign to go beyond equal pay for the same work and to require equal pay for work of equal *value*—what has come to be known as "pay equity." Advocates of pay equity legislation hypothesized that a gender-neutral job evaluation scheme would disclose that many lower-paying jobs done mostly by women required skills, effort, responsibility, and working conditions equivalent to those of higher-paying jobs done mostly by men.

Originally, guarantees of equal pay for men and women doing the same work formed part of human rights and fair employment statutes. Those statutes require individual workers or groups of workers to file complaints of discrimination against their employer. Such complaints can be costly and time-consuming, and they have been criticized as addressing the problem in a piecemeal fashion.

As a result, some provinces have enacted legislation that obliges some or all employers to take measures to attain pay equity between male and female job categories. In Quebec, this legislation applies to all employers; in Ontario, private sector employers with less than 10 employees are exempt. In most other provinces, it applies only in the public and quasi-public sector. The legislation requires employers to submit a pay equity plan in accordance with the specified calculation methods. Employees or unions may bring complaints of non-compliance to a specialized administrative tribunal.

The Conservative government elected in Ontario in 1995 repealed a portion of the *Pay Equity Act*, RSO 1990 c P.7, that dealt with broader public sector workplaces, which were mostly female. Implementing pay equity in these workplaces was difficult, since there was no obvious male-dominated job category that could serve as a comparator. The repealed legislative provisions specified that in such cases, a "proxy comparison method" was to be used to calculate whether pay equity adjustments were called for, and almost all female-dominated workplaces in the public sector had been the subject of proxy comparison orders. (The proxy comparison method was never extended to the Ontario private sector.) A 1996 legislative amendment, Schedule J, capped existing proxy pay equity adjustments at 3 percent of the employer's 1993 payroll and prohibited any further use of the proxy comparison method. As a result, the women affected had only 22 percent of their pay differential corrected.

A union representing 5,200 Ontario broader public-sector workers argued that Schedule J violated section 15(1) of the *Charter*. Their application for a declaration of invalidity was granted in *Service Employees International Union, Local 204 v Ontario (AG)* (1997), 35 OR (3d) 508 (Gen Div). Justice O'Leary said:

> There is no doubt that the applicants are members of the disadvantaged group the *Pay Equity Act* was designed to benefit and that they have been excluded from its reach by the Schedule J amendment. Accordingly, their claim of discrimination must succeed unless the government can justify the exclusion under s. 1 of the *Charter*.

Justice O'Leary went on to hold that the Ontario government had failed to provide an adequate justification under section 1 of the *Charter* for its legislative action. Specifically, he rejected its expert evidence that the proxy method was not a valid way of quantifying gender-based systemic wage discrimination in the female-dominated broader public sector. Therefore, the government did not have a pressing and substantial objective in enacting Schedule J. Justice O'Leary continued:

> I point out there was no attempt by the respondent to establish that in order to live within the $500 million cap government placed on pay equity spending, the government had to remove the proxy method and throw the full weight of the funding reduction on those working in the proxy sector. It was not explained why the burden could not have been apportioned equitably amongst all workers in the broader public sector who benefited from the $380 million still paid annually by government towards the cost of wage adjustments in that sector.
>
> It must also be noted that the Schedule J amendment cannot be justified as an incremental approach to pay equity. It is not a matter of putting off to another day, when the same can be afforded, the correction of the gender-based systemic wage inequity from which women in the proxy sector undoubtedly suffer. Schedule J and the government's position on this application tells proxy sector women they are not and cannot be covered under the *Pay Equity Act* even though other women in the broader public sector have had their systemic gender-based wage inequity 100 percent cured.

CONCLUSION

It is a matter of choice for government as to whether or not it legislates to remove inequity. When, however, government decides to legislate and identifies the disadvantaged group the legislation is intended to benefit, then it must, subject to s. 1 of the *Charter*, make the legislation apply fairly and equally to all within the group or government itself is guilty of discriminating. This is especially so where government itself picks up the cost of removing the inequality that is the focus of the legislation. Where legislation discriminates against a portion of the group the legislation is designed to help, the legislation contravenes s. 15(1) of the *Charter* and so is *ultra vires* unless the discrimination is demonstrably justified under s. 1 of the *Charter*.

The *Pay Equity Act*, because of the 1996 Schedule J amendment, discriminates against proxy sector women by denying them the opportunity of quantifying and correcting the systemic gender-based wage inequity from which they suffer, a benefit the *Act* grants to other women working in the broader public sector.

The discrimination has not been justified under s. 1 of the *Charter*, in that the stated objective of the Schedule J amendment does not warrant overriding the constitutional right of equal benefit of the law. Indeed, the stated objective—the restoring of the *Pay Equity Act* to true pay equity principles—I find to be mistaken. Proxy method was and is an appropriate pay equity tool in keeping with the intent of the *Pay Equity Act* to relieve women, including those working in female-segregated workplaces in the broader public sector, from systemic gender-based wage discrimination.

Since it was the 1996 Schedule J amendment that created the discrimination, I declare that Schedule J of the *Savings and Restructuring Act, 1996*, amending the *Pay Equity Act*, is unconstitutional and of no force and effect.

* * * * *

Walden v Canada (Social Development), 2007 CHRT 56

[Sections 7 and 10 of the *Canadian Human Rights Act* provided as follows:

7. It is a discriminatory practice, directly or indirectly, ...
   (b) in the course of employment, to differentiate adversely in relation to an employee, on a prohibited ground of discrimination.

10. It is a discriminatory practice for an employer, employee organization or employer organization
   (a) to establish or pursue a policy or practice that deprives or tends to deprive an individual or class of individuals of any employment opportunities on a prohibited ground of discrimination.]

[1] ... The Complainants are a group of predominantly female nurses who work as medical adjudicators in the CPP Disability Benefits Program. For 35 years they have worked alongside doctors, a predominantly male group of workers, in a common enterprise—the determination of eligibility for CPP disability benefits.

[2] The Complainants say that the doctors (known as "medical advisors") and nurses (known as "medical adjudicators") do the same work: they apply their medical knowledge to determine eligibility for CPP disability benefits. When medical advisors perform that work, they are classified as health professionals within the Public Service classification system. However, when the medical adjudicators do this work, they are not classified as health professionals. Rather, they are designated as program administrators. As a result of their classification, medical advisors receive better compensation, benefits, training, professional recognition and opportunities for advancement than medical adjudicators.

[3] The Complainants assert that it is discriminatory to treat a female dominated group of workers differently from a male dominated group when they are performing the same or substantially similar work. They seek to be treated the same as medical advisors.

[4] The issues to be determined in this complaint are whether the Respondents have discriminated against the Complainants on the basis of their gender by: (1) treating them differently from the medical advisors contrary to s. 7 of the *Canadian Human Rights Act*; and/or (2) pursuing a practice that deprives the Complainants of employment opportunities, contrary to section 10 of the *CHRA*. ...

[The tribunal went on to discuss the issues of sufficient evidence, comparator groups, differential treatment, and the employer's response to these issues.]

[38] A discriminatory practice is defined under s. 7 of the Act as "adverse differentiation on the basis of a prohibited ground of discrimination." To establish a *prima facie* case under s. 7, the Complainants must present evidence that they are being adversely

differentiated on the basis of their gender. With respect to s. 10(a) of the Act, evidence must be presented of a policy or practice that deprives, or tends to deprive, the Complainants of an employment opportunity based on a prohibited ground of discrimination.

[39] Statistical evidence that apparently neutral conduct negatively affects a disproportionate number of members of a protected group is sufficient to establish a *prima facie* case under sections 7 and 10 . . .

[. . .]

(i) What is the appropriate comparator group?
[42] The appropriate comparator group is implicit in the requirement for establishing a *prima facie* case: it is the group of predominantly male workers who are performing the same or substantially similar work to that of the Complainants. That group is the medical advisors. There is no other group of predominantly male employees in the CPP Disability Benefits program whose work could arguably be described as the same as or substantially similar to that of the adjudicators.

(ii) What is the evidence of gender predominance?
[43] Before they are hired, medical adjudicators are required to provide proof that they are licensed to practice as a Registered Nurse in Canada. There was no dispute that 95% of nurses are women. The predominance of women in nursing and the requirement to produce a nursing license before being hired as an adjudicator results in an overwhelming preponderance of women in the medical adjudicator position. Currently, according to the Respondents, 95% of all medical adjudicators are women.

[44] The Respondents produced evidence that 80% of medical advisors are men. . . .

[67] Based on the foregoing evidence, I am satisfied that the Complainants have established a *prima facie* case that the work they have done since March of 1978, and are still doing at the present time, is the same or substantially similar to the work of the medical advisors. . . .

[81] [Based on evidence of differential professional recognition, salary/benefits, payment of professional fees and continuing education/training, and career advancement,] I find that the Complainants have established a *prima facie* case that since March of 1978, they were, and still are treated differently from the predominantly male group of medical advisors who performed the same or substantially similar work as them in the past and continue to do so in the present. . . .

[The tribunal found that it was of no consequence that the complainants had only recently made the argument that they were doing the same work as medical advisors. On the basis of previous jurisprudence and the French version of the relevant section of the Act, the tribunal found (at paras 97–101) that the term "employment opportunities" referred to conditions enabling employment and the advancement of individuals in their employment, thus including the areas of deprivation alleged by the complainants. These included (para 99): "recognition and classification as health professionals; payment of professional fees and training/educational opportunities on the same basis as the medical advisors; and opportunities for career advancement as health professionals," which all affected their "ability to enhance their earnings and career potential within the Public Service." With respect to the identification of the appropriate comparator group, the tribunal said:]

[107] Moreover, the Respondents' argument that the male medical adjudicators' work should be compared to that of the female medical adjudicators is unreasonable. The male adjudicators are not a separate group, but rather are part of the predominantly female group of medical adjudicators. Therefore, by virtue of their membership in this group, they too are subject to any potential discriminatory difference in treatment vis-à-vis the medical advisors. A comparison of their work with that of the female adjudicators would not be a meaningful indicator of equal treatment of the overwhelmingly female population in the group. The Complainants in this case allege that their inferior working conditions are a function of the strong gender predominance of their occupational group. This allegation cannot be properly tested by examining the working conditions of this small male minority within their ranks.

[108] Therefore, I maintain that the appropriate comparator group is the predominantly male group of medical advisors....

[120] The advisors bring a different kind of knowledge to the program, perform some different tasks and have been given different responsibilities than the adjudicators. This provides a reasonable and non-discriminatory explanation for some of the differences in salary and benefits. It also explains why the advisor and the adjudicator positions might occupy different levels within a classification standard in Health Services.

[121] However, the differences in the work responsibilities of the respective positions are not extensive enough to explain the wide disparity in treatment between the advisors and the adjudicators. In particular, the Respondent has failed to provide a reasonable non-discriminatory response to the following question: why have the advisors been recognized as health professionals, and compensated accordingly, when their primary function is to make eligibility determinations and yet, when the adjudicators perform the same primary function, they are designated as program administrators and are paid half the salary of the advisors? ...

[136] In my view, if the medical advisors are deemed to be applying their medical knowledge to the safety and physical well-being of people and assessing medical fitness for the purpose of determining eligibility, then the adjudicators should also be deemed to be doing the same for the purposes of classification. The Respondents have failed to provide a reasonable, non- discriminatory reason for the differential application of the principles of classification in the Public Service. They have failed to explain their refusal to recognize the professional nature of the work done by a group of predominantly female workers when they are performing essentially the same core function as predominantly male workers whose work receives professional recognition.

[137] Similarly, the Respondents have not provided a reasonable, non-discriminatory explanation for treating the adjudicators differently from the advisors with respect to the payment of professional fees and educational/training opportunities and the provision of career advancement opportunities. The adjudicators use their medical expertise to determine eligibility, just as advisors do. They are health professionals and should be provided with the same employment advantages and opportunities for career development and advancement that other health professionals have in the Public Service....

(iii) Have the Respondents established that the differential treatment is a bona fide occupational requirement?

[139] Subsections 15(1)(a) and 15(2) of the *CHRA* provide a defense to discriminatory conduct and practices where it is established that they are based on a *bona fide*

occupational requirement. To constitute a BFOR, the Respondents must establish that accommodating the needs of the individuals would cause them undue hardship having regard to health, safety and cost.

[140] The only factor that applies in this case is cost. The Respondents did not provide evidence that the cost of treating the adjudicators the same as the advisors with respect to professional recognition, the payment of licensing fees, and the provision of training and educational opportunities would cause them undue hardship.

[141] Marc Thibodeau, a negotiator with the Treasury Board Secretariat, testified that a change in the adjudicators' classification and the resulting impact on salary levels would affect the way that similar positions within the Public Service were classified and remunerated. For example, disability claims adjudication at the Department of Veterans Affairs is done by employees who are also classified as PM-4. The recognition of the medical adjudicators' professional expertise in the present case could result in a review of the classification levels of adjudicators in departments like Veterans Affairs. This, in turn, might cause a significant increase in the Public Service payroll.

[142] Almost invariably there is a cost involved in providing a workplace that is free from discrimination. Often increased cost is provided as a reason for refusing to deal with a problem of discrimination in the workplace. However, it is only when the cost of redressing the discrimination is so high that it would cause the Respondent undue financial hardship that the conduct will be considered a bona fide occupational requirement. The Respondents provided no evidence that the classification of medical adjudicators as health professionals would cause them undue financial hardship....

[143] I find, on a balance of probabilities, that the Complainants have established that the Respondents' refusal since March of 1978, to recognize the professional nature of the work performed by the medical adjudicators in a manner proportionate to the professional recognition accorded to the work of the medical advisors, is a discriminatory practice within the meaning of both ss. 7 and 10. The effects of the practice have been to deprive the adjudicators of professional recognition and remuneration commensurate with their qualifications, and to deprive them of payment of their licensing fees, as well as training and career advancement opportunities on the same basis as the advisors.

[144] Section 53(2)(a) of the *CHRA* provides the Tribunal with the authority to order the Respondents to cease the discriminatory practice and to take measures, in consultation with the Commission, to redress the practice or to prevent the same or a similar practice from occurring in the future. The parties requested that, in the event that I found the complaints to be substantiated, I make an order that the discriminatory practice cease, but that I refrain from specifying the measures that should be taken to redress the practice. They asked to be given an opportunity to negotiate the appropriate measures to be taken with all of the stakeholders. I am in agreement with this request ...

* * * * *

In *Newfoundland (Treasury Board) v Newfoundland and Labrador Assn of Public and Private Employees (NAPE)*, 2004 SCC 66, the Supreme Court of Canada considered a section 15(1) *Charter* challenge to a provincial statute (the *Public Sector Restraint Act*, SN 1991, c 3 [rep and sub 1992, c P-41.1), which delayed the implementation of a pay equity award already granted to female workers in the Newfoundland public sector. The Court held that the statute in question violated section 15(1). "Sex," it noted (at para 43), "is a prohibited ground of discrimination," and "[t]he differential treatment did not arise merely because of the type of job but rather because the job is one that is generally held by women." Also, it said (at para 49), "[l]ow pay often denotes low status jobs, exacting a price in dignity as well as dollars. As such, the interest affected by the Act was of great importance."

However, the Court went on to hold that the impugned statute was justified under section 1 of the *Charter* because the government was in the midst of a severe fiscal crisis. On this, Binnie J, for the Court, said:

> [61] It seems to me the severity of these measures, including the cut to pay equity, corroborates the government's statement that it believed itself, on reasonable grounds, to be in the middle of a fiscal crisis....
>
> [64] ... The spring of 1991 was not a "normal" time in the finances of the provincial government. At some point, a financial crisis can attain a dimension that elected governments must be accorded significant scope to take remedial measures, even if the measures taken have an adverse effect on a *Charter* right, subject, of course, to the measures being proportional both to the fiscal crisis and to their impact on the affected *Charter* interests. In this case, the fiscal crisis was severe and the cost of putting into effect pay equity according to the original timetable was a large expenditure ($24 million) relative even to the size of the fiscal crisis....
>
> [72] [C]ourts will continue to look with strong scepticism at attempts to justify infringements of *Charter* rights on the basis of budgetary constraints. To do otherwise would devalue the *Charter* because there are *always* budgetary constraints and there are *always* other pressing government priorities. Nevertheless, the courts cannot close their eyes to the periodic occurrence of financial emergencies when measures must be taken to juggle priorities to see a government through the crisis. It cannot be said that in weighing a delay in the timetable for implementing pay equity against the closing of hundreds of hospital beds, as here, a government is engaged in an exercise "whose sole purpose is financial." The weighing exercise has as much to do with social values as it has to do with dollars. In the present case, the "potential impact" is $24 million, amounting to more than 10 percent of the projected budgetary deficit for 1991-92. The delayed implementation of pay equity is an extremely serious matter, but so too (for example) is the layoff of 1,300 permanent, 350 part-time and 350 seasonal employees, and the deprivation to the public of the services they provided....
>
> [75] Loss of credit rating, and its impact on the government's ability to borrow, and the added cost of borrowing to finance the provincial debt which, in the case of Newfoundland, requires "[h]undreds of millions of dollars every year in interest" ... are matters of high importance. The President of the Treasury Board told the House of Assembly that "the financial health of the Province was at stake." ... The Newfoundland Government had already experienced a period of trusteeship in the 1930s, a fact glumly referred to by the President of the Treasury Board in his speech. The financial health of the Province is the golden goose on which all else relies. The government in 1991

was not just debating rights versus dollars but rights versus hospital beds, rights versus layoffs, rights versus jobs, rights versus education and rights versus social welfare. The requirement to reduce expenditures, and the allocation of the necessary cuts, was undertaken to promote other values of a free and democratic society ... And, as Sopinka J. pointed out in *Egan v. Canada* ..., "it is not realistic for the Court to assume that there are unlimited funds to address the needs of all." ...

[84] It is therefore recognized that in such cases governments have a large "margin of appreciation" within which to make choices. It seems evident that the scope of that "margin" will be influenced, amongst other things, by the scale of the financial challenge confronting a government and the size of the expenditure required to avoid a *Charter* infringement in relation to that financial challenge ...

[90] The documentary evidence ... demonstrates that other options were also considered and rejected including a hiring freeze, layoffs and cuts to other programs such as social assistance as well as tax increases. In fact, to avoid additional cuts the government also borrowed approximately $50 million to finance its current expenses.

In its analysis under section 1, the Court did not address the argument that the delay and partial denial of the pay equity award meant that female workers in the Newfoundland public service, but not male workers, were required to subsidize the provincial debt.

14:400 THE FUTURE OF EQUALITY

14:410 Economic Inequality

Canadian courts have repeatedly held that equality rights are concerned with the protection of human dignity. However, the courts have frequently excluded economic equality claims either on the basis that the *Charter* is not a guarantor of economic rights or because of the view that such claims engage matters of social and economic policy rather than individual rights. Nor has occupational status or membership in a particular socioeconomic group, such as low-income wage earners or welfare recipients, been found to be a ground "analogous" to those listed in section 15 and thus one which can support a *Charter* challenge. See, for example, *Reference re Workers' Compensation Act, 1983 (Nfld)*, [1989] 1 SCR 922. In general, unless a legislative or administrative action can be characterized as a denial of equal treatment on the basis of a listed or analogous ground, the fact that it creates, perpetuates, or fails to ameliorate an economic disadvantage has so far been held insufficient to bring it within the definition of discrimination.

In *Delisle v Canada (Deputy Attorney General)*, [1999] 2 SCR 989, referred to in Chapter 12, the Supreme Court of Canada reiterated its reluctance to consider occupational status as an analogous ground for the purposes of section 15 of the *Charter*. That case involved the statutory exclusion of Royal Canadian Mounted Police (RCMP) officers from eligibility for collective bargaining. In rejecting the argument of the appellant RCMP officers that the exclusion violated their equality rights under section 15, Bastarache J, for the majority of the Court, said (at para 44):

> In this case the appellant has not established that the professional status or employment of RCMP members are analogous grounds. It is not a matter of functionally immutable

characteristics in a context of labour market flexibility. A distinction based on employment does not identify, here, "a type of decision making that is suspect because it often leads to discrimination and denial of substantive equality" ... in view in particular of the status of police officers in society.

In the later case of *Dunmore v Ontario (Attorney General)*, 2001 SCC 94, excerpted in Chapter 12, agricultural workers had been excluded from collective bargaining by statute, and they were a group that had much lower social status than the RCMP officers in *Delisle*. However, the Supreme Court of Canada did not deal with the claim that their exclusion from collective bargaining violated their equality rights under section 15 of the *Charter*, because the Court held the exclusion to violate their right to freedom of association under section 2(d).

Earlier decisions also show a reluctance on the part of the Supreme Court of Canada to use section 15 of the *Charter* to interfere with the distributive decisions of legislatures, even where there was an arguable connection to a prohibited ground. For example, in *Symes v Canada*, [1993] 4 SCR 695, a female lawyer incurred high childcare costs in order to have time to practice her profession. The *Income Tax Act*, RSC 1985, c 1 (5th Supp), did not allow her to deduct all of those costs as a professional expense, but allowed only the much smaller childcare deduction. The Supreme Court rejected her section 15 claim that this effectively discriminated against women workers. In the view of the majority of the Court, although it was clear that women disproportionately bore the burden of childcare, it was not established that they disproportionately paid the costs of such care.

In general, claims of economic discrimination fare no better under human rights law than under the *Charter*. Quebec and New Brunswick are an exception. Their human rights statutes list "social condition" as a prohibited ground. That term has been held to refer to a combination of objective factors, such as income level or family background, and subjective factors such as unfavourable perceptions held by others. No other jurisdiction includes social condition or the equivalent as a prohibited ground of discrimination, although some prohibit discrimination on the basis of "source of income" or "social origin." Section 7 of the Alberta *Human Rights Act*, RSA 2000, c A-25.5 is an example.

The absence of protection from discrimination on the basis of social condition has been a source of repeated criticism. The Canadian Labour Congress (CLC), in its submissions to the Canadian Human Rights Act Review Panel for its report, *Promoting Equality: A New Vision* (2000), argued that various forms of economic discrimination "in fact impede access to equality of opportunity probably almost as often as any other form of discrimination." It noted that costs associated with obtaining or maintaining employment (such as paying for tests or buying tools) may serve as barriers to employment for the poor. The CLC recommended that "social condition" be added to the federal Act, with a definition similar to that developed in Quebec. It argued that such an amendment to the federal human rights statute would have the added result of encouraging courts and tribunals to treat social condition as an analogous ground when interpreting section 15 of the *Charter*.

Economic inequality, and the resulting problem of social exclusion, is increasing in Canada and almost everywhere else. Wage rates have fallen in real terms in the last generation, and there is more dispersion, or inequality, of wages. Such changes are often attributed to market forces, the effects of technology and greater communication, or simply to globalization. However, the degree of economic inequality varies considerably among industrialized countries, and there is evidence that it is affected by the extent of collective bargaining and the relative strength of unions: see I Bakker, "Globalization and Human Development in the Rich Countries: Lessons from Labour Markets and Welfare States" in *Globalization with a Human Face, Background Papers, vol 2, Human Development Report 1999* (New York: Human Development Report Office, United Nations Development Programme, 1999) 29. In turn, collective bargaining coverage and union density depend on the state of labour market rules and labour relations institutions.

Laws facilitating collective bargaining rules were originally introduced, in part, to address economic equality. However, under the *Wagner Act* [*National Labor Relations Act*, 29 USC §§ 151–169] model which prevails across Canada, collective bargaining is not equally available to all workers, nor is it equally advantageous when it is available. This has become all the more true with the proliferation of atypical forms of work in the new economy. Those in "peripheral" rather than "core" labour markets and those in non-standard forms of work typically face greater difficulties attaining union representation. When they do attain it, they often face poor prospects of gains at the bargaining table, if not imminent decertification. They also benefit less from statutory protections and insurance schemes. For example, relative to full-time workers, part-time workers have greater difficulty achieving the number of hours required to access employment insurance and, although they are required to contribute to the scheme, are often excluded from benefits as a result. Apart from the disadvantage to the growing number of part-time workers, such exclusions may raise additional equality concerns where, for example, part-timers are predominantly women or parents with children. See *Canada (Attorney General) v Lesiuk*, 2003 FCA 3, leave to appeal to SCC refused, [2003] SCCA No 94.

The recently released Ontario *Changing Workplaces Review—Final Report* [C Michael Mitchell & John C Murray, *The Changing Workplaces Review—Final Report* (Ontario: Ministry of Labour, May 2017)] documents the increasing use of precarious part-time work in a number of industries, including "retail, restaurants, food services, child care, custodial services, some parts of the public sector, agriculture and construction." The report notes how the combination of "low income, uncertainty, lack of control over scheduling, lack of benefits such as pensions and health care, personal emergency leave or sick leave, all together or in various combinations, create stress and many other difficulties which affect the quality of life, mental health and overall physical health of many employees." Another stark example of the rise of flexible labour markets is the increasingly widespread use of zero-hour contracts in Britain and other countries across many industries. They demand that workers be available for work, but no work will necessarily be provided. Some research has suggested that such work has detrimental effects on the workers' physical and mental health. For a discussion of its use in higher education, see Ana Lopes & Indra Angeli Dewan, "Precarious Pedagogies? The Impact of Casual and Zero-Hour Contracts in Higher Education" (2014) 7:8 *Journal of Feminist Scholarship* 28.

The *Charter* has not yet been successfully used to force legislatures to address the structural causes of workplace stratification on prohibited grounds, including those that may relate to the design of labour market institutions. For example, it has been suggested that the fragmentation of bargaining units under the *Wagner* model creates an unconstitutional barrier to the attainment of workplace equality by women and ethnic or racial minorities because it precludes them from engaging in effective collective bargaining. Even where governments have repealed existing legislation, such as employment equity laws, that is designed to ameliorate the position of disadvantaged groups in the workplace, the courts have generally refused to find a breach of section 15. See *Ferrell v Ontario (Attorney General)* (1998), 42 OR (3d) 97 (CA), leave to appeal to SCC refused, [1999] SCCA No 79. The only exception is the trial court decision in *SEIU Local 204 v Ontario*, mentioned in Section 14:500. In that case, certain provisions of the Ontario *Pay Equity Act* (the proxy comparison provisions) had made the benefits of that Act accessible to the most economically disadvantaged of the groups of female employees whom the Act was designed to benefit. The repeal of those provisions was held to be a breach of section 15(1) because it "discriminate[d] against a portion of the group the legislation is designed to help...."

Historically, part-time college workers in Ontario had no right to bargain collectively under the *Colleges Collective Bargaining Act*, RSO 1990, c 15. In November 2006, the ILO adopted a report from its Committee on Freedom of Association which found that there was no "reason why ... the basic rights of association and collective bargaining afforded to all workers should not also apply to part-time employees," and which recommended that the Ontario government "rapidly take legislative measures" to rectify the situation (*Report of the Committee on Freedom of Association*, Report No 343, UNILOOR, 297th Session, GB 297/10, (2006) at para 362). Subsequently, the *Colleges Collective Bargaining Act, 2008*, SO 2008, c 15, extended collective bargaining rights to part time and sessional college employees.

In *Confédération des syndicats nationaux v Québec (Procureur général)*, 2008 QCCS 5076, Grenier JCS held (at paras 319–88) that two Quebec statutes excluding homecare workers (nearly all of whom were women) from employee status under the Quebec *Labour Code*, CQLR c 27, violated section 15(1) of the *Charter*. People doing similar work in an institutional setting, rather than in homes, were covered by the *Code*. In Grenier JCS's words (at para 388), the two statutes in question "have the effect of perpetuating unfavourable attitudes toward people who do homecare work, by applying a stereotype that sees it as not being real work" [TRANSLATION].

14:420 Equality in the Interface Between Welfare and Work

Natasha Kim & Tina Piper, "*Gosselin v. Quebec*: Back to the Poorhouse ..." (2003) 48 McGill LJ 749 at 751–55 and 778–79

> The Supreme Court of Canada released its decision in the highly anticipated case of *Gosselin v. Quebec (A.G.)* on 19 December 2002. The reason for the unusually long delay in the release of the judgment is apparent in the final result: a slim five-to-four split, with four separate dissenting judgments and highly divergent positions taken by the two factions of the Court.
>
> The basis of this judicial debate was the court challenge by Louise Gosselin to Quebec's social assistance regulations of the 1980s. Under section 29(a) of the Regulation respecting social aid, social assistance recipients were treated differentially on the basis of age and employability. Single individuals under thirty years old, who were considered employable ("under thirty"), were given approximately one third the assistance of their counterparts thirty years and over ("thirty and over"): only 170 dollars per month.
>
> [...]
>
> As noted above, the *Regulation respecting social aid* limited the amount of social assistance payable to recipients under thirty to one-third of what was available to recipients

thirty and over. The regulation did, however, make it possible for those under thirty to increase their payments to the level of social assistance paid to recipients thirty and over if they participated in one of three programs: On-the-Job-Training, Community Work, or Remedial Education. Ms. Gosselin brought the case as a class action on behalf of all social assistance recipients subject to the differential regime from 1985 to 1989, arguing that the differential regime violated sections 15 and 7 of the *Charter* and section 45 of the *Quebec Charter*. The claim failed on all three grounds at all levels of court.

[...]

The Supreme Court of Canada held, by a slim majority of five to four, that the social assistance scheme established by the *Regulation respecting social aid* did not infringe section 15(1) of the *Charter*. The majority judgment was written by McLachlin C.J. and was concurred in by Gonthier, Iacobucci, Major, and Binnie, JJ. The dissenting judgments held that the regulation violated section 15(1) of the *Charter* and that the infringement was not justified under section 1.

The main area of conflict between the majority and the minority was the application of the *Law* section 15(1) test, in particular, the four contextual factors to be considered under the third branch of the test ...

[...]

McLachlin C.J., writing for the majority, concluded, after an examination of the four factors from *Law*, that there was no support for a finding that there had been discrimination and a denial of human dignity to constitute a violation of section 15(1). First, she held that young people, as a group, had not suffered from historical disadvantage and age distinctions were common and necessary for ordering society. Second, she observed that there was a correspondence between the scheme and the actual circumstances of the social assistance recipients: the provision of education and training provided incentives for young people to work and affirmed their potential and did not undermine their dignity. Third, she noted that the ameliorative purpose factor was neutral in this case since the *Regulation respecting social aid* was not designed to improve the condition of another group (e.g., recipients who are thirty and older). McLachlin C.J. concluded that the impugned law did not adversely affect the appellant's dignity and that any adverse short-term effects were outweighed by the legislation's attempt to improve the self-reliance and dignity of the group.

In dissent, Bastarache J. (Arbour and L'Heureux-Dubé JJ. concurring in the section 15(1) analysis) applied the *Law* criteria to different effect. First, he argued that the majority mischaracterized the group (i.e., young people) and should have considered the special vulnerability of *social assistance recipients* under thirty. Second, he held that there was a lack of correspondence between the differential social assistance scheme and the actual needs, capacities, and circumstances of social assistance recipients under and over thirty. Third, Bastarache J. rejected the ameliorative purpose factor in this case and found that the scheme had a severe effect on an extremely important interest to the claimant by knowingly placing her and others in a precarious and unliveable situation.

Bastarache J. (with the concurrence of LeBel J. in full and Arbour J. in part) then found that the infringement was not justified under section 1 of the *Charter*. Although he accepted that a certain level of deference should be paid to government in reviewing this type of legislation, he held that this does not give the government carte blanche to limit rights. Bastarache found the objectives—to facilitate the integration of youth into the workforce and to "avoid *attracting* them to social assistance" — to be pressing and substantial and also found a rational connection between those objectives and some differential treatment of the under thirty recipients. Bastarache J. concluded, however, that the measures enacted by the government were not minimally impairing of the appellant's rights and suggested less impairing alternatives to achieve the government's goals. He further found that there was no proportionality between the detrimental effects on the appellant's self-worth and equality and the government's objectives.

Arbour J. concurred with this minimal impairment analysis, and further argued that there was no rational connection between denying social assistance recipients the basic means of subsistence and promoting their dignity and liberty.

LeBel J. also dissented from the majority, holding that the differential legislative treatment between social assistance recipients was based on stereotypes of youth and discriminated against young recipients for no valid reason.

Finally, L'Heureux-Dubé J. held that the Court should not consider the legislature's good intentions in determining whether the impugned legislation violated section 15(1) and held that discrimination based on age did not operate only in relation to old age. She found that the legislative distinction was discriminatory, in part, because of the harm to Ms. Gosselin's fundamental interests in physical and psychological integrity, as a result of both a personal characteristic that could not be changed and the pre-existing disadvantage of some members of the group.

[...]

The majority used the term "dignity" freely when supporting its judgment. The concept of dignity, however, is inherently malleable and can be a vessel to be filled by many different concepts, as has been discovered by many common law courts around the world. The majority's conception of dignity in *Gosselin* is particularly challenging. References to the dignity of work and long-term self-sufficiency regardless of whether it means living at home or being unable to survive demonstrate a lack of consideration for the realities of the class before them: there is no discussion of the "dignity" of being compelled to perform the work no one else wants for minimum wage. There is little dignity in the stereotypical assumption that social assistance recipients will not participate in work or training opportunities unless forced through financial deprivation. Fundamentally, the workfare nature of the Quebec legislation removes the *choice* to work and the right to be free from coercion that should be central to human dignity.

Quite apart from a question of whether a minimum level of assistance should be a governmental obligation, discriminatory treatment within a social assistance scheme is particularly egregious because the purported purpose underlying the scheme claims to be highly complementary to that of equality provisions: to promote the equal participation in our society of groups that may be particularly vulnerable to systemic, attitudinal, and other barriers to the realization of their potential or goals as individuals; to promote "a society in which all are secure in the knowledge that they are recognized at law as equal human beings, equally capable, and equally deserving."

[This excerpt has been reproduced with permission from Copibec.]

14:430 Gender and Economic Discrimination

It is relatively uncontroversial that labour markets are gendered in their structure and operation. It is one of the few truly universal gender traits that men and women everywhere do different types of work, although the particular roles that they play vary enormously from society to society. See Gillian Hadfield, "A Coordination Model of the Sexual Division of Labor" (1999) 40 *Journal of Economic Behavior and Organization* 125. It remains the case in all societies that women perform more unpaid work than men; moreover, the allocation of unpaid work between men and women does not necessarily shift appreciably when women enter the labour market. As noted in the United Nations Development Programme's Human Development Report, 1999, this produces a distinct set of burdens and costs for women.

Labour market regulations have traditionally been directed at regulating the conditions of paid work in core industrial sectors. In addition, their reach is by definition limited to the formal rather than the informal sector. The neglect of unpaid work is arguably discriminatory against women as such work significantly constrains labour market participation. More to the point, however, is the discriminatory potential of workplace rules which do not accommodate or compensate for those non-market obligations (such as unpaid domestic work), and which directly or indirectly relegate women to lower occupational status and income. The following excerpt deals with the relationship between paid and unpaid work, and makes the case for seeing it as a labour market issue.

Diane Elson, "Labor Markets as Gendered Institutions: Equality, Efficiency and Empowerment Issues" (1999) 27:3 *World Development* 611 at 612–13

> The most fundamental way in which labor markets are gendered institutions is in the way in which they operate at the intersection of ways in which people make a living and care for themselves, their children, their relatives and friends. Activities which make a living are recognized by economists as economic activities which should in principle be counted as part of national production. For brevity, we might call the sum of this largely market-oriented work the "productive economy." But, as feminist economists have pointed out, unpaid, unjacketed caring activities are also critical for the functioning of the "productive economy," since they reproduce, on a daily and intergenerational basis, the labor force which works in the productive economy. Moreover, feminist economists have argued that unpaid caring activities entail work, even though they are not market-oriented. For brevity, we might call the sum of unpaid, caring work, the "reproductive economy." ...
>
> Labor markets form one of the points of intersection of these two economies ... But they operate in ways that fail to acknowledge the contributions of the reproductive economy. Instead they operate in ways that disadvantage those who carry out most of the work in the reproductive economy: women. Labor market institutions are constructed in ways that represent only the costs to employers of the time that employees spend on unpaid caring for others. The benefits are not represented. Thus, for instance, employees' parenting duties are represented as liabilities and not assets to their employers. Labor market institutions are constructed in ways that reflect only the immediate costs of time off from paid work to have and rear children, and care for sick relatives and

friends. They are not constructed to reflect the benefits of the reproduction and maintenance of a pool of labor from which employers can select their employees. Nor do they reflect the enhanced interpersonal skills which come from parenting and managing a household. In the language of economics, the reproductive economy produces benefits for the productive economy which are externalities, not reflected in market prices and wages. Or, as feminist economist Nancy Folbre puts it, labor market institutions fail to face up to the problem of "who pays for the kids?" ...

Of course, the operation of labor market institutions cannot escape the fact that someone has to pay for the kids. (Just as there is no such thing as a free lunch, there is also no such thing as a free replenishment of the pool of labor.) Most labor market institutions are constructed on the basis that the burdens of the reproductive economy will be, and should be, borne largely by women. For instance, arrangements for paternal leave are far less widespread than maternal leave, and where they do exist, there are many barriers to men taking up their entitlements, because promotion often depends upon showing "commitment" to the job, and taking paternal leave may be interpreted as a sign of weak commitment to the job. Domestic responsibilities penalize women in the labor market and are a key factor in women's weak position in terms of earnings and occupations.

It is sometimes claimed that labor markets adapt so as to allow women to combine paid work with unpaid work—for example, part-time work and home-based work. But, this kind of adaptation is generally one-sided—more designed to allow the productive economy access to workers whose entry into the labor market is constrained by domestic responsibilities than to give weight to the contribution that women's *unpaid* work makes to the productive economy. This is revealed in the way in which these more "informal" types of work typically do not have contracts which give employees any rights to paid time for meeting their responsibilities in the reproductive economy—rights such as maternity leave, and time-off for caring for sick relatives. Nor does such employment cover women's needs when they have retired from paid work, since pension rights are also not covered. Instead, the presumption appears to be that someone else (husband, children) will support such workers in their old age.

Thus labor market institutions are not only bearers of gender, they are also reinforcers of gender inequality. But different institutional configurations give different results: some labor markets are more equal than others. Moreover, improvements can be brought about by public action, i.e. by combined action by the state and by groups of active citizens. Public action can build upon the potential for change in labor market institutions themselves. For such institutions are not like fortresses of stone, rather they are combinations of overlapping and conflicting practices, norms and networks, whose seeming solidity at any moment masks subterranean pressures and fissures.
[Reprinted by permission.]

Richard Posner, *Economic Analysis of Law*, 7th ed (New York: Aspen Publishers, 2007) at 356–58

The central economic question relating to employment discrimination against women is explaining the persistently higher average wages of men; women's wages per hour are on average about two-thirds of men's. Differences in the amount of investment in market-related human capital appear to be the key to understanding this phenomenon. The woman who allocates a substantial part of her working life to household production, including child care, will obtain a substantially lower total return on her market human capital than a man who allocates much less time to such production. She will therefore invest less in her market human capital, and since earnings are in part a return on one's human capital, women's earnings will be lower than men's. Women will therefore be attracted to occupations that don't require much human capital, which is one reason women traditionally were nurses rather than doctors, secretaries rather than executives. But insofar as women devote more time to household production than men do because women's opportunities in the job market are depressed by sex discrimination, the difference in the amount of market human capital that men and women accumulate, and the resulting difference in earnings, is an effect of discrimination, but society-wide discrimination rather than discrimination based on the discriminatory motivations of individual employers. However, with the amount of time that women are devoting to household production declining for the reasons discussed in Chapter 5, both the occupational and the wage differences between men and women would have narrowed even without government intervention. The existence of sex discrimination by employers is a necessary rather than a sufficient condition for a law prohibiting such discrimination to confer a net economic benefit on society as a whole, or even on women as a whole. First, not all employment discrimination on grounds of sex is inefficient. Consider the refusal (which is now unlawful) of employers to pay pregnancy disability benefits. From the standpoint of pricing labor efficiently, to be made to pay a worker who is absent on account of pregnancy makes no more sense than to be made to pay a worker who is absent because he is painting the baby's room. In neither case is the worker conferring a benefit on the employer. (How are paid vacations or paid sick leave different? Read on.)

Second, antidiscrimination laws can boomerang against the protected class as employers take rational measures to minimize the laws' impact. For example, the *Equal Pay Act* requires employers to pay the same wage to men and women doing the same work. If women workers have a lower marginal product, employers will have an incentive to substitute capital for labor inputs in those job classifications in which they employ many women. In addition, having to pay female employees more than their market worth may make employers reluctant to hire women; and though this reluctance may expose the employer to a suit for hiring discrimination, such suits are rare because damage obtaining in such a suit usually are small. The reason is that a job applicant is unlikely to land a job that pays a great deal more than she could get elsewhere, yet her damages if her application is wrongfully denied will be limited to the difference between what her wage would have been in that job and what it is in her existing job, or if she's not employed then in her best alternative employment.

There is a double whammy here. While the expected liability costs of a discriminatory refusal to hire are low, the expected liability costs of a discriminatory firing (call these "firing costs") are high, since a worker's wage in his current job is likely to exceed, often by a considerable margin, the wage in the best alternative job that he could land (why?). These costs are avoided by not hiring a member of a class protected by the employment discrimination law.

Even if the *Equal Pay Act* is fully enforced, women may not benefit. Having to pay them a higher wage will increase the employer's costs and may therefore cause him to reduce the wages of all his employees, male and female, or raise those wages more slowly than he otherwise would, or lay off workers. The larger the fraction of the workforce that is female, the less of the employer's added labor costs will be shifted in these ways to the male workers and so the less the women will benefit form the Act.

Moreover, some of the costs that antidiscrimination laws impose on employers will be passed on to consumers in the form of higher prices, and female consumers will be hurt along with male. The heterogeneity of women's interests, combined with the financial and altruistic interdependence between men and women, creates further uncertainty as to whether women will be net beneficiaries of antidiscrimination laws. Increased labor costs that are due to payment of pregnancy disability benefits are borne in part by all workers, but while pregnant employees obtain an offset from the benefits themselves, women who are either not employed or not fertile are clear losers.

The biggest losers of all are women who are either not employed or not intending to have children but who are married to men who are employed. Their husbands' wages and employment opportunities will shrink as a result of employers' higher labor costs due to mandated employee benefits, and the wives will suffer insofar as household consumption is joint or they are altruistic toward their husbands. In addition, all consumers will have to pay higher prices if labor inputs are used less efficiently as a result of prohibiting efficient discrimination.

"Comparable worth" refers to the policy, which proponents believe should be written into law, of equalizing the wage levels in jobs filled primarily by women and in jobs dominated by men by determining the "true" worth of different jobs and requiring that jobs having the same true worth carry the same wage. As long as employers are forbidden to exclude women from desired job classifications, comparable worth makes no economic sense. For on that assumption, if a truck driver is paid more than a secretary, even though the secretary works just as long hours and has as good an education, the market must be compensating a skill that is in shorter supply, or offsetting a disamenity, rather than making arbitrary distinctions based on fast-vanishing stereotypes.

Under comparable worth, with wages in jobs dominated by women artificially raised, the number of jobs available will shrink as employers seek to substitute other, and now cheaper, inputs and as customers substitute other products for those made by firms whose wage bills and hence prices have risen because of comparable worth.

At the same time, men will start competing more for those jobs, lured by the higher wages. So female employment in a job classification that had been (for whatever reason) congenial to women may (why not will?) drop. Some displaced women will find new employment in the predominantly male occupations such as truck driving—perhaps replacing men who have become secretaries. But these women may not be happier in their new jobs; after all, there is nothing to stop a woman today from becoming a truck driver. Finally, under comparable worth women's incentives to invest in human capital usable in the traditional men's jobs will drop as the relative wages in those jobs drop, so that in the end occupational sex segregation may not be greatly affected.

[Reprinted from *Economic Analysis of Law*, 7th edition, with the permission of Aspen Publishers.]

For further discussion, see Kerry Rittich, "Feminization and Contingency: Regulating the Stakes of Work for Women," in JAF Conaghan et al, *Labour Law in an Era of Globalization* (Oxford: Oxford University Press, 2002) 117–36.

To what extent do we already indemnify unpaid labour through employment insurance and legislated employment standards? Are labour laws and other protective legislation implicated in the economic disadvantage that women face in labour markets? How might existing equality jurisprudence serve to alleviate that disadvantage? Consider, for example, the application to these issues of the holdings in the *Vriend* and *Meiorin* cases, set out earlier in this chapter.

14:440 Evolving Boundaries of Discrimination

14:441 Family Status and Caregiving Responsibilities

While "classical" grounds of discrimination such as sex and race remain important, the law has evolved in response to some topical societal issues and now protects a wider variety of groups and their special needs. This includes, for example, family status and the duty to accommodate caregiving needs. Family status is directly linked to our discussion above. As Elizabeth Shilton argues, "[t]he work/family divide both creates and reinforces gender inequality, and the unequal burden of family care work makes a significant contribution to women's continuing inequality inside and outside the workplace. Accordingly, the issues raised by family status litigation are linked inextricably to the broad issue of gender equality in Canadian workplaces." See Elizabeth Shilton, "'Family Status' Discrimination: New Tool for Transforming Workplaces, or Trojan Horse for Subverting Gender Equality?" (2013) Queen's University Legal Research Paper No 2015-049. For more on the relationship between work and family, see Joanne Conaghan & Kerry Rittich, eds, *Labour Law, Work, and Family: Critical and Comparative Perspectives* (Oxford: Oxford University Press, 2005); and Judy Fudge, "Working-Time Regimes, Flexibility, and Work-Life Balance: Gender Equality and Families" in Catherine Krull & Justyna Sempruch, eds, *A Life in Balance? Reopening the Family-Work Debate* (Vancouver: UBC Press, 2011) 170.

While the Supreme Court of Canada has not yet addressed this issue, there is a debate as to the test for a *prima facie* case of discrimination on the basis of family status. While in British Columbia, the BC Court of Appeal confirmed in *Health Sciences Assn of BC v Campbell River and North Island Transition Society*, 2004 BCCA 260 at para 39 that a *prima facie* case of discrimination on the basis of family status is established when "a change in a term or condition of employment imposed by an employer results in a serious interference with a substantial parental or other family duty" (at para 39), other jurisdictions have followed the test established by the Federal Court of Appeal in *Canada (Attorney General) v Johnstone*.

Canada (Attorney General) v Johnstone, 2014 FCA 110

    Mainville J.A. —

Background and context

[...]

[5] Ms. Johnstone is an employee of the CBSA since 1998. Her husband also works for the CBSA as a supervisor. They have two children. After the eldest was born in January 2003, Ms. Johnstone returned to work from her maternity leave on January 4, 2004. The second child was then born in December 2004, and Ms. Johnstone returned to work on December 26, 2005.

[6] Prior to returning to work from her first maternity leave, Ms. Johnstone asked the CBSA for an accommodation to her work schedule at the Pearson International Airport in Toronto.

[7] The work schedule for full-time CBSA employees occupying positions similar to that of Ms. Johnstone is built around a rotating shift plan referred to as a Variable Shift Scheduling Agreement or VSSA. At the pertinent time, full-time employees rotated through 6 different start times over the course of days, afternoons, and evenings with no predictable pattern, and they worked different days of the week throughout the duration of the schedule. The schedule was based on a 56 day pattern, and employees were given 15 days notice of each new shift schedule, subject to the employer's discretion to change the schedule on 5 days' notice.

[8] Full-time employees such as Ms. Johnstone were required to work 37.5 scheduled hours per week under the VSSA on the basis of an 8 hour day that included a one half hour meal break. Any individual who worked less than 37.5 hours a week was considered a part-time employee. Part-time employees had fewer employment benefits than full-time employees, notably with regard to pension entitlements and promotion opportunities.

[9] It is useful to note that Ms. Johnstone's husband also worked on a variable shift schedule as a customs superintendent. Their work schedules overlapped 60% of the time but were not coordinated. The Tribunal concluded that Ms. Johnstone's husband was facing the same work scheduling problems, and that neither could provide the necessary childcare on a reliable basis.

[10] In the past, the CBSA had accommodated some employees who had medical issues by providing them with a fixed work schedule (static shift) on a full-time basis. The CBSA also accommodated employee work schedules with respect to constraints resulting from religious beliefs. However, the CBSA refused to provide an accommodation to employees with childcare obligations on the ground that it had no legal duty to do so. Instead, the CBSA had an unwritten policy allowing an employee with childcare obligations to work fixed schedules, but only insofar as the employee agreed to be treated as having a part-time status with a maximum work schedule of 34 hours per week.

[11] Prior to returning from her first maternity leave, Ms. Johnstone asked the CBSA to provide her with static shifts on a full-time basis. She wished to work 3 days per week for 13 hours a day (including one half-hour meal break) so that she could remain full-time. She requested this schedule since she only had access to child care arrangements with family members for the three days in question, and was unable to make other childcare arrangements on a reasonable basis. In light of its unwritten policy, CBSA only offered her static shifts for 34 hours per week resulting in her being treated as a part-time employee.

[12] It is useful to note that the CBSA did not refuse to provide static shifts to Ms. Johnstone on a full-time basis on the ground that this would cause it undue hardship.

Rather, it refused the proposed schedule on the ground that it had no legal duty to accommodate Ms. Johnstone's childcare responsibilities.

[13] Ms. Johnstone was not satisfied with the CBSA's unwritten policy that required her to accept part-time employment in return for obtaining static shifts. As a result, she filed a complaint with the Canadian Human Rights Commission on April 24, 2004, alleging discrimination on the basis of family status contrary to sections 7 and 10 of the *Canadian Human Rights Act*. . . .

Procedural history

[...]

[21] Following an extensive review of the case law, the Tribunal held that the prohibited ground of discrimination on family status includes family and parental obligations such as childcare obligations. It consequently rejected the Appellant's definition of family status that limited its scope to the status of being in a family relationship. In this regard, the Tribunal noted the following at paragraph 233 of its decision:

> [233] This Tribunal finds that the freedom to choose to become a parent is so vital that it should not be constrained by the fear of discriminatory consequences. As a society, Canada should recognize this fundamental freedom and support that choice wherever possible. For the employer, this means assessing situations such as Ms. Johnstone's on an individual basis and working together with her to create a workable solution that balances her parental obligations with her work opportunities, short of undue hardship.

[22] With respect to the *prima facie* case of discrimination on the ground of family status, the Tribunal rejected the test set out in Campbell River. It rather followed the test propounded in Hoyt and approved by Barnes J. Under this approach, "an individual should not have to tolerate some amount of discrimination to a certain unknown level before being afforded the protection of the [*Canadian Human Rights*] Act": Tribunal's decision at para. 238.

[23] As a result, the Tribunal held that Ms. Johnstone had made out a case of *prima facie* discrimination in that the "CBSA engaged in a discriminatory practice by establishing and pursuing an unwritten policy communicated to and followed by management that affected Ms. Johnstone's employment opportunities including, but not limited to promotion, training, transfer, and benefits on the prohibited ground of family status": Tribunal decision at para. 242.

[24] The Tribunal further held that the CBSA had not established a defence based on a *bona fide* occupational requirement that would justify its refusal of the work schedule accommodation sought by Ms. Johnstone, nor had it developed a sufficient undue hardship argument to discharge it from its duty of accommodation. The Tribunal noted, at paragraphs 359 and 362 of its decision, that the position advanced on behalf of the CBSA throughout the proceedings was that it had no legal duty to accommodate Ms. Johnstone, rather than whether such an accommodation would lead to undue hardship. . . .

[29] The Attorney General of Canada sought judicial review of the Tribunal's decision . . .

[...]

[31] The Federal Court Judge held that the Tribunal had reasonably concluded that family status includes childcare responsibilities, since that interpretation was well within the scope of the ordinary meaning of the words, was consistent with the opinions of numerous human rights and labour relations adjudicative bodies that have considered the matter, and was consistent with the objectives of the *Canadian Human Rights Act*.

[32] The Judge also held that the test used by the Tribunal for finding a *prima facie* case of discrimination was reasonable, as was its application of that test in this case. In so doing, he specifically discarded the "serious interference" test used in *Campbell River*....

The legal test for finding a *prima facie* case of discrimination on the prohibited ground of family status

[75] There is no fundamental dispute between the parties as to many aspects of the legal test that is used to determine whether there is discrimination on the prohibited ground of family status. All parties agree that the test comprises two parts. First, a *prima facie* case of discrimination must be made out by the complainant. Once that *prima facie* case has been made out, the analysis moves to a second stage where the employer must show that the policy or practice is a *bona fide* occupational requirement and that those affected cannot be accommodated without undue hardship.

[76] The parties also agree that the first part of the test that concerns a *prima facie* case requires complainants to show that they have a characteristic protected from discrimination, that they experienced an adverse impact with respect to employment, and that the protected characteristic was a factor in the adverse impact.

[77] Beyond that however, the parties disagree as to how the *prima facie* part of the test should be defined and applied. The appellant submits that an approach similar to the one used by the British Columbia Court of Appeal in *Campbell River* should be used, while the other parties submit that this would result in imposing a higher *prima facie* threshold for cases based on discrimination on the ground of family status.

[78] *Campbell River* concerned an arbitration award under a collective agreement where the legal issue was the meaning and scope of the expression family status found in subsection 13(1) of the *British Columbia Human Rights Code*, R.S.B.C. 1996, c. 210. The complainant was the mother of a boy then aged thirteen who had severe behavioral problems requiring specific parental and professional attention. Her employer changed her work schedule from an 8am to 3pm shift to an 11:30am to 6pm shift. This shift change impeded the complainant from attending to the needs of her son after his school hours. The arbitrator denied the grievance brought by the complainant to challenge the work schedule change. The arbitrator found that the circumstances involving childcare arrangements did not raise an issue of discrimination based on the prohibited ground of family status. The British Columbia Court of Appeal overturned the arbitrator and remitted the grievance for a new determination. In so doing, the Court made the following conclusions of law:

> [39] [...] Whether particular conduct does or does not amount to *prima facie* discrimination on the basis of family status will depend on the circumstances of each case. In the usual case where there is no bad faith on the part of the employer and no governing provision in the applicable collective agreement or employment contract, it seems to me that

a *prima facie* case of discrimination is made out when a change in a term or condition of employment imposed by an employer results in a serious interference with a substantial parental or other family duty or obligation of the employee. I think that in the vast majority of situations in which there is a conflict between a work requirement and a family obligation it would be difficult to make out a *prima facie* case.

[Emphasis added]

[79] The requirements of a "serious interference" with a "substantial" duty or obligation are the subjects of the controversy between the parties. The appellant invokes the reasoning in Campbell River as a practical approach, and thus proposes to limit *prima facie* cases of discrimination to circumstances where (a) the parental obligation at issue cannot be delegated to a third party, (b) the claimant has tried unsuccessfully to reconcile the non-delegable parental obligation with the employment duties, and (c) the non-delegable parental obligation at issue is substantial.

[80] The other parties to this appeal submit that adopting this approach would entail a higher threshold for a finding of *prima facie* discrimination on the ground of family status than for the other prohibited grounds set out in the *Canadian Human Rights Act*. In their view, a *prima facie* case requires only that a person be differentiated adversely on a prohibited ground in the course of employment. They thus submit that the standard set out in *Campbell River* is wrong in law and fundamentally flawed in that it conflates the issue of *prima facie* discrimination—which is determined at the first stage of the test—and that of undue hardship—which is determined at the second stage of the test. They notably rely on the following criticism of *Campbell River* made by the Tribunal in its *Hoyt* decision:

> [119] A different articulation of the evidence necessary to demonstrate a *prima facie* case is articulated by the British Columbia Court of Appeal in [*Campbell River*]. The Court of Appeal found that the parameters of family status as a prohibited ground of discrimination in the *Human Rights Code* of British Columbia must not be drawn too broadly or it would have the potential to cause 'disruption and great mischief' in the workplace. The Court directed that a *prima facie* case is made out 'when a change in a term or condition of employment imposed by an employer results in serious interference with a substantial parental or other family duty or obligation of the employee." Low, J.A. observed that the *prima facie* case would be difficult to make out in cases of conflict between work requirements and family obligations.
>
> [120] With respect, I do not agree with the Court's analysis. Human rights codes, because of their status as 'fundamental law,' must be interpreted liberally so that they may better fulfill their objectives [...] It would, in my view, be inappropriate to select out one prohibited ground of discrimination for a more restrictive definition.
>
> [121] In my respectful opinion, the concerns identified by the Court of Appeal, being serious workplace disruption and great mischief, might be proper matters for consideration in the *Meiorin* analysis and in particular the third branch of the analysis, being reasonable necessity. When evaluating the magnitude of hardship, an accommodation might give rise to matters such as serious disruption in the workplace, and serious impact on employee morale are appropriate considerations [...] Undue hardship is to be proven by

the employer on a case by case basis. A mere apprehension that undue hardship would result is not a proper reason, in my respectful opinion, to obviate the analysis.

[81] I agree that the test that should apply to a finding of *prima facie* discrimination on the prohibited ground of family status should be substantially the same as that which applies to the other enumerated grounds of discrimination. There should be no hierarchies of human rights. However, though the test should be substantially the same, that test is also necessarily flexible and contextual, as aptly noted by the Canadian Human Rights Commission in its submissions before this Court.

[82] The starting point of the test to establish a *prima facie* case of discrimination is set out in *Ontario Human Rights Commission v. Simpsons-Sears*, above at p. 558, where McIntyre J. noted that the complainant in proceedings before a human rights tribunal must show a *prima facie* case of discrimination, and such a *"prima facie* case in this context is one which covers the allegations made and which, if they are believed, is complete and sufficient to justify a verdict in the complainant's favour in the absence of an answer from the respondent-employer."

[83] The test is necessarily flexible and contextual because it is applied in cases with many different factual situations involving various grounds of discrimination. As noted by Evans J.A. in *Morris v. Canada (Canadian Armed Forces)*, 2005 FCA 154 ... at para. 28, a "flexible legal test of a *prima facie* case is better able than more precise tests to advance the broad purpose underlying the *Canadian Human Rights Act*, namely, the elimination in the federal legislative sphere of discrimination from employment ...".

[84] As a result, a *prima facie* case must be determined in a flexible and contextual way, and the specific types of evidence and information that may be pertinent or useful to establish a *prima facie* case of discrimination will largely depend on the prohibited ground of discrimination at issue....

[86] ... [T]he specific types of evidence and information that may be applied to establish a *prima facie* case of discrimination largely depend on the nature of the prohibited ground of discrimination at issue.

[87] In this case, the Federal Court Judge concluded, at paragraph 121 of his reasons, that "the childcare obligations arising in discrimination claim[s] based on family status must be one of substance and the complainant must have tried to reconcile family obligations with work obligations", adding that "this requirement does not constitute creating a higher threshold test for serious interference." I agree.

[88] Normally, parents have various options available to meet their parental obligations. Therefore, it cannot be said that a childcare obligation has resulted in an employee being unable to meet his or her work obligations unless no reasonable childcare alternative is reasonably available to the employee. It is only if the employee has sought out reasonable alternative childcare arrangements unsuccessfully, and remains unable to fulfill his or her parental obligations, that a *prima facie* case of discrimination will be made out....

[91] This approach is not adding an extra burden on complainants in cases involving family status. As aptly noted in *Alliance Employees Union, Unit 15 v. Customs and Immigrations Union (Loranger Grievance)*, [2011] O.L.A.A. No. 24 at para. 45, complainants in disability cases must first establish that they have a disability and have an ongoing obligation

to notify the employer of changes in their restriction; it is not more onerous to require a parent to establish the nature of the restrictions he or she faces in meeting both parental and employment obligations. ...

[93] I conclude from this analysis that in order to make out a *prima facie* case where workplace discrimination on the prohibited ground of family status resulting from childcare obligations is alleged, the individual advancing the claim must show (i) that a child is under his or her care and supervision; (ii) that the childcare obligation at issue engages the individual's legal responsibility for that child, as opposed to a personal choice; (iii) that he or she has made reasonable efforts to meet those childcare obligations through reasonable alternative solutions, and that no such alternative solution is reasonably accessible, and (iv) that the impugned workplace rule interferes in a manner that is more than trivial or insubstantial with the fulfillment of the childcare obligation.

[94] The first factor requires the claimant to demonstrate that a child is actually under his or her care and supervision. This requires the individual claiming *prima facie* discrimination to show that he or she stands in such a relationship to the child at issue and that his or her failure to meet the child's needs will engage the individual's legal responsibility. In the case of parents, this will normally flow from their status as parents. In the case of de facto caregivers, there will be an obligation to show that, at the relevant time, their relationship with the child is such that they have assumed the legal obligations which a parent would have found.

[95] The second factor requires demonstrating an obligation which engages the individual's legal responsibility for the child. This notably requires the complainant to show that the child has not reached an age where he or she can reasonably be expected to care for himself or herself during the parent's work hours. It also requires demonstrating that the childcare need at issue is one that flows from a legal obligation, as opposed to resulting from personal choices.

[96] The third factor requires the complainant to demonstrate that reasonable efforts have been expended to meet those childcare obligations through reasonable alternative solutions, and that no such alternative solution is reasonably accessible. A complainant will, therefore, be called upon to show that neither they nor their spouse can meet their enforceable childcare obligations while continuing to work, and that an available childcare service or an alternative arrangement is not reasonably accessible to them so as to meet their work needs. In essence, the complainant must demonstrate that he or she is facing a *bona fide* childcare problem. This is highly fact specific, and each case will be reviewed on an individual basis in regard to all of the circumstances.

[97] The fourth and final factor is that the impugned workplace rule interferes in a manner that is more than trivial or insubstantial with the fulfillment of the childcare obligation. The underlying context of each case in which the childcare needs conflict with the work schedule must be examined so as to ascertain whether the interference is more than trivial or insubstantial.

[98] It is not necessary to define in more precise terms the test for *prima facie* discrimination on the ground of family status resulting from childcare obligations. The test itself must be sufficiently flexible so as to advance the broad purpose of the *Canadian Human Rights Act* as set out in section 2 of that Act, notably the principle that individuals

should have the opportunity equal with other individuals to make for themselves the lives they are able and wish to have and to have their needs accommodated, consistent with their duties and obligations as members of society, without being hindered in or prevented from doing so by discriminatory practices based on family status.

[99] Consequently, deciding what specific types of evidence are required to meet all four factors of the above test for a *prima facie* case of discrimination in any given context will vary with the facts of each case, and is better left to be determined on a case-by-case basis.

Application to the circumstances of Ms. Johnstone

[100] Applying the proper legal test, I can find no reviewable error in the Tribunal's conclusion that Ms. Johnstone has made out a *prima facie* case of adverse discrimination by the CBSA on the basis of family status.

[101] *First*, it is not disputed that Ms. Johnstone had one and then two children under her care and supervision during the times pertinent to her complaint. Though this responsibility was shared with her husband, this does not detract from Ms. Johnstone's shared responsibility for the care and supervision of her two children. As a result, she satisfied the first leg of the test outlined above for establishing a *prima facie* case.

[102] *Second*, both children were toddlers for which she and her husband were legally responsible. She and her husband could not leave the children on their own without adult supervision during their working hours without breaching their legal obligations towards them. As a result, they were legally required to provide their children with some form of childcare arrangement while they were away to attend to their work with the CBSA. As a result, Ms. Johnstone's childcare obligations engaged her legal responsibilities as a parent towards her children, as opposed to a personal choice. As such, Ms. Johnstone satisfied the second leg of the test.

[103] *Third*, the Tribunal found as a matter of fact that Ms. Johnstone had made serious but unsuccessful efforts to secure reasonable alternative childcare arrangements: Tribunal's decision at paras. 187,188, 193 and 194. The Tribunal outlined the significant efforts of Ms. Johnstone to secure childcare arrangements that would allow her to continue to work the rotating and irregular schedule set out in her VSSA.

[104] In particular, the Tribunal noted that Ms. Johnstone had investigated numerous regulated childcare providers, both near her home and near her work, but that none of these provided services outside standard work hours: Tribunal's decision at para. 79. The Tribunal also noted her efforts with unregulated childcare providers, including family members, as well as the broader inquiries she made to secure flexible childcare arrangements that would meet her work schedule: Tribunal's decision at paras. 80-81. The Tribunal found that the work schedules of Ms. Johnstone and of her husband were such that neither could provide the childcare needed on a reliable basis: Tribunal's decision at para. 82. The Tribunal further noted that the alternative of a live-in nanny was not an appropriate option in the circumstances, since Ms. Johnstone's family would have had to move into a home that could accommodate another adult person: Tribunal's decision at para. 83.

[105] Consequently, Ms. Johnstone clearly satisfied the third leg of the test for a *prima facie* case, in that she made reasonable efforts to meet her childcare obligations through reasonable alternative solutions, but no such alternative solution was reasonably available.

[106] Fourth, the Tribunal found that Ms. Johnstone's regular work schedule based on the VSSA interfered in a manner that was more than trivial or insubstantial with the fulfillment of her childcare obligations.

[107] The Tribunal notably relied on the evidence of Martha Friendly, who was qualified as an expert on childcare policy in Canada, including childcare availability for people who work rotating and fluctuating shifts on an irregular basis: Tribunal's decision at paras. 174 to 195. Ms. Friendly testified that unpredictability in work hours was the most difficult factor in accommodating childcare, and that it made finding a paid third-party provider of childcare, regulated or unregulated, almost impossible: Tribunal's decision at paras. 178 and 179. She also testified that the next most difficult factor was the need for extended work hours outside standard operating hours, which also rendered childcare availability virtually impossible to find: Tribunal's decision at para. 180. She concluded that Ms. Johnstone's situation was "one of the most difficult childcare situations that she could imagine" based on different shifts at different times and different days including weekends, overtime, shifts at all hours of the day or night, and the fact her husband worked a similar type of job schedule: Tribunal's decision at para. 195.

[108] As a result, Ms. Johnstone clearly made out a *prima facie* case of discrimination on the ground of family status resulting from childcare obligations, and the Tribunal committed no reviewable error in so finding.

[109] Since the appellant is not asserting any *bona fide* occupational requirement or an undue burden in providing Ms. Johnstone fixed shifts on a full-time basis, the Tribunal's ruling that Ms. Johnstone's complaint under the *Canadian Human Rights Act* was substantiated must be upheld.

A recent decision by the Ontario Human Rights Tribunal suggests that this test is far from being settled. See *Misetich v Value Village Stores Inc*, 2016 HRTO 1229 at paras 54–57:

[54] In order to establish family status discrimination in the context of employment, the employee will have to do more than simply establish a negative impact on a family need. The negative impact must result in real disadvantage to the parent/child relationship and the responsibilities that flow from that relationship, and/or to the employee's work. For example, a workplace rule may be discriminatory if it puts the employee in the position of having to choose between working and caregiving or if it negatively impacts the parent/child relationship and the responsibilities that flow from that relationship in a significant way.

[55] Assessing the impact of the impugned rule is done contextually and may include consideration of the other supports available to the applicant. These supports are relevant to assessing both the family-related need and the impact of the impugned rule on that need. For instance, if the applicant is a single parent, both the family-related need and the impact of the impugned rule on the family-related need may be greater.

[56] Considering the supports available to an applicant may appear to some to be akin to considering whether an applicant can self-accommodate. It is different in a fundamental

way. Requiring an applicant to self-accommodate as part of the discrimination test means the applicant bears the onus of finding a solution to the family/work conflict; it is only when he/she cannot that discrimination is established. This is different than considering the extent to which other supports for family-related needs are available in the overall assessment of whether an applicant has met his/her burden of proving discrimination.

[57] Once the applicant proves discrimination, the onus shifts to the respondent to establish that the applicant cannot be accommodated to the point of undue hardship.

14:442 Gender Identity and Gender Expression

Another example of evolving boundaries is the growing legal protection for discrimination on grounds of sexual orientation, gender identity, and gender expression. The Supreme Court of Canada has held that sexual orientation constituted an analogous prohibited ground under section 15 of the *Charter* in 1995 (see *Egan v Canada*, [1995] 2 SCR 513). It has ordered the government of Alberta to read into its protection against discrimination the ground of sexual orientation in *Vriend*, discussed above in Section 14:220. Some Canadian jurisdictions have also added sexual identity and expression into their human rights acts (see, for example, *Ontario Human Rights Code*, RSO 1990, c H.19 s 5; and Canada, Bill C-16, *An Act to Amend the Canadian Human Rights Act and the Criminal Code of Canada*, 2017). Still, discrimination against members of the LGBTQ community has been increasingly documented in the literature (see, for example, Jonathan Eaton, "Transitions at Work: Industrial Relations Responses to the Emerging Rights of Transgender Workers" (2004) 11 *Canadian Labour and Employment Law Journal* 113–41) and recognized in the caselaw (see, for example, *Dawson v Vancouver Police Board (No 2)*, 2015 BCHRT 54, where discrimination against transgender workers was successfully argued as discrimination on the basis of sex).

14:443 Accommodation of Age-Related Needs

Another topical issue is that of the aging workers. While age as a ground of discrimination is not new, it receives growing attention. Canadians are living longer and staying healthier for longer. Many of them wish to, or have to, work longer as their retirement savings are often inadequate. Since mandatory retirement has been abolished across Canada (with some statutory exceptions and exemptions), and labour force participation rate of older workers has increased, issues around unequal treatment on the basis of age and the duty to accommodate age-related needs has become more acute. See, for example, Pnina Alon-Shenker, "The Duty to Accommodate Senior Workers: Its Nature, Scope and Limitations" (2012) 38:1 *Queen's Law Journal* 165.

14:444 Intersectionality

Finally, there is a growing recognition of the complexities of discrimination experienced by individuals who belong to more than one historically disadvantaged group. In response, there have been strong calls to develop an intersectional approach to discrimination, which takes into account the lived realities of individuals and the social context of discrimination. See, for example, Ontario Human Rights Commission, *An Intersectional Approach to Discrimination: Addressing Multiple Grounds in Human Rights Claims* (Toronto: Human Rights Commission 2001); and Dianne Pothier, "Connecting Grounds of Discrimination to Real People's Real Experiences" (2001) 13:2 *Canadian Journal of Women and the Law* 37.

14:450 Questions of Scope, Coverage, and Classifications

Who is protected under human rights acts? Is "employment" under human rights acts limited to the traditional contractual relationship between an "employer" and an "employee," which meets the common law tests for vicarious liability (i.e. control and dependency)? Or should questions of scope be determined given the quasi-constitutional nature and broad public and remedial purposes of human rights acts? Here are three examples (excerpted below): In the first case, an employee of the Department of National Defence is sexually harassed by her supervisor and files a human rights complaint against her employer. In this case, the Supreme Court ruled that employers are responsible for unauthorized discriminatory acts of their employees conducted in the course of employment because the purpose of the human rights act is to remove discrimination and harassment regardless of motive or intention, and because the employer is in the best position to take effective remedial action to remove undesirable conditions. In the second case, the BC Human Rights Tribunal denied an application to dismiss a human rights complaint against Tim Hortons, the franchisor. In the last case, a law firm partner in British Columbia, who was required to retire at the age of sixty-five, files an age discrimination complaint against his law firm. The Supreme Court dismissed his complaint, holding that in most cases the BC *Human Rights Code* would not apply to the relationship between a partner and a law firm. For a critique of this last judgment, see Brian Langille & Pnina Alon-Shenker, "Law Firm Partners and the Scope of Labour Laws" (2015) 4:2 *Canadian Journal of Human Rights* 211.

Robichaud v Canada (Treasury Board), [1987] 2 SCR 84

1. LA FOREST J.—The issue in this case is whether an employer is responsible for the unauthorized discriminatory acts of its employees in the course of their employment under the *Canadian Human Rights Act*, S.C. 1976–77, c. 33, as amended, as it stood before the enactment in 1983 of ss. 48(5) and (6) of the Act which now deal specifically with the issue; see S.C. 1980–81–82–83, c. 143, s. 23.

Background

2. ... Mrs. Bonnie Robichaud filed a complaint with the Canadian Human Rights Commission dated January 26, 1980 that she had been sexually harassed, discriminated against and intimidated by her employer, the Department of National Defence, and that Dennis Brennan, her supervisor, was the person who had sexually harassed her....

4. A Human Rights Tribunal was appointed under s. 39 of the *Canadian Human Rights Act* to inquire into Robichaud's complaint. The Tribunal found that a number of encounters of a sexual nature had occurred between her and Brennan, but dismissed the complaint against Brennan and against the employer. However, an appeal to a Review Tribunal was allowed. The Review Tribunal found that Brennan had sexually harassed Robichaud and that the Department of National Defence was strictly liable for the actions of its supervisory personnel. However, it postponed the assessment of damages until further argument was heard.

5. Both Brennan and The Queen, as represented by the Treasury Board (for the Department of National Defence), filed applications under s. 28 of the *Federal Court Act*,

R.S.C. 1970 (2nd Supp.), c. 10, requesting the Federal Court of Appeal to review and set aside the decision of the Review Tribunal. Both applications were heard at the same time. Brennan's application was dismissed, but that of The Queen was allowed, MacGuigan J. dissenting. The court set aside the decision of the Review Tribunal, and referred the matter back to it on the basis that Robichaud's complaint against the Crown was not sustainable. The latter decision was appealed to this Court.

Preliminary Observations

6. As is well-known, the *Canadian Human Rights Act* prohibits discriminatory practices in, among other activities, employment on a number of grounds, including sex (s. 3). Specifically, the present case is alleged to fall under s. 7 of the Act which reads as follows:

> 7. It is a discriminatory practice, directly or indirectly,
> (a) to refuse to employ or continue to employ any individual, or
> (b) *in the course of employment, to differentiate adversely in relation to an employee*, on a prohibited ground of discrimination. [Emphasis added.]

In this Court, it was not questioned that sexual harassment in the course of employment constituted discrimination on the ground of sex or that the actions of Brennan amounted to sexual harassment. The sole question for this Court, therefore, is whether such actions can be attributed to the employer, here the Crown, to which the Act applies by virtue of s. 63(1).

Analysis

7. In the Court of Appeal and in the arguments before this Court, considerable attention was given to various theories supporting the liability of an employer for the acts of its employees, such as vicarious liability in tort and strict liability in the quasi-criminal context. As Thurlow C.J. notes, however, the place to start is necessarily the Act, the words of which, like those of other statutes, must be read in light of its nature and purpose.

8. The purpose of the Act is set forth in s. 2 as being to extend the laws of Canada to give effect to the principle that every individual should have an equal opportunity with other individuals to live his or her own life without being hindered by discriminatory practices based on certain prohibited grounds of discrimination, including discrimination on the ground of sex. As McIntyre J., speaking for this Court, recently explained in Ontario Human Rights Commission and *O'Malley v. Simpsons-Sears Ltd.*, [1985] 2 S.C.R. 536, the Act must be so interpreted as to advance the broad policy considerations underlying it. That task should not be approached in a niggardly fashion but in a manner befitting the special nature of the legislation, which he described as "not quite constitutional"; see also *Insurance Corporation of British Columbia v. Heerspink*, [1982] 2 S.C.R. 145, per Lamer J., at pp. 157–58. By this expression, it is not suggested, of course, that the Act is somehow entrenched but rather that it incorporates certain basic goals of our society. More recently still, Dickson C.J. in *Canadian National Railway Co. v. Canada (Canadian Human Rights Commission) (the Action Travail des Femmes case)*, [1987] 1 S.C.R. 1114, emphasized that the rights enunciated in the Act must be given full recognition

and effect consistent with the dictates of the Interpretation Act that statutes must be given such fair, large and liberal interpretation as will best ensure the attainment of their objects.

9. It is worth repeating that by its very words, the Act (s. 2) seeks "to give effect" to the principle of equal opportunity for individuals by eradicating invidious discrimination. It is not primarily aimed at punishing those who discriminate. McIntyre J. puts the same thought in these words in *O'Malley* at p. 547:

> The Code aims at the removal of discrimination. This is to state the obvious. Its main approach, however, is not to punish the discriminator, but rather to provide relief for the victims of discrimination. It is the result or the effect of the action complained of which is significant.

10. Since the Act is essentially concerned with the removal of discrimination, as opposed to punishing antisocial behaviour, it follows that the motives or intention of those who discriminate are not central to its concerns. Rather, the Act is directed to redressing socially undesirable conditions quite apart from the reasons for their existence. O'Malley makes it clear that "an intention to discriminate is not a necessary element of the discrimination generally forbidden in Canadian human rights legislation" (at p. 547). This legislation creates what are "essentially civil remedies" (p. 549). McIntyre J. there explains that to require intention would make the Act unworkable. He has this to say at p. 549:

> To take the narrower view and hold that intent is a required element of discrimination under the Code would seem to me to place a virtually insuperable barrier in the way of a complainant seeking a remedy. It would be extremely difficult in most circumstances to prove motive, and motive would be easy to cloak in the formation of rules which, though imposing equal standards, could create, as in *Griggs v. Duke Power Co.*, 401 U.S. 424 (1971), injustice and discrimination by the equal treatment of those who are unequal (*Dennis v. United States*, 339 U.S. 162 (1950), at p. 184).

The foregoing remarks were made in the context of a provincial human rights code, but they are equally applicable to the federal Act; see *Bhinder v. Canadian National Railway Co.*, [1985] 2 S.C.R. 561, at p. 586, per McIntyre J. In the latter case, similar views to those of McIntyre J. in *O'Malley* were expressed, albeit in dissent, by Dickson C.J., at pp. 569 and 571. The same approach is again inherent in the Chief Justice's judgment in *Canadian National Railway Co. (Action Travail des Femmes), supra.*

11. The interpretative principles I have set forth seem to me to be largely dispositive of this case. To begin with, they dispose of the argument that one should have reference to theories of employer liability developed in the context of criminal or quasicriminal conduct. These are completely beside the point as being fault oriented, for, as we saw, the central purpose of a human rights Act is remedial to eradicate antisocial conditions without regard to the motives or intention of those who cause them.

12. The last observation also goes some way towards disposing of the theory that the liability of an employer ought to be based on vicarious liability developed under the law of tort. On this issue, counsel for the Crown placed considerable reliance on the

requirement in s. 7(b) that the act complained of must have been done in the course of employment. It is clear, however, that that limitation, as developed under the doctrine of vicarious liability in tort cannot meaningfully be applied to the present statutory scheme. For in torts what is aimed at are activities somehow done within the confines of the job a person is engaged to do, not something, like sexual harassment, that is not really referable to what he or she was employed to do. The purpose of the legislation is to remove certain undesirable conditions, in this context in the workplace, and it would seem odd if under s. 7(a) an employer would be liable for sexual harassment engaged in by an employee in the course of hiring a person, but not be liable when that employee does so in the course of supervising another employee, particularly an employee on probation. It would appear more sensible and more consonant with the purpose of the Act to interpret the phrase "in the course of employment" as meaning work or job-related, especially when that phrase is prefaced by the words "directly or indirectly". Interestingly, in adding "physical handicap" as a prohibited ground of discrimination in the workplace (s. 3), the phrase used is "in matters related to employment".

13. Any doubt that might exist on the point is completely removed by the nature of the remedies provided to effect the principles and policies set forth in the Act. This is all the more significant because the Act, we saw, is not aimed at determining fault or punishing conduct. It is remedial. Its aim is to identify and eliminate discrimination. If this is to be done, then the remedies must be effective, consistent with the "almost constitutional" nature of the rights protected.

14. What then are the remedies provided by the Act? Section 4, after providing that a discriminatory practice may be the subject of a complaint under the Act, goes on to say that anyone who is found to be engaging or to have engaged in such a practice may be made subject to an order under ss. 41 and 42. Subsections 41(2) and (3) are particularly relevant; they read as follows:

> 41. ... (2) If, at the conclusion of its inquiry, a Tribunal finds that the complaint to which the inquiry relates is substantiated, subject to subsection (4) and section 42, it may make an order against the person found to be engaging or to have engaged in the discriminatory practice and include in such order any of the following terms that it considers appropriate:
> (a) that such person cease such discriminatory practice and, in consultation with the Commission on the general purposes thereof, take measures, including adoption of a special program, plan or arrangement referred to in subsection 15(1), to prevent the same or a similar practice occurring in the future;
> (b) that such person *make available to the victim of the discriminatory practice on the first reasonable occasion such rights*, opportunities or privileges as, in the opinion of the Tribunal, are being or were denied the victim as a result of the practice;
> (c) that such person compensate the victim, as the Tribunal may consider proper, *for any or all of the wages* that the victim was deprived of and *any expenses incurred* by the victim as a result of the discriminatory practice; and
> (d) that such person compensate the victim, as the Tribunal may consider proper, for any or all additional cost of obtaining alternative goods, services, facilities or accommodation and any expenses incurred by the victim as a result of the discriminatory practice.

(3) *In addition* to any order that the Tribunal may make pursuant to subsection (2), if the Tribunal finds that

(a) a person is engaging or has engaged in a discriminatory practice *wilfully or recklessly*, or

(b) the victim of the discriminatory practice has suffered in respect of feelings or self-respect as a result of the practice, the Tribunal may order the person to pay such compensation to the victim, not exceeding five thousand dollars, as the Tribunal may determine. [Emphasis added.]

15. It is clear to me that the remedial objectives of the Act would be stultified if the above remedies were not available as against the employer. As MacGuigan J. observed in the Court of Appeal, [1984] 2 F.C. 799, at p. 845:

> The broad remedies provided by section 41, the general necessity for effective follow-up, including the cessation of the discriminatory practice, imply a similar responsibility on the part of the employer. That is most clearly the case with respect to the requirement in paragraph 41(2)(a) that the person against whom an order is made "take measures, including the adoption of a special program, plan or arrangement ... to prevent the same or a similar practice occurring in the future". Only an employer could fulfil such a mandate.

MacGuigan J.'s comment equally applies to an order to make available the rights denied to the victims under para. (b). Who but the employer could order reinstatement? This is true as well of para. (c) which provides for compensation for lost wages and expenses. Indeed, if the Act is concerned with the *effects* of discrimination rather than its *causes* (or motivations), it must be admitted that only an employer can remedy undesirable effects; only an employer can provide the most important remedy a healthy work environment. The legislative emphasis on prevention and elimination of undesirable conditions, rather than on fault, moral responsibility and punishment, argues for making the Act's carefully crafted remedies effective. It indicates that the intention of the employer is irrelevant, at least for purposes of s. 41(2). Indeed, it is significant that s. 41(3) provides for *additional* remedies in circumstances where the discrimination was reckless or wilful (i.e., intentional). In short, I have no doubt that if the Act is to achieve its purpose, the Commission must be empowered to strike at the heart of the problem, to prevent its recurrence and to require that steps be taken to enhance the work environment.

16. Not only would the remedial objectives of the Act be stultified if a narrower scheme of liability were fashioned; the educational objectives it embodies would concomitantly be vitiated. If, as was suggested by the Court of Appeal, society must wait for a Minister (who is already subject to public scrutiny) to discriminate before the Act comes into operation, how effective can the educational function of the Act be? More importantly, the interpretation I have proposed makes education begin in the workplace, in the micro democracy of the work environment, rather than in society at large.

17. Hence, I would conclude that the statute contemplates the imposition of liability on employers for all acts of their employees "in the course of employment", interpreted in the purposive fashion outlined earlier as being in some way related or associated with the employment. It is unnecessary to attach any label to this type of liability; it is purely statutory. However, it serves a purpose somewhat similar to that of vicarious liability in tort, by placing responsibility for an organization on those who control it and are in

a position to take effective remedial action to remove undesirable conditions. I agree with the following remarks of Marshall J., who was joined by Brennan, Blackmun and Stevens JJ., in his concurring opinion in the United States Supreme Court decision in *Meritor Savings Bank, FSB v. Vinson*, 106 S.Ct. 2399 (1986), at pp. 2410–11 concerning sexual discrimination by supervisory personnel:

> An employer can act only through individual supervisors and employees; discrimination is rarely carried out pursuant to a formal vote of a corporation's board of directors. Although an employer may sometimes adopt company-wide discriminatory policies violative of Title VII, acts that may constitute Title VII violations are generally effected through the actions of individuals, and often an individual may take such a step even in defiance of company policy. Nonetheless, Title VII remedies, such as reinstatement and back-pay, generally run against the employer as an entity.
>
> ...
>
> A supervisor's responsibilities do not begin and end with the power to hire, fire, and discipline employees, or with the power to recommend such actions. Rather, a supervisor is charged with the day-to-day supervision of the work environment and with ensuring a safe, productive, workplace. There is no reason why abuse of the latter authority should have different consequences than abuse of the former. In both cases it is the authority vested in the supervisor by the employer that enables him to commit the wrong: it is precisely because the supervisor is understood to be clothed with the employer's authority that he is able to impose unwelcome sexual conduct on subordinates.

18. In the light of these conclusions, it is unnecessary for me to examine the allegations that the Crown would, in any event, be directly liable for management's failure to adequately investigate Robichaud's complaints, thereby perpetuating the poisoned work environment. At all events, this, too, involves the acts of employees.

19. I should perhaps add that while the conduct of an employer is theoretically irrelevant to the imposition of liability in a case like this, it may nonetheless have important practical implications for the employer. Its conduct may preclude or render redundant many of the contemplated remedies. For example, an employer who responds quickly and effectively to a complaint by instituting a scheme to remedy and prevent recurrence will not be liable to the same extent, if at all, as an employer who fails to adopt such steps. These matters, however, go to remedial consequences, not liability.

United Steelworkers obo others v Tim Hortons and others (No 2), 2015 BCHRT 168

[1] The United Steelworkers (the "USWA" or the "Union") has filed a representative complaint on behalf of a group described as "all workers from the Philippines currently and formerly employed through the temporary foreign worker program at 658380 B.C. Ltd. doing business as Tim Hortons in Fernie, B.C. (the "Complainant Group").

[2] The Respondents are 658380 B.C. Ltd. ("658380"), who is the franchisee which operated the Tim Hortons in Fernie at all relevant times; Pierre Joseph Pelletier and Kristin Hovind-Pelletier (together the "Pelletiers"), a husband and wife who are the principals of 658380 B.C. Ltd. (collectively the "Franchisee Group").

[3] The complaint is also brought against Tim Hortons, Inc. ("THI") and TDL Group Corp. ("TDL") (collectively the "Tim Hortons Respondents"). According to the Tim Hortons Respondents, TDL is in the business of licensing the right to operate Tim Hortons restaurants in Canada. As most Canadians will know, Tim Hortons restaurants are ubiquitous in Canada selling coffee, donuts, soup, sandwiches and other food and beverages.

[4] Within the Tim Hortons Respondents, TDL is indirectly a wholly owned subsidiary of THI. TDL entered into a franchise agreement with 658380.

[5] The complaint alleges that the Respondents discriminated against the Complainant Group in their employment contrary to s. 13 of the *Human Rights Code* because of the Complainants' race, colour, ancestry and place of origin.

[6] Specifically, the Complainant Group alleges that its members were denied overtime premiums, given less desirable shifts and threatened with being returned to the Philippines, while this was not the case with workers who were not foreigners.

[7] The Franchisee Group says that the USWA does not have the authority to represent the members of the Complainant Group. They deny that they have discriminated against the Complainant Group as alleged and say that they allowed banking of overtime and assisted members of the Complainant Group with immigration and other issues.

[8] The Tim Hortons Respondents, for their part, deny that they employed any of the members of the Complainant Group. Rather, they say that TDL entered into a licensing agreement with 658380 to operate a Tim Hortons restaurant, but that 658380 operated as an independent contractor with regard to the employment of the Complainant Group and others.

[9] More particularly, the Tim Hortons Respondents say that, while they had authority to determine certain aspects of 658380's business, such as prices, menus and branding, they were not party to any employment contracts with any members of the Complainant Group, had no control over any terms of employment and had no ability to influence the employment relationship between members of the Complainant Group and 658380....

II APPLICATION TO DISMISS

[11] The Tim Hortons Respondents have brought an application to dismiss the complaint against them, pursuant to s. 27(1)(b) and (c) of the *Human Rights Code*.

[12] The relevant parts of s. 27 (1) state:

> (1) A member or panel may, at any time after a complaint is filed and with or without a hearing, dismiss all or part of the complaint if that member or panel determines that any of the following apply: ...
> (b) the acts or omissions alleged in the complaint or that part of the complaint do not contravene this Code;
> (c) there is no reasonable prospect that the complaint will succeed; ...

[...]

[31] THI is a publicly-traded federally-incorporated company. TDL is a Nova Scotia company extra-provincially registered in Alberta and engaged in the business of developing, opening and licensing the rights to operate Tim Hortons restaurants. TDL is said to be an "indirectly but wholly owned subsidiary of the Respondent THI"....

[33] In support of their application to dismiss pursuant to s. 27(1)(c), the Tim Hortons Respondents rely on the agreement entered into between TDL and 658380 (the "Franchise Agreement")....

[36] In the Franchise Agreement, TDL grants a license to 658380 to operate a Tim Hortons restaurant in Fernie. B.C. and, in connection with that restaurant, to use the Tim Hortons Trademarks and the "Tim Hortons System", which, among other things, includes "the Licensor's Confidential Operating Manual" (the "Manual")....

[...]

[62] However, even if that were not the case, considering all of the material submitted, I am not convinced that there is no reasonable likelihood the complaint will succeed.

[63] I start with several propositions that are clear. First, and to reiterate, despite what the law may be in other jurisdictions, discrimination under s. 13 of the *Code* is not limited to employers or persons who attract vicarious liability.

[64] The Tim Hortons Respondents rely on decisions of the Ontario Divisional Court in *Toshi Enterprises Ltd. v. Coffee Time Donuts Inc.*, 2008 Carswell Ontario 7954 and of the Queen's Bench of Saskatchewan in *Youngblut and others v. Jim and Jaklen Holdings Ltd.*, 2002 SKQB 463.

[65] One should approach decisions in this area from other jurisdictions with some caution because of the different wording of their statutes and the emphasis in those jurisdictions on establishing an employment or employment-like relationship.

[66] In British Columbia, the *Code* prohibition in s. 13 is of a person, not an "employer". The test, as noted in *Chárthaigh*, is whether the franchisor exercises sufficient control over the franchisee to influence its behaviour and unreasonably failed to exercise that control in circumstances where the *Code* was being violated.

[67] Second, the question of the liability of a franchisor for the conduct of its franchisee will typically be fact-based. In that respect, I agree with the approach in *Chárthaigh* and *Philip* that a determination of whether a franchisor exercises sufficient control over the actions of a franchisee to attract liability is typically best left to an evidentiary hearing on the merits.

[68] The test that a complainant must meet to implicate a franchisor in a human rights complaint is not entirely developed. There are cases which suggest or even find that control must be such as to find that the franchisor is in fact the employer. This is the approach taken by the Tribunal in *Maycock v. Canadian Tire Corp.*, 2004 BCHRT 33 following a decision of the Saskatchewan Court of Queen's Bench in *Youngblut v. Jim and Jaklen Holding Ltd.*, 2002 SKQB 463.

[69] *Maycock* was followed in *Boyetchko v. Home Hardware Stores Ltd.*, 2004 BCHRT 421 (CanLII), 2004 BCHRT421 where the Tribunal said (at para. 5):

> A franchisor may be a proper respondent to a human rights complaint arising out of its franchisee's employment relationships or services: *Maycock v. Canadian Tire Corporation Limited and another*, 2004 BCHRT 33. A franchisor may be liable if it exercises such a degree of control over the acts or omissions alleged in the complaint that it can be said that the franchisor is itself providing a service or employing the employees in question: *Maycock* at para. 46.

[70] In *Maycock*, however, the Tribunal began with but then arguably ignored the directive of the Supreme Court of Canada in *Robichaud v. Canada (Treasury Board)*, [1987] 2

S.C.R. 84 where the Court addressed the issue of liability of an employer for the unauthorized discriminatory acts of its employees. The Court noted that liability in a human rights context should not be determined on the basis of principles brought from other areas but with regard to the remedial purposes of such legislation. In finding that the educational and remedial aspects of human rights legislation would be stultified if a remedy could not be provided against an employer for the discriminatory actions of its employees, the Court stated:

> It is unnecessary to attach any label to this type of liability; it is purely statutory. However, it serves a purpose somewhat similar to that of vicarious liability in tort, by placing responsibility for an organization on those who control it and are in a position to take remedial effective action to remove undesirable conditions. (para. 17)

[71] More recently, in *Chárthaigh* the Tribunal said (at para. 20):

> I am satisfied that if Blenz has sufficient control over the operations of the franchise location where the alleged harassment incidents occurred to influence the response of the franchisee to Ms. Chárthaigh's allegations, and they were as indifferent to the allegations as alleged, they could be found in violation of the Code.

[72] The principal underlying *Chárthaigh* appears more in line with decisions of the Tribunal in other situations, not involving franchisees. In *Vetro v. Greater Vancouver Transportation Authority*, 2005 BCHRT 383, a Handy Dart driver employed by a co-operative under contract with a transit authority alleged discrimination and named both the transit authority and the co-operative which directly employed him. The complaint against the transit authority alleged that, once it had positive notice of the circumstances of the employer's termination of Mr. Vetro and its retaliatory acts, it had an obligation under the *Code* to ensure that the service which was being conducted for it, in its name, with its money, and to fulfill its statutory duty, was not done in a manner which contravenes the *Code*.

[73] The Tribunal denied the application to dismiss stating (at para. 13):

> In this context, the issue of whether TransLink was Mr. Vetro's employer is not determinative of the issue. Section 13(1) does not require that "a person" be "an employer" in order for its provisions to apply. The section provides that "a person" must not discriminate "regarding" employment. Several decisions by the Tribunal have contemplated a contravention of s. 13(1) in situations where there was no direct employment relationship between the complainant and the respondent, but where the respondent has the ability to interfere with or influence the employment relationship: see, for example, *Middlemiss v. Norske Canada Ltd.*, 2002 BCHRT 5; and *Pettie v. Canada Safeway Limited and Gavin (No. 2)*, 2004 BCHRT 440.

[74] The Tribunal noted that human rights law was not static and that a determination of whether the transit authority had any liability in the circumstances would require not only consideration of the contractual arrangement but the actual practices that were at issue. To similar effect was the decision of the Tribunal in *Hunter v. British Columbia (Ministry of Health)*, 2005 BCHRT 408. The parties did not fully argue the law on this

application and I make no final determination about the legal analysis that may apply in this context.

[75] In my view, regardless of whether the standard for finding a franchisor liable for the discriminatory acts of its franchisee is as set out in *Maycock* and *Boyetchko* or the approach in *Chárthaigh* and in *Vetro*, I am unconvinced that there is no reasonable prospect that this complaint will succeed. In this case, in addition to the provisions of the Franchise Agreement, the actual conduct of the Tim Hortons Respondents could demonstrate the requisite control over the employment relationship between the Franchisee Group and the Complainant Group. This includes, among other things, carrying out extended and seemingly extensive audits of 658780, appearing to require substantial remediation and seemingly cancelling the Franchise Agreements and leases when 658780 failed to remedy its apparent violation of local employment standards legislation, particularly with regard to the temporary foreign workers. I have also considered that the Tim Hortons Respondents did not produce the "Confidential Operating Manual" when it is clearly relevant and is deemed to be part of the Franchise Agreement, suggesting that provisions in the manual may go to the degree of control by the Tim Hortons Respondents of the franchisee.

[76] As well, the Tim Hortons Respondents played a role in the franchisee's participation in the Temporary Foreign Worker program and appeared to mandate a Tim Hortons-wide harassment policy.

[77] I cannot say, and it is not my role at this stage to determine, that the agreement and the actual manner of the relationship between the Tim Hortons Respondents and the Franchisee Group is sufficient to attach liability to the Tim Hortons Respondents for the alleged misconduct of the franchisee and its principals. What I can and do say at this preliminary stage is that, based on the materials before me (and also because not all of the relevant materials were placed before me), I am not prepared to exercise my discretion to dismiss the complaint without a hearing. I am not persuaded that there is no reasonable prospect that the complaint will succeed.

[78] The Tim Hortons Respondents' application to dismiss the Complainant Group's complaint pursuant to s. 27(1)(c) is denied.

McCormick v Fasken Martineau DuMoulin LLP, 2014 SCC 39

[1] Abella J.: John Michael McCormick became an equity partner at Fasken Martineau DuMoulin LLP in 1979. In the 1980s, the equity partners — those partners with an ownership interest in the firm — voted to adopt a provision in their Partnership Agreement whereby equity partners were to retire as equity partners and divest their ownership shares in the partnership at the end of the year in which they turned 65. A partner could make individual arrangements to continue working as an employee or as a "regular" partner without an equity stake, but such arrangements were stated in the Agreement to be "the exception".

[2] In 2009, when he was 64, Mr. McCormick brought a claim alleging that this provision in the Partnership Agreement constituted age discrimination contrary to s. 13(1) of the British Columbia *Human Rights Code*.

[3] Fasken applied to have the claim dismissed on the grounds that the complaint was not within the jurisdiction of the tribunal and that there was no reasonable prospect that the complaint would succeed. In its view, Mr. McCormick, as an equity partner, was not in the type of workplace relationship covered by the *Code*.

[4] The issue before this Court, therefore, is how to characterize Mr. McCormick's relationship with his firm in order to determine if it comes within the jurisdiction of the *Code* over employment. That requires us to examine the essential character of the relationship and the extent to which it is a dependent one.

[5] At the time this complaint was brought, Fasken had 650 lawyers worldwide, of whom 260 were equity partners. There were about 60 equity partners in Fasken's Vancouver office. Responsibility for the day-to-day running of the partnership is delegated through the Partnership Agreement to the Partnership Board, consisting of 13 equity partners, including three from the British Columbia region, elected to three-year terms by the equity partners. Before the creation of the Board, this responsibility had been given to the "Executive Committee". In 1998-1999, Mr. McCormick served for a year on that committee.

[6] The Board determines the compensation criteria for equity partners. The compensation criteria in place at the relevant time included the quality of the legal work, teamwork, generation of profitable business from new and existing clients, profitable maintenance of existing clients, contribution to the firm's image, reputation and seniority, profitable personal production, businesslike personal practice management, contribution to firm activities, ancillary income generated for the firm, and peer review. A regional compensation committee, comprised of equity partners, allocates the firm's profits to the equity partners in the region based on these criteria. There is a limited right of appeal back to the committee based on information not available at the time the initial allocation was made.

[7] The Board appoints and gives direction to the firm's managing partner, who is responsible for the overall management of the firm and who is accountable to the Board. The duties of the managing partner include "managing and structuring the human resources of the Firm, including Partners, associates and staff" and "delegat[ing] specific functions, responsibilities, authorities and accountabilities to Regional Managing Partners, committees, task forces, individual Partners or associates, as appropriate, and supervis[ing] the execution of those tasks". Within the firm, all management and support staff report directly or indirectly to a chief operating officer. The chief operating officer reports through the firm's managing partner to the Board.

[8] All written opinions given to a client are the opinion of the firm, and must be reviewed and approved by a partner other than the partner who prepared it. The firm appoints a "client manager" for each client, who may not be the lawyer who brought the client to the firm. Each matter the firm handles for a client is overseen by a "file manager", who is responsible for ensuring that the matter is efficiently and properly dealt with. The client manager monitors the performance of the file manager for each matter. All content produced by lawyers, including equity partners, becomes the property of the firm. Any income earned by a partner that relates in any manner to the practice of law is deemed to be property of the firm. Partners are prohibited from entering into financial arrangements or contracts in the name of the firm without the authorization of the firm's managing partner, Board Chair, regional managing partner or two members of the Board.

[9] A vote of the equity partnership as a whole is required for such matters as an amendment to the Partnership Agreement, the admission of a new equity partner, the expulsion of an equity partner, the dissolution of the firm, the removal of the managing partner, the opening of a new office, as well as the approval of certain significant expenses or debts.

[10] An equity partner also has a capital account with the firm, which is paid out when he or she leaves the firm. The aggregate of the partners' capital accounts represents the funding of the partnership. Partners are liable for the debts of the partnership to the extent that they are not covered by insurance or which the Board elects to treat as an expense, and as limited by s. 104 of the *Partnership Act*. If the partnership is dissolved, partners are entitled to receive a share of the assets remaining after all of the partnership's debts and obligations are satisfied.

[11] An equity partner like Mr. McCormick has an ownership interest in the firm. The terms of the Partnership Agreement require that equity partners divest their ownership shares in the partnership at the end of the year in which they turn 65. All equity partners are subject to this time limit on their ownership interests in the firm. A partner may make individual arrangements to continue working as an employee or as a "regular" partner without an equity stake, but such arrangements are stated in the Agreement to be "the exception rather than the rule".

[12] Mr. McCormick brought a complaint to the British Columbia Human Rights Tribunal, arguing that this provision of the Partnership Agreement constituted age discrimination in employment, contrary to s. 13(1) of the *Code*. Fasken brought an application to dismiss Mr. McCormick's claim on the grounds that the Tribunal did not have jurisdiction over the claim because Fasken was not in an employment relationship with Mr. McCormick....

[23] Deciding who is in an employment relationship for purposes of the *Code* means, in essence, examining how two synergetic aspects function in an employment relationship: control exercised by an employer over working conditions and remuneration, and corresponding dependency on the part of a worker. In other words, the test is who is responsible for determining working conditions and financial benefits and to what extent does a worker have an influential say in those determinations? The more the work life of individuals is controlled, the greater their dependency and, consequently, their economic, social and psychological vulnerability in the workplace....

[24] The test applied by the Human Rights Tribunal in British Columbia for determining whether someone is in an employment relationship under the *Code* was developed in *Crane*, where it identified the following indicia:

a. "Utilization"—this ... looks to the question of whether the alleged employer "utilized" or gained some benefit from the employee in question;
b. Control—did the alleged employer exercise control over the employee, whether in relation to the determination of his or her wages or other terms and conditions of employment, or in relation to their work more generally, such as the nature of the work to be performed or questions of discipline and discharge?
c. Financial burden—did the alleged employer bear the burden of remuneration of the employee? and

d. Remedial purpose—does the ability to remedy any discrimination lie with the alleged employer? [para. 79]

This test too is, in essence, a control/dependency test. The concepts of utilization, control, financial burden, as well as the ability of the employer to remedy any discrimination, all ultimately relate to whether the employer controls working conditions and remuneration, resulting in dependency on the part of the employee.

[25] Placing the emphasis on control and dependency in determining whether there is an employment relationship is consistent with approaches taken to the definition of employment in the context of protective legislation both in Canada and internationally.... The Ontario Labour Relations Board, for example, uses a seven-factor test for determining if an employment relationship exists, based on indicia that relate mainly to control and economic dependency. Among other criteria, the Board asks whether the alleged employer exercises direction and control over the performance of work; imposes discipline; has the authority to dismiss employees; bears the burden of remuneration; and is perceived to be the employer.... That said, while significant underlying similarities may exist across different statutory schemes dealing with employment, it must always be assessed in the context of the particular scheme being scrutinized....

[39] Turning to Mr. McCormick's relationship with his partnership and applying the control/dependency test, based on his ownership, sharing of profits and losses, and the right to participate in management, I see him more as someone in control of, rather than subject to, decisions about workplace conditions. As an equity partner, he was part of the group that controlled the partnership, not a person vulnerable to its control.

[40] It is true that Fasken had certain administrative rules to which Mr. McCormick was subject, but they did not transform the substance of the relationship into one of subordination or dependency. Management and compensation committees are necessary mechanisms to implement and coordinate the firm's policies, not limitations on a partner's autonomy. Fasken's Board, regional managing partners, and compensation committees were all directly or indirectly accountable to, and controlled by, the partnership as a whole, of which Mr. McCormick was a full and equal member. Under the Partnership Agreement, most major decisions, *including those relating to the firm's mandatory retirement* policy, were subject to a vote of the partnership, in which all partners, including Mr. McCormick, had an equal say. Mr. McCormick was an equity partner when the current retirement policy was adopted, and was entitled to vote on the very policy that he is now challenging.

[41] In addition to the right to participate in the management of the partnership, as an equity partner Mr. McCormick benefited from other control mechanisms, including the right to vote for—and stand for election to—the firm's Board; the duty that the other partners owed to him to render accounts; the right not to be subject to discipline or dismissal; the right, on leaving the firm, to his share of the firm's capital account; and the protection that he could only be expelled from the partnership by a special resolution passed by a meeting of all equity partners and a regional resolution in his region, arguably giving him tenure since there is no evidence of any equity partners being expelled from this partnership.

[42] Nor was Mr. McCormick dependent on Fasken in a meaningful sense. It is true that his remuneration came exclusively from the partnership, but this remuneration

represented his share of the profits of the partnership in accordance with his ownership interest. The partnership was run for the economic benefit of the partners, including Mr. McCormick. While the financial proceeds of Mr. McCormick's work were pooled with those of other lawyers in the firm, and the distribution of profits was ultimately determined by internal committees, these committees applied criteria that were designed to measure the partner's contribution to the firm. Mr. McCormick drew his income from the profits of the partnership and was liable for its debts and losses. In addition, he had a capital account and was entitled to share in the partnership's assets if it dissolved. In effect, Mr. McCormick was not working for the benefit of someone else, as the Tribunal's reasons suggest, he was, as an equity partner, in a common enterprise with his partners for profit, and was therefore working for his own benefit.

[43] Finally, it must be observed that in order to change the firm's mandatory retirement policy, all of Fasken's equity partners would have been entitled to vote. Responsibility for remedying any alleged inequity thus lay in the hands of Mr. McCormick as much as any other equity partner. Instead, he financially benefited for over 30 years from the retirement of the other partners. In fact, in no material way was Mr. McCormick structurally or substantively ever in a subordinate relationship with the other equity partners....

[45] In the absence of any genuine control over Mr. McCormick in the significant decisions affecting the workplace, there cannot, under the *Code*, be said to be an employment relationship with the partnership. Far from being subject to the control of Fasken, Mr. McCormick was among the partners who controlled it from 1979, when he became an equity partner, until he left in 2012. The Tribunal therefore erred in concluding that it had jurisdiction over his relationship with the partnership.

14:500 SOME OTHER HUMAN RIGHTS ISSUES IN THE WORKPLACE

In addition to entitlements to equality and non-discrimination, there is growing recognition that workers may have other concerns at work that merit protection, especially where rules and practices at work touch on employee behaviour outside the workplace, where they raise issues of employee civil liberties, or where breaches on the part of employers endanger employees in the workplace. Some of the most contentious issues involve drug testing, privacy concerns, and employee whistleblowing. Although courts and adjudicators have moved to circumscribe employer use of random alcohol and drug tests, the legal limits of such testing and the extent of employer defences of its use are still unclear. At the same time, both the federal government and provincial legislatures have implemented new statutory rights to privacy that have an impact on the collection and use of information in the workplace.

14:510 Drug Testing

What is an employer entitled to do in order to maintain a drug-free workplace? For example, to what extent may it rely upon random drug and alcohol testing? Can employees be required to disclose all past drug and alcohol abuse?

CHAPTER 14: EQUALITY AND HUMAN RIGHTS IN EMPLOYMENT

***Entrop v Imperial Oil Ltd* (2000), 50 OR (3d) 18 (ONCA)**

[The employer introduced a rigorous drug and alcohol testing policy in the wake of the Exxon Valdez oil spill disaster. The complainant employee was a recovered alcoholic. Although he had not had a drink for seven years, he was transferred from a safety-sensitive position to a less desirable one after he disclosed his prior history of alcohol abuse in accordance with the employer's policy. A Board of Inquiry held that the policy violated the Ontario *Human Rights Code*, and the Ontario Court of Appeal upheld that decision. Relying on the three-part test in the Supreme Court of Canada decision in *Meiorin*, excerpted in Section 14:240, and having found that the policy was both rationally connected to job performance and adopted honestly and in good faith, Laskin JA considered whether the testing provisions were reasonably necessary to achieve their purpose.]

Laskin J.A.:

[...]

98 ... As the Board held, Imperial Oil has the right to assess whether its employees are capable of performing their essential duties safely. An employee working in a safety-sensitive position while impaired by alcohol or drugs presents a danger to the safe operation of Imperial Oil's business. Therefore, as the Board found, "freedom from impairment" by alcohol or drugs is a BFOR. An employee impaired by alcohol or drugs is incapable of performing or fulfilling the essential requirements of the job. The contentious issue is whether the means used to measure and ensure freedom from impairment—alcohol and drug testing with sanctions for a positive test—are themselves BFORs. Are they reasonably necessary to achieve a work environment free of alcohol and drugs?

99 I deal with drug testing first. The drugs listed in the Policy all have the capacity to impair job performance, and urinalysis is a reliable method of showing the presence of drugs or drug metabolites in a person's body. But drug testing suffers from one fundamental flaw. It cannot measure present impairment. A positive drug test shows only past drug use. It cannot show how much was used or when it was used. Thus, the Board found that a positive drug test provides no evidence of impairment or likely impairment on the job. It does not demonstrate that a person is incapable of performing the essential duties of the position. The Board also found on the evidence that no tests currently exist to accurately assess the effect of drug use on job performance and that drug testing programs have not been shown to be effective in reducing drug use, work accidents or work performance problems. On these findings, random drug testing for employees in safety-sensitive positions cannot be justified as reasonably necessary to accomplish Imperial Oil's legitimate goal of a safe workplace free of impairment.

100 The random drug testing provisions of the Policy suffer from a second flaw: the sanction for a positive test is too severe, more stringent than needed for a safe workplace and not sufficiently sensitive to individual capabilities. This aspect of the Policy's provisions on random drug testing was not addressed by the Board. However, the Administrative Guidelines specify the consequences of a Policy violation. Employees in non-safety-sensitive jobs who test positive are subject to progressive discipline, which consists of a warning, a three-to-five day suspension without pay, and termination. But

for employees in safety-sensitive positions who test positive for drugs or alcohol, the Guidelines provide only one sanction: termination of employment. . . .

106 The provisions for random alcohol testing for employees in safety-sensitive positions stand on a different footing. Breathalyzer testing can show impairment . . .

[. . .]

110 Imperial Oil can legitimately take steps to deter and detect alcohol impairment among its employees in safety-sensitive jobs. Alcohol testing accomplishes this goal. For employees in safety-sensitive jobs, where supervision is limited or non-existent, alcohol testing is a reasonable requirement. . . .

112 However, random alcohol testing though reasonable for employees in safety-sensitive jobs, will not satisfy the third step of the *Meiorin* test unless Imperial Oil has met its duty to accommodate the needs of those who test positive. The Policy's Guidelines provide for dismissal from employment following a single positive test. The Board did not discuss the question of individual accommodation following a positive breathalyser test. However, for the reasons I discussed in connection with drug testing, dismissal in all cases is inconsistent with Imperial Oil's duty to accommodate. To maintain random alcohol testing as a BFOR, Imperial Oil is required to accommodate individual differences and capabilities to the point of undue hardship. That accommodation should include consideration of sanctions less severe than dismissal and, where appropriate, the necessary support to permit the employee to undergo a treatment or a rehabilitation program.

113 I would therefore set aside the Board's conclusion that random alcohol testing for employees in safety-sensitive positions breaches the Code and in its place hold that this testing is a BFOR provided the sanction for an employee testing positive is tailored to the employee's circumstances. . . .

115 Entrop's original complaint of discrimination was directed at the Policy provisions for mandatory disclosure, reassignment and reinstatement. The Board concluded that the mandatory disclosure, reassignment and reinstatement provisions violated the Code. She concluded that alcohol and drug testing for certification for safety-sensitive positions and post-reinstatement may be permissible if Imperial Oil "can establish that testing is necessary as one facet of a larger process of assessment" of alcohol or drug abuse. The Divisional Court upheld her conclusions and I would too.

(a) Are the provisions for mandatory disclosure, reassignment and reinstatement *prima facie* discriminatory?

116 The Policy requires any employee in a safety-sensitive position to disclose a current or past substance abuse problem. On disclosure, that employee is automatically reassigned to a non-safety-sensitive job. The employee can only be reinstated to a safety-sensitive position by undergoing two years of rehabilitation, followed by five years of abstinence and by agreeing to a set of post-reinstatement controls. . . .

120 The contentious question is whether Imperial Oil has shown that the Policy provisions for mandatory disclosure, automatic reassignment and reinstatement are reasonably necessary to ensure that employees working in safety-sensitive jobs are not

impaired by alcohol or drugs. In my view, the provisions as drafted are not reasonably necessary to accomplish Imperial Oil's purpose. The provisions fail the third step in the *Meiorin* test for at least four reasons.

121 First, requiring an employee to disclose a past substance abuse problem, no matter how far in the past, is an unreasonable requirement. As the Commission acknowledged, Imperial Oil is entitled to require disclosure of a current substance abuse problem and a past substance abuse problem to a point. That point is reached when the risk of relapse or recurrence is no greater than the risk a member of the general population will suffer a substance abuse problem. On the expert evidence before her, the Board found that the cut-off point is five to six years of successful remission for a person with a previous alcohol abuse problem and six years of successful remission for a person with a previous drug abuse problem. Had the Policy provisions on mandatory disclosure been tailored to these cut-off points, I would have found them unobjectionable.

122 Second, automatic reassignment out of a safety-sensitive position following disclosure of a past substance abuse problem is not reasonably necessary either. Automatic reassignment cannot be justified because it follows a mandatory disclosure obligation that itself is too broad. More important, automatic reassignment fails to accommodate individual differences and capabilities. Although Imperial Oil may be justified in temporarily removing an employee with an active or recently-active substance abuse problem from a safety-sensitive job, it failed to establish that a single rule, automatic reassignment, was reasonably necessary in all cases. To use the words in *Meiorin* at p. 37 ... Imperial Oil failed to show that it could not accommodate "individual testing against a more individually sensitive standard" without imposing undue hardship on the company.

123 Entrop's case is a good example of why the Policy provisions for mandatory disclosure and automatic reassignment are not reasonably necessary. The evidence showed that his risk of relapse was extremely low and that his past alcohol abuse had not adversely affected his performance as a control board operator. In short, he was not incapable of performing his job because of his past alcohol abuse ...

124 A third and related reason why these Policy provisions are not reasonably necessary is that the requirement of two years' rehabilitation followed by five years' abstinence is overly broad. The Board concluded that "a minimum seven year period between the date of reassignment and potential reinstatement" contravenes the Code "because this length of time is not necessary in all cases." I agree with that conclusion, which again is supported by the expert evidence led at the hearing. Indeed, the seven year period is required even for those who have successfully completed a treatment program because "substance abuse problem" as defined in the Policy includes participation in a "structured program of counselling, therapy or other treatment." Imperial Oil did not show that a single seven year rule was needed and that it could not without undue hardship accommodate differences in how quickly individuals recover from a substance abuse problem.

125 Fourth, as the Board also concluded, "the mandatory conditions and undertakings for reinstatement are unlawful since the evidence shows this is more than is necessary in certain instances." Imperial Oil may legitimately insist on placing special controls for a period of time on an employee with a previous substance abuse problem

who is returned to a safety-sensitive position. But the controls must be tailored to the individual's circumstances to meet the accommodation requirement.

126 The controls initially demanded by Imperial Oil apply to all employees reinstated to a safety-sensitive position after disclosure of a past substance abuse problem. Many are onerous. For example, the employee must attend a self-help group (apparently indefinitely), must commit "to report to Imperial Oil's Occupational Health Division any changes in his/her circumstances that may significantly increase the risk of relapse," must commit "to report to his/her supervisor/manager compliance with the above conditions on a periodic basis to be determined by the review panel," and must commit "to undergo annual medical examinations, including screening for alcohol and drug abuse, conducted by Imperial's Occupational Health Division." These controls can be modified over time but to require them at all for employees like Entrop cannot be justified.

127 For these reasons, Imperial Oil has failed to meet the third step of the *Meiorin* test. The provisions for mandatory disclosure, reinstatement and reassignment cannot, therefore, be justified as BFORs.

In its recent decision in *Stewart v Elk Valley Coal Corp*, 2017 SCC 30, the Supreme Court upheld the termination of a cocaine-addicted employee who worked in a safety-sensitive job. The majority of justices found that he was not terminated because of his addiction, but rather because he breached the employer's drug and alcohol policy which required the disclosure of any addiction issues. The majority found that the complainant had not proven a *prima facie* case of discrimination because he had not established that his addiction, which on the evidence was not severe, was a factor in his failure to disclose. The majority stressed that it could not be assumed but rather had to be demonstrated on the basis of evidence that the employee's addiction was a factor in his termination, in that it diminished his ability to comply with the terms of the employer's policy. Two concurring justices and one dissenting justice viewed the facts differently, holding that the real reason for his termination was his addiction (that is, a *prima facie* case was established). In his dissenting opinion, Gascon J stressed that "[a] drug policy that, in application, automatically terminates employees who use drugs *prima facie* discriminates against individuals burdened by drug dependence" (at para 60). The concurring and dissenting opinions were divided on the question of whether the employer could have accommodated the employee short of undue hardship or not.

By contrast, in another recent case, *Communications, Energy and Paperworkers Union, Local 30 v Irving Pulp & Paper, Ltd*, 2013 SCC 34, the Supreme Court upheld a long line of arbitral jurisprudence requiring that employer searches conducted on the basis of management rights under a collective agreement be reasonable. The decision restricted the unilateral imposition of "mandatory, random and unannounced testing for all employees," even in a dangerous workplace, to cases where there was "reasonable cause, such as a general problem of substance abuse in the workplace" (at para 6). In this case, the Court held that "the expected safety gains to the employer ... range 'from uncertain ... to minimal at best,' while the impact on employee privacy was ... more severe" and that eight incidents of alcohol consumption or impairment at the workplace over a period of fifteen years did not reflect a significant problem with workplace alcohol use" sufficient to justify an "affront to the dignity and privacy of employees" (at paras 6, 47, and 51).

14:520 The Right to Privacy at Work

Employers inevitably gather sensitive information about their workers. This may occur at the point of hiring, in the ordinary course of employment (for example, in meeting employer obligations to provide information to tax authorities), or when employees become ill or disabled. In addition, outside actors such as creditors, landlords, and insurance companies may approach employers for references and other information about workers in their employ. How employers collect and use such information is of vital interest to workers, particularly where (as in the case of health or family data) it is inherently personal or otherwise touches on the private lives of employees. The growing ease with which information can be disseminated and reproduced—by fax, by email, and over the internet—has heightened long-standing employee concerns about their capacity to control information that might have implications for their security, reputation, and well-being. New instruments of surveillance, from cameras to computer programs, allow closer scrutiny of employees at work. Practices such as subcontracting also raise concerns about privacy, as they make it more likely that types of data which once remained within the control of the employer will get passed on to outside entities. Finally, there is a growing market for commercially valuable information which can tempt those who have it to sell it. On the other hand, the risks arising from new technology and new workplace practices are intertwined with (and may contribute to) a normative and cultural shift toward more insistence on privacy. Employers, for their part, are also concerned about the challenges that new technology adds to their ability to control corporate information and to manage their reputation.

In the last decade, both federal and provincial governments have passed legislation that limits the use of information in the workplace. The key statute is the federal *Personal Information Protection and Electronic Documents Act*, SC 2000, c 5 [PIPEDA]. PIPEDA governs information management within federally regulated entities. It also applies to private sector organizations in the course of their commercial activities, unless the particular province has enacted "substantially similar" legislation—which Quebec, Alberta, and British Columbia have done. PIPEDA sets limits on the collection, use, and disclosure of information, and calls for more transparency and accountability in how information is managed. A key provision, section 5(3), is the requirement that information may only be collected, used, and disclosed for purposes that a "reasonable person" would consider appropriate. Moreover, the purposes for which information is being collected must be disclosed to the employee at the time of collection, and any later uses for other purposes require further consent by the employee. PIPEDA also gives employees a right of access to their personal information, and a right to have any errors corrected.

Employees who believe that their employer has contravened their rights under PIPEDA may bring complaints to the Privacy Commissioner. In one case (or "finding"), the commissioner held that the installation of cameras in the employer's railway yard for the purposes of reducing vandalism and theft and ensuring safety did not fall within what a reasonable person would consider appropriate, given the minor nature of past incidents of vandalism, even though the employer had told employees about the camera system and had taken measures to protect their privacy. The complainant had argued that the cameras could be used to monitor employee conduct and work performance, and that information gleaned in this manner could have disciplinary consequences. See *Employee objects to company's use of digital video surveillance cameras*, Office of the Privacy Commissioner of Canada, *PIPEDA Case Summary #2003-114*. The Federal Court reached a different conclusion, although it applied the same four-stage test for section 5(3) of PIPEDA: (1) Is camera surveillance and recording necessary to meet a specific need? (2) Is camera surveillance and recording likely to be effective in meeting that need? (3) Is the loss of privacy proportional to the benefit gained? (4) Is there a less privacy-invasive way of achieving the same end? As new evidence became available, the Court found that the loss of privacy was proportional to the benefit gained because warning signs were displayed in the yard; the collection of personal information was brief, capturing only a person's image when that person was close to the camera; the recordings were kept locked up, were only accessed if an incident was reported, and were otherwise destroyed; and employees had a low expectation of privacy in public places. Also, there was no other less privacy-invasive way to meet the goal as the employer had examined and ruled out alternatives that were not cost-effective, such as fencing and the use of security guards. See *Eastmond v Canadian Pacific Railway*, 2004 FC 852.

A number of provinces have also passed statutes that bear on workplace privacy. In Ontario, for example, those statutes include the following: *Freedom of Information and Protection of Privacy Act*, RSO 1990, c F.31; *Municipal Freedom of Information and Protection of Privacy Act*, RSO 1990, c M.56; and *Personal Health Information Protection Act, 2004*, SO 2004, c 3 Schedule A. Privacy rights are also set out in some employment standards statutes, and may be the subject of grievances under collective agreements. For example, the arbitration award in *Hamilton Health Sciences v Ontario Nurses' Association (2007)*, 2007 CanLII 73923 Ont Lab Arb, concerned privacy rights under Ontario's *Personal Health Information Protection Act, 2004*, SO 2004, c 3, Schedule A [PHIPA], and under section 63 of its *Occupational Health and Safety Act*, RSO 1990, c 0.1 [OHSA]. Arbitrator Surdykowski dealt with the statutory and collective agreement privacy rights of nurses seeking short-term disability (STD) benefits through a third-party provider to which the hospital-employer had outsourced its STD application, assessment, and adjudication functions. A union policy grievance took issue with the third party provider's medical consent form. The union argued that in seeking consent that was coerced, overly broad, and improper for the purposes of short-term sickness benefits, the provider, and by extension the hospital, were in violation of collective agreement and statutory privacy rights.

Referring to both the PHIPPA and the OHSA, the arbitrator noted that employers can only invade employee privacy and compel the disclosure of personal medical information where expressly permitted by statute or by the collective agreement, or where the disclosure was demonstrably required and permitted by law for the particular purpose. Because the parties cannot contract out of legislation, such as the privacy and occupational health and safety statutes, those statutes and the collective agreement govern the information that employees must share, on the least intrusive basis possible, in satisfying the burden of proving their entitlement to sick leave benefits. In arbitrator Surdykowski's words (at para 27):

> The employer's desire for more information, or its genuine concern for an employee's well-being or desire to assist the employee, do not trump the employee's privacy rights. Nor do questions of expediency or efficiency. In the absence of a collective agreement

provision or legislation that provides otherwise the employer is entitled to know only that the employee is unable to work because she is ill or injured, the expected return date to work, and what work the employee can or cannot do.

The arbitrator went on to find that the employer had no right to information about a diagnosis; nor could it seek overly broad consent in the first instance or withhold benefits when employees refused to provide such consent. The mere assertion by the employer or third party that the information would be treated with heightened confidentiality did not by itself expand the employer's entitlement to personal medical information: "Either an employee has privacy rights or she does not," the arbitrator said, and went on: "A right that cannot be exercised is no right at all" (para 45). Given the comprehensive and clear instructions in both the PHIPPA (ss 18, 30, and 37) and OHSA (s 63) on the need for an employee's consent, given the revocable nature of such consent, and given the limitations of the employer's health insurance plan, the arbitrator concluded that the third party consent form was overly broad.

As technology advances and personal information can now be accessed, collected and disclosed by others more easily than in the past, the law of privacy, and privacy in the workplace continues to evolve. Below are two examples. The first decision deals with informational privacy and privacy expectations of employees using a company computer. While the second decision is not an employment case, it may be applicable and exemplifies how common law evolves in response to changes in society. In this case, a new tort was established — intrusion upon seclusion.

R v Cole, 2012 SCC 53

[A high-school teacher was charged with possession of child pornography and unauthorized use of a computer. He was permitted to use his work-issued laptop computer for incidental and personal purposes, which he did. While performing maintenance activities, a technician found on his laptop a hidden folder containing nude photographs of an underage female student. The technician notified the principal, and copied the photographs to a compact disc. The principal seized the laptop, and school board technicians copied the temporary internet files onto a second disc. The laptop and both discs were handed over to the police, who, without a warrant, reviewed their contents. While the issue was whether this evidence was admissible for the criminal trial, the Supreme Court of Canada made some comments with regards to the way the employer handled the issue.]

Fish J.:

[1] The Court left no doubt in *R. v. Morelli*, 2010 SCC 8, [2010] 1 S.C.R. 253, that Canadians may reasonably expect privacy in the information contained on their own *personal* computers. In my view, the same applies to information on *work* computers, at least where personal use is permitted or reasonably expected.

[2] Computers that are reasonably used for personal purposes — whether found in the workplace or the home — contain information that is meaningful, intimate, and touching on the user's biographical core. *Vis-à-vis* the state, everyone in Canada is constitutionally entitled to expect privacy in personal information of this kind.

[3] While workplace policies and practices may diminish an individual's expectation of privacy in a work computer, these sorts of operational realities do not in themselves remove the expectation entirely: The nature of the information at stake exposes the likes, interests, thoughts, activities, ideas, and searches for information of the individual user....

[39] Whether Mr. Cole had a reasonable expectation of privacy depends on the "totality of the circumstances" (*R. v. Edwards*, [1996] 1 S.C.R. 128, at para. 45).

[40] The "totality of the circumstances" test is one of substance, not of form. Four lines of inquiry guide the application of the test: (1) an examination of the subject matter of the alleged search; (2) a determination as to whether the claimant had a direct interest in the subject matter; (3) an inquiry into whether the claimant had a subjective expectation of privacy in the subject matter; and (4) an assessment as to whether this subjective expectation of privacy was objectively reasonable, having regard to the totality of the circumstances (*Tessling*, at para. 32; *Patrick*, at para. 27). I will discuss each in turn.

[41] In this case, the subject matter of the alleged search is the data, or informational content of the laptop's hard drive, its mirror image, and the Internet files disc—not the devices themselves.

[42] Our concern is thus with *informational privacy*: "[T]he claim of individuals, groups, or institutions to determine for themselves when, how, and to what extent information about them is communicated to others" (*Tessling*, at para. 23, quoting A. F. Westin, *Privacy and Freedom* (1970), at p. 7).

[43] Mr. Cole's direct interest and subjective expectation of privacy in the informational content of his computer can readily be inferred from his use of the laptop to browse the Internet and to store personal information on the hard drive.

[44] The remaining question is whether Mr. Cole's subjective expectation of privacy was objectively reasonable.

[45] There is no definitive list of factors that must be considered in answering this question, though some guidance may be derived from the relevant case law. As Sopinka J. explained in *R. v. Plant*, [1993] 3 S.C.R. 281, at p. 293:

> In fostering the underlying values of dignity, integrity and autonomy, it is fitting that s. 8 of the *Charter* should seek to protect a biographical core of personal information which individuals in a free and democratic society would wish to maintain and control from dissemination to the state. This would include information which tends to reveal intimate details of the lifestyle and personal choices of the individual.

[46] The closer the subject matter of the alleged search lies to the biographical core of personal information, the more this factor will favour a reasonable expectation of privacy. Put another way, the more personal and confidential the information, the more willing reasonable and informed Canadians will be to recognize the existence of a constitutionally protected privacy interest.

[47] Computers that are used for personal purposes, regardless of where they are found or to whom they belong, "contain the details of our financial, medical, and personal situations" (*Morelli*, at para. 105). This is particularly the case where, as here, the computer is used to browse the Web. Internet-connected devices "reveal our specific

interests, likes, and propensities, recording in the browsing history and cache files the information we seek out and read, watch, or listen to on the Internet" (*ibid.*).

[48] This sort of private information falls at the very heart of the "biographical core" protected by s. 8 of the *Charter*.

[49] Like *Morelli*, this case involves highly revealing and meaningful information about an individual's personal life—a factor strongly indicative of a reasonable expectation of privacy. Unlike in *Morelli*, however, this case involves a *work-issued* laptop and not a personal computer found in a private residence.

[50] The Policy and Procedures Manual of the school board asserted ownership over not only the hardware, but also the data stored on it: "Information technology systems and all data and messages generated on or handled by board equipment are considered to be the property of [the board], and are not the property of users of the information technology".

[51] While the ownership of property is a relevant consideration, it is not determinative (*R. v. Buhay*, 2003 SCC 30, [2003] 1 S.C.R. 631, at para. 22). Nor should it carry undue weight within the contextual analysis. As Dickson J. (later C.J.) noted in *Hunter*, at p. 158, there is "nothing in the language of [s. 8] to restrict it to the protection of property or to associate it with the law of trespass".

[52] The *context* in which personal information is placed on an employer-owned computer is nonetheless significant. The policies, practices, and customs of the workplace are relevant to the extent that they concern the use of computers by employees. These "operational realities" may diminish the expectation of privacy that reasonable employees might otherwise have in their personal information (*O'Connor v. Ortega*, 480 U.S. 709 (1987), at p. 717, *per* O'Connor J.).

[53] Even as modified by practice, however, written policies are not determinative of a person's reasonable expectation of privacy. Whatever the policies state, one must consider the *totality* of the circumstances in order to determine whether privacy is a reasonable expectation in the particular situation (*R. v. Gomboc*, 2010 SCC 55, [2010] 3 S.C.R. 211, at para. 34, *per* Deschamps J.).

[54] In this case, the operational realities of Mr. Cole's workplace weigh both for and against the existence of a reasonable expectation of privacy. *For*, because written policy and actual practice permitted Mr. Cole to use his work-issued laptop for personal purposes. *Against*, because both policy and technological reality deprived him of exclusive control over—and access to—the personal information he chose to record on it.

[55] As mentioned earlier, the Policy and Procedures Manual stated that the school board owned "all data and messages generated on or handled by board equipment". Moreover, the principal reminded teachers, annually, that the Acceptable Use Policy applied to them. This policy provided that "[t]eachers and administrators may monitor all student work and e-mail including material saved on laptop hard drives", and warned that "[u]sers should NOT assume that files stored on network servers or hard drives of individual computers will be private".

[56] Though Mr. Cole's laptop was equipped with a password, the contents of his hard drive were thus available to all other users and technicians with domain administration rights—at least when the computer was connected to the network. And even if the Acceptable Use Policy did not directly apply to teachers, as Mr. Cole maintains, he

and other teachers were in fact put on notice that the privacy they might otherwise have expected in their files was limited by the operational realities of their workplace.

[57] The "totality of the circumstances" consists of many strands, and they pull in competing directions in this case. On balance, however, they support the objective reasonableness of Mr. Cole's subjective expectation of privacy.

[58] The nature of the information in issue heavily favours recognition of a constitutionally protected privacy interest. Mr. Cole's personal use of his work-issued laptop generated information that is meaningful, intimate, and organically connected to his biographical core. Pulling in the other direction, of course, are the ownership of the laptop by the school board, the workplace policies and practices, and the technology in place at the school. These considerations diminished Mr. Cole's privacy interest in his laptop, at least in comparison to the personal computer at issue in *Morelli*, but they did not eliminate it entirely.

Jones v Tsige, 2012 ONCA 32

[1] SHARPE J.A.: — Does Ontario law recognize a right to bring a civil action for damages for the invasion of personal privacy?

[2] In July 2009, the appellant, Sandra Jones, discovered that the respondent, Winnie Tsige, had been surreptitiously looking at Jones' banking records. Tsige and Jones did not know each other despite the fact that they both worked for the same bank and Tsige had formed a common-law relationship with Jones' former husband. As a bank employee, Tsige had full access to Jones' banking information and, contrary to the bank's policy, looked into Jones' banking records at least 174 times over a period of four years.

[3] The central issue on this appeal is whether the motion judge erred by granting summary judgment and dismissing Jones' claim for damages on the ground that Ontario law does not recognize the tort of breach of privacy.

Facts

[4] Jones and Tsige worked at different branches of the Bank of Montreal ("BMO"). Jones maintains her primary bank account there. Jones and Tsige did not know or work with each other. However, Tsige became involved in a relationship with Jones' former husband. For about four years, Tsige used her workplace computer to access Jones' personal BMO bank accounts at least 174 times. The information displayed included transactions details as well as personal information, such as date of birth, marital status and address. Tsige did not publish, distribute or record the information in any way.

[5] Jones became suspicious that Tsige was accessing her account and complained to BMO. When confronted by BMO, Tsige admitted that she had looked at Jones' banking information, that she had no legitimate reason for viewing the information and that she understood it was contrary to BMO's code of business conduct and ethics and her professional responsibility. Tsige explained then, and maintains in this action, that she was involved in a financial dispute with the appellant's former husband and accessed the accounts to confirm whether he was paying child support to the appellant. Jones does not accept that explanation as she says it is inconsistent with the timing and frequency of Tsige's snooping.

[6] Tsige has apologized for her actions and insists that she has ceased looking at Jones' banking information. Tsige is contrite and embarrassed by her actions. BMO disciplined Tsige by suspending her for one week without pay and denying her a bonus.

[7] In her statement of claim, Jones asserts that her privacy interest in her confidential banking information has been "irreversibly destroyed" and claims damages of $70,000 for invasion of privacy and breach of fiduciary duty, and punitive and exemplary damages of $20,000.

1. Motions for summary judgment

[8] Jones proceeded under the simplified procedure of Rule 76 of the *Rules of Civil Procedure*, R.R.O. 1990, Reg. 194 and moved for summary judgment. Tsige brought a cross-motion for summary judgment to dismiss the action.

[9] The motion judge found that Tsige did not owe Jones a fiduciary obligation and dismissed that claim. Jones has not appealed that finding.

[10] The motion judge then reviewed the jurisprudence concerning the existence of a tort of invasion of privacy. He observed that recent Superior Court decisions have refused to strike out such claims at the pleading stage and that some academic writing indicates that the tort may exist.

[11] The motion judge concluded, however, that the statement of Cronk J.A. in *Euteneier v. Lee* (2005), 77 O.R. (3d) 621, [2005] O.J. No. 3896 (C.A.), at para. 63, leave to appeal to S.C.C. refused [2005] S.C.C.A. No. 516 is, in his words, "binding and dispositive of the question" of whether the tort of invasion of privacy exists at common law in Ontario. Euteneier concerned a lawsuit brought by a woman whose clothes were forcibly removed by police following her suicide attempt while she was detained in a holding cell. In considering whether the trial judge had accurately described the plaintiff's privacy and dignity interests, Cronk J.A. observed, at para. 63, "[the plaintiff] properly conceded in oral argument before this court that there is no 'free-standing' right to dignity or privacy under the *Charter* or at common law".

[12] The motion judge added that given the existence of privacy legislation protecting certain rights, any expansion of those rights should be dealt with by statute rather than common law.

[13] The motion judge dismissed Jones' motion for summary judgment and granted the motion brought by Tsige. He rejected Jones' submission that costs should be denied on the ground that the issue was novel and that Tsige's conduct was objectionable. The motion judge felt that Jones had pursued the litigation aggressively and failed to accept reasonable settlement offers. He awarded costs fixed at $35,000.

Issues

[14] Jones appeals to this court, raising the following issues:

1. Did the motion judge err in holding that Ontario law does not recognize a cause of action for invasion of privacy?
2. Did the motion judge err with respect to costs?

[. . .]

Issue 1. Does Ontario law recognize a cause of action for invasion of privacy?

(a) Introduction

[15] The question of whether the common law should recognize a cause of action in tort for invasion of privacy has been debated for the past 120 years. Aspects of privacy have long been protected by causes of action such as breach of confidence, defamation, breach of copyright, nuisance and various property rights. Although the individual's privacy interest is a fundamental value underlying such claims, the recognition of a distinct right of action for breach of privacy remains uncertain. As Adams J. stated in Ontario (Attorney General) v. Dieleman (1994), 20 O.R. (3d) 229, [1994] O.J. No. 1864, 117 D.L.R. (4th) 449 (Gen. Div.), at p. 688 D.L.R., after a comprehensive review of the case law, "invasion of privacy in Canadian common law continues to be an inceptive, if not ephemeral, legal concept, primarily operating to extend the margins of existing tort doctrine".

[16] Canadian, English and American courts and commentators almost invariably take the seminal articles of S.D. Warren and L.D. Brandeis, "The Right to Privacy" (1890), 4 Harv. L. Rev. 193 and William L. Prosser, "Privacy" (1960), 48 Cal. L. Rev. 383 as their starting point.

[17] Warren and Brandeis argued for the recognition of a right of privacy to meet the problems posed by technological and social change that saw "instantaneous photographs" and "newspaper enterprise" invade "the sacred precincts of private life" (at p. 195). They identified the "general right of the individual to be let alone", the right to "inviolate personality" (at p. 205), "the more general right to the immunity of the person" and "the right to one's personality" (at p. 207) as fundamental values underlying such well-known causes of action as breach of confidence, defamation and breach of copyright. They urged that open recognition of a right of privacy was well-supported by these underlying legal values and required to meet the changing demands of the society in which they lived.

[18] Professor Prosser's article picked up the threads of the American jurisprudence that had developed in the 70 years following the influential Warren and Brandeis article. Prosser argued that what had emerged from the hundreds of cases he canvassed was not one tort, but four, tied together by a common theme and name, but comprising different elements and protecting different interests. Prosser delineated a four-tort catalogue, summarized as follows, at p. 389:

1. Intrusion upon the plaintiff's seclusion or solitude, or into his private affairs.
2. Public disclosure of embarrassing private facts about the plaintiff.
3. Publicity which places the plaintiff in a false light in the public eye.
4. Appropriation, for the defendant's advantage, of the plaintiff's name or likeness.

[19] Most American jurisdictions now accept Prosser's classification and it has also been adopted by the *Restatement (Second) of Torts* (2010). The tort that is most relevant to this case, the tort of "intrusion upon seclusion", is described by the *Restatement*, at §652B as:

> One who intentionally intrudes, physically or otherwise, upon the seclusion of another or his private affairs or concerns, is subject to liability to the other for invasion of his privacy, if the invasion would be highly offensive to a reasonable person.

[20] The comment section of the *Restatement* elaborates this proposition and explains that the tort includes physical intrusions into private places as well as listening or looking, with or without mechanical aids, into the plaintiff's private affairs. Of particular relevance to this appeal is the observation that other non-physical forms of investigation or examination into private concerns may be actionable. These include opening private and personal mail or examining a private bank account, "even though there is no publication or other use of any kind" of the information obtained.

[21] If Jones has a right of action, it falls into Prosser's first category of intrusion upon seclusion. While I will make some reference to the fourth category of appropriation of the plaintiff's name or likeness in my discussion below, I will focus primarily on intrusion upon seclusion. I do so for two reasons. First, I accept Prosser's insight that the general right to privacy embraces four distinct torts, each with its own considerations and rules, and that confusion may result from a failure to maintain appropriate analytic distinctions between the categories. Second, as a court of law, we should restrict ourselves to the particular issues posed by the facts of the case before us and not attempt to decide more than is strictly necessary to decide that case. A cause of action of any wider breadth would not only over-reach what is necessary to resolve this case, but could also amount to an unmanageable legal proposition that would, as Prosser warned, breed confusion and uncertainty.

[22] The following discussion will examine whether the common law recognizes a cause of action for invasion of privacy. I will canvass case law from Ontario and other provinces and examine federal and provincial legislation relating to privacy. For completeness, I will also discuss the state of the law in foreign jurisdictions.

(b) Case law

[23] Reflecting on Canadian jurisprudence, Allen M. Linden and Bruce Feldthusen, *Canadian Tort Law*, 9th ed. (Toronto: LexisNexis, 2011) observed, at p. 59, that "[w]e seem to be drifting closer to the American model"....

[24] My analysis of the case law supports the same conclusion: Ontario has already accepted the existence of a tort claim for appropriation of personality and, at the very least, remains open to the proposition that a tort action will lie for an intrusion upon seclusion.

(i) Ontario case law

[25] In Canada, there has been no definitive statement from an appellate court on the issue of whether there is a common law right of action corresponding to the intrusion on seclusion category. Ontario trial judges have, however, often refused to dismiss such claims at the pleading stage as disclosing no cause of action and some have awarded damages for claims based on violations of the right to be free of intrusion upon seclusion. The clear trend in the case law is, at the very least, to leave open the possibility that such a cause of action does exist....

[29] There are also several Ontario cases in which the trial judge refused to strike pleadings alleging the tort of invasion of privacy as disclosing no cause of action.

[30] *Somwar v. McDonald's Restaurants of Canada Ltd.* (2006), 79 O.R. (3d) 172, [2006] O.J. No. 64 (S.C.J.) contains perhaps the most coherent and definitive pronouncement

in Ontario jurisprudence of the existence of a common law tort of invasion of privacy corresponding to the intrusion upon seclusion category. Somwar accused his employer, McDonald's Restaurants, of unlawfully invading his privacy by conducting a credit bureau check on him without his consent. The plaintiff claimed damages for invasion of privacy and for punitive damages. The defendant moved to strike the statement of claim and dismiss the plaintiff's action on the basis that it did not disclose a reasonable cause of action under rule 21.01(1)(b) of the *Rules of Civil Procedure*.

[31] Stinson J. reviewed the Ontario case law and observed that while the cases were not entirely consistent, even where the courts did not accept the existence of a privacy tort, they rarely went so far as to rule out the potential of such a tort. The body of case law, together with the recognition by the Supreme Court of Canada of the protection of privacy under s. 8 of the *Canadian Charter of Rights and Freedoms*, led him to conclude, at paras. 29 and 31:

> With advancements in technology, personal data of an individual can now be collected, accessed (properly and improperly) and disseminated more easily than ever before. There is a resulting increased concern in our society about the risk of unauthorized access to an individual's personal information. The traditional torts such as nuisance, trespass and harassment may not provide adequate protection against infringement of an individual's privacy interests. Protection of those privacy interests by providing a common law remedy for their violation would be consistent with Charter values and an "incremental revision" and logical extension of the existing jurisprudence. . . .
>
> Even if the plaintiff's claim for invasion of privacy were classified as "novel" (which, in any event, is not a proper basis for dismissing it), the foregoing analysis leads me to conclude that the time has come to recognize invasion of privacy as a tort in its own right. It therefore follows that it is neither plain nor obvious that the plaintiff's action cannot succeed on the basis that he has not pleaded a reasonable cause of action.

[...]

(ii) Provincial case law

[33] While there appears to be no appellate decision from another province definitively establishing a common law right of action for intrusion upon seclusion, dicta in at least two cases support the idea. In *Motherwell v. Motherwell*, [1976] A.J. No. 555, 73 D.L.R. (3d) 62 (S.C. App. Div.), a case involving harassing telephone calls, the court held the plaintiff had a right of action in nuisance but added, at para. 25, that "the interests of our developing jurisprudence would be better served by approaching invasion of privacy by abuse of the telephone system as a new category, rather than seeking by rationalization to enlarge" the existing categories of nuisance.

[...]

(c) Charter jurisprudence

[39] *Charter* jurisprudence identifies privacy as being worthy of constitutional protection and integral to an individual's relationship with the rest of society and the state. The Supreme Court of Canada has consistently interpreted the *Charter*'s s. 8 protection against unreasonable search and seizure as protecting the underlying right to privacy.

In *Hunter v. Southam Inc.*, 1984] 2 S.C.R. 145, [1984] S.C.R. No. 36, at pp. 158–59 S.C.R., Dickson J. adopted the purposive method of *Charter* interpretation and observed that the interests engaged by s. 8 are not simply an extension of the concept of trespass, but rather are grounded in an independent right to privacy held by all citizens.

[40] In *R. v. Dyment*, [1988] 2 S.C.R. 417, [1988] S.C.J. No. 82, at p. 427 S.C.R., La Forest J. characterized the s. 8 protection of privacy as "[g]rounded in a man's physical and moral autonomy" and stated that "privacy is essential for the well-being of the individual. For this reason alone, it is worthy of constitutional protection, but it also has profound significance for the public order." La Forest J. added, at p. 429 S.C.R.:

> In modern society, especially, retention of information about oneself is extremely important. We may, for one reason or another, wish or be compelled to reveal such information, but situations abound where the reasonable expectations of the individual that the information shall remain confidential to the persons to whom, and restricted to the purposes for which it is divulged, must be protected.

[41] *Charter* jurisprudence has recognized three distinct privacy interests: *Dyment*, at pp. 428–29 S.C.R.; *R. v. Tessling*, [2004] 3 S.C.R. 432, [2004] S.C.J. No. 63, at paras. 19–23. The first two interests, personal privacy and territorial privacy, are deeply rooted in the common law. Personal privacy, grounded in the right to bodily integrity, protects "the right not to have our bodies touched or explored to disclose objects or matters we wish to conceal". Territorial privacy protects the home and other spaces where the individual enjoys a reasonable expectation of privacy. The third category, informational privacy, is the interest at stake in this appeal. In *Tessling*, Binnie J. described it, at para. 23:

> Beyond our bodies and the places where we live and work, however, lies the thorny question of how much information about ourselves and activities we are entitled to shield from the curious eyes of the state (*R. v. S.A.B.*, [2003] 2 S.C.R. 678). This includes commercial information locked in a safe kept in a restaurant owned by the accused (*R. v. Law*, [2002] 1 S.C.R. 227, at para. 16). Informational privacy has been defined as "the claim of individuals, groups, or institutions to determine for themselves when, how, and to what extent information about them is communicated to others": A. F. Westin, *Privacy and Freedom* (1970), at p. 7. Its protection is predicated on the assumption that all information about a person is in a fundamental way his own, for him to communicate or retain ... as he sees fit.

> (Report of a Task Force established jointly by Department of Communications/Department of Justice, *Privacy and Computers* (1972), at p. 13).

[42] This characterization would certainly include Jones' claim to privacy in her banking records.

[43] In *Hill v. Church of Scientology of Toronto* (1995), 24 O.R. (3d) 865, [1995] 2 S.C.R. 1130, [1995] S.C.J. No. 64, Cory J. observed, at para. 121, that the right to privacy has been accorded constitutional protection and should be considered as a *Charter* value in the development of the common law tort of defamation. In *Hill*, Cory J. stated, at para. 121: "reputation is intimately related to the right to privacy which has been accorded constitutional protection". See, also, *R. v. O'Connor*, [1995] 4 S.C.R. 411, [1995] S.C.J. No. 98, at

para. 113, per L'Heureux-Dubé J.: identifying privacy as "an essential component of what it means to be 'free'".

[44] The *Charter* treatment of privacy accords with art. 12 of the *Universal Declaration of Human Rights*, G.A. Res. 271(III), UNGAOR, 3d Sess., Supp. No. 13, UN. Doc. A/810 (1948) 71, which provides that "[n]o one shall be subjected to arbitrary interference with his privacy, home or correspondence" and proclaims that "[e]veryone has the right to the protection of the law against such interference or attacks". Privacy is also recognized as a fundamental human right by art. 17 of the *International Covenant on Civil and Political Rights*, 19 December 1966, 999 U.N.T.S. 171.

[45] While the *Charter* does not apply to common law disputes between private individuals, the Supreme Court has acted on several occasions to develop the common law in a manner consistent with *Charter* values: see *R.W.D.S.U., Local 580 v. Dolphin Delivery Ltd.*, [1986] 2 S.C.R. 573, [1986] S.C.J. No. 75, at p. 603 S.C.R.; *R. v. Salituro*, [1991] 3 S.C.R. 654, [1991] S.C.J. No. 97, at pp. 666 and 675 S.C.R.; *Hill v. Scientology*, at p. 1169 S.C.R.; *R.W.D.S.U., Local 558 v. Pepsi-Cola Canada Beverages (West) Ltd.*, [2002] 1 S.C.R. 156, [2002] S.C.J. No. 7; *Grant v. Torstar Corp.*, [2009] 3 S.C.R. 640, [2009] S.C.J. No. 61.

[46] The explicit recognition of a right to privacy as underlying specific *Charter* rights and freedoms, and the principle that the common law should be developed in a manner consistent with *Charter* values, supports the recognition of a civil action for damages for intrusion upon the plaintiff's seclusion: see John D.R. Craig, "Invasion of Privacy and *Charter* Values: The Common-Law Tort Awakens" (1997), 42 McGill L.J. 355.

(d) Legislation

(i) Acts relating to private information

[47] The federal and Ontario governments have enacted a complex legislative framework addressing the issue of privacy. These include *Personal Information Protection and Electronic Documents Act*, S.C. 2000, c. 5 ("PIPEDA"); *Personal Health Information Protection Act, 2004*, S.O. 2004, c. 3, Sch. A; *Freedom of Information and Protection of Privacy Act*, R.S.O. 1990, c. F.31; *Municipal Freedom of Information and Protection of Privacy Act*, R.S.O. 1990, c. M.56; *Consumer Reporting Act*, R.S.O. 1990, c. C.33.

[48] Tsige argues that it is not open to this court to adapt the common law to deal with the invasion of privacy on the ground that privacy is already the subject of legislation in Ontario and Canada that reflects carefully considered economic and policy choices. It is submitted that expanding the reach of the common law in this area would interfere with these carefully crafted regimes and that any expansion of the law relating to the protection of privacy should be left to Parliament and the legislature.

[49] I am not persuaded that the existing legislation provides a sound basis for this court to refuse to recognize the emerging tort of intrusion upon seclusion and deny Jones a remedy. In my view, it would take a strained interpretation to infer from these statutes a legislative intent to supplant or halt the development of the common law in this area: see Robyn Bell, "Tort of Invasion of Privacy—Has its Time Finally Come?" in Archibald and Cochrane, eds., *Annual Review of Civil Litigation* (Toronto: Carswell, 2005), at p. 225.

[50] PIPEDA is federal legislation dealing with "organizations" subject to federal jurisdiction and does not speak to the existence of a civil cause of action in the province.

While BMO is subject to PIPEDA, there are at least three reasons why, in my view, Jones should not be restricted to the remedy of a PIPEDA complaint against BMO. First, Jones would be forced to lodge a complaint against her own employer rather than against Tsige, the wrongdoer. Second, Tsige acted as a rogue employee contrary to BMO's policy and that may provide BMO with a complete answer to the complaint. Third, the remedies available under PIPEDA do not include damages, and it is difficult to see what Jones would gain from such a complaint.

[51] The Ontario legislation essentially deals with freedom of information and the protection of certain private information with respect to government and other public institutions. Like PIPEDA, it has nothing to do with private rights of action between individuals.

(ii) Provincial Privacy Acts

[52] Four common law provinces currently have a statutorily created tort of invasion of privacy: British Columbia, *Privacy Act*, R.S.B.C. 1996, c. 373; Manitoba, *Privacy Act*, R.S.M. 1987, c. P125; Saskatchewan, *Privacy Act*, R.S.S. 1978, c. P-24; and Newfoundland, *Privacy Act*, R.S.N.L., 1990, c. P-22. All four Privacy Acts are similar. They establish a limited right of action, whereby liability will only be found if the defendant acts wilfully (not a requirement in Manitoba) and without a claim of right. Moreover, the nature and degree of the plaintiff's privacy entitlement is circumscribed by what is "reasonable in the circumstances".

[53] Under Quebec law, the right to privacy is explicitly protected both by arts. 3 and 35–37 of the *Civil Code of Québec*, S.Q. 1991, c. 64 and by s. 5 of the *Charter of Human Rights and Freedoms*, R.S.Q. c. C-12. See *Robbins v. Canadian Broadcasting Corp.* (1957), 12 D.L.R. (2d) 37 (Que. S.C.); *Aubry v. Éditions Vice-Versa*, [1998] 1 S.C.R. 591, [1998] S.C.J. No. 30; H. Patrick Glenn, "The Right to Privacy in Quebec Law" in Dale Gibson, ed., *Aspects of Privacy Law: Essays in Honour of John M. Sharp* (Toronto: Butterworths, 1980), at ch. 3.

[54] Significantly, however, no provincial legislation provides a precise definition of what constitutes an invasion of privacy. The courts in provinces with a statutory tort are left with more or less the same task as courts in provinces without such statutes. The nature of these acts does not indicate that we are faced with a situation where sensitive policy choices and decisions are best left to the legislature. To the contrary, existing provincial legislation indicates that when the legislatures have acted, they have simply proclaimed a sweeping right to privacy and left it to the courts to define the contours of that right.

(e) Other jurisdictions

(i) United States

[55] As already indicated, most American states have recognized a right of action for invasion of privacy rights as defined by the four categories identified by Prosser and now adopted by the *Restatement*.

[56] Generally speaking, to make out cause of action for intrusion upon seclusion, a plaintiff must show

1. an unauthorized intrusion;
2. that the intrusion was highly offensive to the reasonable person;

3. the matter intruded upon was private; and
4. the intrusion caused anguish and suffering.

See William Prosser, *Law of Torts*, 4th ed. (West Publishing Company, 1971), at pp. 808–12.

[57] The first element indicates that the tort focuses on the act of intrusion, as opposed to dissemination or publication of information: *Roe v. Cheyenne Mt. Conf. Resort, Inc.*, 124 F.3d 1221 (10th Cir. 1997), at p. 1236 F.3d. The focus of the court in determining whether this element is satisfied is on "the type of interest involved and not the place where the invasion occurs": *Evans v. Detlefsen*, 857 F.2d 330 (6th Cir. 1988), at p. 338 F.2d.

[58] With regard to the second element, factors to be considered in determining whether a particular action is highly offensive include the degree of intrusion, the context, conduct and circumstances of the intrusion, the tortfeasor's motives and objectives and the expectations of those whose privacy is invaded: see J.D. Lee and Barry A. Lindahl, *Modern Tort Law: Liability & Litigation*, 2nd ed., looseleaf (West Group, 2002), at 48:6.

[59] In determining the third element, the plaintiff must establish that the expectation of seclusion or solitude was objectively reasonable. The courts have adopted the two-prong test used in the application of the Fourth Amendment of the United States Constitution. The first step is demonstrating an actual subjective expectation of privacy, and the second step asks if that expectation is objectively reasonable: *Katz v. United States*, 389 U.S. 347, 88 S. Ct. 507 (1967), at p. 361 U.S.

[60] The fourth element has received considerably less attention as anguish and suffering are generally presumed once the first three elements have been established.
[...]

2. Defining the tort of intrusion upon seclusion

(a) Introduction
[65] In my view, it is appropriate for this court to confirm the existence of a right of action for intrusion upon seclusion. Recognition of such a cause of action would amount to an incremental step that is consistent with the role of this court to develop the common law in a manner consistent with the changing needs of society.

(b) Rationale
[66] The case law, while certainly far from conclusive, supports the existence of such a cause of action. Privacy has long been recognized as an important underlying and animating value of various traditional causes of action to protect personal and territorial privacy. *Charter* jurisprudence recognizes privacy as a fundamental value in our law and specifically identifies, as worthy of protection, a right to informational privacy that is distinct from personal and territorial privacy. The right to informational privacy closely tracks the same interest that would be protected by a cause of action for intrusion upon seclusion. Many legal scholars and writers who have considered the issue support recognition of a right of action for breach of privacy: see, e.g., P. Winfield, "Privacy" (1931), 47 Law Q. Rev. 23; D. Gibson, "Common Law Protection of Privacy: What to do Until the Legislators Arrive" in Lewis Klar, ed., *Studies in Canadian Tort Law* (Toronto: Butterworths, 1977) 343; Robyn M. Ryan Bell, "Tort of Invasion of Privacy—Has its

Time Finally Come?" in Todd Archibald and Michael Cochrane, eds., *Annual Review of Civil Litigation* (Toronto: Carswell, 2005) 225; Peter Burns, "The Law and Privacy: The Canadian Experience" (1976), 54 Can. Bar Rev. 1; John D.R. Craig, "Invasion of Privacy and *Charter* Values: The Common-Law Tort Awakens" (1997), 52 McGill L.J. 355.

[67] For over 100 years, technological change has motivated the legal protection of the individual's right to privacy. In modern times, the pace of technological change has accelerated exponentially. Legal scholars such as Peter Burns have written of "the pressing need to preserve 'privacy' which is being threatened by science and technology to the point of surrender": "The Law and Privacy: the Canadian Experience", at p. 1. See, also, Alan Westin, *Privacy and Freedom* (New York: Atheneum, 1967). The Internet and digital technology have brought an enormous change in the way we communicate and in our capacity to capture, store and retrieve information. As the facts of this case indicate, routinely kept electronic databases render our most personal financial information vulnerable. Sensitive information as to our health is similarly available, as are records of the books we have borrowed or bought, the movies we have rented or downloaded, where we have shopped, where we have travelled and the nature of our communications by cellphone, e-mail or text message.

[68] It is within the capacity of the common law to evolve to respond to the problem posed by the routine collection and aggregation of highly personal information that is readily accessible in electronic form. Technological change poses a novel threat to a right of privacy that has been protected for hundreds of years by the common law under various guises and that, since 1982 and the *Charter*, has been recognized as a right that is integral to our social and political order.

[69] Finally, and most importantly, we are presented in this case with facts that cry out for a remedy. While Tsige is apologetic and contrite, her actions were deliberate, prolonged and shocking. Any person in Jones' position would be profoundly disturbed by the significant intrusion into her highly personal information. The discipline administered by Tsige's employer was governed by the principles of employment law and the interests of the employer and did not respond directly to the wrong that had been done to Jones. In my view, the law of this province would be sadly deficient if we were required to send Jones away without a legal remedy.

(c) Elements

[70] I would essentially adopt as the elements of the action for intrusion upon seclusion the *Restatement (Second) of Torts* (2010) formulation which, for the sake of convenience, I repeat here:

> One who intentionally intrudes, physically or otherwise, upon the seclusion of another or his private affairs or concerns, is subject to liability to the other for invasion of his privacy, if the invasion would be highly offensive to a reasonable person.

[71] The key features of this cause of action are, first, that the defendant's conduct must be intentional, within which I would include reckless; second, that the defendant must have invaded, without lawful justification, the plaintiff's private affairs or concerns; and third, that a reasonable person would regard the invasion as highly offensive

causing distress, humiliation or anguish. However, proof of harm to a recognized economic interest is not an element of the cause of action. I return below to the question of damages, but state here that I believe it important to emphasize that given the intangible nature of the interest protected, damages for intrusion upon seclusion will ordinarily be measured by a modest conventional sum.

(d) Limitations

[72] These elements make it clear that recognizing this cause of action will not open the floodgates. A claim for intrusion upon seclusion will arise only for deliberate and significant invasions of personal privacy. Claims from individuals who are sensitive or unusually concerned about their privacy are excluded: it is only intrusions into matters such as one's financial or health records, sexual practises and orientation, employment, diary or private correspondence that, viewed objectively on the reasonable person standard, can be described as highly offensive.

[73] Finally, claims for the protection of privacy may give rise to competing claims. Foremost are claims for the protection of freedom of expression and freedom of the press. As we are not confronted with such a competing claim here, I need not consider the issue in detail. Suffice it to say, no right to privacy can be absolute and many claims for the protection of privacy will have to be reconciled with, and even yield to, such competing claims. A useful analogy may be found in the Supreme Court of Canada's elaboration of the common law of defamation in *Grant v. Torstar* where the court held, at para. 65, that "[w]hen proper weight is given to the constitutional value of free expression on matters of public interest, the balance tips in favour of broadening the defences available to those who communicate facts it is in the public's interest to know."

3. Damages

(a) Introduction

[74] As I have indicated, proof of actual loss is not an element of the cause of action for intrusion upon seclusion. However, the question necessarily arises: what is the appropriate approach to damages in cases, like the present, where the plaintiff has suffered no pecuniary loss?

[75] Where the plaintiff has suffered no provable pecuniary loss, the damages fall into the category of what Professor Stephen M. Waddams, *The Law of Damages*, looseleaf (Toronto: Canada Law Book, 2011), at para. 10.50, describes as "symbolic" and others have labelled as "moral" damages: see *Dulude v. Canada*, [2000] F.C.J. No. 1454, 192 D.L.R. (4th) 714 (C.A.), at para. 30. They are awarded "to vindicate rights or symbolize recognition of their infringement": Waddams, at para. 10.50. I agree with Prof. Waddams' observation that a conventional range of damages is necessary to maintain "consistency, predictability and fairness between one plaintiff and another".

[76] Guidance in determining an appropriate range of damages can be gleaned from existing case law from Ontario as well as from the provinces where there is a statutory cause of action.

[...]

3. Application to this case

[89] It is my view that, in this case, Tsige committed the tort of intrusion upon seclusion when she repeatedly examined the private bank records of Jones. These acts satisfy the elements laid out above: the intrusion was intentional, it amounted to an unlawful invasion of Jones' private affairs, it would be viewed as highly offensive to the reasonable person and caused distress, humiliation or anguish.

[90] In determining damages, there are a number of factors to consider. Favouring a higher award is the fact that Tsige's actions were deliberate and repeated and arose from a complex web of domestic arrangements likely to provoke strong feelings and animosity. Jones was understandably very upset by the intrusion into her private financial affairs. On the other hand, Jones suffered no public embarrassment or harm to her health, welfare, social, business or financial position and Tsige has apologized for her conduct and made genuine attempts to make amends. On balance, I would place this case at the mid- point of the range I have identified and award damages in the amount of $10,000. Tsige's intrusion upon Jones' seclusion, this case does not, in my view, exhibit any exceptional quality calling for an award of aggravated or punitive damages.

14:530 Off-Duty Conduct on Social Media

Another issue we can only treat selectively is that of off-duty conduct; specifically, posting racist or sexist messages on social media that may warrant discipline from an employer. In such cases, employers must balance the privacy and freedom of expression interests of the employee against the employer's interest in maintaining productivity and its reputation. However, some jurisdictions have legislation on harassment. In Ontario, there is *Occupational Health and Safety Amendment Act (Violence and Harassment in the Workplace)*, 2009, SO 2009, c 23, which may further shape the employer's response and mandate intervention to prevent online bullying of coworkers. In *Toronto (City) v Toronto Professional Fire Fighters' Association, Local 3888*, 2014 CanLII 76886 (Ont Lab Arb), a firefighter was terminated for his two-year-long series of sexist, misogynistic, and racist tweets in which he identified as a Toronto firefighter with a picture in uniform. Arbitrator Elaine Newman upheld his termination, citing the long-standing test for off-duty conduct established in *Millhaven Fibres Ltd v OCAW, Local 9-670*, [1967] OLAA No 4. According to this test, off-duty conduct warrants termination if: (1) the conduct harms the employer's reputation or product; (2) the grievor's conduct renders them unable to perform their duties; (3) the grievor's conduct leads to refusal, reluctance or inability of other employees to work with them; (4) the grievor has been guilty of a serious breach of the *Criminal Code* or the applicable human rights code injurious to the general reputation of the company and its employees; or (5) the conduct places difficulty in the way of the company properly carrying out its functions of efficiently managing its works and efficiently directing its workforce. However, another firefighter who was involved in a similar incident was reinstated, and a three-day unpaid suspension was substituted for his termination. Arbitrator Gail Misra held that the employer's policies regarding the use of social media were not made public, that the tweet was an isolated incident and was not directed at anyone in the workplace, that the grievor had a clean record, and that no employee had complained about his tweets (*Toronto (City) v Toronto Professional Fire Fighters' Association, Local 3888*, 2014 CanLII 62879 (Ont Lab Arb)). In both cases, it was held that the employee's expectation of privacy when engaging in social media is low and that employers can use employee's activity on social media as evidence of misconduct.

14:540 Freedom from Bullying and Psychological Harassment

More attention has recently been paid, both domestically and internationally, to the issue of psychological harassment and bullying in the workplace. Four elements of psychological harassment have been identified in the literature: (1) recurring and persistent unwelcome behaviour; (2) conduct that may be subtle or obvious; (3) conduct that is not restricted to harassment on an enumerated ground such as race or gender; and (4) behaviour identified through the psychological and emotional effects on the victim rather than the intention of the aggressor. (See Carla Gonçalves Gouveia, "From Laissez-faire to Fair Play: Workplace Violence & Psychological Harassment" (2007) 65:2 *University of Toronto Faculty of Law Review* 137. See also David J Doorey, "Employer 'Bullying': Implied Duties of Fair Dealing in Canadian Employment Contracts" (2005) 30 *Queen's Law Journal* 500, for a comprehensive discussion of the differences between characterizing bullying as a repudiation by breach of the contract and as a repudiation without a breach.) The issue of psychological harassment or bullying thus reaches beyond the limits of equality law.

Toronto Transit Commission v ATU (2004), 132 LAC (4th) 225 (Ont Lab Arb), involved a grievance where the employee, Vito Stina, alleged that his supervisor had engaged in a sustained course of harassment and abuse causing him physical illness and psychological harm. Arbitrator Shime found that he had jurisdiction to hear the grievance, for the following reasons:

1) The collective agreement had an implied term that a supervisor must act in a non-abusive, non-harassing manner.
2) The agreement's provisions on health and safety monitoring and consultation implied that the management rights clause had to be exercised with a view to employee safety, including psychological safety.
3) The *Occupational Health and Safety Act*, RSO 1990, c 0.1 s 21(2)(1), in expressly requiring supervisors to take "every reasonable precaution ... for the protection of a worker," implicitly restrained managerial authority to act inconsistently with that requirement.
4) The Supreme Court of Canada in *Weber*, excerpted at Section 9:410, held that where the essential character of a dispute arose under the collective agreement, the dispute should be dealt with in arbitration rather than in the courts.

Arbitrator Shime went on to hold that workplace abuse and harassment by a supervisor constituted bad faith, was contrary to the management rights clause of the collective agreement, and was the proper subject matter of a grievance. The award went on to define abuse and harassment, to find that it had occurred in this case, and to set forth an extensive remedy, including significant monetary damages and workplace immunity for the grievor from the abusive supervisor.

Among other remedies, Arbitrator Shime ordered: (1) restoration of the grievor's sick leave credits, with compensation for the difference in sick pay and regular salary; (2) $25,000 in general damages against the supervisor and the employer; (3) the provision of a harassment-free workplace to the grievor, including no communication with him by the supervisor; (4) that the grievor be allowed to move freely among the employer's various workplaces, and that the supervisor be moved when needed to keep him away from the grievor; and (5) the provision of anti-abuse and anti-harassment training for all of the employer's managers.

For a narrower approach, see *Cara Operations Ltd v Teamsters Chemical, Energy and Allied Workers Union, Local 647 (Palmieri Grievance)*, [2005] OLAA No 302 (Luborsky).

In *Severance v Oliver*, 2007 PESCAD 2, the appellate court found that it lacked jurisdiction to hear a tort action for harassment and sexual harassment in a case where harassment was covered by the collective agreement and by the employer's duty to provide a safe and healthy workplace.

Different provinces have responded to workplace harassment in various ways. Quebec has been the first Canadian jurisdiction to introduce legislation on psychological harassment in the workplace in 2002. This legislation goes beyond the protection of employees from harassment on the basis of enumerated grounds. For a discussion of psychological harassment under the Quebec *Labour Standards Act* and the procedural and jurisdictional complexity of the legal framework, see Rachel Cox, "Psychological Harassment Legislation in Québec: The First Five Years" (2010) 32:1 *Comparative Labor Law & Policy Journal* 55.

Table of Cases

This table of cases contains only those cases discussed or mentioned in the Group's commentary, or those cases from which excerpts have been included. Excerpts are marked in bold.

683481 Ontario Ltd v Beattie et al (1990), 73 DLR (4th) 346 (Ont HCJ) 662

Acrow (Automation) Ltd v Rex Chainbelt, [1971] 3 All ER 1175 (CA) 630
Addis v Gramophone Co Ltd, [1909] AC 488 (HL) 318
Air Canada v CALPA (1997), 28 BCLR (3d) 159 (SC) 663
Ajax (Town) v National Automobile, Aerospace and Agricultural Implement
    Workers Union of Canada (CAW-Canada), Local 222 (1998),
    41 OR (3d) 426 (Ont CA), aff'd 2000 SCC 23) 396
Alberta (Attorney General) v Retail Wholesale Canada, Local 285
    (Brewers Distributors), [2001] 6 WWR 643 (Alta QB) 669
Alberta (Information and Privacy Commissioner) v United Food and
    Commercial Workers, Local 401, 2013 SCC 62, [2013] 3 SCR 733 17
Alberta Reference. See Reference Re Public Service Employee Relations Act (Alberta)
Allen v Alberta, 2003 SCC 13 .... 753, 785
Allsco Building Products Ltd v United Food and Commerce Workers,
    Local 1288p, [1999] 2 SCR 1136 16–17
American Airlines Incorporated (1981) 43 di 114, [1981] 3 CLRBR 90
    (CLRB no 301) 450
Anderson v Haakon Industries (Canada) Ltd (1987), 48 DLR (4th) 235,
    [1987] BCJ No 2721 (CA) **308**
Andrews v Law Society of British Columbia, [1989] 1 SCR 143 .... 1066, 1067, 1086
Association des cadres de la Société des casinos du Québec et Société des
    casinos du Québec inc, 2016 QCTAT 6870 371
Association professionnelle des cadres de premier niveau d'Hydro-Québec
    (APCPNHQ) et Hydro-Québec, 2016 QCTAT 6871 371
Atkinson v CLAC, Local 66, [2003] BCLRBD No 422 .... **798**, 828
Attorney General for Newfoundland v Newfoundland Association of Public
    Employees (1977), 74 DLR (3d) 195 645
Attorney General for Ontario v OTF (1997), 36 OR (3d) 367 (SCJ) 634, 644

Bank of Nova Scotia, Vancouver Heights Branch, [1978] 2 CLRBR 181 497

Bardal v Globe & Mail Ltd (1960), 24 DLR (2d) 140 (Ont SCJ) **297**, 311
Baron Metal Industries, [2001] OLRD No 1210 459
Bartlam v Saskatchewan Crop Insurance Corp (1993), 49 CCEL 141 (Sask QB) **304**
BC Health. See Health Services and Support — Facilities Subsector Bargaining Assn v
    British Columbia
Bell Canada, et al v Attorney General of Canada, 2018 CanLII 40808 (SCC) 774
Bernard v Canada (Attorney General), 2014 SCC 13 .... **866**
Berry v Pulley, [2002] 2 SCR 493 .... 632, **830**
Better Value Furniture v Vancouver Distribution Centre Ltd (1981),
    122 DLR (3d) 12 (BCCA) 637
Bhasin v Hrynew, 2014 SCC 71 .... 264, **265**, 267
Bingley (Re), 2004 CIRB 291 812
Birch v Union of Taxation Employees, Local 70030, 2008 ONCA 809 .... **851**
Bisaillon v Concordia University, 2006 SCC 19, [2006] SCJ No 19 .... 757, 758, **785**
Bliss v Attorney General of Canada, [1979] 1 SCR 183 1086
Body v Murdoch, [1954] OWN 658 633
Bowes v Goss Power Products Ltd, 2012 ONCA 425 253
British Columbia (Public Service Employee Relations Commission) v BCGSEU,
    [1999] 3 SCR 3 [the **Meiorin** case] **1075**, 1094, 1140
British Columbia (Workers' Compensation Board) v Figliola, 2011 SCC 52 .... 765, 766, 769, 768
British Columbia Hydro and Power Authority and International Brotherhood of
    Electrical Workers, Local 258 and Local 213, [1976] 2 CLRBR 410 615
British Columbia Public School Employers' Assn v British Columbia Teachers'
    Federation (Head Grievance) (2010), 193 LAC (4th) 65 (BCLRB) **841**
British Columbia Public School Employers' Association v British Columbia
    Teachers' Federation, 2005 BCSC 1490 .... 634, 687
British Columbia Teachers' Federation v British Columbia Public School
    Employers' Assn, 2009 BCCA 39, leave to appeal to SCC refused,
    2009 CanLII 44624 615
British Columbia Teachers' Federation v British Columbia, 2014 BCSC 121,
    rev'd 2015 BCCA 184, aff'd 2016 SCC 49 .... 987, **988**
British Columbia Terminal Elevator Operators' Association on Behalf of the
    Saskatchewan Wheat Pool v Grain Workers' Union, Local 333 (1994),
    94 CLLC para 16,060 (CLRB) **610**
British Columbia Transit and Transit Management Assn (1990), 6 CLRBR
    (2d) 1 (BCLRB) 382
Brooks v Canada Safeway, [1989] 1 SCR 1219 .... 1086, 1087
Brown v Waterloo Regional Board of Commissioners of Police (1983),
    43 OR (2d) 113 (CA) **264**
Bukvich v Canadian Union of United Brewery, Flour, Cereal, Soft Drink and
    Distillery Workers, Local 304 and Dufferin Aggregates (1982), 82 CLLC
    para 16,156 (OLRB) **793**, 800

Cabiakman v Industrial Alliance Life Insurance Co, 2004 SCC 55 288

Cadillac Fairview Corporation v Retail, Wholesale and Department Store
  Union (1989), 71 OR (2d) 200 .... **456**
Canada (Attorney General) v Johnstone, 2014 FCA 110 .... **1140**
Canada (Attorney General) v Lesiuk, 2003 FCA 3, leave to appeal to SCC refused 1132
Canada (Director of Investigation and Research) v Southam Inc,
  [1997] 1 SCR 748 .... 769, 773
Canada Post Corp and CUPW (Condon), Re. See Re Canada Post Corp and CUPW
Canada Post Corporation (1995), 95 CLLC para 220-042 (CIRB) **450**
Canada Safeway Ltd v Retail, Wholesale and Department Store Union, Local 454,
  [1997] 1 SCR 1079 769
Canadian Air Line Pilots' Association [CALPA] v Eastern Provincial Airways Ltd
  (1983), 5 CLRBR (NS) 368 .... **675**
Canadian Association of Industrial, Mechanical and Allied Workers v Noranda
  Metal Industries Ltd, [1975] 1 CLRBR 145 (BC) **545**
Canadian Association of Industrial, Mechanical and Allied Workers, Local 14 v
  Paccar of Canada Ltd, [1989] 2 SCR 983 .... 616, 620
Canadian Association of Smelter and Allied Workers v Royal Oak Mines et al and
  British Columbia Federation of Labour (1993), 21 CLRBR (2d) 55,
  93 CLLC para 16,063 (CLRB) 517, 678
Canadian Broadcasting Corp v Canada (Labour Relations Board), [1995] 1 SCR 157 .... **423**
Canadian Fabricated Products Ltd (1954), 54 CLLC para 17,090 (OLRB) 456
Canadian Imperial Bank of Commerce (Powell River Branch) v British Columbia
  Government Employees' Union (1992), 15 CLRBR (2d) 86 .... **489**
Canadian Merchant Service Guild v Gagnon et al, [1984] 1 SCR 509 792
Canadian National Railway Co v Canada (Canadian Human Rights Commission),
  [1987] 1 SCR 1114 .... **1115**, 1121
Canadian National Railways Co and Council of Railway Unions (1993)
  23 CLRBR (2d) 122 620
Canadian Paperworkers Union, Canadian Labour Congress and Its Local 305 v
  International Wallcoverings, a Division of International Paints (Canada) Limited,
  [1983] OLRB Rep 1316 .... **416**
Canadian Union of Public Employees v Labour Relations Board (Nova Scotia),
  [1983] 2 SCR 311 [the Digby School Board case] 539
Canadian Union of Public Employees, Local 1251 v Her Majesty in Right of
  the Province of New Brunswick, 21 December 2009, 2009 CanLII 74885
  (NBLEB) 583
Canadian Union of Public Employees, Local 963 v New Brunswick Liquor Corporation,
  [1979] 2 SCR 227 769
Canadian Union of Public Employees, Metropolitan Toronto Civic Employees' Union,
  Local 43 v Metropolitan Toronto (Municipality of) (1990), 74 OR (2d) 239 (CA) 712
Canadian Union of United Brewery, Flour, Cereal, Soft Drink & Distillery Workers,
  Local No 304 v Canada Trustco Mortgage Company, [1984] OLRB Rep 1356 .... **559**
CanAero v O'Malley, [1974] SCR 592 272
Cancoil Thermal Corp v Abbot et al, [2004] CLLC ¶220-045 (Ont SCJ) **656**, 659

Canex Placer Limited (Endako Mines Division) v Canadian Association of Industrial, Mechanical and Allied Workers, Local 10, [1975] 1 CLRBR 269 (BCLRB) **650**, 656
Captains and Chiefs Association v Algoma Central Marine, 2010 CIRB 531 .... **352**, 363, 364
Cara Operations Ltd v Teamsters Chemical, Energy and Allied Workers Union, Local 647 (Palmieri Grievance), [2005] OLAA No 302 (Luborsky) 1186
Carewest v Health Sciences Association of Alberta (2001), 93 LAC (4th) 129 1087
Carter v Bell & Sons (Canada) Ltd, [1936] OR 290, [1936] OR 290 (CA) **235**, **264**
CAW, Local 222 v Charterways Transportation Ltd. See Ajax (Town) v National Automobile, Aerospace and Agricultural Implement Workers Union of Canada (CAW-Canada), Local 222
Ceccol v Ontario Gymnastic Federation (2001), 55 OR (3d) 614 (CA) **248**, 311
Central Okanagan School District No 23 v Renaud, [1992] 2 SCR 970 .... 1105, **1106**
CEP, Local 911 and ISM Information Systems Management Corp, [1998] Sask LRBR 352 .... **840**
Chevron Corp v Yaiguaje, 2015 SCC 42 .... **208**
Children's Aid Society of Metropolitan Toronto, [1977] 1 CLRBR 129 (OLRB) 381
Children's Aid Society of Ottawa-Carleton, [2001] OLRD No 1234 (OLRB) 364
Christie v York Corp, [1940] SCR 139 .... **224**
CN v THE UNITED KINGDOM, No 4239/08 (2013), 56 EHRR 24 189
Coleman and Office and Technical Employees' Union, Local 738. See Office and Technical Employees' Union, Local 378
Communications, Electronic, Electrical, Technical and Salaried Workers of Canada v Graham Cable TV/FM (1986), 12 CLRBR (NS) 1 606
Communications, Energy and Paperworkers Union of Canada, Local 87-M v Ming Pao Newspapers (Canada) Ltd, 2011 CanLII 77758 (OLRB) 594
Communications, Energy and Paperworkers Union, Local 30 v Irving Pulp & Paper, Ltd, 2013 SCC 34, [2013] 2 SCR 458 ....712, 1167
Compagnie Minière Quebec Cartier v Quebec (Grievances Arbitrator), [1995] 2 SCR 1095 749
Conféderation des syndicats nationaux v Québec (Procureur général), 2008 QCCS 5076 1133
Consolidated Bathurst Packaging Ltd v Canadian Paperworkers Union, Local 595, [1982] 3 CLRBR 324 662
CPR Co v Zambri. See R v Canadian Pacific Railway Co
Crevier v Attorney-General of Quebec, [1981] 2 SCR 220 110
Crewdson and Stebeleski v International Brotherhood of Electrical Workers, Local 1541 (1992), 18 CLRBR (2d) 107 811–12
Crofter Hand Woven Harris Tweed Co v Veitch, [1942] AC 435 (HL) 629
Cronk v Canadian General Insurance Co (1994), 19 OR (3d) 515 (Gen Div), rev'd (1995), 128 DLR (4th) 147 (CA) **298**

Danyluk v Ainsworth Technologies Inc, 2001 SCC 44, [2001] 2 SCR 460 1063
Dawson v Vancouver Police Board (No 2), 2015 BCHRT 54 1149

Delisle v Canada (Deputy Attorney General), [1999] 2 SCR 989 ....947, 1130, 1131
Di Tomaso v Crown Metal Packaging Canada LP, 2011 ONCA 469 304
Digby School Board. *See Canadian Union of Public Employees v Labour Relations Board (Nova Scotia)*
Domglas Ltd (1976), 76 CLLC para 16,050 (OLRB), upheld (1978), 78 CLLC para 14,135 (Ont Div Ct) 615
Douglas/Kwantlen Faculty Assn v Douglas College, [1990] 3 SCR 570...734
Downtown Eatery (1993) Ltd v Her Majesty the Queen in Right of Ontario (2001), 54 OR (3d) 161 (CA)... **244**, 247
Dunmore v Ontario (Attorney General) (1997), 37 OR (3d) 287, 1997 CanLII 16229 (Ont SCJ) **891**
Dunmore v Ontario (Attorney General), [2001] 3 SCR 1016, 2001 SCC 94 ....871, **893**, 1131
Dunsmuir v New Brunswick, 2008 SCC 9, [2008] 1 SCR 190 ....110, **771**, 774, 775

Eastmond v Canadian Pacific Railway, 2004 FC 852 11697
Eaton's, [1985] OLRB Rep March 491 562
Egan v Canada, [1995] 2 SCR 513 1149
Ellison v Burnaby Hospital Society (1992), 42 CCEL 239 (BCSC)...**253**, 255
Elsley v JG Collins Ins Agencies, [1978] 2 SCR 916 ....**256**
Employees of Kelly's Ambulance (1982) Ltd and Canadian Union of Public Employees v Kelly's Ambulance (1982) Ltd (NSLRB), 19 August 1993 ....**514**
Entrop v Imperial Oil Ltd (2000), 50 OR (3d) 18 (CA) **1164**
Evans v Teamsters Local Union No 31, [2008] 1 SCR 661, 2008 SCC 20..**312**

Falconbridge Ltd v Sudbury Mine, Mill, & Smelter Workers Union, Local 598, [2000] OJ No 4168 (SCJ) 636
Ferrell v Ontario (Attorney General) (1998), 42 OR (3d) 97 (CA), leave to appeal to SCC refused 1114–15, 1133
Ford Motor Co of Canada v UAW-CIO, reprinted in 1 CLLR 1245 846
Fownes Construction Co (Re), [1974] 1 CLRBR 510 (BCLRB) **347–48**
Fraser v Ontario (Attorney General), 2008 ONCA 760, rev'd 2011 SCC 20........................**925, 931**
Fresco v Canadian Imperial Bank of Commerce, 2012 ONCA 444 1048
Fulawka v Bank of Nova Scotia, 2012 ONCA 443 1048
Fullowka v Pinkerton's of Canada Ltd, 2010 SCC 5 ....**825**

Gagnon v Foundation Maritime Ltd (1961), 28 DLR (2d) 174 631
Garcia v Tahoe Resources Inc, 2017 BCCA 39..**207**
GasTOPS Ltd v Forsyth, [2009] OJ No 3969 (SC)...**268**
General Motors of Canada Limited, [1996] OLRB Rep May/June 409 623
Girex Bancorp Inc v Lynette Hsieh, 2004 CanLII 24679 (OLRB) 1004, **1009**
Globex Foreign Exchange Corporation v Kelcher, 2005 ABCA 419..260
Goudie v Ottawa (City), 2003 SCC 14..785
Gould (Re), [2010] BCLRB No B3/2010..**843**

Graham Cable TV/FM, Toronto v Cable Television Workers Association (1987),
    14 CLRBR (NS) 250 378
Grande Prairie Roman Catholic Separate School District No 28 v CEP,
    Local Union No 328 (2011), 198 CLRBR (2d) 106 (Alta LRB) 372
Graphic Arts International Union Local 12-L v Graphic Centre (Ontario) Inc,
    [1976] OLRB Rep 221 544
Hamilton Health Sciences v Ontario Nurses' Association (2007),
    2007 CanLII 73923 (ONLA) 1169
Harrison v Carswell, [1976] 2 SCR 200 654
Health Sciences Assn of BC v Campbell River and North Island Transition Society,
    2004 BCCA 260 1140
Health Services and Support—Facilities Subsector Bargaining Assn v
    British Columbia, 2007 SCC 27, [2007] 2 SCR 391 .... 17, 351, 871, **900**
Hersees of Woodstock Ltd v Goldstein (1963), 38 DLR (2d) 449 (Ont CA) **660**, 661
Hill v Peter Gorman Ltd (1957), 9 DLR (2d) 124 (ONCA) 289
Honda Canada Inc v Keays, 2008 SCC 39 326
Hospitality & Service Trades Union, Local 261 v Service Star Building Cleaning Inc,
    2013 CanLII 34400 (OLRB) 397
Howard v Benson Group Inc (The Benson Group Inc), 2016 ONCA 256 253
Humpty Dumpty Foods Ltd, [1977] 2 CLRBR 248 (OLRB) 616
Hydro-Québec v Syndicat des employées de techniques professionnelles et
    de bureau d'Hydro-Québec, section locale 2000 (SCFP-FTQ),
    2008 SCC 43 1099

*Imbleau v Laskin. See Re Polymer Corporation & Oil, Chemical & Atomic Workers
    International Union, Local 16-14*
Imperial Sheet Metal v Landry, 2007 NBCA 51 272
Industrial Hardwood Products (1996) Ltd v International Wood and Allied Workers
    of Canada, Local 2693 (2001), 52 OR (3d) 694 (CA) 659
Industrial Hardwood Products (1996) Ltd v IWAWC, Local 2963 (2000),
    62 CLRBR (2d) 98 (Ont SCJ) 627
Insurance Corp of British Columbia and CUPE, [1974] 1 CLRBR 403 481
International Alliance of Theatrical Stage Employees, Local 849 v Egg Films, Inc,
    2015 NSLB 213 589
International Alliance of Theatrical Stage Employees, Moving Picture Technicians,
    Artists and Allied Crafts, Local 849 v Egg Films Inc (2012), 2012 NSLB 120,
    application for judicial review refused (**sub nom Egg Films Inc v Nova Scotia
    (Labour Board)**), 2013 NSSC 123, aff'd 2014 NSCA 33 340
International Association of Machinists and Aerospace Workers and Courtesy
    Chrysler (NSLRB), 5 September 2001 517
International Association of Machinists v John Bertram & Sons Co (1967),
    18 LAC 362 719
International Brotherhood of Boilermakers v Sheafer-Townsend Ltd (1953),
    53 CLLC 17,058 (OLRB) 780

International Brotherhood of Electrical Workers v Winnipeg Builders Exchange,
[1967] SCR 628 631
International Brotherhood of Teamsters v Therien, [1960] SCR 265 .... **632**, 633, **830**
**International Woodworkers of America, Local 2-69 v Consolidated Bathurst
Packaging Ltd**, [1983] OLRB Rep 1411 ....**578**, 583, 662
Isidore Garon ltée v Tremblay; Fillion et Frères (1976) inc v Syndicat national
des employés de garage du Québec inc, 2006 SCC 2 ....760, 764, 765, 785
Ivanhoe Inc v UFCW, Local 500, 2001 SCC 47, [2001] 2 SCR 565.......................................400

Janzen v Platy Enterprises Ltd, [1989] 1 SCR 1252 .... **1088**, 1089
JI Case Co v National Labor Relations Board, 321 US 332 (1944) 780
Jones v Tsige, 2012 ONCA 32...**1173**
Judd v CEP, Local 2000 (2000), 91 CLRBR (2d) 33 (BCLRB) **816**

K Mart Canada Ltd v United Food and Commercial Workers, Local 1518,
[1999] 2 SCR 1083..670
Karmel v Calgary Jewish Academy, 2015 ABQB 731 ....253, 268
Kennedy Lodge Inc, [1984] OLRB Rep 931..431
Kennedy Lodge Nursing Home (1980), 81 CLLC para 16,078 (OLRB).................................429

Labour Relations Board of Saskatchewan v John East Iron Works Ltd, [1949] AC 134 110
Lavigne v Ontario Public Service Employees' Union, [1991] 2 SCR 211 ....734, 846, **857**
Law Society of Upper Canada v Rovet, [1992] LSDD No 24...**471**
Limo Jet Gold Express (2008), 171 LAC (4th) 28...646
Liquor Distribution Branch v Hiram Walker & Sons Limited, [1978]
2 CLRBR 334 (BCLRB) 663
Lloyd v Imperial Parking Ltd (1996), [1997] 3 WWR 697,
46 Alta LR (3d) 220 (QB) **290**, 294
**Local 273, International Longshoremen's Association et al v Maritime Employers'
Association et al**, [1979] 1 SCR 120 ....**611**
Loeb Highland v United Food and Commercial Workers Union, [1993]
OLRB Rep March 197...463
London Civic Employees Local Union No 107 v London (City), [2010] OLAA
No 270 (Snow) **749**
Love v Acuity Investment Management Inc, 2011 ONCA 130 304
Lucyshyn v Amalgamated Transit Union, Local 615 (2010), 178 CLRBR (2d) 96
(Sask LRB) **806**
Lyons v Multari (2000), 50 OR (3d) 526 (CA) 260

Macaraeg v E Care Contact Centers Ltd, 2008 BCCA 182, leave to appeal to
SCC refused, [2008] SCCA No 293 ....1048, 1063
MacGregor v National Home Services, 2012 ONSC 2042 ....**253**
Machtinger v HOJ Industries Ltd, [1992] 1 SCR 986....................................261, 297, **1031**
Mackie Moving Systems Corp (Re) (2002), 80 CLRBR (2d) 195, [2002] CIRB No 156................349

MacMillan Bloedel Ltd and Pulp, Paper & Woodworkers of Canada, Local 8
   (1986), 2 CLAS 52...646
Maple Leaf Sports & Entertainment (1999), 49 CLRBR (2d) 285
   (Ont Ct J (Gen Div))...661
McCormick v Fasken Martineau DuMoulin LLP, 2014 SCC 39 ....**1159**
McGavin Toastmaster Ltd v Ainscough, [1976] 1 SCR 718 .... 678 764, **781**, 784
McIntyre v Hockin, (1889), 16 OAR 498 (CA) **294–95**
McKee v Reid's Heritage Homes Ltd, 2009 ONCA 916... **236**
McKinlay Transport v Goodman (1978), 78 CLLC para 14,161 (FC) 634
McKinley v BC Tel, [2001] 2 SCR 161..262, **274**
McKinnon v Ontario (Ministry of Correctional Services) (No 3), [1998]
   OHRBID No 10 ....**1091**
McKinnon v Ontario (Ministry of Correctional Services), 2010 HRTO 1521 1093
McRae Jackson v CAW, [2004] CIRB No 290 819
Meiorin. See British Columbia (Public Service Employee Relations Commission) v BCGSEU
MEP Environmental Products Ltd v Hi.Performance Coatings Company Limited
   et al, 2006 MBQB 119, aff'd 2007 MBCA 71 272
Meredith v Canada (Attorney General), 2015 SCC 2 .... xxvi, 869, **984**
Metroland Printing, Publishing and Distributing Ltd, [2003] OLRD No 514 (OLRB)...........**484**, 489
Metropolitan Life Insurance Co v International Union of Operating Engineers,
   [1970] SCR 425..769
Mifsud v MacMillan Bathurst Inc (1989), 70 OR (2d) 701 (CA) 312
Millhaven Fibres Ltd and Ontario OCAW, Local 9-670, [1967] OLAA No 4................1184
Milnet Mines Ltd (1953), 53 CLLC para 17,063 (OLRB)...456
Mini-Skool Ltd (1983), 5 CLRBR (NS) 211.. 677
Misetich v Value Village Stores Inc, 2016 HRTO 1229... **1148**
Mississaugas of Scugog Island First Nation v AG Canada and AG Ontario (2007),
   287 DLR (4th) 452, 2007 ONCA 814, leave to appeal to SCC refused,
   [2008] SCCA No 35, 2008 CanLII 18945 117
Moore v British Columbia (Education), 2012 SCC 61 ....**1074**, 1121
Morgan v Fry, [1968] 2 QB 710 (CA) 630
Mount Allison University (Re), [1982] 3 CLRBR 284 363
Mounted Police Association of Ontario v Canada (Attorney General),
   2015 SCC 1 ....695, 871, **947**

**National Automobile, Aerospace Transportation and General Workers Union of
   Canada (CAW-Canada) and its Local 2224 v Buhler Versatile Inc**, [2001]
   MLBD No 9 (QL) (Man LB) **568**, 589
National Bank of Canada and Retail Clerks' International Union, [1982]
   3 CLRBR 1..**460**
National Bank of Canada v Retail Clerks' International Union et al,
   [1984] 1 SCR 269..**461**
National Gallery of Canada v Public Service Alliance of Canada (2001)
   Ontario Court (Gen Div) [unreported].. 653

National Harbours Board (Re), [1979] 3 CLRBR 86.. **626**
National Harbours Board v Syndicat national des employés du Port de Montréal,
  [1979] 3 CLRBR 502...**624**, 634
National Labor Relations Board v Exchange Parts Co, 375 US 405 (1964) **439**
National Labor Relations Board v Federbush Co, 121 F2d 954
  (US 2nd Circuit Court of Appeals) (1941)... **439**
National Labor Relations Board v Yeshiva University, 100 S Ct 856 (1980) 363
Nelson Crushed Stone and United Cement, Lime & Gypsum Workers' International
  Union, Local Union 494 v Martin, [1978] 1 CLRBR 115 (OLRB) **613**
New Brunswick v O'Leary, [1995] 2 SCR 967..785
New Dominion Stores (cob Great Atlantic & Pacific Co of Canada) v
  Retail Wholesale Canada Canadian Service Sector, Division of USWA,
  Local 414 (McCaul Grievance) (1997), 60 LAC (4th) 308 (Beck) **744**
New Jenny Nail & Spa v Qiurong Cao Jane and Director of Employment
  Standards, 2016 CanLII 28478 (OLRB) 1004, **1012**
Newfoundland (Treasury Board) v Newfoundland and Labrador Assn of
  Public and Private Employees (NAPE), 2004 SCC 66,
  [2004] 3 SCR 381 ....1128, **1129**
Nieman's Pharmacy. See Canada Post Corporation v CUPW
NLRB v General Electric Co, 418 F2d 736 (1969), certiorari denied
  397 US 965 (1970).. 571
Nor-Man Regional Health Authority Inc v Manitoba Association of
  Health Care Professionals, 2011 SCC 59.. 696, **720**, 736, 739, 768
Nova Scotia (Workers' Compensation Board) v Martin, 2003 SCC 54 ....**735**

O'Malley. See Ontario (Human Rights Commission) v Simpsons Sears Ltd
Office and Technical Employees' Union, Local 378 (1995), 28 CLRBR (2d) 1 ....842, **843**
Ontario (Attorney General) v Fraser, 2011 SCC 20 ....xxv, 871, **933**
Ontario (Director of Disability Support Program) v Tranchemontagne,
  2010 ONCA 593 1073
Ontario (Human Rights Commission) v Simpsons Sears Ltd, [1985] 2 SCR 536
  [the **O'Malley** case].. **1071**
Ontario Public Service Employees Union v Family Services of
  Hamilton-Wentworth Inc, [1980] 2 CLRBR 76 371
Ontario Public Service Employees Union v Royal Ottawa Health Care Group,
  [1999] OLRB Rep July/August 711...**436**, 438
Ontario Workers' Union v Humber River Regional Hospital (2011),
  195 CLRBR (2d) 286 (OLRB) **375**
Orchard v Tunney, [1957] SCR 436... 8292
OSSTF v Toronto (City) Board of Education, [1994] OLRB Rep August 1098 381
OSSTF. See also Ontario Secondary School Teachers' Federation
Ouellet v Syndicat des travailleurs et travailleuses de Deauville (1983),
  83 CLLC 14,054 (Que Lab Ct) 800
Overwaitea Food Group (2003), 102 CLRBR (2d) 211 (BCLRB) 670

Parry Sound (District) Social Services Administration Board v
Ontario Public Service Employees Union, Local 324,
2003 SCC 42 .... xxv, **722**, 758, 764, 812
Penner v Niagara (Regional Police Services Board), 2013 SCC 19 .... 765, 766, 767, 768
Plastics CMP Limited, [1982] OLRB Rep May 726 576
Plourde v Wal-Mart Canada Corp, 2009 SCC 54, [2009] 3 SCR 465 .... 164, 468, 469
PN v FR & MR and another (No 2), 2015 BCHRT 60 .... **214**
Pointe-Claire (City) v Quebec (Labour Court), [1997] 1 SCR 1015,
97 CLLC para 220-039 .... **385**
Pomietlarz v UFCW, Local 1000A, [2013] OLRB Rep March/April 231 798
Potter v New Brunswick Legal Aid Services Commission, 2015 SCC 10,
[2015] 1 SCR 500 .... 267, **284**, 289, **294**
Prince Rupert Grain v Grain Workers Union, Local 333 (2002),
8 BCLR (4th) 91 (CA) 634
Professional Institute of the Public Service of Canada v Canada
(Attorney General) (2002), 222 DLR (4th) 438
(Ont CA) 633
PSAC v Canada, [1987] 1 SCR 424 .... 17, 870
PSAC v NAV Canada (2002), 212 DLR (4th) 68 749

**Quebec (Commission des droits de la personne et des droits de la jeunesse) v
Bombardier Inc (Bombardier Aerospace Training Centre)**, 2015 SCC 39 1074–75
**Quebec (Commission des droits de la personne et des droits de la jeunesse
on behalf of Morin et al) v Quebec (Attorney General)**, 2004 SCC 39,
[2004] 2 SCR 185 758
**Québec (Commission des droits de la personne et des droits de la jeunesse) c
Centre maraîcher Eugène Guinois JR inc**, 2005 CanLII 11754 (QC TDP) **140**
Quebec (Commission des normes du travail) v Asphalte Desjardins Inc,
2014 SCC 51, [2014] 2 SCR 514 311
Quintette Operating Corp v United Steelworkers of America, Local 9113,
[1997] BCCAAA No 619 (BCDLA) 1087
Quong-Wing v R (1914), 49 SCR 440 1066

R v Advance Cutting and Coring Ltd, 2001 SCC 70, [2001] 3 SCR 209 860
R v Canadian Pacific Railway Co (1962), 31 DLR (2d) 209 (Ont HC), aff'd (**sub nom
CPR Co v Zambri**) (1962), 34 DLR (2d) 654 (Ont CA) [the **Royal York** case] **673, 674**
R v Cole, 2012 SCC 53 .... **1170**
R v K-Mart Canada Ltd, [1982] OJ No 54, 82 CLLC para 14,185 (CA) **469**
R v Van der Peet, [1996] 2 SCR 507 117
Rasanen v Rosemount Instruments Ltd (1994), 17 OR (3d) 267 (CA) 1063
Rayonier Canada (BC) Ltd v International Woodworkers of America, Local 1-217,
[1975] 2 CLRBR 196, [1975] BCLRBD No 42 .... **801**
Re Burnaby (District) and CUPE, Local 23, [1974] 1 CLRBR 1 (BCLRB) **351**
Re Canada Post Corp and CUPW (2013), 116 CLAS 137, 2013 CIRB 672 .... **401**, 841

Re Council of Printing Industries of Canada and Toronto Printing Pressmen and Assistants' Union No 10 et al (1983), 42 OR (2d) 404 (CA) (leave to appeal to SCC refused (1983), 52 NR 308n 711
Re Metropolitan Toronto Board of Commissioners of Police and Metropolitan Toronto Police Ass'n (1972), 26 DLR (3d) 672 (CA), aff'd on other grounds by the SCC 749
Re Metropolitan Toronto Board of Commissioners of Police v Metropolitan Toronto Police Association (1981), 33 OR (2d) 476, 124 DLR (3d) 684 (Ont CA) 711
Re Noranda Metal Industries Ltd, Fergus Division v International Brotherhood of Electrical Workers (1983), 44 OR (2d) 529 (CA) **716**, 719
Re Oil, Chemical & Atomic Workers & Polymer Corporation (1958), 10 LAC 31 644
Re Polymer Corp and Oil, Chemical & Atomic Workers (1959), 10 LAC 51 736
Re Polymer Corporation & Oil, Chemical & Atomic Workers International Union, Local 16-14, [1961] OR 176 (HCJ), affirmed by [1961] OR 438 (CA), and further affirmed (sub nom Imbleau v Laskin) [1962] SCR 338 739
Re Robb Engineering and United Steelworkers of America, Local 4122 (1978), 86 DLR (3d) 307 (NSCA) 615
Re Tandy Electronics and United Steelworkers of America (1980), 115 DLR (3d) 197 (Ont Div Ct) 459
Re United Steelworkers of America and Russelsteel Ltd (1966), 17 LAC 253 .... **708**, 711
Red Deer College v Michaels, [1976] 2 SCR 324 311
Reference Re Public Service Employee Relations Act (Alberta), [1987] 1 SCR 313, 87 CLLC para 14,021 .... 17, 870, **871**
Reference re Workers' Compensation Act, 1983 (Nfld), [1989] 1 SCR 922 1130
Renaud (Re), [1999] BCESTD No 462 1004
Rescare Premier Canada, [2003] OLRB Rep Nov/Dec 1077 678
Retail, Wholesale and Department Store Union, Local 558 v Pepsi-Cola Canada Beverages (West) Ltd, 2002 SCC 8, 208 DLR (4th) 385, [2002] 1 SCR 156 .... xxv, 17, 632, 649, 653, **663**, 669, 670, 671
RJR-MacDonald Inc v Canada (AG), [1994] 1 SCR 311 635
RMH Teleservices International Inc, BCLRB Decision No B345/2003 (reconsidered in BCLRB Decision No B188/2005, and returned to original panel for remedies in BCLRB Decision No B280/2005 449
Robichaud v Canada (Treasury Board), [1987] 2 SCR 84 1150
Rogers Cable TV (British Columbia) Ltd, Vancouver Division et al v International Brotherhood of Electrical Workers, Local 213 (1987), 16 CLRBR (NS) 71 647
Rookes v Barnard, [1964] AC 1129 .... 629, 630, 631
Royal Oak Mines v Canada (Labour Relations Board), [1996] 1 SCR 369 ..... **457**, 539, **566**, **584**, 678
Royal York. See R v Canadian Pacific Railway Co
RWDSU v Saskatchewan, [1987] 1 SCR 460 .... 17, 870, 871

Sadyathasan v United Food and Commercial Workers International Union Canada Local 175, 2015 CanLII 21273 (OLRB) 678

Saskatchewan Federation of Labour v Saskatchewan,
  2015 SCC 4 ....17, **183**, 779, 869, 970, **972**
School District No 54 v Bulkley Valley Teachers' Ass'n (1993),
  19 CLRBR 269 (BCLRB)... 686–87
Secretary of State for Employment v Associated Society of Locomotive
  Engineers and Firemen and Others (No 2), [1972] 2 All ER 949 (CA) 262
Seneca College of Applied Arts and Technology v Bhadauria,
  [1981] 2 SCR 181, 124 DLR (3d) 193...631, 1066
Sept-Îles (City) v Quebec (Labour Court), 2001 SCC 48, [2001] SCJ No 48................400
Service Employees International Union, Local 204 v Ontario (AG) (1997),
  35 OR (3d) 508 (Gen Div) **1123**, 1133
Service, Office and Retail Workers' Union of Canada [SORWUC] v
  Canadian Imperial Bank of Commerce, [1977]
  2 CLRBR 99 493
Severance v Oliver, [2007] SCCA No 74..1186
Shah v Xerox Canada Ltd (2000), 131 OAC 44 294
Shaw v Levac Supply Ltd, (1991), 91 CLLC 17,007 (Ont Bd Inq).................................**1090**
Shaw-Almex Industries Ltd (1986), 15 CLRBR (NS) 23 677
Shuswap Lake General Hospital v British Columbia Nurses' Union, [2002]
  BCCAAA No 21 [the **Lockie** Grievance] **1094**
Simon Fraser University v CUPE, Local 3338, 2013 CanLII 2940 (BCLRB) 548
Simpsons Limited v Canadian Union of Brewery, Flour, Cereal, Soft Drink and
  Distillery Workers (1985), 9 CLRBR (NS) 343 433
Slaight Communications Inc v Davidson, [1989] 1 SCR 1038,
  59 DLR (4th) 416, 93 NR 183..733
Smith & Rhuland Ltd v Nova Scotia, [1953] 2 SCR 95, 53 CLLC 15,057 ....**379**
Speckling v Communications, Energy and Paperworkers' Union of Canada,
  Local 76, BCLRB Decision No B333/2003 ....**847**
Speckling v Local 76 of the Communications, Energy and Paperworkers'
  Union of Canada, 2006 BCCA 203 851
St Anne Nackawic Pulp & Paper Co Ltd v Canadian Paper Workers Union,
  Local 219, [1986] 1 SCR 704... 634, **637**, 643, 644, 739, 750, 764
Steele v Louisville & Nashville Railroad Co, 323 US 192 (1944)............................**790**, 792
Stein v British Columbia (Housing Management Commission) (1992),
  65 BCLR (2d) 181 (CA).. 263
Stevens v The Globe and Mail (1996), 28 OR (3d) 481 (CA) 1061
Stewart v Elk Valley Coal Corp, 2017 SCC 30 1167
Stratford v Lindley, [1965] AC 269 (HL) 630
Sunnycrest Nursing Homes Limited, [1982] 2 CLRBR 51 (OLRB) 576
Symes v Canada [1993] 4 SCR 695... 1131
Syndicat catholique des employés de magasins de Québec Inc v Compagnie
  Paquet Ltée, [1959] SCR 206..**780**
Syndicat de la fonction publique du Québec v Quebec (Attorney General),
  2010 SCC 28 765

T Eaton Co, [1985] OLRB Rep June 491 ....456, 656
Taylor-Baptiste v Ontario Public Service Employees Union, 2015 ONCA 495 842
Techform Products v Wolda (2001), 56 OR (3d) 1 (CA) 255
Telus Communications Inc v Telecommunications Workers' Union,
    2007 BCCA 413 ....**671**
Telus Communications v TWU (2005), 385 AR 43 (QB) 670
Telus Communications, [2004] CIRBD No 12 684
Tessier Ltée v Quebec (Commission de la santé et de la sécurité du travail),
    2012 SCC 23, [2012] 2 SCR 3 ....**112**
Thomson v Deakin, [1952] Ch 646 (CA) 630
Toronto (City) Board of Education v OSSTF, District 15, [1997] 1 SCR 487..........................**748**, 749
Toronto (City) v CUPE, Local 79, 2003 SCC 63..765
Toronto (City) v Professional Fire Fighters' Association, Local 3888,
    2014 CanLII 62879 (ONLA)... 1185
Toronto (City) v Toronto Professional Fire Fighters' Association, Local 3888,
    2014 CanLII 76886 (ON LA).. 1184
Toronto Jewellery Manufacturers Association, [1979] OLRB Rep July 719 539
Toronto Transit Commission v ATU (2004), 132 LAC (4th) 225 (Ont Lab Arb) 1185
Toronto Transit Commission, [1996] OLRB Rep Sept/Oct 889 652
Torquay Hotel Co v Cousins, [1969] 2 Ch 106 (CA) 630
Tranchemontagne v Ontario (Director, Disability Support Program), 2006 SCC 14 766
Travailleurs et travailleuses unis de l'alimentation et du commerce,
    section locale 501 (TUAC-FTQ) et Savoura, 2014 CanLII 76230
    (QC SAT) **213**

Unilux Boiler Corp v United Steelworkers of America, Local 3950, [2005]
    OLRD No 2471 (OLRB)...**613**
Union Colliery Co v Bryden, [1899] AC 580 (PC)..1066
United Electrical, Radio and Machine Workers of America v DeVilbiss (Canada) Ltd
    (1976), 76 CLLC 16,009 (OLRB) **543**
United Food & Commercial Workers Canada, Local 175 v WHL Management
    Limited Partnership, 2014 CanLII 76990 (ON LRB)..**571**, 677
United Food and Commercial Workers, Local 1518 v Kmart Canada Ltd, [1999]
    2 SCR 1083 .... 16, 649, 670
United Food and Commercial Workers, Local 401 v Alberta Human Rights and
    Citizenship Commission, 2003 ABCA 246 1111
United Food and Commercial Workers, Local 503 v Wal-Mart Canada Corp,
    [2014] 2 SCR 232, 2014 SCC 45 .... 164, 431, **465**, 469
United Rubber, Cork, Linoleum & Plastic Workers of America, Local 1028 v
    Michelin Tires (Canada) Ltd, [1979] 3 CLRBR 429...**503**
United Steelworkers 1-2693 v Neenah Paper Company of Canada,
    2006 CanLII 9888, [2006] OLRD No 1132... 541, **616**, 620
United Steelworkers obo others v Tim Hortons and others (No 2),
    2015 BCHRT 168 ....**1155**

United Steelworkers of America v Gaspé Copper Mines Ltd,
 [1970] SCR 362, 10 DLR (3d) 443 634
United Steelworkers of America v Radio Shack, [1980] 1 CLRBR 99 (OLRB)...............459, **552**, 584
United Steelworkers of America v TD Canada Trust in the Greater City of
 Sudbury, 2005 CIRB 316 (CanLII).. **498**
United Steelworkers of America v Wal-Mart Canada, [1997] OLRD No 207,
 aff'd **(sub nom Wal-Mart Canada Inc v United Steelworkers of America)**
 [1997] OJ No 3063 (Div Ct) leave to appeal refused, [1999] OJ No 2995 (CA)) **440**

Victoria Times Colonist v CEP, Local 25-G, 2008 BCSC 109..614
Vladyslav Logvynosky v Milk and Bread Drivers, 2016 CanLII 20059 (OLRB)...........................798
Vriend v Alberta, [1998] 1 SCR 493... **1067, 1140, 1149**

W Harris & Company (1953), 4 LAC 1531...749
Walden v Canada (Social Development), 2007 CHRT 56 .... **1125**
Wallace v United Grain Growers Ltd, [1997] 3 SCR 701 .... 264, **318**
Walter LM Speckling v Labour Relations Board of British Columbia, 2006 BCSC 285 851
Walters v CUPE, Local 5089, [2014] OLRB Rep July/August 700 798
Watson v Moore Corp (1996), 134 DLR (4th) 252 (BCCA) 255
Weber v Ontario Hydro, [1995]
 2 SCR 929... xxvi, 643, **734**, 736, **750**, 753, 754, 757, 758, 764, 784, 1185
Westinghouse Canada Ltd, [1980] 2 CLRBR 469
 (OLRB) 429, 459, 465, 575, 576, 578, 583
**Westroc Industries Ltd v United Cement, Lime and Gypsum Workers
 International Union,** [1981] 2 CLRBR 315 (OLRB) **620**
White Spot Ltd v British Columbia (Labour Relations Board),
 [1997] BCJ No 1440 (SC).. **392**
**William Scott & Company Ltd v Canadian Food and Allied Workers Union,
 Local P-162,** [1977] 1 CLRBR 1 (BCLRB) **740**
Wilson v Atomic Energy of Canada Ltd, [2016] 1 SCR 770 ....**1039**

Yarrow Lodge Ltd v Hospital Employees' Union et al (1993)
 BCLRB No B444/93 (BCLRB) 592, **593**
Young v Canadian Northern Railway, [1931] 1 DLR 645 (PC) **694**